UNIVERSITY CASEBOOK SERIES®

LAND USE REGULATION

SECOND EDITION

STEWART E. STERK
H. Bert and Ruth Mack Professor of Law
Benjamin Cardozo School of Law, Yeshiva University

EDUARDO M. PEÑALVER
Allan R. Tessler Dean and Professor of Law
Cornell Law School

SARA C. BRONIN
Professor of Law and Faculty Director, Center for Energy and
Environmental Law
University of Connecticut School of Law

FOUNDATION
PRESS

University Casebook Series is a trademark registered in the U.S. Patent and Trademark Office.

© 2011 by THOMSON REUTERS/FOUNDATION PRESS
© 2016 LEG, Inc. d/b/a West Academic
    444 Cedar Street, Suite 700
    St. Paul, MN 55101
    1-877-888-1330

Printed in the United States of America

ISBN: 978-1-62810-129-4

PREFACE

Legal doctrine plays an important but peripheral role in the practice of Land Use law. Statutory and constitutional provisions become critical once land use disputes reach litigation, but most land use disputes are not resolved in court. Rather, they are resolved in front of city councils or local zoning boards or planning commissions composed of laymen who may know little about constitutional and statutory interpretation or about common law principles. Representing clients before part-time volunteer decisionmakers presents challenges different from those that arise in ordinary litigation.

This book is designed to prepare students for the various roles land use lawyers must play: zealous advocate, good listener, calm conciliator, wise counselor. Although the book—like most law school casebooks—includes leading appellate cases, our focus is on the relevance of those cases for a land use practitioner. The book's extensive questions and problems are designed to explore how lawyers should advise and represent their clients in light of the issues raised by the decided cases.

In the preparation of this Second Edition we were fortunate to receive a stream of extraordinarily valuable suggestions from our colleague, Michael Herz. We are grateful for his help. Thanks are also due for the student help we received from Sara Barlowe, Stephanie Brenner, Ali Claus, Alex Deutsch, Kseniya Lezhnev, Giovanna Marchese, Jenna Montesano, and Carl Rizzi. In addition, the contributions made to the First Edition by Emily Bayer-Pacht, Jonathan Rohr, Brian Steinwascher, Laura Tam, and Robert Tricchinelli continue to enrich this edition.

STEWART E. STERK
EDUARDO M. PEÑALVER
SARA C. BRONIN

May 2016

SUMMARY OF CONTENTS

TABLE OF CONTENTS

TABLE OF CASES

The principal cases are in bold type.

UNIVERSITY CASEBOOK SERIES®

LAND USE REGULATION

SECOND EDITION

CHAPTER ONE

INTRODUCTION

I. WHY REGULATE LAND USE

Land use law makes critical decisions about the way most of us are able to conduct our lives, including determining the locations at which we are able to conduct basic human activities such as eating, working, and sleeping. We begin this casebook by considering a few reasons why a government would use the law to order the way people use their land.

A. EFFICIENCY CONCERNS

The owner of an estate situated on a 10-acre parcel of land has just died. The parcel lies on the outskirts of a medium-size city that has experienced considerable growth over the past decade. The owner's estate has just sold the parcel to a developer, who is considering potential uses for the parcel.

The parcel fronts on the west side of a wide, heavily traveled street. Across the street is a public elementary school. Single-family homes on one-quarter acre lots are located to the south and west of the subject parcel. Immediately north of the parcel is another large estate. The developer believes that estate will be sold and devoted to another use within the next few years.

The developer has not yet settled on a use for the parcel. Among the options the developer is considering are a retail shopping center, a condominium development, and a single-family subdivision.

NOTES AND QUESTIONS

1. Assume that the municipality has not enacted any land use regulations. In choosing among alternatives for the site, what factors would you expect the developer to consider? Suppose the construction costs for a condominium complex would be $5,000,000, and the developer expects the units to sell for $8,000,000. By contrast, the shopping center would cost $3,000,000 and the expected sale price would be $5,000,000. Will the developer inevitably prefer the condominium complex over the shopping center? What other factors might be relevant to the developer's choice?

2. Will neighboring landowners care which use the developer selects? Why? Suppose, for instance, a 100-unit condominium complex would be expected to include 50 school-age children each year, and it costs the local school system an average of $8,000 to educate a child. If the complex would generate $200,000 in tax revenue, would you expect neighbors to be indifferent to construction of the complex?

Suppose the retail shopping center would generate the same $200,000 in tax revenue, and would generate no new expenditures for schools. Would you expect neighbors to oppose the shopping center? Why or why not?

3.   In the absence of regulation, does the developer have any reason to take neighbor concerns into account in choosing among competing uses?

4.   Suppose the developer concluded that building a retail shopping center would generate $1,000,000 more in profit than building a 30-unit subdivision of single-family homes on quarter-acre lots. If the neighbors were concerned that the shopping center would diminish their property values, could they offer to pay the developer if the developer agreed to build the subdivision instead of the shopping center? Would the developer care whether profit came from the neighbors or from the shopping center?

What reasons are there to believe that negotiations between the developer and the neighbors might not ensure efficient use of land in the area? Even if negotiations would prevent inefficient uses, are there reasons—grounded in efficiency or fairness—why the neighbors should not have to pay the developer to desist from making uses that would generate external costs? To what extent can public regulation of land use solve these problems?

B. AESTHETIC CONCERNS

Consider the following description of South Broadway in Saratoga Springs, N.Y.:

> By any standard, South Broadway looks terrible. No thought has gone into the relationship between things—the buildings to each other, the buildings to the street, the pedestrian to the buildings. The detailing of the street is a mess . . . the absence of trees planted along the sides of the street lends it a bleak, sun-blasted look, which the clutter of signs only aggravates. Even experienced from inside a car, the place is depressing.

James Howard Kunstler, The Geography of Nowhere (1993) at 138. Kunstler's theme finds echoes throughout the literature on American cities and suburbs.

NOTES AND QUESTIONS

1.   What incentives do developers have for creating aesthetically pleasing buildings and spaces? Who derives benefit from attractively planned spaces, and who bears the costs of ugly ones?

2.   What training do developers have that would enable them to gauge the aesthetic preferences of potential customers and of the broader community at large?

In Salt Lake City, as part of a broad planning effort called "Envision Utah," residents were shown photographs of various streetscapes and asked to rate them on a scale of −5 to +5. The more walkable environments were consistently rated higher than suburban alternatives. In particular, participants pointed to visual interest and human scale features of pedestrian friendly streets. Peter Calthorpe and William Fulton, The Regional City (2001). If developers choose not to incorporate insights like these into their projects, is it because they are ill-informed, or because consumer purchasing decisions reflect preferences different from those they express in response to surveys?

3. How well do developers' customers (and other community residents) understand their own aesthetic preferences? To what extent do customers subordinate aesthetics to functional considerations, especially when aesthetics and function are "bundled" into a single package—a home, an office building, or a retail shopping center? If customers consider aesthetic issues relatively unimportant, should regulators impose aesthetic choices on developers and their customers?

4. *Externalities Again.* Even if developers are sensitive to aesthetic concerns, should we expect developers to worry about how well their projects "fit" with others in the community? Is a mish-mash of contrasting styles just as problematic as simple ugliness?

C. COMMUNITY CONCERNS

Some theorists believe that land use decisions affect the way people interact with one another. If developers build, and consumers buy, single-family homes on large lots, residents of those homes will not interact with their neighbors on sidewalks or streets. If retail stores are all located in indoor shopping malls, fewer residents will have chance encounters with other community residents on downtown streets. Consumers do not actively choose a more isolated lifestyle; a conglomeration of factors—many of them related to land use planning— thrust that lifestyle upon them.

For many theorists, better land use planning can help restore a sense of community to American life. In the words of one proponent of the "New Urbanism"—a contemporary approach to land use planning about which you will learn more in later chapters:

> Community is what America has most conspicuously lost, and community is precisely what the canonical Modern architecture and planning of the middle years of this century were totally unable to provide.

Vincent Scully, The Architecture of Community, in The New Urbanism (Peter Katz ed. 1994) at 221–30.

In effect, these theorists argue that the whole is greater than the sum of the parts. Aggregating the preferences of current residents to determine what land use is most efficient ignores the ways in which existing land use laws constrain the options among which consumers can choose and, moreover, fails to take note of the impact that current land use regimes have on consumer preferences.

Another strain of "communitarian" land use thought does not so much prefer land use law that fosters community to land use law that breeds individualism or alienation. Rather, it is concerned with how the law might foster one model of community over another. Thinkers in this mode worry about the use of land use regulation, whether private covenants or public zoning codes, to avoid redistributive policies or to create homogeneous communities that are segregated by income and race. These critics of "exclusionary" land use regulation draw extensively on arguments framed in terms of efficiency, fairness, and democratic values to make their case. We will discuss the problem of exclusionary land uses in more depth in Chapter Nine.

NOTES AND QUESTIONS

1. Are you convinced that design of physical space has such a direct impact on the formation of community? Manhattan, the core of New York City, is one of the most walkable environments in the United States. Are Manhattanites noted for their sense of community? Perhaps Manhattanites' reputation for aloofness or individualism derives from an overly narrow conception of "community." Consider this excerpt from Jane Jacobs's classic book, The Death and Life of Great American Cities (1961):

> Reformers have long observed city people loitering on busy corners, hanging around in candy stores and bars and drinking soda pop on stoops, and have passed a judgment, the gist of which is: "This is deplorable! If these people had decent homes and a more private or bosky outdoor place, they wouldn't be on the street!"

> This private judgment represents a profound misunderstanding of cities. . . . [Sidewalks] bring together people who do not know each other in an intimate, private social fashion and in most cases do not care to know each other in that fashion.

> Nobody can keep open house in a great city. Nobody wants to. And yet if interesting, useful and significant contacts among the people of cities are confined to acquaintances suitable for private life, the city becomes stultified. Cities are full of people with whom, from your viewpoint, or mine, or any other individual's, a certain degree of contact is useful or enjoyable; but you do not want them in your hair. And they do not want you in theirs either. . . .

> The trust of a city street is formed over time from many, many little public sidewalk contacts. It grows out of people stopping by at the bar for a beer, getting advice from the grocer and giving advice to the newsstand man, comparing opinions with other customers at the baker and nodding hello to the two boys drinking pop on the stoop, eyeing the girls while waiting to be called for dinner, admonishing the children, hearing about a job from the hardware man and borrowing a dollar from the druggist, admiring the new babies and sympathizing over the way a coat faded. Customs vary: in some neighborhoods people compare

notes on their dogs; in others they compare notes on their landlords.

Most of it is ostensibly utterly trivial but the sum is not trivial at all. The sum of such casual, public contact at a local level—most of it fortuitous, most of it associated with errands, all of it metered by the person concerned and not thrust upon him by anyone—is a feeling for the public identity of people, a web of public respect and trust, and a resource in time of personal or neighborhood need. The absence of this trust is a disaster to a city street.

2. What role, if any, can land use law play in fostering (or impeding) the sort of casual social interactions that Jacobs describes as essential to the health of a city sidewalk?

3. Suppose the right physical environment would increase community and decrease isolation. What kind of land use regulation would produce that environment? Would municipalities have to prohibit traditional suburban development even though residents (perhaps mistakenly) believe they prefer large houses on large lots? How politically feasible would such an approach be? Alternatively, would cities merely need to rescind the sorts of single-use, low-density zoning regimes that operate in most suburban municipalities?

4. Consider this statement by Andres Duany, Elizabeth Plater-Zyberk, and Jeff Speck, in their book, Suburban Nation (2000):

> Boston's Beacon Hill, Nantucket, Santa Fe, Carmel—all of these well-known places, many of which have become tourist destinations, exist in direct violation of current zoning ordinances. Even the classic American main street, with its mixed-use buildings right up against the sidewalk, is now illegal in most municipalities. Somewhere along the way, through a series of small and well-intentioned steps, traditional towns became a crime in America. At the same time, one of the largest segments of our economy, the homebuilding industry, developed a comprehensive system of land development practices based upon sprawl, practices that have become so ingrained as to be second nature. It is these practices, and the laws that encourage them, which must be overcome if good growth is to become a viable alternative.

Are Duany, Plater-Zyberk and Speck calling for more regulation of land use, less regulation, or both? Are the sorts of single-use, low-density zoning regimes to which they refer the cause of sprawl or do they merely represent the effort by local communities to lock in development patterns that they prefer?

II. REGULATING THE REGULATORS

A. WHO ARE THE REGULATORS?

Some land use regulation involves no governmental intervention. As we shall see in Chapter Eight, developers often create mechanisms that allow community residents to regulate land use through private associations.

The primary focus of this course, however, is on public regulation designed to address the efficiency, aesthetic, and communitarian issues raised in the preceding section. Although state and federal governments play a role in the regulatory process, local governments—villages, towns, cities, and counties—bear the primary responsibility for land use regulation.

Because they have knowledge about local conditions and preferences, local government officials enjoy significant advantages as land use regulators. But how are they to assess the wisdom of particular regulatory choices? Elected officials and citizen volunteers— who have ultimate decision-making authority on most regulatory issues—have little basis for determining whether existing transportation systems can support 500 or 5,000 new residents. They are unlikely to have the expertise to assess the environmental impact of wetlands development, or to estimate accurately the impact a new shopping center would have on existing downtown stores.

For advice on these and many other regulatory issues, local officials turn to professional planners and other experts. Larger municipalities may have a planning staff, while smaller ones may have a single salaried planner or may instead employ outside planning consultants.

B. PLANNERS AND PLANNING

1. SOME HISTORY AND THEORY

What do planners do? One image of the planner is that of the master designer who lays out an entire city from soup to nuts. The "City Beautiful" movement, launched at the 1893 World's Fair in Chicago, popularized that image. Architect Daniel Burnham, the fair's director of works, provided what might have served as the credo for the movement: "Make no little plans, they have no magic to stir men's blood."

During the post-World War II era, Edward Banfield and others developed the "rational planning model." The model focused on breaking the planning process into steps. The first step was to identify and elaborate goals and objectives. Once those objectives were articulated, planners would design courses of action that could achieve those objectives. Planners would then evaluate the consequences of each potential course of action, setting the stage for a choice among those alternatives. The rational planning model attempted to place planning on a scientific foundation. In effect, Banfield and the rational planning model described a logical problem-solving framework for dealing with complex interactions.

At about the same time, planning as a profession received a major boost when Congress required local governments to develop workable programs for community improvement in order to qualify for certain kinds of federal funding. Local governments responded to this federal prod by drafting "comprehensive plans" that often followed the rational planning model.

Within planning circles, however, the rational planning model, like the City Beautiful model before it, has been discredited—in part for the same reason: the model was too ambitious to be practical. Comparing all possible alternatives and assessing the impact of each on all relevant factors exceeds human capacities. Charles Lindblom, a political scientist who studies government decision-making, has suggested that it is more realistic for cities to engage in a modest and incremental planning process, rather than a comprehensive one. Charles E. Lindblom, The Science of "Muddling Through," 19 Pub. Admin. Rev. 79 (1959). Most planners today recognize that unforeseen circumstances arise and tastes and preferences evolve, and there is increased focus on neighborhood planning and specific goal-setting—even if and as they work through the traditional framework of the comprehensive plan.

2. PLANNING ON THE GROUND: THE ROLE OF PLANS AND PLANNERS
    IN THE REGULATORY PROCESS

Comprehensive Plans. Planners are involved in the regulatory process at multiple stages. First, statutes in many states obligate municipalities to develop "comprehensive plans" (and, as we have already noted, the federal government has at various times provided incentives for municipalities to do so). These plans do not generally have the force of law with respect to any parcel of land, but they nevertheless play an important role in setting goals and objectives for future municipal development.

Often, the plan will be drafted in the form of a series of goals, objectives, and policies. Consider a hypothetical example with respect to one goal a municipality might advance:

Goal 1: The City shall increase the economic vitality of the Downtown Future Land Use District.

  Objective 1.1: Support local businesses by creating a 24-hour downtown.

    Policy 1.1.1. The City shall adopt land development regulations that provide incentives for the development of housing in the Downtown Future Land Use District. These incentives may include, but are not limited to, height bonuses and fee waivers.

Objective 1.2: Enhance Downtown's role as a popular tourist destination.

Policy 1.2.1: The City shall adopt design standards to maintain vernacular architecture. These standards shall address, but are not limited to: building height, building setbacks, ground floor fenestration, parking standards and the location of parking, balconies, overhangs and awnings, and building material.

Policy 1.2.2: The City shall provide incentives for maintaining and rehabilitating historic structures. These incentives may include, but are not limited to, expedited permitting and reduced parking standards.

Policy 1.2.3: Through the capital budget process, the City shall fund streetscape improvements in the Downtown to improve pedestrian safety and comfort.

Wendy Grey, The Comprehensive Plan and Land Development Regulations, 82 Plan. Comm'rs J. at 2 (Spr. 2011). A plan would, of course, include a variety of other goals. Some might be of relevance to every area of the municipality, while others would be of relevance only in particular areas.

It probably does not take a professional planner to identify a goal like "increase the economic vitality of downtown." What, then, does a planner contribute? Primarily, knowledge about what strategies might be helpful in achieving the goal. That knowledge, derived from study of the experiences in other municipalities, enables the planner to help formulate the kinds of objectives and policies articulated in the sample excerpt above.

Although planners work with other municipal officials, consultants, and citizen volunteers in developing the comprehensive plan, planners typically play the principal role in drafting the plan.

As we shall see, the legal effect of the plan varies from state to state. In a few states, zoning ordinances may be invalid if they are not consistent with the plan as drafted—which imbues the plan with legal significance. But even in states where the plan has no binding effect, it serves as a guide for regulators in drafting zoning ordinances and other regulatory provisions. As a matter of practice, regulators may evaluate regulatory proposals to ensure that they are consistent with the goals and objectives set out in the comprehensive plan.

Beyond the Comprehensive Plan. Although planners in many municipalities continue to prepare and revise comprehensive plans, planners often have more impact on concrete proposals for incremental changes in land use. Suppose, for instance, a municipality considers zoning a particular district to permit multi-family housing. What impact would the zoning change have on traffic, schools, parking, municipal infrastructure, and environmental conditions? Municipal officials might look to planners to conduct studies that might answer those questions. Planners will be able to estimate, given the number and configuration of apartments, how many children and how many cars development would generate. That data should prove useful to municipal officials in evaluating proposed zoning amendments and in evaluating other development proposals.

NOTES AND QUESTIONS

1. In practice, would you expect planners to exert more influence on municipal officials than those officials exert on planners? Why or why not? What incentives do planners have to make recommendations that are likely to displease municipal officials? How about planners' accountability to the general public? Should planners be obligated to incorporate input received by the public during the planning process or during the process of evaluating specific projects? If so, how?

2. Developers often employ planners. Why? Might the work a planner does for developers—or the work a planner hopes to do for a developer in the future—affect the positions or advice the planner advances in discussions with municipal officials?

3. Planners bring expertise to the development process. On the other hand, they have little personal financial stake in the outcomes generated by their advice. Unlike a developer, a planner does not have to "put his money where his mouth is." How should decision-makers balance expertise and lack of incentive in evaluating the recommendations of planners?

4. Is deference to the recommendations of planners anti-democratic? What justifications are there for conferring power on "experts" to decide what physical environment will be most attractive for the residents of a particular municipality?

C. THE POLITICAL ECONOMY OF LAND USE REGULATION

As we have seen, private developers often have little incentive to account for the adverse impact their development will generate— whether measured in terms of efficiency, aesthetics, or community. Public regulation can limit the developer's ability to generate adverse effects. Recall the potential developer choosing among uses for a 10-acre estate. Suppose a proposed retail shopping center would devalue 100 neighboring parcels by an average of $1,000 each—a $100,000 devaluation that the developer has no reason to consider if the developer operates in the absence of regulatory constraints. But suppose the shopping center land itself is worth $1,000,000 more as a shopping center than as a single-family subdivision. Is it clear that the developer should not build the center? If the municipality prohibits construction of a shopping center on the site, the municipality is imposing costs of $900,000—costs nine times greater than the devaluation the municipality is ostensibly trying to avoid.

Would municipal officials act that way? One thing to keep in mind is that the efficiency implications of a particular land use decision are rarely cut and dry. Using current market value to measure efficiency can be misleading. Today's market value measures the price private actors are willing to pay for land developed in a particular way. But land use decisions may have a very long lifespan, and today's market value may not accurately reflect future value, even though it is undoubtedly true that the price buyers are willing to pay today is determined in part by the price they expect to receive in the future.

First, today's market participants may not be able to anticipate consequences that may occur decades into the future. Lack of foresight may lead to decisions that prove, ultimately, to be inefficient.

Second, today's actors—private and public—inevitably have to make tradeoffs between short-term costs (or benefits) and long-term costs (or benefits). Economists refer to parties' weighting of temporal impacts as their "discount rate." Parties who value the short term over the long term are said to have a "high" discount rate whereas parties who weigh the long term more heavily are said to have a "low" discount rate.

Public officials might reach a decision that differs from the short-term evaluation of market participants because they are better (or worse) at predicting the future or, alternatively, because they are using a different discount rate to evaluate how much weight to give to short and long-term consequences of a land use decision. Questions about the right discount rate to apply in the evaluation of land use decisions are very difficult to resolve and often implicate deep moral commitments.

Another explanation for why public officials might opt for a land use decision that appears to be less than optimal focuses on the indisputable fact that municipal officials are not disinterested parties objectively tallying costs and benefits. They may have the "public interest" in mind, but they also have an interest in re-election or reappointment—which may lead them to favor the interests of particular individuals and groups. Unregulated land use may lead to inefficiency, to ugliness, and to isolation, but to endorse public regulation on that ground alone is to ignore the flaws within the public decision-making process. The question is not whether there are flaws in private (or public) decision-making but whether a public (or private) regulatory system can be harnessed to address those imperfections without introducing even greater evils.

If municipal officials were responsive primarily to the 100 resident voters, the officials might ignore the magnitude of the loss and prohibit the shopping center. (After all, the developer might be a non-resident and a non-voter.) On the other hand, officials might be responsive to the concerns of the developer—especially if the developer were a generous campaign contributor. Which surmise is more likely to reflect the behavior of actual municipal officials? It's hard to say. Some scholars have suggested that suburban officials are more likely to be captured by resident-voters, while urban officials may be more responsive to developer interests, but there is no universal answer. The important point—emphasized in the "public choice" literature—is that treating a government entity as a disinterested or neutral arbiter ignores the reality that government decisions are made by individuals, all of whom have incentives to advance the interests of particular groups, even if the resulting decisions are inefficient.

The incentives and constraints that public officials face will turn in large part on countless subtleties in the institutional context within which they operate, including the rules governing elections, administrative appointments, campaign finance, municipal incorporation and annexation, district boundary-setting, judicial review, as well as cultural expectations and many, many other variables. Trying to determine whether a public regulatory regime—in some form (and not necessarily the existing one)—will be better at evaluating the efficiency of a particular land use than the private market is therefore an enormously complicated undertaking. The key question for land use lawmaking is whether one particular decision-making structure, however imperfect, is likely to reliably yield better (i.e., less imperfect) decisions than another. In the (not infrequent) event that we cannot even answer that question with any confidence, should we opt for one mode of decision-making over another because, notwithstanding uncertainty about whether it will yield better decisions in the short or even medium-term, we prefer that mode of decision-making for *other* reasons (e.g., because it is more consistent with freedom or because it is more likely to be self-correcting when better information becomes available)?

The same point holds even if we focus on other goals of land use law, such as fostering aesthetic or communitarian values. Are government officials likely to be particularly good judges of architectural style, design function, or historical importance? Might they be unduly cautious in their judgments, stifling creative design in favor of conventional and "safe" projects? What constraints to place on the regulatory power of municipal officials or how to use institutional design to structure their incentives are central problems for assessing the proper domain and content of land use regulation. Are regulations justified only to remedy defects in market processes, which we should assume to be the default mode of decision-making? And, if so, how should the legal system minimize the risk of error or distortions introduced by the regulatory process itself?

III. THE DOCTRINAL STARTING POINT: VILLAGE OF EUCLID

The most familiar and traditional technique for land use regulation is zoning: division of the municipality's land area into separate zones for different uses. (We study the details of zoning in Chapter Two.) Zoning originated in the early part of the 20th century. The early ordinances were largely promulgated in cities and other already-developed areas. Can you imagine why? Nevertheless, zoning's legal foundation was uncertain until the Supreme Court's decision in the following case:

Village of Euclid v. Ambler Realty Co.

Supreme Court of the United States, 1926
272 U.S. 365

■ MR. JUSTICE SUTHERLAND delivered the opinion of the Court.

The Village of Euclid is an Ohio municipal corporation. It adjoins and practically is a suburb of the City of Cleveland. Its estimated population is between 5,000 and 10,000, and its area from twelve to fourteen square miles, the greater part of which is farm lands or unimproved acreage. It lies, roughly, in the form of a parallelogram measuring approximately three and one-half miles each way. East and west it is traversed by three principal highways: Euclid Avenue, through the southerly border, St. Clair Avenue, through the central portion, and Lake Shore Boulevard, through the northerly border in close proximity to the shore of Lake Erie. The Nickel Plate railroad lies from 1,500 to 1,800 feet north of Euclid Avenue, and the Lake Shore railroad 1,600 feet farther to the north. The three highways and the two railroads are substantially parallel.

Appellee is the owner of a tract of land containing 68 acres, situated in the westerly end of the village, abutting on Euclid Avenue to the south and the Nickel Plate railroad to the north. Adjoining this tract, both on the east and on the west, there have been laid out restricted residential plats upon which residences have been erected.

On November 13, 1922, an ordinance was adopted by the Village Council, establishing a comprehensive zoning plan for regulating and restricting the location of trades, industries, apartment houses, two-family houses, single family houses, etc., the lot area to be built upon, the size and height of buildings, etc.

The entire area of the village is divided by the ordinance into six classes of use districts, denominated U–1 to U–6, inclusive; three classes of height districts, denominated H–1 to H–3, inclusive; and four classes of area districts, denominated A–1 to A–4, inclusive. The use districts are classified in respect of the buildings which may be erected within their respective limits, as follows: U–1 is restricted to single family dwellings, public parks, water towers and reservoirs, suburban and interurban electric railway passenger stations and rights of way, and farming, non-commercial greenhouse nurseries and truck gardening; U–2 is extended to include two-family dwellings; U–3 is further extended to include apartment houses, hotels, churches, schools, public libraries, museums, private clubs, community center buildings, hospitals, sanitariums, public playgrounds and recreation buildings, and a city hall and courthouse; U–4 is further extended to include banks, offices, studios, telephone exchanges, fire and police stations, restaurants, theatres and moving picture shows, retail stores and shops, sales offices, sample rooms, wholesale stores for hardware, drugs and groceries, stations for gasoline and oil (not exceeding 1,000 gallons storage) and for ice delivery, skating rinks and dance halls, electric substations, job and newspaper printing, public garages for motor vehicles, stables and wagon sheds (not exceeding five horses, wagons or motor trucks) and distributing stations for central store and commercial enterprises; U–5 is further extended to include billboards and advertising signs (if permitted), warehouses, ice and ice cream manufacturing and cold storage plants, bottling works, milk bottling and central distribution stations, laundries, carpet cleaning, dry cleaning and dyeing establishments, blacksmith, horseshoeing, wagon and motor vehicle repair shops, freight stations, street car barns, stables and wagon sheds (for more than five horses, wagons or motor trucks), and wholesale produce markets and salesrooms; U–6 is further extended to include plants for sewage disposal and for producing gas, garbage and refuse incineration, scrap iron, junk, scrap paper and rag storage, aviation fields, cemeteries, crematories, penal and correctional institutions, insane and feeble minded institutions, storage of oil and gasoline (not to exceed 25,000 gallons), and manufacturing and industrial operations of any kind other than, and any public utility not included in, a class U–1, U–2, U–3, U–4 or U–5 use. There is a seventh class of uses which is prohibited altogether.

Class U–1 is the only district in which buildings are restricted to those enumerated. In the other classes the uses are cumulative; that is to say, uses in class U–2 include those enumerated in the preceding class, U–1; class U–3 includes uses enumerated in the preceding classes, U–2 and U–1; and so on. In addition to the enumerated uses, the ordinance provides for accessory uses, that is, for uses customarily incident to the principal use, such as private garages. Many regulations are provided in respect of such accessory uses.

Appellee's tract of land comes under U–2, U–3 and U–6. The first strip of 620 feet immediately north of Euclid Avenue falls in class U–2, the next 130 feet to the north, in U–3, and the remainder in U–6. The uses of the first 620 feet, therefore, do not include apartment houses, hotels, churches, schools, or other public and semi-public buildings, or other uses enumerated in respect of U–3 to U–6, inclusive. The uses of the next 130 feet include all of these, but exclude industries, theatres, banks, shops, and the various other uses set forth in respect of U–4 to U–6, inclusive.

* * *

VILLAGE OF EUCLID
1922 ZONING MAP

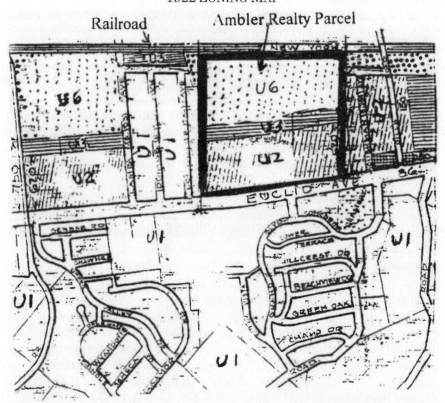

The lands lying between the two railroads for the entire length of
the village area and extending some distance on either side to the north
and south, having an average width of about 1,600 feet, are left open,
with slight exceptions, for industrial and all other uses. This includes
the larger part of appellee's tract. Approximately one-sixth of the area
of the entire village is included in U–5 and U–6 use districts. That part
of the village lying south of Euclid Avenue is principally in U–1
districts. The lands lying north of Euclid Avenue and bordering on the
long strip just described are included in U–1, U–2, U–3 and U–4
districts, principally in U–2.

The ordinance is assailed on the grounds that it is in derogation of
§ 1 of the Fourteenth Amendment to the Federal Constitution in that it
deprives appellee of liberty and property without due process of law and
denies it the equal protection of the law, and that it offends against
certain provisions of the Constitution of the State of Ohio. The prayer of
the bill is for an injunction restraining the enforcement of the ordinance
and all attempts to impose or maintain as to appellee's property any of
the restrictions, limitations or conditions. The court below held the
ordinance to be unconstitutional and void, and enjoined its enforcement.
297 Fed. 307.

Before proceeding to a consideration of the case, it is necessary to determine the scope of the inquiry. The bill alleges that the tract of land in question is vacant and has been held for years for the purpose of selling and developing it for industrial uses, for which it is especially adapted, being immediately in the path of progressive industrial development; that for such uses it has a market value of about $10,000 per acre, but if the use be limited to residential purposes the market value is not in excess of $2,500 per acre; that the first 200 feet of the parcel back from Euclid Avenue, if unrestricted in respect of use, has a value of $150 per front foot, but if limited to residential uses, and ordinary mercantile business be excluded therefrom, its value is not in excess of $50 per front foot.

It is specifically averred that the ordinance attempts to restrict and control the lawful uses of appellee's land so as to confiscate and destroy a great part of its value; that it is being enforced in accordance with its terms; that prospective buyers of land for industrial, commercial and residential uses in the metropolitan district of Cleveland are deterred from buying any part of this land because of the existence of the ordinance and the necessity thereby entailed of conducting burdensome and expensive litigation in order to vindicate the right to use the land for lawful and legitimate purposes; that the ordinance constitutes a cloud upon the land, reduces and destroys its value, and has the effect of diverting the normal industrial, commercial and residential development thereof to other and less favorable locations.

The record goes no farther than to show, as the lower court found, that the normal, and reasonably to be expected, use and development of that part of appellee's land adjoining Euclid Avenue is for general trade and commercial purposes, particularly retail stores and like establishments, and that the normal, and reasonably to be expected, use and development of the residue of the land is for industrial and trade purposes. Whatever injury is inflicted by the mere existence and threatened enforcement of the ordinance is due to restrictions in respect of these and similar uses; to which perhaps should be added—if not included in the foregoing—restrictions in respect of apartment houses.

Building zone laws are of modern origin. They began in this country about twenty-five years ago. Until recent years, urban life was comparatively simple; but with the great increase and concentration of population, problems have developed, and constantly are developing, which require, and will continue to require, additional restrictions in respect of the use and occupation of private lands in urban communities. Regulations, the wisdom, necessity and validity of which, as applied to existing conditions, are so apparent that they are now uniformly sustained, a century ago, or even half a century ago, probably would have been rejected as arbitrary and oppressive. Such regulations are sustained, under the complex conditions of our day, for reasons analogous to those which justify traffic regulations, which, before the advent of automobiles and rapid transit street railways, would have been condemned as fatally arbitrary and unreasonable. And in this there is no inconsistency, for while the meaning of constitutional guaranties never varies, the scope of their application must expand or contract to meet the new and different conditions which are constantly coming within the field of their operation. In a changing world, it is impossible that it should be otherwise. But although a degree of elasticity is thus imparted, not to the *meaning*, but to the *application* of constitutional principles, statutes and ordinances, which, after giving due weight to the new conditions, are found clearly not to conform to the Constitution, of course, must fall.

The ordinance now under review, and all similar laws and regulations, must find their justification in some aspect of the police power, asserted for the public welfare. The line which in this field separates the legitimate from the illegitimate assumption of power is not capable of precise delimitation. It varies with circumstances and conditions. A regulatory zoning ordinance, which would be clearly valid as applied to the great cities, might be clearly invalid as applied to rural communities. In solving doubts, the maxim *sic utere tuo ut alienum non laedas*, which lies at the foundation of so much of the common law of nuisances, ordinarily will furnish a fairly helpful clew. And the law of nuisances, likewise, may be consulted, not for the purpose of controlling, but for the helpful aid of its analogies in the process of ascertaining the scope of, the power. A nuisance may be merely a right thing in the wrong place, like a pig in the parlor instead of the barnyard. If the validity of the legislative classification for zoning purposes be fairly debatable, the legislative judgment must be allowed to control. Radice v. New York, 264 U.S. 292, 294.

There is no serious difference of opinion in respect of the validity of laws and regulations fixing the height of buildings within reasonable limits, the character of materials and methods of construction, and the adjoining area which must be left open, in order to minimize the danger of fire or collapse, the evils of over-crowding, and the like, and excluding from residential sections offensive trades, industries and structures likely to create nuisances. See Welch v. Swasey, 214 U.S. 91; Hadacheck v. Los Angeles, 239 U.S. 394; Reinman v. Little Rock, 237 U.S. 171; Cusack Co. v. City of Chicago, 242 U.S. 526, 529–530.

Here, however, the exclusion is in general terms of all industrial establishments, and it may thereby happen that not only offensive or dangerous industries will be excluded, but those which are neither offensive nor dangerous will share the same fate. But this is no more than happens in respect of many practice—forbidding laws which this Court has upheld although drawn in general terms so as to include individual cases that may turn out to be innocuous in themselves. Hebe Co. v. Shaw, 248 U.S. 297, 303; Pierce Oil Corp. v. City of Hope, 248 U.S. 498, 500. The inclusion of a reasonable margin to insure effective enforcement, will not put upon a law, otherwise valid, the stamp of invalidity. Such laws may also find their justification in the fact that, in some fields, the bad fades into the good by such insensible degrees that the two are not capable of being readily distinguished and separated in terms of legislation. In the light of these considerations, we are not prepared to say that the end in view was not sufficient to justify the general rule of the ordinance, although some industries of an innocent character might fall within the proscribed class. It can not be said that the ordinance in this respect "passes the bounds of reason and assumes the character of a merely arbitrary fiat." Purity Extract Co. v. Lynch, 226 U.S. 192, 204. Moreover, the restrictive provisions of the ordinance in this particular may be sustained upon the principles applicable to the broader exclusion from residential districts of all business and trade structures, presently to be discussed.

It is said that the Village of Euclid is a mere suburb of the City of Cleveland; that the industrial development of that city has now reached and in some degree extended into the village and, in the obvious course of things, will soon absorb the entire area for industrial enterprises; that the effect of the ordinance is to divert this natural development elsewhere with the consequent loss of increased values to the owners of the lands within the village borders. But the village, though physically a suburb of Cleveland, is politically a separate municipality, with powers of its own and authority to govern itself as it sees fit within the limits of the organic law of its creation and the State and Federal Constitutions. Its governing authorities, presumably representing a majority of its inhabitants and voicing their will, have determined, not that industrial development shall cease at its boundaries, but that the course of such development shall proceed within definitely fixed lines. If it be a proper exercise of the police power to relegate industrial establishments to localities separated from residential sections, it is not easy to find a sufficient reason for denying the power because the effect of its exercise is to divert an industrial flow from the course which it would follow to the injury of the residential public if left alone, to another course where such injury will be obviated. It is not meant by this, however, to exclude the possibility of cases where the general public interest would so far outweigh the interest of the municipality that the municipality would not be allowed to stand in the way.

We find no difficulty in sustaining restrictions of the kind thus far reviewed. The serious question in the case arises over the provisions of the ordinance excluding from residential districts, apartment houses, business houses, retail stores and shops, and other like establishments. This question involves the validity of what is really the crux of the more recent zoning legislation, namely, the creation and maintenance of residential districts, from which business and trade of every sort, including hotels and apartment houses, are excluded. Upon that question, this Court has not thus far spoken.

The matter of zoning has received much attention at the hands of commissions and experts, and the results of their investigations have been set forth in comprehensive reports. These reports, which bear every evidence of painstaking consideration, concur in the view that the segregation of residential, business, and industrial buildings will make it easier to provide fire apparatus suitable for the character and intensity of the development in each section; that it will increase the safety and security of home life; greatly tend to prevent street accidents, especially to children, by reducing the traffic and resulting confusion in residential sections; decrease noise and other conditions which produce or intensify nervous disorders; preserve a more favorable environment in which to rear children, etc. With particular reference to apartment houses, it is pointed out that the development of detached house sections is greatly retarded by the coming of apartment houses, which has sometimes resulted in destroying the entire section for private house purposes; that in such sections very often the apartment house is a mere parasite, constructed in order to take advantage of the open spaces and attractive surroundings created by the residential character of the district. Moreover, the coming of one apartment house is followed by others, interfering by their height and bulk with the free circulation of air and monopolizing the rays of the sun which otherwise would fall upon the smaller homes, and bringing, as their necessary accompaniments, the disturbing noises incident to increased traffic and business, and the occupation, by means of moving and parked automobiles, of larger portions of the streets, thus detracting from their safety and depriving children of the privilege of quiet and open spaces for play, enjoyed by those in more favored localities,—until, finally, the residential character of the neighborhood and its desirability as a place of detached residences are utterly destroyed. Under these circumstances, apartment houses, which in a different environment would be not only entirely unobjectionable but highly desirable, come very near to being nuisances.

If these reasons, thus summarized, do not demonstrate the wisdom or sound policy in all respects of those restrictions which we have indicated as pertinent to the inquiry, at least, the reasons are sufficiently cogent to preclude us from saying, as it must be said before the ordinance can be declared unconstitutional, that such provisions are clearly arbitrary and unreasonable, having no substantial relation to the public health, safety, morals, or general welfare. Cusack Co. v. City of Chicago, supra, pp. 530–531; Jacobson v. Massachusetts, 197 U.S. 11, 30–31.

It is true that when, if ever, the provisions set forth in the ordinance in tedious and minute detail, come to be concretely applied to particular premises, including those of the appellee, or to particular conditions, or to be considered in connection with specific complaints, some of them, or even many of them, may be found to be clearly arbitrary and unreasonable.

What would be the effect of a restraint imposed by one or more of the innumerable provisions of the ordinance, considered apart, upon the value or marketability of the lands is neither disclosed by the bill nor by the evidence, and we are afforded no basis, apart from mere speculation, upon which to rest a conclusion that it or they would have any appreciable effect upon those matters. Under these circumstances, therefore, it is enough for us to determine, as we do, that the ordinance in its general scope and dominant features, so far as its provisions are here involved, is a valid exercise of authority, leaving other provisions to be dealt with as cases arise directly involving them.

Decree reversed.

■ MR. JUSTICE VAN DEVANTER, MR. JUSTICE MCREYNOLDS and MR. JUSTICE BUTLER dissent.

NOTES AND QUESTIONS

1.   Before the Village of Euclid enacted its zoning ordinance, did the village face an externality problem? If so, what externality problem was the ordinance designed to address? The Court refers repeatedly to the law of nuisance. Is a zoning code enacted in advance by a legislative body a better way of dealing with externalities than the common law of nuisance? Do you agree with the Court that the increased complexity of modern cities necessitates a new approach to land use governance?

2.   Do you think the ordinance enacted by the village maximized land values within the village's borders? Why or why not? If the ordinance did not maximize land values, why would the village enact it? Who do you think supported an ordinance that would diminish the value of land within the village?

3.   The Court says that "[i]f the validity of the legislative classification for zoning purposes be fairly debatable, the legislative judgment must be allowed to control." Is the Court right to defer so strongly to the expertise of the village government in enacting the zoning code? Why or why not? For further discussion, see Chapter Six, Section II.

4.   Note the emphasis the Court places on Euclid's status as an autonomous municipality, notwithstanding the fact that it is, in effect, part of the greater Cleveland community. In light of Euclid's connections to (dependence on?) Cleveland, does it make sense for the Court to defer so strongly to Euclid's status as an independent municipal entity? What obligations (if any) do Euclid's decisionmakers have towards neighboring municipalities and towards the metropolitan area as a whole? By diverting industrial development outside of Euclid, is the village shirking those obligations? The Court says that it does not mean to "exclude the possibility of cases where the general public interest would so far outweigh the interest of the municipality that the municipality would not be allowed to stand in the way." It obviously thinks this is not such a case. Can you imagine a scenario in which the public interest would outweigh the municipality's own decisions about what land uses to allow? For further discussion of these issues, see Chapter Nine, Section II.

5.   The Village of Euclid's zoning scheme was "cumulative": only one use was permitted in a U–1 district; the U–2 district permitted all of the uses in a U–1 district, but added new permitted uses. Similarly, the U–6 district permitted all of the uses authorized in U–5 districts, together with additional uses. As a result, an owner of land in a U–6 district, which permitted industrial uses, would have been permitted to build a single-family residence in that district. Given the likely conflict between single-family residences and industrial uses, why would the ordinance have permitted such a use? Can you imagine why a lawyer for the village might have advised the village to adopt a cumulative zoning ordinance?

Consider the rationale the court offered for sustaining the zoning ordinance. Would the rationale have justified excluding residential uses from U–6 districts? Why or why not?

6.   The village zoned some of Ambler's land U–2 and U–3 even though the land was adjacent to the railroad. Was that land well-suited for residential use? For industrial use? Why did the village prohibit industrial use in the area?

7.   As the opinion notes, Ambler Realty contended that the ordinance significantly reduced the value of its land. Did Ambler challenge the application of the ordinance to its own parcel? Do you think such a challenge would have met with more success? Note that in Nectow v. City of Cambridge, 277 U.S. 183 (1928), decided only two years after *Euclid*, the landowner prevailed on such an "as applied challenge."

What reasons might the lawyer for Ambler Realty have had for neglecting to advance an "as applied" challenge to the village's ordinance?

8.   Suppose a municipal official (from someplace other than Euclid) approached you in 1930. The official wanted help in drafting a zoning ordinance for his municipality, and had been told by a planner that it made no sense to permit residential uses in industrial zones. The municipal official agreed with the planner, and has asked you whether there is any reason not to provide strict segregation between residential and industrial uses. How would you respond? Does your answer explain why so many ordinances across the country resemble the ordinance in *Euclid* (hence the name "Euclidean zoning," which has nothing to do with Euclidean geometry)?

9.   The Court observes a conflict between single-family dwellings and apartment houses, which it says come close to being nuisances. Do you agree with its assessment? The Court also refers repeatedly to the interests of children in the separation of uses, and even of housing types. What sorts of land use systems are best for children and families? The kinds of stand-alone neighborhoods of single-family dwellings envisioned by the Euclid zoning ordinance and the Supreme Court—or the sorts of dense, mixed-use neighborhoods praised by Jane Jacobs in the excerpt above? Even if the Court is right about what is best for the children who can afford to live in a detached single-family home, what about the interests of those children whose parents can only afford to live in a rented apartment? Does the separation of uses benefit them? Does the village have an obligation to look out for their interests as well? Should the village be permitted to exclude apartments altogether? For further discussion, see Chapter Nine, Section II.

CHAPTER TWO

ZONING BASICS

I. THE ZONING ENABLING ACT

In the United States, zoning is principally the province of municipalities. The local power to zone, however, was not always uncontested. "Dillon's rule," articulated by a 19th century Iowa Supreme Court justice, held that local governments had only those powers expressly granted to them by state statute or state constitution. Today, many states have reversed Dillon's rule, and have granted "home rule," enabling municipalities to exercise the powers of government even without specific state statutory or constitutional authority. But the practice of zoning developed at a time when Dillon's rule remained an important constraint on local government. As a result, early efforts by some municipalities to enact zoning ordinances were thwarted when courts concluded that the state had not conferred zoning power on the municipality.

In response, virtually every state has enacted one or more zoning enabling acts. These statutes confer on localities the power to zone. Even in home rule states, zoning ordinances may not conflict with the terms of the enabling act.

II. THE ZONING ORDINANCE OR ITS EQUIVALENT

In the vast majority of jurisdictions, the locality's legislative body enacts the local zoning ordinance. That body may have a variety of different names—city council, board of trustees, board of aldermen, etc.—but it is almost invariably an elected body. Of course, the legislative body will typically have help in drafting the ordinance. The local legislature might appoint a zoning or planning commission to serve in an advisory capacity, and may also engage consultants for advice about zoning matters. In a small minority of jurisdictions, the zoning commission or planning and zoning commission has the power to enact the local zoning ordinance. Many cities and towns in Connecticut, for example, have appointed or elected commissions that serve as the final authority on the zoning law. In such cases, the zoning law takes the form of regulations rather than ordinances, although for ease of reference, this casebook usually refers to all zoning laws as zoning ordinances.

The typical zoning ordinance includes a number of standard features. First, the ordinance creates a variety of zoning districts, and lists the permitted uses in each of those districts. Second, the ordinance incorporates a map of the municipality. The map correlates each parcel of land with one of the zoning districts. Third, the ordinance includes provisions regulating enforcement of the ordinance.

A. DIVISION INTO DISTRICTS

Like the ordinance at issue in *Village of Euclid v. Ambler Realty*, supra p. 12, most zoning ordinances impose restrictions on use, area, and height of buildings within municipal borders.

1. USE RESTRICTIONS

Traditional ordinances separated residential, commercial, and industrial uses. Although mixed-use districts have become more common in recent years, separation remains the norm, despite growing criticism. For an argument that separation of residential from commercial uses places particularly significant hurdles in front of African-American entrepreneurs, *see* Stephen Clowney, Invisible Businessman: Undermining Black Enterprise with Land Use Rules, 2009 U. Ill. L. Rev. 1061 (2009).

A municipality may have several different residential districts, some permitting only single-family houses, others permitting two-family houses, and others permitting apartment buildings of different size and organization. Similarly, the municipality may have several different commercial and industrial districts. For instance, the municipality may want to keep fast-food restaurants out of downtown, but may zone another area to permit those restaurants.

2. AREA & BULK RESTRICTIONS

Within a residential district, a municipality may have concerns about the density of development. In order to preserve open space, to avoid congestion, or to limit demands on municipal infrastructure, the zoning ordinance will typically include provisions that limit the number and arrangement of homes in the area. These limitations take a number of forms. Among the most common are minimum lot size requirements, together with minimum frontage and setback requirements.

Traditional setback requirements in effect mark off a rectangle in which homeowners or builders could build their home. For instance, if the zoning district permitted single-family homes on lots with a minimum frontage of 60 feet, a minimum depth of 100 feet, a 25-foot front yard setback, a 35-foot rear yard setback, and 8 and 10-foot side yard setbacks, the builder could locate a home anywhere within a rectangle 42 feet wide and 40 feet deep.

Many municipalities have enacted additional restrictions to ensure that the bulk of a building is proportional to the existing fabric. First, floor area ratios ("FARs") limit the total square footage a builder can build on a particular lot. For instance, on a 6,000 square-foot parcel, a FAR of .5 means that the builder cannot build a home larger than 3,000 square feet. Second, some municipalities have enacted maximum lot coverage provisions, limiting the percentage of the lot that may be covered with improvements.

Area and bulk restrictions are not limited to residential districts. FARs have become common in commercial and industrial districts, and zoning ordinances may also require other forms of restrictions; for instance, an ordinance might require that the developer set aside some number of parking spaces for each square foot of commercial or industrial space.

3.   HEIGHT RESTRICTIONS

To preserve light, air, and view, most municipalities also impose height limitations on buildings within each zoning district. Building height restrictions may limit the number of stories a building may have, or may limit the number of feet from the ground, or, in most cases, both. Additional height restrictions may be placed on accessory structures, such as rooftop solar collectors, or architectural features, such as turrets.

PROBLEMS

For each of the following problems, assume the schedule of minimum requirements set forth on page 26 is in effect.

1. Landowner owns a lot measuring 60 feet wide and 100 feet deep fronting on a street in an R–6 zoning district. Landowner wants to build a rectangular house on the lot. Which of the following houses would the zoning restrictions permit? For those houses permitted by the ordinance, what restrictions are there on where the landowner can locate the house?

    a.   A single-story house measuring 44 feet wide and 40 feet deep.

    b.   A single-story house measuring 40 feet wide and 55 feet deep.

    c.   A two-story house measuring 30 feet wide and 60 feet deep.

    d.   A two-story house measuring 30 feet wide and 50 feet deep.

    e.   A single-story house measuring 40 feet wide and 25 feet deep.

2. Landowner owns a parcel measuring 120 feet wide and 200 feet deep in an RM–3 zoning district. Landowner wants the answer to two questions:

    a.   What is the maximum number of apartments she can build on the parcel?

    b.   What is the maximum number of square feet she can include in the building (assume the building is not on a "wide street")?

District	Min Lot Area (sq ft)	Min Lot Width/ Frontage (ft)	Min Lot Depth (ft)	Min Habitable Floor Area (sq ft)	Max Height of Principal Bldg		Min Required Yards				Max Coverage All Buildings (% lot area)	Max Floor Area Ratio
					Stories	Ft	Front (ft)	Lesser Side (ft)	2 Sides Combined (ft)	Rear (ft)		
R-20 1-Fam	20,000	100	100	2-story: 1,800; 1-story: 1,650	2.5	35	25	20	45	10	35%	0.30
R-15 1-Fam	15,000	100	100	2-story: 1,800; 1-story: 1,650	2.5	35	25	15	35	30	35%	0.35
R-10 1-Fam	10,000	100	100	2-story: 1,600; 1-story: 1,400	2.5	35	25	10	25	30	35%	0.40
R-6 1-Fam	6,000	60	100	2-story: 1,500; 1-story: 1,300	2.5	35	20	8	18	25	35%	0.50
R-2F 1/2-Fam	3,750/dwelling unit	75	100	Each dwelling unit: 900	2.5	35	20	6	16	25	35%	0.65
RM-1 Multi-Unit	40,000 but not less than 2,500/dwelling unit	150	150		2.5	35	40	30	60	25	25%	0.50
RM-2 Multi-Unit	20,000 but not less than 1,500/dwelling unit	150	150		3 (3.5 on wide streets)	40	25	25	50	25	30%	0.80
RM-3 Multi-Unit	20,000 but not less than 1,000/dwelling unit	100	130		4 (4.5 on wide streets)	50	25	25	50	30	35%	1.20

B. THE ZONING MAP

The zoning map correlates each parcel in the municipality with one of the districts created in the ordinance. Sometimes, a zoning map is a mishmash of colors, with multiple districts coexisting on the same block—a telltale sign that the zoning ordinance was passed after a city was already developed. Other times, the zoning map appears to be the result of an orderly process—a sign that the city may have been a planned community, with zoning restrictions anticipated at the outset.

Below is a sample of a zoning map of Mamaroneck, a town on Long Island Sound, just outside of New York City, which was founded in 1788:

Village of Mamaroneck Zoning Map

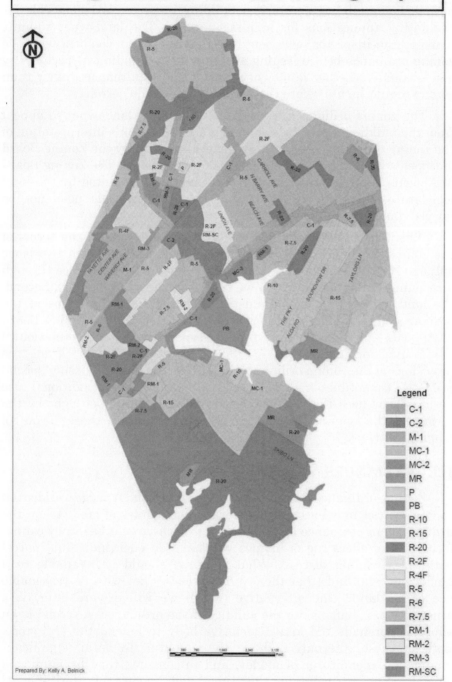

Legend

- C-1
- C-2
- M-1
- MC-1
- MC-2
- MR
- P
- PB
- R-10
- R-15
- R-20
- R-2F
- R-4F
- R-5
- R-6
- R-7.5
- RM-1
- RM-2
- RM-3
- RM-SC

Prepared By: Kelly A. Belnick

C. ADMINISTRATIVE PROVISIONS

Suppose a landowner owns a parcel and wants to build a building that she believes conforms with the zoning ordinance. Can the landowner simply build the building? In general, the answer is no. The zoning ordinance will typically require landowner to obtain a building permit. Generally, the municipal building inspector is responsible for evaluating applications for building permits. The landowner submits plans to the inspector, who confirms that the plans conform with the zoning ordinance before issuing a permit. (The building inspector may also evaluate whether landowner must meet requirements other than zoning requirements before the inspector issues the permit).

The zoning ordinance will typically permit a landowner to appeal from the building inspector's or zoning administrator's interpretation of the zoning ordinance. Appeals are generally heard by the Zoning Board of Appeals (sometimes called a Board of Adjustment). The Zoning Board of Appeals is an administrative body, generally appointed by the local legislature. Members of the Zoning Board of Appeals need not be lawyers (and generally are not).

When the landowner's project does not comply with the terms of the zoning ordinance, the ordinance leaves landowner with two basic options. First, the landowner can seek to amend the ordinance through a rezoning (an option to which we return in the next chapter). Second, the landowner can seek administrative relief from the terms of the ordinance. The zoning ordinance typically confers on the Zoning Board of Appeals—the same body typically responsible for interpretation of the zoning ordinance—the power to issue "variances" from the provisions of the zoning ordinance, as well as the power to issue "special permits" (sometimes called "special exceptions" or "conditional use permits") for uses that are not permitted as a matter of right by the terms of the zoning ordinance. We now examine these forms of administrative relief.

III. Variances

Zoning ordinances paint with a broad brush. A large residential zoning district may encompass several square miles of land. When the drafters of an ordinance attempt to cover such large areas, they cannot focus on the effect the ordinance will have on each individual parcel within the zoning district. What recourse should be available to a landowner who finds that the ordinance leaves her with no reasonable use of his land? One alternative (which we will explore later) is a constitutional challenge to the validity of the ordinance. A second is an effort to persuade the local legislative body to amend the ordinance. Both of these alternatives have the potential to entail significant municipal expenditures of money, and to consume time by municipal officials (not to mention the time and money of the affected landowners).

In an effort to avoid these two alternatives, the drafters of early zoning ordinances provided an administrative "safety valve." A landowner whose project does not strictly comply with the provisions of the zoning ordinance can bypass both litigation and legislation in favor of administrative relief: the landowner can apply to the Zoning Board of Appeals for a variance from the terms of the ordinance. Variances come in two varieties, corresponding to the two broad ways in which zoning codes regulate land use: use variances, which exempt a particular parcel from a regulation of the sorts of uses permitted on the land, and area variances, which exempt a particular parcel from some part of the zoning code's spatial regulation. But what restrictions are there on the power of the Zoning Board of Appeals to grant a variance? And what are the differences in the law's treatment of use variances and area variances? Consider the following case:

Sasso v. Osgood

New York Court of Appeals, 1995
86 N.Y.2d 374, 657 N.E.2d 254, 633 N.Y.S.2d 259

■ SIMONS, J.

This appeal requires us to interpret the provisions of recently enacted Town Law § 267–b(3) regulating area variances. Specifically, the question is whether the provisions of the statute are exclusive or whether an applicant for an area variance must make a showing of "practical difficulties." The Appellate Division came to the latter conclusion that, the provisions of the statute notwithstanding, an applicant must show "practical difficulties" before being entitled to an area variance. We disagree, and reverse the order of that Court.

I

In 1989, intervenor Gerald Speach purchased a waterfront parcel of land situated on Graham's Creek, a man-made canal in the Town of Henderson. The creek is located on the eastern end of Lake Ontario near the mouth of the St. Lawrence River and is lined with commercial and private boathouses. Speach's property, undeveloped but for an existing single slip boathouse, is located within a "lakefront district" as designated by local ordinances adopted in 1991 and is a "special permit" use. It has an area of 5,200 square feet and is approximately 50 feet wide along the road that is its northern border and 72 feet wide at the waterfront. The Town of Henderson zoning ordinances require a minimum lot area of 12,000 square feet and minimum lot width of 100 feet. Thus Speach's property is substandard in both area and width.

In 1990, Speach applied to the Town of Henderson Zoning Board of Appeals for area variances to allow him to demolish the existing structure and build a larger boathouse. At that time, the local ordinances required a minimum lot size of 7,500 square feet. Petitioners Sasso and Edney, who own adjacent lots developed with boathouses and residences, objected to the application. They contended that Speach's proposed boathouse would obstruct their access to light, air and view, and that the foundations of their structures and their septic systems would be damaged by construction and altered water drainage patterns. The Zoning Board granted the variances, and petitioners commenced a CPLR article 78 proceeding to annul that determination. Supreme Court dismissed the petition, but on appeal, the Appellate Division reversed and granted it. The Appellate Division determined that Speach had failed to demonstrate "practical difficulties sufficient to justify an area variance" primarily because he had not shown that "'strict enforcement of the [zoning] ordinance will cause him a significant economic injury'" (Matter of Sasso v. Gamble, 181 A.D.2d 988).

In 1993, Speach submitted a new application for area variances to the Zoning Board based on changed circumstances since his 1990 application. Speach had altered the design of the boathouse and its method of construction to address the concerns of petitioners, and he argued that local redistricting of the property in 1991 supported his application. Speach also relied on newly enacted Town Law § 267–b(3) which, he contended, no longer required him to show economic hardship or practical difficulties. Applying the criteria set forth in the new statute, the Zoning Board granted Speach's application for a variance. Supreme Court denied petitioners' ensuing article 78 petition to annul the determination of the Zoning Board, but on appeal to the Appellate Division, that Court annulled the determination of the Zoning Board and granted the petition. The Court noted that the standards for granting area variances under the former test of practical difficulties and the new statutory criteria are not appreciably different, and held that "an applicant still must demonstrate that strict compliance with the zoning ordinance will result in practical difficulties" (Matter of Sasso v. Osgood, 206 A.D.2d 837, 838). We granted intervenor's motion for leave to appeal to this Court.

II

Prior to July 1, 1992, the authority of Town Zoning Boards of Appeal to grant variances from local zoning ordinances was defined in Town Law former § 267. The boards were authorized to grant variances "[w]here there are practical difficulties or unnecessary hardships in the way of carrying out the strict letter of [local] ordinances" provided that "the spirit of the ordinance shall be observed, public safety and welfare secured and substantial justice done" (Town Law former § 267[5]). Although the former statute did not distinguish between "use" and "area" variances or assign the specific tests to them, court decisions generally applied the "unnecessary hardship" test in use variance cases, while requiring a demonstration of "practical difficulties" in area variance cases (see, Matter of Village of Bronxville v. Francis, 1 A.D.2d 236, 238, aff'd 1 N.Y.2d 839; see also, Matter of Hoffman v. Harris, 17 N.Y.2d 138, 144; Dauernheim, Inc. v. Town Bd., 33 N.Y.2d 468, 471; Matter of Off Shore Rest. Corp. v. Linden, 30 N.Y.2d 160, 168).

A three-pronged test of "unnecessary hardship" was clearly articulated more than 50 years ago (see, Matter of Otto v. Steinhilber, 282 N.Y. 71, 76) and that test, now embodied in Town Law § 267–b(2), has been applied in use variance cases without substantial difficulty (see, e.g., Matter of Village Bd. v. Jarrold, 53 N.Y.2d 254; see also, Holy Sepulchre Cemetery v. Board of Appeals, 271 App. Div. 33; Matter of Fasani v. Rappaport, 30 A.D.2d 588; Matter of Swartz v. Wallace, 87 A.D.2d 926; Matter of Varley v. Zoning Bd. of Appeals, 131 A.D.2d 905; Matter of Dwyer v. Polsinello, 160 A.D.2d 1056; Matter of Drake v. Zoning Bd. of Appeals, 183 A.D.2d 1031). The definition and application of the "practical difficulties standard" has proven far more troublesome.

Lacking a statutory definition, we have recognized the existence of "practical difficulties" where the unusual topography of the subject parcel interfered with construction of a building (see, Matter of Wilcox v. Zoning Bd. of Appeals, 17 N.Y.2d 249, 255), and where area variances were required to build a house on an amply sized but oddly shaped parcel that did not meet frontage and side yard requirements (Conley v. Town of Brookhaven Zoning Bd. of Appeals, 40 N.Y.2d 309, 316). We have also suggested that an area variance could be granted upon a showing of "significant economic injury" (Matter of Fulling v. Palumbo, 21 N.Y.2d 30, 33; see also, Matter of Cowan v. Kern, 41 N.Y.2d 591, 596). In Matter of National Merritt v. Weist (41 N.Y.2d 438) we considered both unique topography and economic injury relevant to the application for an area variance. These cases are only illustrative. We have noted several times that there is no precise definition of the term "practical difficulties" (Matter of Doyle v. Amster, 79 N.Y.2d 592, 595; Matter of Fuhst v. Foley, 45 N.Y.2d 441, 445), observing that "[t]he basic inquiry at all times is whether strict application of the ordinance in a given case will serve a valid public purpose which outweighs the injury to the property owner" (Matter of De Sena v. Board of Zoning Appeals, 45 N.Y.2d 105, 108).

Without any legislative guidance defining the requirements for an area variance, the courts began to develop a list of considerations to be applied under Town Law former § 267 (see, Matter of Wachsberger v. Michalis, 19 Misc. 2d 909, aff'd 18 A.D.2d 921; see also, Matter of Friendly Ice Cream Corp. v. Barrett, 106 A.D.2d 748; Human Dev. Servs. v. Zoning Bd. of Appeals, 110 A.D.2d 135, aff'd 67 N.Y.2d 702). Although originally offered as guidance for determining whether "the spirit of the ordinance [is] observed, public safety and welfare secured and substantial justice done" (see, Matter of Wachsberger v. Michalis, 19 Misc. 2d, at 912 [Meyer, J.], *supra*), these criteria came to be known as the "practical difficulties" test (*see,* 2 Anderson, New York Zoning Law and Practice § 23.34, at 208–209 [3d ed.]). The criteria notwithstanding, however, precise and concise definition of "practical difficulties" never emerged from the case law. In particular, it remained unclear whether a showing of "significant economic injury" was part of the "practical difficulties" test (see, e.g., Matter of Doyle v. Amster, 79 N.Y.2d 592, *supra*; Matter of Orchard Michael, Inc. v. Falcon, 65 N.Y.2d 1007; Matter of Children's Hosp. v. Zoning Bd. of Appeals, 181 A.D.2d 1056; Matter of Stengel v. Town of Woodstock Zoning Bd. of Appeals, 155 A.D.2d 854; Matter of Salierno v. Briggs, 141 A.D.2d 547).

Effective July 1, 1992, the Legislature repealed former section 267 of the Town Law, and enacted comprehensive provisions governing Zoning Boards of Appeals (L. 1991, ch. 692). Unlike the former section 267, the new statute defines "use" and "area" variances, as well as the criteria to be evaluated in determining applications for each. Use variances may be granted upon an applicant's showing "that applicable zoning regulations and restrictions have caused unnecessary hardship," expressly incorporating that phrase as it existed in former section 267 of the Town Law. The statute defines the elements of proof necessary to establish unnecessary hardship, essentially codifying the criteria originally set forth in Matter of Otto v. Steinhilber (282 N.Y. 71, 76, *supra*), with the added requirement that the applicant prove that "the alleged hardship has not been self-created" (Town Law § 267–b[2][b][4]).

The standard for area variances is contained in section 267–b(3) of the Town Law in a provision that does not expressly require the applicant to prove "practical difficulties." It states:

> In making its determination [whether to grant an area variance], the zoning board of appeals shall take into consideration *the benefit to the applicant if the variance is granted, as weighed against the detriment to the health, safety and welfare of the neighborhood or community by such grant*. In making such determination the board shall also consider: (1) whether an undesirable change will be produced in the character of the neighborhood or a detriment to nearby properties will be created by the granting of the area variance; (2) whether the benefit sought by the applicant can be achieved by some other method, feasible for the applicant to pursue, other than an area variance; (3) whether the requested area variance is substantial; (4) whether the proposed variance will have an adverse effect or impact on the physical or environmental conditions in the neighborhood or district; and (5) whether the alleged difficulty was self-created, which consideration shall be relevant to the decision of the board of appeals, but shall not necessarily preclude the granting of the area variance.

(Town Law § 267–b[3][b] [emphasis added].)

The five factors listed parallel the criteria previously used by the lower courts and identified by Professor Anderson as the "practical difficulties" test (2 Anderson, New York Zoning Law and Practice § 23.34, *op. cit.*; see, e.g., Matter of Friendly Ice Cream Corp. v. Barrett,

106 A.D.2d 748, *supra*; Human Dev. Servs. v. Zoning Bd. of Appeals, 110 A.D.2d 135, *supra;* Matter of Wachsberger v. Michalis, 19 Misc. 2d 909, aff'd 18 A.D.2d 921, *supra*).

III

The precise question posed on this appeal is whether by failing to include the phrase "practical difficulties" in the new statute, the Legislature has eliminated the requirement that the applicant for an area variance make that showing.

Intervenor Speach argues that the court may look only to the plain and unambiguous language of the statute when construing it (see, Sega v. State of New York, 60 N.Y.2d 183, 190–191). He asserts that while Town Law former § 267 required a showing of practical difficulties or unnecessary hardship before an area or use variance was granted, the new statute incorporates only unnecessary hardship for use variances (Town Law § 256–b[2]) and fails to incorporate the old practical difficulties standard in subdivision (3), the provision which now regulates area variances. Thus, he maintains, a showing of "practical difficulties" is not an element of an application for an area variance. Notwithstanding the absence of any explicit reference to "practical difficulties" in Town Law § 267–b(3), however, the subdivision is ambiguous because it requires the Zoning Board to consider whether "the alleged *difficulty* was self-created" (Town Law § 267–b[3][b][5] [emphasis added]). Accordingly, we must examine the Legislature's intent in amending the statute.

Reference to the Bill Jacket for chapter 692 of the Laws of 1991 supports intervenor's contention that an applicant for an area variance need not show "practical difficulties" as required under Town Law former § 267 and prior case law. Documents in the Bill Jacket make clear that the statute was enacted to clarify existing law by setting forth readily understandable guidelines for both Zoning Boards of Appeal and applicants for variances and to eliminate the confusion that then surrounded applications for area variances. Thus one memorandum states:

> The rules governing the granting of area variances that have been established by the courts are not nearly as clear as those governing use variances, and the result has been a great deal of confusion by boards of appeals, with a high degree of potential exposure to litigation. The new Town Law, section 267–b(3) and Village Law, section 7–712–b(3) resolve this problem by establishing a statutory test for the issuance of area variances which is flexible and which incorporates what we believe are the best features of the court decisions in order to protect the community.

(Bill Jacket, L. 1991, ch. 692, at 26, Mem. of Executive Deputy Secretary of State James Baldwin).

The same intent may be found in several other memoranda and establish that the legislation was enacted to aid laypersons—both applicants and lay members of Zoning Boards of Appeal—in understanding and implementing the existing case law; it was intended to have "little impact on existing laws since the main thrust of the legislation is to clarify and establish, in statute, the powers of the Zoning Board as already defined by jurisprudence."

We conclude Town Law § 267–b(3)(b) requires the Zoning Board to engage in a balancing test, weighing "the benefit to the applicant" against "the detriment to the health, safety and welfare of the neighborhood or community" if the area variance is granted, and that an applicant need not show "practical difficulties" as that test was formerly applied.

IV

Applying the new statute we conclude that the action of the Henderson Zoning Board was rational and not arbitrary and capricious (see, Matter of Cowan v. Kern, 41 N.Y.2d 591, 599, *supra*; McGowan v. Cohalan, 41 N.Y.2d 434, 438). As required by Town Law § 267–b(3)(b), the Zoning Board addressed five specific criteria. First, it determined that no undesirable change would be produced in the character of the neighborhood, because Graham's Creek serves primarily as a site for boathouses and commercial marinas, and that the addition of intervenor's proposed three-slip boathouse will not result in a significant increase in boat traffic or noise. The Zoning Board's conclusion that the variance will have minimal impact on nearby properties is supported by evidence that intervenor's boathouse will comply with all setback and height restrictions imposed by local ordinances. In making this finding, the Board had before it and considered the conditions imposed on intervenor's construction by the Town Planning Board which mitigated concerns voiced by petitioners (see, Town Law § 267–b[3][b][1]).

Next, the Zoning Board concluded that no alternatives other than the grant of area variances existed, because intervenor's lot is of substandard size, and *no* improvement to the property could be made without the requested lot size and width variances (*id.*, subd. [3][b][2]). The Zoning Board then acknowledged that the variances sought were substantial, but that there was no available adjacent land for intervenor to purchase so that he could meet the zoning requirements, and granting the variances would merely permit intervenor to use his property for a permitted use equal to all other neighboring lots (*id.*, subd. [3][b][3]). The Zoning Board's conclusion under subdivision (3)(b)(4) that granting the variances would lead to no adverse effect or impact on the neighborhood other than the previously discussed effect on petitioners is also supported by the record.

The only determination of the Zoning Board not supported by the record is its conclusion that intervenor's difficulty was not self-created.

The record reveals that the parcel was of substandard lot size when intervenor purchased it in 1989 and it is well established that, in such circumstances, the variance applicant's difficulty or hardship is self-created (see, Matter of Doyle v. Amster, 79 N.Y.2d 592, 597, *supra*; Conley v. Town of Brookhaven Zoning Bd. of Appeals, 40 N.Y.2d 309, 315, *supra*). Nevertheless, the statute expressly states that the fact that the applicant's difficulty was self-created does not necessarily preclude the granting of the area variance (Town Law § 267–b[3][b][5]). Under all the circumstances presented, the Board did not act arbitrarily in granting a variance notwithstanding the applicant's self-created difficulty.

In sum, the Zoning Board weighed the benefit to intervenor—the opportunity to fully use his property for a permitted use—against any detriment to the health, safety and welfare of the neighborhood or community, and determined to grant the variance. Its conclusions find ample support from the photographs and other materials in the record, and its determination was not irrational, arbitrary or capricious. Thus, the Appellate Division erred in reversing the order of Supreme Court confirming the determination.

Accordingly, the order of the Appellate Division should be reversed, with costs to intervenor against petitioners, and the judgment of Supreme Court, Jefferson County, reinstated.

■ CHIEF JUDGE KAYE and JUDGES TITONE, BELLACOSA, SMITH, LEVINE and CIPARICK concur.

NOTES AND QUESTIONS

1. How did this case get to court? Who brought the proceeding? Against whom? On what ground?

2. Does the Court of Appeals hold that the Zoning Board of Appeals was obligated to grant a variance to Speach? If the ZBA had denied Speach a variance, concluding that the boathouse would increase traffic and noise, and noting that the variance from the terms of the ordinance was substantial, would the Court of Appeals have overturned the denial of the variance?

3. Suppose Speach had sought to build a "boatel" on his land (three boat slips, with rooms above the slips for the boaters to sleep). What kind of variance would Speach have needed? Suppose Speach offered the same evidence before the ZBA as he offered in the *Sasso* case. If the ZBA had granted a variance, could the neighbors have succeeded in having it overturned? If the ZBA had denied a variance, could Speach have succeeded in having it overturned?

The applicable New York statute is as follows:

N.Y. TOWN LAW SEC. 267–b

2.   Use variances.

(a) The board of appeals, on appeal from the decision or determination of the administrative official charged with the enforcement of such ordinance or local law, shall have the power to grant use variances, as defined herein.

(b) No such use variance shall be granted by a board of appeals without a showing by the applicant that applicable zoning regulations and restrictions have caused unnecessary hardship. In order to prove such unnecessary hardship the applicant shall demonstrate to the board of appeals that for each and every permitted use under the zoning regulations for the particular district where the property is located, (1) the applicant cannot realize a reasonable return, provided that lack of return is substantial as demonstrated by competent financial evidence; (2) that the alleged hardship relating to the property in question is unique, and does not apply to a substantial portion of the district or neighborhood; (3) that the requested use variance, if granted, will not alter the essential character of the neighborhood; and (4) that the alleged hardship has not been self-created.

(c) The board of appeals, in the granting of use variances, shall grant the minimum variance that it shall deem necessary and adequate to address the unnecessary hardship proven by the applicant, and at the same time preserve and protect the character of the neighborhood and the health, safety and welfare of the community.

4.   Suppose Speach were seeking to build a boatel, and could prove that he could not recover a positive return on the cost of constructing any improvement permitted on his parcel under the existing ordinance. If the ZBA were to grant him a use variance, would the neighbors be successful in challenging the variance? Would the neighbors' challenge have a better chance of success, or a weaker chance, if the rest of the area faced the same difficulties that led Speach to seek the variance? *See* Osborne M. Reynolds, Jr., The "Unique Circumstances" Rule in Zoning Variances—An Aid in Achieving Greater Prudence and Less Leniency, 31 Urb. Law. 127 (1999).

Suppose the ZBA were to deny Speach a use variance for construction of a boatel. Would Speach be successful in challenging the denial?

5.   Why would the New York legislature reject application of use variance standards to cases involving area variances? Why should Speach be entitled to an area variance even without proving that compliance with the ordinance would cause hardship? Consider the following:

Use variances by their nature have the potential to bring about great changes in neighborhood character, but area variances usually do not have this effect. While area variances provide an increment of relief (normally small) from a physical dimensional restriction such as building height, setback, and so forth, use variances permit wholesale deviation from the way in which land in the zone is used. Accordingly, the measure of unnecessary hardship for use and area variances is different.

Ziervogel v. Washington County Bd. of Adjustment, 269 Wis.2d 549, 563–64, 676 N.W.2d 401, 408 (2004). Are you persuaded? Note that many jurisdictions, unlike New York, continue to require an applicant to prove some modicum of hardship as a prerequisite for obtaining an area variance. *See, e.g.,* Kans. Stat. Ann. § 12–759(e)(1)(C).

6. *Use Variance or Area Variance?* Statutes and cases mandate different standards for area variances and use variances. In most cases, there is little dispute about what type of variance a landowner needs. On the margins, however, disputes may arise about what kind of variance is at issue (and therefore, about what standard applies). In the following circumstances, what kind of variance does landowner need?

   a.   Landowner, who owns a gas station, wants to post a sign identifying the brand of gasoline on a pole visible from neighboring streets. The local ordinance prohibits pole signs. *See* City of Olathe v. Bd. of Zoning Appeals, 10 Kan.App.2d 218, 696 P.2d 409 (1985).

   b.   Landowner wants to convert an existing building to restaurant use. Restaurants are permitted uses within the zoning district, but only if they provide off-street parking for patrons. Landowner's parcel has no room for off-street parking. *See* Colin Realty Co, LLC v. Town of North Hempstead, 24 N.Y.3d 96, 21 N.E.3d 188 (2014).

Would the following definitions, drawn from the New York statute, resolve these questions?

   (a)   "Use variance" shall mean the authorization by the zoning board of appeals for the use of land for a purpose which is otherwise not allowed or is prohibited by the applicable zoning regulations.

   (b)   "Area variance" shall mean the authorization by the zoning board of appeals for the use of land in a manner which is not allowed by the dimensional or physical requirements of the applicable zoning regulations.

7.   Two neighbors, Sasso and Edney, appeared at a public hearing to object to Speach's variance application. The ZBA granted the variance over their objections. Would the ZBA have made the decision if ten neighbors had objected? Should the strength of the opposition matter in evaluating a variance application, or should the ZBA dispassionately evaluate the statutory factors without regard to that opposition? Consider the conclusions accompanying a survey of variance practices in Wisconsin:

   If four or more persons appear at the ZBA variance hearing in person or in writing objecting to the application, then the variance is always denied. The objectors don't have to be neighbors. They can live across town. There were only one or two exceptions to this rule in 85 communities over four years. . . . On the other hand, having fewer than four people appear at the hearing and object to the variance does not guarantee that the variance will be granted. As the survey concludes, "If three or fewer objectors appear at a ZBA variance application hearing, there is no rhyme or reason whether a variance application is or is not granted."

Alan R. Madry, Judging Ziervogel: The Twisted Path of Recent Zoning Variance Decisions in Wisconsin, 91 Marq. L. Rev. 485 (2007) (quoting study; footnotes omitted). What does the survey suggest about how a lawyer for a landowner should proceed when applying for a variance? A lawyer for objecting neighbors?

Land use lawyers must always keep two objectives in mind: how do I persuade local decision-makers to provide my client with the relief she needs, and how do I pave the way for obtaining judicial relief if I fail to persuade those local decision-makers? The first objective is often the more important one. See Craig Anthony Arnold, The Structure of the Land Use Regulatory System in the United States, 22 J. Land Use & Envtl. L. 441, 492 (2007):

> The real "law" of land use regulation exists mostly in zoning codes and regulatory procedures, as well as in the actions or decisions of local land use regulatory bodies. Consider all the planning, zoning, and regulatory permitting decisions (e.g., conditional use permits, variances, subdivision maps or plats, site plans, planned unit developments, development agreements) that are made every week throughout the year, in comparison to the number of reported judicial opinions or even lawsuits that are resolved by the courts on the merits on land use issues in any given year. For example, in 2000, the Anaheim (California) Planning Commission considered and made one or more decisions (in many cases multiple decisions) on 225 land use projects. In the same year, no reported judicial opinions addressed land use issues in Anaheim.

8.   Suppose Speach had built a boatel on his land without obtaining a variance or a building permit. Suppose he then sought a variance to legalize the boatel, contending that without the variance, he would suffer hardship—loss of his investment in the boatel. If the ZBA were to grant a variance, would the neighbors succeed in upsetting the grant of the variance? What ground would they advance?

Suppose instead that Speach had built his three-slip boathouse without obtaining a variance (in violation of the minimum lot size requirement in the ordinance). If he then sought a variance to legalize the boathouse, and the ZBA granted the variance, would the neighbors succeed in upsetting the grant of the variance? How, if at all, are the cases different?

9.   Suppose Speach had bought the parcel knowing that a boathouse, by itself, would not generate a return on construction costs, let alone on the price of the land. If the ZBA granted a use variance to permit construction

of a boatel, would the neighbors succeed in challenging the variance on the ground that any hardship was self-created? Why or why not?

10. Variance standards are not consistent from state to state. In Virginia, for instance, the state supreme court has held that a zoning board of appeals may only grant a variance when strict application of the ordinance to the landowner's parcel would effect an unconstitutional taking. Cochran v. Fairfax County Bd. of Zoning Appeals, 267 Va. 756, 594 S.E.2d 571 (2004).

11. *Fees.* Applying for variances and other development permits is not free. Although members of the Zoning Board of Appeals will typically be unpaid volunteers, municipal employees receive and process applications, and planning consultants may provide professional guidance to the municipality. Most municipalities attempt to recover some of the costs by imposing fees on applicants. The fees differ markedly among jurisdictions, and vary depending on the nature of the application. For an argument that application fees create daunting barriers for black firms, *see* Stephen Clowney, Invisible Businessman: Undermining Black Enterprise with Land Use Rules, 2009 U. Ill. L. Rev. 1061, 1075 (2009).

IV. TOOLS FOR INCREASING THE FLEXIBILITY OF ZONING ORDINANCES

As one court has put it, traditional Euclidean zoning has "the virtue of certainty and the handicap of rigidity." Lutz v. City of Longview, 83 Wash.2d 566, 568, 520 P.2d 1374 (1974). In order to reduce the potential for wasteful land use resulting from inflexible regulation, zoning authorities have developed a series of tools, in addition to the variance (which we have already discussed), whose purpose is to soften the impact of zoning classifications. Conditional use zoning, incentive zoning, and performance zoning, each of which we will discuss in greater detail in this chapter, all aim to solve the same problem of excessive inflexibility within zoning ordinances. Efforts to mitigate the rigidity of traditional zoning ordinances, however, also have the impact of reducing certainty and predictability for landowners and their neighbors. As we will see, they also generate the possibility of new forms of unfairness.

A. SPECIAL EXCEPTIONS OR CONDITIONAL USES

Consider a problem common to many municipalities: where should churches and schools be located? It often makes little sense to restrict these facilities to industrial or commercial districts, where children and parishioners may be confronted with excessive traffic. At the same time, demand for churches and schools will not generally be large enough to merit creation of separate districts. For the most part, churches and schools can co-exist in harmony with residential uses, but they may raise traffic, parking, noise, and lighting concerns different from those presented by typical residential uses.

Municipalities often deal with these issues by permitting churches and schools in residential districts, but only after the proposed church or school has received a "special permit" or "special exception" or "conditional use permit." This procedure allows the Zoning Board of Appeals or the Planning and Zoning Commission to review the specific proposal to minimize its impact on the community.

The special permit procedure extends beyond schools and churches to a variety of other uses. A common question, however, involves the scope of the decision-making body's discretion in evaluating special permit applications. Consider the following case:

Petition of Skeen
Supreme Court of Appeals of West Virginia, 1994
190 W.Va. 649, 441 S.E.2d 370

■ NEELY, J.

G. Samuel Skeen and Jeanne C. Skeen appeal from a 9 November 1992 order of the Circuit Court of Mercer County affirming the decision of the Zoning Board of Adjustment for the City of Bluefield that denied their application for a special use exemption to operate a babysitting service in their Bluefield home.

Mrs. Skeen operated the babysitting service in her home on Marmont Drive in Mercer County from 1981 through fall 1991. The service was properly licensed and supervised by both the State of West Virginia and the Mercer County Economic Opportunity Corporation. When the Skeens' house was purchased and destroyed to construct a new shopping center complex in fall 1991, the Skeens purchased their present residence on Ridgecrest Road in the City of Bluefield.

The Ordinances of the City of Bluefield classify Ridgecrest Road as an R–1 residence district. Pursuant to the ordinance, no business may be located or prosecuted in an R–1 residence district without application and permission by city zoning authorities. At the suggestion of an official from the City of Bluefield, the Skeens applied for a permit to have a babysitting service in their new home on 21 November 1991. That application was refused on the same day.

Pursuant to the provisions of W. Va. Code 8–24–51 through 8–24–65 [1969], the City of Bluefield maintains a Zoning Board of Adjustment ("the Board") whose function is to hear appeals from the strict application of the City's zoning ordinance and authorize special exceptions or conditional uses[1] to the ordinance. One such special

---

[1]   In zoning law, a special exception is commonly understood to be synonymous with a conditional use. As A.H. Rathkopf in footnote one of chapter three in *The Law of Zoning and Planning* 54–1 (3d ed. 1972) explains:

Although in this chapter we adhere to ordinary terminology and use the term "special exception use" or "special exception permit," it should be pointed out in the beginning that this term is a misnomer. As will be made clear in this chapter, no "exception" is made to the provisions of the ordinance in permitting such use; the permit granted is

exception listed in section 23–32 of the Code of Ordinances of the City of
Bluefield (City Code) is for a "home occupation."

The Board heard the Skeens' appeal on 27 January 1992. Notice of
such hearing, by letter and by publication, was given to all adjoining
landowners and interested persons as required by law. Following an
extensive hearing, the Board made findings of fact and conclusions of
law denying the Skeens' application. From the Board's denial, the
Skeens sought a writ of certiorari to the Circuit Court of Mercer County
to reverse the Board's decision. By order entered on 9 November 1992,
the Circuit Court affirmed the Board's decision. On 21 December 1992,
the Circuit Court denied the Skeens' motion to alter or amend its order
affirming the Board's decision.

Section 23–30 of the City Code divides residence districts into four
classes varying as to the number of family dwellings allowable on each
separate lot. An R–1 residence district provides minimum standards for
the development and use of single-family detached housing built on
separate lots. Section 23–31 of the Code sets out the "permitted uses"
for land and structures in each residential district. Although section
23–31 does not include babysitting services as one of the "permitted
uses" in an R–1 residence district, section 23–32 lists certain "special
exceptions" allowed within an R–1 residence district upon authorization
by the Board. Special exception number 12 provides that "home
occupations" are allowable as a special exception. Section 23–3 of the
Code defines "home occupation" as "an occupation conducted in a
dwelling unit" and sets out the requisite elements of a "home
occupation." Such elements, in summary, are as follows:

(a) no person other than members of the family are engaged
in the occupation;

(b) the home occupation is subordinate to and incidental to
home use for residential purposes and uses not more than 25%
of the floor area;

(c) there is no change in the outside appearance of the
building or premises;

(d) the home occupation is not conducted in any accessory
building;

(e) no excess traffic or any need for parking is generated by
the conduct of the home occupation;

(f) no equipment or process is used creating noise, vibration,
glare, fumes, odors and like nuisances.

At the Board's hearing on 27 January 1992, the Skeens
demonstrated that their babysitting service fully complies with the

---

for a use specifically provided for in the ordinance in the case in which conditions,
legislatively prescribed, are also found. A much more accurate description would be
"conditional use" permit.

requirements set forth for a "home occupation." The Skeens' satisfaction of these requirements notwithstanding, the Board denied the application. The Skeens contend that the Circuit Court erred in affirming the Board's denial of their application because the Board failed to apply the principle of law appropriate to finding whether a special exception or conditional use exists.

In Syllabus point 1 of Harding v. Bd., etc., City of Morgantown, 159 W. Va. 73, 219 S.E.2d 324 (1975), this Court distinguished between a special exception or conditional use and a variance:

> A special exception or conditional use, unlike a variance, does not involve the varying of an ordinance, but rather compliance with it. When it is granted, a special exception or conditional use permits certain uses which the ordinance authorizes under stated conditions.[2]

In other words, whereas a variance relates primarily to the allowance of a use of a particular property *prohibited* in the particular zone, the right to a special exception or conditional use automatically exists if the Board finds compliance with the standards or requisites set forth in the ordinance. *Id.*

In order for this Court to determine whether the conditional use sought by the applicant before the Board violated any of the conditions required before the granting of such a conditional use, the Board must make written findings of fact. 159 W. Va. 73 at 82. Such facts determine whether the particular conditional use applied for is consistent with the spirit, purpose and intent of the ordinance. *Id.* at 83. On appeal a board of zoning appeals is presumed to have acted correctly. However, a reviewing court should reverse the administrative decision where the board has applied an erroneous principle of law, was plainly wrong in its factual findings, or has acted beyond its jurisdiction. Wolfe v. Forbes, 159 W. Va. 34, 217 S.E.2d 899 (1975).

No evidence was introduced at the hearing that the requirements for a home occupation special exception set forth in City Code section 23–3 were not met. Indeed, the Board based its denial on a ground wholly separate from the requirements set out in section 23–3, namely

---

[2] In Tullo v. Millburn Township, 54 N.J.Super. 483, 149 A.2d 620 (App.Div.1959), the court further illustrates the distinction of a conditional use or special exception from a variance:

> The theory is that certain uses, considered by the local legislative body to be essential or desirable for the welfare of the community and its citizenry or substantial segments of it, are entirely appropriate and not essentially incompatible with the basic uses in any zone (or in certain particular zones), but not at every or any location therein or without restrictions or conditions being imposed by reason of special problems the use or its particular location in relation to neighboring properties presents from a zoning standpoint, such as traffic congestion, safety, health, noise, and the like. The enabling act therefore permits the local ordinance to require approval of the local administrative agency as to the location of such use within the zone.

See also Yokley, *Zoning Law and Practice* § 15–4 (3rd ed. 1965).

the virtual unanimous opposition of the neighboring landowners. Pursuant to the rule articulated in *Harding,* if the Board finds compliance with the standards or requisites set forth in the ordinance, the right to the exception exists. Because the Board was plainly wrong in failing to apply its factual findings to the *Harding* standard, the Circuit Court's affirmation of its decision must be reversed.

We note that the Board's finding that no unnecessary hardship will redound to the Skeens in being deprived of the opportunity to conduct a babysitting service within their home was also in error. Mrs. Skeen depends on the service to maintain herself both financially and emotionally. Her service is substantially funded by the State of West Virginia, which has been endorsing this service for the benefit of underprivileged citizens within the City of Bluefield since 1981 and is currently conducting the service in 63 other residential locations.

Furthermore, as admitted by the Board, refusal of the Skeens' application will set a precedent based on which the Board can refuse other home occupation applications for babysitting services in other neighborhoods. Such a precedent not only undermines the good intentions of the Skeens and future applicants for such home occupation permits; it also adds further financial strain to other families in the City of Bluefield with two working parents who rely on such babysitting services.

Accordingly, for the foregoing reasons, we reverse.

NOTES AND QUESTIONS

1. In light of the court's opinion in *Skeen*, what was the purpose of review by the ZBA? If the applicant satisfied the elements for home occupation enumerated in the Bluefield City Code, did the ZBA have power to deny the special exception application?

2. Why would the city enumerate the criteria for a home occupation use, and also provide for review by the ZBA? If all the user has to do is meet the enumerated criteria, is the home occupation a conditional use or an "as-of-right" use (a use to which the applicant is entitled without obtaining a variance or conditional use permit)?

3. The ZBA in *Skeen* found that the applicants had not demonstrated that they would suffer unnecessary hardship if their application for a special exception were denied. The West Virginia Supreme Court concluded that the ZBA's finding was erroneous. Was the finding relevant? Should an applicant have to establish hardship to obtain a special use permit?

Although the West Virginia ordinance is silent on the relevance of hardship, consider the theory of the special use permits, as elucidated in the *Tullo* case quoted in the *Skeen* opinion. Given that theory, should hardship be relevant?

4. Suppose the Bluefield City Code had not listed home occupations as special exceptions. If the Skeens had wanted to operate a babysitting service, what options would have been open to them? Professor Nicole Garnett questions current prohibitions on home occupations:

> There are strong reasons to reconsider zoning restrictions on working from home: not only are many millions of people already violating zoning laws by working from home, but technological advances are making it easier for more to do so every day. Furthermore, working at home is often a viable solution to the dilemmas faced by parents struggling to balance work and family, could enable low-income individuals to achieve economic self-sufficiency, and might help alleviate the social and environmental problems caused by suburban sprawl.

Nicole Stelle Garnett, On Castles and Commerce: Zoning Law and the Home-Business Dilemma, 42 Wm. & Mary L. Rev. 1191, 1197–98 (2001).

5.   Suppose the Skeens had applied to operate a dog grooming business in their garage, asserting that they were operating a "home occupation." If the ZBA had denied the special permit application, would the court have overturned the denial? Why or why not? *Cf.* Lowney v. Zoning Bd. of Appeals, 71 A.3d 670 (2013).

6.   Suppose you had been consulted by the Skeens' neighbors, who sought advice about the steps they should take to minimize the chance that the ZBA would grant a special permit to the Skeens. What advice would you have given?

Suppose instead you had been consulted by the Skeens, who sought advice about how they might maximize the chance that the ZBA would grant the permit. What advice would you have given?

7.   Suppose the local zoning ordinance permits "places of worship" and "nursery schools" in residential districts, subject to special permit requirements. If a landowner applies for a special permit to operate a nursery school, may the municipality impose conditions on approval of the special permit application? What limits are there on the conditions the municipality may impose? Why impose limits?

Consider the following:

(a)   A condition that the nursery school provides one on-site parking space for each five students;

(b)   A condition that the nursery school encloses the school and playground with a wrought-iron fence;

(c)   A condition that the nursery school pays for private trash removal;

(d)   A condition that the nursery school pays to upgrade the sewer line in the street in front of the school.

In *Skeen*, the court overturned the board's determination for exceeding its authority. What happens if the body charged with reviewing special permit applications does not exercise all of the authority granted to it? Consider the following case:

917 Lusk, LLC v. City of Boise

Supreme Court of Idaho, 2015
158 Idaho 12, 343 P.3d 41

■ HORTON, J.

This case arises from 917 Lusk, LLC's (Lusk) petition for judicial review of the Boise City Council's (City Council) decision granting a conditional use permit for Royal Boulevard Associates, LP (Royal) to build an apartment complex. The Ada County district court affirmed the City Council's decision and Lusk timely appealed. We reverse the decision of the district court.

FACTUAL AND PROCEDURAL BACKGROUND

In the fall of 2011, Royal's predecessor in interest applied for permission to build a 352,000 square foot, five-story, multi-family apartment complex called River Edge Apartments (River Edge) at 1004 West Royal Boulevard in Boise. The site of the proposed construction is near Boise State University, adjacent to the Boise River, east of Ann Morrison Park, and west of property owned by Lusk. Multi-family housing is an allowed use for this location. However, the Boise City Code (BCC) requires a conditional use permit (CUP) in order to construct a building more than 35 feet tall in an R–OD zone. If constructed as planned, River Edge will be between 59 and 63 feet tall.

Lusk was entitled to notice of the application for a CUP due to the proximity of its property to the proposed project. Lusk owns the Keynetics, Inc., building located immediately east and south of River Edge's proposed building site.

On March 5, 2012, the Boise Planning and Zoning Commission (Commission) held a hearing on the River Edge application, receiving testimony from City staff, the applicant team, and members of the public. The Commission unanimously approved granting the River Edge application for a CUP and variance[1] allowing the height exception. The following day, the Commission provided a written explanation for its decision as to the variance and the CUP. This document set forth the conditions of approval, including twelve site-specific conditions.

Lusk appealed the Commission's decision to the City Council, contending that the Commission's decision failed to address the

---

[1] [On January 25, 2012, a little more than a month before the Commission's hearing, the Idaho Supreme Court had held that a municipality could exempt a project from height limitations only by granting a variance, not a conditional use permit. As a result, Royal sought both a variance and a conditional use permit. After the Commission's decision, but before the City Council's decision in this case, the Idaho Legislature amended its statute to make it clear that a municipality could provide for waiver of height limitations by conditional use permit. The new statute made Royal's variance application unnecessary and irrelevant to the case].

requirements for a CUP. In a 15-page letter, Lusk outlined its claims of error. Of particular importance to this appeal is the focus that Lusk placed on the impact of constructing a 622-bedroom apartment complex with 280 automobile parking spaces, given that River Edge's plans were to lease the bedrooms on an individual basis to students. Lusk asserted that "the proposed project will place an undue burden on transportation and other public facilities in the vicinity" and "the proposed project will adversely affect other property in the vicinity."

On April 17, 2012, the City Council upheld the Commission's approval of the River Edge CUP and denied Lusk's appeal. In addition to adopting the Commission's reasons for its decision, the City Council directly addressed Lusk's concern regarding parking: "The Council also found that the public record from the Planning and Zoning Commission meeting revealed a robust discussion regarding parking. The Commission determined that the project was correctly designated as multi-family and that the level of provided automobile parking was sufficient."

Lusk appealed to the district court, which affirmed the City Council's decision. Lusk timely appealed to this Court.

ANALYSIS

Lusk appeals the City Council's decision affirming the Commission's grant of a CUP allowing Royal, the intervenor in this appeal, to construct a building taller than the applicable zoning height limitation. Lusk argues that because the Commission did not follow the correct procedure for granting a CUP, the City Council erred in affirming the Commission's decision. Lusk contends that the City Council's decision violated its substantial rights, and asks this Court to remand this case back to the Commission for a new public hearing to fully consider all of the criteria required for conditional use approval under the BCC.

Lusk argues that the BCC "clearly and unambiguously" requires any request for a height increase to only be granted when all of the BBC's criteria governing a CUP application are considered and met. Lusk argues that BCC sections 11–06–04.13 and 11–06–04.14 require the Commission to make a thorough review to determine whether parking will be adequate for the proposed project before granting a CUP. Royal responds that the plain language of these ordinances does not require consideration of parking requirements beyond those in the Parking Chapter of the BCC and that the City Council's interpretation of them was reasonable.

The BCC provides that height exceptions in an R–OD district "require a commission-level conditional use permit in accordance with the provisions of [BCC] section 11–06–06.13." BCC section 11–06–04.13 states in relevant part:

The Commission, following the procedures outlined below, may approve a conditional use permit when the evidence presented at the hearing is such as to establish: . . .

C. That the site is large enough to accommodate the proposed use and all yards, open spaces, pathways, walls and fences, parking, loading, landscaping and other features as are required by this title; and

D. That the proposed use, if it complies with all conditions imposed, will not adversely affect other property of the vicinity; . . . .

BCC § 11–06–04.13.

Lusk argues that Section 11–06–04.13 requires the Commission to make a thorough review to determine whether planned parking is adequate for the proposed project before granting a conditional use permit.

BCC section 11–06–04.13.D requires that the Commission find that "the evidence presented at the hearing is such as to establish . . . [t]hat the proposed use . . . will not adversely affect other property of the vicinity." BCC § 11–06–04.13.D. Idaho Code section 67–6512(d)(7) provides that "conditions may be attached" to a CUP "[r]equiring more restrictive standards than those generally required in an ordinance." The critical inquiry is not whether there was "robust discussion" of parking issues before the Commission, as the City Council found to have occurred. Rather, the appropriate inquiry is whether the Commission recognized that it possessed the discretionary authority to impose parking requirements beyond the minimum established by the Parking Chapter. The record unambiguously demonstrates that the Commission failed to perceive that it had discretion to require additional parking as a condition of approval of the CUP.

On March 5, 2012, Joshua Johnson, a staff member of Boise City Planning and Development Services, provided a staff report to the Commission. In that report, he stated:

Finally, the landowner who testified in opposition to the height also brought up a perceived shortage of parking as a further point of opposition. The project meets City parking standards for multi-family units and this issue is not before the Commission. The only two items that should be considered are the Variance for a height exception and the Boise River System Permit.

At the March 5, 2012, hearing before the Commission, Johnson advised the Commission that Royal's project "meets our Parking Code. This issue is not before the Commission tonight. The application tonight only concerns the additional height requested by the applicant." Following substantial testimony relating to parking concerns, Commissioner Stevens informed the Commission that it lacked authority to impose additional requirements for parking beyond those found in the Parking Chapter:

> I want to remind the Commissioners that the parking issue tonight is not actually before us. This Commission is not in position to make findings that require our applicant to be held to standards above that which is in our code. That would be arbitrary and would make the City be in some serious hot water, so I want to make sure that when we have our discussion tonight, that we keep the parking out of it. It is not before us. They have met code and to require that is above and beyond what we are allowed to do.

Commissioner Story then echoed this view, stating: "Like you said parking is off the table. This complies. I can't say our code is correct on parking and the way it should be handled, but I think the rubber meets the road where we're talking about height and that's really the only thing we have before us." Thereafter, the Commission unanimously approved the CUP.

Following Lusk's appeal to the City Council, Hal Simmons, Planning Director with Boise City Planning and Development Services, sent a memorandum to the City Council, outlining staff recommendations regarding the appeal. In that memorandum, he reiterated the erroneous legal premise advanced in the staff report and accepted by the Commission: "While parking was discussed, the Commission correctly observed that the project meets established zoning ordinance standards and that it was not in their purview to require additional parking."

He later stated:

> The appellant states that parking problems associated with the high density project will overburden public facilities. This sentence highlights two fundamental flaws in the appeal: As proposed, the project meets density and parking requirements of Boise City Code. These standards are outlined in detail within the staff report and are discussed in the minutes from the March 5, 2012 hearing. Commissioner Stevens stated at the beginning of the deliberation, *"I want to remind the Commissioners that the parking issue tonight is not actually before us. This Commission is not in position to make findings that require our applicant to be held to standards above that which is in our code. That would be arbitrary and would make the City be in some serious hot water."*

(emphasis in original). Although the record reflects the City Council's unanimous denial of Lusk's appeal, it is silent as to any discussion as to whether the Commission had the right to require additional parking as a condition for approving the CUP.

Idaho Code section 67–6512(d)(7) provides that "conditions may be attached" to a CUP "[r]equiring more restrictive standards than those generally required in an ordinance." BCC section 11–06–04.13.D requires that the Commission determine "[t]hat the proposed use . . . will not adversely affect other property of the vicinity." BCC § 11–06–04.13.D. The testimony before the Commission related the potential for adverse effects to the vicinity due to automobile parking needs that would result from the project. The Commission failed to recognize that Idaho law and the BCC provided it with discretion to require the project to provide on-site automobile parking beyond the minimum required by the Parking Chapter. As a result of this failure to apply governing legal standards, the Commission refused to consider the adverse effects on property in the vicinity. Thus, we find that the decision reflected an abuse of discretion. Dunagan v. Dunagan, 147 Idaho 599, 603, 213 P.3d 384, 388 (2009) (error found when trial court failed to recognize grounds for exercise of discretion).

CONCLUSION

We reverse the decision of the district court affirming the City Council's approval of the Commission's decision to grant the CUP to Royal. We award costs on appeal, but not attorney fees, to Lusk.

■ JUSTICES EISMANN, J. JONES and JUSTICE PRO TEM WALTERS concur.

■ CHIEF JUSTICE BURDICK Dissents without opinion.

NOTES AND QUESTIONS

1. Why would the City of Boise use the conditional use permit device to permit escape from the zoning ordinance's height restrictions? Consider two alternatives: (1) increase the permissible height of buildings throughout the zoning district; or (2) require developers to seek variances if they want to exceed the ordinance's limitations. Why might the city prefer the conditional use permit device to those two alternatives?

2. *Parking Requirements Generally.* The Boise City Code, like most zoning ordinances, imposes minimum parking requirements for many uses, including multi-family dwellings. Boise's parking requirements (like many others) are based on a combination of number of dwelling units and number of bedrooms. The Boise Code generally requires 1 parking space for each one-bedroom dwelling unit, 1.25 parking spaces for each two-bedroom unit, and 1.5 parking spaces for each unit with three or more bedrooms. The Code also requires 1 guest parking space for each 10 dwelling units. So, if a developer like Royal contemplated building 150 four-bedroom units, the developer would have to provide 240 parking spaces (150 x 1.5 plus 150 x .1). If the developer instead contemplated building 300 two-bedroom units, the developer would have to provide 405 parking spaces (300 x 1.25 plus 300 x .1).

Why would a zoning ordinance include minimum parking requirements? Wouldn't one expect the developer to include adequate parking in any project in order to make the project marketable to potential residents (or commercial purchasers or tenants)?

Increasingly, localities are adopting maximum parking requirements. Why would a city adopt maximum parking requirements?

3. If Royal had proposed to build the same 622 units in a 3-story, 35-foot high building that met the Code's parking requirements, would Royal have needed a conditional use permit? Would there have been any opportunity for the Commission to review parking issues directly?

4. What position do you think Royal's lawyer took with respect to parking in his application to the Planning and Zoning Commission? Do you think Royal's lawyer argued that the Commission had discretion to review the adequacy of parking?

If the Commission had reviewed the adequacy of parking, and concluded that Royal's project included adequate parking, would Lusk have prevailed in this case? Does that mean that Royal's lawyer pursued the wrong strategy? What risks would Royal have faced if its lawyer had conceded that the Commission had discretion?

5. Suppose Lusk had not raised the parking issue before the Commission or the City Council. Would the Idaho Supreme Court have overturned the grant of the conditional use permit? Why or why not?

6. Suppose Lusk had raised a laundry list of objections to Royal's project. In light of the language of the ordinance and the court's holding, would the Commission have to consider all of them? If you were representing the Commission, how would you advise the Commission to proceed?

7. Note that in Boise, the determination of the Planning and Zoning Commission was not final. Instead, the Boise City Council had to review the grant of a conditional use permit. In many states and municipalities, the determination of the administrative body is final, subject only to judicial review, but not review by the local legislative body.

The drafters of traditional zoning ordinances regarded variances and special use permits as safety valves that enabled local officials to consider relatively unusual uses and circumstances that did not easily fit into the rigid classifications that characterized the typical Euclidean ordinance. What objections might there be to an ordinance that includes none of the pre-set standards of the typical zoning ordinance, and instead confers broad discretion on local officials to react to development proposals as they are made? Consider the following case:

Chrismon v. Guilford County

Supreme Court of North Carolina, 1988
322 N.C. 611, 370 S.E.2d 579

■ MEYER, J.

In 1964, Guilford County adopted a comprehensive zoning ordinance. The ordinance zoned Mr. Clapp's 3.18-acre tract, as well as an extensive area surrounding his tract, as "A–1 Agricultural" (hereinafter "A–1"). Under this particular zoning classification, one element of the business—namely, the grain drying and storing operation—constituted a permitted use. Significantly, however, the sale and distribution of the lime, fertilizer, pesticides, and other agricultural chemicals were not uses permitted by the A–1 classification. However, because this latter activity pre-existed the ordinance, Mr. Clapp was allowed to continue to sell agricultural chemicals on the 3.18-acre tract adjacent to his own home. Under the ordinance, though such sales constituted a nonconforming use, the sales could be carried on, so long as they were not expanded.

Beginning in 1980, however, Mr. Clapp moved some portion of his business operation from the 3.18-acre tract north of Gun Shop Road to the 5.06-acre tract south of Gun Shop Road, directly adjacent to plaintiffs' lot. Subsequently, Mr. Clapp constructed some new buildings on this larger tract, erected several grain bins, and generally enlarged his operation. Concerned by the increased noise, dust, and traffic caused by Mr. Clapp's expansion, plaintiffs filed a complaint with the Guilford County Inspections Department. The Inspections Department subsequently notified Mr. Clapp, by letter dated 22 July 1982, that the expansion of the *agricultural chemical operation* to the larger tract adjacent to plaintiffs' lot constituted an impermissible expansion of a nonconforming use. The same letter informed Mr. Clapp further that, though his activity was impermissible under the ordinance, should he so desire, he could request a rezoning of the property.

Shortly thereafter, Mr. Clapp applied to have both of the tracts in question, the 3.18-acre tract north of Gun Shop Road and the 5.06-acre tract south of Gun Shop Road, rezoned from A–1 to "Conditional Use Industrial District" (hereinafter CU–M–2). He also applied for a conditional use permit, specifying in the application that he would use the property as it was then being used and listing those improvements he would like to make in the next five years. Under the CU–M–2 classification, Clapp's agricultural chemical operation would become a permitted use upon the issuance of the conditional use permit. The Guilford County Planning Board met on 8 September 1982 and voted to approve the recommendation of the Planning Division that the property be rezoned consistent with Mr. Clapp's request.

On 20 December 1982, pursuant to appropriate notice, the Guilford County Board of Commissioners held a public hearing concerning Mr.

Clapp's rezoning application. Members of the Board heard statements from Mr. Clapp, from plaintiffs, and, also, from plaintiffs' attorney. Several additional persons had previously spoken in favor of Mr. Clapp's rezoning request at earlier Board meetings, stating that Mr. Clapp's business provided a service to the farmers in the immediate vicinity. The Board had also been presented with a petition signed by eighty-eight persons favoring the rezoning. Having considered the matter, the Board members voted to rezone the tracts in question from A–1 to CU–M–2, and as a part of the same resolution, they also voted to approve the conditional use permit application.

Pursuant to this decision by the County to rezone the property in question, plaintiffs brought this action seeking to have both the zoning amendment and the conditional use permit declared invalid.

[T]he Court of Appeals reversed the decision of the trial court.

The questions plainly before us are these: first, did the rezoning of defendant Clapp's tract from A–1 to CU–M–2 by the Guilford County Board of Commissioners constitute illegal spot zoning; and second, did the same rezoning constitute illegal contract zoning. The Court of Appeals answered each question in the affirmative. We conclude that the correct answer to both questions is "no."

I.

The practice of conditional use zoning—like that used by Guilford County in this case—is one of several vehicles by which greater zoning flexibility can be and has been acquired by zoning authorities. Conditional use zoning anticipates that when the rezoning of certain property within the general zoning framework described above would constitute an unacceptably drastic change, such a rezoning could still be accomplished through the addition of certain conditions or use limitations. Specifically, conditional use zoning occurs when a governmental body, without committing its own authority, secures a given property owner's agreement to limit the use of his property to a particular use or to subject his tract to certain restrictions as a precondition to any rezoning. D. Hagman & J. Juergensmeyer, *Urban Planning and Land Development Control Law* § 5.5 (2d ed. 1986); Shapiro, *The Case For Conditional Rezoning*, 41 Temp.L.Q. 267 (1968).

It is indeed generally agreed among commentators that, because it permits a given local authority greater flexibility in balancing conflicting demands, the practice of conditional use zoning is exceedingly valuable. Before the now-disputed zoning occurred, the tracts of land in question, and all of the surrounding land for some miles, were classified under the comprehensive zoning plan as A–1. While the A–1 classification allowed Mr. Clapp to engage in the storage and sale of grain, it did not allow him to store and sell agricultural chemicals, which was his desire. While the rezoning of the two tracts to M–2 Industrial would clearly allow the desired agricultural chemical operation, it would also clearly allow for activities substantially inconsistent with the surrounding A–1 areas. Herein lies the usefulness of conditional use zoning. By rezoning these tracts CU–M–2, the desired activity becomes a conforming use, but by virtue of the attendant conditions, uses undesirable under these circumstances can be limited or avoided altogether.

Notwithstanding the manifest benefits of conditional use zoning, there has, over the course of time, been some divergence of opinion amongst courts and commentators alike as to the legal status of the practice. In fact, the initial judicial response to conditional use zoning was to condemn the practice as invalid per se. Those courts falling into this category have objected to conditional use zoning on the several grounds that it constitutes illegal spot zoning; that it is not, on the specific facts, authorized by the state's zoning enabling legislation; and that it results in an improper and illegal abandonment of the local government's police powers.

The benefits of the additional zoning and planning flexibility inherent in conditional use zoning have apparently not escaped the attention of jurisdictions which have addressed the issue more recently. Many jurisdictions now approve of the practice of conditional use zoning, so long as the action of the local zoning authority in accomplishing the zoning is reasonable, neither arbitrary nor unduly discriminatory, and in the public interest. These jurisdictions, which comprise a growing trend, have concluded, among other things, that zoning legislation provides ample authority for the practice; that the use under the practice of carefully tailored restraints advanced, rather than injured, the interests of adjacent landowners; and that the practice is an appropriate means of harmonizing private interests in land and thus of benefitting the public interest. Wegner, *Moving Toward the Bargaining Table: Contract Zoning, Development Agreements, and the Theoretical Foundations of Government Land Use Deals,* 65 N.C.L.Rev. 957, 983–84 (1987).

Today, we join this growing trend of jurisdictions in recognizing the validity of properly employed conditional use zoning. Like the jurisdictions we expressly join today, we are persuaded that the practice, when properly implemented, will add a valuable and desirable flexibility to the planning efforts of local authorities throughout our state. In our view, the "all or nothing" approach of traditional zoning techniques is insufficient in today's world of rapid industrial expansion and pressing urban and rural social and economic problems. See Bartram v. Zoning Commission, 136 Conn. 89, 68 A.2d 308 (1949); Shapiro, *The Case For Conditional Zoning,* 41 Temp.L.Q. 267 (1968).

Having so stated, we hasten to add that, just as this type of zoning can provide much-needed and valuable flexibility to the planning efforts of local zoning authorities, it could also be as easily abused. We recognize that critics of the practice are to a limited extent justified in their concern that the unrestricted use of conditional use zoning could lead to private or public abuse of governmental power. We have said, however, that, in order to be legal and proper, conditional use zoning, like any type of zoning, must be reasonable, neither arbitrary nor unduly discriminatory, and in the public interest. In re Ellis, 277 N.C. 419, 178 S.E.2d 77. It goes without saying that it also cannot constitute illegal spot zoning or illegal contract zoning as those two concepts are developed in the pages which follow. The benefits of the flexibility of conditional use zoning can be fairly achieved only when these limiting standards are consistently and carefully applied.

III.

We turn ... to the question of contract zoning. [T]he Court of Appeals also held that the rezoning in question constituted illegal "contract zoning" and was therefore invalid and void for that alternative reason. In the view of this Court, the Court of Appeals, in its approach to the question of whether the rezoning at issue in this case constituted illegal contract zoning, improperly considered as equals two very different concepts—namely, valid conditional use zoning and illegal contract zoning. By virtue of this treatment of the two quite distinguishable concepts, the Court of Appeals has, for all intents and purposes, outlawed conditional use zoning in North Carolina by equating this beneficial land planning tool with a practice universally considered illegal.

Illegal contract zoning properly connotes a transaction wherein both the landowner who is seeking a certain zoning action and the zoning authority itself undertake reciprocal obligations in the context of a *bilateral* contract. [C]ontract zoning of this type is objectionable primarily because it represents an abandonment on the part of the zoning authority of its duty to exercise independent judgment in making zoning decisions.

As we indicated in Part I above, valid conditional use zoning, on the other hand, is an entirely different matter. Conditional use zoning, to repeat, is an outgrowth of the need for a compromise between the interests of the developer who is seeking appropriate rezoning for his tract and the community on the one hand and the interests of the neighboring landowners who will suffer if the most intensive use permitted by the new classification is instituted. One commentator has described its mechanics as follows:

> An orthodox conditional zoning situation occurs when a zoning authority, *without committing its own power,* secures a property owner's agreement to subject his tract to certain restrictions as a prerequisite to rezoning. These restrictions may require that the rezoned property be limited to just one of the uses permitted in the new classification; or particular physical improvements and maintenance requirements may be imposed.

Shapiro, *The Case For Conditional Zoning,* 41 Temp. L.Q. 267, 270–71 (1968) (emphasis added).

In our view, therefore, the principal differences between valid conditional use zoning and illegal contract zoning are related and are essentially two in number. First, valid conditional use zoning features merely a unilateral promise from the landowner to the local zoning authority as to the landowner's intended use of the land in question, while illegal contract zoning anticipates a bilateral contract in which the landowner and the zoning authority make reciprocal promises. Second, in the context of conditional use zoning, the local zoning authority maintains its independent decision-making authority, while in the contract zoning scenario, it abandons that authority by binding itself contractually with the landowner seeking a zoning amendment.

We conclude that the zoning authority neither entered into a bilateral contract nor abandoned its position as an independent decision-maker. Therefore, we find what occurred in the case before us to constitute valid conditional use zoning and *not* illegal contract zoning.

First, having carefully reviewed the record in the case, we find no evidence that the local zoning authority—here, the Guilford County Board of Commissioners—entered into anything approaching a bilateral contract with the landowner—here, Mr. Clapp. The facts of the case reveal that, pursuant to a filed complaint from the Chrismons, the Guilford County Inspections Department, by a letter dated 22 July 1982, notified Mr. Clapp that his expansion of the agricultural chemical operation to the tract adjacent to plaintiffs' lot constituted an impermissible expansion of a nonconforming use. More important for purposes of this issue, the letter informed Mr. Clapp of his various options in the following manner:

> Mr. Clapp, there are several courses of action available to you in an effort to resolve your Zoning Ordinance violations:
>
> 2.   You may request rezoning of that portion of your land involved in the violations. *This is not a guaranteed option.*

[W]e are quite satisfied that the only promises made in this case were unilateral—specifically, those from Mr. Clapp to the Board in the form of the substance of his conditional use permit application. As the letter excerpted above makes clear, no promises whatever were made by the Board in exchange, and this rezoning does not therefore fall into the category of illegal contract zoning.

Second, and perhaps more important, the Board did not, by virtue of its actions in this case, abandon its position as an independent decision-maker. On the contrary, we find that the Board made its decision in this matter only after a lengthy deliberation completely consistent with both the procedure called for by the relevant zoning ordinance and the rules prohibiting illegal contract zoning.

The Guilford County Zoning Ordinance provides appropriate procedures to be used by landowners wishing to apply for rezonings to a conditional use district and for conditional use permits. Pursuant to the ordinance, a landowner must apply separately for rezoning to the appropriate conditional use district and for the conditional use permit. This second petition—that for the conditional use permit—must provide specific details of the applicant's proposed use of the land affected by the potential permit. Petitions are directed to the Guilford County Board of Commissioners and are filed initially in the office of the Planning Department. The Planning Director submits the petition and the Planning Department's recommendation to the Planning Board. The Planning Board subsequently makes advisory recommendations to the Board of County Commissioners, which, following a public hearing held pursuant to proper notice, makes the final decision as to whether the rezoning application and the permit will be approved or disapproved.

IV.

In conclusion, this Court has carefully reviewed the record in its entirety and all of the contentions of the parties to this action. Consistent with the above, we hold as follows: (1) the practice of conditional use zoning, insofar as it is reasonable, neither arbitrary nor unduly discriminatory, and in the public interest and, subject to our discussions of spot zoning and contract zoning above, is an approved practice in this state; (2) the rezoning in this case, while clearly spot zoning, was not *illegal* spot zoning in that it was done pursuant to a clear showing of a reasonable basis; and (3) the rezoning in this case, because the Board neither entered into a bilateral agreement nor abandoned its place as the independent decision-maker, was not illegal contract zoning.

REVERSED.

■ MITCHELL, J., dissenting.

The zoning amendment and conditional use permit in this case amounted to written *acceptance* by Guilford County of Clapp's *offer*—by written application—to use his property only in certain ways. Thus, for reasons fully discussed in the opinion of the Court of Appeals, 85 N.C.App. 211, 354 S.E.2d 309 (1987), Guilford County's actions in the present case also amounted to illegal "contract zoning."

NOTES AND QUESTIONS

1. *Conditional Use Zoning or Spot Zoning or Contract Zoning?* The tools we discuss in this chapter for increasing flexibility within zoning regimes have a double-edged quality. At the same time that they make zoning ordinances more supple, they run the risk of increasing the opportunity for impropriety or favoritism in the application of zoning laws to individual landowners. Courts have therefore shown a degree of ambivalence in their

review of the use of these tools. Courts have employed two doctrines in particular, spot zoning and contract zoning, to limit the discretion of zoning authorities. We discuss spot zoning claims in Chapter Six. In a portion of the opinion not included above, the *Chrismon* court rejected a spot zoning challenge. Contract zoning is typically understood to involve situations in which the zoning authority promises to alter the zoning treatment of a particular parcel in exchange for bargained-for concessions by the regulated landowner. The challenge for courts attempting to distinguish contract zoning, on the one hand, from legitimate efforts by zoning authorities to increase flexibility within a zoning ordinance (such as conditional-use zoning), on the other, is to develop clear and predictable standards for putting a particular exercise of zoning flexibility in one box rather than another. In many cases, judicial reasoning in this area begins to look somewhat arbitrary or conclusory. If the standards for determining contract zoning are so unclear, how much protection can the contract zoning doctrine offer against the potential for arbitrariness or unfairness introduced by conditional use zoning?

2.   The court in *Chrismon* emphasizes the fact that Clapp submitted two applications, one for a rezoning, and one for a conditional use permit, and that the zoning authorities considered these separately, in two steps. What is the relevance of this two-step process for the court? Does the court mean to suggest that, had the Board granted Clapp both a rezoning and a conditional use permit on the basis of a single application, the Board would have been engaged in illegal contract zoning? In other words, should it make any difference to the question whether a municipality has engaged in contract zoning whether the municipality proceeds via a two-step or a one-step process?

3.   Suppose Clapp had applied for a rezoning to a district that permitted sale of agricultural chemicals. Suppose further that the Board of Commissioners had denied the application, but had written to Clapp proposing that "if you agree not to expand your current sale of agricultural chemicals, we will approve a rezoning application." Clapp writes back to the Board agreeing to those terms, and submitting a recorded covenant barring expanded sale of agricultural chemicals.

    a.   Is the Board bound to approve the rezoning application? In other words, if it did not approve the application, would Clapp have a claim against the Board? Could he remove the covenant?

    b.   Could neighbors successfully challenge approval of a rezoning application as impermissible contract zoning?

    c.   Are the dangers associated with the hypothetical transaction any different from the dangers posed by the actual transaction in *Chrismon?* If not, does the distinction between contract zoning and conditional zoning make sense?

4. Consider the following description by one court of the standard development process for the Ballston area in Arlington, Virginia:

> The County has adopted a General Land Use Plan ("GLUP") as part of its Comprehensive Plan enacted pursuant to Section 15.2–2223 of the Virginia Code. The GLUP sets forth the County's vision for desired development and growth in the County.

> Through its land use regulations the County has planned for and encouraged the concentration of development within two corridors commonly referred to as the "Metro Corridors." The Rosslyn-Ballston corridor refers to the area roughly coinciding with the Metro orange line from Rosslyn to Glebe Road. The County structured its Comprehensive Plan to allow the highest densities in the Metro corridors.

> The County has also adopted "Sector Plans" for specific areas surrounding the Metro stations in the Rosslyn-Ballston Metro corridor. The Sector Plan provides a more detailed development plan for the particular area in order to implement the Comprehensive Plan. The County's Sector Plan for the Virginia Square sector is the plan applicable to Complainant's property which is the subject of this suit.

> While the GLUP and Sector Plans set forth the County's vision and desired development, zoning establishes specific permitted uses and restrictions for particular properties. Each zoning classification has permitted, or "by-right" use, which allows a property owner to develop property in accordance with the restrictions and limitations set forth in the classification without further review by the County Board. A "by-right" development receives administrative review by County staff and, if the proposed development meets the zoning classification, approval is granted by the County Board.

> The "by-right" uses of the existing zoning classification of parcels within the Rosslyn-Ballston corridor would not allow the development planned for and desired by the County in the GLUP. The GLUP envisions greater development and density than would be allowed "by-right" under the zoning classifications for the property.

> Beyond the "by-right" uses, a property owner may seek a more dense development or greater uses of property by seeking approval of a site plan which calls for such a special exception use. In order to develop property in the Rosslyn-Ballston corridor in accordance with the County's goals and desires planned for in the GLUP, a property owner must utilize the site plan process to obtain a special exception.

> The basic elements of the site plan process used by the County require rezoning in order to develop according to the GLUP. The rezoning can only be accomplished through this

process because the site plan allows significantly higher density and height than the underlying zoning. The special exception site plan process is a lengthy, comprehensive review because of the intensity of development allowed by site plan. The developer in this process has an incentive to rezone in order to obtain increased density; the County gets property in the corridor developed in accordance with the GLUP. Nearly all development within the Rosslyn-Ballston corridor has been by site plan approval.

See Kansas-Lincoln, L.C. v. County Bd. of Arlington, 66 Va. Cir. 274 (2004). Does conditional use zoning, and the power it grants the local government to extract concessions from developers, encourage zoning authorities to intentionally zone land for a lower-than-desirable levels of development in order to create bargaining power in the inevitable negotiations with developers over conditional use permits?

B. INCENTIVE ZONING

In a number of jurisdictions, zoning authorities permit developers to exceed normal zoning limits in exchange for including certain specified "amenities," broadly construed, as part of the development project. These amenities might include items like a public atrium or park, low-income housing units or contributions to a low-income housing fund, child-care facilities, or landscaping or architectural details. Typically, provision of the amenities will permit the developer to include some percentage of additional square footage or building height or bulk beyond what is permitted according to the applicable zoning provisions.

Case Study: Incentive Zoning in Downtown Seattle

Some form of Incentive Zoning has been employed in downtown Seattle since the 1960s. Recent downtown rezoning included an update to this program, and its current form presents one example of what Seattle can do. While the final regulations for the area remain extremely complicated, a simplified version exists below. The City developed a program for commercial buildings in the 1980s; residential buildings were added in 2006.

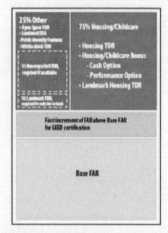

Commercial Buildings

In key Downtown zones, the following rules apply: to receive the first bonus increment of FAR above the base, developers must agree to build a LEED Silver certified structure. After that, developers are able to acquire additional square footage, up to a maximum established by the code, by participating in a combination bonus/TDR options. 75 percent of the additional floor area must be earned through affordable housing/child care options, and the remaining 25 percent through other menu options as shown above.

Residential Buildings

In the Downtown Mixed Commercial Zone, the following rules apply (similar programs exist in other downtown zones); developers may build to 290'. Between 85' and 290', developers are able to acquire additional square footage, to a maximum established by code, by participating in a bonus program. They can also build higher than 290' (up to a maximum height of 400') by participating in a bonus program. To participate in the program, developers must first commit to building a LEED Silver certified structure. Developers can either build affordable housing on site as part of the bonus program or contribute to an affordable housing fund at a certain cost per square foot.

Source: Seattle Planning Commission

Taking advantage of the Seattle incentives zoning scheme, the builders of the 55-story Washington Mutual Tower in downtown Seattle were able to double the square footage permitted as of right. (The zoning code permitted 27 stories as of right.) The list of incentives the building's developers took advantage of was detailed in Barry D. Yatt, Cracking the Codes (1998). They include:

- 13 stories for contributions to off-site low-income housing
- 2.5 stories for including a public escalator
- 2 stories for an urban plaza
- 2 stories compensating for the square footage lost by the distinctive profile of the upper floors

- 2 stories compensating for the space taken up by the building's mechanical equipment

- 2 stories for including retail space in the building

- 1.5 stories for a public atrium

- 1 story for an underground bus tunnel connection

- 1 story for a ground-floor day care facility

- 0.5 story for a public flowered terrace

As Yatt notes, these incentives were not placed on top of the zoning code as it had previously existed. Instead, when the City of Seattle made them available, it simultaneously reduced the as-of-right development that was permitted in the area. The floor area ratio (FAR) for the zone was decreased from 10 to 5, and the maximum height was reduced from 400 feet to 200 feet. *See id.* at 154. In other words, the incentives that the Washington Mutual developers took advantage of merely got them back to where they would have been as of right under the prior zoning regime.

A number of municipalities have focused their use of incentive zoning on a single objective: generating more "affordable housing." In many municipalities, ordinances authorize developers to increase building height or overall FAR if they agree to build a specified number or specified percentage of "affordable" units. Some ordinances require the developer to build the affordable units on site; others allow the developer to build the affordable units elsewhere.

When municipalities use these density bonuses to generate affordable housing, two issues arise:

(1) are the bonuses effective—do they generate more affordable units?

(2) are they consistent with overall land use policy objectives?

In evaluating the second issue, consider the following critique of incentive zoning:

East Midtown Rezoning: Looking for Extra Zoning Rights? They're for Sale

Michael Gruen, Juan Rivero
Copyright © 2013 by Center for New York City Law; Michael Gruen, Juan Rivero

A disarmingly simple plan for rezoning Manhattan's office district running from Grand Central Terminal north to about 58th Street has been approved by the Planning Commission and will come to a Council vote around the time of the November election.

It has three key components: 1) The City almost doubles the allowable floor area for new buildings on large sites along the major thoroughfares; 2) it sells to the landowner the right to build the increased space at the estimated market value of development rights (a base price of $250 per square foot); and 3) it applies the proceeds to unspecified transportation and pedestrian circulation improvement projects likely, when selected, to be located at Grand Central.

The City Club of New York has asserted that the scheme thinly disguises an illegal sale of zoning rights. It exceeds the permissible scope of zoning power, which is to regulate land use. Instead, it monetizes the very power to zone, breaching the constitutional line between fair, planning-oriented regulation, and taking.

The Planning Commission (CPC) defends the legality of the proposal, arguing that it is consistent with incentives that have been offered to developers since 1961 and frequently used to promote many types of public benefits, including plazas, subway stations improvements, and affordable housing, a strategy often described as "incentive zoning." CPC also argues that the property owner has free choice not to build beyond current zoning limits and, if he chooses to do so, his payment of the applicable charge is purely voluntary.

From a policy standpoint, the scheme looks bad. It looks like the planning process has been turned upside down. That process would normally focus on planning issues such as anticipating an impending weak office rental market in East Midtown because of obsolescent buildings, and planning solutions such as using up zoning to encourage new construction. That is what CPC is empowered to do. But its chain of reasoning appears rather to have focused on financial issues such as how to finance essential improvements to remedy an existing transportation mess, and how to tap the financial resources of building owners so as to avoid spending general funds or raising taxes. Only then does it reach a solution ostensibly, but not actually, within its authority: upzone and sell the new zoning rights, which the City can mint as easily as the Treasury can mint money.

This is not an appearance that builds respect for the Planning Commission nor for the integrity of government in general. That the motives of the Commission may be pure is immaterial. Appearance drives impressions and voters.

If, as appears, money is the motivating factor, the scheme is risky. If it is found illegal, the court would most likely void the financial transaction but leave the upzoning in place, at least for projects already in development at that time.

NOTES AND QUESTIONS

1. Can incentive zoning work without first (as Seattle did) reducing the development permitted as-of-right to a level well below what the market demands? Is there anything unfair about doing this?

2. Are incentive zoning schemes any different from a tax on development? If they operate just like a tax, why might a municipality favor achieving the same goals through incentive zoning? Do you think most developers would have a preference as between a tax or an incentive zoning scheme, or would most be indifferent between the two?

3.   Are incentive or inclusionary zoning schemes only effective during a building boom? What would be the likely impact of incentive zoning during a real estate downturn?

C. TRANSFERABLE DEVELOPMENT RIGHTS

Suppose I buy a parcel of land in a single-family residential district and want to build a house that exceeds the floor area ratio ("FAR") permitted by the zoning ordinance. Can I approach my neighbor, who owns a modest home that does not use all of her available FAR, and ask her to sell me her unused FAR to expand the size of my proposed house? The general answer is no. Our lots are treated as separate, and all of the constraints of the zoning ordinance are measured separately for each lot. If one of the goals of the zoning ordinance is to promote uniformity of buildings within the district, that rule makes some sense; a McMansion on my lot won't be any more palatable to the rest of the neighborhood just because my next door neighbor has a smaller than average home.

Are there circumstances, however, where transfer of development rights makes sense? If the primary reason for limiting the size of buildings is to restrict density of development (as may be the case in some urban areas), how much does it matter whether a given city block has 1 large building or 10 smaller ones? As long as the same overall square footage generates the same burden on sidewalks, streets, and public transportation systems, one might argue that landowners ought to be able to transfer unused development rights.

Zoning Lot Merger in New York City

New York City, where land values are among the highest in the world, pioneered the concept of the "zoning lot merger," which permits one landowner to transfer unused development rights from one parcel to an adjoining parcel. Imagine, for instance, a developer who wants to build on a 50 x 100 parcel with an FAR of 5. The developer is entitled to build 25,000 square feet of floor area. But suppose the parcel immediately to the west of the developer's parcel is the same size as developer's parcel, but uses only 10,000 square feet. If the owner of that parcel does not immediately contemplate expanding her own building, the neighbor might be willing to sell the developer her unused 15,000 square feet of FAR—enabling the developer to build 40,000 square feet on his own parcel. New York City's zoning ordinance permits the two owners to merge their lots for zoning purposes without merging them for other purposes, and then measures FAR for the merged lot. In effect, the neighbor has transferred her development rights to the developer. Because the two lots are treated as a single zoning lot, the developer does not need any sort of special permit or variance to exceed the FAR ordinarily permitted.

Moreover, the New York City ordinance permits merger of multiple lots, not just two. And because the ordinance focuses on FAR, not on building height, as the primary limit on building size, a developer who obtains development rights from a large number of neighboring parcels can build a skyscraper on a parcel initially zoned for a much more modest FAR. The developer of One57, currently New York City's second tallest residential building, used zoning lot mergers to build the 90-story tower, in which a single apartment has reportedly sold for $90 million.

Selling the Sky: Katz's Delicatessen and the Sale of Air Rights

Ali Lake
Columbia Spectator, September 25, 2014

Katz's Delicatessen, of *When Harry Met Sally* fame, is no longer dealing only in pastrami sandwiches and fake orgasms. Of late, its owners have been selling air.

Air rights, more formally known as transferable development rights, are essentially rights to the air above a lot. Sometimes these rights are bought and sold so that one building can be cantilevered over a shorter neighbor, but more often they are traded to get around zoning restrictions.

New York zoning law dictates a maximum allowable floor area for each lot, which in practice limits the height of any building on that lot—but a developer can buy up surplus space from adjacent buildings in order to build above the cap. With the high demand for real estate and, in particular, for apartments with a view, developers are buying up air rights all over Manhattan to construct lucrative developments like the towering One57 in midtown.

Katz's Deli recently sold its air rights for an undisclosed sum. The purchase will likely go toward enabling the construction of a high-rise building in one of the deli's two neighboring lots, both of which were recently purchased by developer Ben Shaoul.

But the buying and selling of air rights may undermine the very purpose of New York's zoning laws. Elliott Sclar, the director of the Center for Sustainable Urban Development and a professor of urban planning and international affairs at Columbia, says that developers have taken what was "of a public purpose—zoning for light and air and health and a lot of other good reasons" and made it into a commodity. With the advent of zoning lot mergers and TDRs, he also warns that the city may not have the carrying capacity to accommodate the influx of people that towering residential buildings will bring. "By carrying capacity I mean the ability for service. For people to walk on the street, for cars to park. These buildings create a lot of need. Taxicabs have to pull up, buses have to serve things," he says.

But for Jake Dell, proprietor of Katz's Deli, selling the air rights was a matter of preservation.

"I think that people get confused with the concept of air rights, so I think what's easiest to say is that we removed them, basically," he says. "So now no one can build on top of Katz's. There's no cantilevering over the building. There's no plopping a building on this lot, there's nothing like that. It's very much a way to protect who we are. People come to us with a certain expectation, and this is done to protect that reality."

And if you've come to Katz's with the expectation of fake-orgasm-worthy food, don't worry; that's still very much preserved as well.

Transferable Development Rights as a Regulatory Tool

Suppose a municipality wants to restrict development in an environmentally-sensitive area, or to ensure that a landmark building is maintained in its current state, despite development pressures to demolish it. The municipality could simply rezone the environmental area to prohibit intensive development, or prohibit demolition of the landmark, but that might cause serious financial hardship to the affected landowners. Alternatively, the municipality could take the affected land and pay compensation, but that would be unattractive to municipal officials trying to keep taxes low. Transferable Development Rights (or TDRs) are a legal tool that planners can use to address these problems. The idea, in a nutshell, is to give owners of restricted land the power to exceed development restrictions on other parcels.

TDR schemes typically involve two categories of parcels: sending parcels and receiving parcels. "Sending" parcels are those burdened by the restrictive land use regulations. The owners of such restricted parcels are given the right to exceed land use restrictions elsewhere in the jurisdiction on eligible, so-called "receiving" parcels. Depending on the details and scale of the particular TDR program, making these development rights alienable can give them substantial market value.

TDRs are especially useful where adverse impacts from development require particularly severe restrictions in a localized area within a jurisdiction but where there is ample demand for development elsewhere in the jurisdiction that would not cause the same harmful impacts. Properly designed, a TDR scheme can help spread the costs of restricting development in ways that avoid unfairly burdening individual landowners. As with incentive zoning, however, TDRs likely work best when demand for relief from land use restrictions on the receiving parcels is strong. (Do you see why?) The value of TDRs would, therefore, be undermined if developers of eligible receiving parcels could easily obtain variances. Consequently, TDR programs often make it difficult for developers to obtain variances for parcels eligible to receive TDRs.

TDRs in the New Jersey Pinelands

One particularly comprehensive TDR program is the Pinelands Development Credit (PDC) program in New Jersey. The PDC program exists as one part of the Pinelands Comprehensive Management Plan ("Pinelands Plan"), which was adopted by the New Jersey Pinelands Commission in 1981. The Pinelands Plan covers 53 municipalities in four counties, an area of over 1 million acres. It designates land within that region as either subject to severe development restrictions (the sending area for this TDR scheme) designed to preserve the pinelands ecosystem or as part of "Regional Growth Areas," the receiving area.

PDCs are awarded to owners of parcels of at least 10 acres of restricted land. One PDC allows the owner of the credit to exceed applicable development limits on an eligible receiving parcel by up to four dwellings, and to exceed the density provided for in the local zoning laws by up to 50%. The number of PDCs awarded to a restricted parcel depends on its precise characteristics. The owner of a 40 acre upland parcel, for example, will typically be eligible to receive a full credit, but owners of smaller parcels—or wetland parcels—will receive fractional credits. See NJAC 7:50–5.43(b)I.iii & iv (a quarter credit would allow the construction of one extra dwelling on a receiving parcel). In order to sell a PDC, the credit must first be certified by the Pinelands Development Credit Bank, which was established by the New Jersey legislature in 1985 to administer the program. The bank maintains a list of available PDCs, but it generally does not sell PDCs itself. Those sales are private transactions between PDC owners and landowners in receiving areas. In order to prevent the variance process from undermining the value of PDCs, the Pinelands TDR program imposes the requirement that, where a proposed development would otherwise require a variance from bulk or area standards, the developer must acquire the requisite number of PDCs before the local government may approve the requested variance. When the program began, it was estimated that PDCs would be worth $10,000 each. As of 2014, transactions indicated a value of about $38,000 per PDC. As of the end of 2014, more than 2800 PDCs have been allocated to owners of restricted land under the program, and over 600 projects using PDCs—involving roughly 1200 PDCs—have been built or approved.

TDRs as a Landmarks Preservation Tool in New York City

In the 1960s, New York City embraced the use of TDRs as a tool for preservation of landmarks. Once the city landmarks preservation commission designates a landmark, the owner of the site faces significant restrictions on altering existing structures. To soften the blow of such restrictions, the city's zoning ordinance authorizes the transfer of development rights from designated landmarks to other sites in the vicinity of the landmark, but not necessarily on the same block. In this respect, landmark owners have a broader right to transfer development rights than would otherwise be permitted through the zoning lot merger process. However, transfer of development rights associated with a landmark requires a special permit, while zoning lot mergers can be accomplished as a matter of right, without any special permit. As a result, landmark transfers are far less common; one study found that between 2003 and 2011, only two transfers occurred.

NOTES AND QUESTIONS

1. As with incentive zoning, does the connection between the success of TDRs and demand for regulatory relief by owners of receiving parcels create incentives for land use policymakers to regulate receiving parcels for less development than they actually want to see?

2. Are TDRs fair to neighbors of receiving parcels, who now must cope with more intensive development than would have been possible in the absence of a TDR scheme?

3. In order to obtain a PDC, owners of restricted land in the New Jersey pinelands must agree to insert a no-development restriction into their property's deeds, and that restriction will thereafter run with title to their land. What does the deed restriction add to the limitations already imposed by the applicable land use regulations? Why would New Jersey impose such a requirement?

4. New York City has expanded the use of TDRs in a number of special districts to influence the course of development within those districts. For more detailed discussion, see Vicki Been & John Infranca, Transferable Development Rights Programs, 78 Brooklyn L. Rev. 435, 446–455 (2013).

V. ACCESSORY USES

Most zoning ordinances would prohibit a landowner from using a parcel located in a residential district to build a law office or a three-car garage. But suppose the landowner wants to include a law office or a three-car garage as part of a single-family house she intends to build on the parcel. Should landowner now be permitted to use the garage or the law office? Most ordinances make provisions for "accessory uses"—uses that would not be permitted by themselves but which are permitted in conjunction with the permitted principal use of the parcel. How far should accessory use protection extend? Consider the following case:

Matter of New York Botanical Garden v. Board of Standards and Appeals

Court of Appeals of New York, 1998
91 N.Y.2d 413, 694 N.E.2d 424, 671 N.Y.S.2d 423

■ WESLEY, J.

In 1993, Fordham University applied to the New York City Department of Buildings (DOB) for a permit to build a new broadcasting facility and attendant tower as an accessory use on its

Rose Hill campus. The DOB issued Fordham a building permit. After construction began, the New York Botanical Garden objected to the issuance of the permit. The DOB Commissioner determined that the radio station and accompanying tower together were an accessory use within the meaning of section 12–10 of the New York City Zoning Resolution. The Botanical Garden appealed to the Board of Standards and Appeals (BSA) which, after reviewing numerous submissions from both parties and holding two public hearings, unanimously confirmed the Commissioner's determination. The issue before this Court is whether that determination was arbitrary or capricious; we agree with both lower courts that it was not.

Fordham University was founded in 1841, at the site of the current main campus, as St. John's College. Shortly thereafter, the Jesuits assumed administration of the institution; it took its current name in 1907. The main campus is situated on approximately 80 acres in the Rose Hill section of the North Bronx, directly adjacent along its eastern border to the Botanical Garden. The campus falls within an R6 zoning district (medium density residential). The University offers a wide variety of graduate and undergraduate studies, including degree programs in communications and media studies. As part of these programs, the University offers courses such as "Introduction to Radio," "Radio News Techniques," "Broadcast News Operations" and an internship at the University's radio station, WFUV.

Fordham has operated WFUV as an on-campus, noncommercial, educational radio station since 1947. WFUV is affiliated with National Public Radio and has operated at its current signal strength of 50,000 watts since 1969. The station's current antenna extends 190 feet above ground level and is situated atop the University's Keating Hall, which also houses WFUV's broadcast studio. In 1983, Fordham explored new sites for the antenna. On February 17, 1993, it filed an application with the DOB to construct a new one-story radio transmitting building and an accessory 480-foot (approximately 45-story) radio tower midway along the eastern border of the campus. The application correctly identified the University as a Use Group 3 facility, a permitted use within R6 zoning districts (see, NY City Zoning Resolution § 22–13), and described the tower and radio station as an accessory use to the principal use of the property as an educational institution. DOB approved the project and issued a building permit on March 1, 1994; construction began shortly after the permit was renewed on May 13, 1994.

By letter to the DOB Commissioner dated June 30, 1994, the Botanical Garden, which is located across a four-lane thoroughfare from the tower site, objected to the construction and its classification as an "accessory use" under the Zoning Resolution. By that time, construction of the tower was partially complete, at a cost to Fordham of $800,000.

On July 1, 1994, the DOB Commissioner issued a stop work order pending resolution of the objection.

By letter of September 12, 1994, the Commissioner informed Fordham that the DOB had determined that the tower did in fact constitute an accessory use within the meaning of Zoning Resolution § 12–10. In response to the Botanical Garden's request, the Commissioner issued a final determination confirming the decision on November 7, 1994. The Botanical Garden filed an administrative appeal with the BSA on December 6, 1994. After reviewing substantial submissions, and holding two public hearings, the BSA affirmed the Commissioner's determination. The BSA found that Fordham's operation of a radio station of this size and power was "clearly incidental to the educational mission of the University," and that it was "commonplace" for universities to operate stations "at or near the same power level." The BSA expressly ruled that "the sole issue ... is whether the proposed tower is 'incidental to' and 'customarily found' in connection with the University and not whether the tower could be smaller or relocated to another site."

The Botanical Garden then commenced this CPLR article 78 proceeding to annul the BSA's determination that the radio station and tower constituted an accessory use of Fordham's property. The trial court dismissed the petition, holding that the BSA's determination was rational and supported by substantial evidence. The court noted that aesthetics appeared to be at the heart of petitioner's concerns, and implicitly rejected this as a valid basis for labeling the BSA's determination arbitrary and capricious.

The Appellate Division unanimously affirmed.

This Court has frequently recognized that the BSA is comprised of experts in land use and planning, and that its interpretation of the Zoning Resolution is entitled to deference. So long as its interpretation is neither "irrational, unreasonable nor inconsistent with the governing statute," it will be upheld (Matter of Trump-Equitable Fifth Ave. Co. v. Gliedman, 62 N.Y.2d 539, 545). Of course, this principle does not apply to purely legal determinations; where "the question is one of pure legal interpretation of statutory terms, deference to the BSA is not required" (Matter of Toys "R" Us v. Silva, 89 N.Y.2d 411, 419). However, "when applying its special expertise in a particular field to interpret statutory language, an agency's rational construction is entitled to deference" (Matter of Raritan Dev. Corp. v. Silva, 91 N.Y.2d 98, 102).

Here, the BSA determined that Fordham's radio station and tower constituted an "accessory use" within the meaning of Zoning Resolution § 12–10. That section provides that an accessory use:

(a) Is a *use* conducted on the same *zoning lot* as the principal *use* to which it is related (whether located within the same or an *accessory building or other structure,* or as an *accessory use* of land) . . . and

(b) Is a *use* which is clearly incidental to, and customarily found in connection with, such principal *use;* and

(c) Is either in the same ownership as such principal *use,* or is operated and maintained on the same *zoning lot* substantially for the benefit or convenience of the owners, occupants, employees, customers, or visitors of the principal *use.*

Thus, Zoning Resolution § 12–10 sets forth a three-prong test for determining whether a use qualifies as an accessory one: first, it must be conducted on the same zoning lot as the principal use; second, it must be "clearly incidental to, and customarily found in connection with" the principal use; and third, there must be unity of ownership, either legal or beneficial, between the principal and accessory uses. Petitioner acknowledges that the first and third prongs are satisfied here. It takes issue, however, with the BSA's determination that a tower of this size is clearly incidental to, and customarily found in connection with, the principal use of this land as a university campus. Petitioner also maintains that this question, particularly the "customarily found" inquiry, presents an issue of pure statutory construction and therefore this Court should not give any deference to the BSA determination. We disagree.

Whether a proposed accessory use is clearly incidental to and customarily found in connection with the principal use depends on an analysis of the nature and character of the principal use of the land in question in relation to the accessory use, taking into consideration the over-all character of the particular area in question (see, Matter of Hassett v. Horn, 23 N.Y.2d 745, rev'g 29 A.D.2d 945 on the dissent below). This analysis is, to a great extent, fact-based (Matter of Exxon Corp. v. Board of Stds. & Appeals, 128 A.D.2d 289, 298 ["the requirement that the proposed use be one customarily found in connection with, and incidental to (the principal use) poses a factual issue for Board resolution"]). Moreover, such an analysis is one that will clearly benefit from the expertise of specialists in land use planning. Pursuant to section 659(b) of the New York City Charter, the BSA includes a city planner, an engineer and an architect. These professionals unanimously determined that the radio station and the proposed tower are incidental to, and customarily found in connection with, an educational institution. This Court may not lightly disregard that determination.

The Botanical Garden nonetheless argues that the "customarily found" element of the definition of accessory use itself poses a purely legal question, relying on Matter of Teachers Ins. & Annuity Ass'n v. City of New York (82 N.Y.2d 35). We did hold in *Teachers* that, in an appropriate case, this Court will parse various sections of a statute or regulation, and identify certain sections as requiring deference to agency experts, while other sections present questions of pure legal interpretation. In *Teachers* we noted that whether a restaurant was of "special historical or aesthetic interest" (Administrative Code of City of NY § 25–301[b]) to justify its designation as a landmark was an interpretation and application of the Landmarks Law better left to the expertise of the Landmarks Preservation Commission. However, the "jurisdictional predicate" that the restaurant would only be given landmark status if it was "'customarily open or accessible to the public'" was a matter of pure legal interpretation (*id.,* at 41–42). The Court in *Teachers* was not called upon to examine whether there was record support for deciding the "jurisdictional predicate." The issue was a straightforward legal one: does a restaurant fall within the coverage of the statute—i.e., areas that are customarily open or accessible to the public.

In this case, there is no dispute that radio stations and their attendant towers are clearly incidental to and customarily found on college campuses in New York and all over the United States. The issue before the BSA was: is a station of this particular size and power, with a 480-foot tower, customarily found on a college campus or is there something inherently different in this radio station and tower that would justify treating it differently. This is clearly a fact-based determination substantially different from the law issue presented in *Teachers*.

Granting the BSA's determination its appropriate weight, we cannot say that its classification of the tower as an accessory use is arbitrary or capricious, or not supported by substantial evidence. It must be noted that the Botanical Garden's initial objection was to the over-all size of Fordham's radio operations. Petitioner argued before the DOB Commissioner and the BSA that it was not customary, but rather highly unusual, for a university to operate a station which is affiliated with National Public Radio and which broadcasts at a signal strength of 50,000 watts. It argued that the "sheer extent of the operations," which reached "far beyond the immediate college community" showed that the station was not being operated as an adjunct to University programs, but that it was essentially a commercial enterprise.

In response, Fordham established that it is commonplace for stations affiliated with educational institutions to operate on the scale of WFUV. The University submitted evidence showing that 180 college or university radio stations are affiliated with National Public Radio. (This represents 58% of all NPR affiliates.) Of these, slightly more than half operate at a signal strength of 50,000 watts. Fordham also presented proof that the station was an integral part of the University's communications curriculum. Finally, Fordham introduced evidence that building this tower was a practical necessity, in order for the station to comply with FCC regulations. This evidence provides a substantial basis for the BSA's determination that Fordham's radio operations are of a type and character customarily found in connection with an educational institution.

The Botanical Garden nonetheless maintains that it is not customary for universities to build radio towers of this height in connection with their radio operations. This argument ignores the fact that the Zoning Resolution classification of accessory uses is based upon functional rather than structural specifics. The use found to be accessory here is the operation of a 50,000-watt university radio station. As set forth above, there was more than adequate evidence to support the conclusion that such a use is customarily found in connection with a college or university.

The specifics of the proper placement of the station's antenna, particularly the height at which it must be placed, are dependent on site-specific factors such as the surrounding geography, building density and signal strength. This necessarily means that the placement of antennas will vary widely from one radio station to another. Thus, the fact that this specific tower may be somewhat different does not render the Board's determination unsupported as a matter of law, since the use itself (i.e., radio operations of this particular size and scope) is one customarily found in connection with an educational institution. Moreover, Fordham did introduce evidence that a significant number of other radio stations affiliated with educational institutions in this country utilize broadcast towers similar in size to the one it proposes.

Separation of powers concerns also support the decision we reach today. Accepting the Botanical Garden's argument would result in the judicial enactment of a new restriction on accessory uses not found in the Zoning Resolution. Zoning Resolution § 12–10 (accessory use) (q) specifically lists "*[a]ccessory* radio or television towers" as examples of permissible accessory uses (provided, of course, that they comply with the requirements of Zoning Resolution § 12–10 [accessory use] [a], [b] and [c]). Notably, no height restriction is included in this example of a permissible accessory use. By contrast, other examples of accessory uses contain specific size restrictions. For instance, Zoning Resolution § 12–10 defines a "home occupation" as an accessory use which "[o]ccupies not more than 25 percent of the total *floor area* . . . and in no event more than 500 square feet of *floor area*" (§ 12–10 [home occupation] [c]) and the accessory use of "[l]iving or sleeping accommodations for caretakers" is limited to "1200 square feet of *floor area*" (§ 12–10 [accessory use] [b][2]). The fact that the definition of accessory radio towers contains no such size restrictions supports the conclusion that the size and scope of these structures must be based upon an individualized assessment of need. The BSA is the body designated to make this determination, and courts may intervene only if its determination is arbitrary or capricious.

Matter of Presnell v. Leslie (3 N.Y.2d 384), relied upon heavily by petitioner, does not dictate a contrary result. The petitioner in *Presnell,* an amateur radio operator, applied for a building permit to construct a 44-foot radio tower. He claimed that he was entitled to a permit as of right, because the tower was an accessory use to the principal use of the lot as his residence. The Village Board of Trustees denied the application, finding that the tower was neither an accessory building nor use customary to a residential dwelling. Presnell challenged this determination. The trial court dismissed the petition and the Appellate Division affirmed. This Court affirmed, holding that "it cannot be said as a matter of law that the erection of a 44-foot steel tower in a compact residential area of a suburban community, where dwellings are restricted in height to 35 feet . . . is a customarily incidental use of residential property, or one which might commonly be expected by neighboring property owners" (*id.*, at 388).

Presnell is distinguishable because there, the municipality had denied the permit. Thus, we specifically limited our scope of review to whether that determination was unsupported "as a matter of law" (3 N.Y.2d, at 388). We did not hold that the municipality could not have determined that the tower was a permissible accessory use. We afforded its determination the proper level of respect, reviewable only for clear legal error. While we did not articulate this as an arbitrary and capricious or substantial evidence question, this was the standard effectively employed. Here, the BSA determined that the station and tower did constitute an accessory use. Thus, rather than mandating reversal, *Presnell* actually lends support to Fordham's position that the BSA's determination should be upheld as an appropriate and well-supported exercise of its power to decide what does or does not constitute an accessory use under the pertinent zoning ordinance.

Accordingly, the order of the Appellate Division should be affirmed, with costs.

■ CHIEF JUDGE KAYE and JUDGES TITONE, BELLACOSA and CIPARICK concur; JUDGES SMITH and LEVINE taking no part.

NOTES AND QUESTIONS

1. Why would the New York City Zoning Resolution prohibit a radio tower operated by a commercial radio station while permitting an identical tower, used for precisely the same purpose, when operated as a use accessory to a university? Isn't the effect on neighboring owners precisely the same?

2. Fordham's radio tower was never completed. After the tower was half-built, Fordham agreed with the Botanical Garden and Montefiore Medical Center to place a smaller tower atop an apartment building owned by Montefiore. The Botanical Garden agreed to share some of the costs of removing the half-built tower, and agreed to some of the rental payments at the tower's new location.

3. The New York City Zoning Resolution at issue in the Botanical Garden case provided that to qualify as a permitted accessory use, the use had to be "incidental to, and customarily found in connection with" the principal use of the parcel. The requirements that an accessory use be "incidental" and "customary" are common to many ordinances. Some ordinances require that the accessory use be "subordinate" to the principal use. If an ordinance includes the New York City language, which of the following would qualify as a permitted accessory use? Justify your conclusions:

a.   Rooftop solar collectors designed to provide heat and electrical power for a residential home?

b.   A backyard wind turbine designed to provide the same heat and power? *See* Tink-Wig Mountain Lake Forest Prop. Owners Ass'n v. Lackawaxen Twp. Zoning Hearing Bd., 986 A.2d 935 (Pa. Cmwlth. 2009).

c.   A backyard dog house?

d.   A backyard pigeon coop? *See* DaPurificacao v. Zoning Bd. of Adjustment, 377 N.J.Super. 436, 873 A.2d 582 (App. Div. 2005). What if the pigeon coop houses 40 racing pigeons? *See* La Russo v. Neuringer, 105 A.D.3d 743 (App. Div. 2013).

e.   A storage building in back of a single-family residence? Does the size of the building matter? Does it matter what the owner stores in the building? *See* DeVoe v. City of Missoula, 274 P.3d 752 (Mont. 2012).

f.   An encampment for homeless citizens on a parcel owned by a church and used for religious services? *See* City of Woodinville v. Northshore United Church of Christ, 162 P.3d 427, 139 Wash.App. 639 (2007).

g.   A campground (with parking lot for recreational vehicles) on a "campus" used by a church as a church and worship center? *See* City of Hope v. Sadsbury Twp. Zoning Hearing Bd., 890 A.2d 1137 (Pa. Cmwlth. 2006).

4.   In determining whether a use is a permitted accessory use, should the relative sizes of the principal and accessory uses matter? Suppose, for instance, that a district permits use for recreational clubs. A club seeks to build 30 residential units on the site, contending that seasonal residences for club members are an accessory use. If the residential units occupy 60% of the club site, can the residences qualify as "incidental" to the principal use? *See* Matter of Mamaroneck Beach & Yacht Club, Inc. v. Zoning Bd. of Appeals, 53 A.D.3d 494, 862 N.Y.S.2d 81 (2008) (holding that the zoning board of appeals, in "engrafting area requirements upon provisions defining a permissive accessory use, based upon the square footage of other building structures on the property, was irrational and unreasonable."). In light of that holding, are all uses "incidental"?

5.   *Evidence.* If you represent a landowner seeking to establish that a use qualifies as an accessory use, what sort of evidence would you present to the zoning board of appeals? What evidence did Fordham present to the board in the *Botanical Garden* case? Suppose you represent neighbors objecting to a proposed accessory use. What evidence would you present?

6. *Standard of Review.* In the *Botanical Garden* case, suppose the Board of Standards and Appeals had decided that the radio tower was not an accessory use because it was not incidental to operation of the university. If Fordham had sought judicial review, how would the Court of Appeals have decided the case? Suppose the Board had decided that the radio tower was not customary, and therefore not a permitted accessory use. In each case, is the board's determination a determination of fact or a determination of law? What significance might the distinction have?

VI. ZONING AMENDMENTS

As we have seen, the municipal legislature generally enacts the initial zoning ordinance, which specifies the permitted uses within each district, and incorporates a map of the various districts. The municipal legislature cannot always anticipate the effect the ordinance will have on every parcel within the municipal borders. Variances and special use permits enable the municipal legislature to delegate to an administrative body the power to make adjustments that do not alter the basic legislative decisions. This basic scheme is good for the municipal legislature, because it conserves legislative resources for the other issues on the legislature's agenda. It also has advantages for landowners and neighbors, because the zoning board of appeals will generally have more time and more expertise to devote to the problems facing those landowners and neighbors.

Variances and special use permits, however, are of no value to a landowner who wants to make use of her land in a way that is patently inconsistent with the existing zoning ordinance. The administrative process is equally useless for neighbors who are unhappy with the classifications codified in the existing ordinance. When landowners or neighbors seek more basic changes in the structure of the zoning ordinance, or in the zoning map, they must approach the municipal legislature to seek a zoning amendment—what many people have in mind when they refer to a "rezoning."

As with most legislation on the state and federal level, zoning amendments rarely spring full-blown from the mind of a local legislator who is reconsidering the policy issues that were addressed in the existing zoning ordinance. Instead, landowners or neighbors typically initiate the amendment process to achieve private objectives. These interest groups try to persuade local legislators to amend the ordinance, just as interest groups try to persuade congressmen and state legislators. Later, we will study criticisms of analogies between the local legislative process and the state and federal process, but for now, we will focus on the basics.

Most statutes require the local legislature to conduct a public hearing on proposed amendments to the zoning ordinance. Interested parties are typically free to appear at the hearing to voice their opinions, and to submit written materials in support of (or in opposition to) any proposed amendment.

Zoning amendments generally come in two basic forms. The first is a **text amendment**, which modifies the restrictions applicable in a particular zoning district, or in all zoning districts. The amendment is a "text amendment" because the amendment modifies the text of the ordinance; the legislature adds or subtracts words from the existing ordinance to achieve the desired result. For instance, if the ordinance imposes a 50 foot height limitation on all buildings within a district, or on all buildings within the municipality, a group of developers who want to build taller buildings might seek a text amendment that substitutes 80 feet for 50 feet in some or all of the districts within the municipality.

The second form of amendment is a **map amendment,** which does not modify the restrictions applicable in any zoning district, but instead alters the map to change the district in which a particular parcel of land is located. For instance, if a developer is perfectly happy to comply with the current ordinance's restrictions on apartment houses, but the developer's land is located in a district that permits only single-family homes, the developer would typically seek a map amendment that places his parcel in a district that permits multiple-family residences.

VII.   NON-CONFORMING USES

To some extent, zoning provides a blueprint for future development. But what effect does zoning have on existing development? In most states, newly enacted ordinances do not prohibit landowners from operating pre-existing non-conforming uses, although they do prohibit expansion of those uses. This exception for non-conforming uses rests on two foundations. First, changing the rules of the game for landowners who made significant expenditures in reliance on existing law might be unfair, and, in some circumstances, unconstitutional. (More on constitutional issues later.) Second, the hope was that over time, non-conforming uses would fade away because they would be inconsistent with new development in the area. Against that background, consider the following two cases:

Cleveland MHC, LLC v. City of Richland

Supreme Court of Mississippi, 2015
163 So.3d 284

■ COLEMAN, J.

The City of Richland began enforcing a zoning ordinance that regulated nonconforming uses and prohibited Cleveland MHC, LLC from replacing mobile homes that were removed from its property. The Rankin County Circuit Court upheld the City's decision, and Cleveland

MHC appealed. The Court of Appeals reversed. The City petitioned the Court for certiorari, which we granted.

Facts and Procedural History

Cleveland Mobile Home Community has been operating in Rankin County since the 1950s. It includes spaces for 138 mobile homes and seventeen campers or recreational vehicles, and the spaces are rented to tenants. When the City of Richland incorporated in 1975, the mobile-home park became part of the City and was zoned "I–1, Light Industrial Zoning." The City's ordinances prohibit industrial property being used for residential purposes. Thus, use of the property as a mobile-home park was a nonconforming use. Regarding nonconforming uses, the City ordinances provide that nonconforming lots, uses, or structures are allowed "to continue until they are removed" but the "survival" of the nonconformity is not encouraged. Further, nonconformities "shall not be enlarged upon, expanded[,] or extended, [nor] be used as grounds for adding other [s]tructures or uses prohibited elsewhere in the same district."

The mobile-home park was a nonconforming use for many years, and mobile homes were removed from the property and replaced over the years. Cleveland MHC, LLC purchased the mobile-home park in 2008 and claims that it received assurance from the City's zoning administrator that it would be allowed to continue operating and moving mobile homes in and out without restriction. However, in April 2011, apparently due to deterioration of the property, the City informed Cleveland MHC that it would begin enforcing the zoning ordinance and, when an existing mobile home was removed, it could not be replaced. Cleveland MHC appealed to the Board of Aldermen in July 2011. The Board upheld the City's decision and voted unanimously to adopt the following resolution: "That in the event a mobile home or similar vehicle is removed from its then present location in the Cleveland Mobile Home Park, another mobile home or similar vehicle shall not be placed on the vacated site.

Analysis

Cleveland MHC claims that its replacing existing mobile homes with new ones is "a lawful continuation of the property's nonconforming use, not an enlargement of that use." The issue at hand is a matter of first impression for the Court.

The Court of Appeals held that the nonconforming use ordinance applied to the "mobile-home park as a whole," not to individual lots within the park, such that, as long as Cleveland MHC used the property as a mobile-home park and did not expand, its operation was a permitted use. The City asserts that the Court of Appeals' decision effectively gives Cleveland MHC a perpetual right to continue its nonconformity. The City claims that the Court of Appeals' decision is not in line with the majority of courts that have ruled on the issue.

However, as the Court of Appeals discussed, several courts have come down on the opposite side of the issue.

We agree with the Court of Appeals that the nature of the nonconforming use must be defined before the issue can be resolved. Cleveland MHC owns the entire property and operates a mobile-home park thereon. The individual lots in the mobile-home park are rented to tenants; the lots are not owned individually. Thus, the nonconforming use belongs to Cleveland MHC, and the nonconformity is Cleveland MHC's use of the land as a mobile-park home. While the individual structures thereon are nonconformities in themselves, they make up parts of the whole. Therefore, we hold that the Court of Appeals correctly determined that the nonconforming use relates to the mobile-home park as a whole, not to individual lots.

The City claims that "it has long been a standard feature of municipal zoning law in Mississippi and elsewhere that a property owner cannot rebuild or replace one non-conforming structure with another," citing Palazzola v. City of Gulfport, 211 Miss. 737, 52 So.2d 611 (1951), and Pelham Esplanade, Inc. v. Board of Trustees, 77 N.Y.2d 66, 563 N.Y.S.2d 759, 565 N.E.2d 508 (1990). These cases are distinguishable. The issue in Palazzola and Pelham Esplanade was whether nonconformities could be replaced after they burned down or were destroyed. The nonconformity at issue was the structure itself. Once the structure was destroyed, it could not be rebuilt. In the instant case, the nonconformity is the use of the property as a mobile-home park, and that use has not been destroyed or changed.

Because the nature of the nonconforming use is Cleveland MHC's use of the property as mobile-home park, we hold that the Court of Appeals was correct in determining that the City's interpretation of the nonconforming use ordinance to apply on a lot-by-lot basis is arbitrary, capricious, and illegal. First, the City's resolution deprives Cleveland MHC of its constitutional right to enjoy its property, as the resolution effectively would destroy the mobile-home park—as well as Cleveland MHC's investment—by attrition. Cleveland MHC relied on the City's course of conduct, and possibly assurance from the zoning administrator, when it purchased the property with the understanding that it could continue operating as the mobile-home park had in the past. The mobile-home park had been in operation for more than fifty years, much of that time subject to the zoning ordinance and operating as a nonconforming use. For more than thirty years, the City did not enforce the nonconforming use ordinance as to each pad on the property. For three years under the new ownership, the City said nothing about the removal and replacement of mobile homes on the property. The Court of Appeals correctly noted that "[a] citizen's right to be protected in 'the lawful use of his property is one of the most sacred rights reserved to him under our Constitution.' "

Conclusion

We affirm the judgment of the Court of Appeals.

NOTES AND QUESTIONS

1. Suppose a landowner purchases vacant land in an area where mobile homes are in great demand. If the municipality subsequently enacts an ordinance zoning the land for light industrial uses, can the landowner challenge the ordinance based on the landowner's expectation that it would use the land for mobile home purposes?

How, if at all, was Cleveland MHC's position different? What investment (other than its investment in the land) was jeopardized by the city's prohibition?

2. What improvements would Cleveland MHC be entitled to make to the mobile home park?

a. Could it permit larger homes (double-wides instead of single-wides)?

b. Could it increase the number of homes on the site?

c. Could it offer new services and amenities—a swimming pool? A workout room?

What arguments would you make for Cleveland MHC? For the city or any disgruntled neighbors?

3. More generally, when does a change in a pre-existing non-conforming use constitute an impermissible expansion? Suppose, for instance, that Landowner has long operated a marina, and that the municipality recently rezoned the area to permit only residential uses. Which of the following changes in use constitutes an impermissible expansion of the pre-existing non-conforming use?

a. Landowner contracts with a boating company to store its boats, doubling the number of boats in the marina at any one time. *Cf.* Jahnigen v. Staley, 245 Md. 130, 225 A.2d 277 (Md. 1967);

b. Landowner builds a new dock, enabling it to accommodate twice as many boats;

c. Landowner adds lights to the marina, making it easier for boaters to find the marina at night;

d. Landowner adds a retail store inside the marina, selling snacks, sunglasses, and other items designed for use on the water. *Cf.* City of Okoboji v. Okoboji Barz, Inc., 717 N.W.2d 310 (Iowa 2006);

e. Landowner adds a bar inside the principal marina building, featuring activities that include karaoke, live music, hog roasting, and monthly full moon parties. *See id.*

4. Suppose Cleveland MHC had sold the individual pads on which buyers located their own mobile homes. When a buyer sold her pad and moved her home, could the purchaser install a new mobile home on the pad? Why or why not?

5. If the City's Board of Aldermen—its "legislative" body—approved a resolution precluding addition of a new mobile home, what basis did the court have for upsetting that legislative determination?

Trip Associates, Inc. v. Mayor and City Council of Baltimore

Court of Appeals of Maryland, 2006
392 Md. 563, 898 A.2d 449

■ BELL, C. J.

The question this case presents is whether the Board of Municipal and Zoning Appeals ("the Board") erred when it restricted the number of days per week the appellants could operate a valid nonconforming use. The appellants' property, located in the B–5–1 Zoning District in Baltimore City, is being used for the operation of "Club Choices," a nightclub and after-hours establishment that sometimes features adult entertainment. The Club is owned by the appellant, Anthony Dwight Triplin ("Triplin"), who also is the owner of Triplin Associates, Inc. ("Trip"), the other appellant.

Triplin purchased 1815–17 North Charles Street, the property at issue, in 1983. Prior to his purchase, the property had been a nightclub featuring adult entertainment, including male and female exotic dancing. The adult entertainment had been presented up to five nights a week since 1979. When Triplin purchased the property, the applicable zoning ordinance did not prohibit the use of the property as an adult entertainment facility. Nevertheless, Triplin reduced the number of nights of nude or exotic dancing from five to two nights per week, featuring music and comedy on the other nights. The Board approved his use of the premise as an "after hours establishment" in 1992. With this approval, the adult entertainment was presented after hours, exclusively.

On December 15, 1994, Ordinance No. 443 was enacted. That ordinance, codified at Baltimore City Code, Art. 30, § 8.0–6l, regulated adult entertainment businesses, "where persons appear in a state of total or partial nudity." It also provided that "any adult entertainment business existing on September 10, 1993 is considered a nonconforming use, subject to all Class III regulations." Baltimore City Zoning Code § 13–609. After this Ordinance was passed, Triplin continued to use the facility as a club that provided adult entertainment after hours. That use was unchallenged until April 14, 2000, when a Baltimore City zoning inspector issued a "Code Violation Notice and Order" to the Club. The violation notice charged:

ZONING VIOLATION

1. Using portion of premises for adult entertainment without first obtaining proper Adult Entertainment Ordinance and Adult Entertainment License. DISCONTINUE SAID USE. REMOVE ALL STOCK, MATERIAL, EQUIPMENT, AND ANY ADVERTISING SIGNS ASSOCIATED WITH SAID USE. OBTAIN CERTIFICATE OF OCCUPANCY BEFORE RE-ESTABLISHING ANY USE.

Triplin appealed to the Board. On appeal, Triplin testified that Club Choices featured exotic dancing and adult entertainment two times a week, Wednesdays and Fridays, for two hours each night. That testimony was confirmed by employees, who offered further that such dancing with partial nudity has been presented two nights per week since 1983.

The Board ruled:

1. ... Adult entertainment may be continued two nights during the week.

The Board finds that a non-conforming use of the premises for adult entertainment had been established prior to Ordinance 443 (adult entertainment business approved December 15, 1994) and may be continued under Subsection 13–402 of the Zoning Code. The Board finds that with the above condition that the request would not be detrimental to or endanger the public health, security, general welfare, or morals or be injurious to the use and enjoyment of other property in the immediate vicinity, nor substantially diminish and impair property values in the neighborhood. Further, and as agreed by the appellant that this is specifically for the appellant Mr. Triplin, the owner and operator of the subject site and a copy of the resolution/decision is to be recorded in the land records of Baltimore City and the appellant is to provide to the Board a court certified copy to be placed in the file ... as part of the record. The purpose of the recording requirement is to give the Charles North Community Association legal standing to enjoin any uses as adult entertainment to a subsequent purchaser, owner, lessee or operator. ...

In accordance with the above facts and findings and subject to the aforementioned condition, (adult entertainment two nights a week only) the Board approves the application.

Board of Municipal and Zoning Appeals, Appeal No. 327–00X, October 12, 2000. Thus, the Board, despite finding that Club Choices was a valid nonconforming use, limited that use, based on the testimony, to two nights per week.

Triplin petitioned the Circuit Court for Baltimore City for judicial review of the Board's decision. That court affirmed the Board's decision and, in addition, ruled that Triplin needed to "apply for and obtain all necessary and relevant licenses required by the City for the operation of an adult entertainment business."

Triplin noted an appeal to the Court of Special Appeals, Trip Assoc. Inc. v. Mayor & City Council of Baltimore, 151 Md. App. 167, 824 A.2d 977 (2003), in which he challenged the Board's power temporally to restrict the nonconforming use and the ruling by the Circuit Court that he obtain an adult entertainment license in order to avoid abandonment of the nonconforming use. The intermediate appellate court . . . affirmed the judgment . . . insofar as the Board's power to restrict the nonconforming use was concerned.

Triplin filed a petition with this Court for a writ of certiorari, which we granted. Trip v. Baltimore, 377 Md. 112, 832 A.2d 204 (2003). We shall reverse.

A.

Title 13 of the Baltimore City Zoning Code establishes the zoning districts in Baltimore, and "provides for the regulation of nonconforming uses and noncomplying structures existing in the various districts." Baltimore City Zoning Code § 13–102. Under the Baltimore City Zoning Code, a "nonconforming use" is defined as "any lawfully existing use of a structure or of land that does not conform to the applicable use regulations of the district in which it is located." Baltimore City Zoning Code § 13–101(c). A valid and lawful nonconforming use is established if a property owner can demonstrate that before, and at the time of, the adoption of a new zoning ordinance, the property was being used in a then-lawful manner for a use that, by later legislation, became non-permitted. *See, e.g.*, Chayt v. Board of Zoning Appeals of Baltimore City, 177 Md. 426, 434, 9 A.2d 747, 750 (1939) (concluding that, to be a nonconforming use, an existing business use must have been known in the neighborhood as being employed for that given purpose); Lapidus v. Mayor and City Counsel of Baltimore, 222 Md. 260, 262, 159 A.2d 640, 641 (1960) (noting that an applicant claiming that a nonconforming use had been established before the effective date of the city zoning ordinance needed to prove that the use asserted existed prior to the date of the ordinance); Vogl v. City of Baltimore, 228 Md. 283, 288, 179 A.2d 693, 696 (1962) (holding that the party claiming the existence of a nonconforming use has the burden of establishing the existence of the use at the time of the passage of the prohibiting zoning ordinance). See also Lone v. Montgomery County, 85 Md. App. 477, 496, 584 A.2d 142, 151 (1991).

As the Court of Special Appeals recognized, nonconforming uses are not favored. County Council v. Gardner, Inc., 293 Md. at 268, 443 A.2d at 119 ("These local ordinances must be strictly construed in order to effectuate the purpose of eliminating nonconforming uses."); Grant v.

Mayor and City Council of Baltimore, 212 Md. 301, 308, 129 A.2d 363, 365 (1957) ("Indeed, there is general agreement that the fundamental problem facing zoning is the inability to eliminate the nonconforming use."); Colati v. Jirout, 186 Md. 652, 657, 47 A.2d 613, 615 (1946) (noting that the spirit of the Baltimore City Zoning Ordinance is against the extension of non-conforming uses). Indeed, in *Grant*, this Court stated, "The earnest aim and ultimate purpose of zoning was and is to reduce nonconformance to conformance as speedily as possible with due regard to the legitimate interests of all concerned." 212 Md. at 307, 129 A.2d at 365. The context for this conclusion was the historical development of the nonconforming use, which the Court also detailed:

> Nonconforming uses have been a problem since the inception of zoning. Originally they were not regarded as serious handicaps to its effective operation; it was felt they would be few and likely to be eliminated by the passage of time and restrictions on their expansion. For these reasons and because it was thought that to require immediate cessation would be harsh and unreasonable, a deprivation of rights in property out of proportion to the public benefits to be obtained and, so, unconstitutional, and finally a red flag to property owners at a time when strong opposition might have jeopardized the chance of any zoning, most, if not all, zoning ordinances provided that lawful uses existing on the effective date of the law could continue although such uses could not thereafter be begun.

Id.

Nevertheless, a "nonconforming use is a vested right entitled to constitutional protection." Amereihn v. Kotras, 194 Md. 591, 601, 71 A.2d 865, 869 (1950). The Court in *Amereihn* made that point forcefully. There, after the area in which a light manufacturing plant was located was zoned as residential, the neighbors brought a complaint, praying that the new owners of the plant be restrained from using the property for manufacturing purposes. This Court, in ruling against the neighbors, pointed out:

> If a property is used for a factory, and thereafter the neighborhood in which it is located is zoned residential, if such regulations applied to the factory it would cease to exist, and the zoning regulation would have the effect of confiscating such property and destroying a vested right therein of the owner. Manifestly this cannot be done, because it would amount to a confiscation of the property.

194 Md. at 601, 71 A.2d at 869 (citations omitted).

A nonconforming use may be reduced to conformance or eliminated in two ways: by "amortization," that is, requiring its termination over a reasonable period of time, and by "abandonment," *i.e.* non-use for a specific of time. Thus, in *Grant*, the Court held that an amortization period of five years to remove nonconforming billboards was valid, and that a five-year period was not an arbitrary time period. 212 Md. at 316, 129 A.2d at 370. *See* Donnelly Advertising Corp. of Maryland v. Mayor and City Council of Baltimore, 279 Md. 660, 671, 370 A.2d 1127, 1134 (1977). *See also* Chesapeake Outdoor Enterprises, Inc. v. Mayor and City Council of Baltimore, 89 Md. App. 54, 597 A.2d 503 (1991) (holding that even assuming a valid nonconforming use, municipality was nonetheless entitled to summary judgment requiring that signs be taken down, because ordinances contained amortization periods, validated by court decisions, requiring that such signs be taken down over a period of time even if constituting nonconforming uses, and all such amortization periods had long since expired); Harris v. Mayor and City Council of Baltimore, 35 Md. App. 572, 371 A.2d 706 (1977) (holding that a court is not restricted, in determining constitutional reasonableness of amortization provision, to consideration of the original amortization period or its later extension, due to the passage of time since the enactment of those provisions). So long as it provides for a reasonable relationship between the amortization and the nature of the nonconforming use, an ordinance prescribing such amortization is not unconstitutional. Gough v. Board of Zoning Appeals for Calvert County, 21 Md. App. 697, 704–705, 321 A.2d 315, 319 (1974). See also Grant, 212 Md. at 316, 129 A.2d at 370; Colati, 186 Md. at 657, 47 A.2d at 615.

The Baltimore City ordinance takes the "abandonment" approach. Section 13–406, as we have seen, prohibits the expansion of any nonconforming use, except as authorized by the Board. Under § 13–407, "Discontinuance or abandonment," the failure actively and continuously to operate the nonconforming use results in its abandonment.

Abandonment . . . focuses not on the owner's intent, but rather, on whether the owner failed to use the property as a nonconforming use in the time period specified in the zoning ordinance. See Catonsville Nursing Home, Inc. v. Loveman, 349 Md. 560, 581, 709 A.2d 749, 759 (1998) ("There is no hard and fast rule in nonconforming use abandonments that intent to abandon must be actually shown when the zoning ordinance or statute utilizes the word 'abandonment' ").

On the other hand, the abandonment or discontinuance must be active and actual.

There is no issue with regard to Club Choices' status; it is a valid Class III nonconforming use property under § 13–609 of the Zoning Code. It is an adult-entertainment business, presently existing, that was also operating as such on September 10, 1993, as § 13–609 specifies. As to that status, there is no contention that Triplin has abandoned or discontinued it, at least in whole. The issue is, as the Court of Special Appeals has framed it, whether using the valid nonconforming use more frequently than it was being used when the use became nonconforming—presenting adult entertainment more than two nights per week—would be a prohibited expansion of the use or a mere intensification of the use.

B.

Despite Maryland's well settled policy against nonconforming use, and the Baltimore City Zoning Code's explicit prohibition against expansion of those uses, Baltimore City Zoning Code § 13–406, Maryland recognizes, and our cases have held, that an intensification of a nonconforming use is permissible, so long as the nature and character of that use is unchanged and is substantially the same. *See* Feldstein v. Zoning Board, 246 Md. 204, 211, 227 A.2d 731, 734; Jahnigen v. Staley, 245 Md. 130, 137, 225 A.2d 277, 281; Nyburg v. Solmson, 205 Md. 150, 161, 106 A.2d 483, 488; Green v. Garrett, 192 Md. 52, 63, 63 A.2d 326, 330. See also Kastendike v. Baltimore Ass'n for Retarded Children, Inc., 267 Md. 389, 396–98, 297 A.2d 745, 749–50 (1972); Parr v. Bradyhouse, 177 Md. 245, 247, 9 A.2d 751, 752 (1939) (determining that rental of tract of land formerly used for a dairy business for riding academy did not affect the right to use the land as a non-conforming use, as it was simply a change from cows to horses).

In *Green,* citizens of Baltimore City sought to enjoin the Department of Recreation and Parks of Baltimore City and the Baltimore Baseball and Exhibition Company from allowing professional baseball to be played at Baltimore Stadium, and further to enjoin the use of the loud speaker system, the flood lights, and the parking facilities nearby. Baltimore Stadium was constructed prior to 1931, when the district in which it was located was rezoned residential, after which it was used infrequently for football games, track meets and civic events. It was used more frequently after 1939, when lights were installed, a speaker system having been installed earlier. That increased use consisted mainly of football games and other events, not baseball games. In 1944, however, a fire destroyed the baseball stadium, then known as Oriole Park. This resulted in more baseball games being played at Baltimore Stadium. 192 Md. at 57–58, 63 A.2d at 328.

When that occurred, neighboring citizens contended that the use of the Stadium for baseball games for a considerable portion of the year was an enlargement of the valid nonconforming use of the Stadium and, therefore, contravened the zoning ordinance. They pointed out that, when the zoning ordinance was enacted, the nonconforming use consisted of professional football games and the infrequent, at best, baseball game. This Court disagreed. Acknowledging that the "spirit of the zoning ordinance is against the extension of non-conforming uses and that such uses should not be perpetuated any longer than necessary," we observed:

> We have never held that the more frequent use of a property
> for a purpose which does not conform to the ordinary

restrictions of the neighborhood is an extension of an infrequent use of the same building for a similar purpose. We do not think such a contention is tenable. Nor does it seem to us that a different use is made of the Stadium when the players of games there are paid. The use of the property remains the same.

192 Md. at 63, 63 A.2d at 330. This Court concluded, "we find that the Department had and has power to lease the Stadium ... for the purposes of professional baseball, and that such use is not an extension of the non-conforming use heretofore existing ... " 192 Md. at 63–64, 63 A.2d at 330–331.

Jahnigen v. Staley, 245 Md. 130, 225 A.2d 277 (1967), is similarly instructive. There, a decree by the Circuit Court for Anne Arundel County, in addition to restrictions related to and involving expansions of physical facilities, including the extension of a pier, occurring after the zoning which prohibited any non-conforming use to those uses in effect prior to the date of its adoption, 245 Md. at 133, 225 A.2d at 279, restricted the nonconforming use of marina property to the rental of seven rowboats. The waterfront property had been used by its previous owners as a boat rental property dating from 1946, when a pier was attached to the land, and continuing after 1949, when a comprehensive zoning ordinance rezoned the land and placed the property into an agricultural classification.

On appeal, this Court reaffirmed the principle that although the purpose of zoning regulations is to restrict rather than to expand nonconforming uses, Phillips v. Zoning Commissioner, 225 Md. 102, 169 A.2d 410 (1961), an intensification of a non-conforming use is permissible so long as the nature and character of the use is unchanged and substantially the same facilities are used. 245 Md. at 137, 225 A.2d at 281; see also Nyburg, 205 Md. 150, 106 A.2d 483. While physical expansions like constructing a new pier and use of the land for services other than what was already present prior to the effective date of the ordinance were held to be invalid extensions of the nonconforming use, this Court decided that "any increase in the number of rowboats rented would be an intensification of [the] non-conforming use and would not be an extension." 245 Md. at 138, 225 A.2d at 282. The intensification of a non-conforming use, in short, is permissible so long as the nature and character of the use is unchanged and substantially the same facilities are used. 245 Md. at 137, 225 A.2d at 281.

In these cases, we have consistently held that merely increasing the frequency of a nonconforming use did not constitute an unlawful extension; rather, it was but an intensification of the use.

Nor are we persuaded by the out-of-state cases upon which the appellees and the Court of Special Appeals relied. Garb-Ko v. Carrollton Township, 86 Mich. App. 350, 272 N.W.2d 654 supports the proposition for which it is offered, the Court of Appeals of Michigan having answered in the affirmative the question, "whether the extension of hours of a grocery store operating as a nonconforming use constitutes an expansion of the nonconforming use which can be lawfully restricted by the defendant township." 86 Mich. App. at 352–353, 272 N.W.2d at 655. It did so, however, on the basis of the following Michigan policies: "that the continuation of a nonconforming use must be substantially of the same size and same essential nature as the use existing at the time of passage of a valid zoning ordinance" and that "the policy of the law is against the extension or enlargement of nonconforming uses, and zoning regulations should be strictly construed with respect to expansion." *Id.* at 353, 272 N.W.2d at 655, quoting Norton Shores v. Carr, 81 Mich. App. 715, 720, 265 N.W.2d 802, 805 (1978).

Judgment of the Court of Special Appeals reversed.

NOTES AND QUESTIONS

1. How did this case arise? Who made the initial determination that the adult use was in violation of the zoning ordinance? How did the lawyers for Trip Associates respond?

2. What investment, if any, did Trip Associates make that would have been lost if the prohibition on adult entertainment had applied retroactively? Was there any evidence that Trip Associates had altered the premises in some way to accommodate adult entertainment? If not, then why protect Trip Associates against application of the ordinance?

Note that the courts in *Cleveland MHC* and *Trip Associates*, like many other courts, discuss a constitutional basis for protection of non-conforming uses. Some courts explicitly rely on state constitutional provisions. *See, e.g.,* Pa. Nw. Distribs., Inc. v. Zoning Hearing Bd., 526 Pa. 186, 584 A.2d 1372 (1991). Other courts, like the courts in *Cleveland MHC* and *Trip Associates*, are less precise about the source of constitutional protection for non-conforming uses. One possible source is the federal constitution's Takings Clause. But the Supreme Court has upheld, in numerous cases, the right of a municipality to prohibit an existing use when the prohibition is designed to prevent harm to neighbors. *See, e.g.,* Hadacheck v. Sebastian, 239 U.S. 394 (1915) (upholding zoning provision prohibiting brickyards in residential district, even though brickyard predated zoning ordinance); Miller v. Schoene, 276 U.S. 272 (1928) (upholding regulation requiring removal of existing cedar trees to protect local apple industry). In light of *Hadachek* and *Miller*, would Trip Associates have succeeded on a takings claim if the city had prohibited adult uses? If the city had imposed a closing time of 2 a.m.?

3. In *Trip Associates*, the zoning ordinance restricted the uses of a building that conformed with the provisions of the zoning ordinance. In other cases, the structure itself might not conform to the ordinance because it violates height limitations, or setback requirements, or floor area ratios. Should the protection extended to non-conforming structures be different from the protection extended to non-conforming uses?

4. In light of the court's holding, is Trip Associates now better off or worse off than it was before the city enacted the prohibition on adult entertainment? In light of your answer, do you understand why non-conforming uses tend not to disappear over time?

5. The Baltimore City Code, like most zoning ordinances, prohibits expansion of non-conforming uses; in *Trip Associates*, the court distinguished between impermissible expansion of a non-conforming use, and protected "intensification" of a non-conforming use. Why distinguish between the two? Doesn't intensification permit the owner to obtain a greater return on its investment than it was realizing before the ordinance was enacted? Isn't the non-conforming use doctrine designed only to preserve the existing return on investment?

6. Landowner operates a drug store in an area that has been rezoned for residential use only. Faced with competition from a major chain, the drug store has begun losing money. Landowner asks whether he can convert the drug store into a fast food outlet, a supermarket, or a bank branch. What advice would you give to the landowner?

7. As the court indicates in *Trip Associates*, once a landowner abandons a pre-existing non-conforming use, future uses must conform to the current ordinance. Some ordinances require abandonment for a specified period of time, often one year. But what constitutes abandonment? Suppose, for instance, landowner has operated a warehouse for 25 years. Five years ago, the area was rezoned to prohibit commercial uses. Landowner stopped using the warehouse for 10 months. Then, fearful of losing the right to use the building for commercial purposes, landowner stores 10 crates in the building, occupying one-tenth of one percent of the building's area. Has landowner abandoned the pre-existing non-conforming use? *See* Toys "R" Us v. Silva, 89 N.Y.2d 411, 676 N.E.2d 862, 654 N.Y.S.2d 100 (1996).

Suppose a state or municipal entity wants to terminate a non-conforming use like the ones at issue in *Cleveland MHC* and *Trip Associates*. Would the termination be permissible if the government gave the landowner time to recoup its investment? Consider the following case:

Modjeska Sign Studios, Inc. v. Berle

Court of Appeals of New York, 1977
43 N.Y.2d 468, 402 N.Y.S.2d 359, 373 N.E.2d 255

■ JASEN, J.

At issue on this appeal is whether the State, having enacted legislation regulating advertising signs and structures in the Catskill and Adirondack Parks, may, after the expiration of a six and one-half year amortization period, require the removal of nonconforming signs without compensation.

ECL 9–0305 (subd. 1) provides that to ensure the natural beauty of the Catskill and Adirondack Parks, advertising signs and structures, for which a permit is not obtained, are prohibited except accessory signs and signs located within the Catskill Park limits of an incorporated village. Any signs erected within the Catskill Park as of May 26, 1969, which are not in conformance with the regulations promulgated to implement ECL 9–0305 (see 6 NYCRR Part 195), were required to be removed by January 1, 1976. (ECL 9–0305, subd. 1.)

Plaintiff owns approximately 96 outdoor advertising signs or billboards situated within the Catskill Park. Admittedly, none of these signs conforms to the regulations promulgated pursuant to ECL 9–0305. Seeking therefore to enjoin the removal of its signs, plaintiff, only two weeks before the expiration of the amortization period, commenced the present action to declare ECL 9–0305 unconstitutional on the ground that it constitutes a taking for which compensation must be provided.

Special Term denied plaintiff's motion for a preliminary injunction and granted summary judgment for the defendant, declaring ECL 9–0305 to be constitutional. The Appellate Division unanimously affirmed.

Having reaffirmed today our prior decisions holding aesthetics to be a valid basis for the exercise of the police power (see Suffolk Outdoor Adv. Co. v. Hulse, 43 N.Y.2d 483 [decided herewith]), we proceed to a consideration of plaintiff's contention that ECL 9–0305 constitutes a taking requiring that monetary compensation be given to owners of nonconforming signs removed from the Catskill Park.

In contrast to a safety-motivated exercise of the police power, a regulation enacted to enhance the aesthetics of a community generally does not provide a compelling reason for immediate implementation with respect to existing structures or uses. True, the public will benefit from a more aesthetically beautiful community, but absent the urgency present in a safety-motivated regulation, the immediate benefit gained does not outweigh the loss suffered by those individuals adversely affected. As always, an exercise of the police power must be reasonable. While we do not believe that compensation is required, we do believe that it would have been unreasonable to require, solely for aesthetic purposes, the immediate removal of the billboards prohibited in the present case.

Fortunately, rather than adopting a regulation requiring the immediate removal of nonconforming billboards without compensation, the Legislature has chosen to provide an amortization period as a means of ameliorating the burden cast upon affected billboard owners. The concept of amortization evolved as a hoped for solution to the tension between the ideal of comprehensive zoning and contemporary notions of due process. At the outset, even zoning laws prospective in operation only were looked at with a jaundiced eye. Understandably, attempts to apply a zoning ordinance retroactively faced far greater resistance. (See Comment, The Abatement of Pre-existing Nonconforming Uses under Zoning Laws: Amortization, 57 N.W. L. Rev. 323.) Consequently, zoning ordinances were enacted to control only new land uses. As for existing nonconforming uses, it was hoped that they would gradually disappear. However, as Professor Anderson has observed: "It became axiomatic that old uses never die." (Anderson, Amortization of Nonconforming Uses—A Preliminary Appraisal of Harbison v. City of Buffalo, 10 Syracuse L. Rev. 44; see Comment, The Abatement of Pre-existing Nonconforming Uses Under Zoning Laws: Amortization, 57 N.W. L. Rev. 323.)

As a middle ground between prospectively and retroactively applied zoning laws, the concept of amortization emerged. By limiting the period during which an existing nonconforming use may be continued, a balance is struck between an individual's interest in maintaining the present use of his property and the general welfare of the community sought to be advanced by the zoning ordinance. Thus, by permitting a limited period during which an existing nonconforming use may be continued, rather than requiring its termination immediately, amortization provides an owner with an opportunity to recoup his investment and avoid substantial financial loss. (See generally, ALI Model Land Development Code, art. 4, Discontinuance of Existing Land Uses [1975], 142, 146; 1 Anderson, New York Zoning Law and Practice [2d ed.], § 6.47; Nonconforming Uses—Amortization, Ann., 22 A.L.R.3d 1134; Anderson, Amortization of Nonconforming Uses—A Preliminary Appraisal of Harbison v. City of Buffalo, 10 Syracuse L. Rev. 44; Holme, Billboards and On-Premises Signs: Regulation and Elimination Under the Fifth Amendment, 1974 Institute on Planning, Zoning, and Eminent Domain 247; Comment, The Abatement of Pre-existing Nonconforming Uses Under Zoning Laws: Amortization, 57 N.W. L. Rev. 323.)

In Matter of Harbison v. City of Buffalo (4 N.Y.2d 553), involving an ordinance requiring the termination of a cooperage business within a period of three years, we sustained the constitutionality of the concept of amortization. As long as the amortization period is reasonable, it should be upheld. (See Nonconforming Uses—Amortization, Ann., 22 A.L.R.3d 1134; 82 Am. Jur. 2d, Zoning and Planning, § 188.) Whether an amortization period is reasonable is a question which must be answered in light of the facts of each particular case. (See Nonconforming Uses—Amortization, Ann., 22 A.L.R.3d 1134.) Certainly, a critical factor to be considered is the length of the amortization period in relation to the investment. (See City of Los Angeles v. Gage, 127 Cal. App. 2d 442; National Adv. Co. v. County of Monterey, 1 Cal. 3d 875, cert. den. 398 U.S. 946.) Naturally, as the financial investment increases in dimension, the length of the amortization period should correspondingly increase. Similarly, another factor considered significant by some courts is the nature of the nonconforming activity prohibited. Generally a shorter amortization period may be provided for a nonconforming use as opposed to a nonconforming structure. (See, e.g., Village of Gurnee v. Miller, 69 Ill. App. 2d 248.)

In essence, however, we believe the critical question which must be asked is whether the public gain achieved by the exercise of the police power outweighs the private loss suffered by owners of nonconforming uses. (See, e.g., Grant v. Mayor & City Council of Baltimore, 212 Md. 301.) While an owner need not be given that period of time necessary to permit him to recoup his investment entirely (see Comment, The Abatement of Pre-existing Nonconforming Uses Under Zoning Laws: Amortization, 57 N.W. L. Rev. 323, 332), the amortization period should not be so short as to result in a substantial loss of his investment. (See Matter of Harbison v. City of Buffalo, 4 N.Y.2d 553, 563, supra; People v. Miller, 304 NY 105, 109.) If an owner can show that the loss he suffers as a result of the removal of a nonconforming use at the expiration of an amortization period is so substantial that it outweighs the public benefit gained by the legislation, then the amortization period must be held unreasonable.

In determining what constitutes a substantial loss, a court presented with a challenge to a prohibition of billboards similar to the statute in this case should look to, for example, such factors as: initial capital investment, investment realization to date, life expectancy of the investment, the existence or nonexistence of a lease obligation, as well as a contingency clause permitting termination of the lease. As a general rule, most regulations requiring the removal of nonconforming billboards and providing a reasonable amortization period should pass constitutional muster. In concluding as we do, we note that courts in a number of other jurisdictions have passed favorably upon legislative pronouncements requiring removal of nonconforming billboards within amortization periods of varying lengths. (See, e.g., Murphy Inc. v. Board of Zoning Appeals, 147 Conn. 358 [2 years]; National Adv. Co. v. County of Monterey, 1 Cal. 3d 875, cert. den. 398 U.S. 946, supra [1 year]; Western Outdoor Adv. Co. v. City of Miami, 256 So. 2d 556 [Fla.] [5 years]; Art Neon Co. v. City & County of Denver, 488 F.2d 118, cert. den. 417 U.S. 932 [2 to 5 years].)

Because of the procedural posture in which this case comes to us, we are unable to determine whether, as applied, the six and one-half year amortization period provided in ECL 9–0305 is unreasonable. It is clear that in granting summary judgment for the defendant, both the trial court and the Appellate Division concluded, as a matter of law, that the Legislature may constitutionally require the removal of billboards pursuant to the police power without compensating those owners adversely affected. As a result, the reasonableness of the amortization period, as a question of fact, was never addressed by either the parties in opposition to or support of the cross motion for summary judgment or by the courts. For this reason, we believe a remand for an immediate hearing is required to provide plaintiff with an opportunity to establish, if it can, that the statutory amortization period of six and one-half years is unreasonable, as applied.

Accordingly, the order of the Appellate Division should be reversed and the case remanded to Supreme Court, Albany County, for further proceedings in accordance with this opinion.

NOTES AND QUESTIONS

1. Who enacted the amortization provision in *Modjeska*? Suppose instead that the amortization provision had been enacted by a town board. If you represented a landowner, what challenges, other than the federal constitutional challenge advanced in *Modjeska*, would you have considered? In other cases, landowners have successfully challenged amortization provisions on the following grounds:

    a.   Amortization violates the state constitution. *See* Pa. Nw. Distrib., Inc. v. Zoning Hearing Bd., 526 Pa. 186, 584 A.2d 1372 (1991).

    b.   A state statute protecting pre-existing non-conforming uses precludes municipalities from enacting amortization provisions. *See* United Adver. Corp. v. Borough of Raritan, 11 N.J. 144, 93 A.2d 362 (1952).

    c.   Because state legislation does not explicitly authorize municipalities to enact amortization provisions, municipalities have no power to enact such provisions. *See* State v. Bates, 305 N.W.2d 426 (Iowa 1981).

How would you decide which of these challenges to advance in any particular case?

2. In *Modjeska*, the challenged legislation included a single amortization period for all signs subject to the ordinance. Some amortization ordinances authorize municipal officials to compute amortization periods based on the investment the landowner has made in the non-conforming use or structure. *See, e.g.,* M & S Cox Invs., LLC v. Provo City Corp., 169 P.3d 789 (Utah 2007). Thus, a landowner with a newer or more expensive sign might enjoy a longer amortization period than a landowner whose sign is older or cheaper.

3. Suppose you are Modjeska's lawyer, and you are preparing for the hearing on remand. Investigation has revealed the following facts: (1) Modjeska purchased a parcel of land in Catskill Park three years ago for $30,000; (2) Modjeska immediately erected a sign on that parcel at a cost of $40,000; (3) Modjeska then leased the sign space for a two-year period at $7,000 per year; (4) a year ago, at the expiration of the original lease, Modjeska leased the sign space at $10,000 per year; and (5) signs usually do not require replacement or significant repair for 20 years. Assume the ordinance has just been enacted, and requires removal of the sign six years from now.

How would you argue that the amortization provision is unreasonable? What additional facts, if any, would be helpful in crafting your argument?

Now, suppose you represent the state. How would you argue that the amortization provision is reasonable?

4. Suppose now that the sign prohibition and the amortization provision applied not to signs in Catskill and Adirondack Parks, but to signs within 200 feet of any state highway. Assume the facts are otherwise the same as in Question 3. In light of the opinion in *Modjeska*, would the arguments about reasonableness, and the likely outcome, be any different from the arguments and outcome in Question 3? Why or why not?

5. Return to the facts in the *Trip Associates* case. Suppose the Baltimore City Council approached you about including an amortization provision designed to phase out adult entertainment uses in a particular district. What advice would you give the Council? Would the amortization technique be useful to the Council? If so, how long would you suggest the amortization period should be? *Cf.* Stringfellow's of New York, Ltd. v. City of New York, 91 N.Y.2d 382, 694 N.E.2d 407, 671 N.Y.S.2d 406 (N.Y. 1998).

Should it be easier or harder to use amortization to phase out non-conforming uses than to phase out non-conforming structures?

VIII. NEW URBANIST ZONING

In recent years, New Urbanists like Andres Duany and Elizabeth Plater-Zyberk have taken the lead in criticizing the sorts of land use patterns generated by traditional Euclidean zoning: they favor density over dispersion, community over privacy, and mixed uses over separation of uses. Innovations within Euclidean zoning, like mixed use districts and Planned Unit Developments have addressed some of these criticisms, for example, by permitting increased density through clustering. But Euclidean zoning by and large remains wedded to the logic of separation of uses and ceilings on density and bulk. New Urbanists have proposed alternative models of zoning that break entirely with the Euclidean forms.

The defining feature of New Urbanist thought is its orientation towards historic patterns of development, particularly the small town and the city of the early twentieth century, before the rise of the automobile. At its core, New Urbanism is an anti-sprawl movement, a reaction to the patterns of development that took hold in the United States in the years following World War II. New Urbanists are fond of arguing that the urban places most people think work the best are illegal in most of the country. As Andres Duany has put it, "the vast majority of conventional zoning codes prohibit the replication of our best examples of urbanism, places like Nantucket, Williamsburg, or even Main Street USA in Disneyland." Our current zoning laws, they say, are profoundly anti-urban—"they separate land uses, decrease densities, and increase the amount of land devoted to car travel, prohibiting the kind of urbanism that typifies our most beloved urban places."[2] Although they blame land use law for the situation we face,

---

[2] Duany & Talen, Making the Good Easy: The Smart Code Alternative, 29 Fordham Urb. L.J. 1445 (2002).

they do not reject land use regulations altogether. Indeed, they turn to zoning-type ordinances to accomplish their goals.

Although hardly monolithic, New Urbanists subscribe to a number of principles. First, they advocate planning on the level of metropolitan regions, a topic to which we will return in later chapters. They conceive of the metropolitan region as a cluster of well-structured cities and towns, which are themselves composed of coherent neighborhoods with identifiable centers and edges. Second, they favor compact, relatively high-density development, which preserves farmland and environmentally sensitive areas and is friendly to mass transit. Third, within these high-density communities, New Urbanists favor mixed land uses rather than single-use zones. Such a mixture of uses promotes walkability and reduces reliance on automobiles, which New Urbanists view as inhibiting social interaction and vibrant street (i.e., sidewalk) life. In addition to mixing uses, New Urbanists promote walkability through a pedestrian friendly street design, including such features as a grid or modified grid street structure, short blocks, and the discreet placement of garages and parking spaces to avoid auto-dominated landscapes. Fourth, New Urbanists focus less on the use of zoning codes to discipline uses and more on the use of codes to mandate building and street/building typologies in an effort to create coherent urban form at a human scale.

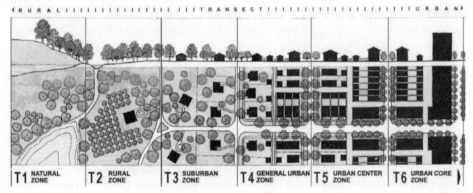

The central concept within new urbanist zoning is the "transect." According to DPZ & Co., "[a] transect of nature is a geographical cross-section of a region intended to reveal a sequence of environments. It helps study the many symbiotic elements that contribute to habitats where certain plants and animals thrive." The transect is normative, not purely descriptive—it is a cross section of metropolitan areas as New Urbanists would like it to be. Part of the New Urbanist critique of traditional zoning is that it has made such a transect impossible to accomplish. The New Urbanist rural-to-urban transect is divided into a series of T-Zones for application within zoning codes. These six habitats vary by the ratio and level of intensity of their natural and social components.

In keeping with their particular goals, proposed New Urbanist zoning ordinances have a distinctive look and feel. Following from their support for mixed use and their concern with the building form, New Urbanist zoning codes are typically more focused on building form than use. In addition, they frequently incorporate graphical elements rather than being primarily textual. See, for example, the one-page "Urban Code" for Seaside, Florida, an early New Urbanist development on Florida's gulf coast.

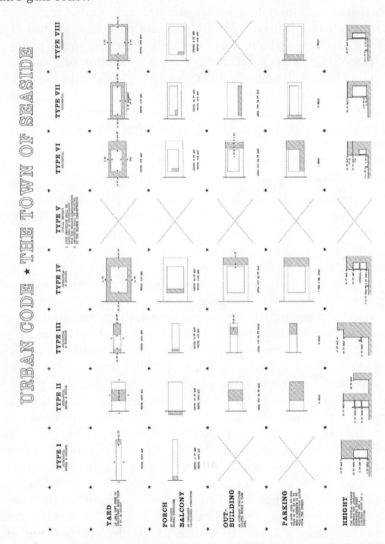

New Urbanists are as interested in the underuse of land as they are with development that is too intensive for the surrounding community. Thus, their codes typically include things like *minimum* building heights. This is in stark contrast with the "outer envelope" approach typical of Euclidean zoning, which is criticized by New Urbanists as excessively vague. New Urbanist zoning laws emphasize the relationship of buildings to the street and the importance of this relationship in the creation of a pedestrian friendly streetscape through a high-density mixture of uses and attention to vertical architectural elements that create a coherent street line. New Urbanists therefore specify design elements included within zoning code with a great deal of precision. On the other hand, they are far less rigorous than traditional zoning codes in their regulation of use. New Urbanists are typically open to mixed use in virtually any built areas, particularly the mixture of commercial and residential uses. They look especially favorably on the location of commercial uses at street level, where they stimulate pedestrian interest. Finally, New Urbanists pay close attention to the location of parking, which they see as interfering with pedestrians' enjoyment of the street. While traditional zoning ordinances often require commercial developers to set aside a great deal of space for off-street parking (often located between the street and the store front, in order to comply with onerous set-back requirements), New Urbanist zoning codes typically reduce off-street parking requirements and move parking behind buildings and away from frontages (either above or below ground, in the case of garages), in order to prioritize the immediate relationship between buildings and sidewalks.

New Urbanism is not without its critics. Objections have been levied against New Urbanism on a number of fronts. First, some commentators question whether it can deliver on its promise of reduced car dependence. Empirical evidence on this front is mixed. Several studies have shown reduced vehicle miles traveled within traditional neighborhoods (not just New Urbanist developments), but those that focus on New Urbanist developments have presented a mixed record. New Urbanists respond to this mixed record, by noting that the impact of individual developments on transportation choices cannot be judged in isolation from what is going on in the rest of society. Second, some critics accuse New Urbanists of being nostalgic and conservative. They argue that New Urbanists want us to return to a past that never really existed. They also allege that New Urbanists overlook the negative characteristics of small-town life and turn-of-the-century cities. Finally, defenders of existing land use patterns frequently accuse New Urbanist planners of being elitists who ignore the reality of the American housing market. These critics emphasize that consumers prefer the suburban patterns of development reinforced by Euclidean zoning practices. They also emphasize the high cost of housing in many New Urbanist developments. New Urbanism might be a nice boutique product, they suggest, but it is unable to deliver housing that is affordable to the middle and working classes.

QUESTIONS

1.   Are the goals of the New Urbanists fundamentally inconsistent with the tools of Euclidean zoning, as we have described them in this chapter, or

can New Urbanist ideals be implemented through the standard zoning tools?

2. Can transect-based zoning be implemented at the municipal level? Does your answer have any effect on your attitude concerning the appropriate level of government for making land-use decisions?

3. Is New Urbanist hostility to the automobile admirable, or merely anachronistic or nostalgic?

4. For a more extensive comparison between traditional and New Urbanist zoning codes, *see* Michael Lewyn, New Urbanist Zoning for Dummies, 58 Ala. L. Rev. 257 (2006).

IX. REVIEW PROBLEMS

1. Landowner owns a 110 acre parcel of land in an area zoned "rural residential." The ordinance permits "a mixture of agriculture and low-density rural living" and explicitly lists agriculture and uses accessory to agriculture as permitted uses. The ordinance also permits, by special exception, "Home business/retail" and "Bed & Breakfast Homes." The ordinance defines agriculture by referring to a state statute that lists a number of uses including "commercial Christmas tree operation" as an agricultural operation.

Landowner, who operates a Christmas tree farm, has recently refurbished an old barn on the parcel and has advertised the farm as a venue for weddings and other celebrations. (Landowner got the idea from a friend of his, who has done the same thing on his own farm elsewhere in the state.) Landowner's immediate neighbor has complained about the 10 events Landowner has already held on the farm. Landowner wants to know whether she needs any approvals to continue to sponsor weddings, and if so, what approvals are necessary. Advise Landowner. *See* Forster v. Town of Henniker, 118 A.3d 1016 (N.H. 2015).

2. In 2005, Homeowner began maintaining exotic animals, including three tigers and two leopards, in cages in his backyard. Later that year, the town enacted its first zoning ordinance. The ordinance permits home occupations as specially permitted uses in residential districts. (Homeowner's home is located in a residential district.) The ordinance defines home occupations as "businesses where the activities of the business are conducted inside the residence, a legally constructed accessory building, or at off-site locations." Homeowner obtained a state license to maintain the animals in 2006 and a federal license in 2007.

Homeowner does not have any employees, does not pay business taxes or have business insurance, and makes no profit. He does, however, invite people to see his animals, and he maintains a donation box for visitors. Donations are used to feed and maintain the animals. Neighbors have complained about the traffic and about the possibility of escape by the animals. The neighbors want to know whether they can stop Homeowner from maintaining the animals. Advise them. *See* Salton v. Town of Mayfield Zoning Bd. of Appeals, 983 N.Y.S.2d 656 (N.Y. App. 2014).

CHAPTER THREE

BEYOND ZONING: LARGE DEVELOPMENTS, HISTORIC PROPERTIES, AND AESTHETICS

I. REGULATING LARGE DEVELOPMENTS

Chapter Two primarily dealt with the way zoning codes regulated single buildings on single lots. We start this chapter by envisioning a scenario in which a developer finds a large piece of property—a property of a few acres, or perhaps hundreds of acres, in size—on which he hopes to build more than one building, perhaps involving more than one use. In order to do so, the developer will review the options offered by both the zoning code and the subdivision regulations. If the developer wants to keep the land as one legal parcel, he may choose to apply for a special zoning approval that allows for denser development than would otherwise be allowed as of right. If the developer wants to divide the parcel up into ownership among many, then he may choose to undertake the process outlined in the subdivision regulations. He may combine subdivision with one of the special zoning procedures that allow greater density or different configurations (such as clustering). Whatever route the developer chooses to take, it is likely he will have to submit an application for site plan review.

Not every locality has zoning codes, much less the special zoning techniques described below—and not every locality has subdivision regulations. For those that do, wide variety exists among them.

A. SPECIAL ZONING TECHNIQUES

As we have seen, in a typical zoning ordinance, each zoning district specifies uses and imposes restrictions on minimum lot size, street frontage, and setbacks—largely to protect neighbors against incompatible uses and congestion. Suppose, however, a developer wants to put together a large-scale project that departs from many of the requirements in the applicable zoning district. The developer is unlikely to design the development in a way that would be unattractive to prospective buyers, because the developer will bear much of the cost of buyer dissatisfaction. Should the developer have to seek a zoning amendment to develop in accordance with her plan?

Several special zoning techniques—the floating zone, the planned unit development, and cluster zoning—allow developers to design large-scale projects that might not fit within the straitjacket imposed by traditional zoning requirements.

1. FLOATING ZONES AND PLANNED UNIT DEVELOPMENTS

A floating zone provides development standards that deviate from the traditional code, usually to incentivize desirable development. It is created in the text of the ordinance first and later "lands" on a particular parcel upon application. Planned unit developments—also called planned area developments or planned developments—offer a flexible framework within which property owners may negotiate mixed-use or other unique arrangements on large lots.

The ordinance in New Haven, the subject of the next case, included the following provisions for planned developments:

Section 65.A. Objectives. The provisions of this section are to be applied in instances where tracts of land of considerable size are developed, redeveloped or renewed as integrated and harmonious units, and where the overall design of such units is so outstanding as to warrant modification of the standards contained elsewhere in this ordinance. A planned development, to be eligible under this section, must be:

1.   in accordance with the comprehensive plans of the City, including all plans for redevelopment and renewal;

2.   composed of such uses, and in such proportions, as are most appropriate and necessary for the integrated functioning of the planned development and for the city;

3.   so designed in its space allocation, orientation, texture, materials, landscaping and other features as to produce an environment of stable and desirable character, complementing the design and values of the surrounding neighborhood, and showing such unusual merit as to reflect credit upon the developer and upon the city; and

4.   so arranged as to provide a minimum of 250 square feet of usable open space per dwelling unit on the tract, except 125 square feet in the case of elderly housing units, subject to the specific minimum standards enumerated in section 15.A.1.g of this ordinance.

Section 65.B. Tract. The tract for which application is made must have the following minimum area:

1.   For a Planned Development Unit under paragraph D.1 below, one-half acre in the case of dwellings only, and one acre in all other cases.

2.   For a Planned Development District under paragraph D.2 below, one acre in the case of dwellings only, and two acres in all other cases.

Section 65.C. Who may apply. An Application may be filed by (1) the owner or owners or lessee or lessees of all land and structures included within the tract, or (2) any governmental agency including the New Haven Redevelopment Agency. . . .

Section 65.D. Application and General Plans. Each Application shall state the proposed modifications of existing zoning, and shall be accompanied by General Plans, including contoured site plans. The General Plans shall show the improvements to be erected upon the tract, the open spaces to be provided, the nature and location of the proposed use or uses, the relationship of the proposed development to surrounding properties, and other pertinent information.

Traffic Impact Study. All applications filed pursuant to this section shall be referred to the Department of Traffic and Parking for an advisory report on the traffic impact. The traffic impact study shall show the amount and direction of traffic to be generated by the proposed development and shall estimate the effect of such traffic on the roadway capacity and safety.

The Application and General Plans shall be sufficient in scope and character to determine that the Objectives stated in subsection A above will be met. Any proposed division of the tract into separately owned and operated units shall be indicated. The Application and General Plans shall be filed and acted upon in the following manner:

1. Where the proposed modifications of existing zoning concern only the bulk and placement of structures and the size and shape of lots (regulation of lot area, average lot width, distance between buildings, size of courts, yards, gross floor area, building height, and/or building coverage), or involve a reduction of lot area per dwelling unit of no more than 33 percent, such Application and General Plans shall be filed with the Board of Zoning Appeals and acted upon as a special exception under subsection 63.D of this ordinance. . . .

2. In any other case, the Application and General Plans shall be filed with the Board of Aldermen and acted upon as a proposed amendment to this ordinance. If such Application and General Plans are approved by the Board of Aldermen, following a favorable recommendation by the City Plan Commission and after an advisory report from the Department of Traffic and Parking regarding the traffic impact study, upon specific findings that each of the objectives stated in the subsection 65.A above will be met, such approval shall be construed to amend this ordinance insofar (and only insofar) as specific deletions, additions and changes are made which are related to the land and structures in the tract, and the tract shall be designated as a separate Planned Development District provided that the requirements of subsection 65.E below are met.

3. All applications filed under this section may be referred by the Board of Zoning Appeals in the case of Planned Development Units, and by the Board of Aldermen in the case of Planned Development Districts, to any Neighborhood Planning Agency (NPA) of jurisdiction as defined in Section 1 of this Ordinance, which may issue an advisory report on the proposed zoning designation to the Board of Zoning Appeals or Board of Aldermen, as appropriate.

What objections might there be to such a provision for planned development districts? Consider the following case:

Campion v. Board of Aldermen
of the City of New Haven

Supreme Court of Connecticut, 2006
278 Conn. 500, 899 A.2d 542

■ BORDEN, J.

The sole issue in this certified appeal is whether any enabling authority exists for § 65 of the New Haven zoning ordinance, which provides for the creation of planned development districts.

The underlying facts, as set forth by the Appellate Court, are as follows: "In an application dated April 16, 2001, the [DelMonaco] partnership requested the creation of a planned development district that would consolidate all six parcels. The size of the planned development district would be 4.04 acres and would be carved out of the surrounding RS–2 zoning district. In the application, the [DelMonaco] partnership proposed a two phase plan for the implementation of the planned development district. During the first phase, certain structures, including the Cove Manor Convalescent Nursing Home (convalescent home), a preexisting, nonconforming use, and three residential structures would be demolished. Furthermore, enlargements and renovations to the catering facility would be completed, including the construction of a new parking facility and a garden reception area. During the second phase, a new residence would be constructed for the DelMonaco family.

"The [commission] held public hearings on the [DelMonaco] partnership's application on June 13 and July 25, 2001. The plans for the planned development district, as submitted by the [DelMonaco] partnership, included a structure to enclose the garden at the catering facility and the reconfiguration of the existing parking lot. The capacity of the catering facility would be increased from 299 persons to 470 persons with the addition of a garden pavilion. Additionally, nearly 100 new parking spaces would be created.

"On September 19, 2001, the commission approved the application and imposed certain conditions, including a limitation of the size of the new building, the number of parking spaces, the hours of operation and project phasing. The commission forwarded its report and approval to the board of aldermen. On February 19, 2002, the board of aldermen [approved, but] substantially amended the conditions of approval for the planned development district. Specifically, the board of aldermen made the following amendments: (1) no change to the size of the catering facility was permitted at that time; (2) the number of parking spaces was limited to 199; (3) the maximum occupancy was limited to 299 persons; (4) separate functions in the garden area were prohibited; (5) the 0.67 acres for the DelMonaco family residence was excluded from the planned development district; (6) the permitted hours of operation were established; (7) a five year moratorium was placed on expansion, improvement or modification within the district; and (8) the board of aldermen reserved the right to extend and to review the five year moratorium." *Id.*, at 822–25, 859 A.2d 586.

By approving the DelMonaco partnership's application subject to the previously identified conditions, the board of aldermen created a new zoning district that amended the New Haven zoning ordinance, as well as the zoning map, to designate the combined parcels of property as a planned development district. As part of its decision to approve the DelMonaco partnership's application, the board of aldermen also made several findings regarding the planned development district, namely, that: (1) it was in accordance with the city's comprehensive plan; (2) it reduced traffic from the catering facility in the surrounding neighborhood; (3) it minimized conflict with the surrounding residential community; and (4) it was designed in such a way as to meet all the objectives of § 65.A of the New Haven zoning ordinance.

The plaintiffs appealed from the board of aldermen's decision to the trial court, which dismissed the plaintiffs' appeal.

We begin our analysis with a brief discussion of the history of the source of the city's zoning authority. That history makes clear that the city's source of zoning power is a special act passed by the General Assembly in 1925.

Section 1 of the 1925 Special Act provides the board of aldermen with the broad power to "divide the city of New Haven into districts of such number, shape and area as may be best suited to carry out the provisions of [the] act. . . . [Additionally, § 1 requires that the zoning] regulations shall be uniform for each class of buildings or structures throughout any district . . . [and that] [r]egulations in one or more districts may differ from those in another district." Furthermore, § 5 of the 1925 Special Act provides that "[t]he regulations imposed and the districts created under the provisions of this act may be changed or altered from time to time by ordinance, but no such change or alteration shall be made until the proposed change shall have been referred to the zoning commission for a hearing . . . [and the commission has reported] to said board of aldermen its recommendations in the matter. . . ."

[T]he creation of planned development districts pursuant to § 65 of the New Haven zoning ordinance is comparable to the creation of floating zones,[11] which is a practice that we have deemed authorized by enabling legislation similar to the 1925 Special Act. In Sheridan v. Planning Board, 159 Conn. 1, 17, 266 A.2d 396 (1969), we concluded that floating zones were authorized under the special act conferring zoning authority on the city of Stamford even though the term "floating zone" was not specifically mentioned in the special act.

In searching for enabling authority for Stamford's floating zone regulation, our analysis in *Sheridan* centered on the substance and function of the regulation as it related to the broad authority conferred by the relevant special act. We also note certain characteristics specific to Stamford's floating zone regulation that bear similarities to the city's use of planned development districts pursuant to § 65 of the New Haven zoning ordinance. Specifically, in *Sheridan* we stated that, "[u]nlike the special exception, when a zoning board grants an application requesting it to apply a floating zone to a particular property, *it alters the zone boundaries of the area by carving a new zone out of an existing one. . . .* This legislative function meets the *need for flexibility in modern zoning ordinances* since the exact location of the new zone is left for future determination, as the demand develops, and applications are granted which meet all conditions specified by the board." (Citations omitted; emphasis added.) *Id.*, at 17, 266 A.2d 396.

In sum, like a floating zone, a planned development district "alters the zone boundaries of the area by carving a new zone out of an existing one," and, consequently, represents a legitimate legislative act by the city to regulate growth and meet the "need for flexibility in modern zoning ordinances. . . ." *Id.* Similar to our conclusion in *Sheridan* with respect to the permissibility of floating zones, therefore, we conclude that the language of the 1925 Special Act is sufficiently broad to permit the creation of planned development districts pursuant to § 65 of the New Haven zoning ordinance.

---

[11] "A floating zone is a special detailed use district of undetermined location in which the proposed kind, size and form of structures must be preapproved. It is legislatively predeemed compatible with the area in which it eventually locates if specified standards are met and the particular application is not unreasonable. . . . It differs from the traditional Euclidean zone in that it has no defined boundaries and is said to float over the entire area where it may eventually be established. . . . The legality of this type of zoning, when properly applied, has been recognized by this court." (Citations omitted; internal quotation marks omitted.) *Schwartz v. Plan & Zoning Commission*, 168 Conn. 20, 22, 357 A.2d 495 (1975). Additionally, our courts have noted that "[w]hile the concept of a floating zone is similar to the established power of a zoning board to grant special exceptions, the two types of regulation may be distinguished. The special exception is the product of administrative action, while the floating zone is the product of legislative action. . . . Further, if a landowner meets the conditions set forth for a special exception, the board is bound to grant one, but in the case of a floating zone discretion is maintained and additional limitations may be imposed—more control is retained by the zoning board because it is acting legislatively." (Internal quotation marks omitted.) *Homart Development Co. v. Planning & Zoning Commission*, 26 Conn.App. 212, 215–16, 600 A.2d 13 (1991).

[W]e acknowledge that a floating zone differs from a planned development district in certain respects. We conclude, however, that these differences are largely procedural in nature and are not significant enough to invalidate planned development districts that derive their authority from the city's 1925 Special Act. For example, a floating zone is approved in two discrete steps—first, the zone is created in the form of a text amendment, but without connection to a particular parcel of property—and second, the zone is later landed on a particular property through a zoning map amendment. In short, with respect to floating zones, development plans for specific properties within a district are approved separately from the zoning map amendment. Planned development districts established pursuant to § 65 of the New Haven zoning ordinance, however, combine into a single step the approval of a zoning map amendment and a general development plan for the district. This procedural discrepancy does not change the fact that both floating zones and planned development districts have the effect of "alter[ing] the zone boundaries of [an] area by carving a new zone out of an existing one." *Id.*

Additionally, the fact that a floating zone has established standards for the kind, size and form of the structures eventually to be applied to a particular area, while § 65 of the New Haven zoning ordinance does not contain uniform and identified standards that would apply to each planned development district, does not warrant different treatment when searching for enabling authority in the 1925 Special Act. By definition, a floating zone does not apply to a specific piece of property. River Bend Associates, Inc. v. Zoning Commission, 271 Conn. 1, 30 n. 20, 856 A.2d 973 (2004). Indeed, it has been described as "another device to allow individual treatment of properties. . . . Since the floating zone regulations establish a zone for a type of use with an undetermined location, the zone can technically be applied anywhere in the municipality. It can result in individual preferences and respond to development pressures rather than considering the best area for location of particular uses." R. Fuller, 9 Connecticut Practice Series: Land Use Law and Practice (2d ed. 1999) § 3.8, at. 32–33. Furthermore, a "floating zone is normally used to benefit a single landowner" and "[i]t is this potential for favoritism that is the real issue raised by the device." T. Tondro, Connecticut Land Use Regulation (2d ed. 1992), at 72.

Despite these concerns, which are still present even though floating zones contain preapproved specifications for the use of land, we concluded that floating zones were authorized by the broad language in the Stamford Special Act, and we approved the enhanced discretion that they give to municipal zoning boards due to a recognized need for flexibility in modern zoning practices. See Sheridan v. Planning Board, supra, 159 Conn. at 17, 266 A.2d 396. The same concerns are present with respect to planned development districts. Such concerns do not change the fact, however, that the 1925 Special Act contains similarly broad language that authorizes the board of aldermen to create new zoning districts and make alterations to existing districts. Accordingly, in searching for the required enabling authority in the 1925 Special Act, we view § 65 of the New Haven zoning ordinance in the same manner and provide the same treatment as a floating zone.

The plaintiffs further contend that § 65 of the New Haven zoning ordinance lacks sufficient standards in order to be deemed valid and that its provisions are unreasonably vague. Specifically, the plaintiffs argue that a delegation of authority from the legislature to municipalities may be challenged for vagueness on due process grounds if the regulation does not give an individual of ordinary intelligence sufficient notice of what the law is so that the individual has a reasonable opportunity to comply with it. Accordingly, the plaintiffs reason, if a zoning regulation lacks specific standards for its application by an administrative body, it thereby results in an impermissible delegation to that administrative body of the power to decide basic policy matters on a subjective basis. We disagree.

Section 65 of the New Haven zoning ordinance does not lack adequate standards and is not impermissibly vague. A planned development, to be eligible under this section, must be: "1. in accordance with the comprehensive plans of the City, including all plans for redevelopment and renewal; 2. composed of such uses, and in such proportions, as are most appropriate and necessary for the integrated functioning of the planned development and for the city; [and] 3. so designed in its space allocation, orientation, texture, materials, landscaping and other features as to produce an environment of stable and desirable character, complementing the design and values of the surrounding neighborhood, and showing such unusual merit as to reflect credit upon the developer and upon the city. . . ." Additionally, § 65.B of the New Haven zoning ordinance specifies the minimum area necessary for a planned development district, § 65.C discusses who may file a planned development district application, and § 65.D requires that a traffic impact study be completed. Prior to approval of the planned development district application, § 65.D also requires a specific finding, following public hearing, that the objectives outlined in § 65.A have been met.

These requirements provide adequate notice, both to the individuals requesting the creation of the new zone as well as to the opponents of the planned development district application, of the standards and the procedure utilized by the board of aldermen to evaluate a request for a planned development district. In order to pass constitutional muster, a zoning ordinance need not contain detailed and rigid standards that anticipate every conceivable factual situation.

Second, as we already have discussed, the approval of a planned development district creates a new zoning district, and like any other adoption of a new zone, is legislative in nature and must be enacted by the board of aldermen. Conversely, when a legislative body delegates authority to an administrative agency, that agency must be given specific guidance as to the standards for its decision. See Sonn v. Planning Commission, 172 Conn. 156, 159, 374 A.2d 159 (1976).

Finally, the plaintiffs argue that § 65 of the New Haven zoning ordinance provides the commission and the board of aldermen with unlimited discretion as to what to allow as a planned development district, resulting in impermissible spot zoning and contract zoning. We disagree.

Section 65 of the New Haven zoning ordinance does not confer unlimited discretion to the commission and the board of aldermen. Indeed, "[t]he discretion of a legislative body, because of its constituted role as formulator of public policy, is much broader than that of [a zoning board acting in an administrative capacity]. . . ." (Internal quotation marks omitted.) *Id.*, at 416, 788 A.2d 1239. [T]he board of aldermen's discretion is still subject to well established checks on its ability to take legislative acts, namely, judicial review on a case-by-case basis as to whether: (1) the action is in accord with the city's comprehensive plan; and (2) the action is reasonably related to the normal police power purposes enumerated in the 1925 Special Act. Both of these standards were met in the present case.

These same standards also place a check on the city's ability to engage in spot zoning or contract zoning. The record simply does not support the plaintiffs' allegations that the board of aldermen utilized such mechanisms when reviewing the DelMonaco partnership's application. In particular, spot zoning requires a change in zone that affects a small area and is out of harmony with the municipality's comprehensive plan. We previously have concluded that a parcel of land as small as 2.5 acres was not so small that it properly could not be considered a separate zone. See Kutcher v. Town Planning Commission, 138 Conn. 705, 710, 88 A.2d 538 (1952). The DelMonaco partnership's application for a planned development district pertains to a parcel that is more than four acres in size. Furthermore, in the present case the board of aldermen specifically concluded that the new zone was in conformance with the city's comprehensive plan and that the planned development district would benefit the community as a whole. "The courts must be cautious about disturbing the decisions of a local legislative zoning body familiar with the circumstances of community concern. . . ." Spada v. Planning & Zoning Commission, 159 Conn. 192, 199, 268 A.2d 376 (1970).

Similarly, with respect to contract zoning, the principal concern is that, by individually contracting with a zoning authority, an applicant may be able to gain some favor not available to all other applicants and, therefore, bypass the municipality's established process for gaining approval for a change in zone. The plaintiffs suggest that, as applied in this case, § 65 of the New Haven zoning ordinance facilitated contract zoning because the DelMonaco partnership and the board of zoning appeals had entered into a stipulation to settle a zoning appeal involving a request for a special exception to expand parking at the catering facility, with the understanding that a planned development district application subsequently would be filed. The implication that there was some type of nefarious connection between the settlement of the DelMonaco partnership's zoning appeal, with its decision to file an application for a planned development district, ignores the facts that the application was subject to a total of five public hearings before the commission and the board of aldermen, that the commission issued a detailed report with its recommendations, and that the commission's report imposed several conditions for approval of the application. Additionally, the board of aldermen properly considered and made further modifications to the commission's recommendation before approving the application and also made all of the findings required by § 65 of the New Haven zoning ordinance. In short, rather than suggesting any impropriety or that the DelMonaco partnership obtained special privilege not available to others, the record reflects that all of the usual procedures required to create a new zone pursuant to § 65 were followed as part of the DelMonaco's application process.

The plaintiffs repeatedly have insinuated, both in their brief and at oral argument before this court, that the board of aldermen's granting of the DelMonaco partnership's application for a planned development district was the result of political lobbying, improper negotiation, and corruption that allowed the partnership to curry favor with the city's legislative body. There is no support for these allegations in the record. The mere possibility that § 65 of the New Haven zoning ordinance could be misused in a particular case does not mean, in the absence of any evidence to the contrary, that it was misused in this case, or that authority for the ordinance is not present in the city's enabling legislation. The plaintiffs' claim is based on nothing more than unsupported conjecture and innuendo.

The judgment of the Appellate Court is reversed and the case is remanded to that court with direction to affirm the judgment of the trial court.

NOTES

1. *Planned Developments (Including Cluster Zoning).* A "planned development district," the term used in the New Haven ordinance at issue in *Campion*, is more commonly referred to as a planned unit development, or "PUD." PUDs entered the land use lexicon in the 1950s and 60s. Although defined in various ways by different jurisdictions, PUDs are typically a mechanism for permitting developers of large residential projects to deviate from the limited menu of options available under a municipality's zoning code. For example, a PUD provision in a zoning code

might permit the developer of a large residential project to include mixed uses in the development or to exceed the density restrictions imposed by the zoning code in a particular part of the development in exchange for open space in another part of the project. It may also allow for or require "cluster zoning," a technique we explore in Section 2. Cluster zoning permits a developer to group dense construction in a smaller area than would otherwise be allowed, while leaving larger portions of the parcel or parcels undeveloped. A PUD proposal will typically include a map and a proposal specifying the details of the project, such as infrastructure layout, building design, open space, and regulations governing future development within the boundaries of the project. Although they have faced legal challenges, such as those leveled against the provision in *Campion*, courts have frequently, though not always, upheld PUD provisions against this sort of challenge. Compare Cheney v. Village 2 at New Hope, Inc., 429 Pa. 626, 241 A.2d 81 (1968) (upholding PUD provision), with Lutz v. City of Longview, 83 Wash.2d 566, 520 P.2d 1374 (1974) (striking down a PUD provision).

2. *Floating Zones.* Some zoning ordinances make provisions for floating zones instead of or in addition to PUDs. A floating zone resembles an ordinary zoning district in that it is first created by amending the text of a zoning ordinance to set forth certain development standards for setbacks, height, bulk, lot coverage, and the like. When it is first created in the text, the zone is not automatically mapped on to any land within the municipality. Instead, if a developer wants to develop in accordance with the requirements of the floating zone (rather than the standards for the district in which the developer's land is located), the developer applies for a map amendment, which would place the floating zone on his land. If a municipal official consulted you about the relative advantages of including a PUD provision and a floating zone provision in the local ordinance, what advice would you give to the official?

3. How much notice does the existence of a floating zone or planned development district (such as the one at issue in the *Campion* case) provide to the neighboring landowners of potential developments? From the standpoint of neighbors, does one device provide more protection than the other? Is the use of such flexibility-enhancing devices for large projects inconsistent with the other goals of traditional Euclidean zoning?

4. Do you agree with the *Campion* court's reasoning that the planned development district provision does not violate the principle that properties within a particular zone must be treated uniformly? Can you think of a counterargument?

5. Why would the DelMonaco partnership have used the PDD provisions in the New Haven ordinance rather than applying for a zoning amendment? What advantages, if any, does § 65 confer on an applicant?

Does § 65 provide adequate standards to constrain the discretion of the board of aldermen and the city's planning commission in its consideration of proposed planned development districts? Would the court have applied the same standard of review to a simple rezoning in the absence of § 65? If so, what is the benefit, if any, of having on the books a provision like § 65?

6. Should a resident landowner be permitted to challenge a municipality's creation of a "floating zone" before that zone has "landed" on any particular parcel? See Schwartz v. Town Plan & Zoning Comm'n, 168 Conn. 20, 357 A.2d 495 (1975). Suppose the floating zone required the parcels on which it lands to be at least 3 acres in size and that only one or two parcels in the municipality fit those conditions. Should the owners of those parcels be able to launch a challenge against the floating zone's provisions? Should the neighbors of those parcels? See Harris v. Zoning Comm'n, 259 Conn. 402, 788 A.2d 1239 (2002).

7. Suppose a New Haven developer acquired a 50,000 square foot parcel in a district zoned for single-family homes on lots no smaller than 50 feet wide and 100 feet deep (with typical setback requirements). If the developer wanted to build 10 attached town houses on lots far smaller than 50 feet wide, reserving the remainder of the parcel for recreational open space, what steps would landowner have to take to build the town house project? Would a zoning amendment be necessary, or does § 65 offer an avenue for relief? How, if at all, would the developer be better off invoking § 65?

In many zoning ordinances, the PUD provisions resemble those in § 65(D)(1) of the New Haven ordinance, giving an administrative body (rather than the local legislature) power to approve projects that do not precisely comply with the minimum requirements of the zoning ordinance, so long as the projects do not vary too substantially from the overall density requirements imposed by the ordinance.

2.   CLUSTER ZONING

Planned unit developments and floating zones often (but not always) enable a developer to build more intensively than the zoning ordinance would otherwise permit. While municipal decision-makers may be unwilling to permit increased density, they may be willing to relax lot size and setback restrictions in order to preserve open space or to achieve other environmental or aesthetic objectives. Consider the two development alternatives below, each of which would generate the same number of residential units:

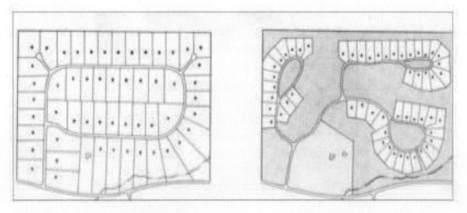

Conventional Subdivision   **Cluster Subdivision**

Which of the two layouts preserves more open space? Developers often prefer cluster subdivisions because roads and utilities are less expensive to build when homes are clustered. They may not be preferable, however, to homeowners seeking more space.

Many state statutes authorize municipalities to make provisions for cluster subdivisions. Municipalities, in turn, typically require that cluster subdivisions, like other subdivisions, obtain municipal approval (the subject of the next section). In considering a proposed cluster subdivision, the developer and the municipality face a preliminary question: how many units may the developer build? As you read the next case, consider the Massachusetts statute reproduced in footnote 1 of the court's opinion, and the Framingham bylaws reproduced in footnote 3.

Nexum Development Corp. v. Planning Board of Framingham

Massachusetts Appeals Court, 2011
943 N.E.2d 965

■ MILLS, J.

Nexum Development Corp. (Nexum) proposes to develop a thirty-two acre tract of land (property) as a residential cluster development[1] in Framingham. The planning board of Framingham (board) denied Nexum's applications for a special permit and the resulting cluster

---

[1] A "cluster development" is "a residential development in which the buildings and accessory uses are clustered together into one or more groups separated from adjacent property and other groups within the development by intervening open land. A cluster development shall be permitted only on a plot of land of such minimum size as a zoning ordinance or by-law may specify which is divided into building lots with dimensional control, density and use restrictions of such building lots varying from those otherwise permitted by the ordinance or by-law and open land. Such open land when added to the building lots shall be at least equal in area to the land area required by the ordinance or by-law for the total number of units or buildings contemplated in the development." G.L. c. 40A, § 9, inserted by St.1975, c. 808, § 3.

subdivision plan necessary to construct the project. Nexum appealed these two adverse decisions to the Superior Court pursuant to G.L. c. 40A, § 17, and G.L. c. 41, § 81BB. Following a bench trial, the judge denied the appeals. We affirm.

1. *Background.* The property fronts Nixon Road, a public way, and is largely wooded, with a small area of wetlands. The property features a large, 150-foot high hill and has no connection to any municipal water supply or sewer system. Nexum proposed to build twenty-four detached single-family residences in a condominium development on the property, reserving the remainder of the property for open space managed by a local conservation organization. Nexum planned to construct a common well and a common septic system for use by the condominium residences.

Nexum sought, in two separate but necessarily parallel applications, (1) a special permit for cluster development pursuant to Framingham's open space residential development (OSRD) provisions in its zoning by-law, and (2) approval of the resulting definitive subdivision plan. Nexum proceeded through the permitting process from December, 2001, until the board's ultimate votes on March 25, 2004. The board denied the applications.

Nexum appealed from the denial of the special permit pursuant to G.L. c. 40A, § 17. Nexum also appealed from the board's decision denying approval of the definitive subdivision plan pursuant to G.L. c. 41, § 81BB. The consolidated matters proceeded to trial in March, 2009. The judge issued a thoughtful memorandum of decision, denying Nexum's appeals, on June 30, 2009. He concluded that the by-law and applicable regulations required the denial of the applications because (1) Nexum failed to comply with by-law requirements to establish the permissible density of the project,[3] and (2) Nexum could not comply with conditions imposed by the Framingham board of health related to on-site water supply.

Nexum appeals, arguing [that] Nexum's density calculation was valid without soils tests on each lot shown on the preliminary subdivision density yield plan, and [that] the judge erroneously upheld the board's denials on the basis of inadequate water supply.

3. *Density.* The judge concluded that the language of the by-law, § IV(M)(4)(c)(1) (see note 3, supra), is clear and unambiguous as matter of law and requires an applicant (where the project is not served by public sewer) to "certify that each lot identified on the plan is buildable, as evidenced by a soils test, consistent with Title 5 [of the State

---

[3]   The by-law, in § IV(M)(4)(c)(1), requires that the number of dwelling units in a cluster development not exceed the number of lots which the by-law, and "all applicable land use regulations in the district (including wetlands protection), and . . . the [town's subdivision regulations]," would permit in a conventional subdivision. The by-law also requires that for parcels unserved by public sewer, an applicant "must certify that each lot identified on the plan is buildable, as evidenced by a soils test, consistent with Title 5 [of the State environmental code, 310 Code Mass. Regs. §§ 15.000 et seq.]."

environmental code, 310 Code Mass. Regs. §§ 15.000 et seq.]." He determined that this language required Nexum to conduct a Title 5 soils test on each lot identified in its preliminary subdivision density yield plan. Because Nexum had not done so, he concluded, the by-law constrained the board to deny the applications. We agree.

The by-law section at issue clearly imposes a cap on the number of dwelling units which a developer can permissibly build in an OSRD cluster development: the number of "buildable" lots which the land could support if developed under a conventional subdivision plan. The by-law specifies that a soils test on each lot on the preliminary subdivision density yield plan will determine whether the lot is "buildable." Because the by-law therefore requires a soils test on each lot shown on the preliminary subdivision density yield plan, and because Nexum did not comply with this requirement, Nexum did not properly establish the project's permissible density, and the board properly denied the applications.

The language of the by-law does not permit Nexum's interpretation that a single soils test for a common septic system serving the development would comply with the by-law. Nexum, in effect, argues that the relevant "plan" referred to in this section of the by-law is the cluster plan, not the preliminary subdivision density yield plan. Because this section of the by-law is entitled "Density Yield Plan" and only discusses the requirements for submission of the preliminary subdivision density yield plan, Nexum's interpretation does not persuade us.

Nexum further argues that the tentative approval by the board of the preliminary subdivision density yield plan should have been conclusive on the issue of compliance with the density yield plan section of the by-law. We disagree. The board's September, 2002, "determination," in which it "accept[ed]" Nexum's proposed density of twenty-four units, was made as part of a pre-application conference procedure described under § IV(M)(5) of the by-law as "optional and . . . advisory only." The board expressly conditioned this "accept[ance]" as "[b]ased on the pre-application plans and materials" and "subject to the [b]oard's normal discretion as provided for in the OSRD [b]y-[l]aw and [s]pecial [p]ermit process." Because this "accept[ance]" resulted from an "optional" and "advisory" process in which the board preserved its discretion to deny the applications for nonconformity with the by-law, the "accept[ance]" did not bind the board, and subsequent denial of the applications was proper.

4. *Water supply*. Here, the BOH conditioned approval of the special permit on future satisfaction of water supply issues. The record establishes, and the judge correctly found, that Nexum could not achieve compliance with the conditions. The BOH conditioned its approval of the project on a showing that the water supply could suffice during peak summer usage and that the water supply would not have a

significant effect on the wells of abutting owners. Thus, as the judge correctly put it, the BOH approval was tied to "several conditions subsequent that were beyond Nexum's control and could be impossible to satisfy." It follows that no amendment to the applications could, as a practical matter, satisfy the BOH conditions and that the board had no choice but to deny the applications.

In addition, the board was required to find that a proposed development has made adequate provisions for water supply in order to approve both a special permit and a definitive subdivision plan. The record discloses various studies by the parties, dialogue among them, and theories as to various tests and standards for determining adequacy of water for the project. The judge, on this competent record evidence concluded that the proposed water supply was inadequate. The board therefore had a legal obligation to deny the applications on the additional ground that the project had inadequate water supply provisions.

Judgment affirmed.

NOTES AND QUESTIONS

1. What approvals did Nexum have to obtain in order to develop a cluster subdivision? Why would Framingham have required a special permit for a cluster subdivision?

2. Did all of Nexum's proposed lots pass the soils test required by the state environment code? If your answer is yes, what was the basis for the board's decision?

3. What plans were required of a Framingham developer seeking to build a cluster subdivision? What provisions in the Massachusetts statute and the Framingham bylaws led the planning board to require those plans? What was missing from Nexum's plans?

4. Why did Nexum choose to litigate rather than seeking approval for a conventional subdivision plan?

5. Suppose a Framingham developer has acquired a rectangular parcel of land measuring 1,000 feet by 300 feet, for a total of 300,000 square feet. The parcel is in a district requiring a minimum lot size of 10,000 square feet and minimum lot frontage of 100 square feet. Developer submits an application to build a cluster subdivision with 30 homes clustered on 100,000 square feet of the parcel, and proposes to leave the remainder of the parcel as open space. There are no water supply or septic problems in the area. The Planning Board finds the cluster subdivision attractive and seeks the advice of you, the Board's counsel. In light of the Framingham bylaws, can the Planning Board approve the cluster subdivision? Why or why not?

B. SUBDIVISION REGULATION

Consider a developer who has purchased a substantial parcel in a zoning district permitting single-family homes on lots with a minimum size of 50 feet by 100 feet. The ordinance has no cluster provisions like those in Framingham. Developer wants to build as many homes as possible, and wants to economize on the cost of road construction. Developer's parcel fronts on public roads on the north and south, but not on the east and west. Developer wants to subdivide his parcel into 25 lots, all of which conform to the municipal zoning ordinance, in the configuration illustrated below:

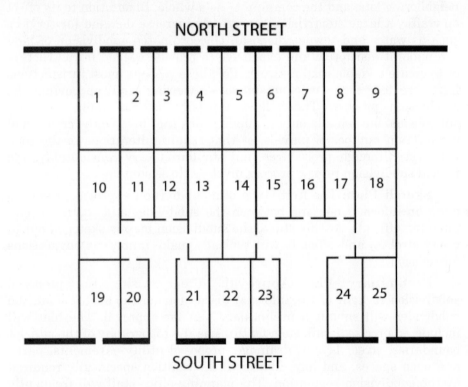

Should municipal officials have any concerns about the configuration? Suppose, for instance, traffic on North Street is extraordinarily busy. Might the addition of nine new curb cuts, to accommodate driveways for purchasers of lots 1 through 9, increase the potential for traffic accidents? Even on South Street, the proposed subdivision will, at a minimum, add five curb cuts—two for roads, and three for driveways (for lots 19, 22, and 25).

Will fire trucks be able to navigate the roads that provide access to lots 10 through 18? And if there are no other nearby roads that connect North Street and South Street, will fire trucks from a fire station on South Street be delayed in reaching lots 1 through 9 in case of emergency? Moreover, if the developer sells off the subdivided lots, what guarantee does the municipality have that the developer will ever build the roads that service lots 10 through 18?

Finally, has sufficient provision been made for connecting all of the new lots to sewer, water, and electric utility lines? Concerns about lot sizes may arise where lots are not connected to local utilities and septic systems (requiring ample space to function) must be used. In such cases, the use of cluster development is less likely.

As these questions illustrate, the subdivision of a large parcel into several smaller parcels can have dramatic implications for future residents of the subdivision, current residents, and future developers of neighboring lots, and the community as a whole. In addition to its effect on traffic, a large subdivision can greatly increase demand for services such as water and sewage disposal. Uncoordinated subdivision of land can make it disruptive and expensive to provide needed infrastructure or to create a viable road network. For these reasons, most jurisdictions have created some mechanism for reviewing and approving the subdivision process. These laws typically do not apply to every subdivision, but usually only to subdivisions that involve the creation of a minimum number of parcels, or that require alterations to the road network. Although procedures and standards vary considerably, the typical subdivision review process involves three steps:

Sketch Plan: The first stage of a subdivision approval process is often an informal meeting between the subdivider and county or city planning officials. At this stage, the subdivision map is sketched out in broad strokes, and officials will typically make numerous suggestions for revision.

Preliminary Plat Approval: After revising the proposed subdivision in light of the informal discussions of the sketch plan, the subdivider will submit a preliminary plat for approval. The plat will include, in precise detail, such features as the topography of the site, lot boundaries, street layout, drainage, proposed utility easements, parks and open spaces, and any additional information specifically required by the subdivision regulation. The planning office staff will frequently review the submission for facial consistency with the requirements of the subdivision regulation and may refer the plan over to environmental review bodies (including local wetlands commissions), the city engineer, and others. Then staff will pass it on to the local planning commission (or whatever body is designated by the subdivision regulation to make subdivision decisions) for review. The commission will usually hold a public hearing to discuss the proposal and then render a decision. Both the staff and the commission are looking to ensure compliance with the subdivision regulations, the zoning lot size requirements of the zoning code, traffic and pedestrian safety, street layout and naming, and adequacy of the proposed infrastructure. At this stage, the commission can (and frequently does) demand additional changes to the preliminary plat before granting its preliminary approval. Once it is satisfied with the preliminary plat, the commission specifies what must be done in order to receive final approval of the subdivision. In many jurisdictions, among the conditions the commission may impose on the subdivider is a requirement that he dedicate (i.e., give) streets and sidewalks within the subdivision to the public, or at least give easements to the general public, held by the local government.

Final Plat Approval: Once the subdivider has received approval of the preliminary plat, the clock begins ticking for the completion of the conditions for final plat approval. In California, for example, the conditions for final approval must normally be satisfied within 24 months of approval of the preliminary plat. In many states, including California, obtaining final approval of the subdivision is a ministerial task as long as the final plat corresponds to the preliminary plat and the conditions imposed for final approval. It is at this stage that the public officially accepts the dedicated streets and sidewalks in the subdivision.

Every state has passed an enabling act that allows local governments to regulate how a property owner can subdivide a single parcel into many parcels. These enabling acts typically require that a locality have a consistent process for evaluating each subdivision application, and authorize or require the municipality to adopt reasonable rules and regulations. The statutes often require that any subdivision be coordinated with existing state or local comprehensive plans, and provide adequate water supply, utilities, and trees. Many subdivision statutes also authorize the municipality to impose exactions and take contributions from the subdivider as a condition for subdivision approval. Ordinarily, statutes and local ordinances delegate the task of reviewing subdivision proposals to an administrative body— either a zoning and planning commission, as in the case that follows, or to a planning board. Some statutes, however, provide for subdivision review by the local legislative body, unless that body delegates the responsibility to an administrative body. *See, e.g.*, Cal. Gov't Code § 66452.2.

How much authority should the administrative body have to regulate subdivisions? Consider the following case:

Andrews v. Planning and Zoning Commission of the Town of Wallingford

Appellate Court of Connecticut, 2006
97 Conn.App. 316, 904 A.2d 275

■ DiPentima, J.

The plaintiffs, Lynn Andrews and Jeff Andrews, submitted an application to the commission seeking to subdivide property that they owned in Wallingford. Access to the proposed subdivision was to be by way of an existing road in North Branford. Subsequent to the plaintiffs' submission of their application, the commission applied to amend its subdivision regulations to add the following requirement: "All proposed streets shall be connected to existing public roads within the Town of Wallingford." A public hearing on the amendment was held on October 15, 2003. At that hearing, the only comment or explanation from the commission was made by Linda Bush, the town planner, who stated that she always had believed that this requirement was in the regulations until the commission had received the plaintiffs' subdivision application. She further stated that this would, "put it on the books that if you are going to build a road, it has to be connected to an existing road so that police, fire and school buses can get there from Wallingford." No one from the public had a comment or question, and the amendment was then approved. The plaintiffs appealed to the trial court from the commission's decision amending the subdivision regulations. The court found that the public hearing on the amendment could not have lasted more than three minutes, failed to provide any indication as to how many parcels of land would be affected, and was without input from the fire department, police department or the board of education. The court held that the commission had exceeded its statutory authority under § 8–25, sustained the plaintiffs' appeal and declared the amendment null and void. This appeal followed.

On appeal, the commission's sole claim is that § 8–25 authorizes a regulation requiring new subdivision streets to be connected to existing Wallingford streets. General Statutes § 8–25 provides a planning commission with the authority to establish subdivision regulations. The scope of the commission's authority is detailed specifically in the statute. "As a creature of the state, the [town] can exercise only such powers as are expressly granted to it, or such powers as are necessary to enable it to discharge the duties and carry into effect the objects and purposes of its creation." (Internal quotation marks omitted.) Avonside, Inc. v. Zoning & Planning Commission, 153 Conn. 232, 236, 215 A.2d 409 (1965). Therefore, a subdivision regulation can be adopted only with positive statutory authorization. Sonn v. Planning Commission, 172 Conn. 156, 159, 374 A.2d 159 (1976). "In other words, in order to determine whether the regulation in question was within the authority of the commission to enact, we do not search for a statutory prohibition against such an enactment; rather, we must search for statutory authority for the enactment." Avonside, Inc. v. Zoning & Planning Commission, supra, at 236, 215 A.2d 409.

Section 8–25(a) provides in relevant part: "Before exercising the powers granted in this section, the commission shall adopt regulations covering the subdivision of land. . . . Such regulations shall provide that the land to be subdivided shall be of such character that it can be used for building purposes without danger to health or the public safety . . . and that the proposed streets are in harmony with existing or proposed principal thoroughfares shown in the plan of conservation and development as described in section 8–23, especially in regard to safe intersections with such thoroughfares, and so arranged and of such width, as to provide an adequate and convenient system for present and prospective traffic needs. . . .”

No provision in § 8–25 gives the commission the specific authority to require that proposed streets connect with existing roads within the town of the subdivision. See Finn v. Planning & Zoning Commission, supra, 156 Conn. at 545, 244 A.2d 391. With respect to roads, the statute authorizes a town to ensure only that proposed subdivision roads are in harmony with existing roads in the plan of development, form safe intersections with existing roads, and are arranged and of adequate width to handle the existing and proposed traffic on such road. The commission's regulation, without more, does not satisfy any of these specifically referenced purposes.

The commission seems to suggest that the language of § 8–25 that subdivided land "be of such character that it can be used for building purposes without danger to health or the public safety" authorizes the regulation. It made no showing, however, as to how or why requiring proposed streets to connect to existing Wallingford roads is necessary for health and public safety. The only basis in the record for such a nexus is the town planner's statement that "if you are going to build a road, it has to be connected to an existing road so that police, fire and school buses can get there from Wallingford." No evidence was provided in support of this statement and, as indicated by the court, there was no input from the municipal departments allegedly affected by the failure to have such a regulation in place. In light of the limitations on a planning commission's legislative authority, we conclude that this solitary statement is insufficient to show that the regulation was required for health and public safety and therefore authorized by § 8–25.

That the commission must provide some connection to the enabling statute for its legislative action finds support in our case law reviewing similar limitations on subdivision development. We find particularly informative our Supreme Court's decisions in Crescent Development Corp. v. Planning Commission, 148 Conn. 145, 168 A.2d 547 (1961), and Smith v. Zoning Board of Appeals, supra, 227 Conn. at 71, 629 A.2d 1089.

In *Crescent Development Corp.,* the proposed subdivision was located in both New Canaan and Stamford, but the only access road to the public highway for both towns was through New Canaan. Crescent Development Corp. v. Planning Commission, supra, 148 Conn. at 147, 168 A.2d 547. Our Supreme Court upheld the New Canaan planning and zoning commission's approval of the subdivision, which was conditioned on the construction of an access road from the developer's land to an established or public road in Stamford. *Id.,* at 152–53, 168A.2d 547. Such a requirement comported with the enabling act, which explicitly authorizes the commission to regulate for traffic needs. On the basis of the record of the hearing on the subdivision application, the commission was able to express a sufficient connection between its regulation and the enabling statute. Specifically, the commission articulated that its purpose in requiring the condition was to prevent great traffic density at the proposed road's intersection, which would cause the proposed road not to be in harmony with the existing public road "in regard to safe intersections. . . ." (Internal quotation marks omitted.) *Id.*, at 150, 168A.2d 547. In contrast, no such connection to the enabling statute was made in this case.

Similarly, in *Smith,* the defendant zoning board of appeals had made a strong showing in support of the commission's regulation. At issue in *Smith* was a developer's appeal from a denial of a subdivision application on the basis of consideration of historical factors. Smith v. Zoning Board of Appeals, supra, 227 Conn. at 77, 629 A.2d 1089. Our Supreme Court concluded that the regulation was not beyond the scope of § 8–25 after agreeing with the board that the provision for health and public safety includes protection of the environment, which, in turn, encompasses historic preservation. *Id.*, at 84, 629 A.2d 1089. In support of its argument, the board demonstrated that the regulation comported with a number of other generally accepted requirements: The preservation of historic resources was listed among the basic objectives in the town plan, a provision of the Greenwich land use regulations specifically permitted an evaluation of historical factors in subdivisions located within the coastal zone, General Statutes § 7–147a et seq. expresses a public policy favoring historic preservation, and the developer's deed contained a restriction subjecting the land to regulations imposed because it was located in a historic district. Smith v. Zoning Board of Appeals, supra, 227 Conn. at 78–79, 629 A.2d 1089. Unlike in *Smith,* the commission in the present case did not show that its regulation accorded with any other established requirements.

Because nothing in § 8–25 expressly authorizes the commission to require that any proposed subdivision street connect to an existing Wallingford road, and because the commission made no showing that such a regulation is necessary for health and public safety, we conclude that the commission exceeded its statutory authority and the amendment is therefore null and void.

The judgment is affirmed.

NOTES AND QUESTIONS

1.   Apart from the question of authority discussed in *Andrews,* does Wallingford have a legitimate interest in ensuring that roads in new subdivisions connect up with existing roads within Wallingford? If you think there is such an interest, how would you characterize it?

2.   Suppose the town planner had asked for your advice before proposing that the commission promulgate the regulation. What advice would you

have given to the planner? Do you think that advice would have made a difference in the outcome of the litigation?

3.   An excerpt from Conn. Gen. Stat. § 8–25 follows:

> [T]he [planning] commission shall adopt regulations covering the subdivision of land. No such regulations shall become effective until after a public hearing held in accordance with the provisions of section 8–7d. Such regulations shall provide that the land to be subdivided shall be of such character that it can be used for building purposes without danger to health or the public safety, that proper provision shall be made for water, sewerage and drainage, including the upgrading of any downstream ditch, culvert or other drainage structure which, through the introduction of additional drainage due to such subdivision, becomes undersized and creates the potential for flooding on a state highway, and, in areas contiguous to brooks, rivers or other bodies of water subject to flooding, including tidal flooding, that proper provision shall be made for protective flood control measures and that the proposed streets are in harmony with existing or proposed principal thoroughfares shown in the plan of conservation and development as described in section 8–23, especially in regard to safe intersections with such thoroughfares, and so arranged and of such width, as to provide an adequate and convenient system for present and prospective traffic needs. Such regulations shall also provide that the commission may require the provision of open spaces, parks and playgrounds when, and in places, deemed proper by the planning commission, which open spaces, parks and playgrounds shall be shown on the subdivision plan. Such regulations may, with the approval of the commission, authorize the applicant to pay a fee to the municipality or pay a fee to the municipality and transfer land to the municipality in lieu of any requirement to provide open spaces.

In light of the statute, would the Town of Wallingford have exceeded its authority if it promulgated a regulation that required all roads within the subdivision to connect "to existing public roads adequate to provide for the health and safety of residents of the subdivision"?

Suppose the Town had promulgated such a regulation, and then denied subdivision approval due to inadequate street connections, focusing on access by fire trucks and school buses. If you represented the landowner, how would you frame a challenge to the denial? Would the challenge succeed?

4.   Who should have standing to challenge a board's *denial* of a subdivision application? An environmental organization advocating for increased density? A neighboring municipality? Residents of the neighboring municipality? Who should have standing to challenge a board's *grant* of a subdivision application?

5.   What is the difference between a subdivision regulation and a Planned Unit Development provision in a zoning code? Would a municipality need to

adopt both kinds of provision in order to achieve the different outcomes anticipated by each? *See* City of Urbana v. Champaign County, 76 Ill. 2d 63, 27 Ill. Dec. 777, 389 N.E.2d 1185 (1979) (finding that the power of a city to authorize a Planned Unit Development did not derive from its ability to subdivide, because the city wrote its subdivision ordinance to only apply to tracts of land divided into two or more parcels).

6.   The conformity between roads within a new subdivision and the existing road network is often a central focus of subdivision review. In fact, the concern with that conformity is often specifically mentioned in subdivision statutes as an issue planning boards should address in evaluating subdivision proposals. *See, e.g.,* N.J. Stat. Ann. § 40.55(D)–38. Without some entity coordinating the design of roads within subdivisions, a coherent, efficient road network would be impossible to create in the first instance. And retrofitting such a network onto subdivisions, once they have been created, is likely to be far more expensive and disruptive than putting the roads in the right place to begin with.

More on Street Layouts—To Grid or Not to Grid?

Enthusiasm for orderliness in street design has waxed and waned and waxed again through the years. Consider the history of the famous Manhattan street grid, as told by Hendrik Hartog, in his book Public Property and Private Power (1983). Most land in New York City was originally owned by the Corporation of the City of New York. After independence from England, New York aimed to dispose of its public lands with more of an eye towards raising revenue than controlling the use to which the land was put. In addition, the dominant ideology of the time favored the relatively rapid transfer of public lands into private hands. The result of this was the steady transfer of publicly owned lands in Manhattan to private owners, often without any significant deed restrictions.

By the turn of the 19th century, New York City's leaders sought to take more of a leadership role in guiding the development of private lands. They complained, for example, that "the arrangement of the original or lower part of the city . . . *is essentially defective.* Beauty, order, and convenience seem to have been little valued by our ancestors." Most of the streets, they worried, "were constructed according to the fancy or interest of some obstinate or inexperienced landholders, without regard to uniformity, health, or beauty." Hartog at 159 (quoting Thomas Stanford, A Concise Description of the City of New York (1814)). Thus, in 1807, the city council presented a bill to the state legislature seeking the authority to draw a map that would fix the future development of the streets and roads of Manhattan north of the settled city. Reflecting the preferences of the time, it called for the imposition of a uniform grid over the entire remaining undeveloped portion of Manhattan. The grid would be made up of 155 east-west streets, 60 feet in width and 200 feet apart, crossed by 12 north-south avenues, each one 100 feet wide. Topography was ignored. Mappers assumed (correctly, as it turned out) that the land could simply be flattened as development proceeded.

Frederick Law Olmsted detested the proposed map, reportedly saying that there was "good authority for the story that the system of 1807 was hit upon by the chance occurrence of a mason's sieve near a map of the ground to be laid out. It was taken up and placed on the map, and the question being asked, 'what do you want better than that?' no one was able to answer." Initially, the decision to impose the grid without regard to topography or private boundaries generated a great deal of controversy. In one case, an old woman threw artichokes and cabbages at surveyors. Despite this initial opposition, the publication of the grid map in 1811 was ultimately embraced by private landowners, who came to appreciate the predictability it offered them.

The Manhattan grid continues to be a source of debate, among planners and lay people alike. Cornell planning professor John Reps, for example, argues that the grid leaves insufficient sites for public buildings, contributes to congestion at the frequent intersections, and leads to overbuilding on narrow lots that result from the shallow blocks. Others have objected to the monotony of the grid on aesthetic grounds. The goals of the grid's proponents, however, were largely utilitarian and minimalist—to provide predictability for landowners, and to leave as much to private initiative as possible.

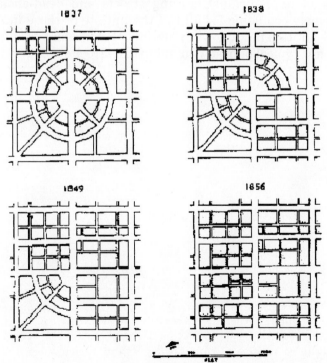

The Evolution of the Street Grid of Circleville, Ohio. Source: John William Reps, The Making of Urban America 490, fig. 291 (1992).

Another, less well-known, city struggled with its own efforts to studiously avoid and then create a street grid. The town of Circleville, Ohio, was founded in 1810. Its original street layout involved a series of concentric circles, with an octagonal courthouse at the city's center. Residents became disaffected with the circular pattern, however, which produced awkward, wedge-shaped lots and, residents believed, hindered development. In one of the first instances of urban redevelopment in the United States, in 1837, the Ohio legislature empowered the Circleville Squaring Company to retrofit the town with a more conventional grid. Without the power of eminent domain, the Company needed the consent of each property owner in order to reconfigure their property lines to permit the shift from circular streets to a grid. The process was lengthy, but over a period of several years, the Squaring Company went about its task, ultimately completing the job by 1856.

Most post-World War II street design in the United States has tended to reject the rigidity of the grid in favor of curvilinear streets arranged on a hierarchical model, with limited access highways at the top leading to "arterial" roads from which branch "collector" streets, which gather the traffic from "local" streets, which are often loops or cul-de-sacs. In order to get from one destination to another, suburban residents must frequently drive up and down the entire street hierarchy. Walking is virtually out of the question, and alternative routes tend to be few and far between. The result has been a suburban crazy quilt of unpredictably curving streets and dead-ends that are often extremely confusing for all but the initiate or those in possession of a GPS unit. The following aerial photograph, from Puyallup, Washington is typical of post-War suburban street design:

In recent years, however, the rise of New Urbanism has led to a revival of interest in grids. The New Urbanist development of Seaside, Florida, provides a typical example of New Urbanist street layouts. Although not the unrelenting gridiron pattern of Manhattan, New Urbanist street layouts are far more enthusiastic about the grid than their suburban counterparts. Where used, curves tend to follow more predictable semi-circular patterns that are easier for first-time users to visualize and navigate. New Urbanists also eschew the rigid street hierarchy and attempt to design street networks in ways that permit travelers, and particularly pedestrians, to choose between a number of alternative routes to get from one point to another.

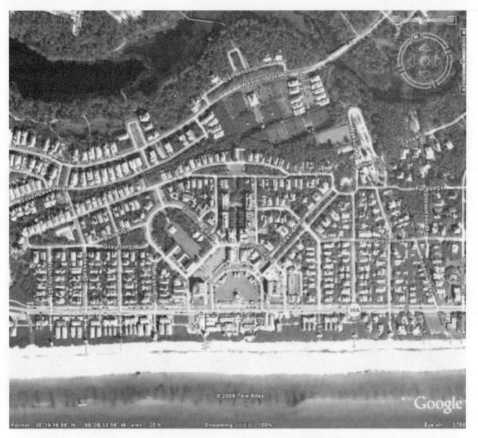

Street Names. In addition to coordinating the layout of the street network, regulation of the subdivision process provides an opportunity for local governments to coordinate street names. Typically, the proposed names for new streets to be built as part of a subdivision must be approved by the planning board responsible for approving the subdivision plan. Frequently, that board will delegate street naming to a special street names committee. The goal of street name approval is to prevent the adoption of inappropriate or confusing names and avoid the duplication of names. For example, a new street that is merely the continuation of an existing street is usually required to adopt the name of the existing street, thereby preventing street names from changing from block to block. And a new street should not be given a name that is confusingly similar to the name of a street in a different part of town. Confusing or duplicate street names can be inconvenient. They can also be unsafe, slowing the response times for emergency vehicles. Should street names be coordinated on a regional, rather than merely municipal, scale?

Infrastructure Coordination and Cost

Streets are just one example of the sort of infrastructural coordination beyond the scale of the individual subdivision that is a central concern of subdivision regulation. Sewers can also frequently be built more efficiently when they are laid out to take into account the existing network of pipes and the needs of existing and future subdivisions.

The desire to take into account the fit between the needs of the proposed subdivision and those of the larger community leads many municipalities to use the subdivision approval process as an opportunity for bargaining with developers over who will pay the costs for shared infrastructure. Local governments routinely require developers to build out or pay for the infrastructural elements specified by the planning authority. And in many jurisdictions, though not all, planning authorities are empowered to condition subdivision approval on the developer's dedication of infrastructural elements, such as sidewalks, roads, and even parks or schools, to the public. This common practice raises the question of the proper allocation of costs of infrastructure improvements between the subdividing developer and the community as a whole. This question is particularly important where the infrastructure within the proposed subdivision would generate benefits for the public as a whole. For example, when an arterial road serving multiple neighborhoods passes the proposed subdivision, who should pay to construct the portion of the road as it passes the subdivision? The subdivider? The town? Both? If both, how should the cost be allocated between the two entities? *See, e.g.,* Briar West, Inc. v. City of Lincoln, 206 Neb. 172, 291 N.W.2d 730 (1980) (noting that "reasonableness is the essential requirement in determining what costs may be legally imposed as a condition of subdivision approval" and rejecting imposition on subdivider of costs for paving an arterial road that abutted the proposed subdivision but to which the subdivision's lots would not have direct access). This question is a species of the broader problem of the limits on government's power to impose exactions on developers, which we will discuss at greater length in Chapter Five.

New Urbanist Subdivisions: The Transit Oriented Development

Peter Calthorpe, a leading New Urbanist, has advocated orienting new subdivisions towards regional transit networks in order to minimize dependence on automobiles, with their attendant environmental costs, and to foster a richer social experience within newly developed communities. *See* Peter Calthorpe, The Next American Metropolis: Ecology, Community, and the American Dream (1993). He encapsulates his ideas under the rubric of Transit Oriented Developments ("TODs"), a category that extends beyond new subdivisions to include urban infill and large-scale redevelopment. Calthorpe's TODs are characterized by four features: (1) orientation towards regional transit networks; (2) a commitment to a mixture of uses; (3) high density; and (4) pedestrian-friendly design.

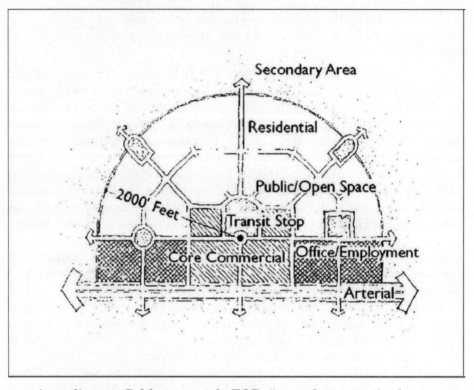

According to Calthorpe, each TOD "must have a mixed-use core commercial area located adjacent to the transit stop." Everything within a TOD should be within roughly 2,000 feet (roughly a 10-minute walk) of a transit stop. At a minimum, it should provide convenience retail and local-serving offices; larger core areas should include supermarkets, restaurants, service commercial, entertainment, comparison retail, second floor residential, and employment-intensive office and light residential uses. Mixed-use development within the neighborhood reduces the need for automobile trips for convenience shopping, and proximity to transit links permits residents to access broader regional facilities without relying on their private cars.

Urban TODs should have a density of 18 dwelling units per net acre (yielding a population density of over 20,000 people per square mile). Although density can vary across an individual TOD, minimum density of any given area within a TOD should be 7 units per net acre. This density should be achieved through a mixture of residential forms, including detached single-family homes on small lots, attached town houses and duplexes, and apartment buildings and condominiums as well as liberal rules permitting the building of residential units accessory to single-family dwellings, such as "granny" and "in-law" apartments.

Within a TOD, street layout is designed to maximize walkability. Streets must be lined by sidewalks and trees. Building entries must face the street, to enhance the pedestrian experience. Calthorpe favors narrow streets with on-street parking, to slow traffic to a speed that does not menace pedestrians. In addition, Calthorpe, like most New Urbanists, favors a street system arranged in a simple and memorable pattern, such as a grid. Streets should converge on transit stops, core commercial areas, schools and parks. The street system should provide multiple and parallel routes between the TOD's core commercial area and its residential and employment areas.

C. SITE PLAN REVIEW

The subdivision review process gives municipal officials a measure of control over developments when a landowner proposes to subdivide a parcel into individual lots. Often, however, a developer plans a large project that does not require subdivision into lots. Whether or not a developer plans to subdivide a parcel, municipalities often require review and approval of a developer's plans for the layout of buildings, parking, landscaping, and utility provisions within a large development project. Typically referred to as "site plan" approval, the process is not usually applied to the construction of single-family dwellings, but tends to be reserved for multi-family units and commercial developments. The purpose of such a review process is to ensure that the new development makes adequate provision for the increased demand for services and infrastructure that the development generates and that the structures built in conjunction with the new development operate in harmony with the surrounding community.

The site plan review process varies among the states and localities. In some jurisdictions, site plan review requirements must largely be set out in advance in the zoning code. In other jurisdictions, decision-makers may be given more discretion to balance different interests against each other. In such jurisdictions, additional discretionary power is put in the hands of land use regulators. In this respect, subdivision review and site plan review share many common characteristics, as the following case illustrates:

Derry Senior Development, LLC v. Town of Derry

Supreme Court of New Hampshire, 2008
157 N.H. 441, 951 A.2d 170

■ DUGGAN, J.

On August 8, 2006, the plaintiff applied for final site plan approval to construct an independent adult community development on its property. The proposed project consisted of, among other things: (1) thirty-six two-bedroom single family detached residences, with "35 units to be located on a new private way to be called Kimball's Lane, [and] one additional unit to be accessed from Drew Road"; (2) six community septic systems, each with four-inch sewage collection pipes;

(3) thirty-six individual water wells; and (4) approximately forty acres of open space.

Before submitting the application to the board, the plaintiff obtained approval for its project from, among other entities, the [New Hampshire Department of Environmental Services] DES. *See generally* RSA ch. 485–A (2001 & Supp. 2007). The Town of Derry Department of Public Works (DPW), however, opposed the proposed development. It requested that: "all sewer collection system components upstream of the septic tank(s) . . . be built according to [the higher standards found in the] Town of Derry Sewer Division Regulations"; that is, "the collection system . . . be comprised of 8 [inch] sewer mains, 6 [inch] sewer services and precast concrete manholes at intersecting pipes or at the end of a sewer main," not, as the plaintiff proposed, "4 [inch] pipes with cleanouts."

The town's engineer also reviewed the application, and recommended, among other things, that "[a]lthough the content of the [septic system design] plans [wa]s statutorily within the purview of the NHDES, . . . all 'common' sewage collection lines be constructed of SDR 35 PVC, having a minimum diameter of six (6) inches for improved serviceability and performance."

[At a December 6, 2006 hearing], the DPW reiterated that it required, among other things, that Kimball Lane be twenty-four feet wide, and that the sewer collection system be "buil[t] to town standards as required of the Indian Hill Estates," another independent adult community previously approved by the board.

[A]fter acknowledging that the plan met DES requirements, the board voted to disapprove the application partly because the proposed sewage system did not have "larger piping to eliminate the failure that [the town previously] experienced" with community septic systems.

The plaintiff appealed to the superior court. *See* RSA 677:15 (Supp. 2007). The superior court affirmed.

On appeal, the plaintiff argues that the town has enacted "no site plan regulations that specifically address septic systems or septic set back requirements," and, "[t]herefore, DES approval should be *prima facie* proof that an applicant's design and setbacks are safe and sufficient."

The town counters that the board properly relied upon "the testimony and comments of . . . two individuals who are qualified in th[e] area" of septic systems in requiring larger piping. The town maintains that the "board's concerns were not *ad hoc* but were legitimate in light of the proposal and its experience with community septic systems," and that the board "had persuasive evidence before it that supported its denial of . . . the septic plan as designed."

Our review of the trial court's decision is deferential. We will uphold the decision on appeal unless it is unsupported by the evidence or legally erroneous.

"Site plan review is designed to insure that uses permitted by a zoning ordinance are constructed on a site in such a way that they fit into the area in which they are being constructed without causing drainage, traffic, or lighting problems." Summa Humma Enters. v. Town of Tilton, 151 N.H. 75, 78, 849 A.2d 146 (2004) (quotation omitted). It is "also designed to assure that sites will be developed in a safe and attractive manner and in a way that will not involve danger or injury to the health, safety, or prosperity of abutting property owners or the general public." *Id.* (quotation omitted). To accomplish these purposes, a plan is "subject[ed] . . . to the very expertise expected of a planning board in cases where it would not be feasible to set forth in the ordinance a set of specific requirements upon which a building inspector could readily grant or refuse a permit." *Id.* (quotation omitted). The planning board "review[s] site plans to determine if they properly address such issues as surface and sanitary drainage, the effect on ground water, and the creation of pollution sources," 15 P. Loughlin, *New Hampshire Practice, Land Use Planning and Zoning* § 30.02, at 427 (2000), and, thus, has the authority "to impose requirements and conditions that are reasonably related to land use goals and considerations within its purview," Summa Humma Enters., 151 N.H. at 78, 849 A.2d 146 (citations omitted).

Although "[s]ite review can be an extremely useful and powerful tool for municipalities . . . , there are definite limits to its use." . . . "For example, site plans may only be reviewed after the local legislative body has specifically authorized the planning board to exercise site plan control and only communities which have adopted valid zoning ordinances may grant site review control to their planning boards." 15 P. Loughlin, *supra* § 30.09, at 436–37; see RSA 674:43, I (Supp. 2007). Further, "[s]ite review statutes are not self-executing, but rather, the local planning board must adopt specific site review regulations before exercising authority." 15 P. Loughlin, *supra* § 30.09, at 437; see RSA 674:44, I (Supp. 2007); RSA 675:6 (1996) (setting forth method of adoption of site plan regulations). These regulations must, among other things, "[d]efine the purposes of site plan review" and "[s]pecify the general standards and requirements with which the proposed development shall comply, including appropriate reference to accepted codes and standards for construction." RSA 674:44, III(b), (c). The regulations that the planning board adopts may, among other things, "stipulate, as a condition precedent to the approval of the plat, the extent . . . to which water, sewer, and other utility mains, piping, connections, or other facilities shall be installed." RSA 674:44, IV.

Relevant to this case is a regulation governing "[s]anitary sewer construction," which provides, in pertinent part:

In areas where municipal sewer is not available, an on-site subsurface sewage disposal system may be designed and constructed *as long as said design and construction fully complies with all applicable requirements of the New Hampshire Code of Administrative Rules; and the applicant has secured appropriate permits for the same from the [DES].*

[Derry, N.H. Land Development Control Regulations (LDCR), part 3, art. VII,] § 170–66(A)(1) (emphasis added).

The New Hampshire Code of Administrative Rules sets forth comprehensive rules for the design of sewage disposal systems. *See N.H. Admin. Rules,* Env-Ws 1000–1025. The purpose of these rules is "to prevent pollution of all public or private water supplies, whether underground or surface sources," *Id.* 1001.01, and "to prevent nuisances and potential health hazards," RSA 485–A:1 (2001).

In this case, the DES' approval states that the plaintiff's proposed development meets these rules, which include requirements concerning pipe size and the distance of the system from wells and property lines. Relying upon this approval and Smith v. Town of Wolfeboro, 136 N.H. 337, 615 A.2d 1252 (1992), the plaintiff argues that, because the board has not enacted more stringent standards for septic systems than those set forth in the administrative rules, the "DES permit creates a presumption that [the proposed] septic plan is safe and adequate."

In *Smith,* we noted that "a planning board is entitled to rely in part on its own judgment and experience in acting upon applications for subdivision approval[,] . . . is not bound by a determination of another agency, such as the WSPCD, and is free to enact more exacting or protective standards." *Id.* at 343, 615 A.2d 1252 (quotation omitted). "In th[at] case, however, there [we]re no local standards to guide applicants as to what, beyond WSPCD approval, [wa]s required for septic system approval." *Id.*

Instead, the regulations "authorize[d] the board to disapprove a plan for 'land of such character as cannot be safely used for building purposes because of exceptional danger to health.' " *Id.* As to sewage disposal systems, the regulation stated:

That in areas not currently served by public sewer systems it is the responsibility of the subdivider to provide adequate information to prove that the area of each lot is adequate to permit the installation and operation of an individual sewage disposal system. . . . Such information may consist of the report of the . . . [WSPCD].

Id. Based upon this regulation, we held that, "although the developer ha[d] the initial burden of proving adequate sewage disposal, there [wa]s a presumption under this regulation that WSPCD approval of an on-site sewage system [wa]s adequate proof of a safe septic system." *Id.* at 344, 615 A.2d 1252. Thus, "[o]nce the owners produced the WSPCD's report, the lots should have been approved, in the absence of other evidence that the septic systems still posed an 'exceptional danger to health.'" *Id.*

We agree with the plaintiff that the present case is strikingly similar to *Smith.*

As in *Smith,* the board here has enacted no other septic system standards guiding applicants as to what, beyond DES approval, is required to ensure the safety and adequacy of the proposed sewage disposal system. Although the board could have enacted more stringent standards, *see* RSA 485–A:32, I (2001); RSA 674:44, II, IV, the site plan regulations it chose to enact direct that an applicant is permitted to design and construct a sewage disposal system "as long as" the proposed system fully complies with DES regulations.

[But] the presumption created by the regulation and DES' approval was rebuttable. If other evidence demonstrated that, notwithstanding DES' approval, the proposed system would "involve danger or injury to health, safety, or prosperity" because, for example, it would "inadequate[ly] protect[ ] . . . the quality of groundwater," or result in "pollution . . . which might prove harmful to persons, structures, or adjacent properties," LDCR § 170–47(A)(1), the board had the authority to deny site plan approval.

Here, the town asserts, testimony that community septic systems had failed in the past, combined with the location of four abutters' wells down-gradient of the proposed sewage disposal system, constitutes legitimate and persuasive evidence supporting the board's decision to deny the plaintiff's application. We disagree.

The proposed system approved by the DES was comprised of four-inch piping. The town's engineer recommended that all common sewage collection lines be six inches in diameter. The board denied the plaintiff's application subject to the condition that all such lines have a minimum diameter of six inches.

The board denied approval because it presumably agreed with the DPW that the eight-inch sewer mains that are required for municipal sewers were also necessary for the proposed community septic system. Although the board is entitled to rely upon its own judgment and experience in acting upon applications for site plan review, the board may not deny approval on an *ad hoc* basis because of vague concerns. Further, the board's decision must be based upon more than the mere personal opinion of its members. Where, as here, another agency's approval creates a presumption that the proposal protects the public interest, the record must show specific facts justifying rejection of the agency's determination; that is, concrete evidence indicating that

following the agency's determination in the particular circumstances
would pose a real threat to the public interest.

[N]o evidence in the record explains why the plaintiff's proposed
system, upgraded with six-inch piping, did not adequately protect
against such failure. [In addition, nothing] in the record suggests that
the proposed system created an identifiable danger to the four down-
gradient wells. For example, no evidence indicates that the wells are
located at such a severe slope or short distance from the system that,
although the DES' minimum setback requirements are met, these
individual wells are particularly vulnerable to contamination. In the
absence of any specific facts suggesting that the plaintiff's system was
constructed or located in such a fashion as to pose a safety risk to the
four down-gradient wells, the board could not reasonably deny site plan
approval based upon its vague concern that the down-gradient wells
might be in danger. To conclude otherwise would allow the board to
deny approval of any proposed plan simply because a well is located
down-gradient from a septic system, regardless of whether the well at
issue is so far removed from the system that there is no danger of
contamination.

Accordingly, we reverse the trial court's ruling upholding the
board's decision to deny site plan approval because the sewage pipe
design was inadequate to protect the health and safety of the residents
and because four abutters' wells are located down-gradient of the septic
site. We remand to the trial court for review of the board's remaining
reasons for denying the plaintiff's application for site plan approval.

Reversed and remanded.

NOTES AND QUESTIONS

1.   If you had represented the developer in the *Derry* case, how would you
have responded to the concerns expressed by the Town's Department of
Public Works at the public hearing? What advice would you have given to
the developer? Does the New Hampshire Supreme Court's decision
vindicate the strategy the actual developer employed in the *Derry* case?

2.   Did the Town of Derry lose because its site-plan approval regulations
were too vague or too specific? If you were advising the town on how to
rewrite its regulations in the wake of this case, in order to allow the town to
impose sewage disposal requirements that go beyond the state's
environmental regulations, what would you recommend?

3.   How does the town's zoning code interact with its site-plan review
process? Must proposed site-plans (or subdivisions) comply with the
applicable zoning regulations? What consequences follow if a municipality
approves a site plan that does not comply? Suppose a municipality
threatens to reject a proposed site-plan or subdivision unless the developer
agrees to accept use or bulk restrictions that go beyond what is required by
the zoning law. How would you advise the developer to respond? If the
developer refuses to modify the site plan, and the municipality issues a

disapproval, should a court uphold the municipality's decision? How would you expect the *Derry* court to respond?

4. In addition to wastewater treatment, what other sorts of consequences of development should a municipality routinely consider as part of its site-plan or subdivision approval processes?

5. During its site-plan or subdivision approval process, should a municipality be required to consider consequences that will occur outside of its own boundaries? We will discuss municipalities' regional obligations at greater length in Chapter Nine.

II. HISTORIC PRESERVATION

Suppose the owners of an elegant Victorian home want to tear it down to build a modernist mansion better suited to the needs of their family. Or suppose a commercial developer proposes to significantly modify the façade of the municipality's first department store—an icon of the town's main street—in order to attract a new retail chain as a tenant. Or suppose a renowned architect plans to build her own home in a style distinctly different from those of her suburban neighbors. Assume that each of these proposals conforms completely with the local zoning ordinance. Despite that conformity, each of these proposals could have a significant impact on the community—aesthetically, culturally, or both. Neighbors might regard the proposed change as unattractive, either absolutely or by comparison with the building it replaced or modified. Even if the change is aesthetically pleasing, it may disrupt the area's cultural identity, making the neighborhood less attractive to existing and potential residents.

To weigh the balance between development and preservation, communities around the country have enacted historic preservation laws that complement zoning laws. In contrast to zoning, which applies land use development principles to all properties within a jurisdiction, local historic preservation law focuses on the protection and enhancement of historic properties. Local historic preservation laws are authorized by state enabling statutes that are independent of, but have similarities to, the standard zoning enabling acts adopted by every state. These state statutes may allow a local government to engage in a range of administrative and regulatory activities involving preservation.

For a property to be subject to a local regulatory regime, it must be formally "designated" historic by a local, state, or federal governmental body. The designation process entails a formal review as to whether a property is "significant" enough to merit listing on a register of historic places. Significance is most often determined on the basis of the property's association with an important past event or an important historical figure, or on whether the property has special architectural or engineering characteristics. *See, e.g.*, 36 C.F.R. § 60.4 (outlining federal criteria for significance). The property must have integrity—that is, it must be intact enough to convey its significance. And it must be of a certain age—usually around 50 years or more—although exceptionally important properties may be designated before the 50-year mark. *See, e.g.*, 36 C.F.R. § 60.4 (describing the federal process). Properties designated historic by the federal government are listed on the National Register of Historic Places; state and local governments have registers of historic places that use similar criteria. Properties may be listed individually or may be listed as part of a historic district.

Once a property is designated historic, a local regulatory scheme may require that a review by a historic commission take place before the designated property can be demolished or altered. New construction within a historic district can also be regulated. As noted above, the key concept in such reviews is compatibility with existing or surrounding historic properties. Property owners who want to prove compatibility will seek a "certificate of appropriateness" from the historic commission. These historic commissions typically consist of between 5 and 10 volunteers, some of whom may have special expertise in architectural history or urban planning.

With that brief introduction to historic preservation law, we focus on the big-picture issues. How should government protect historic properties? Who should serve as the arbiter of aesthetic or historic significance? How should aesthetic and historic values be balanced against autonomy concerns and economic factors? The materials in this section explore these questions, and examine how land use law addresses them.

A. DESIGNATION

Billy Graham Evangelistic Association v. City of Minneapolis

Supreme Court of Minnesota, 2003
667 N.W.2d 117

■ MEYER, JUSTICE.

In this case we decide whether the City of Minneapolis (the City) acted unreasonably, arbitrarily, or capriciously in designating an area near downtown Minneapolis as an historic preservation district. Respondent, Billy Graham Evangelistic Association (BGEA), owns four buildings in the designated district. By writ of certiorari, BGEA challenged the City's designation and the court of appeals granted relief to BGEA. The City appeals.

Minnesota Statutes § 471.193 announces a state policy that the "historical, architectural, archaeological, engineering, and cultural heritage of this state is among its most important assets." Minn. Stat. § 471.193, subd. 1 (2002). In order to promote the conservation of historic properties, the legislature granted local governments the power to establish commissions to designate districts or buildings of historic significance and to preserve those assets. *Id.*, subds. 2, 3.

The City exercised the authority granted by the legislature and formed the Heritage Preservation Commission of the City of Minneapolis (HPC) under chapter 599 of the City code. Minneapolis, Minn., Code of Ordinances (Code), ch. 599 (2001). The commission is made up of ten members, chosen for their knowledge and expertise in the field of historic preservation. *See* Code § 599.120(c) (2001). The commission considers seven criteria in determining whether a property is worthy of designation as a landmark or historic district.

In November of 1999, a neighborhood group, the Citizens for a Loring Park Community, asked the HPC to study whether an area on and around Harmon Place, from Loring Park to 11th Street South, merited a designation as historic. The citizens' group liked the mini-downtown feel of the area, with its eclectic group of businesses in one-to four-story buildings and pedestrian-friendly streets. In 2000, the HPC asked the City planning department to commission a study of the area for possible historic designation. The planning department contracted with Carole Zellie of Landscape Research to conduct the designation study. Zellie presented her report to the planning department in April of 2001. She concluded that an area comprising ten city blocks (see map appended to this opinion) merited historic designation for its role in the City's historic automotive industry and met criteria 1 and 4 of the Code. The Zellie report concluded that the area could be designated for protection because of its past association as the hub of the automotive sales district in Minneapolis at the beginning of the 20th century.

The Zellie report explained that "the automobile dealership evolved into a prominent and very specialized building type" and that the Harmon Place area showed "some of the best efforts of local architects." Various architectural styles for these buildings were "all arranged around the important display windows." Zellie concluded that:

> Harmon Place was synonymous with the Minneapolis automotive industry for fifty years, from the birth of the local and national industry to its dispersal to the suburbs. Twenty-two automotive buildings from the dozens which once lined Hennepin Avenue and Harmon Place survive in the ten-block [area]. Most of the contributing buildings still embody a good sense of an important era in the city's growth, and illustrate a chapter of its transportation, economic, and social history.

Having determined that the area met two of the criteria for designation, Zellie analyzed each of the individual buildings in the area. Of the 42 buildings comprising the proposed District, Zellie found 26 were "contributing," i.e., met criteria 1 and/or 4 of the ordinance, and 22 of those 26 fit the additional unifying characteristics Zellie identified: buildings constructed between 1907–1930 with some relation to the automobile industry. The remaining 16 properties were designated as "noncontributing."

After Zellie's study recommended historic designation for the Harmon Place Historic District (the District), the proposed designation began working its way through the approval process required by city ordinance. *See* Code §§ 599.200–.300 (2001). First, the HPC forwarded the Zellie report to the state historic preservation officer, who concurred that the District was eligible for preservation under criteria 1 and 4. Then the City Planning Department sent a letter to property owners in the District, informing them that a consultant had recommended historic designation, that they could access the report, and there would be a public hearing likely held in August of 2001. The City Planning Commission adopted the findings of the planning department and approved the designation on August 6, 2001. The proposed designation included five buildings owned by BGEA at that time: buildings 11, 12, 13, 25, and 27 (see map).

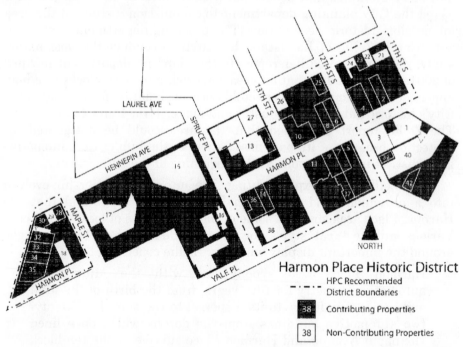

Harmon Place Historic District

- - - - HPC Recommended District Boundaries

▮38 Contributing Properties

│38│ Non-Contributing Properties

Meanwhile, in July 2001, the HPC denied a request from the University of St. Thomas to demolish five buildings that St. Thomas owned within the proposed District.[4] St. Thomas appealed to the city council, which, on August 10, 2001, granted permission for the demolition of the requested buildings, including four buildings designated as contributing properties.

---

4   St. Thomas owned buildings 1, 2, 3, 39, 40, 41, and 42, but the HPC only denied the demolition of buildings 2, 39, 40, 41, and 42.

Before the first public hearing on the District's historic designation, BGEA hired Charlene Roise, of Hess, Roise and Company, to conduct an independent study of the proposed District. Roise concluded that the Fawkes block, at the westernmost end of the proposed District, bordered by Hennepin Avenue, Harmon Place, and Maple Street, fit the criteria for designation as an historic district. She disagreed with the designation of the remainder of the nine blocks, however.

Apparently in response to Roise's report, the planning department revised the proposed District to exclude (1) the large "superblock" containing the Minneapolis Community College, the Minneapolis Area Vocational Technical Institute, and the H. Alden Smith house (buildings 15, 16, and 17), because the buildings did not contribute to the proposed District; (2) the frontage along Hennepin Avenue, because the character of the buildings did not reflect the character of the District and the only contributing properties had been extensively remodeled; and (3) all of the property owned by the University of St. Thomas.

The HPC held a public hearing on September 25, 2001, and in response to the significant interest in the designation, the HPC scheduled a second public hearing on October 16, 2001. At both meetings, there was significant opposition to the area's historic designation by local property owners. The owners complained that they had not had enough input in the process, that the designation would decrease their buildings' value, that the auto industry was not significant enough in the history of Minneapolis, and that the buildings had already been altered too much to merit designation. Additionally, Roise and Marjorie Pearson (also a consultant for BGEA) spoke on behalf of BGEA and urged limiting the historic designation to the Fawkes block and four individual buildings in the northeast portion.

Residents of the neighborhood spoke in favor of the designation at the public hearings, mentioning that they wanted to save the character of the area, its historic value, and the pedestrian-friendly nature of the District. City Council Member Lisa Goodman opined: "This is about preserving one of the last, very unique architectural areas in the city." At the October 16 HPC meeting a motion to approve the two subdistricts was amended to include five properties facing Hennepin Avenue (buildings numbered 21–25). The commissioners discussed why the HPC staff had recommended excluding them, and reasons for keeping them in the District. Finally, the HPC approved the designation of the two subdistricts, with the inclusion of the five buildings facing Hennepin Avenue. The HPC did not make written findings to support its inclusion of the Hennepin Avenue properties.

On October 31, the City's Zoning and Planning Committee (Zoning) heard public testimony and then adopted the findings of the planning department, requested findings to support the inclusion of the Hennepin Avenue properties, and approved the designation. Zoning then passed the recommendation on to the city council for final approval, together with findings that the inclusion of the Hennepin Avenue properties helped to preserve the integrity of the contributing properties and the character of the District. On November 9, 2001, the city council passed two resolutions, designating the southwest portion (Fawkes block) and the northeast portion (which included respondent BGEA's four properties) as the Harmon Place Historic District.

On a writ of certiorari to the court of appeals, BGEA challenged the designation of the northeast portion of the District, claiming that the City acted arbitrarily, capriciously, or unreasonably. The court of appeals agreed with some of BGEA's claims as to how the City's action was arbitrary, and did not address the remainder. The court focused on three aspects of the designation that it characterized as arbitrary: the inclusion of the properties facing Hennepin Avenue, the fact that only that portion of building 13 facing Harmon Place is included within the District, and the inconsistent use of an alley as a boundary. Billy Graham Evangelistic Ass'n v. City of Minneapolis, 653 N.W.2d 638, 644–46 (Minn. App. 2002). The court reversed the City's designation of the northeast portion of the District, finding it to be arbitrary and capricious. *Id.* at 646.

The City claims the court of appeals misstated the record and substantially departed from the usual course of justice in its standard of review of quasi-judicial decisions. BGEA reasserts the two broad claims it made to the court of appeals. First, BGEA argues that the City erred as a matter of law in interpreting the heritage preservation ordinance to permit inclusion of noncontributing properties in an historic district. Second, BGEA contends that the City's designation of the District was arbitrary or capricious in various substantive and procedural ways.

I.

We begin with BGEA's argument that the City erred as a matter of law in interpreting the heritage preservation ordinance to permit inclusion of noncontributing properties in a district. The Code defines an historic district as "*all* property within a defined area designated as an historic district by the city council because of the historical, cultural, architectural, archaeological or engineering significance of the district, or designated as an historic district by state law." Code § 599.110 (2001) (emphasis added). The ordinance says the seven different "criteria shall be considered in determining whether *a property* is worthy of designation" and defines property as "*any* land, building, structure or object, surface or subsurface area, natural or landscape feature." Code §§ 599.210, 599.110 (2001) (emphasis added). BGEA interprets the word property to mean a singular structure, i.e., one building or parcel; and argues that each singular property must possess the required historical, cultural, or architectural significance. We do not read the ordinance so narrowly. The ordinance permits *any* building, structure, surface area, or landscape feature to be included in an historic district. The ordinance does not limit properties to those with historical significance. We conclude that the plain language of the ordinance allows for the inclusion of noncontributing properties within an historic district and the City did not err as a matter of law in permitting inclusion of some noncontributing properties in the District.

II.

We turn to the central question in this case, whether the City acted arbitrarily or capriciously in designating the northeast portion of the District. Recently we ruled that cities are engaged in quasi-judicial action when they designate buildings for heritage preservation. Handicraft Block Ltd. Partnership v. City of Minneapolis, 611 N.W.2d 16, 24 (Minn. 2000). Because they are quasi-judicial acts, we affirm decisions to designate property as historic unless we make an independent determination that the decisions are unreasonable, arbitrary, or capricious. *See* Honn v. City of Coon Rapids, 313 N.W.2d 409, 416–17 (Minn. 1981).

In this case, the City did make contemporaneous findings to support its decision. Various levels of city government made formal, written findings concerning the District. The final written findings came from Zoning, which made findings of fact after its October 30 meeting. Looking at the record as a whole, including hearing transcripts and written memoranda, the City made its reasoning clear and public as to the District. Therefore, BGEA bears the burden of proving that the City acted arbitrarily, capriciously, or unreasonably in designating the District as historic.

BGEA asserts that the City's designation of the District's boundaries was arbitrary or capricious because specific properties were treated arbitrarily, expert testimony was arbitrarily dismissed, the City did not comply with its own ordinance, and the City treated BGEA differently than the University of St. Thomas.

Specific Properties

BGEA argues that the City gave no reason for including certain noncontributing properties in the District, while other noncontributing properties were excluded; that apartment buildings and surface parking lots should not have been included in the District; that the inclusion of only the part of building 13 facing Harmon Place was indicative of arbitrariness; and that no reasons were given to support the inclusion of the properties facing Hennepin Avenue.

Based upon our independent review of the record in this case, we cannot conclude that the City acted unreasonably, arbitrarily, or capriciously in designating properties to be included in the District. The City gave contemporaneous rationale to support the inclusion and exclusion of all the properties that BGEA contests. The findings issued by Zoning detail the reasons for including the properties facing Hennepin Avenue, designating the block including building 13, and retaining certain noncontributing properties in the District. The Zellie report supports the District's overall historic value and its comportment with the criteria in the ordinance. All necessary levels of city and state agencies approved the designation of this area as historic. The full District encompasses 31 buildings, the majority of which (23) an expert has deemed are contributing to the historic character of the area. Even the disputed northeast portion of the District has a reasonable number of contributing buildings (15 out of 20).

Some of BGEA's complaints stem from changes in the District's boundaries that were made by the City as the proposed historic designation made its way through various levels of city government. After receiving critiques of its larger, original proposed District, the City acted to ameliorate the economic effects of the designation on local property owners by splitting the District into two sections, whose combined area was significantly smaller than the original proposal. Downsizing the District and redrawing its boundaries was a rational response to the issues raised by property owners. In addition, it was rational for the City to include the areas with the highest concentration of contributing buildings (especially the buildings facing Harmon Avenue, the heart of the District) and to attempt to achieve recognizable boundaries for the historic District. We are concerned about the sufficiency of the reasons given for the inclusion in the District of only the part of building 13 facing Harmon Place and the Hennepin Avenue properties, given the somewhat marginal historic value of the northeast portion of the District. Nevertheless, evaluating the City's determinations in the light of an ordinance with subjective and broadly-defined criteria for designation, we cannot conclude that the City's decision-making was not rational. Therefore, we conclude that the City's decision to include or exclude certain properties within the District was supported by legally sufficient reasons and was not unreasonable, arbitrary, or capricious.

Expert Evidence

Next, BGEA criticizes the City's treatment of experts in the hearing process. It asserts that the City ignored Roise's opinions and that the City's failure to rebut Roise's report is evidence of an arbitrary decision. BGEA refers specifically to Roise's opinion that apartment buildings should not be included in the District, that vacant lots destroyed the cohesion of the District, and that many of the contributing buildings had undergone significant changes.

We recently touched upon the issue of experts in Schwardt v. County of Watonwan, 656 N.W.2d 383 (Minn. 2003), and noted that local decisionmakers have discretion in weighing evidence. *Id. at 388.* Upon review, courts should not attempt to weigh the credibility of conflicting experts, but instead review the record to ensure that the decision was "legally sufficient," i.e., had support in the record. *See*

Barton Contracting Co. v. City of Afton, 268 N.W.2d 712, 718 (Minn. 1978).

In this case the record shows that the City accepted all expert evidence that was proffered and took the experts' opinions into consideration, in addition to the opinion of its staff. The experts gave conflicting testimony about the inclusion of various properties. For example, Zellie had included the Hennepin Avenue properties in her single district proposal while Roise had excluded them. Despite BGEA's contention that the HPC did not consider Roise's testimony, the record indicates that the planning department altered its recommendation for the District's boundaries in response to Roise's alternative proposal. Following Roise's lead, the planning department recommended the alley between Harmon Place and Hennepin Avenue as a boundary, excluded a significant number of noncontributing buildings, and carved out two smaller subdistricts. With the recommendations of Roise, Zellie, and the planning department in hand, the commissioners voiced their reasons for drawing the District's final boundaries. We conclude that the City acted appropriately in accepting and considering all expert testimony before reaching its decision, and there are sufficient facts in the record to support the City's decision.

HPC's Obligation Under the City Ordinance

BGEA alleges that procedural irregularities are evidence that the City acted arbitrarily. Primarily, BGEA asserts the HPC failed to make findings sufficient to satisfy its obligation under the city ordinance. BGEA argues that all findings should have come from the HPC, instead of from Zoning. Because some findings originated with Zoning, BGEA asserts the entire designation should fail for arbitrariness.

The HPC is required to make findings under Code § 599.280 (2001). The HPC adopted some of the findings of the planning department, but did not add findings to justify including the Hennepin Avenue properties. Instead, Zoning developed findings to support the inclusion of the Hennepin Avenue properties. Thus, all findings did not originate with the HPC. We do not think the remedy for that failure, however, should be a judicial reversal of an historic designation that was approved by all levels of city government. There is no evidence that HPC's failure to make findings prejudiced BGEA. It was clear at the public meeting of the HPC on October 16 that the commission had voted to add the Hennepin Avenue properties back into the District; BGEA had notice of the HPC's recommendation to Zoning. Indeed, a lawyer from BGEA spoke at the Zoning meeting on October 30. There is nothing more BGEA could have done to voice its opinion, even if the HPC had included specific findings about the Hennepin Avenue buildings' historic merit. Therefore, we conclude that the findings were sufficiently contemporaneous and adequate to support designating the entire northeast portion of the District.

The University of St. Thomas

BGEA alleges they were situated similarly to another property owner, the University of St. Thomas (St. Thomas), whose properties within the originally proposed District were approved for demolition. BGEA notes that four of St. Thomas's buildings that were described as "contributing" in the Zellie report are now demolished, while the four BGEA buildings, three of which were "contributing," are still standing and part of the District. BGEA asserts that St. Thomas received vastly different treatment at the hands of the City than did BGEA, with no rationale for doing so in the record, a practice that is prohibited by our holdings in Northwestern College, 281 N.W.2d at 869, and Hay v. Township of Grow, 296 Minn. 1, 7–8, 206 N.W.2d 19, 23–24 (1973).

We have held in multiple cases that "[a] zoning ordinance must operate uniformly on those similarly situated." *Northwestern College*, 281 N.W.2d at 869; accord *Hay*, 296 Minn. at 7–8, 206 N.W.2d at 24. Disparate treatment of two similarly-situated property owners may be an indication that the local government is acting unreasonably or arbitrarily. *See Northwestern College*, 281 N.W.2d at 868–69.

We do not agree that BGEA and St. Thomas were similarly-situated property owners who received disparate treatment. There were more similarities between Northwestern College and Bethel College than there are between BGEA and St. Thomas. In *Northwestern*, both applicants were Christian colleges, in the same type of zoned area, applying for very similar types of permits, and the city council approved one and denied the other within a span of two months. St. Thomas and BGEA are both nonprofit entities that owned contributing properties within the large district that Zellie originally proposed, but the similarities end there. BGEA chose to challenge the designation of the District in the first instance, which the City determines using the criteria in Code § 599.210. St. Thomas did not challenge the inclusion of its property within the District, but instead requested a "certificate of appropriateness" from the HPC, which the City determines using criteria in Code § 599.350(b) (2001). The standards involved in deciding the two questions are divergent and make these property owners dissimilar in the type of relief sought. Because the appropriateness of demolition considers factors other than the contributing status of the property, these properties were not similarly situated.

In addition to the City reviewing BGEA's and St. Thomas's requests using different criteria, the properties of BGEA and St. Thomas were situated differently within the Harmon Place area. St. Thomas's buildings were concentrated on a block in which a very small area was taken up by contributing buildings, while BGEA's buildings, were in the heart of the northeast subdistrict. We conclude that the City did not act arbitrarily in treating BGEA's and St. Thomas's buildings differently.

We conclude that the City of Minneapolis did not act arbitrarily or capriciously in designating the contested northeast portion of the District as historic. Under a higher standard of review we might reach a different result, given the somewhat marginal historic value of this area. Our decision is constrained by the significant deference that we accord the quasi-judicial actions of local governments and the broad and subjective criteria for historic designation set out in the ordinance. Because the historic designation meets the criteria in the ordinance, the City made findings in favor of its decision, and the City's findings are supported by the record, we conclude the designation of the Harmon Place Historic District is neither unreasonable, arbitrary, nor capricious.

Reversed.

■ GILBERT, JUSTICE (concurring in part, dissenting in part).

I concur that a historical district can include some noncontributing properties and that the standard of review is arbitrary and capricious. However, I respectfully dissent from the majority's holding that the City did not act arbitrarily or capriciously in this case and would affirm the court of appeals.

This designation procedure hinges on a report (Zellie Report) prepared by the City's commissioned consultant, Carole Zellie (consultant). This consultant studied a section on the southern edge of downtown Minneapolis, where the City's automotive industry flourished from around the turn of the century to the 1950s. The consultant ultimately recommended that the area be designated a historic district. However, the Zellie Report contains a significant flaw—it ignores the historical and physical change that has occurred in this district since the late 1950s when the auto industry vacated this area. While the Zellie Report concedes that the auto industry era began in 1907 and ended in 1957 with "its dispersal to the suburbs," the report represents a nostalgic summary of a bygone era and is written as if there had been no change in this area since the 1950s. The Zellie Report carries forward the history of this bygone era without taking into consideration the end of the era and the transformation of the district by the time it was being considered for historical designation.

Considerable changes have taken place in the northeast section of the district since the late 1950s. For instance, substantial religious institutions emerged in this area. In 1914, across the street from this designated area, the Basilica of St. Mary's Church was constructed. At the north end is the First Baptist Church. Then, the Northwestern Bible and Training School was developed here in the 1940s and 1950s. Subsequently, the Billy Graham Association purchased and occupied five buildings in the district beginning in 1950 (buildings 11, 12, 13, 25 and 27). Finally, to complete this cycle, the University of St. Thomas (St. Thomas) campus acquired large portions of the historically designated district and was permitted to demolish five buildings in this area and expanded the downtown campus. This activity began in 2001 and continued through the final historical designation process.

As pointed out by a unanimous panel of the court of appeals, the City's planning commission essentially redrew the boundaries that were recommended by the paid consultant and by the City planning department staff. See Billy Graham Evangelistic Assoc. v. City of Minneapolis, 653 N.W.2d 638, 645 (Minn. App. 2002). It is in redrawing these boundaries that the City acted in an arbitrary and capricious manner.

The majority admits that the northeast portion has a "somewhat marginal historic value." Thus, this "combination of danger signals"—ignoring its own committee's recommendation, lack of findings and marginal historical value suggest that the City acted arbitrarily when it included the Hennepin Avenue properties in the district. *See* Cable Communications Bd. v. Nor-West Cable Communications P'ship, 356 N.W.2d 658, 669 (Minn. 1984)

Finally, although I agree that some noncontributing property can be included within a historical district, those properties should not predominate over contributing properties. Further, noncontributing properties should only be included when they add value or support the architecture of the district. This arbitrary and capricious action of the City should not be condoned by this court nor should we give our approval to this unbounded exercise of significant governmental power just short of a "taking" in an eminent domain context. The "constraint" and "deference" the majority accords the City in this appeal amounts to an abdication of our judicial power. The majority's decision rubber stamps a defective, disparate and improper use of governmental power. If this action by the City is not arbitrary and capricious, what is? We must draw the line somewhere. In doing so, we are not substituting "our own judgment about the historic value of the District" as the majority opinion states, but rather exercising our independent legal judgment to ensure that another branch of government conducts its business according to the law, rather than according to its whim or wishes.

NOTES AND QUESTIONS

1. What buildings and structures should a municipality try to preserve? Why not preserve all structures? Some structures are notorious architectural flops. If they endure for long enough, should they be preserved because of their unique ugliness? *Cf.* In re Vermont National Bank, 157 Vt. 306, 597 A.2d 317 (1991), in which Burlington, Vermont, sought—unsuccessfully—to preserve an "international style" glass façade on a bank building over the bank's objection that the façade was "cold, outdated, and uninviting." The building was located between a department store and a McDonald's.

Why should Minneapolis want to preserve an area previously devoted to automobile dealerships at a time when there is no longer a market for automobiles in downtown Minneapolis? If dealership buildings are poorly suited for other uses, does it make sense to preserve them?

What about tenement buildings notorious for their unsafe design and unpleasant environment? If they played a significant role in the city's development, should the city protect them against demolition? If so, how many should the city protect, and which ones? *Cf.* State by Powderly v. Erickson, 285 N.W.2d 84 (Minn. 1979) (upholding preservation of row houses plagued with building code and fire safety regulations).

2. The *Billy Graham* opinion notes that the City of Minneapolis had established a Heritage Preservation Commission to make initial determinations about what should be preserved. Many other cities have similar commissions that play a significant role in designating landmarks and historic districts. Would you expect these commissions to be representative of the public at large? Of business interests in the community? Or would you expect them to be heavily populated with people committed to preservation? If such a commission were dominated by preservationists, what implications would that have for legislative or judicial review of the commission's decisions?

Does a landowner derive any benefit from the designation of its parcel as a landmark? From the designation of its parcel as part of a historic district? What is the difference—from the point of view of the landowner—between the two (landmark designations of individual parcels and inclusion within historic districts)? Might landowners in some historic districts support the designation? Suppose, for instance, you owned property in New Orleans' French Quarter. If you knew that some of your neighbors were planning to replace their early 19th century homes with modern apartment buildings, would you be in favor of creation of a historic district that restricted your own right (and your neighbors' rights) to alter existing structures? *Cf.* Maher v. City of New Orleans, 516 F.2d 1051 (5th Cir. 1975). Is a landowner likely to have similar incentives to support designation of his building as a stand-alone landmark?

3. Typically, a landmark or historic district designation imposes restrictions on alterations to the premises, and subjects the landowner to a bureaucratic process if the landowner wants to deviate from the restrictions. Does that explain why the Billy Graham Evangelistic Association opposed the designation of its parcels?

4. Under the Minneapolis City Code, the designation process included the following steps: (1) someone nominates the property to the historic preservation commission; (2) the preservation commission may direct the planning director to study the property; (3) the planning director submits all proposed sites to the state historic preservation officer for review and comment; (4) the city planning commission reviews the designation, holding public hearings with proper notice to affected parties; (5) the planning commission makes findings and submits them to the zoning and planning committee of the city council; (6) the zoning and planning committee submits the proposed designation to the city council, which has the final decision. Of course, not every proposed designation will make it to the city council, because, for instance, the preservation commission, or the planning commission, may not recommend designation.

Suppose Billy Graham Evangelistic Association had retained you to represent its interest in avoiding designation of its property. At which stages of the process would you have taken any action, and what action would you have taken?

5. *Vagueness Challenges.* The City of Chicago enacted a landmark ordinance that listed seven criteria the commission should consider in deciding whether to designate a landmark. The Illinois Supreme Court characterized these criteria as: "(1) critical part of the City's heritage, (2) significant historic event, (3) significant person, (4) important architecture, (5) important architect, (6) distinctive theme as a district, and (7) unique visual feature." The ordinance went on to require that the commission, in making a designation, had to rely on at least two of the criteria in determining that the designated property had "significant historic, community, architectural, or aesthetic interest or value." Preservationists around the country were alarmed when an Illinois court found that a property owner challenging this ordinance for vagueness had a cause of action. Hanna v. City of Chicago, 388 Ill.App.3d 909, 329 Ill.Dec. 799, 907 N.E.2d 390 (2009). They breathed a sigh of relief when, on remand, the trial court found that the words used "provide[d] a description of the observable historic character of the districts" and were not void for vagueness. Hanna v. City of Chicago, No. 06 CH 19422 (Cook County, Ill. Chancery Div. May 2, 2012). In the *Handicraft* case mentioned in *Billy Graham*, the property owners employed the opposite argument of the *Hanna* property owner—that the local ordinance was sufficiently determinate to permit judicial review. *See* Handicraft Block Ltd. Partnership v. City of Minneapolis, 611 N.W.2d 16 (Minn. 2000).

6. *The Unequal Treatment Problem.* It can be difficult for property owners to challenge historic preservation laws under unequal treatment or equal protection principles, because of the unique nature of real property being regulated. In the *Billy Graham* case, BGEA had argued that the University of St. Thomas was a similarly situated property owner treated differently in the historic designation process. The court, by contrast, concluded that there were significant differences between the two non-profit entities. Which of the differences cited by the court is persuasive? Why would the planning commission have excluded the university's properties from the historic district?

Courts are split, however, on the propriety of local governments exempting particular property owners from regulation, when such decisions are not made on the basis of architectural or historical merit. For an example of a historic district ordinance that explicitly exempted properties owned by particular owners—here, the city library and museum association and the Roman Catholic Church—see Springfield Preservation Trust, Inc. v. Springfield Library and Museums Ass'n, 447 Mass. 408, 852 N.E.2d 83 (2006) (upholding exclusion of properties owned by church and association at the time of designation but construing the ordinance not to exempt properties in the district subsequently acquired by the church and the association). Is there any justification for explicit exclusions based on the identity of the property owner?

In Native American Rights Fund, Inc. v. City of Boulder, 97 P.3d 283 (Colo. App. 2004), the court struck down a historic district ordinance on due process grounds because the city had reserved the right to bypass the ordinance's procedures altogether by entering into private agreements with landowners to exclude their properties from the district. The city had entered into a memorandum of agreement with the University of Colorado exempting university structures, and the court concluded that the city would not have enacted the ordinance without the bypass provision. As a result, the court held the entire ordinance invalid.

If city officials had approached you about how to proceed in light of the university's expressed willingness to litigate inclusion of its property in the historic district, what advice would you have given the city?

B. REGULATION

Once a municipality creates a historic district, or designates an individual building as a landmark, what restrictions does the designation impose on a landowner's ability to make changes to the property? A prohibition on all changes would defeat the purpose of the ordinance, because it would lead to decay of the historically significant structure. Most ordinances create an administrative structure that requires a landowner who wants to make changes to a designated building to obtain a "certificate of appropriateness" from a local historic commission before making alterations to the building. Many localities have adopted the U.S. Secretary of the Interior Standards for the Treatment of Historic Properties, see 36 C.F.R. § 68, to help historic commissions weigh what kinds of treatments are appropriate. How should commissions evaluate applications for certificates of appropriateness, and how should courts review commission decisions? Consider the following case:

Norton v. City of Danville
Supreme Court of Virginia, 2004
268 Va. 402, 602 S.E.2d 126

■ AGEE, J.

In this appeal, we consider whether the Danville City Council (the "city council") acted contrary to law or so arbitrarily as to constitute an abuse of discretion when it affirmed the decision of the Danville Commission of Architectural Review (the "commission") not to grant a certificate of appropriateness. Carl T. Norton, appellant, also argues that the city ordinances at issue creating the commission exceed the power granted by Virginia Code § 15.2–2306, and are therefore *ultra vires* and void.

I.   BACKGROUND AND PROCEEDINGS BELOW

Norton owns a home on Main Street in the historic district of the City of Danville on what is commonly referred to as "Millionaires Row." Norton's house, constructed in 1884, is described as an outstanding example of the Italianate style of architecture. Across Main Street from Norton's house is the Sutherlin mansion which is considered to be the best example of Italianate architecture in the city.

During the spring and summer of 2001, Norton's house was burglarized on three separate occasions. That fall, upon the recommendation of Danville police, Norton replaced the existing wooden front door of his home with a door containing glass panes to help officers patrolling Norton's neighborhood see into the house.

Approximately four months after the installation of the new glass door, Kenneth C. Gillie, Jr. ("Gillie"), the director of the Danville Planning Division and the city's zoning administrator, drove by Norton's home and saw the new door. Gillie sent a letter to Norton informing him that he would need to obtain a certificate of appropriateness from the commission if he wanted to keep the glass-paned front door. Otherwise, Norton would have to reinstall a wooden door or be subject to a criminal charge.

The city council established the seven-member commission pursuant to Code § 15.2–2306 to review improvements made in the Danville historic district within view of a public right-of-way or place. For any such improvement to be lawful, the commission must issue a certificate of appropriateness.

In March 2002, the commission denied Norton's application for a certificate of appropriateness for the glass-paned front door. The commission instructed Norton to restore the front door to its "original condition," which the commission determined to be a wooden door with no glass panes. Norton reapplied for a certificate of appropriateness which the commission again denied in May 2002 with a commission member stating the Norton home was "perhaps one of the few remaining original wooden door houses in this City."

Norton appealed the commission's decision to the city council, which affirmed the commission's decision, noting "the CAR [the commission] feels the door was wooden when it was built." Neither the commission nor the city council recited a factual basis for determining the appearance or composition of the original door or whether it was indeed a solid wooden door at the time the house was built.

As authorized by the city code, Norton appealed to the Circuit Court of the City of Danville, arguing the commission's action was "arbitrary." Norton also averred the applicable municipal ordinances exceeded the power granted by state statute rendering those ordinances, and the actions taken under them, *ultra vires* and void. In affirming the city council decision, the trial court ruled that the issue of whether Norton's home should have a glass front door was fairly debatable and therefore "the Court cannot substitute its judgment for that of City Council." We awarded Norton this appeal.

II. ANALYSIS

A. Validity of the Municipal Ordinances

Virginia Code § 15.2–2306(A)(3) and Danville City Code § 41–109 authorize a limited appeal from the city council's decision regarding historic preservation matters. In pertinent part, Virginia Code § 15.2–2306(A)(3), states:

> The court may reverse or modify the decision of the governing body, in whole or in part, if it finds upon review that the decision of the governing body is contrary to law or that its decision is arbitrary and constitutes an abuse of discretion, or it may affirm the decision of the governing body.

Code § 15.2–2306(A)(3).

The historical preservation area statute, Code § 15.2–2306(A)(3), limits judicial review of a governing body's decision to whether that decision is "arbitrary and constitutes an abuse of discretion," or "is contrary to law," similar to the standards applied by the courts in reviewing zoning decisions under Code § 15.2–2314. Norton's challenge to the underlying ordinance as *ultra vires* and violative of the Dillon rule, is barred from consideration in judicial review of the city council's action concerning the certificate of appropriateness. Code § 15.2–2306(A)(3), and the derivative municipal ordinance, grant the trial court authority to review the city council's specific act under the ordinance, not the validity of the ordinance itself. Therefore, we do not consider Norton's initial assignments of error because they are beyond the scope of review authorized by Code § 15.2–2306.

B. The City Council's Actions as Arbitrary and Unreasonable

Norton's remaining assignment of error challenges the city council's action on the certificate of appropriateness as "arbitrary and unreasonable." He contends his evidence showing city council's action was unreasonable was not met by evidence of reasonableness by the city council so as to make the issue fairly debatable. Norton avers the trial court's holding to the contrary is reversible error. For the reasons discussed below, we agree with Norton.

"When a governing body of any locality reserves unto itself the right to issue special exceptions, the grant or denial of such exceptions is a legislative function." Board of Supervisors v. McDonald's Corp., 261 Va. 583, 589, 544 S.E.2d 334, 338 (2001) (citing Cole v. City Council of Waynesboro, 218 Va. 827, 837, 241 S.E.2d 765, 771 (1978)). Such legislative actions are presumptively correct. *Id.*; see also County of

Lancaster v. Cowardin, 239 Va. 522, 525, 391 S.E.2d 267, 269, 6 Va. Law Rep. 2078 (1990). The city council's legislative action regarding Norton's application for a certificate of appropriateness is analogous and subject to the same presumption and standard of review.

"Legislative action is reasonable if the matter in issue is fairly debatable." Board of Supervisors v. Lerner, 221 Va. 30, 34, 267 S.E.2d 100, 102 (1980). An issue may be said to be "fairly debatable when the evidence offered in support of the opposing views would lead objective and reasonable persons to reach different conclusions." Board of Supervisors v. Williams, 216 Va. 49, 58, 216 S.E.2d 33, 40 (1975). "The burden of proof is on him who assails it to prove that it is clearly unreasonable, arbitrary or capricious, and that it bears no reasonable or substantial relation to the public health, safety, morals, or general welfare." Turner v. Board of Supervisors, 263 Va. 283, 288, 559 S.E.2d 683, 686 (2002).

As the applicant for a certificate of appropriateness, Norton bore the burden of presenting evidence that the city council's actions were unreasonable. If Norton presented such evidence, the burden shifted to the city council to produce some evidence that its actions were reasonable thereby rendering the issue fairly debatable. In this case, the city council failed to meet its evidentiary burden.

Norton presented evidence to the trial court that many other houses in the historic preservation district had glass doors. A house of similar Italianate style, the Sutherlin mansion, directly across the street from Norton's home, had a wooden door facing Main Street but commercial glass doors on a side entrance visible from a public street. He also produced evidence showing his home has three other glass doors, besides the front door at issue, which are visible from the street.

Norton called Gillie as a witness during the trial, who testified as follows on direct examination:

Q. What evidence do you have to show that the initial door was all wood?

A. We have seen photos of the door that was all wood. I have seen the door personally and it was all wood.

Q. Well, when was the house built?

A. In the 1880s.

Q. 1884?

A. Somewhere around that.

Q. So you weren't around in 1884, you didn't see the doors?

A. No, sir.

Q. When you say "initially," you mean the way it was when you first saw it?

A. Yes.

Q. You don't know what it was initially?

A. No.

Q. But you're saying the reason that you eliminated the glass part was that initially it had wooden doors.

A. To the best of my knowledge, it had wooden doors.

Q. And that's to your knowledge?

A. Yes.

Q. And you first saw it when?

A. 1992.

Norton thus met his burden to show probative evidence of unreasonableness in the city council's action to compel him to install a wooden door. Norton's evidence reflected that the commission and the city council acted to compel him to install a wooden door on the unsupported supposition such a door existed in 1884, although no evidence directly established that the house featured a wooden door before 1992.

To meet Norton's evidence of unreasonableness, the city council was obligated to put forth some evidence of reasonableness for its decision in order to carry its burden to render the matter fairly debatable. Despite this low threshold, the city council failed to present evidence demonstrating that its decision was reasonable. This is due, in large part, to the fact that the city council presented no witnesses and offered no exhibits to demonstrate there was a wooden door before 1992, such as demonstrative historical photographs or similar items of evidence.

No witness testified for the city council to verify how the original nature of the door was determined. Although Norton was ordered to restore the door to its deemed original condition, the commission and the city council admitted in their proceedings that they did not know what type of door was on the house when it was originally constructed. Similarly, the city council offered no explanation why its mandate that Norton's house have a wooden front door was reasonable, when other glass-paned doors on the house are clearly viewable by the public.

The city council did not meet Norton's evidence that its actions were unreasonable with evidence of reasonableness. The trial court thus erred in concluding the issue was fairly debatable because the city council failed to meet its burden of proof. As a matter of law, the trial court could not conclude the issue was fairly debatable because the city council adduced no evidence of reasonableness.

III. CONCLUSION

For these reasons, we conclude the trial court could not in this proceeding consider Norton's challenges to the validity of the Danville

City ordinances. We also conclude that the city council failed to meet its evidentiary burden to demonstrate that its actions were reasonable in affirming the commission's refusal to grant the certificate of appropriateness. Accordingly, the trial court erred in holding the city council's action to be fairly debatable. The judgment of the trial court will be reversed and final judgment will be entered.

NOTES AND QUESTIONS

1. In *Norton*, as in most land use cases, the court started by presuming that the council's decision was valid, and it imposed on the landowner the obligation to establish that the decision was unreasonable. Once Norton established that many other Italianate buildings in the area had glass doors, the burden shifted to the city to defend its decision requiring a wooden door. Suppose the city had established that the building had a wooden front door in 1950, or 1920. Would that proof have been sufficient to satisfy the city's burden? Why or why not? Is there a reason to require the city to prove that the house had wooden doors when it was built, or can an architectural feature have historic significance even if the feature was not original to the house?

2. Suppose the city had established that Norton's house had a wooden front door when it was built in the 1880s. Suppose, though, that the current doors had decayed, and Norton wanted to replace them. Could the commission have required that Norton replace the doors with the same wood used on the original house? Or suppose the windows had rotted, and Norton sought to replace them with windows of identical size and shape, but with insulated double-pane glass. Should a commission withhold a certificate? If the commission did withhold a certificate, should a court uphold the commission's determination? *See* Ex Parte Duncan, 1 So.3d 15 (Ala. 2008), in which the Montgomery Historic Preservation Commission denied a certificate of appropriateness to a landowner who had replaced wooden windows with vinyl windows. Landowner challenged the determination, arguing that the change in windows was beyond the commission's authority to regulate, because the change resulted in no change in the building's exterior appearance. The Alabama Supreme Court reversed the trial court's grant of summary judgment to the city, holding that the landowner had raised a triable issue of fact about whether replacement of the windows constituted a change in exterior appearance. Would the court have reached the same result if the landowner had replaced wood siding with vinyl siding?

3. Landowner owns a parcel in a historic district. Landowner proposes an alteration that would clearly change the exterior appearance of the parcel, but the change has no impact on any element of historic significance. Is landowner entitled to a certificate of appropriateness, or may the commission deny a certificate on the ground that the change would compromise the aesthetic character of the district? *See* Gibbons v. Historic District Commission, 285 Conn. 755, 941 A.2d 917 (2008) (holding that commission's denial of a certificate permitting landowner to move an outbuilding was arbitrary when based only on aesthetic rather than historic concerns).

4.   *The Role of Hardship in Historic Preservation.* A requirement that renovations be appropriate to the historic site will impose some administrative costs on the landowner, because obtaining approvals takes time and possibly additional payments to architects and other consultants. Some of these administrative costs may be offset where a historic commission encourages repairs of historic fabric, instead of replacement, and where construction labor is inexpensive. In other situations, regulatory requirements to use materials appropriate to the period may add some costs. For example, wooden windows or siding may be more expensive to install than vinyl windows or siding. And historically appropriate materials may be less energy efficient. How should these costs be factored into the preservation process?

Most preservation enabling statutes have hardship provisions, which authorize commissions to relieve landowners of restrictions that might otherwise apply. *See, e.g.,* Conn. Gen. Stat. § 7–147g. This differs from the way the typical zoning enabling statute deals with variances in that the historic commission may both apply its rules and authorize variances from them; in the zoning context, a zoning commission may only apply the rules, and must leave variances to the zoning board of appeals. If you represented a landowner subject to historic preservation laws, would you make hardship arguments to the commission, or would you reserve them for judicial review of the commission's determination? Why?

The landowner who relies on hardship faces an uphill battle. Consider City of Pittsburgh v. Weinberg, 544 Pa. 286, 676 A.2d 207 (1996). In 1986, the city designated the Gateway House, a 2 ½ story residence built in 1860, as a historic structure. Because the house was in dilapidated condition, landowners sought permission to conduct restoration work, but landowners could not obtain a mortgage to finance the cost of rehabilitation because the cost of necessary renovations would exceed the fair market value of the house after completion of the renovations. The commission nevertheless denied a certificate of appropriateness because the house was not structurally unsound, and because landowners knew of the historic designation and its ramifications at the time they purchased the house. Although two lower courts held that the record did not support the commission's rejection of the hardship claim, the Pennsylvania Supreme Court reinstated the commission's decision, relying on testimony by landowners' real estate expert that the house—unrenovated—could be sold for a price comparable to the price landowners paid for the house. The court concluded that the fact that landowners "did not engage the services of an architect or contractor to estimate the cost or feasibility of restoring the Gateway House cannot serve as a basis for their claims of economic hardship after the fact." *Id.* at 297, 676 A.2d 213. How would you respond to the Pennsylvania Supreme Court's argument?

5.   The typical state enabling statute allows for local governments to regulate only the exteriors of buildings. However, some enabling statutes allow for the regulation of interiors. New York City's Landmarks Law, for example, regulates interiors—including Broadway theaters and banks—and even requires property owners to include language in leases about prohibitions on changing interior landmarks. *See* N.Y.C. Landmarks Law, § 25–301 & 25–322. Should designation of a building as a historic landmark prevent an owner from making changes to the interior of the building not visible from the outside? *Compare* Teachers Ins. and Annuity Ass'n of America v. City of New York, 82 N.Y.2d 35, 603 N.Y.S.2d 399, 623 N.E.2d 526 (1993), *with* United Artists' Theater Circuit, Inc. v. City of Philadelphia, 535 Pa. 370, 635 A.2d 612 (1993). Does it make a difference if the public has a right to access the interior of the building? *See* Weinberg v. Barry, 634 F.Supp. 86 (D.D.C. 1986).

6.   In some localities, property owners and neighbors dissatisfied with the decision of a historic commission may be required to appeal to a local administrative body before going to court. For example, Washington, D.C. has a Mayor's Agent who serves as a one-person appeals board to review decisions of the city's Historic Preservation Review Board. The Mayor's Agent is appointed by the Mayor and need not have any special expertise in preservation. In Philadelphia, the Board of License and Inspection Review hears appeals from local historic commission decisions, but again has no special expertise in preservation as it hears appeals from a range of other municipal decisions. In other places, appeals must be made to a legislative body. Do you have concerns about each of these types of administrative review?

III. Aesthetic Regulation

In the *Billy Graham* and *Norton* cases, historic preservation played a significant role in the restrictions placed on the landowner. What if the municipality enacts controls designed solely to generate aesthetically pleasing buildings? Although in the early days of zoning, courts questioned whether municipalities had power to regulate for aesthetic purposes, most courts today concede that municipalities have a legitimate interest in promoting an aesthetically pleasing environment. To that end, many municipalities have established architectural review boards to consider design issues associated with large projects or sensitive areas. Other municipalities entrust some design issues to the local planning board. How much guidance must municipal regulations provide to developers? The following case addresses that issue:

Anderson v. City of Issaquah
Court of Appeals of Washington, Division One, 1993
70 Wn. App. 64, 851 P.2d 744

■ Kennedy, J.

Appellants M. Bruce Anderson, Gary D. LaChance, and M. Bruce Anderson, Inc. (hereinafter referred to as Anderson), challenge the denial of their application for a land use certification, arguing, inter alia, that the building design requirements contained in Issaquah Municipal Code (IMC) 16.16.060 are unconstitutionally vague.

Facts

Anderson owns property located at 145 N.W. Gilman Boulevard in the city of Issaquah (City). In 1988, Anderson applied to the City for a land use certification to develop the property. The property is zoned for general commercial use. Anderson desired to build a 6,800-square-foot commercial building for several retail tenants.

After obtaining architectural plans, Anderson submitted the project to various City departments for the necessary approvals. The process went smoothly until the approval of the Issaquah Development Commission (Development Commission) was sought. This commission was created to administer and enforce the City's land use regulations. It has the authority to approve or deny applications for land use certification.

Section 16.16.060 of the IMC enumerates various building design objectives which the Development Commission is required to administer and enforce. Insofar as is relevant to this appeal, the Development Commission is to be guided by the following criteria:

IMC 16.16.060(B). Relationship of Building and Site to Adjoining Area.

1. Buildings and structures shall be made compatible with adjacent buildings of conflicting architectural styles by such means as screens and site breaks, or other suitable methods and materials.

2. Harmony in texture, lines, and masses shall be encouraged.

IMC 16.16.060(D). Building Design.

1. Evaluation of a project shall be based on quality of its design and relationship to the natural setting of the valley and surrounding mountains.

2. Building components, such as windows, doors, eaves and parapets, shall have appropriate proportions and relationship to each other, expressing themselves as a part of the overall design.

3. Colors shall be harmonious, with bright or brilliant colors used only for minimal accent.

4. Design attention shall be given to screening from public view all mechanical equipment, including refuse enclosures, electrical transformer pads and vaults, communication equipment, and other utility hardware on roofs, grounds or buildings.

5. Exterior lighting shall be part of the architectural concept. Fixtures, standards and all exposed accessories shall be harmonious with the building design.

6. Monotony of design in single or multiple building projects shall be avoided. Efforts should be made to create an interesting project by use of complimentary details, functional orientation of buildings, parking and access provisions and relating the development to the site. In multiple building projects, variable sitting of individual buildings, heights of buildings, or other methods shall be used to prevent a monotonous design.

As initially designed, Anderson's proposed structure was to be faced with off-white stucco and was to have a blue metal roof. It was designed in a "modern" style with an unbroken "warehouse" appearance in the rear, and large retail-style windows in the front. The City moved a Victorian era residence, the "Alexander House", onto the neighboring property to serve as a visitors' center. Across the street from the Anderson site is a gasoline station that looks like a gasoline station. Located nearby and within view from the proposed building site are two more gasoline stations, the First Mutual Bank Building built in the "Issaquah territorial style", an Elks hall which is described in the record by the Mayor of Issaquah as a "box building", an auto repair shop, and a veterinary clinic with a cyclone-fenced dog run. The area is described in the record as "a natural transition area between old downtown Issaquah and the new village style construction of Gilman [Boulevard]."

The Development Commission reviewed Anderson's application for the first time at a public hearing on December 21, 1988. Commissioner Nash commented that "the facade did not fit with the concept of the surrounding area." Commissioner McGinnis agreed. Commissioner Nash expressed concern about the building color and stated that he did not think the building was compatible with the image of Issaquah. Commissioner Larson said that he would like to see more depth to the building facade. Commissioner Nash said there should be some interest created along the blank back wall. Commissioner Garrison suggested that the rear facade needed to be redesigned.

At the conclusion of the meeting, the Development Commission voted to continue the hearing to give Anderson an opportunity to modify the building design.

On January 18, 1989, Anderson came back before the Development Commission with modified plans which included changing the roofing from metal to tile, changing the color of the structure from off-white to "Cape Cod" gray with "Tahoe" blue trim, and adding brick to the front facade. During the ensuing discussion among the commissioners, Commissioner Larson stated that the revisions to the front facade had not satisfied his concerns from the last meeting. In response to

Anderson's request for more specific design guidelines, Commissioner McGinnis stated that the Development Commission had "been giving direction; it is the applicant's responsibility to take the direction/suggestions and incorporate them into a revised plan that reflects the changes." Commissioner Larson then suggested that "the facade can be broken up with sculptures, benches, fountains, etc." Commissioner Nash suggested that Anderson "drive up and down Gilman and look at both good and bad examples of what has been done with flat facades."

As the discussion continued, Commissioner Larson stated that Anderson "should present a [plan] that achieves what the Commission is trying to achieve through its comments/suggestions at these meetings" and stated that "architectural screens, fountains, paving of brick, wood or other similar methods of screening in lieu of vegetative landscaping are examples of design suggestions that can be used to break up the front facade." Commissioner Davis objected to the front facade, stating that he could not see putting an expanse of glass facing Gilman Boulevard. "The building is not compatible with Gilman." Commissioner O'Shea agreed. Commissioner Nash stated that "the application needs major changes to be acceptable." Commissioner O'Shea agreed. Commissioner Nash stated that "this facade does not create the same feeling as the building/environment around this site."

Commissioner Nash continued, stating that he "personally liked the introduction of brick and the use of tiles rather than metal on the roof." Commissioner Larson stated that he would like to see a review of the blue to be used: "Tahoe blue may be too dark." Commissioner Steinwachs agreed. Commissioner Larson noted that "the front of the building could be modulated [to] have other design techniques employed to make the front facade more interesting."

With this, the Development Commission voted to continue the discussion to a future hearing.

On February 15, 1989, Anderson came back before the Development Commission. In the meantime, Anderson's architects had added a 5-foot overhang and a 7-foot accent overhang to the plans for the front of the building. More brick had been added to the front of the building. Wood trim and accent colors had been added to the back of the building and trees were added to the landscaping to further break up the rear facade.

Anderson explained the plans still called for large, floor to ceiling windows as this was to be a retail premises: "[A] glass front is necessary to rent the space. . . ." Commissioner Steinwachs stated that he had driven Gilman Boulevard and taken notes. The following verbatim statement by Steinwachs was placed into the minutes:

*My General Observation From Driving Up and Down
Gilman Boulevard.*

I see certain design elements and techniques used in various
combinations in various locations to achieve a visual effect that
is sensitive to the unique character of our Signature Street. I
see heavy use of brick, wood, and tile. I see minimal use of
stucco. I see colors that are mostly earthtones, avoiding
extreme contrasts. I see various methods used to provide
modulation in both horizontal and vertical lines, such as
gables, bay windows, recesses in front faces, porches, rails,
many vertical columns, and breaks in roof lines. I see long,
sloping, conspicuous roofs with large overhangs. I see windows
with panels above and below windows. I see no windows that
extend down to floor level. This is the impression I have of
Gilman Boulevard as it relates to building design.

Commissioner Nash agreed stating, "There is a certain feeling you
get when you drive along Gilman Boulevard, and this building does not
give this same feeling." Commissioner Steinwachs wondered if the
applicant had any option but to start "from scratch." Anderson
responded that he would be willing to change from stucco to wood facing
but that, after working on the project for 9 months and experiencing
total frustration, he was not willing to make additional design changes.

At that point, the Development Commission denied Anderson's
application, giving four reasons:

1. After four [sic] lengthy review meetings of the
Development Commission, the applicant has not been
sufficiently responsive to concerns expressed by the
Commission to warrant approval or an additional continuance
of the review.

2. The primary concerns expressed relate to the building
architecture as it relates to Gilman Boulevard in general, and
the immediate neighborhood in particular.

3. The Development Commission is charged with protecting,
preserving and enhancing the aesthetic values that have
established the desirable quality and unique character of
Issaquah. . .

4. We see certain design elements and techniques used in
various combinations in various locations to achieve a visual
effect that is sensitive to the unique character of our Signature
Street. On Gilman Boulevard we see heavy use of brick, wood
and tile. We see minimal use of stucco. We see various methods
used to provide both horizontal and vertical modulation,
including gables, breaks in rooflines, bay windows, recesses
and protrusions in front face. We see long, sloping, conspicuous
roofs with large overhangs. We see no windows that extend to

ground level. We see brick and wood panels at intervals between windows. We see earth tone colors avoiding extreme contrast.

Anderson, who by this time had an estimated $250,000 into the project, timely appealed the adverse ruling to the Issaquah City Council (City Council). After a lengthy hearing and much debate, the City Council decided to affirm the Development Commission's decision by a vote of 4 to 3.

The City Council considered formal written findings and conclusions on April 3, 1989. The City Council verbally adopted its action on that date but required that certain changes be made to the proposed findings and conclusions. Those changes were made and the final findings and conclusions were signed on April 5, 1989 (backdated to April 3). On April 5, a notice of action was issued to Anderson, stating that he had 14 days *from the date of that notice* in which to file any appeal.

Thirteen days later, on April 18, 1989, Anderson filed a complaint in King County Superior Court.

Discussion

In the area of land use, a court looks not only at the face of the ordinance but also at its application to the person who has sought to comply with the ordinance and/or who is alleged to have failed to comply. Burien Bark Supply, 106 Wash. 2d at 871; Grant Cy. v. Bohne, 89 Wash. 2d 953, 955, 577 P.2d 138 (1978). The purpose of the void for vagueness doctrine is to limit arbitrary and discretionary enforcements of the law. Burien Bark Supply, 106 Wash. 2d at 871.

Looking first at the face of the building design sections of IMC 16.16.060, we note that an ordinary citizen reading these sections would learn only that a given building project should bear a good relationship with the Issaquah Valley and surrounding mountains; its windows, doors, eaves and parapets should be of "appropriate proportions", its colors should be "harmonious" and seldom "bright" or "brilliant;" its mechanical equipment should be screened from public view; its exterior lighting should be "harmonious" with the building design and "monotony should be avoided." The project should also be "interesting." IMC 16.16.060(D)(1)–(6). If the building is not "compatible" with adjacent buildings, it should be "made compatible" by the use of screens and site breaks "or other suitable methods and materials." "Harmony in texture, lines, and masses [is] encouraged." The landscaping should provide an "attractive ... transition" to adjoining properties. IMC 16.16.060(B)(1)–(3).

As is stated in the brief of amicus curiae, we conclude that these code sections "do not give effective or meaningful guidance" to applicants, to design professionals, or to the public officials of Issaquah who are responsible for enforcing the code. Brief of Amicus Curiae, at 1.

Although it is clear from the code sections here at issue that mechanical equipment must be screened from public view and that, probably, earthtones or pastels located within the cool and muted ranges of the color wheel are going to be preferred, there is nothing in the code from which an applicant can determine whether his or her project is going to be seen by the Development Commission as "interesting" versus "monotonous" and as "harmonious" with the valley and the mountains. Neither is it clear from the code just what else, besides the valley and the mountains, a particular project is supposed to be harmonious with, although "harmony in texture, lines, and masses" is certainly encouraged. IMC 16.16.060(B)(2).

In attempting to interpret and apply this code, the commissioners charged with that task were left with only their own individual, subjective "feelings" about the "image of Issaquah" and as to whether this project was "compatible" or "interesting". The commissioners stated that the City was "making a statement" on its "signature street" and invited Anderson to take a drive up and down Gilman Boulevard and "look at good and bad examples of what has been done with flat facades." One commissioner drove up and down Gilman, taking notes, in a no doubt sincere effort to define that which is left undefined in the code.

The point we make here is that neither Anderson nor the commissioners may constitutionally be required or allowed to guess at the meaning of the code's building design requirements by driving up and down Gilman Boulevard looking at "good and bad" examples of what has been done with other buildings, recently or in the past. We hold that the code sections here at issue are unconstitutionally vague on their face. The words employed are not technical words which are commonly understood within the professional building design industry. Neither do these words have a settled common law meaning.

As they were applied to Anderson, it is also clear the code sections at issue fail to pass constitutional muster. Because the commissioners themselves had no objective guidelines to follow, they necessarily had to resort to their own subjective "feelings." The "statement" Issaquah is apparently trying to make on its "signature street" is not written in the code. In order to be enforceable, that "statement" must be written down in the code, in understandable terms. See, e.g., Morristown Road Assocs. v. Mayor & Common Coun. & Planning Bd., 163 N.J. Super. 58, 394 A.2d 157 (1978). The unacceptable alternative is what happened here. The commissioners enforced not a building design code but their own arbitrary concept of the provisions of an unwritten "statement" to be made on Gilman Boulevard. The commissioners' individual concepts were as vague and undefined as those written in the code. This is the very epitome of discretionary, arbitrary enforcement of the law.

As well illustrated by the appendices to the brief of amicus curiae, aesthetic considerations are not impossible to define in a code or ordinance.

We believe the issue of whether a community can exert control over design issues based solely on accepted community aesthetic values is far from "settled" in Washington case law. The possibility certainly has not been foreclosed by our Supreme Court. *See Polygon,* 90 Wash. 2d at 70 ("While this court has not held that aesthetic factors alone will support an exercise of the police power, such considerations taken together with other factors can support such action."). *See also Duckworth,* 91 Wash. 2d at 30 ("While we have indicated that aesthetic considerations alone *may* not support invocation of the police powers. . . ." (Italics ours.))

Clearly, however, aesthetic standards are an appropriate *component* of land use governance. Whenever a community adopts such standards they can and must be drafted to give clear guidance to all parties concerned. Applicants must have an understandable statement of what is expected from new construction. Design professionals need to know in advance what standards will be acceptable in a given community. It is unreasonable to expect applicants to pay for repetitive revisions of plans in an effort to comply with the unarticulated, unpublished "statements" a given community may wish to make on or off its "signature street". It is equally unreasonable, and a deprivation of due process, to expect or allow a design review board such as the Issaquah Development Commission to create standards on an *ad hoc* basis, during the design review process.

Conclusion

It is not disputed that Anderson's project meets all of the City's land use requirements except for those unwritten and therefore unenforceable requirements relating to building design which the Development Commission unsuccessfully tried to articulate during the course of several hearings. We order that Anderson's land use certification be issued, provided however, that those changes which Anderson agreed to through the hearing before the City Council may validly be imposed.

NOTES AND QUESTIONS

1.   In State ex rel. Stoyanoff v. Berkeley, 458 S.W.2d 305 (Mo. 1970), landowner owned a parcel of land in an exclusive suburb of St. Louis. Almost all neighboring homes were "two-story houses of conventional architectural design, such as Colonial, French Provincial or English." Landowner sought to build a home "of a pyramid shape, with a flat top, and with triangular shaped windows or doors at one or more corners." The proposed building satisfied all applicable zoning requirements. If the landowner had advanced the same proposal in the City of Issaquah, and the Issaquah ordinance had been in effect, would the court have upheld the

city's refusal to approve landowner's architectural design? Or does the court's opinion mean that the city would have to enact a new ordinance before disapproving any architectural design?

If you were redrafting the Issaquah ordinance to deal with the prospect of a home like the one in *Stoyanoff*, how would you draft it? Are you convinced that you could draft an ordinance that escapes vagueness difficulties but allows the architectural review board to disapprove the *Stoyanoff* house?

2. The *Anderson* case is not alone in holding architectural review standards void for vagueness. *See also* Waterfront Estates Dev. Inc. v. City of Palos Hills, 232 Ill.App.3d 367, 173 Ill.Dec. 667, 597 N.E.2d 641 (1992) (citing earlier Illinois cases); Morristown Road Assocs. v. Mayor, 163 N.J.Super. 58, 394 A.2d 157 (1978). Other courts have rejected vagueness challenges or challenges that the city has unconstitutionally delegated power to an architectural review board. *See, e.g.,* Vill. of Hudson v. Albrecht, 9 Ohio St.3d 69, 458 N.E.2d 852 (1984); People v. Stoyanoff, supra. In some of the cases that have been decided, landowners eschewed vagueness challenges in favor of the contention that the municipality's determination was not supported by substantial evidence. See, e.g., Breneric Associates v. City of Del Mar, 69 Cal.App.4th 166, 81 Cal.Rptr.2d 324 (1998) (rejecting challenge, emphasizing deferential nature of review).

3. What was the developer in *Anderson* trying to build? Do you think the developer had strong commitments to a particular architectural style? In light of the developer's objectives, what advice would you have given the developer for his appearances before the Development Commission? For his appearance before the City Council?

4. Architectural review boards have become common even in relatively small municipalities, yet the volume of litigation challenging review board determinations remains quite small. What explanations might there be for the disparity?

5. Are architectural review boards a good idea? Why not rely on markets to guard against ugly buildings, or those that do not harmonize well with neighboring buildings? Don't developers have more incentive to weed out unattractive (and therefore unmarketable) buildings than do local bureaucrats? And if a grotesque building slips through occasionally—as it surely will—is that worse than a bureaucratic system that discourages innovation in order to preserve "harmony?"

6. Although courts (like the court in *Anderson*) have sometimes questioned whether aesthetic considerations could ever, by themselves, justify land use regulation, the more recent decisions have tended to hold that aesthetic goals are an adequate justification for the exercise of the police power. *See* Oregon City v. Hartke, 240 Or. 35, 400 P.2d 255 (1965). The challenge, as illustrated in the *Anderson* case, is to craft aesthetic regulations that are sufficiently clear so as not to give unbridled discretion to land use decisionmakers.

7. The amicus brief in the case, which argued that the Issaquah ordinance was unconstitutionally vague, was filed by the Seattle Chapter of the American Institute of Architects, the Washington Council of the American Institute of Architects, and the Washington Chapter of the American Society of Landscape Architects. What interests did these groups have in the outcome of this litigation? If they opposed the Issaquah ordinance, why were they nonetheless favorably disposed towards aesthetic regulation in general?

8. In addition to giving rise to the sorts of due process problems identified by the *Anderson* court, such vague regulation may also raise significant First Amendment questions. *See, e.g.*, Lamar Corp. v. City of Twin Falls, 133 Idaho 36, 981 P.2d 1146 (1999). Many of the cases raising the First Amendment argument have involved attempts by municipalities to regulate billboards, often on aesthetic grounds. *See, e.g.*, Metromedia, Inc. v. City of San Diego, 453 U.S. 490 (1981). Does the regulation of building design itself implicate expressive freedoms protected by the First Amendment? The Nazis famously denounced flat roofs as "degenerate." See Richard Pommer, The Flat Roof: A Modernist Controversy in Germany, 43 Art. J. 158 (1983). Could a city ban a particular architectural style, such as modernism, on aesthetic grounds, or would such a ban violate the First Amendment? Could it ban all but one particular architectural style? What if the ban were part of an historic preservation district?

Getting Specific: Form-Based Coding

The *Anderson* case highlighted that, sometimes, local laws aiming to regulate aesthetics may not provide sufficient guidance to property owners, developers, and design professionals. Localities have responded by getting more specific about the types of building forms that are allowed within their jurisdiction. This may include regulation of building shapes, heights, ground coverage, entrance types, and rooflines. The broad term for this new crop of rules is form-based coding (or form-based zoning). Communities have been understandably resistant to shift their entire zoning scheme into a pure form-based code that dispenses with considerations about uses. Rather, communities have layered form-based coding principles on top of rules about land uses—the traditional topic of zoning regulations.

Consider the following excerpt from the aesthetic regulations of Puyallup, Washington, which have been layered atop a traditional, use-based regulatory scheme:

20.26.300 Nonresidential design review standards.

Any nonresidential structures constructed, or subject to major expansion and/or extensive exterior remodeling, and located in any zone except the ML, CBD-Core or CBD zone shall be subject to the following design review standards:

(1) Building Wall and Roof Modulation. All buildings which contain two or more stories or have a building footprint of more than 10,000 square feet or which have

any facade length greater than 100 feet, and which will be visible from a public street or residential zone for more than three years beyond the date of construction completion, shall use the following elements and features in design and construction of the building:

(a) Wall Plane Proportions. No wall plane visible from any public right-of-way shall be wider than 2.5 times the height of the wall plane. (A wall plane is a flat vertical surface on a building facade, which may include doors, windows, openings, or other incidental recessions that do not extend through to the roofline.)

(b) Horizontal Modulation. All building walls shall provide horizontal modulation consistent with the following standards:

(i) The maximum allowable horizontal length of a building wall between modulations is 100 feet;

(ii) The minimum depth of each modulation is 10 feet; and

(iii) The minimum width of each modulation is 15 feet. As an alternative treatment, horizontal modulation may be provided by installation of one stand of trees for each required modulation, located within 20 feet of that portion of the building wall requiring modulation. Each stand of trees must have a canopy of at least 1,000 square feet (as measured in frontal view rather than top view) and may include existing trees or planted trees arranged as a massing. The stand of trees shall provide year-round screening through a combination of evergreen and not more than 25 percent deciduous trees and may include existing trees, or planted trees. Stands of trees intended to meet modulation requirements shall be in addition to required perimeter landscaping.

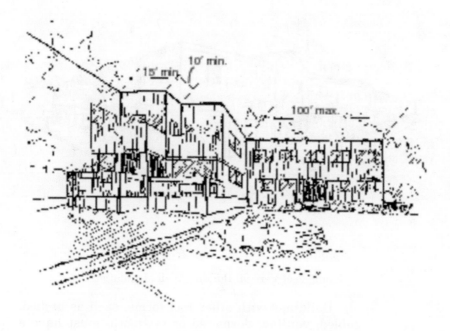

Example of Horizontal Building Wall Modulation

(c) Roofline Modulation. For buildings with flat, gabled, hipped or similar roofs, with slopes of less than three feet vertical to 12 feet horizontal, the maximum length of any continuous roofline is 50 feet without being modulated. If the continuous roofline exceeds 50 feet in length, the following methods must be used:

(i) The height of the visible roofline must change at least four feet if the adjacent roof segments are less than 50 feet in length.

(ii) The height of the visible roofline must change at least eight feet if the adjacent roof segments are 50 feet or more in length.

(iii) The length of a sloped or gabled roofline must be at least 20 feet, with a minimum slope of three feet vertical to 12 feet horizontal.

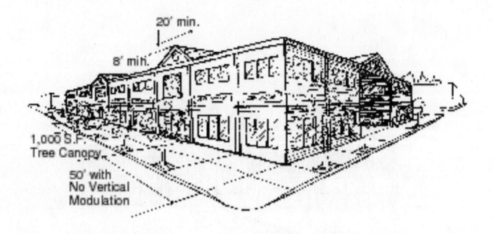

Example of Vertical Building Wall Modulation

(d) Buildings with other roof forms, such as arched, gabled, vaulted, dormered or sawtooth, must have a significant change in slope or significant change in roof line at least every 100 feet.

(2) Building Wall and Facade Articulation. All buildings which contain two or more stories or have a building footprint of more than 10,000 square feet or which have any facade length greater than 100 feet and which are visible from a public street for more than three years beyond the date of construction completion or located within 100 feet of a residential zone shall use the following elements and features in design and construction of the building:

(a) Any wall or portion of a wall which is visible from a public street or residential zone and contains at least 400 square feet of surface area without any window, door, building wall modulation or other architectural feature shall screen or treat the wall using at least two of the following methods or techniques:

(i) Installation of a vertical trellis with climbing vines or plant material in front of the blank wall;

(ii) Providing a landscaped strip at least 10 feet in width in front of the blank wall and planted with plant materials which will obscure or screen at least 50 percent of the blank wall within three years;

(iii) Use of alternate building materials or wall textures in the exterior treatment of the blank wall; or

(iv) Use of functional or nonfunctional architectural features such as windows, doors, pillars, columns, awnings, roofs, etc., which cover at least 25 percent of the wall surface.

CHAPTER FOUR

DEVELOPER CHALLENGES: STATE LAW

In this chapter, we explore several state law doctrines that developers frequently use to challenge adverse decisions by local governments: (1) the argument that a municipality has exceeded its delegated powers, including claims that the conditions a municipality has placed on a regulatory approval constitute an unlawful exaction; (2) the assertion by a developer that it has a "vested right" to proceed under a prior regulatory regime, or, relatedly, that a municipality is estopped from denying regulatory permission for some reason; (3) the contention that the municipal action violates "public policy"; and, finally, (4) the claim that a particular land use regulation is so vague that it fails to provide adequate notice to landowners or to sufficiently constrain governmental decisionmaking. Though the legal foundations of these arguments are often unstated, many of these doctrines find echoes in federal constitutional norms. Despite this conceptual overlap with federal law, however, it is important to recognize these state law arguments as distinct legal doctrines with their own, sometimes idiosyncratic, characteristics. Indeed, applying these doctrines, state courts often prove far more willing to wade into aggressive review of local government land use decisionmaking than the federal courts.

I. MUNICIPALITY HAS EXCEEDED ITS POWERS

Municipalities exercise power by virtue of a delegation of power from states. As you will see, different states apply different standards in interpreting those delegations. Most states now grant localities broad power to legislate pursuant to the general welfare or allow for "home rule" jurisdictions to set some of their own powers, bounded only loosely by state law. Some states, however, continue to apply a more stringent rule, "Dillon's Rule," which will find a municipality to possess only those powers expressly delegated to it by the state and those powers necessary or indispensable to either the powers expressly granted or the essential nature of the municipality.

Corresponding with these differences, there are two ways in which a municipality can exceed its delegated powers. First, a municipality might exercise a power that has been affirmatively preempted by state law. Second, a municipality might attempt to exercise a power that a state has not delegated to it.

A. STATE PREEMPTION OF MUNICIPAL POWERS

City of Springfield v. Goff

Supreme Court of Missouri, 1996
918 S.W.2d 786

■ ROBERTSON, J.

Section 89.060, RSMo 1994, permits thirty percent of the landowners affected by a zoning change to file a petition protesting the change to the legislative body of a municipality. In that event, the zoning ordinance does not take effect unless two-thirds of the members of the municipality's legislative body vote in favor of the change. The City of Springfield, Missouri, a charter city, adopted charter section 11.18. The charter provision recognizes as valid a protest petition signed by ten percent of the affected landowners and requires that three-quarters of the members of the Springfield city council vote in favor of a change to override the protest petition. * * * *

Respondents Dorothy and Genevieve Haydon asked the City to rezone a parcel of land to permit a bed and breakfast in an area previously zoned for single-family residences. More than ten percent, but less than thirty percent, of the affected landowners opposed the zoning change and filed a petition with the city council before the council considered the zoning change request. When the zoning change did not receive a three-quarter's majority, the council declared that the request for a change in zoning failed.

Respondents Lon and Debora Goff sought a change in zoning to permit a small motel in place of the car wash or self-service storage units previously approved. Affected landowners filed a timely protest petition with the city council, which met the requirements of charter section 11.18, but not section 89.060. The council received the petition and voted 5–3 in favor of the change. Because the zoning change did not receive the three-quarter's majority required by section 11.18 following the filing of a protest, the council declared the zoning-change request defeated.

Springfield filed a declaratory judgment action against the Goffs, seeking a declaration of the validity of section 11.18. The Goffs filed a motion for summary judgment. The trial court permitted the Haydons to intervene as defendants and entered judgment in favor of the Goffs and Haydons. The trial court's order declared that section 11.18 of the Springfield charter conflicted with section 89.060 in violation of article VI, section 19(a). Springfield appealed.

Section 89.060, RSMo 1994, relates to changes in zoning regulations and provides:

> Such regulations, restrictions, and boundaries may from time
> to time be amended, supplemented, changed, modified or

repealed. In case, however, of a protest against such change duly signed and acknowledged by the owners of *thirty percent or more,* either of the areas of the land (exclusive of streets and alleys) included in such proposed change or within an area determined by lines drawn parallel to and one hundred and eighty-five feet distant from the boundaries of the district proposed to be changed, such amendment shall not become effective except by the favorable vote of *two-thirds* of all the members of the legislative body of such municipality. . . .

(Emphasis added.) Prior to 1988, section 89.060 required only ten percent of the affected landowners to sign a protest petition and required a three-quarter's vote of the members of the municipal legislative body to override the protest. *See* § 89.060, RSMo 1986. Until 1988, Springfield, had no independent charter provision concerning zoning protest petitions. Instead, its charter reflected the language and requirements of section 89.060.

Following the 1988 amendments, Springfield initially adopted zoning protest petition requirements identical to those contained in the new section 89.060. However, on April 4, 1989, Springfield's voters approved an amendment to the city's charter, adopting section 11.18, which restored the right of ten percent of affected landowners to file a valid protest against a proposed zoning change, and required a three-quarter's majority of the city council to override a valid protest petition and to approve a zoning change. Section 11.18 provides:

Notwithstanding any other law to the contrary, whenever a valid protest petition is filed in opposition to the rezoning of land, the zoning change shall not become effective except by the favorable vote of *three fourths* of all the members of the City Council. In order for a protest petition to be valid against the change, it shall be duly signed and acknowledged by the owners of *ten percent* or more, either of the areas of the land (exclusive of streets and alleys) included in such proposed change, or within an area determined by lines drawn parallel to and one hundred and eighty-five feet distant from the boundaries of the land proposed to be changed. In the event it is determined that this provision is invalid, then the city council shall have the authority to determine the percentage for a protest petition and to require more than a simple majority of the full council to rezone property when a valid protest petition is filed in opposition to the rezoning.

(Emphasis added.)

Springfield first urges that section 89.060 violates article VI, section 22. That constitutional provision states: "No law shall be enacted creating or fixing the powers, duties or compensation of any municipal office or employment for any city . . . adopting its own charter. . . ." Springfield argues that any attempt by the legislature to establish procedures that cities must follow to effect zoning changes is "an attempt to define the powers of municipal officers."

The constitutional authority to cities to adopt and amend a charter, Mo. Const. Art. VI, §§ 19–22, intends to grant cities broad authority to tailor a form of government that its citizens believe will best serve their interests. State ex rel. St. Louis Fire Fighters Ass'n Local No. 73, AFL-CIO v. Stemmler, 479 S.W.2d 456, 458–59 (Mo. 1972) (en banc). While the power of charter cities is not without boundaries—article VI, section 19(a), requires that charter city ordinances be consistent with the constitution and "not limited or denied" by state statutes—the General Assembly is expressly prohibited from dictating the types of municipal offices and employment charter cities must establish or the powers or compensation of officers and employees of charter cities. Art. VI, § 22.

Springfield argues that the General Assembly's establishment of the majority by which the members of the city council must vote to approve a zoning change over a protest petition is tantamount to fixing the powers of a municipal office. We do not read section 22 so broadly. Instead, by its plain language, section 22 is limited to prohibiting the General Assembly from enacting state laws prescribing the individual offices of a charter city and the duties and compensation of the officers holding those offices. Section 22 applies only to individual offices. In other words, the General Assembly may not tell the officers of a charter city what they must do; it may, however, limit the powers a charter city may exercise through its officers. Consistent with this understanding of section 22, the constitution does not prohibit the legislature from establishing procedures by which charter cities may make substantive determinations regarding the uses of private property through zoning regulation.

Section 89.060 does not violate article VI, section 22. It neither creates a municipal office or employment, nor fixes the powers, duties or compensation of a municipal office or employment. Rather, section 89.060 places limitations upon the exercise of powers by the governing bodies of municipalities. The statute, a provision of the Missouri Zoning Enabling Act, section 89.010, et seq., RSMo 1994, requires legislative bodies to follow certain procedures for rezoning land in the face of a valid protest petition, i.e., one signed by thirty percent of affected landowners. Section 89.060 is constitutional.

The second issue is whether the adoption of section 11.18 of Springfield's charter purports to grant the city a power denied it by state statute in violation of article VI, section 19(a). A charter provision that conflicts with a state statute is void. A conflict exists where a charter "permits what the statute prohibits" or "prohibits what the statute permits." Cape Motor Lodge, Inc. v. City of Cape Girardeau, 706 S.W.2d 208, 211 (Mo. 1986) (en banc).

Sections 89.010 to 89.140 constitute the sole source of authority for cities in zoning matters. Consequently, a city must conform to the terms of the state's grant of authority when exercising its powers relating to zoning. A city follows the terms of the grant of zoning authority by adhering to all of the procedures set forth in sections 89.050 to 89.070.

Section 89.060 permits a protest against a zoning change by the owners of "thirty percent or more" of the affected property. Section 11.18 reduces the statutory percentage to ten percent. Section 89.060 does not permit a protest by less than thirty percent of the owners.

Section 89.060 also requires that upon the filing of a valid protest petition a zoning change must be approved by two-thirds of a municipality's legislative body. Section 11.18 requires a three-quarter's super-majority of the Springfield city council to approve a zoning change over a protest petition. Section 89.060 does not permit approval by more than two-thirds of a legislative body.

In permitting protests by a lower percentage of owners and requiring a greater percentage of votes by members of the city council to override protests, section 11.18 allows what section 89.060 prohibits. Therefore, section 11.18 violates article VI, section 19(a) of the constitution. Section 11.18 is void.

The judgment of the trial court is affirmed.

NOTES AND QUESTIONS

1.   What interests, if any, are protected by preventing the state from "creating or fixing the powers, duties or compensation of any municipal office or employment for any city," but permitting the state to substantively regulate municipal lawmaking procedures?

2.   Do you agree with the Missouri Supreme Court that, by making it easier for citizens to challenge zoning changes, Springfield has exceeded its municipal powers by acting contrary to state law?

3.   The Court in *Goff* says that a charter provision conflicts with a state statute when it "permits what the statute prohibits" or "prohibits what the statute permits." What does Section 89.060 forbid? What does it permit? What does Section 11.18 forbid? What does it permit? How does Section 11.18 of the city charter permit what Section 89.060 forbids or prohibit what Section 89.060 permits?

4.   What do you think motivated voters in Springfield to enact the 1989 amendment to the city charter, reverting to the pre-1988 protest provision? Which interest groups do you suppose supported the 1989 amendment? Which groups opposed it?

5.   The state legislature enacts a statute providing that in deciding an application for an area variance, a zoning board of appeals "shall take into consideration the benefit to the applicant if the variance is granted, as weighed against the detriment to the health, safety and welfare of the neighborhood or community by such grant." The state statute also lists five factors to be considered in evaluating an area variance application. If a municipality's local ordinance provides that an area variance shall be

denied if the landowner's hardship is self-created, can the developer challenge the ordinance as pre-empted by state law? If you represented the municipality, how would you respond? *See* Cohen v. Board of Appeals, 100 N.Y.2d 395, 764 N.Y.S.2d 64, 795 N.E.2d 619 (2003).

B. EXTENT OF MUNICIPALITY'S DELEGATED POWERS

City of Ocean Springs v. Homebuilders Association of Mississippi

Supreme Court of Mississippi, 2006
932 So.2d 44

■ RANDOLPH, J.

The Mayor and Board of Aldermen of the city of Ocean Springs (collectively "City") adopted a Comprehensive Plan, which included separate impact fee ordinances which authorized the assessment, collection, and expenditure of "development impact fees" for various municipal improvements, services, equipment, and vehicles. In its Development Impact Fee Procedures Ordinance, the City defined a development impact fee as:

> A fee relating to a capital expenditure or service provided by the City which is imposed on new development as a condition of approval of such development as a prerequisite to obtaining development approval and which is calculated to defray all or a portion of the costs of capital improvements required to accommodate new land development at city-designated level of service standards and which reasonably benefits the new land development.

The impact fees were to be paid in addition to any and all other applicable land use, zoning, planning, adequate public facilities, platting, or other related fees, requirements, standards, and conditions imposed by the City.

After the City's adoption of the ordinances, the Appellees filed a Bill of Exceptions appealing the adoption of the impact fee ordinances. Appellees claimed that the impact fees constituted facial and per se illegal taxes which the City did not have the power to enact. The City filed a Receipt and Addendum to the Bill of Exceptions, objecting to certain alleged facts and law asserted in the Bill of Exceptions.

The parties submitted the case to the Jackson County Circuit Court ("Circuit Court"), and after briefing and oral argument, the Circuit Court held the impact fees to be a void taxing measure. By subsequent order, the Circuit Court denied the City's Motion for a Stay and enjoined further collection of impact fees by the City. The City was directed to submit an accounting of fees already collected and a plan for their refund. The City appeals the ruling of the Circuit Court.

The City submits that adoption of impact fee ordinances are permissible as a police power measure, and are reasonably authorized by the City's Home Rule authority under Miss. Code Ann. Section 21–17–5; or, in the alternative, by general planning and zoning statutes. The City argues the regulations are reasonably related and roughly proportional to the need generated by the development, and the City submits the impact fee ordinances are reasonable and proportionate to the needs of Ocean Springs.

Appellees contend that the City officials assumed authority in violation of Article 4, Section 80 of the Mississippi Constitution and that regardless of how reasonable the City's fees are, the City was without authority to adopt the fees, and whether the impact fees are reasonably related or roughly proportional to the needs of Ocean Springs is of no import. Appellees specifically contend Miss. Code Ann. Section 21–17–5 does not bestow authority upon the City to implement impact fees.

The State of Mississippi does not have a specific constitutional provision or statute regarding implementation of development impact fees, nor can authority be found in the common law.

There are twenty-seven (27) states which have adopted development impact fee statutes, although five of the states' statutes related exclusively to roads.[4]

Four additional states have determined, in the absence of specific impact fee legislation, that such fees are otherwise authorized. Courts in Kansas, Wyoming, Florida and Ohio have held that municipalities have the authority to adopt impact fees, even though there is not a specific statute to allow for it.

Article IV, Section 80 of the Mississippi Constitution declares, "[p]rovision shall be made by general laws to prevent the abuse by cities, towns, and other municipal corporations of their powers of assessment, taxation, borrowing money, and contracting debts." Appellees argue this provision of the Mississippi Constitution prohibits assessments or taxation, unless there is specific statutory authority allowing the City to do so. In Adams v. Kuykendall, 83 Miss. 571, 35 So. 830, 835 (1904), this Court stated, "[w]e hold the taxing power of the sovereign is vested solely in the State and its relinquishment is never to be inferred."

The City argues the authority to adopt impact fees is derived from Mississippi general planning and zoning statutes, as well as Miss. Code Ann. Section 21–17–5, the Home Rule statute. Appellees counter that, "Mississippi municipalities are creatures of the state, and they have

---

4   The following states have adopted development impact fees: AR, AZ, CA, CO, DE, GA, HI (roads only), ID, IL (roads only), IN, MT, NV, NH, NM, NJ (roads only), PA (roads only), RI, SC, TX, UT, VA (roads only), VT, WV, WA and WI.

only those powers delegated to them by statute," otherwise the City has no legal authority with which to adopt these fees.

Miss. Code Ann. Section 17–1–11(1)(a) provides, "[t]he governing authority of each municipality and county may provide for the preparation, adoption, amendment, extension and carrying out of a comprehensive plan for the purpose of bringing about coordinated physical development in accordance with present and future needs. . . ." The City argued a Comprehensive Plan was adopted by the City in 2001 and contained, as a condition to development approval, a provision for payment of impact fees. The City argues Miss. Code Ann. Section 17–1–11 grants authority for the City to impose impact fees even absent Home Rule authority.

Miss. Code Ann. Section 17–1–11 has been interpreted as applying primarily to zoning ordinances and enacted Planning statutes. We agree. Under the Municipal Planning Statutes, Miss. Code Ann. Section 17–1–1, *et seq.*, there are no provisions which grant authority to adopt impact fees or other revenue raising mechanisms to implement the City's Comprehensive Plan.

The City further urges the authority to impose impact fees exists under Miss. Code Ann. Section 21–17–5, commonly known as the Home Rule Statute. The City relies on the language of Section 21–17–5(1), "[e]xcept as otherwise provided in subsection (2) of this section, the powers granted to governing authorities of municipalities in this section are complete without the existence of or reference to any specific authority granted in any other statute or law of the state of Mississippi" as its authority, and does not require a specific legislative mandate. In part, we agree. Consistent with our holding in Maynard v. City of Tupelo, 691 So.2d 385 (Miss. 1997), we find that Home Rule authority grants municipalities authority to impose *fees,* as long as the imposition is not inconsistent with legislative mandate or the Mississippi Constitution, and is a fee, as opposed to a tax, as discussed *infra.*

We conclude there is no constitutional basis, legislative enactment, or common law doctrine, which empowers cities to adopt and impose development impact fees.

The Circuit Court held, "[t]he fact that the City labeled this exaction 'fee' rather than 'tax' is not important; the purpose of the enactment governs over terminology." The City argues that because the impact fees were reasonably related to the infrastructure needs created by new development and the fees were earmarked and deposited into a special fund, the impact fees meet the criteria for fees. Appellees successfully argued before the Circuit Court that the City was utilizing the fees for general municipal purposes and as a revenue-raising mechanism, therefore they were a tax. The United States Supreme Court addressed the distinction between a tax and a fee in Illinois Cent. R. Co. v. City of Decatur, 147 U.S. 190, 198–99, 13 S.Ct. 293, 37 L.Ed.132 (1893) (quoting Cooley on Taxation, at 416), and held:

> Special assessments are a peculiar species of taxation, standing apart from the general burdens imposed for state and municipal purposes, and governed by principles that do not apply generally. The general levy of taxes is understood to exact contributions in return for the general benefits of government and it promises nothing to the persons taxed beyond what may be anticipated from an administration of the laws for individual protection and the general public good. Special assessments, on the other hand, are made upon the assumption that a portion of the community is to be especially and peculiarly benefited, in the enhancement of the value of the property peculiarly situated as regards a contemplated expenditure of public funds; and, in addition to the general levy, they demand that special contributions, in consideration of the special benefit, shall be made by the persons receiving it.

More recently, the United States Court of Appeals for the Fifth Circuit was called upon to address the distinction between a tax and a fee in Home Builders Ass'n of Miss. v. City of Madison, Miss., 143 F.3d 1006, 1011 (5th Cir. 1998), and held:

> Workable distinctions emerge from the relevant case law, however: the classic tax sustains the essential flow of revenue to the government, while the classic fee is linked to some regulatory scheme. The classic tax is imposed by a state or municipal legislature, while the classic fee is imposed by an agency upon those it regulates. The classic tax is designed to provide benefit for the entire community, while the classic fee is designed to raise money to help defray an agency's regulatory expenses.

The State of Mississippi has adopted similar distinctions stating, "[t]he chief distinction is that a tax is an exaction for public purposes while a fee relates to an individual privilege or benefit to the payer." Miss. Att'y Gen. Op. 1996–0425 (1996) (quoting United States v. River Coal Co., 748 F.2d 1103, 1106 (6th Cir. 1984)).

"Properly understood, regulatory fees are charges to cover the cost of the state's use of its regulatory powers which can be allocated to those who are either voluntarily or involuntarily receiving special attention from government regulators." Hugh Spitzer, Taxes v. Fees: A Curious Confusion, 38 Gonz. L. Rev. 335, 353 (2003) (quoting Covell v. City of Seattle, 127 Wash. 2d 874, 879, 905 P.2d 324, 327 (1995)). "Such fees cover public expenditures on inspection, record-keeping, and processing, and are correctly limited to the proportionate cost of giving the fee payer that special attention." Id. (quoting Teter v. Clark County, 104 Wash. 2d 227, 234, 704 P.2d 1171, 1177 (1985)).

The fees at issue do not qualify as regulatory in nature. These fees cannot be said to cover "administrative expenses" incurred by the City. In order to obtain a building permit, these fees must be paid; however, the fees are not based on the administrative expense the City incurs in issuing the building permit.

Further, to be regulatory in nature, there must be a specific benefit conferred on the payer of the fee. The Circuit Court found the City's impact fees did not provide any special benefit to the parties paying the fees. The City submits, "[b]enefit is guaranteed by earmarking impact fee revenue in a separate fund from the general fund and restricting the use of impact fee revenue to new infrastructure that will benefit new development." The parties agree the fees were deposited into a separate account from the City's general municipal fund. However, to be determined is whether the developers upon whom the impact fees were imposed were receiving the benefit or if the benefit of the fees was being received by the municipality as a whole.

The learned trial judge observed, "[t]his is little, if any, assurance that such funds provide a special benefit to the class upon whom the burden is imposed. Simply opening a special account earmarked for particular city services or facilities is insufficient to provide a 'special' benefit to those utilizing the service or facility."

In conjunction with the City's Procedures Ordinance, the six Ordinances were adopted for general municipal purposes, fire department purposes, park and recreation purposes, police department purposes, major roadways and water facility purposes. At a 2002 public hearing, Bruce Peshoff, the principal in the design of the City's impact fees, stated the "first round" of impact fees were being developed for fire, parks and for *general municipal services*.

The public services identified in the Ordinances have traditionally been funded by tax revenues. The City is responsible for general municipal services that benefit the City as a whole.

It is the opinion of this Court that the Circuit Court in the matter *sub judice* did not err in holding the City's impact fees constituted an illegal tax. Impact fees are not per se illegal; however, the authority to implement the fees rests with the Legislature.

"The county and city are not authorized to impose taxes without direct authorization from the Legislature. Even under home rule provisions ... the city and county are explicitly barred from levying taxes other than those authorized by statute." Miss. Att'y Gen. Op. 1989–124 (1989). In City of Jackson v. Freeman-Howie, Inc., 239 Miss. 84, 121 So.2d 120, 123 (1960) we held, "[a] city derives its existence and powers by its charter from the State, and can perform the acts for which it has authority thereunder except such as may be in conflict with the Constitution."

CONCLUSION

Courts cannot fault the logic or the foresight that induces the municipality to consider the long-term impact of permitted development on municipal resources and public facilities. However, in the absence of legislative intent, municipalities cannot depart from traditionally authorized methods of financing public facilities so as to allocate the costs of substantial public projects among new developments on the basis of their anticipated impact.

NOTES AND QUESTIONS

1. Why do you think the homebuilders challenged these impact fees? Given the choice, do you think most developers would rather pay an impact fee or be forced to hand over a certain quantity of land for infrastructure development or open space?

2. Suppose a Mississippi state statute had authorized municipalities to impose impact fees to cover road construction. Would the developer's argument in the *Ocean Springs* case have been stronger or weaker? Why?

3. *Dillon's Rule*: The court in *Ocean Springs* rested its decision in part on something called "Dillon's Rule." The following excerpt from McQuillin, *The Law of Municipal Corporations*, explains the origins and meaning of the rule, which continues to operate in a number of jurisdictions:

> § 4:11 "Dillon's Rule" is a canon of statutory construction from common law that calls for the strict and narrow construction of local governmental authority. Dillon's Rule, propagated by Iowa Supreme Court Justice John F. Dillon over 100 years ago is as follows: a municipal corporation possesses and can exercise only the following powers: (1) those granted in express words; (2) those necessarily or fairly implied in or incident to the powers expressly granted; and (3) those essential to the accomplishment of the declared objects and purposes of the corporation—not simply convenient, but indispensable. Any fair, reasonable, substantial doubt concerning the existence of power is resolved by the courts against the corporation, and the power is denied. Today, home rule authority reverses Dillon's Rule, however, the rule remains the most important factor in deciding the powers of non-home rule local governments. Though under Illinois Constitution home rule units of local government may enact regulations when the state has not specifically declared its exercise to be exclusive, non-home-rule units of local government are governed by Dillon's Rule, under which non-home-rule units possess only the powers that are specifically conveyed by the Constitution or statute. Mississippi still operates entirely under this regime, and a few other states incorporate aspects of this regime into their delegation of municipal powers. For example, under Dillon's Rule, a municipality can regulate wages only if a state statute explicitly grants specific municipal authority over wage regulation. California is the only state in the union that explicitly gives statutory authority to local governments over minimum wage regulation, and it has rejected Dillon's Rule.

4. The majority of states have moved away from Dillon's Rule by granting broad powers to local governments or by enacting home-rule statutes that allow localities to establish their own rules within loose state limits. Still, municipalities continue to be understood by many courts and commentators as creatures of the state government, whose powers can be freely curtailed by the state legislature within the limits of state and federal constitutional law. There have been some signs that this traditional understanding of cities as exclusively creatures of the *state* government has been giving way to a more complicated view of the place of cities within the federal framework. In one case, for example, the U.S. Supreme Court held that Congress could directly grant municipalities the power to condemn state land, even over the objection of the state government, of whom the municipality is supposedly a creature. *See* City of Tacoma v. Taxpayers of Tacoma, 357 U.S. 320 (1958). A few federal laws implicating local land use controls, such as the Religious Land Use and Institutionalized Persons Act of 2000, 42 U.S.C. § 2000cc et seq., also reflect this trend. On the other hand, the Supreme Court has rejected, on federalism grounds, the notion of "sovereign" cities. *See* Community Commc'n Co. v. City of Boulder, 455 U.S. 40 (1982).

5. As the court in the *Ocean Springs* case makes clear, a majority of states grant municipalities the power to impose impact fees. But many states, like Mississippi, restrict the ability of municipalities to impose "taxes" absent specific legislative approval. The question then becomes whether an "impact fee" is a "tax" such that it is beyond the power of the local government to impose without specific legislative approval. Do you agree with the court in *Ocean Springs* that the provision in question was really a tax and not a fee? Should a tax be distinguished from a fee based on how it is assessed and collected? How the revenues are used? Both?

6. Should local governments enjoy unfettered discretion (within constitutional limits) in determining how to raise their revenues? *See* Clayton Gillette, *Fiscal Home Rule*, 86 Denv. U. L. Rev. 1241 (2009). Is there any reason to be particularly mistrustful of the ways local governments might use the power to tax?

7. In some states, local governments are required by state law to create comprehensive plans and to conform their individual zoning decisions with those plans, a topic we cover more fully in Part II of Chapter Six. In these states, developers frequently challenge a permit denial or unfavorable zoning action as inconsistent with the governing comprehensive plan. An action inconsistent with the comprehensive plan exceeds the power of the local government and therefore constitutes grounds for relief. *See, e.g.,* Marion County Hous. Auth. v. City of Woodburn, 8 Or. LUBA 285 (1983). In other states, however, denying a permit for a use that is allowed under the applicable zoning ordinance merely because the development appears to conflict with the comprehensive plan is seen as improperly elevating the comprehensive plan to the status of a zoning code and constitutes grounds for relief. *See* Urrutia v. Blaine County, 134 Idaho 353, 2 P.3d 738 (2000).

8. A handful of states impose on municipalities the obligation to accept their "fair share" of certain types of development that are necessary for the health of the region as a whole but that many municipalities find undesirable, either for fiscal reasons or because of the impact the land use might have on the quality of life of the municipalities' residents. Low-income, multi-family dwellings are an example. In these jurisdictions, developers may be empowered to challenge an adverse land use decision on the grounds that it violates a municipality's regional obligations. This is sometimes referred to as a "builder's remedy." We will discuss regional obligations in depth in Chapter Nine.

NOTE ON SPECIAL ASSESSMENTS

In *Ocean Springs*, the city sought to escape the conclusion that the impact fee was an unauthorized tax by analogizing the fee to a "special assessment" which the United States Supreme Court (in the *Illinois Central* case cited in *Ocean Springs*) has distinguished from an ordinary tax. Other courts have also held that a special assessment is not a tax within the meaning of state statutes and constitutional provisions requiring that real estate taxes be assessed uniformly on all property within the municipality.

A special assessment is a fee imposed by the municipality on landowners to pay for improvements that disproportionately benefit those landowners. Historically, special assessments were imposed on only a subset of the municipality's landowners, but in recent years, some special assessments have been imposed on all municipal landowners. *See generally* Laurie Reynolds, Taxes, Fees, Assessments, Dues, and the "Get What You Pay For" Model of Local Government, 56 Fla. L. Rev. 373, 397–404 (2004).

Suppose residents of a particular neighborhood want the municipality to build storm sewers to relieve localized flooding conditions that arise during major storms. Holdout and free-rider problems might prevent neighborhood residents from making private arrangements to build the storm sewers. Residents might instead lobby municipal officials to install the sewers and then assess the landowners whose parcels abut the streets under which the municipality installs the sewers.

Would municipal residents be better off if state law prohibited special assessments and instead required municipalities to raise all revenue through general taxation? Consider the storm sewer hypothetical. Would municipal residents not affected by localized flooding be likely to support installation of the storm sewers if they were financed through general taxation? Why might their position change if the sewers were financed by a special assessment?

When a municipality imposes a special assessment, it can choose from a number of formulas for determining how much each benefited landowner should pay. The municipality might assess in proportion to the square footage of land benefited by the improvement, or it might assess in proportion to frontage on a street benefited by the improvement, or in proportion to the value of the benefited property. So long as the formula the municipality chooses has a rational basis, courts are unlikely to overturn the formula.

How was the impact fee imposed in *Ocean Springs* different from a special assessment? If the justification for authorizing special assessments rests on the holdout and free-rider costs that make it impossible for private parties to agree to improvements that benefit all of them, does the same justification apply when the municipality imposes a fee on a single private developer? Or is it more likely that the impact fee is designed to benefit residents other than those paying the fee? *See* Ronald H. Rosenberg, The Changing Culture of American Land Use Regulation: Paying for Growth With Impact Fees, 59 SMU L. Rev. 177, 216–220 (2006).

C. UNLAWFUL EXACTIONS

520 Victor Street Condominium Ass'n v. Plaza

Superior Court of New Jersey, Appellate Division, 2013
2013 WL 5525719

■ PER CURIAM.

Plaintiffs appeal from a judgment of the Law Division affirming the resolution of approval by Defendant, the Zoning Board of Adjustment ("Board") of the Township of Saddle Brook ("Township"), of an application for variances and development by Defendant, Mr. Raymond Plaza ("Plaza" or "the Applicant"). Plaintiffs raise numerous challenges to the Board's resolution, including its requirement of a $400,000 contribution by Plaza.

We conclude that the Board did not comply with *N.J.S.A.* 40:55D–42 or the pertinent Township ordinance when it required the $400,000 contribution. Accordingly, we reverse the Law Division's judgment in part, vacate the Board's approval of Plaza's application, and remand to the Board for reconsideration.

Plaza's 2006 application sought permission to develop three multi-story residential buildings on a property on Fifth Street in the Township. He amended his application to limit eighty percent of the condominium units to persons at least fifty-five years old. Plaza's application was opposed by Plaintiff 520 Victor Street Condominium Association ("Plaintiff"), which operated an adjacent multi-family residential development called Saw Mill Commons.

Plaza sought to build these condominium buildings in the Township's Industrial Zoning District, which did not permit multi-family residential housing. Accordingly, Plaza's application sought a use variance as well as other variances.

The Board conducted hearings on Plaza's application throughout 2007. On December 11, 2007, the Board voted to approve the application. On March 3, 2008, the Board adopted a Resolution of Approval, making findings on fact and conclusions of law. The Board granted a use variance and other variances, and approved the site plan. The Board made the approval subject to sixteen conditions, one of which was that Plaza make the $400,000 contribution.

Plaintiffs filed in the Law Division a complaint in lieu of prerogative writs, seeking to void the Board's resolution. On June 17, 2011, after a two-day trial, the judge issued an order for judgment with a lengthy opinion dismissing the complaint with prejudice and affirming the Board's actions, finding they were not arbitrary, capricious, or unreasonable. * * *

The $400,000 contribution raises the concerns that underlie the strict requirements of the [Municipal Land Use Law] ("MLUL") and Ordinance § 206–111. *See Nunziato v. Planning Bd. of Edgewater*, 225 *N.J.Super.* 124, 134 (App. Div. 1988) ("The intolerable spectacle of a planning board haggling with an applicant over money too strongly suggests that variances are up for sale."). First, those requirements are designed to "safeguard against municipal duress to procure otherwise unlawful exactions" from developers. *Toll Bros., supra,* 194 *N.J.* at 251. Second, the requirements recognize that "[a] developer's voluntary contribution to defray the cost of a municipal obligation, should not be permitted to influence or affect municipal zoning decisions." *Id.* at 250. Accordingly, courts must be "extremely sensitive to the threat presented by unlawful exactions imposed by a municipality on developers whether the developers are reluctant or enthusiastic participants in the transaction." *Ibid.*

The Law Division judge, after reviewing the record before the Board and listening to counsel's arguments, distinguished *Nunziato* and concluded that the $400,000 was not an improper offer and that the Board and Plaza "acted in good faith in negotiating this contribution." We need not determine the accuracy of that conclusion because the Board, in mandating the $400,000 contribution, did not comply with several key requirements of the MLUL and Ordinance § 206–111. *See Pond Run Watershed Ass'n v. Twp. of Hamilton Zoning Bd. of Adjustment*, 397 *N.J.Super.* 335, 361–64 (App. Div. 2008) (vacating a zoning approval because of an improper contribution even though "the parties had acted in good faith").

A.

First, the Board never determined that any sewerage and drainage improvements were "necessitated" by the proposed development. *N.J.S.A.* 40:55D–42; Ordinance § 206–111A(2)(a). Instead, the Board agreed with its engineer's opinion that:

> The Applicant has met or exceeded all existing, state, county and local requirements with regard to the provision of adequate sanitary sewer and water utility connections to the site. The Applicant has met an additional requirement to have no additional impact on the current drainage concerns in the neighborhood. The Applicant has met all State stormwater design requirements. Any continued flooding will not affect any of the residents in the neighborhood any worse than currently.

The Board further found that "the proposed development will not impact the flooding in the area," and noted that the increased sanitary sewer flow from the development would be de minimis for the area, and would not warrant a flow study. The Board's engineer testified that the development would have no negative impact on stormwater drainage, and that the Township had adequate sewer design capacity for the proposed development.

Instead of basing the contribution on the impact of the development, the Board justified the contribution primarily on preexisting flooding and sewage problems.

The Board's engineer . . . focused on the preexisting flooding and sewer problems in the area. He stressed that stormwater inflow, infiltration of ground water into deteriorating sewer lines, and sump pumps emptying ground water into the sanitary sewers had already caused "the failure of the sanitary sewer collection system." He stated that Plaza "has provided the necessary sanitary sewer capacity and public water capacity assurances but these do not resolve the localized flooding and inflow and infiltration sewer concerns experienced in the area during heavy rain events," which "is not a condition that was created by this applicant." He also detailed issues with the existing stormwater drainage system, which was affected by sediment buildup and prone to flooding.

To address the sanitary sewer problem, the Board's engineer recommended that Plaza construct an extension of the North Fifth Street pump station force main from Sylvan Street to Market Street, to eliminate three ninety-degree turns and "enable the force main to operate at peak capacity," at a total estimated cost of $275,000. To address the stormwater drainage problem, the engineer recommended that Plaza provide a "donation of $125,000 to the Township of Saddle Brook for the design and construction of 'future' stormwater improvements and stormwater maintenance activities." The Board determined that Plaza would not construct the sanitary sewer improvement, but instead:

> shall make a contribution of $400,000 to the Township of Saddle Brook for its pro rata share of off-site tract improvements, to include: (i) $275,000 to fund the design and construction of an off-site sanitary sewer improvement to provide for an extension of the North Fifth Street pump station force main from Sylvan Street to a point on the northern side of Market Street; and (ii) $125,000 for the design and construction of off-tract* stormwater improvements and stormwater maintenance activities.

---

*   Eds: New Jersey statutes define "off-tract" as "not located on the property which is the subject of a development application nor on the closest half of the abutting street or right-of-way." N.J.S.A. 40:55D–5.

These improvements were largely justified to fix the preexisting flooding and sewage problems.

The Board required Plaza to fund these improvements, moreover, even as it acknowledged the testimony of Plaza's expert that the development would alleviate rather than exacerbate the existing problems. Plaza's expert described how the development would reduce impervious coverage, restore the wetland buffer area, filter sediment, increase stormwater storage, and reduce stormwater flow. Plaza also offered to use a camera to inspect the sewers and water-jet them to remove sediment, increasing their capacity.

"[A] municipality may only demand contributions for off-tract improvements 'that [are] necessitated by the development itself, or [are] a direct consequence of the development." *Toll Bros., supra,* 194 *N.J.* at 244. Indeed, courts "have traditionally required a strong, almost but-for, causal nexus between off-site public facilities and private development in order to justify exactions." *Ibid.* "It follows that a planning board violates the MLUL when a condition unrelated to the needs generated by a development is imposed. . . ." *Id.* at 230. To the extent the Board required Plaza to fix preexisting problems and pay for repairs to the Township infrastructure not necessitated by the development itself, the Board's resolution "exceeds [its] authority under the MLUL and is therefore invalid." *N.J. Builders Ass'n v. Bernards Twp.,* 108 *N.J.* 223, 224 (1987).

We recognize that the Board need not "compute with precision" the extent to which off-tract improvements are a direct consequence of a development. *F & W Assocs. v. Cnty. of Somerset,* 276 *N.J.Super.* 519, 528–29 (App. Div. 1994). However, the Board failed to make any computation of the extent to which these improvements were necessitated by the development, rather than by the preexisting problems.

It is conceivable that replacing the warehouses currently occupying the property with a condominium complex containing a hundred or more residents might necessitate greater control over any flooding and sewage backups affecting the property. However, the Board made no findings that the development would itself be affected by flooding and sewage backup, or that the improvements to be funded by the $400,000 were necessary to prevent such impact on the development itself. The Board thus failed to establish the required "causal nexus between the conditions imposed and the needs created by the development." *Toll Bros., supra,* 194 *N.J.* at 246.

B.

Second, in ordering Plaza to pay "$125,000 for the design and construction of off-tract stormwater improvements and stormwater maintenance activities," the Board failed to "specify the off-tract improvements which are necessary," or to "specify[] . . . the estimated cost of" those improvements. Ordinance § 206–111A(2)(a), (b). The Board's engineer conceded that the choice had not yet been made which of the potential "future" stormwater improvements would be funded, and that he could provide no cost estimates for those improvements. The Board's lack of specificity regarding the "future" stormwater improvements, and the absence of proof of how the $125,000 contribution was calculated, violates Ordinance § 206–111, and fails to show that the unspecified improvements are "reasonable and necessary" under *N.J.S.A.* 40:55D–42. *See Pond Run, supra,* 397 *N.J.Super.* at 360.

C.

Third, the Board did not apply Ordinance § 206–111's "fair and reasonable standards to determine the proportionate or pro-rata amount of the cost of such facilities that shall be borne by each developer or owner within a related and common area." *N.J.S.A.* 40:55D–42. Rather, the Board simply found that Plaza's $400,000 contribution "is a fair and reasonable estimate of its pro-rata share . . . based upon the recommendations of the Board's Engineer and the [2004 and 2005] reports." As noted above, those reports predated Plaza's application, so they could not estimate the development's pro-rata share. The Board's engineer also did not estimate the pro-rata share of these improvements by allocating their total costs between Plaza and other owners of land who will benefit from the improvements. Neither the Board nor its engineer used the formulas specified in Ordinance § 206.111A(3)(d) to determine "[t]he applicant's proportionate share" for sewer, stormwater, or drainage improvements, or to "determine the pro-rata amount of cost to be borne by other owners of lands which will be benefitted by the proposed improvements."

Under the MLUL, it is "impermissible to saddle the developer with the full cost where other property owners receive a special benefit from the improvement." *Toll Bros., supra,* 194 *N.J.* at 245. Furthermore, the pro-rata shares of the developer and other landowners must be calculated both to "protect[ ] a developer from paying a disproportionate share of the cost of improvements that also benefit other persons," and "to insure that other landowners do not enjoy a free ride at the expense of another's toil." *Toll Bros., supra,* 194 *N.J.* at 244–45. We acknowledge that the municipality has a degree of flexibility in determining the cost of improvements. *Id.* at 245. However, the Board failed to apportion the costs between Plaza and other landowners benefitting from the improvements, and thus violated the MLUL and Ordinance § 206–111.

Thus, we find that the Board violated these requirements of the MLUL and the Township ordinance in requiring the $400,000 contribution. We therefore conclude that the $400,000 contribution is invalid.

We must next consider the effect of the invalidity of the contribution on the Board's approvals.

The Board's resolution provided:

In the event that any conditions are held to be invalid, unenforceable, or unlawful, the entire approval granted herein shall be unenforceable. It is the intent of the Board that the approval granted herein shall not be approved if any condition is invalid, and that the conditions are not severable from the approvals granted herein.

Therefore, we must vacate the Board's approval of Plaza's application.

Accordingly, we remand the matter for reconsideration by the Board, to make a new determination on the merits of Plaza's application. In making that determination, the Board may utilize the record generated in its 2007 hearings, with all parties having an opportunity to supplement that record to reflect any developments since December 11, 2007.

As noted above, there were indications in the reports and testimony of the Board's engineer that the proposed development would necessitate some off-tract improvements. Accordingly, we will permit the Board to reconsider whether any improvements are necessitated by the development, to receive additional evidence on such improvements, and to determine whether a contribution may be required, but it must do so only in strict compliance with *N.J.S.A.* 40:55D–42 and Ordinance § 206–111.

The Law Division's judgment is reversed in part, the Board's approval is vacated, and the matter is remanded to the Board for further consideration of Plaza's application in accordance with this opinion.

NOTES AND QUESTIONS

1. "Exactions" occur when a land use regulator conditions regulatory approval it has the discretion to grant or deny on the property owner's conveyance of some property interest to the government. That exacted property interest could take the form of a parcel of land for a park or sidewalk, an easement for utility rights of way, or the payment of cash for off-site improvements (or even for the municipality's general fund). Although not all exactions are unlawful, courts are suspicious of them, and some states have enacted statutes to regulate them. The formulations vary but, typically, exactions statutes require courts to scrutinize whether there is some reasonable connection between the likely impacts of a proposed development and the substance and scale of the exaction.

2. In its own series of "exactions" cases, Nollan v. California Coastal Commission, 483 U.S. 825 (1987), Dolan v. City of Tigard, 512 U.S. 374 (1994), and Koontz v. St. Johns River Water Management District, 133 S.Ct. 2586 (2012), the U.S. Supreme Court has constitutionalized a version of exaction review under the auspices of the Takings Clause of the Fifth Amendment. (For a more detailed discussion of this area of federal constitutional law, *see* Part I.G. of Chapter Five.) Despite this growing body of federal constitutional law, the states remain free to scrutinize exactions more closely than the Supreme Court has required. Because of the continued relevance of state law in this area, land use lawyers are wise to be attentive to it.

3. Notice who the plaintiffs were in this case. Why should neighbors have standing to object to the amount of money a developer is required to pay to the municipality to offset the impacts of development approval? Should it make a difference whether the neighbors are arguing that the municipality has demanded too much from the developer or should they only be able to argue that the municipality has demanded too little? Which argument are the neighbors making in this case?

4. The Court in *520 Victor Street* cites *Nunziato v. Planning Bd. of Edgewater,* 225 N.J.Super. 124, 134 (App. Div. 1988), a case in which the court referred to "[t]he intolerable spectacle of a planning board haggling with an applicant over money," which, in its view, "too strongly suggests that variances are up for sale." What are the dangers of permitting municipalities and developers from bargaining with one another over the terms of development approval? Are those dangers greater when the payment of money is involved than when the payment from the developer is through the in-kind dedication of property? *See* Lee Anne Fennell, Hard Bargains and Real Steals: Land Use Exactions Revisited, 86 Iowa L. Rev. 1, 17–41 (2000) (discussing some potential benefits of bargaining between land use regulators and developers).

5. If you were the counsel for the municipality, what sorts of arguments would you make on remand? In supplementing the record, what kinds of evidence would you present?

6. Apart from the law, what constrains the sorts of conditions municipalities are likely to impose on developers seeking regulatory approval? *See generally* Vicki Been, "Exit" as a Constraint on Land Use Exactions: Rethinking the Unconstitutional Conditions Doctrine, 91 Colum. L. Rev. 473 (1991).

II. VESTED RIGHTS

A. ESTABLISHING VESTED RIGHTS

Metro Dev. Comm'n of Marion County v. Pinnacle Media, LLC

Supreme Court of Indiana
836 N.E.2d 422 (2006), *aff'd on rehearing* 846 N.E.2d 654 (2006)

■ SULLIVAN, JUSTICE.

Pinnacle Media, LLC, seeks a declaration that a change in the zoning ordinance of the City of Indianapolis concerning billboard location permits is not applicable to its plan to erect 10 billboards in Indianapolis. Because no construction or other work that gave Pinnacle a vested interest in the billboard project had begun on the billboards at the time of the ordinance change, the ordinance change did apply to the 10 billboards.

Background

Pinnacle Media, LLC, erects and leases advertising billboards. In July, 1999, after some period of discussion, the City of Indianapolis advised Pinnacle in writing that the City's billboard location permit regulation did not apply with respect to billboards proposed to be erected in interstate highway rights-of-way because those rights-of-way were not covered by the City's zoning ordinance.

Pinnacle thereupon embarked on a plan to erect billboards without applying to the City for a permit. Its plan consisted of three steps. First, it would lease land for this purpose from Hoosier Heritage Port Authority, an entity that owned abandoned railroad rights-of-way at points where the abandoned railroad rights-of-way intersected with or were otherwise coextensive with interstate highway rights-of-way. Second, it would seek permits from State government, specifically, the Indiana Department of Transportation ("INDOT"), which is responsible for interstate highways. Third, it would erect the billboards without seeking any approval from the City. Following this plan, Pinnacle erected two billboards in 1999, after leasing rights-of-way and obtaining INDOT permits.

Shortly thereafter, Pinnacle initiated efforts to erect 15 additional billboards by securing additional leases and submitting additional applications to INDOT. The last of these applications was submitted on April 19, 2000. A period of negotiation with the State followed during which INDOT initially denied all 15 of the applications. Pinnacle appealed the denials and ultimately entered into a settlement with the State. Well over a year later, on June 18, 2001, INDOT approved 10 of the applications and Pinnacle abandoned its request for the other five in accordance with the settlement.

Meanwhile, following the erection of the two initial billboards, the City re-examined its policy in respect of excluding interstate highway rights-of-way from the coverage of its zoning ordinance. On April 26, 2000, the City officially proposed an amendment to this effect to its zoning ordinance. Pinnacle and other interested parties received notice of the proposed amendment on April 28, and were given the opportunity to appear at a public hearing on the matter on May 17. On July 10, 2000, the City–County Council enacted into law an amendment to the zoning ordinance, assigning zoning classifications to the previously un-zoned land occupied by interstate highways. Indianapolis/Marion County Rev.Code §§ 730–100 through –103. This had the effect of making the City's billboard location permit applicable to billboards proposed to be erected in interstate highway rights-of-way.

Following receipt of the INDOT approvals in 2001, Pinnacle began erecting one of the billboards. The City issued a stop work order on grounds that Pinnacle had not obtained the permit for the billboard required by the amended zoning ordinance. Pinnacle ceased construction and subsequently filed suit against the City, seeking a declaration that the amendment to the zoning ordinance was inapplicable to the 10 permits and that the stop work order was void and unenforceable. The City filed a motion to dismiss, which the trial court denied, and both parties subsequently filed for summary judgment. The trial court granted summary judgment in favor of Pinnacle and also concluded that Pinnacle was entitled to attorney fees because the City engaged in "frivolous, unreasonable, or groundless litigation." Appellant's App. at 9–10. The Court of Appeals affirmed the determination of the trial court that the amendment to the zoning ordinance was inapplicable to the 10 permits but reversed the trial court on the attorney fees issue. *Metro. Dev. Comm'n v. Pinnacle Media, LLC,* 811 N.E.2d 404, 414 (Ind.Ct.App.2004). We now grant transfer and reverse the judgment of the trial court.

Discussion

The question of whether Pinnacle's 10 billboards are subject to the 2000 zoning ordinance amendment implicates two disparate lines of Indiana cases. Both lines employ the term "vested rights" and generally stand for the proposition that a person's "vested rights" are protected against retroactive application of a change in law. But each line takes a quite different approach to defining or determining when a "vested right" exists, and these approaches can lead to different results.

The first line of cases arises under a zoning law principle called "nonconforming use." . . . The general rule is that a nonconforming use may not be terminated by a new zoning enactment. . . . In these situations, it is often said that the landowner had a "vested right" in the use of the property before the use became nonconforming, and because the right was vested, the government could not terminate it without implicating the Due Process or Takings Clauses of the Fifth Amendment of the federal constitution, applicable to the states through the Fourteenth Amendment. *See generally,* John J. Delaney and Emily J. Vaias, *Recognizing Vested Development Rights as Protected Property in Fifth Amendment Due Process and Takings Claims,* 49 Wash. U.J. Urb. & Contemp. L. 27, 31–35 (1996).

A relatively frequent subject of land use litigation is whether a developer can have a "vested interest" in a nonconforming use that is only intended—construction has not yet begun at the time of the new enactment—such that the government cannot terminate it. *See* Linda S. Tucker, Annotation, *Activities in Preparation for Building as Establishing Valid Nonconforming Use or Vested Right to Engage in Construction for Intended Use,* 38 A.L.R.5th 737, 752 (1996 & Supp. 2005).

As a general proposition, the courts have been willing to hold that the developer acquires a "vested right" such that a new ordinance does not apply retroactively if, but only if, the developer "(1) relying in good faith, (2) upon some act or omission of the government, (3) . . . has made substantial changes or otherwise committed himself to his substantial disadvantage prior to a zoning change." Delaney & Vaias, *supra,* at 31–35 (citing *Sgro v. Howarth,* 54 Ill.App.2d 1, 203 N.E.2d 173, 177 (1964)).

Indiana law, as enunciated in *Lutz,* is consistent with these principles. In that case, the developer acquired real estate pursuant to an option agreement that required the seller to demolish a house on the property and clear the lots for construction of a gasoline service station. The developer secured a mortgage commitment to finance the construction and entered into an agreement by which a petroleum concern would lease and operate the service station when built. After all of these actions had been taken but before construction of the service station itself began, the city enacted a zoning ordinance that did not permit the erection of gasoline service stations on the real estate in question. *Lutz,* 230 Ind. at 78–79, 101 N.E.2d at 189.

When the developer's application for a zoning variance was denied by the Board of Zoning Appeals, the developer appealed, contending that by entering into the lease and proceeding to convert the real estate to a service station prior to the passage of the zoning ordinance, his rights to use of the property in that way had become vested and that the application of the zoning ordinance to him was unconstitutional. *Id.* at 77, 101 N.E.2d at 188. The trial court affirmed the decision of the Board of Zoning Appeals, as did this Court:

> The zoning ordinance herein is, of course, subject to any vested rights in the property of appellants acquired prior to the enactment of the zoning law. But where no work has been commenced, or where only preliminary work has been done without going ahead with the construction of the proposed building, there can be no vested rights. The fact that ground had been purchased and plans had been made for the erection of the building before the adoption of the zoning ordinance prohibiting the kind of building contemplated, is held not to exempt the property from the operation of the zoning ordinance. Structures in the course of construction at the time of the enactment or the effective date of the zoning law are exempt from the restrictions of the ordinance. The service station was not in the course of construction so as to give to appellants vested rights, and was not a nonconforming use existing at the time of passage of the ordinance.

Id. at 81–82, 101 N.E.2d at 190.

The second line of cases traces its origin in Indiana law to zoning law but has over the years been invoked more generally when a person has an application for a government permit pending at the time a law governing the granting of the permit changes.

The lead case in this line illustrates the point. In *Knutson v. State ex rel. Seberger,* 239 Ind. 656, 160 N.E.2d 200 (1959) (on reh'g), this Court held that an application for approval of a subdivision plat was not subject to the provisions of a subdivision control ordinance enacted by a town council after the date on which the application was first filed.

The Court in *Knutson* said that "a municipal council may not, by the enactment of an emergency ordinance, give retroactive effect to a pending zoning ordinance thus depriving a property owner of his right to a building permit in accordance with a zoning ordinance in effect at the time of the application of such permit." *Id.* at 667, 160 N.E.2d at 201.

Knutson has been relied upon by the Court of Appeals in a number of cases for the proposition that a change in law cannot be applied retroactively in respect of a permit application on file with a permitting agency at the time of the change.

. . . *Lutz* and *Knutson* lie in uneasy tension with one another. If the land acquisition, demolition, and site preparation work in *Lutz* is not enough to establish a vested interest, how can it be that the mere filing in *Knutson* of a building permit (when, by definition, no construction has yet begun) is enough to do so? In the words of one commentator, "[i]t is difficult to see how the theoretically distinguishable concept of nonconforming use, protecting owners of developed property from the provisions of subsequently enacted zoning regulations, could logically be applied to protect a landowner who has only reached the stage of applying for a building permit." Roland F. Chase, Annotation, *Retroactive Effect of Zoning Regulation, in Absence of Saving Clause, on Pending Application for Building Permit,* 50 A.L.R.3d 596, 607 (1973, Supp. 2005).

Pinnacle argues adamantly that this is not a nonconforming use case for which *Lutz* is precedent but a permit application case controlled by *Knutson.* While for reasons we will set forth in a moment we think this is a nonconforming use case, we also think, at least in respect of building permits, the *Knutson* rule should be revisited.

To repeat, the Court in *Lutz* held that "[t]he zoning ordinance herein is, of course, subject to any vested rights in the property of appellants acquired prior to the enactment of the zoning law. But where no work has been commenced, or where only preliminary work has been done without going ahead with the construction of the proposed building, there can be no vested rights." *Lutz,* 230 Ind. at 81, 101 N.E.2d at 190. We think this is the correct rule for nonconforming uses, one that is the rule of most jurisdictions.

With respect to building permits, then, *Knutson*'s suggestion that having a building permit on file creates a vested right that cannot be overcome by a change in zoning law is overruled.

Regardless of *Knutson*'s viability, we do not believe its rule is available to Pinnacle in this case. While Pinnacle argues vehemently that this is not a nonconforming use case, we believe that it is properly analyzed under *Lutz*'s principles. When Pinnacle set out to erect the 10 (initially 15) billboards, there was no location permit required by the City. This is exactly the position the developer in *Lutz* was in when it started out to develop the gasoline service station. The question there—as we find it to be here—was whether, at the time of the change in the zoning ordinance, construction had proceeded on the project to the point that the developer had a vested interest. As discussed, the Court held that the construction had not. *Lutz,* 230 Ind. at 81, 101 N.E.2d at 190.

In this case, no construction of any kind had proceeded on the 10 billboards as of April 26, 2000, the date the ordinance change was officially proposed, or even July 10, 2000, the date it was enacted. Pinnacle does not present us with any argument that it made construction expenditures before the enactment of the zoning ordinance change.[6] Nor could it. It was not until 11 months later, June 18, 2001, that Pinnacle received the separate approvals required by the State.

Pinnacle argues that its filing of applications for permits with the State on April 19, 2000, immunized it from the City's zoning change but we see no basis in law or logic for this proposition. While we acknowledge that at times, state law can pre-empt local law, *see, e.g.,* Ind. Code § 36–1–3–5(a) (2005), Pinnacle provides us with no authority that there is state pre-emption here. Local government enjoys wide latitude from the State in land use regulation. Its authority includes "not only all powers granted it by statute, but also all other powers necessary or desirable in the conduct of its affairs." *Ind. Dep't of Natural Res. v. Newton County,* 802 N.E.2d 430, 432 (Ind. 2004) (quotations and citations omitted). And while here the City has imposed burdens in addition to those of the State for a party seeking to erect billboards in interstate rights-of-way, state law has not been frustrated by the city zoning ordinance. *See id* at 433. In other words, this is not a

---

[6]   *Compare with State ex rel. Great Lakes Pipe Line Co. v. Hendrickson,* 393 S.W.2d 481, 484 (Mo.1965). In *Hendrickson,* a public utility company had acquired land in a village for the purpose of installing a pumping station. After having been advised by the village that it had no zoning regulations, the utility had entered into a contract for the construction of the station. After the utility's contractors began work, the village enacted a zoning ordinance that restricted the erection of pumping stations. Before the ordinance was enacted, the utility had spent or committed itself to a total of over $64,000 in addition to the amount that it had paid for the land. *Id.* at 482–83. The court found that "[a] structure in the course of construction at the time of the enactment of the ordinance is protected as a nonconforming use, but mere preliminary work which is not of a substantial nature does not constitute a nonconforming use." *Id.* at 484. The court then held that because the utility had completed a portion of the structure and had obligated itself to a great extent of money before the zoning ordinance was passed, the utility had established a non-conforming use of the land for the purpose of a pumping station prior to the enactment of the ordinance and had a vested right thereto. *Id.*

case where anything the City has done interferes with State prerogatives. Furthermore, common experience tells us that permits and approvals from different agencies and levels of government are often required for a single project. Compliance with one agency's or level's requirements simply does not constitute compliance with another's.

Most telling in this respect is the fact that regardless of what the City's billboard location regulation was, or even whether it had one, Pinnacle would still have been required to obtain State approval for its project. State approval was in addition to, and not a substitute for, local approval. That being so, Pinnacle cannot use its compliance with State requirements as a substitute for compliance with local requirements.

Geisler v. City Council of Cedar Falls

Supreme Court of Iowa, 2009
769 N.W.2d 162

■ BAKER, J.

In 2004, Geisler purchased real estate located in the Overlay District of Cedar Falls, Iowa, for the purpose of developing an eight-unit apartment complex. In May of 2005, he submitted a site plan for redevelopment of the land to the Cedar Falls Planning and Zoning Commission. At the Commission's May 18, 2005, meeting, city planner Martin Ryan stated that the site plan met all the basic ordinance requirements. However, there was a large amount of resident opposition to the proposed development, and the Commission voted to deny approval of Geisler's site plan.

The regular Cedar Falls City Council meeting was held on May 23, 2005. At the meeting, the Council considered Geisler's proposed site plan. Several Overlay District residents expressed concerns about the plan, including the increase in traffic it would generate and the detrimental effect to single-family homes in the area. The Council denied the site plan under Cedar Falls City Ordinance No. 29–160(f) because it was "inconsistent with the character of the neighborhood due to architectural design . . . [and was] not of comparable scale and character in relation to adjoining properties." Under the ordinance in effect in May of 2005, the Council had the discretion to determine whether the site plan was compatible with surrounding buildings.

At the May 23, 2005, meeting, a motion also passed to discuss a temporary moratorium to study the issue of multi-family unit construction in the Overlay District. At the next City Council meeting on June 13, 2005, the City Council passed a resolution imposing a moratorium on all development or construction of multi-family housing in the Overlay District.

Also on this date, Geisler submitted a revised site plan to the City Department of Development. It was not processed in time to be discussed at the meeting. Later, on July 11, 2005, a city official refused to consider Geisler's revised site plan, effectively denying the project. After further study of a proposed zoning amendment, the City Council passed a resolution on December 12, 2005, down-zoning the Overlay District, prohibiting all development or construction of multi-family housing. Geisler did not resubmit the site plan after the enactment of the ordinance.

On June 22, 2005, Geisler filed a petition for writ of certiorari in the district court alleging that the City acted illegally by denying his site plan and subsequently passing the moratorium on development in the Overlay District. On July 25, 2005, the City filed a motion to dismiss Geisler's petition for lack of subject matter jurisdiction.

On February 6, 2006, the district court issued an order overruling in part and granting in part the City's motion to dismiss. The trial court overruled the City's motion with regard to denial of the site plan because the record was not sufficient to conclude the City denied the plan because it intended to impose a moratorium on development. The court granted the City's motion as to Geisler's claim that the City acted illegally in imposing the moratorium, ruling the City was within its legislative authority to do so. Subsequently, the City filed a motion for summary judgment on the remaining claim, which the court granted because the December 2005 ordinance that prohibited the project was under discussion at the time Geisler submitted his initial site plan in May 2005. Geisler appeals.

A.   *Legality of Moratorium.* A writ of certiorari will not lie against the City if it was exercising a legislative function at the time it enacted the moratorium; such actions are not reviewable by the courts. In enacting the moratorium until a revised zoning ordinance could be reviewed, the City was performing a traditional legislative function. To the extent Geisler disagrees with the City's exercise of this legislative function, his recourse is "review by the electorate at the next election." Stream v. Gordy, 716 N.W.2d 187, 192 (Iowa 2006).

B.   *Legality of Site Plan Denial.* In his original petition, Geisler also challenged the City's denial of his proposed site plan. There was a change in the Overlay District's zoning ordinance from the time Geisler submitted his project and it was denied in May of 2005, to the time the City's refusal to approve his site plan was reviewed by the district court. The district court granted summary judgment to the City on Geisler's claim that the City illegally denied his site plan. In granting the City's motion for summary judgment, the district court applied what has been referred to as the pending ordinance rule concluding that "at the time the site plan was denied there was pending concern, discussion and intention to amend the zoning ordinance and the site plan was denied for reasons that fueled the moratorium and zoning changes." Because the district court believed there was a pending ordinance at the time of Geisler's application, the court applied the new ordinance in effect at the time of the court's decision, which ordinance prohibited multi-family housing, and found the City's denial was appropriate. We must determine whether the district court was correct in applying the pending ordinance rule to Geisler's claim.

We have recognized two exceptions to the rule that the reviewing court applies the law in effect at the time of its review. First, a developer may acquire a vested right because of substantial expenditures made in reliance on the previously existing ordinance, thereby precluding application of the new ordinance. Second, a reviewing court will not apply a new ordinance if officials acted in bad faith by denying or delaying approval of a properly submitted and conforming site plan in order to alter a zoning ordinance to bar the prospective development.

We have previously discussed the substantial expenditure exception. In Quality Refrigerated Servs. Inc. v. City of Spencer, 586 N.W.2d 202 (Iowa 1998), we noted that an affected landowner may acquire vested rights under certain circumstances:

> The only vested right that a property owner may acquire is the right *to complete* the development of his property in accordance with his plans as of the effective date of the new ordinance. . . .

> To determine whether a property owner has acquired a vested right, we engage in a two-part analysis: (1) did the property owner make substantial expenditures toward the use in question prior to the zoning change; and (2) were the expenditures made by the property owner lawful.

Quality Refrigerated Servs., 586 N.W.2d at 206. We held that without the required building permit, the landowner's expenditures were illegal and, therefore, could not be relied upon to acquire a vested right. *Quality Refrigerated Servs.*, 586 N.W.2d at 207.

At the point when Cedar Falls rezoned Geisler's property, effectively stopping the project, no building permit had been issued. Because only expenditures made pursuant to a validly issued permit will support the vested rights exception, U.S. Cellular v. Bd. of Adjustment, 589 N.W.2d 712, 718 (Iowa 1999), Geisler had acquired no vested rights and cannot rely upon this exception.

We also discussed the bad-faith exception in *U.S. Cellular*. The Board of Adjustment for the City of Des Moines denied U.S. Cellular's request to construct a cell phone tower in an area that permitted such use but required a special permit. After the site plan's denial, the Board rezoned the area to prohibit the requested use. This court affirmed the ruling of the district court finding bad faith on behalf of the Board. To find bad faith, we required illegality of the denial coupled with an improper purpose.

In the context of a zoning decision, " '[a]n illegality is established if the board has not acted in accordance with a statute; if its decision was not supported by substantial evidence; or if its actions were unreasonable, arbitrary, or capricious.'" Perkins v. Bd. of Supervisors, 636 N.W.2d 58, 64 (Iowa 2001) (quoting Norland v. Worth County Comp. Bd., 323 N.W.2d 251, 253 (Iowa 1982)). In *U.S. Cellular,* we found that the application was denied without any legal justification even though it met all of the requirements of the then existing ordinance. U.S. Cellular, 589 N.W.2d at 718–19. We specifically noted that the Board's professed reasons for denial were not based on either the ordinance in effect at the time of application or the ordinance that was subsequently passed. *Id.* at 718. Further, the Board misrepresented both the facts allegedly supporting the application's original denial and the facts allegedly supporting the change in ordinance. *Id.* Under those circumstances, we found the Board's actions "patently illegal." *Id.*

Of course, not every erroneous denial of a permit is done in bad faith. The decisionmaker must act with an improper purpose for the denial to be in bad faith. *See id.* at 717. The Board's improper purpose in *U.S. Cellular* was illegally denying the application to produce a delay thereby giving the Board time "to enact the new ordinance prohibiting the requested use." *Id.* at 719.

Other states have discussed the issue of what constitutes an improper purpose in finding bad faith. Certain examples are clear, such as punishing a political opponent or denying a barber shop license to protect the decisionmaker's competing shop. Brady v. Town of Colchester, 863 F.2d 205, 216 (2d Cir. 1988); Wilkerson v. Johnson, 699 F.2d 325, 328–29 (6th Cir. 1983). Other examples are less clear. In New Jersey, the court found bad faith because, after concluding the change in the zoning ordinance seemed to bear no relation to public health, safety, morals, or general welfare and was arbitrary, it found the change was "for no other purpose than to preclude a use which for seventeen years has been lawful." Brown v. Terhune, 125 N.J.L. 618, 18 A.2d 73, 74 (N.J. 1941).

Courts have also found bad faith when municipalities attempt "to zone out a use" or stop a particular project. State ex. rel. Humble Oil & Refining Co. v. Wahner, 25 Wis. 2d 1, 130 N.W.2d 304, 311 (Wis. 1964). In *Humble Oil,* this conclusion was based upon the fact that "town officials were trying to keep one jump ahead of Humble and were attempting to change the rules after they had been hailed into court" by Humble. *Id.* From these cases it can be discerned that an improper purpose exists when a zoning authority adopts a new zoning regulation designed to frustrate a particular applicant's plans for development.

We find that the district court erred in relying on the pending ordinance rule rather than applying the legal principles set out in *U.S. Cellular.* Because the district court did not consider whether the site plan denial was done in bad faith, we remand the issue of bad faith to the district court to determine whether the City illegally denied the site plan and whether an improper purpose existed.

NOTES AND QUESTIONS

1. Why should a landowner ever acquire vested rights to develop in accordance with a particular zoning ordinance? When a municipality enacts an ordinance, the drafters will generally be unable to foresee all problems the ordinance might generate. Why shouldn't the municipality be able to react to a development proposal—which makes potential problems concrete—by changing the ordinance to protect the public?

2. *Substantial Expenditures.* What constitutes a "substantial expenditure" that would give rise to a vested right to complete the project? For most courts, the mere purchase or leasing of land in contemplation of a project is not sufficient. *See, e.g.*, Lutz v. City of New Albany Plan Comm'n, 230 Ind. 74, 101 N.E.2d 187 (1951). The initiation of construction, such as laying a foundation or installing pipes in the ground, is usually recognized as giving rise to vested rights. But courts will also look to other financial commitments, such as architectural fees, the purchase of equipment, or contracts that make the developer liable to third parties. For most courts, it is the financial scope of the investment, rather than the particular details of those expenses, that gives rise to the vested right. *See, e.g.*, Town of Hillsborough v. Smith, 276 N.C. 48, 170 S.E.2d 904 (1969). Under the Indiana Supreme Court's decision in the *Pinnacle* case, would a developer who spent a great deal of money to obtain a permit be able to argue that it had obtained vested rights by virtue of those expenses?

3. A claim of vested rights can arise whenever a municipality changes the land use regulations that apply to a particular project, whether they be zoning ordinances, building codes, subdivision or site-plan regulations, etc. Although each regulatory context raises its own particular line-drawing problems, state courts typically apply the same general standard in each context, asking whether the landowner has invested sufficient resources in the project to be entitled to lock in the prior regulatory regime. Is the Court's decision in *Pinnacle* consistent with this approach? Was the approach of the court in *Knutson* (discussed at length in the *Pinnacle* case)?

4. If vested rights doctrine is designed to protect substantial expenditures made by a developer in reliance on an existing ordinance, why should bad faith be relevant? So long as the developer has not yet made substantial expenditures, why shouldn't the municipality be entitled to amend the ordinance to block a particular project that has engendered community opposition?

5. How would you rate the likelihood that Geisler will succeed in showing bad faith on remand? If you were Geisler's lawyer, what facts would you point to in support of your argument that the city acted in bad faith?

6. *Vested Rights Statutes.* The outcome of the common law "substantial expenditures" vesting test can be very difficult to predict. In an effort to provide some clarity in a murky area of law, at least eighteen states have enacted legislation dealing with the question of vested rights. *See* J.

Spencer Hall, State Vested Rights Statutes, 50 Urb. Law. 451, 459 (2009). Of these, roughly half provide for vesting upon filing of a development application and roughly half provide for vesting upon receipt of some form of preliminary development approval. *See id.*; *see also* Brian K. Steinwascher, Statutory Development Rights: Why Implementing Vested Rights Through Statute Serves the Interests of the Developer and Government Alike, 32 Cardozo L. Rev. 265 (2010).

What justification is there for each approach? Which approach is preferable? In states that provide for vesting upon filing of an application, how should courts treat applications that are incomplete or otherwise deficient when filed?

7. *Subdivision Applications: When Do Rights Vest?* Because of its protracted nature, the subdivision process poses particular challenges for courts considering claims of vested rights. At what point in the lengthy subdivision process (described in Chapter Three) should a developer be protected against subsequent changes in the substantive law? When the sketch plan is submitted? *See* In re Champlain Oil Co., 176 Vt. 458, 852 A.2d 622 (2004) (sketch plan not sufficient). When the preliminary plat is submitted for review? *See* Rev. Code Wash. 58.17.033; Noble Manor Co. v. Pierce County, 133 Wash.2d 269, 943 P.2d 1378 (1997). When the preliminary plat is approved? *See* City of West Hollywood v. Beverly Towers, Inc., 52 Cal.3d 1184, 278 Cal. Rptr. 375, 805 P.2d 329 (1991) (preliminary plat approval vests where no further discretionary approvals are required and final approval is a ministerial act). When the developer begins to invest in satisfying the conditions for final approval? Upon final plat approval?

8. *Multi-Phase Projects More Generally.* Suppose a developer proposes a complex, multi-phase project under an existing zoning regime, obtains all of the required permits, but has only begun construction work on the first phase of the project when the zoning law is amended in ways that would detrimentally impact later phases of the project. Can the developer claim a vested right in the completion of the entire project, or just in the phase on which work has begun? What if work on the first phase included work on infrastructure that would benefit the project as a whole, including subsequent phases? Consider this discussion by the Third Department of New York's Appellate Division of the so-called "single integrated project theory":

> Pursuant to that theory an owner might acquire vested rights to a site where substantial construction had not been undertaken where the site is but a part of a single project and where, prior to the more restrictive amendment, substantial construction had been commenced and substantial expenditures had been made in connection with other phases of the integrated project which also benefited or bore some connection to the affected site.

Schoonmaker Homes-John Steinberg, Inc., Matter of v. Vill. of Maybrook, 178 A.D.2d 722, 576 N.Y.S.2d 954 (1991).

9. Suppose the developer of a large shopping center, shortly after obtaining a building permit, catches wind of public opposition to the project and learns that a resolution is pending in the city council to rezone his property for residential use. The developer then accelerates its construction schedule in order to break ground on the project before the city council can act on the resolution. Does the developer have a vested right? *See* Stowe v. Burke, 255 N.C. 527, 122 S.E.2d 374 (1961) (no).

10. Can a neighbor challenge a zoning board's conclusion that a developer has a vested right to proceed under a prior zoning ordinance? *See* Hale v. Bd. of Zoning Appeals, 277 Va. 250, 673 S.E.2d 170 (2009).

B. DETERMINING THE SCOPE OF VESTED RIGHTS

New Castle Investments v. City of LaCenter

Court of Appeals of Washington
98 Wash.App. 224 (1999)

■ BRIDGEWATER, C.J.

New Castle Investments (NCI) applied to the City of LaCenter for preliminary plat approval on April 7, 1996. Two days later, on April 9, LaCenter adopted its [transportation impact fee ("TIF")] ordinance, LCMC 17.07. LaCenter's TIF became effective on April 16.

A hearing on the preliminary plat was held before a city hearings examiner. The hearings examiner issued an order granting approval of the preliminary plat and found that LaCenter's TIF did not apply to the NCI's proposed development because it became effective after the preliminary plat application was perfected.

LaCenter appealed the hearings examiner's decision and a hearing was held before the LaCenter City Council. The Council affirmed the examiner's decision except with respect to his conclusion that the TIF did not apply, which the Council reversed.

NCI then appealed the Council's decision to the Clark County Superior Court. The court reversed the Council's decision and reinstated the hearings examiner's order, finding that the TIF did not apply to the development.

LaCenter appeals the superior court's order and seeks the reinstatement of the Council's order. Three amici curiae briefs have been filed in this case: (1) by the City of Vancouver and the Washington State Association of Municipal Attorneys; (2) by the Building Industry Association; and (3) by the Washington Cities Insurance Authority and the Cities of Battle Ground, Camas, and Washougal. For convenience, references made to the arguments of the City of LaCenter and the two amici briefs from the City of Vancouver, et al, and the Washington Cities Insurance Authority, et al, will be collectively attributed to "the Cities," and references made to the arguments of NCI or the Building Industry Association will be attributed to "the Developers."

The only issue in this case is whether the land use vesting statute, RCW 58.17.033, applies to TIFs assessed on new development. The vesting statute, RCW 58.17.033(1), provides:

A proposed division of land, as defined in RCW 58.17.020, shall be considered under the subdivision or short subdivision ordinance, and zoning or *other land use control ordinances,* in effect on the land at the time a fully completed application for preliminary plat approval of the subdivision, or short plat approval of the short subdivision, has been submitted to the appropriate county, city, or town official.

The resolution of this case depends upon the meaning of the phrase "land use control ordinances," which is not defined in the statute. Specifically, the issue is whether that term can be used to describe a fee used to pay for city facilities, such as traffic signals or a park, that may be indirectly impacted by new development. . . . The Cities assert that TIFs are not land use control ordinances because the Legislature never intended the vesting statute to apply to TIFs and because, as a tax, TIFs do not fall within the definition of land use control ordinance. The Developers contend that TIFs are land use ordinances and are not taxes.

The Developers claim that this case can be resolved simply by a plain reading of the statute. But the statute does not define "other land use control ordinances." The Developers assert that a TIF is a land use *control* ordinance because it is a land use ordinance. TIFs were authorized by the Growth Management Act (GMA), which regulates land use, and TIFs apply only to land use projects. But the Cities argue that a TIF does not "control" development, in the sense that it limits or changes the development in any way. TIFs do not exercise a restraining or directing influence over land use; they only increase the cost. Therefore, if we look only at the individual meaning of the word control, TIFs do not "control" land use. But the dictionary definition of one word does not decide this case, for our primary goal is to ascertain the Legislature's intended meaning of the term. * * *

The Cities contend that applying the vesting statute to TIFs would be contrary to legislative intent. The Cities believe that the Legislature did not intend that TIFs would be calculated until the building permit is issued.

The Legislature addressed the time for vesting of TIFs in the original version of the creating legislation.

(5) Notwithstanding any other provision of sections 43 through 48 of this act, that portion of a project for which a valid building permit has been issued prior to the effective date of a county, city, or town impact fee ordinance, adopted pursuant to sections 43 through 48 of this act, shall not be subject to impact fees under such ordinance so long as the building

permit remains valid and construction is commenced and is pursued according to the terms of the permit.

Laws of 1990, 1st Ex.Sess., ch. 17, § 45. (CP 128) Thus, the Legislature expressly stated that the impact fees vested upon the issuance of a building permit (rather than upon filing the application). Unfortunately for our purposes, this section was vetoed by the Governor for reasons unrelated to the time for vesting.[1] Nevertheless, the Cities argue that the presence of this provision within the original legislation shows that the Legislature did not intend TIFs to vest at the time of application.

The Developers contend that section five cannot be considered legislative intent because it was vetoed. The general rule is: "In exercising the veto power, the governor acts as a part of the legislative bodies and the act is to be considered now just as it would have been if the vetoed provisions had never been written into the bill at any stage of the proceedings." *Shelton Hotel Co. v. Bates,* 4 Wash.2d 498, 506, 104 P.2d 478 (1940). But in this case, the Governor's veto statement made clear that it was not section five that he objected to, but another section. The Governor's veto statement is a part of legislative intent. *State, Dep't of Ecology v. Theodoratus,* 135 Wash.2d 582, 594, 957 P.2d 1241 (1998). Therefore, section five is a reflection of legislative intent and it does indicate that the Legislature intended that TIFs vest at the time the permit is issued, rather than at the time of application.

At common law, "[t]he purpose of the vested rights doctrine [was] to provide a measure of certainty to developers and to protect their expectations against fluctuating land use policy." *Noble Manor Co. v. Pierce County,* 133 Wash.2d 269, 278, 943 P.2d 1378 (1997). The common law purpose is consistent with the Legislature's expressed purpose for the vesting statute. The Final Legislative Report on the bill enacting RCW 58.17.033 stated, in part, that the statute was intended to prevent a project from being "obstructed by enacting new zoning ordinances or building codes."

But although the vested rights doctrine was to protect developers, there are "important competing policy concerns regarding vested rights for land use":

> [D]evelopment interests protected by the vested rights doctrine come at a cost to the public interest because the practical effect of recognizing a vested right is to sanction the creation of a new nonconforming use. If a vested right is too easily granted, the public interest is subverted. * * *

Noble Manor, 133 Wash.2d at 280, 943 P.2d 1378. With these concerns in mind, it is important that the vested rights doctrine not be applied more broadly than its intended scope. The cost of a development, which

---

[1] The Governor objected to subsection one, which he felt would limit "substantive authority under the State Environmental Policy Act." Laws of 1990, 1st Ex. Sess, ch. 17, § 45, comments following act.

is the only aspect of development affected by TIFs, is a large part of the developer's decision making. Certainly it is to the developer's advantage if the cost can be determined early in the process and with some degree of certainty. But it does not necessarily follow that the cost of development is the type of expectation the vested rights doctrine was intended to protect.

At its core, a TIF is a fee charged to new development. The Court of Appeals has held in a somewhat different context that "it is inappropriate to apply the vesting doctrine to fees." *Lincoln Shiloh Assocs. v. Mukilteo Water Dist.*, 45 Wash.App. 123, 128, 724 P.2d 1083, 742 P.2d 177, *review denied*, 107 Wash.2d 1014 (1986). *Lincoln* held that there is no vested right to lower fees charged for connecting to a water system:

> Lincoln is not being forced to use its land or build differently from that which Lincoln was able to do at the time its plans were approved by the District. Instead, the cost is increased. Lincoln had no more than an expectation that the connecting charges would remain at $6,400. There is no vested right here to the connection fee remaining $6,400.

45 Wash.App. at 128–29, 724 P.2d 1083. Although the fees addressed in *Lincoln* are in a different category than TIFs, the reasoning in that case is equally applicable here.

Therefore, it would be inconsistent with the purpose behind the vested rights doctrine and the vesting statute to apply it to fees such as TIFs.

The Cities also argue that the definition of "land use control ordinance" does not reasonably include taxes, and that TIFs are taxes. The Developers dispute that TIFs are taxes, arguing instead that they are regulatory fees. Whether a charge imposed by a governmental entity is a tax or a regulatory fee depends upon three factors: (1) whether the primary purpose is to raise revenue (tax) or to regulate (regulatory fee); (2) "whether the money collected must be allocated only to the authorized regulatory purpose;" and (3) "whether there is a direct relationship between the fee charged and the service received by those who pay the fee or between the fee charged and the burden produced by the fee payer." *Covell v. City of Seattle*, 127 Wash.2d 874, 879, 905 P.2d 324 (1995).

In *Hillis Homes, Inc. v. Snohomish County*, 97 Wash.2d 804, 805, 650 P.2d 193 (1982), the court determined that county ordinances that impose fees on new residential subdivisions and housing proposals to fund public infrastructure are taxes rather than regulatory fees. * * *

Like the fees in *Hillis Homes*, there can be no question that the purpose of TIFs is to finance public facilities and system improvements, in other words, to raise revenue. Although these fees may have some land-use related objectives, such as ensuring orderly growth, these fees are not "merely tools in the regulation of land subdivision." *Hillis Homes,* 97 Wash.2d at 809, 650 P.2d 193. The primary purpose of the fees is to raise money. Under *Hillis Homes,* the determination that the purpose is fiscal is sufficient to support the determination that the fees are taxes.

TIFs also resemble taxes according to the other two *Covell* factors. TIFs serve a public purpose or to "pay for public facilities." RCW 82.02.090(3); RCW 82.02.050(1)(a). And there is no *direct* relationship between the fees charged and the particular development. Although impact fees must be "reasonably related" to the impact of new development on the public infrastructure, they are not individually calculated for each new development, but rather are based on a general calculation that applies to all new development.

But the Developers contend that TIFs are not taxes because, unlike taxes, there are restrictions placed on the handling and use of the money.[2] This argument is not persuasive. Similar restrictions were placed on the fees considered in *Hillis Homes,* yet the court still found them to be taxes. Also, the statute authorizing TIFs requires a nexus between the fee charged and the use made of the money, which the Developers argue is not the character of a tax. However, as the Cities point out, an even greater nexus requirement is placed on special assessment taxes, where the assessed property must be specially benefited by the improvements, as distinguished from a general benefit to the entire district. Thus, the nature of TIFs is not inherently inconsistent with their characterization as taxes.

But their resemblance to taxes is inconsistent with placing TIFs within the definition of "land use control ordinance." The placement of TIFs among tax statutes, rather than land use regulations, indicates that they are in a different category from other land use statutes. RCW 82.02.050 through RCW 82.02.090 (the "GMA Impact Fee Statute") was adopted as part of the GMA in 1990. But it was not placed in the RCW chapters governing land use control or development regulation; instead, it was codified among excise taxes in RCW 82.

We do not hold that these fees are taxes, but only that these fees do not fall within the vesting statute as "land use control ordinances." By their nature, TIFs are fees that augment tax dollars; they are another source of revenue for improvements that benefit the public in general, and they are not intended to regulate the particular development. Thus, we are satisfied through our analysis of the *Covell* factors and *Hillis Homes* that TIFs have characteristics that distinguish them from regulations. The statutory character of TIFs indicates that the impact

---

[2]   TIF fees must be retained in a special account (RCW 82.02.070); the interest must be spent only on system improvements (RCW 82.02.070); the funds must be spent in conformance with the municipality's growth management plan (RCW 82.02.070); and the funds must be spent within five years of collection or be returned to the payor (RCW 82.02.080).

fee is in a different category from other land use statutes and does not fall within the definition of "land use control ordinance."

The TIFs do not affect the physical aspects of development (i.e., building height, setbacks, or sidewalk widths) or the type of uses allowed (i.e., residential, commercial, or industrial). If they did, then TIFs would be subject to the vested rights doctrine. In other words, "[the developer] is not being forced to use its land or build differently from that which [the developer] was able to do at the time its plans were approved. . . . Instead, the cost is increased." *Lincoln Shiloh Assoc.,* 45 Wash.App. at 128, 724 P.2d 1083. To freeze the calculation of the impact fee at the time of application would disconnect planning and financing from the actual effects of growth. The Legislature has stated that the indirect effects of growth can be recovered. If the fee were frozen, then new growth could take place without the developer paying its fair share for improving public facilities. The developer could be paying an impact fee that reflects a planning effort and a cost that is no longer relevant. The TIFs must be calculated when the growth is to occur, at the time of the building permits; otherwise cities would be underfunded to pay for the indirect costs of new growth.

Because TIFs do not "control" land use, do not affect the developer's rights with regard to the physical use of his or her land, and are best characterized as revenue raising devises rather than land use regulation, we hold that the definition of "land use control ordinances" does not include TIFs. This holding is consistent with legislative intent and public policy behind the TIF and the vesting statute. The vesting statute does not apply to TIFs.

Reversed.

NOTES AND QUESTIONS

1.   Could you imagine an impact fee that would also operate as a "land use control" in the sense of aiming to channel development in preferred directions?

2.   *Subdivision Approvals:* Suppose landowner applies to subdivide her parcel into 50 separate lots in preparation for development. Landowner has received both preliminary and final subdivision approval.

   a.   Before the landowner sells off any of the parcels, the municipality rezones the area to increase minimum lot size, making it unlawful to build on any of the 50 subdivided lots. Will the developer be successful if she challenges application of the zoning amendment to her parcel?

   b.   Instead of increasing minimum lot size, the municipality decreases the permissible FAR on all lots in the area from 0.5 to 0.35. Will the developer be successful if she challenges application of the amendment to her parcel?

Is there any reason to treat (a) differently from (b)?

3. Suppose that, after a developer has obtained development approval and expended substantial resources preparing a site for construction, a municipality dramatically increases its property taxes in a way that would render the development unprofitable for the developer. Should the doctrine of vested rights protect the developer against such non-regulatory changes?

C. TERMINATING VESTED RIGHTS

Fountain Village Development Co.
v. Multnomah County
Court of Appeals of Oregon, 2001
176 Or.App. 213, 31 P.3d 458

■ HASELTON, P. J.

In 1985, the landowner constructed a concrete bunker for the purpose of growing marijuana plants on 38 acres in east Multnomah County. At that time, the property was zoned for Multiple Use Forest (MUF). MUF zoning permitted a dwelling on a parcel of 38 acres or more.

The owner began construction of a log cabin on top of the bunker sometime before March 1987. Because the owner lacked a building permit for the construction, Multnomah County issued a "stop work order." By March 10, 1987, the landowner applied for, and was issued, a building permit for the log cabin construction. Work on the cabin continued, but it was not finished. After 1987, there was no further construction, and there were no further expenditures toward construction. In 1991, a renewed building permit issued, but no construction was undertaken under the renewed permit. LUBA [eds.— the Land Use Board of Appeals] characterized the 1987 permit as having expired.

In 1992, federal agents found marijuana on the property and subsequently seized the property, apparently because it was purchased with the proceeds of illegal drug trafficking. Multnomah County then acquired title to the property. On January 7, 1993, the county changed the zoning from MUF to Commercial Forest Use (CFU). In the CFU zone, a single-family dwelling is a conditional use, not an outright permitted use. MCC 11.15.2050(B). The effect of the zone change was that a person who sought to build a dwelling on the property would have to obtain specific permission for the dwelling subject to county conditions.

The former landowner reacquired the 38-acre property, and, in a series of transactions in 1993 and 1994, the present petitioner, Fountain Village Development Company, purchased it. Petitioner paid some $25,000 for the two-acre portion upon which the cabin is sited. In 1994, the county approved a lot line adjustment that reduced the portion of the property housing the cabin to 2.96 acres. The remainder of the property was sold.

In 1995, petitioner spent some $3,000 to clear soil off the bunker, construct a road to the site, and hire an engineer to review the integrity of the uncompleted log cabin. Petitioner made no efforts to complete the cabin for occupancy because interest rates for second-home loans were then unfavorable. Between 1995 and 1998, petitioner cleared brush, replaced broken windows, and maintained the roof, but did not perform any work to complete the cabin. Petitioner applied for a loan to complete the cabin in 1998 when interest rates fell.

On September 24, 1999, petitioner asked the county for a legal status determination regarding the cabin. The county issued an administrative decision, which concluded that petitioner had no vested right to complete and use the cabin. The administrative decision treated the residential use as a nonconforming use and said the use had been abandoned or discontinued under the county code. The decision relied on MCC 11.15.8805(B), which provides:

> If a non-conforming structure or use is abandoned or discontinued for any reason for more than two years, it shall not be re-established unless the resumed use conforms with the requirements of this code at the time of the proposed resumption.

Petitioner sought review before a hearing officer. The hearing officer considered the matter and concluded that any vested right to complete and use the cabin as a nonconforming use had been abandoned or discontinued. Petitioner took the matter to the Board of Commissioners, which affirmed the hearing officer's decision.

Before LUBA, petitioner attacked the county's application of its code provisions addressing abandonment and discontinuance of a nonconforming use. Petitioner asserted that the county code could not possibly be applied to its circumstance because the code at MCC 11.15.8805 governs "uses," and, in this case, no "use" had been established. In other words, to petitioner, a vested right to complete a use is not a nonconforming use and could not be treated as such.

In the alternative, petitioner argued that, because the county code expressly provides that "a nonconforming structure or use may be maintained with ordinary care," MCC 11.15.8805(C), the county could not conclude that petitioner had lost its vested right through abandonment or discontinuance. Petitioner also contended that the county's ostensible reliance on a "substantial effort" standard for discontinuance was erroneous as inconsistent with the "ordinary care" language of MCC 11.15.8805(C). Petitioner also pointed to facts showing that it maintained the cabin during the same years that the county relied on in finding that the use had been abandoned or discontinued.

LUBA did not address whether petitioner, in fact, had a vested right in completing and using the cabin. Rather, LUBA concluded that, even assuming that such a vested right had ever existed: (1) It could be lost in the same manner as nonconforming use—i.e., through abandonment or discontinuance, MCC 11.15.8805(B); and (2) substantial evidence supported the county's finding of discontinuance.

LUBA's fundamental holding is that "vested rights, like nonconforming use rights, may be lost where the holder fails to diligently exercise those rights." By extension, LUBA rejected petitioner's assertion that the only restrictions applicable to continuance of a vested right are equitable defenses, such as laches. Indeed, LUBA observed that it would be incongruous to confer greater protection on the vested right to create a use than on the eventual use itself.

Petitioner argued, nonetheless, that abandonment requires proof of an intent to abandon the putative use, and that here there was no evidence of such an intent. Petitioner pointed specifically to its maintenance of the unfinished structure from 1995 to 1998, and asserted that it was reasonable to delay finishing the cabin because of unfavorable interest rates at the time. That determination did not end the matter, however, because MCC 11.15.8805(B) provides that a nonconforming use may be lost by *either* abandonment *or* discontinuance and, while the former requires proof of intent to relinquish a known right, the latter does not. Consequently, LUBA next considered whether the petitioner's failure to continue development of the cabin resulted in loss through "discontinuance."

In that regard, petitioner argued that its maintenance of the cabin precluded any finding of discontinuance. LUBA rejected that argument and, in doing so, apparently sustained the county's determination that there was a "discontinuance of substantial effort to finish the development" over the requisite two-year period:

> According to petitioner, because MCC 11.15.8805(C) allows a nonconforming use or structure to be "maintained with ordinary care," such maintenance during a period of time negates a finding of discontinuance during that period. We disagree. The county's decision views a vested right to complete a partially completed building to be lost if there is "discontinuance of substantial effort to finish the development" over the requisite two-year period. There is no dispute that petitioner's actions in maintaining the site over the period 1995 to 1998 did nothing to finish the development.[7]

---

[7] LUBA also rejected petitioner's contention that it was reasonably justified in deferring completion of the structure because of disadvantageous interest rates. In so holding, LUBA emphasized that MCC 11.15.8805(B) provides that a nonconforming use that is discontinued *"for any reason"* for more than two years cannot be resumed unless it conforms with the county zoning ordinance.

On review, petitioner reiterates its arguments before LUBA. We begin with petitioner's core contention that statutes and local laws governing nonconforming uses do not apply to vested rights generally, much less to petitioner's circumstances specifically.[8]

Petitioner asserts, in effect, that if the legislature had wanted to include vested rights within the scope of the laws governing nonconforming uses, it could have, and would have, said so explicitly. Instead, in petitioner's view, the legislature enacted "vesting statutes" that give landowners a right to develop their property under regulations existing when the right vested. As an example of such a "vesting statute," petitioner points to ORS 215.427(3), which requires that, in certain circumstances, approval or denial of a land use application "shall be based upon the standards and criteria that were applicable at the time the application was first submitted." Thus, in petitioner's view, as long as a vested right has not been realized through actual use (here, the completion of the cabin), it is not subject to nonconforming use treatment.

We reject petitioner's proposed mutually exclusive dichotomization of "vested rights" and "nonconforming uses." Nothing in Oregon's case law or statutes precludes subjecting vested rights to develop property to the same limitations that apply to nonconforming uses generally—and, indeed, as addressed below, not to do so would yield incongruous results. Just as the regulation of existing nonconforming uses is a matter within a county's authorized land use purview, so too is the regulation of vested rights to develop—which are, in effect, inchoate nonconforming uses.

In *Milcrest Corp. v. Clackamas County,* 59 Or. App. 177, 650 P.2d 963 (1982), a developer had sought approval of a planned unit development and had made expenditures and performed work toward completion of that project. The county's new comprehensive plan made the development nonconforming. We concluded that the developer had, as a result of its actions, "acquired a vested right *in* a nonconforming use." *Milcrest,* 59 Or. App. at 181, 650 P.2d 963 (emphasis added). We also found, given the facts, that the developer did not abandon its right by applying for and obtaining approval of a revised planned unit development.

One final, practical consideration buttresses our conclusion that LUBA was correct in concluding that vested rights may be lost by abandonment or discontinuance. As LUBA observed:

> We can conceive of no reason why a vested right should be treated more favorably than a nonconforming use with respect to the duration of that right or the requirement for diligent exercise. If petitioner's view were correct, the holder of a

---

[8]   In so framing our analysis, we imply no view as to whether petitioner ever had a vested right to build and complete the cabin.

vested right is in a considerably more secure position than the holder of a nonconforming use, even though the latter may have invested far more capital to complete the use, and may have more to lose if that use is terminated. Further, under petitioner's view, the holder of a vested right can allow the land or structure to sit idle for an extended, perhaps unlimited, period of time, while the owner of a nonconforming use must employ the land or structure even under adverse economic conditions, to avoid loss of that right through discontinuance.

We agree with LUBA that there is no reason to afford the "inchoate" entitlement to a use greater protection from loss than the actual use would ultimately enjoy.

Notwithstanding that conclusion, a remand is required. LUBA does not appear to have addressed petitioner's threshold argument that the applicable standard, if any, is "ordinary care" and not "substantial efforts" to complete. MCC 11.15.8805(C) provides that a "nonconforming structure or use may be maintained with ordinary care." Conversely, neither ORS 215.130 nor MCC 11.15.8805 uses the term "substantial efforts." We do not understand LUBA to have explained why "ordinary care" is not the controlling standard or why—given the appropriate relationship between subsections (B) and (C)—"substantial efforts" can or should be the standard. Because that question is central to the inquiry, we remand to LUBA to, at a minimum, explain why "substantial efforts" and not "ordinary care" is the controlling standard for purposes of loss of a vested right pursuant to MCC 11.15.8805.

NOTES AND QUESTIONS

1.   Do you agree with the Oregon Court of Appeals that the doctrines of vested rights and prior nonconforming uses are addressed to the same fundamental issue? If you think the two situations are different, which sort of claim (a claim of vested right or of a prior nonconforming use) do you think is entitled to greater solicitude from the courts?

2.   The court in *Fountain Village* remanded the case to the LUBA to determine which standard should be applied to the determination whether a "vested right" or "prior nonconforming use" has been abandoned. The two options it identified were "ordinary care" and "substantial efforts." Which standard should the LUBA apply? Would it make sense to apply the "ordinary care" standard to a claim for vested rights?

3.   Why shouldn't passage of time without completion itself be sufficient to cause a loss of vested rights? In the subdivision review context, some statutes provide that approval of a subdivision insulates the lots in the subdivision from the effect of a subsequently enacted ordinance increasing minimum lot size or setback requirements only for a specific period of time (e.g., three years). *See, e.g.,* N.Y. Vill. L., § 7–709. Does that approach make sense? Should it be limited to the subdivision context? Why or why not?

4. Why protect vested rights and prior nonconforming uses at all? Why not simply apply existing law to all existing and planned land uses? For one argument that we should not provide any special protection to existing land uses or vested rights, *see* Christopher Serkin, Existing Uses and the Limits of Land Use Regulations, 84 NYU L. Rev. 1222 (2009).

III. ZONING ESTOPPEL

West End Citizens Association v. District of Columbia Bd. of Zoning Adjustment

District of Columbia Court of Appeals, 2015
112 A.3d 900

■ GLICKMAN, ASSOCIATE JUDGE:

This is round two in an appeal by the West End Citizens Association ("WECA") of a Certificate of Occupancy ("C of O") granted to intervenor, Foggy Bottom Grocery, LLC. Intervenor does business under the name FoBoGro. The C of O allowed FoBoGro to operate a grocery in a residentially zoned neighborhood of the District of Columbia known as Foggy Bottom. In round one, the Board of Zoning Adjustment ("BZA") concluded that the proposed grocery business would not constitute an improper expansion of a nonconforming use and therefore upheld the C of O. This court reversed that decision. On remand, the BZA again rejected WECA's appeal of the C of O, this time on equitable estoppel grounds. Before us now is WECA's petition for review of that determination. For the reasons that follow, we affirm.

I.

The building at the center of this controversy is a three-story row house located at 2140 F Street, N.W. It has been the site of a grocery store since 1946. The operation of that grocery on one floor of the building has been a lawful nonconforming use in a residentially zoned area since at least May 12, 1958, when the modern zoning map became effective.

In 2008, FoBoGro became interested in acquiring and modernizing the grocery business there. Before doing so, it applied for a new C of O to allow the entire building to be used for a grocery store and what its application referred to as a "sandwich shop." The Zoning Administrator approved the application and issued the requested C of O on August 21, 2008. The C of O provided that the total area of the building that could be devoted to the approved uses was 1,835 square feet, which encompassed all three floors. After receiving this C of O, FoBoGro purchased the business, leased the building from George Washington University, and eventually began renovating the property.

WECA did not learn of FoBoGro's August 2008 C of O until around August 2009. It then complained to the Zoning Administrator that the C of O improperly expanded a nonconforming use in two respects: by allowing the operation of a grocery to expand from one floor of the building to all three floors, and by permitting the operation of a sandwich shop at the location in addition to a grocery. In response to WECA's complaints, the Zoning Administrator sent a revocation notice to FoBoGro on October 14, 2009. "Because you changed the prior use of the Property in your application by the adding of a proposed 'sandwich shop use,'" the notice stated, "the C of O . . . was issued in error." The notice did not cite the alleged expansion of the grocery store use from one to three floors as a basis for revocation.[1]

FoBoGro opposed the threatened revocation. It explained that it merely intended to sell sandwiches and other prepared foods for off-premises consumption only, as a component of its grocery business. This explanation satisfied the Zoning Administrator that no expansion of the nonconforming use was planned. On November 4, 2009, he issued a new C of O to FoBoGro to replace the August 2008 C of O. The new C of O continued to permit a grocery business to be conducted in the 1,835 square foot space at 2140 F Street. The only differences were that it described the authorized use as including an "accessory prepared food shop" instead of a "sandwich shop," and it stated explicitly that the approved occupancy comprised three floors of the building.

WECA promptly appealed the November 2009 C of O to the BZA. It contended that the C of O impermissibly expanded the existing nonconforming grocery use by permitting FoBoGro to use the entire building in the grocery business instead of only one floor, and by permitting the operation of an accessory prepared foods shop. FoBoGro disputed these contentions and asserted affirmative equitable defenses of laches and estoppel.

After a hearing at which the Zoning Administrator and other witnesses testified, the BZA rendered its initial decision in this case. It ruled that the C of O did not authorize an impermissible expansion of the nonconforming grocery store use, because that use had not been limited in the past to only one floor of the building, and because the incidental sale of prepared food for off-site consumption was part of the grocery business. The BZA therefore denied WECA's appeal of the C of O without finding it necessary to address FoBoGro's equitable defenses.

WECA sought review in this court. In an unpublished memorandum opinion, we affirmed the BZA's determination that the sale of prepared food was encompassed in the grocery use. We held, however, that the nonconforming grocery use at 2140 F Street had been

---

[1]   Although prior C of O's had authorized use of the first floor as a grocery store without mentioning the other two floors of the building, the Zoning Administrator determined that those other floors always had been utilized to provide storage and office space for the grocery. This was permissible in the Zoning Administrator's view because C of O's for commercial establishments typically did not mention parts of the premises that were not open to the public. The Zoning Administrator therefore concluded that FoBoGro's use of the floors in its grocery business did not constitute an expansion of the nonconforming use of the premises, even though FoBoGro planned to repurpose the floors for retail use.

limited by the terms of earlier C of O's to one floor of the building, and that it was improper for the November 2009 C of O to permit the expansion of such use to the rest of the building. We remanded the record to the BZA for it to consider three remaining issues: the timeliness of WECA's appeal of the Zoning Administrator's approval of the expanded grocery use, and FoBoGro's laches and estoppel defenses to the revocation of its C of O.

In its decision on remand, the BZA ruled that FoBoGro had forfeited a challenge to the timeliness of WECA's appeal and had not established a laches defense. The BZA concluded, however, that FoBoGro's equitable estoppel defense to revocation of its C of O was meritorious. Accordingly, the BZA dismissed the remaining portion of WECA's appeal.

II.

Because of the public interest in enforcement of the zoning laws, stringent conditions are placed on the assertion of an equitable estoppel defense against the government, and "its application is limited to situations when the equities are strongly in favor of the party invoking the doctrine." [*Sisson v. District of Columbia Bd. Of Zoning Adjustment*, 805 A.2d 964, 972 (D.C. 2002).] Thus, as the BZA correctly recognized, we typically have said that to make out a case of estoppel, a party must show that "(1) acting in good faith, (2) on affirmative acts of [the zoning authority], (3) he made expensive and permanent improvements in reliance thereon, and (4) the equities strongly favor him." [*Id.*] For the equities to favor the party claiming an estoppel, any injury to the public that would flow from the non-enforcement of the zoning law must be minimal and outweighed by the injury estoppel would avoid.[8]

The BZA concluded the requirements of equitable estoppel were satisfied in this case because it found that (1) the Zoning Administrator's 2008 C of O permitted the entire building to be used for the operation of a grocery; (2) FoBoGro proceeded reasonably and in good faith, having no reason to believe the 2008 C of O impermissibly expanded the nonconforming grocery use; (3) FoBoGro relied on the 2008 C of O by spending "considerable sums" to purchase the grocery business, lease the building, enter into various contracts, renovate the building, and incur other business expenses; and (4) the equities favored FoBoGro, because of its good faith and objectively reasonable

---

[8]   We note that an estoppel of government action to enforce the zoning laws does not necessarily foreclose private enforcement of rights under those laws—for example, where an adjoining property owner whose "interest is distinct from and greater than that of the community as a whole" complains in a timely manner of special damages attributable to an erroneously issued building permit or C of O. *Garrou v. Teaneck Tryon Co.*, 11 N.J. 294, 94 A.2d 332, 335 (1953). The availability of private relief when the government is estopped from revoking a permit or a C of O, or from otherwise enforcing the zoning laws, is a question our court has yet to resolve or examine in detail. Given the absence of any convincing showing of prejudice to WECA, as we discuss below, we conclude in the present case only that the BZA permissibly relied on estoppel principles to foreclose WECA's challenge to the issuance of the 2009 C of O to FoBoGro.

reliance on the 2008 C of O, and because the BZA found "no evidence" that the neighborhood would be harmed by the continued operation of "a grocery store that has been a neighborhood institution for over 60 years."

WECA's principal argument on appeal is that FoBoGro "could not have relied justifiably or reasonably" on the 2008 C of O when it incurred the bulk of its renovation expenses, because it did so *after* WECA commenced its attack on the C of O in August 2009.[10] But as the BZA appreciated, FoBoGro relied on the 2008 C of O to its considerable financial detriment in other ways well before it learned of WECA's challenge to the legality of its C of O, for example by purchasing the grocery business and entering into a lease of the building. Although our cases in the zoning context have focused on whether the party invoking estoppel made expensive and permanent improvements in reliance on the erroneous governmental decision, we see no reason in principle why other forms of reliance cannot equally support an estoppel. Any error by the BZA in taking FoBoGro's renovation costs into account strikes us as surely inconsequential.

Furthermore, contrary to WECA's contention, the BZA's finding that FoBoGro acted in good faith is not undermined by the fact that its principal (Mr. Hart) identified himself as the business owner in the application for the 2008 C of O before FoBoGro actually purchased the grocery. This fact was not concealed and there is no indication that the Zoning Administrator was misled in any way or that WECA or any other party was prejudiced by the irregularity.

Finally, regarding the BZA's assessment of the competing equities, WECA disagrees with the finding that the expansion of the nonconforming grocery store use from one to three floors will not harm the surrounding neighborhood. WECA appears to complain that the BZA failed to address its claims of prejudice. However, WECA does not even attempt to demonstrate that the BZA's finding lacks substantial support in the record, nor does it point us to evidence of any actual harm flowing from the grocery store operation. WECA's expressed concerns about possible adverse effects on the area's tranquility, traffic, and property values were speculative and unsubstantiated. In our view, the BZA's dismissal of those concerns—it found "no evidence" of harm and stated that "[i]n fact, WECA has never argued that it has been harmed in any way by the operations of the grocery store"—was within the ambit of its discretion as fact finder.

In sum, we are not persuaded that the BZA materially erred in finding on the record before it that FoBoGro satisfied all the requirements for an equitable estoppel of the revocation of its C of O. We likewise are not persuaded that the BZA misunderstood or

---

[10] FoBoGro was not issued a building permit authorizing renovations until August 16, 2009, and construction at the property did not begin until late September or early October 2009.

misapplied the law, that it acted arbitrarily or capriciously, or that it abused its discretion. Accordingly, we uphold the determination that FoBoGro established its estoppel defense and affirm the BZA's order of December 8, 2014, dismissing the remainder of WECA's appeal of the November 2009 C of O issued to FoBoGro.

So ordered.

Town of West Hartford v. Rechel

Supreme Court of Connecticut, 1983
190 Conn. 114, 459 A.2d 1015

■ PETERS, J.

The principal issue in this case is whether a municipality can be estopped from enforcing its zoning regulations because of a longstanding pattern of conduct permitting unauthorized uses of private property. The plaintiff town of West Hartford, acting by its building inspector, Edward A. Dombroskas, sued to enjoin the defendants Joseph P. Rechel and Shirley T. Rechel from operating two rooming houses in the town. After a court trial, a permanent injunction was issued, from which the defendants have appealed.

The underlying facts found by the trial court in its memorandum of decision are essentially undisputed. The two properties owned by the defendants are located at 55 Highland Street and 739 Prospect Avenue, in an area zoned by the town of West Hartford as an R–10 district, which is a one-family residential district. In such a district, rooming or boarding houses are permitted only as accessory uses, if the owner uses the premises as his own residence and limits the number of roomers to three or less. Rooming houses as main uses, without an owner in residence, are now and have been, since at least 1925, totally forbidden. Even as accessory uses, rooming houses require appropriate town licenses. These zoning regulations, although adopted in their present form in 1968, do not vary materially from regulations first adopted in 1945. Before 1945, rooming houses were permitted as accessory uses without any limit on the number of roomers who might share the houses with their resident owners.

The history of the disputed properties reveals that, prior to 1941, they were used for single-family purposes. At some time during the early 1940s, both properties were converted into rooming houses, in which substantial numbers of boarders received room and board, with the owner retaining an apartment on the premises. Thereafter, the properties became rooming houses without an owner in residence, and were so operated by the defendants, who bought the house on Highland Street in 1962 and the other, on Prospect Avenue, in 1965.

From 1949 to 1967, the town issued rooming house licenses to the defendants and their predecessors in title. Despite the receipt of properly submitted applications for subsequent years, the town refused thereafter to take any action to issue further licenses. The building inspector wrote the defendants in 1969 to inform them that their rooming houses, since they rented to more than three roomers, were not allowable uses in the town. The following year, however, town corporation counsel gave a formal opinion that the defendants' properties, because of their history of continuing use as boarding houses, qualified as legal nonconforming uses. Despite that opinion, the town brought the present lawsuit in 1975.

The trial court, upon reviewing this finding of facts, came to the following conclusions of law. The properties were not, and never had been, operated as legal accessory uses. When first converted to rooming house use, the number of boarders was so disproportionate to the residential uses of the principal occupants that the uses did not qualify as accessory uses. Furthermore, even if the early uses had been accessory in nature, they had thereafter lost their accessory character by abandonment. The defendants, having themselves never resided on the properties and having operated them as businesses for the generation of income from roomers, could no longer rely on the prior uses. After abandonment, a prior legal use is lost and cannot be revived. Blum v. Lisbon Leasing Corp., 173 Conn. 175, 181, 377 A.2d 280 (Conn. 1977). The defendants had therefore failed to prove their special defense of "prior legal nonconforming use."

The trial court further concluded that the defendants could not prevail on their equitable defenses of laches and estoppel. With respect to laches, the court determined that the town had not unreasonably delayed its enforcement of its 1968 ordinances. With respect to estoppel, the court expressed doubt about the availability of such a defense against a municipality and found an absence of "hard evidence" that the defendants had suffered any loss "because of any action of the town."

Finally, the trial court rejected the defendants' argument that the town had so far abandoned its zoning plan in the immediate area of the defendants' properties that enforcement of its regulations against the defendants was arbitrary and capricious. Having viewed the properties and the neighborhood, the court found no evidence either of abandonment of the town plan or of arbitrariness in its enforcement.

In their appeal from the trial court's order permanently enjoining their use of 55 Highland Street and 739 Prospect Avenue as rooming or boarding houses in violation of Article 4 of the town zoning regulations, the defendants rely principally on their arguments of estoppel and laches although they also contest the conclusion that they had not proven their acquisition of a nonconforming use. We shall consider these claims in the reverse order, taking up first the question of legal nonconforming use.

With regard to the legal status of their properties, the defendants now concede that they can prevail only if they can establish that the houses were actually used as accessory rooming houses before 1945.

They dispute the trial court's contrary finding by pointing to evidence that the houses were in fact used as rooming houses in 1943 and 1948. This evidence is supported, they claim, by the town's subsequent issuance of rooming house licenses, which creates a presumption that the houses complied with the town's zoning ordinances.

The fallacy in this argument is that it fails to overcome the trial court's finding that the rooming houses were being operated illegally as main uses, rather than legally as accessory uses, in the years at issue. It was not sufficient to establish that the owners then resided in the rooming houses. The defendants have not directly challenged the trial court's factual finding that there was a disproportion between the number of boarders and the resident owners but dispute instead its consequent conclusion that such a disproportion prevented the boarding uses from being "accessory." The defendants argue that such disproportion is irrelevant since it was not until 1945 that the town limited to three the number of roomers who could legally be housed in a residential accessory rooming house. It does not, however, follow that accessory use had no numerical limitation whatsoever before 1945. The trial court was, in our view, entirely within its province in inferring that the concept of accessory use necessarily required an inquiry into the extent to which actual uses were incidental to the underlying permitted residential uses of the property. We therefore find no error in the trial court's conclusion that the properties, while they became rooming houses, were never operated as accessory uses in conformity with applicable town regulations.

We turn then to the defendants' claim that the equitable principle of laches makes it improper for the town to enjoin their rooming houses even if these rooming houses are otherwise unauthorized under town regulations. The defendants acknowledge that Bianco v. Darien, 157 Conn. 548, 556, 254 A.2d 898 (1969), permitting a town to enforce its zoning ordinances after a thirty-six year lapse, stands in the way of their recovery on this theory. Whether we conclude, as did the trial court, that the town is enforcing its 1968 zoning enactments or, as the defendants maintain, its similar 1924 and 1945 ordinances, we are not prepared, in the circumstances of this case, to overrule our holding in *Bianco* that "[a] zoning commission 'is not estopped by laches from enforcing its zoning laws.'" *Id.; see* 3 Rathkopf, LAW OF ZONING AND PLANNING (4th ed. 1982) § 45.05(2).

A defense based on laches would have us focus on the effect of inaction, of the mere passage of time. *See* 9 McQuillin, MUNICIPAL CORPORATIONS (3d rev. ed. 1978) § 27.56. The defendants' final argument, however, focuses on affirmative conduct of the town which, they maintain, was of such a character as now to estop the town from obtaining an equitable remedy against them.

This court has recently restated the law of municipal estoppel. In Zoning Comm'n v. Lescynski, 188 Conn. 724, 731–32, 453 A.2d 1144

(Conn. 1982), we held that, in special circumstances, a municipality may be estopped from enforcing its zoning regulations. We recognized that estoppel always requires "proof of two essential elements: the party against whom estoppel is claimed must do or say something calculated or intended to induce another party to believe that certain facts exist and to act on that belief; and the other party must change its position in reliance on those facts, thereby incurring some injury." In municipal zoning cases, however, estoppel may be invoked "(1) only with great caution, (2) only when the resulting violation has been unjustifiably induced by an agent having authority in such matters, and (3) only when special circumstances make it highly inequitable or oppressive to enforce the regulations."

Lescynski puts to rest some of the controversy surrounding zoning estoppel. Contrary to the view of the plaintiff, a municipality can be estopped by erroneous acts of its officers from enforcing its zoning ordinances, as long as those officers act within the scope of their authority. The determination that the town's building inspector (who was also its zoning enforcement officer) acted erroneously in issuing rooming house licenses for the premises in question does not, therefore, defeat the defendants' claim of estoppel. The building inspector was, pursuant to town ordinances, the proper person to issue such licenses and the proper person to certify that the rooming house was or would be in compliance with existing zoning regulations. Any other construction of who is "an agent having authority in such matters," *Lescynski, supra,* would entirely defeat any and all claims of estoppel. Had the municipal agent's conduct been in conformity with zoning regulations, his legally authorized acts would automatically have conferred indefeasible rights upon the claimant. It is only when the municipal agent acts in good faith, within the scope of his authority, but in error, that the occasion for invocation of estoppel can arise.

The defendants therefore have a right, pursuant to *Lescynski,* to a defense based upon estoppel, if they can factually demonstrate its remaining components. The final question before us, therefore, is whether they have satisfied this substantial burden of proof. The defendants were required to show that the agents of the town acted to induce their reliance and that the defendants relied on the town's actions to their detriment to such an extent that enforcement of the town's zoning regulations would be "highly inequitable or oppressive." Zoning Comm'n v. Lescynski, *supra,* 188 Conn. 732, 453 A.2d 1144.

The facts upon which the defendants rely to show inducement are the rooming house licenses issued from 1949 to 1966, whose legitimacy was attested by two separate opinions of two town corporation counsel, one in 1957 and one in 1970. The defendants testified without contradiction that they inquired into the availability of rooming house licenses before they bought their properties. They applied for a license for one of the houses in 1962 while they were still negotiating its purchase. Even though the building inspector had no personal contact with the defendants, he was fully aware of the uses to which the defendants and their predecessors in title intended to put the property. In these circumstances the pattern of officially licensing the properties as rooming houses constituted an inducement to the defendants to purchase them for the same purpose. Inducement for the purposes of estoppel requires a mental state which is a general intent to act rather than a special intent to mislead. It is sufficient if actions are taken with an awareness that they would be relied upon; it is not necessary to prove that the actions were intended knowingly to mislead the party claiming estoppel. *See* Evanston v. Robbins, 117 Ill. App. 2d 278, 286, 254 N.E.2d 536 (Ill. 1969). The trial court's ruling to the contrary was therefore in error.

The facts found by the trial court similarly establish that the defendants did not fail to exercise due diligence when they relied upon the conduct of the town. While it may be true, as the plaintiff argues, that the relevant town ordinances were available for the defendants' inspection, it is equally true that the defendants, as lay persons, could not reasonably be expected to detect problems with apparent prior conforming uses that two separate corporation counsel had been unable to uncover. In the circumstances, it was not unreasonable for the defendants to assume that the rooming houses which they were purchasing constituted legal rather than illegal nonconforming uses. This element of estoppel is therefore also proven.

The final element of estoppel which the trial court did not reach cannot however be determined on the present record. As we have previously noted, the defendants must show not only unjustifiable inducement but also reliance of such a nature that it would be "highly inequitable or oppressive to enforce the [town's zoning] regulations." Zoning Comm'n v. Lescynski, 188 Conn. 724, 732, 453 A.2d 1144 (Conn. 1982). On the issue of reliance, the record discloses testimony by the defendants that the market value of their properties reflected their assumed rooming house status, and that their properties had been altered by substantial expenditures consistent with their boarding house use. The record further discloses a neighborhood which, despite some nonresidential uses, the trial court, after inspection, found not inconsistent with town enforcement of rooming house zoning regulations. There is, however, nothing before us to show that in granting the injunction, the trial court undertook the process of weighing competing equitable considerations to determine whether the town's conduct, the extent of the defendants' reliance and the condition of the neighborhood, warranted the equitable relief sought by the town. Such a weighing process involves the exercise of discretion by the trier of fact and not by an appellate tribunal. Because we cannot tell whether this is one of the special cases in which zoning estoppel, although only invoked with great caution, is appropriate, there must be a new trial on this remaining aspect of the defense of estoppel.

There is error, the judgment is set aside, and the case is remanded for further proceedings in accordance with this opinion.

NOTES AND QUESTIONS

1. Compare the *West End* case with Parkview Assocs. v. City of New York, 71 N.Y.2d 274, 525 N.Y.S.2d 176, 519 N.E.2d 1372 (1988). The language of the applicable zoning ordinance made it clear that landowner was not entitled to build higher than 19 stories on its entire parcel, but the zoning map was less than clear. If one had read only the map, and not the language enacted by the city council, one could have concluded that landowner was entitled to build 31 stories on part of the parcel. Landowner applied for, and received, a building permit to build 31 stories. After substantial construction, the commissioner of buildings discovered the mistake and issued a stop work order on all construction above 19 stories. Landowner contended that as a result of issuance of the building permit, the city should be estopped from enforcing the 19-story limit. The New York Court of Appeals disagreed. The court wrote:

> Insofar as estoppel is not available to preclude a municipality from enforcing the provisions of its zoning laws and the mistaken or erroneous issuance of a permit does not estop a municipality from correcting errors, even where there are harsh results, the City should not be estopped here from revoking that portion of the building permit which violated the long-standing zoning limits imposed by the applicable P.I.D. resolution. Even if there was municipal error in one map and in the mistaken administrative issuance of the original permit, those factors would be completely outweighed in this case by the doctrine that reasonable diligence would have readily uncovered for a good-faith inquirer the existence of the unequivocal limitations of 150 feet in the original binding metes and bounds description of the enabling legislation, and that this boundary has never been changed by the Board of Estimate.

71 N.Y.2d at 282, 519 N.E.2d at 1375 (citations omitted).

Can you reconcile *West End* with *Parkview*? If not, which approach is preferable? Why?

2. Why couldn't landowners in *Rechel* and *Parkview* rely on the vested rights doctrine? What is the difference, if any, between the doctrines of zoning estoppel and vested rights?

3. Once FoBoGro purchased the property at 2140 F. Street NW, was there any way for the City (or the neighbors) to obtain judicial review of the erroneous Certificate of Occupancy? Would the same have been true for an erroneous denial of FoBoGro's request for a Certificate of Occupancy?

4. If, at the time they purchased their property, the Rechels knew that the permits to operate their rooming house had been issued in error, could they still have raised a claim of zoning estoppel?

5. Suppose you are a developer planning an industrial project that is permitted under the applicable zoning ordinance, but that nevertheless requires a permit from the city. In the past, this permit has always been granted for projects similar to yours. You carefully research the zoning ordinance and, confident that you will be granted a permit, begin spending money in preparation for the project before the permit is actually issued. To your surprise, the permit is denied. Do you have a claim for zoning estoppel? *See* Pure Oil Div. v. City of Columbia, 254 S.C. 28, 173 S.E.2d 140 (1970) (yes).

6. Suppose the same facts as Note 5, except that, in addition to studying the zoning code, you consult with the building inspector, who assures you that the permit will be issued after the planning board expressly authorizes him to do so. Do you have a strong claim for zoning estoppel?

7. Suppose the same facts as Note 5, except that, after the city denies the permit, the developer proceeds to complete the project, and the city waits nearly 25 years before bringing an action to enforce the zoning code. *See* City of Evanston v. Robbins, 117 Ill.App.2d 278, 254 N.E.2d 536 (1969).

IV. PUBLIC POLICY

Gangemi v. Zoning Board of Appeals of the Town of Fairfield

Supreme Court of Connecticut, 2001
255 Conn. 143, 763 A.2d 1011

■ BORDEN, J.

The dispositive issue in this certified appeal is whether the continued maintenance of a certain "no rental" condition imposed on a zoning variance granted to the plaintiffs in 1986 by the defendant, the zoning board of appeals of the town of Fairfield (board), which the plaintiffs did not challenge by direct appeal at that time, violates the public policy against restraints against alienation of property. The plaintiffs, Sebastian Gangemi and Rebecca J. Gangemi, appeal, pursuant to our grant of certification, from the judgment of the Appellate Court affirming the judgment of the trial court. The trial court dismissed the plaintiffs' appeal from the defendant's denial of their application to invalidate the no rental condition for lack of subject matter jurisdiction. The plaintiffs claim that the trial court improperly dismissed their appeal because the continued maintenance of the condition violates the strong public policy against restraints on the alienation of property. We agree. Accordingly, we reverse the judgment of the Appellate Court.

In 1986, the plaintiffs secured a zoning variance from the board, one condition of which was "[o]wner occupancy only." In 1996, the Fairfield zoning enforcement officer determined that the plaintiffs were violating the condition by renting their property, and he ordered them to comply with the condition. The plaintiffs applied to the board requesting that it invalidate the condition. The board denied the application. The plaintiffs appealed to the trial court, which rendered judgment dismissing the appeal. The plaintiffs appealed to the Appellate Court, which affirmed the trial court's judgment. The variance permitted the plaintiffs to reduce the required side setback line from 7 feet to 3.2 feet, thus giving them an additional 3.8 feet of footprint and adding 59.6 square feet to their house. In this connection, we note that the variance also gave the plaintiffs permission to convert the house from a seasonal cottage to a year-round dwelling by enclosing the open porch and adding a one-story addition in order to enlarge the bathroom and construct a furnace room. At oral argument before this court, the parties informed us that, at the time the variance was granted, applicable zoning regulations permitted only seasonal use of the plaintiffs' property. The parties further informed us, however, that the zoning regulations have since been amended to eliminate the prior seasonal restriction, thereby permitting year-round use. Thus, under the current zoning regulations, the plaintiffs' house, as well as all of the other houses in the Fairfield beach district, may now be used year-round irrespective of the variance and its original conditions.

[T]he property in question is located within the Fairfield beach district, which is subject to § 11.1.1 of the Fairfield zoning regulations. Section 11.1.1 of the Fairfield zoning regulations imposes the following limitations: "A single detached dwelling for one family ... [and] no dwelling or dwelling unit in the Beach District may be occupied by more than four (4) unrelated persons." Thus, there is nothing in the zoning regulations that prohibits either the plaintiffs or any other property owners in the beach district from renting their houses to others. Moreover, there is nothing in our zoning statutes that, at least specifically, permits such a flat prohibition.

It is undisputable that "[i]t is the policy of the law not to uphold restrictions upon the free and unrestricted alienation of property unless they serve a legal and useful purpose." Peiter v. Degenring, 136 Conn. 331, 336, 71 A.2d 87 (Conn. 1949). It is also undisputable that this policy is strong and deeply rooted. J. Dukeminier & J. Krier, Property (3d ed. 1993) 223 ("[T]he rule against direct restraints on alienation is an old one, going back to the fifteenth century or perhaps even earlier."). Moreover, it is undisputable that the right of property owners to rent their real estate is one of the bundle of rights that, taken together, constitute the essence of ownership of property. See, e.g., id. at 86 ("[Property] consists of a number of disparate rights, a 'bundle' of them: the right to possess, the right to use, the right to exclude, the right to transfer."). The question that the present case poses, therefore, is whether, under the facts of this case, the continued maintenance of the no rental condition serves "a legal and useful purpose." Peiter v. Degenring, *supra,* at 336, 71 A.2d 87; see also T. Tondro, *Connecticut Land Use Regulation* (2d ed. 1992) 89, n. 185 ("[T]he real question is whether a valid zoning objective is being served."). We conclude that it does not.

Owners of a single-family residence can do one of three economically productive things with the residence: (1) live in it; (2) rent it; or (3) sell it. Thus, if the owners of a single-family residence do not choose, for reasons of family size or other valid reasons, to live in the house they own, their only viable options are to rent it or to divest themselves entirely of their ownership by selling it. Stripping the plaintiffs of essentially one-third of their bundle of economically productive rights constituting ownership is a very significant restriction on their right of ownership. In addition, when the variance was granted in 1986, the no rental condition deprived the plaintiffs only of the right to rent their property on a seasonal basis. With the change in the zoning regulations, however, the plaintiffs now also have lost the more significant right to rent their property on a year-round basis, resulting in a total loss of the right to rent.

Furthermore, the maintenance of the no rental condition in the present case not only strips the plaintiffs of one of those three options, it also significantly reduces the value of the third because when they do put the house on the market it will necessarily bring significantly less than the fair market value that it would have commanded without the condition. Finally, insofar as this record discloses, the condition limiting the plaintiffs' economic use of the house to occupancy, and prohibiting their economic use of it by renting it, is a limitation that does not adhere to the rest of the property owners in the beach district. Thus, the most obvious consequence of the continued maintenance of the no rental condition on the plaintiffs' property is to give those other property owners a grossly unfair advantage over the plaintiffs in the marketplace. A house, particularly a house located in a beach district, that can never be rented obviously would be significantly less desirable to a potential purchaser than the rest of the houses in the beach district, which do not have such a drastic limitation on their economic use.

Neither the state zoning statutes nor the local zoning regulations place any such limitation on those other property owners. Thus, whatever adverse consequences to other properties may be imagined to flow from occupancy of the houses in the beach district by *renters* as opposed to *owners* cannot be reasonably attributable to the plaintiffs' use of their property, because presumably no other properties are so encumbered. Put another way, if all or most of the other houses in the beach district legally can be rented to any group of four or fewer unrelated persons, we fail to see how this condition on this one house conceivably may serve any legal or useful purpose—except to maintain the unfair market advantage that the other unencumbered houses have, a purpose that the law should hardly label as "legal and useful." Peiter v. Degenring, *supra,* 136 Conn. at 336, 71 A.2d 87.

Finally, the continued maintenance of this no rental condition violates another strong and deeply rooted policy, namely, the policy against economic waste. Our law has long recognized such a policy. *See* Levesque v. D & M Builders, Inc., 170 Conn. 177, 181–82, 365 A.2d 1216 (1976). By artificially and significantly devaluing the plaintiffs' property, as compared to the value of the surrounding parcels, the continued maintenance of the condition in question removes from the marketplace, and thereby from the economy, that significant differential in value. We can see no legal or useful purpose in doing so. The consequence of such conduct is economic waste.

We acknowledge that permitting the plaintiffs to challenge the condition now means that they will receive what could be regarded as a windfall, because they secured a variance in 1986 coupled with the no rental condition, and it is possible that, had the condition not been imposed, either the zoning authority might not have granted the variance or an aggrieved neighbor might have successfully challenged the granting of the variance by way of appeal at that time. Moreover, for the period between 1986, when they secured the variance, and whenever the zoning regulations were amended to eliminate the seasonal use restriction on the beach district, the plaintiffs had the full benefit of the variance. That, however, does not alter our conclusion, however, for two reasons.

First, whenever the law permits a previously imposed condition to be challenged collaterally . . . some similar windfall is afforded the property owner. . . . Against this, however, must be balanced the current effects of the condition. Those effects are: (1) the drastic and direct restriction on the alienability of the plaintiffs' property; (2) its grossly unfair consequence, when compared with the freedom of alienability of the other property owners in the beach district; and (3) the fact that the restriction is, unlike the second part of the windfall, temporally unlimited—in fact, permanent. This balance leads us to conclude that the no rental condition is so restrictive of the plaintiffs' ability to alienate their property that it outweighs the public policy considerations underlying the bar on collateral attacks. We need not, and do not, decide whether a no rental condition may never be valid in the zoning context. Compare Kirsch Holding Co. v. Manasquan, 59 N.J. 241, 281 A.2d 513 (1971) (invalidating regulation prohibiting rental to groups of persons not meeting statutory definition of family), United Property Owners Ass'n of Belmar v. Belmar, 185 N.J. Super. 163, 447 A.2d 933 (1982) (invalidating regulation prohibiting rental for one year or less when residence not intended to be permanent residence of renter), Kulak v. Zoning Hearing Bd., 128 Pa. Commw. 457, 563 A.2d 978 (1989) (condition to special exception requiring apartment building owner to reside in one apartment did not serve any valid zoning purpose, but owner nonetheless bound because not appealed from when imposed), *and* 5 A. Rathkopf & D. Rathkopf, THE LAW OF ZONING AND PLANNING (4th ed. Ziegler 2000) § 56A.02 (1)(e) 56A–8 ("[T]he principle that zoning enabling acts authorize local regulation of 'land use' and not regulation of the 'identity or status' of owners or persons who occupy the land would likely be held to apply to invalidate zoning provisions distinguishing between owner-occupied and rental housing."), *with* Ewing v. Carmel-by-the-Sea, 234 Cal. App. 3d 1579, 286 Cal. Rptr. 382 (1991), *cert. denied,* 504 U.S. 914, 112 S.Ct. 1950, 118 L.Ed.2d 554 (1992) (upholding constitutionality of ordinance prohibiting rental of residential property for fewer than thirty days), *and* Kasper v. Brookhaven, 142 App. Div. 2d 213, 535 N.Y.S.2d 621 (1988) (upholding ordinance requiring homeowners who apply for accessory rental apartments to occupy principal residence).

It may be that where such a condition is imposed by virtue of a statute or regulation that is of district-wide application and is tailored to a specific land use policy, *see, e.g.,* Ewing v. Carmel-by-the-Sea, *supra,* 234 Cal. App. 3d at 1590, 286 Cal. Rptr. 382 (maintenance of residential character of district by prohibiting very short term rentals), such a condition might be valid. Where, however, as in the present case, the no rental condition is not district-wide and therefore presumably applies only to the property at issue, thereby affording the other property owners in the beach district a distinct market advantage, and there is no other regulation even approaching its scope or purpose, the continued maintenance of the no rental condition serves no valid purpose, and violates the strong and deeply rooted public policy in favor of the free and unrestricted alienability of property.

The judgment of the Appellate Court is reversed and the case is remanded to that court with direction to remand the case to the trial court for further proceedings according to law.

NOTES AND QUESTIONS

1.   What is the legal foundation of the public policy the Connecticut Supreme Court found the no-rental provision to violate? The U.S. Constitution? The state constitution? The common law? Some other source?

2.   The court suggests that a district-wide no-rental policy might withstand challenge. But if the application of the no-rental provision to a single property violates the public policy in favor of free alienation of property, why would a district-wide restraint on alienation be any better? Does the court's suggestion to the contrary say anything about the concerns actually motivating its decision?

V. VAGUENESS

Kosalka v. Town of Georgetown

Supreme Judicial Court of Maine, 2000
752 A.2d 183

■ DANA, J.

On February 21, 1997, Eric and Patricia Kosalka submitted an application to the Georgetown Planning Board (GPB) for a permit to construct a nine-trailer recreational vehicle campground on property owned by Eric's mother, Ruth Kosalka.

The Ordinance . . . provides that campgrounds are allowed, as a conditional use, in both the General Development and the Limited Residential–Recreational Districts. To qualify as a conditional use, a proposed campground must: (1) "not result in unsafe or unhealthy conditions"; (2) "not result in erosion or sedimentation"; (3) "not result in pollution"; (4) "not result in damage to spawning grounds, fish, aquatic life, bird and other wildlife habitat"; (5) "conserve shoreland vegetation"; (6) "conserve visual points of access to waters"; (7) "conserve actual points of public access to waters"; (8) "conserve natural beauty"; and (9) "avoid problems associated with flood plain development and use."

The GPB . . . found that the proposed campground did not satisfy the conditional use guidelines because it did not "conserve the natural beauty" of the area.

The Kosalkas appealed the GPB's decision to the Georgetown Board of Zoning Appeals (ZBA). The ZBA partially reversed the GPB, finding that the proposed campground was located in the Limited Residential–Recreational District because the lot was "actually developed." Nevertheless, the ZBA denied the Kosalkas' application because it concluded that it did not have jurisdiction to consider whether the "conserve natural beauty" requirement was constitutional.

The Kosalkas filed a complaint in the Superior Court pursuant to M.R. Civ. P. 80B, challenging the constitutionality of the "natural beauty" requirement. [T]he Court affirmed the ZBA's conclusion that the proposed development is located in the Limited Residential–Recreational District, and found that the Kosalkas "failed to demonstrate that [the natural beauty language] is unconstitutional on its face." The Superior Court remanded the case to the ZBA to consider whether the proposed campground satisfied the Ordinance's natural beauty requirement.

On remand, the ZBA held public hearings, visited the site, viewed pictures and plans, and concluded that the proposed campground would not conserve the area's natural beauty. The ZBA, therefore, affirmed the Planning Board's denial of a campground permit. The Kosalkas again appealed to the Superior Court, which affirmed. This appeal followed.[2]

DISCUSSION

[T]he Kosalkas bear the burden of demonstrating that the Ordinance is unconstitutional. See Gorham v. Town of Cape Elizabeth, 625 A.2d 898, 900 (Me. 1993). The Kosalkas argue that the "conserve natural beauty" requirement is an unconstitutional delegation of legislative authority because it fails to "furnish a guide which will enable those to whom the law is to be applied to reasonably determine their rights." Stucki v. Plavin, 291 A.2d 508, 510 (Me. 1972). We agree.

We have noted in the conditional use context that "in order to withstand attack as an impermissible legislative delegation of authority, ordinances that establish criteria for acceptance of a conditional use must specify sufficient reasons why such a use may be denied." *Gorham,* 625 A.2d at 900. Developers are entitled to know with reasonable clarity what they must do under state or local land use control laws to obtain the permits or approvals they seek. Waterville Hotel Corp. v. Bd. of Zoning Appeals, 241 A.2d 50 (Me. 1968).

In *Stucki v. Plavin,* we held unconstitutional a zoning ordinance that allowed lots that straddled district lines to be governed by the less restrictive district, "provided, however, that such extension of use into the more restrictive portion shall meet the approval of the Zoning Board of Appeals." *Stucki,* 291 A.2d at 509. In striking down that provision, we noted that the ZBA was forced to consider, "Under what set of facts do we grant or withhold approval?" and the applicant had to ask, "What must I present to gain the Board's approval?" *Id.* at 511. We concluded that "[i]f there is no language in the ordinance, which, by reasonable interpretation answers these questions, the [ordinance] . . . is void on its face." *Id.*

Additionally, in Wakelin v. Town of Yarmouth, 523 A.2d 575, 576 (Me. 1987), we struck down a zoning ordinance that gave the ZBA the discretion to deny special exception applications because the proposed use was not "compatible with the existing uses in the neighborhood, with respect to . . . intensity of use . . . and density of development." *Id.* We concluded that the ordinance "fails to articulate the quantitative standards necessary to transform the unmeasured qualities 'intensity of use' and 'density of development' into specific criteria objectively useable by both the Board and the applicant." *Id.* at 577. Without such specific objective criteria, the ZBA was "free to express a legislative-type opinion about what is appropriate for the community." *Id.*

---

[2] Because we conclude that the "conserve natural beauty" requirement is an unconstitutional delegation of legislative authority, we need not discuss the Kosalkas' alternative argument that the Georgetown Zoning Board erred in concluding that the Kosalkas' proposed campground did not, in fact, conserve natural beauty.

Here, the Georgetown Ordinance requires that all development "conserve natural beauty." However, all development, to some extent, destroys or impairs "natural beauty." If the provision means that *all* natural beauty must be conserved, then *all* development must be banned. Because the provision cannot reasonably be interpreted to ban all development, the question becomes: How much destruction is okay? Or, put another way: How much conservation is required? On this question, however, the Georgetown Ordinance, like the ordinance in *Stucki,* is silent. Neither developers nor the ZBA are given any guidance on how to interpret the "conserve natural beauty" requirement. Instead, developers are left guessing at how much conservation is necessary, and the ZBA is free to grant or deny permits as it sees fit.

No one can adequately advise the Kosalkas (or any other Georgetown developer) how to create a development plan that will satisfy the requirement because, without guidance in the Ordinance, the ZBA is free to grant or deny permits on whatever set of facts it sees fit. This is precisely the problem we sought to avoid in *Wakelin.* Under the Georgetown Ordinance, a developer can bury all utilities, maintain the site's vegetation, and even plant additional trees, and still fall short in the minds of ZBA members, who are free to make legislative-type decisions based on any factor they independently deem appropriate.

Because the condition that all proposed developments "conserve natural beauty" is an unmeasurable quality, totally lacking in cognizable, quantitative standards, this condition is an unconstitutional delegation of legislative authority and violative of the due process clause. Additionally, because the Georgetown Planning Board concluded that the proposed campground satisfied all other requirements found in the Ordinance, we vacate the judgment of the Superior Court and remand to the ZBA with instructions to grant the conditional use permit.

SP Star Enterprises, Inc. v. City of Los Angeles

Court of Appeal of California, Second District, Division 3, 2009
173 Cal. App.4th 459, 93 Cal.Rptr.3d 152

■ KLEIN, P.J.

Appellant SP Star Enterprises, Inc. (Star) holds a certificate of occupancy from the City of Los Angeles (the City) permitting Star to operate an adult club featuring nude entertainment in a two-story, 7,000-square-foot converted warehouse/manufacturing facility zoned M3–1 on Ducommun Street north of Little Tokyo. Star also holds a franchise to operate a Penthouse branded adult cabaret. This case involves Star's application for a conditional use permit for the sale and on-site consumption of alcohol at the club.

The City's Zoning Administrator granted Star's application for one year. The Los Angeles Hompa Hongwanji Buddhist Temple (the

Temple) and the Fukui Mortuary appealed the approval to the City's Central Area Planning Commission (APC). The appeal was supported by the Los Angeles Police Department, two city council members, the Central City East Association and numerous private citizens who argued the proposed use is not compatible with the religious and community uses in the area or the redevelopment of the area north of Little Tokyo.

Star responded its upscale business would improve tourism in the area as Penthouse cabarets had in other cities and would have no adverse impact on the neighborhood. Further, Star already was licensed to offer fully nude dancing and issuance of the conditional use permit would trigger Alcoholic Beverage Control (ABC) regulations which limit adult entertainment to topless dancing on stages at least six feet from the nearest patron.

The APC conducted a public hearing at which it upheld the appeal, resulting in the denial of the conditional use permit. Star then sought a writ of mandate. The trial court denied Star's writ petition, indicating it would uphold the APC's ruling whether it applied a substantial evidence or a *de novo* standard of review. This appeal followed.

The thrust of Star's attack on the APC's ruling and the trial court's denial of its writ petition is that Star is entitled to preferential treatment because it engages in a disfavored form of protected expression. Thus, the standards under which the APC operated must be strictly scrutinized to avoid giving the APC unbridled discretion to regulate speech. Star also contends the APC's findings were a pretext for discriminating against disfavored speech and were not supported by substantial evidence.

We conclude the case does not involve free speech but the right to sell alcohol, which is not a protected activity and does not involve a fundamental vested right. Yu v. Alcoholic Bev. etc. Appeals Bd., 3 Cal. App. 4th 286, 297, 4 Cal. Rptr. 2d 280 (1992). Thus, the standards under which the APC upheld the appeal need not reflect the " 'precision of regulation' " required when a municipality regulates protected activity. Burton v. Municipal Court, 68 Cal. 2d 684, 691, 68 Cal. Rptr. 721, 441 P.2d 281 (1968). Rather, because the standards applied by the APC are not vague or arbitrary and the APC's decision finds substantial support in the record, we affirm the trial court's order denying Star's writ petition.*

---

*   Eds. Note: In a footnote to a portion of the opinion not reproduced, the court set out the following provisions of the Los Angeles Municipal Code (LAMC):

LAMC section 12.24, subdivision E requires the APC to make the following findings before a conditional use permit may be approved: "[T]he proposed location will be desirable to the public convenience or welfare, is proper in relation to adjacent uses or the development of the community, will not be materially detrimental to the character of development in the immediate neighborhood, and will be in harmony with the various elements and objectives of the General Plan." LAMC, § 12.24, subd. E.

Because this case involves the on-site sale and consumption of alcohol, we do not subject the LAMC to the strict level of scrutiny applicable in cases involving freedom of speech. "[T]he rule announced in *Burton* [requiring precision in the standards under which a permit may be issued] applies only to those situations in which the operation of a licensing ordinance impinges upon the exercise of First Amendment activities, rather than ordinary commercial enterprises." Sunset Amusement Co. v. Board of Police Comm'rs, 7 Cal. 3d 64, 72, 101 Cal. Rptr. 768, 496 P.2d 840 (1972) (citation omitted). Absent an ascertainable effect upon First Amendment activities, the provisions of the LAMC provide an adequate standard to guide the APC's discretion, namely, that it must exercise its power in a reasonable, rather than arbitrary, manner to promote the interest of the public. *Id.*

The provisions of the LAMC relating to the issuance of a conditional use permit based on a finding the " 'proposed location will be desirable to the public convenience or welfare and will be in harmony with the various elements and objectives of the Master Plan' " specifically have been upheld against challenges of vagueness. Stoddard v. Edelman, 4 Cal. App. 3d 544, 548, 84 Cal. Rptr. 443 (1970); Case v. City of Los Angeles, 218 Cal. App. 2d 36, 42, 32 Cal. Rptr. 271 (1963); Wheeler v. Gregg, 90 Cal. App. 2d 348, 203 P.2d 37 1949).

"In fact, a substantial amount of vagueness is permitted in California zoning ordinances: [I]n California, the most general zoning standards are usually deemed sufficient. The standard is sufficient if the administrative body is required to make its decision in accord with the general health, safety, and welfare standard." *Id.* at 682, 215 Cal. Rptr. 439 (citation omitted); Higgins v. City of Santa Monica, 62 Cal. 2d 24, 30, 41 Cal. Rptr. 9, 396 P.2d 41 (1964).

In sum, the provisions of the LAMC in issue must be upheld as a reasonable exercise of the City's police power to license and regulate business activities.

NOTES AND QUESTIONS

1. What is the harm of an excessively vague land use provision? Can the harm be mitigated through procedural safeguards?

2. Do you agree with the Maine Supreme Court that a rule must be reducible to quantitative measurement in order to provide sufficient

---

LAMC section 12.24, subdivision W.1 requires additional findings by the APC for approval of a conditional use permit to sell alcohol. Specifically, the APC must find: "(1) that the proposed use will not adversely affect the welfare of the pertinent community; [¶] (2) that the granting of the application will not result in an undue concentration of premises for the sale or dispensing for consideration of alcoholic beverages . . . ; and [¶] (3) that the proposed use will not detrimentally affect nearby residentially zoned communities in the area of the City involved, after giving consideration to the distance of the proposed use from residential buildings, churches, schools, hospitals, public playgrounds and other similar uses. . . ." LAMC, § 12.24, subd. W.1(a).

certainty to decisionmakers and landowners? Can a legal standard guide behavior or constrain discretion without such a quantitative metric?

3. Could architectural review or historic preservation survive the Maine court's standards for excessive vagueness? Could any aesthetic regulation survive? See Part II of Chapter Three for more on this topic.

4. Can you imagine a land use provision that would fail under the California Court of Appeals' standard of review?

CHAPTER FIVE

DEVELOPER CHALLENGES: FEDERAL LAW

I. TAKINGS

A. HISTORICAL BACKGROUND

The last clause of the federal constitution's Fifth Amendment provides, "nor shall private property be taken for public use without just compensation." The clause was directed at limiting governmental power to confiscate private property without paying compensation. But the Takings Clause, like the rest of the Bill of Rights, was initially designed to constrain the power of the federal government; the federal Takings Clause had no application to actions taken by state or local governments—although many state constitutions included parallel restrictions on governmental power to "take" property without paying just compensation.

The Supreme Court has read the Fourteenth Amendment's Due Process Clause to "incorporate" most of the Bill of Rights, including the Takings Clause. Thus, any action that would violate the Fifth Amendment if done by the federal government is deemed to violate the Fourteenth Amendment when done by state or local officials. The Supreme Court has considered the scope of the constitutional prohibition in a number of important cases (including the *Euclid* case, discussed in Chapter Two). Consider the following two cases:

Mugler v. Kansas
Supreme Court of the United States, 1887
123 U.S. 623

■ JUSTICE HARLAN delivered the opinion of the court.

These cases involve an inquiry into the validity of certain statutes of Kansas relating to the manufacture and sale of intoxicating liquors.

[I]n 1880, the people of Kansas ... ratified an amendment to the state constitution, which declared that the manufacture and sale of intoxicating liquors should be forever prohibited in that State, except for medical, scientific, and mechanical purposes.

In order to give effect to that amendment, the legislature repealed the act of 1868, and passed an act, approved February 19, 1881, to take effect May 1, 1881, entitled "An act to prohibit the manufacture and sale of intoxicating liquors, except for medical, scientific, and mechanical purposes, and to regulate the manufacture and sale thereof for such excepted purposes." The thirteenth section declares, among other things, all places where intoxicating liquors are manufactured, sold, bartered, or given away, or are kept for sale, barter, or use, in violation of the act, to be common nuisances; and provides that upon the judgment of any court having jurisdiction finding such place to be a nuisance, the proper officer shall be directed to shut up and abate the same.

The facts necessary to a clear understanding of the questions, common to these cases, are the following: Mugler and Ziebold & Hagelin were engaged in manufacturing beer at their respective establishments (constructed specially for that purpose), for several years prior to the adoption of the constitutional amendment of 1880. They continued in such business in defiance of the statute of 1881. . . .

The buildings and machinery constituting these breweries are of little value if not used for the purpose of manufacturing beer; that is to say, if the statutes are enforced against the defendants the value of their property will be very materially diminished.

The general question in each case is, whether the foregoing statutes of Kansas are in conflict with that clause of the Fourteenth Amendment, which provides that "no State shall make or enforce any law which shall abridge the privileges or immunities of citizens of the United States; nor shall any State deprive any person of life, liberty, or property, without due process of law."

It is . . . contended, that, although the State may prohibit the manufacture of intoxicating liquors for sale or barter within her limits, for general use as a beverage, "no convention or legislature has the right, under our form of government, to prohibit any citizen from manufacturing for his own use, or for export, or storage, any article of food or drink not endangering or affecting the rights of others."

It will be observed that the proposition, and the argument made in support of it, equally concede that the right to manufacture drink for one's personal use is subject to the condition that such manufacture does not endanger or affect the rights of others. If such manufacture does prejudicially affect the rights and interests of the community, it follows, from the very premises stated, that society has the power to protect itself, by legislation, against the injurious consequences of that business.

But by whom, or by what authority, is it to be determined whether the manufacture of particular articles of drink, either for general use or for the personal use of the maker, will injuriously affect the public? Power to determine such questions, so as to bind all, must exist somewhere; else society will be at the mercy of the few, who, regarding only their own appetites or passions, may be willing to imperil the peace and security of the many, provided only they are permitted to do as they please. Under our system that power is lodged with the legislative branch of the government. It belongs to that department to exert what are known as the police powers of the State, and to determine, primarily, what measures are appropriate or needful for the protection of the public morals, the public health, or the public safety.

Keeping in view these principles, as governing the relations of the judicial and legislative departments of the government with each other, it is difficult to perceive any ground for the judiciary to declare that the prohibition by Kansas of the manufacture or sale, within her limits, of intoxicating liquors for general use there as a beverage, is not fairly adapted to the end of protecting the community against the evils which confessedly result from the excessive use of ardent spirits.

This conclusion is unavoidable, unless the Fourteenth Amendment of the Constitution takes from the States of the Union those powers of police that were reserved at the time the original Constitution was adopted. But this court has declared, upon full consideration, in Barbier v. Connolly, 113 U.S. 27, 31, that the Fourteenth Amendment had no such effect.

The principle, that no person shall be deprived of life, liberty, or property, without due process of law, was embodied, in substance, in the constitutions of nearly all, if not all, of the States at the time of the adoption of the Fourteenth Amendment; and it has never been regarded as incompatible with the principle, equally vital, because essential to the peace and safety of society, that all property in this country is held under the implied obligation that the owner's use of it shall not be injurious to the community.

It is supposed by the defendants that the doctrine for which they contend is sustained by Pumpelly v. Green Bay Co., 13 Wall. 166. But in that view we do not concur. That was an action for the recovery of damages for the overflowing of the plaintiff's land by water, resulting from the construction of a dam across a river. The defence was that the dam constituted a part of the system adopted by the State for improving the navigation of Fox and Wisconsin rivers; and it was contended that as the damages of which the plaintiff complained were only the result of the improvement, under legislative sanction, of a navigable stream, he was not entitled to compensation from the State or its agents. The case, therefore, involved the question whether the overflowing of the plaintiff's land, to such an extent that it became practically unfit to be used, was a taking of property, within the meaning of the constitution of Wisconsin, providing that "the property of no person shall be taken for public use without just compensation therefor." This court said it would be a very curious and unsatisfactory result, were it held that, "if the government refrains from the absolute conversion of real property to the uses of the public, it can destroy its value entirely, can inflict irreparable and permanent injury to any extent, can, in effect, subject it to total destruction, without making any compensation, because, in the narrowest sense of that word, it is not taken for the public use. Such a construction would pervert the constitutional provision into a restriction upon the rights of the citizen, as those rights stood at the common law, instead of the government, and make it an authority for the invasion of private right under the pretext of the public good, which had no warrant in the laws or practices of our ancestors." *Id.* at 177, 178.

These principles have no application to the case under consideration. The question in Pumpelly v. Green Bay Co. arose under the State's power of eminent domain; while the question now before us arises under what are, strictly, the police powers of the State, exerted for the protection of the health, morals, and safety of the people. It was a case in which there was a "permanent flooding of private property," a "physical invasion of the real estate of the private owner, and a practical ouster of his possession." His property was, in effect, required to be devoted to the use of the public, and, consequently, he was entitled to compensation.

As already stated, the present case must be governed by principles that do not involve the power of eminent domain, in the exercise of which property may not be taken for public use without compensation. A prohibition simply upon the use of property for purposes that are declared, by valid legislation, to be injurious to the health, morals, or safety of the community, cannot, in any just sense, be deemed a taking or an appropriation of property for the public benefit. Such legislation does not disturb the owner in the control or use of his property for lawful purposes, nor restrict his right to dispose of it, but is only a declaration by the State that its use by any one, for certain forbidden purposes, is prejudicial to the public interests. Nor can legislation of that character come within the Fourteenth Amendment, in any case, unless it is apparent that its real object is not to protect the community, or to promote the general well-being, but, under the guise of police regulation, to deprive the owner of his liberty and property, without due process of law. The power which the States have of prohibiting such use by individuals of their property as will be prejudicial to the health, the morals, or the safety of the public, is not—and, consistently with the existence and safety of organized society, cannot be—burdened with the condition that the State must compensate such individual owners for pecuniary losses they may sustain, by reason of their not being permitted, by a noxious use of their property, to inflict injury upon the community. The exercise of the police power by the destruction of property which is itself a public nuisance, or the prohibition of its use in a particular way, whereby its value becomes depreciated, is very different from taking property for public use, or from depriving a person of his property without due process of law. In the one case, a nuisance only is abated; in the other, unoffending property is taken away from an innocent owner.

It is true, that, when the defendants in these cases purchased or erected their breweries, the laws of the State did not forbid the manufacture of intoxicating liquors. But the State did not thereby give any assurance, or come under an obligation, that its legislation upon that subject would remain unchanged. Indeed, as was said in Stone v. Mississippi, 101 U.S. 814, the supervision of the public health and the public morals is a governmental power, "continuing in its nature," and "to be dealt with as the special exigencies of the moment may require;" and that, "for this purpose, the largest legislative discretion is allowed, and the discretion cannot be parted with any more than the power itself." So in Beer Co. v. Massachusetts, 97 U.S. 32: "If the public safety or the public morals require the discontinuance of any manufacture or traffic, the hand of the legislature cannot be stayed from providing for its discontinuance by any incidental inconvenience which individuals or corporations may suffer."

For the reasons stated, we are of opinion that the judgments of the Supreme Court of Kansas have not denied to Mugler, the plaintiff in error, any right, privilege, or immunity secured to him by the Constitution of the United States, and its judgment, in each case, is, accordingly, affirmed. We are, also, of opinion that the Circuit Court of the United States erred in dismissing the bill of the State against Ziebold & Hagelin. The decree in that case is reversed, and the cause remanded, with directions to enter a decree granting to the State such relief as the act of March 7, 1885, authorizes.

Pennsylvania Coal Co. v. Mahon

Supreme Court of the United States, 1922
260 U.S. 393

■ MR. JUSTICE HOLMES delivered the opinion of the Court.

This is a bill in equity brought by the defendants in error to prevent the Pennsylvania Coal Company from mining under their property in such way as to remove the supports and cause a subsidence of the surface and of their house. The bill sets out a deed executed by the Coal Company in 1878, under which the plaintiffs claim. The deed conveys the surface, but in express terms reserves the right to remove all the coal under the same, and the grantee takes the premises with the risk, and waives all claim for damages that may arise from mining out the coal. But the plaintiffs say that whatever may have been the Coal Company's rights, they were taken away by an Act of Pennsylvania, approved May 27, 1921, P.L. 1198, commonly known there as the Kohler Act.

The statute forbids the mining of anthracite coal in such way as to cause the subsidence of, among other things, any structure used as a human habitation, with certain exceptions, including among them land where the surface is owned by the owner of the underlying coal and is distant more than one hundred and fifty feet from any improved property belonging to any other person. As applied to this case the statute is admitted to destroy previously existing rights of property and contract. The question is whether the police power can be stretched so far.

Government hardly could go on if to some extent values incident to property could not be diminished without paying for every such change in the general law. As long recognized, some values are enjoyed under an implied limitation and must yield to the police power. But obviously the implied limitation must have its limits, or the contract and due process clauses are gone. One fact for consideration in determining such limits is the extent of the diminution. When it reaches a certain magnitude, in most if not in all cases there must be an exercise of eminent domain and compensation to sustain the act. So the question depends upon the particular facts. The greatest weight is given to the judgment of the legislature, but it always is open to interested parties to contend that the legislature has gone beyond its constitutional power.

This is the case of a single private house. No doubt there is a public interest even in this, as there is in every purchase and sale and in all that happens within the commonwealth. Some existing rights may be modified even in such a case. Rideout v. Knox, 148 Mass. 368. But usually in ordinary private affairs the public interest does not warrant much of this kind of interference. A source of damage to such a house is not a public nuisance even if similar damage is inflicted on others in different places. The damage is not common or public. Wesson v. Washburn Iron Co., 13 Allen, 95, 103. The extent of the public interest is shown by the statute to be limited, since the statute ordinarily does not apply to land when the surface is owned by the owner of the coal. Furthermore, it is not justified as a protection of personal safety. That could be provided for by notice. Indeed the very foundation of this bill is that the defendant gave timely notice of its intent to mine under the house. On the other hand the extent of the taking is great. It purports to abolish what is recognized in Pennsylvania as an estate in land—a very valuable estate—and what is declared by the Court below to be a contract hitherto binding the plaintiffs. If we were called upon to deal with the plaintiffs' position alone, we should think it clear that the statute does not disclose a public interest sufficient to warrant so extensive a destruction of the defendant's constitutionally protected rights.

But the case has been treated as one in which the general validity of the act should be discussed. The Attorney General of the State, the City of Scranton, and the representatives of other extensive interests were allowed to take part in the argument below and have submitted their contentions here. It seems, therefore, to be our duty to go farther in the statement of our opinion, in order that it may be known at once, and that further suits should not be brought in vain.

It is our opinion that the act cannot be sustained as an exercise of the police power, so far as it affects the mining of coal under streets or cities in places where the right to mine such coal has been reserved. As said in a Pennsylvania case, "For practical purposes, the right to coal consists in the right to mine it." Commonwealth v. Clearview Coal Co., 256 Pa. St. 328, 331. What makes the right to mine coal valuable is that it can be exercised with profit. To make it commercially impracticable to mine certain coal has very nearly the same effect for constitutional purposes as appropriating or destroying it. This we think that we are warranted in assuming that the statute does.

It is true that in Plymouth Coal Co. v. Pennsylvania, 232 U.S. 531, it was held competent for the legislature to require a pillar of coal to be left along the line of adjoining property, that, with the pillar on the other side of the line, would be a barrier sufficient for the safety of the employees of either mine in case the other should be abandoned and allowed to fill with water. But that was a requirement for the safety of employees invited into the mine, and secured an average reciprocity of advantage that has been recognized as a justification of various laws.

The rights of the public in a street purchased or laid out by eminent domain are those that it has paid for. If in any case its representatives have been so short sighted as to acquire only surface rights without the right of support, we see no more authority for supplying the latter without compensation than there was for taking the right of way in the first place and refusing to pay for it because the public wanted it very much. The protection of private property in the Fifth Amendment presupposes that it is wanted for public use, but provides that it shall not be taken for such use without compensation. A similar assumption is made in the decisions upon the Fourteenth Amendment. Hairston v. Danville & Western Ry. Co., 208 U.S. 598, 605. When this seemingly absolute protection is found to be qualified by the police power, the natural tendency of human nature is to extend the qualification more and more until at last private property disappears. But that cannot be accomplished in this way under the Constitution of the United States.

The general rule at least is, that while property may be regulated to a certain extent, if regulation goes too far it will be recognized as a taking. It may be doubted how far exceptional cases, like the blowing up of a house to stop a conflagration, go—and if they go beyond the general rule, whether they do not stand as much upon tradition as upon principle. Bowditch v. Boston, 101 U.S. 16. In general it is not plain that a man's misfortunes or necessities will justify his shifting the damages to his neighbor's shoulders. Spade v. Lynn & Boston R.R. Co., 172 Mass. 488, 489. We are in danger of forgetting that a strong public desire to improve the public condition is not enough to warrant achieving the desire by a shorter cut than the constitutional way of paying for the change. As we already have said, this is a question of degree—and therefore cannot be disposed of by general propositions. But we regard this as going beyond any of the cases decided by this Court.

We assume, of course, that the statute was passed upon the conviction that an exigency existed that would warrant it, and we assume that an exigency exists that would warrant the exercise of eminent domain. But the question at bottom is upon whom the loss of the changes desired should fall. So far as private persons or communities have seen fit to take the risk of acquiring only surface rights, we cannot see that the fact that their risk has become a danger warrants the giving to them greater rights than they bought.

Decree reversed.

■ JUSTICE BRANDEIS, dissenting.

Every restriction upon the use of property imposed in the exercise of the police power deprives the owner of some right theretofore enjoyed, and is, in that sense, an abridgment by the State of rights in property without making compensation. But restriction imposed to protect the public health, safety or morals from dangers threatened is not a taking. The restriction here in question is merely the prohibition of a noxious use. The property so restricted remains in the possession of its owner. The State does not appropriate it or make any use of it. The State merely prevents the owner from making a use which interferes with paramount rights of the public.

It is said that one fact for consideration in determining whether the limits of the police power have been exceeded is the extent of the resulting diminution in value; and that here the restriction destroys existing rights of property and contract. But values are relative. If we are to consider the value of the coal kept in place by the restriction, we should compare it with the value of all other parts of the land. That is, with the value not of the coal alone, but with the value of the whole property. The rights of an owner as against the public are not increased by dividing the interests in his property into surface and subsoil. The sum of the rights in the parts can not be greater than the rights in the whole. The estate of an owner in land is grandiloquently described as extending *ab orco usque ad coelum*. But I suppose no one would contend that by selling his interest above one hundred feet from the surface he could prevent the State from limiting, by the police power, the height of structures in a city. And why should a sale of underground rights bar the State's power? For aught that appears the value of the coal kept in place by the restriction may be negligible as compared with the value of the whole property, or even as compared with that part of it which is represented by the coal remaining in place and which may be extracted despite the statute.

A prohibition of mining which causes subsidence of such structures and facilities is obviously enacted for a public purpose; and it seems, likewise, clear that mere notice of intention to mine would not in this connection secure the public safety. Yet it is said that these provisions of the act cannot be sustained as an exercise of the police power where the right to mine such coal has been reserved. The conclusion seems to rest upon the assumption that in order to justify such exercise of the police power there must be "an average reciprocity of advantage" as between the owner of the property restricted and the rest of the community; and that here such reciprocity is absent. Reciprocity of advantage is an important consideration, and may even be an essential, where the State's power is exercised for the purpose of conferring benefits upon the property of a neighborhood, as in drainage projects, Wurts v. Hoagland, 114 U.S. 606; Fallbrook Irrigation District v. Bradley, 164 U.S. 112; or upon adjoining owners, as by party wall provisions, Jackman v. Rosenbaum Co., 260 U.S. 22. But where the police power is exercised, not to confer benefits upon property owners, but to protect the public from detriment and danger, there is, in my opinion, no room for considering reciprocity of advantage. There was no reciprocal advantage to the owner prohibited from using his oil tanks in 248 U.S. 498; his brickyard, in 239 U.S. 394; his livery stable, in 237 U.S. 171; his billiard hall, in 225 U.S. 623; his oleomargarine factory, in 127 U.S. 678; his brewery, in 123 U.S. 623; unless it be the advantage of living and doing business in a civilized community. That reciprocal advantage is given by the act to the coal operators.

NOTES AND QUESTIONS

1. Did the Court in *Mugler* treat the landowners' constitutional challenge as a takings challenge? If not, why not?

How does the Court distinguish *Mugler* from *Pumpelly v. Green Bay Co.,* in which a dam built under state auspices caused the flooding of the landowner's land, making it unusable? If the state's action in *Pumpelly* constituted a taking, why not the state's action in *Mugler*?

2. Suppose the state's prohibitions reduced the value of the brewery equipment to nearly zero. Why should the brewery owner have to bear that loss? Wouldn't it be fairer to spread that loss among the public at large? Would the Supreme Court have accomplished that result by holding the state's action unconstitutional?

Who should bear the loss if a state imposes emissions limits that require certain factories to close? Mileage requirements that render certain automobile technologies obsolete? Is that a decision that should be made by courts or legislatures? What does the Court in *Mugler* say about that issue?

3. Suppose a blight attacks trees within the state. The blight infests ornamental cedar trees, causing no damage to those trees, but destroys commercially valuable apple trees. If you were a state legislator faced with the problem, which of these alternatives seems preferable:

a. Do nothing and allow cedar tree and apple tree owners to negotiate to a solution;

b. Require removal of all cedar trees, and compensate the cedar tree owners with tax monies;

c. Require removal of all cedar trees, and require apple tree owners to compensate cedar tree owners;

d. Require removal of all cedar trees, and provide no compensation to cedar tree owners?

In light of *Mugler*, would any of these alternatives be unconstitutional? *Cf.* Miller v. Schoene, 276 U.S. 272 (1928) (upholding legislation requiring removal of cedar trees without providing compensation to tree owners).

4. How is *Pennsylvania Coal* different from *Mugler*? If mining coal threatened to cause subsidence of soil, why would the Court hold the Kohler Act unconstitutional? Isn't it up to the legislature to decide whether the coal's company's activities were sufficiently harmful to warrant prohibition? And if the activities were harmful, why would compensation be due?

5. Does *Pennsylvania Coal* hold that the Kohler Act violates the Takings Clause? The Due Process Clause? The Contracts Clause? Does it matter? If so, why?

6. *The Denominator Problem.* The most famous phrase in the *Pennsylvania Coal* is Justice Holmes' statement that "while property may be regulated to a certain extent, if regulation goes too far it will be recognized as a taking." How can a court tell whether regulation has gone too far? Is the issue a relative one—what percentage of the property's value has the landowner lost? If so, how should a court define the landowner's property? For instance, should it be all of the coal mining rights owned by the coal company, or should it be the right to cause subsidence of the surface? How would Justice Brandeis, who dissented in *Pennsylvania Coal*, resolve this issue? The issue, often dubbed "the denominator problem," remains a difficult one for takings jurisprudence.

B. THEORETICAL PERSPECTIVES.

In 1967, in one of the most influential law review articles in history, Professor Frank Michelman tackled the takings issue. He started by recognizing that government regulation often generates efficiency gains, and then turned to a basic question: why not always require those benefited by the regulation to compensate those who have suffered losses as a result of the regulation? He identified the impracticality of full compensation:

[T]o insist on full compensation to every interest which is disproportionately burdened by a social measure dictated by efficiency would be to call a halt to the collective pursuit of efficiency. It would require a tracing of all impacts, no matter how remote, speculative, or arguable, and a valuation of all burdens, no matter how idiosyncratic or imponderable. . . . The expense of maintaining and operating whatever settlement machinery was deemed adequate would more than eat up the gains which seemed to make the measure efficient.

Frank I. Michelman, Property, Utility, and Fairness: Comments on the Ethical Foundations of "Just Compensation" Law, 80 Harv. L. Rev. 1165, 1178–79 (1967). Michelman argued that from a utilitarian perspective, property owners should be compensated for losses resulting from efficiency-promoting regulations whenever the "demoralization costs" generated by not compensating would exceed the "settlement costs" associated with compensation. Demoralization costs are typically higher when a property owner's losses result from purposive human action. As Michelman notes:

[E]ven though people can adjust satisfactorily to random uncertainty, which can be dealt with through insurance, including self-insurance, they will remain on edge when contemplating the possibility of strategically determined losses. For when the bearing of strategy is evident, one faces the risk of being *systematically* imposed upon, which seems a risk of a very different order from the risk of occasional, accidental injury.

Capricious redistributions will not be tolerated, even as accidental adjuncts of efficiency-dictated measures, when compensation settlements can be reached without much trouble, that is, when settlement costs are low. The clearer it is that the claimant has sustained an injury distinct from those sustained by the generality of persons in society, and the more obviously there appears to be some objectively satisfactory measure of his disproportionate or distinctive injury, the more compelling will his claim to compensation become.

Id. at 1217. Michelman then turned to the question of fairness:

A decision not to compensate is not unfair as long as the disappointed claimant ought to be able to appreciate how such decisions might fit into a consistent practice which holds forth a lesser long-run risk to people like him than would any consistent practice which is naturally suggested by the opposite decision. . . .

If we set about to make practical use of this approach, we shall find ourselves asking much the same questions to determine whether a compensability decision is fair as were suggested by the utilitarian approach. The relevant risks plainly are minimized by insistence on compensation when settlement costs are low, when efficiency gains are dubious, and when the harm concentrated on one individual is unusually great. They are also minimized if insistence on compensation is relaxed when there are visible reciprocities of burden and benefit, or when burdens similar to that for which compensation is denied are concomitantly imposed on many other people (indicating that settlement costs are high and that those sustaining the burden are probably incurring relatively small net losses— else, being many, they probably could have been mobilized to deflect the measure which burdens them).

Id. at 1223.

NOTES AND QUESTIONS

1.   Reconsider the following cases:

Village of Euclid v. Ambler Realty (p. 12 *supra*).

Mugler v. Kansas (p. 235 *supra*).

Pennsylvania Coal Co. v. Mahon (p. 239 *supra*).

Miller v. Schoene (see Note 3, *supra*).

In each case, consider how you would use Michelman's analytical framework to argue (a) that the landowner is entitled to compensation, and (b) that the landowner is not entitled to compensation. In each case, which argument is more persuasive?

2.   Michelman also argued that, from a utilitarian perspective, regulation is undesirable when the regulation's efficiency gains are smaller than settlement costs—"the dollar value of the time, effort and resources which would be required to reach compensation settlements adequate to avoid demoralization costs." 80 Harv. L. Rev. 1165, 1214–15. Are government entities more likely to enact regulations Michelman would consider undesirable when those entities are freed of the obligation to pay compensation?

Consider the following analysis offered by Richard Epstein in Takings: Private Property and the Power of Eminent Domain (1985) at 263–65:

The need for diligent supervision in land use cases derives in large measure from the persistent risk of faction in local government politics. . . . [T]here are easily exploitable gains to be made under public control, both from the owners of undeveloped plots and from those who wish to acquire them.

In the usual land use controversy, the participants press for their immediate advantage, and their zeal may be heightened if their successful maneuvers frighten off others who wish to challenge local domination.

The political process is directly connected to the problem of takings. Local boards may take private rights of use and disposition into the public domain without compensation, then parcel them out again to others by majority rule.... Where property rights are enforced, owners can make choices on efficient land use without having to overcome the conundrums of collective choice.... Land use regulation places the land back into a modified common pool, where many persons can limit the future use of the land, even though only one person, the owner, can actually use it. Ill-defined rights replace well-defined ones, and transaction cost barriers are likely to exceed the gains that otherwise are obtainable from any shift in land use or ownership.

Strict judicial supervision of the zoning process is therefore appropriate to correct the unstable political situation.

Epstein argued that government should be required to compensate landowners for losses due to government regulation unless the regulation is designed to control nuisances, or where the restricted property owners receive "implicit in-kind compensation" because "the restrictions imposed by the general legislation upon the rights of others serve as compensation for the property taken." *Id.* at 195

How do you think Epstein would have decided *Euclid*? *Miller v. Schoene*?

3. Should takings law require governmental entities to honor particular legal rights, or should takings law protect landowners against *changes* in legal rights? Do the excerpts from Professors Michelman and Epstein shed any light on that question?

C. *PENN CENTRAL* BALANCING

In *Nectow v. City of Cambridge*, 277 U.S. 183 (1928), decided six years after *Pennsylvania Coal*, the Supreme Court invalidated a local zoning regulation (invoking the Due Process clause). For the next 50 years, the Court did not invalidate a local land use regulation, and provided little guidance in the few cases that did challenge local regulations. In the meanwhile, state courts grappled with the content of the Takings Clause. The Supreme Court returned to the scene in the following case:

Penn Central Transportation Co. v. New York City

Supreme Court of the United States, 1978
438 U.S. 104

■ JUSTICE BRENNAN delivered the opinion of the Court.

The question presented is whether a city may, as part of a comprehensive program to preserve historic landmarks and historic districts, place restrictions on the development of individual historic landmarks—in addition to those imposed by applicable zoning ordinances—without effecting a "taking" requiring the payment of "just compensation." Specifically, we must decide whether the application of New York City's Landmarks Preservation Law to the parcel of land occupied by Grand Central Terminal has "taken" its owners' property in violation of the Fifth and Fourteenth Amendments.

I

A

New York City adopted its Landmarks Preservation Law in 1965.

The operation of the law can be briefly summarized. The primary responsibility for administering the law is vested in the Landmarks Preservation Commission (Commission), a broad based, 11-member agency assisted by a technical staff. If the Commission determines, after giving all interested parties an opportunity to be heard, that a building or area satisfies the ordinance's criteria, it will designate a building to be a "landmark situated on a particular 'landmark site,' or will designate an area to be a 'historic district.' " Thus far, 31 historic districts and over 400 individual landmarks have been finally designated, and the process is a continuing one.

Final designation as a landmark results in restrictions upon the property owner's options concerning use of the landmark site.

In the event an owner wishes to alter a landmark site, three separate procedures are available through which administrative approval may be obtained. First, the owner may apply to the Commission for a "certificate of no effect on protected architectural features": that is, for an order approving the improvement or alteration on the ground that it will not change or affect any architectural feature of the landmark and will be in harmony therewith.

Second, the owner may apply to the Commission for a certificate of "appropriateness." Such certificates will be granted if the Commission concludes—focusing upon aesthetic, historical, and architectural values—that the proposed construction on the landmark site would not unduly hinder the protection, enhancement, perpetuation, and use of the landmark. Again, denial of the certificate is subject to judicial review. Moreover, the owner who is denied either a certificate of no exterior effect or a certificate of appropriateness may submit an alternative or modified plan for approval. The final procedure—seeking a certificate of appropriateness on the ground of "insufficient return."

Although the designation of a landmark and landmark site restricts the owner's control over the parcel, designation also enhances the economic position of the landmark owner in one significant respect. Under New York City's zoning laws, owners of real property who have not developed their property to the full extent permitted by the applicable zoning laws are allowed to transfer development rights to contiguous parcels on the same city block. *See* New York City, Zoning Resolution Art. I, ch. 2, § 12–10 (1978) (definition of "zoning lot").

B

This case involves the application of New York City's Landmarks Preservation Law to Grand Central Terminal (Terminal). The Terminal, which is owned by the Penn Central Transportation Co. and its affiliates (Penn Central), is one of New York City's most famous buildings. Opened in 1913, it is regarded not only as providing an ingenious engineering solution to the problems presented by urban railroad stations, but also as a magnificent example of the French beaux-arts style.

On August 2, 1967, following a public hearing, the Commission designated the Terminal a "landmark" and designated the "city tax block" it occupies a "landmark site."

On January 22, 1968, appellant Penn Central, to increase its income, entered into a renewable 50-year lease and sublease agreement with appellant UGP Properties, Inc. (UGP), a wholly owned subsidiary of Union General Properties, Ltd., a United Kingdom corporation. Under the terms of the agreement, UGP was to construct a multi-story office building above the Terminal. UGP promised to pay Penn Central $1 million annually during construction and at least $3 million annually thereafter. The rentals would be offset in part by a loss of some $700,000 to $1 million in net rentals presently received from concessionaires displaced by the new building.

Appellants UGP and Penn Central then applied to the Commission for permission to construct an office building atop the Terminal. Two separate plans, both designed by architect Marcel Breuer and both apparently satisfying the terms of the applicable zoning ordinance, were submitted to the Commission for approval. The first, Breuer I, provided for the construction of a 55-story office building, to be cantilevered above the existing facade and to rest on the roof of the Terminal. The second, Breuer II Revised, called for tearing down a portion of the Terminal that included the 42d Street facade, stripping off some of the remaining features of the Terminal's facade, and constructing a 53-story office building. The Commission denied a certificate of no exterior effect on September 20, 1968. Appellants then applied for a certificate of "appropriateness" as to both proposals. After four days of hearings at which over 80 witnesses testified, the Commission denied this application as to both proposals.

Appellants did not seek judicial review of the denial of either certificate. Further, appellants did not avail themselves of the opportunity to develop and submit other plans for the Commission's consideration and approval. Instead, appellants filed suit in New York Supreme Court, Trial Term, claiming, *inter alia*, that the application of the Landmarks Preservation Law had "taken" their property without just compensation in violation of the Fifth and Fourteenth Amendments and arbitrarily deprived them of their property without due process of law in violation of the Fourteenth Amendment. Appellants sought a declaratory judgment, injunctive relief barring the city from using the Landmarks Law to impede the construction of any structure that might otherwise lawfully be constructed on the Terminal site, and damages for the "temporary taking" that occurred between August 2, 1967, the designation date, and the date when the restrictions arising from the Landmarks Law would be lifted

II

The issues presented by appellants are (1) whether the restrictions imposed by New York City's law upon appellants' exploitation of the Terminal site effect a "taking" of appellants' property for a public use within the meaning of the Fifth Amendment, which of course is made applicable to the States through the Fourteenth Amendment, *see* Chicago, B. & Q. R. Co. v. Chicago, 166 U.S. 226, 239 (1897), and, (2), if so, whether the transferable development rights afforded appellants constitute "just compensation" within the meaning of the Fifth Amendment. We need only address the question whether a "taking" has occurred.

A

The question of what constitutes a "taking" for purposes of the Fifth Amendment has proved to be a problem of considerable difficulty. While this Court has recognized that the "Fifth Amendment's guarantee . . . [is] designed to bar Government from forcing some people alone to bear public burdens which, in all fairness and justice, should be borne by the public as a whole," Armstrong v. United States, 364 U.S. 40, 49 (1960), this Court, quite simply, has been unable to develop any "set formula" for determining when "justice and fairness" require that economic injuries caused by public action be compensated by the government, rather than remain disproportionately concentrated on a few persons. *See* Goldblatt v. Hempstead, 369 U.S. 590, 594 (1962). Indeed, we have frequently observed that whether a particular restriction will be rendered invalid by the government's failure to pay for any losses proximately caused by it depends largely "upon the particular circumstances [in that] case." United States v. Central Eureka Mining Co., 357 U.S. 155, 168 (1958); *see* United States v. Caltex, Inc., 344 U.S. 149, 156 (1952).

In engaging in these essentially ad hoc, factual inquiries, the Court's decisions have identified several factors that have particular significance. The economic impact of the regulation on the claimant and, particularly, the extent to which the regulation has interfered with distinct investment-backed expectations are, of course, relevant considerations. *See* Goldblatt v. Hempstead, *supra*, at 594. So, too, is the character of the governmental action. A "taking" may more readily be found when the interference with property can be characterized as a physical invasion by government, *see, e.g.*, United States v. Causby, 328 U.S. 256 (1946), than when interference arises from some public program adjusting the benefits and burdens of economic life to promote the common good.

"Government hardly could go on if to some extent values incident to property could not be diminished without paying for every such change in the general law," Pennsylvania Coal Co. v. Mahon, 260 U.S. 393, 413 (1922), and this Court has accordingly recognized, in a wide variety of contexts, that government may execute laws or programs that adversely affect recognized economic values. Exercises of the taxing power are one obvious example. A second are the decisions in which this Court has dismissed "taking" challenges on the ground that, while the challenged government action caused economic harm, it did not interfere with interests that were sufficiently bound up with the reasonable expectations of the claimant to constitute "property" for Fifth Amendment purposes. *See, e.g.*, United States v. Willow River Power Co., 324 U.S. 499 (1945) (interest in high-water level of river for runoff for tailwaters to maintain power head is not property); United States v. Chandler-Dunbar Water Power Co., 229 U.S. 53 (1913) (no property interest can exist in navigable waters); *see also* Demorest v. City Bank Co., 321 U.S. 36 (1944); Muhlker v. Harlem R. Co., 197 U.S. 544 (1905); Sax, Takings and the Police Power, 74 Yale L. J. 36, 61–62 (1964).

More importantly for the present case, in instances in which a state tribunal reasonably concluded that "the health, safety, morals, or general welfare" would be promoted by prohibiting particular contemplated uses of land, this Court has upheld land-use regulations that destroyed or adversely affected recognized real property interests. *See* Nectow v. Cambridge, 277 U.S. 183, 188 (1928). Zoning laws are, of course, the classic example, *see* Euclid v. Ambler Realty Co., 272 U.S. 365 (1926) (prohibition of industrial use); Gorieb v. Fox, 274 U.S. 603, 608 (1927) (requirement that portions of parcels be left unbuilt); Welch v. Swasey, 214 U.S. 91 (1909) (height restriction), which have been viewed as permissible governmental action even when prohibiting the most beneficial use of the property. *See* Goldblatt v. Hempstead, *supra*, at 592–593, and cases cited; *see also* Eastlake v. Forest City Enterprises, Inc., 426 U.S. 668, 674, n. 8 (1976).

Zoning laws generally do not affect existing uses of real property, but "taking" challenges have also been held to be without merit in a wide variety of situations when the challenged governmental actions prohibited a beneficial use to which individual parcels had previously been devoted and thus caused substantial individualized harm. Miller v. Schoene, 276 U.S. 272 (1928), is illustrative. In that case, a state entomologist, acting pursuant to a state statute, ordered the claimants to cut down a large number of ornamental red cedar trees because they produced cedar rust fatal to apple trees cultivated nearby. Although the statute provided for recovery of any expense incurred in removing the cedars, and permitted claimants to use the felled trees, it did not provide compensation for the value of the standing trees or for the resulting decrease in market value of the properties as a whole. A unanimous Court held that this latter omission did not render the statute invalid. The Court held that the State might properly make "a choice between the preservation of one class of property and that of the other" and since the apple industry was important in the State involved, concluded that the State had not exceeded "its constitutional powers by deciding upon the destruction of one class of property [without compensation] in order to save another which, in the judgment of the legislature, is of greater value to the public." *Id.*, at 279.

Pennsylvania Coal Co. v. Mahon, 260 U.S. 393 (1922), is the leading case for the proposition that a state statute that substantially furthers important public policies may so frustrate distinct investment-backed expectations as to amount to a "taking." Because the statute made it commercially impracticable to mine the coal, *id.*, at 414, and thus had nearly the same effect as the complete destruction of rights claimant had reserved from the owners of the surface land, see *id.*, at 414–415, the Court held that the statute was invalid as effecting a "taking" without just compensation. *See also* Armstrong v. United States, 364 U.S. 40 (1960) (Government's complete destruction of a materialman's lien in certain property held a "taking"); Hudson Water Co. v. McCarter, 209 U.S. 349, 355 (1908) (if height restriction makes property wholly useless "the rights of property . . . prevail over the other public interest" and compensation is required). *See generally* Michelman, Property, Utility, and Fairness: Comments on the Ethical Foundations of "Just Compensation" Law, 80 Harv. L. Rev. 1165, 1229–1234 (1967).

Finally, government actions that may be characterized as acquisitions of resources to permit or facilitate uniquely public functions have often been held to constitute "takings." United States v. Causby, 328 U.S. 256 (1946), is illustrative. In holding that direct overflights above the claimant's land, that destroyed the present use of the land as a chicken farm, constituted a "taking," *Causby* emphasized that Government had not "merely destroyed property [but was] using a part of it for the flight of its planes." *Id.*, at 262–263, n. 7.

B

In contending that the New York City law has "taken" their property in violation of the Fifth and Fourteenth Amendments, appellants make a series of arguments, which, while tailored to the facts of this case, essentially urge that any substantial restriction imposed pursuant to a landmark law must be accompanied by just compensation if it is to be constitutional. They accept for present purposes both that the parcel of land occupied by Grand Central Terminal must, in its present state, be regarded as capable of earning a reasonable return, and that the transferable development rights afforded appellants by virtue of the Terminal's designation as a landmark are valuable, even if not as valuable as the rights to construct above the Terminal. In appellants' view none of these factors derogate from their claim that New York City's law has effected a "taking."

They first observe that the airspace above the Terminal is a valuable property interest, citing United States v. Causby, *supra.* They urge that the Landmarks Law has deprived them of any gainful use of their "air rights" above the Terminal and that, irrespective of the value of the remainder of their parcel, the city has "taken" their right to this superjacent airspace, thus entitling them to "just compensation" measured by the fair market value of these air rights.

"Taking" jurisprudence does not divide a single parcel into discrete segments and attempt to determine whether rights in a particular segment have been entirely abrogated. In deciding whether a particular governmental action has effected a taking, this Court focuses rather both on the character of the action and on the nature and extent of the interference with rights in the parcel as a whole—here, the city tax block designated as the "landmark site."

Secondly, appellants, focusing on the character and impact of the New York City law, argue that it effects a "taking" because its operation has significantly diminished the value of the Terminal site. Appellants concede that the decisions sustaining other land-use regulations, which, like the New York City law, are reasonably related to the promotion of the general welfare, uniformly reject the proposition that diminution in property value, standing alone, can establish a "taking," *see* Euclid v. Ambler Realty Co., 272 U.S. 365 (1926) (75% diminution in value caused by zoning law); Hadacheck v. Sebastian, 239 U.S. 394 (1915) (87 1/2% diminution in value); *cf.* Eastlake v. Forest City Enterprises, Inc., 426 U.S., at 674, n. 8, and that the "taking" issue in these contexts is resolved by focusing on the uses the regulations permit. *See also* Goldblatt v. Hempstead, *supra.* Appellants, moreover, also do not dispute that a showing of diminution in property value would not establish a "taking" if the restriction had been imposed as a result of historic-district legislation, *see generally* Maher v. New Orleans, 516 F.2d 1051 (CA5 1975), but appellants argue that New York City's regulation of individual landmarks is fundamentally different from zoning or from historic-district legislation because the controls imposed by New York City's law apply only to individuals who own selected properties.

It is true, as appellants emphasize, that both historic-district legislation and zoning laws regulate all properties within given physical communities whereas landmark laws apply only to selected parcels.

But, contrary to appellants' suggestions, landmark laws are not like discriminatory, or "reverse spot," zoning: that is, a land-use decision which arbitrarily singles out a particular parcel for different, less favorable treatment than the neighboring ones. *See* 2 A. Rathkopf, The Law of Zoning and Planning 26–4, and n. 6 (4th ed. 1978). In contrast to discriminatory zoning, which is the antithesis of land-use control as part of some comprehensive plan, the New York City law embodies a comprehensive plan to preserve structures of historic or aesthetic interest wherever they might be found in the city, and as noted, over 400 landmarks and 31 historic districts have been designated pursuant to this plan.

Next, appellants observe that New York City's law differs from zoning laws and historic-district ordinances in that the Landmarks Law does not impose identical or similar restrictions on all structures located in particular physical communities. It follows, they argue, that New York City's law is inherently incapable of producing the fair and equitable distribution of benefits and burdens of governmental action which is characteristic of zoning laws and historic-district legislation and which they maintain is a constitutional requirement if "just compensation" is not to be afforded. It is, of course, true that the Landmarks Law has a more severe impact on some landowners than on others, but that in itself does not mean that the law effects a "taking." Legislation designed to promote the general welfare commonly burdens some more than others. For example, the property owner in *Euclid* who wished to use its property for industrial purposes was affected far more severely by the ordinance than its neighbors who wished to use their land for residences.

In any event, appellants' repeated suggestions that they are solely burdened and unbenefited is factually inaccurate. This contention overlooks the fact that the New York City law applies to vast numbers of structures in the city in addition to the Terminal—all the structures contained in the 31 historic districts and over 400 individual landmarks, many of which are close to the Terminal. Unless we are to reject the judgment of the New York City Council that the preservation of landmarks benefits all New York citizens and all structures, both economically and by improving the quality of life in the city as a whole—which we are unwilling to do—we cannot conclude that the owners of the Terminal have in no sense been benefited by the Landmarks Law. Doubtless appellants believe they are more burdened than benefited by the law, but that must have been true, too, of the property owners in *Miller*, *Hadacheck*, *Euclid*, and *Goldblatt*.

C

Rejection of appellants' broad arguments is not, however, the end of our inquiry, for all we thus far have established is that the New York City law is not rendered invalid by its failure to provide "just compensation" whenever a landmark owner is restricted in the exploitation of property interests, such as air rights, to a greater extent than provided for under applicable zoning laws. We now must consider whether the interference with appellants' property is of such a magnitude that "there must be an exercise of eminent domain and compensation to sustain [it]." Pennsylvania Coal Co. v. Mahon, 260 U.S., at 413. That inquiry may be narrowed to the question of the severity of the impact of the law on appellants' parcel, and its resolution in turn requires a careful assessment of the impact of the regulation on the Terminal site.

Unlike the governmental acts in *Goldblatt*, *Miller*, *Causby*, *Griggs*, and *Hadacheck*, the New York City law does not interfere in any way with the present uses of the Terminal. Its designation as a landmark not only permits but contemplates that appellants may continue to use the property precisely as it has been used for the past 65 years: as a railroad terminal containing office space and concessions. So the law does not interfere with what must be regarded as Penn Central's primary expectation concerning the use of the parcel. More importantly, on this record, we must regard the New York City law as permitting Penn Central not only to profit from the Terminal but also to obtain a "reasonable return" on its investment.

Appellants, moreover, exaggerate the effect of the law on their ability to make use of the air rights above the Terminal in two respects. First, it simply cannot be maintained, on this record, that appellants have been prohibited from occupying *any* portion of the airspace above the Terminal. While the Commission's actions in denying applications to construct an office building in excess of 50 stories above the Terminal may indicate that it will refuse to issue a certificate of appropriateness for any comparably sized structure, nothing the Commission has said or done suggests an intention to prohibit *any* construction above the Terminal. The Commission's report emphasized that whether any construction would be allowed depended upon whether the proposed addition "would harmonize in scale, material, and character with [the Terminal]." Record 2251. Since appellants have not sought approval for the construction of a smaller structure, we do not know that appellants will be denied any use of any portion of the airspace above the Terminal.

Second, to the extent appellants have been denied the right to build above the Terminal, it is not literally accurate to say that they have been denied *all* use of even those pre-existing air rights. Their ability to use these rights has not been abrogated; they are made transferable to at least eight parcels in the vicinity of the Terminal, one or two of which have been found suitable for the construction of new office buildings. Although appellants and others have argued that New York City's transferable development-rights program is far from ideal, the New

York courts here supportably found that, at least in the case of the Terminal, the rights afforded are valuable. While these rights may well not have constituted "just compensation" if a "taking" had occurred, the rights nevertheless undoubtedly mitigate whatever financial burdens the law has imposed on appellants and, for that reason, are to be taken into account in considering the impact of regulation. *Cf.* Goldblatt v. Hempstead, 369 U.S., at 594, n. 3.

On this record, we conclude that the application of New York City's Landmarks Law has not effected a "taking" of appellants' property. The restrictions imposed are substantially related to the promotion of the general welfare and not only permit reasonable beneficial use of the landmark site but also afford appellants opportunities further to enhance not only the Terminal site proper but also other properties.

Affirmed.

■ JUSTICE REHNQUIST, with whom THE CHIEF JUSTICE and JUSTICE STEVENS join, dissenting.

Of the over one million buildings and structures in the city of New York, appellees have singled out 400 for designation as official landmarks. The owner of a building might initially be pleased that his property has been chosen by a distinguished committee of architects, historians, and city planners for such a singular distinction. But he may well discover, as appellant Penn Central Transportation Co. did here, that the landmark designation imposes upon him a substantial cost, with little or no offsetting benefit except for the honor of the designation. The question in this case is whether the cost associated with the city of New York's desire to preserve a limited number of "landmarks" within its borders must be borne by all of its taxpayers or whether it can instead be imposed entirely on the owners of the individual properties.

Only in the most superficial sense of the word can this case be said to involve "zoning." Typical zoning restrictions may, it is true, so limit the prospective uses of a piece of property as to diminish the value of that property in the abstract because it may not be used for the forbidden purposes. But any such abstract decrease in value will more than likely be at least partially offset by an increase in value which flows from similar restrictions as to use on neighboring properties. All property owners in a designated area are placed under the same restrictions, not only for the benefit of the municipality as a whole but also for the common benefit of one another. In the words of Mr. Justice Holmes, speaking for the Court in Pennsylvania Coal Co. v. Mahon, 260 U.S. 393, 415 (1922), there is "an average reciprocity of advantage."

Where a relatively few individual buildings, all separated from one another, are singled out and treated differently from surrounding buildings, no such reciprocity exists. The cost to the property owner which results from the imposition of restrictions applicable only to his property and not that of his neighbors may be substantial—in this case, several million dollars—with no comparable reciprocal benefits. And the cost associated with landmark legislation is likely to be of a completely different order of magnitude than that which results from the imposition of normal zoning restrictions.

I

B

Appellees have thus destroyed—in a literal sense, "taken"—substantial property rights of Penn Central. Because "not every destruction or injury to property by governmental action has been held to be a 'taking' in the constitutional sense," Armstrong v. United States, 364 U.S., at 48, however, this does not end our inquiry. But an examination of the two exceptions where the destruction of property does *not* constitute a taking demonstrates that a compensable taking has occurred here.

1

As early as 1887, the Court recognized that the government can prevent a property owner from using his property to injure others without having to compensate the owner for the value of the forbidden use.

Thus, there is no "taking" where a city prohibits the operation of a brickyard within a residential area, *see* Hadacheck v. Sebastian, 239 U.S. 394 (1915), or forbids excavation for sand and gravel below the water line, *see* Goldblatt v. Hempstead, 369 U.S. 590 (1962). Nor is it relevant, where the government is merely prohibiting a noxious use of property, that the government would seem to be singling out a particular property owner. *Hadacheck, supra,* at 413.

Appellees are not prohibiting a nuisance. The record is clear that the proposed addition to the Grand Central Terminal would be in full compliance with zoning, height limitations, and other health and safety requirements. Instead, appellees are seeking to preserve what they believe to be an outstanding example of beaux arts architecture. Penn Central is prevented from further developing its property basically because *too good* a job was done in designing and building it. The city of New York, because of its unadorned admiration for the design, has decided that the owners of the building must preserve it unchanged for the benefit of sightseeing New Yorkers and tourists.

2

Even where the government prohibits a noninjurious use, the Court has ruled that a taking does not take place if the prohibition applies over a broad cross section of land and thereby "[secures] an average reciprocity of advantage." Pennsylvania Coal Co. v. Mahon, 260 U.S., at 415. It is for this reason that zoning does not constitute a "taking." While zoning at times reduces *individual* property values, the burden is shared relatively evenly and it is reasonable to conclude that on the whole an individual who is harmed by one aspect of the zoning will be benefited by another.

Here, however, a multimillion dollar loss has been imposed on appellants; it is uniquely felt and is not offset by any benefits flowing from the preservation of some 400 other "landmarks" in New York City. Appellees have imposed a substantial cost on less than one one-tenth of one percent of the buildings in New York City for the general benefit of all its people. It is exactly this imposition of general costs on a few individuals at which the "taking" protection is directed.

As Mr. Justice Holmes pointed out in Pennsylvania Coal Co. v. Mahon, "the question at bottom" in an eminent domain case "is upon whom the loss of the changes desired should fall." 260 U.S., at 416. The benefits that appellees believe will flow from preservation of the Grand Central Terminal will accrue to all the citizens of New York City. There is no reason to believe that appellants will enjoy a substantially greater share of these benefits. If the cost of preserving Grand Central Terminal were spread evenly across the entire population of the city of New York, the burden per person would be in cents per year—a minor cost appellees would surely concede for the benefit accrued. Instead, however, appellees would impose the entire cost of several million dollars per year on Penn Central. But it is precisely this sort of discrimination that the Fifth Amendment prohibits.

NOTES AND QUESTIONS

1.   Among the factors the Court treats as relevant in determining whether a regulation should be deemed a taking is the regulation's interference with investment-backed expectations. Whose expectations were relevant in *Penn Central*? Penn Central's expectations? UGP Properties' expectations?

What were UGP's investment-backed expectations at the time it entered into a lease with Penn Central? How much did the landmark regulation interfere with those expectations? What were the expectations of Penn Central (or its railroad predecessors) at the time those predecessors acquired the terminal property? How much did the landmark regulation interfere with those expectations? Why should Penn Central's expectations be more relevant than UGP's? Does the issue raise the same "denominator problem" as the regulation of subsidence rights in *Pennsylvania Coal?* Does the Court resolve the issue the same way?

2.   How can a court tell whether a landowner will actually build the structure the landowner contends it will build? If the landowner would have built the structure were it not for the challenged regulation, why didn't the landowner build the structure before the regulation was enacted? Does that explain, at least in part, why the *Penn Central* majority suggests that a regulation is more likely to be deemed a taking when the regulation interferes with an existing use than with a prospective use?

Is a regulation always a taking when it interferes with an existing use? Suppose, for instance, a zoning regulation prohibits brickyards in an area newly zoned for residential use. Would the owner of an existing brickyard be entitled to compensation if not exempted from the new ordinance? *See Hadacheck v. Sebastian*, 239 U.S. 394 (1915) (discussed in *Penn Central*).

3. Recall Professor Michelman's concern that requiring compensation would cripple regulation when "settlement costs" are high and the regulation's harm is spread among many landowners, but that compensation is generally appropriate when losses are concentrated on a small number of parties, and where settlement costs are low. Were the losses imposed by New York's Landmarks Preservation Law concentrated on a small number of landowners? Do the majority and dissent disagree about how to answer that question?

4. The *Penn Central* dissenters distinguished New York's landmark preservation ordinance from zoning by noting that zoning—and not landmark regulation—creates an "average reciprocity of advantage" that justifies leaving adversely affected landowners without compensation. How does the Court's majority respond to this argument?

5. *TDRs*. Transferable Development Rights (TDRs), discussed in Chapter Three, played a role in the New York City landmark preservation scheme, and in the Supreme Court's opinion. Many jurisdictions have authorized the use of TDRs to accomplish a variety of land use planning ends, including agricultural and historic preservation.

If a municipality wants to preserve an existing use on a site where development pressures make the site more valuable for a different use, the municipality can enact a TDR program that authorizes a parcel owner to sell, on the market, development rights not used on the existing site. The purchaser of the rights then becomes entitled to use the rights to build more intensively on the "receiving parcel" than the zoning ordinance would otherwise permit.

Typically, an ordinance limits the geographical area in which the TDRs can be used. Most ordinances also limit the maximum permissible density on any individual receiving parcel. For instance, the New York ordinance permitted use of TDRs to increase permissible density on a receiving site by a maximum of 20%. For a discussion of the restrictions applicable to New York City landmarks at the time of the *Penn Central* decision, *see* Norman Marcus, Air Rights in New York City: TDR, Zoning Lot Merger and the Well-Considered Plan, 50 Brook. L. Rev. 867, 878–881 (1984). Why would a municipality impose these limits? What effect would limits like these have on the market value of TDRs?

The advantages of TDR schemes are evident. They enable municipalities to preserve existing uses without depriving the site owner of all economic return. What disadvantages are there to TDR schemes? Who might object to TDRs?

In evaluating a landowner's takings claim, should TDRs be considered in determining whether a regulation (like New York City's landmark preservation scheme) unduly interferes with a landowner's investment-backed expectations, or should they be considered only in determining whether the landowner has received just compensation? Do the majority and the dissent in *Penn Central* agree on that issue? Who has the better of the argument?

6. *The Denominator Problem, Revisited.* In *Penn Central*, the landowner argues that it has suffered a total deprivation of its "air rights" over the terminal. This argument reintroduces the "denominator problem" we mentioned in our discussion of *Pennsylvania Coal*. The Court rejects Penn Central's narrow characterization of the denominator as the restricted space above the terminal. " 'Taking' jurisprudence does not divide a single parcel into discrete segments and attempt to determine whether rights in a particular segment have been entirely abrogated. In deciding whether a particular government action has effected a taking, this Court focuses . . . on the nature and extent of interference with rights in the parcel as a whole." The Court thought it obvious that "parcel as a whole" at issue in *Penn Central* was "the city tax block designated as the 'landmark site.' " But is that so obvious? The Grand Central Terminal property was built on the site of an earlier New York Central Railroad terminal (called "Grand Central Depot"). That terminal and its associated rail yard to the north stretched nearly from Madison to Lexington Avenues and from 42nd Street north to 49th Street. *See* William D. Middleton, Grand Central 25–30 (1977). When the current Grand Central Terminal was built, the New York Central Railroad (the predecessor of Penn Central) decided to bury the large rail yard. This allowed it to erect buildings on steel platforms over the tracks and connect its land to the existing street network, turning a rail yard into incredibly valuable real estate, which the railroad referred to in promotional material as "the Terminal City . . . a city within a city, occupying an area of thirty blocks." *Id.* at 91.

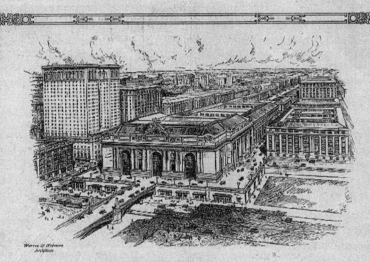

THE TERMINAL CITY

THE GREATEST CIVIC DEVELOPMENT EVER UNDERTAKEN—INCIDENT TO THE
NEW GRAND CENTRAL TERMINAL IN NEW YORK CITY, WHICH WILL BE

OPENED FEBRUARY, 1913

This vast undertaking comprehends the erection of a great Terminal City, a city within a city, occupying an area of thirty blocks, in New York City.

It will embrace hotels and modern apartment houses, convention and exhibition halls, clubs and restaurants, and department stores and specialty shops. In short, practically every sort of structure or enterprise incident to the modern city.

These features are all in addition to post office, express buildings and other natural adjuncts of the up-to-date terminal—to expeditiously handle diverse traffic.

All these structures will be erected over the tracks about the terminal itself, while a plaza will surround the Terminal building, reached on the North and South by a new Boulevard, hiding all trace of the railroad yard.

THE NEWLY COMPLETED
GRAND CENTRAL TERMINAL

Will provide every detail essential to the comfort and convenience of its patrons. The Terminal itself is the physical embodiment of the latest and the highest ideal of service. Its adequate description is impossible here. It must be seen to be fully appreciated—or indeed to be completely comprehended.

The Main Terminal alone is 722 feet long and 301 feet wide on the surface, and half again as wide below the street level. It will accommodate comfortably 30,000 people at one time.

Through and suburban service occupy different levels approached by inclines, avoiding stairways, so that each level may be reached without confusion. Incoming and outgoing traffic is segregated and the two currents of travel separated. Every facility is progressively arranged so that no step need be retraced, no time lost.

There are 42 tracks for through travel and 25 tracks for local trains, 33 miles in all, within the Terminal, accommodating over 1000 cars at one time. Dedicated to the Public Service, February, 1913.

NEW YORK CENTRAL LINES

In its consideration of Penn Central's takings claim, the New York Court of Appeals treated as the relevant "denominator" this larger "Terminal City" parcel, from which Penn Central was deriving considerable income, much of it related to the proximity to Grand Central Terminal. *See*

Penn Central Transp. Co. v. New York City, 42 N.Y.2d 324, 333–34 (1977). In Lucas v. South Carolina Coastal Council, 505 U.S. 1003 (1992), the U.S. Supreme Court ridiculed the New York court's choice of a denominator as "extreme" and "unsupportable." In light of the New York Central's own references to the area as a single planned community—a "city within a city"—do you agree?

D. PER SE RULES

Although *ad hoc*, balancing approaches like the one the Court adopted in *Penn Central* allow courts to focus on the unique facts of each case, those balancing approaches also generate uncertainty, and invite litigation. As a result, it is not surprising that the Supreme Court would try to carve out some areas in which takings cases might be resolved by application of clear legal rules. Consider, in light of the following case, whether a rule-based approach to takings law would be more satisfactory.

Lucas v. South Carolina Coastal Council
Supreme Court of the United States, 1992
505 U.S. 1003

■ JUSTICE SCALIA delivered the opinion of the Court.

In 1986, petitioner David H. Lucas paid $975,000 for two residential lots on the Isle of Palms in Charleston County, South Carolina, on which he intended to build single-family homes. In 1988, however, the South Carolina Legislature enacted the Beachfront Management Act, S. C. Code Ann. § 48–39–250 *et seq.* (Supp. 1990), which had the direct effect of barring petitioner from erecting any permanent habitable structures on his two parcels. *See* § 48–39–290(A). A state trial court found that this prohibition rendered Lucas's parcels "valueless." App. to Pet. for Cert. 37. This case requires us to decide whether the Act's dramatic effect on the economic value of Lucas's lots accomplished a taking of private property under the Fifth and Fourteenth Amendments requiring the payment of "just compensation." U.S. Const., Amdt. 5.

I

A

In the late 1970's, Lucas and others began extensive residential development of the Isle of Palms, a barrier island situated eastward of the city of Charleston. Toward the close of the development cycle for one residential subdivision known as "Beachwood East," Lucas in 1986 purchased the two lots at issue in this litigation for his own account. No portion of the lots, which were located approximately 300 feet from the beach, qualified as a "critical area" under the 1977 Act; accordingly, at the time Lucas acquired these parcels, he was not legally obliged to obtain a permit from the Council in advance of any development activity. His intention with respect to the lots was to do what the owners of the immediately adjacent parcels had already done: erect single-family residences. He commissioned architectural drawings for this purpose.

The Beachfront Management Act brought Lucas's plans to an abrupt end. Under that 1988 legislation, the Council was directed to establish a "baseline" connecting the landwardmost "points of erosion . . . during the past forty years" in the region of the Isle of Palms that includes Lucas's lots. S. C. Code Ann. § 48–39–280(A)(2) (Supp. 1988). In action not challenged here, the Council fixed this baseline landward of Lucas's parcels. That was significant, for under the Act construction of occupyable improvements was flatly prohibited seaward of a line drawn 20 feet landward of, and parallel to, the baseline. § 48–39–290(A). The Act provided no exceptions.

B

Lucas promptly filed suit in the South Carolina Court of Common Pleas, contending that the Beachfront Management Act's construction bar effected a taking of his property without just compensation. Lucas did not take issue with the validity of the Act as a lawful exercise of South Carolina's police power, but contended that the Act's complete extinguishment of his property's value entitled him to compensation regardless of whether the legislature had acted in furtherance of legitimate police power objectives. Following a bench trial, the court agreed. Among its factual determinations was the finding that "at the time Lucas purchased the two lots, both were zoned for single-family residential construction and . . . there were no restrictions imposed upon such use of the property by either the State of South Carolina, the County of Charleston, or the Town of the Isle of Palms." App. to Pet. for Cert. 36. The trial court further found that the Beachfront Management Act decreed a permanent ban on construction insofar as Lucas's lots were concerned, and that this prohibition "deprived Lucas of any reasonable economic use of the lots, . . . eliminated the unrestricted right of use, and rendered them valueless." *Id.*, at 37. The court thus concluded that Lucas's properties had been "taken" by operation of the Act, and it ordered respondent to pay "just compensation" in the amount of $1,232,387.50. *Id.*, at 40.

The Supreme Court of South Carolina reversed. It found dispositive what it described as Lucas's concession "that the Beachfront Management Act [was] properly and validly designed to preserve . . . South Carolina's beaches." 304 S.C. 376, 379, 404 S.E.2d 895, 896 (1991). Failing an attack on the validity of the statute as such, the court believed itself bound to accept the "uncontested . . . findings" of the South Carolina Legislature that new construction in the coastal zone—such as petitioner intended—threatened this public resource. *Id.*, at

383, 404 S.E.2d at 898. The court ruled that when a regulation respecting the use of property is designed "to prevent serious public harm," *id.*, at 383, 404 S.E.2d at 899 (citing, *inter alia*, Mugler v. Kansas, 123 U.S. 623, 31 L. Ed. 205, 8 S. Ct. 273 (1887)), no compensation is owing under the Takings Clause regardless of the regulation's effect on the property's value.

We granted certiorari. 502 U.S. 966 (1991).

* * *

III

A

[W]e have generally eschewed any " 'set formula' " for determining how far is too far, preferring to "engage in . . . essentially ad hoc, factual inquiries." Penn Central Transportation Co. v. New York City, 438 U.S. 104, 124, 57 L. Ed. 2d 631, 98 S. Ct. 2646 (1978) (quoting Goldblatt v. Hempstead, 369 U.S. 590, 594, 8 L. Ed. 2d 130, 82 S. Ct. 987 (1962)). *See* Epstein, Takings: Descent and Resurrection, 1987 S. Ct. Rev. 1, 4. We have, however, described at least two discrete categories of regulatory action as compensable without case-specific inquiry into the public interest advanced in support of the restraint. The first encompasses regulations that compel the property owner to suffer a physical "invasion" of his property. In general (at least with regard to permanent invasions), no matter how minute the intrusion, and no matter how weighty the public purpose behind it, we have required compensation. For example, in Loretto v. Teleprompter Manhattan CATV Corp., 458 U.S. 419, 73 L. Ed. 2d 868, 102 S. Ct. 3164 (1982), we determined that New York's law requiring landlords to allow television cable companies to emplace cable facilities in their apartment buildings constituted a taking, *id.*, at 435–440, even though the facilities occupied at most only 1 1/2 cubic feet of the landlords' property, *see id.*, at 438, n.16.

The second situation in which we have found categorical treatment appropriate is where regulation denies all economically beneficial or productive use of land.

We have never set forth the justification for this rule. Perhaps it is simply, as Justice Brennan suggested, that total deprivation of beneficial use is, from the landowner's point of view, the equivalent of a physical appropriation. *See* San Diego Gas & Electric Co. v. San Diego, 450 U.S. at 652 (dissenting opinion). "For what is the land but the profits thereof[?]" 1 E. Coke, Institutes, ch. 1, § 1 (1st Am. ed. 1812). Surely, at least, in the extraordinary circumstance when *no* productive or economically beneficial use of land is permitted, it is less realistic to indulge our usual assumption that the legislature is simply "adjusting the benefits and burdens of economic life," Penn Central Transportation Co., 438 U.S. at 124, in a manner that secures an "average reciprocity of advantage" to everyone concerned, Pennsylvania Coal Co. v. Mahon, 260 U.S. at 415. And the *functional* basis for permitting the government, by regulation, to affect property values without compensation—that "Government hardly could go on if to some extent values incident to property could not be diminished without paying for every such change in the general law," *id.*, at 413—does not apply to the relatively rare situations where the government has deprived a landowner of all economically beneficial uses.

On the other side of the balance, affirmatively supporting a compensation requirement, is the fact that regulations that leave the owner of land without economically beneficial or productive options for its use—typically, as here, by requiring land to be left substantially in its natural state—carry with them a heightened risk that private property is being pressed into some form of public service under the guise of mitigating serious public harm.

We think, in short, that there are good reasons for our frequently expressed belief that when the owner of real property has been called upon to sacrifice *all* economically beneficial uses in the name of the common good, that is, to leave his property economically idle, he has suffered a taking.

B

The trial court found Lucas's two beachfront lots to have been rendered valueless by respondent's enforcement of the coastal-zone construction ban. Under Lucas's theory of the case, which rested upon our "no economically viable use" statements, that finding entitled him to compensation. Lucas believed it unnecessary to take issue with either the purposes behind the Beachfront Management Act, or the means chosen by the South Carolina Legislature to effectuate those purposes. The South Carolina Supreme Court, however, thought otherwise. In its view, the Beachfront Management Act was no ordinary enactment, but involved an exercise of South Carolina's "police powers" to mitigate the harm to the public interest that petitioner's use of his land might occasion.

It is correct that many of our prior opinions have suggested that "harmful or noxious uses" of property may be proscribed by government regulation without the requirement of compensation. For a number of reasons, however, we think the South Carolina Supreme Court was too quick to conclude that that principle decides the present case. The "harmful or noxious uses" principle was the Court's early attempt to describe in theoretical terms why government may, consistent with the Takings Clause, affect property values by regulation without incurring an obligation to compensate—a reality we nowadays acknowledge explicitly with respect to the full scope of the State's police power. *See, e.g.,* Penn Central Transportation Co., 438 U.S. at 125 (where State "reasonably concludes that 'the health, safety, morals, or general welfare' would be promoted by prohibiting particular contemplated uses of land," compensation need not accompany prohibition).

"Harmful or noxious use" analysis was, in other words, simply the progenitor of our more contemporary statements that "land-use regulation does not effect a taking if it 'substantially advances legitimate state interests'. . . ." Nollan v. California Coastal Comm., 483 U.S. 825, at 834 (quoting Agins v. Tiburon, 447 U.S. at 260); *see also* Penn Central Transportation Co., *supra*, at 127; Euclid v. Ambler Realty Co., 272 U.S. 365, 387–388, 71 L. Ed. 303, 47 S. Ct. 114 (1926).

The transition from our early focus on control of "noxious" uses to our contemporary understanding of the broad realm within which government may regulate without compensation was an easy one, since the distinction between "harm-preventing" and "benefit-conferring" regulation is often in the eye of the beholder. It is quite possible, for example, to describe in *either* fashion the ecological, economic, and esthetic concerns that inspired the South Carolina Legislature in the present case. One could say that imposing a servitude on Lucas's land is necessary in order to prevent his use of it from "harming" South Carolina's ecological resources; or, instead, in order to achieve the "benefits" of an ecological preserve. A given restraint will be seen as mitigating "harm" to the adjacent parcels or securing a "benefit" for them, depending upon the observer's evaluation of the relative importance of the use that the restraint favors. *See* Sax, Takings and the Police Power, 74 Yale L. J. 36, 49 (1964) ("The problem [in this area] is not one of noxiousness or harm-creating activity at all; rather it is a problem of inconsistency between perfectly innocent and independently desirable uses"). Whether Lucas's construction of single-family residences on his parcels should be described as bringing "harm" to South Carolina's adjacent ecological resources thus depends principally upon whether the describer believes that the State's use interest in nurturing those resources is so important that *any* competing adjacent use must yield.

When it is understood that "prevention of harmful use" was merely our early formulation of the police power justification necessary to sustain (without compensation) *any* regulatory diminution in value; and that the distinction between regulation that "prevents harmful use" and that which "confers benefits" is difficult, if not impossible, to discern on an objective, value-free basis; it becomes self-evident that noxious-use logic cannot serve as a touchstone to distinguish regulatory "takings"— which require compensation—from regulatory deprivations that do not require compensation. *A fortiori* the legislature's recitation of a noxious-use justification cannot be the basis for departing from our categorical rule that total regulatory takings must be compensated. If it were, departure would virtually always be allowed.

Where the State seeks to sustain regulation that deprives land of all economically beneficial use, we think it may resist compensation only if the logically antecedent inquiry into the nature of the owner's estate shows that the proscribed use interests were not part of his title to begin with.

Where "permanent physical occupation" of land is concerned, we have refused to allow the government to decree it anew (without compensation), no matter how weighty the asserted "public interests" involved, Loretto v. Teleprompter Manhattan CATV Corp., 458 U.S. at 426—though we assuredly *would* permit the government to assert a permanent easement that was a pre-existing limitation upon the landowner's title. We believe similar treatment must be accorded confiscatory regulations, i.e., regulations that prohibit all economically beneficial use of land: Any limitation so severe cannot be newly legislated or decreed (without compensation), but must inhere in the title itself, in the restrictions that background principles of the State's law of property and nuisance already place upon land ownership. A law or decree with such an effect must, in other words, do no more than duplicate the result that could have been achieved in the courts—by adjacent landowners (or other uniquely affected persons) under the State's law of private nuisance, or by the State under its complementary power to abate nuisances that affect the public generally, or otherwise.[16]

On this analysis, the owner of a lakebed, for example, would not be entitled to compensation when he is denied the requisite permit to engage in a landfilling operation that would have the effect of flooding others' land. Nor the corporate owner of a nuclear generating plant, when it is directed to remove all improvements from its land upon discovery that the plant sits astride an earthquake fault. Such regulatory action may well have the effect of eliminating the land's only economically productive use, but it does not proscribe a productive use that was previously permissible under relevant property and nuisance principles. The use of these properties for what are now expressly prohibited purposes was *always* unlawful, and (subject to other constitutional limitations) it was open to the State at any point to make the implication of those background principles of nuisance and property law explicit. *See* Michelman, Property, Utility, and Fairness, Comments on the Ethical Foundations of "Just Compensation" Law, 80 Harv. L. Rev. 1165, 1239–1241 (1967). In light of our traditional resort to "existing rules or understandings that stem from an independent source such as state law" to define the range of interests that qualify for

---

[16] The principal "otherwise" that we have in mind is litigation absolving the State (or private parties) of liability for the destruction of "real and personal property, in cases of actual necessity, to prevent the spreading of a fire" or to forestall other grave threats to the lives and property of others. Bowditch v. Boston, 101 U.S. 16, 18–19, 25 L. Ed. 980 (1880); *see* United States v. Pacific R. Co., 120 U.S. 227, 238–239, 30 L. Ed. 634, 7 S. Ct. 490 (1887).

protection as "property" under the Fifth and Fourteenth Amendments, this recognition that the Takings Clause does not require compensation when an owner is barred from putting land to a use that is proscribed by those "existing rules or understandings" is surely unexceptional. When, however, a regulation that declares "off-limits" all economically productive or beneficial uses of land goes beyond what the relevant background principles would dictate, compensation must be paid to sustain it.

The "total taking" inquiry we require today will ordinarily entail (as the application of state nuisance law ordinarily entails) analysis of, among other things, the degree of harm to public lands and resources, or adjacent private property, posed by the claimant's proposed activities, *see, e.g.*, Restatement (Second) of Torts §§ 826, 827, the social value of the claimant's activities and their suitability to the locality in question, *see, e.g., id.*, §§ 828(a) and (b), 831, and the relative ease with which the alleged harm can be avoided through measures taken by the claimant and the government (or adjacent private landowners) alike, *see, e.g., id.*, §§ 827(e), 828(c), 830. The fact that a particular use has long been engaged in by similarly situated owners ordinarily imports a lack of any common-law prohibition (though changed circumstances or new knowledge may make what was previously permissible no longer so, *see id.*, § 827, Comment g). So also does the fact that other landowners, similarly situated, are permitted to continue the use denied to the claimant.

It seems unlikely that common-law principles would have prevented the erection of any habitable or productive improvements on petitioner's land; they rarely support prohibition of the "essential use" of land, Curtin v. Benson, 222 U.S. 78, 86, 56 L. Ed. 102, 32 S. Ct. 31 (1911). The question, however, is one of state law to be dealt with on remand. We emphasize that to win its case South Carolina must do more than proffer the legislature's declaration that the uses Lucas desires are inconsistent with the public interest, or the conclusory assertion that they violate a common-law maxim such as *sic utere tuo ut alienum non laedas*. As we have said, a "State, by *ipse dixit*, may not transform private property into public property without compensation. . . ." Webb's Fabulous Pharmacies, Inc. v. Beckwith, 449 U.S. 155, 164, 66 L. Ed. 2d 358, 101 S. Ct. 446 (1980). Instead, as it would be required to do if it sought to restrain Lucas in a common-law action for public nuisance, South Carolina must identify background principles of nuisance and property law that prohibit the uses he now intends in the circumstances in which the property is presently found. Only on this showing can the State fairly claim that, in proscribing all such beneficial uses, the Beachfront Management Act is taking nothing.

* * *

The judgment is reversed, and the case is remanded for proceedings not inconsistent with this opinion.

■ JUSTICE BLACKMUN, dissenting.

Today the Court launches a missile to kill a mouse.

The State of South Carolina prohibited petitioner Lucas from building a permanent structure on his property from 1988 to 1990. Relying on an unreviewed (and implausible) state trial court finding that this restriction left Lucas' property valueless, this Court granted review to determine whether compensation must be paid in cases where the State prohibits all economic use of real estate. According to the Court, such an occasion never has arisen in any of our prior cases, and the Court imagines that it will arise "relatively rarely" or only in "extraordinary circumstances." Almost certainly it did not happen in this case.

My fear is that the Court's new policies will spread beyond the narrow confines of the present case. For that reason, I, like the Court, will give far greater attention to this case than its narrow scope suggests—not because I can intercept the Court's missile, or save the targeted mouse, but because I hope perhaps to limit the collateral damage.

The Court recognizes that "our prior opinions have suggested that 'harmful or noxious uses' of property may be proscribed by government regulation without the requirement of compensation," *ante*, 505 U.S. at 1022, but seeks to reconcile them with its categorical rule by claiming that the Court never has upheld a regulation when the owner alleged the loss of all economic value. Even if the Court's factual premise were correct, its understanding of the Court's cases is distorted. In none of the cases did the Court suggest that the right of a State to prohibit certain activities without paying compensation turned on the availability of some residual valuable use. Instead, the cases depended on whether the government interest was sufficient to prohibit the activity, given the significant private cost.

These cases rest on the principle that the State has full power to prohibit an owner's use of property if it is harmful to the public. "Since no individual has a right to use his property so as to create a nuisance or otherwise harm others, the State has not 'taken' anything when it asserts its power to enjoin the nuisance-like activity." Keystone Bituminous Coal, 480 U.S. at 491, n. 20. It would make no sense under this theory to suggest that an owner has a constitutionally protected right to harm others, if only he makes the proper showing of economic loss. *See* Pennsylvania Coal Co. v. Mahon, 260 U.S. 393, 418, 67 L. Ed. 322, 43 S. Ct. 158 (1922) (Brandeis, J., dissenting) ("Restriction upon [harmful] use does not become inappropriate as a means, merely because it deprives the owner of the only use to which the property can then be profitably put").

B

Ultimately even the Court cannot embrace the full implications of its *per se* rule: It eventually agrees that there cannot be a categorical rule for a taking based on economic value that wholly disregards the public need asserted. Instead, the Court decides that it will permit a State to regulate all economic value only if the State prohibits uses that would not be permitted under "background principles of nuisance and property law." *Ante*, 505 U.S. at 1031.

Until today, the Court explicitly had rejected the contention that the government's power to act without paying compensation turns on whether the prohibited activity is a common-law nuisance. The brewery closed in *Mugler* itself was not a common-law nuisance, and the Court specifically stated that it was the role of the legislature to determine what measures would be appropriate for the protection of public health and safety. *See* 123 U.S. at 661. In upholding the state action in *Miller*, the Court found it unnecessary to "weigh with nicety the question whether the infected cedars constitute a nuisance according to common law; or whether they may be so declared by statute." 276 U.S. at 280. *See also Goldblatt*, 369 U.S. at 593; *Hadacheck*, 239 U.S. at 411. Instead the Court has relied in the past, as the South Carolina court has done here, on legislative judgments of what constitutes a harm.

The Court rejects the notion that the State always can prohibit uses it deems a harm to the public without granting compensation because "the distinction between 'harm-preventing' and 'benefit-conferring' regulation is often in the eye of the beholder." *Ante*, 505 U.S. at 1024. Since the characterization will depend "primarily upon one's evaluation of the worth of competing uses of real estate," *ante*, 505 U.S. at 1025, the Court decides a legislative judgment of this kind no longer can provide the desired "objective, value-free basis" for upholding a regulation, *ante*, 505 U.S. at 1026. The Court, however, fails to explain how its proposed common-law alternative escapes the same trap.

The Court makes sweeping and, in my view, misguided and unsupported changes in our takings doctrine. While it limits these changes to the most narrow subset of government regulation—those that eliminate all economic value from land—these changes go far beyond what is necessary to secure petitioner Lucas' private benefit. One hopes they do not go beyond the narrow confines the Court assigns them to today.

I dissent.

■ JUSTICE STEVENS, dissenting.

The Court's holding today effectively freezes the State's common law, denying the legislature much of its traditional power to revise the law governing the rights and uses of property. Until today, I had thought that we had long abandoned this approach to constitutional law. More than a century ago we recognized that "the great office of statutes is to remedy defects in the common law as they are developed, and to adapt it to the changes of time and circumstances." Munn v. Illinois, 94 U.S. 113, 134, 24 L. Ed. 77 (1877).

Arresting the development of the common law is not only a departure from our prior decisions; it is also profoundly unwise. The human condition is one of constant learning and evolution—both moral and practical. Legislatures implement that new learning; in doing so they must often revise the definition of property and the rights of property owners. Thus, when the Nation came to understand that slavery was morally wrong and mandated the emancipation of all slaves, it, in effect, redefined "property." On a lesser scale, our ongoing self-education produces similar changes in the rights of property owners: New appreciation of the significance of endangered species, *see, e.g.,* Andrus v. Allard, 444 U.S. 51, 62 L. Ed. 2d 210, 100 S. Ct. 318 (1979); the importance of wetlands, *see, e.g.,* 16 U.S.C. § 3801 *et seq.*; and the vulnerability of coastal lands, *see, e.g.,* 16 U.S.C. § 1451 *et seq.,* shapes our evolving understandings of property rights.

Of course, some legislative redefinitions of property will effect a taking and must be compensated—but it certainly cannot be the case that every movement away from common law does so. There is no reason, and less sense, in such an absolute rule. We live in a world in which changes in the economy and the environment occur with increasing frequency and importance. If it was wise a century ago to allow government " 'the largest legislative discretion' " to deal with " 'the special exigencies of the moment,' " *Mugler*, 123 U.S. at 669, it is imperative to do so today. The rule that should govern a decision in a case of this kind should focus on the future, not the past.

The Court's categorical approach rule will, I fear, greatly hamper the efforts of local officials and planners who must deal with increasingly complex problems in land-use and environmental regulation. As this case—in which the claims of an *individual* property owner exceed $1 million—well demonstrates, these officials face both substantial uncertainty because of the ad hoc nature of takings law and unacceptable penalties if they guess incorrectly about that law.

NOTES AND QUESTIONS

1.   In *Lucas*, the Court identified two *per se* takings rules. The first, not at issue in *Lucas* itself, is the rule that a permanent physical invasion constitutes a taking without regard to the harm to the landowner. What makes permanent physical invasions special? How many parcels of land is any municipality likely to invade physically and permanently? If the answer is "not so many," are permanent physical invasions particularly likely to single out affected landowners for unfavorable treatment? Similarly, if any permanent physical invasion affects relatively few

landowners, how difficult will it be for a municipality or other governmental entity to identify and compute the losses to affected landowners? Put in other terms, will settlement costs typically be high or low in cases of permanent physical invasion?

Loretto v. Teleprompter Manhattan CATV Corp., 458 U.S. 419 (1982), tests most of the generalizations about permanent physical invasions. New York City had authorized a cable television company to place small cable boxes on the real property of every New York landlord; no landlord was singled out, and the number of affected landlords was large. As a result, settlement costs were likely to be large compared to the harm inflicted by the cable boxes. The court nevertheless applied the *per se* rule. Was *Loretto* a misapplication of the rule, or is an occasionally perverse result the price of having rules rather than standards?

2. How significant is the permanent physical invasion rule for land use planning? How often will a municipality need to physically invade a landowner's parcel?

Suppose a municipality were to enact an ordinance requiring homeowners to install sidewalks, open to the public at large, in front of their homes. Would *Loretto* render the ordinance unconstitutional unless the municipality compensated the homeowners? *Cf.* Bonito Partners, LLC v. City of Flagstaff, 229 Ariz. 75, 270 P.3d 902 (Ariz. App. 2012) (sustaining obligation of abutting owners to repair city-owned sidewalks). Suppose, instead, that the municipality requires developers to install streets and sidewalks as a condition of subdivision approval. Is the developer entitled to compensation? Why or why not?

In Horne v. Department of Agriculture, 133 S.Ct. 2053 (2015), a case involving personal property rather than land, the Court held that a federal statute requiring raisin growers to set aside a percentage of their crop for the federal government's account worked a *per se* physical taking under *Loretto*. But the Court also conceded that the government would have been able to prohibit all sale of the raisins (creating the same economic effect for the grower) without effecting a *per se* taking. The Court's explanation: "The Constitution . . . is concerned with means as well as ends." *Id.* at 2428. Does *Horne* suggest an answer to the sidewalk hypotheticals?

3. Suppose a municipality zones a large tract of land for agricultural use. Does *Lucas* enable landowner to advance a *per se* takings claim? *See generally* Mark W. Cordes, Takings Fairness, and Farmland Preservation, 60 Ohio St. L.J. 1033 (1999) (answering no). Does it matter whether the land in question is arable? Whether the potential value of any crops grown on the land exceeds the cost of growing the crops?

4. Suppose a landowner has owned a vacant beachfront lot for 30 years. During that time, applicable zoning regulations have consistently limited the parcel to single-family residential use, but have required a 20-foot setback from the road, and a 100-foot setback from the mean high water mark. Landowner's parcel measured 150 feet from road to mean high water mark until last year, when a hurricane caused massive beach erosion, and left landowner with only 110 feet from road to mean high water mark. Landowner unsuccessfully applied for a building permit, and subsequently a zoning variance. If the landowner then brings a takings claim, citing *Lucas*, should the landowner succeed?

5. In 1969, a landowner bought a parcel of land adjacent to a parcel used for disposal of large canisters of toxic waste. Landowner used the land for a sand and gravel mining operation, and for its offices. Landowner knew of the toxic wastes on the neighboring parcel. Thirty years later, government officials learn that the wastes have been leaking from the canisters, and have contaminated the soil on landowner's parcel. As part of the cleanup process, officials prohibit all use of the landowner's land and buildings, and install a number of monitoring stations on the landowner's land. Landowner brings a takings claim. Does *Lucas* entitle landowner to relief? Does *Loretto* entitle landowner to relief?

Would the landowner's position be materially different if the landowner had, in 1970, brought a nuisance action against the neighbor, seeking to enjoin disposal of toxic wastes, and the neighbor prevailed? *Cf.* John R. Sand & Gravel Co. v. United States, 62 Fed. Cl. 556 (2004), *vac.* 457 F.3d 1345 (Fed. Cir. 2006).

6. Justice Scalia's opinion in *Lucas* emphasizes that if a state regulation prevents a landowner from making any economic use of his land, the regulation constitutes a taking unless the state can identify "background principles of nuisance and property law that prohibit the uses" the landowner now intends to make of the land. Must those background principles be common law principles, or may they be statutory or regulatory principles? Is there a principle of federal constitutional law that requires states to use the common law to develop legal principles? For a discussion of the background principles courts have used to avoid compensating a landowner who has been left with no economically valuable use of land, *see* Michael C. Blumm, Lucas's Unlikely Legacy: The Rise of Background Principles as Categorical Takings Defenses, 29 Harv. Envtl. L. Rev. 321 (2005).

7. Suppose you represent a municipality. Your client wants to prevent development in an area of the town but wants to avoid a *Lucas* challenge. What advice would you give to municipal officials about how to proceed? What advantages, if any, are there to avoiding a *Lucas* challenge if the affected landowners could still advance a challenge pursuant to the *Penn Central* balancing test?

NOTE ON JUDICIAL TAKINGS

State and local administrative agencies, together with local legislatures, implement most land use regulation. But courts play a role as well. Consider a variation on the facts in Note 4, *supra*. Landowner brings an action in 1970, seeking to require cleanup of toxic wastes on neighboring land, and loses. The court concludes, in effect, that maintenance of the toxic wastes did not constitute a nuisance—giving the neighbor a property right to maintain those wastes on the land. Forty years later, landowner's successor brings a similar action against neighbor's successor, and the court issues an injunction, concluding that maintenance of the wastes does constitute a nuisance. Can the neighbor bring an action against the state, claiming that the nuisance determination constituted a "judicial taking" of property without just compensation?

The Supreme Court addressed, but did not resolve, the status of judicial takings in Stop the Beach Renourishment, Inc. v. Florida Dep't of Envt'l Protection, 560 U.S. 702 (2010). Pursuant to a state statute, a state agency issued permits to deposit dry sand on the lake shore as an erosion control measure. The deposited sand would not belong to the lakefront owners, and would eliminate contact between the water and the land owned by lakefront owners. The deposit of sand would also make it impossible for natural forces to deposit sand adjacent to land owned by the lakefront owners; under Florida common law, such "accretions" would belong to the lakefront owners. When lakefront owners contended that approval of the permits worked an unconstitutional taking, the Florida Supreme Court upheld the permits, concluding that the statute authorizing deposit of the sand would not infringe on the owners' right of access to the lake. That court also held that the right to accretions was not a vested property right. Lakefront owners then sought review in the United States Supreme Court, contending that the Florida Supreme Court's decision itself effected a taking of lakefront property rights.

The Supreme Court unanimously rejected the takings claim, but divided on whether a judicial decision could effect a taking. Justice Scalia, writing for a four-judge plurality, concluded that the Takings Clause "is not addressed to the action of a specific branch or branches. It is concerned simply with the act, and not with the governmental actor." For the plurality, the Takings Clause "bars *the State* from taking private property without paying for it, no matter which branch is the instrument of the taking." *Id.* at 715 (emphasis in original). On the facts of the case, however, the plurality concluded that the Florida Supreme Court's decision was consistent with prior Florida property law, and therefore did not work a taking. In two separate concurrences, Justices Kennedy and Breyer concluded that the Court should not reach the "judicial taking" issue, because the case could be resolved without reaching that issue. Justice Kennedy, in particular, suggested that cases raising "judicial taking" claims would be better resolved using a due process analysis.

If the Court were ultimately to endorse the Scalia position, would judicial taking doctrine open the door to a federal claim for any party who thinks a state court got the law wrong, if the result of the new legal rule would be an award of damages or injunctive relief against the claimant? If not, what limits would the Court impose on judicial takings claims?

Despite the academic interest generated by *Stop the Beach Renourishment*, and by judicial takings generally, the issue may be of limited practical importance to developers and municipalities. Courts do not initiate legal proceedings. In cases like *Stop the Beach Renourishment*, where the court decision arises out of an action by some other branch of government, aggrieved landowners can always proceed against that other government actor rather than the court. If the agency's action would not constitute a taking, it will generally be unlikely that a court decision upholding that action would constitute a taking.

E. NOTICE (AND THE DENOMINATOR PROBLEM, REVISITED)

If a landowner buys a parcel of land knowing that regulations seriously limit its use, can the landowner nevertheless challenge those regulations? Consider the following case:

Palazzolo v. Rhode Island
Supreme Court of the United States, 2001
533 U.S. 606

■ JUSTICE KENNEDY delivered the opinion of the Court.

Petitioner Anthony Palazzolo owns a waterfront parcel of land in the town of Westerly, Rhode Island. Almost all of the property is designated as coastal wetlands under Rhode Island law. After petitioner's development proposals were rejected by respondent Rhode Island Coastal Resources Management Council (Council), he sued in state court, asserting the Council's application of its wetlands regulations took the property without compensation in violation of the Takings Clause of the Fifth Amendment, binding upon the State through the Due Process Clause of the Fourteenth Amendment. Petitioner sought review in this Court, contending the Supreme Court of Rhode Island erred in rejecting his takings claim. We granted certiorari. 531 U.S. 923, 148 L. Ed. 2d 238, 121 S. Ct. 296 (2000).

I

The town of Westerly is on an edge of the Rhode Island coastline.

Westerly today has about 20,000 year-round residents, and thousands of summer visitors come to enjoy its beaches and coastal advantages.

One of the more popular attractions is Misquamicut State Beach, a lengthy expanse of coastline facing Block Island Sound and beyond to the Atlantic Ocean. The primary point of access to the beach is Atlantic Avenue, a well-traveled 3-mile stretch of road running along the coastline within the town's limits. At its western end, Atlantic Avenue is something of a commercial strip, with restaurants, hotels, arcades, and other typical seashore businesses. The pattern of development becomes more residential as the road winds eastward onto a narrow spine of land bordered to the south by the beach and the ocean, and to the north by Winnapaug Pond, an intertidal inlet often used by residents for boating, fishing, and shellfishing.

In 1959 petitioner, a lifelong Westerly resident, decided to invest in three undeveloped, adjoining parcels along this eastern stretch of Atlantic Avenue. To the north, the property faces, and borders upon, Winnapaug Pond; the south of the property faces Atlantic Avenue and the beachfront homes abutting it on the other side, and beyond that the dunes and the beach. To purchase and hold the property, petitioner and associates formed Shore Gardens, Inc. (SGI). After SGI purchased the property petitioner bought out his associates and became the sole shareholder. In the first decade of SGI's ownership of the property the corporation submitted a plat to the town subdividing the property into 80 lots; and it engaged in various transactions that left it with 74 lots, which together encompassed about 20 acres. During the same period SGI also made initial attempts to develop the property and submitted intermittent applications to state agencies to fill substantial portions of the parcel. Most of the property was then, as it is now, salt marsh subject to tidal flooding. The wet ground and permeable soil would require considerable fill—as much as six feet in some places—before significant structures could be built. SGI's proposal, submitted in 1962 to the Rhode Island Division of Harbors and Rivers (DHR), sought to dredge from Winnapaug Pond and fill the entire property. The application was denied for lack of essential information. A second, similar proposal followed a year later. A third application, submitted in 1966 while the second application was pending, proposed more limited filling of the land for use as a private beach club. These latter two applications were referred to the Rhode Island Department of Natural Resources, which indicated initial assent. The agency later withdrew approval, however, citing adverse environmental impacts. SGI did not contest the ruling.

No further attempts to develop the property were made for over a decade. Two intervening events, however, become important to the issues presented. First, in 1971, Rhode Island enacted legislation creating the Council, an agency charged with the duty of protecting the State's coastal properties. 1971 R. I. Pub. Laws ch. 279, § 1 *et seq.* Regulations promulgated by the Council designated salt marshes like those on SGI's property as protected "coastal wetlands," Rhode Island Coastal Resources Management Program (CRMP) § 210.3 (as amended, June 28, 1983) (lodged with the Clerk of this Court), on which development is limited to a great extent. Second, in 1978 SGI's corporate charter was revoked for failure to pay corporate income taxes; and title to the property passed, by operation of state law, to petitioner as the corporation's sole shareholder.

In 1983 petitioner, now the owner, renewed the efforts to develop the property. An application to the Council, resembling the 1962 submission, requested permission to construct a wooden bulkhead along the shore of Winnapaug Pond and to fill the entire marsh land area. The Council rejected the application, noting it was "vague and inadequate for a project of this size and nature." Petitioner went back to the drawing board, this time hiring counsel and preparing a more specific and limited proposal for use of the property. The new application, submitted to the Council in 1985, echoed the 1966 request to build a private beach club. The details do not tend to inspire the reader with an idyllic coastal image, for the proposal was to fill 11 acres of the property with gravel to accommodate "50 cars with boat trailers, a dumpster, port-a-johns, picnic tables, barbecue pits of concrete, and other trash receptacles." *Id.* at 25.

The application fared no better with the Council than previous ones. Under the agency's regulations, a landowner wishing to fill salt marsh on Winnapaug Pond needed a "special exception" from the Council. CRMP § 130. In a short opinion the Council said the beach club proposal conflicted with the regulatory standard for a special exception. *See* App. 27. To secure a special exception the proposed activity must serve "a compelling public purpose which provides benefits to the public as a whole as opposed to individual or private interests." CRMP § 130A(1). This time petitioner appealed the decision to the Rhode Island courts, challenging the Council's conclusion as contrary to principles of state administrative law. The Council's decision was affirmed. Petitioner filed an inverse condemnation action in Rhode Island Superior Court, asserting that the State's wetlands regulations, as applied by the Council to his parcel, had taken the property without compensation in violation of the Fifth and Fourteenth Amendments. *See* App. 45. The suit alleged the Council's action deprived him of "all economically beneficial use" of his property, *ibid.* resulting in a total taking requiring compensation under Lucas v. South Carolina Coastal Council, 505 U.S. 1003, 120 L. Ed. 2d 798, 112 S. Ct. 2886 (1992). He sought damages in the amount of $3,150,000, a figure derived from an appraiser's estimate as to the value of a 74-lot residential subdivision. The State countered with a host of defenses. After a bench trial, a justice of the Superior Court ruled against petitioner, accepting some of the State's theories.

The Rhode Island Supreme Court affirmed. 746 A.2d 707 (2000). Like the Superior Court, the State Supreme Court recited multiple grounds for rejecting petitioner's suit. The court held, first, that petitioner's takings claim was not ripe, *id.* at 712–715; second, that petitioner had no right to challenge regulations predating 1978, when he succeeded to legal ownership of the property from SGI, *id.* at 716; and third, that the claim of deprivation of all economically beneficial use was contradicted by undisputed evidence that he had $200,000 in development value remaining on an upland parcel of the property, *id.* at 715. In addition to holding petitioner could not assert a takings claim based on the denial of all economic use the court concluded he could not recover under the more general test of Penn Central Transp. Co. v. New York City, 438 U.S. 104, 57 L. Ed. 2d 631, 98 S. Ct. 2646 (1978). On this claim, too, the date of acquisition of the parcel was found determinative, and the court held he could have had "no reasonable investment-backed expectations that were affected by this regulation" because it predated his ownership, 746 A.2d at 717; *see also Penn Central, supra*, at 124.

We disagree with the Supreme Court of Rhode Island as to the first two of these conclusions; and, we hold, the court was correct to conclude that the owner is not deprived of all economic use of his property because the value of upland portions is substantial. We remand for further consideration of the claim under the principles set forth in *Penn Central*.

II

A

[In this section, the Court concludes that the landowner's claim was ripe for adjudication.]

B

We turn to the second asserted basis for declining to address petitioner's takings claim on the merits. When the Council promulgated its wetlands regulations, the disputed parcel was owned not by petitioner but by the corporation of which he was sole shareholder. When title was transferred to petitioner by operation of law, the wetlands regulations were in force. The state court held the postregulation acquisition of title was fatal to the claim for deprivation of all economic use, 746 A.2d at 716, and to the *Penn Central* claim, *id.* at 717. While the first holding was couched in terms of background principles of state property law, see *Lucas*, 505 U.S. at 1015, and the second in terms of petitioner's reasonable investment-backed expectations, see *Penn Central*, 438 U.S. at 124, the two holdings together amount to a single, sweeping, rule: A purchaser or a successive title holder like petitioner is deemed to have notice of an earlier-enacted restriction and is barred from claiming that it effects a taking.

The theory underlying the argument that post-enactment purchasers cannot challenge a regulation under the Takings Clause seems to run on these lines: Property rights are created by the State. *See, e.g.*, Phillips v. Washington Legal Foundation, 524 U.S. 156, 163, 141 L. Ed. 2d 174, 118 S. Ct. 1925 (1998). So, the argument goes, by prospective legislation the State can shape and define property rights and reasonable investment-backed expectations, and subsequent owners cannot claim any injury from lost value. After all, they purchased or took title with notice of the limitation.

The State may not put so potent a Hobbesian stick into the Lockean bundle. The right to improve property, of course, is subject to the reasonable exercise of state authority, including the enforcement of valid zoning and land-use restrictions. *See Pennsylvania Coal Co.*, 260 U.S. at 413 ("Government hardly could go on if to some extent values incident to property could not be diminished without paying for every such change in the general law"). The Takings Clause, however, in certain circumstances allows a landowner to assert that a particular exercise of the State's regulatory power is so unreasonable or onerous as to compel compensation. Just as a prospective enactment, such as a new zoning ordinance, can limit the value of land without effecting a taking because it can be understood as reasonable by all concerned, other enactments are unreasonable and do not become less so through passage of time or title. Were we to accept the State's rule, the post-enactment transfer of title would absolve the State of its obligation to defend any action restricting land use, no matter how extreme or unreasonable. A State would be allowed, in effect, to put an expiration date on the Takings Clause. This ought not to be the rule. Future generations, too, have a right to challenge unreasonable limitations on the use and value of land.

Nor does the justification of notice take into account the effect on owners at the time of enactment, who are prejudiced as well. Should an owner attempt to challenge a new regulation, but not survive the process of ripening his or her claim (which, as this case demonstrates, will often take years), under the proposed rule the right to compensation may not by asserted by an heir or successor, and so may not be asserted at all. The State's rule would work a critical alteration to the nature of property, as the newly regulated landowner is stripped of the ability to transfer the interest which was possessed prior to the regulation. The State may not by this means secure a windfall for itself. . . . A blanket rule that purchasers with notice have no compensation right when a claim becomes ripe is too blunt an instrument to accord with the duty to compensate for what is taken.

In *Lucas* the Court observed that a landowner's ability to recover for a government deprivation of all economically beneficial use of property is not absolute but instead is confined by limitations on the use of land which "inhere in the title itself." *Id.* at 1029. This is so, the Court reasoned, because the landowner is constrained by those "restrictions that background principles of the State's law of property and nuisance already place upon land ownership." *Id.* at 1029. It is asserted here that *Lucas* stands for the proposition that any new regulation, once enacted, becomes a background principle of property law which cannot be challenged by those who acquire title after the enactment.

We have no occasion to consider the precise circumstances when a legislative enactment can be deemed a background principle of state law or whether those circumstances are present here. It suffices to say that a regulation that otherwise would be unconstitutional absent compensation is not transformed into a background principle of the State's law by mere virtue of the passage of title.

For reasons we discuss next, the state court will not find it necessary to explore these matters on remand in connection with the claim that all economic use was deprived; it must address, however, the merits of petitioner's claim under *Penn Central*. That claim is not barred by the mere fact that title was acquired after the effective date of the state-imposed restriction.

III

As the case is ripe, and as the date of transfer of title does not bar petitioner's takings claim, we have before us the alternative ground relied upon by the Rhode Island Supreme Court in ruling upon the merits of the takings claims. It held that all economically beneficial use was not deprived because the uplands portion of the property can still be improved. On this point, we agree with the court's decision. Petitioner accepts the Council's contention and the state trial court's finding that his parcel retains $200,000 in development value under the State's wetlands regulations. He asserts, nonetheless, that he has suffered a total taking and contends the Council cannot sidestep the holding in *Lucas* "by the simple expedient of leaving a landowner a few crumbs of value." Brief for Petitioner 37.

Assuming a taking is otherwise established, a State may not evade the duty to compensate on the premise that the landowner is left with a token interest. This is not the situation of the landowner in this case, however. A regulation permitting a landowner to build a substantial residence on an 18-acre parcel does not leave the property "economically idle." *Lucas, supra*, at 1019.

In his brief submitted to us petitioner attempts to revive this part of his claim by reframing it. He argues, for the first time, that the upland parcel is distinct from the wetlands portions, so he should be permitted to assert a deprivation limited to the latter. This contention asks us to examine the difficult, persisting question of what is the proper denominator in the takings fraction. *See* Michelman, Property, Utility, and Fairness: Comments on the Ethical Foundations of "Just Compensation Law," 80 Harv. L. Rev. 1165, 1192 (1967). Some of our cases indicate that the extent of deprivation effected by a regulatory action is measured against the value of the parcel as a whole, *see, e.g.,* Keystone Bituminous Coal Ass'n v. DeBenedictis, 480 U.S. 470, 497, 94 L. Ed. 2d 472, 107 S. Ct. 1232 (1987); but we have at times expressed discomfort with the logic of this rule, *see Lucas, supra*, at 1016–1017, n. 7, a sentiment echoed by some commentators, *see, e.g.,* Epstein, Takings: Descent and Resurrection, 1987 Sup. Ct. Rev. 1, 16–17 (1987); Fee, Unearthing the Denominator in Regulatory Takings Claims, 61 U. Chi. L. Rev. 1535 (1994). Whatever the merits of these criticisms, we will not explore the point here. Petitioner did not press the argument in the state courts, and the issue was not presented in the petition for certiorari. The case comes to us on the premise that petitioner's entire parcel serves as the basis for his takings claim, and, so framed, the total deprivation argument fails.

* * *

For the reasons we have discussed, the State Supreme Court erred in finding petitioner's claims were unripe and in ruling that acquisition of title after the effective date of the regulations barred the takings claims. The court did not err in finding that petitioner failed to establish a deprivation of all economic value, for it is undisputed that the parcel retains significant worth for construction of a residence. The claims under the *Penn Central* analysis were not examined, and for this purpose the case should be remanded.

The judgment of the Rhode Island Supreme Court is affirmed in part and reversed in part, and the case is remanded for further proceedings not inconsistent with this opinion.

It is so ordered.

■ JUSTICE O'CONNOR, concurring.

I join the opinion of the Court but with my understanding of how the issues discussed in Part II–B of the opinion must be considered on remand.

Part II–B of the Court's opinion addresses the circumstance, present in this case, where a takings claimant has acquired title to the regulated property after the enactment of the regulation at issue. As the Court holds, the Rhode Island Supreme Court erred in effectively adopting the sweeping rule that the preacquisition enactment of the use restriction *ipso facto* defeats any takings claim based on that use restriction. Accordingly, the Court holds that petitioner's claim under Penn Central Transp. Co. v. New York City, 438 U.S. 104, 57 L. Ed. 2d 631, 98 S. Ct. 2646 (1978), "is not barred by the mere fact that title was acquired after the effective date of the state-imposed restriction." *Ante,* at 21.

The more difficult question is what role the temporal relationship between regulatory enactment and title acquisition plays in a proper *Penn Central* analysis. Today's holding does not mean that the timing of the regulation's enactment relative to the acquisition of title is immaterial to the *Penn Central* analysis. Indeed, it would be just as much error to expunge this consideration from the takings inquiry as it would be to accord it exclusive significance. Our polestar instead remains the principles set forth in *Penn Central* itself and our other cases that govern partial regulatory takings. Under these cases, interference with investment-backed expectations is one of a number of factors that a court must examine. Further, the regulatory regime in place at the time the claimant acquires the property at issue helps to shape the reasonableness of those expectations.

The Rhode Island Supreme Court concluded that, because the wetlands regulations predated petitioner's acquisition of the property at issue, petitioner lacked reasonable investment-backed expectations and hence lacked a viable takings claim. 746 A.2d 707, 717 (2000). The court erred in elevating what it believed to be "[petitioner's] lack of reasonable investment-backed expectations" to "dispositive" status. *Ibid.* Investment-backed expectations, though important, are not talismanic under *Penn Central*. Evaluation of the degree of interference with investment-backed expectations instead is *one* factor that points toward the answer to the question whether the application of a particular regulation to particular property "goes too far." Pennsylvania Coal Co. v. Mahon, 260 U.S. 393, 415, 67 L. Ed. 322, 43 S. Ct. 158 (1922).

Further, the state of regulatory affairs at the time of acquisition is not the only factor that may determine the extent of investment-backed expectations. For example, the nature and extent of permitted development under the regulatory regime vis-a-vis the development sought by the claimant may also shape legitimate expectations without vesting any kind of development right in the property owner. We also have never held that a takings claim is defeated simply on account of the lack of a personal financial investment by a postenactment acquirer of property, such as a donee, heir, or devisee. *Cf.* Hodel v. Irving, 481 U.S. 704, 714–718, 95 L. Ed. 2d 668, 107 S. Ct. 2076 (1987). Courts instead must attend to those circumstances which are probative of what fairness requires in a given case.

If investment-backed expectations are given exclusive significance in the *Penn Central* analysis and existing regulations dictate the reasonableness of those expectations in every instance, then the State wields far too much power to redefine property rights upon passage of title. On the other hand, if existing regulations do nothing to inform the analysis, then some property owners may reap windfalls and an important indicium of fairness is lost. As I understand it, our decision today does not remove the regulatory backdrop against which an owner takes title to property from the purview of the *Penn Central* inquiry. It simply restores balance to that inquiry. Courts properly consider the effect of existing regulations under the rubric of investment-backed expectations in determining whether a compensable taking has occurred. As before, the salience of these facts cannot be reduced to any "set formula." *Penn Central*, 438 U.S. at 124 (internal quotation marks omitted). The temptation to adopt what amount to *per se* rules in either direction must be resisted. The Takings Clause requires careful examination and weighing of all the relevant circumstances in this context. The court below therefore must consider on remand the array of relevant factors under *Penn Central* before deciding whether any compensation is due.

■ JUSTICE SCALIA, concurring.

I write separately to make clear that my understanding of how the issues discussed in Part II–B of the Court's opinion must be considered on remand is not Justice O'Connor's.

The principle that underlies her separate concurrence is that it may in some (unspecified) circumstances be "unfai[r]," and produce unacceptable "windfalls," to allow a subsequent purchaser to nullify an unconstitutional partial taking (though, inexplicably, not an unconstitutional total taking) by the government. *Ante*, at 4. The polar horrible, presumably, is the situation in which a sharp real estate developer, realizing (or indeed, simply gambling on) the unconstitutional excessiveness of a development restriction that a naive landowner assumes to be valid, purchases property at what it would be worth subject to the restriction, and then develops it to its full value (or resells it at its full value) after getting the unconstitutional restriction invalidated.

This can, I suppose, be called a windfall—though it is not much different from the windfalls that occur every day at stock exchanges or antique auctions, where the knowledgeable (or the venturesome) profit at the expense of the ignorant (or the risk averse). There is something to be said (though in my view not much) for pursuing abstract "fairness" by requiring part or all of that windfall to be returned to the naive original owner, who presumably is the "rightful" owner of it. But there is nothing to be said for giving it instead to the *government*—which not only did not lose something it owned, but is both the *cause* of the miscarriage of "fairness" and the only one of the three parties involved in the miscarriage (government, naive original owner, and sharp real estate developer) which *acted unlawfully*—indeed *unconstitutionally*. Justice O'Connor would eliminate the windfall by giving the malefactor the benefit of its malefaction. It is rather like eliminating the windfall that accrued to a purchaser who bought property at a bargain rate from a thief clothed with the indicia of title, by making him turn over the "unjust" profit *to the thief*.

In my view, the fact that a restriction existed at the time the purchaser took title (other than a restriction forming part of the "background principles of the State's law of property and nuisance," Lucas v. South Carolina Coastal Council, 505 U.S. 1003, 1029, 120 L. Ed. 2d 798, 112 S. Ct. 2886 (1992)) should have no bearing upon the determination of whether the restriction is so substantial as to constitute a taking. The "investment-backed expectations" that the law will take into account do not include the assumed validity of a restriction that in fact deprives property of so much of its value as to be unconstitutional. Which is to say that a *Penn Central* taking, *see* Penn Central Transp. Co. v. New York City, 438 U.S. 104, 57 L. Ed. 2d 631,

98 S. Ct. 2646 (1978), no less than a total taking, is not absolved by the transfer of title.

NOTES AND QUESTIONS

1.   Five justices, including Justices Scalia and O'Connor, joined Justice Kennedy's opinion. As a result, the votes of both Justice Scalia and Justice O'Connor were necessary to form a majority. What implications does that have for the importance of their respective concurring opinions?

2.   When a municipality learns that Owner is planning to develop its parcel for residential use, the municipality seeks to prevent development of Owner's parcel by rezoning the land to permit only agricultural uses, even though the soil is infertile, the climate is dry, and Owner has no source of irrigation. Owner becomes disenchanted with development, and sells the parcel to Buyer, who purchases with notice of the zoning amendment. If Buyer brings a claim contending that the zoning ordinance, as applied to its land, constitutes a taking, how would Justice Kennedy have decided the case? Justice Scalia? Justice O'Connor? The Rhode Island Supreme Court?

    What reason would there be to permit Buyer's takings challenge to succeed if Buyer purchased with notice of the zoning restriction? Would the price Buyer paid to Owner matter? Should it matter?

3.   Owner purchased a building, currently used as single-room-occupancy hotel, for $2,000,000, expecting to rehabilitate the building and convert it to condominium ownership. The municipality then enacts an ordinance requiring owners of SRO hotel buildings to maintain those buildings as SRO hotels. If the building is limited to use as an SRO, its market value is $600,000. What basis, if any, does Owner have for a takings challenge? *Cf.* Seawall Assocs. v. City of New York, 74 N.Y.2d 92, 542 N.E.2d 1059, 544 N.Y.S.2d 542 (1989). Would you expect the challenge to succeed?

    Instead of litigating the takings claim, Owner sells the building to Buyer, who knows of the restriction, and pays $800,000 for the building. If Buyer now brings a takings challenge, is Buyer's litigation position weaker than Owner's? The same as Owner's? Should there be a difference between Owner's position and Buyer's?

4.   Return to the facts in *Lucas*. Suppose, however, that Lucas had owned 5 beachfront lots, and that the development baseline fixed by the Coastal Council had left Lucas without any economic use for three of the parcels, but with a right to build residential homes on the other two. How would the Court analyze a takings claim by Lucas? Does *Palazzolo* shed any light on that question?

    What if Lucas had owned only one lot, and that one lot was on the "wrong" side of the line dividing the area in which development was permitted from the area in which development was prohibited (as it was in *Lucas* itself). Would a purchase by Lucas of a lot on the "right" side of the dividing line defeat the takings claim Lucas would otherwise have? Why or why not?

Is the "denominator problem" relevant to *Lucas* claims as well as *Penn Central* claims?

5. In *Palazzolo* itself, suppose the landowner had sold the upland parcel before the Coastal Resources Management Council had enacted its wetlands regulation. Would the Court's analysis of the landowner's takings claim have been different? How?

What if the sale had taken place after enactment of the regulation, but before landowner brought his takings claim? For a discussion of the effect of market transactions on the denominator problem, *see* Patrick Wiseman, May the Market Do What Taking Jurisprudence Does Not: Divide a Single Parcel Into Discrete Segments, 19 Tul. Envtl. L.J. 269 (2006) and Mark W. Cordes, The Effect of Palazzolo v. Rhode Island on Takings and Environmental Land Use Regulation, 43 Santa Clara L. Rev. 337, 364–65 (2003).

For arguments that the Court's focus on the "parcel as a whole" is misguided, *see* Steven J. Eagle, Property Tests, Due Process Tests and Regulatory Takings Jurisprudence, 2007 B.Y.U. L. Rev. 899, 939–943; John Fee, The Takings Clause as a Comparative Right, 76 S. Cal. L. Rev. 1003, 1029–32 (2003) (describing the denominator problem as a "conceptual black hole").

6. State regulations promulgated in 1920 prohibit development on land adjacent to a lake that serves as the village's principal water source. Landowner buys a 16.8-acre lakefront parcel in 2005, and seeks to develop three single-family homes. The village planning board denies the subdivision application, relying on the state regulations. Can the landowner prevail on a takings claim? *See* Monroe Equities LLC v. State, 47 Misc.3d 747, 4 N.Y.S.3d 816 (N.Y. Ct. Cl. 2014) (answering no).

7. *Statutes of Limitations.* Suppose a state imposes a statute of limitations on challenges to zoning amendments, and measures the statutory period from the moment of the ordinance's enactment. If the person who owns the land at the time of enactment fails to challenge the ordinance, can the state apply the statute of limitations to bar claims by future owners?

In Travis v. County of Santa Cruz, 33 Cal.4th 757, 94 P.3d 538, 16 Cal.Rptr.3d 404 (2004), a county ordinance imposed restrictions on second dwelling units on residential property. A California statute required any challenges to a zoning amendment to be brought within 90 days of the amendment's enactment. Long after the 90-day period had expired, the landowner sought a permit to build a second dwelling unit. When the permit was denied, the landowner advanced a takings claim, and was met by a statute of limitations defense. The California Supreme Court held that the 90-day statute did not bar a takings claim, relying on language in *Palazzolo* emphasizing that "[f]uture generations, too, have a right to challenge unreasonable limitations on the use and value of land." *Id.* at 770, 94 P.3d at 545, 16 Cal. Rptr. 3d at 412–13.

F. MORATORIA

Municipalities sometimes enact moratoria on development, ostensibly to permit more careful study of regulatory alternatives. If those moratoria last long enough, or if the municipality extends those moratoria, the economic impact on landowners can be serious. Can a moratorium give rise to a takings claim?

Tahoe-Sierra Preservation Council, Inc. v. Tahoe Regional Planning Agency

United States Supreme Court, 2002
535 U.S. 302

■ JUSTICE STEVENS delivered the opinion of the Court.

The question presented is whether a moratorium on development imposed during the process of devising a comprehensive land-use plan constitutes a *per se* taking of property requiring compensation under the Takings Clause of the United States Constitution. This case actually involves two moratoria ordered by respondent Tahoe Regional Planning Agency (TRPA) to maintain the status quo while studying the impact of development on Lake Tahoe and designing a strategy for environmentally sound growth. The first, Ordinance 81–5, was effective from August 24, 1981, until August 26, 1983, whereas the second more restrictive Resolution 83–21 was in effect from August 27, 1983, until April 25, 1984. As a result of these two directives, virtually all development on a substantial portion of the property subject to TRPA's jurisdiction was prohibited for a period of 32 months. Although the question we decide relates only to that 32-month period, a brief description of the events leading up to the moratoria and a comment on the two permanent plans that TRPA adopted thereafter will clarify the narrow scope of our holding.

I

The relevant facts are undisputed. The Court of Appeals, while reversing the District Court on a question of law, accepted all of its findings of fact, and no party challenges those findings. All agree that Lake Tahoe is "uniquely beautiful," [Tahoe-Sierra Pres. Council, Inc. v. Tahoe Reg'l Planning Agency,] 34 F. Supp. 2d 1226, 1230 (Nev. 1999), that President Clinton was right to call it a " 'national treasure that must be protected and preserved,' " *ibid.* and that Mark Twain aptly described the clarity of its waters as " 'not *merely* transparent, but dazzlingly, brilliantly so,' " *ibid.* (emphasis added) (quoting M. Twain, Roughing It 174–175 (1872)).

Lake Tahoe's exceptional clarity is attributed to the absence of algae that obscures the waters of most other lakes. Historically, the lack of nitrogen and phosphorous, which nourish the growth of algae, has ensured the transparency of its waters. Unfortunately, the lake's pristine state has deteriorated rapidly over the past 40 years; increased land development in the Lake Tahoe Basin (Basin) has threatened the " 'noble sheet of blue water' " beloved by Twain and countless others. 34 F. Supp. 2d at 1230. As the District Court found, "dramatic decreases in clarity first began to be noted in the 1950's/early 1960's, shortly after development at the lake began in earnest." *Id.* at 1231. The lake's unsurpassed beauty, it seems, is the wellspring of its undoing.

Those areas in the Basin that have steeper slopes produce more runoff; therefore, they are usually considered "high hazard" lands. Moreover, certain areas near streams or wetlands known as "Stream Environment Zones" (SEZs) are especially vulnerable to the impact of development because, in their natural state, they act as filters for much of the debris that runoff carries. Because "[t]he most obvious response to this problem . . . is to restrict development around the lake—especially in SEZ lands, as well as in areas already naturally prone to runoff," *id.*, at 1232, conservation efforts have focused on controlling growth in these high hazard areas.

In the 1960's, when the problems associated with the burgeoning development began to receive significant attention, jurisdiction over the Basin, which occupies 501 square miles, was shared by the States of California and Nevada, five counties, several municipalities, and the Forest Service of the Federal Government. In 1968, the legislatures of the two States adopted the Tahoe Regional Planning Compact, see 1968 Cal. Stats., ch. 998, p. 1900, § 1; 1968 Nev. Stats. 4, which Congress approved in 1969, Pub. L. 91–148, 83 Stat. 360. The compact set goals for the protection and preservation of the lake and created TRPA as the agency assigned "to coordinate and regulate development in the Basin and to conserve its natural resources." Lake Country Estates, Inc. v. Tahoe Regional Planning Agency, 440 U.S. 391, 394, 59 L. Ed. 2d 401, 99 S. Ct. 1171 (1979).

The 1980 Tahoe Regional Planning Compact (Compact) redefined the structure, functions, and voting procedures of TRPA, App. 37, 94 Stat. 3235–3238; 34 F. Supp. 2d at 1233, and directed it to develop regional "environmental threshold carrying capacities"—a term that embraced "standards for air quality, water quality, soil conservation, vegetation preservation and noise." 94 Stat. 3235, 3239. The Compact provided that TRPA "shall adopt" those standards within 18 months, and that "within 1 year after" their adoption (i.e., by June 19, 1983), it "shall" adopt an amended regional plan that achieves and maintains those carrying capacities. *Id.* at 3240. The Compact also contained a finding by the Legislatures of California and Nevada "that in order to make effective the regional plan as revised by [TRPA], it is necessary to halt temporarily works of development in the region which might otherwise absorb the entire capability of the region for further development or direct it out of harmony with the ultimate plan." *Id.* at

3243. Accordingly, for the period prior to the adoption of the final plan ("or until May 1, 1983, whichever is earlier"), the Compact itself prohibited the development of new subdivisions, condominiums, and apartment buildings, and also prohibited each city and county in the Basin from granting any more permits in 1981, 1982, or 1983 than had been granted in 1978.

During this period TRPA was also working on the development of a regional water quality plan to comply with the Clean Water Act, 33 U.S.C. § 1288 (1994 ed.). Despite the fact that TRPA performed these obligations in "good faith and to the best of its ability," 34 F. Supp. 2d at 1233, after a few months it concluded that it could not meet the deadlines in the Compact. On June 25, 1981, it therefore enacted Ordinance 81–5 imposing the first of the two moratoria on development that petitioners challenge in this proceeding. The ordinance provided that it would become effective on August 24, 1981, and remain in effect pending the adoption of the permanent plan required by the Compact. App. 159, 191.

The District Court made a detailed analysis of the ordinance, noting that it might even prohibit hiking or picnicking on SEZ lands, but construed it as essentially banning any construction or other activity that involved the removal of vegetation or the creation of land coverage on all SEZ lands, as well as on class 1, 2, and 3 lands in California. 34 F. Supp. 2d at 1233–1235. Some permits could be obtained for such construction in Nevada if certain findings were made. *Id.* at 1235. It is undisputed, however, that Ordinance 81–5 prohibited the construction of any new residences on SEZ lands in either State and on class 1, 2, and 3 lands in California.

Given the complexity of the task of defining "environmental threshold carrying capacities" and the division of opinion within TRPA's governing board, the District Court found that it was "unsurprising" that TRPA failed to adopt those thresholds until August 26, 1982, roughly two months after the Compact deadline. *Ibid.* Under a liberal reading of the Compact, TRPA then had until August 26, 1983, to adopt a new regional plan. 94 Stat. 3240. "Unfortunately, but again not surprisingly, no regional plan was in place as of that date." 34 F. Supp. 2d at 1235. TRPA therefore adopted Resolution 83–21, "which completely suspended all project reviews and approvals, including the acceptance of new proposals," and which remained in effect until a new regional plan was adopted on April 26, 1984. Thus, Resolution 83–21 imposed an 8-month moratorium prohibiting all construction on high hazard lands in either State. In combination, Ordinance 81–5 and Resolution 83–21 effectively prohibited all construction on sensitive lands in California and on all SEZ lands in the entire Basin for 32 months, and on sensitive lands in Nevada (other than SEZ lands) for eight months. It is these two moratoria that are at issue in this case.

On the same day that the 1984 plan was adopted, the State of California filed an action seeking to enjoin its implementation on the ground that it failed to establish land-use controls sufficiently stringent to protect the Basin. *Id.* at 1236. The District Court entered an injunction that was upheld by the Court of Appeals and remained in effect until a completely revised plan was adopted in 1987. Both the 1984 injunction and the 1987 plan contained provisions that prohibited new construction on sensitive lands in the Basin. As the case comes to us, however, we have no occasion to consider the validity of those provisions.

II

Approximately two months after the adoption of the 1984 Plan, petitioners filed parallel actions against TRPA and other defendants in federal courts in Nevada and California that were ultimately consolidated for trial in the District of Nevada. The petitioners include the Tahoe Sierra Preservation Council, a nonprofit membership corporation representing about 2,000 owners of both improved and unimproved parcels of real estate in the Lake Tahoe Basin, and a class of some 400 individual owners of vacant lots located either on SEZ lands or in other parts of districts 1, 2, or 3. Those individuals purchased their properties prior to the effective date of the 1980 Compact, App. 34, primarily for the purpose of constructing "at a time of their choosing" a single-family home "to serve as a permanent, retirement or vacation residence," *id.* at 36. When they made those purchases, they did so with the understanding that such construction was authorized provided that "they complied with all reasonable requirements for building." *Ibid.*

Petitioners' complaints gave rise to protracted litigation that has produced four opinions by the Court of Appeals for the Ninth Circuit and several published District Court opinions. For present purposes, however, we need only describe those courts' disposition of the claim that three actions taken by TRPA—Ordinance 81–5, Resolution 83–21, and the 1984 regional plan—constituted takings of petitioners' property without just compensation. Indeed, the challenge to the 1984 plan is not before us because both the District Court and the Court of Appeals held that it was the federal injunction against implementing that plan, rather than the plan itself, that caused the post-1984 injuries that petitioners allegedly suffered, and those rulings are not encompassed within our limited grant of certiorari. Thus, we limit our discussion to the lower courts' disposition of the claims based on the 2-year moratorium (Ordinance 81–5) and the ensuing 8-month moratorium (Resolution 83–21).

Although [the district court] was satisfied that petitioners' property did retain some value during the moratoria, it found that they had been temporarily deprived of "all economically viable use of their land." *Id.* at

1245. The court concluded that those actions therefore constituted "categorical" takings under our decision in Lucas v. South Carolina Coastal Council, 505 U.S. 1003, 120 L. Ed. 2d 798, 112 S. Ct. 2886 (1992). It rejected TRPA's response that Ordinance 81–5 and Resolution 83–21 were "reasonable temporary planning moratoria" that should be excluded from *Lucas'* categorical approach.

Contrary to the District Court, the Court of Appeals held that because the regulations had only a temporary impact on petitioners' fee interest in the properties, no categorical taking had occurred.

Faced squarely with the question whether a taking had occurred, the court held that *Penn Central* was the appropriate framework for analysis. Petitioners, however, had failed to challenge the District Court's conclusion that they could not make out a taking claim under the *Penn Central* factors.

We now affirm.

IV

The text of the Fifth Amendment itself provides a basis for drawing a distinction between physical takings and regulatory takings. Its plain language requires the payment of compensation whenever the government acquires private property for a public purpose, whether the acquisition is the result of a condemnation proceeding or a physical appropriation. But the Constitution contains no comparable reference to regulations that prohibit a property owner from making certain uses of her private property. Our jurisprudence involving condemnations and physical takings is as old as the Republic and, for the most part, involves the straightforward application of *per se* rules. Our regulatory takings jurisprudence, in contrast, is of more recent vintage and is characterized by "essentially ad hoc, factual inquiries," *Penn Central*, 438 U.S. at 124, designed to allow "careful examination and weighing of all the relevant circumstances." *Palazzolo*, 533 U.S. at 636 (O'Connor, J., concurring).

This longstanding distinction between acquisitions of property for public use, on the one hand, and regulations prohibiting private uses, on the other, makes it inappropriate to treat cases involving physical takings as controlling precedents for the evaluation of a claim that there has been a "regulatory taking," and vice versa. For the same reason that we do not ask whether a physical appropriation advances a substantial government interest or whether it deprives the owner of all economically valuable use, we do not apply our precedent from the physical takings context to regulatory takings claims. Land-use regulations are ubiquitous and most of them impact property values in some tangential way—often in completely unanticipated ways. Treating them all as *per se* takings would transform government regulation into a luxury few governments could afford. By contrast, physical appropriations are relatively rare, easily identified, and usually represent a greater affront to individual property rights. "This case does not present the 'classic taking' in which the government directly appropriates private property for its own use," Eastern Enterprises v. Apfel, 524 U.S. 498, 522, 141 L. Ed. 2d 451, 118 S. Ct. 2131 (1998); instead the interference with property rights "arises from some public program adjusting the benefits and burdens of economic life to promote the common good," *Penn Central*, 438 U.S. at 124.

Perhaps recognizing this fundamental distinction, petitioners wisely do not place all their emphasis on analogies to physical takings cases. Instead, they rely principally on our decision in Lucas v. South Carolina Coastal Council, 505 U.S. 1003, 120 L. Ed. 2d 798, 112 S. Ct. 2886 (1992)—a regulatory takings case that, nevertheless, applied a categorical rule—to argue that the *Penn Central* framework is inapplicable here.

Petitioners seek to bring this case under the rule announced in *Lucas* by arguing that we can effectively sever a 32-month segment from the remainder of each landowner's fee simple estate, and then ask whether that segment has been taken in its entirety by the moratoria. Of course, defining the property interest taken in terms of the very regulation being challenged is circular. With property so divided, every delay would become a total ban; the moratorium and the normal permit process alike would constitute categorical takings. Petitioners' "conceptual severance" argument is unavailing because it ignores *Penn Central*'s admonition that in regulatory takings cases we must focus on "the parcel as a whole." 438 U.S. at 130–131. We have consistently rejected such an approach to the "denominator" question. *See* Keystone, 480 U.S. at 497. *See also* Concrete Pipe & Products of Cal., Inc. v. Construction Laborers Pension Trust for Southern Cal., 508 U.S. 602, 644, 124 L. Ed. 2d 539, 113 S. Ct. 2264 (1993) ("To the extent that any portion of property is taken, that portion is always taken in its entirety; the relevant question, however, is whether the property taken is all, or only a portion of, the parcel in question"). Thus, the District Court erred when it disaggregated petitioners' property into temporal segments corresponding to the regulations at issue and then analyzed whether petitioners were deprived of all economically viable use during each period. 34 F. Supp. 2d at 1242–1245. The starting point for the court's analysis should have been to ask whether there was a total taking of the entire parcel; if not, then *Penn Central* was the proper framework.

An interest in real property is defined by the metes and bounds that describe its geographic dimensions and the term of years that describes the temporal aspect of the owner's interest. *See* Restatement of Property §§ 7–9 (1936). Both dimensions must be considered if the interest is to be viewed in its entirety. Hence, a permanent deprivation of the owner's use of the entire area is a taking of "the parcel as a whole," whereas a temporary restriction that merely causes a diminution in value is not. Logically, a fee simple estate cannot be rendered valueless by a temporary prohibition on economic use, because the property will recover value as soon as the prohibition is lifted. Mere fluctuations in value during the process of governmental decisionmaking, absent extraordinary delay, are "incidents of ownership. They cannot be considered as a 'taking' in the constitutional sense" (quoting Danforth v. United States, 308 U.S. 271, 285, 84 L. Ed. 240, 60 S. Ct. 231 (1939)).

V

Considerations of "fairness and justice" arguably could support the conclusion that TRPA's moratoria were takings of petitioners' property based on any of seven different theories. First, even though we have not previously done so, we might now announce a categorical rule that, in the interest of fairness and justice, compensation is required whenever government temporarily deprives an owner of all economically viable use of her property. Second, we could craft a narrower rule that would cover all temporary land-use restrictions except those "normal delays in obtaining building permits, changes in zoning ordinances, variances, and the like" which were put to one side in our opinion in *First English*, 482 U.S. at 321. Third, we could adopt a rule like the one suggested by an amicus supporting petitioners that would "allow a short fixed period for deliberations to take place without compensation—say maximum one year—after which the just compensation requirements" would "kick in." Fourth, with the benefit of hindsight, we might characterize the successive actions of TRPA as a "series of rolling moratoria" that were the functional equivalent of a permanent taking. Fifth, were it not for the findings of the District Court that TRPA acted diligently and in good faith, we might have concluded that the agency was stalling in order to avoid promulgating the environmental threshold carrying capacities and regional plan mandated by the 1980 Compact. *Cf.* Monterey v. Del Monte Dunes at Monterey, Ltd., 526 U.S. 687, 698, 143 L. Ed. 2d 882, 119 S. Ct. 1624 (1999). Sixth, apart from the District Court's finding that TRPA's actions represented a proportional response to a serious risk of harm to the lake, petitioners might have argued that the moratoria did not substantially advance a legitimate state interest, *see Agins* and *Monterey*. Finally, if petitioners had challenged the application of the moratoria to their individual parcels, instead of making a facial challenge, some of them might have prevailed under a *Penn Central* analysis.

As the case comes to us, however, none of the last four theories is available. The "rolling moratoria" theory was presented in the petition for certiorari, but our order granting review did not encompass that issue, 533 U.S. 948, 121 S. Ct. 2589, 150 L. Ed. 2d 749 (2001); the case was tried in the District Court and reviewed in the Court of Appeals on the theory that each of the two moratoria was a separate taking, one for a 2-year period and the other for an 8-month period. 216 F.3d at 769. And, as we have already noted, recovery on either a bad faith theory or a theory that the state interests were insubstantial is foreclosed by the District Court's unchallenged findings of fact. Recovery under a *Penn Central* analysis is also foreclosed both because petitioners expressly disavowed that theory, and because they did not appeal from the District Court's conclusion that the evidence would not support it. Nonetheless, each of the three *per se* theories is fairly encompassed within the question that we decided to answer.

With respect to these theories, the ultimate constitutional question is whether the concepts of "fairness and justice" that underlie the Takings Clause will be better served by one of these categorical rules or by a *Penn Central* inquiry into all of the relevant circumstances in particular cases. From that perspective, the extreme categorical rule that any deprivation of all economic use, no matter how brief, constitutes a compensable taking surely cannot be sustained. Petitioners' broad submission would apply to numerous "normal delays in obtaining building permits, changes in zoning ordinances, variances, and the like," 482 U.S. at 321, as well as to orders temporarily prohibiting access to crime scenes, businesses that violate health codes, fire-damaged buildings, or other areas that we cannot now foresee. Such a rule would undoubtedly require changes in numerous practices that have long been considered permissible exercises of the police power. As Justice Holmes warned in *Mahon*, "government hardly could go on if to some extent values incident to property could not be diminished without paying for every such change in the general law." 260 U.S. at 413. A rule that required compensation for every delay in the use of property would render routine government processes prohibitively expensive or encourage hasty decisionmaking. Such an important change in the law should be the product of legislative rulemaking rather than adjudication.

In rejecting petitioners' *per se* rule, we do not hold that the temporary nature of a land-use restriction precludes finding that it effects a taking; we simply recognize that it should not be given exclusive significance one way or the other.

A narrower rule that excluded the normal delays associated with processing permits, or that covered only delays of more than a year, would certainly have a less severe impact on prevailing practices, but it would still impose serious financial constraints on the planning process. Unlike the "extraordinary circumstance" in which the government deprives a property owner of all economic use, *Lucas*, 505 U.S. at 1017, moratoria like Ordinance 81–5 and Resolution 83–21 are used widely among land-use planners to preserve the status quo while formulating a more permanent development strategy. In fact, the consensus in the planning community appears to be that moratoria, or "interim development controls" as they are often called, are an essential tool of successful development. Yet even the weak version of petitioners' categorical rule would treat these interim measures as takings regardless of the good faith of the planners, the reasonable expectations of the landowners, or the actual impact of the moratorium on property values.

The interest in facilitating informed decisionmaking by regulatory agencies counsels against adopting a *per se* rule that would impose such severe costs on their deliberations. Otherwise, the financial constraints of compensating property owners during a moratorium may force officials to rush through the planning process or to abandon the practice altogether. To the extent that communities are forced to abandon using moratoria, landowners will have incentives to develop their property quickly before a comprehensive plan can be enacted, thereby fostering inefficient and ill-conceived growth. A finding in the 1980 Compact itself, which presumably was endorsed by all three legislative bodies that participated in its enactment, attests to the importance of that concern. 94 Stat. 3243 ("The legislatures of the States of California and Nevada find that in order to make effective the regional plan as revised by the agency, it is necessary to halt temporarily works of development in the region which might otherwise absorb the entire capability of the region for further development or direct it out of harmony with the ultimate plan").

It may well be true that any moratorium that lasts for more than one year should be viewed with special skepticism. But given the fact that the District Court found that the 32 months required by TRPA to formulate the 1984 Regional Plan was not unreasonable, we could not possibly conclude that every delay of over one year is constitutionally unacceptable. Formulating a general rule of this kind is a suitable task for state legislatures.[37] In our view, the duration of the restriction is one of the important factors that a court must consider in the appraisal of a regulatory takings claim, but with respect to that factor as with respect to other factors, the "temptation to adopt what amount to *per se* rules in either direction must be resisted." *Palazzolo*, 533 U.S. at 636 (O'Connor, J., concurring). There may be moratoria that last longer than one year

---

[37] Several States already have statutes authorizing interim zoning ordinances with specific time limits. *See* Cal. Govt. Code Ann. § 65858 (West Supp. 2002) (authorizing interim ordinance of up to two years); Colo. Rev. Stat. § 30–28–121 (2001) (six months); Ky. Rev. Stat. Ann. § 100.201 (2001) (one year); Mich. Comp. Laws Ann. § 125.215 (2001) (three years); Minn. Stat. § 394.34 (2000) (two years); N. H. Rev. Stat. § 674:23 (2001) (one year); Ore. Rev. Stat. Ann. § 197.520 (1997) (10 months); S. D. Codified Laws § 11–2–10 (2001) (two years); Utah Code Ann. § 17–27–404 (1995) (18 months); Wash. Rev. Code § 35.63.200 (2001) Wis. Stat. § 62.23(7)(d) (2001) (two years). Other States, although without specific statutory authority, have recognized that reasonable interim zoning ordinances may be enacted. *See, e.g.*, S. E. W. Friel v. Triangle Oil Co., 76 Md. App. 96, 543 A.2d 863 (1988); New Jersey Shore Builders Ass'n v. Dover Twp. Comm., 191 N.J. Super. 627, 468 A.2d 742 (1983); SCA Chemical Waste Servs., Inc. v. Konigsberg, 636 S.W.2d 430 (Tenn. 1982); Sturges v. Chilmark, 380 Mass. 246, 402 N.E.2d 1346 (1980); Lebanon v. Woods, 153 Conn. 182, 215 A.2d 112 (1965).

which interfere with reasonable investment-backed expectations, but as the District Court's opinion illustrates, petitioners' proposed rule is simply "too blunt an instrument," for identifying those cases. *Id.* at 628. We conclude, therefore, that the interest in "fairness and justice" will be best served by relying on the familiar *Penn Central* approach when deciding cases like this, rather than by attempting to craft a new categorical rule.

Accordingly, the judgment of the Court of Appeals is affirmed.

It is so ordered.

■ CHIEF JUSTICE REHNQUIST, with whom JUSTICE SCALIA and JUSTICE THOMAS join, dissenting.

For over half a decade petitioners were prohibited from building homes, or any other structures, on their land. Because the Takings Clause requires the government to pay compensation when it deprives owners of all economically viable use of their land, *see* Lucas v. South Carolina Coastal Council, 505 U.S. 1003, 120 L. Ed. 2d 798, 112 S. Ct. 2886 (1992), and because a ban on all development lasting almost six years does not resemble any traditional land-use planning device, I dissent.

Lucas reaffirmed our "frequently expressed" view that "when the owner of real property has been called upon to sacrifice *all* economically beneficial uses in the name of the common good, that is, to leave his property economically idle, he has suffered a taking." 505 U.S. at 1019. *See also* Agins v. City of Tiburon, 447 U.S. 255, 258–259, 65 L. Ed. 2d 106, 100 S. Ct. 2138 (1980). The District Court in this case held that the ordinances and resolutions in effect between August 24, 1981, and April 25, 1984, "did in fact deny the plaintiffs all economically viable use of their land." 34 F. Supp. 2d 1226, 1245 (Nev. 1999). The Court of Appeals did not overturn this finding. And the 1984 injunction, issued because the environmental thresholds issued by respondent did not permit the development of single-family residences, forced petitioners to leave their land economically idle for at least another three years. The Court does not dispute that petitioners were forced to leave their land economically idle during this period. *See ante*, at 7. But the Court refuses to apply *Lucas* on the ground that the deprivation was "temporary."

Neither the Takings Clause nor our case law supports such a distinction. For one thing, a distinction between "temporary" and "permanent" prohibitions is tenuous. The "temporary" prohibition in this case that the Court finds is not a taking lasted almost six years. The "permanent" prohibition that the Court held to be a taking in *Lucas* lasted less than two years. *See* 505 U.S. at 1011–1012. The "permanent" prohibition in *Lucas* lasted less than two years because the law, as it often does, changed. The South Carolina Legislature in 1990 decided to amend the 1988 Beachfront Management Act to allow the issuance of

" 'special permits' for the construction or reconstruction of habitable structures seaward of the baseline." *Id.* at 1011–1012. Land-use regulations are not irrevocable. Under the Court's decision today, the takings question turns entirely on the initial label given a regulation, a label that is often without much meaning. There is every incentive for government to simply label any prohibition on development "temporary," or to fix a set number of years. As in this case, this initial designation does not preclude the government from repeatedly extending the "temporary" prohibition into a long-term ban on all development. The Court now holds that such a designation by the government is conclusive even though in fact the moratorium greatly exceeds the time initially specified. Apparently, the Court would not view even a 10-year moratorium as a taking under *Lucas* because the moratorium is not "permanent."

The *Lucas* rule is derived from the fact that a "total deprivation of use is, from the landowner's point of view, the equivalent of a physical appropriation." 505 U.S. at 1017. The regulation in *Lucas* was the "practical equivalence" of a long-term physical appropriation, i.e., a condemnation, so the Fifth Amendment required compensation. The "practical equivalence," from the landowner's point of view, of a "temporary" ban on all economic use is a forced leasehold. For example, assume the following situation: Respondent is contemplating the creation of a National Park around Lake Tahoe to preserve its scenic beauty. Respondent decides to take a 6-year leasehold over petitioners' property, during which any human activity on the land would be prohibited, in order to prevent any further destruction to the area while it was deciding whether to request that the area be designated a National Park.

Surely that leasehold would require compensation. In a series of World War II-era cases in which the Government had condemned leasehold interests in order to support the war effort, the Government conceded that it was required to pay compensation for the leasehold interest.

Instead of acknowledging the "practical equivalence" of this case and a condemned leasehold, the Court analogizes to other areas of takings law in which we have distinguished between regulations and physical appropriations, *see ante*, at 17–19. But whatever basis there is for such distinctions in those contexts does not apply when a regulation deprives a landowner of all economically beneficial use of his land. In addition to the "practical equivalence" from the landowner's perspective of such a regulation and a physical appropriation, we have held that a regulation denying all productive use of land does not implicate the traditional justification for differentiating between regulations and physical appropriations. In "the extraordinary circumstance when *no* productive or economically beneficial use of land is permitted," it is less likely that "the legislature is simply 'adjusting the benefits and burdens of economic life' in a manner that secures an 'average reciprocity of advantage' to everyone concerned," *Lucas*, 505 U.S. at 1017–1018 (quoting Penn Central Transp. Co. v. New York City, 438 U.S. 104, 124, 57 L. Ed. 2d 631, 98 S. Ct. 2646 (1978), and Pennsylvania Coal Co. v. Mahon, 260 U.S. at 415), and more likely that the property "is being pressed into some form of public service under the guise of mitigating serious public harm," *Lucas*, *supra*, at 1018.

* * *

III

When a regulation merely delays a final land use decision, we have recognized that there are other background principles of state property law that prevent the delay from being deemed a taking. Thus, the short-term delays attendant to zoning and permit regimes are a longstanding feature of state property law and part of a landowner's reasonable investment-backed expectations. *See Lucas*, 505 U.S. at 1034 (Kennedy, J., concurring in judgment).

But a moratorium prohibiting all economic use for a period of six years is not one of the longstanding, implied limitations of state property law. Moratoria are "interim controls on the use of land that seek to maintain the status quo with respect to land development in an area by either 'freezing' existing land uses or by allowing the issuance of building permits for only certain land uses that would not be inconsistent with a contemplated zoning plan or zoning change." 1 E. Ziegler, Rathkopf's The Law of Zoning and Planning § 13:3, p. 13–6 (4th ed. 2001). Typical moratoria thus prohibit only certain categories of development, such as fast-food restaurants, *see* Schafer v. New Orleans, 743 F.2d 1086 (CA5 1984), or adult businesses, *see* Renton v. Playtime Theatres, Inc., 475 U.S. 41, 89 L. Ed. 2d 29, 106 S. Ct. 925 (1986), or all commercial development, *see* Arnold Bernhard & Co. v. Planning & Zoning Comm'n, 194 Conn. 152, 479 A.2d 801 (1984). Such moratoria do not implicate *Lucas* because they do not deprive landowners of all economically beneficial use of their land. As for moratoria that prohibit all development, these do not have the lineage of permit and zoning requirements and thus it is less certain that property is acquired under the "implied limitation" of a moratorium prohibiting all development.

Because the prohibition on development of nearly six years in this case cannot be said to resemble any "implied limitation" of state property law, it is a taking that requires compensation.

* * *

NOTES AND QUESTIONS

1. Suppose a municipality has enacted a two-year moratorium on development in an outlying area of town to study how much additional development the municipality's infrastructure will be able to support in the foreseeable future. Anti-development forces within the municipality raised objections to a number of firms who have bid for the right to conduct the study. At the expiration of two years, municipal officials were not yet able to agree on who should conduct the study, so the municipality extended the moratorium for an additional two years. Now, almost four years later, a landowner who owns a parcel within the area subject to the moratorium seeks advice about its legal position.

In light of *Tahoe-Sierra*, does the landowner have a plausible takings claim? How would the landowner frame a takings claim? Why didn't the landowners in *Tahoe-Sierra* frame their claim that way?

The Court's opinion in *Tahoe-Sierra* suggests a number of constitutional attacks a landowner might advance against a moratorium. For discussion of the Court's "roadmap," *see* Steven J. Eagle, Planning Moratoria and Regulatory Takings: The Supreme Court's Fairness Mandate Benefits Landowners, 31 Fla. St. U. L. Rev. 429 (2004).

2. Suppose the municipality imposes a moratorium not for a specified period of time, but until a permit applicant satisfied municipally-imposed conditions. Does the moratorium constitute a *Lucas* taking if there is no reasonable prospect that the permit applicant will be able to satisfy the conditions? *See* Monks v. City of Rancho Palos Verdes, 167 Cal. App.4th 263, 84 Cal.Rptr.3d 75 (2008) (In area subject to landslides, municipality imposed moratorium unless landowner could establish that its lot was more stable than industry standard of "safety factor 1.5." The court held that the moratorium constituted a taking when previous reports established that no parcel in the area was likely to be above safety factor 1.2, and there was no evidence that development on individual lots would destabilize the area and cause harm).

3. A municipality controlled by anti-development forces seeks advice, in light of *Tahoe-Sierra*, about the potential use of a moratorium. What limits are there on a municipality's power to impose a moratorium on new development in particular areas of the municipality, or in the municipality as a whole? Do municipalities have inherent power to impose moratoria, or must state law explicitly authorize moratoria? *See* Droste v. Board of County Comm'rs, 159 P.3d 601 (Colo. 2007) (holding that general grant of land use authority conferred on municipality power to enact moratoria); but *cf.* Biggers v. City of Bainbridge Island, 162 Wash.2d 683, 169 P.3d 14 (2007) (holding that imposition of rolling moratoria on shoreline development exceeded municipality's authority when state law did not give municipalities power to regulate shorelines).

4. *The Role of State Legislatures and State Courts.* The majority opinion in *Tahoe-Sierra* suggested that state legislatures were particularly well-equipped to develop and impose time limits on development moratoria, and cited a number of state statutes that regulate the duration of interim zoning ordinances. Should the potential for state regulation play a role in defining the scope of federal constitutional rights? Why or why not?

Do state legislatures and courts have particular advantages in regulating moratoria, as distinguished from other local government limits on development? Or would we be better off leaving most regulation of land use practices to state courts and legislatures?

5. *The Claim that the Regulation Does Not "Substantially Advance" a State Interest.* In *Tahoe-Sierra*, Justice Stevens offers seven suggestions for claims a landowner might make in attacking a moratorium. The sixth of the claims is that the moratorium does not substantially advance a legitimate state interest. The availability of such a claim had its roots in dictum in Agins v. City of Tiburon, 447 U.S. 255 (1980), and the Court reasserted the availability of a "substantially advance" claim in a number of subsequent cases, including *Tahoe-Sierra*. But in Lingle v. Chevron, U.S.A., Inc., 544 U.S. 528 (2005), where the Court was squarely presented with a claim that a regulation did not substantially advance a state interest, the Court held "that the 'substantially advances' formula is not a valid takings test, and indeed conclude[d] that it has no proper place in our takings jurisprudence." *Id.* at 540.

Justice O'Connor's opinion noted that "the 'substantially advances' formula was derived from due process, not takings, precedents" and concluded that the inquiry was ill-suited to takings cases because it

> reveals nothing about the *magnitude or character of the burden* a particular regulation imposes on private property rights. Nor does it provide any information about how any regulatory burden is *distributed* among property owners. In consequence, this test does not help to identify those regulations whose effects are functionally comparable to government appropriation or invasion of private property; it is tethered neither to the text of the Takings Clause nor to the basic justification for allowing regulatory actions to be challenged under the Clause.

544 U.S. at 542.

G. UNCONSTITUTIONAL CONDITIONS: LIMITING MUNICIPAL POWER TO EXACT BENEFITS FROM LANDOWNERS

As the materials on incentive zoning and subdivision controls indicate, municipalities frequently seek to extract significant public benefits from developers. Although developers may be significant campaign contributors, they do not have much voting power in local elections, and even pro-development municipal officials will want to take credit for municipal benefits generated by new development, whether those benefits come in the form of cash or ancillary public improvements. In many states, statutes limit the power of local zoning authorities to extract payments from developers. In the following two cases, landowners argued, successfully, that the Takings Clause limits municipal power to impose exactions on developers.

Nollan v. California Coastal Commission

Supreme Court of the United States, 1987
483 U.S. 825

■ JUSTICE SCALIA delivered the opinion of the Court.

I

The Nollans own a beachfront lot in Ventura County, California. A quarter-mile north of their property is Faria County Park, an oceanside public park with a public beach and recreation area. Another public beach area, known locally as "the Cove," lies 1,800 feet south of their lot. A concrete seawall approximately eight feet high separates the beach portion of the Nollans' property from the rest of the lot. The historic mean high tide line determines the lot's oceanside boundary.

The Nollans originally leased their property with an option to buy. The building on the lot was a small bungalow, totaling 504 square feet, which for a time they rented to summer vacationers. After years of rental use, however, the building had fallen into disrepair, and could no longer be rented out.

The Nollans' option to purchase was conditioned on their promise to demolish the bungalow and replace it. In order to do so, under Cal. Pub. Res. Code Ann. §§ 30106, 30212, and 30600 (West 1986), they were required to obtain a coastal development permit from the California Coastal Commission. On February 25, 1982, they submitted a permit application to the Commission in which they proposed to demolish the existing structure and replace it with a three-bedroom house in keeping with the rest of the neighborhood.

The Nollans were informed that their application had been placed on the administrative calendar, and that the Commission staff had recommended that the permit be granted subject to the condition that they allow the public an easement to pass across a portion of their property bounded by the mean high tide line on one side, and their seawall on the other side. This would make it easier for the public to get to Faria County Park and the Cove. The Nollans protested imposition of the condition, but the Commission overruled their objections and granted the permit subject to their recordation of a deed restriction granting the easement. App. 31, 34.

On June 3, 1982, the Nollans filed a petition for writ of administrative mandamus asking the Ventura County Superior Court to invalidate the access condition. They argued that the condition could not be imposed absent evidence that their proposed development would have a direct adverse impact on public access to the beach. The court agreed, and remanded the case to the Commission for a full evidentiary hearing on that issue. *Id.*, at 36.

On remand, the Commission held a public hearing, after which it made further factual findings and reaffirmed its imposition of the condition. It found that the new house would increase blockage of the view of the ocean, thus contributing to the development of "a 'wall' of residential structures" that would prevent the public "psychologically . . . from realizing a stretch of coastline exists nearby that they have every right to visit." *Id.*, at 58. The new house would also increase private use of the shorefront. *Id.*, at 59. These effects of construction of the house, along with other area development, would cumulatively "burden the public's ability to traverse to and along the shorefront." *Id.*, at 65–66. Therefore the Commission could properly require the Nollans to offset that burden by providing additional lateral access to the public beaches in the form of an easement across their property. The Commission also noted that it had similarly conditioned 43 out of 60 coastal development permits along the same tract of land, and that of the 17 not so conditioned, 14 had been approved when the Commission did not have administrative regulations in place allowing imposition of the condition, and the remaining 3 had not involved shorefront property. *Id.*, at 47–48.

The Nollans filed a supplemental petition for a writ of administrative mandamus with the Superior Court, in which they argued that imposition of the access condition violated the Takings Clause of the Fifth Amendment, as incorporated against the States by the Fourteenth Amendment.

II

Had California simply required the Nollans to make an easement across their beachfront available to the public on a permanent basis in order to increase public access to the beach, rather than conditioning their permit to rebuild their house on their agreeing to do so, we have no doubt there would have been a taking. To say that the appropriation of a public easement across a landowner's premises does not constitute the taking of a property interest but rather (as Justice BRENNAN contends) "a mere restriction on its use," *post*, at 848–849, n. 3, is to use words in a manner that deprives them of all their ordinary meaning. We think a "permanent physical occupation" has occurred, for purposes of that rule, where individuals are given a permanent and continuous right to pass to and fro, so that the real property may continuously be traversed, even though no particular individual is permitted to station himself permanently upon the premises.

Given, then, that requiring uncompensated conveyance of the easement outright would violate the Fourteenth Amendment, the question becomes whether requiring it to be conveyed as a condition for issuing a land-use permit alters the outcome. We have long recognized that land-use regulation does not effect a taking if it "substantially advance[s] legitimate state interests" and does not "den[y] an owner economically viable use of his land," Agins v. Tiburon, 447 U.S. 255, 260 (1980). *See also* Penn Central Transportation Co. v. New York City, 438

U.S. 104, 127 (1978) ("[A] use restriction may constitute a 'taking' if not reasonably necessary to the effectuation of a substantial government purpose"). Our cases have not elaborated on the standards for determining what constitutes a "legitimate state interest" or what type of connection between the regulation and the state interest satisfies the requirement that the former "substantially advance" the latter. They have made clear, however, that a broad range of governmental purposes and regulations satisfies these requirements. *See* Agins v. Tiburon, *supra*, at 260–262 (scenic zoning); Penn Central Transportation Co. v. New York City, *supra* (landmark preservation); Euclid v. Ambler Realty Co., 272 U.S. 365 (1926) (residential zoning); Laitos & Westfall, Government Interference with Private Interests in Public Resources, 11 Harv. Envtl. L. Rev. 1, 66 (1987). The Commission argues that among these permissible purposes are protecting the public's ability to see the beach, assisting the public in overcoming the "psychological barrier" to using the beach created by a developed shorefront, and preventing congestion on the public beaches. We assume, without deciding, that this is so—in which case the Commission unquestionably would be able to deny the Nollans their permit outright if their new house (alone, or by reason of the cumulative impact produced in conjunction with other construction) would substantially impede these purposes, unless the denial would interfere so drastically with the Nollans' use of their property as to constitute a taking. *See* Penn Central Transportation Co. v. New York City, *supra*.

The Commission argues that a permit condition that serves the same legitimate police-power purpose as a refusal to issue the permit should not be found to be a taking if the refusal to issue the permit would not constitute a taking. We agree. Thus, if the Commission attached to the permit some condition that would have protected the public's ability to see the beach notwithstanding construction of the new house—for example, a height limitation, a width restriction, or a ban on fences—so long as the Commission could have exercised its police power (as we have assumed it could) to forbid construction of the house altogether, imposition of the condition would also be constitutional. Moreover (and here we come closer to the facts of the present case), the condition would be constitutional even if it consisted of the requirement that the Nollans provide a viewing spot on their property for passersby with whose sighting of the ocean their new house would interfere. Although such a requirement, constituting a permanent grant of continuous access to the property, would have to be considered a taking if it were not attached to a development permit, the Commission's assumed power to forbid construction of the house in order to protect the public's view of the beach must surely include the power to condition construction upon some concession by the owner, even a concession of property rights, that serves the same end. If a prohibition designed to accomplish that purpose would be a legitimate exercise of the police power rather than a taking, it would be strange to conclude that providing the owner an alternative to that prohibition which accomplishes the same purpose is not.

The evident constitutional propriety disappears, however, if the condition substituted for the prohibition utterly fails to further the end advanced as the justification for the prohibition. When that essential nexus is eliminated, the situation becomes the same as if California law forbade shouting fire in a crowded theater, but granted dispensations to those willing to contribute $100 to the state treasury. While a ban on shouting fire can be a core exercise of the State's police power to protect the public safety, and can thus meet even our stringent standards for regulation of speech, adding the unrelated condition alters the purpose to one which, while it may be legitimate, is inadequate to sustain the ban. Therefore, even though, in a sense, requiring a $100 tax contribution in order to shout fire is a lesser restriction on speech than an outright ban, it would not pass constitutional muster. Similarly here, the lack of nexus between the condition and the original purpose of the building restriction converts that purpose to something other than what it was. The purpose then becomes, quite simply, the obtaining of an easement to serve some valid governmental purpose, but without payment of compensation. Whatever may be the outer limits of "legitimate state interests" in the takings and land-use context, this is not one of them. In short, unless the permit condition serves the same governmental purpose as the development ban, the building restriction is not a valid regulation of land use but "an out-and-out plan of extortion." J. E. D. Associates, Inc. v. Atkinson, 121 N. H. 581, 584, 432 A. 2d 12, 14–15 (1981); *see* Brief for United States as Amicus Curiae 22, and n. 20. *See also* Loretto v. Teleprompter Manhattan CATV Corp., 458 U.S., at 439, n. 17.[5]

III

The Commission claims that it concedes as much, and that we may sustain the condition at issue here by finding that it is reasonably related to the public need or burden that the Nollans' new house creates or to which it contributes. We can accept, for purposes of discussion, the Commission's proposed test as to how close a "fit" between the condition and the burden is required, because we find that this case does not meet even the most untailored standards. The Commission's principal contention to the contrary essentially turns on a play on the word "access." The Nollans' new house, the Commission found, will interfere

---

[5]   One would expect that a regime in which this kind of leveraging of the police power is allowed would produce stringent land-use regulation which the State then waives to accomplish other purposes, leading to lesser realization of the land-use goals purportedly sought to be served than would result from more lenient (but nontradeable) development restrictions. Thus, the importance of the purpose underlying the prohibition not only does not *justify* the imposition of unrelated conditions for eliminating the prohibition, but positively militates against the practice.

with "visual access" to the beach. That in turn (along with other shorefront development) will interfere with the desire of people who drive past the Nollans' house to use the beach, thus creating a "psychological barrier" to "access." The Nollans' new house will also, by a process not altogether clear from the Commission's opinion but presumably potent enough to more than offset the effects of the psychological barrier, increase the use of the public beaches, thus creating the need for more "access." These burdens on "access" would be alleviated by a requirement that the Nollans provide "lateral access" to the beach.

Rewriting the argument to eliminate the play on words makes clear that there is nothing to it. It is quite impossible to understand how a requirement that people already on the public beaches be able to walk across the Nollans' property reduces any obstacles to viewing the beach created by the new house. It is also impossible to understand how it lowers any "psychological barrier" to using the public beaches, or how it helps to remedy any additional congestion on them caused by construction of the Nollans' new house. We therefore find that the Commission's imposition of the permit condition cannot be treated as an exercise of its land-use power for any of these purposes.

We are left, then, with the Commission's justification for the access requirement unrelated to land-use regulation:

"Finally, the Commission notes that there are several existing provisions of pass and repass lateral access benefits already given by past Faria Beach Tract applicants as a result of prior coastal permit decisions. The access required as a condition of this permit is part of a comprehensive program to provide continuous public access along Faria Beach as the lots undergo development or redevelopment." App. 68.

That is simply an expression of the Commission's belief that the public interest will be served by a continuous strip of publicly accessible beach along the coast. The Commission may well be right that it is a good idea, but that does not establish that the Nollans (and other coastal residents) alone can be compelled to contribute to its realization. Rather, California is free to advance its "comprehensive program," if it wishes, by using its power of eminent domain for this "public purpose," *see* U.S. Const., Amdt. 5; but if it wants an easement across the Nollans' property, it must pay for it.

Reversed.

■ JUSTICE BRENNAN, with whom JUSTICE MARSHALL joins, dissenting.

Appellants in this case sought to construct a new dwelling on their beach lot that would both diminish visual access to the beach and move private development closer to the public tidelands. The Commission reasonably concluded that such "buildout," both individually and cumulatively, threatens public access to the shore. It sought to offset this encroachment by obtaining assurance that the public may walk along the shoreline in order to gain access to the ocean. The Court finds this an illegitimate exercise of the police power, because it maintains that there is no reasonable relationship between the effect of the development and the condition imposed.

The first problem with this conclusion is that the Court imposes a standard of precision for the exercise of a State's police power that has been discredited for the better part of this century. Furthermore, even under the Court's cramped standard, the permit condition imposed in this case directly responds to the specific type of burden on access created by appellants' development. Finally, a review of those factors deemed most significant in takings analysis makes clear that the Commission's action implicates none of the concerns underlying the Takings Clause. The Court has thus struck down the Commission's reasonable effort to respond to intensified development along the California coast, on behalf of landowners who can make no claim that their reasonable expectations have been disrupted. The Court has, in short, given appellants a windfall at the expense of the public.

Dolan v. City of Tigard
Supreme Court of the United States, 1994
512 U.S. 374

■ CHIEF JUSTICE REHNQUIST delivered the opinion of the Court.

Petitioner challenges the decision of the Oregon Supreme Court which held that the city of Tigard could condition the approval of her building permit on the dedication of a portion of her property for flood control and traffic improvements. 317 Ore. 110, 854 P.2d 437 (1993). We granted certiorari to resolve a question left open by our decision in Nollan v. California Coastal Comm'n, 483 U.S. 825, 97 L. Ed. 2d 677, 107 S. Ct. 3141 (1987), of what is the required degree of connection between the exactions imposed by the city and the projected impacts of the proposed development.

I

Pursuant to the State's requirements, the city of Tigard, a community of some 30,000 residents on the southwest edge of Portland, developed a comprehensive plan and codified it in its Community Development Code (CDC). The CDC requires property owners in the area zoned Central Business District to comply with a 15% open space and landscaping requirement, which limits total site coverage, including all structures and paved parking, to 85% of the parcel. CDC, ch. 18.66, App. to Pet. for Cert. G–16 to G–17. After the completion of a transportation study that identified congestion in the Central Business District as a particular problem, the city adopted a plan for a pedestrian/bicycle pathway intended to encourage alternatives to automobile transportation for short trips. The CDC requires that new development facilitate this plan by dedicating land for pedestrian pathways where provided for in the pedestrian/bicycle pathway plan.

The city also adopted a Master Drainage Plan (Drainage Plan). The Drainage Plan noted that flooding occurred in several areas along Fanno Creek, including areas near petitioner's property. Record, Doc. No. F, ch. 2, pp. 2–5 to 2–8; 4–2 to 4–6; Figure 4–1. The Drainage Plan also established that the increase in impervious surfaces associated with continued urbanization would exacerbate these flooding problems. To combat these risks, the Drainage Plan suggested a series of improvements to the Fanno Creek Basin, including channel excavation in the area next to petitioner's property. App. to Pet. for Cert. G–13, G–38. Other recommendations included ensuring that the floodplain remains free of structures and that it be preserved as greenways to minimize flood damage to structures. Record, Doc. No. F, ch. 5, pp. 5–16 to 5–21. The Drainage Plan concluded that the cost of these improvements should be shared based on both direct and indirect benefits, with property owners along the water-ways paying more due to the direct benefit that they would receive. *Id.*, ch. 8, p. 8–11. CDC Chapters 18.84 and 18.86 and CDC § 18.164.100 and the Tigard Park Plan carry out these recommendations.

Petitioner Florence Dolan owns a plumbing and electric supply store located on Main Street in the Central Business District of the city. The store covers approximately 9,700 square feet on the eastern side of a 1.67-acre parcel, which includes a gravel parking lot. Fanno Creek flows through the southwestern corner of the lot and along its western boundary. The year-round flow of the creek renders the area within the creek's 100-year floodplain virtually unusable for commercial development. The city's comprehensive plan includes the Fanno Creek floodplain as part of the city's greenway system.

Petitioner applied to the city for a permit to redevelop the site. Her proposed plans called for nearly doubling the size of the store to 17,600 square feet and paving a 39-space parking lot. The existing store, located on the opposite side of the parcel, would be razed in sections as construction progressed on the new building. In the second phase of the project, petitioner proposed to build an additional structure on the northeast side of the site for complementary businesses and to provide more parking. The proposed expansion and intensified use are consistent with the city's zoning scheme in the Central Business District. CDC § 18.66.030, App. to Brief for Petitioner C–1 to C–3.

The City Planning Commission (Commission) granted petitioner's permit application subject to conditions imposed by the city's CDC. The CDC establishes the following standard for site development review approval:

> Where landfill and/or development is allowed within and
> adjacent to the 100-year floodplain, the City shall require the
> dedication of sufficient open land area for greenway adjoining
> and within the floodplain. This area shall include portions at a
> suitable elevation for the construction of a pedestrian/bicycle
> pathway within the floodplain in accordance with the adopted
> pedestrian/bicycle plan.

CDC § 18.120.180.A.8, App. to Brief for Respondent B–45 to B–46.

Thus, the Commission required that petitioner dedicate the portion
of her property lying within the 100-year floodplain for improvement of
a storm drainage system along Fanno Creek and that she dedicate an
additional 15-foot strip of land adjacent to the floodplain as a
pedestrian/bicycle pathway. The dedication required by that condition
encompasses approximately 7,000 square feet, or roughly 10% of the
property. In accordance with city practice, petitioner could rely on the
dedicated property to meet the 15% open space and landscaping
requirement mandated by the city's zoning scheme. App. to Pet. for
Cert. G–28 to G–29. The city would bear the cost of maintaining a
landscaped buffer between the dedicated area and the new store. *Id.*, at
G–44 to G–45.

Petitioner requested variances from the CDC standards. Variances
are granted only where it can be shown that, owing to special
circumstances related to a specific piece of the land, the literal
interpretation of the applicable zoning provisions would cause "an
undue or unnecessary hardship" unless the variance is granted. CDC
§ 18.134.010, App. to Brief for Respondent B–47. Rather than posing
alternative mitigating measures to offset the expected impacts of her
proposed development, as allowed under the CDC, petitioner simply
argued that her proposed development would not conflict with the
policies of the comprehensive plan. *Id.*, at E–4. The Commission denied
the request.

The Commission made a series of findings concerning the
relationship between the dedicated conditions and the projected impacts
of petitioner's project. First, the Commission noted that "it is reasonable
to assume that customers and employees of the future uses of this site
could utilize a pedestrian/bicycle pathway adjacent to this development
for their transportation and recreational needs." City of Tigard
Planning Commission Final Order No. 91–09 PC, App. to Pet. for Cert.
G–24. The Commission noted that the site plan has provided for bicycle
parking in a rack in front of the proposed building and "it is reasonable
to expect that some of the users of the bicycle parking provided for by
the site plan will use the pathway adjacent to Fanno Creek if it is
constructed." *Ibid.* In addition, the Commission found that creation of a
convenient, safe pedestrian/bicycle pathway system as an alternative

means of transportation "could offset some of the traffic demand on [nearby] streets and lessen the increase in traffic congestion." *Ibid.*

The Commission went on to note that the required floodplain dedication would be reasonably related to petitioner's request to intensify the use of the site given the increase in the impervious surface. The Commission stated that the "anticipated increased storm water flow from the subject property to an already strained creek and drainage basin can only add to the public need to manage the stream channel and floodplain for drainage purposes." *Id.*, at G–37. Based on this anticipated increased storm water flow, the Commission concluded that "the requirement of dedication of the floodplain area on the site is related to the applicant's plan to intensify development on the site." *Ibid.* The Tigard City Council approved the Commission's final order, subject to one minor modification; the city council reassigned the responsibility for surveying and marking the floodplain area from petitioner to the city's engineering department. *Id.*, at G–7.

Petitioner appealed to the Land Use Board of Appeals (LUBA) on the ground that the city's dedication requirements were not related to the proposed development, and, therefore, those requirements constituted an uncompensated taking of her property under the Fifth Amendment. In evaluating the federal taking claim, LUBA assumed that the city's findings about the impacts of the proposed development were supported by substantial evidence. Given the undisputed fact that the proposed larger building and paved parking area would increase the amount of impervious surfaces and the runoff into Fanno Creek, LUBA concluded that "there is a 'reasonable relationship' between the proposed development and the requirement to dedicate land along Fanno Creek for a greenway." *Id.*, at D–16. With respect to the pedestrian/bicycle pathway, LUBA noted the Commission's finding that a significantly larger retail sales building and parking lot would attract larger numbers of customers and employees and their vehicles. It again found a "reasonable relationship" between alleviating the impacts of increased traffic from the development and facilitating the provision of a pedestrian/bicycle pathway as an alternative means of transportation. *Ibid.*

The Oregon Court of Appeals affirmed, rejecting petitioner's contention that in Nollan v. California Coastal Comm'n, 483 U.S. 825, 97 L. Ed. 2d 677, 107 S. Ct. 3141 (1987), we had abandoned the "reasonable relationship" test in favor of a stricter "essential nexus" test. 113 Ore. App. 162, 832 P.2d 853 (1992). The Oregon Supreme Court affirmed. 317 Ore. 110, 854 P.2d 437 (1993). The court also disagreed with petitioner's contention that the *Nollan* Court abandoned the "reasonably related" test.

II

The Takings Clause of the Fifth Amendment of the United States Constitution, made applicable to the States through the Fourteenth Amendment, Chicago, B. & Q. R. Co. v. Chicago, 166 U.S. 226, 239, 17 S. Ct. 581, 41 L. Ed. 979 (1897), provides: "Nor shall private property be taken for public use, without just compensation." One of the principal purposes of the Takings Clause is "to bar Government from forcing some people alone to bear public burdens which, in all fairness and justice, should be borne by the public as a whole." Armstrong v. United States, 364 U.S. 40, 49, 4 L. Ed. 2d 1554, 80 S. Ct. 1563 (1960). Without question, had the city simply required petitioner to dedicate a strip of land along Fanno Creek for public use, rather than conditioning the grant of her permit to redevelop her property on such a dedication, a taking would have occurred. *Nollan, supra*, at 831. Such public access would deprive petitioner of the right to exclude others, "one of the most essential sticks in the bundle of rights that are commonly characterized as property." Kaiser Aetna v. United States, 444 U.S. 164, 176, 62 L. Ed. 2d 332, 100 S. Ct. 383 (1979).

On the other side of the ledger, the authority of state and local governments to engage in land use planning has been sustained against constitutional challenge as long ago as our decision in Village of Euclid v. Ambler Realty Co., 272 U.S. 365, 71 L. Ed. 303, 47 S. Ct. 114 (1926). "Government hardly could go on if to some extent values incident to property could not be diminished without paying for every such change in the general law." Pennsylvania Coal Co. v. Mahon, 260 U.S. 393, 413, 67 L. Ed. 322, 43 S. Ct. 158 (1922). A land use regulation does not effect a taking if it "substantially advances legitimate state interests" and does not "deny an owner economically viable use of his land." Agins v. City of Tiburon, 447 U.S. 255, 260, 65 L. Ed. 2d 106, 100 S. Ct. 2138 (1980).

The sort of land use regulations discussed in the cases just cited, however, differ in two relevant particulars from the present case. First, they involved essentially legislative determinations classifying entire areas of the city, whereas here the city made an adjudicative decision to condition petitioner's application for a building permit on an individual parcel. Second, the conditions imposed were not simply a limitation on the use petitioner might make of her own parcel, but a requirement that she deed portions of the property to the city. In *Nollan, supra*, we held that governmental authority to exact such a condition was circumscribed by the Fifth and Fourteenth Amendments. Under the well-settled doctrine of "unconstitutional conditions," the government may not require a person to give up a constitutional right—here the right to receive just compensation when property is taken for a public use—in exchange for a discretionary benefit conferred by the government where the benefit sought has little or no relationship to the property. Petitioner contends that the city has forced her to choose between the building permit and her right under the Fifth Amendment to just compensation for the public easements. Petitioner does not quarrel with the city's authority to exact some forms of dedication as a condition for the grant of a building permit, but challenges the showing made by the city to justify these exactions. She argues that the city has identified "no special benefits" conferred on her, and has not identified any "special quantifiable burdens" created by her new store that would justify the particular dedications required from her which are not required from the public at large.

III

In evaluating petitioner's claim, we must first determine whether the "essential nexus" exists between the "legitimate state interest" and the permit condition exacted by the city. *Nollan*, 483 U.S. at 837. If we find that a nexus exists, we must then decide the required degree of connection between the exactions and the projected impact of the proposed development. We were not required to reach this question in *Nollan*, because we concluded that the connection did not meet even the loosest standard. 483 U.S. at 838. Here, however, we must decide this question.

A

We addressed the essential nexus question in *Nollan*. We agreed that the Coastal Commission's concern with protecting visual access to the ocean constituted a legitimate public interest. 483 U.S. at 835. We also agreed that the permit condition would have been constitutional "even if it consisted of the requirement that the Nollans provide a viewing spot on their property for passersby with whose sighting of the ocean their new house would interfere." 483 U.S. at 836. We resolved, however, that the Coastal Commission's regulatory authority was set completely adrift from its constitutional moorings when it claimed that a nexus existed between visual access to the ocean and a permit condition requiring lateral public access along the Nollans' beachfront lot. 483 U.S. at 837. How enhancing the public's ability to "traverse to and along the shorefront" served the same governmental purpose of "visual access to the ocean" from the roadway was beyond our ability to countenance. The absence of a nexus left the Coastal Commission in the position of simply trying to obtain an easement through gimmickry, which converted a valid regulation of land use into " 'an out-and-out plan of extortion.' " *Ibid.*, quoting J. E. D. Associates, Inc. v. Atkinson, 121 N.H. 581, 584, 432 A.2d 12, 14–15 (1981).

No such gimmicks are associated with the permit conditions imposed by the city in this case. Undoubtedly, the prevention of flooding along Fanno Creek and the reduction of traffic congestion in the Central Business District qualify as the type of legitimate public purposes we have upheld. *Agins*, 447 U.S. at 260–262. It seems equally obvious that a nexus exists between preventing flooding along Fanno Creek and limiting development within the creek's 100-year floodplain. Petitioner proposes to double the size of her retail store and to pave her now-gravel parking lot, thereby expanding the impervious surface on the property and increasing the amount of storm water runoff into Fanno Creek.

The same may be said for the city's attempt to reduce traffic congestion by providing for alternative means of transportation. In theory, a pedestrian/bicycle pathway provides a useful alternative means of transportation for workers and shoppers: "Pedestrians and bicyclists occupying dedicated spaces for walking and/or bicycling . . . remove potential vehicles from streets, resulting in an overall improvement in total transportation system flow." A. Nelson, Public Provision of Pedestrian and Bicycle Access Ways: Public Policy Rationale and the Nature of Private Benefits 11, Center for Planning Development, Georgia Institute of Technology, Working Paper Series (Jan. 1994).

B

The second part of our analysis requires us to determine whether the degree of the exactions demanded by the city's permit conditions bears the required relationship to the projected impact of petitioner's proposed development.

The city required that petitioner dedicate "to the City as Greenway all portions of the site that fall within the existing 100-year floodplain [of Fanno Creek] . . . and all property 15 feet above [the floodplain] boundary." *Id.*, at 113, n. 3, 854 P.2d at 439, n. 3. In addition, the city demanded that the retail store be designed so as not to intrude into the greenway area. The city relies on the Commission's rather tentative findings that increased storm water flow from petitioner's property "can only add to the public need to manage the [floodplain] for drainage purposes" to support its conclusion that the "requirement of dedication of the floodplain area on the site is related to the applicant's plan to intensify development on the site." City of Tigard Planning Commission Final Order No. 91–09 PC, App. to Pet. for Cert. G–37.

The city made the following specific findings relevant to the pedestrian/bicycle pathway:

> In addition, the proposed expanded use of this site is anticipated to generate additional vehicular traffic thereby increasing congestion on nearby collector and arterial streets. Creation of a convenient, safe pedestrian/bicycle pathway system as an alternative means of transportation could offset some of the traffic demand on these nearby streets and lessen the increase in traffic congestion.

Id., at G–24.

The question for us is whether these findings are constitutionally sufficient to justify the conditions imposed by the city on petitioner's building permit. Since state courts have been dealing with this question a good deal longer than we have, we turn to representative decisions made by them.

In some States, very generalized statements as to the necessary connection between the required dedication and the proposed development seem to suffice. *See, e.g.*, Billings Properties, Inc. v. Yellowstone County, 144 Mont. 25, 394 P.2d 182 (1964); Jenad, Inc. v. Scarsdale, 18 N.Y.2d 78, 218 N.E.2d 673, 271 N.Y.S.2d 955 (1966). We think this standard is too lax to adequately protect petitioner's right to just compensation if her property is taken for a public purpose.

Other state courts require a very exacting correspondence, described as the "specific and uniquely attributable" test. The Supreme Court of Illinois first developed this test in Pioneer Trust & Savings Bank v. Mount Prospect, 22 Ill. 2d 375, 380, 176 N.E.2d 799, 802 (1961). Under this standard, if the local government cannot demonstrate that its exaction is directly proportional to the specifically created need, the exaction becomes "a veiled exercise of the power of eminent domain and a confiscation of private property behind the defense of police regulations." *Id.*, at 381, 176 N.E.2d at 802. We do not think the Federal Constitution requires such exacting scrutiny, given the nature of the interests involved.

A number of state courts have taken an intermediate position, requiring the municipality to show a "reasonable relationship" between the required dedication and the impact of the proposed development. Typical is the Supreme Court of Nebraska's opinion in Simpson v. North Platte, 206 Neb. 240, 245, 292 N.W.2d 297, 301 (1980), where that court stated:

> The distinction, therefore, which must be made between an appropriate exercise of the police power and an improper exercise of eminent domain is whether the requirement has some reasonable relationship or nexus to the use to which the property is being made or is merely being used as an excuse for taking property simply because at that particular moment the landowner is asking the city for some license or permit.

Thus, the court held that a city may not require a property owner to dedicate private property for some future public use as a condition of obtaining a building permit when such future use is not "occasioned by the construction sought to be permitted." *Id.*, at 248, 292 N.W.2d at 302.

We think the "reasonable relationship" test adopted by a majority of the state courts is closer to the federal constitutional norm than either of those previously discussed. But we do not adopt it as such, partly because the term "reasonable relationship" seems confusingly similar to the term "rational basis" which describes the minimal level of scrutiny under the Equal Protection Clause of the Fourteenth Amendment. We think a term such as "rough proportionality" best encapsulates what we hold to be the requirement of the Fifth Amendment. No precise mathematical calculation is required, but the city must make some sort of individualized determination that the required dedication is related both in nature and extent to the impact of the proposed development.

We turn now to analysis of whether the findings relied upon by the city here, first with respect to the floodplain easement, and second with respect to the pedestrian/bicycle path, satisfied these requirements.

It is axiomatic that increasing the amount of impervious surface will increase the quantity and rate of storm water flow from petitioner's property. Therefore, keeping the floodplain open and free from development would likely confine the pressures on Fanno Creek created by petitioner's development. In fact, because petitioner's property lies within the Central Business District, the CDC already required that petitioner leave 15% of it as open space and the undeveloped floodplain would have nearly satisfied that requirement. App. to Pet. for Cert. G–16 to G–17. But the city demanded more—it not only wanted petitioner not to build in the floodplain, but it also wanted petitioner's property along Fanno Creek for its greenway system. The city has never said why a public greenway, as opposed to a private one, was required in the interest of flood control.

The difference to petitioner, of course, is the loss of her ability to exclude others. As we have noted, this right to exclude others is "one of the most essential sticks in the bundle of rights that are commonly characterized as property." *Kaiser Aetna*, 444 U.S. at 176. It is difficult to see why recreational visitors trampling along petitioner's floodplain easement are sufficiently related to the city's legitimate interest in reducing flooding problems along Fanno Creek, and the city has not attempted to make any individualized determination to support this part of its request.

The city contends that the recreational easement along the greenway is only ancillary to the city's chief purpose in controlling flood hazards. It further asserts that unlike the residential property at issue in *Nollan*, petitioner's property is commercial in character and, therefore, her right to exclude others is compromised. Brief for Respondent 41, quoting United States v. Orito, 413 U.S. 139, 142, 37 L. Ed. 2d 513, 93 S. Ct. 2674 (1973) (" 'The Constitution extends special safeguards to the privacy of the home' "). The city maintains that "there is nothing to suggest that preventing [petitioner] from prohibiting [the easements] will unreasonably impair the value of [her] property as a [retail store]." PruneYard Shopping Center v. Robins, 447 U.S. 74, 83, 64 L. Ed. 2d 741, 100 S. Ct. 2035 (1980).

Admittedly, petitioner wants to build a bigger store to attract members of the public to her property. She also wants, however, to be able to control the time and manner in which they enter. The recreational easement on the greenway is different in character from the exercise of state-protected rights of free expression and petition that we permitted in *PruneYard*. In *PruneYard*, we held that a major private shopping center that attracted more than 25,000 daily patrons had to provide access to persons exercising their state constitutional rights to distribute pamphlets and ask passers-by to sign their petitions. *Id.*, at 85. We based our decision, in part, on the fact that the shopping center "may restrict expressive activity by adopting time, place, and manner regulations that will minimize any interference with its commercial functions." *Id., at 83.* By contrast, the city wants to impose a permanent recreational easement upon petitioner's property that borders Fanno Creek. Petitioner would lose all rights to regulate the time in which the public entered onto the greenway, regardless of any interference it might pose with her retail store. Her right to exclude would not be regulated, it would be eviscerated.

If petitioner's proposed development had somehow encroached on existing greenway space in the city, it would have been reasonable to require petitioner to provide some alternative greenway space for the public either on her property or elsewhere. *See Nollan*, 483 U.S. at 836 ("Although such a requirement, constituting a permanent grant of continuous access to the property, would have to be considered a taking if it were not attached to a development permit, the Commission's assumed power to forbid construction of the house in order to protect the public's view of the beach must surely include the power to condition construction upon some concession by the owner, even a concession of property rights, that serves the same end"). But that is not the case here. We conclude that the findings upon which the city relies do not show the required reasonable relationship between the floodplain easement and the petitioner's proposed new building.

With respect to the pedestrian/bicycle pathway, we have no doubt that the city was correct in finding that the larger retail sales facility proposed by petitioner will increase traffic on the streets of the Central Business District. The city estimates that the proposed development would generate roughly 435 additional trips per day. Dedications for streets, sidewalks, and other public ways are generally reasonable exactions to avoid excessive congestion from a proposed property use. But on the record before us, the city has not met its burden of demonstrating that the additional number of vehicle and bicycle trips generated by petitioner's development reasonably relate to the city's requirement for a dedication of the pedestrian/bicycle pathway easement. The city simply found that the creation of the pathway "could offset some of the traffic demand . . . and lessen the increase in traffic congestion."

As Justice Peterson of the Supreme Court of Oregon explained in his dissenting opinion, however, "the findings of fact that the bicycle pathway system '*could* offset some of the traffic demand' is a far cry from a finding that the bicycle pathway system *will*, or is *likely to*, offset some of the traffic demand." 317 Ore. at 127, 854 P.2d at 447 (emphasis in original). No precise mathematical calculation is required, but the city must make some effort to quantify its findings in support of the dedication for the pedestrian/bicycle pathway beyond the conclusory statement that it could offset some of the traffic demand generated.

IV

Cities have long engaged in the commendable task of land use planning, made necessary by increasing urbanization, particularly in metropolitan areas such as Portland. The city's goals of reducing flooding hazards and traffic congestion, and providing for public greenways, are laudable, but there are outer limits to how this may be done. "A strong public desire to improve the public condition [will not] warrant achieving the desire by a shorter cut than the constitutional way of paying for the change." *Pennsylvania Coal*, 260 U.S. at 416.

The judgment of the Supreme Court of Oregon is reversed, and the case is remanded for further proceedings not inconsistent with this opinion.

It is so ordered.

NOTES AND QUESTIONS

1. On what basis could the landowner in *Nollan* have advanced a takings claim if the coastal commission had simply declared that members of the public had a right to walk along the beach between the mean high tide line and the seawall? Would the landowner have had a claim under *Penn Central?* Under *Lucas?*

Consider now the bicycle pathway in *Dolan*. How would the landowner argue that the requirement that she provide a pathway constitutes a taking?

2. In *Nollan* and *Dolan,* government decision-makers imposed conditions tailored to the individual circumstances of each landowner's application (although in *Nollan,* the coastal commission had imposed similar conditions on nearly all coastal development permits in the area).

What if a municipality instead enacted an ordinance providing that whenever an applicant seeks approval for a development permit, any permit issued is conditioned on the applicant's dedication of 10 square feet of land for each square foot of floor area, or on the applicant's payment of $20 to the municipality for every square foot of floor area? Would the applicant be entitled to challenge the ordinance under *Nollan* and *Dolan?* Put in other terms, do *Nollan* and *Dolan* apply only to individualized determinations, or do they also apply to exactions imposed by local legislation?

A number of courts have held that the *Nollan/Dolan* analysis does not apply to legislative determinations, relying in part on language in *Dolan* itself distinguishing between "legislative" and "adjudicative" decisions. *See e.g.*, Krupp v. Breckenridge Sanitation Dist., 19 P.3d 687 (Colo. 2001); Home Builders Ass'n of Central Arizona v. City of Scottsdale, 187 Ariz. 479, 930 P.2d 993 (1997). Dictum in Lingle v. Chevron, U.S.A., Inc., 544 U.S. 528 (2005), lends inconclusive support to this view. In the course of reaffirming *Nollan* and *Dolan,* the Court described the cases as involving "takings challenges to adjudicative land-use exactions." 544 U.S. at 546. One might read the language merely as accurate description of the cases themselves, but it is also possible to read the language as an indication that *Nollan* and *Dolan* do not apply to legislatively-imposed exactions. For criticism of the legislative/adjudicative distinction, *see* Carlos A. Ball & Laurie Reynolds, Exactions and Burden Distribution in Takings Law, 47 Wm. & Mary L. Rev. 1513, 1561–68 (2006).

Some courts have distinguished between legislatively mandated fees that confer discretion on administrative decision-makers and those that do not. *See* Dudek v. Umatilla County, 187 Or. App. 504, 69 P.3d 751, 756 (2003). Some judges think the legislative/adjudicative distinction doesn't make sense. In the words of one who questioned the ability of courts to distinguish between legislative and adjudicative categories, "[a] municipality should not be able to insulate itself from a takings challenge merely by utilizing a different bureaucratic vehicle when expropriating a citizen's property." B.A.M. Dev., L.L.C. v. Salt Lake County, 87 P.3d 710, 728 (2004) (Orme, J., dissenting) (quoting Amoco Oil Co. v. Village of Schaumburg, 277 Ill.App.3d 926, 214 Ill.Dec. 526, 661 N.E.2d 380 (1995)).

What are the best arguments for distinguishing between across-the-board exactions and those imposed on a case-by-case basis? The best arguments against drawing that distinction? *See generally* Jane C. Needleman, Exactions: Exploring Exactly When *Nollan* and *Dolan* Should be Triggered, 28 Cardozo L. Rev. 1563 (2006).

3. *Proportionality to What?* For an exaction to be sustained, the exaction must be designed to account for the impact proposed development might have on the community. *Dolan* requires that the exaction be "roughly proportional" to that impact. But what must be proportional to the impact of the development? Consider some alternatives: (1) the effectiveness of the exaction; (2) the cost of the exaction to the developer; (3) both; and (4) some combination of the two.

In *Dolan*, the city estimated that the new development would generate 435 additional trips each day. Consider the following scenarios:

a.   A bikeway would reduce street traffic by 435 cars a day, eliminating all external effects imposed by the development, and would cost $300,000 (about 1/3 the cost of the proposed development). Studies show that in the absence of the bikeway, the additional 435 trips would require drivers to spend, on average, an extra two seconds a trip in traffic; many drivers would not be delayed at all, while at peak times, the maximum delay would be twenty seconds. The bikeway would be used by 3,000 bikers a day, and its existence would reduce the number of accidents and injuries by about 5 per year, but the city can't prove that the development itself would increase the number of accidents or injuries.

b.   Same facts as (a), except the bikeway would cost $30,000.

c.   A bikeway would only reduce street traffic by 100 cars a day, which would save drivers an average of about one second per trip, and the bikeway would cost $30,000.

4.   Suppose the municipal code requires site plan approval for apartment developments larger than 10 units. In response to a developer proposal to build a 100-unit apartment complex, the planning board grants approval, conditioned on developer's agreement to set aside 20 of the units for "affordable" housing units that will sell or rent for below-market rates, and on which developer will make no profit. Developer seeks to challenge the constitutionality of the condition. How would you frame the developer's argument? The municipality's response?

How, if at all, would the arguments change if the local code included a provision requiring that 20% of all units in new developments be devoted to affordable housing?

5.   Many scholars have argued that *Nollan* and *Dolan* prevent municipalities and developers from reaching mutually beneficial agreements. *See, e.g.*, Mark Fenster, Regulating Land Use in a Constitutional Shadow: The Institutional Contexts of Exactions, 58 Hastings L.J. 729, 747 (2007); Lee Ann Fennell, Hard Bargains and Real Steals: Land Use Exactions Revisited, 86 Iowa L. Rev. 1, 27–33 (2000). For instance, in *Nollan* itself, once the coastal commission understands that it cannot condition the Nollans' permit on grant of the easement, might not the commission deny the permit altogether? Wouldn't that leave everyone worse off, because both the Nollans and the commission would prefer a regime in which the Nollans get the permit and give up the easement? That is, even if the condition imposed is unrelated to the reason for requiring the permit, an agreement that includes the permit and the easement grant will leave both parties better off; a restriction on such agreements creates potential inefficiencies. How would Justice Scalia respond to this efficiency critique of *Nollan*?

6.   *Competition as a Constraint on Exactions.* How serious is the concern that, absent doctrinal constraint, municipal officials will impose exactions that deter socially beneficial development and that unfairly redistribute wealth from outsiders to insiders? Professor Vicki Been has argued that market forces—competition among municipalities for development— provide adequate constraints against excessive exactions. Vicki Been, "Exit" as a Constraint on Land Use Exactions: Rethinking the Unconstitutional Conditions Doctrine, 91 Colum. L. Rev. 473 (1991). For a response, *see* Stewart E. Sterk, Competition Among Municipalities as a Constraint on Land Use Exactions, 45 Vand. L. Rev. 831 (1992).

Nollan and *Dolan* left open some critical questions about the scope of exactions doctrine. In the following case, the Court addressed two of them:

Koontz v. St. Johns River Water Management District

Supreme Court of the United States, 2013
133 S.Ct. 2586

■ JUSTICE ALITO delivered the opinion of the Court.

Our decisions in Nollan v. California Coastal Comm'n, 483 U.S. 825 (1987), and Dolan v. City of Tigard, 512 U.S. 374 (1994), provide important protection against the misuse of the power of land-use regulation. In those cases, we held that a unit of government may not condition the approval of a land-use permit on the owner's relinquishment of a portion of his property unless there is a "nexus" and "rough proportionality" between the government's demand and the effects of the proposed land use. In this case, the St. Johns River Water Management District (District) believes that it circumvented Nollan and Dolan because of the way in which it structured its handling of a permit application submitted by Coy Koontz, Sr., whose estate is represented in this Court by Coy Koontz, Jr. The District did not approve his application on the condition that he surrender an interest in his land. Instead, the District, after suggesting that he could obtain approval by signing over such an interest, denied his application because he refused to yield. The Florida Supreme Court blessed this maneuver and thus effectively interred those important decisions. Because we conclude that Nollan and Dolan cannot be evaded in this way, the Florida Supreme Court's decision must be reversed.

I

[Koontz owned an undeveloped 14.9 acre parcel, some of which was subsequently classified as wetlands. Florida law required owners who wanted to develop wetlands to obtain permits from the water management district in the area, and also required owners to offset any environmental damage from development by creating, enhancing, or preserving wetlands elsewhere. In 1994, Koontz sought a permit to develop 3.7 acres of his parcel, and offered to convey a conservation easement to the St. Johns River Water District over the remaining 11 acres. The District informed Koontz that it would not approve the project, but that it would approve development if he agreed to one of two concessions: (1) reducing the development plan to one acre, installing a more costly stormwater system, and conveying a conservation easement over the remaining 13.9 acres; or (2) developing all 3.7 acres, and paying to make improvements to district-owned land several miles away.

The District's policy is not to require any particular offsite improvement project. Instead, the District said that it "would also favorably consider" alternatives to its suggested alternatives if Koontz proposed something "equivalent."

Koontz then brought an action in state court seeking relief under a Florida statute authorizing compensation for takings. A trial court held that the District's actions were unlawful under *Nollan* and *Dolan*—eds.]

The Florida District Court affirmed, but the State Supreme Court reversed. A majority of that court distinguished Nollan and Dolan on two grounds. First, the majority thought it significant that in this case, unlike Nollan or Dolan, the District did not approve petitioner's application on the condition that he accede to the District's demands; instead, the District denied his application because he refused to make concessions. Second, the majority drew a distinction between a demand for an interest in real property (what happened in Nollan and Dolan) and a demand for money. The majority acknowledged a division of authority over whether a demand for money can give rise to a claim under Nollan and Dolan, and sided with those courts that have said it cannot.

Recognizing that the majority opinion rested on a question of federal constitutional law on which the lower courts are divided, we granted the petition for a writ of certiorari, and now reverse.

II

A

We have said in a variety of contexts that "the government may not deny a benefit to a person because he exercises a constitutional right." Regan v. Taxation With Representation of Wash., 461 U.S. 540, 545 (1983).

Nollan and Dolan "involve a special application" of this doctrine that protects the Fifth Amendment right to just compensation for property the government takes when owners apply for land-use permits. Lingle v. Chevron U.S.A. Inc., 544 U.S. 528, 547 (2005); Dolan, 512 U.S., at 385 (invoking "the well-settled doctrine of 'unconstitutional conditions' "). Our decisions in those cases reflect two realities of the permitting process. The first is that land-use permit applicants are especially vulnerable to the type of coercion that the unconstitutional conditions doctrine prohibits because the government often has broad discretion to deny a permit that is worth far more than property it would like to take. By conditioning a building permit on the owner's deeding over a public right-of-way, for example, the government can pressure an owner into voluntarily giving up property for which the Fifth Amendment would otherwise require just compensation. See *id.*, at 384; Nollan, 483 U.S., at 831. So long as the building permit is more valuable than any just compensation the owner could hope to receive for the right-of-way, the owner is likely to accede to the government's demand, no matter how unreasonable. Extortionate demands of this sort frustrate the Fifth Amendment right to just compensation, and the unconstitutional conditions doctrine prohibits them.

A second reality of the permitting process is that many proposed land uses threaten to impose costs on the public that dedications of property can offset. Where a building proposal would substantially increase traffic congestion, for example, officials might condition permit approval on the owner's agreement to deed over the land needed to widen a public road. Respondent argues that a similar rationale justifies the exaction at issue here: petitioner's proposed construction project, it submits, would destroy wetlands on his property, and in order to compensate for this loss, respondent demands that he enhance wetlands elsewhere. Insisting that landowners internalize the negative externalities of their conduct is a hallmark of responsible land-use policy, and we have long sustained such regulations against constitutional attack. See Village of Euclid v. Ambler Realty Co., 272 U.S. 365 (1926).

Nollan and Dolan accommodate both realities by allowing the government to condition approval of a permit on the dedication of property to the public so long as there is a "nexus" and "rough proportionality" between the property that the government demands and the social costs of the applicant's proposal. Dolan, supra, at 391; Nollan, 483 U.S., at 837. Our precedents thus enable permitting authorities to insist that applicants bear the full costs of their proposals while still forbidding the government from engaging in "out-and-out . . . extortion" that would thwart the Fifth Amendment right to just compensation. *Ibid.* (internal quotation marks omitted). Under Nollan and Dolan the government may choose whether and how a permit applicant is required to mitigate the impacts of a proposed development, but it may not leverage its legitimate interest in mitigation to pursue governmental ends that lack an essential nexus and rough proportionality to those impacts.

B

The principles that undergird our decisions in Nollan and Dolan do not change depending on whether the government approves a permit on the condition that the applicant turn over property or denies a permit because the applicant refuses to do so.

A contrary rule would be especially untenable in this case because it would enable the government to evade the limitations of Nollan and Dolan simply by phrasing its demands for property as conditions precedent to permit approval. Under the Florida Supreme Court's approach, a government order stating that a permit is "approved if" the owner turns over property would be subject to Nollan and Dolan, but an identical order that uses the words "denied until" would not. Our unconstitutional conditions cases have long refused to attach significance to the distinction between conditions precedent and conditions subsequent. To do so here would effectively render Nollan and Dolan a dead letter.

The Florida Supreme Court puzzled over how the government's demand for property can violate the Takings Clause even though " 'no property of any kind was ever taken,' " 77 So.3d, at 1225 (quoting 5 So.3d, at 20 (Griffin, J., dissenting)); see also 77 So.3d, at 1229–1230, but the unconstitutional conditions doctrine provides a ready answer. Extortionate demands for property in the land-use permitting context run afoul of the Takings Clause not because they take property but because they impermissibly burden the right not to have property taken without just compensation. As in other unconstitutional conditions cases in which someone refuses to cede a constitutional right in the face of coercive pressure, the impermissible denial of a governmental benefit is a constitutionally cognizable injury.

That is not to say, however, that there is no relevant difference between a consummated taking and the denial of a permit based on an unconstitutionally extortionate demand. Where the permit is denied and the condition is never imposed, nothing has been taken. While the unconstitutional conditions doctrine recognizes that this burdens a constitutional right, the Fifth Amendment mandates a particular remedy—just compensation—only for takings. In cases where there is an excessive demand but no taking, whether money damages are available is not a question of federal constitutional law but of the cause of action—whether state or federal—on which the landowner relies. Because petitioner brought his claim pursuant to a state law cause of action, the Court has no occasion to discuss what remedies might be available for a Nollan/Dolan unconstitutional conditions violation either here or in other cases.

C

Finally, respondent argues that we need not decide whether its demand for offsite improvements satisfied Nollan and Dolan because it gave petitioner another avenue for obtaining permit approval. Specifically, respondent said that it would have approved a revised permit application that reduced the footprint of petitioner's proposed construction site from 3.7 acres to 1 acre and placed a conservation easement on the remaining 13.9 acres of petitioner's land. Respondent argues that regardless of whether its demands for offsite mitigation satisfied Nollan and Dolan, we must separately consider each of petitioner's options, one of which did not require any of the offsite work the trial court found objectionable.

Respondent's argument is flawed because the option to which it points—developing only 1 acre of the site and granting a conservation easement on the rest—involves the same issue as the option to build on 3.7 acres and perform offsite mitigation. We agree with respondent that, so long as a permitting authority offers the landowner at least one alternative that would satisfy Nollan and Dolan, the landowner has not been subjected to an unconstitutional condition. But respondent's suggestion that we should treat its offer to let petitioner build on 1 acre as an alternative to offsite mitigation misapprehends the governmental benefit that petitioner was denied. Petitioner sought to develop 3.7 acres, but respondent in effect told petitioner that it would not allow him to build on 2.7 of those acres unless he agreed to spend money improving public lands. Petitioner claims that he was wrongfully denied a permit to build on those 2.7 acres. For that reason, respondent's offer to approve a less ambitious building project does not obviate the need to determine whether the demand for offsite mitigation satisfied Nollan and Dolan.

III

We turn to the Florida Supreme Court's alternative holding that petitioner's claim fails because respondent asked him to spend money rather than give up an easement on his land. A predicate for any unconstitutional conditions claim is that the government could not have constitutionally ordered the person asserting the claim to do what it attempted to pressure that person into doing. For that reason, we began our analysis in both Nollan and Dolan by observing that if the government had directly seized the easements it sought to obtain through the permitting process, it would have committed a per se taking. See Dolan, 512 U.S., at 384; Nollan, 483 U.S., at 831. The Florida Supreme Court held that petitioner's claim fails at this first step because the subject of the exaction at issue here was money rather than a more tangible interest in real property. Respondent and the dissent take the same position.

We note as an initial matter that if we accepted this argument it would be very easy for land-use permitting officials to evade the limitations of Nollan and Dolan. Because the government need only provide a permit applicant with one alternative that satisfies the nexus and rough proportionality standards, a permitting authority wishing to exact an easement could simply give the owner a choice of either surrendering an easement or making a payment equal to the easement's value. Such so-called "in lieu of" fees are utterly commonplace, Rosenberg, The Changing Culture of American Land Use Regulation: Paying for Growth with Impact Fees, 59 S.M.U. L.Rev. 177, 202–203 (2006), and they are functionally equivalent to other types of land use exactions. For that reason and those that follow, we reject respondent's argument and hold that so-called "monetary exactions" must satisfy the nexus and rough proportionality requirements of Nollan and Dolan.

A

The demand for money at issue here "operate[d] upon . . . an identified property interest" by directing the owner of a particular piece of property to make a monetary payment. The fulcrum this case turns on is the direct link between the government's demand and a specific parcel of real property. Because of that direct link, this case implicates the central concern of Nollan and Dolan: the risk that the government may use its substantial power and discretion in land-use permitting to pursue governmental ends that lack an essential nexus and rough proportionality to the effects of the proposed new use of the specific property at issue, thereby diminishing without justification the value of the property.

B

Respondent and the dissent argue that if monetary exactions are made subject to scrutiny under Nollan and Dolan, then there will be no principled way of distinguishing impermissible land-use exactions from property taxes. We think they exaggerate both the extent to which that problem is unique to the land-use permitting context and the practical difficulty of distinguishing between the power to tax and the power to take by eminent domain.

It is beyond dispute that "[t]axes and user fees . . . are not 'takings.' " [citations omitted].

[O]ur cases show that teasing out the difference between taxes and takings is more difficult in theory than in practice.

This case does not require us to say more. We need not decide at precisely what point a land-use permitting charge denominated by the government as a "tax" becomes "so arbitrary . . . that it was not the exertion of taxation but a confiscation of property." Brushaber v. Union Pacific R. Co., 240 U.S. 1, 24–25 (1916). For present purposes, it suffices to say that despite having long recognized that "the power of taxation should not be confused with the power of eminent domain," Houck v. Little River Drainage Dist., 239 U.S. 254, 264 (1915), we have had little trouble distinguishing between the two.

C

Finally, we disagree with the dissent's forecast that our decision will work a revolution in land use law by depriving local governments of the ability to charge reasonable permitting fees. Numerous courts—including courts in many of our Nation's most populous States—have confronted constitutional challenges to monetary exactions over the last two decades and applied the standard from Nollan and Dolan or something like it. Yet the "significant practical harm" the dissent predicts has not come to pass. That is hardly surprising, for the dissent is correct that state law normally provides an independent check on excessive land use permitting fees.

We hold that the government's demand for property from a land-use permit applicant must satisfy the requirements of Nollan and Dolan even when the government denies the permit and even when its demand is for money. The Court expresses no view on the merits of petitioner's claim that respondent's actions here failed to comply with the principles set forth in this opinion and those two cases. The Florida Supreme Court's judgment is reversed, and this case is remanded for further proceedings not inconsistent with this opinion.

It is so ordered.

■ JUSTICE KAGAN, with whom JUSTICE GINSBURG, JUSTICE BREYER, and JUSTICE SOTOMAYOR join, dissenting.

Our core disagreement concerns the second question the Court addresses. The majority extends Nollan and Dolan to cases in which the government conditions a permit not on the transfer of real property, but instead on the payment or expenditure of money. The boundaries of the majority's new rule are uncertain. But it threatens to subject a vast array of land-use regulations, applied daily in States and localities throughout the country, to heightened constitutional scrutiny. I would not embark on so unwise an adventure, and would affirm the Florida Supreme Court's decision.

The majority's approach . . . threatens significant practical harm. By applying Nollan and Dolan to permit conditions requiring monetary payments—with no express limitation except as to taxes—the majority extends the Takings Clause, with its notoriously "difficult" and "perplexing" standards, into the very heart of local land-use regulation and service delivery. 524 U.S., at 541. Cities and towns across the nation impose many kinds of permitting fees every day. Some enable a government to mitigate a new development's impact on the community, like increased traffic or pollution—or destruction of wetlands. See, e.g., Olympia v. Drebick, 156 Wash.2d 289, 305, 126 P.3d 802, 809 (2006). Others cover the direct costs of providing services like sewage or water to the development. See, e.g., Krupp v. Breckenridge Sanitation Dist., 19 P.3d 687, 691 (Colo.2001). Still others are meant to limit the number of landowners who engage in a certain activity, as fees for liquor licenses do. See, e.g., Phillips v. Mobile, 208 U.S. 472, 479 (1908); BHA Investments, Inc. v. Idaho, 138 Idaho 348, 63 P.3d 474 (2003). All now must meet Nollan and Dolan's nexus and proportionality tests. The Federal Constitution thus will decide whether one town is overcharging for sewage, or another is setting the price to sell liquor too high. And the flexibility of state and local governments to take the most routine actions to enhance their communities will diminish accordingly.

That problem becomes still worse because the majority's distinction between monetary "exactions" and taxes is so hard to apply.

In sum, *Nollan* and *Dolan* restrain governments from using the permitting process to do what the Takings Clause would otherwise prevent—i.e., take a specific property interest without just compensation. Those cases have no application when governments impose a general financial obligation as part of the permitting process.

NOTES AND QUESTIONS

1.   Reconsider *Nollan*. Suppose the California Coastal Commission had denied Nollan's permit altogether, but indicated that it would approve his permit to expand his house if Nollan "volunteered" to grant the Coastal Commission a lateral access easement. Would Nollan have had a takings claim? In *Koontz,* the Court was unanimous in holding that denial of a permit for failure to consent to a taking would fall within the scope of the unconstitutional conditions doctrine developed in *Nollan* and *Dolan.*

But what if the Coastal Commission, educated by *Koontz,* never articulates any demands. Suppose, instead, the board denies the permit outright. Nollan advances a takings claim, alleging that the Commission was waiting for him to offer a lateral access easement (or some other concession). Would Nollan's claim survive a motion to dismiss? If the answer to that question is yes, what evidence would Nollan have to produce to support his claim that the board was waiting for an offer from him? Would it be enough to show that the board had, in the past, granted permits to other owners who had offered the Commission a lateral access easement or some other concession? Does *Koontz* answer these questions?

2.   In holding that *Nollan* and *Dolan* apply to monetary exactions, the Court in *Koontz* resolved an issue that had previously divided lower courts. *Koontz* also effectively rejects the position that *Nollan* and *Dolan* are inapplicable when the municipality conditions development approval on the developer's grant of a conservation easement (which effectively prevents the developer from building on the property, but which does not permit anyone else to occupy the property. *See* In re Smith v. Town of Mendon, 4 N.Y.3d 1, 789 N.Y.S.2d 696, 822 N.E.2d 1214 (2004).

Are the reasons for the *Nollan* rule more or less applicable when the municipality conditions approval on the payment of cash instead of conditioning approval on dedication of an easement? *See* Michael B. Kent, Jr., Theoretical Tension and Doctrinal Discord: Analyzing Development Impact Fees as Takings, 51 Wm. & Mary L. Rev. 1833 (2010); Jane C. Needleman, Exactions: Exploring Exactly When *Nollan* and *Dolan* Should be Triggered, 28 Cardozo L. Rev. 1563 (2006).

3.   Assuming an exaction triggers the unconstitutional conditions analysis, when has the municipality established a significant "nexus" to support the exaction? Suppose the municipality imposes a "sanitation fee," a "police protection fee," and a "school fee" on a new residential development, contending that the additional residents will require additional personnel, and therefore additional cost to the municipality.

Would a developer succeed in a constitutional challenge to those fees? What arguments would you make on behalf of the developer?

4. The City of San Francisco imposes a rent control ordinance to deal with a persistent "shortage" of housing affordable to most residents. The city then enacts an ordinance permitting a landlord to withdraw apartments from the rental market only if the landlord pays existing tenants amounts equal to 24 times the difference between the fair market rent for the apartment and tenant's existing rent. Does the city's ordinance work a taking under *Nollan, Dolan*, and *Koontz*? See Levin v. City and County of San Francisco, 71 F.Supp.3d 1072 (N.D. Cal. 2014).

5. *Dollars and Cents.* A beachfront condominium complex, suffering from serious erosion, seeks a permit to build a seawall to protect the structural integrity of the complex. The seawall itself, while protecting the complex, will redirect the erosion rather than eliminating it altogether. The coastal commission plans to grant a permit for the seawall, but on condition that the condominium pay a fee to compensate for the loss of recreational space at neighboring beaches. The commission seeks advice about how to assess as large a fee as possible that will not violate *Dolan's* rough proportionality standard. What advice would you give the commission? *See* Ocean Harbor House Homeowners Ass'n v. California Coastal Comm'n, 163 Cal.App.4th 215, 77 Cal.Rptr.3d 432 (2008).

How much dollars-and-cents evidence should courts require municipalities to provide to justify imposition of impact fees? Should a municipality's use of a formula for calculation of the fee help the municipality in litigation even if the data that goes into the formula is highly speculative? In the *Ocean Harbor House* case, part of the formula used by the commission assumed that consumers derived $13 of surplus value from each beachfront visit. How would you assess the reliability of that figure? On the other hand, if a court suspects the accuracy of the figure, what should the court do? Invalidate the fee altogether? Sustain it without numerical justification? Is that why the Court in *Dolan* requires only "rough" proportionality?

6. *Settlement.* Suppose a municipality, after *Koontz*, avoids imposition of all impact fees. Instead, the municipality routinely denies zoning amendments, subdivisions, etc. When the landowner brings a takings claim (or raises a state law challenge), the municipality offers to settle the claim by giving the landowner the permit the landowner wants in return for payment of a sum of money, or in return for grant of an easement. By the terms of the settlement agreement, the landowner waives all claims against the municipality. Has there been any constitutional violation? If a municipality can use this device, how much have *Nollan, Dolan*, and *Koontz* accomplished?

7. *State Law Restrictions on Exactions.* A developer seeking to challenge a municipal exaction is not limited to constitutional challenges. As noted in Chapter Four, state statutes may limit the purposes and scope of impact fees, and may specify procedures municipalities must follow. *See, e.g.*, 53 Penn. Stat. § 10503–A. Some statutes expressly authorize impact fees for particular purposes, leading to the inference that municipalities may not authorize fees for other purposes. *See, e.g.,* N.Y. Vill. Law § 7–730(4)(c) (expressly authorizing planning board to require developer to pay a sum of money in lieu of provision of parkland).

H. REMEDIES

What remedies are available to a landowner when a court concludes that a land use regulation constitutes a taking of property without just compensation? The landowner is certainly entitled to a declaration that the regulation, as enacted, is unconstitutional. At that point, the municipality faces a choice: the municipality can enact a less restrictive, constitutional regulation, or the municipality can exercise its eminent domain power, and pay compensation to the landowner for the value of the land.

Does declaratory relief make the landowner whole? What about the time and money the landowner has lost during the litigation? Should the landowner be compensated for that? Consider the following case:

First English Evangelical Lutheran Church of Glendale v. County of Los Angeles

Supreme Court of the United States, 1987
482 U.S. 304

■ CHIEF JUSTICE REHNQUIST delivered the opinion of the Court.

In this case the California Court of Appeal held that a landowner who claims that his property has been "taken" by a land-use regulation may not recover damages for the time before it is finally determined that the regulation constitutes a "taking" of his property. We disagree, and conclude that in these circumstances the Fifth and Fourteenth Amendments to the United States Constitution would require compensation for that period.

In 1957, appellant First English Evangelical Lutheran Church purchased a 21-acre parcel of land in a canyon along the banks of the Middle Fork of Mill Creek in the Angeles National Forest. The Middle Fork is the natural drainage channel for a watershed area owned by the National Forest Service. Twelve of the acres owned by the church are flat land, and contained a dining hall, two bunkhouses, a caretaker's lodge, an outdoor chapel, and a footbridge across the creek. The church operated on the site a campground, known as "Lutherglen," as a retreat center and a recreational area for handicapped children.

In July 1977, a forest fire denuded the hills upstream from Lutherglen, destroying approximately 3,860 acres of the watershed area and creating a serious flood hazard. Such flooding occurred on February 9 and 10, 1978, when a storm dropped 11 inches of rain in the watershed. The runoff from the storm overflowed the banks of the Mill Creek, flooding Lutherglen and destroying its buildings.

In response to the flooding of the canyon, appellee County of Los Angeles adopted Interim Ordinance No. 11,855 in January 1979. The ordinance provided that "[a] person shall not construct, reconstruct, place or enlarge any building or structure, any portion of which is, or will be, located within the outer boundary lines of the interim flood protection area located in Mill Creek Canyon. . . ." App. to Juris. Statement A31. The ordinance was effective immediately because the county determined that it was "required for the immediate preservation of the public health and safety. . . ." *Id.*, at A32. The interim flood protection area described by the ordinance included the flat areas on either side of Mill Creek on which Lutherglen had stood.

The church filed a complaint in the Superior Court of California a little more than a month after the ordinance was adopted. As subsequently amended, the complaint alleged two claims against the county and the Los Angeles County Flood Control District. The first alleged that the defendants were liable under Cal. Govt. Code Ann. § 835 (West 1980) for dangerous conditions on their upstream properties that contributed to the flooding of Lutherglen. As a part of this claim, appellant also alleged that "Ordinance No. 11,855 denies [appellant] all use of Lutherglen." App. 12, 49. The second claim sought to recover from the Flood Control District in inverse condemnation and in tort for engaging in cloud seeding during the storm that flooded Lutherglen.

In Agins v. Tiburon, *supra*, the California Supreme Court decided that a landowner may not maintain an inverse condemnation suit in the courts of that State based upon a "regulatory" taking. 24 Cal. 3d, at 275–277, 598 P. 2d, at 29–31. In the court's view, maintenance of such a suit would allow a landowner to force the legislature to exercise its power of eminent domain. Under this decision, then, compensation is not required until the challenged regulation or ordinance has been held excessive in an action for declaratory relief or a writ of mandamus and the government has nevertheless decided to continue the regulation in effect. Based on this decision, the trial court in the present case granted the motion to strike the allegation that the church had been denied all use of Lutherglen. It explained that "a careful rereading of the *Agins* case persuades the Court that when an ordinance, even a non-zoning ordinance, deprives a person of the total use of his lands, his challenge to the ordinance is by way of declaratory relief or possibly mandamus." App. 26. Because the appellant alleged a regulatory taking and sought only damages, the allegation that the ordinance denied all use of Lutherglen was deemed irrelevant.

On appeal, the California Court of Appeal read the complaint as one seeking "damages for the uncompensated taking of all use of

Lutherglen by County Ordinance No. 11,855. . . ." App. to Juris. Statement A13–A14. It too relied on the California Supreme Court's decision in *Agins* in rejecting the cause of action. . . It accordingly affirmed the trial court's decision to strike the allegations concerning appellee's ordinance. The California Supreme Court denied review.

This appeal followed, and we noted probable jurisdiction. 478 U.S. 1003 (1986). Appellant asks us to hold that the California Supreme Court erred in Agins v. Tiburon in determining that the Fifth Amendment, as made applicable to the States through the Fourteenth Amendment, does not require compensation as a remedy for "temporary" regulatory takings—those regulatory takings which are ultimately invalidated by the courts. Four times this decade, we have considered similar claims and have found ourselves for one reason or another unable to consider the merits of the *Agins* rule. *See* MacDonald, Sommer & Frates v. Yolo County, 477 U.S. 340 (1986); Williamson County Regional Planning Comm'n v. Hamilton Bank, 473 U.S. 172 (1985); San Diego Gas & Electric Co., *supra*; Agins v. Tiburon, *supra*. For the reasons explained below, however, we find the constitutional claim properly presented in this case, and hold that on these facts the California courts have decided the compensation question inconsistently with the requirements of the Fifth Amendment.

I

Concerns with finality left us unable to reach the remedial question in the earlier cases where we have been asked to consider the rule of *Agins*. *See* MacDonald, Sommer & Frates, *supra*, at 351 (summarizing cases). In each of these cases, we concluded either that regulations considered to be in issue by the state court did not effect a taking, Agins v. Tiburon, 447 U.S., at 263, or that the factual disputes yet to be resolved by state authorities might still lead to the conclusion that no taking had occurred. MacDonald, Sommer & Frates, *supra*, at 351–353; Williamson County, *supra*, at 188–194; San Diego Gas & Electric Co., *supra*, at 631–632. Consideration of the remedial question in those circumstances, we concluded, would be premature.

The posture of the present case is quite different. The California Court of Appeal has . . . held that, regardless of the correctness of appellant's claim that the challenged ordinance denies it "all use of Lutherglen," appellant may not recover damages until the ordinance is finally declared unconstitutional, and then only for any period after that declaration for which the county seeks to enforce it. The constitutional question pretermitted in our earlier cases is therefore squarely presented here.

We reject appellee's suggestion that, regardless of the state court's treatment of the question, we must independently evaluate the adequacy of the complaint and resolve the takings claim on the merits before we can reach the remedial question. However "cryptic"—to use appellee's description—the allegations with respect to the taking were, the California courts deemed them sufficient to present the issue. We accordingly have no occasion to decide whether the ordinance at issue actually denied appellant all use of its property or whether the county might avoid the conclusion that a compensable taking had occurred by establishing that the denial of all use was insulated as a part of the State's authority to enact safety regulations. *See, e.g.*, Goldblatt v. Hempstead, 369 U.S. 590 (1962); Hadacheck v. Sebastian, 239 U.S. 394 (1915); Mugler v. Kansas, 123 U.S. 623 (1887). These questions, of course, remain open for decision on the remand we direct today. We now turn to the question whether the Just Compensation Clause requires the government to pay for "temporary" regulatory takings.

II

Consideration of the compensation question must begin with direct reference to the language of the Fifth Amendment, which provides in relevant part that "private property [shall not] be taken for public use, without just compensation." As its language indicates, and as the Court has frequently noted, this provision does not prohibit the taking of private property, but instead places a condition on the exercise of that power. *See Williamson County*, 473 U.S., at 194; Hodel v. Virginia Surface Mining & Reclamation Ass'n, Inc., 452 U.S. 264, 297, n. 40 (1981); Hurley v. Kincaid, 285 U.S. 95, 104 (1932); Monongahela Navigation Co. v. United States, 148 U.S. 312, 336 (1893); United States v. Jones, 109 U.S. 513, 518 (1883). This basic understanding of the Amendment makes clear that it is designed not to limit the governmental interference with property rights *per se*, but rather to secure *compensation* in the event of otherwise proper interference amounting to a taking. Thus, government action that works a taking of property rights necessarily implicates the "constitutional obligation to pay just compensation." Armstrong v. United States, 364 U.S. 40, 49 (1960).

We have recognized that a landowner is entitled to bring an action in inverse condemnation as a result of " 'the self-executing character of the constitutional provision with respect to compensation. . . .' " United States v. Clarke, 445 U.S. 253, 257 (1980), quoting 6 P. Nichols, Eminent Domain § 25.41 (3d rev. ed. 1972). As noted in JUSTICE BRENNAN's dissent in *San Diego Gas & Electric Co.*, 450 U.S., at 654–655, it has been established at least since Jacobs v. United States, 290 U.S. 13 (1933), that claims for just compensation are grounded in the Constitution itself:

> "The suits were based on the right to recover just compensation for property taken by the United States for public use in the exercise of its power of eminent domain. *That right was guaranteed by the Constitution.* The fact that condemnation proceedings were not instituted and that the

right was asserted in suits by the owners did not change the essential nature of the claim. The form of the remedy did not qualify the right. It rested upon the Fifth Amendment. Statutory recognition was not necessary. A promise to pay was not necessary. Such a promise was implied because of the duty to pay imposed by the Amendment. *The suits were thus founded upon the Constitution of the United States.*"

Id., at 16. (Emphasis added.)

It has also been established doctrine at least since Justice Holmes' opinion for the Court in Pennsylvania Coal Co. v. Mahon, 260 U.S. 393 (1922), that "the general rule at least is, that while property may be regulated to a certain extent, if regulation goes too far it will be recognized as a taking." *Id.*, at 415. While the typical taking occurs when the government acts to condemn property in the exercise of its power of eminent domain, the entire doctrine of inverse condemnation is predicated on the proposition that a taking may occur without such formal proceedings.

While the California Supreme Court may not have actually disavowed this general rule in *Agins*, we believe that it has truncated the rule by disallowing damages that occurred prior to the ultimate invalidation of the challenged regulation. The California Supreme Court justified its conclusion at length in the *Agins* opinion, concluding that:

> "In combination, the need for preserving a degree of freedom in the land-use planning function, and the inhibiting financial force which inheres in the inverse condemnation remedy, persuade us that on balance mandamus or declaratory relief rather than inverse condemnation is the appropriate relief under the circumstances."

24 Cal. 3d, at 276–277, 598 P. 2d, at 31.

We, of course, are not unmindful of these considerations, but they must be evaluated in the light of the command of the Just Compensation Clause of the Fifth Amendment. The Court has recognized in more than one case that the government may elect to abandon its intrusion or discontinue regulations. *See, e.g.,* Kirby Forest Industries, Inc. v. United States, *supra*; United States v. Dow, 357 U.S. 17, 26 (1958). Similarly, a governmental body may acquiesce in a judicial declaration that one of its ordinances has effected an unconstitutional taking of property; the landowner has no right under the Just Compensation Clause to insist that a "temporary" taking be deemed a permanent taking. But we have not resolved whether abandonment by the government requires payment of compensation for the period of time during which regulations deny a landowner all use of his land.

In considering this question, we find substantial guidance in cases where the government has only temporarily exercised its right to use private property. In United States v. Dow, *supra*, at 26, though rejecting a claim that the Government may not abandon condemnation proceedings, the Court observed that abandonment "results in an alteration in the property interest taken—from [one of] full ownership to one of temporary use and occupation. . . . In such cases compensation would be measured by the principles normally governing the taking of a right to use property temporarily. *See* Kimball Laundry Co. v. United States, 338 U.S. 1 [1949]; United States v. Petty Motor Co., 327 U.S. 372 [1946]; United States v. General Motors Corp., 323 U.S. 373 [1945]."

These cases reflect the fact that "temporary" takings which, as here, deny a landowner all use of his property, are not different in kind from permanent takings, for which the Constitution clearly requires compensation. *Cf. San Diego Gas & Electric Co.*, 450 U.S., at 657 (Brennan, J., dissenting) ("Nothing in the Just Compensation Clause suggests that 'takings' must be permanent and irrevocable"). It is axiomatic that the Fifth Amendment's just compensation provision is "designed to bar Government from forcing some people alone to bear public burdens which, in all fairness and justice, should be borne by the public as a whole." Armstrong v. United States, 364 U.S., at 49. See also Penn Central Transportation Co. v. New York City, 438 U.S. 104, 123–125 (1978); Monongahela Navigation Co. v. United States, 148 U.S., at 325. In the present case the interim ordinance was adopted by the County of Los Angeles in January 1979, and became effective immediately. Appellant filed suit within a month after the effective date of the ordinance and yet when the California Supreme Court denied a hearing in the case on October 17, 1985, the merits of appellant's claim had yet to be determined. The United States has been required to pay compensation for leasehold interests of shorter duration than this. The value of a leasehold interest in property for a period of years may be substantial, and the burden on the property owner in extinguishing such an interest for a period of years may be great indeed. *See, e.g.*, United States v. General Motors, *supra*. Where this burden results from governmental action that amounted to a taking, the Just Compensation Clause of the Fifth Amendment requires that the government pay the landowner for the value of the use of the land during this period. *Cf.* United States v. Causby, 328 U.S., at 261 ("It is the owner's loss, not the taker's gain, which is the measure of the value of the property taken"). Invalidation of the ordinance or its successor ordinance after this period of time, though converting the taking into a "temporary" one, is not a sufficient remedy to meet the demands of the Just Compensation Clause.

Nothing we say today is intended to abrogate the principle that the decision to exercise the power of eminent domain is a legislative function "'for Congress and Congress alone to determine.'" Hawaii Housing Authority v. Midkiff, 467 U.S. 229, 240 (1984), quoting Berman v. Parker, 348 U.S. 26, 33 (1954). Once a court determines that a taking has occurred, the government retains the whole range of options already available—amendment of the regulation, withdrawal of the invalidated regulation, or exercise of eminent domain. Thus we do not, as the Solicitor General suggests, "permit a court, at the behest of a private person, to require the . . . Government to exercise the power of eminent domain. . . ." Brief for United States as Amicus Curiae 22. We merely hold that where the government's activities have already worked a taking of all use of property, no subsequent action by the government can relieve it of the duty to provide compensation for the period during which the taking was effective.

We also point out that the allegation of the complaint which we treat as true for purposes of our decision was that the ordinance in question denied appellant all use of its property. We limit our holding to the facts presented, and of course do not deal with the quite different questions that would arise in the case of normal delays in obtaining building permits, changes in zoning ordinances, variances, and the like which are not before us. We realize that even our present holding will undoubtedly lessen to some extent the freedom and flexibility of land-use planners and governing bodies of municipal corporations when enacting land-use regulations. But such consequences necessarily flow from any decision upholding a claim of constitutional right; many of the provisions of the Constitution are designed to limit the flexibility and freedom of governmental authorities, and the Just Compensation Clause of the Fifth Amendment is one of them.

Here we must assume that the Los Angeles County ordinance has denied appellant all use of its property for a considerable period of years, and we hold that invalidation of the ordinance without payment of fair value for the use of the property during this period of time would be a constitutionally insufficient remedy. The judgment of the California Court of Appeal is therefore reversed, and the case is remanded for further proceedings not inconsistent with this opinion.

It is so ordered.

■ JUSTICE STEVENS, with whom JUSTICE BLACKMUN and JUSTICE O'CONNOR join as to Parts I and III, dissenting.

One thing is certain. The Court's decision today will generate a great deal of litigation. Most of it, I believe, will be unproductive. But the mere duty to defend the actions that today's decision will spawn will undoubtedly have a significant adverse impact on the land-use regulatory process. The Court has reached out to address an issue not actually presented in this case, and has then answered that self-imposed question in a superficial and, I believe, dangerous way.

The Court's reasoning also suffers from severe internal inconsistency. Although it purports to put to one side "normal delays in obtaining building permits, changes in zoning ordinances, variances and the like," *ante*, at 321, the Court does not explain why there is a constitutional distinction between a total denial of all use of property during such "normal delays" and an equally total denial for the same length of time in order to determine whether a regulation has "gone too far" to be sustained unless the government is prepared to condemn the property. Precisely the same interference with a real estate developer's plans may be occasioned by protracted proceedings which terminate with a zoning board's decision that the public interest would be served by modification of its regulation and equally protracted litigation which ends with a judicial determination that the existing zoning restraint has "gone too far," and that the board must therefore grant the developer a variance. The Court's analysis takes no cognizance of these realities. Instead, it appears to erect an artificial distinction between "normal delays" and the delays involved in obtaining a court declaration that the regulation constitutes a taking.

In my opinion, the question whether a "temporary taking" has occurred should not be answered by simply looking at the reason a temporary interference with an owner's use of his property is terminated. Litigation challenging the validity of a land-use restriction gives rise to a delay that is just as "normal" as an administrative procedure seeking a variance or an approval of a controversial plan. Just because a plaintiff can prove that a land-use restriction would constitute a taking if allowed to remain in effect permanently does not mean that he or she can also prove that its temporary application rose to the level of a constitutional taking.

The policy implications of today's decision are obvious and, I fear, far reaching. Cautious local officials and land-use planners may avoid taking any action that might later be challenged and thus give rise to a damages action. Much important regulation will never be enacted,[17] even perhaps in the health and safety area. Were this result mandated by the Constitution, these serious implications would have to be

---

[17] It is no answer to say that "after all, if a policeman must know the Constitution, then why not a planner?" San Diego Gas & Electric Co. v. San Diego, 450 U.S. 621, 661, n. 26 (1981) (Brennan, J., dissenting). To begin with, the Court has repeatedly recognized that it itself cannot establish any objective rules to assess when a regulation becomes a taking. *See* Hodel v. Irving, 481 U.S. 704, 713–714 (1987); Andrus v. Allard, 444 U.S. 51, 65 (1979); *Penn Central*, 438 U.S., at 123–124. How then can it demand that land planners do any better? However confusing some of our criminal procedure cases may be, I do not believe they have been as open-ended and standardless as our regulatory takings cases are. As one commentator concluded: "The chaotic state of taking law makes it especially likely that availability of the damages remedy will induce land-use planning officials to stay well back of the invisible line that they dare not cross." Johnson, Compensation for Invalid Land-Use Regulations, 15 Ga. L. Rev. 559, 594 (1981); *see also* Sallet, The Problem of Municipal Liability for Zoning and Land-Use Regulation, 31 Cath. U. L. Rev. 465, 478 (1982); Charles v. Diamond, 41 N. Y. 2d 318, 331–332, 360 N. E. 2d 1295, 1305 (1977); Allen v. City and County of Honolulu, 58 Haw. 432, 439, 571 P. 2d 328, 331 (1977).

ignored. But the loose cannon the Court fires today is not only unattached to the Constitution, but it also takes aim at a long line of precedents in the regulatory takings area. It would be the better part of valor simply to decide the case at hand instead of igniting the kind of litigation explosion that this decision will undoubtedly touch off.

NOTES AND QUESTIONS

1. If municipalities did not have to compensate landowners for the harm they suffer while challenging regulations that amount to unconstitutional takings, what incentive would municipal officials have to avoid unconstitutional regulations? Is that what provoked Justice Brennan's question: "if a policeman must know the Constitution, then why not a planner?" Is Justice Stevens' response persuasive?

2. What effect does the *First English* rule have on the position of developers seeking development approvals? What leverage, if any, does *First English* provide to developers, and how can they use it?

3. Suppose a landowner applies for a variance to build on a substandard parcel. The zoning board of appeals determines that he's not entitled to a variance. If a court concludes that the landowner has met the standards for obtaining a variance, and that the zoning board of appeals erred in denying the variance, is the landowner entitled to compensation for delays due to the erroneous variance denial? How, if at all, is this problem different from the one in *First English?*

4. If a landowner is entitled to compensation for a temporary taking in a case like *First English,* why weren't the landowners entitled to compensation in *Tahoe-Sierra*? Wasn't the harm to the landowners the same?

5. *Historical Background.* State courts had long been resistant to awarding money damages to landowners even after finding regulations unconstitutional. For instance, the New York courts had held the state's police power and the state's eminent domain power were distinct. As a result, if a municipality acted pursuant to its police power, but exceeded the bounds of that power, the constitutional violation was a deprivation of property without due process, not a taking without just compensation. If, after judicial invalidation of the regulation, the municipality wanted to continue to restrict the landowner, it could only do so by exercising its condemnation power, and paying compensation, but the municipality would not be liable for any losses incurred during the period before judicial invalidation. *See* Fred F. French Investing Co. v. City of New York, 39 N.Y.2d 587, 593–94, 350 N.E.2d 381, 384–85, 385 N.Y.S.2d 5, 8 (1976); *cf.* HFH Ltd. v. Superior Court, 15 Cal.3d 508, 542 P.2d 237, 125 Cal.Rptr. 365 (1975) (remedy for improper legislation is a mandamus action to undo the government's action).

As the Court noted in *First English*, the Supreme Court had, on several prior occasions, declined to address the availability of a damage remedy against municipalities for enacting unconstitutional land use regulations. Justice Brennan's dissent in San Diego Gas & Electric Co. v. San Diego, 450 U.S. 621 (1981), however, signaled that the Court would ultimately reject the prevalent state court approach in favor of a requirement that municipalities pay damages for losses incurred during the course of a successful takings challenge.

6.   Suppose that after *First English*, a landowner challenges an onerous land use regulation as a taking. The state court that hears the claim believes that the regulation "goes too far," but wants to avoid imposing financial liability on the municipality. Can the court conclude that the municipality had no authority, under state law, to impose the regulation, and thereby avoid municipal liability by holding that the regulation was of no effect under state law? *See, e.g.*, Pheasant Bridge Corp. v. Township of Warren, 169 N.J. 282, 777 A.2d 334 (2001); Torromeo v. Town of Fremont, 148 N.H. 640, 813 A.2d 389 (2002); Landgate, Inc. v. California Coastal Comm'n, 17 Cal.4th 1006, 73 Cal.Rptr.2d 841, 953 P.2d 1188 (1998). *See generally* Thomas E. Roberts, An Analysis of *Tahoe-Sierra* and Its Help or Hindrance in Understanding the Concept of a Temporary Regulatory Taking, 25 U. Haw. L. Rev. 417, 440–47 (2003).

If the municipality is not liable for interim damages in cases where municipalities had no authority to impose the regulation, has *First English* merely encouraged state courts to invalidate regulations on state law grounds rather than relying on the Takings Clause?

The Measure of Damages

The Court in *First English* held that in a takings case, "invalidation of the ordinance without payment of fair value for the use of the property" during the period between enactment and invalidation "would be a constitutionally insufficient remedy." If damages must be awarded to a successful takings claimant, how are damages to be computed? Will the answer be the same when the invalidated ordinance left the owner with no economic use of the land (the Court's view of the facts in *First English)* and when the ordinance left the landowner with some use, but a use much less valuable than permitted before enactment of the ordinance?

Computing damages is fraught with difficulties, most of which courts have not yet had the opportunity to explore fully. First, what is the period for which the landowner is entitled to damages? Does the taking begin as soon as the municipality enacts the challenged regulation? Does it begin when landowner applies for a permit? When landowner is denied a permit? *See generally* Gregory M. Stein, Pinpointing the Beginning and Ending of a Temporary Regulatory Taking, 70 Wash. L. Rev. 953 (1995) (suggesting a presumption that the period begins when a permit is denied). Should the landowner have to seek a permit when the ordinance would leave permitting officials no power to grant the permit?

Second, assuming the period of the taking is clear, how much compensation should the landowner receive for that period? One measure is the market rate return on the difference between the fair market value of the property without the regulatory restriction and the fair market value with the restriction. *See* Wheeler v. Pleasant Grove, 833 F.2d 267, 271 (11th Cir. 1987). But suppose the landowner cannot make use of the property with the restriction unless the landowner spends money developing the property. Should the landowner be penalized for not spending the money while challenging the restriction? Conversely, if the landowner purchased the property with knowledge that its development proposal might not be approved, does the *Wheeler* formula overcompensate the landowner? In Herrington v. County of Sonoma, 790 F.Supp. 909 (N.D. 1991), aff'd 12 F.3d 901 (9th Cir. 1993), the court suggested that the probability of approval was a relevant factor in assessing damages. The *Herrington* court offered the following formula for computing damages:

$$[(aX + bY) - Y] \, Rt + ac$$

In which:

a = probability of approval of the developer's proposal

b = probability that the developer's proposal would not be approved

(a + b = 100%)

X = value of the land with the proposed development

Y = value of the land with no development

(aX + bY) = weighted probability of approval of developer's proposal

R = rate of interest

t = duration of the delay

c = increased costs of development resulting from the delay

Consider how the *Herrington* formula differs from the *Wheeler* formula. What objections might be raised against the *Herrington* formula? In light of *Wheeler* and *Herrington*, consider the following problems:

PROBLEMS

1. Landowner purchased a parcel of vacant land zoned for residential purposes in 2012 at a price of $5,000,000. After a significant flood in 2013, the municipality rezoned all land within 300 feet of a river as a "flood plain," and prohibited all development within that flood plain. Landowner's parcel lies within the flood plain.

Landowner immediately challenged the regulation, citing *Lucas v. South Carolina Coastal Council*. Does the municipality have any response?

In 2016, a court concluded that the regulation works a taking, and that the landowner is entitled to compensation. The court has asked the parties for briefs on how much compensation should be awarded.

a.   If you represent the landowner, how much would you seek, and how would you justify your request?

b.   If you represent the municipality, how would you respond, and how would you justify your response?

c.   How much compensation should the court award?

Suppose now that the landowner does not challenge the regulation until 2015, and the court does not decide the case until 2018. Which of your answers would change, and why?

2.   Landowner purchases a parcel of vacant land zoned for residential purposes in 2012 at a price of $5,000,000. Landowner has plans to develop the parcel in accordance with the zoning ordinance. Those plans would require landowner to spend $15,000,000 in construction costs, but the landowner projects that it will be able to sell the finished homes for $30,000,000 by 2016 (assuming the landowner obtains the required subdivision approval from the municipality). In 2013, the municipality rezones the land for recreational purposes only. The amended ordinance would permit the landowner to build docks along the river, to build tennis and squash courts, and to build campsites. Landowner's parcel would be worth $1,000,000 for those purposes. (It would cost the landowner $500,000 to build facilities that would have a market value of $1,500,000 when completed.)

Landowner immediately challenges the regulation. What defenses would the municipality raise? Suppose a court were to conclude that the regulation works a taking, and were to ask the parties for briefs on how much compensation landowner should receive.

a.   If you represent the landowner, how much would you seek, and how would you justify your request?

b.   If you represent the municipality, how would you respond?

c.   Is there any additional information you might want in representing either party?

d.   How much compensation should the court award?

I.   RIPENESS AND LIMITATIONS ON ACCESS TO FEDERAL COURT

What steps must a landowner take before bringing a court challenge to a local land use regulation? The impact of a regulation often depends on how the regulation is administered by local land use authorities. Can a landowner bring an action before trying, and failing, to persuade local officials to permit development?

Williamson County Regional Planning Commission v. Hamilton Bank

Supreme Court of the United States, 1985
473 U.S. 172

■ JUSTICE BLACKMUN delivered the opinion of the Court.

I

A

[In 1973, developer sought preliminary subdivision plat approval for a 736-unit residential development on a 676-acre parcel. The County Planning Commission approved the preliminary plat, which included 260 acres of open space in the form of a golf course. Lot lines were drawn for 469 units, and the rest of the area was labeled "not to be developed until approved by the planning commission." The density calculation that would have permitted 736 units was apparently inconsistent with the zoning regulations then in effect, which required deductions for land lying in flood plains and for land with a grade in excess of 25%.

Developer then spent $3.5 million on the golf course and on sewer and water facilities. Developer then obtained final plat approval for 212 units in 1979. Meanwhile, the county amended its zoning ordinance to change the permissible density, and the planning commission concluded that the new provisions should be applicable to pending applications. When the developer submitted a revised preliminary plat for approval, the planning commission disapproved the application because, in computing density, there had been no deduction for roads and steep slopes. The developer then appealed to the Board of Zoning Appeals, which determined that the Commission should apply the 1973 regulations, and that the Commission should define slopes differently.

Respondent bank then acquired 257 of the original developer's undeveloped acres through foreclosure. The bank's land included many of the parcels left blank in the 1973 plat. The new plat proposed development of 688 units in total (inclusive of the 212 units for which developer had obtained final plat approval—many of which were already developed). The Commission disapproved the plat, raising eight objections. The Commission declined to follow the decision of the Board of Zoning Appeals because that Board had no jurisdiction to hear appeals from the Commission.—eds.]

B

Respondent then filed this suit in the United States District Court for the Middle District of Tennessee, pursuant to 42 U.S.C. § 1983, alleging that the Commission had taken its property without just compensation and asserting that the Commission should be estopped under state law from denying approval of the project. Respondent's expert witnesses testified that the design that would meet each of the

Commission's eight objections would allow respondent to build only 67 units, 409 fewer than respondent claims it is entitled to build, and that the development of only 67 sites would result in a net loss of over $1 million. App. 377. Petitioners' expert witness, on the other hand, testified that the Commission's eight objections could be overcome by a design that would allow development of approximately 300 units. Tr. 1467–1468.

[After a 3-week trial, the jury found a taking and awarded $350,000 in damages. The trial court entered a permanent injunction requiring application of the ordinance in effect in 1973, but granted judgment n.o.v. on the damage claim, holding that temporary deprivations could not constitute a taking. The Sixth Circuit reversed, holding that damages are required for a temporary taking—the position subsequently taken by the Supreme Court in *First English.*—eds.]

III

Because respondent has not yet obtained a final decision regarding the application of the zoning ordinance and subdivision regulations to its property, nor utilized the procedures Tennessee provides for obtaining just compensation, respondent's claim is not ripe.

A

As the Court has made clear in several recent decisions, a claim that the application of government regulations effects a taking of a property interest is not ripe until the government entity charged with implementing the regulations has reached a final decision regarding the application of the regulations to the property at issue.

Respondent has submitted a plan for developing its property. But respondent did not then seek variances that would have allowed it to develop the property according to its proposed plat, notwithstanding the Commission's finding that the plat did not comply with the zoning ordinance and subdivision regulations. It appears that variances could have been granted to resolve at least five of the Commission's eight objections to the plat. The Board of Zoning Appeals had the power to grant certain variances from the zoning ordinance, including the ordinance's density requirements and its restriction on placing units on land with slopes having a grade in excess of 25%. Tr. 1204–1205; *see* n. 3, *supra.* The Commission had the power to grant variances from the subdivision regulations, including the cul-de-sac, road-grade, and frontage requirements. Nevertheless, respondent did not seek variances from either the Board or the Commission.

Respondent argues that it "did everything possible to resolve the conflict with the commission," Brief for Respondent 42, and that the Commission's denial of approval for respondent's plat was equivalent to a denial of variances. The record does not support respondent's claim, however. There is no evidence that respondent applied to the Board of

Zoning Appeals for variances from the zoning ordinance. As noted, the developer sought a ruling that the ordinance in effect in 1973 should be applied, but neither respondent nor the developer sought a variance from the requirements of either the 1973 or 1980 ordinances.

Indeed, in a letter to the Commission written shortly before its June 18, 1981, meeting to consider the preliminary sketch, respondent took the position that it would not request variances from the Commission until *after* the Commission approved the proposed plat.

The Commission's regulations clearly indicated that unless a developer applied for a variance in writing and upon notice to other property owners, "any condition shown on the plat which would require a variance will constitute grounds for disapproval of the plat." CA App. 933. Thus, in the face of respondent's refusal to follow the procedures for requesting a variance, and its refusal to provide specific information about the variances it would require, respondent hardly can maintain that the Commission's disapproval of the preliminary plat was equivalent to a final decision that no variances would be granted.

Our reluctance to examine taking claims until such a final decision has been made is compelled by the very nature of the inquiry required by the Just Compensation Clause. Although "[the] question of what constitutes a 'taking' for purposes of the Fifth Amendment has proved to be a problem of considerable difficulty," Penn Central Transp. Co. v. New York City, 438 U.S., at 123, this Court consistently has indicated that among the factors of particular significance in the inquiry are the economic impact of the challenged action and the extent to which it interferes with reasonable investment-backed expectations. *Id.*, at 124. *See also* Ruckelshaus v. Monsanto Co., 467 U.S., at 1005; PruneYard Shopping Center v. Robins, 447 U.S., at 83; Kaiser Aetna v. United States, 444 U.S., at 175. Those factors simply cannot be evaluated until the administrative agency has arrived at a final, definitive position regarding how it will apply the regulations at issue to the particular land in question.

Respondent asserts that it should not be required to seek variances from the regulations because its suit is predicated upon 42 U.S.C. § 1983, and there is no requirement that a plaintiff exhaust administrative remedies before bringing a § 1983 action. Patsy v. Florida Board of Regents, 457 U.S. 496 (1982). The question whether administrative remedies must be exhausted is conceptually distinct, however, from the question whether an administrative action must be final before it is judicially reviewable. While the policies underlying the two concepts often overlap, the finality requirement is concerned with whether the initial decisionmaker has arrived at a definitive position on the issue that inflicts an actual, concrete injury; the exhaustion requirement generally refers to administrative and judicial procedures by which an injured party may seek review of an adverse decision and obtain a remedy if the decision is found to be unlawful or otherwise inappropriate. *Patsy* concerned the latter, not the former.

The difference is best illustrated by comparing the procedure for seeking a variance with the procedures that, under *Patsy*, respondent would not be required to exhaust. While it appears that the State provides procedures by which an aggrieved property owner may seek a declaratory judgment regarding the validity of zoning and planning actions taken by county authorities, *see* Fallin v. Knox County Bd. of Comm'rs, 656 S. W. 2d 338 (Tenn. 1983); Tenn. Code Ann. §§ 27–8–101, 27–9–101 to 27–9–113, and 29–14–101 to 29–14–113 (1980 and Supp. 1984), respondent would not be required to resort to those procedures before bringing its § 1983 action, because those procedures clearly are remedial. Similarly, respondent would not be required to appeal the Commission's rejection of the preliminary plat to the Board of Zoning Appeals, because the Board was empowered, at most, to review that rejection, not to participate in the Commission's decisionmaking.

Resort to those procedures would result in a judgment whether the Commission's actions violated any of respondent's rights. In contrast, resort to the procedure for obtaining variances would result in a conclusive determination by the Commission whether it would allow respondent to develop the subdivision in the manner respondent proposed. The Commission's refusal to approve the preliminary plat does not determine that issue; it prevents respondent from developing its subdivision without obtaining the necessary variances, but leaves open the possibility that respondent may develop the subdivision according to its plat after obtaining the variances. In short, the Commission's denial of approval does not conclusively determine whether respondent will be denied all reasonable beneficial use of its property, and therefore is not a final, reviewable decision.

B

A second reason the taking claim is not yet ripe is that respondent did not seek compensation through the procedures the State has provided for doing so. The Fifth Amendment does not proscribe the taking of property; it proscribes taking without just compensation. If a State provides an adequate procedure for seeking just compensation, the property owner cannot claim a violation of the Just Compensation Clause until it has used the procedure and been denied just compensation.

Under Tennessee law, a property owner may bring an inverse condemnation action to obtain just compensation for an alleged taking of property under certain circumstances. Tenn. Code Ann. § 29–16–123 (1980). The statutory scheme for eminent domain proceedings outlines the procedures by which government entities must exercise the right of eminent domain. §§ 29–16–101 to 29–16–121. The State is prohibited from "[entering] upon [condemned] land" until these procedures have been utilized and compensation has been paid the owner, § 29–16–122, but if a government entity does take possession of the land without following the required procedures, "the owner of such land may petition for a jury of inquest, in which case the same proceedings may be had, as near as may be, as hereinbefore provided; or he may sue for damages in the ordinary way. . . ." § 29–16–123.

The Tennessee state courts have interpreted § 29–16–123 to allow recovery through inverse condemnation where the "taking" is effected by restrictive zoning laws or development regulations. *See* Davis v. Metropolitan Govt. of Nashville, 620 S. W. 2d 532, 533–534 (Tenn. App. 1981); Speight v. Lockhart, 524 S. W. 2d 249 (Tenn. App. 1975). Respondent has not shown that the inverse condemnation procedure is unavailable or inadequate, and until it has utilized that procedure, its taking claim is premature.

We therefore reverse the judgment of the Court of Appeals and remand the case for further proceedings consistent with this opinion.

NOTES AND QUESTIONS

1. At the time the Court decided *Williamson County*, the Court had not yet decided *First English*. Whether landowners should be entitled to money damages as a remedy was the subject of fierce debate among academics and practitioners. The general assumption was that the Court had taken certiorari in *Williamson County* to resolve the issue. Instead, the Court used ripeness as a basis for postponing decision on that issue. But the Court's treatment of ripeness remained significant even after the Court decided that landowners were entitled to a damage remedy when government regulation works a taking. *See, e.g.*, Peters v. Clifton, 498 F.3d 727 (7th Cir. 2007) (holding that *Williamson County*'s ripeness requirements are applicable to claims for injunctive relief as well as claims for money damages).

2. In *Williamson County,* the bank brought its action in federal district court. Did that play a role in the Court's decision? Suppose the bank had brought the same action in Tennessee state court. Would either prong of the Court's ripeness doctrine prevent a Tennessee state court from entertaining a claim brought pursuant to 42 U.S.C. § 1983?

With respect to the finality prong, *see* Casey v. Mayor & City Council of Rockville, 400 Md. 259, 929 A.2d 74 (2007) (holding that a takings challenge to a historic preservation ordinance was unripe because no final determination had been made on landowner's application for a permit to demolish the building). On the availability of state relief prong, *see* MC Assocs. v. Town of Cape Elizabeth, 773 A.2d 439 (Me. 2001) (holding that landowner can proceed simultaneously on state and federal takings claims in state court, and that federal takings claim is ripe even if state claim has not yet been resolved); Giovanella v. Conservation Comm'n, 447 Mass. 720, 857 N.E.2d 451 (2006) (holding that landowner need not bring state inverse condemnation claim before bringing state court takings claim).

If ripeness doctrine precluded a landowner from bringing a § 1983 claim in Tennessee state court, could the landowner bring any other action in Tennessee state court to avoid the ripeness issues discussed in *Williamson County?*

3.   Landowner paid $5,000,000 for an undeveloped 6-acre parcel of land. At the time of purchase, the applicable zoning ordinance required a minimum lot size of a quarter acre. Landowner expected to build about 20 homes on the parcel (leaving room for roads and other public facilities). After the purchase, the municipality amended the zoning ordinance to require a minimum lot size of three acres. The new ordinance would permit the landowner to build only one home (given the configuration of the lot and contiguous roads).

Can the landowner bring a takings claim in federal court? State court? How would the municipality respond?

Suppose the zoning ordinance precludes the Zoning Board of Appeals from granting a variance unless the landowner can show that its hardship is unique. The new ordinance affected 30 acres of land, and 8 different landowners. Would the landowner have to seek a variance before proceeding to state court? Federal court?

Would the landowner ever have to seek a zoning amendment before proceeding to court?

4.   Suppose now that the landowner in Question 3 has unsuccessfully sought a zoning variance. Can the landowner now bring a takings claim in federal court? In light of *Williamson County,* can a landowner ever bring a takings claim in federal court? Would an absolute bar make sense?

5.   Suppose a landowner can demonstrate that, although the state constitution has a provision authorizing the award of money damages for any taking of property, no court in the state has ever awarded damages for an unconstitutional taking. Has the landowner met *Williamson County's* second prong? *See* Peters v. Clifton, 498 F.3d 727 (7th Cir. 2007) (holding that discussion of precedent is insufficient to establish that a state remedy would be "unavailable or inadequate").

Suppose state law does not directly provide a damage remedy, but instead limits a landowner to a mandamus proceeding to force a government actor to bring an appropriation proceeding against the private owner. Has the landowner established that no adequate state remedy is available? *See* River City Capital, L.P. v. Board of County Comm'rs, 491 F.3d 301, 307–09 (6th Cir. 2007) (holding claim unripe).

6.   Suppose a property owner brings a taking claim in federal court, and the federal court, on examining the complaint, concludes that property owner's claim is devoid of merit. Must the court dismiss the claim on ripeness grounds (effectively sending the parties back to state court to litigate the claim), or may the federal court dismiss the claim on the merits? A number of federal courts have concluded, relying on dictum in Supreme Court cases, that *Williamson County's* ripeness requirement is prudential rather than jurisdictional. As a result, these courts have dismissed taking claims on the merits to avoid relitigation in state courts. *See* Wilkins v. Daniels, 744 F.3d 409 (6th Cir. 2014) (concluding that Ohio statute requiring microchip in wild animals did not work a taking of animal owners' property, and noting that ripeness dismissal would do a disservice to federalism principles by requiring state court to adjudicate a claim, already before federal court, that has no merit); MHC Financing, Ltd. v. City of San Rafael, 714 F.3d 1118 (9th Cir. 2013); Guggenheim v. City of Goleta, 638 F.3d 1111 (9th Cir. 2010).

7. Educated by *Williamson County,* landowner brings a takings claim in state court. The municipality removes the case to federal court, and then moves to dismiss on ripeness grounds. Should the municipality prevail? *See* Sherman v. Town of Chester, 752 F.3d 554 (2d Cir. 2014) and Sansotta v. Town of Nags Head, 724 F.3d 533 (4th Cir. 2013) (both concluding that municipality waived its ripeness defense when it removed state case to federal court).

First English establishes that a landowner who challenges a state or local land use regulation as a taking can seek damage relief pursuant to 42 U.S.C. § 1983. Ordinarily, a victim of unconstitutional action by state or local officials can choose between state and federal court. *Williamson County* presents a problem, however, for the plaintiff who wants to proceed in federal court: the Supreme Court has held that the takings claim is not ripe until a state court has denied just compensation. If the landowner first seeks relief in state court, and the effort proves unsuccessful, can the landowner now proceed to federal court? Consider the following case:

San Remo Hotel, L.P. v. City and County of San Francisco

Supreme Court of the United States, 2005
545 U.S. 323

■ JUSTICE STEVENS delivered the opinion of the Court.

This case presents the question whether federal courts may craft an exception to the full faith and credit statute, 28 U.S.C. § 1738, for claims brought under the Takings Clause of the Fifth Amendment.

I

In 1979, San Francisco's Board of Supervisors responded to "a severe shortage" of affordable rental housing for elderly, disabled, and low-income persons by instituting a moratorium on the conversion of residential hotel units into tourist units

The genesis of this protracted dispute lies in the 1981 HCO's requirement that each hotel "file an initial unit usage report containing" the "number of residential and tourist units in the hotel[s] as of September 23, 1979." § 41.6(b)(1), App. to Pet. for Cert. 206a. Jean

Iribarren was operating the San Remo Hotel, pursuant to a lease from petitioners, when this requirement came into effect. Iribarren filed the initial usage report for the hotel, which erroneously reported that all of the rooms in the hotel were "residential" units. The consequence of that initial classification was that the City zoned the San Remo Hotel as "residential hotel"—in other words, a hotel that consisted entirely of residential units. And that zoning determination ultimately meant that, despite the fact that the San Remo Hotel had operated in practice as a tourist hotel for many years, 145 F.3d, at 1100, petitioners were required to apply for a conditional use permit to do business officially as a "tourist hotel," San Remo Hotel, L.P. v. City and County of San Francisco, 27 Cal. 4th 643, 654, 117 Cal. Rptr. 2d 269, 41 P.3d 87, 94 (2002).

After the HCO was revised in 1990, petitioners applied to convert all of the rooms in the San Remo Hotel into tourist use rooms under the relevant HCO provisions and requested a conditional use permit under the applicable zoning laws. In 1993, the City Planning Commission granted petitioners' requested conversion and conditional use permit, but only after imposing several conditions, one of which included the requirement that petitioners pay a $567,000 "in lieu" fee. Petitioners appealed, arguing that the HCO requirement was unconstitutional and otherwise improperly applied to their hotel. *See id.*, at 656, 41 P.3d, at 95. The City Board of Supervisors rejected petitioners' appeal on April 19, 1993.

Petitioners filed in federal court for the first time on May 4, 1993. Petitioners' first amended complaint alleged four counts of due process (substantive and procedural) and takings (facial and as-applied) violations under the Fifth and Fourteenth Amendments to the United States Constitution, one count seeking damages under Rev. Stat. § 1979, 42 U.S.C. § 1983, for those violations, and one pendent state-law claim. The District Court granted respondents summary judgment. As relevant to this action, the court found that petitioners' facial takings claim was untimely under the applicable statute of limitations, and that the as-applied takings claim was unripe under *Williamson County*, 473 U.S. 172, 87 L. Ed. 2d 126, 105 S. Ct. 3108.

On appeal to the Court of Appeals for the Ninth Circuit, petitioners took the unusual position that the court should not decide their federal claims, but instead should abstain under Railroad Comm'n of Tex. v. Pullman Co., 312 U.S. 496, 85 L. Ed. 971, 61 S. Ct. 643 (1941), because a return to state court could conceivably moot the remaining federal questions. The [Ninth Circuit] affirmed the District Court's determination that petitioners' as-applied takings claim—the claim that the application of the HCO to the San Remo Hotel violated the Takings Clause—was unripe. Because petitioners had failed to pursue an inverse condemnation action in state court, they had not yet been denied just compensation as contemplated by *Williamson County*. 145 F.3d, at 1105.

At the conclusion of the Ninth Circuit's opinion, the court appended a footnote stating that petitioners would be free to raise their federal takings claims in the California courts. If, however, they wanted to "retain [their] right to return to federal court for adjudication of [their] federal claim, [they] must make an appropriate reservation in state court." *Id.*, at 1106, n. 7. That is precisely what petitioners attempted to do when they reactivated the dormant California case. Yet petitioners advanced more than just the claims on which the federal court had abstained, and phrased their state claims in language that sounded in the rules and standards established and refined by this Court's takings jurisprudence. Petitioners claimed, for instance, that "imposition of the fee 'fails to substantially advance a legitimate government interest' and that 'the amount of the fee imposed is not roughly proportional to the impact' of the proposed tourist use of the San Remo Hotel." 27 Cal. 4th, at 656, 41 P.3d, at 95 (quoting petitioners' second amended state complaint).

The California Supreme Court [held that the trial court had properly dismissed the complaint—eds.] The court initially noted that petitioners had reserved their federal causes of action and had sought no relief for any violation of the Federal Constitution. *Id.*, at 649, n. 1, 41 P.3d, at 91, n. 1. In the portion of its opinion discussing the Takings Clause of the California Constitution, however, the court noted that "we appear to have construed the clauses congruently." *Id.*, at 664, 41 P.3d, at 100–101 (citing cases). Accordingly, despite the fact that petitioners sought relief only under California law, the state court decided to "analyze their takings claim under the relevant decisions of both this court and the United States Supreme Court." *Ibid.*, 41 P.3d, at 101.

Petitioners did not seek a writ of certiorari from the California Supreme Court's decision in this Court. Instead, they returned to Federal District Court by filing an amended complaint based on the complaint that they had filed prior to invoking *Pullman* abstention. The District Court held that petitioners' facial attack on the HCO was not only barred by the statute of limitations, but also by the general rule of issue preclusion.

The Court of Appeals affirmed. The court rejected petitioners' contention that general preclusion principles should be cast aside whenever plaintiffs "must litigate in state court pursuant to *Pullman* and/or *Williamson County*." We granted certiorari and now affirm.

II

Article IV, § 1, of the United States Constitution demands that "Full Faith and Credit shall be given in each State to the public Acts, Records, and judicial Proceedings of every other State. And the Congress may by general Laws prescribe the Manner in which such

Acts, Records and Proceedings shall be proved, and the Effect thereof." In 1790, Congress responded to the Constitution's invitation by enacting the first version of the full faith and credit statute. *See* Act of May 26, 1790, ch. 11, 1 Stat. 122. The modern version of the statute, 28 U.S.C. § 1738, provides that "judicial proceedings . . . shall have the same full faith and credit in every court within the United States and its Territories and Possessions as they have by law or usage in the courts of such State. . . ." This statute has long been understood to encompass the doctrines of res judicata, or "claim preclusion," and collateral estoppel, or "issue preclusion." *See* Allen v. McCurry, 449 U.S. 90, 94–96, 66 L. Ed. 2d 308, 101 S. Ct. 411 (1980).

The general rule implemented by the full faith and credit statute—that parties should not be permitted to relitigate issues that have been resolved by courts of competent jurisdiction—predates the Republic. It "has found its way into every system of jurisprudence, not only from its obvious fitness and propriety, but because without it, an end could never be put to litigation." Hopkins v. Lee, 19 U.S. 109, 6 Wheat. 109, 114, 5 L. Ed. 218 (1821).

As this case is presented to us, under our limited grant of certiorari, we have only one narrow question to decide: whether we should create an exception to the full faith and credit statute, and the ancient rule on which it is based, in order to provide a federal forum for litigants who seek to advance federal takings claims that are not ripe until the entry of a final state judgment denying just compensation. *See Williamson County*, 473 U.S. 172, 87 L. Ed. 2d 126, 105 S. Ct. 3108.

The essence of petitioners' argument is as follows: because no claim that a state agency has violated the federal Takings Clause can be heard in federal court until the property owner has "been denied just compensation" through an available state compensation procedure, *id.*, at 195, 87 L. Ed. 2d 126, 105 S. Ct. 3108, "federal courts [should be] required to disregard the decision of the state court" in order to ensure that federal takings claims can be "considered on the merits in . . . federal court," Brief for Petitioners 8, 14. Therefore, the argument goes, whenever plaintiffs reserve their claims under England v. Louisiana Bd. of Medical Examiners, 375 U.S. 411, 11 L. Ed. 2d 440, 84 S. Ct. 461 (1964), federal courts should review the reserved federal claims *de novo*, regardless of what issues the state court may have decided or how it may have decided them.

We reject petitioners' contention.

III

[The Court rejected the argument that *England v. Louisiana Bd. of Medical Exam'rs*, 375 U.S. 411, entitled petitioners to reserve all of their federal law claims while litigating state takings claims in state court].

IV

Petitioners' ultimate submission, however, does not rely on *England* alone. Rather, they argue that federal courts simply should not apply ordinary preclusion rules to state-court judgments when a case is forced into state court by the ripeness rule of *Williamson County*. For support, petitioners rely on the Court of Appeals for the Second Circuit's decision in *Santini*, 342 F.3d, at 130.

In *Santini*, the Second Circuit held that parties "who litigate state-law takings claims in state court involuntarily" pursuant to *Williamson County* cannot be precluded from having those very claims resolved "by a federal court." 342 F.3d, at 130. The court did not rest its decision on any provision of the federal full faith and credit statute or our cases construing that law. Instead, the court reasoned that "it would be both ironic and unfair if the very procedure that the Supreme Court required [plaintiffs] to follow before bringing a Fifth Amendment takings claim . . . also precluded [them] from ever bringing a Fifth Amendment takings claim." *Ibid*. We find this reasoning unpersuasive for several reasons.

First, both petitioners and *Santini* ultimately depend on an assumption that plaintiffs have a right to vindicate their federal claims in a federal forum. We have repeatedly held, to the contrary, that issues actually decided in valid state-court judgments may well deprive plaintiffs of the "right" to have their federal claims relitigated in federal court. *See, e.g.*, Migra v. Warren City School Dist. Bd. of Ed., 465 U.S. 75, 84, 79 L. Ed. 2d 56, 104 S. Ct. 892 (1984); Allen, 449 U.S., at 103–104, 66 L. Ed. 2d 308, 101 S. Ct. 411. This is so even when the plaintiff would have preferred not to litigate in state court, but was required to do so by statute or prudential rules. *See id.*, at 104, 66 L. Ed. 2d 308, 101 S. Ct. 411. The relevant question in such cases is not whether the plaintiff has been afforded access to a federal forum; rather, the question is whether the state court actually decided an issue of fact or law that was necessary to its judgment.

As in *Allen*, we are presently concerned only with issues *actually decided* by the state court that are dispositive of federal claims raised under § 1983. And, also as in *Allen,* it is clear that petitioners would have preferred not to have been forced to have their federal claims resolved by issues decided in state court. Unfortunately for petitioners, it is entirely *unclear* why their preference for a federal forum should matter for constitutional or statutory purposes.

The second reason we find petitioners' argument unpersuasive is that it assumes that courts may simply create exceptions to 28 U.S.C. § 1738 wherever courts deem them appropriate. Even conceding, *arguendo,* the laudable policy goal of making federal forums available to deserving litigants, we have expressly rejected petitioners' view. "Such a fundamental departure from traditional rules of preclusion, enacted into federal law, can be justified only if plainly stated by Congress." Kremer v. Chemical Constr. Corp., 456 U.S. 461, 485, 72 L. Ed. 2d 262, 102 S. Ct. 1883 (1982).

The same concerns animate our decision here. Congress has not expressed any intent to exempt from the full faith and credit statute federal takings claims. Consequently, we apply our normal assumption that the weighty interests in finality and comity trump the interest in giving losing litigants access to an additional appellate tribunal.

With respect to those federal claims that did require ripening, we reject petitioners' contention that *Williamson County* prohibits plaintiffs from advancing their federal claims in state courts. The requirement that aggrieved property owners must seek "compensation through the procedures the State has provided for doing so," 473 U.S., at 194, 87 L. Ed. 2d 126, 105 S. Ct. 3108, does not preclude state courts from hearing simultaneously a plaintiff's request for compensation under state law and the claim that, in the alternative, the denial of compensation would violate the Fifth Amendment of the Federal Constitution. Reading *Williamson County* to preclude plaintiffs from raising such claims in the alternative would erroneously interpret our cases as requiring property owners to "resort to piecemeal litigation or otherwise unfair procedures." MacDonald, Sommer & Frates v. Yolo County, 477 U.S. 340, 350, n. 7, 91 L. Ed. 2d 285, 106 S. Ct. 2561 (1986).

It is hardly a radical notion to recognize that, as a practical matter, a significant number of plaintiffs will necessarily litigate their federal takings claims in state courts. It was settled well before *Williamson County* that "a claim that the application of government regulations effects a taking of a property interest is not ripe until the government entity charged with implementing the regulations has reached a final decision regarding the application of the regulations to the property at issue." 473 U.S., at 186, 87 L. Ed. 2d 126, 105 S. Ct. 3108. As a consequence, there is scant precedent for the litigation in federal district court of claims that a state agency has taken property in violation of the Fifth Amendment's Takings Clause. To the contrary, most of the cases in our takings jurisprudence, including nearly all of the cases on which petitioners rely, came to us on writs of certiorari from state courts of last resort.

State courts are fully competent to adjudicate constitutional challenges to local land-use decisions. Indeed, state courts undoubtedly have more experience than federal courts do in resolving the complex factual, technical, and legal questions related to zoning and land-use regulations.

At base, petitioners' claim amounts to little more than the concern that it is unfair to give preclusive effect to state-court proceedings that are not chosen, but are instead *required* in order to ripen federal takings claims. Whatever the merits of that concern may be, we are not free to disregard the full faith and credit statute solely to preserve the availability of a federal forum. The Court of Appeals was correct to decline petitioners' invitation to ignore the requirements of 28 U.S.C. § 1738. The judgment of the Court of Appeals is therefore affirmed.

It is so ordered.

■ CHIEF JUSTICE REHNQUIST, with whom JUSTICE O'CONNOR, JUSTICE KENNEDY, and JUSTICE THOMAS join, concurring in the judgment.

As the Court recognizes, *ante*, at 346–347, 162 L. Ed. 2d, at 339, *Williamson County* all but guarantees that claimants will be unable to utilize the federal courts to enforce the Fifth Amendment's just compensation guarantee. The basic principle that state courts are competent to enforce federal rights and to adjudicate federal takings claims is sound, *see ante*, at 347, 162 L. Ed. 2d, at 339, and would apply to any number of federal claims But that principle does not explain why federal takings claims in particular should be singled out to be confined to state court, in the absence of any asserted justification or congressional directive.

I joined the opinion of the Court in *Williamson County*. But further reflection and experience lead me to think that the justifications for its state-litigation requirement are suspect, while its impact on takings plaintiffs is dramatic. Here, no court below has addressed the correctness of *Williamson County*, neither party has asked us to reconsider it, and resolving the issue could not benefit petitioners. In an appropriate case, I believe the Court should reconsider whether plaintiffs asserting a Fifth Amendment takings claim based on the final decision of a state or local government entity must first seek compensation in state courts.

NOTES AND QUESTIONS

1.   Which prong of the *Williamson County* ripeness test prevents plaintiff from proceeding first in federal court? Recall that the Court developed the ripeness tests in *Williamson County* at least in part to avoid deciding whether landowners could obtain money damages as a remedy for a taking—a question that was not yet resolved at the time. Do you think the Court in *Williamson County* focused on the impact its ripeness doctrine would have on a taking plaintiff's right to seek redress from a federal court?

2.   In *San Remo*, the hotel raised only state constitutional claims in state court. Why? Suppose the plaintiff had raised only state claims, and had not cited any U.S. Supreme Court cases. Would the plaintiff then have been entitled to raise its federal takings claim in federal court? Does it matter whether the plaintiff "actually litigated" the federal claims in state court?

3.   The Court in *San Remo* focused on issue preclusion (often called collateral estoppel). Was the plaintiff also barred by claim preclusion (often called *res judicata*)? If the plaintiff could have raised federal claims in state court, would ordinary claim preclusion principles hold that plaintiff forfeited a right to bring the claim anywhere if plaintiff failed to raise them at the same time it raised its state law claims?

In Adam Bros. Farming, Inc. v. County of Santa Barbara, 604 F.3d 1142 (9th Cir. 2010), plaintiffs initially sued in California state court to challenge a wetlands designation as a violation of the Equal Protection, Due Process, and Takings Clauses. When the state court concluded that the takings claim was not ripe, plaintiffs amended their complaint to delete that claim. A state appeals court overturned a jury award of damages, concluding that plaintiffs lacked standing and that the statute of limitations had run. Plaintiff then brought a takings claim in federal court. Although the Ninth Circuit held that the takings claim was ripe, the court also held that *res judicata* barred plaintiff's federal claim, because it sought recovery for the same primary right as the prior state court claim. According to the court, "[f]or purposes of *res judicata*, it is irrelevant that Adam Bros. attempts to recover under different legal theories." *Id.* at 1149. *See generally* Stewart E. Sterk, The Demise of Federal Takings Litigation, 48 Wm. & Mary L. Rev 251, 276–83 (2006).

4.   In a portion of the opinion not reproduced here, the Court held that a taking plaintiff could raise a "facial" takings challenge in federal court, and then ask the federal court to abstain from deciding the issue until after the state court resolved the plaintiff's state law claims. According to the Court, "facial" challenges are not subject to the *Williamson County* ripeness doctrine. But what is a "facial" takings challenge? When would a local ordinance ever work a "taking" on its face, without regard to the state administrative and judicial relief available to the affected landowner? Note that *San Remo* was decided simultaneously with Lingle v. Chevron U.S.A., Inc., 544 U.S. 528 (2005), in which the Court held that a claim that a regulation does not substantially advance a legitimate state interest is not cognizable as a takings claim. Is a "substantially advances" challenge a facial takings claim? Once the Court has precluded "substantially advances" challenges, is there anything left that constitutes a facial takings claim?

5.   *San Remo* effectively channels all takings litigation into state court. Is that a bad thing? What advantages are there to the Court's approach (other than the obvious one of relieving federal courts of the burden of hearing takings cases)? Which courts, state or federal, are more likely to be in tune with the dynamics of local land use regulation?

6.   Even if state courts hear all takings cases in the first instance, landowners always have the potential for relief from the United States Supreme Court. As the Court notes in *San Remo*, most of the Court's leading takings decisions have reached the Court from state supreme courts. How effective a monitor would you expect the Supreme Court to be in this area? Why? *See generally* Stewart E. Sterk, The Federalist Dimension of Regulatory Takings Jurisprudence, 114 Yale L. J. 203 (2004).

J. PROPERTY RIGHTS LEGISLATION

Developers and property rights advocates have not been content to rely on Supreme Court adjudication as the primary bulwark against what they regard as overzealous land use regulation. Stymied by the Court's takings jurisprudence, property rights advocates have lobbied for legislation at the state level. In a number of states, they have persuaded state legislatures to restrict the power of municipalities to enact regulations that diminish the value of a landowner's land. In other states, they have made property protection an issue on ballot initiatives; in some states, voters have defeated these initiatives, in others, voters have enacted them but state courts have invalidated the initiatives on state law grounds, and in still other states, the initiatives have been enacted into law.

The substance of these statutes varies considerably. Consider the following two examples:

FLORIDA STATUTES

Section 70.001   Private property rights protection

(2) When a specific action of a governmental entity has inordinately burdened an existing use of real property or a vested right to a specific use of real property, the property owner of that real property is entitled to relief, which may include compensation for the actual loss to the fair market value of the real property caused by the action of government, as provided in this section.

(3) For purposes of this section:

(a) The existence of a "vested right" is to be determined by applying the principles of equitable estoppel or substantive due process under the common law or by applying the statutory law of this state.

(b) The term "existing use" means:

1. An actual, present use or activity on the real property, including periods of inactivity which are normally associated with, or are incidental to, the nature or type of use; or

2. Activity or such reasonably foreseeable, nonspeculative land uses which are suitable for the subject real property and compatible with adjacent land uses and which have created an existing fair market value in the property greater than the fair market value of the actual, present use or activity on the real property.

(d) The term "action of a governmental entity" means a specific action of a governmental entity which affects real property, including action on an application or permit.

(e) The terms "inordinate burden" or "inordinately burdened":

1. Mean that an action of one or more governmental entities has directly restricted or limited the use of real property such that the property owner is permanently unable to attain the reasonable, investment-backed expectation for the existing use of the real property or a vested right to a specific use of the real property with respect to the real property as a whole, or that the property owner is left with existing or vested uses that are unreasonable such that the property owner bears permanently a disproportionate share of a burden imposed for the good of the public, which in fairness should be borne by the public at large.

2. Do not include temporary impacts to real property; impacts to real property occasioned by governmental abatement, prohibition, prevention, or remediation of a public nuisance at common law or a noxious use of private property; or impacts to real property caused by an action of a governmental entity taken to grant relief to a property owner under this section. However, a temporary impact on development, as defined in s. 380.04, that is in effect for longer than 1 year may, depending upon the circumstances, constitute an "inordinate burden" as provided in this paragraph.

TEXAS GOVERNMENT CODE

Section 2007.002   Definitions

In this chapter:

(5) "Taking" means:

(A) a governmental action that affects private real property, in whole or in part or temporarily or permanently, in a manner that requires the governmental entity to compensate the private real property owner as provided by the Fifth and Fourteenth Amendments to the United States Constitution or Section 17 or 19, Article I, Texas Constitution; or

(B) a governmental action that:

(i) affects an owner's private real property that is the subject of the governmental action, in whole or in part or temporarily or permanently, in a manner that restricts or limits the owner's right to the property that would otherwise exist in the absence of the governmental action; and

(ii) is the producing cause of a reduction of at least 25 percent in the market value of the affected private real property, determined by comparing the market value of the property as if the governmental action is not in effect and the market value of the property determined as if the governmental action is in effect.

Section 2007.003   Applicability

(a) This chapter applies only to the following governmental actions:

(1) the adoption or issuance of an ordinance, rule, regulatory requirement, resolution, policy, guideline, or similar measure;

(2) an action that imposes a physical invasion or requires a dedication or exaction of private real property;

(3) an action by a municipality that has effect in the extraterritorial jurisdiction of the municipality, excluding annexation, and that enacts or enforces an ordinance, rule, regulation, or plan that does not impose identical requirements or restrictions in the entire extraterritorial jurisdiction of the municipality; and

(4) enforcement of a governmental action listed in Subdivisions (1) through (3), whether the enforcement of the governmental action is accomplished through the use of permitting, citations, orders, judicial or quasi-judicial proceedings, or other similar means.

(b) This chapter does not apply to the following governmental actions:

(1) an action by a municipality except as provided by Subsection (a)(3);

(5) the discontinuance or modification of a program or regulation that provides a unilateral expectation that does not rise to the level of a recognized interest in private real property;

(6) an action taken to prohibit or restrict a condition or use of private real property if the governmental entity proves that the condition or use constitutes a public or

private nuisance as defined by background principles of nuisance and property law of this state;

(7) an action taken out of a reasonable good faith belief that the action is necessary to prevent a grave and immediate threat to life or property;

(8) a formal exercise of the power of eminent domain;

(9) an action taken under a state mandate to prevent waste of oil and gas, protect correlative rights of owners of interests in oil or gas, or prevent pollution related to oil and gas activities;

(10) a rule or proclamation adopted for the purpose of regulating water safety, hunting, fishing, or control of nonindigenous or exotic aquatic resources;

(11) an action taken by a political subdivision:

(A) to regulate construction in an area designated under law as a floodplain;

(B) to regulate on-site sewage facilities;

(C) under the political subdivision's statutory authority to prevent waste or protect rights of owners of interest in groundwater; or

(D) to prevent subsidence;

(12) the appraisal of property for purposes of ad valorem taxation;

(13) an action that:

(A) is taken in response to a real and substantial threat to public health and safety;

(B) is designed to significantly advance the health and safety purpose; and

(C) does not impose a greater burden than is necessary to achieve the health and safety purpose; or

Section 2007.023   Entitlement to Invalidation of Governmental Action

(a) Whether a governmental action results in a taking is a question of fact.

(b) If the trier of fact in a suit or contested case filed under this subchapter finds that the governmental action is a taking under this chapter, the private real property owner is only entitled to, and the governmental entity is only liable for, invalidation of the governmental action or the part of the governmental action resulting in the taking.

NOTES AND QUESTIONS

1. How would *Palazzolo* have been decided if the Florida statute had been in effect? The Texas statute? What about *Williamson County*?

2. Suppose a municipality were to enact new subdivision regulations requiring cul-de-sacs to be larger in order to accommodate new, larger (and presumably, more effective) fire trucks. The regulations, together with other density and frontage requirements, limit a residential developer to six homes on a particular site, while the developer could have built nine homes before the new regulations were enacted. Does the developer have a claim under the *Penn Central* test? The Florida statute? The Texas statute?

3. How would you expect municipalities to change their behavior in light of property rights statutes like those enacted in Florida and Texas? Would such changes be desirable?

The Oregon Experience

Beginning in the 1970s, Oregon pioneered land use planning at the state level. The state channeled development within urban growth boundaries, acted to preserve rural forests and farmland, and worked to encourage efficient infrastructure planning. This activism generated a response both from libertarian groups and from the state's timber industry. After a number of unsuccessful initiatives to curb land use regulation, Oregon voters approved a citizen initiative to amend the state's constitutional takings provision. When the state supreme court invalidated the amendment on procedural grounds, opponents of regulation launched a new campaign to enact a statutory amendment that would curb state regulation. In 2004, Oregon voters approved Ballot Measure 37 by a landslide margin of 61 to 39 percent. Although the timber industry provided significant funding to the campaign for Measure 37, the measure's ballot success cannot be explained as the triumph of money: opponents of Measure 37 outspent proponents three to one. *See* Bethany R. Berger, What Owners Want and Governments Do: Evidence from the Oregon Experiment, 78 Fordham L. Rev. 1281, 1286 (2009).

Measure 37's takings provisions were more far-reaching than those embodied in the Florida and Texas statutes reproduced above:

> The right to compensation created by Measure 37 is extraordinarily broad. First, the measure requires compensation for any regulation that in any way diminishes the value of a particular property. On its face, no alleged diminution in value is too small to support a claim. Second, the measure has potentially far-reaching retroactive effect. A present landowner is potentially entitled to compensation for any regulation imposed upon her land after the time she or a family member acquired the property. A landowner therefore

may reach back generations to determine the date upon which she acquired her property for purposes of asserting a Measure 37 claim ... Third, the measure calculates the amount of compensation that is due in a highly speculative manner, which several commentators have criticized for potentially creating large windfall gains for individual claimants.

Measure 37 exempts five categories of land use regulations from its compensation requirement. First, land use regulations passed before the present owner, or her family, as defined in the measure, acquired the property are exempt from compensation. Second, land use regulations "restricting and prohibiting activities commonly and historically recognized as public nuisances under common law" are exempt. The measure further directs that this exemption "shall be construed narrowly in favor of a finding of compensation under this act." Third, land use regulations "restricting or prohibiting activities for the protection of public health and safety, such as fire and building codes, health and sanitation regulations, solid or hazardous waste regulations, and pollution control regulations" are exempt from compensation. Fourth, "to the extent land use regulation is required to comply with federal law," it is exempt. Fifth, regulations "restricting or prohibiting the use of the property for the purpose of selling pornography or performing nude dancing," are also exempt from compensation, provided that the provision is not "intended to affect or alter rights provided by the Oregon or United States Constitutions."

Michael C. Blumm & Eric Grafe, Enacting Libertarian Property: Oregon's Measure 37 and Its Implications, 85 Denv. U. L. Rev. 279, 309–10 (2007). By 2007, Measure 37 had generated more than 7,500 compensation claims covering over 750,000 acres and seeking over $10 billion in compensation. Id. at 358. Perhaps for that reason, in 2007, Oregon voters approved Measure 49, which limited the scope of Measure 37. The statute made it significantly more difficult for landowners to obtain relief from restrictions enacted before 2007, and limited, to a lesser extent, the power of landowners to obtain relief from regulations enacted after January 1, 2007. Nevertheless, Measure 49 retained the heart of Measure 37, entitling landowners to compensation, or to a waiver from regulation, when a government enacts a regulation restricting residential development, agriculture or forestry practices. Id. at 365. Although a number of other states have rejected property-rights initiatives like those embodied in Measure 37, Arizona's voters have approved a similar initiative.

QUESTION

While Measure 37 was in effect, Oregon municipalities faced by Measure 37 claims decided, in all but one case, to waive enforcement of the restrictions rather than paying compensation to the restricted landowner. Professor Berger notes that one of the justifications for requiring municipalities to compensate landowners for deprivation of property rights is that compensation leads government to internalize the costs of its restrictions on property. Bethany R. Berger, What Owners Want and Governments Do: Evidence from the Oregon Experiment, 78 Fordham L. Rev. 1281, 1290 (2009). She argues that the Oregon practice undercuts this justification:

> Contrary to the cost-internalization theory, government faced with compensation requirements did not choose between efficient and inefficient regulation—in all but one case, they simply waived all land use restrictions on qualifying Measure 37 claimants.

Id. at 1290. If you represented a property rights group, how would you respond to Professor Berger's argument?

II. THE DUE PROCESS CLAUSE

The federal constitution's Fifth Amendment provides that "[n]o person shall be ... deprived of life, liberty, or property, without due process of law; nor shall private property be taken for public use without just compensation." The Fourteenth Amendment provides due process protection against the States: "nor shall any State deprive any person of life, liberty, or property, without due process of law."

For many years, courts treated land use regulations that significantly reduced land values as potential due process violations. Indeed, some courts concluded that what we now call takings claims should have been treated instead as due process claims. The argument ran like this: when the government enacts land use regulations, the government is acting pursuant to its police power, not pursuant to its eminent domain power. The government's police power, however, is not unconstrained. But when the government exceeds the permissible scope of the police power, its action is not transformed into an exercise of the eminent domain power; instead, the limit on the government's police power flows from the Due Process Clause. As a result, when a regulation goes "too far," the regulation deprives the landowner of property without due process of law; it doesn't "take" property within the meaning of the Eminent Domain Clause. *See, e.g.*, Fred F. French Investing Co., Inc. v. City of New York, 39 N.Y.2d 587, 385 N.Y.S.2d 5, 350 N.E.2d 381, 384–85 (1976).

In recent decades, the Supreme Court has made it clear that the federal constitutional protections against regulations that interfere with a landowner's investment-backed expectations are grounded in the Eminent Domain Clause, not the Due Process Clause. Nevertheless, due process continues to play a role in policing local land use regulations.

In *Village of Euclid v. Ambler Realty*, the Supreme Court acknowledged the broad police power enjoyed by states and municipalities, and indicated that when a municipality enacts pursuant to its police power, before the ordinance can be declared unconstitutional, it must be established "that such provisions are clearly arbitrary and unreasonable, having no substantial relation to the public health, safety, morals, or general welfare." 272 U.S. 365 at 395. Today, this constitutional restriction on the police power is rooted in the Due Process Clause. The landowner's right is

> the Due Process Clause right not to have his use of the land restricted arbitrarily and capriciously, which is a right not to have his use of his land restricted for reasons having no substantial relation to the public health, safety, morals, or general welfare (a "substantive due process" or "arbitrary and capricious due process" claim).

Corn v. City of Lauderdale Lakes, 997 F.2d 1369, 1374 (11th Cir. 1993).

Suppose, however, a landowner applies for approval of a site plan, or for a zoning amendment, and the responsible municipal officials deny the application. If the landowner contends that the municipal officials denied the application out of personal animus, has the landowner stated a due process claim? If so, does every permit denial enable the landowner to sue in federal court? Would that transform federal courts into zoning boards of appeals? Consider the following case:

United Artists Theatre Circuit, Inc. v. Township of Warrington

United States Court of Appeals for the Third Circuit, 2003
316 F.3d 392

■ ALITO, CIRCUIT JUDGE.

United Artists Theatre Circuit, Inc. ("United Artists"), an owner and operator of movie theaters, sought land development approval from Warrington Township Pennsylvania, ("Township"), to construct and operate a multiplex theater on land that United Artists owned. United Artists claims that Warrington Township and its Board of Supervisors (the "Board") complicated and delayed approval of United Artists' development plan, and thereby allowed a competitor to beat United Artists in a race to build a movie theater in the Township, which is too small to support two theaters. United Artists alleges that the Township and individual members of the Board engaged in this conduct because they wanted the Township to receive an improper "impact fee" from the competing developer. In this appeal, the defendant Supervisors contest the District Court's denial of their qualified-immunity-based motion for summary judgment. We vacate and remand.

I.

A.

The dispute underlying this case arises out of a development race between United Artists' proposed multiplex and a competing multiplex theater development proposed by Regal Cinema and developer Bruce Goodman. The record shows that the two companies were competing to obtain approval of their plans by the Township because the market could support only one of the theaters. Goodman agreed to pay the Township an annual "impact fee" of $100,000, but United Artists refused the Township's repeated requests for such a payment. United Artists asserts that, because of Goodman's promise to pay this fee, the Township allowed his project to "sail through the land development process," while United Artists' proposal was repeatedly stalled.

The Board of Supervisors' review process consisted of two phases, preliminary approval and final approval. In January 1996, United Artists submitted a preliminary plan for its theater to the Township Planning Commission, an independent body of local officials that makes recommendations regarding land-use plans to the Board of Supervisors. Along with the preliminary plan, United Artists submitted a traffic impact study, which led the Township to require, as a precondition to the issuance of an occupancy permit, the installation of a separate left-turn lane into the theater. United Artists failed to acquire the property necessary to make this improvement and expressed its intention to request a waiver of the condition or to sue for relief. United Artists claims that its failure to construct the road improvement was a mere pretext for the Township's refusal to support its theater proposal and that this refusal was actually motivated by the Township's desire to obtain an impact fee from Goodman and Regal Cinema.

After granting preliminary approval of United Artists' proposal, the Township attempted to change the terms of that approval by requiring United Artists to obtain an easement for the road improvement and to complete the installation of signals before construction could begin, rather than before the time of occupancy, as was originally provided in the preliminary approval. United Artists then brought suit against the Township in the Court of Common Pleas of Bucks County, and that court found the change in conditions to be unlawful under the Pennsylvania Municipalities Planning Code. On appeal, the Commonwealth Court agreed. After succeeding in this state court litigation and eliminating the building permit condition, United Artists began this action against the Township and the Supervisors in federal court.

In the meantime, the Board granted preliminary approval of the Goodman proposal on February 4, 1997—one month after the initial application was submitted—and final approval was granted on May 21, 1997. By contrast, United Artists, did not receive preliminary approval until March 18, 1997, 14 months after submitting its initial application. The Board then tabled its vote on United Artists' application for final approval on three occasions, each time asking if United Artists would pay an impact fee. The Board granted final approval of the United Artists proposal on September 16, 1997. The Goodman/Regal Cinema multiplex was completed in 1999; United Artists never built a theater in Warrington.

B.

United Artists' complaint in this case asserted procedural and substantive due process claims under 42 U.S.C. § 1983, as well as supplementary state law claims. As defendants, the complaint named the Township and the members of the Board of Supervisors—Gerald Anderson, Joseph Lavin, Douglas Skinner, Wayne Bullock, and Katherine Watson ("Supervisors")—in both their official and individual capacities. * * *

III.

B.

In County of Sacramento v. Lewis, 523 U.S. 833, 140 L. Ed. 2d 1043, 118 S. Ct. 1708 (1998), the Supreme Court explained the standard that applies when a plaintiff alleges that an action taken by an executive branch official violated substantive due process. The Court observed that "the core of the concept" of due process is "protection against arbitrary action" and that "only the most egregious official conduct can be said to be 'arbitrary in the constitutional sense.'" *Id.* at 845–46 (citation omitted). After noting its long history of speaking of "the cognizable level of executive abuse of power as that which shocks the conscience," *id.* at 846 (citing Rochin v. California, 342 U.S. 165, 96 L. Ed. 183, 72 S. Ct. 205 (1952)), the Court continued:

> Most recently, in Collins v. Harker Heights, [503 U.S. 115, 128, 117 L. Ed. 2d 261, 112 S. Ct. 1061 (1992)], we said again that the substantive component of the Due Process Clause is violated by executive action only when it "can properly be characterized as arbitrary, or conscience shocking, in a constitutional sense."

Lewis, 523 U.S. at 847 (emphasis added). *See also* Fagan v. City of Vineland, 22 F.3d 1296, 1303 (3d Cir. 1994) (en banc) ("The substantive component of the Due Process Clause can only be violated by governmental employees when their conduct amounts to an abuse of official power that 'shocks the conscience.' "). At the same time, however, the *Lewis* Court acknowledged that "the measure of what is conscience-shocking is no calibrated yard stick," *Lewis,* 523 U.S. at 847, and that "deliberate indifference that shocks in one environment may not be so patently egregious in another." *Id.* at 850.

Despite *Lewis* . . . , United Artists maintains that this case is not governed by the "shocks the conscience" standard, but by the less demanding "improper motive" test that originated with Bello v. Walker, 840 F.2d 1124 (3d Cir. 1988), and was subsequently applied by our court in a line of land-use cases. In these cases, we held that a municipal land use decision violates substantive due process if it was made for any reason "unrelated to the merits," Herr v. Pequea Township, 274 F.3d 109, 111 (3d Cir. 2001) (citing cases), or with any "improper motive." *See, e.g.,* Woodwind Estates, Ltd. v. Gretkowski, 205 F.3d 118 (3d Cir. 2000); Blanche Road Corp. v. Bensalem Township, 57 F.3d 253 (3d Cir. 1995); DeBlasio v. Zoning Board of Adjustment, 53 F.3d 592 (3d Cir. 1995); Parkway Garage, Inc. v. City of Philadelphia, 5 F.3d 685 (3d Cir. 1993); Midnight Sessions, Ltd. v. City of Philadelphia, 945 F.2d 667 (3d Cir. 1991).

These cases, however, cannot be reconciled with *Lewis*'s explanation of substantive due process analysis. Instead of demanding conscience-shocking conduct, the *Bello* line of cases endorses a much less demanding "improper motive" test for governmental behavior. Although the District Court opined that there are "few differences between the [shocks the conscience] standard and improper motive standard," we must respectfully disagree. 2001 U.S. Dist. LEXIS 12189 at *12 n. 5, Aug. 15, 2001 order, in App. at 11a. The "shocks the conscience" standard encompasses "only the most egregious official conduct." *Lewis*, 523 U.S. at 846. In ordinary parlance, the term "improper" sweeps much more broadly, and neither Bello nor the cases that it spawned ever suggested that conduct could be "improper" only if it shocked the conscience. We thus agree with the Supervisors that the *Bello* line of cases is in direct conflict with *Lewis*.

In sum, we see no reason why the present case should be exempted from the *Lewis* shocks-the-conscience test simply because the case concerns a land use dispute. Such a holding would be inconsistent with the plain statements in *Lewis* and our own post-*Lewis* cases that we have already noted. Since *Lewis*, our court has applied the "shocks the conscience" standard in a variety of contexts. *See, e.g.,* Boyanowski v. Capital Area Intermediate Unit, 215 F.3d 396 (3d Cir. 2000) (applying the "shocks the conscience" test to a claim of civil conspiracy); Fuentes v. Wagner, 206 F.3d 335 (3d Cir. 2000) (finding the "shocks the conscience" standard appropriate in an excessive force claim in the context of a prison disturbance); Miller v. City of Philadelphia, 174 F.3d 368 (3d Cir. 1999) (applying the "shocks the conscience" standard in the child custody context). There is no reason why land use cases should be treated differently. We thus hold that, in light of *Lewis*, *Bello* and its progeny are no longer good law.

We note that our holding today brings our Court into line with several other Courts of Appeals that have ruled on substantive due process claims in land-use disputes. *See, e.g.*, Chesterfield Development Corp. v. City of Chesterfield, 963 F.2d 1102, 1104–05 (8th Cir. 1992) (holding that allegations that the city arbitrarily applied a zoning ordinance were insufficient to state a substantive due process claim, and stating in dicta that the "decision would be the same even if the City had knowingly enforced the invalid zoning ordinance in bad faith. . . . A bad-faith violation of state law remains only a violation of state law."); PFZ Properties, Inc. v. Rodriguez, 928 F.2d 28, 32 (1st Cir. 1991) ("Even assuming that ARPE engaged in delaying tactics and refused to issue permits for the Vacia Talega project based on considerations outside the scope of its jurisdiction under Puerto Rico law, such practices, without more, do not rise to the level of violations of the federal constitution under a substantive due process label.").

Application of the "shocks the conscience" standard in this context also prevents us from being cast in the role of a "zoning board of appeals." Creative Environments, Inc. v. Estabrook, 680 F.2d 822, 833 (1st Cir. 1982) (quoting Village of Belle Terre v. Boraas, 416 U.S. 1, 13, 39 L. Ed. 2d 797, 94 S. Ct. 1536 (1974) (Marshall, J., dissenting)); *see also* Nestor Colon Medina & Sucesores, Inc. v. Custodio, 964 F.2d 32, 45–46 (1st Cir. 1992) (disagreeing with *Bello* and stating that "we have consistently held that the due process clause may not ordinarily be used to involve federal courts in the rights and wrongs of local planning disputes"). The First Circuit in *Estabrook* observed that every appeal by a disappointed developer from an adverse ruling of the local planning board involves some claim of abuse of legal authority, but "it is not enough simply to give these state law claims constitutional labels such as 'due process' or 'equal protection' in order to raise a substantial federal question under section 1983." *Estabrook*, 680 F.2d at 833. Land-use decisions are matters of local concern and such disputes should not be transformed into substantive due process claims based only on allegations that government officials acted with "improper" motives.

■ COWEN, CIRCUIT JUDGE, dissenting.

I agree with the Majority that land use decisions are generally issues of "local concern." But those very same decisions necessarily assume constitutional dimension when the calculated, intentional and deliberate abuse of government power is at hand. *See Lewis*, 523 U.S. at 846 ("the Due Process Clause was intended to prevent government officials from abusing [their] power. . . .") (citations omitted); *Id.* at 848–49 (intentional conduct by government official falls at the polar end of Tort law's "culpability spectrum" in substantive Due Process cases); Daniels v. Williams, 474 U.S. 327, 331, 88 L. Ed. 2d 662, 106 S. Ct. 662 (1986) ("Historically, [the] guarantee of due process has been applied to deliberate decisions of government officials to deprive a person of life, liberty or property") (emphasis in original) (citations omitted); Wolff v. McDonnell, 418 U.S. 539, 558, 41 L. Ed. 2d 935, 94 S. Ct. 2963 (1974) ("The touchstone of due process is protection of the individual against arbitrary action of government") (citations omitted). The concern that the federal Judiciary will become a local zoning board takes a permanent back seat to the federal Judiciary's obligation to protect the core constitutional freedoms of the American public from deliberate and intentional governmental deprivation.

In sum, I would hold fast to the scheme that is already firmly entrenched in this Circuit: In land use constitutional tort cases, the government's conduct may be judged under an "improper motive" framework. The evisceration of this standard by the Majority today is a most unfortunate step backwards in the evolution of § 1983 as the legislative guardian of bedrock constitutional rights. I am deeply concerned that there will be consequences.

NOTES AND QUESTIONS

1. What property interest did United Artists have in this case? If United Artists had no property interest, how could municipal action deprive it of property without due process?

The Third Circuit had earlier held that a landowner's ownership interest in land constitutes "property" for due process purposes; the landowner does not have to show a more specific property interest interfered with by the municipal action. *See* DeBlasio v. Zoning Bd. of Adjustment, 53 F.3d 592, 601 (3d. Cir. 1995). Not all federal courts have agreed. In some circuits, if municipal officials have broad discretion to deny the requested permit, the landowner has no property in the permit, and a denial cannot constitute a deprivation of property without due process. For instance, in EJS Properties, LLC v. City of Toledo, 698 F.3d 845 (6th Cir. 2012), the court granted summary judgment dismissing a substantive due process claim by a landowner who contended that his proposed zoning amendment was rejected because he refused to make a "donation" sought by a council member. The court concluded that because the landowner had no property interest in the amendment, landowner could not prevail on the due process claim even if the council member's action were to shock the court's conscience. By contrast, if state law significantly constrains the power of officials to deny the permit, the landowner has a property interest in the permit sufficient to serve as a foundation for a due process claim. For a general discussion, *see* George Washington University v. District of Columbia, 318 F.3d 203 (D.C. Cir. 2003).

If the Third Circuit had adopted a more limited definition of property, would it have been necessary to embrace such a constrained view of what constitutes a deprivation?

2. Suppose the municipality in *United Artists* had conceded that it had delayed approval of the United Artists development plan in order to obtain an illegal impact fee from Goodman. Would that have shocked the conscience of the court? If so, then shouldn't United Artists have had the opportunity to prove that the municipal officials were motivated by the desire to obtain the illegal fee? If not, then what would shock the court's conscience? Outright bribery? Consider the Sixth Circuit's response to a claim that Council Member McCloskey voted against a zoning amendment because the applicant refused to contribute $100,000 to a pet charity in his district:

> Perhaps it is unfortunate that the solicitation of a bribe by a public official does not shock our collective conscience the way that pumping a detainee's stomach does. But, although we can condemn McCloskey for his misconduct, we simply cannot say that his behavior is so shocking as to shake the foundations of this country.

EJS Properties, LLC v. City of Toledo, 698 F.3d 845, 862 (6th Cir. 2012).

3. Land use issues often provoke considerable public concern and outcry. If municipal officials respond to that outcry, and enact an ordinance not because they can discern some public purpose served by the ordinance, but solely to pacify resident voters, do adversely affected landowners have a due process claim?

> Nothing is more common in zoning disputes than selfish opposition to zoning changes. The Constitution does not forbid government to yield to such opposition; it does not outlaw the characteristic operations of democratic . . . government, operations which are permeated by pressure from special interests. . . . The fact 'that town officials are motivated by parochial views of local interests which work against plaintiffs' plan and which may contravene state subdivision laws' . . . does not state a claim of denial of substantive due process.

Greenbriar, Ltd. v. City of Alabaster, 881 F.2d 1570, 1579 (11th Cir. 1989) (quoting other cases). *See also* CEnergy-Glenmore Wind Farm No. 1, LLC v. Town of Glenmore, 769 F.3d 485, 488 (7th Cir. 2014):

> As far as the Constitution is concerned, popular opposition to a proposed land development plan is a rational and legitimate reason for a legislature to delay making a decision.

4. Assume for the moment that the allegations in United Artists' complaint were true—that the municipality delayed approval of United Artists' application in order to obtain an illegal impact fee from Goodman. If United Artists was not entitled to recover for a violation of due process, what other alternatives, if any, were available to United Artists? What check is there on this form of illegal municipal behavior?

5. *Ripeness.* Sometimes, landowners raise due process claims on facts that might also give rise to taking claims. A number of courts have held that *Williamson County's* ripeness rules apply to substantive and procedural due process claims that arise out of regulatory overreaching. Thus, in Kurtz v. Verizon New York, Inc., 758 F.3d 506 (2d Cir. 2014), the Second Circuit, in dismissing a due process claim on ripeness grounds, noted that applying *Williamson County* to due process claims "prevents evasions of the ripeness test by artful pleading of a takings claim as a due process claim." *Id.* at 516.

The Seventh Circuit, without explicitly discussing *Williamson County's* ripeness rules, has held that "regardless of how a plaintiff labels an objectionable land-use decision (i.e. as a taking or as a deprivation without substantive or procedural due process), recourse must be made to state rather than federal court." CEnergy-Glenmore Wind Farm No. 1, LLC v. Town of Glenmore, 769 F.3d 485, 489 (7th Cir. 2014).

Why wasn't ripeness an issue in *United Artists?*

When a landowner invokes the federal constitution's Due Process Clause to challenge a municipality's zoning actions, the landowner typically has a choice of forum: state or federal court. Although the Due Process Clause binds both federal and state courts, state courts often (but not always) construe the constitutional provision more broadly than do federal courts. In considering the due process challenge raised in the following case, consider how the *United Artists* court would have dealt with the due process claim:

Town of Rhine v. Bizzell

Supreme Court of Wisconsin, 2008
311 Wis.2d 1, 751 N.W.2d 780

■ ZIEGLER, J.

On October 1, 2003, the Manitowoc Area Off Highway Vehicle Club, Inc., (hereinafter "the Club") purchased 77.2 acres of land in section twelve of the Town of Rhine, Sheboygan County. The zoning classification of this land has been "B–2 Commercial Manufacturing or Processing" for 20 years. Within this classification, "[t]here are no permitted uses in the B–2 District, except that those uses permitted in the Agricultural Land Districts A–1, A–2 and A–3 may be authorized in conjunction with any conditional uses. . . . All uses are conditional and shall comply with the provisions of Section 4.09 [Conditional Uses] of this ordinance." Town of Rhine, Wis., Municipal Code § 4.08(2)(a). Conditional uses in the "B–2 Commercial Manufacturing or Processing" district include: (1) fabrication of consumer or industrial commodities; (2) garbage, rubbish, offal, industrial waste and dead animal reduction or disposal; (3) quarrying; (4) mining and ore processing; (5) salvage yards for wood, metals, papers and clothing; and (6) stockyards.

After purchasing the property in 2003, club members used the property for riding all-terrain vehicles (ATVs) and hunting. On January 6, 2004, pursuant to a request by the Town of Rhine, the Club's president appeared at a Town of Rhine board meeting. At the meeting, the Club president was asked what activities were occurring on the property. The Club president responded that members "are a group of families that live in the city limits and don't own enough property to enjoy outdoor recreation such as hunting, horseback riding, bicycling, ATV riding, etc."

Chairman Sager then related that B–2 zones require a conditional use permit "for any use of the land." He further stated that "an application should be directed to the Plan Commission for either a CUP [conditional use permit] or rezoning."

On May 19, 2004, the Club applied for a conditional use permit. In the conditional use application, the Club stated that it wanted to use the property for recreational activities, such as hunting and riding ATVs. The application stated, "[t]his IS NOT a request for a commercial or industrial operation." The conditional use permit was denied on September 7, 2004. Although the record is unclear as to when, the Club also applied for the B–2 zone to be rezoned to a B–1, "Neighborhood Business" district. That rezoning request was also denied, but it is unclear from the record when it was denied.

On October 10, 2004, the Elkhart Lake Police Department issued citations to six club members for violating the Town of Rhine's Public Nuisance Ordinance. [The Club challenged the citations, contending that the ordinance itself was unconstitutional, while the town sought an order enjoining the Club from operating ATVs on the property. The trial court held that the zoning ordinance was unconstitutional, and the court of appeals certified the case to the Wisconsin Supreme Court— eds.]

ANALYSIS

The Club argues that Municipal Code § 4.08(2)(a), the B–2 District, is unconstitutional on its face because it violates due process in that any use of the property is prohibited unless the landowner obtains a conditional use permit. It further argues that there are no clear and objective standards for the landowner to obtain a conditional use permit. The Town of Rhine, on the other hand, argues that Municipal Code § 4.08(2)(a) is constitutional. It argues that the B–2 District does allow for certain uses of the property under a conditional use permit, and therefore, it is inaccurate to assert that B–2 zoning does not allow any use. The Town of Rhine also argues that Municipal Code § 4.01 sets forth adequate standards for obtaining a conditional use permit, and it asserts that a number of other municipalities have conditional use provisions similar to the Town of Rhine. We conclude that § 4.08(2)(a) is unconstitutional on its face.

A. Zoning Principles

A conditional use permit allows a property owner "to put his property to a use which the ordinance expressly permits when certain conditions [or standards] have been met." *Skelly Oil Co.,* 58 Wis.2d at

701, 207 N.W.2d 585. The degree of specificity of these standards may vary from ordinance to ordinance. 3 E.C. Yokley, Zoning Law and Practice § 21–1, at 21–4 (4th ed. 2002) (2002 revision by Douglas Scott MacGregor).

Allowing for conditional uses, in addition to permitted uses as of right, makes sense when one considers the purpose of the conditional use permit. First, conditional uses are flexibility devices, "which are designed to cope with situations where a particular use, although not inherently inconsistent with the use classification of a particular zone, may well create special problems and hazards if allowed to develop and locate as a matter of right in [a] particular zone." *Id.* at 701, 207 N.W.2d 585; *see also* Gail Easley, Conditional Uses: Using Discretion, Hoping for Certainty, American Planning Association Zoning Practice, May 2006, at 2 (identifying conditional uses as flexibility devices).

Second, conditional use permits are appropriate for "certain uses, considered by the local legislative body to be essential or desirable for the welfare of the community . . . , but not at every or any location . . . or without conditions being imposed. . . ." Mandelker, Land Use Law, § 6.54, at 6–61 (5th ed. 2003) (citation omitted). Thus, those uses subject to a conditional use permit are necessary to the community, but because they often represent uses that may be problematic, their development is best governed more closely rather than as of right.

"Conditional use permits"—also referred to as "conditional uses"—however, should not be confused with "conditional-use district zoning" or "conditional zoning." In "conditional-use district zoning," "a landowner requests that some property be placed in a new zoning district that has no permitted uses, only special or conditional uses." David W. Owens, Legislative Zoning Decisions 93 (2d ed. 1999).

B.   Constitutional Principles

"The Due Process Clause of the Fourteenth Amendment prohibits a state from depriving 'any person of life, liberty, or property without due process of law.' " Penterman v. Wisconsin Elec. Power Co., 211 Wis.2d 458, 480, 565 N.W.2d 521 (1997) (citation omitted); *see also* Laughter v. Board of County Comm'rs for Sweetwater County, 110 P.3d 875, 887–88 (Wyo. 2005). "The substantive component of the Due Process Clause protects individuals from certain arbitrary, wrongful actions 'regardless of the fairness of the procedures used to implement them.' " *Penterman,* 211 Wis.2d at 480, 565 N.W.2d 521 (citations omitted). "Substantive due process forbids a government from exercising 'power without any reasonable justification in the service of a legitimate governmental objective.' " Thorp v. Town of Lebanon, 2000 WI 60, ¶ 45, 235 Wis.2d 610, 612 N.W.2d 59 (citation omitted).

The United States Supreme Court has recognized a landowner's right to substantive due process in zoning cases. *See Pearson*, 961 F.2d at 1217, 1220 (citing to Village of Arlington Heights v. Metropolitan

Hous. Dev. Corp., 429 U.S. 252, 263, 97 S.Ct. 555, 50 L.Ed.2d 450 (1977); Nectow v. City of Cambridge, 277 U.S. 183, 187, 48 S.Ct. 447, 72 L.Ed.842 (1928); [Village of] Euclid v. Ambler Realty Co., 272 U.S. 365, 373, 47 S.Ct. 114, 71 L.Ed.303 (1926)). The Supreme Court has stated, "a zoning ordinance is unconstitutional when its 'provisions are clearly arbitrary and unreasonable having no substantial relation to the public health, safety, morals or general welfare.'" *Thorp,* 235 Wis.2d 610, ¶ 45, 612 N.W.2d 59 (quoting *Euclid,* 272 U.S. at 395, 47 S.Ct. 114).

However, when evaluating a claim that a landowner's substantive due process rights have been violated, a plaintiff must show that he or she has been deprived of a property interest that is constitutionally protected. *Thorp,* 235 Wis.2d 610, ¶ 46, 612 N.W.2d 59 (citing *Penterman,* 211 Wis.2d at 480, 565 N.W.2d 521). "A property interest is constitutionally protected if 'state law recognizes and protects that interest.'" *Thorp,* 235 Wis.2d 610, ¶ 46, 612 N.W.2d 59. "[I]t is well settled that the rights of ownership and use of property have long been recognized by this state." *Penterman,* 211 Wis.2d at 480, 565 N.W.2d 521. Additionally, Wis. Stat. § 62.23(7)(b) provides that "[a]ll such regulations shall be uniform . . . for the use of land throughout each district, but the regulations in one district may differ from those in other districts."

C.   Town of Rhine's B–2 District and Conditional Use Ordinance

Certainly, municipalities may regulate where and under what circumstances certain less desirable uses, such as salvage yards and stockyards, may be developed. However, here no justification exists for precluding all uses in the B–2 District and only providing the landowner with the possibility of obtaining a conditional use permit. Ordinances can be drafted so the acceptable uses as of right do not conflict with the conditional uses. Municipalities have the power to zone property and restrict where particular undesirable uses may be developed within the municipality. However, zoning that restricts the land such that the landowner has no permitted use as of right must bear a substantial relation to the health, safety, morals or general welfare of the public in order to withstand constitutional scrutiny. In this case, the restricted use of the B–2 District land does not bear a substantial relation to the public health, safety, morals or general welfare.

Cases from Wisconsin and other jurisdictions support the conclusion that the common, accepted practice is to first outline permitted uses and then, in addition to permitted uses, the ordinance may provide for conditional uses. A number of cases illustrate this point, but they do not address the merits of a "no permitted uses zone." However, in Sheerr v. Township of Evesham, the Superior Court of New Jersey evaluated and applied the substantive due process standard to a parcel that provided no permitted uses and allowed use only when the landowner obtained a conditional use permit. 184 N.J. Super. 11, 445 A.2d 46, 60–65 (Law Div. 1982). The *Sheerr* court concluded that the ordinance was unconstitutional as applied to the plaintiff's property. *Id.*

Here, we conclude that the B–2 District can be appropriately described as a "no permitted uses" zone, and we conclude that the no permitted uses B–2 District is arbitrary and unreasonable because it bears no substantial relation to public health, safety, morals or general welfare. However, we do recognize that there may be limited circumstances in which a "no permitted uses" zone is a valid exercise of power because the restriction bears substantial relation to the public health, safety, morals or general welfare. For example, in Dur-Bar Realty Co. v. City of Utica, 57 A.D.2d 51, 394 N.Y.S.2d 913, 918 (1977), the New York Supreme Court, Appellate Division, concluded that a "no permitted uses" zone was constitutional as the parcel at issue was in a "Land Conservation District and represented a zone located in the flood plain." *Id.* at 915–16, 918. The "Land Conservation District" "aimed to regulate the use" of land in a "flood prone area." *Id.* at 918. The ordinance at issue today does not include a similar purpose as in *Dur-Bar Realty.*

The court in *Dur-Bar Realty* identified several policy objectives for restricting use in a flood plain:

> (1) the protection of individuals who might choose, despite the flood dangers, to develop or occupy land on a flood plain; (2) the protection of other landowners from damages resulting from the development of a flood plain and the consequent obstruction of the flood flow; (3) the protection of the entire community from individual choices of land use which require subsequent public expenditures for public works and disaster relief.

Id. The court concluded, "[i]t is beyond question that these objectives, which correspond closely to the stated purposes of the present ordinance, may be the subject of a legitimate exercise of the police power." *Id.* The court further stated that, " 'Land Conservation District' provisions do bear a substantial relation to legitimate governmental purpose and a reasonable relation to the goal of flood safety.' " *Id.* Thus, since the limitations related to flood safety, the restriction satisfied the relationship to the public health, safety, morals or general welfare.

In its analysis, the *Dur-Bar Realty* court contrasted the "flood plain" ordinance in that case with the ordinance at issue in Marshall v. Village of Wappingers Falls, 28 A.D.2d 542, 279 N.Y.S.2d 654 (1967). In *Wappingers Falls,* there were no permitted uses as of right in the "Planned Residential District" but twelve uses were available through a special permit. *Id.* at 655–56. The court in *Wappingers Falls* concluded that the "Planned Residential District was *ultra vires* because it was not zoning in accordance with a comprehensive plan." *Id.* The court in

Dur-Bar Realty stated that the Planned Residential District in *Wappingers Falls* did not appear "in any way unusual in topography or location so as to justify the subjection of all use proposals to case by case decision." *Dur-Bar Realty,* 394 N.Y.S.2d at 916. In contrast, the court in *Dur-Bar Realty* concluded that the flood plain ordinance was "a product of assessment of the character of the land in light of the public health and safety interests in being protected against flooding and other hazards that would result from building in an area unsuitable for intensive development." *Id.*

To be clear, after today, municipalities still have ample authority to regulate land use—and they should. Such regulation is an appropriate legislative function; it can serve to protect the health, safety and welfare of the public, and it encourages well reasoned growth. The issuance of conditional use permits also is an appropriate function for municipalities. Municipalities certainly have broad authority to restrict land use, but the district at issue today provides for no permitted use as of right, and the only use is garnered through the possibility of obtaining a conditional use permit. No reasonable justification exists for such excessive government control and restriction—especially when that government control is set against land use rights, and the control bears no substantial relation to the public health, safety, morals or general welfare.

Precluding any permitted use and then only providing generalized standards for obtaining a conditional use permit opens the door to favoritism and discrimination. Under this scenario, a town, pursuant to the ordinance, may arbitrarily preclude any activity on the land in question because (1) there are no permitted uses as a matter of right; and (2) if obtaining a conditional use permit is completely within the discretion of a town, judicial review of a denial is significantly limited because of the non-specific nature of the conditional use standards. As a result, if such an ordinance was deemed acceptable, towns could preclude all uses at will and in a manner that virtually precludes any meaningful judicial review. Such a determination could open the door to abuse. If permitted uses exist as of right, the impact of denying conditional uses is significantly decreased because the landowner has permitted uses as of right.

The facial, constitutional challenge here is sustained. This ordinance is not in balance with the rights of landowners. Because the landowners have demonstrated beyond a reasonable doubt that the ordinance at issue does not provide for any uses as of right, and this restriction in the B–2 District is arbitrary and unreasonable in the sense that it does not bear a substantial relation to public health, safety, morals or general welfare, we conclude that Municipal Code § 4.08(2)(a), the B–2 District, is unconstitutional on its face.

NOTES AND QUESTIONS

1. Does the town's action satisfy the *United Artists'* "shock the conscience" test? Doesn't a municipality always have a plausible justification for reserving judgment about a particular development until after it knows the details of the landowner's proposal?

2. In *Town of Rhine*, the court suggests that a zoning ordinance violates a landowner's substantive due process rights if the ordinance "bears no substantial relation to the public health, safety, morals or general welfare." That formulation has a lengthy pedigree. During the late 19th and early 20th centuries, the United States Supreme Court held that purely economic regulation exceeded the "police power" of the state, and therefore violated the federal constitution's Due Process Clause. Only if regulation promoted the safety, health, morals and general welfare was the regulation within the scope of the state's police power. In Lochner v. New York, 198 U.S. 45 (1905), perhaps the Supreme Court's most infamous substantive due process case, the Court struck down a state statute imposing a maximum hour limitation on bakery workers, concluding that the legislation did not promote safety, health, morals, or general welfare.

Although the Supreme Court has largely repudiated *Lochner*'s approach to due process, state courts continue to invoke the "health, safety, morals or general welfare" formulation when considering due process challenges to zoning regulations. The judicial tendency to hew to that old formula undoubtedly stems, in part, from the inclusion of similar language in many state zoning enabling statutes. Section 1 of the Standard State Zoning Enabling Act, drafted in 1926 under the auspices of the United States Department of Commerce and adopted by many states, started by granting zoning power to municipal legislative bodies "[f]or the purpose of promoting health, safety, morals, or the general welfare of the community." As a result, the old due process limitation has become, in many states, a statutory limitation on municipal zoning power.

3. *Facial Challenges v. As Applied Challenges.* In *Town of Rhine*, the landowner attacked the ordinance on its face, contending that an ordinance that permits no uses as a matter of right violates the Due Process Clause without regard to the ordinance's effect on any particular landowner. Are there circumstances in which a landowner would be better advised to raise an "as applied" due process challenge?

Suppose, for instance, that a municipality enacts an ordinance that bans all banks on the ground floor of buildings in the municipality's downtown business district. The municipality's stated reason for the ordinance is that banks, unlike retail stores, generate no sales tax revenue for the municipality. Landowner owns a number of buildings, and knows that banks will pay twice the rent for ground floor space as other prospective tenants. Does it matter whether the landowner advances a facial attack on the exclusion of banks, or instead argues that the ordinance, as applied to its parcels, violates the Due Process clause?

In Napleton v. Village of Hinsdale, 229 Ill.2d 296, 891 N.E.2d 839 (2008), the Illinois Supreme Court upheld such an ordinance against a facial challenge, holding that the municipality's effort to generate sales tax revenues precluded a determination that the ordinance was invalid on its face. The court, however, suggested (relying on past Illinois cases) that in the case of an as-applied challenge, courts would be required to balance "the gain to the public against the specific burdens experienced by an individual property owner." *Id.* at 318, 891 N.E.2d at 852. If one adopts the approach articulated by the Illinois Supreme Court, what is the difference between an "as applied" due process challenge and a takings challenge?

4.   Should a lawyer in a case like *Town of Rhine* rely exclusively on the Due Process Clause in challenging an ordinance that, at least arguably, does not promote health, safety, morals, or general welfare? What other claims might be available to the landowner? Even the cases cited in *Town of Rhine* do not rely exclusively on the Due Process Clause. *See* Sheerr v. Township of Evesham, 184 N.J.Super. 11, 445 A.2d 46 (1982) (relying in part on the Takings Clause and in part on substantive due process); Marshall v. Village of Wappingers Falls, 28 A.D.2d 542, 279 N.Y.S.2d 654 (1967) (relying on statutory requirement that zoning be in conformity with a comprehensive plan).

Suppose you were representing a landowner today who wanted to challenge an ordinance like the one enacted by the Town of Rhine. Would you advance a takings claim? A substantive due process claim? A claim that the ordinance exceeds the town's zoning power under the state enabling act? A claim that the ordinance is not in accordance with a comprehensive plan? *Cf.* Napleton v. Village of Hinsdale, 229 Ill.2d 296, 322 Ill.Dec. 548, 891 N.E.2d 839 (2008) (combining facial due process challenge with complaint that ordinance was not enacted pursuant to a comprehensive plan).

What obstacles might there be to advancing any of these claims? Can the landowner advance them all in the same case?

5.   *Arbitrariness as a Zoning Concept.* Note that in the last paragraph of the opinion in *Town of Rhine*, the court labels the ordinance as "arbitrary and unreasonable." Other courts use the terminology "arbitrary and capricious." Those labels are closely tied to the "health, safety, morals, or general welfare" formulation; if an ordinance does not promote health, safety, morals, or general welfare, then the municipality had no good reason for enacting it, and as a result, the ordinance was arbitrary.

6.   Consider now the substance of the landowner's claim in *Town of Rhine.* Why would the town enact an ordinance that permits no uses? Would the court have reached a different result if the ordinance had permitted agricultural uses without a conditional use permit, but authorized other uses only with a permit? If so, why?

Does the court hold that due process requires every ordinance to permit at least one use without a conditional use permit? If not, how can the court conclude that the town's ordinance is invalid on its face (as opposed to being invalid as applied to landowner's parcel)?

7. Although state courts have often been more hospitable to substantive due process claims than federal courts, even in state courts, due process challenges face an uphill battle. The California courts are notorious for taking a deferential approach to local zoning decisions. For an argument that state courts should take an expansive view of the Due Process Clause in land use cases, *see* J. Peter Byrne, Due Process Land Use Claims After Lingle, 34 Ecology L.Q. 471 (2007).

8. Return to the *United Artists* case. In light of the typical hostility federal courts have displayed toward substantive due process claims involving local zoning actions, why did United Artists bring suit in federal court?

What remedy did United Artists seek? Would United Artists have been content with a declaration that it was entitled to development approval? Why not? If United Artists would have been content with an award of declaratory or injunctive relief, would United Artists have been better off advancing its due process claim in state or federal court?

How likely is it that a state court would have awarded money damages against the municipality? Does that explain United Artists' decision to proceed in federal court?

III. DISCRIMINATION CLAIMS: EQUAL PROTECTION AND THE FAIR HOUSING ACT

The United States Constitution's Equal Protection Clause provides that "[n]o state shall . . . deny to any person within its jurisdiction the equal protection of the laws." Equal protection claims generally involve questions of classification. An equal protection plaintiff typically argues that a government official (or a legislative body) has drawn distinctions that discriminated against persons in a particular class without adequate justification. The focus on classification is what distinguishes equal protection claims from due process claims.

Classification plays a central role in the process of regulating land use. Drafting a zoning ordinance requires line-drawing; the ordinance will permit some uses and prohibit others. An ordinance may permit sit-down restaurants downtown, but not take out restaurants. It may permit single-family homes but prohibit two-family homes. Those whose uses are prohibited may challenge the lines the ordinance has drawn. Moreover, sometimes landowners may allege unequal treatment not in the language of the ordinance, but in individualized determinations on permits and variances. Often, unhappy landowners allege equal protection violations; on other occasions, they invoke federal statutes—particularly the Fair Housing Act. This section considers the issues raised by those challenges.

In theory, all land use restrictions are subject to equal protection challenge. But most challenges will fail because equal protection doctrine generally upholds governmental distinctions when the governmental body offers a rational basis for the challenged distinction. Almost all governmental distinctions satisfy the rational basis test.

By contrast, when the governmental distinction disadvantages a suspect class (for example, a racial minority group), or restricts a fundamental right, the governmental body must meet a higher standard. Typically, the government's interest must be "compelling" and the regulation must be closely related (narrowly tailored) to that governmental interest.

The Supreme Court does not, however, apply an "all or nothing" approach. Sometimes, for instance, courts classify a class not as "suspect" but as "quasi-suspect" (gender is the archetypal example), and apply an intermediate level of scrutiny. Much of the focus in equal protection litigation generally is on establishing what level of scrutiny applies. Keep this oversimplified framework in mind as you consider the materials in this section.

A. DISCRIMINATORY LINE-DRAWING

Hernandez v. City of Hanford

Supreme Court of California, 2007
41 Cal.4th 279, 159 P.3d 33, 59 Cal.Rptr.3d 442

■ GEORGE, C. J.

This case involves a constitutional challenge to a zoning ordinance enacted by the City of Hanford in 2003. In order to protect the economic viability of Hanford's downtown commercial district—a prominent feature of which is a large number of regionally well-regarded retail furniture stores—the challenged ordinance generally prohibits the sale of furniture in another commercial district in Hanford (currently designated the Planned Commercial or PC district) that contains a large shopping mall in which several department stores as well as other retail stores are located. At the same time, the ordinance creates a limited exception to the general prohibition on the sale of furniture in the PC district, permitting large department stores (those with 50,000 or more square feet of floor space) located within that district to sell furniture within a specifically prescribed area (occupying no more than 2,500 square feet of floor space) within the department store.

The owners of a "stand-alone" home furnishings and mattress store located within the PC district, who wished to sell bedroom furniture along with mattresses and home accessories (such as lamps and carpets) in their store, brought this action contesting the validity of the foregoing provisions of the zoning ordinance.

I

In 1989, the City of Hanford amended its general plan to provide for a new commercial district in the vicinity of 12th Avenue and Lacey Boulevard. This new district originally was designated the "Regional Commercial" district but later was renamed the Planned Commercial or PC district. The district encompassed several hundred acres of land and was intended to accommodate the location of malls, large "big box" stores, and other retail uses.

At trial, Jim Beath, the city's community development director, testified regarding the background of the city's adoption of the new district in 1989. (Beath had been the city's community development director in 1989 and continued to occupy that position at the time of trial in 2005.) Beath explained that when the city was considering the creation of the new district in 1989, it was concerned that the extent of anticipated commercial development in the proposed district might well have a negative effect on the city's downtown commercial district. In light of that concern, the city council appointed the Retail Strategy Development Committee (the Committee) "made up of people from the mall area as well as the downtown district and other citizens." The Committee was asked to propose land use rules for the new district that would "provide for the large box and other kinds of retail use that the City ... had grown to need and yet still make sure that [the new district] didn't have a negative impact on the downtown district."

The Committee ultimately recommended that certain designated uses generally not be permitted in the new district, and Beath testified that those uses "were ones that were already established in the downtown district that they didn't want to see removed from the downtown district and relocate[d] out at the planned commercial district, and those were car dealerships, banks, professional offices, and furniture stores." In establishing the new district, the city council limited the uses that were to be permitted in that district in line with the Committee's recommendations.

[After the city created the new PC district, Hernandez, who owned a furniture store in downtown Hanford, sought to establish a new business in the district. Questions arose about the meaning of the ordinance, which prohibited sale of furniture, but permitted sale of "home furnishings." City officials notified Hernandez that the city had uniformly interpreted the ordinance to permit lamps, wall hangings, and other accessories, but not furniture. Hernandez nevertheless opened a "home furnishings" store, selling mattresses and some bedroom furniture. A city inspector cited Hernandez for a zoning violation, prompting Hernandez to complain to the city that the zoning code was being applied in a discriminatory fashion because department stores were selling furniture and had not been cited by the city. As a result, the city considered amendments to clarify the ordinance—eds.]

Ultimately, on July 15, 2003, the city council adopted the amendment to the city zoning provisions relating to the sale of furniture in the PC district that is challenged in this case, Hanford Ordinance 03–03 (Ordinance No. 03–03).

Section 1 of Ordinance No. 03–03 adds definitions of "department store," "furniture," and "home furnishing accessories" to the general zoning provisions of the Hanford Municipal Code. "Department store" is defined as a retail store of at least 50,000 square feet "within which a variety of merchandise is displayed . . . for sale in departments," and the section further provides that a department store within the PC district may display and sell furniture in only one location (and on only one level within that location) having a total floor space of no more than 2,500 square feet. "Furniture" is defined as "the things placed in a room which equips it for living," but "[h]ome appliances, outdoor/patio furniture, wall cabinets, garage storage units and home furnishing accessories as defined in this [s]ection" are excluded from the definition of furniture for purposes of the zoning law. "Home furnishing accessories," in turn, are defined as "compl[e]mentary or decorative items placed in a room to accentuate the furniture," such as "curtains, draperies, blinds, . . . mirrors, pictures, . . . rugs, vases, . . . floor lamps, [and] table lamps," but as not including furniture.

Section 2 of Ordinance No. 03–03 adds as permissible uses within the PC district: "Department Stores" as defined in the ordinance, "Home Furnishing Accessories" as defined in the ordinance, and "Stores, which sell mattresses and metal bed frames with basic headboards and footboards that do not include shelves, drawers or sitting areas." Finally, section 3 of the ordinance adds a paragraph to the PC zoning provisions that specifically states: "The sale of furniture is prohibited in the PC zone district except by Department Stores in accordance with the definition of Department Stores" as set forth in the ordinance.

Accordingly, the ordinance in question generally prohibits the sale of furniture in the PC district, but at the same time creates a limited exception permitting a large department store within the PC district to display and sell furniture within a single location in the store measuring no more than 2,500 square feet.

Shortly after the ordinance was enacted, plaintiffs filed the present action against the city, challenging the validity of the ordinance on a number of grounds. Plaintiffs' complaint contended that the ordinance was invalid (1) because it was enacted for the primary purpose of regulating economic competition, and (2) because it violated the equal protection clauses of the federal and state Constitutions.

II

Before reaching the equal protection issue . . . we turn first to the more general (and more sweeping) contention that plaintiffs raised below and upon which they continue to rely in this court—that the zoning ordinance at issue is invalid because the "primary purpose" of the ordinance's general prohibition of the sale of furniture in the PC district assertedly was to "regulat[e] economic competition."

Our court has not previously had occasion to address the question whether a municipality, in order to protect or preserve the economic viability of its downtown business district or neighborhood shopping areas, may enact a zoning ordinance that regulates or controls competition by placing limits on potentially competing commercial activities or development in other areas of the municipality. More than a half-century ago, however, this court explained that "[i]t is well settled that a municipality may divide land into districts and prescribe regulations governing the uses permitted therein, and that zoning ordinances, when reasonable in object and not arbitrary in operation, constitute a justifiable exercise of police power." Lockard v. City of Los Angeles (1949) 33 Cal. 2d 453, 460 [202 P.2d 38]; *see also* Associated Home Builders etc., Inc. v. City of Livermore (1976) 18 Cal. 3d 582, 604–605 [135 Cal. Rptr. 41, 557 P.2d 473]; *see generally* Cal. Const., art. XI, § 7; Gov. Code, § 65800 *et seq.* [E]ven when the regulation of economic competition reasonably can be viewed as a direct and intended effect of a zoning ordinance or action, so long as the primary purpose of the ordinance or action—that is, its principal and ultimate objective—is not the impermissible *private* anticompetitive goal of protecting or disadvantaging a particular favored or disfavored business or individual, but instead is the advancement of a legitimate *public* purpose—such as the preservation of a municipality's downtown business district for the benefit of the municipality as a whole—the ordinance reasonably relates to the general welfare of the municipality and constitutes a legitimate exercise of the municipality's police power. *Accord*, Lockard v. City of Los Angeles, *supra*, 33 Cal. 2d 453, 466 ["in determining what uses should be permitted in the 12-block strip, the legislative body was, of course, entitled to consider the effect of such uses on the surrounding areas, and to weigh the possibility of injury to those areas by reason of permitting various types of activity as against the desirability of allowing such uses"]; *see generally* 1 Rathkopf, The Law of Zoning and Planning (rev. ed. 1998) § 2:20, pp. 2–59 to 2–61; Strom, Land Use Controls: Effects on Business Competition II (1980) 6 Zoning & Planning L. Rep. 41, 46.

In the present case, it is clear that the zoning ordinance's general prohibition on the sale of furniture in the PC district—although concededly intended, at least in part, to regulate competition—was adopted to promote the legitimate public purpose of preserving the economic viability of the Hanford downtown business district, rather than to serve any impermissible private anticompetitive purpose. Furthermore, as in *Ensign Bickford, supra*, 68 Cal. App. 3d 467, here the zoning ordinance's restrictions are aimed at regulating *"where,"* within the city," *id.* at p. 477, a particular type of business generally may be located, a very traditional zoning objective. Under these circumstances, we agree with the lower court's conclusion that the zoning ordinance cannot be found invalid as an improper limitation on competition.

III

As noted above, although the Court of Appeal agreed that the challenged zoning ordinance's general prohibition on the sale of furniture in the PC district is permissible, that court concluded the ordinance in question violates the equal protection clause by limiting the exception created by the ordinance to only the sale of furniture by large department stores, and not making the exception available to other retail stores wishing to sell furniture within the same amount of square footage permitted for furniture sales by large department stores. The Court of Appeal found that, in this context, the ordinance's disparate treatment of large department stores and other retail stores is not constitutionally permissible.

In evaluating the Court of Appeal's resolution of this issue, we begin with the question of the appropriate equal protection standard applicable in this case. As explained in Warden v. State Bar (1999) 21 Cal. 4th 628 [88 Cal. Rptr. 2d 283, 982 P.2d 154], there are "two principal standards or tests that generally have been applied by the courts of this state and the United States Supreme Court in reviewing classifications that are challenged under the equal protection clause of the Fourteenth Amendment of the United States Constitution or article I, section 7, of the California Constitution. . . . The first is the basic and conventional standard for reviewing economic and social welfare legislation in which there is a "discrimination" or differentiation of treatment between classes or individuals. It manifests restraint by the judiciary in relation to the discretionary act of a co-equal branch of government; in so doing it invests legislation involving such differentiated treatment with a presumption of constitutionality and "requir[es] merely that distinctions drawn by a challenged statute bear some rational relationship to a conceivable legitimate state purpose." This first basic equal protection standard generally is referred to as the "rational relationship" or "rational basis" standard.

As further explained in Warden v. State Bar, *supra*, 21 Cal. 4th at p. 641, the second equal protection standard is "[a] more stringent test [that] is applied . . . in cases involving 'suspect classifications' or touching on 'fundamental interests.'" Here the courts adopt "an attitude of active and critical analysis, subjecting the classifications to strict scrutiny. Under the strict standard applied in such cases, *the state* bears the burden of establishing not only that it has a *compelling* interest which justifies the law but that the distinctions drawn by the law are *necessary* to further its purpose." [Citation omitted.] *Warden, supra*, 21 Cal. 4th at p. 641. This second standard generally is referred to as the "strict scrutiny" standard.

The zoning ordinance at issue in the present case does not involve suspect classifications or touch upon fundamental interests and thus, as the Court of Appeal recognized and as all parties agree, the applicable standard under which plaintiffs' equal protection challenge properly must be evaluated is the rational relationship or rational basis standard.

As noted above, in finding the exception set forth in the ordinance invalid under the rational relationship test, the Court of Appeal reasoned that "with the blanket 2,500-square-foot restrictions on furniture in the PC zone, the small retailer poses the same potential threat, if any, to the downtown merchants as the larger store. Thus, limiting the furniture sales exception to stores with more than 50,000 square feet is arbitrary. A rational relationship between the size classification and the goal of protecting downtown simply does not exist."

We disagree with the Court of Appeal's determination that the ordinance violates the equal protection clause. The Court of Appeal's conclusion effectively rests on the premise that there was only a single purpose underlying the challenged ordinance—the protection of furniture stores located in the downtown business district from potential competition by retail establishments conducting business within the PC district. Because the Court of Appeal was of the view that the disparate treatment in the ordinance's exception of large department stores and other stores was not rationally related to *that* purpose, the appellate court concluded the exception was invalid.

Both the terms and legislative history of the measure at issue disclose, however, that the ordinance was intended to serve *multiple* purposes: to protect the economic health and viability of the city's downtown furniture stores, but to do so in a manner that did not threaten or detract from the city's ability to attract and retain large department stores in the PC district. Past cases establish that the equal protection clause does not preclude a governmental entity from adopting a legislative measure that is aimed at achieving multiple objectives, even when such objectives in some respects may be in tension or conflict.

[T]he Hanford ordinance challenged here clearly was intended to serve multiple purposes. The city desired to protect the economic viability of its downtown business district, but at the same time it did not wish to diminish the financial benefits of the PC district for the large department stores that it wanted to attract and maintain in that district. Because the city viewed large department stores as particularly significant elements of the PC district, and because the management of those stores had made clear the importance to them of retaining their ability to offer furniture sales that typically were offered by their sister stores in other locations, it was rational for the city to decide to provide an exception from the general prohibition on furniture sales in the PC district for such large department stores and only such stores. The circumstance that the city also decided to limit the exemption afforded to department stores by placing a square-foot limit on the area within each store in which furniture could be displayed does not in any manner detract from the rationality of limiting the exception to large department stores.

Accordingly, contrary to the Court of Appeal's determination, we conclude that the ordinance's differential treatment of large department stores and other retail stores is rationally related to one of the legitimate legislative purposes of the ordinance—the purpose of attracting and retaining large department stores within the PC district. The Court of Appeal's resolution of this issue, which would have required the city to extend the ordinance's 2,500-square-foot exception for furniture sales to *all* retail stores within the PC district, would have undermined the ordinance's overall objective of permitting the sale of furniture in the PC district only to the extent such activity is necessary to serve the city's interest in attracting and retaining large department stores in that district.

IV

In sum, the Court of Appeal erred in invalidating the ordinance at issue. The judgment of the Court of Appeal is reversed.

■ KENNARD, J., BAXTER, J., WERDEGAR, J., CHIN, J., MORENO, J., and CORRIGAN, J., concurred.

NOTES AND QUESTIONS

1.   A municipality enacts a zoning ordinance that requires a minimum square footage of 3,000 feet per store for all stores in a new retail district. A group of small retailers complains that the ordinance violates the Equal Protection Clause by arbitrarily excluding them from operating within the district. How should the municipality respond to the complaint? Would the municipality prevail?

2.   What justification did the court in *Hernandez* find persuasive in rejecting the equal protection challenge? Is there any ordinance that would *not* be sustained on a justification similar to the one offered in *Hernandez?*

3.   The court in *Hernandez* investigates legislative history and considers the city's actual intent. In a case that does not involve a suspect class, should actual intent matter, or should it be enough if the city could come up with some rational basis for its classification?

4.   Size restrictions are not limited to commercial districts. Suppose a municipality's zoning ordinance imposes a minimum lot size of three acres for each home. How could a municipality defend the minimum lot size?

What strategies would you recommend to a developer who wants to challenge the minimum lot size?

5. Suppose a municipality imposes a minimum square footage for all homes within a district (or within the entire municipality). Municipal officials make it clear that the square footage requirement is designed to ensure that all new development "pays for itself"—that is, that the new residents are wealthy enough that taxes they pay will more than cover for all of the services they consume. Does this sort of fiscal zoning constitute an equal protection violation? Should it?

Zoning as a Restraint on Competition

The court in *Hernandez* concluded that a significant purpose of Hanford's ordinance was a desire to preserve the downtown business district (presumably by protecting it from competition in the newly created PC district). Why is that a permissible governmental purpose? Shouldn't government provide a level playing field for new businesses and existing businesses? If consumers are unhappy with the service and amenities provided downtown, why should the municipality prevent competition from challenging the predominance of downtown?

Does municipal protection of existing businesses raise federal antitrust claims? At one time, local governments feared antitrust liability, but the Supreme Court effectively closed the door on that possibility in City of Columbia v. Omni Outdoor Advertising, Inc., 499 U.S. 365 (1991). In that case, the city had enacted an ordinance restricting the size, location, and spacing of billboards shortly after an out-of-state billboard company entered the local market, which had long been dominated by a local company. The ordinance disproportionally harmed new competitors, because the market leader already had billboards in place, and was less affected by the ordinance's spacing requirements. The out-of-state competitor brought suit, contending that city officials and the local company had engaged in an anticompetitive conspiracy. Although a number of federal courts of appeals had previously held that local governments could be liable for antitrust violations in cases of conspiracy, the Supreme Court rejected "any interpretation of the Sherman Act that would allow plaintiffs to look behind the actions of state sovereigns to base their claims on 'perceived conspiracies to restrain trade' " *Id.* at 378 (citations omitted).

QUESTIONS

1. In light of *City of Columbia*, what was the basis for the anti-competition claim in *Hernandez?*

2. Why did the California Supreme Court reject the claim advanced in *Hernandez* that the ordinance restricted competition in violation of state law?

3. In light of *Hernandez*, when, if ever, would you expect a state law claim to succeed? What does a municipality have to prove to defeat a claim that the ordinance constitutes an invalid restraint on competition?

B. "Class of One" Claims

In *Hernandez*, as in most equal protection cases, the landowner objected to a classification—the zoning ordinance permitted furniture sales in stores larger than 50,000 square feet, but not in stores measuring 50,000 square feet or less. Landowner identified herself as a member of a group—persons seeking to sell furniture in small stores—that was disadvantaged by the classification in the zoning ordinance.

Suppose, however, the landowner does not identify herself as a member of a group, but instead contends that she was singled out for unfavorable treatment. Does that allegation suffice to state an equal protection claim? The next two cases consider that issue:

Village of Willowbrook v. Olech

Supreme Court of the United States, 2000
528 U.S. 562

■ Per Curiam.

Respondent Grace Olech and her late husband Thaddeus asked petitioner Village of Willowbrook to connect their property to the municipal water supply. The Village at first conditioned the connection on the Olechs granting the Village a 33-foot easement. The Olechs objected, claiming that the Village only required a 15-foot easement from other property owners seeking access to the water supply. After a 3-month delay, the Village relented and agreed to provide water service with only a 15-foot easement.

Olech sued the Village claiming that the Village's demand of an additional 18-foot easement violated the Equal Protection Clause of the Fourteenth Amendment. Olech asserted that the 33-foot easement demand was "irrational and wholly arbitrary"; that the Village's demand was actually motivated by ill will resulting from the Olechs' previous filing of an unrelated, successful lawsuit against the Village; and that the Village acted either with the intent to deprive Olech of her rights or in reckless disregard of her rights. App. 10, 12.

The District Court dismissed the lawsuit pursuant to Federal Rule of Civil Procedure 12(b)(6) for failure to state a cognizable claim under the Equal Protection Clause. Relying on Circuit precedent, the Court of Appeals for the Seventh Circuit reversed, holding that a plaintiff can allege an equal protection violation by asserting that state action was motivated solely by a " 'spiteful effort to "get" him for reasons wholly unrelated to any legitimate state objective.' " 160 F.3d 386, 387 (CA7 1998) (quoting Esmail v. Macrane, 53 F.3d 176, 180 (CA7 1995)). It determined that Olech's complaint sufficiently alleged such a claim. 160 F.3d at 388. We granted certiorari to determine whether the Equal Protection Clause gives rise to a cause of action on behalf of a "class of one" where the plaintiff did not allege membership in a class or group.

Our cases have recognized successful equal protection claims brought by a "class of one," where the plaintiff alleges that she has been intentionally treated differently from others similarly situated and that there is no rational basis for the difference in treatment. *See* Sioux City Bridge Co. v. Dakota County, 260 U.S. 441, 67 L. Ed. 340, 43 S. Ct. 190 (1923); Allegheny Pittsburgh Coal Co. v. Commission of Webster Cty., 488 U.S. 336, 102 L. Ed. 2d 688, 109 S. Ct. 633 (1989). In so doing, we have explained that " 'the purpose of the equal protection clause of the Fourteenth Amendment is to secure every person within the State's jurisdiction against intentional and arbitrary discrimination, whether occasioned by express terms of a statute or by its improper execution through duly constituted agents.' " *Sioux City Bridge Co., supra*, at 445 (quoting Sunday Lake Iron Co. v. Township of Wakefield, 247 U.S. 350, 352, 62 L. Ed. 1154, 38 S. Ct. 495 (1918)).

That reasoning is applicable to this case. Olech's complaint can fairly be construed as alleging that the Village intentionally demanded a 33-foot easement as a condition of connecting her property to the municipal water supply where the Village required only a 15-foot easement from other similarly situated property owners. *See* Conley v. Gibson, 355 U.S. 41, 45–46, 2 L. Ed. 2d 80, 78 S. Ct. 99 (1957). The complaint also alleged that the Village's demand was "irrational and wholly arbitrary" and that the Village ultimately connected her property after receiving a clearly adequate 15-foot easement. These allegations, quite apart from the Village's subjective motivation, are sufficient to state a claim for relief under traditional equal protection analysis. We therefore affirm the judgment of the Court of Appeals, but do not reach the alternative theory of "subjective ill will" relied on by that court.

It is so ordered.

■ JUSTICE BREYER, concurring in the result.

The Solicitor General and the village of Willowbrook have expressed concern lest we interpret the Equal Protection Clause in this case in a way that would transform many ordinary violations of city or state law into violations of the Constitution. It might be thought that a rule that looks only to an intentional difference in treatment and a lack of a rational basis for that different treatment would work such a transformation. Zoning decisions, for example, will often, perhaps almost always, treat one landowner differently from another, and one might claim that, when a city's zoning authority takes an action that fails to conform to a city zoning regulation, it lacks a "rational basis" for its action (at least if the regulation in question is reasonably clear).

This case, however, does not directly raise the question whether the simple and common instance of a faulty zoning decision would violate the Equal Protection Clause. That is because the Court of Appeals found that in this case respondent had alleged an extra factor as well— a factor that the Court of Appeals called "vindictive action," "illegitimate animus," or "ill will." 160 F.3d 386, 388 (CA7 1998). And, in that respect, the court said this case resembled Esmail v. Macrane, 53 F.3d 176 (CA7 1995), because the Esmail plaintiff had alleged that the municipality's differential treatment "was the result not of prosecutorial discretion honestly (even if ineptly—even if arbitrarily) exercised but of an illegitimate desire to 'get' him." 160 F.3d at 388.

In my view, the presence of that added factor in this case is sufficient to minimize any concern about transforming run-of-the-mill zoning cases into cases of constitutional right. For this reason, along with the others mentioned by the Court, I concur in the result.

Loesel v. City of Frankenmuth

United States Court of Appeals for the Sixth Circuit, 2012
692 F.3d 452

■ RONALD LEE GILMAN, CIRCUIT JUDGE.

This appeal concerns the legality of actions taken by the City of Frankenmuth (the City) to keep a Wal-Mart supercenter from being built on land owned by the Loesel family in Frankenmuth Township (the Township). As the result of a post purchase-agreement ordinance that restricted the size of any new buildings on the property to 65,000 square feet or less, Wal-Mart Real Estate Business Trust (Wal-Mart) terminated its conditional agreement to purchase the Loesels' land for $4 million.

The Loesels sued the City for damages, claiming that the selective zoning ordinance violated their rights under the Equal Protection Clause of the Fourteenth Amendment to the U.S. Constitution. A jury agreed, awarding the Loesels $3.6 million in damages. For the reasons set forth below, we **REVERSE** the judgment of the district court and **REMAND** the case for further proceedings consistent with this opinion.

I. BACKGROUND

A. Factual background

Frankenmuth, "Michigan's Little Bavaria," is one of the top tourist destinations in Michigan. Despite its popularity with tourists, Frankenmuth maintains a small town atmosphere with a population of 4,838 in the City and 2,049 in the Township, according to the 2000 U.S. Census (the last Census taken before the events relevant to this case occurred). The City is famous for its Bavarian-themed stores, restaurants such as the Bavarian Inn and Zehnder's serving family-style chicken dinners, and its gift shops. Bronner's Christmas

Wonderland, the world's largest year-round Christmas store, draws over two million visitors annually.

The plaintiffs (collectively, the Loesels), are the co-owners of a 37-acre tract of land that borders Main Street just outside the Frankenmuth city limits. They inherited the property from their mother when she died in 2003. A 2003 property-tax appraisal valued the land at $95,000.

The Loesels' property has been used as farmland for nearly 100 years. Although not within the City's boundaries, the property is within the urban growth area that was established jointly by the City and the Township in 1985 to confine and guide urban growth in order to retain the character of the Frankenmuth community. The City's and the Township's growth is guided by their Joint Growth Management Plan (the Plan) that sets forth the goals for Frankenmuth's expansion. In 1985, the first version of the Plan was drafted and, in June 2005, the second version of the Plan was formally adopted.

The two governments agreed as part of the Plan that they should "[p]romote compact residential and commercial development inside the urban limit line," which included the Loesels' property. To promote growth, the western portion of the Loesels' property along Main Street, approximately 15 acres in size, was zoned as Commercial Local Planned Unit Development (CL–PUD), with the remaining 22 acres to the east designated as Residential Planned Unit Development (R–PUD). Permitted uses for CL–PUD-zoned properties include developments that "provide principally for sale of goods and services to meet the general needs of the residents of the Frankenmuth community, including but not limited to grocery, department, drug and hardware stores, financial institutions, professional and personal service offices and transportation sale and service businesses." City of Frankenmuth, Mich., Zoning & Planning Code § 5.241.3(1) (2009).

At the time the Loesels inherited the property, the land was being leased to a tenant farmer. In 2004, however, the Loesels were approached by a real-estate broker who told them he had a client interested in purchasing their property. The Loesels met with the broker and discovered that he represented Wal-Mart. Because the western portion of the Loesels' property abuts Main Street and is commercially zoned, Wal-Mart was interested in buying the property to build a store.

In early 2005, City officials became aware that Wal-Mart was interested in purchasing and developing the Loesels' property. [The Loesels entered into an agreement to sell to Wal-Mart, conditioned on feasibility of the project. Under the terms of the agreement, Wal-Mart had 180 days to withdraw without penalty. Meanwhile, City Manager Charles Graham quickly expressed opposition, as did a number of local business people. The city enacted a moratorium on construction of any facility with an area of 70,000 square feet or more in order to consider legislation. Graham then introduced the idea of an ordinance limiting retail establishments to 65,000 square feet, but the tourist-oriented businesses in the area, including the Bavarian Mall and Bronner's Christmas Wonderland, were concerned about the potential effect of a 65,000 square foot limitation—eds.]

As a result of these and other concerns, Graham, with the assistance and input of others, decided to shrink the size of the area affected by the proposed ordinance even further, to include only CL–PUD-zoned properties. This meant that the only properties affected by the ordinance were the Loesels' property and a handful of much smaller parcels in its immediate vicinity. The proposed ordinance excluded the part of the town immediately south of the Loesels' property, including the Bavarian Mall and Bronner's.

This version of the ordinance was ultimately adopted on December 7, 2005 as Ordinance No.2005–10. It established the "Commercial Local Planned Unit Development Overlay Zone (CL–PUDOZ) encompassing all CL–PUD (Commercial Local Planned Unit Development) zoning districts in the City of Frankenmuth" and required that the floor area of any retail building in the CL–PUDOZ "shall not exceed sixty-five thousand (65,000) square feet."

Wal-Mart and the Loesels, apparently unaware of the ordinance's passage, amended their purchase agreement on the same date to state that Wal-Mart would buy all 37 acres of the Loesels' property for $4 million. The amendment also provided that Wal-Mart had to put a $5,000 nonrefundable deposit into escrow.

Wal-Mart continued for the time being to move forward with the project and attended a pre-application meeting with the City and the Township on January 13, 2006. Following the meeting, the City sent a list of additional items that would be needed for Wal-Mart to proceed with the application process, such as traffic-impact and economic-impact studies and a landscaping plan that complied with storm-water drainage regulations. Wal-Mart was directed to submit these items before a second pre-application meeting was scheduled. In light of the new size-cap ordinance, however, Wal-Mart declined to continue with the approval process and never again communicated with the City about the proposal.

In a letter dated March 16, 2006, Wal-Mart informed the Loesels that it intended to terminate the purchase agreement pursuant to the "feasibility" clause. The Loesels received the $5,000 from the escrow account and Wal-Mart recovered its $50,000 deposit. A representative from Wal-Mart testified (in a deposition that was read into the record at trial) that the agreement was terminated because Wal-Mart would not have been able to build its proposed supercenter on the Loesels' property given the 65,000-square-foot restriction.

B.   Procedural background

In March 2008, the Loesels filed a complaint against the City. They brought suit under 42 U.S.C. § 1983, alleging that the City's 65,000-square-foot zoning restriction violated their rights under the Equal Protection, Due Process, Privileges or Immunities, and Commerce Clauses of the U.S. Constitution. As a remedy, they sought $4 million in compensatory damages, attorney fees under 42 U.S.C. § 1988, costs, and an order declaring that the ordinance is unconstitutional.

The district court granted summary judgment for the City on all but the Loesels' equal protection claim.

A trial was held on the Loesels' facial equal protection claim in February and March 2010. The City moved for judgment as a matter of law following the close of the Loesels' case-in-chief and again at the close of its own proof. Both times the district court declined to rule, taking the matter "under advisement pending the determination of the jury." The jury then returned a verdict for the Loesels and awarded them $3.6 million in damages.

Shortly thereafter, the City filed a renewed motion for judgment as a matter of law or, in the alternative, for a new trial or remittitur, which the district court denied in September 2010.

II. ANALYSIS

A.   Judgment as a matter of law

Here, the City argues that there was insufficient evidence for the jury to reasonably conclude that the 65,000-square-foot size restriction violated the Equal Protection Clause.

In this case, the Loesels pursued their equal protection claim under the "class-of-one" theory recognized by the Supreme Court in *Village of Willowbrook v. Olech,* 528 U.S. 562, 120 S.Ct. 1073, 145 L.Ed.2d 1060 (2000) (per curiam) (holding that the Olechs sufficiently stated an equal protection claim where they alleged that, as a condition of being connected to the municipal water supply, the village demanded a 33-foot easement from the Olechs but required an easement of only 15 feet from similarly situated neighbors). Class-of-one claims are generally viewed skeptically because such claims have the potential to turn into an exercise in which juries are second-guessing the legislative process:

> In the wake of *Olech,* the lower courts have struggled to define the contours of class-of-one cases. All have recognized that, unless carefully circumscribed, the concept of a class-of-one equal protection claim could effectively provide a federal cause of action for review of almost every executive and administrative decision made by state actors. It is always possible for persons aggrieved by government action to allege, and almost always possible to produce evidence, that they were treated differently from others, with regard to everything from

zoning to licensing to speeding to tax evaluation. It would become the task of federal courts and juries, then, to inquire into the grounds for differential treatment and to decide whether those grounds were sufficiently reasonable to satisfy equal protection review. This would constitute the federal courts as general-purpose second-guessers of the reasonableness of broad areas of state and local decisionmaking: a role that is both ill-suited to the federal courts and offensive to state and local autonomy in our federal system.

Jennings v. City of Stillwater, 383 F.3d 1199, 1210–11 (10th Cir. 2004) (footnote omitted).

That is why a plaintiff must overcome a "heavy burden" to prevail based on the class-of-one theory. The Loesels must show that they were treated differently than those similarly situated in all material respects. In addition, they

must show that the adverse treatment they experienced was so unrelated to the achievement of any combination of legitimate purposes that the court can only conclude that the government's actions were irrational. This showing is made either by negativing every conceivable reason for the government's actions or by demonstrating that the actions were motivated by animus or ill-will.

Rondigo, L.L.C. v. Twp. of Richmond, 641 F.3d 673, 682 (6th Cir. 2011). (citations and internal quotation marks omitted).

1. Similarly situated

The Loesels have the burden of demonstrating that they were treated differently than other property owners who were similarly situated in *all material respects.*

"In determining whether individuals are 'similarly situated,' a court should 'not demand exact correlation, but should instead seek relevant similarity.'" *Bench Billboard v. City of Cincinnati,* 675 F.3d 974, 987 (6th Cir. 2012) (quoting *Perry v. McGinnis,* 209 F.3d 597, 601 (6th Cir. 2000) (citation omitted)). Furthermore, "determining whether individuals are similarly situated is generally a factual issue for the jury." *Eggleston v. Bieluch,* 203 Fed.Appx. 257, 264 (11th Cir. 2006).

The Loesels asserted at trial that the two local properties containing the area's largest retail establishments—the Bavarian Mall and Bronner's—were similarly situated to their property. But the City contends that, as a matter of law, there are material differences between the Loesels' property and the other two properties. The district court disagreed with the City and ruled that sufficient evidence existed for a jury to reasonably conclude that the Bavarian Mall and Bronner's were similarly situated to the store that Wal-Mart proposed to build on the Loesels' property:

> [The City] contend[s] that Plaintiffs are not similarly situated to Bronner's and Kroger because the stores sell different products than Wal-Mart and because the properties are zoned differently. [The City] has not explained how any differences between the products to be sold by Wal-Mart and those sold by either Bronner's or Kroger is relevant and material to the enactment of a size-cap and the equal protection analysis.

The district court's analysis implies that the proper comparison is between the stores on the properties (or, in the case of the Loesels, the store proposed for their property), rather than between the property owners or the properties themselves. And at times the court conflated the Loesels with Wal-Mart. The relevant question, however, should be framed in terms of the properties and their owners, not in terms of the stores located on those properties. In other words, the proper comparison is not between the supercenter that Wal-Mart wanted to develop, on the one hand, and the Bavarian Mall and Bronner's on the other, but between the Loesels' property and the properties on which the Bavarian Mall and Bronner's sit.

The first property that the Loesels assert is similarly situated to theirs is the parcel on which the Bavarian Mall is located. This strip mall is the second-largest commercial development in Frankenmuth, located on the east side of Main Street just south of the Loesels' property. The properties are in fact so close that only two small parcels of land separate them. Originally constructed in 1973, the Bavarian Mall has retail space measuring 104,000 square feet. Its tenants include a Kroger grocery store and a gas station.

Two brothers, Dave and Tom Johnston, own a controlling interest in the Bavarian Mall. Dave was a member of the Downtown Development Authority (DDA) in 2005, and Tom had previously been on the City Council. Tom was the person who filed the articles of incorporation for Citizens for Frankenmuth First in August 2005.

The 45-acre parcel on which Bronner's Christmas Wonderland sits is the other property that the Loesels assert is similarly situated to theirs. Located at the southern end of Main Street, two miles south of the Loesels' property, the parcel contains a 400,000 square-foot retail store. The owner of Bronner's is the Bronner family. Wayne Bronner, president and chief executive officer of Bronner's, was chairman of the DDA board of directors in 2005.

According to the City, the district court should have ruled as a matter of law that the Loesels' property is not similarly situated to the Bavarian Mall and Bronner's properties because of three alleged distinctions between them. The first alleged difference concerns the zoning classification: both the Bavarian Mall and Bronner's are located on B–3-zoned properties, whereas the portion of the Loesels' parcel affected by the ordinance is zoned CL–PUD.

The Loesels' respond by pointing out that this distinction is not a material one. Indeed, even City Manager Graham conceded that there was "no difference in terms of how the zoning treated the CL–PUD and the B–3" and that "essentially the same regulations" apply to both zones. He also acknowledged that, had the Loesels' property been inside the City limits in 1985 when the zones were first applied, "It would probably have been designated as B–3." The jury could therefore have reasonably concluded that the difference in "labels" for these commercially zoned properties is not material.

This leads to the City's second alleged distinction: that the Loesels' property differs from the Bavarian Mall and Bronner's properties because the Loesels' property is vacant land, whereas the properties containing the Bavarian Mall and Bronner's were already developed. The City's argument would have more force had it not previously designated the Loesels' property as CL–PUD. As part of the City's Plan, however, the promotion of commercial development is encouraged on the CL–PUD properties. Accordingly, the jury could have reasonably concluded that the developed/undeveloped distinction is not material.

The City's last alleged difference between the Loesels' property and the other two properties that it contends is material relates to their traffic capacities. Main Street is five lanes wide at the entrances to both the Bavarian Mall and Bronner's, but narrows to three lanes at the Loesels' property. The City contends that a three-lane road does not provide adequate traffic capacity for a store with over 65,000 square feet of sales space. Traffic-capacity considerations, however, are typically deferred until the development-application process. To prevent a development from being built where traffic capacity is inadequate, the City did not have to enact a size-restriction ordinance; it could have simply rejected the application on the basis of inadequate traffic capacity. Moreover, Main Street in front of the Loesels' property would have the same traffic capacity as at the other two locations simply by extending the extra two lanes the length of the property. These facts lessen the importance of the difference in traffic capacity to the point where the jury could have reasonably concluded that it is not material.

In sum, there is a genuine dispute of material fact as to whether the three properties are similarly situated. This means that the district court did not err in denying the City's renewed motion for judgment as a matter of law on this issue.

2. *Rational basis*

The City next contends that it is entitled to judgment as a matter of law on the issue of whether the zoning ordinance had a rational basis. Under rational basis review, the defendant "has no obligation to produce evidence to sustain the rationality of its actions; its choice is presumptively valid and may be based on rational speculation unsupported by evidence or empirical data." *TriHealth, Inc. v. Bd. of Comm'rs, Hamilton Cnty., Ohio,* 430 F.3d 783, 790 (6th Cir. 2005). The burden instead falls on the Loesels to "demonstrate that a government action lacks a rational basis . . . either by negativing every conceivable basis which might support the government action or by demonstrating that the challenged government action was motivated by animus or ill-will." *Warren v. City of Athens, Ohio,* 411 F.3d 697, 711 (6th Cir. 2005) (brackets and internal quotation marks omitted).

a. No-conceivable-basis theory

The City contends that the Loesels did not present evidence sufficient to refute every possible nondiscriminatory reason for enacting the 65,000 square-foot size restriction. It argues that the testimony of its municipal-land-use expert Donald Wortman demonstrated that a rational basis existed for applying the size limit to only CL–PUD-zoned properties. Wortman testified that several characteristics of the Loesels' property made it unsuitable for a large big-box retail store, including the parcel's inadequate depth (the CL–PUD portion of the Loesels' property is only 660 feet deep as opposed to the typical 1,000 feet or more of depth typical of large retail developments), its close vicinity to residential property, its inadequate traffic capacity and space for parking, and its potential storm-water retention issues.

Wortman then identified about one dozen parcels of land within Frankenmuth's urban growth area that he believed were better suited for the development of a big-box store than was the Loesels' property. He further reasoned that the ordinance bolstered the City's desire to maintain "a compact commercial core" in the downtown city center that is "pedestrian friendly [and] a benefit to the residents."

The Loesels respond by arguing that the jury correctly rejected Wortman's opinions because his testimony was undercut on cross-examination and by the testimony of City Manager Graham. Wortman conceded, for example, that he had no idea whether the parcels that he identified in the southern end of the City were available for sale, what the current uses of those properties were, or whether any of the parcels contained undeveloped wetlands or had appropriate road access.

Moreover, City Manager Graham contradicted Wortman's opinion that the Plan called for growth in the southern end of Frankenmuth rather than in the northern end. Graham testified that the Plan made no distinction between the two areas of the City.

In sum, a genuine dispute exists as to whether the ordinance lacked a rational basis. The jury could therefore have rejected Wortman's testimony in finding for the Loesels on this issue.

b. Animus or ill will

Finally, the City contends that the district court should have granted the City judgment as a matter of law on the issue of whether animus or ill will against the Loesels motivated the enactment of the 65,000-square-foot size restriction. The district court determined that a reasonable jury could conclude that the City harbored animus against the Loesels because no invitations or notices were sent to the Loesels concerning the city council meeting at which the proposed size-limitation ordinance was discussed. But the fact that the City was not cognizant of or proactively seeking the Loesels' opinions is a far cry from harboring animus or ill will. Animus is defined as "ill will, antagonism, or hostility usually controlled but deep-seated and sometimes virulent." *Webster's Third New International Dictionary, Unabridged* (2002). Similarly, ill will is defined as an "unfriendly feeling: animosity, hostility." *Id.* These definitions indicate that a showing of animus or ill will (hereinafter collectively referred to as "animus") requires more than simply failing to invite the Loesels to a meeting.

Although the Loesels presented abundant evidence showing that certain City officials, such as City Manager Graham, strongly opposed having a Wal-Mart supercenter in Frankenmuth, the animus had to be directed against the Loesels to be relevant to their claim. *See Taylor Acquisitions, L.L.C., v. City of Taylor,* 313 Fed.Appx. 826, 838 (6th Cir. 2009) (holding that the plaintiff had to show in its class-of-one equal protection claim that government officials expressed animus against the plaintiff, not against the development it was proposing); *see also Ziss Bros. Constr. Co. v. City of Independence, Ohio,* 439 Fed.Appx. 467, 479 (6th Cir. 2011) (concluding that the plaintiff failed to allege an equal protection violation based on animus where the plaintiff alleged that the animus of the defendant-city was directed at the plaintiff's proposed development plan and not at the plaintiff itself); *McDonald v. Vill. of Winnetka,* 371 F.3d 992, 1001 (7th Cir. 2004) (holding that a class-of-one claim may be established by showing that there "is a totally illegitimate animus toward the *plaintiff* by the defendant" (emphasis added) (internal quotation marks omitted)). The district court, therefore, should have granted the City's motion for judgment as a matter of law on the animus theory of liability.

This leaves us with the question of whether the district court's error requires that we remand the case for a new trial. Before deliberations, the jury was instructed that it could find the City liable under either the no-conceivable-basis or the animus theory of liability. The jury returned a general verdict form answering "Yes" to the following question of liability: "Did the plaintiff[s] prove their equal protection claim by a preponderance of the evidence?" But as determined above, only the no-conceivable-basis theory was properly submitted to the jury. Because nothing on the verdict form indicated which theory formed the basis for the jury's decision, the question is whether we may presume that the jury found for the Loesels' under the factually sufficient no-conceivable-basis theory or whether we must vacate the verdict and remand for a new trial.

[The court decided that it could not presume that the jury decided the case only on the no-conceivable-basis theory]. We therefore must vacate the judgment for the Loesels and remand this case for a new trial.

III. CONCLUSION

For all of the reasons set forth above, we **REVERSE** the judgment of the district court and **REMAND** the case for further proceedings consistent with this opinion.

NOTES AND QUESTIONS

1. Note the procedural posture of the *Olech* case. The Court held that the district court had improperly dismissed the complaint for failure to state a cognizable equal protection claim. Did the Court hold that Olech should succeed on her claim? The Court did not explain what Olech would have to prove in order to prevail on her equal protection claim. Courts have struggled with that issue since *Olech* was decided, as the *Loesel* case illustrates.

2. Suppose Mrs. Olech brings forth evidence that the village required a 15-foot easement from ten other landowners seeking access to the municipal water supply, while requiring a 33-foot easement of her. Has she made out a *prima facie* case of an equal protection violation? If not, what would she have to prove? Would her case be better (or worse), if she could prove that the village had required a 33-foot easement of two other landowners?

3. Reconsider the *United Artists* case. If United Artists had established that the township had delayed approval of its development plan, while acting expeditiously on its competitor's plan, would United Artists have made out a *prima facie* case that the township had deprived United Artists of equal protection? What else would United Artists have had to prove?

Suppose a homeowner seeking a side yard variance can prove that the zoning board of appeals denied her application after granting a side yard variance to several neighbors over the past three years. Has the homeowner made out a *prima facie* case for an equal protection claim? Does *Olech* create an opportunity for a creative lawyer to transform every permit denial into an equal protection claim?

4. Why did Justice Breyer write a concurrence in *Olech*? Would his approach significantly reduce the incidence of equal protection claims? If the court had adopted his position, would United Artists have been able to make out an equal protection claim? A homeowner complaining of a variance denial?

Under Justice Breyer's approach, what is a court to do if landowner's lawyer introduces evidence of illegitimate animus, and the municipality offers a plausible and facially neutral basis for distinguishing landowner's application from other applications the municipality has granted? What does illegitimate animus have to do with equal protection?

5. *Similarity.* The Loesels claimed that the new zoning ordinance treated them differently from the owners of specified other parcels in the city. Don't all zoning ordinances draw lines between districts permitting different uses? On the *Loesel* court's analysis, does every spot zoning claim satisfy the "similarity" threshold for an equal protection claim?

Other courts have been insisted on higher thresholds of similarity as a mechanism for avoiding "class of one" claims. The Second Circuit, for instance, has said that

> [T]o succeed on a class-of-one claim, a plaintiff must establish that (i) no rational person could regard the circumstances of the plaintiff to differ from those of a comparator to a degree that would justify the differential treatment on the basis of a legitimate government policy; and (ii) the similarity in circumstances and difference in treatment are sufficient to exclude the possibility that the defendants acted on the basis of a mistake.

Clubside, Inc. v. Valentin, 468 F.3d 144, 159 (2d Cir. 2006). The Second Circuit applied that standard to dismiss a "class of one" claim by a developer whose subdivision application was frustrated by the village's refusal to permit sewer hook-ups. Ruston v. Town Board, 610 F.3d 55 2d Cir. 2010). Although the developer in *Ruston* pointed to other owners who had been permitted to connect to the village sewer system, the court held— apparently as a matter of law, not a matter of fact for the jury—that none of those applications were sufficiently similar to trigger an equal protection claim. *See also* Snyder v. Gaudet, 756 F.3d 30 (1st Cir. 2014) (reversing denial of summary judgment motion by local officials because applicant had not demonstrated sufficient similarity).

6. *Rational Basis.* In *Loesel*, the court held that whether the city had a rational basis for the ordinance was a question of fact for the jury. What was the question of fact? Whether Wortman (the city's expert) had articulated a rational basis for the ordinance? Whether the city acted for the reasons Wortman articulated? If the focus is on whether city officials acted on the rational basis the city has now articulated, won't every "class of one" case present a question of fact about the municipality's rational basis?

The Seventh Circuit, which has been relatively lenient about the need to prove similarity, has taken a much harder line about the need to plead and prove that the municipality lacked a rational basis, holding that "even at the pleadings stage, '[a]ll it takes to defeat [a class-of-one] claim is a *conceivable* rational basis for the difference in treatment.'" Miller v. City of Monona, 784 F.3d 1113 (7th Cir. 2015), (quoting D.B. ex rel. Kurtis B. v.

Kopp, 725 F.3d 681, 686 (7th Cir. 2013)). In *Miller*, the plaintiff's complaint alleged that the city had improperly impeded her development project "for the stated reason of asbestos debris and interior asbestos." The court held that because she pleaded "rational bases for the actions of local officials, Miller pleaded herself out of court." 784 F.3d at 1122. Do you think the *Loesel* court would have reached the same result? Why or why not? Which approach makes more sense?

7. *Animus.* Suppose Wal-Mart had completed its purchase from the Loesels before the city rezoned the property. Would the court have overturned a jury verdict in favor of Wal-Mart? Was there evidence in the record to support a finding of animus against Wal-Mart? If the answer is yes, why should it matter that, in this case, the animus was directed against the prospective purchaser of the property rather than the current owner?

If you represented a landowner advancing a "class of one" claim, what kinds of evidence would you seek to present as proof of animus towards your client? Would it be enough to show that the landowner opposed the current mayor in the most recent election? *Cf.* Sacher v. Vill. of Old Brookville, 967 F.Supp.2d 663, 672 (E.D.N.Y. 2013). To show that the landowner had fired a member of the City Council? *See* Snyder v, Gaudet, 756 F.3d 30 (1st Cir. 2014)?

Should animus alone be enough to ensure that the landowner prevails if there is also a rational basis for the municipality's decision? *Cf.* Miller v. City of Monona, 784 F.3d 1113 at 1123: "to succeed on a class-of-one claim, Miller had to do more than merely allege facts casting the actions of Monona officials as being motivated by animus; she needed to exclude possible rational explanations for their actions."

8. How important is *Olech*? If a municipality faced with a "class of one" equal protection claim can overcome the claim by establishing a rational basis for its decision, why would a landowner bother bringing an equal protection claim?

Suppose the landowner brings a "class of one" claim in federal court, and also raises various state law claims. If the federal court ultimately dismisses the class of one claim, must it also dismiss the state law claims, or does *Olech* provide a vehicle for access to federal courts on claims that would otherwise be limited to state court?

C. DISCRIMINATION AGAINST RACIAL AND ETHNIC MINORITIES

Background

Urban Neighborhood Regeneration and the Phases of Community Evolution After World War II in the United States

James A. Kushner

41 Ind. L. Rev. 575, 577–79, 590–91 (2008)

At the end of World War II, pent-up housing demand and returning soldiers sent the public looking for new housing in the newly developing suburbs. The period between 1945 and 1968 was marked by extraordinary national investment in suburban infrastructure including federally subsidized highways, utility extension, and rapid suburbanization. Suburbanization resulted from demand fueled by the availability of low-interest loans for the purchase of modestly priced houses in new suburban subdivisions. Loans were insured by the Federal Housing Administration and often made through the Veterans Administration. During this period, development was strictly segregated on the basis of race as mandated by federal government loan requirements, i.e., the federal government conditioned the availability of mortgage insurance to entire housing developments on the adoption of racial covenants or equitable servitudes—covenants inserted into subdivision deeds or in the subdivision plat filed with the deed and binding future lot purchasers as compared to covenants entered into between neighbors or those attached to deeds—and often local zoning, private covenants, or simply violence by local police or white supremacists. The basis of the requirement was the belief that a one-race community would stabilize housing values and assure marketability by adhering to the American custom of racial segregation. The principal regulatory mechanism used was zoning, particularly suburban exclusionary zoning requiring detached, single-family homes on relatively large lots. Communities often required in excess of an acre per home with broad street setbacks for lawns. Virtually no lots were zoned for mobile homes or apartments. Where apartments were provided, sites were often unattractive, and bedrooms were limited to exclude families and attract senior citizens and single adults.

"Between 1960 and 2000, the number of African Americans living in suburbs grew by approximately 9 million, representing a migration as large as the exodus of African Americans from the rural South in the mid-twentieth century. More than one-third of African Americans-almost 12 million people-lived in suburbs." The divide between many minority communities, which were now in the city and the older suburbs, and the more affluent communities, predominantly in white newer suburbs, became more pronounced despite back-to-the-city moves, investment, the gentrification of attractive neighborhoods, and despite the fact that segregation between blacks and non-blacks is at its lowest level since 1920. Although minorities increased their presence in the suburbs and the affluent were returning to certain neighborhoods in the city, the divide between neighborhoods during this period was still characterized by hyper-segregation. Thus, while black-white segregation in metropolitan areas has declined in the past two decades and diversity has increased, the nation must nevertheless be characterized as having a high degree of racial separation. Majority-black suburban neighborhoods generally provide fewer economic opportunities in terms of rising home values and access to good schools and jobs, making it harder for blacks to catch up and keep up financially with whites. In 2005, "the average white person in the United States live[d] in a neighborhood that [was] more than 80 percent white, while the average black person live[d] in one that [was] mostly black." African Americans are the most residentially segregated group in the United States.

As Professor Kushner notes, federal housing policy and zoning law have played a role in patterns of segregation within the United States. What recourse is available to a prospective resident, developer, or community group who contends that municipal officials have engaged in racially discriminatory practices?

Doctrinally, a plaintiff has two principal alternatives: a constitutional equal protection claim, and a statutory Fair Housing Act challenge. If the plaintiff establishes that municipal officials have discriminated based on race, the plaintiff is likely to prevail on both the constitutional and the statutory challenge. The problem for the plaintiff is establishing discrimination. On that issue, equal protection doctrine is quite different from Fair Housing Act doctrine. Consider first the leading equal protection case:

Village of Arlington Heights v. Metropolitan Housing Development Corp.

Supreme Court of the United States, 1977
429 U.S. 252

■ MR. JUSTICE POWELL delivered the opinion of the Court.

In 1971 respondent Metropolitan Housing Development Corporation (MHDC) applied to petitioner, the Village of Arlington Heights, Ill., for the rezoning of a 15-acre parcel from single-family to multiple-family classification. Using federal financial assistance, MHDC planned to build 190 clustered townhouse units for low- and moderate-income tenants. The Village denied the rezoning request.

MHDC, joined by other plaintiffs who are also respondents here, brought suit in the United States District Court for the Northern District of Illinois. They alleged that the denial was racially discriminatory and that it violated, inter alia, the Fourteenth Amendment and the Fair Housing Act of 1968, 82 Stat. 81, 42 U.S.C. § 3601 *et seq.*

I

Arlington Heights is a suburb of Chicago, located about 26 miles northwest of the downtown Loop area. Most of the land in Arlington Heights is zoned for detached single-family homes, and this is in fact the prevailing land use. The Village experienced substantial growth during the 1960's, but, like other communities in northwest Cook County, its population of racial minority groups remained quite low. According to the 1970 census, only 27 of the Village's 64,000 residents were black.

The Clerics of St. Viator, a religious order (Order), own an 80-acre parcel just east of the center of Arlington Heights. Part of the site is occupied by the Viatorian high school, and part by the Order's three-story novitiate building, which houses dormitories and a Montessori school. Much of the site, however, remains vacant. Since 1959, when the Village first adopted a zoning ordinance, all the land surrounding the Viatorian property has been zoned R–3, a single-family specification with relatively small minimum lot-size requirements. On three sides of the Viatorian land there are single-family homes just across a street; to the east the Viatorian property directly adjoins the backyards of other single-family homes.

The Order decided in 1970 to devote some of its land to low- and moderate-income housing. Investigation revealed that the most expeditious way to build such housing was to work through a nonprofit developer experienced in the use of federal housing subsidies under § 236 of the National Housing Act, 48 Stat. 1246, as added and amended, 12 U.S.C. § 1715z–1.

MHDC is such a developer. It was organized in 1968 by several prominent Chicago citizens for the purpose of building low- and moderate-income housing throughout the Chicago area. In 1970 MHDC was in the process of building one § 236 development near Arlington Heights and already had provided some federally assisted housing on a smaller scale in other parts of the Chicago area.

After some negotiation, MHDC and the Order entered into a 99-year lease and an accompanying agreement of sale covering a 15-acre site in the southeast corner of the Viatorian property. MHDC became the lessee immediately, but the sale agreement was contingent upon MHDC's securing zoning clearances from the Village and § 236 housing assistance from the Federal Government. If MHDC proved unsuccessful in securing either, both the lease and the contract of sale would lapse.

The agreement established a bargain purchase price of $300,000, low enough to comply with federal limitations governing land-acquisition costs for § 236 housing.

MHDC engaged an architect and proceeded with the project, to be known as Lincoln Green. The plans called for 20 two-story buildings with a total of 190 units, each unit having its own private entrance from the outside. One hundred of the units would have a single bedroom, thought likely to attract elderly citizens. The remainder would have two, three, or four bedrooms. A large portion of the site would remain open, with shrubs and trees to screen the homes abutting the property to the east.

The planned development did not conform to the Village's zoning ordinance and could not be built unless Arlington Heights rezoned the parcel to R–5, its multiple-family housing classification. Accordingly, MHDC filed with the Village Plan Commission a petition for rezoning, accompanied by supporting materials describing the development and specifying that it would be subsidized under § 236. The materials made clear that one requirement under § 236 is an affirmative marketing plan designed to assure that a subsidized development is racially integrated. MHDC also submitted studies demonstrating the need for housing of this type and analyzing the probable impact of the development. To prepare for the hearings before the Plan Commission and to assure compliance with the Village building code, fire regulations, and related requirements, MHDC consulted with the Village staff for preliminary review of the development. The parties have stipulated that every change recommended during such consultations was incorporated into the plans.

During the spring of 1971, the Plan Commission considered the proposal at a series of three public meetings, which drew large crowds. Although many of those attending were quite vocal and demonstrative in opposition to Lincoln Green, a number of individuals and representatives of community groups spoke in support of rezoning. Some of the comments, both from opponents and supporters, addressed what was referred to as the "social issue"—the desirability or undesirability of introducing at this location in Arlington Heights low- and moderate-income housing, housing that would probably be racially integrated.

Many of the opponents, however, focused on the zoning aspects of the petition, stressing two arguments. First, the area always had been zoned single-family, and the neighboring citizens had built or purchased there in reliance on that classification. Rezoning threatened to cause a measurable drop in property value for neighboring sites. Second, the Village's apartment policy, adopted by the Village Board in 1962 and amended in 1970, called for R–5 zoning primarily to serve as a buffer between single-family development and land uses thought incompatible, such as commercial or manufacturing districts. Lincoln Green did not meet this requirement, as it adjoined no commercial or manufacturing district.

At the close of the third meeting, the Plan Commission adopted a motion to recommend to the Village's Board of Trustees that it deny the request. The motion stated: "While the need for low and moderate income housing may exist in Arlington Heights or its environs, the Plan Commission would be derelict in recommending it at the proposed location." Two members voted against the motion and submitted a minority report, stressing that in their view the change to accommodate Lincoln Green represented "good zoning." The Village Board met on September 28, 1971, to consider MHDC's request and the recommendation of the Plan Commission. After a public hearing, the Board denied the rezoning by a 6–1 vote.

The following June MHDC and three Negro individuals filed this lawsuit against the Village, seeking declaratory and injunctive relief. A second nonprofit corporation and an individual of Mexican-American descent intervened as plaintiffs. The trial resulted in a judgment for petitioners. Assuming that MHDC had standing to bring the suit, the District Court held that the petitioners were not motivated by racial discrimination or intent to discriminate against low-income groups when they denied rezoning, but rather by a desire "to protect property values and the integrity of the Village's zoning plan." 373 F. Supp. at 211. The District Court concluded also that the denial would not have a racially discriminatory effect.

A divided Court of Appeals reversed. It first approved the District Court's finding that the defendants were motivated by a concern for the integrity of the zoning plan, rather than by racial discrimination. Deciding whether their refusal to rezone would have discriminatory effects was more complex. The court observed that the refusal would have a disproportionate impact on blacks. Based upon family income, blacks constituted 40% of those Chicago area residents who were eligible to become tenants of Lincoln Green, although they composed a far lower percentage of total area population.

There was another level to the court's analysis of allegedly discriminatory results. Invoking language from Kennedy Park Homes Ass'n v. City of Lackawanna, 436 F. 2d 108, 112 (CA2 1970), *cert. denied*, 401 U.S. 1010 (1971), the Court of Appeals ruled that the denial of rezoning must be examined in light of its "historical context and ultimate effect." 517 F. 2d, at 413. Northwest Cook County was enjoying rapid growth in employment opportunities and population, but it continued to exhibit a high degree of residential segregation. The court held that Arlington Heights could not simply ignore this problem. Indeed, it found that the Village had been "exploiting" the situation by allowing itself to become a nearly all-white community. *Id*., at 414. The

Village had no other current plans for building low- and moderate-income housing, and no other R–5 parcels in the Village were available to MHDC at an economically feasible price.

Against this background, the Court of Appeals ruled that the denial of the Lincoln Green proposal had racially discriminatory effects and could be tolerated only if it served compelling interests. Neither the buffer policy nor the desire to protect property values met this exacting standard. The court therefore concluded that the denial violated the Equal Protection Clause of the Fourteenth Amendment.

II

At the outset, petitioners challenge the respondents' standing to bring the suit.

A

Here there can be little doubt that MHDC meets the constitutional standing requirements. The challenged action of the petitioners stands as an absolute barrier to constructing the housing MHDC had contracted to place on the Viatorian site. If MHDC secures the injunctive relief it seeks, that barrier will be removed. An injunction would not, of course, guarantee that Lincoln Green will be built. MHDC would still have to secure financing, qualify for federal subsidies, and carry through with construction. But all housing developments are subject to some extent to similar uncertainties. When a project is as detailed and specific as Lincoln Green, a court is not required to engage in undue speculation as a predicate for finding that the plaintiff has the requisite personal stake in the controversy. MHDC has shown an injury to itself that is "likely to be redressed by a favorable decision." Simon v. Eastern Ky. Welfare Rights Org., *supra*, at 38.

Petitioners nonetheless appear to argue that MHDC lacks standing because it has suffered no economic injury. MHDC, they point out, is not the owner of the property in question. Its contract of purchase is contingent upon securing rezoning. MHDC owes the owners nothing if rezoning is denied.

We cannot accept petitioners' argument. In the first place, it is inaccurate to say that MHDC suffers no economic injury from a refusal to rezone, despite the contingency provisions in its contract. MHDC has expended thousands of dollars on the plans for Lincoln Green and on the studies submitted to the Village in support of the petition for rezoning. Unless rezoning is granted, many of these plans and studies will be worthless even if MHDC finds another site at an equally attractive price.

Petitioners' argument also misconceives our standing requirements. It has long been clear that economic injury is not the only kind of injury that can support a plaintiff's standing. United States v. SCRAP, *supra*, at 686–687; Sierra Club v. Morton, 405 U.S. 727, 734

(1972); Data Processing Service v. Camp, 397 U.S. 150, 154 (1970). MHDC is a nonprofit corporation. Its interest in building Lincoln Green stems not from a desire for economic gain, but rather from an interest in making suitable low-cost housing available in areas where such housing is scarce. This is not mere abstract concern about a problem of general interest. *See* Sierra Club v. Morton, *supra*, at 739. The specific project MHDC intends to build, whether or not it will generate profits, provides that "essential dimension of specificity" that informs judicial decisionmaking. Schlesinger v. Reservists to Stop the War, 418 U.S. 208, 221 (1974).

B

As a corporation, MHDC has no racial identity and cannot be the direct target of the petitioners' alleged discrimination. In the ordinary case, a party is denied standing to assert the rights of third persons. Warth v. Seldin, 422 U.S., at 499. But we need not decide whether the circumstances of this case would justify departure from that prudential limitation and permit MHDC to assert the constitutional rights of its prospective minority tenants. *See* Barrows v. Jackson, 346 U.S. 249 (1953); *cf.* Sullivan v. Little Hunting Park, 396 U.S. 229, 237 (1969); Buchanan v. Warley, 245 U.S. 60, 72–73 (1917). For we have at least one individual plaintiff who has demonstrated standing to assert these rights as his own.

Respondent Ransom, a Negro, works at the Honeywell factory in Arlington Heights and lives approximately 20 miles away in Evanston in a 5-room house with his mother and his son. The complaint alleged that he seeks and would qualify for the housing MHDC wants to build in Arlington Heights. Ransom testified at trial that if Lincoln Green were built he would probably move there, since it is closer to his job.

Ransom has adequately averred an "actionable causal relationship" between Arlington Heights' zoning practices and his asserted injury. Warth v. Seldin, *supra*, at 507. We therefore proceed to the merits.

III

Our decision last Term in Washington v. Davis, 426 U.S. 229 (1976), made it clear that official action will not be held unconstitutional solely because it results in a racially disproportionate impact. "Disproportionate impact is not irrelevant, but it is not the sole touchstone of an invidious racial discrimination." *Id.*, at 242. Proof of racially discriminatory intent or purpose is required to show a violation of the Equal Protection Clause.

Davis does not require a plaintiff to prove that the challenged action rested solely on racially discriminatory purposes. Rarely can it be said that a legislature or administrative body operating under a broad mandate made a decision motivated solely by a single concern, or even that a particular purpose was the "dominant" or "primary" one. In fact, it is because legislators and administrators are properly concerned with balancing numerous competing considerations that courts refrain from reviewing the merits of their decisions, absent a showing of arbitrariness or irrationality. But racial discrimination is not just another competing consideration. When there is a proof that a discriminatory purpose has been a motivating factor in the decision, this judicial deference is no longer justified.

Determining whether invidious discriminatory purpose was a motivating factor demands a sensitive inquiry into such circumstantial and direct evidence of intent as may be available. The impact of the official action—whether it "bears more heavily on one race than another," Washington v. Davis, *supra*, at 242—may provide an important starting point. Sometimes a clear pattern, unexplainable on grounds other than race, emerges from the effect of the state action even when the governing legislation appears neutral on its face. Yick Wo v. Hopkins, 118 U.S. 356 (1886); Guinn v. United States, 238 U.S. 347 (1915); Lane v. Wilson, 307 U.S. 268 (1939); Gomillion v. Lightfoot, 364 U.S. 339 (1960). The evidentiary inquiry is then relatively easy. But such cases are rare. Absent a pattern as stark as that in *Gomillion* or *Yick Wo*, impact alone is not determinative, and the Court must look to other evidence.

The historical background of the decision is one evidentiary source, particularly if it reveals a series of official actions taken for invidious purposes. For example, if the property involved here always had been zoned R–5 but suddenly was changed to R–3 when the town learned of MHDC's plans to erect integrated housing, we would have a far different case. Departures from the normal procedural sequence also might afford evidence that improper purposes are playing a role. Substantive departures too may be relevant, particularly if the factors usually considered important by the decisionmaker strongly favor a decision contrary to the one reached.

The legislative or administrative history may be highly relevant, especially where there are contemporary statements by members of the decisionmaking body, minutes of its meetings, or reports. In some extraordinary instances the members might be called to the stand at trial to testify concerning the purpose of the official action, although even then such testimony frequently will be barred by privilege. *See* Tenney v. Brandhove, 341 U.S. 367 (1951); United States v. Nixon, 418 U.S. 683, 705 (1974); 8 J. Wigmore, Evidence § 2371 (McNaughton rev. ed. 1961).

The foregoing summary identifies, without purporting to be exhaustive, subjects of proper inquiry in determining whether racially discriminatory intent existed. With these in mind, we now address the case before us.

IV

The impact of the Village's decision does arguably bear more heavily on racial minorities. Minorities constitute 18% of the Chicago area population, and 40% of the income groups said to be eligible for Lincoln Green. But there is little about the sequence of events leading up to the decision that would spark suspicion. The area around the Viatorian property has been zoned R–3 since 1959, the year when Arlington Heights first adopted a zoning map. Single-family homes surround the 80-acre site, and the Village is undeniably committed to single-family homes as its dominant residential land use. The rezoning request progressed according to the usual procedures. The Plan Commission even scheduled two additional hearings, at least in part to accommodate MHDC and permit it to supplement its presentation with answers to questions generated at the first hearing.

The statements by the Plan Commission and Village Board members, as reflected in the official minutes, focused almost exclusively on the zoning aspects of the MHDC petition, and the zoning factors on which they relied are not novel criteria in the Village's rezoning decisions. There is no reason to doubt that there has been reliance by some neighboring property owners on the maintenance of single-family zoning in the vicinity. The Village originally adopted its buffer policy long before MHDC entered the picture and has applied the policy too consistently for us to infer discriminatory purpose from its application in this case. Finally, MHDC called one member of the Village Board to the stand at trial. Nothing in her testimony supports an inference of invidious purpose.

In sum, the evidence does not warrant overturning the concurrent findings of both courts below. Respondents simply failed to carry their burden of proving that discriminatory purpose was a motivating factor in the Village's decision. This conclusion ends the constitutional inquiry. The Court of Appeals' further finding that the Village's decision carried a discriminatory "ultimate effect" is without independent constitutional significance.

V

Respondents' complaint also alleged that the refusal to rezone violated the Fair Housing Act, 42 U.S.C. § 3601 *et seq*. They continue to urge here that a zoning decision made by a public body may, and that petitioners' action did, violate § 3604 or § 3617. The Court of Appeals, however, proceeding in a somewhat unorthodox fashion, did not decide the statutory question. We remand the case for further consideration of respondents' statutory claims.

Reversed and remanded.

NOTES AND QUESTIONS

1. *Standing.* As the Court observes in its opinion, standing is a constitutional requirement for suit in federal court. Suppose a private developer had applied for a zoning amendment to place the Lincoln Green property in an R–5 zone, which would permit multiple-family housing. If the village had denied the application, would the developer have had standing to bring the action on equal protection grounds? How, if at all, is the MHDC's case different?

If the private developer's application had been denied, would MHDC have had standing to challenge the denial? Why or why not? How did the structure of the transaction in *Arlington Heights* surmount the constitutional standing issue? What burden does that place on organizational plaintiffs?

Why did Ransom have standing in this case? Will it always be possible to identify an individual with standing to challenge a zoning decision? If so, why does it matter whether private developers or community organizations have standing?

The constitutional standing requirements discussed by the court in *Arlington Heights* do not apply in state court. But state legislatures or courts may impose their own standing requirements.

2. *Proving Intent.* If the members of the Arlington Heights Village Board had announced, in unison, at a village board meeting, that they were all voting against the proposed zoning amendment because they did not want more African-Americans in the village, discriminatory motive would have been easy to establish. Rarely, however, are courts confronted with such unequivocal evidence. In each of the following scenarios, identify arguments a plaintiff might make in advancing a claim that the board acted out of discriminatory motive, and the arguments the village board might make in response:

a. One member of the village board expressed concern that an increase in African-American students in local schools would result in lower test scores. Five other members repudiate the comments, and indicate that their votes against the amendment reflect only concerns about maintaining the single-family character of the neighborhood. (Recall that the village board voted 6–1 against the amendment.)

b. Two or three members of the board expressed the same concerns.

c. At the board meeting, numerous members of the audience angrily express opposition to the amendment because they do not want more African-Americans in the village. Members of the board do not repudiate the comments and then proceed to vote against the application.

d.   The village board approves a zoning amendment permitting multi-family housing, but requires that the housing be limited to studio and one-bedroom apartments.

3.   In *Arlington Heights*, the Court noted that the situation would have been different if the Lincoln Green property had been zoned R–5, and the village board had amended the ordinance to place the property in an R–3 zone. How likely a scenario is that? Won't municipalities typically place undeveloped property in restrictive zones so that the municipality can exercise more control over the pattern of development?

In *Arlington Heights,* the Court rejected the plaintiffs' constitutional claim. But the plaintiffs had also claimed that the village's action violated the Fair Housing Act, a federal statute enacted primarily to root out discrimination by landlords, real estate brokers, and other private parties. The Supreme Court did not reach the Fair Housing Act issue in *Arlington Heights*, and instead remanded to the Seventh Circuit for consideration of plaintiffs' statutory claim. Consider the operative statutory language. 42 U.S.C. § 3604(a) makes it unlawful:

To refuse to sell or rent after the making of a bona fide offer, or to refuse to negotiate for the sale or rental of, or otherwise make unavailable or deny, a dwelling to any person because of race, color, religion, sex, familial status, or national origin.

If you had been plaintiffs' lawyer in the *Arlington Heights* case, what language would you have relied upon to claim that the village's zoning ordinance had violated the statute? What would plaintiffs have to prove in order to make out a *prima facie* case of a statutory violation? If plaintiffs had made out a *prima facie* case, what evidence would the village have had to introduce to rebut that case? Consider those questions in light of the following case:

Texas Department of Housing and Community Affairs v. Inclusive Communities Project, Inc.

Supreme Court of the United States, 2015
___ U.S. ___, 135 S.Ct. 2507

■ JUSTICE KENNEDY delivered the opinion of the Court.

The underlying dispute in this case concerns where housing for low-income persons should be constructed in Dallas, Texas—that is, whether the housing should be built in the inner city or in the suburbs. This dispute comes to the Court on a disparate-impact theory of liability. In contrast to a disparate-treatment case, where a "plaintiff must establish that the defendant had a discriminatory intent or motive," a plaintiff bringing a disparate-impact claim challenges practices that have a "disproportionately adverse effect on minorities" and are otherwise unjustified by a legitimate rationale. *Ricci v. DeStefano,* 557 U.S. 557, 577 (2009). The question presented for the Court's determination is whether disparate-impact claims are cognizable under the Fair Housing Act (or FHA), 82 Stat. 81, as amended, 42 U.S.C. § 3601 *et seq.*

I

[The federal government provides tax credits for developers who build low-income housing, and provides criteria to guide state agencies charged with administering the program. The criteria favor building the housing in low-income areas. The Inclusive Communities Project (ICP) challenged administration of the program by the Texas Department of Housing, contending that the Department violated the Fair Housing Act by disproportionately awarding credits for use in predominantly black inner-city areas rather than predominantly white suburban areas—eds.]

The District Court concluded that the ICP had established a prima facie case of disparate impact. It relied on two pieces of statistical evidence. First, it found "from 1999–2008, [the Department] approved tax credits for 49.7% of proposed non-elderly units in 0% to 9.9% Caucasian areas, but only approved 37.4% of proposed non-elderly units in 90% to 100% Caucasian areas." Second, it found "92.29% of [low-income housing tax credit] units in the city of Dallas were located in census tracts with less than 50% Caucasian residents."

The District Court then placed the burden on the Department to rebut the ICP's prima facie showing of disparate impact. After assuming the Department's proffered interests were legitimate, the District Court held that a defendant—here the Department—must prove "that there are no other less discriminatory alternatives to advancing their proffered interests." Because, in its view, the Department "failed to meet [its] burden of proving that there are no less discriminatory alternatives," the District Court ruled for the ICP.

The District Court's remedial order required the addition of new selection criteria for the tax credits. For instance, it awarded points for units built in neighborhoods with good schools and disqualified sites that are located adjacent to or near hazardous conditions, such as high crime areas or landfills. The remedial order contained no explicit racial targets or quotas.

While the Department's appeal was pending, the Secretary of Housing and Urban Development (HUD) issued a regulation interpreting the FHA to encompass disparate-impact liability. See Implementation of the Fair Housing Act's Discriminatory Effects Standard, 78 Fed.Reg. 11460 (2013). The regulation also established a burden-shifting framework for adjudicating disparate-impact claims. Under the regulation, a plaintiff first must make a prima facie showing of disparate impact. That is, the plaintiff "has the burden of proving that a challenged practice caused or predictably will cause a discriminatory effect." 24 CFR § 100.500(c)(1) (2014). If a statistical discrepancy is caused by factors other than the defendant's policy, a plaintiff cannot establish a prima facie case, and there is no liability. After a plaintiff does establish a prima facie showing of disparate impact, the burden shifts to the defendant to "prov[e] that the challenged practice is necessary to achieve one or more substantial, legitimate, nondiscriminatory interests." § 100.500(c)(2). HUD has clarified that this step of the analysis "is analogous to the Title VII requirement that an employer's interest in an employment practice with a disparate impact be job related." 78 Fed.Reg. 11470. Once a defendant has satisfied its burden at step two, a plaintiff may "prevail upon proving that the substantial, legitimate, nondiscriminatory interests supporting the challenged practice could be served by another practice that has a less discriminatory effect." § 100.500(c)(3).

The Court of Appeals for the Fifth Circuit held, consistent with its precedent, that disparate-impact claims are cognizable under the FHA. 747 F.3d 275, 280 (2014). On the merits, however, the Court of Appeals reversed and remanded. Relying on HUD's regulation, the Court of Appeals held that it was improper for the District Court to have placed the burden on the Department to prove there were no less discriminatory alternatives for allocating low-income housing tax credits. *Id.*, at 282–283. In a concurring opinion, Judge Jones stated that on remand the District Court should reexamine whether the ICP had made out a prima facie case of disparate impact. She suggested the District Court incorrectly relied on bare statistical evidence without engaging in any analysis about causation. She further observed that, if the federal law providing for the distribution of low-income housing tax credits ties the Department's hands to such an extent that it lacks a meaningful choice, then there is no disparate-impact liability.

The Department filed a petition for a writ of certiorari on the question whether disparate-impact claims are cognizable under the FHA.

II

The issue here is whether, under a proper interpretation of the FHA, housing decisions with a disparate impact are prohibited. Before turning to the FHA, however, it is necessary to consider two other antidiscrimination statutes that preceded it.

[The Court observed that in *Griggs v. Duke Power Co.*, 401 U.S. 424 (1971), it had interpreted Title VII of the Civil Rights Act to authorize disparate impact liability and that, in *Smith v. City of Jackson,* 544 U.S. 228 (2005), it had interpreted the Age Discrimination in Employment Act to authorize disparate impact liability—eds.]

Turning to the FHA, the ICP relies on two provisions. Section 804(a) provides that it shall be unlawful:

"To refuse to sell or rent after the making of a bona fide offer, or to refuse to negotiate for the sale or rental of, or otherwise

make unavailable or deny, a dwelling to any person because of
race, color, religion, sex, familial status, or national origin." 42
U.S.C. § 3604(a).

Here, the phrase "otherwise make unavailable" is of central importance
to the analysis that follows.

Section 805(a), in turn, provides:

"It shall be unlawful for any person or other entity whose
business includes engaging in real estate-related transactions
to discriminate against any person in making available such a
transaction, or in the terms or conditions of such a transaction,
because of race, color, religion, sex, handicap, familial status,
or national origin." § 3605(a).

Applied here, the logic of *Griggs* and *Smith* provides strong support
for the conclusion that the FHA encompasses disparate-impact claims.
Congress' use of the phrase "otherwise make unavailable" refers to the
consequences of an action rather than the actor's intent. See *United
States v. Giles,* 300 U.S. 41 (1937) (explaining that the "word 'make' has
many meanings, among them '[t]o cause to exist, appear or occur'"
(quoting Webster's New International Dictionary 1485 (2d ed. 1934))).
This results-oriented language counsels in favor of recognizing
disparate-impact liability. See *Smith, supra,* at 236, 125 S.Ct. 1536. The
Court has construed statutory language similar to § 805(a) to include
disparate-impact liability. See, *e.g., Board of Ed. of City School Dist. of
New York v. Harris,* 444 U.S. 130, 140–141 (1979) (holding the term
"discriminat[e]" encompassed disparate-impact liability in the context of
a statute's text, history, purpose, and structure).

Recognition of disparate-impact claims is consistent with the FHA's
central purpose. See *Smith, supra,* at 235 (plurality opinion); *Griggs,*
401 U.S., at 432. The FHA, like Title VII and the ADEA, was enacted to
eradicate discriminatory practices within a sector of our Nation's
economy. See 42 U.S.C. § 3601 ("It is the policy of the United States to
provide, within constitutional limitations, for fair housing throughout
the United States"); H.R. Rep., at 15 (explaining the FHA "provides a
clear national policy against discrimination in housing").

These unlawful practices include zoning laws and other housing
restrictions that function unfairly to exclude minorities from certain
neighborhoods without any sufficient justification. Suits targeting such
practices reside at the heartland of disparate-impact liability. The
availability of disparate-impact liability, furthermore, has allowed
private developers to vindicate the FHA's objectives and to protect their
property rights by stopping municipalities from enforcing arbitrary and,
in practice, discriminatory ordinances barring the construction of
certain types of housing units. Recognition of disparate-impact liability
under the FHA also plays a role in uncovering discriminatory intent: It
permits plaintiffs to counteract unconscious prejudices and disguised

animus that escape easy classification as disparate treatment. In this way disparate-impact liability may prevent segregated housing patterns that might otherwise result from covert and illicit stereotyping.

But disparate-impact liability has always been properly limited in key respects that avoid the serious constitutional questions that might arise under the FHA, for instance, if such liability were imposed based solely on a showing of a statistical disparity. Disparate-impact liability mandates the "removal of artificial, arbitrary, and unnecessary barriers," not the displacement of valid governmental policies. *Griggs, supra,* at 431. The FHA is not an instrument to force housing authorities to reorder their priorities. Rather, the FHA aims to ensure that those priorities can be achieved without arbitrarily creating discriminatory effects or perpetuating segregation.

Unlike the heartland of disparate-impact suits targeting artificial barriers to housing, the underlying dispute in this case involves a novel theory of liability. See Seicshnaydre, Is Disparate Impact Having Any Impact? An Appellate Analysis of Forty Years of Disparate Impact Claims Under the Fair Housing Act, 63 Am. U. L. Rev. 357, 360–363 (2013) (noting the rarity of this type of claim). This case, on remand, may be seen simply as an attempt to second-guess which of two reasonable approaches a housing authority should follow in the sound exercise of its discretion in allocating tax credits for low-income housing.

An important and appropriate means of ensuring that disparate-impact liability is properly limited is to give housing authorities and private developers leeway to state and explain the valid interest served by their policies. This step of the analysis is analogous to the business necessity standard under Title VII and provides a defense against disparate-impact liability. See 78 Fed.Reg. 11470 (explaining that HUD did not use the phrase "business necessity" because that "phrase may not be easily understood to cover the full scope of practices covered by the Fair Housing Act, which applies to individuals, businesses, nonprofit organizations, and public entities"). Just as an employer may maintain a workplace requirement that causes a disparate impact if that requirement is a "reasonable measure[ment] of job performance," *Griggs, supra,* at 436 so too must housing authorities and private developers be allowed to maintain a policy if they can prove it is necessary to achieve a valid interest. To be sure, the Title VII framework may not transfer exactly to the fair-housing context, but the comparison suffices for present purposes.

It would be paradoxical to construe the FHA to impose onerous costs on actors who encourage revitalizing dilapidated housing in our Nation's cities merely because some other priority might seem preferable. Entrepreneurs must be given latitude to consider market factors. Zoning officials, moreover, must often make decisions based on a mix of factors, both objective (such as cost and traffic patterns) and, at least to some extent, subjective (such as preserving historic architecture). These factors contribute to a community's quality of life and are legitimate concerns for housing authorities. The FHA does not decree a particular vision of urban development; and it does not put housing authorities and private developers in a double bind of liability, subject to suit whether they choose to rejuvenate a city core or to promote new low-income housing in suburban communities. As HUD itself recognized in its recent rulemaking, disparate-impact liability "does not mandate that affordable housing be located in neighborhoods with any particular characteristic." 78 Fed.Reg. 11476.

In a similar vein, a disparate-impact claim that relies on a statistical disparity must fail if the plaintiff cannot point to a defendant's policy or policies causing that disparity. A robust causality requirement ensures that "[r]acial imbalance . . . does not, without more, establish a prima facie case of disparate impact" and thus protects defendants from being held liable for racial disparities they did not create. *Wards Cove Packing Co. v. Atonio,* 490 U.S. 642, 653 (1989), superseded by statute on other grounds, 42 U.S.C. § 2000e–2(k). Without adequate safeguards at the prima facie stage, disparate-impact liability might cause race to be used and considered in a pervasive way and "would almost inexorably lead" governmental or private entities to use "numerical quotas," and serious constitutional questions then could arise. 490 U.S., at 653.

The litigation at issue here provides an example. From the standpoint of determining advantage or disadvantage to racial minorities, it seems difficult to say as a general matter that a decision to build low-income housing in a blighted inner-city neighborhood instead of a suburb is discriminatory, or vice versa. If those sorts of judgments are subject to challenge without adequate safeguards, then there is a danger that potential defendants may adopt racial quotas—a circumstance that itself raises serious constitutional concerns.

Courts must therefore examine with care whether a plaintiff has made out a prima facie case of disparate impact and prompt resolution of these cases is important. A plaintiff who fails to allege facts at the pleading stage or produce statistical evidence demonstrating a causal connection cannot make out a prima facie case of disparate impact. For instance, a plaintiff challenging the decision of a private developer to construct a new building in one location rather than another will not easily be able to show this is a policy causing a disparate impact because such a one-time decision may not be a policy at all. It may also be difficult to establish causation because of the multiple factors that go into investment decisions about where to construct or renovate housing units. And as Judge Jones observed below, if the ICP cannot show a causal connection between the Department's policy and a disparate impact—for instance, because federal law substantially limits the Department's discretion—that should result in dismissal of this case.

The FHA imposes a command with respect to disparate-impact liability. Here, that command goes to a state entity. In other cases, the command will go to a private person or entity. Governmental or private policies are not contrary to the disparate-impact requirement unless they are "artificial, arbitrary, and unnecessary barriers." *Griggs,* 401 U.S., at 431. Difficult questions might arise if disparate-impact liability under the FHA caused race to be used and considered in a pervasive and explicit manner to justify governmental or private actions that, in fact, tend to perpetuate race-based considerations rather than move beyond them. Courts should avoid interpreting disparate-impact liability to be so expansive as to inject racial considerations into every housing decision.

The limitations on disparate-impact liability discussed here are also necessary to protect potential defendants against abusive disparate-impact claims. If the specter of disparate-impact litigation causes private developers to no longer construct or renovate housing units for low-income individuals, then the FHA would have undermined its own purpose as well as the free-market system. And as to governmental entities, they must not be prevented from achieving legitimate objectives, such as ensuring compliance with health and safety codes. The Department's *amici,* in addition to the well-stated principal dissenting opinion in this case (opinion of Alito, J.), call attention to the decision by the Court of Appeals for the Eighth Circuit in *Gallagher v. Magner,* 619 F.3d 823 (2010). Although the Court is reluctant to approve or disapprove a case that is not pending, it should be noted that *Magner* was decided without the cautionary standards announced in this opinion and, in all events, the case was settled by the parties before an ultimate determination of disparate-impact liability.

Were standards for proceeding with disparate-impact suits not to incorporate at least the safeguards discussed here, then disparate-impact liability might displace valid governmental and private priorities, rather than solely "remov[ing] . . . artificial, arbitrary, and unnecessary barriers." *Griggs,* 401 U.S., at 431. And that, in turn, would set our Nation back in its quest to reduce the salience of race in our social and economic system.

It must be noted further that, even when courts do find liability under a disparate-impact theory, their remedial orders must be consistent with the Constitution. Remedial orders in disparate-impact cases should concentrate on the elimination of the offending practice that "arbitrar[ily] . . . operate[s] invidiously to discriminate on the basis of rac[e]." *Ibid.* If additional measures are adopted, courts should strive to design them to eliminate racial disparities through race-neutral means. See *Richmond v. J.A. Croson Co.,* 488 U.S. 469, 510 (1989) (plurality opinion) ("[T]he city has at its disposal a whole array of race-neutral devices to increase the accessibility of city contracting opportunities to small entrepreneurs of all races"). Remedial orders that impose racial targets or quotas might raise more difficult constitutional questions.

While the automatic or pervasive injection of race into public and private transactions covered by the FHA has special dangers, it is also true that race may be considered in certain circumstances and in a proper fashion When setting their larger goals, local housing authorities may choose to foster diversity and combat racial isolation with race-neutral tools, and mere awareness of race in attempting to solve the problems facing inner cities does not doom that endeavor at the outset.

The Court holds that disparate-impact claims are cognizable under the Fair Housing Act.

The judgment of the Court of Appeals for the Fifth Circuit is affirmed, and the case is remanded for further proceedings consistent with this opinion.

It is so ordered.

■ JUSTICE ALITO, with whom THE CHIEF JUSTICE, JUSTICE SCALIA, and JUSTICE THOMAS join, dissenting.

No one wants to live in a rat's nest. Yet in *Gallagher v. Magner,* 619 F.3d 823 (2010), a case that we agreed to review several Terms ago, the Eighth Circuit held that the Fair Housing Act (or FHA), 42 U.S.C. § 3601 *et seq.,* could be used to attack St. Paul, Minnesota's efforts to combat "rodent infestation" and other violations of the city's housing code. 619 F.3d, at 830. The court agreed that there was no basis to "infer discriminatory intent" on the part of St. Paul. *Id.,* at 833. Even so, it concluded that the city's "aggressive enforcement of the Housing Code" was actionable because making landlords respond to "rodent infestation, missing dead-bolt locks, inadequate sanitation facilities, inadequate heat, inoperable smoke detectors, broken or missing doors," and the like increased the price of rent. *Id.,* at 830, 835. Since minorities were statistically more likely to fall into "the bottom bracket for household adjusted median family income," they were disproportionately affected by those rent increases, *i.e.,* there was a "disparate impact." *Id.,* at 834. The upshot was that even St. Paul's good-faith attempt to ensure minimally acceptable housing for its poorest residents could not ward off a disparate-impact lawsuit.

Today, the Court embraces the same theory that drove the decision in *Magner*. This is a serious mistake. The Fair Housing Act does not create disparate-impact liability, nor do this Court's precedents. And today's decision will have unfortunate consequences for local government, private enterprise, and those living in poverty. Something has gone badly awry when a city can't even make slumlords kill rats without fear of a lawsuit. Because Congress did not authorize any of this, I respectfully dissent.

Not only is the decision of the Court inconsistent with what the FHA says and our precedents, it will have unfortunate consequences. Disparate-impact liability has very different implications in housing and employment cases.

Disparate impact puts housing authorities in a very difficult position because programs that are designed and implemented to help the poor can provide the grounds for a disparate-impact claim. As *Magner* shows, when disparate impact is on the table, even a city's good-faith attempt to remedy deplorable housing conditions can be branded "discriminatory." 619 F.3d, at 834. Disparate-impact claims thus threaten "a whole range of tax, welfare, public service, regulatory, and licensing statutes." *Washington v. Davis,* 426 U.S. 229 (1976).

This is not mere speculation. Here, one respondent has sued the Department for not allocating enough credits to higher income areas. But *another* respondent argues that giving credits to wealthy neighborhoods violates "the moral imperative to improve the substandard and inadequate affordable housing in many of our inner cities." This latter argument has special force because a city can build more housing where property is least expensive, thus benefiting more people. In fact, federal law often favors projects that revitalize low-income communities.

No matter what the Department decides, one of these respondents will be able to bring a disparate-impact case. And if the Department opts to compromise by dividing the credits, both respondents might be able to sue. Congress surely did not mean to put local governments in such a position.

The Solicitor General's answer to such problems is that HUD will come to the rescue. In particular, HUD regulations provide a defense against disparate-impact liability if a defendant can show that its actions serve "substantial, legitimate, nondiscriminatory interests" that "necessar[ily]" cannot be met by "another practice that has a less discriminatory effect." 24 CFR § 100.500(b) (2014). (There is, of course, no hint of anything like this defense in the text of the FHA. But then, there is no hint of disparate-impact liability in the text of the FHA either.)

The effect of these regulations, not surprisingly, is to confer enormous discretion on HUD—without actually solving the problem. What is a "substantial" interest? Is there a difference between a "legitimate" interest and a "nondiscriminatory" interest? To what degree must an interest be met for a practice to be "necessary"? How are parties and courts to measure "discriminatory effect"?

Because HUD's regulations and the Court's pronouncements are so "hazy," courts—lacking expertise in the field of housing policy—may inadvertently harm the very people that the FHA is meant to help. Local governments make countless decisions that may have some disparate impact related to housing. Certainly Congress did not intend to "engage the federal courts in an endless exercise of second-guessing" local programs. *Canton v. Harris,* 489 U.S. 378, 392 (1989).

Even if a city or private entity named in a disparate-impact suit believes that it is likely to prevail if a disparate-impact suit is fully litigated, the costs of litigation, including the expense of discovery and experts, may "push cost-conscious defendants to settle even anemic cases." *Bell Atlantic Corp. v. Twombly,* 550 U.S. 544, 559 (2007). And parties fearful of disparate-impact claims may let race drive their decisionmaking in hopes of avoiding litigation altogether. *Cf. Ricci,* 557 U.S., at 563, 129 S.Ct. 2658. All the while, similar dynamics may drive litigation against private actors

This is not the Fair Housing Act that Congress enacted.

NOTES AND QUESTIONS

1. *Inclusive Communities* was not itself a case involving zoning or other traditional regulatory measures. Nevertheless, as the Court's opinion indicates, disparate impact analysis does apply to zoning measures and other regulations that limit the availability of housing to members of protected classes. The *Arlington Heights* provided an early example. On remand from the Supreme Court, the Seventh Circuit held that the plaintiffs could prevail on a Fair Housing Act claim without establishing discriminatory intent by village officials, but ultimately remanded to the District Court to determine whether the village's decision had discriminatory effect. *See* Metropolitan Housing Dev. Corp. v. Vill. of Arlington Heights, 558 F.2d 1283 (7th Cir. 1977).

2. *The Structure of Fair Housing Act Litigation Against Local Regulators.* As the Court's opinion in *Inclusive Communities* indicates, a plaintiff challenging a determination by a government decision-maker makes out a *prima facie* case by identifying a policy or practice that has a "disparate impact" or "discriminatory effect" on members of a class protected by the statute. If the plaintiff makes out a *prima facie* case, the burden shifts to the government to justify the policy as necessary to achieve some legitimate government objective.

3. *Making Out a Prima Facie Case.* Much Fair Housing Act litigation turns on the plaintiff's ability to make out a *prima facie* case. If plaintiff cannot make out a *prima facie* case, defendant need not offer justifications for its zoning decisions.

Reconsider *Arlington Heights*. If you had been the lawyer for the plaintiffs, what facts would you have relied upon to make out a *prima face* case?

In *Inclusive Communities*, the Court cautioned that a Fair Housing Act plaintiff must establish that the challenged policy or practice *caused* a disparate impact. Consider whether plaintiff has made out a *prima facie* case in the following instances:

a.   The municipality has increased minimum lot size in an undeveloped area from ½ acre to 1 acre. Both before and after the ordinance, development in the area was limited to single-family homes. A private developer challenges the ordinance, and establishes that the mean household income of African-American households in the county is $30,000 less than the mean household income of white households, and that the increase in minimum lot size will lead to an increase of $30,000—from $150,000 to $180,000—in the value (and therefore price) of the average home built in the area. *See* Reinhart v. Lincoln County, 482 F.3d 1225 (10th Cir. 2007).

b.   Same facts as (a), but plaintiff also demonstrates (1) that the population of the municipality is 5% African-American, and (2) that the municipality's work force is 30% African-American.

c.   Same facts as (a) and (b), but plaintiff also demonstrates that 20% of the African-American workforce would be able to afford $150,000 homes, but only 5% would be able to afford $180,000 homes.

d.   Same facts as (a) and (b), but plaintiff also demonstrates that 50% of the white workforce would be able to afford $150,000 homes, and 45% would be able to afford $180,000 homes.

e.   Despite a private developer's request, a municipality declines to zone any land (outside of a small urban renewal area) for multiple-family housing. The developer has proposed to build multiple-family housing, and to permit occupancy by tenants receiving federal rent subsidies. The developer demonstrates that 28% of African-American town residents would qualify for rent subsidies, while only 11% of white town residents would qualify, although in actual numbers, many more white residents than African-American residents would qualify for the subsidies. *See* Huntington Branch, National Assoc. for the Advancement of Colored People v. Town of Huntington, 844 F.2d 926 (2d Cir. 1988).

f.   The city doubles its funding for housing code enforcement in order to prevent neighborhood deterioration. The result is an increase in rents in low income areas disproportionately occupied by members of minority groups. *See* Gallagher v. Magner, 619 F.3d 823 (8th Cir. 2011).

g.   The town seeks to condemn and redevelop a concededly blighted area that serves as home for most of the town's minority residents. *See* Mt. Holly Gardens Citizens in Action, Inc. v. Twp. of Mount Holly, 658 F.3d 375 (3d Cir. 2011).

4. *Rebutting the Prima Facie Case.* Suppose the plaintiff in a Fair Housing Act case establishes that the municipality's ordinance will have a disparate impact on members of a protected class. What sort of proof by the municipality would overcome a showing of disparate impact? Would it be enough for the municipality to prove that the more intensive development proposed by the plaintiff would overburden the municipality's already overcrowded schools? That the more intensive development would clog the existing road system? In other words, is it enough for the municipality to establish that its zoning decision advanced significant non-discriminatory municipal objectives? Or should the municipality also have to prove that it cannot achieve those objectives without creating a disparate impact on members of a protected class?

Reconsider the facts in the *Mt. Holly* case discussed in note 2(g), supra. Would the desire to remove blight from the municipality suffice to rebut the *prima facie* case?

Does the Court's opinion in *Inclusive Communities* answer these questions? How, if at all, do the HUD regulations discussed in *Inclusive Communities* address these questions?

Does the Fair Housing Act make the municipality's intent irrelevant, or does it merely relieve the plaintiff of the burden of proving discriminatory intent, and shift to defendant the burden of proving that it acted for non-discriminatory reasons?

5. *Remedies.* Suppose a court concludes that a municipality's decision not to rezone land (as in *Arlington Heights)* constitutes a violation of the Fair Housing Act. What remedies are available to the plaintiff (whether the plaintiff be a developer or a public-interest organization)? If a court concludes that the ordinance violates the statute, (a) should the court declare the ordinance wholly invalid, and permit the developer to build free of all restrictions, or (b) should the developer be entitled to the rezoning the developer sought, or (c) should the court give the municipality time to redraft the ordinance to make it constitutional?

In addition to declaratory or injunctive relief, should the plaintiff be entitled to recover damages from the municipality? From the municipal officials who enacted the ordinance? What arguments are there for making damage relief available? For denying a damage remedy?

6. In light of the Fair Housing Act, is there any reason for a plaintiff to advance an equal protection challenge to a zoning ordinance that has a disparate impact on members of a group protected by the statute?

7. *Discrimination in Private Housing Markets.* Uncovering racial discrimination in private housing markets is a difficult task. Most attempts to measure the incidence of racial discrimination in private residential markets use paired testers. Paired testers are actors who assume identities that are carefully crafted to ensure that the only difference between the two testers is race. If a landlord or agent or property owner treats the minority tester differently than the white tester in any respect (e.g., by denying that a unit is available, by refusing to show a unit; by showing fewer units, by offering less favorable terms, etc.), this is carefully recorded. Elaborate studies using this demanding methodology have found racial discrimination to be a persistent feature of private housing markets in the United States. John Yinger, an expert on housing discrimination, has concluded that "African American and Hispanic households are very likely to encounter discrimination when they search for housing. This discrimination occurs throughout the country; it severely limits the information minority households receive about available housing; and it adds annoyance, complexity, and expense to their housing search process." John Yinger, Closed Doors, Opportunities Lost (1995). Although studies show improvement over time, progress has been slow and uneven, and, consequently, discrimination remains common. What impact, if any, does private housing discrimination have on land use patterns? Does the pattern of discrimination in private markets put any special duty on local governments to design land use policies that will work to counteract its effects? What might such policies look like?

8. *Federal Funding as a Spur to "Fair Housing."* Congress has used the availability of federal funding as a carrot to induce local government to promote fair housing. To qualify for certain community development grants, local government must certify to the Department of Housing and Urban Development (HUD) that that the recipient "will affirmatively further fair housing." 42 U.S.C. §5304. HUD regulations require recipients to submit annual action plans that identify impediments to fair housing choice in the area, and to take actions to overcome those impediments.

In one high-profile lawsuit, an anti-discrimination group brought an action alleging that Westchester County, New York, had filed false certifications to obtain grant funding. HUD intervened in the action, resulting in a consent decree requiring the county to repay $30 million in grants, while also taking steps to further fair and affordable housing. The litigation has generated multiple judicial opinions. *See, e.g.,* County of Westchester v. Dep't of Housing and Urban Dev., 778 F.3d 412 (2d Cir. 2015).

PROBLEM

An affluent local municipality, concerned about rising housing prices, wants to enable young adult children of existing residents, to remain in town. The town amends its zoning ordinance to expand the permissible density of new development if a developer sets aside affordable units for first-time homebuyers whose incomes are between 80 and 120 percent of the median town income. In choosing among applicants for the "affordable" units, the town gives first priority to town residents and their children.

You work at the Justice Department and have been asked to evaluate the zoning amendment to determine whether it violates the Fair Housing Act. How would you analyze the issue? Would any data be useful in making your evaluation?

What defenses would you expect the town to advance, and how would you deal with those defenses? *See* United States v. Town of Oyster Bay, 66 F. Supp. 3d 285 (E.D.N.Y. 2014).

D. DISCRIMINATION BASED ON DISABILITY

The Fair Housing Act

Since its enactment, the Fair Housing Act has prohibited discrimination based on race, color, religion, and national origin. In 1974, the FHA was amended to prohibit discrimination on the basis of sex. In 1988, the statute was amended to prohibit discrimination based on "familial status" and "handicap." The 1988 Fair Housing Act Amendments include a comprehensive definition of discrimination against individuals with a handicap, and that definition has served as the foundation for numerous challenges of local zoning decisions. The statute includes a "refusal to make reasonable accommodations in rules" as a form of discrimination. Limitations imposed by zoning ordinances constitute "rules" within the meaning of the statute. The relevant statutory provisions are as follows:

42 U.S.C. § 3604. Discrimination in the sale or rental of housing and other prohibited practices.

As made applicable by section 803 [42 U.S.C. § 3603] and except as exempted by sections 803(b) and 807 [42 U.S.C. §§ 3603(b), 3607], it shall be unlawful—

. . .

(f)(1)   To discriminate in the sale or rental, or to otherwise make unavailable or deny, a dwelling to any buyer or renter because of a handicap of—

(A) that buyer or renter,[;]

(B) a person residing in or intending to reside in that dwelling after it is so sold, rented, or made available; or

(C) any person associated with that buyer or renter.

(2) To discriminate against any person in the terms, conditions, or privileges of sale or rental of a dwelling, or in the provision of services or facilities in connection with such dwelling, because of a handicap of—

(A) that person; or

(B) a person residing in or intending to reside in that dwelling after it is so sold, rented, or made available; or

(C) any person associated with that person.

(3) For purposes of this subsection, discrimination includes—

(A) a refusal to permit, at the expense of the handicapped person, reasonable modifications of existing premises occupied or to be occupied by such person if such modifications may be necessary to afford such person full enjoyment of the premises except that, in the case of a rental, the landlord may where it is reasonable to do so condition permission for a modification on the renter agreeing to restore the interior of the premises to the condition that existed before the modification, reasonable wear and tear excepted.[;]

(B) a refusal to make reasonable accommodations in rules, policies, practices, or services, when such accommodations may be necessary to afford such person equal opportunity to use and enjoy a dwelling.

In light of the statute, what limitations may a municipality place on location of facilities for the disabled? The issue arises most frequently when a municipality withholds permission to operate a group home in an established residential neighborhood, an issue we will take up shortly. But the issue also arises when a developer seeks to build a larger project designed, in part or in whole, to serve disabled residents. The following case is illustrative:

Cinnamon Hills Youth Crisis Center, Inc.
v. Saint George City

United States Court of Appeals for the Tenth Circuit, 2012
685 F.3d 917

■ GORSUCH, CIRCUIT JUDGE.

For years Cinnamon Hills has run a residential treatment facility in St. George, Utah for young people with mental and emotional disorders. Now, it wants to expand its operations with a new "step-down" program. Participants would live in a separate facility with more responsibility and autonomy than other students, all to help prepare them for reentry into society. Cinnamon Hills hopes to house its new operation on the top floor of the Ambassador Inn, a local motel it happens to own. At the same time, it wants to continue operating the ground floor as a motel open to the traveling public. Aware its unusual plan violates various city zoning ordinances, Cinnamon Hills sought a variance. When the city demurred, Cinnamon Hills brought this lawsuit alleging unlawful discrimination against the disabled. Unable to discern material facts suggestive of discrimination, the district court granted summary judgment to the city, a conclusion we ultimately find persuasive.

Cinnamon Hills's suit invokes three separate federal statutes: the Fair Housing Act (FHA), the Americans with Disabilities Act (ADA), and the Rehabilitation Act (RA). Whatever the statutory rubric, though, everyone agrees that to avoid summary judgment Cinnamon Hills must present facts suggesting that the city either (1) intentionally discriminated against the disabled, (2) engaged in conduct that had an unlawful disparate impact on the disabled, or (3) failed to provide a reasonable accommodation for the disabled. Accordingly, we organize our discussion around those theories and discuss each in its turn.

Intentional Discrimination. There are two ways to prove intentional discrimination (or "disparate treatment"), and Cinnamon Hills attempts both. First, it says it has direct proof of the city's discriminatory intent. Second, it points to circumstantial evidence and invokes the familiar *McDonnell Douglas* burden shifting scheme originally spawned in the Title VII arena but long since equally entrenched in the FHA, ADA, and RA contexts.

For direct evidence of discrimination, Cinnamon Hills points to various restrictions in § 10–5–3 of the city code, restrictions requiring residential treatment centers to locate in rural areas (among other things). Cinnamon Hills says the restrictions embodied in § 10–5–3 discriminate on their face against the disabled. But whatever else § 10–5–3 may be, it isn't *direct* evidence of discrimination against the disabled in *this* case.

Direct evidence of discrimination is evidence which, if believed, proves that the decision in the case at hand was discriminatory—and does so without depending on any further inference or presumption. So if a city zoning official explicitly relies on a discriminatory policy in making the challenged policy decision, or if he makes discriminatory comments about the disabled while explaining his basis for the contested decision, that is direct evidence of discrimination. *See EEOC v. Wiltel, Inc.,* 81 F.3d 1508, 1514 (10th Cir. 1996).

But in this case, the city did no such thing. It never invoked § 10–5–3 or its restrictions when rejecting Cinnamon Hill's request. Neither has the city ever sought to rely on § 10–5–3 after the fact, during the course of this litigation. Instead, the city has always and exclusively said its decision to deny the requested variance rested (and so was to stand or fall) on two distinct code provisions: a rule limiting stays in motels to 29 days, codified at § 3–2P–3, and a rule against residential uses in a designated commercial (or "C–3") zone, codified at § 10–10–2. And even Cinnamon Hills does not purport to identify anything discriminatory about *those* rules, which make no mention of disabled persons, let alone discriminate against disabled persons on their face.

Turning to [circumstantial evidence], we agree with the district court that the circumstantial evidence Cinnamon Hills does present is insufficient as a matter of law to satisfy the first step of *McDonnell*

Douglas. At that first step, Cinnamon Hills bears the obligation of coming forward with a *prima facie* case of discrimination, a case that must include evidence suggesting the city denied the variance *because of* the disability of Cinnamon Hills's residents. *Butler v. City of Prairie Village,* 172 F.3d 736, 748 (10th Cir. 1999). To meet this burden, Cinnamon Hills must produce evidence suggesting that the city denied to it zoning relief granted to similarly situated applicants without disabilities. Or, if there are no similarly situated non-disabled applicants, Cinnamon Hills must show the circumstances surrounding the denial of the variance support a reasonable inference that the city would have granted to an applicant without disabilities the relief it denied Cinnamon Hills.

We agree with the district court that Cinnamon Hills has failed to show a similarly situated group has been granted zoning relief remotely like the requested variance. In fact, the only relief the city has granted from the 29 day motel stay rule according to Cinnamon Hills itself is for law enforcement, emergency personnel, and 24-hour business caretakers. No one else, with or without a disability, is exempt. And we agree with the district court that "[n]o reasonable jury could conclude that law enforcement and emergency personnel [or motel caretakers] are similarly situated to disabled youth. To be sure, Cinnamon Hills points out that *some* people are allowed to live in C–3 zones: hospitals and nursing homes can locate there, and some buildings may be converted wholesale into condominiums. But there's no evidence the city has ever allowed hospitals, nursing homes, or condominiums to open up for business on the top floor of an operating motel in violation of the 29 day rule. Without that, Cinnamon Hills lacks evidence that others have been granted the relief it was denied.

Neither has Cinnamon Hills presented evidence suggesting a reasonable likelihood that the city would grant a group of non-disabled applicants the relief it denied in this case. Cinnamon Hills argues that several other residential treatment facilities faced obstacles to establishing operations within St. George. But it fails to mention the city ultimately approved most of those facilities. Alternatively, Cinnamon Hills cites a limited number of statements by city officials expressing concern that too many residential youth facilities exist in the city. Some of these officials, however, had no known role in the variance decision in this case. Some of the statements are fifteen or more years old. Such general statements suggesting bias, unattached to the variance at issue and made long ago, bear at best limited probative inferential value under our precedents

Disparate Impact. Unlike a claim for disparate treatment, a claim for disparate impact doesn't require proof of intentional discrimination. *Mountain Side Mobile Estates P'ship v. Sec'y of Hous. & Urban Dev.,* 56 F.3d 1243, 1252 (10th Cir. 1995). Even so, it has challenges of its own.

To prove a case of disparate impact discrimination, the plaintiff must show that "a specific policy caused a significant disparate effect on a protected group." *Reinhart v. Lincoln Cnty.*, 482 F.3d 1225, 1229 (10th Cir. 2007) (quotation omitted). This "is generally shown by statistical evidence ... involv[ing] the appropriate comparables" necessary to create a reasonable inference that any disparate effect identified was caused by the challenged policy and not other causal factors. *Mountain Side Mobile Estates,* 56 F.3d at 1253.

The district court held that Cinnamon Hills has produced no evidence of disparate impact, and again we agree. Cinnamon Hills offers no formal statistics or other evidence that might serve that need. It points again to the 29 day rule's exception for law enforcement, and the limited exceptions we've already identified to the ban on residences in C–3 zones. But even putting aside whether the individuals covered by these exceptions are meaningful comparators, Cinnamon Hills faces a more fundamental problem. It has not identified any evidence that disabled individuals are less able to avail themselves of these exceptions than the non-disabled. And of course without evidence of a *disparity,* Cinnamon Hills cannot make out a disparate impact claim. *See Reinhart,* 482 F.3d at 1230.

Failure to Accommodate. A claim for reasonable accommodation is yet a different sort of animal. It does not require the plaintiff to prove that the challenged policy intended to discriminate or that in effect it works systematically to exclude the disabled. Instead, in the words of the FHA, a reasonable accommodation is required whenever it "may be *necessary* to afford [a disabled] person equal opportunity to use and enjoy a dwelling." 42 U.S.C. § 3604(f)(3)(B) (emphasis added).

What does it mean to be "necessary"? The word implies more than something merely helpful or conducive. It suggests instead something "indispensable," "essential," something that "cannot be done without." Oxford English Dictionary, vol. X at 276 (2d ed. 1989). What's more, the FHA's necessity requirement doesn't appear in a statutory vacuum, but is expressly linked to the goal of "afford[ing] ... equal opportunity to use and enjoy a dwelling." 42 U.S.C. § 3604(f)(3)(B). And this makes clear that the object of the statute's necessity requirement is a level playing field in housing for the disabled. Put simply, the statute requires accommodations that are necessary (or indispensable or essential) to achieving the objective of equal housing opportunities between those with disabilities and those without.

Of course, in some sense *all* reasonable accommodations treat the disabled not just equally but preferentially. *U.S. Airways, Inc. v. Barnett,* 535 U.S. 391, 397–98, 122 S.Ct. 1516, 152 L.Ed.2d 589 (2002). Think of the blind woman who obtains an exemption from a "no pets" policy for her seeing eye dog, or the paraplegic granted special permission to live on a first floor apartment because he cannot climb the stairs. But without an accommodation, those individuals cannot take advantage of the opportunity (available to those without disabilities) to live in those housing facilities. And they cannot *because* of conditions created by their disabilities. These examples show that under the FHA it is sometimes necessary to dispense with formal equality of treatment in order to advance a more substantial equality of opportunity. And that is precisely the point of the reasonable accommodation mandate: to require changes in otherwise neutral policies that preclude the disabled from obtaining "the *same* ... *opportunities* that those without disabilities automatically enjoy." *Id.* (second emphasis added).

But while the FHA requires accommodations necessary to ensure the disabled receive the *same* housing opportunities as everybody else, it does not require *more* or *better* opportunities. The law requires accommodations overcoming barriers, imposed by the disability, that prevent the disabled from obtaining a housing opportunity others can access. But when there is no comparable housing opportunity for non-disabled people, the failure to create an opportunity for disabled people cannot be called necessary to achieve equality of opportunity in any sense. So, for example, a city need not allow the construction of a group home for the disabled in a commercial area where nobody, disabled or otherwise, is allowed to live. *See Bryant Woods Inn,* 124 F.3d at 604; *Wisconsin Cmty. Serv., Inc. v. City of Milwaukee,* 465 F.3d 737, 752 (7th Cir. 2006) (en banc); *Forest City Daly Hous., Inc. v. Town of North Hempstead,* 175 F.3d 144, 152 (2d Cir. 1999).

And recognizing this necessarily marks the end of the road for Cinnamon Hills's reasonable accommodation request. As we have already seen, no one, disabled or otherwise, is generally allowed to stay in a motel for more than 29 days or to reside in a C–3 commercial zone. [T]he evidence shows that in seeking to occupy the top floor of a motel in a commercial zone, Cinnamon Hills is seeking an opportunity that isn't available to others rather than one that is. And that's a result the statute does not compel.

Cinnamon Hills does not so much dispute this analysis on its own terms as to ask us to adopt an entirely different and more lenient legal standard. In its view, an accommodation should be held "necessary" anytime it would "provide [ ] direct amelioration of a disability's effect." Aplt. Br. at 54 (quoting *Bryant Woods Inn,* 124 F.3d at 604). And in this sense, Cinnamon Hills argues, the step-down facility is "necessary" because it would ease the transition of emotionally and mentally troubled youth from residential treatment back into society.

This interpretation, however, overlooks the statute's language linking a defendant's accommodation obligations to the goal of providing "equal opportunity to enjoy a dwelling." On Cinnamon Hills's view, defendants would be required to ameliorate *any* effect of a disability—even if doing so only affects the disabled person's chances of getting a job or playing a sport and has nothing to do with enjoying a home. Under Cinnamon Hills's reading, the Fair Housing Act would require landlords not just to accommodate disabilities affecting housing opportunities but to operate as a sort of clinic seeking to cure all ills. And that is not what the text or purpose of this statute requires.

So it is that, in the end and after independent examination of the record and the law and each of the plaintiff's three theories of relief, we find ourselves in agreement with the district court's disposition and conclude as a matter of law Cinnamon Hills has failed to adduce evidence sufficient to withstand summary judgment. The judgment of the district court is affirmed.

NOTES AND QUESTIONS

1. In *Cinnamon Hills*, the court outlines three separate theories the developer advanced in making its Fair Housing Act claim. How are the three theories different?

2. Suppose Saint George City had recently granted a variance to a developer who sought to build residential apartments above retail stores in a C–3 zone. Would Cinnamon Hills have had a better claim? On which theory or theories?

3. Suppose Saint George's ordinance had provided that motels could permit occupants to stay for longer than 29 days upon obtaining a special permit. If Cinnamon Hills sought a special permit to operate its facility and was denied, could Cinnamon Hills prevail on a Fair Housing Act claim? Which theory or theories would you rely upon if you represented Cinnamon Hills?

PROBLEMS

1. Applicant buys a 13-acre parcel located in a "Community Facilities" zoning district. Hospitals are specially permitted uses in Community Facilities district; residential uses are not permitted. Applicant seeks to build a 300-bed residential treatment facility offering behavioral and mental health services like substance abuse treatment, detoxification, and trauma resolution. The applicant applies for a special permit, characterizing the facility as a hospital.

The Community Facilities district abuts a single-family residential district, and residents of that district appear at the hearing to oppose the special permit application. Some of the residents make discriminatory remarks about the likely residents of the proposed facility. The City Commission denies the special permit application, concluding that the facility would constitute a prohibited residential use, not a permitted hospital.

If you represented the applicant, what theories would you advance in making a Fair Housing Act claim? What facts would you look for that might be helpful to your claim? Conversely, if you represented the City Commission, what facts would you seek to support your defense? *See* Palm Partners, LLC v. City of Oakland Park, 102 F.Supp.3d 1334 (S.D. Fla. 2015).

2. Applicant seeks to build a three-story apartment building to provide permanent supportive housing to individuals with disabilities. Applicant proposes to include 30 residential units in the building, along with on-site counseling and related support services for persons with disabilities. The application requires multiple variances. Under existing zoning, (a) the minimum lot size for 30 residential units would be 73,800 square feet while applicant's parcel includes only 40,451 square feet (which would accommodate only 16 units); (b) 60 parking units would be required, while applicant proposes to provide only 15; and (c) the minimum unit size per apartment is larger than applicant has proposed. If the municipality denies the variance, has the municipality violated the Fair Housing Act? *See* Nikolich v. Vill. of Arlington Heights, 870 F.Supp.2d 556 (N.D. Ill. 2012).

Turn now to the problem of group homes in residential areas. An exemption provided in 42 U.S.C. § 3607(b) provides that "[n]othing in this subchapter limits the applicability of any reasonable local, State, or Federal restrictions regarding the maximum number of occupants permitted to occupy a dwelling."

Courts have taken it as a given that, in light of the statute, a municipality may not enforce an outright ban on group homes for persons with disabilities. But how much control does the statute permit municipalities to exert over group homes located in single-family residential areas?

In City of Edmonds v. Oxford House, 514 U.S. 725 (1995), the Supreme Court held that the exemption in § 3607 for restrictions setting a "maximum number of occupants" does not apply to a restriction limiting the maximum number of unrelated individuals who may live together as a "family." In *City of Edmonds*, the municipal zoning ordinance defined "family" for purposes of single-family zoning districts, as "persons [without regard to number] related by genetics, adoption, or marriage, or a group of five or fewer [unrelated] persons." When the city issued violations to Oxford House for operating a group home for 10 to 12 adults recovering from alcoholism and drug addiction, Oxford House contended that application of the ordinance to its facility violated the Fair Housing Act. The city relied on the § 3607 exemption, but the Supreme Court disagreed, holding that:

> rules that cap the total number of occupants in order to prevent overcrowding of a dwelling "plainly and unmistakably," ... fall within § 3607(b)(1)'s absolute exemption from the FHA's governance; rules designed to preserve the family character of a neighborhood, fastening on

the composition of households rather than on the total number
of occupants living quarters can contain, do not.

514 U.S. at 735.

The Court in *City of Edmonds* did not decide whether recovering
alcoholics or drug addicts were handicapped persons within the
meaning of the statute; the parties had stipulated to that proposition
for purposes of the litigation.

Note, then, the statutory scheme: the municipality can avoid all
liability if the section 3607(b) exemption applies; if it does not apply, a
plaintiff must surmount two hurdles in order to prevail. Plaintiff must
first establish the existence of a "handicap," and must then establish
that the municipality refused to "make reasonable accommodations" for
that handicap.

PROBLEMS

In light of the statute, consider the statutory arguments each party
would make in the following situations:

1.   Developer seeks to build a complex for senior citizens located in a
district zoned for single-family residences. The complex would include ten
single-family homes, one 20-unit apartment building, and a 10-unit
assisted living facility. The units would all be accessible by the mobility
impaired. Residents would not own their own homes, but would enter into a
contract guaranteeing that when they could no longer live in their own
houses or apartments, they would become entitled to live in the assisted
living facility. If the building inspector concludes that the complex does not
comply with the zoning ordinance, and the zoning board of appeals agrees,
what relief can the developer seek? If the zoning board of appeals does not
provide relief, does the developer have a Fair Housing Act claim? What
provisions of the statute would you expect the municipality to invoke in
response? Who is likely to prevail? *See* Budnick v. Town of Carefree, 518
F.3d. 1009 (9th Cir. 2008).

2.   Developer seeks to locate a group home in a single-family residential
district. The home would house adults who suffer from Alzheimer's disease
and other forms of dementia. A state statute expressly provides that a
licensed residential facility providing supervision or care for 6 or fewer
persons shall constitute a residential use permitted in single-family
districts, and shall not require any form of permit different from those
required of single-family residences. The developer, however, wants to use
a home to house 12 residents. The city, which does not limit the number of
related individuals who may live in a single-family house, has refused to
permit use of the home for 12 residents. If the developer brings a Fair
Housing Act claim, what defense should the municipality advance? Suppose
the developer contends that it is not financially feasible to run the home
with fewer than 12 residents. Must the municipality authorize use by 12
residents? Does the Fair Housing Act require municipalities to
accommodate the financial needs of handicapped citizens? *See* Smith & Lee

Associates v. City of Taylor, 102 F.3d 781 (6th Cir. 1996) (holding that cost of operating facility is relevant to FHA analysis).

If the municipality must accommodate handicapped persons without sufficient resources to pay the cost of care in smaller facilities, is there any size limit the municipality may impose on group homes? In *Smith & Lee*, the court concluded that the accommodation of 9 residents in a group home was reasonable. What is magic about 9? Why not 12 or 15?

If a municipality can prevail on a Fair Housing Act claim by establishing that a smaller group home is not financially feasible, what evidence can the municipality introduce to rebut a claim based on financial need? *See* Bryant Woods Inn, Inc. v. Howard County, 124 F.3d 597 (4th Cir. 1997) (rejecting claim for expansion of a group home from 8 residents to 15, emphasizing evidence that other group homes in the area were able to function with 8 residents).

Is there a reason to accommodate the desire of poor disabled persons to live in single-family neighborhoods when the zoning ordinance does not accommodate the desire of poor but able persons to live in the same neighborhoods?

3.   Developer proposes, in a single-family district, a group home for persons afflicted with Alzheimer's disease. The municipality requires special permits for such group homes, and has granted a number of special permits for similar homes. If the municipality denies the permit for this home on the ground that the other homes have a vacancy rate of 25%, can the developer prevail on a Fair Housing Act challenge to the permit denial? *Cf.* Bryant Woods Inn, Inc. v. Howard County, 124 F.3d 597 (4th Cir. 1997) (citing vacancy rate as a reason for upholding permit denial).

4.   A municipality enacts an ordinance authorizing licensed group homes in single-family districts, but requiring that no group home may be located within 2,500 feet of any other group home, in order to insure that no neighborhood bears more than its fair share of the group homes. Does such a "dispersion" ordinance violate the Fair Housing Act? *See* Oconomowoc Residential Programs, Inc. v. City of Milwaukee, 300 F.3d 775 (2002) (holding that denial of a variance from 2,500-foot requirement violated the FHA).

5.   A municipality treats group homes as a "special permit" use within a single-family residential district. A not-for-profit organization wants to buy an existing home in the district for use as a group home. What risks does the organization take if it buys the home? Should a lawyer advise the organization to buy? Can the organization challenge the permit requirement as a violation of the Fair Housing Act even if the organization has neither sought, nor been denied a permit?

In Pacific Shores Properties, LLC v. City of Newport Beach, 730 F.3d 1142 (9th Cir. 2013), the city, in response to complaints by residents about group homes in the area, enacted an ordinance requiring group homes—including existing group homes—to obtain special permits. City officials made it clear that they took this course because of fears that courts would not uphold an absolute ban on group homes.

In reversing the District Court's grant of summary judgment to the city, the Ninth Circuit wrote:

> "Subjecting an entity protected by anti-discrimination laws to a permit or registration requirement, when the requirement is imposed for a discriminatory purpose, has obvious adverse impacts upon that entity, and being forced to submit to such a regime is sufficient to establish injury in a disparate treatment claim. This would be true even if such permits were granted freely."

Suppose there were no evidence of the city's intent to close down existing group homes. How would you defend a permit requirement against a Fair Housing Act challenge?

Group homes often enjoy protection under state statutes as well as the federal statute. *See, e.g.,* Conn. Gen. Stat. 8–3e(1) and 8–3g (requiring localities to treat group homes with six or fewer residents as equivalent to single-family homes).

Group Homes and Equal Protection

In light of the protections afforded by the Fair Housing Act Amendments, the Equal Protection Clause has receded as an important protection for persons with disabilities. Before enactment of the FHAA, the Supreme Court, in City of Cleburne v. Cleburne Living Center, Inc., 473 U.S. 432 (1985), addressed the constitutionality of a municipality's denial of a special use permit for operation of a group home for the mentally retarded. Although the Court struck down the ordinance requiring permits for such homes, the Court's analysis raised questions about the opinion's scope. The Court declined to hold that mental retardation is a suspect or "quasi-suspect" class triggering strict scrutiny, opting instead for "rational basis" review. Recall that, under almost all circumstances, if a court applies rational basis review to a legislative enactment, the enactment survives. But in *City of Cleburne,* the majority opinion could find no rational basis for permitting apartment houses or multiple dwellings as a matter of right within the zoning district, while requiring special permits for group homes, which the municipality labeled as a "hospital for the feeble minded." As a result, the majority invalidated the permit requirement. Other justices, dissenting in part, would have applied stricter scrutiny to an ordinance discriminating against the retarded.

The majority's reasoning, however, would not have applied as directly to permit requirements in single-family districts, because the majority did not have to decide whether there was a rational basis for distinguishing between single-family homes and group homes for the mentally retarded; the Court only had to decide that there was no basis for permitting apartment houses and not group homes. Once Congress adopted the Fair Housing Act Amendments, however, the constitutional issue became largely moot.

E. DISCRIMINATION BASED ON FAMILY COMPOSITION

Zoning ordinances across the country zone many areas for single-family residential use and others for two-family use. What is a "family" for purposes of these ordinances? The Fair Housing Act and, in many states, state statutes, require municipalities to permit group homes when necessary to accommodate persons with disabilities. Suppose, however, there are no persons with disabilities. What limits are there on the power of a municipality to define a "family"?

Municipalities have a number of concerns about family size and composition within a single-family home. Too many adults may lead to various forms of overcrowding. In extreme cases, overcrowding may lead to fire and safety concerns. Parking congestion is a more common problem: if too many adults live in a house designed for a single family, the number of cars used by those adults may result in overcrowded streets, to the detriment of neighbors. Many municipalities are also concerned about phantom "residents" who use a single-family home as an address in order to qualify children for use of the public schools (at cost to the municipality's taxpayers). Proving that a child does not live at a particular address is easier if the municipality's definition of family would not permit the child to live in the house.

In Village of Belle Terre v. Boraas, 416 U.S. 1 (1974), the United States Supreme Court faced a constitutional challenge to the municipality's definition of family brought by the owner and tenants of a home leased by six college students. The ordinance defined "family" as:

> [o]ne or more persons related by blood, adoption, or marriage, living and cooking together as a single housekeeping unit, exclusive of household servants. A number of persons but not exceeding (2) living and cooking together as a single housekeeping unit through not related by blood, adoption, or marriage shall be deemed to constitute a family.

The owner and tenants raised several grounds in their challenge, but Supreme Court rejected them all. In an opinion by Justice Douglas, the Court saw no interference with the freedom of association because "a 'family' may, so far as the ordinance is concerned, entertain whomever it likes." In oft-quoted language, the Court concluded that "[a] quiet place where yards are wide, people few, and motor vehicles restricted are legitimate guidelines in a land-use project addressed to family needs. . . . The police power is not confined to elimination of filth, stench, and unhealthy places. It is ample to lay out zones where family values, youth values, and the blessings of quiet seclusion and clean air make the area a sanctuary for people."

Three years later, the Supreme Court faced the following case. As you read the case, consider what advice you would give to a municipality about how it should define "family" in its ordinance:

Moore v. City of East Cleveland

Supreme Court of the United States, 1977
431 U.S. 494

■ MR. JUSTICE POWELL announced the judgment of the Court, and delivered an opinion in which MR. JUSTICE BRENNAN, MR. JUSTICE MARSHALL, and MR. JUSTICE BLACKMUN joined.

East Cleveland's housing ordinance, like many throughout the country, limits occupancy of a dwelling unit to members of a single family. § 1351.02. But the ordinance contains an unusual and complicated definitional section that recognizes as a "family" only a few categories of related individuals. § 1341.08. Because her family, living together in her home, fits none of those categories, appellant stands convicted of a criminal offense. The question in this case is whether the ordinance violates the Due Process Clause of the Fourteenth Amendment.[2]

I

Appellant, Mrs. Inez Moore, lives in her East Cleveland home together with her son, Dale Moore, Sr., and her two grandsons, Dale, Jr., and John Moore, Jr. The two boys are first cousins rather than brothers; we are told that John came to live with his grandmother and with the elder and younger Dale Moores after his mother's death.

In early 1973, Mrs. Moore received a notice of violation from the city, stating that John was an "illegal occupant" and directing her to

---

[2] Section 1341.08 (1966) provides:

"Family" means a number of individuals related to the nominal head of the household or to the spouse of the nominal head of the household living as a single housekeeping unit in a single dwelling unit, but limited to the following:

(a) Husband or wife of the nominal head of the household.

(b) Unmarried children of the nominal head of the household or of the spouse of the nominal head of the household, provided, however, that such unmarried children have no children residing with them.

(c) Father or mother of the nominal head of the household or of the spouse of the nominal head of the household.

(d) Notwithstanding the provisions of subsection (b) hereof, a family may include not more than one dependent married or unmarried child of the nominal head of the household or of the spouse of the nominal head of the household and the spouse and dependent children of such dependent child. For the purpose of this subsection, a dependent person is one who has more than fifty percent of his total support furnished for him by the nominal head of the household and the spouse of the nominal head of the household.

(e) A family may consist of one individual.

comply with the ordinance. When she failed to remove him from her home, the city filed a criminal charge. Mrs. Moore moved to dismiss, claiming that the ordinance was constitutionally invalid on its face. Her motion was overruled, and upon conviction she was sentenced to five days in jail and a $25 fine. The Ohio Court of Appeals affirmed after giving full consideration to her constitutional claims, and the Ohio Supreme Court denied review. We noted probable jurisdiction of her appeal, 425 U.S. 949 (1976).

II

The city argues that our decision in Village of Belle Terre v. Boraas, 416 U.S. 1 (1974), requires us to sustain the ordinance attacked here. Belle Terre, like East Cleveland, imposed limits on the types of groups that could occupy a single dwelling unit. Applying the constitutional standard announced in this Court's leading land-use case, Euclid v. Ambler Realty Co., 272 U.S. 365 (1926), we sustained the *Belle Terre* ordinance on the ground that it bore a rational relationship to permissible state objectives.

But one overriding factor sets this case apart from *Belle Terre*. The ordinance there affected only unrelated individuals. It expressly allowed all who were related by "blood, adoption, or marriage" to live together, and in sustaining the ordinance we were careful to note that it promoted "family needs" and "family values." 416 U.S., at 9. East Cleveland, in contrast, has chosen to regulate the occupancy of its housing by slicing deeply into the family itself. This is no mere incidental result of the ordinance. On its face it selects certain categories of relatives who may live together and declares that others may not. In particular, it makes a crime of a grandmother's choice to live with her grandson in circumstances like those presented here.

When a city undertakes such intrusive regulation of the family, neither *Belle Terre* nor *Euclid* governs; the usual judicial deference to the legislature is inappropriate. "This Court has long recognized that freedom of personal choice in matters of marriage and family life is one of the liberties protected by the Due Process Clause of the Fourteenth Amendment." Cleveland Board of Education v. LaFleur, 414 U.S. 632, 639–640 (1974). A host of cases, tracing their lineage to Meyer v. Nebraska, 262 U.S. 390, 399–401 (1923), and Pierce v. Society of Sisters, 268 U.S. 510, 534–535 (1925), have consistently acknowledged a "private realm of family life which the state cannot enter." Prince v. Massachusetts, 321 U.S. 158, 166 (1944). Of course, the family is not beyond regulation. *See* Prince v. Massachusetts, *supra*, at 166. But when the government intrudes on choices concerning family living arrangements, this Court must examine carefully the importance of the governmental interests advanced and the extent to which they are served by the challenged regulation. *See* Poe v. Ullman, *supra*, at 554 (Harlan, J., dissenting).

When thus examined, this ordinance cannot survive. The city seeks to justify it as a means of preventing overcrowding, minimizing traffic and parking congestion, and avoiding an undue financial burden on East Cleveland's school system. Although these are legitimate goals, the ordinance before us serves them marginally, at best. For example, the ordinance permits any family consisting only of husband, wife, and unmarried children to live together, even if the family contains a half dozen licensed drivers, each with his or her own car. At the same time it forbids an adult brother and sister to share a household, even if both faithfully use public transportation. The ordinance would permit a grandmother to live with a single dependent son and children, even if his school-age children number a dozen, yet it forces Mrs. Moore to find another dwelling for her grandson John, simply because of the presence of his uncle and cousin in the same household. We need not labor the point. Section 1341.08 has but a tenuous relation to alleviation of the conditions mentioned by the city.

III

Ours is by no means a tradition limited to respect for the bonds uniting the members of the nuclear family. The tradition of uncles, aunts, cousins, and especially grandparents sharing a household along with parents and children has roots equally venerable and equally deserving of constitutional recognition. Over the years millions of our citizens have grown up in just such an environment, and most, surely, have profited from it. Even if conditions of modern society have brought about a decline in extended family households, they have not erased the accumulated wisdom of civilization, gained over the centuries and honored throughout our history, that supports a larger conception of the family. Out of choice, necessity, or a sense of family responsibility, it has been common for close relatives to draw together and participate in the duties and the satisfactions of a common home. Decisions concerning child rearing, which *Yoder*, *Meyer*, *Pierce*, and other cases have recognized as entitled to constitutional protection, long have been shared with grandparents or other relatives who occupy the same household—indeed who may take on major responsibility for the rearing of the children. Especially in times of adversity, such as the death of a spouse or economic need, the broader family has tended to come together for mutual sustenance and to maintain or rebuild a secure home life. This is apparently what happened here.

Whether or not such a household is established because of personal tragedy, the choice of relatives in this degree of kinship to live together may not lightly be denied by the State. *Pierce* struck down on Oregon law requiring all children to attend the State's public schools, holding that the Constitution "excludes any general power of the State to standardize its children by forcing them to accept instruction from public teachers only." 268 U.S., at 535. By the same token the

Constitution prevents East Cleveland from standardizing its children—and its adults—by forcing all to live in certain narrowly defined family patterns.

Reversed.

■ MR. JUSTICE BRENNAN, with whom MR. JUSTICE MARSHALL joins, concurring.

In today's America, the "nuclear family" is the pattern so often found in much of white suburbia. J. Vander Zanden, Sociology: A Systematic Approach 322 (3d ed. 1975). The Constitution cannot be interpreted, however, to tolerate the imposition by government upon the rest of us of white suburbia's preference in patterns of family living. The "extended family" that provided generations of early Americans with social services and economic and emotional support in times of hardship, and was the beachhead for successive waves of immigrants who populated our cities, remains not merely still a pervasive living pattern, but under the goad of brutal economic necessity, a prominent pattern—virtually a means of survival—for large numbers of the poor and deprived minorities of our society. For them compelled pooling of scant resources requires compelled sharing of a household.

The "extended" form is especially familiar among black families. We may suppose that this reflects the truism that black citizens, like generations of white immigrants before them, have been victims of economic and other disadvantages that would worsen if they were compelled to abandon extended, for nuclear, living patterns. Even in husband and wife households, 13% of black families compared with 3% of white families include relatives under 18 years old, in addition to the couple's own children. In black households whose head is an elderly woman, as in this case, the contrast is even more striking: 48% of such black households, compared with 10% of counterpart white households, include related minor children not offspring of the head of the household.

■ MR. JUSTICE STEVENS, concurring in the judgment.

In my judgment the critical question presented by this case is whether East Cleveland's housing ordinance is a permissible restriction on appellant's right to use her own property as she sees fit.

There appears to be no precedent for an ordinance which excludes any of an owner's relatives from the group of persons who may occupy his residence on a permanent basis. Nor does there appear to be any justification for such a restriction on an owner's use of his property. The city has failed totally to explain the need for a rule which would allow a homeowner to have two grandchildren live with her if they are brothers, but not if they are cousins. Since this ordinance has not been shown to have any "substantial relation to the public health, safety, morals, or general welfare" of the city of East Cleveland, and since it cuts so deeply into a fundamental right normally associated with the ownership of residential property—that of an owner to decide who may reside on his or her property—it must fall under the limited standard of review of zoning decisions which this Court preserved in *Euclid* and *Nectow*. Under that standard, East Cleveland's unprecedented ordinance constitutes a taking of property without due process and without just compensation.

NOTES AND QUESTIONS

1. What critical differences are there between the definition of "family" sustained by the Supreme Court in *Belle Terre* and the definition invalidated in *Moore*?

2. In light of *Moore*, can a municipality impose any limits on the number of persons related by blood or marriage who would be permitted to live in a single-family house? Would it be possible to draft a constitutional ordinance that prohibited four sisters and their respective husbands and children from living together in a single-family house?

3. After *Moore*, can a municipality enact a zoning ordinance that imposes a maximum number of occupants, related or unrelated, who may live in a single-family house? Would you expect any political objections to a maximum occupancy limitation? From whom?

Suppose the municipality limited the number of occupants per square foot, or per room. Would such a restriction fare better?

4. A widowed homeowner lives in a single-family district together with her boyfriend, her daughter, and her daughter's boyfriend. Is the homeowner in violation of the zoning ordinance in *Belle Terre*? If you represented the municipality, how would you draft a definition of "family" that would authorize this group of persons to live together without also permitting the home to be used as a fraternity house?

5. Could a municipality deal with problems of congestion more effectively by omitting a definition of "family," and by instead defining single-family residences by reference to structural components? For instance, could a municipality define a single-family house to be one with no more than one room that includes facilities for cooking and refrigeration? What objections would you expect to such a definition?

6. *Family Composition and the Fair Housing Act.* The Fair Housing Act prohibits discrimination based on "familial status." The statute's inartful definition of "familial status" provides:

> "Familial status" means one or more individuals (who have not attained the age of 18 years) being domiciled with—
>
> (1) a parent or another person having legal custody of such individual or individuals; or
>
> (2) the designee of such parent or other person having such custody, with the written permission of such parent or other person.

Would the definition of "family" in *Moore* have violated the Fair Housing Act? Why not? Would the Fair Housing Act prevent a municipality from excluding foster homes, in which the homeowner acts as custodian for rotating groups of five or six unrelated children?

7.   Modern living arrangements have increasingly challenged the concept of the "traditional" American family, with two married parents, and three or four biologically related children. As the size of nuclear families decreases, Americans have begun to turn to cohousing arrangements involving unrelated adults operating as "functional families." Unlike those living in a dormitory or rooming house, a functional family may share household expenses, participate in collective child-rearing, eat meals together, and share common goals and feelings. Should zoning laws include functional families in their definitions of "family"? How would they do this without opening the door to dormitories and rooming houses?

Litigation involving functional families is on the rise. A growing number of state courts have looked beyond *Belle Terre*—which only interpreted the federal constitution on a set of facts that did not involve a functional family—and rejected strict definitions of family. *See, e.g.,* McMinn v. Town of Oyster Bay, 66 N.Y.2d 544, 498 N.Y.S.2d 128, 488 N.E.2d 1240 (1985) (involving four unrelated men); Charter Tp. of Delta v. Dinolfo, 419 Mich. 253, 351 N.W.2d 831 (1984) (involving members of a religious community living as a family); Children's Home of Easton v. City of Easton, 53 Pa. Commw. 216, 417 A.2d 830 (1980) (involving a foster home); Holy State v. Baker, 81 N.J. 99, 405 A.2d 368 (1979) (involving an "Evangelical Christian family"); Name Hospital v. Montroy, 153 N.J. Super. 181, 379 A.2d 299 (Law Div. 1977) (involving a group of nuns). The basis of such decisions is generally that strict definitions of "family" are not reasonably related to a legitimate zoning purpose. Most of these cases involve the interpretation of state constitutional requirements as they apply to functional families whose makeup differs greatly from the six college students challenging the ordinance in *Belle Terre*.

PROBLEM

A municipality's zoning ordinance defines "family" as "(1) Up to three persons occupying a dwelling unit; or (2) Four or more persons occupying a dwelling unit and living together as a traditional family or the functional equivalent of a traditional family." A nonprofit group wants to purchase a house to provide a home for ten homeless persons between the ages of 16 and 20. The home would have round-the-clock staffing with a rotating group of five houseparents and counselors each of whom live locally. The municipality has indicated that it will issue a violation if the nonprofit group carries through its plans. The nonprofit group asks whether it can mount a challenge to the municipality's position. Advise the group. *See* Westhab, Inc. v. City of New Rochelle, 2004 WL 1171400 (S.D.N.Y. 2004).

IV. FREE SPEECH CLAIMS

A. SIGN REGULATION

Because billboards and other signs are often distracting to drivers and ugly to many residents, municipalities (and, to some extent states and even the federal government in the Highway Beautification Act of 1965) have sought to regulate their use. The Supreme Court has long recognized that public safety provides a justification for land use regulation, and in recent decades, courts have also recognized that aesthetic regulation is within the purview of the municipal police power. For instance, in Cromwell v. Ferrier, 19 N.Y.2d 263, 273, 279 N.Y.S.2d 22, 225 N.E.2d 749, 755 (1967), the New York Court of Appeals recognized that:

> Advertising signs and billboards, if misplaced, often are egregious examples of ugliness, distraction, and deterioration. They are just as much subject to reasonable controls, including prohibition, as enterprises which emit offensive noises, odors, or debris. The eye is entitled to as much recognition as the other senses, but, of course, the offense to the eye must be substantial and be deemed to have material effect on the community or district pattern.

As we have seen, municipalities often use amortization periods to eliminate billboards without forcing immediate loss of the investment their owners have made in building them.

Regulation of signs, however, raises issues beyond the economic claims of sign owners and the merits of esthetic regulation. Landowners have often challenged sign regulation on First Amendment grounds. Several of these challenges have reached the Supreme Court.

1. THE METROMEDIA CASE

In Metromedia, Inc. v. City of San Diego, 453 U.S. 490 (1981), the Supreme Court invalidated a San Diego ordinance prohibiting advertising display signs. The ordinance banned both commercial signs and noncommercial signs, but exempted signs advertising goods and services available on the property where the sign is located. So, for instance, McDonald's could maintain a McDonald's sign on a McDonald's restaurant, but could not maintain a sign a mile away advertising the McDonald's restaurant.

Metromedia, a major player in the billboard business, challenged the ordinance on First Amendment grounds. The case generated five opinions in the Supreme Court, none of which garnered more than four votes.

Justice White's plurality opinion started by acknowledging that restrictions on billboards served legitimate government purposes:

promoting traffic safety and avoiding esthetic harm. The plurality nevertheless concluded that the ordinance was invalid because it preferred some forms of commercial speech (onsite advertising signs) to all forms of noncommercial speech:

> "Insofar as the city tolerates billboards at all, it cannot choose to limit their content to commercial messages; the city may not conclude that the communication of commercial information concerning goods and services connected with a particular site is of greater value than the communication of noncommercial messages."

453 U.S. at 513. The plurality suggested that if the San Diego ordinance had banned commercial billboards while permitting noncommercial billboards, the ordinance would be constitutional.

Justice Brennan's concurrence questioned the proposition that the First Amendment permits a sharp distinction between commercial and noncommercial speech:

> "I would be unhappy to see city officials dealing with the following series of billboards and deciding which ones to permit: the first billboard contains the message "Visit Joe's Ice Cream Shoppe"; the second, "Joe's Ice Cream Shoppe uses only the highest quality dairy products"; the third, "Because Joe thinks that dairy products are good for you, please shop at Joe's Shoppe"; and the fourth, "Joe says to support dairy price supports: they mean lower prices for you at his Shoppe." Or how about some San Diego Padres baseball fans—with no connection to the team—who together rent a billboard and communicate the message "Support the San Diego Padres, a great baseball team." May the city decide that a United Automobile Workers billboard with the message "Be a patriot—do not buy Japanese-manufactured cars" is "commercial" and therefore forbid it? What if the same sign is placed by Chrysler?

453 U.S. at 538. Although he agreed that the San Diego ordinance was unconstitutional, he concluded that an ordinance totally banning commercial billboards but allowing noncommercial billboards would also be unconstitutional.

Chief Justice Burger and Justices Stevens and Rehnquist dissented in separate opinions, and would have upheld the San Diego ordinance.

2.   CITY OF LADUE V. GILLEO

Thirteen years later, the Court dealt with another challenge to a sign ordinance—this one by an individual homeowner seeking to make a political statement. In City of Ladue v. Gilleo, 512 U.S. 43 (1994), the court invalidated an ordinance enacted in response to Margaret Gilleo's

8.5 x 11 inch sign, in her second floor window, proclaiming "For Peace in the Gulf." The ordinance prohibited all signs within a residential district unless those signs fell within one of ten exemptions, including "residential identification" signs and "for sale" signs.

In holding that the ordinance violated the First Amendment, the Court emphasized that:

> Ladue has almost completely foreclosed a venerable means of communication that is both unique and important. It has totally foreclosed that medium to political, religious, or personal messages. Signs that react to a local happening or express a view on a controversial issue both reflect and animate change in the life of a community. Often placed on lawns or in windows, residential signs play an important part in political campaigns.

512 U.S. at 54. Justice Stevens, writing for the Court, emphasized that:

> Residential signs are an unusually cheap and convenient form of communication. Especially for persons of modest means or limited mobility, a yard or window sign may have no practical substitute. Even for the affluent, the added costs in money or time of taking out a newspaper advertisement, handing out leaflets on the street, or standing in front of one's house with a hand-held sign may make the difference between participating and not participating in some public debate.

512 U.S. at 57. The Court noted, too, that the self-interest of residents diminishes the danger of widespread "visual clutter" that served as a foundation for the city's ordinance. The Court also suggested the Ladue could use "more temperate measures" to satisfy its regulatory needs.

Against that background, the Court grappled with signs once again, this time in 2015:

Reed v. Town of Gilbert

Supreme Court of the United States, 2015
___ U.S. ___, 135 S.Ct. 2218

■ JUSTICE THOMAS delivered the opinion of the Court.

The town of Gilbert, Arizona (or Town), has adopted a comprehensive code governing the manner in which people may display outdoor signs. The Sign Code identifies various categories of signs based on the type of information they convey, then subjects each category to different restrictions. One of the categories is "Temporary Directional Signs Relating to a Qualifying Event," loosely defined as signs directing the public to a meeting of a nonprofit group. The Code imposes more stringent restrictions on these signs than it does on signs conveying other messages. We hold that these provisions are content-based regulations of speech that cannot survive strict scrutiny.

I

A

The Sign Code prohibits the display of outdoor signs anywhere within the Town without a permit, but it then exempts 23 categories of signs from that requirement. These exemptions include everything from bazaar signs to flying banners. Three categories of exempt signs are particularly relevant here.

The first is "Ideological Sign[s]." This category includes any "sign communicating a message or ideas for noncommercial purposes that is not a Construction Sign, Directional Sign, Temporary Directional Sign Relating to a Qualifying Event, Political Sign, Garage Sale Sign, or a sign owned or required by a governmental agency." Of the three categories discussed here, the Code treats ideological signs most favorably, allowing them to be up to 20 square feet in area and to be placed in all "zoning districts" without time limits.

The second category is "Political Sign[s]." This includes any "temporary sign designed to influence the outcome of an election called by a public body." The Code treats these signs less favorably than ideological signs. The Code allows the placement of political signs up to 16 square feet on residential property and up to 32 square feet on nonresidential property, undeveloped municipal property, and "rights-of-way." These signs may be displayed up to 60 days before a primary election and up to 15 days following a general election.

The third category is "Temporary Directional Signs Relating to a Qualifying Event." This includes any "Temporary Sign intended to direct pedestrians, motorists, and other passersby to a 'qualifying event.' " A "qualifying event" is defined as any "assembly, gathering, activity, or meeting sponsored, arranged, or promoted by a religious, charitable, community service, educational, or other similar non-profit organization." The Code treats temporary directional signs even less favorably than political signs. Temporary directional signs may be no larger than six square feet. They may be placed on private property or on a public right-of-way, but no more than four signs may be placed on a single property at any time. *Ibid.* And, they may be displayed no more than 12 hours before the "qualifying event" and no more than 1 hour afterward.

B

Petitioners Good News Community Church (Church) and its pastor, Clyde Reed, wish to advertise the time and location of their Sunday church services. The Church is a small, cash-strapped entity that owns no building, so it holds its services at elementary schools or other locations in or near the Town. In order to inform the public about

its services, which are held in a variety of different locations, the
Church began placing 15 to 20 temporary signs around the Town,
frequently in the public right-of-way abutting the street. The signs
typically displayed the Church's name, along with the time and location
of the upcoming service. Church members would post the signs early in
the day on Saturday and then remove them around midday on Sunday.
The display of these signs requires little money and manpower, and
thus has proved to be an economical and effective way for the Church to
let the community know where its services are being held each week.

This practice caught the attention of the Town's Sign Code
compliance manager, who twice cited the Church for violating the Code.
The first citation noted that the Church exceeded the time limits for
displaying its temporary directional signs. The second citation referred
to the same problem, along with the Church's failure to include the date
of the event on the signs. Town officials even confiscated one of the
Church's signs, which Reed had to retrieve from the municipal offices.

Reed contacted the Sign Code Compliance Department in an
attempt to reach an accommodation. His efforts proved unsuccessful.
The Town's Code compliance manager informed the Church that there
would be "no leniency under the Code" and promised to punish any
future violations.

Shortly thereafter, petitioners filed a complaint in the United
States District Court for the District of Arizona, arguing that the Sign
Code abridged their freedom of speech in violation of the First and
Fourteenth Amendments.

[T]the District Court granted summary judgment in favor of the
Town. The Court of Appeals . . . affirmed, holding that the Code's sign
categories were content neutral. The court concluded that "the
distinctions between Temporary Directional Signs, Ideological Signs,
and Political Signs . . . are based on objective factors relevant to
Gilbert's creation of the specific exemption from the permit requirement
and do not otherwise consider the substance of the sign."

We granted certiorari, and now reverse.

II

A

The First Amendment, applicable to the States through the
Fourteenth Amendment, prohibits the enactment of laws "abridging the
freedom of speech." U.S. Const., Amdt. 1. Under that Clause, a
government, including a municipal government vested with state
authority, "has no power to restrict expression because of its message,
its ideas, its subject matter, or its content." Police Dept. of Chicago v.
Mosley, 408 U.S. 92, 95, (1972). Content-based laws—those that target
speech based on its communicative content—are presumptively
unconstitutional and may be justified only if the government proves

that they are narrowly tailored to serve compelling state interests. R.A.V. v. St. Paul, 505 U.S. 377, 395 (1992).

Government regulation of speech is content based if a law applies to particular speech because of the topic discussed or the idea or message expressed. This commonsense meaning of the phrase "content based" requires a court to consider whether a regulation of speech "on its face" draws distinctions based on the message a speaker conveys. Some facial distinctions based on a message are obvious, defining regulated speech by particular subject matter, and others are more subtle, defining regulated speech by its function or purpose. Both are distinctions drawn based on the message a speaker conveys, and, therefore, are subject to strict scrutiny.

Our precedents have also recognized a separate and additional category of laws that, though facially content neutral, will be considered content-based regulations of speech: laws that cannot be " 'justified without reference to the content of the regulated speech,' " or that were adopted by the government "because of disagreement with the message [the speech] conveys," Ward v. Rock Against Racism, 491 U.S. 781, 791 (1989). Those laws, like those that are content based on their face, must also satisfy strict scrutiny.

B

The Town's Sign Code is content based on its face. It defines "Temporary Directional Signs" on the basis of whether a sign conveys the message of directing the public to church or some other "qualifying event." It defines "Political Signs" on the basis of whether a sign's message is "designed to influence the outcome of an election." And it defines "Ideological Signs" on the basis of whether a sign "communicat[es] a message or ideas" that do not fit within the Code's other categories. It then subjects each of these categories to different restrictions.

The restrictions in the Sign Code that apply to any given sign thus depend entirely on the communicative content of the sign. If a sign informs its reader of the time and place a book club will discuss John Locke's Two Treatises of Government, that sign will be treated differently from a sign expressing the view that one should vote for one of Locke's followers in an upcoming election, and both signs will be treated differently from a sign expressing an ideological view rooted in Locke's theory of government. More to the point, the Church's signs inviting people to attend its worship services are treated differently from signs conveying other types of ideas. On its face, the Sign Code is a content-based regulation of speech. We thus have no need to consider the government's justifications or purposes for enacting the Code to determine whether it is subject to strict scrutiny.

C

The Court of Appeals . . . determined that the Sign Code was content neutral because the Town "did not adopt its regulation of speech [based on] disagree[ment] with the message conveyed," and its justifications for regulating temporary directional signs were "unrelated to the content of the sign." In its brief to this Court, the United States similarly contends that a sign regulation is content neutral—even if it expressly draws distinctions based on the sign's communicative content—if those distinctions can be " 'justified without reference to the content of the regulated speech.' "

But this analysis skips the crucial first step in the content-neutrality analysis: determining whether the law is content neutral on its face. A law that is content based on its face is subject to strict scrutiny regardless of the government's benign motive, content-neutral justification, or lack of "animus toward the ideas contained" in the regulated speech. In other words, an innocuous justification cannot transform a facially content-based law into one that is content neutral.

Innocent motives do not eliminate the danger of censorship presented by a facially content-based statute, as future government officials may one day wield such statutes to suppress disfavored speech. That is why the First Amendment expressly targets the operation of the laws—i.e., the "abridg[ement] of speech"—rather than merely the motives of those who enacted them. U.S. Const., Amdt. 1.

III

Because the Town's Sign Code imposes content-based restrictions on speech, those provisions can stand only if they survive strict scrutiny, " 'which requires the Government to prove that the restriction furthers a compelling interest and is narrowly tailored to achieve that interest,' " Arizona Free Enterprise Club's Freedom Club PAC v. Bennett, 564 U.S. ___ (2011). Thus, it is the Town's burden to demonstrate that the Code's differentiation between temporary directional signs and other types of signs, such as political signs and ideological signs, furthers a compelling governmental interest and is narrowly tailored to that end.

The Town cannot do so. It has offered only two governmental interests in support of the distinctions the Sign Code draws: preserving the Town's aesthetic appeal and traffic safety. Assuming for the sake of argument that those are compelling governmental interests, the Code's distinctions fail as hopelessly underinclusive.

Starting with the preservation of aesthetics, temporary directional signs are "no greater an eyesore" than ideological or political ones. Yet the Code allows unlimited proliferation of larger ideological signs while strictly limiting the number, size, and duration of smaller directional ones. The Town cannot claim that placing strict limits on temporary directional signs is necessary to beautify the Town while at the same time allowing unlimited numbers of other types of signs that create the same problem.

The Town similarly has not shown that limiting temporary directional signs is necessary to eliminate threats to traffic safety, but that limiting other types of signs is not. The Town has offered no reason to believe that directional signs pose a greater threat to safety than do ideological or political signs. If anything, a sharply worded ideological sign seems more likely to distract a driver than a sign directing the public to a nearby church meeting.

In light of this underinclusiveness, the Town has not met its burden to prove that its Sign Code is narrowly tailored to further a compelling government interest.

IV

Our decision today will not prevent governments from enacting effective sign laws.

The Town has ample content-neutral options available to resolve problems with safety and aesthetics. For example, its current Code regulates many aspects of signs that have nothing to do with a sign's message: size, building materials, lighting, moving parts, and portability. And on public property, the Town may go a long way toward entirely forbidding the posting of signs, so long as it does so in an evenhanded, content-neutral manner. Indeed, some lower courts have long held that similar content-based sign laws receive strict scrutiny, but there is no evidence that towns in those jurisdictions have suffered catastrophic effects.

We acknowledge that a city might reasonably view the general regulation of signs as necessary because signs "take up space and may obstruct views, distract motorists, displace alternative uses for land, and pose other problems that legitimately call for regulation." City of Ladue v. Gilleo, 512 U.S. 43 at 48 (1994). At the same time, the presence of certain signs may be essential, both for vehicles and pedestrians, to guide traffic or to identify hazards and ensure safety. A sign ordinance narrowly tailored to the challenges of protecting the safety of pedestrians, drivers, and passengers—such as warning signs marking hazards on private property, signs directing traffic, or street numbers associated with private houses—well might survive strict scrutiny. The signs at issue in this case, including political and ideological signs and signs for events, are far removed from those purposes. As discussed above, they are facially content based and are neither justified by traditional safety concerns nor narrowly tailored.

We reverse the judgment of the Court of Appeals and remand the case for proceedings consistent with this opinion.

■ JUSTICE ALITO, with whom JUSTICE KENNEDY and JUSTICE SOTOMAYOR join, concurring.

I join the opinion of the Court but add a few words of further explanation.

As the Court shows, the regulations at issue in this case are replete with content-based distinctions, and as a result they must satisfy strict scrutiny. This does not mean, however, that municipalities are powerless to enact and enforce reasonable sign regulations. I will not attempt to provide anything like a comprehensive list, but here are some rules that would not be content based:

> Rules regulating the size of signs. These rules may distinguish among signs based on any content-neutral criteria, including any relevant criteria listed below.

> Rules regulating the locations in which signs may be placed. These rules may distinguish between free-standing signs and those attached to buildings.

> Rules distinguishing between lighted and unlighted signs.

> Rules distinguishing between signs with fixed messages and electronic signs with messages that change.

> Rules that distinguish between the placement of signs on private and public property.

> Rules distinguishing between the placement of signs on commercial and residential property.

> Rules distinguishing between on-premises and off-premises signs.

> Rules restricting the total number of signs allowed per mile of roadway.

> Rules imposing time restrictions on signs advertising a one-time event. Rules of this nature do not discriminate based on topic or subject and are akin to rules restricting the times within which oral speech or music is allowed.

In addition to regulating signs put up by private actors, government entities may also erect their own signs consistent with the principles that allow governmental speech. See Pleasant Grove City v. Summum, 555 U.S. 460, 467–469 (2009). They may put up all manner of signs to promote safety, as well as directional signs and signs pointing out historic sites and scenic spots.

Properly understood, today's decision will not prevent cities from regulating signs in a way that fully protects public safety and serves legitimate esthetic objectives.

■ JUSTICE KAGAN, with whom JUSTICE GINSBURG and JUSTICE BREYER join, concurring in the judgment.

Countless cities and towns across America have adopted ordinances regulating the posting of signs, while exempting certain categories of signs based on their subject matter. For example, some municipalities generally prohibit illuminated signs in residential neighborhoods, but lift that ban for signs that identify the address of a home or the name of its owner or occupant. In other municipalities, safety signs such as "Blind Pedestrian Crossing" and "Hidden Driveway" can be posted without a permit, even as other permanent signs require one Elsewhere, historic site markers—for example, "George Washington Slept Here"—are also exempt from general regulations And similarly, the federal Highway Beautification Act limits signs along interstate highways unless, for instance, they direct travelers to "scenic and historical attractions" or advertise free coffee. See 23 U.S.C. §§ 131(b), (c)(1), (c)(5).

Given the Court's analysis, many sign ordinances of that kind are now in jeopardy Says the majority: When laws "single[ ] out specific subject matter," they are "facially content based"; and when they are facially content based, they are automatically subject to strict scrutiny. So on the majority's view, courts would have to determine that a town has a compelling interest in informing passersby where George Washington slept. And likewise, courts would have to find that a town has no other way to prevent hidden-driveway mishaps than by specially treating hidden-driveway signs. (Well-placed speed bumps? Lower speed limits? Or how about just a ban on hidden driveways?) The consequence—unless courts water down strict scrutiny to something unrecognizable—is that our communities will find themselves in an unenviable bind: They will have to either repeal the exemptions that allow for helpful signs on streets and sidewalks, or else lift their sign restrictions altogether and resign themselves to the resulting clutter.

Although the majority insists that applying strict scrutiny to all such ordinances is "essential" to protecting First Amendment freedoms, I find it challenging to understand why that is so. This Court's decisions articulate two important and related reasons for subjecting content-based speech regulations to the most exacting standard of review. The first is "to preserve an uninhibited marketplace of ideas in which truth will ultimately prevail." McCullen v. Coakley, 573 U.S. ___, ___ (2014) (internal quotation marks omitted). The second is to ensure that the government has not regulated speech "based on hostility—or favoritism—towards the underlying message expressed." R.A.V. v. St. Paul, 505 U.S. 377, 386 (1992). Yet the subject-matter exemptions included in many sign ordinances do not implicate those concerns. Allowing residents, say, to install a light bulb over "name and address" signs but no others does not distort the marketplace of ideas. Nor does that different treatment give rise to an inference of impermissible government motive.

We apply strict scrutiny to facially content-based regulations of speech, in keeping with the rationales just described, when there is any "realistic possibility that official suppression of ideas is afoot." [Subject-matter regulation, in other words, may have the intent or effect of favoring some ideas over others. When that is realistically possible—when the restriction "raises the specter that the Government may effectively drive certain ideas or viewpoints from the marketplace"—we insist that the law pass the most demanding constitutional test.

But when that is not realistically possible, we may do well to relax our guard so that "entirely reasonable" laws imperiled by strict scrutiny can survive.

And indeed we have done just that: Our cases have been far less rigid than the majority admits in applying strict scrutiny to facially content-based laws. In City of Ladue v. Gilleo, 512 U.S. 43 (1994), the Court assumed arguendo that a sign ordinance's exceptions for address signs, safety signs, and for-sale signs in residential areas did not trigger strict scrutiny. See *id.*, at 46–47, and n. 6; *id.*, at 53, (noting this assumption). We did not need to, and so did not, decide the level-of-scrutiny question because the law's breadth made it unconstitutional under any standard.

The majority could easily have taken Ladue's tack here. The Town of Gilbert's defense of its sign ordinance—most notably, the law's distinctions between directional signs and others—does not pass strict scrutiny, or intermediate scrutiny, or even the laugh test. The Town, for example, provides no reason at all for prohibiting more than four directional signs on a property while placing no limits on the number of other types of signs. Similarly, the Town offers no coherent justification for restricting the size of directional signs to 6 square feet while allowing other signs to reach 20 square feet. The best the Town could come up with at oral argument was that directional signs "need to be smaller because they need to guide travelers along a route." Why exactly a smaller sign better helps travelers get to where they are going is left a mystery. The absence of any sensible basis for these and other distinctions dooms the Town's ordinance under even the intermediate scrutiny that the Court typically applies to "time, place, or manner" speech regulations. Accordingly, there is no need to decide in this case whether strict scrutiny applies to every sign ordinance in every town across this country containing a subject-matter exemption.

I suspect this Court and others will regret the majority's insistence today on answering that question in the affirmative. As the years go by, courts will discover that thousands of towns have such ordinances, many of them "entirely reasonable." And as the challenges to them mount, courts will have to invalidate one after the other. (This Court

may soon find itself a veritable Supreme Board of Sign Review.) And
courts will strike down those democratically enacted local laws even
though no one—certainly not the majority—has ever explained why the
vindication of First Amendment values requires that result. Because I
see no reason why such an easy case calls for us to cast a constitutional
pall on reasonable regulations quite unlike the law before us, I concur
only in the judgment.

NOTES AND QUESTIONS—BILLBOARD REGULATION

1. In light of *Metromedia, Ladue,* and *Reed,* could a municipality impose
a complete ban on billboards? *See* Interstate Outdoor Advertising, L.P. v.
Zoning Bd, 706 F.3d 527 (2013) (upholding a ban and rejecting the
argument that a complete ban leaves potential advertisers, including
noncommercial advertisers, with no alternative means to reach a particular
target audience). Could a municipality place size restrictions on billboards
that made it impossible for anyone to make money erecting them?

2. In *Metromedia,* Justice White suggested that it would be constitutional
to prohibit off-site commercial signs so long as the city also permitted
noncommercial signs. Is that position tenable after *Reed?* Why or why not?

3. How easy would it be to distinguish commercial signs from noncommercial signs? Note the hypotheticals in Justice Brennan's *Metromedia*
concurrence. How would you treat a sign paid for by the United Auto
Workers (or General Motors) saying, "Be a patriot—Don't buy Japanese
cars"? Should the sign be treated differently if it were paid for by the
Democratic Party?

Do the difficulties identified by Justice Brennan support the *Reed*
majority's position that all content-based restrictions are presumptively
unconstitutional?

4. Justice Alito's *Reed* concurrence asserts that the Court's opinion
permits a municipality to distinguish between on-premises signs and off-
premises signs. Is that consistent with Justice Thomas' opinion? Why
would a municipality want to draw such a distinction? What value is there
in protecting on-premises signs?

If an ordinance would permit attorney Alito to hang a shingle saying
"Office of Samuel Alito," but would prohibit him from hanging, at the same
location, a shingle that says "Vote Republican" or "Buy a Ford," isn't that
content-based discrimination?

Even if Justice Alito is right that a municipality may distinguish
between on-premises signs and off-premises signs, how would you draft
such an ordinance?

Suppose an ordinance permitted all on-site signs (both commercial and
non-commercial) while prohibiting all off-site signs. Would the ordinance be
invalid? What arguments would you make for each position? *Compare*
Messer v. City of Douglasville, 975 F.2d 1505 (11th Cir. 1992) (suggesting
such an ordinance would be constitutional), *with* Ackerly Communications

v. City of Cambridge, 88 F.3d 33 (1st Cir. 1996) (holding unconstitutional a distinction between on-site and off-site noncommercial speech). *See also* Vono v. Lewis, 594 F.Supp.2d 189 (D.R.I. 2009).

What does it mean for non-commercial speech to be off-site? *See* Southlake Property Associates v. City of Morrow, 112 F.3d 1114 (11th Cir. 1997) (construing statute to treat all non-commercial speech as on-site).

5. *Digital Billboards vs. Static Billboards.* Can a municipality impose restrictions on digital billboards that are more stringent than those it imposes on static billboards? What justification could a municipality offer for such a distinction? *See* Hucul Adver., LLC v. Charter Twp., 748 F.3d 273 (6th Cir. 2014) (upholding ordinance requiring greater spacing between digital billboards than between static billboards).

6. *Inconsistent Enforcement Claims.* In a number of cases, sign owners have complained that although the municipality's ordinance does not, on its face, discriminate against particular commercial speech, the municipality has applied its ordinance in ways that discriminate against particular speakers and speech. Those claims have not generally been successful. Thus, in World Wide Rush, LLC v. City of Los Angeles, 606 F.3d 676 (9th Cir. 2010), the Ninth Circuit overturned the district court's grant of a preliminary injunction against enforcement of a Los Angeles ordinance. Although the trial court had held that the city had undermined its own interest in banning large signs within 2,000 feet of a highway by authorizing exceptions, the Ninth Circuit concluded that the city was entitled to balance interests in safer and more attractive thoroughfares against other municipal interests. *See also* Clear Channel Outdoor, Inc. v. City of New York, 608 F. Supp.2d 477, 500–01 (S.D.N.Y. 2009), in which the court held that a limited number of exceptions to New York's ban on signs within 200 feet of a highway did not invalidate the prohibition.

NOTES AND QUESTIONS—RESIDENTIAL SIGNS

1. In an effort to accommodate political speech while also responding to the preferences of residents who find lawn signs unattractive, a municipality wants to enact an ordinance permitting lawn signs for 60 days before any election, but requiring a permit for display of lawn signs at all other times. The permit process would review the aesthetics, but not the content, of any sign, and would cost each permit applicant $25. Would the ordinance be constitutional? *See* Fiedorowicz v. City of Pewaukee, 2004 U.S. Dist. LEXIS 30638 (E.D. Wis. 2004); McFadden v. City of Bridgeport, 422 F. Supp.2d 659 (N.D. W.Va. 2006) (both holding such ordinances unconstitutional).

Would the answer be different if the municipality permitted lawn signs without permits so long as signs were displayed for no more than 60 days per year, with the choice of days at the option of the landowner?

2.   Suppose a municipality required no permits for lawn signs, and imposed no limits on when they might be displayed, but limited the total size of any lawn sign to 24 square feet. Would the ordinance be constitutional? What if the size limit were 24 square inches?

3.   Concerned that cardboard signs will blow away and cause debris on neighboring lawns, a municipality enacts an ordinance requiring all lawn signs to be constructed of waterproof material, and to weigh at least ten pounds (or to have anchors that weigh at least ten pounds). Would a landowner who wants to post cardboard signs have any basis for challenging the ordinance?

Suppose, for aesthetic reasons, the municipality required that any words on the sign be professionally printed rather than handwritten?

4.   A political campaign has offered to pay each homeowner in a local community $25 for permission to display campaign signs on their front lawns. The municipality wants to prohibit or discourage this practice. What alternatives, if any, are available to the municipality?

5.   *What Counts as a Sign?* A municipality limits the size of signs in residential districts, but defines signs to exclude flags, clocks, thermometers, and "works of art which in no way identify a product." Landowner, who owns a two-family house, applies for a permit to post a sign saying "End Eminent Domain Abuse." When the municipality denies the permit because the sign exceeds size limitations, landowner challenges the constitutionality of the ordinance. In light of *Reed*, should landowner prevail? *Cf.* Neighborhood Enterprises, Inc. v. City of St. Louis, 644 F.3d 728 (8th Cir. 2011) (holding that the ordinance constitutes impermissible content-based regulation).

Similar issues arise with respect to commercial signs. Suppose a municipality restricts the size of signs on commercial buildings. Landowner, who operates a "doggy daycare" business near a dog park, paints a 960 square foot mural on the rear of her building, facing the dog park. The mural includes no words, but incorporates some of the cartoon dogs that appear in the logo she uses for her business. The municipality demands removal of the mural as an impermissible sign. In Wag More Dogs, Ltd. v. Cozart, 680 F.3d 359 (4th Cir. 2012), the court upheld the municipality's determination. Is the result consistent with *Reed*?

6.   *Restriction on the Number of Signs.* Can a municipality limit the number of signs a residential homeowner can post at any one time? In Hensel v. City of Little Falls, 992 F.Supp.2d 916 (D. Minn. 2014), the court upheld a sign ordinance limiting homeowners to two yard signs. In light of *Reed*, would an address sign (e.g. 512 Oak Street) have to count against the limit? A "for sale" sign?

Would it be constitutional to limit the number of signs a homeowner can erect if the result would be to limit the number of political candidates the homeowner can endorse in a year with many contested elections?

B. ADULT USE REGULATION

Theaters and clubs that feature sexually provocative films and performances draw plenty of paying customers, but they also draw the ire of neighbors concerned about the impact these venues have on the neighborhood (as well as the ire of high-minded citizens concerned about the community's moral values). What many municipalities really want is to ban "adult uses" altogether, but the First Amendment precludes an outright prohibition. As a second-best alternative, municipalities want to limit the location of adult uses. Those limitations are often designed with two goals in mind: first, make it as unprofitable as possible for anyone to open an adult business; and second, minimize the impact on the community of any adult businesses that do open.

The Supreme Court's construction of the First Amendment constrains the power of municipalities to limit the location of adult uses. As you read the opinions, consider what strategies the Court has left open to municipalities, and the attacks available to adult use proprietors.

City of Renton v. Playtime Theaters, Inc.

Supreme Court of the United States, 1986
475 U.S. 41

■ JUSTICE REHNQUIST delivered the opinion of the Court.

The Renton ordinance . . . like the one in *American Mini Theatres*, 427 U.S. 50 (1976), does not ban adult theaters altogether, but merely provides that such theaters may not be located within 1,000 feet of any residential zone, single- or multiple-family dwelling, church, park, or school. The ordinance is therefore properly analyzed as a form of time, place, and manner regulation.

This Court has long held that regulations enacted for the purpose of restraining speech on the basis of its content presumptively violate the First Amendment. *See* Carey v. Brown, 447 U.S. 455, 462–463, and n. 7 (1980); Police Dept. of Chicago v. Mosley, 408 U.S. 92, 95, 98–99 (1972). On the other hand, so-called "content-neutral" time, place, and manner regulations are acceptable so long as they are designed to serve a substantial governmental interest and do not unreasonably limit alternative avenues of communication.

At first glance, the Renton ordinance, like the ordinance in *American Mini Theatres*, does not appear to fit neatly into either the "content-based" or the "content-neutral" category. To be sure, the ordinance treats theaters that specialize in adult films differently from other kinds of theaters. Nevertheless, as the District Court concluded, the Renton ordinance is aimed not at the *content* of the films shown at "adult motion picture theatres," but rather at the *secondary effects* of such theaters on the surrounding community.

In short, the Renton ordinance is completely consistent with our definition of "content-neutral" speech regulations as those that "are *justified* without reference to the content of the regulated speech." Virginia Pharmacy Board v. Virginia Citizens Consumer Council, Inc., 425 U.S. 748, 771 (1976) (emphasis added). The ordinance does not contravene the fundamental principle that underlies our concern about "content-based" speech regulations: that "government may not grant the use of a forum to people whose views it finds acceptable, but deny use to those wishing to express less favored or more controversial views." *Mosley, supra*, at 95–96.

The appropriate inquiry in this case, then, is whether the Renton ordinance is designed to serve a substantial governmental interest and allows for reasonable alternative avenues of communication. It is clear that the ordinance meets such a standard. As a majority of this Court recognized in *American Mini Theatres*, a city's "interest in attempting to preserve the quality of urban life is one that must be accorded high respect." 427 U.S., at 71 (plurality opinion); *see id.,* at 80 (POWELL, J., concurring) ("Nor is there doubt that the interests furthered by this ordinance are both important and substantial"). Exactly the same vital governmental interests are at stake here.

The Court of Appeals ruled, however, that because the Renton ordinance was enacted without the benefit of studies specifically relating to "the particular problems or needs of Renton," the city's justifications for the ordinance were "conclusory and speculative." 748 F.2d, at 537. We think the Court of Appeals imposed on the city an unnecessarily rigid burden of proof. The record in this case reveals that Renton relied heavily on the experience of, and studies produced by, the city of Seattle. In Seattle, as in Renton, the adult theater zoning ordinance was aimed at preventing the secondary effects caused by the presence of even one such theater in a given neighborhood.

We hold that Renton was entitled to rely on the experiences of Seattle and other cities . . . , in enacting its adult theater zoning ordinance. The First Amendment does not require a city, before enacting such an ordinance, to conduct new studies or produce evidence independent of that already generated by other cities, so long as whatever evidence the city relies upon is reasonably believed to be relevant to the problem that the city addresses. That was the case here. Nor is our holding affected by the fact that Seattle ultimately chose a different method of adult theater zoning than that chosen by Renton, since Seattle's choice of a different remedy to combat the secondary effects of adult theaters does not call into question either Seattle's identification of those secondary effects or the relevance of Seattle's experience to Renton.

We also find no constitutional defect in the method chosen by Renton to further its substantial interests. Cities may regulate adult theaters by dispersing them, as in Detroit, or by effectively concentrating them, as in Renton. "It is not our function to appraise the wisdom of [the city's] decision to require adult theaters to be separated rather than concentrated in the same areas.... [The] city must be allowed a reasonable opportunity to experiment with solutions to admittedly serious problems." *American Mini Theatres*, 427 U.S., at 71 (plurality opinion). Moreover, the Renton ordinance is "narrowly tailored" to affect only that category of theaters shown to produce the unwanted secondary effects, thus avoiding the flaw that proved fatal to the regulations in Schad v. Mount Ephraim, 452 U.S. 61 (1981), and Erznoznik v. City of Jacksonville, 422 U.S. 205 (1975).

Finally, turning to the question whether the Renton ordinance allows for reasonable alternative avenues of communication, we note that the ordinance leaves some 520 acres, or more than five percent of the entire land area of Renton, open to use as adult theater sites. The District Court found, and the Court of Appeals did not dispute the finding, that the 520 acres of land consists of "[ample], accessible real estate," including "acreage in all stages of development from raw land to developed, industrial, warehouse, office, and shopping space that is criss-crossed by freeways, highways, and roads." App. to Juris. Statement 28a.

Respondents argue, however, that some of the land in question is already occupied by existing businesses, that "practically none" of the undeveloped land is currently for sale or lease, and that in general there are no "commercially viable" adult theater sites within the 520 acres left open by the Renton ordinance.

That respondents must fend for themselves in the real estate market, on an equal footing with other prospective purchasers and lessees, does not give rise to a First Amendment violation. And although we have cautioned against the enactment of zoning regulations that have "the effect of suppressing, or greatly restricting access to, lawful speech," *American Mini Theatres*, 427 U.S., at 71, n. 35 (plurality opinion), we have never suggested that the First Amendment compels the Government to ensure that adult theaters, or any other kinds of speech-related businesses for that matter, will be able to obtain sites at bargain prices

In sum, we find that the Renton ordinance represents a valid governmental response to the "admittedly serious problems" created by adult theaters. *See id.*, at 71 (plurality opinion). Renton has not used "the power to zone as a pretext for suppressing expression," *id.*, at 84 (POWELL, J., concurring), but rather has sought to make some areas available for adult theaters and their patrons, while at the same time preserving the quality of life in the community at large by preventing those theaters from locating in other areas. This, after all, is the essence of zoning.

Reversed.

■ JUSTICE BLACKMUN concurs in the result.

■ JUSTICE BRENNAN, with whom JUSTICE MARSHALL joins, dissenting.

[T]he circumstances here strongly suggest that the ordinance was designed to suppress expression, even that constitutionally protected, and thus was not to be analyzed as a content-neutral time, place, and manner restriction. The Court allows Renton to conceal its illicit motives, however, by reliance on the fact that other communities adopted similar restrictions. The Court's approach largely immunizes such measures from judicial scrutiny, since a municipality can readily find other municipal ordinances to rely upon, thus always retrospectively justifying special zoning regulations for adult theaters.

City of Los Angeles v. Alameda Books, Inc.

Supreme Court of the United States, 2002
535 U.S. 425

■ JUSTICE O'CONNOR announced the judgment of the Court and delivered an opinion, in which THE CHIEF JUSTICE, JUSTICE SCALIA, and JUSTICE THOMAS join.

In 1977, the city of Los Angeles conducted a comprehensive study of adult establishments and concluded that concentrations of adult businesses are associated with higher rates of prostitution, robbery, assaults, and thefts in surrounding communities. *See* App. 35–162 (Los Angeles Dept. of City Planning, Study of the Effects of the Concentration of Adult Entertainment Establishments in the City of Los Angeles (City Plan Case No. 26475, City Council File No. 74–4521–S.3, June 1977)). Accordingly, the city enacted an ordinance prohibiting the establishment, substantial enlargement, or transfer of ownership of an adult arcade, bookstore, cabaret, motel, theater, or massage parlor or a place for sexual encounters within 1,000 feet of another such enterprise or within 500 feet of any religious institution, school, or public park. *See* Los Angeles Municipal Code § 12.70(C) (1978).

There is evidence that the intent of the city council when enacting this prohibition was not only to disperse distinct adult establishments housed in separate buildings, but also to disperse distinct adult businesses operated under common ownership and housed in a single structure.

Concerned that allowing an adult-oriented department store to replace a strip of adult establishments could defeat the goal of the original ordinance, the city council amended § 12.70(C) by adding a prohibition on "the establishment or maintenance of more than one adult entertainment business in the same building, structure or portion thereof."

Respondents, Alameda Books, Inc., and Highland Books, Inc., are two adult establishments operating in Los Angeles. Neither is located within 1,000 feet of another adult establishment or 500 feet of any religious institution, public park, or school. Each establishment occupies less than 3,000 square feet. Both respondents rent and sell sexually oriented products, including videocassettes. Additionally, both provide booths where patrons can view videocassettes for a fee. Although respondents are located in different buildings, each operates its retail sales and rental operations in the same commercial space in which its video booths are located. There are no physical distinctions between the different operations within each establishment and each establishment has only one entrance. 222 F.3d 719 at 721. Respondents concede they are openly operating in violation of § 12.70(C) of the city's Code, as amended. Brief for Respondents 7; Brief for Petitioner 9.

After a city building inspector found in 1995 that Alameda Books, Inc., was operating both as an adult bookstore and an adult arcade in violation of the city's adult zoning regulations, respondents joined as plaintiffs and sued under 42 U.S.C. § 1983 for declaratory and injunctive relief to prevent enforcement of the ordinance. 222 F.3d at 721.

In Renton v. Playtime Theatres, Inc., *supra*, this Court considered the validity of a municipal ordinance that prohibited any adult movie theater from locating within 1,000 feet of any residential zone, family dwelling, church, park, or school. We held ... that the Renton ordinance was aimed not at the content of the films shown at adult theaters, but rather at the secondary effects of such theaters on the surrounding community, namely at crime rates, property values, and the quality of the city's neighborhoods. Therefore, the ordinance was deemed content neutral. *Renton, supra*, at 47–49. Finally, given this finding, we stated that the ordinance would be upheld so long as the city of Renton showed that its ordinance was designed to serve a substantial government interest and that reasonable alternative avenues of communication remained available. 475 U.S. at 50. We concluded that Renton had met this burden, and we upheld its ordinance. *Id.*, at 51–54.

The Court of Appeals applied the same analysis to evaluate the Los Angeles ordinance challenged in this case. The Court of Appeals noted that the primary evidence relied upon by Los Angeles to demonstrate a link between combination adult businesses and harmful secondary effects was the 1977 study conducted by the city's planning department. The Court of Appeals found, however, that the city could not rely on that study because it did not "support a reasonable belief that [the] combination [of] businesses ... produced harmful secondary effects of the type asserted." 222 F.3d at 724.

The central component of the 1977 study is a report on city crime patterns provided by the Los Angeles Police Department. That report indicated that, during the period from 1965 to 1975, certain crime rates grew much faster in Hollywood, which had the largest concentration of adult establishments in the city, than in the city of Los Angeles as a whole. For example, robberies increased 3 times faster and prostitution 15 times faster in Hollywood than citywide. App. 124–125.

Respondents suggest that the city's prohibition on multiuse establishments will raise crime rates in certain neighborhoods because it will force certain adult businesses to relocate to areas without any other adult businesses. Respondents' claim assumes that the 1977 study proves that all adult businesses, whether or not they are located near other adult businesses, generate crime. This is a plausible reading of the results from the 1977 study, but respondents do not demonstrate that it is a compelled reading. Nor do they provide evidence that refutes the city's interpretation of the study, under which the city's prohibition should on balance reduce crime. If this Court were nevertheless to accept respondents' speculation, it would effectively require that the city provide evidence that not only supports the claim that its ordinance serves an important government interest, but also does not provide support for any other approach to serve that interest.

In *Renton,* we specifically refused to set such a high bar for municipalities that want to address merely the secondary effects of protected speech. We held that a municipality may rely on any evidence that is "reasonably believed to be relevant" for demonstrating a connection between speech and a substantial, independent government interest. 475 U.S. at 51–52; *see also, e.g.*, Barnes v. Glen Theatre, Inc., 501 U.S. 560, 584, 115 L. Ed. 2d 504, 111 S. Ct. 2456 (1991) (SOUTER, J., concurring in judgment) (permitting municipality to use evidence that adult theaters are correlated with harmful secondary effects to support its claim that nude dancing is likely to produce the same effects). This is not to say that a municipality can get away with shoddy data or reasoning. The municipality's evidence must fairly support the municipality's rationale for its ordinance. If plaintiffs fail to cast direct doubt on this rationale, either by demonstrating that the municipality's evidence does not support its rationale or by furnishing evidence that disputes the municipality's factual findings, the municipality meets the standard set forth in *Renton.* If plaintiffs succeed in casting doubt on a municipality's rationale in either manner, the burden shifts back to the municipality to supplement the record with evidence renewing support for a theory that justifies its ordinance. *See, e.g.*, Erie v. Pap's A. M., 529 U.S. 277, 298, 146 L. Ed. 2d 265, 120 S. Ct. 1382 (2000) (plurality opinion). This case is at a very early stage in this process. It arrives on a summary judgment motion by respondents defended only by complaints that the 1977 study fails to prove that the city's justification for its ordinance is necessarily correct. Therefore, we conclude that the city, at this stage of the litigation, has complied with the evidentiary requirement in *Renton*.

Accordingly, we reverse the Court of Appeals' judgment granting summary judgment to respondents and remand the case for further proceedings.

It is so ordered.

■ JUSTICE SCALIA, concurring.

I join the plurality opinion because I think it represents a correct application of our jurisprudence concerning regulation of the "secondary effects" of pornographic speech. As I have said elsewhere, however, in a case such as this our First Amendment traditions make "secondary effects" analysis quite unnecessary. The Constitution does not prevent those communities that wish to do so from regulating, or indeed entirely suppressing, the business of pandering sex. *See, e.g.*, Erie v. Pap's A. M., 529 U.S. 277, 310, 146 L. Ed. 2d 265, 120 S. Ct. 1382 (2000) (SCALIA, J., concurring in judgment); FW/PBS, Inc. v. Dallas, 493 U.S. 215, 256–261, 107 L. Ed. 2d 603, 110 S. Ct. 596 (1990) (SCALIA, J., concurring in part and dissenting in part).

■ JUSTICE KENNEDY, concurring in the judgment.

[A] city may not regulate the secondary effects of speech by suppressing the speech itself. A city may not, for example, impose a content-based fee or tax. *See* Arkansas Writers' Project, Inc. v. Ragland, 481 U.S. 221, 230, 95 L. Ed. 2d 209, 107 S. Ct. 1722 (1987) ("Official scrutiny of the content of publications as the basis for imposing a tax is entirely incompatible with the First Amendment's guarantee of freedom of the press"). This is true even if the government purports to justify the fee by reference to secondary effects. *See* Forsyth County v. Nationalist Movement, 505 U.S. 123, 134–135, 120 L. Ed. 2d 101, 112 S. Ct. 2395 (1992). Though the inference may be inexorable that a city could reduce secondary effects by reducing speech, this is not a permissible strategy. The purpose and effect of a zoning ordinance must be to reduce secondary effects and not to reduce speech.

A zoning measure can be consistent with the First Amendment if it is likely to cause a significant decrease in secondary effects and a trivial decrease in the quantity of speech. It is well documented that multiple adult businesses in close proximity may change the character of a neighborhood for the worse. Those same businesses spread across the city may not have the same deleterious effects. At least in theory, a dispersal ordinance causes these businesses to separate rather than to close, so negative externalities are diminished but speech is not.

The narrow question presented in this case is whether the ordinance at issue is invalid "because the city did not study the negative effects of such combinations of adult businesses, but rather relied on judicially approved statutory precedent from other jurisdictions." Pet.

for Cert. This question is actually two questions. First, what proposition does a city need to advance in order to sustain a secondary-effects ordinance? Second, how much evidence is required to support the proposition? The plurality skips to the second question and gives the correct answer; but in my view more attention must be given to the first.

At the outset, we must identify the claim a city must make in order to justify a content-based zoning ordinance. As discussed above, a city must advance some basis to show that its regulation has the purpose and effect of suppressing secondary effects, while leaving the quantity and accessibility of speech substantially intact. The ordinance may identify the speech based on content, but only as a shorthand for identifying the secondary effects outside. A city may not assert that it will reduce secondary effects by reducing speech in the same proportion. The rationale of the ordinance must be that it will suppress secondary effects—and not by suppressing speech.

The plurality's analysis does not address how speech will fare under the city's ordinance. As discussed, the necessary rationale for applying intermediate scrutiny is the promise that zoning ordinances like this one may reduce the costs of secondary effects without substantially reducing speech. For this reason, it does not suffice to say that inconvenience will reduce demand and fewer patrons will lead to fewer secondary effects. This reasoning would as easily justify a content-based tax: Increased prices will reduce demand, and fewer customers will mean fewer secondary effects. But a content-based tax may not be justified in this manner. *See* Arkansas Writers' Project, Inc. v. Ragland, 481 U.S. 221, 95 L. Ed. 2d 209, 107 S. Ct. 1722 (1987); Forsyth County v. Nationalist Movement, 505 U.S. 123, 120 L. Ed. 2d 101, 112 S. Ct. 2395 (1992). It is no trick to reduce secondary effects by reducing speech or its audience; but a city may not attack secondary effects indirectly by attacking speech.

The analysis requires a few more steps. If two adult businesses are under the same roof, an ordinance requiring them to separate will have one of two results: One business will either move elsewhere or close. The city's premise cannot be the latter. It is true that cutting adult speech in half would probably reduce secondary effects proportionately. But again, a promised proportional reduction does not suffice. Content-based taxes could achieve that, yet these are impermissible.

The premise, therefore, must be that businesses—even those that have always been under one roof—will for the most part disperse rather than shut down.

Only after identifying the proposition to be proved can we ask the second part of the question presented: is there sufficient evidence to support the proposition? As to this, we have consistently held that a city must have latitude to experiment, at least at the outset, and that very little evidence is required.

In this case the proposition to be shown is supported by a single study and common experience. The city's study shows a correlation between the concentration of adult establishments and crime. Two or more adult businesses in close proximity seem to attract a critical mass of unsavory characters and the crime rate may increase as a result. The city, therefore, sought to disperse these businesses. Los Angeles Municipal Code § 12.70(C) (1983), as amended. This original ordinance is not challenged here, and we may assume that it is constitutional.

The city may next infer—from its study and from its own experience—that two adult businesses under the same roof are no better than two next door. The city could reach the reasonable conclusion that knocking down the wall between two adult businesses does not ameliorate any undesirable secondary effects of their proximity to one another. If the city's first ordinance was justified, therefore, then the second is too. Dispersing two adult businesses under one roof is reasonably likely to cause a substantial reduction in secondary effects while reducing speech very little.

IV.

These propositions are well established in common experience and in zoning policies that we have already examined, and for these reasons this ordinance is not invalid on its face. If these assumptions can be proved unsound at trial, then the ordinance might not withstand intermediate scrutiny. The ordinance does, however, survive the summary judgment motion that the Court of Appeals ordered granted in this case.

■ JUSTICE SOUTER, with whom JUSTICE STEVENS and JUSTICE GINSBURG join, and with whom JUSTICE BREYER joins as to Part II, dissenting.

II.

My concern is not with the assumption behind the amendment itself, that a conglomeration of adult businesses under one roof, as in a minimal or adult department store, will produce undesirable secondary effects comparable to what a cluster of separate adult establishments brings about, *ante,* at 8. That may or may not be so. The assumption that is clearly unsupported, however, goes to the city's supposed interest in applying the amendment to the book and video stores in question, and in applying it to break them up. The city, of course, claims no interest in the proliferation of adult establishments, the ostensible consequence of splitting the sales and viewing activities so as to produce two stores where once there was one. Nor does the city assert any interest in limiting the sale of adult expressive material as such, or reducing the number of adult video booths in the city, for that would be clear content-based regulation, and the city was careful in its 1977 report to disclaim any such intent. App. 54.

Rather, the city apparently assumes that a bookstore selling videos and providing viewing booths produces secondary effects of crime, and more crime than would result from having a single store without booths in one part of town and a video arcade in another. But the city neither says this in so many words nor proffers any evidence to support even the simple proposition that an otherwise lawfully located adult bookstore combined with video booths will produce any criminal effects. The Los Angeles study treats such combined stores as one, *see id.,* at 81–82, and draws no general conclusion that individual stores spread apart from other adult establishments (as under the basic Los Angeles ordinance) are associated with any degree of criminal activity above the general norm; nor has the city called the Court's attention to any other empirical study, or even anecdotal police evidence, that supports the city's assumption. In fact, if the Los Angeles study sheds any light whatever on the city's position, it is the light of skepticism, for we may fairly suspect that the study said nothing about the secondary effects of freestanding stores because no effects were observed. The reasonable supposition, then, is that "splitting some of them up will have no consequence for secondary effects whatever."

The inescapable point is that the city does not even claim that the 1977 study provides any support for its assumption.

NOTES AND QUESTIONS

1.   *What is a "Secondary Effect"?* Both *Renton* and *Alameda Books* assume that a municipality may regulate speech only when the municipality can establish that the speech is likely to generate adverse "secondary effects." For a general discussion of the secondary effects doctrine, *see* John Fee, The Pornographic Secondary Effects Doctrine, 60 Ala. L. Rev. 291 (2009). In *Alameda Books*, the Court indicated that secondary effects include effects on "crime rates, property values, and the quality of the city's neighborhoods."

Suppose a municipality conducts a study demonstrating that adult uses have the same impact on neighboring property values as junkyards; value of commercial or residential land within 500 feet of any adult use is, on average, 25% lower than the value of equivalent land not near any adult use. If the study's methodology were beyond reproach, would the study justify exclusion of all adult uses? Would it justify limiting adult uses to industrial areas? If so, would municipalities in areas with traditional moral values have more leeway to prohibit adult uses than municipalities less judgmental about sexually explicit performances?

Suppose a municipality establishes that minors often frequent adult clubs and theaters, and that a requirement that adult theaters check identification for age would limit the number of minors exposed to sexually explicit material. Would the identification requirement be justified as a control on "secondary effects"? *See* U.S. Sound & Service, Inc. v. Township of Brick, 126 F.3d 555 (3d Cir. 1997) (no).

2. *The Significance of Studies.* In *Renton*, at the time the City Council enacted its adult use ordinance, the Council had before it an opinion of the Washington Supreme Court in which that court sustained an ordinance that prohibited adult motion picture theaters in all but three specified zones. Northend Cinema, Inc. v. Seattle, 90 Wn.2d 709, 713, 585 P.2d 1153, 1156 (1978). The Washington Supreme Court had relied on findings by the trial court that adult theaters "contribute to neighborhood blight," based in part on a study prepared by the city's committee on planning and urban development.

Suppose now that a municipality cites to the fact-finding in *Northend*, and enacts an ordinance limiting adult uses to a single commercial district. If an aggrieved landowner challenges the ordinance on First Amendment grounds, but presents no studies of its own, is the municipality entitled to summary judgment? Suppose the municipality cites the same opinion as a basis for an anti-concentration ordinance that prohibits an adult use within 2,500 feet of an existing adult use. If the landowner who challenges the ordinance fails to produce a study of its own, is the municipality entitled to summary judgment? Has the Court effectively provided the municipality with a "road map" for obtaining summary judgment by citing to *Northend*, or to another study reaching similar conclusions?

What happens when the landowners produce their own studies challenging the premise that the regulation enacted will control secondary effects associated with adult uses. Consider the facts in For the People Theatres of N.Y., Inc. v. City of New York, 6 N.Y.3d 63, 843 N.E.2d 1121, 810 N.Y.S.2d 381 (2005). The City of New York had enacted regulations treating an establishment as "adult" when at least 40% of its accessible floor area is used for adult purposes. The city relied on a 1994 study of secondary effects of adult entertainment establishments. In 2001, the city amended its regulations to eliminate the 40% formula based on its conclusion that many establishments were using the formula to evade the adult use limitations in the zoning ordinance. A number of establishments challenged the amendment, and brought forward expert testimony and studies establishing that the presence of 40% uses had no adverse impact on adjacent property values, that no 40% establishments were listed as the police department's hot spots for crime, and that there was no correlation between concentration of these bookstores and the violent felony rate. In light of this data, did *Alameda Books* require the city to generate more studies or data to refute the findings by the owners of adult businesses? If not, what would the city have to establish to avoid invalidation of the ordinance? *See* For the People Theaters of N.Y. Inc. v. City of New York, 131 A.D.3d 279, 14 N.Y.S.3d 338 (2015) (holding, after remand for trial, that the ordinance was unconstitutional because the city had failed to establish that clubs with 40% of their space devoted to adult uses had the same sexual focus as the establishments that served as the focus on the 1994 study). *Cf.* Daytona Grand, Inc. v. City of Daytona Beach, 490 F.3d

860 (11th Cir. 2007) (rejecting notion that *Alameda Books* requires municipality to reply to landowner studies with empirical evidence of scientific studies). For a discussion of the conflicting approach courts have taken to his problem, *see* Daniel R. Aaronson et al., The First Amendment in Chaos: How the Law of Secondary Effects is Applied and Misapplied by the Circuit Courts, 63 U. Miami L. Rev. 741 (2009).

3. *Concentration vs. Dispersion.* Municipalities have pursued two different strategies for minimizing the secondary effects associated with adult uses. One strategy is to prohibit adult uses altogether in most areas of the municipality, concentrating adult uses in particular areas. A second strategy—illustrated in *Alameda Books*—is to separate adult uses from one another. Often, municipalities combine the two strategies, prohibiting adult uses altogether in some areas, while also imposing distance requirements in those areas where adult uses are permitted.

Suppose a study demonstrates that an adult theater typically generates an increase in crime, and diminishes property values in the theater's immediate area. How could a municipality use such a study to support an ordinance that concentrates adult uses? An ordinance that disperses them?

4. In his concurrence in *Alameda Books,* Justice Kennedy suggests that a city may not enact an ordinance that would cut adult speech in half in order to achieve a proportional reduction in secondary effects. What does he mean by that? If a municipality concludes that zoning adult uses out of the central business district will cut crime by half, but will cause half of all adult uses to close because they cannot be as profitable outside the central business district, is the prohibition on adult uses in the central business district unconstitutional? Would such a result be consistent with *Renton*'s conclusion that adult uses must fend for themselves in the real estate market?

5. A municipality's zoning ordinance prohibits adult entertainment in residential districts. A homeowner installs webcams in the house, and charges paying members for viewing the activities of the women in the house, and for speaking with the women. Does the homeowner's activity violate the ordinance? *See* Voyeur Dorm, LC v. City of Tampa, 265 F.3d 1232 (11th Cir. 2001) (construing ordinance not to prohibit the homeowner's use of the house). If it does violate the ordinance, would the ordinance be constitutional as applied to the house?

Suppose now that a municipality seeks to apply its adult use ordinance to DVD rental stores that do not permit on-site viewing of the DVDs. May the municipality do so without producing a study that documents the secondary effects of such establishments? *Compare* Encore Videos, Inc. v. City of San Antonio, 330 F.3d 288 (5th Cir. 2003) *with* Doctor John's Inc. v. City of Roy, 465 F.3d 1150 (10th Cir. 2006).

6. Suppose a municipality enacts an ordinance requiring adult uses to locate more than 500 feet from any residential unit, and more than 1000 feet from any other regulated use. Suppose further that the municipality has conducted (or cited) appropriate studies detailing the secondary effects of adult uses. Is the ordinance constitutional if 20 sites within the municipality's borders would be eligible for adult uses? Would your answer be different if six sites would be eligible? *Compare* Lund v. City of Fall River, 714 F.3d 65 (1st Cir. 2013) (eight sites sufficient) *with* Executive Arts Studio, Inc. v. City of Grand Rapids, 391 F.3d 783 (6th Cir. 2004) (six sites insufficient).

Does demand for the sites matter? In Big Dipper Entertainment, L.L.C. v. City of Warren, 641 F.3d 715 (6th Cir. 2011), the court upheld an ordinance that permitted adult uses on 26 sites when, over the most recent five-year period, only two applications for adult businesses had been filed with the city, noting that "[a] supply of sites more than 13 times greater than the five-year demand is more than ample for constitutional purposes." *Id.* at 720. Is the number of applications a reliable proxy for demand? Might the number of applications reflect the unattractive location of the available sites?

Suppose the zoning ordinance imposes parking requirements that use up much of the square footage of the available sites, effectively limiting the size of the interior of any adult use. Does that make the ordinance invalid? In the *Big Dipper* case, the court concluded that the size of the dance floor "is a commercial concern, not a constitutional one." *Id.* at 720.

What if numerous sites are zoned to permit adult uses, but they are all subject to long-term leases? *See* Lund v. City of Fall River, 714 F.3d 65, 70 (1st Cir. 2013) ("[T]he fact that other competing private parties got ahead of him is not alone of any moment in the constitutional analysis, and the cost of development is nothing more than a business consideration for Lund to weigh"). What if the sites are all owned by the same owner, who may not be willing to lease them for adult uses? What if the eligible sites would require significant environmental cleanup, or development of infrastructure? *See* David Vincent, Inc. v. Broward County, 200 F.3d 1325, 1333–35 (11th Cir. 2000).

New Jersey has enacted a state statute prohibiting operation of a sexually-oriented business within 1,000 feet of a public park or residential zone. In considering whether the statute affords sufficient avenues for expression, what is the relevant geographical area? In Borough of Sayreville v. 35 Club L.L.C., 33 A.3d 1200 (N.J. 2012), the New Jersey Supreme Court held that a municipality seeking to enjoin an adult use in violation of the statute could consider alternative sites in neighboring communities, including communities outside the state.

7. Municipalities often apply adult use ordinances to existing adult uses. Can landowners seeking to continue existing adult uses contend that they have "vested rights" to continue their current uses? *See* Daytona Grand, Inc. v. City of Daytona Beach, 490 F.3d 860 (11th Cir. 2007). Why do you think such claims are typically unsuccessful? Do you think a takings claim by an adult use owner who has been ordered to terminate an existing adult use would be any more successful?

8. *Sensitive Use Vetoes.* Many ordinances require that adult uses be a specified distance from particularly sensitive uses—schools, parks, playgrounds, churches. What secondary effect justifications might be advanced for these sensitive use restrictions? Why are these uses more susceptible to secondary effects from adult uses?

If these uses are more susceptible, can a landowner open up a private school or a church near an adult use just to require the use to close? At what point, if any, would the right to maintain an adult use vest? *See* Young v. City of Simi Valley, 216 F.3d 807 (9th Cir. 2000) (striking down sensitive use veto when religious leader established bible study within 1,000 feet of proposed location for adult use one day before adult use application became complete).

If a municipality identifies secondary effects associated with adult uses, may it ever apply a new ordinance retrospectively to existing uses, or must it limit the effect of its adult use ordinance to new adult uses? If the municipality's power to restrict existing adult uses is limited, does the limitation arise from First Amendment doctrine, or from some other doctrine? If you were representing an adult use owner, what doctrines would you cite to prevent application of a new adult use ordinance to your client's establishment?

V. RELIGIOUS FREEDOM CLAIMS

Many homeowners do not want places of worship or other religious uses in their neighborhoods. Sometimes, this opposition is grounded in traffic and safety concerns: churches and religious schools unquestionably generate more traffic and congestion than single-family homes. Often, however, homeowners are concerned that religiously affiliated uses will change the religious or ethnic composition of the neighborhood. But if residents cannot worship near their homes, they will often find it difficult to worship at all. As a result, courts have historically been skeptical of municipal efforts to exclude religiously affiliated uses from residential districts. For instance, courts have held that an exclusion of churches is not in furtherance of the public health, safety, and general welfare, and that a municipality's exclusion of churches from residential districts exceeds the municipality's zoning power:

> It is true that many people prefer not to reside next door to a church. . . We do not believe it a proper function of government to interfere in the name of the public to exclude churches from residential districts for the purpose of securing to adjacent landowners the benefits of exclusive residential restrictions.

State ex rel. Synod of Ohio v. Joseph, 139 Ohio St. 229, 249, 39 N.E.2d 515, 524 (1942). Other courts explicitly relied on the Free Exercise clause of the federal constitution or of a state constitution:

a court may not permit a municipal ordinance to be so construed that it would appear in any manner to interfere with the "free exercise and enjoyment of religious profession and worship." N. Y. Const., art. I, § 3.

Community Synagogue v. Bates, 1 N.Y.2d 445, 458, 154 N.Y.S.2d 15, 136 N.E.2d 488, 496 (1956).

Most of these cases arose in state courts. The emergence of an enhanced federal role in protecting religious land uses arose almost by accident. In Employment Division v. Smith, 494 U.S. 872 (1990), the United States Supreme Court upheld the constitutionality of a state law banning the possession of peyote, a hallucinogen sometimes used in Native American religious practices. The Court held that when a state law is a "neutral law of general applicability," incidental burdens on free exercise of religion did not violate the federal constitution's Free Exercise Clause. (Do you think most land use laws qualify as "neutral laws of general applicability"?) Congress treated *Smith* as an unwarranted restriction on free exercise, and enacted the Religious Freedom Restoration Act (RFRA), which attempted to overturn *Smith* legislatively by prohibiting states (and the federal government) from placing a "substantial burden" on religious exercise unless the government could demonstrate the existence of a compelling governmental interest and that the burden represented the least restrictive means of furthering that interest.

The Supreme Court's first encounter with RFRA arose in a zoning case, City of Boerne v. Flores, 521 U.S. 507 (1997). In *Boerne,* the city's landmark commission had denied a permit request by a church seeking to expand its facilities, and the church invoked RFRA as support for its challenge to the permit denial. When the case reached the Supreme Court, the Court held RFRA exceeded Congress' Fourteenth Amendment powers, but the case itself brought attention to the zoning problems that faced some churches. As a result, Congress acted again, this time enacting a narrower statute with a different constitutional foundation, the Religious Land Use and Institutionalized Persons Act (RLUIPA). Here is the land use provision of the statute:

42 U.S.C. Section 2000cc. Protection of land use as religious exercise

(a) Substantial burdens.

(1) General rule. No government shall impose or implement a land use regulation in a manner that imposes a substantial burden on the religious exercise of a person, including a religious assembly or institution, unless the government demonstrates that imposition of the burden on that person, assembly, or institution—

(A) is in furtherance of a compelling governmental interest; and

(B) is the least restrictive means of furthering that compelling governmental interest.

(2) Scope of application. This subsection applies in any case in which—

(A) the substantial burden is imposed in a program or activity that receives Federal financial assistance, even if the burden results from a rule of general applicability;

(B) the substantial burden affects, or removal of that substantial burden would affect, commerce with foreign nations, among the several States, or with Indian tribes, even if the burden results from a rule of general applicability; or

(C) the substantial burden is imposed in the implementation of a land use regulation or system of land use regulations, under which a government makes, or has in place formal or informal procedures or practices that permit the government to make, individualized assessments of the proposed uses for the property involved.

(b) Discrimination and exclusion.

(1) Equal terms. No government shall impose or implement a land use regulation in a manner that treats a religious assembly or institution on less than equal terms with a nonreligious assembly or institution.

(2) Nondiscrimination. No government shall impose or implement a land use regulation that discriminates against any assembly or institution on the basis of religion or religious denomination.

(3) Exclusions and limits. No government shall impose or implement a land use regulation that—

(A) totally excludes religious assemblies from a jurisdiction; or

(B) unreasonably limits religious assemblies, institutions, or structures within a jurisdiction.

Section 2000cc–5 includes the following definition of "religious exercise":

(7) Religious exercise.

(A) In general. The term "religious exercise" includes any exercise of religion, whether or not compelled by, or central to, a system of religious belief.

(B) Rule. The use, building, or conversion of real property for the purpose of religious exercise shall be considered to be religious exercise of the person or entity that uses or intends to use the property for that purpose.

RLUIPA has resulted in an increase in federal court challenges to local land use decisions. The Supreme Court has upheld the constitutionality of the statute with respect to institutionalized persons but has not yet addressed the constitutionality of the land use provisions. Nevertheless, the statute's scope remains a subject of controversy. Consider the following case:

Westchester Day School v. Village of Mamaroneck

United States Court of Appeals for the Second Circuit, 2007
504 F.3d 338

■ CARDAMONE, CIRCUIT JUDGE.

The appeal before us is from a judgment entered March 3, 2006 in the United States District Court for the Southern District of New York (Conner, J.) that ordered the defendant Village of Mamaroneck to issue a permit to plaintiff Westchester Day School to proceed with the expansion of its facilities. For nearly 60 years Westchester Day School (plaintiff, WDS, day school, or school) has been operating an Orthodox Jewish co-educational day school with classes from pre-school to eighth grade. Believing it needed to expand, the school submitted construction plans to the Village of Mamaroneck and an application for the required special permit. When the village zoning board turned the application down, the present litigation ensued.

BACKGROUND

A. *Westchester Day School's Property*

Westchester Day School is located in the Orienta Point neighborhood of the Village of Mamaroneck, Westchester County, New York. Its facilities are situated on 25.75 acres of largely undeveloped land (property) owned by Westchester Religious Institute. Westchester Religious Institute allows the school and other entities to use the property.

The Mamaroneck Village Code permits private schools to operate in "R–20 Districts" if the Zoning Board of Appeals of the Village of Mamaroneck (ZBA or zoning board) grants them a special permit. The property is in an R–20 district and WDS operates subject to obtaining such a permit which must be renewed every three years.

B. *Westchester Day School's Aims*

As a Jewish private school, Westchester Day School provides its students with a dual curriculum in Judaic and general studies. Even general studies classes are taught so that religious and Judaic concepts are reinforced. In the nursery and kindergarten classes no distinction exists between Judaic and general studies; the dual curriculum is wholly integrated. In grades first through eighth, students spend roughly half their day on general subjects such as mathematics and social studies and half on Judaic studies that include the Bible, the Talmud, and Jewish history.

In an effort to provide the kind of synthesis between the Judaic and general studies for which the school aims, the curriculum of virtually all secular studies classes is permeated with religious aspects, and the general studies faculty actively collaborates with the Judaic studies faculty in arranging such a Jewish-themed curriculum.

The school's physical education teachers confer daily with the administration to ensure that during physical education classes Jewish values are being inculcated in the students. This kind of integration of Jewish and general culture is made possible when a school actively and consciously designs integrated curricular and extracurricular activities on behalf of its student body. Thus, the school strives to have every classroom used at times for religious purposes, whether or not the class is officially labeled Judaic. A Jewish day school like WDS exists, at least in part, because Orthodox Jews believe it is the parents' duty to teach the Torah to their children. Since most Orthodox parents lack the time to fulfill this obligation fully, they seek out a school like WDS.

C. *The Expansion Project*

By 1998 WDS believed its current facilities inadequate to satisfy the school's needs. The district court's extensive findings reveal the day school's existing facilities are deficient and that its effectiveness in providing the education Orthodox Judaism mandates has been significantly hindered as a consequence.

In October 2001 the day school submitted to the zoning board an application for modification of its special permit to enable it to proceed with this $12 million expansion project. On February 7, 2002 the ZBA voted unanimously to issue a "negative declaration," which constituted a finding that the project would have no significant adverse environmental impact and thus that consideration of the project could proceed. After the issuance of the negative declaration, a small but vocal group in the Mamaroneck community opposed the project. As a result of this public opposition, on August 1, 2002 the ZBA voted 3–2 to rescind the negative declaration. The effect of the rescission was to require WDS to prepare and submit a full Environmental Impact Statement.

D. *Prior Legal Proceedings*

Instead, the school commenced the instant litigation on August 7, 2002 contending the rescission of the negative declaration violated RLUIPA and was void under state law. The suit named as defendants the Village of Mamaroneck, its ZBA, and the members of the zoning board in their official capacities (collectively, the Village or defendant).

On December 4, 2002 the district court granted WDS's motion for partial summary judgment and held that the negative declaration had not been properly rescinded, and therefore remained in full force and effect. *See* Westchester Day Sch. v. Vill. of Mamaroneck, 236 F. Supp. 2d 349 (S.D.N.Y. 2002). The Village did not appeal this ruling. Instead, the ZBA proceeded to conduct additional public hearings to consider the merits of the application. The ZBA had the opportunity to approve the application subject to conditions intended to mitigate adverse effects on public health, safety, and welfare that might arise from the project. Rather, on May 13, 2003 the ZBA voted 3–2 to deny WDS's application in its entirety.

The stated reasons for the rejection included the effect the project would have on traffic and concerns with respect to parking and the intensity of use. Many of these grounds were conceived after the ZBA closed its hearing process, giving the school no opportunity to respond.

On May 29, 2003 the school filed an amended complaint challenging the denial of its application. It asserted claims under RLUIPA, 42 U.S.C. § 1983.

A seven-day bench trial began on November 14, 2005 and resulted in the March 2006 judgment. The district court ordered the Village to issue WDS's special permit immediately, but reserved decision on damages and attorneys' fees pending appellate review. *See* Westchester Day Sch. v. Vill. of Mamaroneck, 417 F. Supp. 2d 477 (S.D.N.Y. 2006). From this ruling the Village appeals.

DISCUSSION

Application of RLUIPA

RLUIPA prohibits the government from imposing or implementing a land use regulation in a manner that

> imposes a substantial burden on the religious exercise of a person, including a religious assembly or institution, unless the government demonstrates that imposition of the burden on that person, assembly, or institution (A) is in furtherance of a compelling governmental interest; and (B) is the least restrictive means of furthering that compelling governmental interest.

42 U.S.C. § 2000cc(a)(1). This provision applies only when the substantial burden imposed (1) is in a program that receives Federal financial assistance; (2) affects commerce with foreign nations, among the several states, or with Indian tribes; or (3) "is imposed in the implementation of a land use regulation or system of land use regulations, under which a government makes, or has in place formal or informal procedures or practices that permit the government to make,

individualized assessments of the proposed uses for the property involved." 42 U.S.C. § 2000cc(a)(2).

A. *Religious Exercise*

Religious exercise under RLUIPA is defined as "any exercise of religion, whether or not compelled by, or central to, a system of religious belief." § 2000cc–5(7)(A). Further, using, building, or converting real property for religious exercise purposes is considered to be religious exercise under the statute. § 2000cc–5(7)(B). To remove any remaining doubt regarding how broadly Congress aimed to define religious exercise, RLUIPA goes on to state that the Act's aim of protecting religious exercise is to be construed broadly and "to the maximum extent permitted by the terms of this chapter and the Constitution." § 2000cc–3(g).

[T]o get immunity from land use regulation, religious schools need to demonstrate more than that the proposed improvement would enhance the overall experience of its students. For example, if a religious school wishes to build a gymnasium to be used exclusively for sporting activities, that kind of expansion would not constitute religious exercise. Or, had the ZBA denied the Westchester Religious Institute's 1986 request for a special permit to construct a headmaster's residence on a portion of the property, such a denial would not have implicated religious exercise. Nor would the school's religious exercise have been burdened by the denial of a permit to build more office space.

[T]he district court . . . made careful factual findings that each room the school planned to build would be used at least in part for religious education and practice, finding that Gordon Hall and the other facilities renovated as part of the project, in whole and in all of their constituent parts, would be used for "religious education and practice." In light of these findings, amply supported in the record, the expansion project is a "building [and] conversion of real property for the purpose of religious exercise" and thus is religious exercise under § 2000cc–5(7)(B).

Hence, we need not now demarcate the exact line at which a school expansion project comes to implicate RLUIPA. That line exists somewhere between this case, where every classroom being constructed will be used at some time for religious education, and a case like the building of a headmaster's residence, where religious education will not occur in the proposed expansion.

B. *Substantial Burden*

RLUIPA's legislative history indicates that Congress intended the term substantial burden to be interpreted "by reference to Supreme Court jurisprudence." 146 Cong. Rec. S7774, S7776 (2000).

Supreme Court precedents teach that a substantial burden on religious exercise exists when an individual is required to "choose between following the precepts of her religion and forfeiting benefits, on the one hand, and abandoning one of the precepts of her religion . . . on the other hand." Sherbert v. Verner, 374 U.S. 398, 404, 83 S. Ct. 1790, 10 L. Ed. 2d 965 (1963).

But in the context of land use, a religious institution is not ordinarily faced with the same dilemma of choosing between religious precepts and government benefits. When a municipality denies a religious institution the right to expand its facilities, it is more difficult to speak of substantial pressure to change religious behavior, because in light of the denial the renovation simply cannot proceed. Accordingly, when there has been a denial of a religious institution's building application, courts appropriately speak of government action that directly *coerces* the religious institution to change its behavior, rather than government action that forces the religious entity to choose between religious precepts and government benefits. *See, e.g., Midrash Sephardi*, 366 F.3d at 1227 ("[A] substantial burden is akin to significant pressure which directly coerces the religious adherent to conform his or her behavior accordingly."). Here, WDS contends that the denial of its application in effect coerced the day school to continue teaching in inadequate facilities, thereby impeding its religious exercise.

Yet, when the denial of a religious institution's application to build is not absolute, such would not necessarily place substantial pressure on the institution to alter its behavior, since it could just as easily file a second application that remedies the problems in the first. As a consequence, as we said when this case was earlier before us, "rejection of a submitted plan, while leaving open the possibility of approval of a resubmission with modifications designed to address the cited problems, is less likely to constitute a 'substantial burden' than definitive rejection of the same plan, ruling out the possibility of approval of a modified proposal." *Westchester Day Sch.*, 386 F.3d at 188. Of course, a conditional denial may represent a substantial burden if the condition itself is a burden on free exercise, the required modifications are economically unfeasible, or where a zoning board's stated willingness to consider a modified plan is disingenuous. *Id.* at 188 n. 3. However, in most cases, whether the denial of the application was absolute is important; if there is a reasonable opportunity for the institution to submit a modified application, the denial does not place substantial pressure on it to change its behavior and thus does not constitute a substantial burden on the free exercise of religion.

We recognize further that where the denial of an institution's application to build will have minimal impact on the institution's religious exercise, it does not constitute a substantial burden, even when the denial is definitive. There must exist a close nexus between the coerced or impeded conduct and the institution's religious exercise for such conduct to be a substantial burden on that religious exercise.

Imagine, for example, a situation where a school could easily rearrange existing classrooms to meet its religious needs in the face of a rejected application to renovate. In such case, the denial would not substantially threaten the institution's religious exercise, and there would be no substantial burden, even though the school was refused the opportunity to expand its facilities.

Note, however, that a burden need not be found insuperable to be held substantial. *See* Saints Constantine and Helen Greek Orthodox Church, Inc. v. City of New Berlin, 396 F.3d 895, 901 (7th Cir. 2005). When the school has no ready alternatives, or where the alternatives require substantial "delay, uncertainty, and expense," a complete denial of the school's application might be indicative of a substantial burden. *See id.*

We are, of course, mindful that the Supreme Court's free exercise jurisprudence signals caution in using effect alone to determine substantial burden. This is because an effect focused analysis may run up against the reality that "[t]he freedom asserted by [some may] bring them into collision with [the] rights asserted by" others and that "[i]t is such conflicts which most frequently require intervention of the State to determine where the rights of one end and those of another begin." Braunfeld v. Brown, 366 U.S. 599, 604, 81 S. Ct. 1144, 6 L. Ed. 2d 563 (1961). Accordingly, the Supreme Court has held that generally applicable burdens, neutrally imposed, are not "substantial." *See* Jimmy Swaggart Ministries v. Bd. of Equalization, 493 U.S. 378, 389–91, 110 S. Ct. 688, 107 L. Ed. 2d 796 (1990).

This reasoning helps to explain why courts confronting free exercise challenges to zoning restrictions rarely find the substantial burden test satisfied even when the resulting effect is to completely prohibit a religious congregation from building a church on its own land.

A number of our sister circuits have applied this same reasoning in construing RLUIPA's substantial burden requirement. For example, the Seventh Circuit has held that land use conditions do not constitute a substantial burden under RLUIPA where they are "neutral and traceable to municipal land planning goals" and where there is no evidence that government actions were taken "*because* [plaintiff] is a *religious* institution." Vision Church v. Vill. of Long Grove, 468 F.3d 975, 998–99 (7th Cir. 2006). Similarly, the Ninth Circuit has held that no substantial burden was imposed, even where an ordinance "rendered [plaintiff] unable to provide education and/or worship" on its property, because the plaintiff was not "precluded from using other sites within the city" and because "there [is no] evidence that the City would not impose the same requirements on any other entity." San Jose Christian Coll., 360 F.3d at 1035. The Eleventh Circuit has also ruled that "reasonable 'run of the mill' zoning considerations do not constitute substantial burdens." *Midrash Sephardi*, 366 F.3d at 1227–28 & n. 11.

The same reasoning that precludes a religious organization from demonstrating substantial burden in the neutral application of legitimate land use restrictions may, in fact, support a substantial burden claim where land use restrictions are imposed on the religious institution arbitrarily, capriciously, or unlawfully. The arbitrary application of laws to religious organizations may reflect bias or discrimination against religion. Where the arbitrary, capricious, or unlawful nature of a defendant's challenged action suggests that a religious institution received less than even-handed treatment, the application of RLUIPA's substantial burden provision usefully "backstops the explicit prohibition of religious discrimination in the later section of the Act." *Saints Constantine and Helen*, 396 F.3d at 900.

Accordingly, we deem it relevant to the evaluation of WDS's particular substantial burden claim that the district court expressly found that the zoning board's denial of the school's application was "arbitrary and capricious under New York law because the purported justifications set forth in the Resolution do not bear the necessary substantial relation to public health, safety or welfare," and the zoning board's findings are not supported by substantial evidence. *Westchester Day Sch.*, 417 F. Supp. 2d at 564. Although the Village disputes this finding, we conclude that it is amply supported by both the law and the record evidence.

For example, the zoning board denied WDS's application based, in part, on an accusation that the school made "a willful attempt" to mislead the zoning board. In fact, the accusation was unsupported by the evidence and based on the zoning board's own error with respect to certain relevant facts. *Westchester Day Sch.*, 417 F. Supp. 2d at 531, 571. The ZBA's allegations of deficiencies in the school's traffic study were also unsupported by the evidence before it. *See id.* at 564–66. The concern about lack of adequate parking was based on the zoning board's own miscalculation. *See id.* at 567. Indeed, the ZBA impermissibly based its decision on speculation about future expansion, without a basis in fact. *See id.* at 568. In each of these instances, the ZBA's assumptions were not only wrong; they were unsupported by its own experts. *See id.* at 532, 566, 567, 569. Indeed, the resolution drafted by the ZBA's consultants, which would have *approved* WDS's application subject to conditions addressing various ZBA concerns, was never circulated to the whole zoning board before it issued the challenged denial. *See id.* at 569. In sum, the record convincingly demonstrates that the zoning decision in this case was characterized not simply by the occasional errors that can attend the task of government but by an arbitrary blindness to the facts.

While the arbitrary and unlawful nature of the ZBA denial of WDS's application supports WDS's claim that it has sustained a substantial burden, two other factors drawn from our earlier discussion must be considered in reaching such a burden determination: (1) whether there are quick, reliable, and financially feasible alternatives WDS may utilize to meet its religious needs absent its obtaining the construction permit; and (2) whether the denial was conditional. These two considerations matter for the same reason: when an institution has a ready alternative—be it an entirely different plan to meet the same needs or the opportunity to try again in line with a zoning board's recommendations—its religious exercise has not been substantially burdened. The plaintiff has the burden of persuasion with respect to both factors. *See* § 2000cc–2 (putting burden on plaintiff to prove that government's action substantially burdened plaintiff's exercise of religion).

Here, the school could not have met its needs simply by reallocating space within its existing buildings. The architectural firm it hired determined that certain essential facilities would have to be incorporated into a new building, because not enough space remained in the existing buildings to accommodate the school's expanding needs. Further, experts hired by WDS determined that the planned location for Gordon Hall was the only site that would accommodate the new building. The answer to the first factor is there were not only no quick, reliable, or economically feasible alternatives, there were no alternatives at all.

In examining the second factor—whether the Village's denial of the school's application was conditional or absolute—we look at several matters: (a) whether the ZBA classified the denial as complete, (b) whether any required modification would itself constitute a burden on religious exercise; (c) whether cure of the problems noted by the ZBA would impose so great an economic burden as to make amendment unworkable; and (d) whether the ZBA's stated willingness to consider a modified proposal was disingenuous. *See Westchester Day Sch.*, 386 F.3d at 188 n. 3.

For any of the following reasons, we believe the denial of WDS's application was absolute. First, we observe that the ZBA could have approved the application subject to conditions intended to mitigate adverse effects on public health, safety, and welfare. Yet the ZBA chose instead to deny the application in its entirety. It is evident that in the eyes of the ZBA's members, the denial was final since all of them discarded their notes after voting on the application. Second, were WDS to prepare a modified proposal, it would have to begin the application process anew. This would have imposed so great an economic burden as to make the option unworkable. Third, the district court determined that ZBA members were not credible when they testified they would give reasonable consideration to another application by WDS. When the board's expressed willingness to consider a modified proposal is insincere, we do not require an institution to file a modified proposal before determining that its religious exercise has been substantially burdened.

Consequently, we are persuaded that WDS has satisfied its burden in proving that there was no viable alternative to achieve its objectives, and we conclude that WDS's religious exercise was substantially burdened by the ZBA's arbitrary and unlawful denial of its application.

C. *Least Restrictive Means to Further a Compelling State Interest*

Under RLUIPA, once a religious institution has demonstrated that its religious exercise has been substantially burdened, the burden of proof shifts to the municipality to prove it acted in furtherance of a compelling governmental interest and that its action is the least restrictive means of furthering that interest. § 2000cc–2(b). The Village claims that it has a compelling interest in enforcing zoning regulations and ensuring residents' safety through traffic regulations. However, it must show a compelling interest in imposing the burden on religious exercise in the particular case at hand, not a compelling interest in general.

The district court's findings reveal the ZBA's stated reasons for denying the application were not substantiated by evidence in the record before it. The court stated the application was denied not because of a compelling governmental interest that would adversely impact public health, safety, or welfare, but was denied because of undue deference to the opposition of a small group of neighbors.

Further, even were we to determine that there was a compelling state interest involved, the Village did not use the least restrictive means available to achieve that interest. The ZBA had the opportunity to approve the application subject to conditions, but refused to consider doing so.

CONCLUSION

Accordingly, for the foregoing reasons, the judgment of the district court is affirmed.

NOTES AND QUESTIONS

1. A religiously affiliated high school perceives that it has been losing students to public schools and other private schools because it has inadequate sports facilities. The school seeks a special permit to expand its facilities by replacing its old gymnasium with a new gym that has better facilities and a seating capacity three times as large as its old gymnasium. If the zoning board of appeals denies the permit, and the school brings an action contending that the denial constitutes a RLUIPA violation, what

statutory defenses might the village's lawyer raise? Would the village prevail on any of those defenses?

Suppose now that the school seeks to build the new gym while converting the old gym to a chemistry lab. Would the school's RLUIPA claim be any stronger or weaker? What if the school plans to convert the old gym to a classroom for religious instruction?

2. The court's opinion in *Westchester Day School* suggests that the arbitrariness of the ZBA's denial of the school's application "supports WDS's claim that it has sustained a substantial burden." Why should that be so? What, if anything, does the arbitrariness of the ZBA's action have to do with the magnitude of the school's burden? Wouldn't the burden on the school have been precisely the same if the ZBA had accurately concluded that the expansion would create significant parking and traffic concerns?

Shouldn't the arbitrariness of the municipality's action become relevant in deciding whether the municipality's action furthered a compelling state interest? Do you see why the court's formulation in *Westchester Day School* is more protective of religious users than a formulation that considered arbitrariness only in deciding whether the action furthered a compelling state interest?

3. *Religious Exercise.* Suppose a church purchases a building in a historic district and seeks permission to demolish the building to erect a new one to host social events including a "Saturday night concert series," to feed its members, and to provide a lounge and meditation room. If the city's landmarks commission denies a permit to demolish the building, and the church brings a RLUIPA claim, can the municipality obtain dismissal by contending that the proposed uses do not constitute "religious exercise"? *See* Episcopal Student Found. v. City of Ann Arbor, 341 F. Supp.2d 691 (E.D. Mich. 2004) (holding that under the statute's broad definition, these uses constitute religious exercise but finding that the city did not violate RLUIPA in denying the permit). Would the result be the same if the church proposes to open a hospital, or a counseling center, or a drug rehabilitation center? Are there any limits on what constitutes religious exercise if a church or religious organization defines particular uses as part of its mission? Suppose the church wanted to build an apartment house. Would that constitute religious exercise? *See* The Greater Bible Way Temple of Jackson v. City of Jackson, 478 Mich. 373, 391–394, 733 N.W.2d 734, 745–47 (2007) (proposed apartment building not a religious exercise).

How much turns on whether a proposed use constitutes "religious exercise"? Even if a court defines "religious exercise" broadly, can't the court hold RLUIPA inapplicable by concluding that the municipality's action does not constitute a "substantial burden" on religious exercise? *Cf. The Greater Bible Way, supra* (holding that even if apartment building were a religious exercise, refusal to rezone would not constitute a substantial burden). Does that explain why few cases turn on "religious exercise"?

4.   *Substantial Burden.* Many RLUIPA cases turn on whether the municipality's action has imposed a "substantial burden" on religious exercise. The statute clearly tolerates land use regulation that imposes *some* burden on religious users. As the Seventh Circuit has noted:

> Application of the substantial burden provision to a regulation inhibiting or constraining *any* religious exercise, including the use of property for religious purposes, would render meaningless the word "substantial," because the slightest obstacle to religious exercise incidental to the regulation of land use—however minor the burden it were to impose—could then constitute a burden sufficient to trigger RLUIPA's requirement that the regulation advance a compelling governmental interest by the least restrictive means.

Civil Liberties for Urban Believers v. City of Chicago, 342 F.3d 752, 761 (7th Cir. 2003).

Do the costs and delays associated with obtaining land use approvals constitute a "substantial burden" within the meaning of RLUIPA? Courts have rejected such claims. As the court put it in rejecting a challenge to Chicago's permit requirements:

> Otherwise, compliance with RLUIPA would require municipal governments not merely to treat religious land uses on an equal footing with nonreligious land uses, but rather to favor them in the form of an outright exemption from land-use regulations. Unfortunately for Appellants, no such free pass for religious land uses masquerades among the legitimate protections RLUIPA affords to religious exercise.

Id. at 762. *See also* San Jose Christian College v. City of Morgan Hill, 360 F.3d 1024 (9th Cir. 2004).

In *Westchester Day School*, the substantial burden on the school was related to the municipality's interference with the school's expansion plans. But the court was careful to indicate that interference with expansion plans does not always constitute a substantial burden on the religious institution. The court noted that if a school "could easily rearrange existing classrooms to meet its religious needs," rejection of an expansion plan would not impose a substantial burden on religious exercise. Other courts have agreed that rejection of an expansion plan does not, by itself, establish a substantial burden. *See, e.g.*, Living Water Church of God v. Charter Twp. of Meridian, 2007 WL 4322157 (6th Cir. 2007) (upholding board decision placing 25,000-square-foot limitation on special permit when church wanted to build extension that would bring total square footage to 39,000).

Suppose the church wants to erect a large sign, visible from neighboring highways, displaying its full name and location. If the municipality refuses to grant a permit, can the church contend that the permit denial imposes a substantial burden on religious exercise? *See* Trinity Assembly of God of Baltimore City, Inc. v. People's Counsel for

Baltimore County, 2008 Md. LEXIS 630 (2008) (no substantial burden). *See* Shelley Ross Saxer, Assessing RLUIPA's Application to Building Codes and Aesthetic Land Use Regulation, 2 Alb. Gov't L. Rev. 623, 637–38 (2009). On RLUIPA's treatment of accessory uses, *see generally* Shelley Ross Saxer, Faith in Action: Religious Accessory Uses and Land Use Regulation, 2008 Utah L. Rev. 593 (2008).

5. *Compelling State Interests and Least Restrictive Means.* In *Westchester Day School*, the village justified its permit denial by citing traffic and parking problems that were not, on the facts of the case, substantiated by the evidence. Suppose, however, the parking and traffic problems had been real. Would those concerns justify the municipality in denying a permit? Does the court in *Westchester Day School* resolve that question? If traffic and safety are not compelling state interests, what does constitute a compelling state interest in a zoning case? Assuming traffic is a compelling state interest, what would be the least restrictive means of advancing that compelling state interest? Suppose, for instance, the village had proven that the increase in traffic due to school expansion would have generated massive traffic jams and frequent accidents at two adjacent corners during peak school hours. If the school had demonstrated that closing two streets during those hours would abate the traffic problems (albeit at significant inconvenience to local residents), would the village have been required to close the streets and grant the permit?

6. *Individualized Assessment.* Suppose a municipality deals with parking and congestion problems by imposing a maximum FAR, a maximum lot coverage requirement, and a requirement of one off-street parking space for each 100 square feet of building floor area. If those requirements preclude a religious organization from expanding a church or religious school, does the organization have a RLUIPA claim? Is 42 U.S.C. § 2000cc(a)(2)(C) relevant? *See* The Greater Bible Way Temple of Jackson v. City of Jackson, 478 Mich. 373, 386–91, 733 N.W.2d 734, 742–44 (2007) (holding that refusal to rezone is not an "individualized assessment," and therefore outside RLUIPA's purview). *See generally* Ashira Pelman Ostrow, Judicial Review of Local Land Use Decisions: Lessons from RLUIPA, 31 Harv. J.L. & Pub. Pol'y 717, 742–52 (2008).

Suppose the municipality has a zoning board of appeals with authority to grant variances? Does that authority improve the organization's RLUIPA claim? Does it matter whether the ZBA gives variances, or how often?

7. *Historic Districts.* Let's say a municipality enacts a historic preservation ordinance that requires landowners within historic districts to obtain approval before making exterior changes to buildings. The Roman Catholic Church, which is seeking to close underutilized churches and sell off the property, contends that the ordinance imposes a substantial burden in violation of RLUIPA. Is enactment of the ordinance an individualized assessment that triggers scrutiny under RLUIPA? *See* Roman Catholic Bishop of Springfield v. City of Springfield, 724 F.3d 78 (1st Cir. 2013) (concluding that enactment itself was not an individualized assessment).

Should it matter that in the *City of Springfield* case, the historic district was comprised of a single property—the church itself?

Denial of an application to modify a building in a historic district does constitute an individualized assessment even if enactment of the ordinance does not. *See* Chabad Lubavitch of Litchfield County Inc. v. Litchfield Historic District Comm'n, 768 F.3d 183 (2d Cir. 2014). The issue then shifts to whether the denial constitutes a substantial burden.

42 U.S.C. § 2000cc(b)(1) provides protection to religious users separate and apart from the protections afforded in § 2000cc(a). The statute's "equal terms" provision prohibits a municipality from implementing a land use regulation in a way that treats religious institutions or assemblies on less than equal terms with non-religious institutions or assemblies. Consider the following case:

Elijah Group, Inc. v. City of Leon Valley

United States Court of Appeals for the Fifth Circuit, 2011
643 F.3d 419

■ WIENER, CIRCUIT JUDGE:

Petitioner–Appellant The Elijah Group, Inc. ("the Church") sued the City of Leon Valley, Texas ("the City"), alleging that the City's prohibition of the Church from performing religious services on certain properties violates the Texas Civil Practice and Remedies Code, the Texas Religious Freedom Restoration Act (TRFRA), the federal Religious Land Use and Institutionalized Persons Act (RLUIPA), and both the Texas and U.S. constitutions. After both parties filed motions for summary judgment, the district court denied the Church's motion and granted the City's, holding that the City did not violate any of the statutes or either constitution relied on by the Church. We disagree with the district court as to one of the Church's RLUIPA claims and hold that the City's imposition of its land use regulation violates the Equal Terms Clause of that statute.

I. FACTS & PROCEEDINGS

A. Facts

The City is a relatively small municipality that is landlocked by the City of San Antonio. Until March 2007, the City had maintained a zoning code that allowed churches to obtain Special Use Permits (SUPs) to operate in business zones designated "B–2." At that time, however, the City amended its zoning code for the announced purpose of stimulating the local economy by creating a retail corridor on Bandera Road. That roadway through the City is lined primarily with B–2 properties. The ordinance's 2007 amendments both reclassified a number of B–2 uses and eliminated the right of churches to obtain SUPs in B–2 zones. The City thereby effectively excluded churches entirely from B–2 zones and relegated them to B–3 zones, which are designated for commercial uses with larger space requirements. By contrast, the City preserved the right of some similarly nonretail but nonreligious institutions to obtain SUPs in B–2 zones.

In January 2008, almost a year after the zoning ordinance was amended, the Church entered into a contract to buy a property on Bandera Road that was zoned B–2. The contract was contingent on the property owner successfully petitioning the City to rezone the property from a B–2 to B–3 so that the Church could occupy the property without restriction in accordance with the amended ordinance. When the City denied that rezoning request, the Church nevertheless agreed to lease the property from the owner until the zoning issue could be resolved.

Despite generally zoning "churches" as B–3s, the City permitted the Church to use the B–2 property for specified nonreligious activities. For example, the Church obtained a Certificate of Occupancy from the City to allow day care services on the B–2 property, but the certificate provides that "[t]he authorized use does not include any church use or any use which is inconsistent with the B–2 zoning classification." Therefore, when the Church later began to hold religious services on that B–2 property, the City obtained a temporary restraining order (TRO) against such activity as violative of the zoning ordinance. Although the TRO has since expired, the City has declined to cite the Church until this lawsuit is resolved.

B. Proceedings

The Church filed suit against the City in state court challenging the amended ordinance's validity and constitutionality under various state and federal laws, including the RLUIPA. The City removed the case to federal court, and the parties filed cross-motions for summary judgment. At the request of the district court, a magistrate judge issued a report, which recommended that the court grant the City's motion for summary judgment and dismiss the Church's motion. The district court adopted the magistrate judge's report in full and entered the recommended judgment in favor of the City, dismissing all of the Church's claims. The Church timely filed a notice of appeal, challenging only the district court's dismissal of its claims under the Equal Terms and Substantial Burden Clauses of the RLUIPA and under the TRFRA.

II. ANALYSIS

The Equal Terms Clause

The Equal Terms Clause of the RLUIPA ("the Clause") states:

> No government shall impose or implement a land use regulation in a manner that treats a religious assembly or institution on less than equal terms with a nonreligious assembly or institution.

When we focus on the text of the Clause, we read it as prohibiting the government from "imposing," i.e., enacting, a facially discriminatory ordinance or "implementing," i.e., enforcing a facially neutral ordinance in a discriminatory manner. Here, issue is not taken with the City's implementation of the zoning ordinance as to the Church; rather, the Church makes a *facial* challenge to the ordinance's treating "churches" less favorably than other nonretail, nonreligious institutions.

In prohibiting the government from treating a religious institution "on less than *equal* terms with *a nonreligious assembly or institution*," the Clause by its nature requires that the religious institution in question be compared to a nonreligious counterpart, or "comparator." Since the enactment of the RLUIPA, four circuits have constructed different tests for applying the Clause, each with varying determinations of which nonreligious assemblies and institutions are proper comparators to the religious assembly or institution that brings the claim.

We turn first to the City's zoning ordinance. In articulating the reasoning behind and criteria to be used for creating the retail corridor on Bandera Road, the text of the ordinance does not mention religion. The City's real problem lies in the ordinance's "Permitted Use Table," which lists many types of buildings by use and then specifies the zone or zones in which each is or is not permitted. Specifically, the use table notes that "Churches" are not allowed in B–2 zones *at all,* but that many nonreligious, *nonretail* buildings, e.g., "Club or Lodge (*private*)," are allowed to request SUPs and, if granted, to occupy a B–2 zone. Try as we may, we cannot reconcile the ordinance's facial treatment of a church differently than a private club in light of the way that B–2 zones are defined.

In assessing the City's ordinance under the Clause, we conclude that the Clause does require the Church to show more than simply that its religious use is forbidden and some other nonreligious use is permitted. The "less than equal terms" must be measured by the ordinance itself and the criteria by which it treats institutions differently. When we analyze the City's ordinance within this framework, we are convinced that it is invalid because it prohibits the Church from even applying for a SUP when, e.g., a nonreligious private club may apply for a SUP despite the obvious conclusion that the Church and a private club must be treated the same, i.e., on "equal terms" by the ordinance, given the similar non-B–2 nature of each.

At bottom, the ordinance treats the Church on terms that are less than equal to the terms on which it treats similarly situated nonreligious institutions. We conclude therefore that the imposition of the City's ordinance violates the RLUIPA's Equal Terms Clause.[20]

---

[20] Because we hold that the City's ordinance violates the Equal Terms Clause, we need not and therefore do not reach the Church's claims brought under the Substantial Burden Clause and the TRFRA.

III. CONCLUSION

For the foregoing reasons, the district court's order granting the City's motion for summary judgment and denying the Church's motion for summary judgment is reversed, and the case is remanded for further proceedings consistent with this ruling.

NOTES AND QUESTIONS

1. Suppose the church had not prevailed on its "equal terms" claim. Would it have been able to prevail on a "substantial burden" claim? What arguments would you have made for the church? For the city?

2. Suppose the city had not permitted other nonreligious, nonretail uses in the B–2 District. A commercial movie theater with 300 seats operated, as a permitted use, in the district. Would the church have been able to prevail on an equal terms claim?

The statute prohibits a government entity from treating a religious assembly or institution "on less than equal terms with a nonreligious assembly or institution." But what is a nonreligious assembly or institution? Is a movie theater a nonreligious institution? A car dealer? In a portion of the *Elijah Group* opinion not reproduced, the court catalogues the struggles other circuits have had in formulating a test to determine what constitutes an appropriate "comparator." Does the opinion in *Elijah Group* succeed in articulating a general test?

Does the purpose of the zoning restriction matter? If the purpose of a prohibition on nonreligious, nonretail uses were to control traffic, and the municipality permitted a commercial movie theater, should the church be in a better position to prevail than if the municipality's purpose were to generate municipal revenue? *See* River of Life Kingdom Ministries v. Village of Hazel Crest, 611 F.3d 367 (7th Cir. 2010) (sustaining ban on all noncommercial uses, but suggesting that the issue might be different if the village's concern were adequacy of parking or traffic capacity).

If a municipality requires a special permit for a religious organization to operate in a residential area, but permits cub scout troops to meet in the home of a troop leader, has the municipality violated the equal terms provision? *See* Konikov v. Orange County, 410 F.3d 1317 (11th Cir. 2005) (yes); *see also* The Lighthouse Institute for Evangelism, Inc. v. City of Long Branch, 510 F.3d 253, 272–73 (3d Cir. 2007) (equal terms provision violated when ordinance permits assembly halls but not churches).

3. What if the city had permitted churches as specially permitted uses in the B–2 district, but had then denied a special permit to the church because of well-documented fears that the number of parishioners would cause traffic congestion and parking nightmares. Would the church be able to prevail on an equal terms claim? A substantial burden claim?

4. Suppose the local zoning ordinance requires churches to obtain a conditional use permit. The ordinance also prohibits establishments with liquor licenses from locating within 300 feet of a church. A religious group

buys property within 300 feet of a bar, and seeks a conditional use permit to operate a church. The city denies the permit, citing the prohibition on proximity between churches and establishments with liquor licenses. Can the church prevail on an equal terms claim? *See* Centro Familiar Cristiano Buenas Nuevas v. City of Yuma, 651 F.3d 1163 (9th Cir. 2011) (holding violation of equal terms provision).

5. Suppose a municipality changes the maximum floor area ratio (FAR) of a particular parcel from .5 to .8. Subsequently, a church seeks a similar increase to the FAR applicable to its parcel. If the municipality fails to approve the amendment, has the municipality violated the equal terms provision?

6. *Ripeness.* Landowner holds prayer meetings in a single-family home, and the municipality issues a cease-and-desist order for violation of the provisions of the zoning ordinance. If landowner brings a RLUIPA claim in federal court without first seeking a variance from the ZBA, should the claim be dismissed as unripe? *See* Murphy v. New Milford Zoning Comm'n, 402 F.3d 342, 348 (2d Cir. 2005) (enumerating reasons for subjecting RLUIPA claims to a "finality" requirement, and holding that dispute is unripe until variance and appeals process has been completed); *but cf.* Konikov v. Orange County, 410 F.3d 1317 (11th Cir. 2005) (holding that ripeness requirement is satisfied once zoning code has been applied to landowner, even if landowner has not sought a special permit to legalize prohibited use).

7. *Judge or Jury?* In a RLUIPA case, which issues are issues of law to be decided by the court, and which issues are issues of fact for a jury? Is determining whether the municipality's enactment imposed a substantial burden on a church a question for the jury? *See* Grace United Methodist Church v. City of Cheyenne, 451 F.3d 643 (10th Cir. 2006) (reviewing jury instructions on the substantial burden issue). What about "equal treatment"?

8. *The Free Exercise Clause.* Where there is ample evidence that a facially neutral land use law was enacted out of religious animus, the Free Exercise Clause is obviously violated, even after Employment Division v. Smith, 494 U.S. 872 (1990). *See* Church of Lukumi Babalu Aye v. City of Hialeah, 508 U.S. 520 (1993). Nevertheless, it would be a rare case in which a landowner would be able to establish a free exercise violation without also establishing a RLUIPA violation. RLUIPA was enacted to provide religious users with protection that might not be available under the First Amendment's Free Exercise Clause. (Recall that Congress enacted RLUIPA's predecessor, RFRA, to undo the Supreme Court's holding in *Smith*). But there are cases outside RLUIPA's scope—particularly cases that do not involve an "individualized assessment" by a local decisionmaker—and in those cases, the availability of a free exercise challenge might remain important. Moreover, because RLUIPA's constitutionality has not yet been definitively established, a prudent landowner would always append a free exercise challenge to a RLUIPA claim.

PROBLEM

A church, which has long held a special permit for operation in a single-family district, has a parking lot much larger than it needs for its dwindling membership. The zoning ordinance, however, requires a church to have one parking space for each 100 square feet of interior space. Because the church has 4,000 square feet of interior space, the ordinance requires 40 spaces. The church has significant financial needs (replacement of its furnace, repair of the building's interior) which are a drain on its small membership. As a result, the church seeks a variance to permit operation with only 15 parking spaces. The variance would allow the church to sell off two residential lots, and devote the proceeds to church needs.

You represent the zoning board of appeals. Its members, who are concerned that the parking lot will be inadequate if the church attracts new parishioners, or if the church eventually sells its building to a different church, are opposed to the variance but concerned about potential RLUIPA liability. What advice would you give to the ZBA?

CHAPTER SIX

NEIGHBOR CHALLENGES TO MUNICIPAL LAND USE DECISIONS

When a landowner seeks legislative or administrative action to permit more intensive development of its land, neighbors who oppose the change may try to mobilize political opposition to the change. Especially in smaller municipalities, neighbors can have significant influence. Suppose, however, that political opposition proves unsuccessful. What judicial recourse is available to the neighbors?

Neighbors typically face an uphill battle in court. When a land use decision-maker takes a legislative or quasi-legislative action, such as a rezoning, courts defer to reasonable exercises of legislative judgment. When a land use decision-maker deals with an administrative or judicial action, courts will review the manner of the proceedings and the nature of the decision, but a judge may be reluctant to substitute her judgment for that of the land use decision-maker.

Nevertheless, neighbors do have a number of grounds on which they may challenge zoning amendments, permits, and variances. This chapter explores those grounds, after first exploring the standing of neighbors to seek any judicial relief at all.

I. STANDING

When a landowner challenges a municipal action that restricts use of her own land, standing is rarely a problem. By contrast, when a neighbor challenges an action that authorizes a landowner to use her land in a particular way, standing presents more of an issue. One alternative would be to give standing to all concerned citizens. But that alternative would enable an isolated disaffected resident to impose costs on the landowner, the municipality, and the judicial system. A second alternative would be to deny standing to all neighbors on the assumption that municipal officials represented the interest of neighbors during the process of evaluating the landowner's application. That alternative, however, would eliminate all judicial policing of municipal officials. In rejecting those two alternatives, courts have struggled to find a middle ground. Consider the court's approach in the following case:

Matter of Sun-Brite Car Wash, Inc.
v. Board of Zoning and Appeals

Court of Appeals of New York, 1987
69 N.Y.2d 406, 508 N.E.2d 130, 515 N.Y.S.2d 418

■ KAYE, C.J.

A property holder in nearby proximity to premises that are the subject of a zoning determination may have standing to seek judicial review without pleading and proving special damage, because adverse effect or aggrievement can be inferred from the proximity. Where, however, petitioner's only substantiated objection is the threat of increased business competition—an interest not within the "zone of interest" protected by the zoning laws—even a close neighbor lacks standing to contest a zoning determination.

In March 1984 respondents Gulf Oil Corp. and Fenley & Nichol Co. (Gulf) applied for a permit to erect a prefabricated metal automatic car wash on their property, which is used as a gas station—a nonconforming legal use. The application was first forwarded to the Planning Commission, and after the plan was amended in accordance with its recommendations, the Board held a public hearing—consisting largely of evidence of competitive business losses that would result from the variance—and granted the variance.

Petitioner, Sun-Brite Car Wash—the long-term lessee of a car wash across the street from Gulf, also a nonconforming legal use—commenced this article 78 proceeding to annul the Board's determination. Supreme Court found, first, that Sun-Brite, as a lessee in the immediate vicinity of the affected property, was as a matter of law "aggrieved" within the meaning of Town Law § 267(7), and therefore had the requisite standing. Second, on the merits, the court vacated the Board's decision, holding that upon review of the administrative record applicants had failed to demonstrate that the property was unsuitable for permitted uses or could not yield a reasonable return. The Appellate Division reversed, concluding that Sun-Brite lacked standing to bring this article 78 proceeding because its only substantiated objection to the variance was that it would result in competition. We granted leave to appeal and now affirm.

DISCUSSION

Central to both appeals [*Sun-Brite* and a companion case] is the issue whether the petitioning parties have standing to assert their claims.

Whether in the form of an article 78 proceeding for review of an administrative determination or an action for an injunction, challenges to zoning determinations may only be made by "aggrieved" persons (see, Town Law § 267[7]; Little Joseph Realty v. Town of Babylon, 41 N.Y.2d 738, 741; 3 Rathkopf, Zoning and Planning § 43.01).

While the immediate parties to an administrative proceeding are aggrieved persons who may seek judicial review, it is less clear what other persons are aggrieved in a sense that entitles them to seek review. Aggrievement warranting judicial review requires a threshold showing that a person has been adversely affected by the activities of defendants (or respondents), or—put another way—that it has sustained special damage, different in kind and degree from the community generally (see, Matter of Douglaston Civic Ass'n v. Galvin, 36 N.Y.2d 1, 5; Cord Meyer Dev. Co. v. Bell Bay Drugs, 20 N.Y.2d 211). Traditionally, this has meant that injury in fact must be pleaded and proved.

Standing principles, which are in the end matters of policy, should not be heavy-handed; in zoning litigation in particular, it is desirable that land use disputes be resolved on their own merits rather than by preclusive, restrictive standing rules (see, Matter of Douglaston Civic Ass'n v. Galvin, *supra*, at 6). Because the welfare of the entire community is involved when enforcement of a zoning law is at stake, there is much to be said for permitting judicial review at the request of any citizen, resident or taxpayer; this idea finds support in the provision for public notice of a hearing. But we also recognize that permitting *everyone* to seek review could work against the welfare of the community by proliferating litigation, especially at the instance of special interest groups, and by unduly delaying final dispositions (see, 4 Anderson, American Law of Zoning § 27.09 [3d ed.]; *but see*, Ayer, Primitive Law of Standing in Land Use Disputes: Some Notes From a Dark Continent, 55 Iowa L. Rev. 344, 360).

While something more than the interest of the public at large is required to entitle a person to seek judicial review—the petitioning party must have a legally cognizable interest that is or will be affected by the zoning determination—proof of special damage or in-fact injury is not required in every instance to establish that the value or enjoyment of one's property is adversely affected (see, Matter of Douglaston Civic Ass'n v. Galvin, 36 N.Y.2d 1, *supra*; Little Joseph Realty v. Town of Babylon, 41 N.Y.2d 738, *supra*). The fact that a person received, or would be entitled to receive, mandatory notice of an administrative hearing because it owns property adjacent or very close to the property in issue gives rise to a presumption of standing in a zoning case. But even in the absence of such notice it is reasonable to assume that, when the use is changed, a person with property located in the immediate vicinity of the subject property will be adversely affected in a way different from the community at large; loss of value of individual property may be presumed from depreciation of the character of the immediate neighborhood. Thus, an allegation of close proximity alone may give rise to an inference of damage or injury that enables a nearby owner to challenge a zoning board decision without proof of actual injury (see, Matter of Prudco Realty Corp. v. Palermo, 93 AD2d

837, *aff'd on other grounds* 60 N.Y.2d 656; Matter of Marasco v. Luney, 99 A.D.2d 492, *lv denied* 63 N.Y.2d 605; *see also*, 4 Anderson, American Law of Zoning § 27.18 [3d ed.]; 3 Rathkopf, Zoning and Planning § 43.04).

The status of neighbor does not, however, automatically provide the entitlement, or admission ticket, to judicial review in every instance. Petitioner, for example, may be so far from the subject property that the effect of the proposed change is no different from that suffered by the public generally (*cf.,* Brechner v. Incorporated Vil. of Lake Success, 23 Misc. 2d 159, 161 [Meyer, J.]; 3 Rathkopf, *op. cit.* § 43.04; ALI Model Land Development Code §§ 9–103, 9–104 [Proposed Official Draft 1975] [property owner within 500 feet has standing]). Moreover, petitioner must also satisfy the other half of the test for standing to seek judicial review of administrative action—that "the interest asserted is arguably within the zone of interest to be protected by the statute." (Matter of Dairylea Coop. v. Walkley, 38 N.Y.2d 6, 9, *supra.*) Petitioner's status may be challenged on the ground that the interest it is asserting is not arguably within the "zone of interest" which the regulation is designed to protect. In such instances, even where petitioner's premises are physically close to the subject property, an ad hoc determination may be required as to whether a particular petitioner itself has a legally protectable interest so as to confer standing.

We next turn to application of these principles to the facts presented.

Sun-Brite's standing is first of all challenged because it is a lessee. A leaseholder may, however, have the same standing to challenge municipal zoning action as the owner. A change in contiguous or closely proximate property obviously can as readily affect the value and enjoyment of a leasehold as the underlying ownership interest (see, Lavere v. Board of Zoning Appeals, 39 A.D.2d 639, *aff'd no opn* 33 N.Y.2d 873 [month-to-month tenant]; Daub v. Popkin, 5 A.D.2d 283, *aff'd no opn* 4 N.Y.2d 1024; Community Planning Bd. No. 2 v. Board of Stds. & Appeals, 43 A.D.2d 670; 4 Anderson, American Law of Zoning § 27.13 [3d ed.]). Sun-Brite's status as a tenant is therefore not an impediment to its right to maintain this proceeding.

However, Sun-Brite lacks standing to seek judicial review because, as established in the administrative proceeding, its only substantiated objection was the threat of increased business competition, which is not an interest protected by the zoning laws (see, Matter of Dairylea Coop. v. Walkley, 38 N.Y.2d 6, 9, *supra*; Cord Meyer Dev. Co. v. Bell Bay Drugs, 20 N.Y.2d, at 211, *supra*; Matter of Paolangeli v. Stevens, 19 A.D.2d 763; *see also*, 4 Anderson, American Law of Zoning § 27.17 [3d ed.]; 3 Rathkopf, Zoning and Planning § 43.06). Individual property owners "have no vested rights to monopolies created by zoning laws or ordinances. These are not enforced at the instance of one competitor in order to prevent or reduce competition." (Cord Meyer Dev. Co. v. Bell Bay Drugs, 20 N.Y.2d, *supra*, at 215.) As we made clear in *Cord Meyer* (20 N.Y.2d, *supra*, at 218), the fact that petitioner is a competitor would not alone deprive it of standing if there were other injury, such as depreciation in the value of the property arising from the manner in which the use is conducted (*see also*, 3 Rathkopf, Zoning & Planning § 43.06, at 43–35). Here, however, the administrative record reveals that the only substantiated objection to the variance was the claim that it would result in increased competition. Zoning laws do not exist to insure limited business competition. Therefore, as the Appellate Division correctly concluded, petitioner lacked standing to maintain this proceeding.

Accordingly, . . . the order of the Appellate Division should be affirmed, with costs.

NOTES AND QUESTIONS

1.   Under the standards articulated in *Sun-Brite*, would a resident who lives across the street from the Gulf station have standing to challenge grant of the special permit if the resident contends that:

a.   the proposed car wash will make it more dangerous to cross the street?

b.   the proposed car wash will increase the level of artificial light on her back porch?

c.   the proposed car wash will reduce her property values?

2.   Which of your answers would be different if the resident lived five blocks away?

3.   In *Sun-Brite*, the court indicates that "an allegation of close proximity alone may give rise to an inference of damage or injury" that confers standing even without "proof of actual injury." But what if the zoning board, or a landowner who has received a permit from the zoning board, introduces evidence to establish that the landowner challenging the zoning board's action was not harmed in any significant way.

In Kenner v. Zoning Board of Appeals, 944 N.E.2d 163 (Mass. 2011), the ZBA granted landowner a special permit authorizing demolition and reconstruction of landowner's existing house. The new house would be seven feet higher than the original house. When landowner's immediate neighbor challenged the permit, alleging that the additional seven feet would interfere with an ocean view, landowner submitted photographs rebutting the claim that the additional seven feet would obstruct the neighbor's ocean view. The Supreme Judicial Court of Massachusetts held that this evidence shifted the burden back to the neighbor to demonstrate harm—a burden the neighbor could not meet. Standing, then, is often treated as a question of fact, not merely a pleading requirement.

4.   Suppose a neighbor does not participate in proceedings before the body charged with making a land use decision. Does failure to participate in the

initial decision deprive the neighbor of standing to challenge the decision once it is made? In Vermont, a statute limits standing to those who have "participated in a municipal regulatory proceeding" and provides that participation "shall consist of offering, through oral or written testimony, evidence or a statement of concern related to the subject of the proceeding." 24 Vt. Stat. Ann. §4471. For application of the statute to bar a challenge by neighbors who did not register their concerns until after the town zoning board had acted, *see* In re Verizon Wireless Barton Permit, 6 A.D.3d 713 (Vt. 2010).

5. *Neighborhood Associations.* Neighborhood associations often challenge land use decisions. In many states, associations have standing when one or more members of the association would have standing to advance the challenge. *See, e.g.*, Center Square Ass'n, Inc. v. City of Albany, 9 A.D.3d 651, 780 N.Y.S.2d 203 (2004). In other states, standing requirements are more difficult for an association to surmount. *See, e.g.*, Northeast Concerned Citizens, Inc. v. City of Hickory, 143 N.C.App. 272, 545 S.E.2d 768, 772 (2001) (suggesting that an organization has standing only when *all* of its members/shareholders would individually have standing); Society Created to Reduce Urban Blight v. Zoning Bd. of Adjustment, 921 A.2d 536, 543 (Pa. Cmwlth. 2007) (construing statute to preclude standing to association when the association cannot prove that it was "detrimentally harmed" by zoning variance while simultaneously concluding that individual plaintiff did have standing).

If you represent a neighbor challenging the grant of a zoning variance, permit, or amendment, what advantages are there in joining a neighborhood or community association as a plaintiff in the litigation?

6. *Environmental Groups.* Suppose an association can establish not that the municipality's action will cause its members *harm* different from that suffered by the community at large, but that it has an *interest* different from the community at large. Should that be sufficient to establish standing? In Save the Homosassa River Alliance, Inc. v. Citrus County, 2 So.3d 329, 340 (Fla. App. 2008), the court held that an environmental group had standing to challenge a zoning decision, despite its inability to prove unique harm, because to require unique harm would "make it impossible in most cases to establish standing."

A dissenting judge responded by offering the following prediction:

> Every gadfly with some amorphous environmental agenda, and enough money to pay a filing fee, will be anointed with status simply because the gadfly wants to "protect the planet."

> The environmental gadfly will win every time, not on the merits, but because, in the words of the trial judge, "[w]hen delay will prevent the construction of an approved but undesired development, then one may win by losing if the losing process is sufficiently long." For those who respect property rights, look out!

Id. at 346. Who has the better of the argument?

7. Suppose a neighbor who lives a block away challenges grant of a zoning variance to permit a bank to operate with fewer parking spaces than required by the zoning ordinance. The neighbor contends that the variance will increase congestion on her street, and make it more difficult for residents to park. How much proof of her contentions must the neighbor offer to establish her standing to challenge the variance? Should the mere allegation of increased congestion be enough? Why or why not?

8. Should the merits of the neighbor's challenge be relevant to the court in considering whether the neighbor has standing to advance the challenge? Why or why not?

9. For additional discussion of standing requirements in land use cases, *see* Mark Bobrowski, The Zoning Act's "Person Aggrieved" Standard: From Barvenik to Marashlian, 18 W. New Eng. L. Rev. 385 (1996).

10. *Standing to Challenge Comprehensive Rezonings.* In *Sun-Brite,* the neighbor was challenging the grant of a zoning variance. Would there be any reason to impose different standing rules for challenges to special permits or to piecemeal zoning amendments?

In Anne Arundel County v. Bell, 442 Md. 539, 113 A.3d 639 (2015), the Maryland Court of Appeals indicated that property owner standing rules similar to those articulated in the *Sun-Brite* case should apply to variances, special permits, and piecemeal zoning amendments, but held that more stringent "taxpayer standing" rules should apply when someone challenges a comprehensive rezoning. The court expressed concern that property owner standing rules would confer standing on all property owners in the county, because every comprehensive rezoning applies to every parcel in the county. As a result, the court held that only landowners who could show a reasonable probability of pecuniary loss or increase in taxes would have standing to challenge a comprehensive rezoning.

II. NEIGHBOR CHALLENGES TO ZONING AMENDMENTS

As we have seen, zoning amendments are typically enacted by the local "legislative" body—the town board, the city council, or another body composed of elected officials. When a landowner challenges an unfavorable amendment, or a refusal to amend the ordinance to permit development, the Takings Clause may provide the landowner with a ground for attack, largely because the legislative action or inaction imposes concentrated harm on the landowner. By contrast, when municipal action benefits the landowner, the harm to neighbors is typically more diffuse, and the federal constitution will be a dead end for neighbor-initiated litigation. Instead, the challenges advanced by neighbors will most often focus on defects in the procedures followed by the municipality. The range of available procedural arguments varies from state to state, and depends heavily on the state's enabling legislation. This section explores some of the most common grounds for challenge.

A. CONFORMITY WITH A PLAN

From its inception, land use regulation rested on the premise that regulation should not be purely a matter of naked politics, but instead should be the product of a planning process which scientifically assesses local needs and objectives, and then regulates land use to achieve those objectives. The rational planning model for zoning and other land use control has been under attack on multiple grounds. First, many scholars—planners among them—have concluded that planning should not be, and cannot be, divorced from politics. Second, others have observed that, whatever its theoretical merits, the rational planning model does not describe regulation "on the ground." Despite these criticisms, many state zoning enabling acts, following the Standard Zoning Enabling Act, require that zoning be "in accordance with a comprehensive plan," and many state statutes mandate that municipalities develop a plan that is separate and apart from its zoning ordinance. As a result, neighbors often challenge zoning amendments on the grounds that they are not consistent with the municipality's plan. Consider the following case:

Griswold v. City of Homer

Supreme Court of Alaska, 2008
186 P.3d 558

■ EASTAUGH, J.

I.   INTRODUCTION

After the Homer City Council passed an ordinance limiting the floor area of stores in three City of Homer zoning districts to between 20,000 and 45,000 square feet, Homer residents passed an initiative that increased the area to 66,000 square feet for all three zoning districts. Homer resident Frank Griswold sued the city and argued that the initiative was invalid for various reasons. The superior court upheld the initiative and granted summary judgment to the city. Griswold appeals, arguing that zoning is not a proper subject for an initiative. Because this zoning initiative impermissibly bypassed the Homer Advisory Planning Commission, and therefore exceeded the city council's own legislative power, we conclude that the initiative was invalid. We consequently remand for entry of judgment for Griswold.

II.   FACTS AND PROCEEDINGS

When Fred Meyer, Inc. publicly announced plans in late 2002 to build a 95,000-square-foot store in Homer, the city began an extensive review of its existing zoning code to determine whether it needed to alter floor area limits for retail and wholesale stores. For two years, beginning in March 2003, the question was considered by a special task force, by the Homer Advisory Planning Commission, and by the Homer City Council in more than a dozen hearings. After analyzing issues including traffic impact, the ideal rate of development, landscaping, maintaining the local character of Homer, and protecting groundwater, the planning commission made a series of recommendations to the city council regarding the appropriate floor area for retail and wholesale stores.

While those hearings were still being conducted, Homer voters in March 2004 filed with the city clerk an initiative petition that proposed a "footprint area" of 66,000 square feet for retail and wholesale business buildings in the Central Business District, General Commercial 1 District, and General Commercial 2 District. On April 12, 2004, the city council passed Ordinance 04–11(A), which set building floor area limits of 35,000 square feet in the Central Business District, 20,000 to 45,000 square feet in the General Commercial 1 District, and 45,000 square feet in the General Commercial 2 District. On the same day, in response to the initiative petition, the city council scheduled an election on the initiative for June 15, 2004. The voters approved the initiative at the June 15 election; the initiative became effective on June 21, 2004 as Ordinance 04–18.

Stating that a change in the zoning code sections was "required to properly convey the will of the voters," and that an ordinance was "necessary to implement the will of the voters," in February 2005 the city council enacted Ordinance 05–02, adopting a maximum floor area of 66,000 square feet for retail and wholesale business buildings in the three affected zoning districts. Ordinance 05–02 amended Ordinance 04–11(A) to reflect the text of the initiative. Ordinance 05–02 also effectively defined "footprint area" as "floor area," meaning "the total area occupied by a building, taken on a horizontal plane at the main grade level, exclusive of steps and any accessory buildings."

Frank Griswold challenged the initiative in the superior court, claiming among other things that the initiative process could not be used to amend the zoning code. The city prevailed on summary judgment.

Griswold appeals.

III. DISCUSSION

Griswold argues that the zoning initiative is invalid for several reasons. He contends, among other things, that the zoning authority delegated to the City of Homer requires it to pass only zoning ordinances that are consistent with the city's comprehensive plan.

The power to initiate cannot exceed the power to legislate. To decide whether Homer voters could invoke the initiative process to amend the City of Homer zoning code we must determine the extent of the city council's zoning power and the explicit and implicit limitations on that power.

We first review the statutory sources of that power. Alaska Statute 29.40.010 requires first and second class boroughs to provide for "planning, platting, and land use regulation on an areawide basis." If a city within a borough consents by ordinance, the borough assembly may delegate any of its land use regulation powers to the city. Alaska Statute 29.40.020(a) provides that the borough "shall establish a planning commission" and AS 29.40.020(b) provides that the planning commission "shall prepare and submit a proposed comprehensive plan in accordance with AS 29.40.030. . . ." Section .030 describes "a comprehensive plan" as "a compilation of policy statements, goals, standards, and maps for guiding the physical, social, and economic development, both private and public, of the first or second class borough."

These statutes require "areawide" planning and creation of a comprehensive plan "for the systematic and organized development" of the community, and they implicitly recognize the importance of the planning commission and the comprehensive plan to the process of regulating land use.

A planning commission has statutory responsibilities beyond drafting the comprehensive plan. Per AS 29.40.020(b)(2), the commission must also "review, recommend, and administer measures necessary to implement the comprehensive plan, including measures provided under AS 29.40.040." Because "zoning regulations" are one of the "measures provided under AS 29.40.040," subsection .020(b)(2) requires the planning commission to "review, recommend, and administer" zoning regulations "necessary to implement the comprehensive plan." The assembly by ordinance "shall adopt or amend" land use provisions "[i]n accordance with a comprehensive plan" and "in order to implement the comprehensive plan."

The statutes therefore expressly require that the planning commission have an active role in creating a comprehensive plan for "systematic and organized" local development, reviewing and recommending zoning regulations, and adopting measures "necessary to implement the comprehensive plan." The statutes implicitly recognize that the planning commission plays an important part in the formation and amendment of local land use regulations by providing assistance to the borough (or city) to ensure that development proceeds in a "systematic and organized" manner.

The relevant state statutes are clear. A borough or a city, having the power possessed by the City of Homer, cannot pass or amend a zoning ordinance without involving its planning commission in reviewing that ordinance. This review includes considering whether a proposed ordinance is consistent with the comprehensive plan. A borough assembly or city council may eventually choose not to follow the recommendations of the planning commission, but the statutes preclude bypassing the planning commission altogether.

Likewise, KPBC 21.01.020(B) gives the city council power to establish a planning commission to hear all requests for amendments to zoning codes. This provision can be read as giving the planning commission the primary authority for initial consideration of zoning amendments. At the very least, this provision confirms the commission's role in considering proposed amendments to an existing zoning code that was itself adopted "[i]n accordance with a comprehensive plan . . . and in order to implement the plan. . . ."

It is for this reason that zoning by initiative is invalid. The Homer City Council does not have the power to pass piecemeal zoning amendments without at least giving the Homer Advisory Planning Commission opportunity to review the proposals and make recommendations. Therefore, voters, who have no obligation to consider the views of the planning commission or be informed by its expertise, cannot use the initiative process to eliminate the planning commission's role in "areawide" land use planning and regulation, and thus potentially undermine the comprehensive plan for "systematic and organized" local development.

The facts in this case illustrate how the initiative process limits or even eliminates the intended role of a planning commission. The planning commission spent many months considering appropriate floor area limits for business buildings in the affected zoning districts. The city council charged the commission with "develop[ing] standards for addressing large retail and wholesale development" and "recommend[ing] a size cap for large retail and wholesale development." To that end, the commission, city council, and a task force conducted more than a dozen hearings. The commission reviewed recommendations from the Large Structure Impact Task Force and the Chamber of Commerce Legislative Committee; researched necessary improvements to lighting, landscaping, stormwater drainage, and parking; and developed standards for traffic and economic impact analyses. The commission explicitly applied the standards found in the Homer Comprehensive Plan in its decision-making process. And before the initiative election, the city council considered the planning commission's recommendations and amended the zoning code, adopting different floor area limitations for the subject zoning districts. The voters then approved the initiative and adopted a single, and greater, limitation for all three districts before the commission completed its findings.

Given the public hearings that were being conducted and the opportunity for public debate, it is logical to ask whether the voters had, in effect, the same access as the council to the recommendations of the planning commission, and thus whether the initiative process did not actually bypass the planning commission. The council was required to consider the commission's recommendations, even if it ultimately rejected them. The council acts as a collegial and public body; it is a matter of public record whether it addresses the commission's recommendations and attempts to reconcile proposed amendments with the comprehensive plan and state and borough ordinances. That is not at all the process an initiative election follows. Just as the council cannot choose to completely ignore the recommendations in adopting a zoning amendment, the voters cannot pass an initiative in which the commission's recommendations play no formal, or perhaps even informal, role at all.

The commission does more than simply give notice of hearings and allow the public to be heard on the subject of zoning ordinances. If a zoning amendment is proposed, the commission's role is to analyze the impact of the proposed changes in light of the city's development goals as stated in the comprehensive plan, and to suggest other changes that should accompany the proposed zoning amendment. Even if a city council chooses to disregard the recommendations of the city planning commission, its decision has been informed by the planning commission's consideration of the potential social and regulatory costs and benefits of the proposed amendment. The city's planning commission's role is not merely "procedural," but is substantive. Homer voters therefore could not bypass the commission by using the initiative power.

We REVERSE the superior court's grant of summary judgment and REMAND for entry of judgment for Griswold.

NOTES AND QUESTIONS

1.   Suppose the Homer Advisory Planning Commission had conducted its study and had recommended limiting the square footage of stores in the downtown area to 66,000 square feet, and the Homer City Council had refused to act on the recommendation. An interested citizen had proposed an initiative amending the zoning ordinance to limit square footage of downtown stores to 66,000—the same limit proposed by the Planning Commission. If the voters passed the initiative, and a neighbor then challenged the amendment, would the challenge have succeeded? What if a store owner, rather than an interested citizen, had challenged the amendment?

Is the court in *Griswold* holding that initiatives are invalid even if consistent with a plan developed by the Planning Commission? If so, why? *See* Marcilynn A. Burke, The Emperor's New Clothes: Exposing the Failures of Regulating Land Use Through the Ballot Box, 84 Notre Dame L. Rev. 1453, 1486 (2009):

> [W]hen voters attempt to amend a comprehensive plan, they do
> not have access to the same quality and quantity of information

that local officials possess. Even if the proponents of the initiative engage a professional planner to assist in the drafting of the measure, the public and government officials likely will not have an opportunity to critique or seek to amend the proposal. Initiatives are blunt instruments. Voters must either decide "yes" or "no."

For a more positive assessment of the prospect of direct democracy in land use decisions, *see* Thomas W. Merrill, Reassessing the State and Local Government Toolkit: Direct Voting by Property Owners, 77 U. Chi. L. Rev. 275, 277 (2010) (invoking the Condorcet Jury Theorem, which holds that under certain conditions, "the larger the group making a decision, the more likely the decision will be correct").

2. Suppose there had been no voter initiative in the *Griswold* case. Suppose instead that the Planning Commission had recommended a limit of 30,000 square feet, and the City Council rejected that recommendation, instead enacting a limit of 66,000 square feet—the same limit approved by the voters in *Griswold* itself. Would neighbors have any ground for challenging the amendment? What responses might the city advance?

3. Suppose the city had not created a planning commission, or suppose the planning commission had not made any recommendations at all. Would the City Council have power to enact a zoning amendment?

4. More than a half century ago, in a landmark article, Professor Charles Haar complained that too many state courts:

> emphasize the question whether the zoning ordinance is a comprehensive plan, not whether it is in accordance with a comprehensive plan. Thus construed, the enabling act demands little more than that zoning be "reasonable," and impartial in treatment, to satisfy the constitutional conditions for exercise of the state's police power.

Charles M. Haar, In Accordance With a Comprehensive Plan, 68 Harv. L. Rev. 1154, 1173 (1955). For more recent cases embracing the position Haar criticized, *see* Apple Group, Ltd. v. Granger Twp. Bd. of Zoning Appeals, 41 N.E.3d 1185 (Ohio 2015) ("A zoning resolution is enacted in accordance with a comprehensive plan . . . if it (1) reflects current land uses, (2) allows for change, (3) promotes public health and safety, (4) uniformly classifies similar areas, (5) clearly defines district locations and boundaries, and (6) identifies the use or uses to which each property may be put."); Remmel v. City of Portland, 102 A.3d 1168 (2014) ("[A] municipality may conclude that a rezoning action is consistent with a comprehensive plan when it is in harmony with some provisions of the plan, even if the action appears inconsistent with other provisions of the plan.").

The New York Court of Appeals has articulated a different position, indicating that the state's comprehensive plan requirement requires more than consistency and rationality, and instead:

> requires that the rezoning should not conflict with the fundamental land use policies and development plans of the

community. These policies may be garnered from any available source, most especially the master plan of the community, if any has been adopted, the zoning law itself and the zoning map.

Udell v. Haas, 21 N.Y.2d 463, 472, 288 N.Y.S.2d 888, 235 N.E.2d 897, 902 (1968). *See also* Konigsberg v. Bd. of Aldermen, 283 Conn. 553, 585, 930 A.2d 1, 19 (2007) (quoting earlier opinion establishing that "the comprehensive plan is to be found in the zoning regulations themselves and the zoning map"). How is this standard different from the one Professor Haar condemned? If the zoning ordinance and zoning map itself provide the "fundamental land use policies of the community," how could any zoning provision ever be out of conformity with a comprehensive plan?

5. Often, it is the developer-landowner, rather than a neighbor, who challenges a zoning determination as inconsistent with the comprehensive plan. A number of courts have rejected these challenges on the ground that the comprehensive plan does not impose mandates on zoning authorities. *See, e.g.*, Nestle Waters North America, Inc. v. Town of Fryeburg, 967 A.2d 702 (Me. 2009); Lamar County v. E.T. Carlyle Co., 277 Ga. 690, 594 S.E.2d 335 (2004). Should these courts apply the same standards to challenges by neighbors? Why or why not?

6. When a court finds that a zoning ordinance is inconsistent with a comprehensive plan, which should the court hold invalid—the plan or the zoning ordinance? In Mendota Golf, LLP v. City of Mendota Heights, 708 N.W.2d 162 (Minn. 2006), a suit brought by a landowner challenging the city's rejection of a subdivision proposal because it was inconsistent with the city's comprehensive plan, the Minnesota Supreme Court concluded that the plan was inconsistent with the zoning ordinance but remanded to the city to reconcile the plan and the zoning ordinance. What problems does the court's approach create?

7. In jurisdictions that hold that any zoning amendment must be consistent with the municipality's plan, how much deviation from the plan justifies a court in invalidating the zoning amendment? Suppose a city's comprehensive plan for a particular neighborhood emphasizes maintaining a sense of history, protecting landmarks, creating a pedestrian-friendly environment, and promoting a residential and small business environment. A hospital proposes a zoning amendment that would permit expansion of the hospital and of a "big-box" grocery store, but would require demolition of an historic city shop building. If the city enacts the amendment, can neighbors establish that the amendment is inconsistent with the plan? *See* Citizen Advocates for a Livable Missoula, Inc. v. City Council, 331 Mont. 269, 130 P.3d 1259 (2006), which upheld the amendment on the ground that it was consistent with some parts of the plan, particularly preservation of anchor institutions like the hospital:

> Surely, not every zoning proposal will be consistent with every goal and objective expressed in a city's growth plan documents. To impose such a requirement would remove flexibility from a city's review of zoning proposals and make growth policies a rigid regulation. . . .

Id. at 1265. Could the court have reached the same result if the hospital's proposed amendment would have permitted the hospital to buy and demolish the entire area to permit hospital expansion and construction of a big-box store?

8. A number of state legislatures have enacted statutes providing explicitly that plans should not be treated as regulatory documents. For instance, at roughly the time the city council granted the zoning amendment in the *Citizen Advocates* case discussed in Note 7, the Montana legislature amended its statute governing "growth policies" (the state's term for plans) to provide that "[a] growth policy is not a regulatory document and does not confer any authority to regulate that is not otherwise specifically authorized by law or regulations adopted pursuant to the law." Mont. Code. Ann. § 76–1–605(2)(a).

What effect would such a statute have on the state's requirement that zoning be "in accordance with a growth policy"? Who would lobby for enactment of such a statute?

B. FAILURE TO COMPLY WITH STATUTORY PROCEDURES

State legislatures have almost universally enacted statutes delegating zoning power to municipalities more familiar with local conditions. The zoning enabling act and other state statutes often describe the process municipalities must follow in enacting zoning "legislation." We shall see that courts in most states tend to defer to the substantive zoning decisions made by local legislatures. By contrast, a municipal legislature risks litigation—and invalidation—if it fails to comply with state-mandated procedures. A neighbor challenging a zoning amendment must scrutinize state statutes to see what avenues of attack might be available. Consider the following case:

Wally v. City of Kannapolis

Supreme Court of North Carolina, 2012
365 N.C. 449, 722 S.E.2d 481

■ TIMMONS-GOODSON, J.

This case involves a dispute between the City of Kannapolis ("defendant"), which rezoned rural land to promote commercial development, and neighboring land owners ("plaintiffs"). At issue is whether defendant approved a statement of reasonableness as required by N.C.G.S. § 160A–383 when adopting the zoning amendment. We hold defendant did not approve such a statement, and therefore, the amendment is invalid. Accordingly, we reverse the opinion of the Court of Appeals and remand for proceedings not inconsistent with this opinion.

The property at issue in this case consists of 75.9 acres owned by Coddle Creek, LLC and the Wallace Charitable Trust (collectively, "the

Owners"). [T]he Owners submitted a zoning request to the Kannapolis Planning and Zoning Commission ("Zoning Commission") seeking a more permissive zoning classification, Campus Development— Conditional Zoning. This classification would permit the Owners to develop a neighborhood office and a light industrial and retail business park on the property. In November 2007, the Zoning Commission approved the request, and plaintiffs, as neighboring property owners, appealed to the Kannapolis City Council ("City Council").

At a public hearing in December 2007, the City Council received a staff report from the Zoning Commission regarding the proposed zoning amendment. The staff report contained an analysis of the proposed amendment, including the compatibility of the proposed zoning designation with the surrounding area and impacts on safety, traffic, parking, the environment, and public facilities. Ultimately, the city staff concluded that the rezoning request was "consistent with the long range goals of the City, and reasonable in light of existing and approved infrastructure." At the December 2007 meeting defendant approved the zoning request. The following month defendant adopted a resolution to designate the property as Campus Development—Conditional Zoning.

In March 2008 plaintiffs filed an amended complaint in Superior Court, Cabarrus County, alleging, inter alia, that defendant failed to "adopt a statement" as required by N.C.G.S. § 160A–383. Plaintiffs asked the court to declare the zoning amendment void and to rezone the property to its previous classification. Both parties filed motions for summary judgment and stipulated that there was no genuine issue of material fact. On 23 February 2009, the trial court entered an order granting defendant's motion for summary judgment on all claims and dismissing plaintiffs' declaratory judgment action.

Plaintiffs appealed to the Court of Appeals. Regarding the section 160A–383 issue, the panel presumed the zoning amendment valid and held that plaintiffs failed to show the City Council did not "approve a statement." The court also held that section 160A–383 prohibits judicial review of whether the City Council's statement was statutorily sufficient.

Analysis

In determining whether defendant complied with N.C.G.S. § 160A–383 when it adopted the subject zoning amendment, we recognize that the amendment is presumed valid "and the burden [is] upon [plaintiffs] to show otherwise." Raleigh v. Morand, 247 N.C. 363, 368, 100 S.E.2d 870, 874 (1957) (citations omitted), appeal dismissed, 357 U.S. 343, 78 S.Ct. 1369, 2 L.Ed.2d 1367 (1958). We conclude that plaintiffs have met their burden and therefore hold that the zoning amendment is invalid.

Zoning ordinances regulate land use, not ownership. See Blades, 280 N.C. at 546, 187 S.E.2d at 43 ("The whole concept of zoning implies a restriction upon the owner's right to use a specific tract. . . ."). "The original zoning power of the State reposes in the General Assembly." Allgood v. Town of Tarboro, 281 N.C. 430, 437, 189 S.E.2d 255, 260 (1972) (citation omitted). The General Assembly, in turn, may delegate zoning authority to the legislative body of a municipality. *Id.* Because zoning authority derives from the state's police power, zoning ordinances are valid only when they "promote the public health, the public safety, the public morals or the public welfare." Zopfi v. City of Wilmington, 273 N.C. 430, 433, 160 S.E.2d 325, 330 (1968). In addition, "[t]he power to zone . . . is subject to the limitations of the enabling act," Schloss v. Jamison, 262 N.C. 108, 114, 136 S.E.2d 691, 695 (1964) (citations omitted), and "[z]oning regulations shall be made in accordance with a comprehensive plan," N.C.G.S. § 160A–383 (2011). Exercise of the zoning power also must comport with certain procedural requirements, such as those provided in section 160A–383.

> When adopting or rejecting any zoning amendment, the governing board shall also approve a statement describing whether its action is consistent with an adopted comprehensive plan and any other officially adopted plan that is applicable, and briefly explaining why the board considers the action taken to be reasonable and in the public interest. That statement is not subject to judicial review.

N.C.G.S. § 160A–383.

By its plain language section 160A–383 states that when the governing board adopts a zoning amendment, the board "shall also" approve a statement. *Id.* Thus, the statute requires that defendant take two actions in this situation: first, adopt or reject the zoning amendment, and second, approve a proper statement. *Id.* The approved statement must describe whether the action is consistent with any controlling comprehensive plan and explain why the action is "reasonable and in the public interest." *Id.* In addition, the statute declares that when such a statement is made, it "is not subject to judicial review."

Defendant asserts that N.C.G.S. § 160A–383 expressly prohibits judicial review of the City Council's statement, and therefore, the trial court did not err by granting summary judgment in its favor. Next, defendant argues that the City Council approved a statement in satisfaction of section 160A–383 by adopting the zoning amendment with the staff report that was before the City Council. Under this theory, the City Council impliedly approved the staff's statement regarding consistency and reasonableness. Finally, defendant contends that the City Council complied with the statute by adopting the following statement: "[T]he Council's final vote conforms to the guidelines under which they are granted final authority to act upon a rezoning petition." We are not persuaded by these arguments.

As a preliminary matter, we disagree with defendant's argument that the statute bars judicial review of this issue. The statute provides, "That statement is not subject to judicial review," and by "[t]hat statement," the statute refers to an approved statement. While an approved statement is not subject to judicial review, the statute does not prohibit review of whether the City Council approved a statement, which is the issue here. Accordingly, we review whether the City Council approved a statement.

Turning to the issue proper, we hold that the City Council did not approve a statement as required by N.C.G.S. § 160A–383. First, while the City Council took the initial step of adopting the zoning amendment, it failed to take the second step and "approve a statement" that addresses consistency, reasonableness, and the public interest. This failure is evidenced by the trial court's uncontested finding of fact that "there was no per se written statement of reasonableness," a fact that is binding on appeal. Morand, 247 N.C. at 365, 100 S.E.2d at 872 (stating that where no challenge is made to the findings of fact, those findings are presumed supported by competent evidence and are binding upon appeal).

Second, we are not persuaded by defendant's argument that it complied with the statute by impliedly approving the staff report by virtue of having the report in hand when adopting the zoning amendment. The language of section 160A–383 does not authorize an implied approval. Defendant cites no authority permitting implied approval in this context, and we have found none. Defendant's argument also fails because, while section 160A–383 requires the approved statement to explain why "the board [the City Council] considers the action taken to be reasonable," the staff report merely states that the staff considers the action reasonable.

Finally, we do not agree that the City Council satisfied the statute by adopting a statement announcing that it acted within the guidelines of its zoning authority. Compliance with section 160A–383 requires more than a general declaration that the action comports with relevant law. Section 160A–383 explains that to meet the statutory requirements, an approved statement must describe whether the zoning amendment is consistent with any controlling land use plan and explain why it is reasonable and in the public interest. The statement adopted by the City Council provides no such explanation or description. Rather, it consists of a general declaration that in adopting the zoning amendment, the City Council acted within the guidelines of its zoning authority.

Conclusion

The zoning amendment at issue is invalid because defendant failed to properly approve a statement under N.C.G.S. § 160A–383.

NOTES AND QUESTIONS

1. Suppose the City Council had, at the time it adopted the zoning amendment, approved the following statement:

STATEMENT OF CONSISTENCY

This petition is found to be consistent with adopted policies and to be reasonable and in the public interest.

If you had represented the neighbors, what attack would you have mounted against the amendment? Would the attack have been successful? *See* Atkinson v. City of Charlotte, 760 S.E.2d 395 (N.C. App. 2014).

2. Suppose now that the zoning commission staff had never analyzed the proposed amendment and had never stated any conclusions. The City Council then approved the amendment, with a statement concluding that the rezoning would increase tax revenue without increasing traffic or degrading the environment. Would neighbors have been able to upset the Council's determination? Why or why not?

In City of Reno v. Citizens for Cold Springs, 236 P.3d 10 (Nev. 2010), the Nevada Supreme Court invalidated a zoning amendment for failure to comply with a statutory requirement that

In approving any zoning map amendment, the planning commission and city council shall find the following:

. . .

b. The change in zoning represents orderly development of the city and there are, or are planned to be adequate services and infrastructure to support the proposed zoning change and existing uses in the area.

When adopting the amendment, the City Council made a finding that:

[W]hile the details of the provision of water and sewer will be required when the development is proposed, there is infrastructure in place that could be expanded, such as an existing sewer plant, and a water purveyor called Utilities, Inc. Alternatively, new utilities could be built by the developer.

What argument do you think the lawyers for the neighbors made to invalidate the amendment?

3. Of what value is the procedural requirement that the Council prepare a statement if the statement is not subject to judicial review?

4. What advice would you have given the developer in the *Wally* case if the developer's goal was to insulate the zoning amendment from attack?

5. Each state's procedural requirements may be different, and a careful lawyer for neighbors will scrutinize state law to find a basis for invaliding an amendment favoring a developer. For instance, the Delaware Supreme Court invalidated a zoning amendment for failure to comply with a statute providing that a local legislature "shall not approve" a zoning amendment reclassifying land without first entering into an agreement with the state

Department of Transportation to conduct a study of traffic impact. Barley Mill, LLC v. Save Our County, Inc., 89 A.3d 51 (Del. 2014).

C. SPOT ZONING

Most proposed zoning amendments do not spring full-blown from the mind of a municipal official. Instead, an interested landowner or developer who wants to develop her land more intensively than the existing zoning ordinance permits may propose an amendment, either to the text of the ordinance, or to the zoning map. The landowner may not be concerned with whether the amendment affects other parcels; her concern is with her plans for her own parcel. If the municipal legislature enacts the amendment, is the amendment suspect if it benefits only the landowner's parcel? Consider the following case:

Little v. Winborn
Supreme Court of Iowa, 1994
518 N.W.2d 384

■ TERNUS, J.

The Scott County Board of Supervisors rezoned a 223-acre parcel of agricultural land. Neighboring landowners filed a petition for writ of certiorari challenging the rezoning. The district court found the rezoning ordinance invalid and the owner of the rezoned property appealed. Because we think the rezoning constituted illegal spot zoning, we affirm.

Background Facts and Procedures

In September 1991, the Davenport Shooting Association (Association) petitioned the Scott County Zoning and Planning Commission (Commission) to consider rezoning a 223-acre parcel of land. The land was zoned Agricultural One—agricultural protection district (A–1)—and the Association wanted it rezoned Agricultural Two—agricultural district (A–2). The 223-acre parcel was surrounded by land zoned A–1. In its rezoning petition the Association stated that it intended to build two uninhabited structures on the land for recreational club use, the balance of the land to remain in its agricultural state.

The Commission held two public hearings to consider the petition. The Association explained that rezoning the property was necessary because the Association planned to build a shooting house and a target house on the property.

Several adjacent property owners addressed the Commission and expressed their opposition to the rezoning. They feared the shooting range would be loud, the noise would bother their livestock, and the shooting range would cause more activity in the area. They argued that the land should stay in tillage and that the two structures proposed to be built on the parcel posed a fire hazard. The Association responded that the two buildings would take less than five acres of land out of agricultural production and would create a minimum fire hazard.

Philip Rovang, the Planning Director, recommended approval of the rezoning petition. After the second public hearing, three members of the Commission voted in favor of rezoning and three members voted against. The Commission forwarded its report to the Board of Supervisors.

The Board of Supervisors held a public hearing on the rezoning petition and received comments similar to those made at the hearings before the Commission. The Board voted 3 to 2 to approve the petition.

A petition for writ of certiorari was filed with the district court by the neighboring landowners. The district court concluded the zoning ordinance was invalid and sustained the writ. The court held that Iowa Code section 358A.8 (1991) required an affirmative recommendation of the rezoning petition by the zoning commission before the petition could be considered by the Board. Because the Commission's tie vote was not an approval under the Commission's bylaws, the court concluded that the Commission had not recommended the rezoning so as to allow the Board to vote on the petition.

The district court also found that the Board's rezoning of the Association's property effectively granted the Association approval for a shooting range. The court concluded that the Board's action did not comply with Iowa Code section 657.9 which sets out the procedure for approval of a shooting range. Consequently, the court invalidated the rezoning for failing to meet the requirements of section 657.9.

The neighboring landowners also contended that the rezoning constituted illegal spot zoning. The district court did not rule on that contention.

The Association appeals from the district court's ruling.

Spot Zoning

In their petition for certiorari and on this appeal, the adjacent landowners argued that the ordinance was invalid spot zoning. Therefore, we now consider this issue.

"Spot zoning results when a zoning ordinance creates a small island of property with restrictions on its use different from those imposed on the surrounding property." Jaffe v. City of Davenport, 179 N.W.2d 554, 556 (Iowa 1970). Spot zoning is not automatically invalid. 8 E. McQuillen, Municipal Corporations § 25.84, at 319 (3rd ed. rev. 1991). If it is germane to an object within the police power and there is a reasonable basis to treat the spot-zoned property differently from the surrounding property, the spot zoning is valid. Montgomery v. Bremer County Bd. of Supervisors, 299 N.W.2d 687, 696 (Iowa 1980); *Jaffe*, 179

N.W.2d at 556. *See generally* 101A C.J.S. Zoning and Planning § 44 (1979).

In determining whether there is a reasonable basis for spot zoning, we consider the size of the spot zoned, the uses of the surrounding property, the changing conditions of the area, the use to which the subject property has been put and its suitability and adaptability for various uses. *Jaffe*, 179 N.W.2d at 556. In rural county zoning, the size of the tract is not very important. *Montgomery*, 299 N.W.2d at 696; Keppy v. Ehlers, 253 Iowa 1021, 1023, 115 N.W.2d 198, 200 (1962). The factor of primary importance is whether the rezoned tract has a peculiar adaptability to the new classification as compared to the surrounding property. *Keppy*, 253 Iowa at 1023, 115 N.W.2d at 200. Spot zoning for the benefit of the owner and contrary to the comprehensive plan is unreasonable. *Jaffe*, 179 N.W.2d at 556.

We conclude that the rezoning of the farmland here is spot zoning. This property is surrounded by land zoned A–1. Rezoning this parcel to A–2 would create an island of property with restrictions on its use different from those imposed on surrounding property.

The next question is whether this spot zoning is valid. We consider (1) whether the new zoning is germane to an object within the police power, (2) whether there is a reasonable basis for making a distinction between the spot-zoned land and the surrounding property, and (3) whether the rezoning is consistent with the comprehensive plan.

We discern no object within the police power that would justify rezoning this property. The rezoning of this parcel is not related to the public health, safety, morals or general welfare designed to serve the best interests of the community as a whole. Only the owner of the property and its members would receive any benefit from rezoning this land.

Nor do we find a reasonable basis for distinguishing this property from the surrounding property. The 223-acre parcel contains farm ground and timber. It has no unique quality that makes it more suitable than the property surrounding it to be zoned A–2.

More important, we do not believe the rezoning is pursuant to the Scott County Comprehensive Zoning Plan or the County's zoning district classifications. One of the main thrusts of the comprehensive plan is to "identify and seek means to protect prime agricultural land from scattered development." To carve out a parcel of land in an A–1 district and zone it A–2 would result in the type of scattered development the comprehensive plan seeks to avoid. Moreover, half of the rezoned property qualifies as "prime" agricultural land. Although the Association says that it will remove only five acres from production, there is nothing in the zoning classification or the rezoning ordinance that would limit the property owner's attempts to use the land in a manner other than farming and yet within the A–2 district restrictions.

Uses permitted in an A–2 district include schools, parks, government buildings, golf courses, churches, cemeteries, and solid waste disposal sites. Thus, rezoning provides less, not more, protection for the prime agricultural land in this parcel.

The A–1 agricultural protection district is designed to "protect agricultural land from encroachment of urban development." The A–2 agricultural district is intended to "act as a holding zone until a compatible urban development proposal is approved." According to the county's zoning policies, new urban development in the rural areas should, among other factors, (1) be on marginal or poor farmland, (2) have access to adequately constructed paved roads, (3) have present or planned water and sanitary sewer systems, and (4) be near existing employment and commercial areas. The proposed rezoning does not meet these criteria. There are no plans to develop this rural area for urban uses. As previously noted, half the land is prime farmland. Access to the property is by a dirt road and the County does not intend to improve this road. In fact, the county engineer disapproved of the rezoning request unless the Association would agree to maintain the road itself. There is no private or public sanitary sewer system on the property. The property is not located near existing employment centers or commercial areas. The zoning commissioners who voted against the rezoning petition were aware of such problems. They opposed the rezoning because they thought it was improper spot zoning and represented a change in the County's policies to preserve agricultural land and check urban encroachment on farmland.

Basically, the Association argues that a change from A–1 to A–2 is not very great and will not really change the use of the property. However, as noted above, many uses are allowed in an A–2 district that are incompatible with the preservation of the property in its present form. Consequently, the Association's argument that rezoning will not change the use of the property is not necessarily true. Even if it were true, however, this argument fails to address why this property should be rezoned to A–2 and the surrounding similar property remain in an A–1 district. *See Keppy*, 253 Iowa at 1023, 115 N.W.2d at 200 ("restrictions not bearing alike on all persons living in *the same territory under similar conditions and circumstances* are discriminatory and will not be upheld").

We conclude that none of the factors that form the basis for valid spot zoning exist in this case. Therefore, the enactment of the ordinance rezoning the 223-acre parcel of land from A–1 to A–2 was invalid spot zoning.

Therefore, we affirm the district court's ruling sustaining the writ of certiorari.

AFFIRMED.

NOTES AND QUESTIONS

1. Suppose the shooting association had obtained a text amendment adding shooting ranges to the list of permissible uses in A–1 districts. Would a spot zoning challenge have succeeded? Why or why not? Should the shooting association's lawyers have advised the association to seek a text amendment rather than a map amendment?

2. The court in *Little* uses "spot zoning" as a description of a zoning amendment that places a parcel in a zoning district different from the district that encompasses surrounding land. Once the court finds spot zoning, the court asks a second question: is the spot zoning valid? Other courts collapse the two issues and treat "spot zoning" as a legal conclusion. In these jurisdictions, the court labels an amendment "spot zoning" only if it decides that the amendment is invalid. *See, e.g.,* Michel v. Planning & Zoning Comm'n, 28 Conn.App. 314, 319, 612 A.2d 778, 781 (1992):

> Our courts consistently have invalidated zoning decisions that have constituted spot zoning. Spot zoning is the reclassification of a small area of land in such a manner as to disturb the tenor of the surrounding neighborhood. Two elements must be satisfied before spot zoning can be said to exist. First, the zone change must concern a small area of land. Second, the change must be out of harmony with the comprehensive plan for zoning adopted to serve the needs of the community as a whole. The comprehensive plan is to be found in the scheme of the zoning regulations themselves.

3. What is the source of the prohibition on spot zoning? If the state zoning enabling act confers on municipalities the power to create zoning districts, on what authority can a lawyer rely when asking a court to invalidate the municipality's exercise of that power? Does the opinion in *Little* provide any guidance on that question?

4. Note the overlap between spot zoning cases and cases attacking amendments as not in accordance with a comprehensive plan. Are there cases in which a spot zoning challenge might be successful when a comprehensive plan challenge would not be? Cases in which a plan challenge might be successful, but not a spot zoning challenge?

5. The neighbor who challenges a zoning amendment as "spot zoning" objects to the lines the municipality draws between zoning districts. But isn't all zoning about line-drawing? Won't there always be boundaries between districts that appear somewhat arbitrary? What is special about "spot zoning" that merits judicial invalidation?

6. Consider the following cases. In each case, what should the neighbors' lawyer emphasize in advancing a "spot zoning" challenge? Would you expect the challenge to succeed?

    a. After a court enjoined the sponsor of a county fair from constructing a race track on a fairground located in a district zoned for agricultural use, the county board amended the ordinance to exempt fairground property during the five days of the annual county fair. *See* Perkins v. Bd. of Supervisors, 636 N.W.2d 58 (Iowa 2001).

b.   Purchasers of 17 acres located in the midst of a residential district sought and obtained a zoning amendment rezoning the 17 acres from residential to commercial to permit operation of a cement-batching plant. One hundred fifty neighbors opposed the plant, but the local board found that construction of the plant would assist in development of the area. *See* Anderson v. Island County, 81 Wash.2d 312, 501 P.2d 594 (1972).

c.   The city's largest employer sought and obtained a zoning amendment rezoning previously residential land for light manufacturing. The city was motivated by the economic and tax benefits associated with development of a business park. *Compare* Save Our Forest Action Coalition, Inc. v. City of Kingston, 246 A.D.2d 217, 675 N.Y.S.2d 451 (1998) *with* Chrobuck v. Snohomish County, 78 Wash.2d 858, 480 P.2d 489 (1971).

d.   A municipality amends its ordinance at the behest of a religious organization seeking to develop a senior housing complex in the midst of a district zoned to permit single-family homes. *See* Foothill Communities Coalition v. County of Orange, 166 Cal.Rptr.3d 627 (Cal. App. 2014).

Would your evaluation of any of these situations change if the municipal planning commission, after study, had recommended approval of the amendment?

7.   Suppose, in each of the cases discussed in the preceding note, you had represented the developer at the time the developer applied for the zoning amendment. What steps would you have recommended the developer take to minimize the risk that a subsequent spot zoning challenge would prove successful?

8.   Although courts consistently condemn spot zoning, the vast majority of spot zoning challenges fail. Is that a good thing? *See generally* Osborne Reynolds, Jr., "Spot Zoning": A Spot that Could Be Removed from the Law, 48 Wash. U. J. Urb. & Contemp. L. 117 (1995). What reasons are there to believe that courts will be better than municipal legislatures at evaluating the wisdom of map amendments?

9.   Sometimes, courts use the spot zoning label to invalidate zoning amendments that impose restrictions on a small area that are more onerous than those applied to the surrounding areas. *See, e.g.,* Avenida San Juan Partnership v. City of San Clemente, 135 Cal.Rptr.3d 570 (Cal. App. 2011) (invalidating a restriction limiting development to one dwelling per 20 acres on a parcel surrounded by residential development). In other states, courts attach labels like "reverse spot zoning" or "inverse spot zoning" to amendments that impose onerous restrictions on a small island of land. *See, e.g.,* Riya Finnegan LLC v. Township Council, 197 N.J. 184, 962 A.2d 484 (2008). In Virginia, courts use the label "piecemeal downzoning" to describe the same problem. *See* Turner v. Bd. of County

Supervisors, 263 Va. 283, 559 S.E.2d 683 (2002). Some states apply reverse spot zoning doctrine more broadly, permitting a landowner to raise a "reverse spot zoning" claim not only when the municipality amends the ordinance to impose new restrictions on landowner, but also when a municipality declines to enact a zoning amendment proposed by the landowner (thus retaining the *status quo*, which may leave landowner more restricted than surrounding land). *See, e.g.*, City Comm'n v. Woodlawn Park Cemetery Co., 553 So.2d 1227 (Fla. App. 1989).

D. STANDARD OF REVIEW

In our democratic system, courts typically interfere with legislation only when the legislature has exceeded its authority. At the federal level, courts strike down congressional enactments only when they violate the federal constitution. At the state level, enactments of state legislatures are supreme unless pre-empted by federal legislation or inconsistent with the state or federal constitutions.

At the municipal level, matters are somewhat more complicated because municipalities are not sovereign entities; in a number of states they enjoy only those powers expressly conferred upon them by the state constitution and statutes. Even in home rule states, municipal "legislative" power is generally subject to whatever constraints states impose by statute. We have seen, in the *Wally* case, that courts are willing to strike down zoning amendments when the local legislature has failed to comply with state statutory requirements. How much second-guessing should courts do when the local legislature crosses all of its "t"s and dots all of its "i"s?

The next three cases illustrate three entirely different judicial responses to piecemeal zoning amendments. We include all three for comparative purposes, but no state embraces more than one of these approaches.

1. THE TRADITIONAL (AND MAJORITY) APPROACH

Traditionally, courts have treated zoning ordinances (and amendments to those ordinances) as a species of local legislation. State law generally confers on an elected body of municipal officials—the municipal "legislature"—the power to enact zoning amendments. In accordance with democratic theory, courts defer to municipal decisions on zoning "legislation" unless those decisions exceed the zoning authority given to the municipal legislature by state statutes or by constitutional law. The following case illustrates the traditional approach embraced by the courts of most states:

DiRico v. Town of Kingston

Supreme Judicial Court of Massachusetts, 2010
458 Mass. 83, 934 N.E.2d 208

■ IRELAND, J.

Background.

The material undisputed facts are as follows. The town is a coastal community in southeastern Massachusetts that, in recent years, has experienced unprecedented development pressures. From 1980 to 2000, the town's population grew by sixty per cent, with the majority of development taking the form of single-family residential homes on large lots. In February, 2006, the town was approached by the defendant Thorndike Development Corporation (Thorndike), about the possibility of adopting a zoning amendment that would create a smart growth zoning district on property located less than one-half mile from the Kingston commuter rail station (property). The property consists of 109 acres and includes an excavated sand pit. Thorndike had acquired an option to purchase the property from its owners, the defendants Mary O'Donnell and Robert Moakley, trustees of the O'Donnell Family Realty Trust, and was interested in developing a smart growth development to be called 1021 Kingston's Place (Kingston's Place). Kingston's Place would consist of up to 730 new residential units, 50,000 square feet of retail space, and 250,000 square feet of commercial space.

In February, 2006, the town requested and received a preliminary determination from the [state department charged with administering smart growth development] that the property would be in an "eligible location" for smart growth development. In June, 2006, the town submitted its application to the department for its proposed smart growth project. Included in the town's application, as required, was a certification of the amount of developable land in the proposed smart growth zoning district. Specifically, the town's application certified that the proposed smart growth zoning district consisted of 109 acres, of which 69.6 acres (or 63.9 per cent of the district) consisted of developable land. The application also identified that the proposed district included 11.2 acres (or 10.3 per cent) of environmentally constrained land, none of which, at the time, included rare species habitat designated under State or Federal law.

Effective October 1, 2006, the Natural Heritage and Endangered Species Program, issued the twelfth edition of its Natural Heritage Atlas (atlas). Pursuant to the atlas, a substantial portion of the land comprising the proposed Kingston's Place development, possibly as much as fifty per cent, was designated as a priority habitat of State-listed rare species (including the eastern box turtle) and an estimated habitat of rare wildlife

The town became aware of the atlas designations in November of 2006. Subsequently, the town did not revise its figures contained in its application to the department concerning the developable land area, environmentally constrained land, or total future zoned incentive units in the proposed smart growth zoning district.

On April 4, 2007, the department issued a letter of eligibility to the town, approving the town's application for the creation of the smart growth zoning district and the underlying zoning amendment, with certain conditions. As relevant here, as part of one of the conditions, the department required annual updates to be filed with the department "[o]n or before July 31 of each year . . . containing . . . a table indicating the total land area, the [d]evelopable [l]and [a]rea, the [s]ubstantially [d]eveloped [l]and [a]rea, the number of [i]ncentive [u]nits, the amount of [d]evelopable and [s]ubstantially [d]eveloped [l]and zoned for each type of residential use allowed under the [smart growth zoning ordinance or bylaw] for the [smart growth zoning district]."

On April 11, 2007, the zoning amendment was adopted by a vote of the Kingston town meeting. The department granted its final approval of the zoning amendment on August 28, 2007. The town received a zoning incentive payment in the amount of $600,000. In its first annual update to the department, dated July 30, 2008, the town did not revise its figures relating to the developable land area, environmentally constrained land, or total future zoned incentive units.

On November 14, 2007, the plaintiffs [neighboring landowners] filed their original complaint in the Land Court seeking to have the zoning amendment invalidated. Specifically, as relevant to this appeal, the plaintiffs claimed that the town failed adequately to consider, and should have informed the department of, the effect of the change in the priority habitat designation to the calculation of developable land for the proposed Kingston's Place development.

In her summary judgment decision, the Land Court judge acknowledged that the town's calculation of the amount of developable land, for summary judgment purposes, was incorrect at the time the department issued its letter of eligibility on April 4, 2007, and when the zoning amendment was adopted by the town meeting on April 11, 2007 (because the atlas containing the priority habitat designation became effective on October 1, 2006). She concluded, however, that the error did not invalidate the zoning amendment. The judge explained that the town's duty to submit its first annual update had not yet arisen when the zoning amendment was adopted by the town, and that thereafter, the motives of the town for failing to update the developable land component of its application, could not be considered by the court. For these reasons, the judge concluded that the plaintiffs had not and could not meet their burden of proving facts that compel a conclusion that the validity of the zoning amendment "is not even fairly debatable," Crall v.

Leominster, 362 Mass. 95, 103, 284 N.E.2d 610 (1972). The judge granted the defendants' motion for summary judgment and entered a judgment dismissing the plaintiffs' complaint.

Discussion.

Whether a smart growth zoning ordinance or bylaw is valid accordingly rests on the settled principles that pertain to zoning ordinances or bylaws enacted under G. L. c. 40A. Under these standards, "[t]he enactment of a zoning bylaw by the voters at town meeting is not only the exercise of an independent police power, it is also a legislative act." Durand v. IDC Bellingham, LLC, 440 Mass. 45, 50, 793 N.E.2d 359 (2003) (Durand). *See* Opinion of the Justices, 358 Mass. 838, 840, 267 N.E.2d 113 (1971). Consequently, a strong presumption of validity is to be afforded to the challenged bylaw or ordinance. *Durand, supra* at 51. The presumption "will not normally be undone unless the plaintiff can demonstrate 'by a preponderance of the evidence that the zoning regulation is arbitrary and unreasonable, or substantially unrelated to the public health, safety . . . or general welfare.'" *Id.*, quoting Johnson v. Edgartown, 425 Mass. 117, 121, 680 N.E.2d 37 (1997). "If the reasonableness of a zoning bylaw is even 'fairly debatable, the judgment of the local legislative body responsible for the enactment must be sustained.'" *Durand, supra*, quoting Crall v. Leominster, *supra* at 101. "Such an analysis is not affected by consideration of the various possible motives that may have inspired legislative action." *Durand, supra*, and cases cited.

There is no question that the duty of a municipality to identify correctly the amount of developable land in a proposed smart growth zoning district takes on great significance under the statutory and regulatory scheme. As has been mentioned, this component affects the permissible density of a smart growth project, as well as the amount of financial incentives to be given a municipality from State funds. Consequently, throughout the lengthy process to create a smart growth zoning district, information concerning the amount of developable land in a proposed or approved smart growth zoning district, when required, should be, to the best of a municipality's ability, current and correct as of the date of a submission. To conclude otherwise, would render the various statutory and regulatory obligations after the submission of the original application superfluous. We also note the absence of any express requirement to use the figure (concerning the amount of developable land) set forth in the original application in submissions following the original application.

When originally submitted on June, 2006, the town's application, regarding the amount of developable land in the proposed smart growth zoning district, was accurate. We find no statutory or regulatory mandate imposed on the town to revise its application (concerning the amount of developable land) *prior to* the department's issuance of a letter of eligibility. The same, however, cannot be said of the town's obligations in connection with seeking final approval for the smart growth zoning district from the department. We agree with the plaintiffs that [the] broad regulatory mandate obligated the town to revise its figures concerning the project's developable land area in its submission seeking the department's final approval of its smart growth zoning district. When the town learned of an event (the atlas designation) that rendered information in its original application (concerning the amount of developable land) incorrect, a change was necessitated and the town, as the applicant, was obligated to bring that change to the department's attention in its submission seeking the department's final approval. Should the change to the original application be insignificant, the department retains the discretion to go forward and need not treat every change as an amendment. However, that determination is one for the department, and not for the town, to make.

We also agree with the plaintiffs and the Land Court judge that the town, in its annual updates, is obligated to set forth the current figures concerning the amount of developable land in the smart growth zoning district. [I]naccurate figures would not assist the department in determining the proper density and corresponding amount of financial incentives to be awarded to the town.

Although we conclude that the town failed to revise its figures concerning the developable land area in accordance with the duties discussed above, we conclude that these omissions are not a basis to invalidate the zoning amendment itself. As relevant to the development of Kingston's Place, the amount of developable land bears on the number of units to be developed and the amount of financial incentives to be paid to the town. Thus, the town's omissions do not invalidate the zoning amendment. Rather, the consequence is one of a financial nature, triggering the suspension or repayment of financial incentives awarded to a municipality. *See* 760 Code Mass. Regs. § 59.06(3)(c) and (d).

For these reasons, we agree with the Land Court judge's determinations that the plaintiffs have not proved "facts which compel a conclusion that the question [of the validity of the zoning amendment] is not even fairly debatable," Crall v. Leominster, 362 Mass. 95, 103, 284 N.E.2d 610 (1972), and that the zoning amendment is valid. The judge was correct to grant summary judgment to the defendants and to direct entry of a judgment dismissing the complaint.

Judgment affirmed.

NOTES AND QUESTIONS

1.   When a lawyer challenges a zoning amendment that removes restrictions on a landowner's land, the lawyer must traditionally rely on

some conflict between the amendment and state law. What conflict did the neighbors' lawyer raise in *DiRico*? How, if at all, was the challenge different from the one raised in *Griswold*? From the challenge raised in *Wally*? From the challenge raised in *Little*?

2. If a court or a board of zoning appeals had based its decision on inaccurate or outdated facts, do you think the Supreme Judicial Court would have upheld the decision of the court or board? Why, if at all, should the court treat the determination of the Kingston Town Meeting any differently?

3. In *DiRico*, the amendment was enacted by a vote of the Town meeting. Do you think the court would have been more or less deferential if the amendment had been enacted by a five-person town board? Why? For another formulation, in a case involving a determination by a town board, *see* Church v. Town of Islip, 8 N.Y.2d 254, 258, 203 N.Y.S.2d 866, 168 N.E.2d 680, 682 (1960) ("We start with the proposition that this zoning being a legislative act (not a variance) is entitled to the strongest possible presumption of validity and must stand if there was any factual basis therefor.").

A number of state courts have rejected the traditional approach—at least with respect to piecemeal zoning amendments—and have become less deferential to zoning amendments than they might be to other forms of legislation. The following sections explore two different approaches, each of which leads to less deferential review of zoning amendments.

2.   THE CHANGE/MISTAKE RULE

Clayman v. Prince George's County

Court of Appeals of Maryland, 1972
266 Md. 409, 292 A.2d 689

■ BARNES, J.

In this appeal, [neighbors] seek the reversal of an order, dated November 11, 1971, of the Circuit Court for Prince George's County, affirming the action of the Board of County Commissioners for Prince George's County, sitting as a District Council (District Council), in granting the application of R. Warren Amman for the rezoning of 6.3545 acres of land in Prince George's County from the R–R zone (Rural Residential) to the C–2 zone (General Commercial).

The land involved in the requested rezoning consists of 7.0645 acres of land in Prince George's County located on the east side of Piscataway Road, north of Windbrook Drive. It fronts 771.47 feet on Piscataway Road and 574.30 feet on Windbrook Drive. The Technical Staff of the Prince George's County Planning Board after deducting .71

acre of land for a right-of-way, leaving 6.3545 acres for the proposed C–2 use, recommended that the application for rezoning to the C–2 zone be denied because such rezoning would be contrary to the General Plan adopted in January 1964; there could likely be some delay in the completion of the necessary water and sewer facilities; there had been no mistake in the original zoning or a change in the character of the neighborhood since the original zoning; and any further use of land for commercial facilities should be where provided in the General Plan, which locations were far more advantageous than the subject property located, as it was, at the intersection of only an arterial and a major road.

The Planning Board, however, did not accept the recommendation of the Technical Staff, but on May 21, 1969, recommended approval of the requested rezoning upon three conditions, i.e. (1) the establishment of a 50-foot buffer along the north property line; (2) that landscaping should be provided along the frontage of Piscataway Road and Windbrook Drive to protect the residential development across these roads; and, (3) that the landscape plan be reviewed by the Planning Board. The reasons for its recommendation of approval of the granting of the application, subject to the conditions mentioned, were (1) it is on the corner of two major roads; (2) it is centrally located to serve as a neighborhood shopping center for the developed area around it; and, (3) the applicant has demonstrated a need. Commissioner Malzone dissented substantially upon the reasons for disapproval set forth in the Technical Staff report.

After hearings on September 9 and October 9, 1970, at which the applicants offered expert and other testimony and exhibits and the protestants offered evidence in opposition and submitted various written protests, the District Council on October 28, 1970, approved the application with three conditions, i.e. (1) a 20-foot buffer strip shall be established along the north property line; (2) landscaping shall be provided along the frontage of Windbrook Drive to protect the residential development across these roads; and, (3) the landscape plan should be reviewed by the Planning Board, subject, however, to the applicants' acceptance of these conditions.

The applicants filed their acceptance of the rezoning conditions on December 23, 1970; and the District Council took final action to approve the conditional rezoning on the 2nd day of February, 1971, setting forth findings of fact and conclusions. In these, the District Council determined that the "neighborhood" of the subject property was "the market area of the proposed shopping center." The District Council also found that within this neighborhood there had been changes indicative of increased density and urbanization. Sewerage became available to the emerging residential subdivisions; Piscataway Road is to be widened; population has increased substantially; traffic has increased on Piscataway Road; and Windbrook Drive is to be extended to Floral Park Road and Thrift Road; and, the applicants had established "a definite need for a shopping center in the area." The District Council concluded that "due to the substantial changes and change in character of this neighborhood that commercial use is now justified."

A notice of appeal was duly noted and, on January 18, 1971, the protestants, Clayman and Mackall, filed their petition for review in the Circuit Court for Prince George's County, setting up many grounds of alleged error.

The matter came on for hearing before Judge Ralph W. Powers on October 1, 1971, and after argument was taken under advisement.

Judge Powers, on November 11, 1971, filed his opinion and an order affirming the action of the District Council.

On the merits of this appeal, the appellants have raised a number of questions, several of which might well require a reversal of the order of November 11, 1971. We only find it necessary, however, to decide one of these questions, i.e., whether there was sufficient evidence before the District Council to make fairly debatable its findings of changes in the "neighborhood" of the subject property since the comprehensive zoning which have resulted in a change in the character of the neighborhood. In our opinion, there was not sufficient evidence, under our prior decision, to make these issues fairly debatable.

In Chevy Chase Village v. Montgomery County Council, 258 Md. 27, 41–2, 264 A. 2d 861, 868 (1970), we stated:

> On innumerable occasions, this Court has held that *"there is a strong presumption of the correctness of original zoning and of comprehensive rezoning, and that to sustain a piecemeal change therefrom, there must be strong evidence of mistake in the original zoning or in the comprehensive rezoning or else a substantial change in conditions."*

(Emphasis in original.)

In Montgomery v. Board of County Commissioners for Prince George's County, 256 Md. 597, 602, 261 A. 2d 447, 450 (1970), it was stated by the Court:

> Inasmuch as there is no contention in the present case that there was a mistake in the original zoning, it was necessary that the applicants establish before the District Council (a) what area reasonably constituted the "neighborhood" of the subject property, (b) the changes which have occurred in that neighborhood since the comprehensive rezoning and (c) that these changes resulted in a change in the character of the neighborhood. These are the "basic facts" and "conclusions" which the District Council must find and express in writing

when it grants or denies a map amendment or special exception.

See also, Harley v. Aluisi, 259 Md. 275, 282, 269 A. 2d 575, 579 (1970), citing *Montgomery* with approval and pointing out that the applicant for rezoning has the burden of proof in establishing these factors.

Although what constitutes the neighborhood of a subject property for the purposes of applying the Maryland "change-mistake" rule "should not be precisely and rigidly defined, but may vary from case to case," Woodlawn Ass'n v. Board of County Commissioners for Prince George's County, 241 Md. 187, 198–199, 216 A. 2d 149, 156–157 (1966), nevertheless, the neighborhood in any area must be an area which *reasonably* constitutes the immediate environs of the subject property. *Montgomery, supra.* In our opinion, the "neighborhood" of an area coinciding with the market area of the proposed Windbrook Shopping Center (which appears as Map 2)—said to contain some 51.6 square miles—is most certainly not an area reasonably constituting the neighborhood of the subject property. The rule requires that the "neighborhood" must be the *immediate* neighborhood of the subject property, not some area miles away; and the changes must occur in that immediate neighborhood of such a nature as to have *affected its character. See* Bauserman v. Barnett, 257 Md. 258, 261, 262 A. 2d 521, 523 (1970) and Randolph Hills v. Whitley, 249 Md. 78, 83, 238 A. 2d 257, 260 (1968), and cases therein cited. In our opinion, the applicant did not establish, and the District Council did not properly make a finding, of what constituted the area which reasonably constituted the neighborhood of the subject property and for this reason appellees' position must fail.

Also, in our opinion, the applicant did not establish changes which, under our decisions, resulted in a change in the character of the "neighborhood" even assuming, arguendo, that a reasonable area constituting the neighborhood had been established. Nor do the changes found by the District Council in its findings of fact meet the test of our decisions.

The District Council first found that sewerage for the emerging subdivision had become available since the comprehensive zoning was adopted in 1960. We have held, however, that the availability of sewer and water services does not result in a change in the character of the neighborhood in that these services are equally important to residential as to commercial development. Chatham Corp. v. Beltram, 252 Md. 578, 585–86, 251 A. 2d 1, 5 (1969) and Smith v. Board of County Commissioners of Howard County, 252 Md. 280, 285, 249 A. 2d 708, 711 (1969), and cases therein cited.

Secondly, the District Council found that Piscataway Road is planned for widening, and the extending of Windbrook Drive is planned. Here again, we have held that these contemplated road improvements do not change the character of a neighborhood. Chatham Corp. v. Beltram, *supra*, 252 Md. 578, 585, 251 A. 2d 1, 5 (1969); Helfrich v. Mongelli, 248 Md. 498, 504, 237 A. 2d 454, 458 (1968) and cases cited in the opinions in those cases.

Thirdly, the District Council found that "traffic has increased on Piscataway Road." This indefinite finding evidences no change in the character of the neighborhood. *See* Hardesty v. Dunphy, 259 Md. 718, 271 A. 2d 152 (1970) and our prior decisions cited in the opinion in that case.

The fourth finding of the District Council was that there had been subdivision growth with increased density and urbanization. The comprehensive zoning placed the area in an R–R zone and thus it was contemplated that single-family residential development would occur. It did, but this contemplated growth does not indicate a change in the character of the immediate neighborhood. Hardesty v. Dunphy, *supra*, and Cabin John Limited Partnership v. Montgomery County Council, 259 Md. 661, 271 A. 2d 174, 179 (1970), and cases therein cited.

Under our decisions, no changes were established by the applicant and found by the District Council, even when all of the alleged indicia of change are considered together, which resulted in a change in the character of the immediate neighborhood so that there was no fairly debatable issue before the District Council which would justify its action in granting the rezoning.

Order reversed.

NOTES AND QUESTIONS

1. The District Council in the *Clayman* case made a number of findings documenting changes in the neighborhood since enactment of the original ordinance. Were those findings based on the work of the county's professional planners? If not, whose efforts generated those findings?

2. The court discounted the changes cited by the District Council because many of those changes did not occur in the immediate neighborhood of the proposed shopping center. Why? If the demand for shopping in the county has increased since enactment of the original ordinance, why shouldn't the council be entitled to rezone to account for that increased demand? If there were, in fact, a county-wide increase in demand for shopping, would the *Clayman* court permit the District Council to rezone *any* land to account for increased demand?

3. The court indicated that "contemplated road improvements do not change the character of a neighborhood." Would the result have been different if the road improvements had already been completed rather than contemplated? Why? *See, e.g.*, Nw. Builders, Inc. v. Moore, 475 So.2d 153 (Miss. 1985).

4. Would the District Council have fared better if it had argued that the original zoning ordinance had been based on a mistake? Maryland courts have upheld a rezoning based on a mistake in the original ordinance when the members of the board that enacted the original ordinance testified that they intended to place the disputed parcel in a C–2 zone (which permitted motels), but actually placed the parcel in a C–1 zone (which did not). *See* Tennison v. Shomette, 38 Md.App. 1, 379 A.2d 187 (1977). Can neighbors advance a "mistake" claim in the absence of the sort of "scrivener's error" in *Tennison*? A Maryland appellate court made the following statement:

> The finding of a mistake or error is not so much concerned with the logical validity or merit of ultimate conclusion-drawing as it is with the adequacy and accuracy of the factual premises that underlie the conclusion-drawing. A conclusion based on a factual predicate that is incomplete or inaccurate may be deemed, in zoning law, a mistake or error; an allegedly aberrant conclusion based on full and accurate information, by contrast, is simply a case of bad judgment, which is immunized from second-guessing.

People's Counsel v. Beachwood I Ltd. P'ship, 107 Md.App. 627, 670 A.2d 484 (1995). In light of that standard, what evidence would have been helpful to the lawyers for the developer in *Clayman* if they had sought to advance a mistake claim?

5. The Maryland Court of Appeals has made it clear that the change/mistake rule applies only to piecemeal rezoning, not to comprehensive rezoning. The court has indicated that comprehensive rezoning should be treated as a "legislative" action, while piecemeal rezoning should be treated as a "quasi-judicial process leading to a technical legislative act." Anne Arundel County v. Bell, 442 Md. 539, 113 A.3d 639, 647 (Md. 2015). With piecemeal rezoning, the local legislature's role is to make a factual determination about whether there has been a change or mistake since the last comprehensive rezoning. *Id.* at 649.

Will it always be clear whether a rezoning is piecemeal or comprehensive? If you represented a developer of a municipality seeking to avoid close judicial scrutiny of piecemeal rezoning, might you seek instead a comprehensive rezoning that makes changes only with respect to a small number of parcels?

6. Although the change/mistake rule is generally associated with the Maryland courts, it has also been embraced in some form by the courts of several other states. *See, e.g.,* Albuquerque Commons P'ship v. City Council, 144 N.M. 99, 184 P.3d 411 (2008); Board of Aldermen v. Conerly, 509 So.2d 877, 883 (Miss. 1987); Board of Supervisors v. Snell Constr. Corp., 214 Va. 655, 202 S.E.2d 889, 893, n. 1 (1974). Other states have rejected the rule outright. *See, e.g.,* Neuzil v. City of Iowa City, 451 N.W.2d 159, 165–66 (Iowa 1990).

7. *Evaluating the Change/Mistake Rule.* Why should courts attach a greater presumption of validity to the provisions of the municipality's original zoning ordinance than to subsequent amendments to that ordinance? One answer lies in an idealized vision of the planning process. Professor Carol Rose has described that vision without endorsing it:

> [The] plan . . . would be created by the local planning commission, whose impartiality and technical expertise would ensure the duration and rationality of the overall plan. The plan, in turn, would ensure the rationality and stability of the ordinances that implemented it. It was widely assumed that localities could indeed set their goals far in advance, that changes in land regulation would therefore seldom be necessary, and that citizens would not face fluctuations in the status of their own or their neighbors' land.

Carol M. Rose, Planning and Dealing: Piecemeal Land Controls as a Problem of Local Legitimacy, 71 Calif. L. Rev. 839, 848–49 (1983). This "rational planning" model assumed that subsequent piecemeal zoning changes would be the product of politics, not planning. This assumption, in turn, justifies what the Maryland courts (as noted in *Clayman*) have called "a strong presumption of correctness of original zoning and of comprehensive rezoning."

What reasons are there to believe that politics will play only a limited role in enactment of a comprehensive zoning scheme? And why should the role of politics be limited in any zoning enactments? If the original ordinance was enacted when voters were opposed to commercial development, but high taxes have led to voter support for limited commercial development, why shouldn't a newly enacted local legislature be entitled to act on voter preferences? Would the court in *Clayman* treat a change in voter preferences as an adequate reason for the municipality to rezone land?

8. In a jurisdiction that has embraced the change/mistake rule, what are the most attractive courses of action for a landowner seeking to put her land to more intensive use?

3.   ARE ZONING AMENDMENTS LEGISLATIVE OR "QUASI-JUDICIAL"?

Fasano v. Board of County Commissioners

Oregon Supreme Court, 1973
264 Or. 574, 507 P.2d 23

■ HOWELL, J.

The plaintiffs, homeowners in Washington county, unsuccessfully opposed a zone change before the Board of County Commissioners of Washington County. Plaintiffs applied for and received a writ of review of the action of the commissioners allowing the change. The trial court found in favor of plaintiffs, disallowed the zone change, and reversed the commissioners' order. The Court of Appeals affirmed, 7 Or. App. 176, 489 P.2d 693 (1971), and this court granted review.

The defendants are the Board of County Commissioners and A.G.S. Development Company. A.G.S., the owner of 32 acres which had been zoned R–7 (Single Family Residential), applied for a zone change to P–R (Planned Residential), which allows for the construction of a mobile home park. The change failed to receive a majority vote of the Planning Commission. The Board of County Commissioners approved the change and found, among other matters, that the change allows for "increased densities and different types of housing to meet the needs of urbanization over that allowed by the existing zoning."

The trial court . . . reversed the order of the commissioners because the commissioners had not shown any change in the character of the neighborhood which would justify the rezoning. The Court of Appeals affirmed for the same reason, but added the additional ground that the defendants failed to show that the change was consistent with the comprehensive plan for Washington county.

According to the briefs, the comprehensive plan of development for Washington county was adopted in 1959 and included classifications in the county for residential, neighborhood commercial, retail commercial, general commercial, industrial park and light industry, general and heavy industry, and agricultural areas.

The land in question, which was designated "residential" by the comprehensive plan, was zoned R–7, Single Family Residential.

Subsequent to the time the comprehensive plan was adopted, Washington county established a Planned Residential (P–R) zoning classification in 1963. The P–R classification was adopted by ordinance and provided that a planned residential unit development could be established and should include open space for utilities, access, and recreation; should not be less than 10 acres in size; and should be located in or adjacent to a residential zone. The P–R zone adopted by the 1963 ordinance is of the type known as a "floating zone," so-called because the ordinance creates a zone classification authorized for future use but not placed on the zoning map until its use at a particular location is approved by the governing body. The R–7 classification for the 32 acres continued until April 1970 when the classification was changed to P–R to permit the defendant A.G.S. to construct the mobile home park on the 32 acres involved.

The defendants argue that (1) the action of the county commissioners approving the change is presumptively valid, requiring plaintiffs to show that the commissioners acted arbitrarily in approving the zone change; (2) it was not necessary to show a change of conditions in the area before a zone change could be accomplished; and (3) the change from R–7 to P–R was in accordance with the Washington county comprehensive plan.

We granted review in this case to consider the questions—by what standards does a county commission exercise its authority in zoning matters; who has the burden of meeting those standards when a request for change of zone is made; and what is the scope of court review of such actions?

Any meaningful decision as to the proper scope of judicial review of a zoning decision must start with a characterization of the nature of that decision. The majority of jurisdictions state that a zoning ordinance is a legislative act and is thereby entitled to presumptive validity. This court made such a characterization of zoning decisions in Smith v. County of Washington, 241 Or 380, 406 P2d 545 (1965):

> Inasmuch as ORS 215.110 specifically grants to the governing board of the county the power to amend zoning ordinances, a challenged amendment is a legislative act and is clothed with a presumption in its favor. Jehovah's Witnesses v. Mullen et al., 214 Or. 281, 292, 330 P.2d 5, 74 ALR2d 347 (1958), *appeal dismissed and cert. denied*, 359 U.S. 436, 79 S. Ct. 940, 3 L. Ed. 2d 932 (1959).

241 Or. at 383.

However, in *Smith* an exception to the presumption was found and the zoning held invalid. Furthermore, the case cited by the *Smith* court, Jehovah's Witnesses v. Mullen et al., *supra*, at least at one point viewed the contested zoning in that case as an administrative as opposed to legislative act.

At this juncture we feel we would be ignoring reality to rigidly view all zoning decisions by local governing bodies as legislative acts to be accorded a full presumption of validity and shielded from less than constitutional scrutiny by the theory of separation of powers. Local and small decision groups are simply not the equivalent in all respects of state and national legislatures. There is a growing judicial recognition of this fact of life:

> It is not a part of the legislative function to grant permits, make special exceptions, or decide particular cases. Such activities are not legislative but administrative, quasi-judicial, or judicial in character. To place them in the hands of legislative bodies, whose acts as such are not judicially reviewable, is to open the door completely to arbitrary government."

Ward v. Village of Skokie, 26 Ill. 2d 415, 186 N.E.2d 529, 533 (1962) (Klingbiel, J., specially concurring).

Ordinances laying down general policies without regard to a specific piece of property are usually an exercise of legislative authority, are subject to limited review, and may only be attacked upon constitutional grounds for an arbitrary abuse of authority. On the other hand, a determination whether the permissible use of a specific piece of property should be changed is usually an exercise of judicial authority and its propriety is subject to an altogether different test. An illustration of an exercise of legislative authority is the passage of the ordinance by the Washington County Commission in 1963 which provided for the formation of a planned residential classification to be located in or adjacent to any residential zone. An exercise of judicial authority is the county commissioners' determination in this particular matter to change the classification of A.G.S. Development Company's specific piece of property. The distinction is stated, as follows, in Comment, Zoning Amendments—The Product of Judicial or Quasi-Judicial Action, 33 Ohio St. L.J. 130 (1972):

> Basically, this test involves the determination of whether action produces a general rule or policy which is applicable to an open class of individuals, interest, or situations, or whether it entails the application of a general rule or policy to specific individuals, interests, or situations. If the former determination is satisfied, there is legislative action; if the latter determination is satisfied, the action is judicial."

33 Ohio St. L.J. at 137.

We reject the proposition that judicial review of the county commissioners' determination to change the zoning of the particular property in question is limited to a determination whether the change was arbitrary and capricious.

In Oregon the county planning commission is required by ORS 215.050 to adopt a comprehensive plan for the use of some or all of the land in the county. Under ORS 215.110(1), after the comprehensive plan has been adopted, the planning commission recommends to the governing body of the county the ordinances necessary to "carry out" the comprehensive plan. The purpose of the zoning ordinances, both under our statute and the general law of land use regulation, is to "carry out" or implement the comprehensive plan. 1 Anderson, American Law of Zoning, § 1.12 (1968). Although we are aware of the analytical distinction between zoning and planning, it is clear that under our statutes the plan adopted by the planning commission and the zoning ordinances enacted by the county governing body are closely related; both are intended to be parts of a single integrated procedure for land use control. The plan embodies policy determinations and guiding principles; the zoning ordinances provide the detailed means of giving effect to those principles.

ORS 215.050 states county planning commissions "shall adopt and may from time to time revise a comprehensive plan." In a hearing of the Senate Committee on Local Government, the proponents of ORS 215.050 described its purpose as follows:

> The intent here is to require a basic document, geared into population, land use, and economic forecasts, which should be

the basis of any zoning or other regulations to be adopted by the county.

In addition, ORS 215.055 provides:

215.055 Standards for plan. (1) The plan and all legislation and regulations authorized by ORS 215.010 to 215.233 shall be designed to promote the public health, safety and general welfare and shall be based on the following considerations, among others: The various characteristics of the various areas in the county, the suitability of the areas for particular land uses and improvements, the land uses and improvements in the areas, trends in land improvement, density of development, property values, the needs of economic enterprises in the future development of the areas, needed access to particular sites in the areas, natural resources of the county and prospective needs for development thereof, and the public need for healthful, safe, aesthetic surroundings and conditions.

We believe that the state legislature has conditioned the county's power to zone upon the prerequisite that the zoning attempt to further the general welfare of the community through consciousness, in a prospective sense, of the factors mentioned above. In other words, except as noted later in this opinion, it must be proved that the change is in conformance with the comprehensive plan.

In proving that the change is in conformance with the comprehensive plan in this case, the proof, at a minimum, should show (1) there is a public need for a change of the kind in question, and (2) that need will be best served by changing the classification of the particular piece of property in question as compared with other available property.

In the instant case the trial court and the Court of Appeals interpreted prior decisions of this court as requiring the county commissions to show a change of conditions within the immediate neighborhood in which the change was sought since the enactment of the comprehensive plan, or a mistake in the comprehensive plan as a condition precedent to the zone change.

In Smith v. Washington County, *supra*, the land in question was designated residential under the comprehensive plan, and the county commissioners enacted an amendatory ordinance changing the classification to manufacturing. This court held that the change constituted spot zoning and was invalid. We stated:

Once a [zoning scheme] is adopted, changes in it should be made only when such changes are consistent with the over-all objectives of the plan *and in keeping with changes in the character of the area or neighborhood to be covered thereby.*

241 Or. at 384 (emphasis added).

Because the action of the commission in this instance is an exercise of judicial authority, the burden of proof should be placed, as is usual in judicial proceedings, upon the one seeking change. The more drastic the change, the greater will be the burden of showing that it is in conformance with the comprehensive plan as implemented by the ordinance, that there is a public need for the kind of change in question, and that the need is best met by the proposal under consideration. As the degree of change increases, the burden of showing that the potential impact upon the area in question was carefully considered and weighed will also increase. If other areas have previously been designated for the particular type of development, it must be shown why it is necessary to introduce it into an area not previously contemplated and why the property owners there should bear the burden of the departure.

Although we have said ... that zoning changes may be justified without a showing of a mistake in the original plan or ordinance, or of changes in the physical characteristics of an affected area, any of these factors which are present in a particular case would, of course, be relevant. Their importance would depend upon the nature of the precise change under consideration.

By treating the exercise of authority by the commission in this case as the exercise of judicial rather than of legislative authority and thus enlarging the scope of review on appeal, and by placing the burden of the above level of proof upon the one seeking change, we may lay the court open to criticism by legal scholars who think it desirable that planning authorities be vested with the ability to adjust more freely to changed conditions. However, having weighed the dangers of making desirable change more difficult against the dangers of the almost irresistible pressures that can be asserted by private economic interests on local government, we believe that the latter dangers are more to be feared.

What we have said above is necessarily general, as the approach we adopt contains no absolute standards or mechanical tests. We believe, however, that it is adequate to provide meaningful guidance for local governments making zoning decisions and for trial courts called upon to review them. With future cases in mind, it is appropriate to add some brief remarks on questions of procedure. Parties at the hearing before the county governing body are entitled to an opportunity to be heard, to an opportunity to present and rebut evidence, to a tribunal which is impartial in the matter—i.e., having had no pre-hearing or ex parte contacts concerning the question at issue—and to a record made and adequate findings executed. Comment, Zoning Amendments—The Product of Judicial or Quasi-Judicial Action, 33 Ohio St. L.J. 130–143 (1972).

When we apply the standards we have adopted to the present case, we find that the burden was not sustained before the commission. The record now before us is insufficient to ascertain whether there was a justifiable basis for the decision. The only evidence in the record, that of the staff report of the Washington County Planning Department, is too conclusory and superficial to support the zoning change. It merely states:

> The staff finds that the requested use does conform to the residential designation of the Plan of Development. It further finds that the proposed use reflects the urbanization of the County and the necessity to provide increased densities and different types of housing to meet the needs of urbanization over that allowed by the existing zoning.

Such generalizations and conclusions, without any statement of the facts on which they are based, are insufficient to justify a change of use. Moreover, no portions of the comprehensive plan of Washington County are before us, and we feel it would be improper for us to take judicial notice of the plan without at least some reference to its specifics by counsel.

As there has not been an adequate showing that the change was in accord with the plan, or that the factors listed in ORS 215.055 were given proper consideration, the judgment is affirmed.

■ BRYSON, J., specially concurring.

The basic facts in this case exemplify the prohibitive cost and extended uncertainty to a homeowner when a governmental body decides to change or modify a zoning ordinance or comprehensive plan affecting such owner's real property.

This controversy has proceeded through the following steps:

1.   The respondent opposed the zone change before the Washington County Planning Department and Planning Commission.

2.   The County Commission, after a hearing, allowed the change.

3.   The trial court reversed (disallowed the change).

4.   The Court of Appeals affirmed the trial court.

5.   We ordered reargument and additional briefs.

6.   This court affirmed.

The principal respondent in this case, Fasano, happens to be an attorney at law, and his residence is near the proposed mobile home park of the petitioner A.G.S. No average homeowner or small business enterprise can afford a judicial process such as described above nor can a judicial system cope with or endure such a process in achieving justice. The number of such controversies is ascending.

In this case the majority opinion, in which I concur, adopts some sound rules to enable county and municipal planning commissions and governing bodies, as well as trial courts, to reach finality in decision. However, the procedure is no panacea and it is still burdensome.

It is solely within the domain of the legislative branch of government to devise a new and simplified statutory procedure to expedite finality of decision.

NOTES AND QUESTIONS

1. On what basis did the trial court invalidate the amendment in *Fasano*? The Oregon Court of Appeals?

2. Suppose the Oregon courts had treated the zoning amendment as "legislative," had definitively rejected the change/mistake rule, and had held that the comprehensive plan requirement did not impose enforceable duties on the Board of County Commissioners. Would the amendment have been beyond judicial scrutiny? Did the Board argue that its action was beyond judicial scrutiny? If not, what did the Board argue?

If Fasano had argued that the Board's action was "arbitrary and capricious," how would the Board have responded? Who would have borne the burden of proof on that issue? Who would have prevailed?

3. In light of the court's opinion in *Fasano,* what must a lawyer for a landowner do when the landowner seeks a zoning amendment? Suppose the landowner in *Fasano* had produced letters and oral testimony from five large Washington County employers complaining about difficulty in attracting employees for low-wage jobs because no low-cost housing was available in the county. Suppose further that the neighbors responded by expressing concerns about the effect of mobile homes on their property values. If the Board of County Commissioners then enacted the zoning amendment, would the Oregon Supreme Court have upheld the amendment?

Suppose now that the neighbors also introduced testimony from economists that unemployment in Washington County was high compared to surrounding counties, and that advertised jobs were filled within an average of 10 days? If the Board still enacted the amendment, would the Oregon Supreme Court have upheld the amendment?

Does the court in *Fasano* leave room for any deference to the Board of County Commissioners? If not, has the Oregon Supreme Court transformed zoning into a judicial function?

Consider the following standard articulated by the Florida Supreme Court, which has labeled actions on piecemeal zoning amendments quasi-judicial:

> [W]e hold that a landowner seeking to rezone property has the burden of proving that the proposal is consistent with the comprehensive plan and complies with all procedural requirements of the zoning ordinance. At this point, the burden shifts to the governmental board to demonstrate that maintaining the existing zoning classification with respect to the property accomplishes a legitimate public purpose. In effect, . . . the board will now have the burden of showing that the refusal to rezone the property is not arbitrary, discriminatory, or unreasonable. If the board carries its burden, the application should be denied.

Bd. of County Comm'rs v. Snyder, 627 So.2d 469 (Fla. 1993). How much discretion does the local "legislature" have in considering zoning amendments in Florida?

4. Suppose the Board of County Commissioners had not altered the zoning map, but had instead enacted a text amendment permitting mobile homes within R–7 districts. If the facts of the case were otherwise the same, how, if at all, would the Oregon Supreme Court's analysis have been different?

5. If a state were to treat zoning amendments as quasi-judicial acts, must elected officials who have campaigned in favor of rezoning (or against rezoning) recuse themselves from participating because they have prejudged the merits of the application? The Oregon courts have faced that issue on multiple occasions. In Columbia Riverkeeper v. Clatsop County, 267 Or. App. 578, 602, 341 P.3d 790, 804 (2014) an Oregon court summarized the results:

> The bar for disqualification is high; no published case has concluded that disqualification was required in quasi-judicial land-use proceedings. An elected local official's "intense involvement in the affairs of the community" or "political predisposition" is not grounds for disqualification. Involvement with other governmental organizations that may have an interest in the decision does not require disqualification. An elected local official is not expected to have no appearance of having views on matters of community interest when a decision on the matter is to be made by an adjudicatory procedure.

6. Are neighbors who are contemplating a challenge to a zoning amendment better off in Maryland or in Oregon? Why?

7. The issue in the *Fasano* case involved the standard of judicial review applicable to zoning amendments. Characterizing a zoning amendment as a "judicial" or "quasi-judicial" action may have implications beyond the standard of review. According to the *Fasano* court, what procedural rights do neighbors have when a court characterizes determination of an application for a zoning amendment as a "judicial" action?

8. More than 40 years after the *Fasano* decision, the court's opinion remains controversial. A number of other states have characterized piecemeal zoning amendments as quasi-judicial actions. *See, e.g.,* Bd. of

County Comm'rs v. Snyder, 627 So.2d 469, 476 (Fla. 1993); Cooper v. Board of County Comm'rs, 101 Idaho 407, 614 P.2d 947, 950–51 (1980). Other states once characterized rezoning actions as quasi-judicial, but later returned to the more traditional legislative characterization. *See, e.g.,* Schanz v. City of Billings, 182 Mont. 328, 597 P.2d 67, 71 (1979), retreating from the Montana Supreme Court's earlier opinion in Lowe v. City of Missoula, 165 Mont. 38, 525 P.2d 551 (1974), and holding that "[a] rezoning ordinance, like a zoning ordinance, is a legislative enactment, and is entitled to the presumptions of validity and reasonableness."

Many other states have consistently adhered to the traditional approach, and treat all zoning amendments as legislative actions entitled to a presumption of validity. *See, e.g.,* State v. City of Rochester, 268 N.W.2d 885 (Minn. 1978); Asian Americans for Equality v. Koch, 72 N.Y.2d 121, 531 N.Y.S.2d 782, 527 N.E.2d 265 (1988).

9. *Evaluating the Quasi-Judicial Characterization.* In the *Fasano* case, the court, relying on a student comment in a law review, indicated that when a zoning amendment "entails the application of a general rule or policy to specific individuals, interests or situations," the action on the amendment should be treated as judicial, and should require closer judicial scrutiny. But many individuals and firms lobby Congress and state legislatures for tax benefits and other subsidies that apply only to a narrow range of "individuals, interests or situations." Courts nevertheless treat state and federal enactments—however narrow their application—as legislative rather than judicial actions. Why should zoning amendments be different?

One answer lies in Madisonian political theory: when a constituency is large enough, domination by one faction is unlikely because action is possible only through a coalition of interest groups. No interest group can risk alienating others, because it may need their support on future issues. The result is a legislative process that necessarily considers the interest of each group. The same protections may not exist at the local level. In Professor Rose's words:

> A legislative body drawn from too small or too homogeneous a constituency may be dominated by a single interest or faction. Factional domination may take varying forms. One is sheer corruption, made possible in smaller representative bodies because a limited number of persons have influence which must be bought. Another possibility is domination by a few who are perceived by others as the powerful. The decisions of these few can affect many within the community; others must curry their favor, and even larger interests find difficulty in organizing against their "cabals." Finally, and perhaps most feared by Madison, is the factional domination created by a popular "passion"—sometimes a sudden whim, sometimes a longstanding prejudice—that carries a majority before it. Under any of these various forms of factional domination, all of which are far more likely to occur in a smaller legislature than in a larger one, a

dominant group may subject others to sudden destruction or to permanent political disability.

Carol M. Rose, Planning and Dealing: Piecemeal Land Controls as a Problem of Local Legitimacy, 71 Cal. L. Rev. 839, 855 (1983).

Professor Rose, however, is unconvinced that expanding judicial review of local land use decisions will solve the problem. She argues that piecemeal zoning changes are no more quasi-judicial than they are legislative (*id.* at 882), and suggests that one might treat local government decisions on zoning issues as a form of mediation. In her view, the goal should be to ensure that citizen participation, combined with the possibility of exit from the municipality, operate to constrain municipal zoning decisions:

> [T]he proper mode of ensuring reasonableness, in the sense of fairness and due consideration, is the refinement of the local potential for exit and voice, rather than the attempt to make a local body act like a court when it cannot act like a large legislature.

Id. at 910.

PROBLEM

An exurban municipality had zoned landowner's ten-acre parcel for single-family homes on two-acre lots. Landowner wants to develop a 50-unit luxury condominium complex on the parcel, and plans to seek a map amendment into a district that permits multi-family construction with a density that will enable him to build his complex.

Landowner expects the neighbors—most of whom own single-family homes on large lots—to oppose the amendment and to challenge it in court if the town board approves the amendment.

> 1. If you represent the landowner, what would you emphasize in your presentation to the town board if the parcel were located in Massachusetts? In Maryland? In Oregon? Why, if at all, would your presentation differ depending on the state in which the parcel is located?

> 2. If you represent the neighbors, and you challenge the amendment after it is enacted, how will your strategy differ depending on the state in which the parcel is located?

III. NEIGHBOR CHALLENGES TO ADMINISTRATIVE DETERMINATIONS

When neighbors challenge a zoning amendment, separation of powers concerns are paramount. In each of the principal cases in the preceding section, the zoning amendment was enacted by an elected body that typically exercises legislative powers. A neighbor seeking to overturn the amendment must argue that the amendment did not meet statutory or constitutional requirements, or must persuade the reviewing court that the zoning amendment should not be treated like ordinary legislation.

Separation of powers concerns fade to the background when neighbors challenge variances, special permits, or other forms of administrative relief granted to a landowner. Rarely does the local legislative body consider applications for variances or special permits. Instead, an appointed body—generally a zoning board of appeals or a planning board—hears those applications. The board does not make an unconstrained "legislative" determination; instead, the state enabling act, the local zoning ordinance (or both) impose requirements with which the board must comply when it decides variance or special permit applications. How much deference courts should accord to "administrative" determinations like these is a central question in administrative law. The following case illustrates how courts approach that question in the land use context:

Bontrager Auto Service, Inc. v. Iowa City Board of Adjustment

Supreme Court of Iowa, 2008
748 N.W.2d 483

■ TERNUS, C.J.

The appellant, Iowa City Board of Adjustment, approved the application of appellant, Shelter House Community Shelter and Transition Services, for a special exception to a local zoning regulation to allow Shelter House to construct transient housing in a commercial district. The appellees, opponents of Shelter House's application, successfully challenged the board's decision in district court. Although the district court rejected the objectors' contention the board had failed to make the necessary factual findings, the court ruled there was not substantial evidence to support the board's finding that the proposed transient housing would not substantially diminish or impair property values in the neighborhood.

The board and Shelter House appeal the district court's reversal of the board's approval of Shelter House's application. We agree with the district court that the board made sufficient factual findings. Because we think there was substantial evidence to support the board's finding that property values would not be adversely affected, we reverse the judgment of the district court and remand this case for entry of a judgment affirming the board's decision.

I.   Background Facts and Proceedings.

Shelter House is a nonprofit corporation that has operated transient housing on North Gilbert Street in Iowa City for approximately twenty years. The facility on Gilbert Street is approved for housing twenty-nine transient persons at one time. It was undisputed the shelter has to turn homeless persons away due to a lack of space.

In 2004 Shelter House sought to build a new two-story facility at 429 Southgate Avenue that would provide transitional housing for up to seventy people. This site is zoned intensive commercial, which permits transient housing by special exception. In order to approve a special exception, the board must find the applicant meets the standards set forth for the specific proposed exception, as well as seven general standards to the extent they are applicable.

The Iowa City Department of Planning and Community Development reviewed Shelter House's application and recommended approval. Subsequently, the board held a well-attended meeting at which approximately thirty-seven persons spoke. The main concern of objectors was the possibility of increased criminal activity in the neighborhood, a concern the proponents of the special exception attempted to refute. There was also some evidence elicited relating to property values, with the witnesses for and against the application disagreeing on whether property values would decrease due to the construction of transient housing in the affected neighborhood. Following public comments, the board approved the special exception on a vote of three to one. A written decision granting the application was filed several days later.

Thereafter, neighboring landowners filed petitions for writ of certiorari in the district court, which were consolidated. They claimed the board acted illegally for several reasons, three of which are pertinent to this appeal:

a. The Board of Adjustment acted arbitrarily and capriciously when it granted the application even though the evidence before the Board was that the requested special use would substantially diminish or impair the property values in the neighborhood of the requested special exception and that the proposed special exception would be injurious to the use and enjoyment of other property in the area. Under these circumstances the actions of the Board are a violation of Iowa City Ordinance 14–6W–2(B)(2)(b).

. . . .

f. The property which is the subject of the special exception does not comply with various provisions of Iowa City zoning law . . . :

a) There is insufficient parking under Ordinance 14–6N–1. . . .

g. The Board has made inadequate findings of fact and conclusions of law, contrary to Ordinance 14–6W–3(D).

The last allegation of illegality—that the board's findings of fact were inadequate—was based on the board's alleged failure to specifically find in its written decision that the proposed exception would not substantially diminish or impair property values in the neighborhood.

In response to the petitions, the board submitted its records to the court, including the application for special exception, the staff report recommending approval of the special exception, written materials and comments received by the board, a transcript of the public hearing, the board's minutes, and the board's written decision. In addition, at the trial on the objectors' petitions, the district court heard further testimony from Robert Miklo, city planner for the City of Iowa City. Miklo testified with respect to the staff report and the board's findings of fact. No other evidence outside the board's records was offered or received.

The court subsequently issued a ruling reversing the board's decision. Although the court decided the board had sufficiently complied with the requirement for written findings of fact, it concluded Shelter House had failed to present substantial evidence the proposed special exception would not substantially diminish or impair property values in the neighborhood. The court also held the board had not correctly interpreted the parking-space requirements of its ordinance. The board had approved the special exception on the basis that eighteen parking spaces would be sufficient; whereas, under the district court's interpretation, the ordinance would require twenty-two parking spaces.

II.   Issues on Appeal.

On appeal, the board contends there was substantial evidence to support its determination that property values would not be substantially diminished or impaired by the location of transient housing at the proposed site. With respect to the court's ruling on the required parking spaces, the board asserts that it correctly interpreted the parking-space requirements of its ordinance.

The objectors disagree, of course, with the arguments asserted by the board on appeal. In addition, they claim that, even if the district court's decision on these issues was incorrect, its ruling can nonetheless be upheld on the basis that the board did not make an adequate factual finding on the property-values issue.

In our review of the record, we have discovered a preliminary issue that must be addressed: whether any error with respect to the board's determination of the required number of parking spaces was preserved by the objectors. *See* Top of Iowa Coop. v. Sime Farms, Inc., 608 N.W.2d 454, 470 (Iowa 2000) (stating "this court will consider on appeal whether error was preserved despite the opposing party's omission in not raising this issue at trial or on appeal"). We will address that issue first.

III. Error Preservation on Parking-Spaces Objection.

The objectors argued in the district court and again on appeal that the board failed to properly interpret the parking-spaces requirement of the applicable city ordinance and, consequently, acted illegally in approving a special exception that did not propose an adequate number of parking spaces. In reviewing the record certified by the board to the district court, we are unable to find any discussion of this issue before the board. No one at the meeting challenged the legality of the proposed exception on the basis that it did not comply with the applicable standard for parking spaces.

"In most jurisdictions a reviewing court will not decide an issue which was not raised in the forum from which the appeal was taken. . . . A reviewing court will not entertain a new theory or a different claim not asserted on the board level." 4 Kenneth H. Young, Anderson's American Law of Zoning § 27:37, at 633–34 (4th ed. 1996). Our court has similarly held that "issues must first be presented to the agency in order to be preserved for appellate review." State ex rel. Miller v. DeCoster, 608 N.W.2d 785, 789 (Iowa 2000). Based upon this principle and the record before us, we conclude the issue concerning the alleged inadequacy of the proposed parking spaces, which was not raised at the hearing before the board of adjustment, has not been preserved for this court's review.

IV. Sufficiency of Board's Factual Finding Regarding Impact on Property Values.

The Iowa City Code requires the Iowa City Board of Adjustment to render its decision in writing, "including findings of fact and conclusions of law." Iowa City Code § 14–6W–3(D). It is undisputed the board failed to make a specific finding or conclusion in its written decision regarding the effect of the proposed special exception on property values. This issue was of critical importance because, before the board may approve an application for a special exception, the board must find the applicant has met several general standards. One of those standards states: "The specific proposed exception will not be injurious to the use and enjoyment of other property in the immediate vicinity and will not substantially diminish or impair property values in the neighborhood." Id. § 14–6W–2(B)(2)(b).

Notwithstanding the board's failure to specifically address this standard in its decision, the district court concluded the board had substantially complied with the requirement of written findings of fact and conclusions of law.

We agree with the district court that substantial—as opposed to literal—compliance with the written-findings requirement is sufficient.

[W]e noted in *Citizens* that a board's findings "must be sufficient to enable a reviewing court to determine with reasonable certainty the factual basis and legal principles upon which the board acted." *Id.*; *accord* Bd. of Dirs. v. Justmann, 476 N.W.2d 335, 340 (Iowa 1991). Here, the objectors appear to claim that, because there is no mention of the property-values issue in the board's written decision, the board failed to make a decision on this issue, thereby rendering its action granting the special exception illegal.

Our review of the record convinces us that neither the objectors nor the district court had to guess whether the board considered and resolved the property-values issue. The board was clearly aware of the requirement that the special exception could not be approved if it substantially impaired neighboring property values. Shelter House addressed this standard in its application, and later, at the meeting scheduled to consider the application, city planner Robert Miklo told the board it must consider, among other items, the requirement that "the proposed special exception will not substantially diminish or impair property values in the neighborhood." In addition, several of the numerous persons who spoke at the hearing addressed the issue of property values.

The board filed a written decision on the Shelter House application that contained findings of fact, conclusions of law, and a disposition. In its conclusions of law, the board concluded "that developing the Shelter House at [the proposed] location will not be detrimental overall to the public health, safety, comfort or general welfare," as required by section 14–6W–2(B)(2), but did not make specific reference to the other portion of section 14–6W–2(B)(2) dealing with property values.

Considering the board's written decision in the context of the meeting at which the vote memorialized in the decision occurred, we are able "to determine with reasonable certainty the factual basis and legal principles upon which the board acted." *Citizens*, 277 N.W.2d at 925. We think it is sufficiently clear that the board considered the general standards, including whether the proposed special exception would "substantially diminish or impair property values in the neighborhood," and concluded by a majority vote that these standards were met. The board's failure to reference the entirety of the general standard appearing in section 14–6W–2(B)(2) in its written conclusions of law is not a fatal flaw that warrants reversal.

V.   Scope and Standard of Review of Property-Values Issue.

Our standard of review of the district court's ruling on the property-values issue is dependent upon resolution of a disagreement between the parties with respect to the proper role of the district court in its review of the board's decision. Shelter House maintains that the district court must conduct a substantial-evidence review of the board's findings. *See generally* Grant v. Fritz, 201 N.W.2d 188, 195 (Iowa 1972) ("The 'substantial evidence rule' is utilized in judicial checking of findings of fact. . . ."). Under that standard of review, the *board's* findings are binding if supported by substantial evidence. In contrast, the opponents claim the district court is entitled to find the facts anew and on appeal to this court, the district court's findings are binding if supported by substantial evidence.

Section 414.18 [of the Iowa Code] states:

> If upon the hearing which *shall be tried de novo* it shall appear to the court that testimony is necessary for the proper disposition of the matter, *it may take evidence* or appoint a referee to take such evidence as it may direct and report the same to the court with the referee's findings of fact and conclusions of law, which shall constitute a part of the proceedings upon which the determination of the court shall be made. The court may reverse or affirm, wholly or partly, or may modify the decision brought up for review.

Id. (emphasis added). This court has attempted over the years to interpret what the legislature intended when it provided for a trial de novo and for the taking of additional necessary evidence by the district court.

[The court then reviewed Iowa case law.]

In considering the scope of review in the present appeal, this court is faced with the problem of ascertaining the meaning of section 414.18 in the face of conflicting case law. It is helpful, then, to examine general authorities in this area of the law. In Rathkopf's Law of Zoning, the authors state the review provision in the standard zoning enabling act "gives the court the power to take evidence when there is an issue raised by the pleadings in the proceeding *other than whether the determination is supported by substantial evidence.*" Rathkopf's Law of Zoning § 62:46, at 62–123 (emphasis added).

> In those cases in which the issue is whether the action of a board is based upon substantial evidence, the determination as to the validity of a board's decision should be based upon the record of the proceedings before the board as supplemented by the testimony taken before the court. It should not decide the case merely on the basis of the testimony taken before it if the facts found by the court therein are materially at variance with those found by the board. The court cannot make new findings *on issues presented below.*

Id. at 62–129 (emphasis added).

The author clarifies that, with respect to issues of substantial evidence, "[i]t is only in those extraordinary cases in which it is not clear from the record what a board considered and how it arrived at its findings that additional testimony will ordinarily be taken in order for a court to evaluate [the board's] determination." *Id.* § 62:46, at 62–130 to–

131. According to this treatise, other claims of illegality more properly give rise to the need for additional testimony in district court:

> Where an issue is raised by the petition and answer as to whether the determination was made in violation of lawful procedure, or was arbitrary and an abuse of discretion, the court should take evidence with respect to the matters thus put in issue, and apply the law thereto. Since such matters would not ordinarily appear in the return and record of the respondent in the proceedings, such authority will be utilized when questions of fact are presented which cannot be summarily decided in the review proceeding on the basis of allegations in the petition, although sworn to, or in affidavits, or on the exhibits and other types of informal evidence which a board of appeals is accustomed to consider.

> Where the person appealing from the action of the administrative body sets forth in his petition sufficient facts to persuade the court that there were "in fact or in all likelihood, factors present, not of record which influenced the action of the council complained of," . . . the court should conduct a hearing and consider evidence not of record before the administrative body since the court could not properly have determined the question from the transcript of the proceedings at the public hearing.

Id. at 62–123 to–124, 62–128.

Thus, with respect to the district court's proper role in taking additional evidence, this authority distinguishes between illegalities that appear in the record made before the board, e.g., insufficiency of the evidence to support the board's findings, and illegalities that are outside the record, e.g., a board member's conflict of interest. Only when the illegality does *not* appear in the record made before the board should the district court take additional evidence. In addition, this authority would limit the court's fact-finding role to issues that were *not* before the board.

Our proposed interpretation of the statute also reflects our traditional deference to the fact-finding role of the local tribunal with respect to the issues of fact essential to its decision by preserving the substantial-evidence rule in the review of board decisions. We think it is simply inconsistent to define an illegality as a lack of substantial evidence to support the board's decision, a rule used to review an inferior tribunal's *fact-finding*, but then place the ultimate fact-finding responsibility on the district court. In other words, a substantial-evidence review makes more sense if the fact-finding relevant to the issues before the board remains with the board.

We also think application of the substantial-evidence rule is more consistent with the principle that the court should not substitute its judgment for that of the board. *See, e.g.*, Helmke v. Bd. of Adjustment, 418 N.W.2d 346, 352 (Iowa 1988). The existence of a particular fact is often outcome determinative, as in the present case. To allow the district court to make this crucial finding of fact necessarily allows the court to substitute its judgment for that of the board.

VI. Substantial Evidence to Support Board's Finding That Property Values Would Not be Substantially Diminished or Impaired.

As noted above, the board could not grant a special exception to Shelter House unless it was satisfied "[t]he specific proposed exception . . . will not substantially diminish or impair property values in the neighborhood." Iowa City Code § 14–6W–2(B)(2)(b). We must determine whether there was substantial evidence to support the board's finding that this standard was met. "Evidence is substantial 'when a reasonable mind could accept it as adequate to reach the same findings.' " City of Cedar Rapids v. Mun. Fire & Police Ret. Sys., 526 N.W.2d 284, 287 (Iowa 1995) (quoting Norland v. Iowa Dep't of Job Serv., 412 N.W.2d 904, 913 (Iowa 1987)).

In concluding Shelter House "failed to present substantial evidence that the proposed Special Exception will not substantially diminish or impair property values in the neighborhood," the district court observed:

> there was no testimony or comment at the public hearing from any real estate assessor, real estate appraiser, realtor or owner of property near the current Shelter House concerning this issue, with the exception of a property manager who commented on the already existing problem of renting out property [in the vicinity of the new location].

The district court also gave little credence to the testimony of an urban planner, who referred to national research that property values located in areas of transient housing do not necessarily go down, because the speaker did not provide any documentation of the research or its source. The court concluded the minutes of the board meeting, the transcript of that meeting, and the board's written decision did not collectively contain substantial evidence to support the board's finding that property values would not be impaired or substantially diminished.

While the issue is close, we conclude there was substantial evidence to support the board's decision. As the district court accurately observed, there was no expert testimony that property values would not be impaired by the location of the transient home. Nonetheless, the absence of such evidence is not fatal, as expert testimony concerning the valuation of property is not required by our cases or by the Iowa City Code. *Cf.* Petersen v. Harrison County Bd. of Supervisors, 580 N.W.2d 790, 796 (Iowa 1998) (noting no requirement under chapter 352, dealing with designation of property as an agricultural area, that expert testimony concerning reduced property values be presented at hearing before the board). *See generally Norland*, 323 N.W.2d at 253 (noting determination of a prevailing wage is not an exact science, and there was no statutory constraint on the type of evidence the board could consider).

One person residing in the vicinity of the current transient house commented that the property values in that neighborhood had not been adversely affected. The board was certainly permitted to rely on such anecdotal evidence. *See* Cambodian Buddhist Soc'y v. Planning & Zoning Comm'n, A.2d, 285 Conn. 381, 941 A.2d 868 (Conn. 2008) (noting "commission was entitled to credit the anecdotal reports that past activities on the society's property had made neighboring properties less desirable" in determining whether proposed construction of temple would impair property values). In addition, the board may rely on commonsense inferences drawn from evidence relating to other issues, such as use and enjoyment, crime, safety, welfare, and aesthetics, to make a judgment as to whether the proposed use would substantially diminish or impair property values in the area. We examine, then, evidence before the board that would permit an inference with respect to property values.

The concern most often voiced by opponents of the special exception was the increased likelihood of criminal acts in the neighborhood. Several witnesses reviewed the statistics concerning the arrest rates for residents of the current shelter house and for residents of Hilltop Mobile Home Court, a mobile home development in the neighborhood of the new location. Although the witnesses differed in their interpretation of this data, a close inspection of these figures reveals that the arrest rate for persons giving Shelter House as their address was likely less than the arrest rate for persons giving Hilltop Mobile Home Court as their address. Moreover, there appeared to be more concern about potential crime due to the number of persons turned away by Shelter House than by the persons who actually stay there. There was testimony that the proposed doubling of capacity at the new facility may offset this negative impact by significantly reducing the number of persons turned away for lack of room. There was also a statement from a neighbor of the current shelter house that he did not observe any "rise or change in the amount of crime in the neighborhood."

In addition to the evidence regarding crime, there was testimony from two persons residing in the neighborhood of the current shelter house that the establishment caused no problems in the neighborhood other than some detrimental aesthetics relating to trash cans and the lawn. These issues were to be addressed at the new transient house through a requirement that the new location have a landscape buffer and an eight-foot privacy fence. Another neighbor at the current location denied there was any increase in vehicular traffic due to the presence of the transient house. There was also evidence that it was already difficult to rent property at any price in the area of the new location, supporting an inference that transient housing would not have much of an effect on the already depressed property values. Finally, notwithstanding a lack of documentation, the board could consider the testimony of the urban planner that national research showed property values do not necessarily go down when such a use is introduced into a neighborhood.

We think this evidence, considered collectively, is adequate to support the board's conclusion that the proposed special exception would not substantially diminish or impair the value of neighboring properties. Although there was evidence to the contrary, the reasonableness of the board's decision is open to a fair difference of opinion, and therefore, the board's decision should have been affirmed on that basis. *See Helmke*, 418 N.W.2d at 352 (stating "whether the evidence in a close case such as this one might well support an opposite finding is of no consequence, for the district court cannot substitute its judgment for that of the board of adjustment").

VII. Disposition

We conclude the board made adequate findings, and its decision was supported by substantial evidence. Accordingly, the district court erred in reversing the board's grant of Shelter House's application for a special exception. We therefore reverse the district court's judgment and remand this case back to the district court for entry of an order affirming the decision of the board of adjustment.

REVERSED AND REMANDED.

NOTES AND QUESTIONS

1. Thirty-seven people spoke at the public hearing before the Board of Adjustment in the *Bontrager* case. Would a neighbor who did not speak, and did not appear, have been entitled to seek judicial review of the variance grant? Who keeps track of participants at a public hearing?

2. Suppose the Iowa City zoning ordinance had authorized the Board of Adjustment to grant special permits for transient housing only when the applicant provides one on-site parking space for every three residents. Applying that standard, Shelter House would be required to provide 24 parking spaces. Suppose, however, Shelter House's proposed facility would include only 18 spaces. At the public hearing, neighbors object to inadequate parking. A board member responds "We don't care about parking; we need transient housing." Two other board members agree. The board then votes, 3–1, to approve the special permit. If neighbors challenge the special permit for inadequacy of parking, will they prevail?

Suppose now that the ordinance includes the same parking requirement, but no one raises the issue before the Board of Adjustment. Would neighbors be successful in challenging the special permit for inadequacy of parking? Should neighbors who were not represented by lawyers during the public hearing (or not adequately represented by lawyers) be barred from raising substantial legal claims in a subsequent judicial proceeding? If so, why?

3. *Findings of Fact.* Neighboring landowners in the *Bontrager* case challenged the permit on the ground that the Board of Adjustment did not make the findings of fact required by the ordinance. Why would an ordinance require findings of fact? What objectives does the municipality advance by requiring an administrative board to make findings of fact?

Suppose a zoning board fails to make one of the findings required by the local ordinance. In light of the opinion in *Bontrager*, should a neighbor challenge the grant of a variance or special permit on the ground that the board failed to make a required finding of fact? What factor should the neighbor's lawyer consider in addressing that question?

Whose responsibility is it to make sure the board makes required findings of fact? What role should the landowner's lawyer play? The neighbors' lawyer?

4. *Scope of Review.* If separation of powers concerns do not mandate deference to administrative determinations, why shouldn't courts engage in *de novo* review of variance and special permit determinations? The court in *Bontrager* articulates the principle "that the court should not substitute its judgment for that of the board." Why not? If the board's assessment of the factors listed in the statute or ordinance is wrong, why shouldn't a court correct that assessment?

Two formulations of the scope of judicial review predominate. The one adopted by the *Bontrager* court requires a court to uphold an administrative determination if there is "substantial evidence" to support the determination. The other requires a court to uphold the administrative determination unless it is "arbitrary and capricious." Courts often use the two formulations interchangeably, suggesting that if a determination is not based on substantial evidence, then it must be arbitrary and capricious.

5. What evidence was there to support the finding by the Board of Adjustment that Shelter House would not substantially impair property values in the neighborhood? Suppose the testimony by proponents of Shelter House had been precisely the same. Consider three alternatives (different from the facts in *Bontrager*):

> a. The neighbors introduced, in district court, testimony by real estate appraisers that construction of a transient home typically diminishes property values within 500 feet of the home by about 20%, but has no effect on property more than 500 feet away. The same appraiser also testified, supported by data, that this 20% reduction had been observed when the North Gilbert Street transient house was built in Iowa City 20 years earlier.

> b. The neighbors introduced the same testimony, by the same appraiser, before the Board of Adjustment.

c.   The neighbors introduced the same testimony, supported by two appraisers and a Ph.D. economist, before the Board of Adjustment.

In which of these cases would the court have upheld the Board's grant of the special permit? If there was substantial evidence to support the Board's determination in *Bontrager* itself, should the introduction of contrary evidence alter the result? If so, why?

6.   In *Bontrager*, the applicable ordinance authorized the Board of Adjustment to grant a special permit only if the applicant met all of the ordinance's criteria. As a result, if the neighbors could prove that there was not substantial evidence with respect to any one of the ordinance's criteria, the neighbors would have been entitled to invalidate the Board's action. But suppose the local ordinance had instead provided a list of factors and instructed the Board to balance those factors in considering variance or special permit applications. How would a court determine whether there was substantial evidence to support the Board's determination?

7.   Suppose a group of neighbors are opposed to a variance or special permit application apparently favored by a number of local officials. The neighbors retain a lawyer to represent their interests before the local zoning board. What, if anything, can the lawyer do to increase the neighbors' likelihood of success in eventual litigation? Assume that the lawyer is convinced that the board will grant the variance or special permit.

IV. ENVIRONMENTAL REVIEW

The National Environmental Policy Act ("NEPA"), enacted in 1970, imposed on federal agencies the obligation to prepare an environmental impact statement ("EIS") before taking any action that might have a significant effect on the environment. A number of states soon followed the congressional lead, enacting "little NEPAs" which require state and local officials to prepare environmental impact statements before taking actions with potential environmental significance. Like NEPA itself, the little NEPAs enacted in a number of states, including New York and California, often require impact statements not only for government-sponsored projects, but also for government issuance of permits for privately-sponsored projects. In these states, environmental review has become an integral component of the land use regulatory scheme.

The details of the environmental review process vary from state to state, but the following basic steps are common to most environmental review statutes:

1.   Deciding Whether Any Environmental Review Is Warranted

Suppose, for instance, a developer seeks a zoning amendment, a special permit, a variance, or subdivision approval. Need the agency charged with deciding on the developer's application conduct environmental review? Some little NEPAs create strong presumptions that certain actions merit environmental review, and strong presumptions that other actions do not. As the flow chart below demonstrates, in New York, "Type II" actions, including most area variances, are not subject to environmental review, while "Type I" actions, including most zoning amendments and large development projects, are presumed to require environmental review. No presumption applies to "unlisted" actions.

2.   Preparation of an Environmental Assessment Form

For those actions that trigger environmental review, that review generally starts with the developer's preparation of an environmental assessment form ("EAF"). The EAF is often little more than a questionnaire or checklist on which the developer indicates whether the project will involve particular issues that could generate environmental concerns.

3.   Agency Evaluation of the Environmental Assessment Form

The board or other agency considering the developer's application will review the EAF in the first instance, and will generally become the "lead agency" for the environmental review process. Based on the EAF, the lead agency will decide whether the developer must prepare a draft environmental impact statement ("DEIS"). If, based on the EAF, the agency sees no potential for adverse environmental impact, the agency issues a "negative declaration"—a determination that no further environmental review is warranted. On the other hand if the EAF reveals the potential for environmental harm, the agency issues a "positive declaration" and requires preparation of a DEIS. In some circumstances, the agency may issue a "conditioned negative declaration," which permits the developer to avoid further environmental review if the developer agrees to take certain steps which will address the environmental issues uncovered by the EAF.

4.   The Scoping Session

Once the lead agency determines that the developer must prepare an environmental impact statement, the developer needs guidance about what issues the statement should address. The agency and the developer then conduct what is called a "scoping session" at which the lead agency indicates what the scope of the EIS should be—what environmental issues should the developer address.

5.   Preparation of the DEIS

The developer then prepares the DEIS, which surveys the environmental impact the project will generate. Typically, the developer hires an environmental consultant to prepare the document, which addresses all of the issues identified in the scoping session, and, with respect to each of those issues, compares the project's impact to the status quo (often called the "no build" alternative). The DEIS also compares the proposed project's impact to other alternatives.

6. Public Hearings

Once the developer has submitted the DEIS, the lead agency conducts public hearings on the content of the DEIS, which becomes a matter of public record. At that point, project opponents and other members of the public can challenge the sufficiency or the findings of the DEIS. These public hearings may or may not cause the lead agency to ask the developer to amend the DEIS to address the concerns raised at the hearings.

The public hearings serve non-legal purposes as well. They often operate to galvanize opposition to the project, and to provide opponents with ammunition that might be useful outside the confines of the environmental review process.

7. Adoption of the FEIS

Although the DEIS is largely the developer's document, the lead agency is typically responsible for the final environmental impact statement ("FEIS"). But the lead agency rarely starts from scratch. Instead, the FEIS typically tracks the DEIS, except that the lead agency may reject or modify some of the factual statements or conclusions included in the DEIS.

8. Action on the Project

Once the lead agency concludes the environmental review process, the agency can make its determination on the developer's proposal, whether that proposal be a zoning amendment, or an application for site plan approval, or any other proposal subject to environmental review. The environmental review process should inform the ultimate determination, and may cause the agency to modify or reject the proposal. In New York, when the agency approves a proposal, it must explicitly find that to the maximum extent possible, adverse environmental impacts have been minimized.

9. As the cases that follow indicate, the determinations of the lead agency are subject to judicial review. Project opponents can contend that an agency improperly failed to prepare an EIS, or that the EIS was inadequate.

The chart below is a pictorial representation of the steps in the New York process:

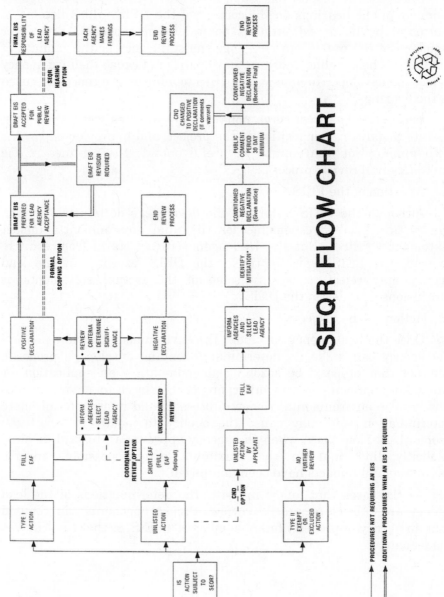

PROBLEM

A developer owns land currently zoned to permit only agricultural uses. Because the parcel is close to a major highway exit, the developer proposes rezoning the land into a business district. The land is already surrounded by business districts on three sides, but the fourth side is zoned agricultural and includes single-family residence parcels.

If the land is rezoned for business use, any construction proposal would require site plan approval from the town planning board. The developer wants your advice about what sort of environmental review will be necessary at the rezoning stage and at the stage when she proposes a concrete development. In light of the SEQR flow chart, advise her. *See* Bergami v. Town Bd., 97 A.D.3d 1018, 949 N.Y.S.2d 245 (2012).

Why an Environmental Review Process?

Land use projects have the potential to affect a community in a variety of ways. The location and design of projects can affect social interactions among community residents. A major project can generate tax revenue or require infrastructure improvements that will have a significant impact on the community's economic well-being. Yet, state statutes do not typically require a separate review of "economic impact" or "social impact." Why, then, impose a separate process for environmental review?

Consider four potential reasons environmental concerns might be undervalued in government decision-making: (1) government officials tend to discount unduly the future effect of their decisions; (2) political pressures cause officials to overvalue concentrated, concrete economic benefits, and to undervalue diffuse environmental benefits; (3) officials are not sufficiently sensitive to environmental issues; and (4) the ordinary political processes do not generate enough information to assure adequate environmental decision-making.

Assume that these problems do lead officials to shortchange environmental concerns in the land use process. Which of them will be mitigated by the environmental review process mandated by a "little NEPA"? And what counts as an environmental issue? Consider those questions in light of the following materials:

Chinese Staff and Workers Association
v. City of New York

Court of Appeals of New York, 1986
68 N.Y.2d 359, 502 N.E.2d 176, 509 N.Y.S.2d 499

■ ALEXANDER, J.

The regulations promulgated by the City of New York (Executive Order No. 91, Aug. 24, 1977, entitled City Environmental Quality Review [CEQR]) as authorized by and in implementation of the State Environmental Quality Review Act (ECL art 8 [SEQRA]) require lead agencies to consider both the short-and long-term and primary and secondary effects of a proposed action in determining whether the action may have a significant effect on the environment so as to require the preparation of an Environmental Impact Statement (EIS). Since respondents' environmental analysis failed to consider the environmental effects required by the regulations, the order of the Appellate Division should be reversed.

This controversy arises out of the proposed construction of Henry Street Tower, a high-rise luxury condominium, on a vacant lot in the Chinatown section of New York City. This building is to be the first construction in the Special Manhattan Bridge District (SMBD), a special zoning district created by the City of New York designed to preserve the residential character of the Chinatown community, encourage new residential development on sites requiring minimal relocation, promote the rehabilitation of existing housing stock, and protect the scale of the community (*see*, New York City Zoning Resolution § 116–00 *et seq.*; Asian Am. for Equality v. Koch, 129 Misc. 2d 67, 71–74*)*. An application for a special permit for Henry Street Tower was submitted by the developer, Henry Street Partners, to the Department of City Planning and the Department of Environmental Protection, the co-lead agencies responsible for implementing SEQRA in the City of New York (*see*, CEQR 1[k]). Following a thorough environmental review of the effects of the project on the physical environment, the agencies issued a conditional negative declaration asserting that the project will not have any significant effect on the environment if certain modifications were adopted by the developer (*see*, CEQR 1[d]; 7[b][2]). The modifications were accepted by the developer and the application for a special permit was thereafter approved by the City Planning Commission and the Board of Estimate.

A combined plenary action and article 78 proceeding was commenced by various members of the Chinatown community challenging the Board of Estimate approval of the special permit.

[P]etitioners argue that the city's environmental review was arbitrary and capricious because of the failure of the lead agencies to consider whether the introduction of luxury housing into the Chinatown community would accelerate the displacement of local low-income residents and businesses or alter the character of the community. Respondents contend that absent a determination that the proposed action will have a significant adverse impact on an area's physical environment, SEQRA and CEQR do not require consideration of any social or economic impacts such as those asserted by petitioners.

II

The initial determination to be made under SEQRA and CEQR is whether an EIS is required, which in turn depends on whether an action may or will not have a significant effect on the environment (ECL 8–0109[2]; CEQR 7[a]). In making this initial environmental analysis, the lead agencies must study the same areas of environmental impacts as would be contained in an EIS, including both the short-term and long-term effects (ECL 8–0109[2][b]) as well as the primary and secondary effects (CEQR 1[g]) of an action on the environment. The threshold at which the requirement that an EIS be prepared is triggered is relatively low: it need only be demonstrated that the action may have a significant effect on the environment (*see*, Oak Beach Inn Corp. v. Harris, 108 A.D.2d 796, 797; H.O.M.E.S. v. New York State Urban Dev. Corp., 69 A.D.2d 222, 232, *supra*).

The dispute here concerns the reach of the term "environment," which is defined as "the *physical conditions* which will be affected by a proposed action, *including* land, air, water, minerals, flora, fauna, noise, objects of historic or aesthetic significance, *existing patterns of population concentration, distribution, or growth, and existing community or neighborhood character*" (ECL 8–0105[6]; CEQR1[f] [emphasis supplied]). Petitioners argue that the displacement of neighborhood residents and businesses caused by a proposed project is an environmental impact within the purview of SEQRA and CEQR, and the failure of respondents to consider these potential effects renders their environmental analysis invalid. Respondents contend that any impacts that are not either directly related to a primary physical impact or will not impinge upon the physical environment in a significant manner are outside the scope of the definition of "environment," and that the lead agencies were therefore not required to investigate the potential effects alleged by petitioners.

Respondents' limited view of the parameters of the term "environment" is contrary to the plain meaning of SEQRA and the city's regulations and must be rejected. It is clear from the express terms of the statute and the regulations that environment is broadly defined (ECL 8–0105[6]; 6 NYCRR 617.2[k]; CEQR1[f]) and expressly includes as physical conditions such considerations as "existing patterns of population concentration, distribution, or growth, and existing community or neighborhood character." Thus, the impact that a project may have on population patterns or existing community character, with or without a separate impact on the physical environment, is a relevant concern in an environmental analysis since the statute includes these concerns as elements of the environment. That these factors might generally be regarded as social or economic is irrelevant in view of this explicit definition. By their express terms, therefore, both SEQRA and CEQR require a lead agency to consider more than impacts upon the physical environment in determining whether to require the preparation of an EIS. In sum, population patterns and neighborhood character are physical conditions of the environment under SEQRA and CEQR regardless of whether there is any impact on the physical environment (*see*, Ulasewicz, Department of Environmental Conservation and SEQRA: Upholding Its Mandates and Charting Parameters For The Elusive Socio-Economic Assessment, 46 Alb. L. Rev. 1255, 1266, 1282).

Turning to the specific allegations in this case, we conclude that under CEQR the potential displacement of local residents and businesses is an effect on population patterns and neighborhood character which must be considered in determining whether the requirement for an EIS is triggered. A significant effect on the environment may be found if a proposed project impairs "the character or quality of existing community or neighborhood character" (CEQR 6[a][5]) or impacts upon "existing patterns of population concentration, distribution, or growth" (ECL 8–0105[6]; *see*, CEQR 6[a][10]). It is not relevant whether the proposed project may effect these concerns primarily or secondarily or in the short term or in the long term since the regulations expressly include all such effects (CEQR 1[g]).

The potential acceleration of the displacement of local residents and businesses is a secondary long-term effect on population patterns, community goals and neighborhood character such that CEQR requires these impacts on the environment to be considered in an environmental analysis. The fact that the actual construction on the proposed site will not cause the displacement of any residents or businesses is not dispositive for displacement can occur in the community surrounding a project as well as on the site of a project. We do not decide whether these impacts will in fact flow from the construction of Henry Street Tower nor do we express any opinion on the merits of the proposed project. Our holding is limited to a determination that existing patterns of population concentration, distribution or growth and existing community or neighborhood character are physical conditions such that the regulations adopted by the City of New York pursuant to SEQRA require an agency to consider the potential long-term secondary displacement of residents and businesses in determining whether a proposed project may have a significant effect on the environment. Since respondents did not consider these potential effects on the environment in their environmental analysis, their determination does not comply with the statutory mandate and therefore is arbitrary and capricious.

III

Respondents have failed to comply with the requirements of SEQRA and CEQR and the appropriate remedy is to grant petitioners' motion for summary judgment declaring the special permit null and void. The suggestion in the dissenting opinion that the omission here can be cured by "an amended negative declaration" (dissenting opn, at p. 371) finds no support in the carefully drafted procedures of the statute and would effectively allow the municipality to comply with SEQRA and CEQR only as an afterthought following a successful challenge to their prior action. Such a result is directly contrary to our holding in Matter of Tri-County Taxpayers Ass'n v. Town Bd. 55 N.Y.2d 41, and moreover, would contravene the important purposes underlying

SEQRA. Indeed, it would allow a project to be initially approved without the benefit of a valid environmental review. In order to further the strong policies served by SEQRA and to not frustrate its important objectives, we hold that the appropriate remedy here is the annulment of the special permit.

IV

Accordingly, the order of the Appellate Division affirming Supreme Court's grant of summary judgment to respondents is reversed and petitioners' cross motion for summary judgment granted.

■ CHIEF JUDGE WACHTLER and HANCOCK, JR., J. (concurring and dissenting in part).

We concur with the majority to the extent that it holds that "under CEQR the potential displacement of local residents and businesses is an effect on population patterns and neighborhood character" (majority opn, at p. 366) which should have been considered by the lead agency before it issued the conditional negative declaration.

We must strongly disagree with so much of the majority decision as may have the effect of invalidating the special permit. Here, under CEQR, we hold merely that certain potential effects should have been considered before the lead agency decided that an EIS was unnecessary. It is not at all certain that these effects will ultimately require anything other than a reiteration that they have no significant effect on the environment as defined in CEQR 1(g). The invalidation of a project, even at great loss to the sponsors, is warranted when, as in Matter of Tri-County Taxpayers Ass'n v. Town Bd. (*supra*), it is clear that the public has been improperly deprived of the "detailed information about the effect which [the] proposed action is likely to have on the environment" (ECL 8–0109[2]) which an EIS would have provided and that the project has proceeded in outright violation of SEQRA. It by no means follows, however, that a project should be nullified when, as here, it may well be concluded that a negative declaration rather than an EIS is the proper course.

NOTES AND QUESTIONS

1. Regulations promulgated under NEPA define human environment "to include the natural and physical environment and the relationship of people with that environment. (See the definition of "effects" in 40 C.F.R. § 1508.8.) This means that economic or social effects are not intended by themselves to require preparation of an environmental impact statement. When an environmental impact statement is prepared and economic or social and natural or physical environmental effects are interrelated, then the environmental impact statement will discuss all of these effects on the human environment." 40 C.F.R. § 1508.14. If the NEPA definition had been in effect, would the proposed development in the *Chinese Staff* case have required an EIS?

The scope of "little NEPAs" varies considerably. For instance, the Minnesota statute protects "air, water, land and other natural resources located within the state from pollution, impairment, or destruction." Minn. Stat. Ann § 116B.01. *See generally* Stansell v. City of Northfield, 618 N.W.2d 814 (Minn. App. 2000) (noting that the Minnesota statute is narrower in scope than the New York statute construed in *Chinese Staff*).

2. In light of the broad definition in the New York statute, how could the developer have believed that the development would generate no environmental impact? What is secondary displacement? If building on a vacant lot generates the potential for secondary displacement, what project does not?

3. What data will be relevant in assessing the demographic impact of the proposed project? How reliable is the data likely to be? What kind of consultant has the expertise to produce the data? Who will choose the expert to make an assessment of the project's likely impact? In light of your answers to these questions, how much confidence would you have in the EIS? In the ability of the lead agency to evaluate the statement?

4. In light of the New York statute, should a project opponent succeed in challenging a project because the environmental review did not include the impact of global warming, and particularly sea level rise, on the project? *See generally* Ballona Wetlands Trust v. City of Los Angeles, 201 Cal.App.4th 455, 473, 134 Cal. Rptr. 194, 206–07 (2012) (sustaining limited treatment of global warming in an environmental impact report because "the purpose of an EIR is to identify the significant effects of a project on the environment, not the significant effects of the environment on the project").

5. In light of *Chinese Staff*, suppose you represent the developer of a project that requires a special permit, or some other zoning approval. Would you advise the developer to seek a positive declaration or a negative declaration? What factors would be relevant in making that determination?

Bakersfield Citizens for Local Control
v. City of Bakersfield

Court of Appeal of California, Fifth Appellate District, 2004
124 Cal.App.4th 1184, 22 Cal.Rptr.3d 203

■ BUCKLEY, ACTING P. J.

INTRODUCTION

Appellant Bakersfield Citizens for Local Control (BCLC) has challenged development of two retail shopping centers in the southwestern portion of the City of Bakersfield (City), alleging violations of the California Environmental Quality Act (CEQA). The shopping centers are located 3.6 miles apart. When complete, they will have a combined total of 1.1 million square feet of retail space. Each shopping center will contain a Wal-Mart Supercenter (Supercenter) plus a mix of large anchor stores, smaller retailers, and a gas station.

An environmental impact report (EIR) was prepared and certified for each project.

FACTUAL OVERVIEW

Real party in interest Panama 99 Properties LLC (P99) is developing a 370,000-square-foot retail shopping center named Panama 99 (Panama) on 35 acres of vacant land located at the northeast corner of Panama Lane and Highway 99. The project site was zoned for mobile home use and its general plan designation was low-density residential/open space.

Real party in interest and appellant Castle and Cooke Commercial–CA, Inc. (C & C), is developing a 700,000-square-foot regional retail shopping center named Gosford Village (Gosford) on 73 acres of vacant land located on the southwest corner of Pacheco Road and Gosford Road. The project site's zoning and general plan land use designation was service industrial.

Panama is located 3.6 miles east of Gosford. The two shopping centers share some arterial roadway links.

Each shopping center will feature a 220,000-square-foot Supercenter as its primary anchor tenant. Supercenters "combin[e] the traditional Wal-Mart discount store with a full-size grocery store." Supercenters compete with large discount stores, traditional department stores, supermarkets and other grocery stores, as well as drug stores and apparel stores. The Supercenter at Panama will replace an existing Wal-Mart store that currently is located 1.4 miles north of the Panama site. In addition to the Supercenter, Panama will contain a Lowe's Home Improvement Warehouse (Lowe's), a gas station and a satellite pad. Gosford will contain a total of 17 retail stores, plus fast food restaurants and a gas station. In addition to the Supercenter, there will be six other anchor tenants, including Kohl's Department Stores (Kohl's) (apparel and home-related items) and Sam's Club (warehouse club selling groceries and a wide array of consumer products).

P99 and C & C (collectively, developers) applied in early 2002 for project approvals and associated zoning changes and general plan amendments. A separate EIR was prepared for each shopping center (hereafter the Panama EIR and the Gosford EIR). The Panama EIR concluded that Panama would have significant and unavoidable direct adverse impacts on air quality and noise. The Gosford EIR concluded that Gosford would have a significant and unavoidable adverse impact on air quality, both individually and cumulatively.

The Panama EIR identified the Supercenter and Lowe's as the two anchor tenants. The Gosford EIR did not identify any tenants. In response to comments questioning the environmental effects resulting from locating two Supercenters in a 3.6-mile radius, the Gosford EIR states that no tenants have been identified. However, it is clear from the administrative record that prior to certification of the Gosford EIR, the public and the City knew that one of Gosford's tenants was going to be a Supercenter.

The planning commission and the City Council considered the two projects at the same meetings. On February 12, 2003, the City Council certified the EIR's and adopted statements of overriding considerations on the nonpublic consent calendar. Then, after public hearing, it approved both projects and granted associated zoning changes and general plan amendments.

In March 2003, BCLC filed two CEQA actions challenging the sufficiency of the EIR's and contesting the project approvals and related land use entitlements (the Panama action and the Gosford action).

Trial was held on the Panama action in November 2003 and on the Gosford action in January 2004. In both actions, the court concluded that CEQA required study of the question whether the two shopping centers, individually or cumulatively, could indirectly trigger a series of events that ultimately result in urban decay or deterioration.

BCLC unsuccessfully sought a temporary restraining order enjoining construction-related activities at the Panama site after the court orally announced its decision in the Panama action.

Argument was held concerning the proper remedy. The trial court concluded that the failure to study urban decay rendered the EIR's inadequate as informational documents and it ordered them decertified. It left the project approvals and associated land use entitlements intact and it severed the Supercenters from the remainder of the projects. It enjoined further construction of the partially built Supercenter buildings but allowed all other construction activities to continue pending full CEQA compliance.

BCLC partially appealed both judgments; C & C partially cross-appealed the judgment in the Gosford action. The appeals were consolidated on our own motion.

DISCUSSION

The applicable standard of review is well established. If the substantive and procedural requirements of CEQA are satisfied, a project may be approved even if it would create significant and unmitigable impacts on the environment. (Fairview Neighbors v. County of Ventura (1999) 70 Cal. App. 4th 238, 242 [82 Cal. Rptr. 2d 436].) Courts are "not to determine whether the EIR's ultimate conclusions are correct but only whether they are supported by substantial evidence in the record and whether the EIR is sufficient as an information document." (Association of Irritated Residents v. County of Madera (2003) 107 Cal. App. 4th 1383, 1391 [133 Cal. Rptr. 2d 718] (Irritated Residents)).

"The EIR must contain facts and analysis, not just the bare conclusions of the agency.' [Citation.] 'An EIR must include detail sufficient to enable those who did not participate in its preparation to understand and to consider meaningfully the issues raised by the proposed project.' " (*Irritated Residents, supra*, 107 Cal. App. 4th at p. 1390.) Failure to comply with the information disclosure requirements constitutes a prejudicial abuse of discretion when the omission of relevant information has precluded informed decisionmaking and informed public participation, regardless whether a different outcome would have resulted if the public agency had complied with the disclosure requirements.

Developers achieved an important practical victory when they convinced the trial court to leave the project approvals in place, sever the Supercenters from the remainder of the projects and allow construction of the rest of the shopping centers to proceed prior to full CEQA compliance. As a result, retail businesses currently are operating at both project sites and nonparties have acquired portions of the project sites. This has generated substantial economic and psychological pressures in favor of the shopping centers as presently approved and partially constructed.

Undoubtedly some would view further environmental study of the partially completed projects as a futile waste of time and money. Since CEQA's purpose is not to generate meaningless paperwork, we were tempted to find the alleged defects in CEQA compliance essentially nonredressable and therefore moot. Yet, after reviewing briefing on this question, we decided not to adopt this rather cynical position.

First, developers expressly recognized that they were proceeding at their own risk when they relied on the contested project approvals during the pendency of this litigation. When an injunction is not granted after commencement of a CEQA action, the agency is to assume that the contested EIR or negative declaration satisfies CEQA's requirements. However, "[a]n approval granted by a responsible agency in this situation provides only permission to proceed with the project at the applicant's risk prior to a final decision in the lawsuit." (Guidelines, § 15233, subd. (b).)

Finally, even at this late juncture full CEQA compliance would not be a meaningless exercise of form over substance. The City possesses discretion to reject either or both of the shopping centers after further environmental study and weighing of the projects' benefits versus their environmental, economic and social costs. As conditions of reapproval, the City may compel additional mitigation measures or require the projects to be modified, reconfigured or reduced. The City can require completed portions of the projects to be modified or removed and it can compel restoration of the project sites to their original condition.

III. *Urban Decay*

Water contamination and air pollution, now recognized as very real environmental problems, initially were scoffed at as the alarmist ravings of environmental doomsayers. Similarly, experts are now warning about land use decisions that cause a chain reaction of store closures and long-term vacancies, ultimately destroying existing neighborhoods and leaving decaying shells in their wake. In this case, the trial court recognized that the shopping centers posed a risk of triggering urban decay or deterioration and it concluded that CEQA required analysis of this potential impact. C & C has challenged this determination. We find C & C's arguments unpersuasive and agree that CEQA requires analysis of the shopping centers' individual and cumulative potential to indirectly cause urban decay.

C & C contends that study is not required because the record does not contain substantial evidence proving that the shopping centers will cause urban decay. This argument founders because it is premised on the wrong standard of review. Substantial evidence is the standard applied to conclusions reached in an EIR and findings that are based on such conclusions. (*Irritated Residents, supra,* 107 Cal. App. 4th at pp. 1390–1391.) BCLC is not challenging a conclusion in the EIR's that the shopping centers would not indirectly cause urban decay or a finding adopted by the City. It is not arguing that the City used the wrong methodology in assessing whether urban decay will be an indirect effect of the project or challenging the validity of an expert's opinion on this topic. Rather, BCLC's argument is that the EIR's failed to comply with the information disclosure provisions of CEQA because they omitted any meaningful consideration of the question whether the shopping centers could, individually or cumulatively, trigger a series of events that ultimately cause urban decay. Neither EIR even contains a statement indicating reasons why it had been determined that urban decay was not a significant effect of the proposed projects. (§ 21100, subd. (c).).

In any event, C & C's position has no substantive merit. There is a great deal of evidence in the record supporting the validity of concerns that the shopping centers could cause a ripple of store closures and consequent long-term vacancies that would eventually result in general deterioration and decay within and outside the market area of the two shopping centers. Although much of BCLC's evidence specifically applied to the Supercenters, the administrative records as a whole contain sufficient indication that addition of 1.1 million square feet of retail space in the shopping centers' overlapping market areas could start the chain reaction that ultimately results in urban decay to necessitate study of the issue with respect to the entirety of the shopping centers.

First, BCLC retained a professor of economics at San Francisco State University, C. Daniel Vencill, to study the cumulative economic effects that will be caused by the two new Supercenters (the Vencill report). Together with two colleagues, Vencill reviewed literature and analyzed the five-mile area surrounding the project sites. Photographs were taken of the sites and "existing blight conditions which have remained unabated for some years in the area surrounding the proposed new sites" were documented. The Vencill report determined that the two shopping centers are in the same shopper catchment area and they will be competing with each other as well as with existing retail establishments. It states that "[t]here are [four] existing shopping centers and malls that will be adversely affected by [Gosford and Panama]. One regional mall is suspected of being in serious decline." The two Supercenters represent significant excess capacity as configured and located. "This will result in oversaturation and fall-out of weaker competitors in the at-risk commercial blight zone the developments will create." The Vencill report identified 29 businesses, primarily but not exclusively grocery stores, that are at direct risk of closure. Two Albertsons are "facing extinction" and a small nursery that is located across the street from Gosford "would certainly become defunct." Additionally, no "alternative plans" were observed for the Wal-Mart building on White Lane that will be vacant when this Wal-Mart store is replaced by the Supercenter at Panama. The Vencill report finds: "It is reasonably probable [that] competition provided by the two proposed [Supercenters] (i.e., the diversion of existing sales from local merchants), individually and especially cumulatively, will have economic impacts on existing businesses triggering a chain of events that may lead to adverse effects on the physical environment in the southern part of Bakersfield. One of the ways this may occur is that smaller retailers in the area, particularly those located within five miles of the sites, and even more specifically those retailers already struggling or on the verge of having to terminate operations, will be unable to compete and will have to go out of business. In turn, this may cause permanent or long-term vacancies of retail space in the area. The result is typically neglect of maintenance and repair of retail facilities, the deterioration of buildings, improvements, and facilities. This may then culminate in physical effects associated with blight-like conditions, which include visual and aesthetic impacts accompanying the physical deterioration."

BCLC also submitted numerous studies and articles analyzing the adverse effects other communities in California (San Diego, Orange County and Calexico), and elsewhere (Oklahoma City, Oklahoma; Bath, Maine; Eastern Pennsylvania; Chicago, Illinois; Syracuse, New York) have experienced as a result of saturation of a market area with super-sized retailers. As relevant here, the authors found numerous adverse effects resulting from saturation of a market area with Supercenters and similar retail facilities, such as SuperTargets and SuperKmarts. These effects include, but are not limited to, physical decay and deterioration resulting from store closures in the same market area or in established areas of the community (i.e., the "traditional downtown area") due to competitive pressures, followed by an inability to easily re-lease the vacated premises. The authors also found that it had been difficult to find tenants for buildings that formerly housed Wal-Mart stores that were replaced by the new Supercenters. Many of the empty buildings physically deteriorated.

Moreover, numerous individuals commented about urban decay during the administrative process. For example, at the planning commission's public hearing on the adequacy of the draft EIR's, Cindy Fabricius stated, "[T]here are 45 empty Wal-Marts in the state of Texas. There are 34 empty standing Wal-Marts in the state of Georgia. There are 27 in Utah. Find them. Go look at them. They are empty. When Wal-Mart moves on they leave their boxes. Those boxes are not bought up by other [businesses]; who can afford that huge of a store; that huge of a rent?" Some comments made at the February 2003 City Council meeting are also relevant. A representative of Save Mart Supermarkets spoke in opposition to the project and submitted the data concerning Oklahoma City. He stated that the addition of the two shopping centers will adversely affect existing shopping centers and asserted that the "[t]he potential for urban blight and decay is a matter which must be considered" in the EIR's. Another commercial property owner wrote that he had been unable to re-lease a building that formerly housed a grocery store and he ended up demolishing the building. When a grocery store closes, the remainder of the stores in the shopping center are likely to close. The center "could end up with many boarded up storefronts." While these individuals are not experts in any sense of the word, their firsthand observations should not casually be dismissed as immaterial because "relevant personal observations are evidence." (*Bishop, supra*, 172 Cal. App. 3d at p. 173; *see also* Ocean View Estates Homeowners Ass'n, Inc. v. Montecito Water Dist. (2004) 116 Cal. App. 4th 396, 402 [10 Cal. Rptr. 3d 451].)

The responses in the EIR's to these and other comments do not meaningfully address the issue of urban decay. The Gosford EIR states that vacant buildings "are part of the evolutional change of the retail environment." It then asserts that further analysis is outside the scope of CEQA because economic and social effects are not considered environmental effects under CEQA. The response in the Panama EIR is similarly incomplete. Ignoring the question of urban decay or deterioration, it simply replies that "blight" is a legal term that does not apply. It also asserts that vacancy rates and business closures are purely economic impacts and therefore outside of CEQA. Finally, it states that a survey of vacant buildings had been prepared and this survey demonstrated that "retailers entering or leaving the market, relocations, re-leasing to new tenants or conversions to other uses is a normal part of a dynamic market."

[I]t is apparent that in this case the shopping centers could, individually and cumulatively, trigger the same downward spiral of business closures, vacancies and deterioration that other communities have experienced when they allowed similar saturation development. Therefore, CEQA requires analysis of this potential environmental impact.

Accordingly, we hold that the omission of analysis on the issue of urban/suburban decay and deterioration rendered the EIR's defective as informational documents. (*Mt. Shasta, supra,* 198 Cal. App. 3d at p. 446.) On remand, the EIR's must analyze whether the shopping centers, individually and/or cumulatively, indirectly could trigger the downward spiral of retail closures and consequent long-term vacancies that ultimately result in decay. (*Ibid.*; *Bishop, supra,* 172 Cal. App. 3d at p. 171.)

IV. *Cumulative Impacts*

The Gosford EIR and the Panama EIR considered each shopping center in isolation. The cumulative impacts sections of each EIR do not reference the other shopping center and neither EIR contains any discussion of or reference to retail development in the area surrounding the project site. BCLC argues that the "failure to treat Panama and Gosford as 'relevant projects' for purposes of evaluating cumulative effects" is "[a]n overarching legal flaw in both EIRs." We agree.

"The significance of a comprehensive cumulative impacts evaluation is stressed in CEQA." (Schoen v. Department of Forestry & Fire Prevention (1997) 58 Cal. App. 4th 556, 572 [68 Cal. Rptr. 2d 343].) Proper cumulative impact analysis is vital "because the full environmental impact of a proposed project cannot be gauged in a vacuum. One of the most important environmental lessons that has been learned is that environmental damage often occurs incrementally from a variety of small sources. These sources appear insignificant when considered individually, but assume threatening dimensions when considered collectively with other sources with which they interact." (Communities for a Better Environment v. California Resources Agency (2002) 103 Cal. App. 4th 98, 114 [126 Cal. Rptr. 2d 441], *fns. omitted*; *see also* Los Angeles Unified School Dist. v. City of Los Angeles (1997) 58 Cal. App. 4th 1019, 1025 [68 Cal. Rptr. 2d 367].) "[C]onsideration of the effects of a project or projects as if no others existed would encourage the piecemeal approval of several projects that, taken together, could overwhelm the natural environment and disastrously overburden the man-made infrastructure and vital community services. This would effectively defeat CEQA's mandate to review the actual effect of the projects upon the environment." (Las

Virgenes Homeowners Federation, Inc. v. County of Los Angeles (1986) 177 Cal. App. 3d 300, 306 [223 Cal. Rptr. 18].)

When faced with a challenge that the cumulative impacts analysis is unduly narrow, the court must determine whether it was reasonable and practical to include the omitted projects and whether their exclusion prevented the severity and significance of the cumulative impacts from being accurately reflected. (Kings County Farm Bureau v. City of Hanford (1990) 221 Cal. App. 3d 692, 723 [270 Cal. Rptr. 650] (Farm Bureau).)

It is beyond dispute that the two shopping centers are both "present" projects within the meaning of Guidelines section 15355, subdivision (b). They were proposed within a month of each other and both shopping centers were considered at the same meetings of the City Planning Commission and the City Council. Many citizens, including BCLC, voiced their opinions about both shopping centers at the same time. Thus, the determinative question is whether Gosford and Panama also are "closely related" within the meaning of Guidelines section 15355, subdivision (b). We answer this question in the affirmative.

First, there is evidence showing that the two shopping centers will compete with each other. The Vencill report states that the market area for stores like Supercenters is about five miles. Since Gosford and Panama are 3.6 miles apart, the two market areas necessarily overlap. As previously discussed, the record contains numerous studies analyzing the adverse effects other communities have experienced when a market area was saturated with large-scale retailers such as traditional Wal-Mart stores and their siblings, Supercenters and Sam's Clubs. Second, the Gosford EIR and the Panama EIR show that the two shopping centers share four arterial roadways: Pacheco Road, Panama Lane, Harris Road and White Lane. A planning commissioner stated that he was concerned that the two projects could have combined, unrecognized adverse impacts on traffic.

Third, ambient air quality is a serious concern. Each of the EIR's concluded that the proposed shopping center would have an unavoidable adverse impact on ambient air quality.

When considered in its entirety, this evidence strongly supports BCLC's position that the two shopping centers are closely related and may have several cumulatively significant adverse impacts. Therefore, CEQA compels assessment and disclosure of these combined environmental effects.

There is no merit to the position of City and developers that cumulative impacts analysis does not require consideration of both shopping centers because, in each case, the other shopping center is outside the radius of the "project area" as defined in EIR's. An EIR is required to discuss significant impacts that the proposed project will cause in the area that is affected by the project. (CEQA Guidelines,

§ 15126.2, subd. (a).) This area cannot be so narrowly defined that it necessarily eliminates a portion of the affected environmental setting. Simply put, selection of "appropriate" geographic areas that just happen to narrowly miss the other large proposed shopping center in every category of impacts despite their overlapping market areas and shared roadways does not constitute the good faith disclosure and analysis that is required by CEQA.

The record raises numerous questions respecting the type and severity of cumulative adverse environmental impacts that likely will result from the two shopping centers. Topics such as traffic, noise, air quality, urban decay and growth inducement immediately surface. City and developers cannot fault BCLC because it does not have evidence answering these and other questions related to the cumulative impacts resulting from construction and operation of both Gosford and Panama. "To conclude otherwise would place the burden of producing relevant environmental data on the public rather than the agency and would allow the agency to avoid an attack on the adequacy of the information contained in the report simply by excluding such information." (*Farm Bureau, supra*, 221 Cal. App. 3d 692, 724.)

On remand, each EIR must analyze the cumulative impacts resulting from construction and operation of the proposed shopping center in conjunction with all other past, present or reasonably foreseeable retail projects that are or will be located within the proposed project's market area. This includes, but is not limited to, analysis of the combined adverse impacts resulting from construction and operation of Gosford and Panama.

* * *

VI. *Prejudice*

In this case, City's failure to assess whether the shopping centers, individually and cumulatively, will indirectly cause urban decay, to evaluate the cumulative impacts of both shopping centers and to correlate the adverse air quality impacts to resulting adverse health consequences, cannot be dismissed as harmless or insignificant defects. As a result of these omissions, meaningful assessment of the true scope of numerous potentially serious adverse environmental effects was thwarted. No discrete or severable aspects of the projects are unaffected by the omitted analyses; the defects relate to the shopping centers in their entirety, not just to one specific retailer. These deficiencies precluded informed public participation and decision making. Therefore, certification of the EIR's was a prejudicial abuse of discretion. (*Peninsula, supra*, 87 Cal. App. 4th at p. 128.)

The Guidelines unequivocally require the lead agency to certify a legally adequate final EIR prior to deciding whether or not to approve or carry out a contested project. (Guidelines, §§ 15089 to 15092.) "[T]he ultimate decision of whether to approve a project, be that decision right or wrong, is a nullity if based upon an EIR that does not provide the decision-makers, and the public, with the information about the project that is required by CEQA." (Santiago County Water Dist. v. County of Orange (1981) 118 Cal. App. 3d 818, 829 [173 Cal. Rptr. 602].) Thus, the project approvals and associated land use entitlements also must be voided. (*See, e.g., Eel River, supra*, 108 Cal. App. 4th at p. 882; *Raptor, supra*, 27 Cal. App. 4th at pp. 742–743.)

DISPOSITION

The judgments are reversed and the actions are remanded to the Superior Court of Kern County.

Upon remand, the superior court is directed as follows in both actions:

(1) To issue new peremptory writs of mandate ordering the City to void its certification of the EIR's and findings of overriding considerations and to void its approval of the projects and associated zoning changes, general plan amendments and other related land use entitlements;

(2) To issue orders, after notice and hearing, that set a date by which the City must certify new EIR's;

(3) To determine, after notice and hearing, whether continuance of construction and retail activities on the project sites prior to full CEQA compliance and reapproval will prejudice the consideration or implementation of particular mitigation measures or alternatives to the project.

NOTES AND QUESTIONS

1.   The EIRs in *Bakersfield* considered a number of issues associated with the two shopping centers, including air quality and noise. How did the developers decide which issues to address in the reports? Why didn't they consider the potential for urban decay?

2.   Once BCLC presented its expert reports and testimony to the planning commission, what steps could the lawyers for the developer have taken to avoid this litigation?

3.   In this case, BCLC presented the planning commission with expert reports to support its conclusion that the new shopping centers would have an economic effect on existing businesses, leading to long-term vacancies of retail space and physical deterioration of buildings. How would the court have reacted to a judicial challenge to the adequacy of the EIR, based on its failure to address issues of urban decay, if:

     a.   BCLC had never raised urban decay before filing a complaint in court, or

b.   BCLC had raised urban decay before the planning commission, but presented no testimony to establish the likelihood of decay?

When should be the last moment at which a project opponent can raise objections to the adequacy of an EIR, or to the validity of approvals granted after making findings premised on the EIR?

4.   Once BCLC presented its reports and testimony at the hearings before the planning commission, what reasons were there to require preparation of a new EIR addressing the same issues? If the planning commission and the city council were already aware of the potential for urban decay, and approved the project anyway, how would a new EIR improve municipal decision-making?

5.   In *Bakersfield,* the EIRs concluded that the shopping center projects would generate a decrease in air quality and an increase in noise, but the planning commission and the city council approved the projects anyway. Why didn't BCLC challenge the environmental review on the ground that municipal officials ignored a documented adverse environmental impact?

When an EIR identifies an adverse impact, and officials approve the project anyway, what challenges, if any, are available to a project opponent? *See* Jackson v. New York State Urban Dev. Corp., 67 N.Y.2d 400, 416, 503 N.Y.S.2d 298, 494 N.E.2d 429, 435–436 (1986):

In a statutory scheme whose purpose is that the agency decision-makers focus attention on environmental concerns, it is not the role of the courts to weigh the desirability of any action or choose among alternatives.

But cf. Matter of AC I Shore Road LLC v. Incorporated Vill. of Great Neck, 43 A.D.3d 439, 841 N.Y.S.2d 344 (2007) (although EIS identified areas of environmental concern, municipal officials failed to take a "hard look" at these issues).

6.   *Mitigating Environmental Impact.* A developer can often reduce the adverse environmental impact of a project by incorporating environment-friendly design features into the project. As part of the environmental review process, a municipality might require the developer to build greener buildings. Even outside of the environmental review process, many municipalities have used standards or incentives to reduce the environmental impact of new construction. Much of the focus has been on incorporating Leadership in Energy and Environmental Design ("LEED") standards into new buildings. Moreover, developers have often found that potential purchasers and tenants will pay more for buildings that comply with LEED standards, which were developed by a private, nonprofit entity committed to promoting and standardizing green construction. As a result, markets as well as regulations now provide incentives for greener construction. *See generally* Matthew J. Parlow, Greenwashed?: Developers, Environmental Consciousness, and the Case of Playa Vista, 35 B.C. Envtl. Aff. L. Rev. 513 (2008).

7. *Cumulative Impact Review.* The *Bakersfield* court concluded that both of the EIRs were inadequate because they failed to consider the cumulative impact of the two shopping centers, instead evaluating the impact of each proposed shopping center in isolation of the other. Although statutes often require review of cumulative impact, determining the scope of that command has generated considerable confusion (and considerable litigation). Suppose, for instance, that there had been proposals for five or six shopping centers in the area, and no certainty that any of them would ultimately be built. How should the EIRs account for the various proposals?

Long Island's Pine Barrens are environmentally sensitive, both because development might threaten the area's water supply and because of a large number of endangered species that call the area home. When 224 separate development proposals, directed to officials in three separate municipalities, all cover land located in the Pine Barrens, must the EIS for each project evaluate the cumulative impact of the various proposals? *See* Long Island Pine Barrens, Inc. v. Planning Bd., 80 N.Y.2d 500, 591 N.Y.S.2d 982, 606 N.E.2d 1373 (1992) ("[T]here is no cohesive framework for relating the 224 projects in issue to each other. The only element they share—their common placement in the Central Pine Barrens—is an insufficient predicate under the present set of administrative regulations for mandatory cumulative impact analyses as preconditions to a myriad of local land use determination.").

8. *Segmentation.* Environmental review statutes typically discourage segmentation of environmental review. In the words of one New York court:

> Segmentation occurs when the environmental review of a single action is broken down into smaller stages or activities, addressed as though they are independent and unrelated, needing individual determinations of significance. . . . The regulations generally prohibiting segmentation are designed to guard against a distortion of the approval process by preventing a project with potentially significant environmental effects from being split into two or more smaller projects, each falling below the threshold requiring full-blown review. Additionally, a project developer is not permitted to exclude certain activities from the definition of a project for the purpose of making it appear that adverse environmental impacts have been minimized for the purpose of circumventing the detailed review called for under SEQRA.

Long Island Pine Barrens, Inc. v. Planning Bd., 204 A.D.2d 548, 551, 611 N.Y.S.2d 917, 919 (1994).

Courts invoke improper segmentation in two circumstances. First, improper segmentation may lead to invalidation of a negative declaration, and to a requirement that developer prepare an environmental impact statement. *See, e.g.,* Defreestville Area Neighborhoods Ass'n, Inc. v. Town Bd., 299 A.D.2d 631, 750 N.Y.S.2d 164 (2002) (town improperly segmented environmental review of zoning amendment when town issued negative declaration based on an EAF that did not consider the development that would follow the zoning change). Second, improper segmentation may lead to a finding that the environmental impact statement was inadequate. *See, e.g.,* Sun Co., Inc. v. City of Syracuse Indus. Dev. Agency, 209 A.D.2d 34, 625 N.Y.S.2d 371 (1995) (EIS for one aspect of lakefront development program is invalid because it failed to consider impact of broader lakefront plan).

9.   *Consideration of Project Alternatives.* State environmental review statutes typically require an environmental impact statement to include an evaluation of the environmental impact of project alternatives, and hold that the statement is deficient if the review of alternatives is inadequate. *See, e.g.,* Laurel Heights Improvement Ass'n v. Regents of the Univ. of Cal., 47 Cal.3d 376, 253 Cal.Rptr. 426, 764 P.2d 278 (1988). Indeed, at the federal level, the NEPA regulations describe the discussion of project alternatives as "the heart of the EIS." 40 C.F.R. § 1502.14. Generally, the EIS will include a review of the proposed project, of the "no-build" alternative (the *status quo*), and of one or two more modest alternative projects that might be appropriate to the site. For instance, in a case like *Bakersfield,* the statement might include a review of a shopping center without a Wal-Mart, or of a center with fewer stores and less traffic.

If you were advising a developer about preparation of the project alternatives section of the EIS, what suggestions would you make about choosing the alternatives to include?

PROBLEM

Dan Developer has bought 50 acres in an area zoned for agricultural development. Developer would like to build a residential subdivision, and plans to apply for a zoning amendment in a state that has enacted a "little NEPA." Developer's preliminary studies reveal:

(1)   that the 140 homes he hopes to build will increase the potential for flooding of neighboring areas, but only in the event of a 40-year storm;

(2)   that building the homes will not cause increased traffic congestion if the roads in the subdivision are designed to direct traffic east of the subdivision, but would cause congestion if the roads are designed to direct traffic west of the subdivision (Developer is not prepared to invest in obtaining subdivision approval until he knows whether the zoning amendment will be approved); and

(3)   in light of the soil conditions in the area, constructing septic systems for waste disposal from the proposed homes creates an identifiable, but small, risk of increased bacterial contamination of the local water supply.

The zoning amendment requires preparation of an environmental impact statement, and the developer seeks advice about how to handle each of these issues in the EIS. How would you advise Developer if you expected the town board to be hostile to the proposed amendment? How, if at all, would your advice change if you expected the town board to be favorably disposed?

CHAPTER SEVEN

DEVELOPMENT PROBLEMS

This chapter provides an opportunity to apply the doctrinal materials developed in preceding chapters to work out three concrete development problems that might face developers and municipal officials.

PROBLEM ONE: EXURBAN SUBDIVISION

In 2006, Developer acquired an eleven acre, largely rectangular parcel of land in a rural part of Orange County, Florida. The parcel is currently covered with mature hardwood trees. Neighboring parcels contain both farmland and low density residential uses. Developer hopes to subdivide the parcel into a number of large residential parcels of one to two acres, build single family homes on each lot and sell the homes for a substantial profit. The comprehensive plan for the area (which, under Florida law is legally binding on the subdivider) calls for density of no greater than one dwelling unit per acre, and the land is zoned RCE, a single family category (see the zoning code excerpts attached to this problem).

In December 2006, Developer submits a preliminary plat subdividing the parcel into seven parcels ranging in size from one to two acres. The subdivision, to be called "Dora Woods," would not include any new streets, but would instead take advantage of existing roadways by having driveways from each parcel exit onto those roads (Franklin Road to the west and Earlwood Avenue to the north). The preliminary plat shows a five-foot sidewalk along the northern and western boundaries of the property, and ten-foot water retention swales, just inside the sidewalk, capable of handling water from a 25 year/24 hour storm event. The plat acknowledges that the nearest municipality will be unable to provide municipal water to the lots, as the local water supply is inadequate. Without water, fire services will be limited.

Upon receiving the first draft of the preliminary plat from Developer, the County's planning staff immediately notices that another subdivision already bears the name Dora Woods. After notifying Developer, Developer changes the name of the subdivision to Tangerine Woods and resubmits the plat, which the County accepts for review.

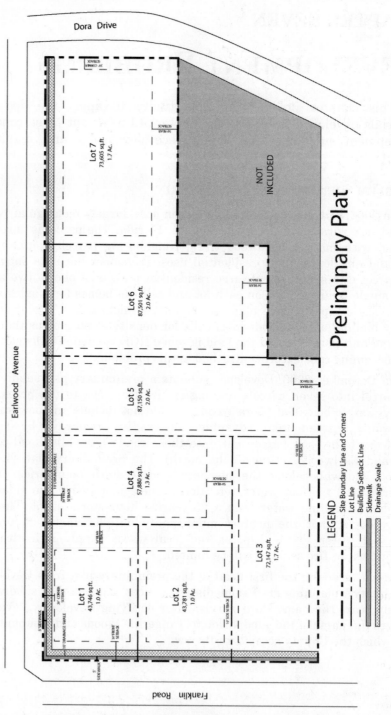

1.   Along with the submission of its Preliminary plat, Developer asks the Development Review Committee ("DRC") for permission to have the lots access existing roads directly rather than being required to provide street access through newly constructed streets within the small subdivision. (The

DRC is a committee made up of representatives from various County departments. It enjoys decision-making power over certain questions. On other issues, it merely offers recommendations that may be accepted or rejected by the Board of County Commissioners. Where the DRC enjoys decision-making power, its decisions are subject to appeal to the Board of County Commissioners.) Does the DRC have the power to grant this request? If so, what considerations should inform its decision whether to exercise that power?

2.   Lot 1 (in the northwest corner of the plat) is 287 feet by 152 feet. It fronts on Franklin Road, which forms the western boundary of the property. Using the zoning code excerpts attached to this problem, what is the buildable area of this lot? How large a home could be built on it? Could the ultimate owner of the property operate an accounting business out of his or her home?

3.   Upon reviewing the drainage plan and site contour map submitted with the preliminary plat, the County planning staff notices that the site slopes down and away from the northeast corner of the parcel. Does this slope make the proposed location of the retention swales improper under the subdivision regulations?

4.   County environmental regulations prohibit the removal of certain tree species without a permit. The county therefore requires subdividers to conduct a survey of the trees on the property to be subdivided and to submit a mitigation plan explaining how the subdivider intends to protect trees from harm during the subdivision process and replace trees that the subdivider intends to remove. The survey of this property reveals hundreds of protected trees. Because many of the trees are located around the periphery of the property, and to minimize disruption to the trees, the Board of County Commissioners conditions its approval of the preliminary plat on Developer's agreement to meander the sidewalks and water retention swales around existing trees. The meander would add about 10% to the length of the sidewalk. Developer objects to the added cost this condition will entail. It seeks permission from the Board to dispense with the sidewalk altogether. The Board replies by insisting that Developer either build the sidewalk as specified in the conditions or pay a fee of $15 per foot (based on how long the Tangerine Woods sidewalk would be with the meandering design) into a County sidewalk fund, which the County may—at its discretion—use to build sidewalks around Tangerine Woods or elsewhere in the County.

   a.   What arguments would you make to the Board that Developer should not be obligated to build a sidewalk at all?

   b.   If the Board continues to insist on the sidewalk or payment of the fee as a condition of subdivision approval, what would your advice be to Developer concerning its obligation to pay the fee? Should Developer challenge the tree protection law? The demand that it build a sidewalk or pay the sidewalk fee? Which would be more likely to prevail?

5.   Under what circumstances would Developer be required to install a wall between the subdivision and Dora Drive, to the east?

6.   After obtaining preliminary plat approval for the subdivision design above, the real estate market in Orange County collapses. Developer no longer thinks there is a market in the short term for seven homes in this part of the County. Rather than throw good money after bad, it wishes to reduce the scope of the planned development, carving off three one-acre parcels in the northwest of the property to develop immediately, while reserving the remaining eight acres for future development. Instead of building the houses itself for resale, Developer plans merely to prepare the land for building, and to sell the subdivided land to a homebuilder. How would you advise Developer to proceed under the subdivision regulations? If the Developer does not want to commit to any development beyond three one-acre lots, how should it craft its proposed revision of the preliminary plat?

7.   Suppose Developer does submit a revised subdivision plan calling for the creation of three one-acre lots, with the remaining eight acres preserved for future development. In early 2010, the County approves the revised plan and, after receiving the necessary construction permits, Developer begins work preparing the three lots for development. By mid-2010, Developer has installed septic systems and driveways for the three lots and is getting ready to install water retention swales. In late 2010, the County amends its zoning code to require 3 acre minimum lot sizes in the RCE zone. Can the County apply this zoning amendment to Developer's three lots? To the remaining eight undeveloped acres?

8.   Assume the same facts as above in (7) except that, after receiving preliminary subdivision approval for the revised plan, Developer does nothing to actually prepare the three lots for development. Two years later, in early 2012, the County amends its zoning code to require 3 acre minimum lot sizes in the RCE zone. Can the County apply this zoning amendment to Developer's three lots? To the remaining eight undeveloped acres?

9.   Could the Board of County Commissioners deny subdivision approval because of the lack of municipal water and the consequent impact on fire department services? If the Board allows the development to proceed, what obligations should the Developer have to alert potential buyers of property within the subdivision about the quality of fire protection services?

10. Developer believes that a system of covenants restricting the land to residential uses and imposing certain design limitations would enhance the value of the property. Developer's market research shows that most new home buyers prefer to live in a community governed by a homeowners' association. In light of the small number of housing units involved, especially since the collapse of the housing market, how would you recommend that Developer proceed? Should it create a homeowners' association? Should it burden the entire property or just the portion it intends to subdivide and sell in the near future?

Subdivision Regulations

Sec. 34–4.—Purpose

This chapter was enacted by the board of county commissioners for the following purposes:

(1) To establish minimum standards of subdivision design.

(2) To ensure an adequate and efficient supply of utilities and services.

(3) To provide for safe and convenient vehicular and pedestrian traffic circulation.

(4) To promote the health, safety and general welfare.

(5) To minimize flooding and promote water management.

(6) To coordinate land development in accordance with the comprehensive policy plan (CCP) policies and other adopted rules and regulations.

(7) To help protect the natural and scenic resources of the county.

(8) To serve as one (1) of the several instruments of land use control authorized by the state legislature for the county.

(9) To ensure the adequate availability of affordable housing in Orange County through the utilization of the expedited permitting process, the housing incentive plan and any existing or adopted policies that encourage the provision of affordable housing units.

Sec. 34–7.—Compliance

(a) *General.* Within the jurisdiction of this chapter, no subdivision shall be made, platted, or recorded, nor shall any building permit be issued, unless such subdivision meets all the requirements of this chapter and has been approved in accordance with the requirements as herein provided. The board of county commissioners or any aggrieved person may have recourse to such remedies in law and equity as may be necessary to insure compliance with the provisions of this chapter, including injunctive relief to enjoin and restrain any person violating the provisions of this chapter, and any rules and regulations adopted under this chapter, and the court shall, upon proof of violation of this chapter have the duty to forthwith issue such temporary and permanent injunctions as are necessary to prevent the violation of this chapter.

(b) *Required improvements.* No subdivision occupancy shall be allowed until all of the improvements have been completed as required by this chapter.

(c) *Erection of buildings.* No building shall be erected on a lot or parcel of land subject to this chapter nor shall any building permit be issued therefor unless one (1) of the following conditions exists:

(1) Such lot or parcel is within a subdivision for which a plat has been recorded (except for a building authorized prior to

platting under section 30–83(b)), and the required improvements have been installed and accepted by the board of county commissioners. Buildings may be erected concurrently with the construction of the required improvements subject to compliance with section 34–133(d). No certificate of occupancy shall be issued until all the required improvements have been completed and duly certified to the board of county commissioners; or

(2) A variance has been granted pursuant to section 34–27.

(d) The provisions of section 34–7(c) shall not apply to the erection of agricultural buildings.

(e) *Violation.* Any person who shall sell any lot, or lay out, construct, open, or dedicate any street, sanitary sewer, storm sewer, water main or drainage structure without having first complied with provisions of this chapter, or otherwise violates this chapter, shall be punished as provided in section 1–9 of the County Code. Each day that the violation continues shall constitute a separate violation.

Sec. 34–27.—Variances to subdivision regulations

(a) Classification of variances.

(1) A request for a variance from the requirements of this chapter as part of a PSP approval shall be reviewed by the DRC.

(2) A proposed variance shall be classified and reviewed as follows:

     a. *Nonsubstantial variance.* A nonsubstantial variance from any of the technical requirements of this chapter may be approved, approved with conditions or denied by the DRC upon compliance with subsection (b) below. The DRC decision may be appealed to the board of county commissioners. The board of county commissioners shall hold a public hearing on the appealed DRC decision. If appealed, the public hearing procedures of section 34–69 shall be followed.

     b. *Substantial variance.* A substantial variance from any of the technical requirements of this chapter shall be reviewed by the DRC and a recommendation for approval, approval with conditions or denial shall be forwarded to the board of county commissioners. The board of county commissioners shall hold a public hearing on the variance request. The public hearing notice procedures set forth in section 34–69 shall be followed.

(3) The determination whether the variance is a substantial or nonsubstantial variance shall be made by the DRC based

upon the scope, nature, density/intensity, consistency with the CPP and location within the boundaries of the property of the proposed variance.

(b) *Review of request; grant.* The DRC may approve a request for a variance from the terms of this chapter when such variance will not be contrary to the public interest and where, owing to special conditions, a literal enforcement of the provisions of this chapter would result in unnecessary hardship. The granting of the variance requested shall not confer on the applicant any special privilege that is denied by this chapter to other lands, structures or required subdivision improvements under similar conditions. Under no circumstances may a nonsubstantial variance be granted if granting such a variance would affect or impact property outside the subdivision, including neighboring lands. No preexisting conditions of neighboring lands which are contrary to this chapter shall be considered grounds for the issuance of a variance. Such variance shall not be granted if it has the effect of nullifying the intent and purpose of these regulations. Furthermore, such variance shall not be granted unless and until:

(1) *Application.* A written application for a variance is submitted demonstrating one (1) of the following:

    a.   That special conditions and circumstances exist which are peculiar to the land, structures, or required subdivision improvements involved and which are not applicable to other lands, structures, or required subdivision improvements.

    b.   That a literal interpretation of the provisions of this chapter would deprive the applicant of rights commonly enjoyed by other properties with similar conditions.

    c.   That special conditions and circumstances exist and do not result from the actions of the applicant.

(2) *Findings.* To approve a variance request the DRC shall make findings that the requirements of this section have been met.

    a.   The DRC shall make a finding that the reasons set forth in the application justify the granting of the variance which would make possible the reasonable use of the land, buildings, or other improvements.

    b.   The DRC shall make further finding that the granting of the variance would be in harmony with the general purpose and intent of these regulations, will not be injurious to the surrounding territory, or otherwise be detrimental to the public welfare.

(3) *Conditions.* Appropriate conditions and safeguards in conformity with this chapter may be prescribed in the granting

of any variance. Violation of such conditions and safeguards, when made a part of the terms under which the variance is granted, shall be deemed a violation of this Code and chapter 30, article III of the County Code.

(4) *Board of county commissioners appeal.* Any decision denying a variance by the DRC may be appealed to the board of county commissioners.

Sec. 34–28.—Variances to zoning code (chapter 38)

(a) The board of county commissioners may grant a variance from the building requirements contained in chapter 38, zoning, which are either specifically listed in section 38–1501 for those districts listed therein or from the types of requirements contained in section 38–1501 for the UR, RCE–2 and RCE–5 Urban Village districts, provided a variance from the section 38–1501 type requirements:

(1) Affects more than one (1) lot; and

(2) May have an effect on the overall site development of the subdivision.

(b) A variance may be granted provided that such variance shall not be contrary to the public interest and where, owing to special conditions, a literal enforcement of the provisions of this chapter and/or the site and building requirements contained in section 38–1501 would result in unnecessary hardship. Such variance shall not be granted if it has the effect of nullifying the intent and purpose of these regulations and/or the site and building requirements contained in section 38–1501. Furthermore, such variance shall not be granted by the board of county commissioners unless and until:

(1) *Application.* A written application for a variance is submitted demonstrating:

    a.   That special conditions and circumstances exist which are peculiar to the land, structures or required improvements involved and which are not applicable to other lands, structures or required improvements.

    b.   That a literal interpretation of the provisions of chapter 34 and/or chapter 38 would deprive the applicant of rights commonly enjoyed by other properties with similar conditions.

    c.   That special conditions and circumstances exist and do not result from the actions of the applicant.

    d.   That the granting of the variance requested will not confer on the applicant any special privilege that is denied by this chapter to other lands, structures or required subdivision improvements under similar conditions. No preexisting conditions of neighboring lands which are contrary to this chapter shall be considered grounds for the issuance of a variance.

e.   That a variance from the provisions of section 38–1501 is in conjunction with either a proposed preliminary subdivision plan or change to an existing preliminary subdivision plan, where the requested variance promotes and makes possible the construction of the project, consistent with the goals of the county, and which would not substantially alter the character of the immediate vicinity. Further, such variance shall not alter the density/intensity of the property upon which the project is located such that the density/intensity upon the varied property would become inconsistent with either the zoning district or comprehensive policy plan.

(2) *Findings.* The board of county commissioners shall make findings that the requirements of this section have been met.

a.   A public hearing on the proposed variance is held. The public hearing may be held prior to or simultaneously with the public hearing for approval of the preliminary subdivision plan when a variance is requested prior to the preliminary subdivision plan approval. When the variance is a change to an approved preliminary subdivision plan, then a specific public hearing to review the variance requesting a change to the preliminary subdivision plan shall be held. The notice requirements of section 34–69 shall be followed.

Sec. 34–67.—Sufficiency review

(a) The developer shall submit to the development engineering division two (2) copies of the preliminary subdivision plan and the receipt for the required fee. This plan shall be prepared as specified in section 34–131 of these regulations.

(b) The county engineer, or authorized representative, shall review the plan for compliance with section 34–131. If pertinent information is missing on the preliminary subdivision plan, the development engineering division shall contact the developer or project engineer. The developer may be required to submit a revised preliminary subdivision plan. If the review by the development engineering division determines that the plan is sufficient, then twelve (12) additional copies shall be submitted to the development engineering division.

Sec. 34–68.—Reviewing agencies

(a) The development engineering division shall distribute copies of the preliminary subdivision plan to the DRC and other advisory staff. Members of the DRC and other interested agencies and departments shall submit written reports to the DRC chairman, who shall prepare a consolidated report. This report will be available in the development engineering division prior to the DRC meeting. Submittal of a written report shall not preclude additional comments at the DRC meeting.

(b) A meeting shall be scheduled between the DRC and the developer and his representatives to review the preliminary subdivision plan for consistency with the provisions of the County Code.

(c) If the review by the DRC determines that a revised plan is necessary, seven (7) copies of the revised plan shall be submitted to the development engineering division.

Sec. 34–69.—Public hearing scheduling

(a) After the DRC reviews the preliminary subdivision plan and makes a recommendation, the chairman of the DRC shall promptly request a public hearing before the board of county commissioners. The public hearing shall be advertised by the clerk of the board of county commissioners and shall be conducted as provided in chapter 30, article III of the County Code. In addition, at least ten (10) days prior to the date of public hearing before the board of county commissioners, the developer shall cause a poster or posters, furnished by the zoning or planning division, to be placed in a conspicuous and easily visible location on the property which is subject to the public hearing. The preliminary subdivision plan, supporting data, and a report from the DRC shall be submitted by the chairman of the DRC to the board of county commissioners at the hearing.

(b) If the plan is recommended for denial by the DRC, the applicant may request in writing, within fifteen (15) days, to the chairman of the DRC that the DRC recommendation not be forwarded to the board of county commissioners for review. The applicant, at his option, may withdraw the application or redesign and resubmit the application to the DRC for further review.

Sec. 34–70.—Action by the board of county commissioners

The board of county commissioners shall approve, approve subject to conditions, or disapprove the preliminary subdivision plan. In disapproving any preliminary subdivision plan, the board of county commissioners shall provide reasons for such action.

Sec. 34–73.—Expiration of approved preliminary subdivision plans and approved development plans

(a) Preliminary subdivision plan approval by the board of county commissioners shall automatically expire if subdivision construction plans are not submitted within one (1) year of preliminary subdivision plan approval and approved within two (2) years of preliminary subdivision plan approval except that the DRC may grant successive one-year extensions if the developer makes written request to the DRC chairman prior to the expiration date.

(b) Development plan approval by the DRC shall automatically expire if the subdivision construction plans are not submitted and approved within two (2) years of development plan (DP) approval by the DRC, except that the DRC may grant successive one (1) year extensions if the developer makes written request to the DRC chairman prior to the expiration date.

Sec. 34–74.—Amendment to preliminary subdivision plan

(a) Submittal and review of request. A request for an amendment to an approved PSP shall be submitted and reviewed in accordance with the provisions of sections 34–67, 34–68 and 34–69.

(b) The DRC shall determine whether the amendment is a substantial or nonsubstantial amendment to the PSP based upon the scope, nature, density/intensity and location of the amendment within the PSP.

> (1) A nonsubstantial amendment shall be reviewed and approved by the DRC.

> (2) A substantial amendment shall be processed, noticed and scheduled for hearing in accordance with the provisions of sections 34–68 and 34–69.

(c) If an applicant contests the DRC determination that a proposed amendment is a substantial change, the amendment shall be processed as a substantial amendment as set forth in subsection (b)(2) above; however, the applicant may present evidence at the public hearing as to why the amendment should be considered nonsubstantial.

(d) At the conclusion of the hearing on a substantial amendment, the board of county commissioners shall approve, approve with conditions or disapprove the amendment to the PSP. In disapproving the amendment to the PSP, the board of county commissioners shall provide reasons for such action. In those situations when the applicant has contested the DRC finding that an amendment is substantial, the board of county commissioners shall also make a finding based on the evidence presented at the hearing whether the proposed amendment is substantial or nonsubstantial.

Sec. 34–91.—General standards

The subdivision construction plans shall conform substantially to the preliminary subdivision plan as approved and may constitute only that phase of the approved preliminary subdivision plan and other necessary improvements which the developer proposes to record and develop. They shall also conform to all requirements of this chapter and any other applicable provisions of the Orange County Code. In seeking approval of the construction plans, a request for a non-substantial variance of the technical requirements of either this chapter or the PSP approval may be approved, approved with conditions, or denied by the county engineer. The county engineer's decision may be appealed to the

DRC, which shall consider the appeal pursuant to the procedure set forth in section 34–27.

Sec. 34–131.—Preliminary subdivision plan and supporting data

(a) *General.* The preliminary subdivision plan shall include the information listed in this section. Notes should be used whenever possible on the preliminary subdivision plan to explain, verify or identify additional information that is important to the understanding of the site and the plan of development. All property being subdivided shall have the appropriate zoning for the land uses being proposed. The preliminary subdivision plan shall be submitted on twenty-four-inch vertical by thirty-six-inch wide sheets.

(b) *Legend and supporting data.* The legend and supporting data of the preliminary subdivision plan shall include:

(1) Title and date of plan.

(2) Name, address, telephone number, FAX and e-mail of the owner/developer (if other than owner), surveyor, engineer and other consultants.

(3) Letter with notarized signature from property owner authorizing the application if owner is not applicant.

(4) Scale of the plan (preferably one (1) inch equals one hundred (100) feet) and north arrow.

(5) Location map showing the site in relation to existing roads, access points and developments.

(6) Legal description and property appraiser's tax identification number of the tract to be subdivided and the approximate acreage.

(7) All contiguous property under ownership or control of the applicant shall be shown, described or noted on the preliminary plan. In some instances, a conceptual master plan may be required where the size or character of the area would dictate a unified planning approach.

(8) Boundary of the tract shown by a heavy line.

(9) The existing zoning, the proposed minimum lot size and width, the proposed residential, commercial and industrial land use type and the residential density.

(10) Names of all abutting subdivisions and location of adjoining platted lots and parcel lines within one hundred (100) feet (if unplatted, so state).

(11) Existing utility transmission and drainage systems, easements and improvements including buildings located on the tract.

(12) Adjacent zoning districts including zoning on opposite side of right-of-way.

(13) All requests for variances shall be noted on plan with appropriate County Code reference and justification.

(14) Number of lots.

(15) Number of dwelling units and the projected school age population.

(16) Lot lines, scaled dimensions and lot numbers.

(17) Where more than one (1) setback applies to a lot, the greater setback distance shall apply.

   a.   Illustrate all setbacks from streets and highways as indicated in chapter 38, article XV of the County Code.

   b.   Indicate by the use of notes the applicable setbacks for the zoning district.

   c.   Illustrate all setbacks on irregular shaped lots.

   d.   Illustrate the fifty-foot building setback from the normal high water elevation of all surface water bodies. Where the normal high water elevation has not been established, the project engineer shall establish it to the satisfaction of the county engineer, prior to subdivision construction plan submission.

   e.   Illustrate the one-hundred-fifty-foot septic tank setback from the normal high-water elevation (NHWE) for all surface water bodies and seventy-five-foot setback from the control elevation for all artificial water bodies.

(18) Approximate phasing of the project, if applicable.

(19) Location of all sites for multifamily, commercial, industrial, utility, institutional or recreational uses and other public and nonpublic uses exclusive of single-family residential lots.

(20) Recreation facilities (to be owned and maintained by a mandatory homeowners association) with the following data:

   a.   Identify the tract(s) proposed for recreation use.

   b.   Type and location of all proposed recreational facilities.

   c.   Setback from all property lines.

   d.   Access and parking.

   e.   Exterior lighting plan (if proposed).

   f.   Landscape and buffer plan.

(c)   To provide flexibility regarding types of facilities to be provided, the following groups shall be established. Uses or their equivalents within a group can be interchangeable and would not require additional review:

Group A: Tennis courts, basketball courts, volleyball courts or other hard court uses.

Group B: Swimming pools, spas.

Group C: Picnic areas, trails, exercise courses, beaches.

Group D: Playfields, playgrounds, tot-lots.

If the recreation facilities are not shown on the preliminary subdivision plan, board of zoning adjustment (BZA) review of these facilities shall be required for conventionally zoned (not planned development) property.

(1)   *Landscape plan.* All preliminary subdivision plans submitted after October 1, 2010, shall include a landscape plan. The landscape plan design for any common or recreation areas lots within the subdivision, but not including stormwater management areas, shall:

a.   Contain no more than sixty (60) percent turf, as defined in section 24–2 of this Code, based upon the total square footage of landscaped and irrigated common areas, but not including qualified retention ponds and stormwater conveyance systems; provided however, that no more than sixty (60) percent of the landscaping on individual residential lots may be turf; and

b.   Conform to the submittal requirements set forth in chapter 24 of this Code.

(2)   In no case shall a landscape plan incorporate the use of prohibited invasive exotic plant species as described in F.S. (2009) § 581.091.

(3)   The landscape plan shall contain certification by the landscape architect or other qualified professional, whichever is appropriate, that the landscape is designed in compliance with this Code. The certification shall be stated directly on the preliminary subdivision plan and shall be submitted to the county as a component of the initial submittal of the preliminary subdivision plan. Furthermore, the landscape plan shall contain certification by the developer that the landscape plan will hereafter be maintained in compliance with this Code and that such maintenance obligations shall be included in the deed restrictions associated with the subdivision.

(4)   The following are exempt from the requirements of chapter 24 of this Code and from this section:

a. Development applications involving one (1) single-family residence or a duplex residential project, on either a single lot or parcel; and

b. Bona fide agricultural activities as defined in the Florida Right to Farm Act (F.S. (2009) § 823.14) provided that fertilizers are applied in accordance with the appropriate best management practices manual adopted by the Florida Department of Agriculture and Consumer Services, Office of Agricultural Water Policy for the crop in question.

(5) Nothing in this article shall be construed to prohibit or be enforced to prohibit any property owner from implementing county-approved low impact development techniques for stormwater management and capture or Florida friendly landscaping on his/her land.

(d) *Physical/environmental conditions.* The following physical and environmental conditions shall be shown on the preliminary subdivision plan:

(1) Existing contours at one-foot intervals based on field surveys or photogrammetric surveys using county datum for the tract to be subdivided. In order to properly assess the drainage impact that the proposed project will have on adjacent properties, the survey shall be extended a minimum of two hundred fifty (250) feet beyond the tract boundary onto adjacent parcels. (Extension across open roadways is not required.) If contours are based upon a field survey, it shall be certified by a land surveyor.

(2) An approved conservation area determination with the identification of all conservation areas.

(3) One-hundred-year flood elevation data for all developments within Zone A as indicated on the county flood insurance rate map, as amended, prepared by the federal emergency management agency. Where the 100-year flood elevation has not been established, the project engineer shall conduct the necessary drainage basin studies to establish the 100-year flood elevation to the satisfaction of the county engineer.

(4) Indicate disposition of any existing structure on-site.

(e) *Required improvements.* The following improvements shall be required and shall be indicated on the preliminary subdivision plans:

(1) *Streets:*

a. The following information shall be provided for existing streets:

1.   The name, location and right-of-way width of all existing streets, access points, rights-of-way and platted streets within five hundred (500) feet in each direction of the proposed entrance to the proposed subdivision;

2.   Right-of-way and setback requirements in chapter 38, article XV of the County Code.

b.   The following information shall be provided for proposed streets:

1.   The name or temporary designation and right-of-way width.

2.   A typical design cross section indicating pavement type, width, drainage features and sidewalks/bikeways. Separate cross sections for all entrance roads featuring medians.

3.   The projected average daily traffic (ADT) from the development based upon trip generation rates contained in the most recent edition of the Institute of Transportation Engineers (ITE) Manual, unless other standards are justified and approved.

4.   Proposed access improvements.

c.   Note explaining any proposed vacation of rights-of-way or easements.

(2) *Water and wastewater systems.* The proposed method and source of water supply and wastewater disposal shall be shown. The developer shall show the points of connection to the existing systems and a schematic layout of the proposed system. If the source is other than Orange County, a letter shall be submitted from the appropriate utility company, confirming that service can be provided. If on-site sewage disposal systems are proposed, supporting calculations shall be provided according to subsection 34–207(2).

(3) *Stormwater management.* A stormwater management plan will be provided with a schematic diagram of the proposed stormwater collection system, method of pollution control and stormwater retention/detention with preliminary calculations as to pond sizing. The direction of flow for all surface drainage and existing storm sewers on or abutting the tract shall be shown. Stormwater retention/detention areas shall be designated as "tracts."

(4) *Screen walls.* Show location of all screen walls which comply with section 34–209. Maintenance responsibility shall

be indicated, but in no case will it be the responsibility of the county.

(5) *Easements.* Show the location, width, purpose and maintenance responsibilities for all proposed easements, facilities, or rights-of-way other than for streets.

(6) *Borrow operations.* If it is anticipated that a borrow operation for export off-site will be undertaken as part of the project, it should be noted on the plans and preliminary grades and quantities shown. An excavation permit (pursuant to chapter 16, Orange County Code) will be required for material removed from the site.

(7) *Finish grade change.* If it is anticipated that finished grades for lots at the perimeter of the property, excluding rights-of-way, will vary more than one (1) foot above or below existing grades, it shall be noted on the preliminary subdivision plan. If the subdivision construction plans result in exceeding these limits without being noted on the preliminary subdivision plan, it shall constitute a substantial change requiring a public hearing.

(8) *Recreation areas/parks.* All recreation areas/parks shall be identified.

(f) *Individual on-site sewage disposal systems (OSDS).* The applicant for any subdivision proposed for development utilizing an OSDS shall submit as part of the preliminary subdivision plan submittal the following soils information prepared by a geotechnical engineer registered to practice in the State of Florida:

(1) At least one (1) boring, a minimum of seven (7) feet deep, for each four (4) lots for residential subdivisions or for each acre proposed for development. The county may require a greater number of soil borings than specified in the preceding sentence in the event that the on-site soils associations are classified as severe by the Soil Conservation Service of the U.S. Department of Agriculture. The county may permit a fewer number of borings where large parcel development is proposed. These borings shall be located throughout the project to provide an accurate characterization of soils and water table conditions.

(2) The following information shall be provided for each boring location:

a. Depth, extent and description of each soil type encountered, consistent with unified soils classification system, and relative density;

b. Depth of water table measured from natural grade; and

c.   Determination of wet season elevation before development.

(3) Sufficient soil samples shall be taken and tested to verify visual soil classifications.

(4) A pre- and post-development groundwater contour map of estimated wet season water table shall be provided together with an indication of direction of flow, flow from off-site and influence upon downstream areas.

(5) A report which summarizes results of investigations, evaluation of soil and groundwater condition for both pre- and post-development conditions, and a statement pertaining to suitability to support an OSDS and special requirements for use of an OSDS including, but not limited to, the following:

a.   Lot sizing in view of soil and water table conditions;

b.   Removal and replacement of marginal low permeability soil underlying the proposed absorption bed area;

c.   Delineation of the need to elevate proposed drainfield areas;

d.   Filling and grading requirements to accomplish a separation of two (2) feet between the bottom of the absorption bed to the estimated wet season water table.

(6) On a site-specific basis, additional information may be required by the county to enable a complete evaluation of conditions.

Sec. 34–151.—General considerations

(a) *Suitability for use.* All lands included within the subdivision shall be suitable for the various purposes proposed in the request for subdivision approval. Further, no subdivision plan shall be approved unless the board of county commissioners finds, after full consideration of all pertinent data, that the subdivision can be served adequately and economically with such normal public facilities and services as are suitable in the circumstances of the particular case.

(b) *Conformance with county policy.* The subdividing and development of any areas subject to this chapter shall conform to the adopted general goals and objectives of the board of county commissioners with respect to the physical development of the county as set forth in various elements of the county comprehensive policy plan, the Orange County Code, and any other applicable adopted ordinances, resolutions and regulations.

Sec. 34–152.—Lots and blocks

(a) *Lot size.* The minimum lot size in a subdivision shall be determined based on the potable water source and wastewater system provided in the subdivision as stated in sections 34–206 and 34–207, respectively, provided that lot dimensions and size shall not be less than the minimum established in chapter 38 of the Orange County Code (zoning).

(b) *Corner lots.* Corner lots shall be at least ten (10) feet greater in width than the minimum established in chapter 38 of the Orange County Code (zoning). Where the minimum width established in chapter 38 exceeds ninety-five (95) feet, no additional width shall be required.

(c) *Access.* Each lot and tract interior to the subdivision shall have a minimum access width of twenty (20) feet to a dedicated public paved street, except in gated communities covered by article VIII of this chapter. The subdivision shall be so designed that remnants and landlocked areas within the subdivision are not created, except access may not be required to parcels identified as conservation areas. All lots shall have access from an internal subdivision street. Access rights to external roads from individual lots shall be dedicated to Orange County. Lots shall not be approved with access on an unpaved right-of-way or with access by any type of easement.

(d) *Flag type lots.* Flag lots shall be designed to minimize safety problems. No more than two (2) flag lots should be located adjacent to each other. The minimum lot width for the narrow extension of the lot to the right-of-way shall be twenty (20) feet.

(e) *Lot lines.* Side lot lines shall be, as nearly as practical, at right angles to straight street lines and radial to curved street lines. In subdivisions which overlap municipal or county boundaries, lot lines shall follow the boundary lines.

Sec. 34–206.—Potable Water and Fire Protection

(a) The development of new facilities and mains and the expansion of existing water systems shall be designed by the engineer in accordance with all applicable state and local criteria.

(1) Water systems designed for connection to or inclusion within the county water system shall be in accordance with the Manual of Standards and Specifications for Wastewater and Water Main Construction.

(2) No construction plans for connection to the county system shall be approved until capacity has been obtained subject to ordinances and applicable agreements.

(b) Where a central water system is required, the system shall be designed and constructed to satisfy the domestic potable, irrigation and fire flow requirements.

(c) Individual potable water supply systems may be permitted when the requirement for a central water system is waived under one (1) of the following conditions, subject to the approval of the Orange County Health Department and other regulatory agencies:

(1) Subdivisions with lots forty-three thousand five hundred sixty (43,560) square feet (one (1) acre) in area or more.

(2) Subdivisions with lots twenty-one thousand seven hundred eighty (21,780) square feet (one-half (½) acre) in area or more, if the subdivision contains fifty (50) lots or less, if such lots have a minimum dimension of one hundred (100) feet, and if satisfactory groundwater can be obtained and all distance and setbacks, soil conditions, water table elevations and other related requirements of F.A.C. chapter 17–22 are met. It is not the intent of this provision to allow sequential development of contiguous subdivisions under single ownership.

(d) Rural fire protection. Multifamily, commercial and industrial/warehousing developments outside the urban service area, where no central water system is available, shall provide either an on-site stored water supply that complies with codes and standards or an alternate method of fire protection that is approved by the county fire official. When required by the county fire official, certain high-risk developments shall provide fire hydrants and other urban fire protection features.

Sec. 34–209.—Roadway screen walls

A six-foot high masonry wall shall be provided to separate residential subdivisions from all adjacent roadways whose average daily traffic volumes are projected to exceed eight thousand (8,000) vehicles within five (5) years of the date of approval of the preliminary subdivision plan. The wall shall not be located within roadway right-of-way.

Sec. 34–226.—Required features

A stormwater management system shall be designed and installed for the development that will contain features to provide for:

(1) *Pollution abatement.* Pollution abatement will be accomplished by retention, or detention with filtration, of one-half (½) inch of runoff from the developed site or the runoff generated from the first one (1) inch of rainfall on the developed site, whichever is greater. The depth of runoff generated from the first inch of rainfall shall be estimated by multiplying the Rational Method Runoff Coefficient (C) for the developed site by one (1) inch of rainfall.

(2) *Recharge where possible.* Recharge in designated areas where the soils are compatible (Hydrologic Soil Group Type "A" soils as indicated on the soils survey map for the county prepared by the U.S.D.A. Soil Conservation Service) will be accomplished by providing for retention of the total runoff generated by a 25-year frequency, 24-hour duration storm event from the developed site. Where a positive outfall is not available, the site shall be designed to retain 100-year frequency/24-hour duration storm on-site.

(3) *Protection from flooding.* Protection from flooding will be accomplished by a design which will provide that:

    a.   The postdevelopment peak rate of discharge permitted from the site will not exceed the predevelopment peak rate of discharge from the site during a 25-year frequency/24-hour duration storm event.

    b.   All residential structures are to be floodfree and all commercial and industrial structures are to be either floodfree or floodproofed (see section 34–228).

Sec. 34–230.—Lot grading and building pad elevation

(a) The lot grading plan shall ensure that stormwater is discharged from each lot to an approved collection system.

(b) The minimum acceptable grade for lots smaller than one (1) acre shall be one (1) percent.

(c) The lot grading plans shall show the elevation of the top of the curb in front of the lot, all property corners and the finished floor.

(d) For lots one-quarter (¼) acre or less, the building envelope must be shown for each lot.

Zoning Law

DIVISION 6.—R–CE COUNTRY ESTATE DISTRICT

Sec. 38–376.—Intent and purpose of district.

Sec. 38–377.—Permitted uses.

Sec. 38–378.—Prohibited uses.

Sec. 38–379.—Special exceptions.

Sec. 38–380.—Site and building requirements.

Sec. 38–381.—Off-street parking.

Secs. 38–382—38–400.—Reserved.

Sec. 38–376.—Intent and purpose of district

The purpose of the country estate district is to establish areas where very low residential densities may be maintained and where investment in homes will be protected from the adverse effects sometimes found in agricultural districts. This district is primarily residential. However, certain uses found only in agricultural districts may be permitted as special exceptions.

Sec. 38–377.—Permitted uses

A use shall be permitted in the R–CE district if the use is identified by the letter "P" in the use table set forth in section 38–77.

Sec. 38–378.—Prohibited uses

A use shall be prohibited in the R–CE district if the space for that use is blank in the use table set forth in section 38–77.

Sec. 38–379.—Special exceptions

(a) A use shall be permitted as a special exception in the R–CE district if the use is identified by the letter "S" in the use table set forth in section 38–77.

(b) Each application for a special exception shall be accompanied by a site plan incorporating the regulations established herein. The site plan shall be drawn to scale indicating property lines, rights-of-way, and the location of buildings, parking areas, curb cuts, and driveways. The site plan shall be submitted to and approved by the board of zoning adjustment prior to the granting of a land use and building permit. Upon such approval, the site plan becomes a part of the land use and building permit and may be amended only by the board of zoning adjustment.

Sec. 38–77.—Uses Per Zoning Code	RCE
Single-family and modular homes with customary accessory uses	P
Principal residence and accessory buildings in excess of size requirements outlined in Condition 114	S
Accessory buildings, uses and structures	P
Screen rooms	P
Screen enclosures	P
Home occupations	P
Temporary mobile homes, travel trailers and recreational vehicles	PS
Chimneys, water & fire towers, church spires, domes, cupolas, stage towers, scenery lofts, cooling towers, elevator bulkheads, smokestacks, flagpoles, and parapet walls	PS
Family foster homes	P
Accessory dwelling unit	S
Swimming pools, jacuzzies, tennis courts, spas, hot tubs, including appurtenances to such uses	P

Community residential homes (max. 6 clients)	P
Family lot provision	S
Guest house	S
Zero side yard development	
Adult/child day care homes	S
Family day care homes	P
Adult/child day care centers	S
Tents	P
Model homes	P
RV or boat storage and parking (residential only)	P
Truck farms	S
Citrus and fruit crops cultivation	P
Commercial plant nurseries and greenhouses (no retailing)	P
Poultry raising or keeping	P
Raising or keeping of cows, horses & ponies for domestic purposes	SP
Parking and storage of dual rear wheel vehicles	P
Limousine service, home-based	PS
Temporary portable storage containers	P
Post office	S
Marinas, commercial boat rentals, airboat rides	S
Airports, airplane landing facilities, aircraft maintenance, seaplane base	S
Helicopter landing facility, Vertiport, airship/blimp hanger facility and hangars	S
Pipeline transportation of petroleum and other commodities, underground pipeline unless required to be above ground due to physical conditions	S
Guyed (Ord. No. 95–23, § 2 8–29–95)	S
Monopole (Ord. No. 95–25, § 2, 8–29–95)	P/S
Substations, telephone switching stations	S
Electrical, gas, sanitary services	S
Temporary sales of Christmas trees, sparklers, and pumpkins	P
Retail sale of products by TV, catalog, mail order, telephone, vending machines, or from other temporary locations	P
Cemeteries, mausoleums	S

Bed and breakfast homestay	S
Parking lots & parking garages for office, commercial or industrial uses	
Stadiums in conjunction with schools	S
Golf courses	S
Indoor clubs, bowling clubs, private indoor clubs, bridge clubs, indoor recreational uses	S
Outdoor clubs, gold and country clubs, private outdoor clubs, tennis clubs, swimming clubs, nonprofit parks and recreation areas, outdoor recreation uses, private recreation areas for single family development	S
Golf driving ranges, golf cart rentals, ski instruction, swimming pools, tennis courts, little league and softball fields, outdoor skating rinks, amusement rides, paintball operations, day camps, rodeos, and go-cart raceway	S
Private kindergarten, elementary, junior high, middle and high schools	S
Charter schools	S
Community centers	S
Churches, mosques, synagogues, temples and other religious institutions with or without attendant schools, educational buildings and/or recreational facilities	S
Highway patrols, sheriffs offices, police depts	P
Fire stations	P
Uses of national defense	S

Zoning Ordinance
Article XII—Site and Building Requirements

District	Min. lot area (sq. ft.) †††	Min. living area (sq. ft.)	Min. lot width (ft.)	*Min. front yard (ft.)	*Min. rear yard (ft.)	Min. side yard (ft.)	Max. building height (ft.)
A–1	21,780 (½ acre)	850	100	35	50	10	35
A–2	21,780 (½ acre)	850	100	35	50	10	35
A–R	108,900 (2½ acres)	1,000	270	35	50	25	35
R–CE	43,560 (1 acre)	1,500	130	35	50	10	35

R–CE–2	2 acres	1,200	250	45	50	30	35
R–CE–5	5 acres	1,200	185	50	50	45	35
R–1AAAA	21,780 (¹/₂ acre)	1,500	110	30	35	10	35
R–1AAA	14,520 (¹/₃ acre)	1,500	95	30	35	10	35
R–1AA	10,000	1,200	85	25‡	30‡	7.5	35
R–1A	7,500	1,200	75	20‡	25‡	7.5	35
R–1	5,000	1,000	50	20‡	20‡	5‡	35
R–2	One-family dwelling, 4,500	1,000	45*****	20‡	20‡	5‡	35

PROBLEM TWO: SUBURBAN MULTI-FAMILY HOUSING

Developer has purchased an 80,000 square foot parcel (about two acres) in a manufacturing district. The parcel had previously been used in a manufacturing operation that discharged petroleum products into the ground; that operation shut down a decade ago, and the parcel has largely been vacant since that time. There is no demand for manufacturing uses on the site.

Because of the parcel's proximity to public transportation, Developer wants to build residential housing on the site. The parcel is roughly triangular in shape. The hypotenuse of the triangle lies on a modest river (with some warehouse buildings on the other side). On the parcel's northern boundary is a paved street. A few modest one and two-family homes are located directly across the street from the parcel; as the road crosses the river and moves further west, a number of warehouse and industrial buildings line the street. On the east, the parcel borders the back of several retail buildings. There is, however, a pedestrian pathway just south of the retail buildings that tracks the river and that provides access to a major retail street and, ultimately, to the railroad station one-half mile away.

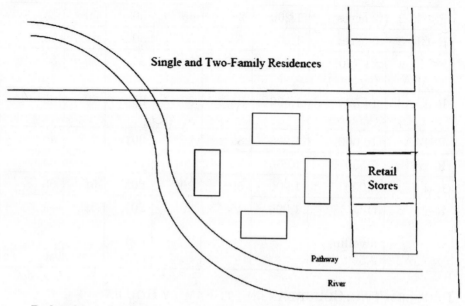

Redevelopment of the parcel will be costly and risky for Developer. The environmental cleanup costs will be significant. No one has yet built multi-family housing in the area, so Developer will be a bit of a pioneer. To recoup her costs, and to obtain compensation for the risks she is taking, Developer wants to build as many units as possible, and also wants to maximize the market value of the units. Ideally, Developer wants to build four separate apartment buildings, each with 32 apartments averaging 1,200 square feet in size. Developer expects these apartments would sell for an average of $200,000.

Developer regularly contributes substantial amounts to campaigns for local legislators (including many of the current members of the village board of trustees). Developer expects that the immediate neighbors will express concerns about traffic, that municipal officials will be concerned about additional burdens on schools and other public facilities, and that other community residents will complain about changes in the character of the community generated by large multi-family housing developments.

In addressing the following questions, assume that the municipality's zoning ordinance includes the provisions that immediately follow question (10).

1. Developer understands that residential uses are not permitted in a manufacturing district, and she consults you about what steps she would need to take to make her development zoning compliant. Advise her about her alternatives, and indicate which alternative you would recommend.

2. Suppose Developer proposes a zoning amendment (1) to create a new RM–4 district that would permit an FAR of 2.0, a maximum building height of 6 stories, and a maximum building coverage of .40, and (2) to place her parcel within the RM–4 district. What steps would you take to persuade the village board to enact the amendment? What arguments would you make in support of the amendment?

3. Suppose now that you serve as the municipal attorney. Members of the board see new residential development as a potential source of tax revenue, and are enthusiastic about the prospect that this polluted and dilapidated site might be cleaned up. They are also favorably disposed to Developer, because of her campaign contributions and her sponsorship of various community charities. At the same time, board members are concerned about the potential impact of an influx of school-age children, about the density in the proposed RM–4 district, and about the precedential effect of creating a new district. (Until now, the board has consistently resisted efforts to increase the density permissible in residential, multi-family developments). The board asks you (a) whether the ordinance can limit, directly or indirectly, the number of school-age children who live in buildings located in an RM–4 district; and (b) whether there is any possibility that residential development might proceed even if the board does not enact the amendment. Advise the board on both issues.

4. Assume the board of trustees decides to go forward with the proposed amendment. What procedural steps must the board take in order to enact the amendment? If the board tells Developer it will only go forward after preparation of an environmental impact statement, and insists that Developer prepare and pay for the statement, what advice would you give to Developer?

5. Suppose that after the environmental impact statement is prepared, the board enacts the amendment. A group of neighbors have approached you about their alternatives. They note that the board never provided reasons for approving the amendment. The neighbors' primary concern is preventing Developer's development; they are less concerned about legal doctrine. What course of action would you advise the neighbors to follow, and why?

6. Suppose now that the board of trustees declines to enact the proposed amendment. The board has made it clear that it will not enact any text amendment that would create a new zoning district. At the same time, in light of the absence of demand for manufacturing uses, the board will consider a map amendment that places Developer's land into another district. Developer would like to have the parcel placed into the district that would permit the most intensive residential development. What relief should Developer seek?

7. Assume the board of trustees, complying with all necessary procedures, enacts an amendment placing Developer's parcel in an RM–3 zone. Developer scales back the proposed development to three buildings, each with 30 units, averaging 1,200 square feet each. Does the proposed development comply with the requirements in an RM–3 zone? If yes, must the director of buildings issue a building permit for the proposed buildings? If no, what further steps must Developer take before obtaining a building permit?

8. Developer now prepares a site plan and seeks approval from the village planning board. At a hearing before the planning board, members of the public and members of the board express concern about the following issues:

    a.   traffic studies indicate that if all 90 units are built, drivers using the abutting street will endure delays of one to two minutes each during rush hours, and the likelihood is great that the incidence of traffic accidents in the area will increase.

    b.   amidst the manufacturing plant and the polluted ground, two 100-year old beech trees managed to survive; Developer's site plan would remove both of them to achieve optimal layout of the buildings.

    c.   because the river blocks one side of each of the proposed buildings from any road or driveway, fire trucks have no way to obtain access to apartments located on the river side of the buildings.

    d.   Developer's proposed development would impose a significant burden on the existing sewer mains running through the street abutting the parcel; as a result, residents in the area might occasionally suffer backups during peak usage periods.

Is the planning board entitled to invoke any or all of these grounds as a basis for denying landowner's application for site plan approval? Suppose the planning board informs Developer of its reservations about approving the project. Developer seeks advice about how to respond. What advice would you give to Developer?

9. Suppose that, after examining the site plan, the planning board would like Developer to construct a public walkway along the riverfront, and would also like Developer to dedicate 20 of the project's 90 units to construction of below-market-rate housing (which would significantly reduce Developer's expected return from the project). Does the planning board have power to mandate the walkway or the below-market-rate housing? If the planning board made Developer's compliance with either or both requests a condition of its approval, what advice would you give to Developer?

Would your advice be the same if the planning board imposed these conditions in exchange for overlooking problems with fire access or traffic congestion?

10. Assume Developer obtains site plan approval, and begins construction of the first building. Midway through construction of that building, the market for residential construction softens. Developer holds off on construction of the other buildings, hoping to sell some of the units in the initial building before incurring new construction costs. Meanwhile, several anti-development candidates win election to the board now seeks to prevent development of the remaining two buildings, and seeks your advice. What options, if any, are open to the board? If you represent Developer, what steps would you advise that she take to protect herself?

ARTICLE V.   RESIDENTIAL DISTRICT REGULATIONS

§ 342–20.   General provision and references

The following are the only uses permitted in residence districts. See Article XI for uses subject to site plan approval. See Article IV for general regulations applying to all districts.

§ 342–24.   Multiple Residence Districts

A. Permitted principal uses. The following are the only principal uses permitted in RM–1, RM–2 and RM–3 Multiple Residence Districts:

  (1) Any uses permitted in a one-family residence district, as permitted therein.

  (2) Dwellings or dwelling groups for three or more families, provided that the entire lot occupied by such dwellings or dwelling groups shall be maintained in single ownership.

  (3) Professional offices or studios, provided that the number of such offices and studios on any lot shall not exceed one for each 25 dwelling units on the lot, and provided that such offices or studios shall be located only on the street floor of any building and shall have access provided thereto from other than a public hall used by residential apartments.

B. Permitted accessory uses. The following accessory uses are permitted in RM–1, RM–2 and RM–3 Multiple Residence Districts only in conjunction with a permitted principal use:

  (1) Any accessory uses permitted in a one-family residence district, as permitted therein.

Schedule of Minimum Requirements for Residential Districts

District	Minimum Lot Area	Maximum Building Height	Maximum Lot Coverage	Maximum FAR
RM–1	40,000 sq. ft	2 stories/35 feet	25%	.5
RM–2	20,000 sq. ft	3 stories/40 feet	30%	1.0
RM–3	20,000 sq. ft.	4 stories/50 feet	35%	1.5

ARTICLE VI.   NONRESIDENTIAL DISTRICT REGULATIONS

§ 342–28.   General provision and references

The following are the only uses permitted in business and industrial districts. See Article XI for uses subject to site plan approval. See Article IV for general regulations applying to all districts.

§ 342–30.   General Commercial Districts

A.   Permitted principal uses.

(1)   The following are the only principal uses permitted in the C–1 General Commercial Districts:

(a)   Business, professional and government offices and banks.

(b)   Retail stores and personal service stores, except those specifically mentioned hereinafter, provided that the area used for sales or personal service purposes does not exceed 3,000 square feet.

(c)   Retail stores and personal service stores, except those specifically mentioned hereinafter, in which the area used for sales or personal service purposes exceeds 3,000 square feet. (This use is subject to the approval procedure set forth in Article X and shall conform to any additional requirements made in connection with such approval.)

(d)   Outlets and pickup stations for laundries and cleaning establishments dealing directly with the public

(e)   Restaurants.

(f)   Funeral establishments.

(g)   Motor vehicle filling/service stations or public garages.

(h)   Motor vehicle sales and rental agencies, with sale of used motor vehicles limited to those traded in on new motor vehicles sold on the premises.

(i)   Residence uses as permitted by § 342–50.

(2)   None of the above uses shall be interpreted as including motor vehicle storage or repair; wholesaling, warehousing or storage; manufacturing, assembling, converting, altering, finishing or any other industrial operation; check-cashing establishments (not including a full-service bank where check cashing is an accessory use); video arcades, betting parlors, billiard or pool parlors or tattoo parlors; unattended businesses (a business with no owner or employee on the premises); or establishments conducting business or the practice of trade as mediums, clairvoyants, soothsayers, fortune-tellers, palmists, reader-advisors or the like.

§ 342–31.   Central Commercial Districts

A. Permitted principal uses.

(1) The following are the only principal uses permitted in C–2 Central Commercial Districts. All uses except those specified in subparagraph (a) are subject to the approval procedure set forth in Article X and shall conform to any additional requirements made in connection with such approval:

(a) Uses permitted in C–1 Districts, as permitted therein.

(b) Theaters, places of public assembly or other places of amusement.

(c) Clubs, without restrictions as to general use and commercial activities.

(d) Residence uses as permitted by § 342–50.

(e) Light manufacturing, assembling, converting, altering, finishing, cleaning or other processing, subject to § 342–47, and provided that goods so produced or processed are to be sold at retail, exclusively on the premises.

Schedule of Minimum Requirements for Non-Residential Districts

District	Minimum Lot Area	Maximum Building Height	Maximum Lot Coverage	Maximum FAR
C–1	None	3 stories/40 feet	50%	1.0
C–2	None	4 stories/45 feet	None	2.0
M–1	10,000 sq. ft	3 stories/45 feet	50%	1.0

ARTICLE VII. STANDARDS FOR USES SUBJECT TO SPECIAL PERMIT PROCEDURES

§ 342–50.   Residence uses in commercial districts

A. Residence uses in C–1 Districts shall meet the following standards:

(1) Site size. The infill provision for housing in C–1 Districts shall apply only to sites under 40,000 square feet, unless a site is to be utilized for below-market housing in accordance with Article XV of this chapter. In cases of the provision of below-market housing, there shall be no restriction on site size.

(2) Floor area ratio. The permitted total floor area ratio (FAR) shall not exceed 0.80. The Planning Board may increase the FAR to 1.0 in accordance with the provisions of Article XV of this chapter for below-market housing.

(3) Height, setback and yard controls. Zoning envelope controls shall be as follows:

(a) Minimum lot width and frontage: 50 feet.

(b) Minimum lot depth: 100 feet.

(c) Minimum habitable floor area (per unit): 450 square feet.

(d) Maximum stories: three.

(e) Maximum height: 40 feet.

(f) Maximum coverage: 30%.

(4) Special permit criteria. The infill housing provision within C–1 Zones shall be allowed only through a special permit granted by the Planning Board. No such permit shall issue unless the following requirements are met, in addition to those of Article X hereof:

(a) Separate entrances. The residentially used portion of any structure shall have an entrance or entrances which do not require access through any nonresidentially used area, other than a common lobby or plaza. The location and design of such entrances shall be subject to approval by the Planning Board as part of the required special permit application.

(b) Reserved parking. Parking for the residences of any mixed structure shall be in a separate lot or in a reserved section of the parking area, which reserved section must be adequately marked, landscaped and otherwise demarcated from commercial parking. For any or all buildings, the Planning Board may require additional parking for visitors up to 15% more than required in Article VIII.

(c) Compatibility of use. The Planning Board shall allow infill housing above commercial uses or in conjunction with commercial uses only if such uses are found to be compatible with such housing. The Planning Board shall consider noise, smell pollution, hours of operation and expected traffic volumes in making this determination.

(d) Building context. The Planning Board shall consider the surrounding scale, height, design and setbacks of existing buildings in its determination of the zoning envelope for infill housing. In undertaking this contextual evaluation, the Planning Board may request building sections and elevations; shadow diagrams, showing the impact of the proposed use on adjacent property; and planimetric context maps, showing all adjacent buildings with street or build-to lines. In order to achieve a compatible building environment, the Planning Board may modify height, setback and yard controls.

B. Residence uses in C–2 Districts shall meet the following standards:

   (1) Residential uses in C–2 Districts shall be allowed only through a special permit granted by the Planning Board.

   (2) No such permit shall issue unless the following requirements are met, in addition to those of Article X hereof and those of Subsection A(4) of this section.

      (a) The residentially used portion of any structure shall have an entrance or entrances which do not require access through any nonresidentially used area, other than a common lobby or plaza. The location and design of such entrances shall be subject to approval by the Planning Board as a part of the required special permit application.

      (b) The maximum permitted floor area ratio for residential uses shall be 2.0. This may be increased in accordance with provisions of Article XV of this chapter for below-market-rate housing.

      (c) The maximum permitted building height shall be 45 feet. This may be increased in accordance with provisions of Article XV of this chapter for below-market-rate housing.

      (d) Parking spaces shall be as provided in Article VIII.

§ 342–52. Planned residential developments

For the purpose of promoting environmental protection, open space preservation and superior design of residential development; encouraging the most appropriate use of land; increasing recreational opportunities; and improving the balance and variety of the Village's existing housing stock, the Planning Board is hereby authorized to approve planned residential developments, subject to site development plan approval in accordance with the standards, procedures and requirements as set forth in Article XI of this chapter.

A. Planned residential development may be permitted only within one-family residence districts.

B. The minimum size of parcel eligible for planned residential development shall be 10 acres. No more than 10% of the total acreage shall be tidal or freshwater wetlands.

C. The maximum permitted number of residential dwelling units within a planned residential development shall be determined by dividing the gross area of the subject parcel by the minimum lot size requirements of the zoning district(s) in which it is located. The Planning Board may, in its discretion, further reduce the maximum permitted density where said Board determines that, because of environmental limitations, traffic access, the use and character of adjoining land or other planning considerations, the maximum permitted density would be inappropriate.

D. The permitted uses within a planned residential development shall be the same as those otherwise permitted in the zoning district(s) in which the property is located, except that attached and semidetached dwellings shall also be permitted.

E. There shall be no more than eight (8) dwelling units in any one dwelling building or attached grouping.

F. The maximum permitted building height shall be the same as permitted for one-family dwellings in the zoning district(s) in which the property is located.

G. In approving a planned residential development, the Planning Board may waive, to the extent determined necessary by said Board to achieve the purposes of this section, all normally applicable lot area, width, frontage, depth, floor area, yard and coverage requirements normally applicable in the zoning district(s) in which the property is located.

H. Notwithstanding the above, the minimum required setback from all perimeter boundaries of the site shall be equal to one and one-half (1 1/2) times the applicable yard requirements for one-family dwellings in the district(s) in which the property is located.

ARTICLE XI.   Site Development Plan Approval

§ 342–74.   Conformity to approved plan required

No building permit may be issued for any building within the purview of this Article, except in conformance with an approved site development plan. No certificate of occupancy may be issued for any building or use of land within the purview of this Article unless the building is constructed or used or the land is developed or used in conformity with an approved site development plan. Every application for site development plan approval shall be accompanied by a certification by the Director of Building, Code Enforcement and Land Use Administration to the effect that said plan meets all the specific applicable requirements of this chapter and a certificate by the Village

Engineer that the plans meet all the applicable standards and requirements established or approved by him.

§ 342–75.   Uses and actions subject to approval

Site development plan approval by the Planning Board shall be required in all districts for:

A. The erection, enlargement or change of use of any building or other structure other than one- or two-family dwellings. Uses subject to Article X and which are reviewed according to that Article's procedure must also follow the site development plan approval process and receive approval from the Planning Board.

B. All proposed uses of open land for which a certificate of occupancy is required.

C. Any proposed clearing of vegetation or earthwork on any property one-half (1/2) acre or larger or any land involving 25% or more of the site.

D. Any amendment of a previously approved site development plan.

§ 342–76.   General criteria and standards of review

The following criteria and standards shall be used by the Planning Board in reviewing applications for site development plan approval. They are intended to provide a framework within which the designer of the site development is free to exercise creativity, invention and innovation. The Planning Board shall not specify or favor any particular architectural style or design or assist in the design of any of the buildings submitted for approval. Participation by the Board shall be restricted to a reasonable, professional review, and, except as otherwise provided in the following subsections, full responsibility for design shall be retained by the applicant.

A. Ecological considerations. The development shall, insofar as practicable:

(1) Result in minimal degradation of unique or irreplaceable land types and in minimal adverse impact upon the critical areas, such as streams, wetlands, areas of aquifer recharge and discharge, steep slopes, highly erodible soils, areas with a high water table, mature stands of mature vegetation and extraordinary wildlife nesting, feeding or breeding grounds.

(2) Conform to existing geological and topographic features to the end that the most appropriate use of land is encouraged.

B. Landscape. The landscape shall be preserved in its natural state, insofar as practicable and environmentally desirable, by minimizing tree and soil removal. If development of the site necessitates the removal of established trees, special attention shall be given to the planting of replacements or to other landscape treatment. Any grade changes shall be in keeping with the general appearance of neighboring developed areas.

C. Relation of proposed structures to environment. Proposed structures shall be related harmoniously to themselves, the terrain and to existing buildings and roads in the vicinity that have a visual relationship to the proposed structures. The achievement of such harmonious relationship may include the enclosure of space in conjunction with other existing buildings or other proposed buildings and the creation of focal points with respect to avenues of approach, terrain features or other buildings.

(1) Proposed structures shall be so sited as to minimize any adverse impact upon the surrounding area and particularly upon any nearby residences by reason of:

(a) Building location, height, bulk and shadows.

(b) Location, intensity, direction and times of use of outdoor lighting.

(c) Likelihood of nuisances.

(d) Other similar considerations.

(2) Appropriate natural or artificial screening may be required to minimize any such adverse impact.

D. Scenic, historic, archaeological and landmark sites. Scenic, historical, archaeological and landmark sites and features that are located on or adjacent to the proposed development shall be preserved and protected insofar as practicable.

E. Surface water drainage. A proposed development shall be designed so as to provide for proper surface water management through a system of controlled drainage that, wherever practicable, preserves existing natural drainage patterns and wetlands and enhances groundwater recharge areas and that protects other properties and existing natural and artificial drainage features from the adverse effects of flooding, erosion and the depositing of silt, gravel or stone.

F. Driveway connections to public streets. All entrance and exit driveways to public streets shall be located with due consideration for traffic flow and so as to afford maximum safety to traffic on the public streets. All such entrances and exits shall be located and designed to:

(1) Conform to municipal sight triangle requirements at corners.

(2) Achieve maximum practicable distance from street intersections and from existing and proposed access connections from adjacent properties.

      (3) Minimize left-hand turns, other turning movements and backing movements.

      (4) Discourage the routing of vehicular traffic to and through local residential streets.

G. Traffic effects. The site development proposal generally shall minimize adverse traffic effects on the road networks serving the area in question.

H. Pedestrian safety. Insofar as practicable, pedestrian and bicycle circulation shall be separated from motor vehicle circulation. Safe and convenient pedestrian circulation, including appropriate sidewalks, shall be provided on the site and its approaches. The pedestrian circulation plan shall be designed to minimize adverse effects of vehicular traffic upon sidewalks and bicycle paths.

I. On-site parking and circulation. The location, width and layout of interior drives shall be appropriate for the proposed interior circulation. The location and layout of accessory off-street parking and loading spaces shall provide for efficient circulation and the safety of pedestrians and vehicles. Insofar as practicable, separate rows or aisles in parking areas shall be divided by trees, shrubbery and other landscaping devices. The location of parking areas shall not detract from the design of proposed buildings and structures or from the appearance of the existing neighboring buildings, structures and landscape. Provision shall be made for access by police, fire and emergency vehicles.

J. Utility services. Electric, telephone and other wire-served utility lines and service connections shall be underground insofar as feasible and subject to state public utilities regulations. Any utility installations remaining above ground shall be located so as to have a harmonious relation to neighboring properties and to the site.

K. Disposal of wastes. There shall be adequate provision for the disposal of all solid, liquid and gaseous wastes and for the avoidance of odors and other air pollutants that may be generated at the site. All applicable federal, state, county and local pollution control standards shall be observed.

L. Noise. All applicable federal, state and local regulations dealing with the control of outside noise which is expected to be generated at the site shall be complied with.

M. Advertising features. The size, location, height, design, color, texture, lighting and materials of permanent signs and outdoor advertising structures or features shall not detract from the design of proposed buildings and structures or of the surrounding properties.

N. Special features. Outside storage areas, service and machinery and structures, service areas, truck loading areas, utility buildings and structures and similar accessory areas and structures shall be subject to such setbacks, screen plantings and other screening methods as shall reasonably be required to prevent any adverse effect upon the environment or nearby property.

§ 342–79.   Planning Board action

The Planning Board shall review the site development plan and act on the application within 45 days from and after the time of submission of the preliminary plan. Failure on the part of the Planning Board to act shall be deemed to constitute approval, unless the time limit is extended by stipulation with the applicant. In reviewing the site development plan, the Planning Board shall take into consideration the public health, safety and general welfare and the comfort and convenience of the public in general and of the residents of the immediate neighborhood in particular and shall set any appropriate conditions and safeguards in harmony with the general purpose and intent of this chapter and according to the general criteria and standards defined in § 342–76.

§ 342–83.   Expiration and demolition

A. A site plan shall be void if construction is not started within one year and completed within two years of the date of the final site plan approval, except that such site plan approval may be renewed by the Planning Board at its discretion.

B. In the interests of public health, safety and general welfare, following final site plan approval pursuant to this article, within 30 days of vacating property, owners must pursue demolition.

ARTICLE XIV.   Amendments

§ 342–95.   General provisions

This chapter or any part thereof may be amended, supplemented or repealed from time to time by the Village Board on its own motion or by petition. Any such proposed amendment may be referred by the Board of Trustees to the Planning Board and the Board of Appeals for advisory reports before public hearing.

ARTICLE XV.   Below-Market-Rate Housing

§ 342–103.   Bonus provisions enumerated; definitions

A. In order to provide a choice of housing opportunities for a variety of income groups within the Village, in accordance with the purposes of this Article and the policies as set forth in the Village Master Plan, bonus provisions for increasing the number of units or floor space devoted to housing shall be allowed, upon a vote of the Planning Board for each specific application, in accordance with the following schedule:

Zoning District	Maximum Coverage	Bonus
C–1	FAR 0.8	0.2 FAR bonus
C–2	FAR 2.0	0.5 FAR bonus
RM–1	2,500 square feet of land/unit	20% unit bonus
RM–2	1,500 square feet of land/unit	20% unit bonus
RM–3	1,000 square feet of land/unit	20% unit bonus

B. For each additional market-rate unit produced as a result of the bonus provision, one comparable below-market-rate unit must be provided. In all cases, 50% of the total number of additional units provided by these bonus provisions must be reserved for below-market-rate families as herein defined.

C. As used in this Article, the following terms shall have the meanings indicated:

BELOW-MARKET-RATE DWELLING UNITS—A dwelling unit, the rental or sales price of which does not exceed the maximum allowable level established by this Article.

BELOW-MARKET-RATE FAMILIES—Families whose aggregate income, including the total of all current annual income of all family members from any source whatsoever at the time of application, but excluding the earnings of those under 21 years of age attending school full time, shall not exceed the following multiple of the median annual Village-paid salaries of all full-time employees of the Village of Mamaroneck, as listed in the Village budget for each year:

(1) One-person family: 1.0.

(2) Two-person family: 1.2.

(3) Three-person family: 1.4.

(4) Four-person family: 1.6.

(5) Five-person family: 1.8.

(6) Six-or-more-person family: 2.0.

PROBLEM THREE: URBAN REDEVELOPMENT I

A New York City agency owns land on two contiguous blocks between 51st and 53rd Streets, and between 10th and 11th Avenues in Manhattan. In Manhattan, streets are typically narrow and generally marked by low rise buildings; avenues are wide and feature more high-rise buildings. The city's land on the northern block occupies 48,000 square feet and stretches from mid-block to 10th Avenue; the city's land on the southern block occupies 22,000 square feet and is entirely a mid-block parcel. Currently, the two parcels are marked by small, underused, and dilapidated structures. Two of those structures currently include theater and administrative space for two not-for-profit theater companies. Both companies have short-term leases on the space. Running underneath both parcels, from south to north, is an open railroad cut operated by Amtrak, which holds an easement entitling it to operate rail lines through the site. The rail line is located 30 feet below the grade of the street, and the railway bed serves as a catch basin for debris from the sidewalk above.

Directly south of the site on 51st Street, are a 38-story residential building and a high school. To the north, on 53rd Street, are a utility building and a parking lot. West of the site on both blocks are 8-story residential buildings. On the southern block, the site is bounded on the east by five-story residential buildings.

EXISTING CONDITIONS

Address the following issues in light of the applicable law provided after problem (12).

1. The city has concluded that the city-owned land constitutes an eyesore that devalues neighboring land, and that the local economy would benefit from redevelopment. A city official approaches you about what course of action the city should take in redeveloping the parcel. Ideally, the city official would like to see two theatres on the parcel, but theatres will not generate enough revenue to support construction costs. The city believes that the area could support more residential units, and would be happy to see affordable housing on the site but, again, affordable housing will generate little revenue. What suggestions would you make to the city official about how the city should deal with the site? Should the city develop the site itself? If not, why not?

2.   Suppose now that the city issues a request for proposals (RFP) seeking bids from private developers to purchase and develop the site. The RFP includes the following requirements: (1) the project must include theatres and administrative space, totaling 60,000 square feet, for the two displaced not-for-profit theatres. The space must be leased to the theater companies or their successors for 30 years at "break even" rents and the developer must contribute $4,000,000 towards build-out of the interior of the theaters; (2) building height must be limited to 19 stories; (3) the project site must include a minimum of 350 residential housing units; and (4) all buildings on the development site must be "green" buildings;

You represent Dump Development, Inc., a developer interested in bidding on the site. Dump seeks your advice about what to propose and how much to bid. Your research reveals that the site currently appears on the zoning map as five separate lots, divided among three separate zoning districts (see map above). The westernmost lot on the northern parcel is located in an M1–5 district, while the westernmost lot on the southern parcel is located in an R–8 district. The other three lots are in a C6–3 district. What advice would you give Dump?

3.   Suppose Dump bids $20,000,000 for the site, proposing to build 650 rental residential apartments in two 24-story mid-block buildings, one located on each city block. For at least 30 years, twenty percent of the units (130 units) will be "affordable" for families earning 80% of the area's median income. The southern tower will also include some commercial space. Dump also proposed to build a seven-story building, fronting on 10th Avenue, to house the requisite theater space.

No other bid exceeds $10,000,000. The other proposals, however, include only 350–400 residential units, and limit building height to 19 stories. If you were advising the city, how would you suggest that the city respond to the various development proposals?

4.   Suppose the city accepts Dump's proposal. Dump wants to know what substantive relief Dump must seek, and what procedural steps Dump must take, in order to develop the parcel. Dump gives you plans which include the following details:

a.   the North parcel includes 48,000 square feet; the South parcel includes 22,000 square feet.

b.   as proposed, the North parcel will include two buildings. The 10th Avenue building will include 60,000 square feet of community facility space to be used by the two theaters and 10,000 square feet of commercial space. The mid-block building will include 280,000 square feet of residential space, divided into 345 units. The 10th Avenue building will be separated from the mid-block building by 30 feet.

c.   as proposed, the South parcel will include a single mid-block building, which will include 245,000 square feet of residential space (divided into 305 units) and 15,000 square feet of commercial space. Most of the commercial space will be located on the ground floor, which will have no residential units, but some commercial space (perhaps including a health club), will be located on the second floor, which will also include residential units.

d.   the North parcel will include 14,000 square feet of ground-level open space, while the South parcel will include 8,000 square feet of ground-level open space. The North parcel will include 6,000 square feet of roof-top open space atop the 10th Avenue building and 6,000 square feet of roof-top open space atop the mid-block building. The South parcel will include 6,000 square feet of roof-top open space atop its mid-block building.

e.   the residential entrances to both mid-block buildings will front on the open space and be accessible from 52nd Street.

f.   the buildings will have no rear yard.

Advise Dump. [You may ignore issues that arise from the fact that the height and shape of the proposed buildings do not conform to New York's extraordinarily complicated building height restrictions].

PROPOSED DEVELOPMENT

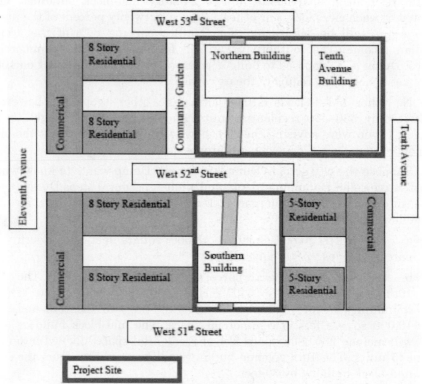

5. After the city accepts Dump's proposal, the theater owners do additional research and discover that build-out of the interior of the theaters will cost $10,000,000, more than twice what they had expected, and more than they can afford (Recall that the RFP had required the developer to contribute $4,000,000 toward build-out). The theater owners consult you for advice. What strategy would you recommend?

6. Just west of the northern parcel, community residents have, for a number of years, operated a "community garden," in which interested residents plant flowers and vegetables each spring, and harvest the vegetables in the fall. Residents have extended the garden to the Amtrak railroad cut, significantly encroaching on the project site. One of the towers would occupy the space on which the garden is located. If the community residents consult you for advice, what strategy would you recommend?

7. Amtrak has developed two concerns about the project. First, Amtrak wants to assure that the project will not in any way affect its ability to run trains under the building. Second, Amtrak wants to make sure that its own operations will not generate lawsuits by occupants of the new buildings unhappy with noise or vibration from Amtrak's operations. If you represent Dump, how would you respond to Amtrak's concerns?

8. Suppose Dump is unwilling to proceed with the project if it has to bear $10,000,000 in theater build-out costs and has to maintain the community garden, which, it believes, will make rental housing in the project less attractive to high-income tenants. What advice would you give to Dump if the theater owners and the neighbors threaten to oppose the project unless Dump makes the concessions they want?

9. Suppose Dump cannot reach any understanding with the theater companies or the residents who want to maintain the community garden. In presenting its application to the local community board, what facts should Dump emphasize? How should the neighbors and the theaters respond?

10. Suppose now that Dump, the neighbors, and the theaters reach an understanding that Dump will contribute $8,000,000 towards build-out costs and relocate the community garden if Dump is permitted to add a four-floor residential tower on top of a portion of the 10th Avenue building, and to sell seven additional condominium units that would allow Dump to recoup most of the expenses associated with build-out and relocation of the gardens. What facts should Dump now emphasize in presenting its application to the community board? Would Dump have to change the relief it seeks from the community board?

11. If the community board recommends that Dump's proposal be disapproved, what alternatives does Dump have? What course of action would you recommend?

12. If the community board recommends approval of Dump's proposal, should Dump alter its presentation before the Borough President, the City Planning Commission, or the City Council?

Applicable Law

New York City zoning regulations are extraordinarily complex. The New York City Charter (excerpted below) establishes a Uniform Land Use Review Procedure (known as ULURP) for many proposed land use changes. The City Planning Commission has also promulgated regulations pursuant to the Charter provisions. For purposes of this problem, you may ignore the CPC regulations. The New York City Zoning Resolution (excerpted below) governs substance (and some procedure) of the city's land use regulation system. To make the problem more accessible, the provisions below represent a simplification of the actual provisions in the Zoning Resolution (believe it or not!).

In addition to the provisions below, you may assume that under the New York City Zoning Resolution (1) neither residential nor commercial uses are permitted in M1–5 Districts; (2) residential and community facility uses are permitted in R–8 Districts, commercial uses are not; and (3) Residential, commercial, and community facility uses are permitted in C6–3 Districts. Theaters are community facility uses.

New York City Charter

Section 197–c.   Uniform land use review procedure

a.   Except as otherwise provided in this charter, applications by any person or agency for changes, approvals, contracts, consents, permits or authorization thereof, respecting the use, development or improvement of real property subject to city regulation shall be reviewed pursuant to a uniform review procedure in the following categories:

(1)   Changes in the city map pursuant to section one hundred ninety-eight and section one hundred ninety-nine;

(2)   Maps of subdivisions or plattings of land into streets, avenues or public places pursuant to section two hundred two;

(3)   Designations of zoning districts under the zoning resolution, including conversion from one land use to another land use, pursuant to sections two hundred and two hundred one;

(4)   Special permits within the jurisdiction of the city planning commission under the zoning resolution, pursuant to sections two hundred and two hundred one;

. . .

b.   The following documents shall be filed with the department of city planning: (1) applications under this section, (2) any amendments thereto that are made prior to approval of such applications pursuant to this chapter, (3) any written information submitted by an applicant for purposes of determining whether an environmental impact statement will be required by law, and (4) documents or records intended to define or substantially redefine the overall scope of issues to be addressed in any draft environmental impact statement required by law. The department of city planning shall forward a copy of any materials it receives pursuant to this subdivision (whether or not such materials have been certified as complete) within five days to each affected borough president, community board or borough board.

. . .

e.   Each affected community board shall, not later than sixty days after receipt of an application that has been certified pursuant to subdivision c of this section,

(1)   notify the public of the application in a manner specified by the city planning commission pursuant to subdivision i of this section, and

(2)   either (a) conduct a public hearing thereon and prepare and submit a written recommendation directly to the city planning commission and to the affected borough president or (b) where authorized by this charter, submit a written waiver of the right to conduct a public hearing and to submit such written recommendations to the commission and the affected borough president.

. . .

g.   Not later than thirty days after the filing of a recommendation or waiver with the borough president by all affected community boards, or, if any affected community board shall fail to act, thirty days after the expiration of the time allowed for such community board to act, the borough president shall submit a written recommendation or waiver thereof to the city planning commission.

h.   Not later than sixty days after expiration of time allowed for the filing of a recommendation or waiver with the city planning commission by a borough president, the commission shall approve, approve with modifications, or disapprove the application. . . . The commission shall conduct a public hearing on all applications that are subject to review and approval by the commission pursuant to this section.

i.   The city planning commission shall establish rules providing (1) guidelines, minimum standards, and procedural requirements for community boards, borough presidents, borough boards and the commission in the exercise of their duties and responsibilities pursuant to this section, (2) minimum standards for certification of applications pursuant to subdivision c of this section, and (3) specific time periods for review of applications pursuant to this section prior to certification.

j.   If a community board, borough president or borough board fails or waives its right to act within the time limits for review pursuant to subdivisions e, f and g of this section, the application shall be referred to the next level of review. If the city planning commission fails to act on an application within the time limit specified in subdivision h of this section, the application shall be deemed to have been denied unless the application (i) is pursuant to paragraph three or four of subdivision a of this section, in which case the application may be forwarded to the council for review pursuant to the provisions of subdivision b of section two hundred, if applicable, or (ii) is pursuant to paragraph eight of subdivision a of this section, in which case the application shall be referred to the council for review and action as provided by state law.

Section 197–d. Council Review

a.   The city planning commission shall file with the council and with the affected borough president a copy of its decisions to approve or approve with modifications (1) all matters described in subdivision a of section one hundred ninety-seven-c, . . . and (3) changes in the text of the zoning resolution pursuant to sections two hundred and two hundred one.

b.   The following decisions filed with the council pursuant to subdivision a of this section, shall be subject to review and action by the council:

(1) any decision of the city planning commission to approve or approve with modifications a matter described in paragraph three or eight of subdivision a of section one hundred ninety-seven-c, . . . or a change in the text of the zoning resolution pursuant to sections two hundred or two hundred one.

(2) any other decision of the city planning commission to approve or approve with modifications a matter described in subdivision a of section one hundred ninety-seven-c, if (i) both an affected community board (after holding a public hearing) and the affected borough president, within the time periods allotted for their reviews pursuant to section one hundred ninety-seven-c, have recommended in writing against approval and (ii) the affected borough president, within five days of receiving a copy of the decision of the commission, files with the commission and the council a written objection to the decision; and

(3) any other decision of the city planning commission to approve or approve with modifications a matter described in subdivision a of section one hundred ninety-seven-c, if within twenty days of the filing of such decision pursuant to subdivision a of this section, the council resolves by the majority vote of all the council members to review the decision of the commission.

c.   Within fifty days of the filing with the council pursuant to subdivision a of this section of any decision of the city planning commission which pursuant to subdivision b of this section is subject to review by the council, the council shall hold a public hearing, after giving public notice not less than five days in advance of such hearing, and the council, within such fifty days, shall take final action on the decision. The affirmative vote of a majority of all the council members shall be required to approve, approve with modifications or disapprove such a decision. If, within the time period provided for in this subdivision and, if applicable, in subdivision d of this section, the council fails to act or fails to act by the required vote on a decision of the city planning commission subject to council review pursuant to subdivision b of this section, the council shall be deemed to have approved the decision of the commission.

. . .

e.   All actions of the council pursuant to this section shall be filed by the council with the mayor prior to the expiration of the time period for council action under subdivisions c and, if applicable, d of this section. Actions of the council pursuant to this section shall be final unless the mayor within five days of receiving a filing with respect to such an action of the council files with the council a written disapproval of the action. Any mayoral disapproval under this subdivision shall be subject to override by a two-thirds vote of all the council members within ten days of such filing by the mayor.

Section 200.   Zoning resolution

a.   Except as provided in subdivision b, any existing resolution or regulation of the council, the board of estimate or of the city planning commission to regulate and limit the height and bulk of buildings, to regulate and determine the area of yards, courts and other open spaces, to regulate density of population or to regulate and restrict the locations of trades and industries and location of buildings designed for specific uses or creating districts for any such purpose, including any such regulation which provides that the board of standards and appeals may determine and vary the application of such resolutions or regulations in harmony with their general purpose and intent and in accordance with general or specific rules contained in such regulations, may be amended, repealed or added to only in the following manner:

1.   The city planning commission may upon its own initiative at any time or upon application as provided in section two hundred one, adopt a resolution to amend the text of the zoning resolution subject to the limitations provided by law. Before adopting any such resolution, the commission shall notify any community board or borough board affected by the resolution and shall afford persons interested an opportunity to be heard at a time and place to be specified in a notice of hearing to be published in the City Record for the ten days of publication of the City Record immediately prior thereto setting forth in general terms the nature of the proposed resolution and a statement of the place at which the entire resolution may be examined.

2.   Any resolution by the commission approving a change in the text of the zoning resolution shall be subject to review and approval by

the council pursuant to section one hundred ninety-seven-d. Any resolution for a zoning text change which the mayor shall have certified to the council as necessary, and which has been disapproved by the commission, may be adopted by the council by a two-thirds vote and, after notice to the parties affected, a public hearing. . . .

3.   In case a protest against such a resolution approved by the city planning commission shall have been presented to the city clerk within thirty days from the date of the filing of such resolution with the council, duly signed and acknowledged by the owners of twenty per centum or more of the area of:

(1) the land included in changes proposed in such proposed resolution, or

(2) the land immediately adjacent extending one hundred feet therefrom, or

(3) the land, if any, directly opposite thereto extending one hundred feet from the street frontage of such opposite land,

such resolution shall not be effective after the filing of such protest unless approved by the council by a three-fourths vote within one hundred eighty days after the filing of said resolution with the city clerk. The effective date of such resolution, if so approved, shall be the date of such approval. A protest duly filed as herein provided may be withdrawn at any time within sixty days from the date of the filing of such resolution.

b.   Designations of zoning districts under the zoning resolution and the issuance of special permits which under the terms of the zoning resolution are within the jurisdiction of the city planning commission shall be subject to review and approval pursuant to the procedures provided in section one hundred ninety-seven-c and section one hundred ninety-seven-d, except that whenever the city planning commission has not recommended approval of a proposed change in the designation of a zoning district or the issuance of a special permit under the zoning resolution or has failed to act on such a matter within the time specified in section one hundred ninety-seven-c, the council by a two-thirds vote may approve such change or the issuance of such permit only if the mayor shall have certified to the council that such change or issuance is necessary. The council shall act upon such designation or permit within fifty days of the filing of the certification of the mayor with the council.

Section 201.   Applications for zoning changes and special permits

a.   Applications for changes in the zoning resolution may be filed by any taxpayer, community board, borough board, borough president, by the mayor or by the land use committee of the council if two-thirds of the members of the committee shall have voted to approve such filing with the city planning commission. All such applications involving changes in the designation of zoning districts under the zoning resolution shall be subject to review and approval pursuant to section one hundred ninety-seven-c, and one hundred ninety-seven-d. For applications involving other changes in zoning resolutions and regulations, the commission prior to taking action upon any such application shall refer it to the affected community boards or borough boards for a public hearing and recommendation.

b.   Applications for special permits within the jurisdiction of the city planning commission under the zoning resolution may be filed by any person or agency. All such applications for the issuance of special permits shall be subject to review and approval pursuant to section one hundred ninety-seven-c and section one hundred ninety-seven-d.

New York City Zoning Resolution

Article I: General Provisions

Section 12–10.   Definitions

Open space. "Open space" is that part of a zoning lot, including courts or yards, which:

(a)   is open and unobstructed from its lowest level to the sky,

(b)   is accessible to and usable by all persons occupying a dwelling unit or a rooming unit on the zoning lot; and

(c)   is not part of the roof of that portion of a building containing dwelling units or rooming units.

Open space ratio. The "open space ratio" of a zoning lot is the number of square feet of open space on the zoning lot, expressed as a percentage of the floor area on that zoning lot. (For example, if for a particular building an open space ratio of 20 is required, 20,000 square feet of floor area in the building would necessitate 4,000 square feet of open space on the zoning lot upon which the building stands; or, if 6,000 square feet of lot area were in open space, 30,000 square feet of floor area could be in the building on that zoning lot.)

Zoning lot. A "zoning lot" is either:

(a)   a lot of record existing on December 15, 1961;

(b)   a tract of land, either unsubdivided or consisting of two or more contiguous lots of record, located within a single block, which, on December 15, 1961, was in single ownership; or

(c)   a tract of land, either unsubdivided or consisting of two or more lots of record contiguous for a minimum of ten linear feet, located within a single block, which at the time of filing for a building permit (or, if no building permit is required, at the time of the filing for a certificate of occupancy) is under single fee ownership.

A zoning lot may be subdivided into two or more zoning lots, provided that all resulting zoning lots and all buildings thereon shall comply with all of the applicable provisions of this Resolution. If such zoning lot, however, is occupied by a non-complying building, such zoning lot may be subdivided provided such subdivision does not create a new non-compliance or increase the degree of non-compliance of such building.

Article II: Residence District Regulations

Chapter 3. Bulk Regulations for Residential Buildings in Residence Districts

23–142. Open Space and floor area regulations in R6, R7, R8 or R9 Districts

Except as otherwise provided, in the districts indicated, the maximum floor area ratio, and minimum required open space ratio for any building on a zoning lot shall be as set forth in the following table:

District	Maximum FAR	Minimum Open Space Ratio
R6	3	2.4
R7	4.5	3.4
R8	6.5	6.0
R9	10	7.5

23–47.   Minimum Required Rear Yards

In all districts, as indicated, a rear yard with a depth of not less than 30 feet shall be provided at every rear lot line on any zoning lot.

23–711. Standard minimum distance between buildings

In all districts, as indicated, the required minimum distance between a residential building and any other building on the same zoning lot shall be 50 feet.

The minimum distance shall be provided at the closest point between buildings.

23–82. Building Walls Regulated by Minimum Spacing Requirements

In all districts, as indicated, at any level at which two portions of a single building are not connected one to the other, such portions shall be deemed to be two separate buildings, and the provisions set forth in Section 23–711 shall apply.

Chapter 4. Bulk Regulations for Community Facility Buildings in Residence Districts

24–11. Maximum Floor Area Ratio and Percentage of Lot Coverage

In all districts, as indicated, for any community facility building or any building used partly for a community facility use on any zoning lot, the maximum floor area ratio and maximum percent of lot coverage shall not exceed the floor area ratio and lot coverage set forth in the table in this Section.

MAXIMUM FLOOR AREA AND MAXIMUM LOT COVERAGE
Lot Coverage as Percent of Lot Area

FAR	Corner Lot	Through Lot	District
4.80	70	65	R6
4.80	70	65	R7–1
6.50	70	65	R7–2
6.50	75	65	R8
10.00	75	65	R9
10.00	75	65	R10

Article III. Commercial District Regulations

Chapter 2. Use Regulations

32–422. Location of floors occupied by non-residential uses

In the districts indicated, in any building, or portion of a building occupied by residential uses, non-residential uses may be located only on a story below the lowest story occupied in whole or in part by such residential uses, except that this limitation shall not preclude the location of any such non-residential use below the level of the first story ceiling, or the extension of a permitted sign accessory to such non-residential use to a maximum height of two feet above the level of the finished floor of the second story, but in no event higher than six inches below the lowest window sill on the second story.

Chapter 3. Bulk Regulations for Commercial or Community Facility Buildings in Commercial Districts

33–122. Commercial buildings

In the districts indicated, the maximum floor area ratio for a commercial building shall not exceed the floor area ratio set forth in the following table:

Districts	Maximum Floor Area
C3	0.5
C4–1, C8–1	1.0
C1–6, C1–7, C1–8, C1–9, C2–6, C2–8, C7, C8–1, C8–3	2.0
C4–2, C4–3, C4–4, C4–5	3.4
C5–1	4.0
C8–4	5.0
C6–1, C6–2, C6–3	6.0

C5–2, C5–4	10.0
C5–3, C5–5	15.0

33–123. Community facility buildings or buildings used for both community facility and commercial uses in all other Commercial Districts

In the districts indicated, the maximum floor area ratio for a community facility building, or for a building used for both commercial and community facility uses, shall not exceed the floor area ratio set forth in the following table:

Districts	Maximum Floor Area
C3	1.0
C4–1	2.0
C8–1	2.4
C4–3	3.0
C1–6, C2–6	4.0
C4–5	4.2
C4–2	4.8
C1–6, C1–7, C2–7, C4–4, C6–1	6.0
C6–2, C8–3, C8–4	6.5
C1–8, C1–9, C2–8, C5–1, C5–2, C5–4, C6–3	10.0
C5–3, C5–5	15.0

In buildings used for both commercial uses and community facility uses, the total floor area used for commercial uses shall not exceed the amount permitted for commercial buildings in Section 33–122.

Chapter 4. Bulk Regulations for Residential Buildings in Commercial Districts

34–11. General Provisions

In the districts indicated, the bulk regulations, including open space regulations, for residential buildings set forth in Article II, Chapter 3, shall apply to all residential buildings in accordance with the provisions of Section 34–112.

34–112. Residential bulk regulations in C3, C4, C5, or C6 Districts

In the districts indicated, the applicable bulk regulations are the bulk regulations for the Residence Districts set forth in the following table:

Districts	Applicable Residence District
C3	R3–2
C4–1	R5
C4–2, C4–3	R6
C4–4, C4–5, C6–1	R7
C6–2	R8
C6–3	R9

Chapter 5. Bulk Regulations for Mixed Buildings in Commercial Districts

35–01. Applicability of this Chapter

The bulk regulations of this Chapter apply to any mixed building located on any zoning lot or portion of a zoning lot in any Commercial District in which such building is permitted. When two or more buildings on a single zoning lot are used in any combination for uses which, if located in a single building would make it a mixed building, the regulations set forth in Sections 35–21 and 35–23 shall apply as if such buildings were a single mixed building.

35–21. General Provisions

In the districts indicated, the bulk regulations, including open space regulations, applicable to residential buildings set forth in Article II, Chapter 3, shall apply to all residential portions of mixed buildings in accordance with the provisions and modifications set forth in the remaining Sections of this Chapter. The purpose of these modifications is to make the regulations set forth in Article II, Chapter 3, applicable to mixed buildings and Commercial Districts.

35–23. Residential Bulk Regulations in C3, C4, C5 or C6 Districts

In the districts indicated, the bulk regulations for residential portions of mixed buildings are the bulk regulations for the Residence Districts set forth in the following table.

Applicable Residence District	District
R3–2	C3
R5	C4–1
R6	C4–2, C4–3
R7	C4–4, C4–5, C6–1
R8	C6–2
R9	C6–3
R10	C5

35–31.   Maximum Floor Area Ratio for Mixed Buildings

In all districts, the provisions of this Section shall apply to any zoning lot containing a mixed building.

The maximum floor area ratio permitted for a commercial or community facility use shall be as set forth in Article III, Chapter 3, and the maximum floor area ratio permitted for a residential use shall be as set forth in Article II, Chapter 3, provided the total of all such floor area ratios does not exceed the greatest floor area ratio permitted for any such use on the zoning lot.

Article VII. Administration

Chapter 2.   Interpretations and Variances

72–21.   Findings Required for Variances

When in the course of enforcement of this Resolution, any officer from whom an appeal may be taken under the provisions of Section 72–11 (General Provisions) has applied or interpreted a provision of this Resolution, and there are practical difficulties or unnecessary hardship in the way of carrying out the strict letter of such provision, the Board of Standards and Appeals may, in accordance with the requirements set forth in this Section, vary or modify the provision so that the spirit of the law shall be observed, public safety secured, and substantial justice done.

Where it is alleged that there are practical difficulties or unnecessary hardship, the Board may grant a variance in the application of the provisions of this Resolution in the specific case, provided that as a condition to the grant of any such variance, the Board shall make each and every one of the following findings:

(a) that there are unique physical conditions, including irregularity, narrowness or shallowness of lot size or shape, or exceptional topographical or other physical conditions peculiar to and inherent in the particular zoning lot; and that, as a result of such unique physical conditions, practical difficulties or unnecessary hardship arise in complying strictly with the use or bulk provisions of the Resolution; and that the alleged practical difficulties or unnecessary hardship are not due to circumstances created generally by the strict application of such provisions in the neighborhood or district in which the zoning lot is located;

(b) that because of such physical conditions there is no reasonable possibility that the development of the zoning lot in strict conformity with the provisions of this Resolution will bring a reasonable return, and that the grant of a variance is therefore necessary to enable the owner to realize a reasonable return from such zoning lot; this finding shall not be required for the granting of a variance to a non-profit organization;

(c) that the variance, if granted, will not alter the essential character of the neighborhood or district in which the zoning lot is located; will not substantially impair the appropriate use or development of adjacent property; and will not be detrimental to the public welfare;

(d) that the practical difficulties or unnecessary hardship claimed as a ground for a variance have not been created by the owner or by a predecessor in title; however where all other required findings are made, the purchase of a zoning lot subject to the restrictions sought to be varied shall not itself constitute a self-created hardship; and

(e) that within the intent and purposes of this Resolution the variance, if granted, is the minimum variance necessary to afford relief; and to this end, the Board may permit a lesser variance than that applied for.

It shall be a further requirement that the decision or determination of the Board shall set forth each required finding in each specific grant of a variance, and in each denial thereof which of the required findings have not been satisfied. In any such case, each finding shall be supported by substantial evidence or other data considered by the Board in reaching its decision, including the personal knowledge of or inspection by the members of the Board. Reports of other City agencies made as a result of inquiry by the Board shall not be considered hearsay, but may be considered by the Board as if the data therein contained were secured by personal inspection.

Chapter 4. Special Permits by the City Planning Commission

74–681. Development within or over a railroad or transit right-of-way or yard

(a) In all districts, when a development or enlargement, including large-scale developments pursuant to Section 74–74, 78–00 et seq. or 79–00 et seq. is located partially or entirely within a railroad or transit right-of-way or yard and/or in railroad or transit air space, the City Planning Commission may permit:

(1) that portion of the railroad or transit right-of-way or yard which will be completely covered over by a permanent platform to be included in the lot area for such development or enlargement;

(2) any portion of the right-of-way or yard where railroad or transit use has been permanently discontinued or terminated to be included in the lot area for such development or enlargement.

(b) As a condition for granting a special permit, the Commission shall find that:

(1) the streets providing access to all uses pursuant to paragraph (a) above are adequate to handle traffic resulting therefrom;

(2) all uses, developments or enlargements located on the zoning lot or below a platform do not adversely affect one another;

(3) if such railroad or transit right-of-way or yard is deemed appropriate for future transportation use, the site plan and structural design of the development does not preclude future use of, or improvements to, the right-of-way for such transportation use.

Prior to granting a special permit, the City Planning Commission shall request the Metropolitan Transportation Authority and the Departments of Transportation of the State of New York and the City of New York to indicate within 30 days whether said agencies have any plan to use that portion of the railroad or transit air space or railroad or transit right-of-way or yard where the railroad or transit use has been permanently discontinued or terminated.

74–74. General Large-Scale Development

For general large-scale developments involving several zoning lots but planned as a unit, the district regulations may impose unnecessary rigidities and thereby prevent achievement of the best possible site plan within the overall density and bulk controls. For these developments, the regulations of this Section are designed to allow greater flexibility for the purpose of securing better site planning, while safeguarding the present or future use and development of the surrounding area.

74–741. Requirements for application

An application to the City Planning Commission for the grant of a special permit pursuant to Section 74–74 (General Large-Scale Development) for a general large-scale development shall include a site plan showing the boundaries of the general large-scale development and the proposed location and use of all buildings or other structures on each zoning lot comprising the general large-scale development.

74–743. Special provisions for bulk modification

(a) For a general large-scale development, the City Planning Commission may permit:

(1) distribution of total allowable floor area, rooming units, dwelling units, lot coverage and total required open space under the applicable district regulations within a general large-scale development without regard for zoning lot lines or district boundaries.

(2)   location of buildings without regard for the applicable yard, court, distance between buildings, or height and setback regulations.

(b)   In order to grant a special permit pursuant to this Section for any general large-scale development, the Commission shall find that:

(1)   the distribution of floor area, open space, dwelling units, rooming units and the location of buildings, primary business entrances and show windows will result in a better site plan and a better relationship among buildings and open areas to adjacent streets, surrounding development, adjacent open areas and shorelines than would be possible without such distribution and will thus benefit both the occupants of the general large-scale development, the neighborhood, and the City as a whole;

(2)   the distribution of floor area and location of buildings will not unduly increase the bulk of buildings in any one block or unduly obstruct access of light and air to the detriment of the occupants or users of buildings in the block or nearby blocks or of people using the public streets.

The Commission may prescribe additional conditions and safeguards to improve the quality of the general large-scale development and to minimize adverse effects on the character of the surrounding area.

74–744. Modification of use regulations

(b)   Location of commercial uses

For any general large-scale development, the City Planning Commission may permit residential and non-residential uses to be arranged within a building without regard for the regulations set forth in Section 32–42 (Location within Buildings), provided the Commission shall find:

(1)   the commercial uses are located in a portion of the mixed building that has separate access to the outside with no opening of any kind to the residential portion of the building at any story;

(2)   the commercial uses are not located directly over any story containing dwelling units; and

(3)   the modifications shall not have any adverse effect on the uses located within the building.

PROBLEM FOUR: URBAN REDEVELOPMENT II

Hartford, Connecticut, is an 18-square-mile city with many physical assets: it boasts a magnificent stock of historic buildings, the beautiful

Connecticut River running along its eastern edge, and an incredible park system designed by Frederick Law Olmsted (born in Hartford!) and his disciples. Unfortunately, since the mid-1950s, the city has experienced population losses, as many residents moved to the surrounding suburbs. This population loss has created a structural deficit that limits the city's ability to invest in major projects and even to conduct basic infrastructure maintenance. Portions of the city have been suffering for decades from disinvestment and decay; too many historic buildings have been demolished, and the land has been either left vacant or used for surface parking lots.

Recently, however, the city's fortunes appear to be changing. Demographic trends favor urban living. A robust historic preservation ordinance now requires citizen review before historic buildings can be destroyed or altered. A form-based zoning code, which aims to preserve neighborhood character and require more compact development, has been adopted by the planning and zoning commission. The federal government has identified land for a national historic park that centers on the legacy of the Colt family, legendary gunmakers. And the State has invested tens of millions of dollars in the construction of downtown housing and of a bus rapid transit system that bisects the city running west to east, connecting to regional points further afield.

Your client is an out-of-state developer, Harriet Bushnell, who is interested in expanding her portfolio into Connecticut. Bushnell does not know Hartford well, but she has been touring a few sites to identify development opportunities. The site that she favors most is a large property on the eastern side of Bartholomew Avenue, currently serving as a surface parking lot and identified on the map with the arrow. As you can see from the map, most of Bartholomew Avenue is lined with large buildings—old factories, in fact. Some of these buildings are being reused for housing or light manufacturing, but the rest sit vacant. The map also indicates the location of the "CTfastrak Busway" Parkville station—right on Park Street, and one block away from Bartholomew Avenue.

Answer the following questions, in light of the material that follows.

1. The State of Connecticut has invested heavily in infrastructure to build the CTfastrak bus rapid transit system. A news report this week highlighted the Governor's plans to expand the capacity of the CTfastrak, both by increasing the number of buses and by increasing the number of stations to outlying suburbs. Harriet Bushnell calls you and asks you to advise her as to whether she should be concerned about this expansion. Can the State take the Bartholomew Avenue site for incorporation into the CTfastrak? Given the conditions you observe on the map, how likely is that to occur?

2. Harriet Bushnell has recently dispatched a surveyor and engineer to review the environmental characteristics of the site. They have told her that the site may have environmental contamination. They further informed her that she may have to conduct a full environmental impact review, complete with public hearings, no matter what kind of construction she does on the site. After reviewing the relevant statutes, does she have to conduct a formal environmental impact review? If your answer is "maybe," how would you recommend she avoid this additional expense?

3. After weighing her options, Bushnell purchased the property and has now completed any required environmental analysis and remediation of the site. Now she is ready to build something. After meeting with the zoning administrator, Bushnell is surprised to learn that Hartford has a citywide form-based zoning code, which dictates not only the uses of particular buildings, but also their forms—including the shapes of roofs, the types of entrances (e.g., whether the façade includes a porch or a stoop), and the minimum and maximum heights of buildings. Bushnell is alarmed: in her view, city officials should feel lucky that anyone has come in to invest in this dilapidated area. She asks you about the likelihood that a challenge to the form-based code will be successful. What body administers the Hartford zoning regulations? How successful do you predict she will be in challenging that body's authority to adopt a form-based code?

4. Having decided not to pursue litigation against the City of Hartford, Harriet Bushnell now hopes to begin construction on a parking garage, to accommodate the cars of people who want to park and ride on the Fastrak. The zoning for the area is the Transit Oriented Development Overlay zone. Can she build a parking garage?

5. Bushnell has put the parking garage idea aside. Her next idea is to build an apartment building, with apartment uses on every floor of the building. Can she do this? If not, can you recommend a minor modification to her plans? In a form-based code, note that having the right to construct a particular "building type" does not necessarily mean that you have the right to any particular use.

6. Harriet Bushnell eventually settles on the construction of a 5,000 square foot retail store on the ground floor and about 30,000 square feet of office space up above. What building type seems to be most appropriate for this use? What advice would you provide regarding the requirements for parking? Let's say it costs $15,000 per automobile parking space located a surface lot, but $40,000 per automobile parking space if she has to build a structured parking garage. Does she have an incentive to reduce the amount of parking? If so, what suggestions would you have if she wants to obtain a reduction?

7. Thanks to your assistance, Harriet Bushnell has cleared all zoning hurdles. But she has one more land use approval to go, as you have just alerted her to the fact that this property is located in the Parkville National Register Historic District. You have read over the National Register nomination form, and Bartholomew Avenue is recognized for its "industrial heritage" character. Is the new construction in that district subject to review by the local historic preservation commission? If so, what are the standards that the commission is required to apply? Will she have any argument to avoid all historic preservation restrictions?

8.   She may also have to finance her development by deploying renewable energy. Given the governmental incentives in place right now, renewable energy will help her significantly offset costs of operating her office building. What incentives does she have to use renewable energy, if any? On which locations on her site could she place renewable energy?

Connecticut General Statutes

Sec. 8–1. Zoning commissions.

(a) Any municipality may, by vote of its legislative body, adopt the provisions of this chapter and exercise through a zoning commission the powers granted hereunder. On and after July 1, 1974, in each municipality, except as otherwise provided by special act or charter provision adopted under chapter 99, the zoning commission shall consist of not less than five nor more than nine members, with minority representation as determined under section 9–167a, who shall be electors of such municipality. * * *

(b) The zoning commission of any town shall have jurisdiction over that part of the town outside of any city or borough contained therein except that the legislative body of any city or borough may, by ordinance, designate the zoning commission of the town in which such city or borough is situated as the zoning commission of such city or borough.

Sec. 8–2. Regulations.

(a) The zoning commission of each city, town or borough is authorized to regulate, within the limits of such municipality, the height, number of stories and size of buildings and other structures; the percentage of the area of the lot that may be occupied; the size of yards, courts and other open spaces; the density of population and the location and use of buildings, structures and land for trade, industry, residence or other purposes, including water-dependent uses, as defined in section 22a–93, and the height, size and location of advertising signs and billboards. Such bulk regulations may allow for cluster development, as defined in section 8–18. Such zoning commission may divide the municipality into districts of such number, shape and area as may be best suited to carry out the purposes of this chapter; and, within such districts, it may regulate the erection, construction, reconstruction, alteration or use of buildings or structures and the use of land. All such regulations shall be uniform for each class or kind of buildings, structures or use of land throughout each district, but the regulations in one district may differ from those in another district, and may provide that certain classes or kinds of buildings, structures or uses of land are permitted only after obtaining a special permit or special exception from a zoning commission, planning commission, combined planning and zoning commission or zoning board of appeals, whichever commission or board the regulations may, notwithstanding any special act to the contrary, designate, subject to standards set forth in the regulations and to conditions necessary to protect the public health, safety, convenience and property values. Such regulations shall be made in accordance with a comprehensive plan and in adopting such regulations the commission shall consider the plan of conservation and development prepared under section 8–23. Such regulations shall be designed to lessen congestion in the streets; to secure safety from fire, panic, flood and other dangers; to promote health and the general welfare; to provide adequate light and air; to prevent the overcrowding of land; to avoid undue concentration of population and to facilitate the adequate provision for transportation, water, sewerage, schools, parks and other public requirements. Such regulations shall be made with reasonable consideration as to the character of the district and its peculiar suitability for particular uses and with a view to conserving the value of buildings and encouraging the most appropriate use of land throughout such municipality. Such regulations may, to the extent consistent with soil types, terrain, infrastructure capacity and the plan of conservation and development for the community, provide for cluster development, as defined in section 8–18, in residential zones. Such regulations shall also encourage the development of housing opportunities, including opportunities for multifamily dwellings, consistent with soil types, terrain and infrastructure capacity, for all residents of the municipality and the planning region in which the municipality is located, as designated by the Secretary of the Office of Policy and Management under section 16a–4a. Such regulations shall also promote housing choice and economic diversity in housing, including housing for both low and moderate income households, and shall encourage the development of housing which will meet the housing needs identified in the housing plan prepared pursuant to section 8–37t and in the housing component and the other components of the state plan of conservation and development prepared pursuant to section 16a–26. Zoning regulations shall be made with reasonable consideration for their impact on agriculture. Zoning regulations may be made with reasonable consideration for the protection of historic factors and shall be made with reasonable consideration for the protection of existing and potential public surface and ground drinking water supplies. On and after July 1, 1985, the regulations shall provide that proper provision be made for soil erosion and sediment control pursuant to section 22a–329. Such regulations may also encourage energy-efficient patterns of development, the use of solar and other renewable forms of energy, and energy conservation. The regulations may also provide for incentives for developers who use passive solar energy techniques, as defined in subsection (b) of section 8–25, in planning a residential subdivision development. The incentives may include, but not be limited to, cluster development, higher density development and performance standards for roads, sidewalks and underground facilities in the subdivision. Such regulations may provide for a municipal system for the creation of development rights and the permanent transfer of such development rights, which may include a system for the variance of density limits in connection with any such transfer. Such regulations may also provide for notice requirements in addition to those required by this chapter. Such regulations may provide for conditions on operations to collect spring water or well water, as defined in section 21a–150, including the time, place and manner of such operations. No such regulations shall prohibit the operation of any family day care home or group day care home in a residential zone. No such regulations shall prohibit the use of receptacles for the storage of items designated for recycling in accordance with section 22a–241b or require that such receptacles comply with provisions for bulk or lot area, or similar provisions, except provisions for side yards, rear yards and front yards. No such regulations shall unreasonably restrict access to or the size of such receptacles for businesses, given the nature of the business and the volume of items designated for recycling in accordance with section 22a–241b, that such business produces in its normal course of business, provided nothing in this section shall be construed to prohibit such regulations from requiring the screening or buffering of such receptacles for aesthetic reasons. Such regulations shall not impose conditions and requirements on manufactured homes having as their narrowest dimension twenty-two feet or more and built in accordance with federal manufactured home construction and safety standards or on lots containing such manufactured homes which are substantially different from conditions and requirements imposed on single-family dwellings and lots containing single-family dwellings. Such regulations shall not impose conditions and requirements on developments to be occupied by manufactured homes having as their narrowest dimension twenty-two feet or more and built in accordance with federal manufactured home construction and safety standards which are substantially different from conditions and requirements imposed on multifamily dwellings, lots containing multifamily dwellings, cluster developments or planned unit developments. Such regulations shall not prohibit the continuance of any nonconforming use, building or structure existing at the time of the adoption of such regulations. Such regulations shall not provide for the termination of any nonconforming use solely as a result of nonuse for a specified period of time without regard to the intent of the property owner to maintain that use. Any city, town or borough which adopts the provisions of this chapter may, by vote of its legislative body, exempt municipal property from the regulations prescribed by the zoning commission of such city, town or borough; but unless it is so voted municipal property shall be subject to such regulations. * * *

Sec. 8–2m. Floating and overlay zones and flexible zoning districts.

The zoning authority of any municipality that (1) was incorporated in 1784, (2) has a mayor and board of alderman form of government, and (3) exercises zoning power pursuant to a special act, may provide for floating and overlay zones and flexible zoning districts, including, but not limited to, planned development districts, planned development units, special design districts and planned area developments. The regulations shall establish standards for such zones and districts. Flexible zoning districts established under such regulations shall be designed for the betterment of the municipality and the floating and overlay zones and neighborhood in which they are located and shall not establish in a residential zone a zone that is less restrictive with respect to uses than the underlying zone of the flexible zoning district. Such regulations shall not authorize the expansion of a pre-existing, nonconforming use. Notwithstanding the provisions of this section, no planned development district shall be approved which would permit a use or authorize the expansion of a pre-existing nonconforming use where the underlying zone is a residential zone.

Sec. 8–4a. Zoning or planning commission may be designated as planning and zoning commission.

Any town, city or borough, unless otherwise provided by special act, may by ordinance or by vote of its legislative body designate its zoning commission or its planning commission as the planning and zoning commission for such municipality, and such commission shall thereupon have all the powers and duties of both a planning commission and a zoning commission and shall supersede any previous planning commission or zoning commission, as the case may be. * * *

Sec. 22a–1b. Evaluation by state agencies of actions affecting the environment. Public scoping process. Environmental monitor.

The General Assembly directs that, to the fullest extent possible: * * *

(c) Each state department, institution or agency responsible for the primary recommendation or initiation of actions which may significantly affect the environment shall in the case of each such proposed action make a detailed written evaluation of its environmental impact before deciding whether to undertake or approve such action. All such environmental impact evaluations shall be detailed statements setting forth the following:

> (1) A description of the proposed action which shall include, but not be limited to, a description of the purpose and need of the proposed action, and, in the case of a proposed facility, a description of the infrastructure needs of such facility,

including, but not limited to, parking, water supply, wastewater treatment and the square footage of the facility;

(2) the environmental consequences of the proposed action, including cumulative, direct and indirect effects which might result during and subsequent to the proposed action;

(3) any adverse environmental effects which cannot be avoided and irreversible and irretrievable commitments of resources should the proposal be implemented;

(4) alternatives to the proposed action, including the alternative of not proceeding with the proposed action and, in the case of a proposed facility, a list of all the sites controlled by or reasonably available to the sponsoring agency that would meet the stated purpose of such facility;

(5) an evaluation of the proposed action's consistency and each alternative's consistency with the state plan of conservation and development, an evaluation of each alternative including, to the extent practicable, whether it avoids, minimizes or mitigates environmental impacts, and, where appropriate, a description of detailed mitigation measures proposed to minimize environmental impacts, including, but not limited to, where appropriate, a site plan;

(6) an analysis of the short term and long term economic, social and environmental costs and benefits of the proposed action;

(7) the effect of the proposed action on the use and conservation of energy resources; and

(8) a description of the effects of the proposed action on sacred sites or archaeological sites of state or national importance. In the case of an action which affects existing housing, the evaluation shall also contain a detailed statement analyzing

(A) housing consequences of the proposed action, including direct and indirect effects which might result during and subsequent to the proposed action by income group as defined in section 8–37aa and by race, and

(B) the consistency of the housing consequences with the long-range state housing plan adopted under section 8–37t. As used in this section, "sacred sites" and "archaeological sites" shall have the same meaning as in section 10–381.

Sec. 22a–1c. Actions which may significantly affect the environment. Definition.

As used in sections 22a–1 to 22a–1i, inclusive, "actions which may significantly affect the environment" means individual activities or a sequence of planned activities proposed to be undertaken by state departments, institutions or agencies, or funded in whole or in part by the state, which could have a major impact on the state's land, water, air, historic structures and landmarks as defined in section 10–410, existing housing, or other environmental resources, or could serve short term to the disadvantage of long term environmental goals. Such actions shall include but not be limited to new projects and programs of state agencies and new projects supported by state contracts and grants, but shall not include (1) emergency measures undertaken in response to an immediate threat to public health or safety; or (2) activities in which state agency participation is ministerial in nature, involving no exercise of discretion on the part of the state department, institution or agency.

Sec. 48–1. United States; ceding jurisdiction to.

(a) The consent of the state of Connecticut is given, in accordance with the seventeenth clause, eighth section, of the first article of the Constitution of the United States, to the acquisition by the United States, by purchase, condemnation or otherwise, of any land in this state required for customhouses, courthouses, post offices, arsenals or other public buildings or for any other purposes of the government. Exclusive jurisdiction in and over any land so acquired by the United States is ceded to the United States for all purposes except the service of all civil and criminal process of the courts of this state and as provided in subsection (b) of this section; but the jurisdiction so ceded shall continue no longer than the United States owns such land. The jurisdiction ceded shall not vest until the United States has acquired the title to such lands by purchase, condemnation or otherwise; and, so long as such lands remain the property of the United States when acquired as aforesaid, the same shall be exempt from all state, county and municipal taxation, assessment or other charges.

(b) The Governor may accept from the appropriate federal authority on behalf of the state retrocession of full or partial jurisdiction over any land provided for in subsection (a) of this section. Documents concerning such retrocession shall be filed in the office of the Secretary of the State and recorded in a like manner as the original land acquisition by the United States.

CHARTER OF THE CITY OF HARTFORD

Ch. 7, § 2(d). Appointive boards and commissions required by Charter. Planning and zoning commission.

Said planning and zoning commission shall be comprised of individuals with skills and knowledge in related fields such as planning (including current involvement in the field), architecture, landscape architecture, real estate, or law. Said commission shall have all the powers and duties of both a planning commission and a zoning commission under the General Statutes and, upon the effective date of this provision, shall supersede the commission on the city plan as the city's planning commission and the council as the city's zoning commission. All ordinances and regulations adopted by the council related to planning and zoning prior to the effective date of this provision shall continue in full force and effect until modified, repealed or superseded in accordance with this Charter and the General Statutes. The decisions of the planning and zoning commission shall be consistent with the plan of conservation and development, as required by the General Statutes, unless the commission concludes that changes in circumstances since the adoption of the plan of development support a deviation from the plan. The commission shall set forth the basis for any deviation from the plan of development in its decision.

CITY OF HARTFORD HISTORIC PROPERTIES COMMISSION ORDINANCE, ARTICLE XII. OF THE MUNICIPAL CODE

Sec. 28–210.—Findings

The court of common council ("council") finds that there exists within the City of Hartford ("city"), many structures, parks, neighborhoods and other areas that have had historic, architectural and economic significance during Hartford's past and which can continue to contribute towards a healthy and thriving future for the city. The council finds that the city's ability to protect, preserve and effectively utilize its architectural and historical heritage and character for aesthetic and economic recovery will be enhanced by an historic preservation ordinance that establishes a mechanism to identify, preserve and enhance distinctive areas, sites, structures and objects that have historic, cultural, architectural and archeological significance. The council finds that the city derives much of its charm and unique appearance from its architecture and from its history, especially as a former center of manufacturing, finances and literature during the Victorian era. The council further finds that historic and architectural preservation is a means of promoting the general welfare of the city and its residents. In furtherance thereof and pursuant to its authority under the Charter of the City of Hartford and under the Home Rule Act, Connecticut General Statutes, section 7–148 the council has enacted this article.

Sec. 28–211.—Purpose

The purpose of this article is to promote the educational, cultural, economic, environmental, and general welfare of the city by:

(a) Strengthening the city's economy by stabilizing and improving property values and economic activity through the adaptive reuse of historic structures;

(b) Creating a mechanism to identify, preserve and enhance distinctive areas, sites, structures, features and objects that have historic, cultural, architectural and archeological significance;

(c) Fostering appropriate use and wider public knowledge and appreciation of such areas, sites, structures, features and objects;

(d) Protecting and enhancing the attractiveness of the city to homebuyers, homeowners, residents, tourists, visitors, businesses and shoppers;

(e) Providing a resource for information, education and expertise to those interested in rehabilitation or construction in a historic district or of an historic structure;

(f) Fostering civic pride in the city's history and development patterns;

(g) Protecting and enhancing neighborhood character;

(h) Fostering and encouraging preservation, restoration and rehabilitation that respects the historic, cultural, architectural and archeological significance of distinctive areas, sites, structures and objects; and

(i) Applying design standards in a reasonable and flexible manner to prevent the unnecessary loss of a community's historical features and to ensure compatible construction and rehabilitation in historic districts while not stifling change and development or forcing modern re-creations of historic styles.

Sec. 28–212.—Established, purposes and duties

There is hereby established a historic preservation commission whose purpose and duty shall be to carry out the purpose and to administer the provisions of this article. * * *

Sec. 28–219.—Review by historic preservation commission

(a) No person or entity may, without first applying and obtaining the approval of the commission, file an application for a demolition permit pursuant to section 9–12 of the Municipal Code, for a building permit pursuant to section 9–15 of the Municipal Code for (1) any demolition of any protected property or part thereof that is listed on the National or State Register of Historic Places, or, in regard to the National Register, for which a National Register application has been approved for study by the State Historic Preservation Office, (2) any alteration of any such protected property or part thereof if that alteration is visible from a street other than a street which faces only the back of the building, or (3) any construction of a new structure in a historic district.

(b) The commission shall adopt the Secretary of the Interior's Standards for Rehabilitation and Guidelines for Rehabilitating Historic Buildings, shall develop rules of procedure and shall publish design guidelines to assist applicants in satisfying these standards. The design guidelines shall provide for flexibility in materials and design to promote economic feasibility. The design guidelines shall describe a variety of methods and designs for preserving the historic architectural character of buildings and neighborhoods. The commission shall make reasonable efforts to guide owners in preserving historic architectural character in a cost-effective manner.

(c) The commission's procedures shall make provision for the consideration of economic hardship, including but not limited to consideration of the cost of historic preservation recommendations, the economic circumstances of the applicant, the availability of other architecturally appropriate alternatives, the relationship of the cost of historic preservation recommendations to the cost of the proposed project as a whole, and the impact of the historic preservation recommendations on the historic district as a whole and on the value of the property. The rules of procedure shall delineate submission requirements for at least four (4) types of hardship applications: (1) a provision for owner-occupied principal residences where exemption is granted based on demonstrated factors, such as age, ability to pay, and length of time living in the neighborhood; (2) a provision for non-owner occupied residential buildings containing six (6) or fewer dwelling units; (3) a provision for all other buildings, including commercial and industrial buildings; and (4) a provision for building demolition where there is no feasible and prudent alternative to demolition. If the applicant objects to compliance with this article because compliance will increase the cost of the alteration subject to review by the commission under this article by more than twenty (20) percent, the applicant shall provide the commission with at least two (2) realistic comparable professional estimates showing the difference in cost between the applicant's proposed alteration and alteration with the modifications requested by the commission. If the commission finds that such difference exceeds twenty (20) percent, the commission shall work with the applicant to find an alternative which will not increase the cost of the alteration by more than twenty (20) percent. The commission shall not require alterations which add more than twenty (20) percent to the cost of the alteration that is subject to review. To assist in the development of design guidelines the commission shall appoint an advisory committee with which it shall consult. The advisory committee shall include, but shall not be limited to, residents, design professionals, city planning, economic development and building code staff, developers, builders, preservation advocates including representatives of the Hartford Preservation Alliance, and such other persons or representatives as the commission may deem appropriate. The advisory committee shall present its recommendations to the commission within six (6) months of its first meeting. The commission shall hold at least one (1) public hearing on the design guidelines prior to voting on its adoption. The commission's procedures and design guidelines shall be subject to council approval prior to implementation. Any commission decision that denies an application or requires a modification of the alteration(s) and/or plan(s) shall state the reason(s) for denial, shall state what modification of the alteration(s) and/or plan(s) would result in approval of the application and shall refer to the relevant section(s) in the design guidelines in which the applicant can find appropriate guidance. * * *

(e) Demolition of a protected property shall be approved by the commission only if the applicant establishes, to the satisfaction of the commission, that (1) there is no economically feasible alternative to demolition or (2) the property, through no fault of any owner of the property after the effective date of this chapter, does not contribute to the architectural or historic character of the district and its demolition will not detract from the architectural or historic character of the district.

CITY OF HARTFORD ZONING REGULATIONS

Figure 3.2–A. Table of Principal Uses

USES	DT-1	DT-2	DT-3	MS-1	MS-2	MS-3	CX-1	CX-2	ID-1	ID-2	MX-1	MX-2	NX-#	N-#-1	N-#-2	N-#-3	OS
Residential & Lodging Category																	
Household Living																	
One-Unit Dwelling	◔	◔	◔	◔	●	◔	◔	◔			●	●	●	●	●	●	
2-Unit Dwelling	◔	◔	◔	◔	◔	●	◔	◔			●	●	●		●	●	
3-Unit Dwelling	◔	◔	◔	◔	◔	●	◔	●			●	●	●			●	
Multi-Unit Dwelling (4+ Units)	◔	●	◔	◔	●	◔	◔	●			●	●	●				
Micro/Efficiency Units	◔	●	◔									◑					
Bed & Breakfast																	
Group Living							○				○	○	○				
Group Living for Health Reasons	○	○	○	○	○	○	○	○	○	○	○	○	○	○	○	○	
Hotel/Apartment Hotel	●	●	●	●	●	●	●	●			●	●					
Residential Care, Large	●	●	●								●	●					
Residential Care, Small	●	●	●				●				●	●	●				
Roominghouse/Boardinghouse									○	○							
Temporary Shelter Facility									◑	◑							
Civic & Institutional Category																	
Assembly, Neighborhood	○	○	○	○	○	○	○	○			○	○	○	○	○	○	○
Assembly, General	○	○	○	○	○	○	○	○	○	○	○						○
Government/Higher Education/Hospital	○	○	○				○	○	○		○	○					
Library/Museum	●	●	●	●	●	●	●	●			●	●	○				
Police/Fire	○	○	○	○	○	○	○	○	○	○	○	○	○				
School: Pre-K, Elementary, Intermediate	○	○	○	○	○	○	○	○			○	○	○	○	○	○	
School: High School, Higher Education	○	○	○	○	○	○	○	○			○	○					
Stadium/Arena	○	○	○				○	○	○	○	○						
Transit Station	○	○	○	○	○	○	○	○	○	○	○	○	○				

KEY: ● = Permitted   ◔ = Permitted in Upper Stories Only   ◑ = Permitted subject to Use-specific conditions   ○ = Requires a Special Permit

USES	DT-1	DT-2	DT-3	MS-1	MS-2	MS-3	CX-1	CX-2	ID-1	ID-2	MX-1	MX-2	NX-#	N-#-1	N-#-2	N-#-3	OS
Open Space Category																	
Community Garden	◐	◐	◐	◐	◐	◐	◐	◐	◐	◐	◐	◐	◐	◐	◐	◐	◐
Honey Beekeeping	◐	◐	◐	◐	◐	◐	◐	◐	◐	◐	◐	◐	◐	◐	◐	◐	◐
Intensive Park Uses									○								○
Park	○	○	○	◐	◐	◐	◐	◐	◐	◐	◐	◐	◐	◐	◐	◐	◐
River Uses	○						○		○	○							○
Urban Farm						○	○	○	○	○	○	○	○	○	○	○	○
Retail Use Category																	
Neighborhood Retail	●	●	●	●	●	●		●				◐					
General Retail	●	●	●			●		●									
Beer/Wine/Liquor Sales	○	○	○	○	○	○		○									
Commercial Equipment & Supply						◐	○	◐	◐	◐							
Convenience Store	◐	◐	◐	◐	◐	◐		◐	◐	◐							
Discount Variety Store									◐	◐							
Outdoor Sales Lot								◐	◐								
Service Use Category																	
Neighborhood Service	◐	◐	◐	◐	◐			◐			◐	◐					
General Service	●							●									
Adult Day Care	●	●	●	●	●			●			◐	◐					
Automobile Fueling & Limited Service						○			●								
Automobile Service/Car Wash							○		●								
Automobile, Truck, Limousine Rental	◐							◐	●	●							
Child Day Care	◐	◐	◐	◐	◐	◐	◐	◐			◐	◐					
Community Service							●	●	●								
Drinking Places	○	○	○	○	○	○		○									
Eating Places	●	●	●	●	●	●		●	●	●		●					
Entertainment Assembly	○	○						○									
Pawn Shop/Check Cashing Establishment									◐								
Private Club	◐	◐	◐	◐	◐	◐	◐	◐				◐					
Smoking Places	○	○	○	○	○	○		○									
Tattoo/Piercing Parlor									◐								

KEY: ● = Permitted ◓ = Permitted in Upper Stories Only ◐ = Permitted subject to Use-specific conditions ○ = Requires a Special Permit

USES	DISTRICTS																
	DT-1	DT-2	DT-3	MS-1	MS-2	MS-3	CX-1	CX-2	ID-1	ID-2	MX-1	MX-2	NX-#	N-#-1	N-#-2	N-#-3	OS
Adult Use Category																	
Adult Establishment									○								
Employment Use Category																	
Office	◓	●	●	◓	●	●	●	●	●	●	●	●	●				
Craftsman/Studio	◐	◐	◐	◐	◐	◐	◐	◐	◐	◐		◐					
Infrastructure Use Category																	
Parking as a Principal Use				○	○	○	○	○	●	●	○	○	○				
Transportation & Utilities	○	○	○	○	○	○	○	○	○	○	○	○					○
Transmission Towers	○	○	○	○	○	○	○	○	○	○	○	○					○
Industrial Use Category																	
Heavy Industry									◐	◐							
Light Industry								◐	◐	◐							
Outdoor Storage Yard									◐	◐							
Transportation Facilities									◐	◐							
Warehouse/Distribution									◐	◐							

KEY: ● = Permitted ◓ = Permitted in Upper Stories Only ◐ = Permitted subject to Use-specific conditions ○ = Requires a Special Permit

Chapter 4—Building Types (Excerpts)

	Downtown Storefront in DT–3	Downtown General in DT–3	Apartment Building in MX–2	Row Building in MX–2
Minimum Primary Front Lot Line Coverage	85%	80%	80%	90%
Primary Build-To Zone	At or max 5' behind Building Line	At or max 15' behind Building Line	Within 5' of Building Line	Within 2' of Building Line
Maximum Building Coverage	100%	100%	65%	70%
Maximum Impervious Coverage (inc. Parking)	100%	100%	80%	80%

Permitted Parking & Loading Locations	Rear yard or internal to building	Rear yard or internal to building	Rear yard or, if 140' or more lot width, side yard	Rear yard
Minimum Height	2 stories & 40'	2 stories & 40'	3 stories	2 stories
Maximum Height (stories)	8	8	6	4.5
Minimum Ground Story Transparency	75%	20%	15%	15%
Street Façade Entrance Type	Storefront, arcade	Stoop, arcade	Stoop, porch	Stoop, porch
Permitted Roof Types	Parapet, pitched, flat, tower	Parapet, pitched, flat, tower	Parapet, pitched, flat, tower	Parapet, flat, tower

4.3.2.E.5 & 4.4.2.E.7. Bonuses for Downtown Storefront and Downtown General Building Types.

Property owners may exceed the maximum overall height set forth for Downtown Storefront and Downtown General Buildings by up to 6 stories by providing the following amenities:

a.   2 additional stories permitted by providing a green roof covering 75 percent of the overall roof surface area.

b.   3 additional stories for providing a functional green roof covering 50 percent of the overall roof surface area.

c.   2 additional stories for providing on-site renewable energy fulfilling at least 25 percent of the energy needs of the building occupants.

d.   3 additional stories for a combined heat and power system (cogeneration) fulfilling at least 50 percent of the heating and cooling needs of the building occupants.

e.   2 additional stories for designating 15 percent of residential units to be affordable.

Figure 4.20–A. Accessory Structure Table.

ACCESSORY STRUCTURES	DT-1	DT-2	DT-3	MS-1	MS-2	MS-3	CX-1	CX-2	ID-1	ID-2	MX-1	MX-2	NX-#	N-#-1	N-#-2	N-#-3	OS	Reference
Accessory Buildings																		4.20.3
Construction Structures	◐	◐	◐	◐	◐	◐	◐	◐	◐	◐	◐	◐	◐	◐	◐	◐	◐	4.20.3.A.
Kiosk				◐	◐	◐	◐	◐	◐	◐	◐	◐	◐				◐	4.20.3.B.
Out Building & Garage				◐	◐	◐	◐	◐	◐	◐	◐	◐	◐	◐	◐	◐	◐	4.20.3.C.
Parking Structure	◐	◐	◐	◐	◐	◐	◐	◐	◐	◐	◐	◐	◐					4.20.3.D.
Temporary Building	◐	◐	◐	◐	◐	◐	◐	◐	◐	◐	◐	◐	◐	◐	◐	◐	◐	4.20.3.E.
Accessory Outdoor Structures																		4.20.4
Ball Court	◐	◐	◐	◐	◐	◐	◐	◐	◐	◐	◐	◐	◐	◐	◐	◐	◐	4.20.4.A.
Deck & Patio	◐	◐	◐	◐	◐	◐	◐	◐	◐	◐	◐	◐	◐	◐	◐	◐	◐	4.20.4.B.
Dog Run							◐	◐	◐								◐	4.20.4.C.
Flag Pole	◐	◐	◐	◐	◐	◐	◐	◐	◐	◐	◐	◐	◐	◐	◐	◐	◐	4.20.4.E.
Fuel Pumps & Canopies					◐				◐									4.20.4.F.
Gazebo											◐	◐	◐	◐	◐	◐	◐	4.20.4.G.
Landscape Features	◐	◐	◐	◐	◐	◐	◐	◐	◐	◐	◐	◐	◐	◐	◐	◐	◐	4.20.4.H.
Temporary Storage Container	◐	◐	◐	◐	◐	◐	◐	◐	◐	◐	◐	◐	◐	◐	◐	◐	◐	4.20.4.I.
Accessory Urban Agriculture Structures																		4.20.5
Accessory Farm Structures	◐	◐	◐	◐	◐	◐	◐	◐	◐	◐	◐	◐	◐	◐	◐	◐	◐	4.20.5.A.
Compost Bins	◐	◐	◐	◐	◐	◐	◐	◐	◐	◐	◐	◐	◐	◐	◐	◐	◐	4.20.5.B.
Henhouses	◐	◐	◐	◐	◐	◐	◐	◐	◐	◐	◐	◐	◐	◐	◐	◐	◐	4.20.5.C.
Accessory Renewable Energy Structures																		4.20.6
Solar - Building-Mounted	◐	◐	◐	◐	◐	◐	◐	◐	◐	◐	◐	◐	◐	◐	◐	◐	◐	4.20.6.A.
Solar - Freestanding						◐	◐	◐	◐	◐	◐	◐	◐	◐	◐	◐	◐	4.20.6.B.
Solar - Parking Lot Canopy				◐	◐	◐	◐	◐	◐	◐	◐	◐						4.20.6.C.
Wind - Freestanding						◐		◐	◐	◐		◐						4.20.6.D.
Wind - Roof-Mounted	◐	◐	◐	◐	◐	◐	◐	◐	◐	◐	◐	◐	◐	◐	◐	◐	◐	4.20.6.E.

● Permitted
◐ Permitted subject to Use-Specific Regulations

Figure 4.20-A Accessory Structure Table

4.20.3.D. Accessory Buildings. Parking Structure.

A stand alone accessory structure for decked, multi-level parking (refer to Figure 4.20–D and Figure 4.20–E). A parking structure is not necessarily fully enclosed.

(1) Location. An accessory parking structure shall be located as follows:

    (a) Parking Structures shall be located in the rear yard only and shall be screened from view from the front of the lot or any Primary Street by the principal building.

(b) Parking Structures shall not extend closer to the front, corner, or side lot line than the principal structure.

(2) Height. The overall height of a Parking Structure shall be one story lower than the majority height of the principal structure, not including the roof type.

Figure 4.20–D & 4.20–E. Plan & Section of Parking Structure.

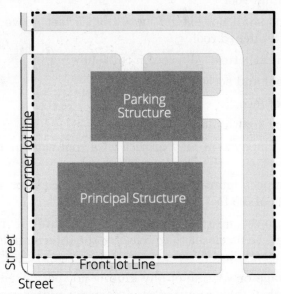

Figure 4.20-D Plan of Parking Structure.

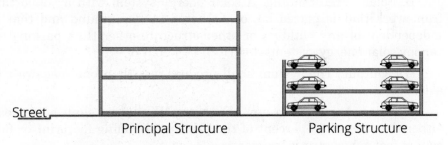

Figure 4.20-E Section of Parking Structure.

4.20.6. Accessory Renewable Energy Structures.

A. Solar—Building-Mounted. A solar energy system that is affixed to or an integral part of a principal or accessory building, including but not limited to photovoltaic or hot water solar energy systems which are contained within roofing materials, windows, skylights, and awnings.

(1) Quantity. The total square footage may not exceed the total area of roof surface of the structure to which the system is attached.

(2)   Flush Mounted System. Systems should be less than 4 inches from the roof surface whenever possible.

(3)   Height

(a)   Systems shall not extend beyond 3 feet parallel to the roof surface of a pitched roof.

(b)   Systems shall not extend beyond 4 feet parallel to the roof surface of a flat roof.

(c)   Systems shall not extend more than 5 feet above the highest peak of a pitched roof.

(4)   Location on Structure. Allowed on the following:

(a)   Principal and accessory structures.

(b)   Any roof face.

(c)   Side and rear building facades.

(5)   Projection. The system may project off a roof edge or building facade as follows.

(a)   May project laterally from a building facade or roof edge a maximum of 3.5 feet.

(b)   May project into an interior side or interior rear setback, but shall be no closer than 5 feet to the interior side or interior rear property line.

(6)   Signs. Signage or writing of any kind is not permitted on any portion of system, other than required manufacturer plates and safety labeling.

B. Solar—Freestanding. A solar energy system with a supporting framework that is placed on, or anchored in, the ground and that is independent of any building or other structure other than parking lot canopy solar energy systems described in 4.20.6.B.

(1)   Output. The system shall produce less than one megawatt of electricity.

(2)   Size. A system in any MX, N, or NX district shall not exceed either the area of 50 percent of the principal building footprint or 600 square feet, whichever is greater.

(3)   Maximum Height. The system shall be as close to the ground as practicable, and not taller than 20 feet on lots of at least 5 acres in the ID districts, 12 feet on lots of at least 5 acres, and 6 feet on all other lots, all measured from the grade at the base of the pole to the highest edge of the system.

(4)   Clearance. Minimum clearance between the lowest point of the system and the surface on which the system is mounted is 3 feet.

(5) Location. Allowed in the interior side yard and interior rear yard only.

(a) For any property designated as historic or located within a historic district, such system shall be located in the rear yard.

(6) Setbacks. All parts of the freestanding system shall be set back a minimum of 5 feet from the interior side and interior rear property lines and shall not be located in a public utility easement.

(7) Appearance. Such system must be gray, natural green, or beige in color, with the exception of the solar photovoltaic panels which are usually black, or system must be screened from view from surrounding residential properties.

(8) Materials. Such system shall not include any unfinished lumber.

C. Solar—Parking Lot Canopy.

A solar energy system with a supporting framework that is placed on, or anchored in, the ground and that is independent of any building or other structure, which is used in a parking lot or the top story of a parking structure to shade vehicles parked in such lot or structure.

(1) Size. A system in any residential district (MX, N, or NX) shall not exceed either the area of 50 percent of the principal building footprint or 600 square feet, whichever is greater.

(2) Maximum Height. The system shall be between 8 and 15 feet in height, so as to provide for parking underneath the system.

(3) Clearance. Minimum clearance between the lowest point of the system and the surface on which the system is mounted is 7.5 feet.

(4) Location. Allowed in the interior side yard and interior rear yard only, if applicable.

(a) For any property designated as historic or located within a historic district, such system shall be located in the rear yard, if applicable. * * *

E. Wind—Roof-Mounted. Wind energy systems that are attached to the roof of a building.

(1) Quantity. One turbine is allowed for every 750 square feet of the combined roof area of all structures on a zoning lot. For a pitched roof, each surface of the roof shall be included in the roof area calculation.

(2) Rated Capacity. A maximum rated capacity of 3 kilowatts per turbine is allowed.

(3) Height

(a) The maximum height of 15 feet is measured from the roof surface on which the system is mounted to the highest edge of the system with the exception of any pitches 10:12 or greater.

(b) The system shall not extend more than 5 feet above the highest peak of a pitched roof.

(4) Location. Roof-mounted wind energy systems are only permitted on structures that are a minimum of 4 stories tall or 40 feet.

(a) Roof-mounted wind energy systems must be set back from the roof or parapet wall one foot for every foot in height of the device above the roof or parapet wall.

(b) Roof-mounted wind energy systems shall only be permitted on roofs with a slope of one inch per foot or less.

(c) A roof-mounted wind energy system shall not be visible from the street when installed on any property designated as historic or located within a historic district.

(5) Installation. Roof-mounted wind energy systems shall be installed only by professional installers certified to install wind turbines, and only pursuant to manufacturer specifications.

4.20.7.B. Accessory Utility Structures. Electric Vehicle Charging Stations.

An electric vehicle charging station is a public or private parking space that is served by battery charging equipment with the purpose of transferring electric energy to a battery or other energy storage device in an electric vehicle.

(1) Types

(a) Level 1, slow charging, operates on a 15 to 20 amp breaker on a 120 volt AC circuit.

(b) Level 2, medium charging, operates on a 40 to 100 amp breaker on a 208 volt or 240 volt AC circuit.

(c) Level 3, fast or rapid charging, operates on a 60 amp or higher breaker on a 480 volt or higher 3-phase circuit with special grounding equipment.

(2) Siting & Setbacks. The siting and setbacks for stations shall be the same as the parking facility within which they are associated. * * *

5.3 Transit Oriented Development Overlay.

5.3.1 General.

A. Intent. The Transit Oriented Development Overlay is intended to allow for greater flexibility and require greater density in the vicinity of fixed nodes of public transportation. Structures that are appropriate for the district are located near transit stations as defined in 3.3.2.H.

B. Applicability. The following regulations apply to all locations noted on the zoning map with the Transit Oriented Development

Overlay, which may be overlain on lots located in any district, other than the DT districts, which are within one-half (1/2) of a mile of any existing or proposed transit station.

5.3.2 Application.

The Transit Oriented Development Overlay requires applicants to file a zoning permit application, unless a special permit application is otherwise required by other provisions in these regulations (for example, in the case of an Assembly Use). The staff or commission may require a transportation management plan to be submitted as part of the application.

5.3.3 Regulations.

Staff or the commission, as applicable, may approve a development with the Transit Oriented Development Overlay which meets the following conditions: * * *

C. Buildings. Permitted building types shall include the following:

(1)   Downtown Storefront Building Type. The requirements for the Downtown Storefront Building Type as defined for the DT–3 district shall be utilized with the bonuses offered by 4.3.2. Note 5.

(2)   Downtown General Building Type. The requirements for the Downtown General Building Type as defined for the DT–3 district shall be utilized with the bonuses offered by 4.4.2. Note 7.

(3)   Apartment Building Type. The requirements of the Apartment Building Type as defined for the MX–2 shall be utilized.

(4)   Row Building. The requirements of the Row Building Type as defined for the MX–2 district shall be utilized.

D. Uses. The uses shall be any of the uses allowed in the DT districts, but not uses allowed in the underlying zoning district which are not also allowed in the DT districts. Such uses are either permitted, permitted with conditions, or special permitted, in the same manner as in the DT districts.

E. Parking. Parking is required per Figure 7.2–A Required Off-Street Automobile Parking. The DT district exemption noted on the table does not apply. Refer to 7.2.4.C. for a transit-related parking credit.

7.2.2. Required Automobile and Bicycle Parking.

A. Organized by Use. The parking requirements are organized by use, in a similar fashion to Figure 3.2–A Table of Principal Uses in 3.0 Uses.

(1)   Parking rates are provided for general use categories; these numbers are applicable for all of the uses within these categories.

(2) If a specific use requires a different parking rate than its use category, it is also listed in Figure 7.2–A Required Off-Street Automobile Parking and Figure 7.2–B Bicycle Parking.

B. Parking Spaces required. The "Required Number of Off-Street Parking Spaces" column indicates the required number of off-street parking spaces in Figure 7.2–A Required Off-Street Automobile Parking, which may be subject to credits and other reductions as are detailed in this section.

C. Maximum allowable Parking Spaces. When a use requires more than 10 spaces and a maximum number is not specified Figure 7.2–A, it is not permitted to provide more than 110 percent of the minimum parking requirement.

D. Required Bicycle Parking.

(1) Purpose. The purpose of this section is to encourage bicycle use as a mode of transportation and lessen the impacts of automobile use, by ensuring quick, convenient and safe access to secure bicycle parking. To achieve this purpose, this section provides for long-term bicycle parking, meant for residents and employees to store bicycles for long periods of time, and short-term bicycle parking, intended to serve users who will quickly store bicycles, for a period of several hours.

(2) Applicability. Bicycle parking requirements apply to the following projects:

(a) Construction of a new building.

(b) Establishment of a new use, on any zoning lot, other than an open-air use such as a farmers' market or bazaar.

(c) Projects that increase the number of residential dwelling units in any building or on any zoning lot by 15 percent or more.

(d) Projects that increase the floor area of non-residential uses in any building or on any zoning lot by 15 percent or more.

(3) Required Quantity of Spaces. Minimum long-term and short-term bicycle parking spaces for specified land uses are set forth in Figure 7.2–B Bicycle Parking.

Figure 7.2–A. Required Off-Street Automobile Parking.

USES	REQUIRED NUMBER OF OFF-STREET PARKING SPACES
Residential & Lodging Uses	
One-Unit Dwelling/Group Living for Health Reasons	Minimum 1 space, maximum 4 spaces per zoning lot. For One-Unit Dwelling Building in N-1-1, maximum 6 spaces per zoning lot
2- & 3- Unit Dwelling	Minimum .5 space, maximum 2 spaces per unit
Multi-Unit Dwelling (4+ Dwelling Units)	Minimum 1 spaces, maximum 3 spaces per unit
Micro/Efficiency Units	Maximum 2 spaces per unit
Bed & Breakfast, Hotel/Apartment Hotel	Minimum 1 space, maximum 2 spaces per 2 guest rooms
Temporary Shelter Facility	Minimum 1 space per 2 employees
Group Living	Minimum 1 space, maximum 1.5 spaces per adult resident. For foster homes and children's homes: minimum 1 space, maximum 2 spaces per 4 children residents
Residential Care, Large	Minimum 1 space, maximum 4 spaces for every 4 beds (excluding bassinets)
Residential Care, Small	Minimum 1 space, maximum 2 spaces per resident
Roominghouse/Boardinghouse	Minimum .5 space, maximum 1 space per rooming unit; plus minimum .5 space, maximum 1.5 spaces per dwelling unit of owner or manager
Civic & Institutional Uses	
Hospital	Minimum 1 space, maximum 4 spaces for every 4 beds (excluding bassinets)
Library/Museum	None
All Other Civic & Institutional Uses	In accordance with special permit review
Open Space Uses	
Park	In accordance with special permit review
Urban Farm	In accordance with special permit review
Retail Uses	
Outdoor Sales Lot for Vehicles	1 space for each unregistered vehicle permitted to be sold, plus 1 additional space per minimum 10, maximum 5 such vehicles, reserved for visitors/employees

USES	REQUIRED NUMBER OF OFF-STREET PARKING SPACES
All Other Retail Uses	Maximum 3 spaces per 1,000 square feet net floor area devoted to retail space
Service Uses	
Automobile Fueling & Limited Service, Automobile Service/Car Wash, Drinking Places, Entertainment Assembly, & Smoking Places	In accordance with special permit review
Eating Places	Maximum 3 spaces for every 5 persons based on maximum capacity
All Other Service Uses	Maximum 3 spaces per 1,000 square foot of net floor area devoted to customer service
Adult Uses	
Adult Establishment	Minimum 1 space, maximum 3 spaces per 600 square feet net floor area devoted to retail space; OR for assembly-type uses: minimum 1 space for every 4 persons based on maximum capacity
Employment Uses	
All Employment Uses	Minimum 1 space, maximum 4 spaces per 1,000 square feet
Infrastructure Uses	
All Infrastructure Uses	In accordance with special permit review
Industrial Uses	
All Industrial & Warehouse Uses	Minimum 1 space per 4 employees, maximum 4 spaces per 4 employees

Notes:
These off-street automobile parking requirements shall not be applied to zoning lots in the DT-1, DT-2, and DT-3 districts.

Where special permit review is required for particular projects, these off-street automobile parking requirements shall be used as guidance but are not binding.

Figure 7.2-A Required Off-Street Automobile Parking

Figure 7.2–B. Bicycle Parking.

BICYCLE PARKING		
Use	Minimum Long-Term Bicycle Spaces	Minimum Short-Term Bicycle Spaces
One-Unit Dwellings, 2- Unit Dwellings 3-Unit Dwellings	No minimum requirement	No minimum requirement
Bed & Breakfast, Hotel/Apartment Hotel	1 per every 60 sleeping rooms	1 per every 30 sleeping rooms, with 4 minimum
All Other Residential Uses	1 per every 30 dwelling units, rooming units, or beds, as applicable	1 per every 15 dwelling units, rooming units, or beds, as applicable, with 4 minimum
Assembly Use & Stadium/Arena	1 per every 500 seats	1 per every 50 seats
Higher Education Facility	1 per every 15,000 square feet of building area	1 per every 5,000 square feet of building area
Transit Station	30 spaces within a .125-mile radius	100 spaces
All Other Civic & Institutional Uses	1 per 15 employees	1 per every 10,000 square feet, with 10 minimum
Parks & Urban Farms	1 per every 15,000 square feet, with 15 minimum	1 per every 15,000 square feet, with 15 minimum
Retail & Service Uses	No minimum requirement	1 per every 3,000 square feet
Office/ Employment Uses	1 per 15 employees	1 per every 10,000 square feet
Commercial parking lots and garages	1 per every 30 automobile parking spaces	1 per every 15 automobile parking spaces

Figure 7.2-B Bicycle Parking

7.2.2.E. Required Automobile and Bicycle Parking. Required Electric Vehicle Charging Stations.

New development shall provide for electric vehicle charging stations designed in accordance with 4.20.7.B. in the following prescribed manner:

(1) For Residential and Lodging Uses, Government/ Higher Education/Hospital Uses, Police/Fire, Schools, Employment Uses, Parking as a Principal Use, and Industrial Uses with 35 or more parking spaces, 3 percent of the total number of parking spaces required shall have Level 1 or Level 2 charging stations.

(2) For Assembly, Library/Museum, Stadiums/Arenas, Transit Station, Retail Uses, and Service Uses with 35 or more parking spaces, at least 3 percent of the total number of parking spaces shall be wired to support a Level 2 charging station, if one is not installed initially, or shall have Level 1 or Level 2 charging stations.

(3) Level 3 charging stations are not required, but may be installed to satisfy the electric vehicle charging station requirements described herein.

7.2.4 Parking Credits.

Vehicular parking standards in Figure 7.2–A Required Off-Street Automobile Parking may be reduced by achieving one or all of the following credits, provided, however, that if any conditions or agreements required by this section are no longer available or in force, then parking must be provided as otherwise required in this chapter.

A. Bicycle Parking Credit. For all uses, the provision of bicycle parking over and above the requirements of Figure 7.2–B Bicycle Parking may be credited against the vehicular parking requirement at a rate of one credit for every 5 bicycle parking spaces.

(1) No fee shall be required for the bicycle parking subject to the credit.

(2) Required parking spaces may be reduced up to 15 percent.

B. Sustainably Designed Parking Facility Credit.

In parking garages or parking lots where over 50 percent of the lot is covered by freestanding solar energy systems (permitted per 4.20.6.B.), the required vehicular parking spaces may be reduced by 15 percent if the applicant achieves 2 of the following measures or 30 percent if the applicant achieves 4 of the following measures:

(1) Applies only low- or no-volatile organic compound coatings to all surfaces and utilizes either an open-air design with no ventilation system in the parking areas or ventilates the decks with variable controlled air flow or sensor-activated technology.

(2) Has a green roof (vegetation) or blue roof (retains water).

(3) Generates more than a de minimis amount of renewable energy through use of solar panels or wind turbines.

(4) Uses exclusively energy-efficient lighting fixtures, as well as lighting controls such as timers, photo sensors, or occupancy sensors.

C. Transit Credit. For all uses, vehicular parking requirements may be reduced with proximity to any transit station as defined in 3.3.2.H. or bus stop served by 2 or more public bus service routes with frequencies every 20 minutes or less. Proximity is measured from any point along the property line to the transit station or bus stop, subject to this section.

(1) Within 1,000 feet of a transit station, a reduction of 50 percent of the required off-street parking.

(2) Within 1,000 feet of a bus stop subject to this section or 2,000 feet of a transit station, a reduction of 20 percent of the required off-street parking.

(3) Within 2,000 feet of a bus stop subject to this section, a reduction of 10 percent of the required off-street parking.

D. Car-Share Parking Credit. For all uses, the vehicular parking requirements may be reduced by designating parking spaces as car-share parking spaces or if an off-site car-share parking facility is located within 800 feet of the site. Car-share parking spaces are defined as spaces that house vehicles owned by a car-share company which can be directly accessed by drivers without the need for a customer service counter, and thus a distinct use from an automobile rental service.

(1) Per each car-share parking space provided, required parking spaces shall be reduced by 4 spaces.

(2) Required parking spaces may be reduced up to 40 percent.

(3) Approval. Applicant must provide documentation of an agreement with a car-share company, providing services to building tenants. If this agreement should terminate at any point, the applicant shall be required to provide parking as otherwise required herein.

E. Transportation Management Reductions. For all uses, when an applicant submits a transportation management plan, the required automobile parking spaces may be reduced by 15 percent if the applicant achieves 2 of the following measures, or 30 percent if the applicant achieves 4 of the following measures:

(1) Ensure that 10 percent of employees participate in a regional ride matching system.

(2) Institute a monthly, market-rate parking charge for all off-street parking, without permitting such charge to be employer-subsidized, with a discount for vehicles containing 3 or more persons.

(3) Provide a vanpool or subscription bus service for at least 10 percent of employees.

(4) Provide subsidized transit passes for 10 percent of employees.

(5) Subsidize at least 25 percent of costs for employee use of high-occupancy motor vehicles such as carpools and vanpools, if there are no parking charges.

(6) Prove that at least 10 percent of employees will walk or bike to work.

CHAPTER EIGHT

PRIVATE RESTRICTIONS ON LAND USE AND THE RISE OF COMMON INTEREST COMMUNITIES

I. INTRODUCTION

Why rely exclusively on government to regulate land use? Indeed, why rely on government at all? Landowners might use private law restrictions to supplement zoning and other public land use controls, and private restrictions might, in some situations, serve as a substitute for government regulation. This chapter explores the promise of—and problems with—private law mechanisms for land use control. These mechanisms include: nuisance litigation; private covenants, and especially the imposition of such covenants through common interest communities; and special districts, such as the business improvement district. This chapter will cover all three of these areas but will focus on the common interest community as the most common private alternative to public land use regulation.

A. NUISANCE

One legal tool for exerting some control over land use is the law of private and public nuisance. We assume that most students have had some exposure to nuisance law in the first-year curriculum, and so we simply summarize key issues here. Both public and private nuisance law are built around the injunction not to use one's land in a way that harms others: *sic utero tuo ut alienam non laedas*. The law of private nuisance empowers an owner to challenge a neighbor's activities where they substantially and unreasonably interfere with the use and enjoyment of the owner's property. *See* Restatement (Second) of Torts § 822 (1979). A public nuisance occurs when a landowner's use unreasonably interferes with "a right common to the general public." *Id.* at § 821B.

Uses that might be unproblematic when conducted separately from one another may be problematic when conducted in close proximity. As the Court put it in *Euclid*, a nuisance "may be merely a right thing in the wrong place, like a pig in the parlor instead of the barnyard." Vill. of Euclid v. Ambler Realty Co., 272 U.S. 365, 388 (1926). Thus, rather than constituting a hypothetical list of land uses that may not be undertaken under any circumstances, the law of nuisance—like zoning law—is concerned with potential conflicts between incompatible land uses. This common focus has led some commentators to suggest that nuisance law might, at least if modified in certain ways, serve as a viable alternative to modern land use regulation. *See, e.g.,* Robert C. Ellickson, Alternatives to Zoning: Covenants, Nuisance Rules, and Fines as Land Use Controls, 40 U. Chi. L. Rev. 681, 719–61 (1973).

Although nuisance law and zoning law address the same concerns about incompatible adjacent uses, nuisance law is unappealing as a primary tool of land use regulation, at least in its present form. For example, courts are reluctant to adjudicate nuisance cases based on anticipated harms from projects that have not yet been undertaken. Typically, courts assign a heavy burden to plaintiffs bringing these "anticipatory nuisance" actions, requiring them to demonstrate that the defendant's use will clearly constitute a nuisance, once completed. *See, e.g.,* Simpson v. Kollasch, 749 N.W.2d 671, 675 (Iowa 2008) ("Relief will usually be denied until a nuisance has been committed where the thing sought to be enjoined may or may not become such, depending on its use or other circumstances."). Once conflicting land uses are fully in place, informally resolving the conflict becomes potentially much more costly since the parties are locked into a bilateral monopoly with one another and since—if the uses are truly incompatible—one of the parties may have to relocate or take expensive measures to mitigate a harm that would not have occurred had the incompatible uses not come into close proximity to one another in the first place. In addition, where a nuisance affects a large number of landowners, those owners may face a collective action problem that delays or deters the filing of a private nuisance action. Finally, nuisance law has no mechanism for regulating building forms and layouts—which, as Chapter Three describes, is increasingly common in twenty-first century zoning laws. All of these limitations of nuisance law make zoning's prospective regulation of land use somewhat more attractive.

B. COVENANTS

Another, perhaps more promising, substitute for public zoning law is provided by the law of private covenants that run with the land. Covenants are a type of servitude—that is, a private arrangement, which is passed on to successors-in-interest, involving rights or obligations tied to land ownership or occupancy.

When zoning emerged in the early 20th century, property law was replete with doctrinal obstacles to enforcement of servitudes. Ill-defined requirements that servitudes have "privity of estate" and "touch or concern" the land made it difficult for landowners to predict whether covenants would be enforced against successors-in-interest. Enforcement against successors is critical to any scheme of private land use regulation, because no servitudes would be worth negotiating if a landowner could escape from its strictures by merely selling his land to a third party. However, courts have significantly relaxed the doctrinal limitations on enforcement of private covenants, a trend recognized and accelerated by the Restatement (Third) of Property, which called for the abandonment of most of the traditional doctrines, substituting instead a "public policy" limit on enforcement of servitudes. Legislative enactment of condominium statutes also set the stage for privately-imposed restrictions in one ownership form. For example, the Uniform Common Interest Ownership Act (UCIOA) has expanded the condominium concept to provide a statutory framework for imposing private restrictions even in communities where individual homes are not held in condominium ownership.

Doctrinal obstacles aside, covenants may nonetheless be a poor substitute for land use regulation in developed areas. Indeed, zoning originated in cities, where land ownership was already fragmented among a large group of property owners. In a world of fragmented ownership, privately-negotiated restrictions are impractical because of high transaction costs associated with obtaining consent from all of the residents of a neighborhood. Suppose, for instance, a group of landowners wanted to prevent the encroachment of industrial uses into their residential neighborhood (the problem in Village of Euclid v. Ambler Realty). Even if the vast majority of landowners supported a restriction on industrial use, and even if doctrine did not preclude enforcement of such a restriction, the restriction would not be of much value if even two or three landowners refused to agree, and built factories or warehouses on their parcels. Public restrictions, through zoning, bypassed the need to obtain unanimous consent of all of the landowners in the area. On the other hand, fragmented ownership is not a problem for a developer with a large tract of land. And it is precisely in the development of subdivisions on new tracts where we have seen significant rise of covenants regulating land use—and serving as a substitute for zoning schemes.

Why would a developer want to impose restrictions on the units within a development? The developer's primary motive is profit, and developers who develop common interest communities typically do so because they believe that the restrictions will increase the market value (and therefore the price) of the units. That is, developers believe that residents will pay more for homes that provide common facilities (and require unit owners to pay assessments for those facilities), for homes bound by architectural controls, and other features. A developer interested in profit would not be likely to impose restrictions that would make the individual units unattractive to potential residents. Of course the developer might be mistaken about consumer demand, and there might be public policy reasons to limit the sort of restrictions a developer might impose, even if those restrictions do reflect consumer demand. This chapter examines first the mechanisms for creating a common interest community, and then turns to some of the problem areas associated with privately-created restrictions on land use. In studying these materials, consider the relative advantages of private and public regulation of land use. In what situations, if any, does the availability of private restrictions make zoning obsolete?

II. THE MECHANICS OF CREATING A COMMON INTEREST COMMUNITY

A developer who plans to create a common interest community starts with an idea about the restrictions that might be attractive to purchasers. But a sensible developer also considers a number of other issues. First, who will manage the community and enforce the restrictions? Once the developer has sold all of the units, the developer has no interest in remaining in the picture. To the extent the development has common areas that need maintenance, the developer will want to create a community association to assess property owners for the costs of maintenance. Also, because no individual unit owner is likely to have enough of an interest in potential violations to bring an action to enforce the restrictions, the developer will typically give the association power to enforce all restrictions.

Second, the developer will want to account for the certainty that conditions will change over the life of the development. The residents may develop different preferences over time. Unforeseen consequences may make some of the restrictions seem unwise and may generate demand for imposition of new restrictions. As a result, the developer will want to make provision for a governance structure that accommodates the community's shifting needs.

Consider, then, the documents the developer will prepare to create the common interest community.

A. THE DECLARATION

The Declaration of Covenants, Conditions and Restrictions (often called the Declaration or the Master Deed) is the foundation for the common interest community. The Declaration includes a number of critical provisions:

1.   The Declaration spells out the geographical boundaries of the community subject to its restrictions;

2.   The Declaration specifies the restrictive covenants imposed on use of land within the community;

3.   If the community is to have a community association, the Declaration requires owners within the community to belong to the association and to pay assessments to the association;

4. In a community with an association, the Declaration identifies the powers and duties of the association, and allocates voting rights within the association. In a purely residential association, the most common allocation is one-unit, one-vote (not one person, one vote), but some associations allocate voting rights based on unit value. In an association with both residential and commercial units, allocation of voting rights may be more complicated.

5. The Declaration will include provisions for its own amendment, and should also give the members of the association power to terminate the covenants in accordance with specified voting procedures.

In an earlier era, many declarations provided that the community's covenants would terminate at a specified date. What difficulties would such a termination provision generate? Can you imagine why most developers do not provide express limits on the duration of covenants?

The developer will record the declaration in the county or local office designated for recording real estate transactions. The declaration will be prepared and recorded before the developer sells any units.

B. THE BYLAWS OF THE COMMUNITY ASSOCIATION

Suppose the declaration requires membership in an association and gives the association power to impose assessments on unit owners. What documents create the association? The developer can choose to incorporate the association, in which case the developer will prepare a certificate of incorporation, or the developer can form the association as an unincorporated association. In either case, the developer will have to prepare bylaws for the association. Although the declaration itself will include fundamental provisions about the association's governance structure, most of the details about the association's operations structure will appear in the bylaws. In some but not all jurisdictions, the developer will have to record the bylaws. In other jurisdictions, the developer has a choice about whether to record. Recording provides notice to prospective purchasers, but makes amendment of the bylaws more cumbersome.

C. THE PLAT MAP

In addition to the declaration, the developer will record a plat map laying out the location of the individual lots within the community. If the development is a condominium, the plat map will also include floor plans for the individual units. The plat map identifies roads and easements within the development. The map enables the developer to sell individual units by referring to the location of those units on the map.

D. THE DEED

The declaration, the association bylaws, and the plat map will be prepared before the developer sells a single unit. Until the developer sells a unit, the developer is free to modify the declaration or the plat map, because the developer is the only party affected by any modification. Once the developer sells off a parcel, however, all of the property within the community becomes bound by the restrictions imposed in the declaration.

The deed is the instrument the developer uses to sell off the individual units. Each deed should refer to the declaration and to the plat map. So long as the deed from the developer to the initial purchaser of an individual lot makes reference to the declaration, the lot becomes bound by the restrictions, and subsequent purchasers remain bound even if the initial purchaser, or some successor, omits reference to the declaration in a subsequent deed.

NOTES AND QUESTIONS

1.   A developer could, of course, impose restrictions on all parcels within a development without creating a community association at all. The developer could record a declaration imposing single-family home restrictions on all lots within the development, or imposing size restrictions on any buildings built, without creating other covenants. Or the developer could impose the restrictions not by recording a single declaration, but by including the covenants in each individual deed as the developer sells off the parcels.

What problems would you foresee if the developer imposes restrictions without creating an association? Who would bear the cost of enforcing the restrictions? Would you expect a freerider problem to develop? Suppose the restrictions were no longer in the interest of the affected lot owners. How could they amend or remove the restrictions if the developer included no provisions for modification or termination? Statutes and common law rules permit parties to seek termination in extreme circumstances, but not without bearing the cost and uncertainty of litigation. *See, e.g.,* N.Y. Real Prop. Acts. Law § 1951 (permitting extinguishment of covenant when court finds that restriction "is of no actual and substantial benefit" to party seeking enforcement); Blakeley v. Gorin, 365 Mass. 590, 313 N.E.2d 903 (1974).

Suppose the developer does not prepare a declaration, and omits the restrictions from the deeds to some of the lots in the development. Can neighbors whose parcels are restricted enforce the restrictions against owners whose lots have never been explicitly restricted? In Sanborn v. McLean, 233 Mich. 227, 206 N.W. 496 (1925), the Michigan Supreme Court held that when, pursuant to the developer's "general plan" of residential development, the developer conveys one lot with a restriction, a "reciprocal negative easement" is impliedly created, and binds the land retained by the developer. *See also* Restatement (Third) of Property (Servitudes) § 2.14. The Sanborn doctrine, however, has been rejected in a number of jurisdictions because of the burden it places on title searchers. *See, e.g.,* Houghton v. Rizzo, 361 Mass. 635, 281 N.E.2d 577 (1972).

2. *Implied Powers.* Suppose the developer creates a community association but fails to confer important powers on the association—such as the power to compel members to join the association, or the power to impose assessments on residents. Does the association have any basis for compelling recalcitrant owners to join, or to pay assessments? A number of courts have held that a person who purchases a lot with knowledge that an association exists and provides services to community residents thereby enters into an implied-in-fact contract to pay a proportionate share of the cost of those services. *See, e.g.,* Seaview Ass'n of Fire Island, N.Y., Inc. v. Williams, 69 N.Y.2d 987, 517 N.Y.S.2d 709, 510 N.E.2d 793 (1987). The Restatement (Third) of Property (Servitudes) § 6.5(1)(a) provides expressly that "a common interest community has the power to raise the funds reasonably necessary to carry out its functions by levying assessments against the individually owned property in the community", and a comment goes on to indicate that the power to levy assessments "will be implied if not expressly granted by the declaration or by statute." *Id.* § 6.5 cmt. b.

Should it matter whether a landowner who refuses to pay the assessment actually uses the service provided by the association? *Cf.* Popponesset Beach Ass'n, Inc. v. Marchillo, 39 Mass. App. Ct. 586, 592, 658 N.E.2d 983, 987 (1996) (holding that "[p]roviding an amenity or service that benefits the land of another, in the absence of invitation therefore, does not compel the owner of the benefited land to pay for it," but also noting that there was no evidence that objecting residents had availed themselves of the association's recreational facilities and services).

3. *Termination Provisions.* If you represented a developer, what provisions would you make for termination of restrictions? Would you permit the association board to terminate restrictive covenants? A majority of residents? Would you require unanimous consent for termination? What problems would each of these alternatives present?

4. *Options Markets as a Mechanism for Facilitating the Creation of Servitudes.* Lee Anne Fennell has argued that lawmakers (or developers) could increase the usefulness of servitudes law as an alternative—or supplement—to public regulation by developing markets for options in servitudes. The problem with public regulation, she argues, is its tendency either to overprotect or underprotect property owners who might, all things being equal, be willing to enter into transactions to permit certain uses or restrain their own use. *See* Lee Anne Fennell, Revealing Options, 118 Harv. L. Rev. 1399, 1450–51 (2005). On the other hand, strategic behavior can make it difficult to reach agreements. This is particularly true when conflicting land uses are already in place. In such situations, each owner can only transact with the other, locking them into what is known as a "bilateral monopoly." Economists believe that bilateral monopolies are particularly likely to generate strategic behavior that drives up transaction costs and prevents people from reaching a mutually beneficial agreement. To try to reduce the problem of strategic behavior, Fennell draws on tools more often associated with financial markets than land use regulation, such as "call" options (options to purchase property at a "strike" price, which itself might either be fixed or determined according to some fixed formula or index) and "put" options (options to sell at some later time). By facilitating the trading of such options, she argues, decision-makers can allocate rights to those who value them most, and keep strategic behavior in check. *See* Lee Anne Fennell, The Unbound Home 96–119 (2009). She proposes, for example, that governments create "entitlements subject to a self-made option" (or "ESSMO"). In an ESSMO, an owner would be able to enjoy an entitlement, but subject to the right of others to exercise a call option at a price set in advance by the owner herself. To discourage the owner from setting the call option price higher than her true valuation, the government might charge the owner a fee based on her stated valuation or use the valuation as the basis for a tax assessment. *See id.* at 106–08.

Another tool she proposes is the "customizable callable call," an option to purchase away from the owner her right to engage in a particular use. This device would have the landowner develop the precise use subject to the option. To prevent strategic valuations, the community might charge the landowner a periodic tax based on her valuation of the option. If the community did not object to the use, it would permit the landowner to continue to engage in it, collecting its tax on the activity. But if it did object, it could buy the landowner out at the price she declared in advance. See *id.* at 111–14.

Both the ESSMO and the "customizable callable call" make it more costly for landowners to exercise the full panoply of use and veto rights that have traditionally gone along with landownership. Owners therefore require some reason to participate in these schemes. This can be accomplished either through coercive mandate (e.g., land use regulations could specify that some uses might only be permitted subject to a self-made option or a "callable call") or through the use of broad financial incentives, such as "flexibility taxes," which charge owners to opt out of the programs, or "put options" against the state, which permit owners to force the state to pay them to opt into the program. Fennell's innovative proposals raise a number of interesting questions. Who should decide the permissible subject matter of these options? For example, should landowners be able to use the sorts of options mechanisms Fennell proposes in order to transact away their rights to object to a nuisance in the future? Could such a result be achieved using existing servitudes mechanisms? Do you think these options mechanisms are too complex for the typical landowner to manage?

III. THE POWER TO LEVY ASSESSMENTS

The declaration of a community association will rarely fix the amount the association may assess against each unit owner. Maintenance and construction costs are unlikely to remain constant, and the community's needs will change over time, which may require the association to confront unanticipated problems. As a result, the declaration will typically give the association the power to determine and collect assessments from individual unit owners. That power, however, can make it difficult for unit owners to plan their annual expenses. What limits, if any, should there be on the power of an association to impose assessments? Consider the following case:

Parker v. Figure "8" Beach Homeowners' Association, Inc.

Court of Appeals of North Carolina, 2005
170 N.C.App. 145, 611 S.E.2d 874

■ HUDSON, JUDGE.

This case concerns a dispute between a coastal homeowner's association and one of its members about the association's authority to levy a special assessment for dredging and maintenance of a waterway. On 21 February 2002, plaintiff Raymond Clifton Parker sued for judgment declaring that a vote on the assessment, the assessment itself, and a contract between defendant New Hanover County ("the county") and defendant Figure "8" Beach Homeowners' Association, Inc. ("HOA") were *ultra vires*, inappropriately obtained, and null and void. Both defendants moved for summary judgment, and by consent of all parties, plaintiff was deemed to have moved for summary judgment. The court denied plaintiff's motion and granted defendants' motions by order entered 16 May 2003. Plaintiff appeals. We affirm.

Plaintiff owns property on Figure 8 Island ("Figure 8"), a privately owned island of 563 lots in New Hanover County. Mason Inlet runs along the south end of the island, separating it from the Town of Wrightsville Beach. Figure 8 is governed pursuant to the HOA bylaws and applicable restrictive covenants. Figure 8 property owners, including plaintiff, are members of the HOA. On 29 January 1993, the covenants were amended to add "channel dredging; beach renourishment" as purposes for which annual assessments could be used. Until 12 April 1993, there were three versions of restrictive covenants on Figure 8 lots, based on their date of sale. On 12 April 1993, the HOA made the 1978 version of the restrictive covenant applicable to all lots. This covenant obligates property owners to pay an annual assessment in an amount fixed by the HOA board, which can also levy additional assessments as it deems necessary. Any assessment for new capital improvements costing more than $60,000 requires approval by a majority of HOA members eligible to vote.

In 1999, the county, the HOA, and several other homeowner associations in the Wrightsville Beach area had been considering measures to deal with erosion, channel dredging and other beach-related maintenance matters. The homeowner associations formed a coalition called the Mason Inlet Preservation Group ("MIPG"), which undertook a project to relocate Mason Inlet. The sand dredged from the project would be used to renourish Figure 8's beaches. The county commissioners voted to sponsor the project and pay for it through a special assessment on the property owners of Wrightsville Beach and Figure 8. Over the next two years, the project moved through the permitting and planning process, and in November 2001, the county obtained from the U.S. Army Corps of Engineers a permit to relocate Mason Inlet. The permit required that the county maintain the relocated inlet for thirty years through regular dredging. On 5 November 2001, the county commission voted 3–2 against the project based on concerns about the cost of maintaining the relocated inlet.

The Figure 8 HOA board quickly developed a plan to seek reversal of the commissioners' vote. Having determined that the costly maintenance was a capital improvement, the board approved immediate solicitation of a vote by HOA members to approve a special assessment covering the maintenance costs of the relocated inlet. On 14 November 2001, the board mailed letters and ballots to all eligible HOA voters. A majority of the ballots returned voted in favor of the special assessment associated with the project.

Plaintiff first argues that the court erred in denying plaintiff's motion for summary judgment and in allowing defendants' motion for summary judgment. We disagree.

This Court has set forth the following standard for interpreting covenants imposing affirmative obligations:

> Covenants that impose affirmative obligations on property owners are strictly construed and unenforceable unless the obligations are imposed in clear and unambiguous language that is sufficiently definite to assist courts in its application. To be enforceable, such covenants must contain some ascertainable standard by which a court can objectively determine both that the amount of the assessment and the purpose for which it is levied fall within the contemplation of the covenant. Assessment provisions in restrictive covenants (1) must contain a sufficient standard by which to measure . . . liability for assessments, . . . (2) must identify with particularity the property to be maintained, and (3) must provide guidance to a reviewing court as to which facilities and properties the . . . association . . . chooses to maintain.

Allen v. Sea Gate Ass'n, 119 N.C. App. 761, 764, 460 S.E.2d 197, 199 (1995) (internal quotation marks omitted) (citing Figure Eight Beach Homeowners' Ass'n, Inc. v. Parker & Laing, 62 N.C. App. 367, 376, 303 S.E.2d 336, 341 (1983) and Beech Mountain Property Owners' Ass'n v. Seifart, 48 N.C. App. 286, 295–96, 269 S.E.2d 178, 183–84 (1980), disc. review denied, 309 N.C. 320, 307 S.E.2d 170 (1983)).

We first consider whether the covenants "contain a sufficient standard by which to measure" the HOA's liability for assessments, and whether the covenants "identify with particularity the property to be maintained," and provide us guidance as to which facilities and properties are to be maintained. Regarding annual assessments, the covenant provides:

> 8(c) The funds arising from such assessment or charges or additional assessment may be used for any or all of the following purposes: Maintaining, operating, improving or replacing the bridges; protection of the property from erosion; collecting and disposing of garbage, ashes, rubbish and the like; *maintenance, improvement* and lighting *of* the streets, roads, drives, rights of way, community land and facilities, tennis courts, *marsh and waterways*; employing watchmen; enforcing these restrictions; paying taxes, indebtedness to the Association, insurance premiums, *governmental charges of all kinds and descriptions* and, in addition, doing any other things necessary or desirable in the opinion of the Association to keep the property in neat and good order and to provide for the health, welfare and safety of owners and residents of Figure Eight Island.

(Emphasis supplied). The 29 January 1993 amendment added the language "channel dredging; beach renourishment" to paragraph 8(c). Taken together, the language of this paragraph provides for assessments to be used for channel dredging and maintenance of marshes and waterways and for payment of governmental charges of all kinds and descriptions. Maps included in the covenants depict and refer to several of the areas which the assessment would be used to dredge and maintain.

One area covered by the assessment which is not immediately adjacent to Figure 8, and thus not depicted in the maps, is that where the to-be-opened Mason Creek would flow into the Atlantic Intracoastal Waterway ("AIW"). This area was of concern to the Army Corp of Engineers and the HOA because the planned relocation of Mason Inlet and the reopening of Mason Creek could create problems with sand build up at this juncture with the AIW. Plaintiff contends that because this area is neither named nor depicted in the covenants, it is not specifically identified and could not have been intended for inclusion in the covenants' maintenance provisions.

Concerning this location the trial court noted in finding 14:

14. Figure Eight Island has a boating community, with a marina near its main clubhouse and with several private docks on the back, or "sound side," of the island. Boating access to the AIW has been enhanced for residents on the southern back side of the island with the dredging and reopening of Mason's

Creek, and the entire island's boating community is benefitted by once again having a navigable inlet on the southern end to the Atlantic Ocean. Periodic dredging of shoaling sands within the intersection of Mason's Creek and the AIW, occurring at a location some 4,500 feet from the southern end of the island proper, nevertheless directly benefits the navigability of channels for the Figure Eight Island boating community and the boaters' access to Mason Inlet, Wrightsville Beach and points both south and north on the AIW.

This finding is supported by the exhibits before the trial court, such as the aerial photo of the island and the environmental assessment report created by the U.S. Army Corp. of Engineers. As several aspects of the overall Mason Inlet relocation plan would have an impact on the confluence of AIW and Mason Creek, we believe that the court's construction of the covenants was reasonable and that the evidence adequately supports this finding, which in turn supports the legal conclusion that the "authority of the Figure 8 HOA to assess its property owners/members upon a vote of the membership is lawfully authorized."

In addition, the HOA ballot clearly specified the possible cost involved and the period of time dredging maintenance could be required. HOA members who voted were informed of the location of the area to be maintained as well as the cost involved and the duration of the commitment upon which they were voting.

Affirmed.

■ JUDGES TIMMONS-GOODSON and STEELMAN concur.

NOTES AND QUESTIONS

1. What constraints did the Figure 8 declaration impose on the association's power to impose assessments? Are there any purposes for which the association would not have been entitled to impose assessments?

2. Suppose the declaration in the *Figure 8* case had conferred no power on the association to make and collect assessments. Would the association have been entitled to assess landowners for dredging? Consider the approach taken by the Restatement (Third) of Property:

Section 6.5—Power to Raise Funds: Assessments, Fees, and Borrowing

  (1) Except as limited by statute or the declaration:

    (a) a common-interest community has the power to raise the funds reasonably necessary to carry out its functions by levying assessments against the individually owned property in the community and by charging fees for services or for the use of common property;

(b) assessments may be allocated among the individually owned properties on any reasonable basis, and are secured by a lien against the individually owned properties.

Is the Restatement's approach consistent with the approach articulated by the North Carolina court in the *Figure 8* case? Under the Restatement approach, if the declaration confers no express power on the association to impose assessments, does the association have implied power to impose assessments? *See also* Meadow Run & Mountain Lake Park Ass'n v. Berkel, 409 Pa.Super. 637, 598 A.2d 1024 (1991) (holding that association has implied authority to collect assessments even when the declaration did not authorize those assessments because unit owner, by using common areas, impliedly agreed to accept responsibility for cost of maintaining and repairing common facilities). Does this approach make more or less sense than the approach articulated by the North Carolina court? Why?

3. Suppose a developer believes that potential customers will balk at buying within a common interest community unless the association is precluded from committing unit owners to new projects that would generate sharp increases in assessments. What language could be included in the declaration to limit the association's power to impose assessments?

4. Real estate taxes are almost always *ad valorem* taxes; that is, all property is subject to the same tax rate, but the tax paid by each property subject to the tax is proportional to the property's value. More expensive properties bear a larger share of the taxes than less expensive properties. Some declarations in community associations use an *ad valorem* approach to assessments, but two other formulas are also common: (1) assessment based on square footage; and (2) equal assessments for each unit.

What advantages does each formula offer? If you were representing a developer, which formula would you recommend? Are there good reasons for treating real estate taxes differently from association assessments?

5. How likely is it that an association will impose an assessment that does not provide unit owners with benefits that are at least equal to the amount of the assessment? What checks are there against inefficient assessments? Against unfair assessments? Are those checks more or less likely to be effective than when local taxes are imposed by local governments?

6. *Collecting Assessments.* What happens if a unit owner doesn't pay the assessment imposed by the association? The obligation to pay is both a personal obligation of the unit owner and an obligation that "runs with the land." Moreover, the declaration will typically give the association a lien right against a unit when the owner has become delinquent in paying assessments. As a result, the association may bring an action against the unit owner personally, or may perfect the lien against the unit owner's property, and then foreclose on the lien. Courts have uniformly rejected the argument, sometimes advanced by unit owners, that homestead laws or other statutory protections prevent community associations from foreclosing against delinquent owners. *See, e.g.,* Inwood N. Homeowners'

Ass'n v. Harris, 736 S.W.2d 632 (Tex. 1987); Bessemer v. Gersten, 381 So.2d 1344 (Fla. 1980). Consider the following news story:

HOA Foreclosed on home of Frisco soldier while he was serving in Iraq

Valerie Wigglesworth Dallas Morning News, June 28, 2010

The case, which has boiled over to involve a federal judge, a publicist and death threats, began when Michael and May Clauer lost their $315,000 home to foreclosure in May 2008 after falling behind on their association dues.

The Heritage Lakes Homeowners Association was initially owed $977.55 and sent multiple notices by certified mail demanding payment. All went unanswered.

The problem, according to a lawyer for the Clauers, was that Michael Clauer—U.S. Army National Guard Capt. Michael Clauer—was deployed to Iraq.

His wife, suffering from depression over her husband's absence, had let mail pile up and didn't open any of the certified letters. May Clauer and her parents owned the house mortgage-free.

It was purchased at auction for $3,201 by Mark DiSanti of Dallas and Steeplechase Productions. Neither DiSanti nor his attorney could be reached for comment.

The house was sold in May 2009 for $135,000 to Jad Aboul-Jibin of Plano.

The Clauers have been allowed to continue living in the house under a judge's order. And this week, a federal district judge ordered all the parties involved to get together to try to reach a settlement on the question of ownership.

Supporters of the state law allowing foreclosures for nonpayment of homeowners association dues argue that people agree to abide by HOA rules, including the fees, when they purchase their homes. Foreclosure is the only way that HOAs can compel people to pay their dues, they argue. Attempts to provide more protections to homeowners have failed in past legislative sessions and may be brought up again when Texas lawmakers convene in January.

For the first seven months of this year, homeowners associations in Dallas, Tarrant, Denton and Collin counties posted 1,625 properties for foreclosure, according to George Roddy of Foreclosure Listing Service. Associations can foreclose on a property for any rule violation, but typically it's for not paying dues.

That posting "is the ultimate threat," Roddy said, noting that most homeowners make arrangements to pay so they don't lose their homes. If they do, a six-month grace period allows them to pay the debt and get the house back.

Should associations be entitled to foreclose for nonpayment of assessments? Should foreclosures require judicial process?

For most associations, lien foreclosure is a last resort. Associations may try instead to provide incentives for payment, such as withdrawing the delinquent owner's privileges to use common facilities, or imposing late fees on delinquent owners. Moreover, because the lien for unpaid assessments runs with the land, the association might simply wait until the delinquent owner seeks to sell the unit, and then collect the unpaid proceeds out of the purchase price. (Because the purchaser would be liable for unpaid assessments, the purchaser will not pay the delinquent seller without assuring that the association's lien is satisfied out of the purchase price.)

By waiting for payment, the association avoids the costs associated with foreclosure, and the personal animosity that would result from foreclosing on a neighbor. What disadvantages are there to waiting for payment? Are those disadvantages more serious in an era of declining real estate prices?

Suppose the association decides to impose late fees on delinquent assessments. Can the delinquent owner challenge the fees on the ground that the association lacked authority to impose them? *See, e.g.,* Villas at Hidden Lakes Condo. Ass'n v. Geupel Constr. Co., 174 Ariz. 72, 847 P.2d 117 (1992) (holding that association could not collect late fees from unit owner when the association had not adopted late fees at the time the assessments became delinquent).

7. *Comparing Public and Private Financing of Amenities.* What advantages can you identify for private provision and financing of facilities like roads, parks, swimming pools, and other facilities whose use is shared by many members of a community? Are private associations likely to be better or worse at gauging the preferences of community members? Are they likely to be better or worse at keeping costs down?

Is private provision and financing likely to have adverse social consequences? Does the existence and importance of community associations lead residents to focus more of their attention on the local community and less on the broader polity? Is that a good result or a bad one? *See* Sherryl D. Cashin, Privatized Communities and the "Secession of the Successful": Democracy and Fairness Behind the Gate, 28 Fordham Urb. L.J. 1675 (2001).

IV. PRIVATE ARCHITECTURAL CONTROLS

Homeowners are often concerned about the impact of new construction on the appearance and value of their own homes. Where there is a public regulatory scheme, localities may regulate building appearance through either zoning or through aesthetic controls. Within common interest communities, many developers deal with this problem by using the declaration or bylaws to establish review boards or architectural control committees to review applications for new construction, and for modifications to existing construction.

How should those committees exercise their powers, and what recourse should be available to unit owners unhappy with committee decisions? Consider the following case:

Valenti v. Hopkins

Supreme Court of Oregon, 1996
324 Or. 324, 926 P.2d 813

■ VAN HOOMISSEN, JUDGE.

This is an action to enforce restrictive covenants in a residential subdivision. After the subdivision's architectural control committee (ACC) approved defendants' house plans, plaintiffs brought this action, asserting that defendants' construction would obstruct plaintiffs' view in violation of the subdivision's restrictive covenants. The trial court denied injunctive relief. The Court of Appeals gave no deference to the ACC's determination and, on *de novo* review, held that defendants had violated the restrictive covenants. The Court of Appeals, therefore, reversed and remanded the case to the trial court to fashion a remedy. The issue is whether the decision of a contractually created private architectural control committee is reviewable *de novo* by the courts, with no deference being given to the committee's interpretation of the enabling restrictive covenants or to its conclusions on the merits. For the reasons that follow, we reverse the decision of the Court of Appeals.

In 1988, plaintiffs purchased their two-story home in the West Ridge Subdivision in Deschutes County. At that time, plaintiffs had an unobstructed view of the Cascade mountains to the west and of the Paulina and Ochoco mountains to the east. At the time plaintiffs purchased their home, the subdivision's restrictive covenants provided that "the height of improvements on a lot shall not materially restrict the view of other lot owners" and that the ACC "shall be the sole judge of the suitability of such heights."

In 1989, the owners of the lots in the subdivision approved amended covenants that control the design of newly constructed homes. Article I of the amended covenants provides in part:

"Section 2. Architectural Control Committee Consent.

"Consent of the Architectural Control Committee is required for all new construction, exterior remodel, landscaping, and any major improvements upon the lot."

Article III (Architectural Rules) provides in part:

"Section 4. View and Building Height.

"The height of improvements or vegetation and trees on a lot shall not materially obstruct the view of adjacent lot owners. The Architectural Control Committee shall judge the suitability of such heights and may impose restrictions."

Plaintiffs' lot and house are on the east side of West Ridge Avenue. In 1990, defendants purchased a lot across West Ridge Avenue to the west of plaintiffs' home. In March 1990, defendants submitted their house plans to the ACC. Plaintiffs objected on the ground that defendants' proposed house would obstruct their view of the mountains to the west. Plaintiffs understood that the view from their first floor would be obstructed by any house built on defendants' lot; however, they expected the ACC to protect the view from their second floor. The ACC rejected defendants' plans for reasons unrelated to plaintiffs' objection. Defendants then submitted alternate plans for a two-story house, which the ACC approved. Defendants later withdrew those plans and, instead, proposed to build another type of house of the same basic design. With some alterations unrelated to height, the ACC approved those plans. Most importantly, the ACC interpreted the subdivision's amended covenants to mean that, because plaintiffs' home was located on the east side of West Ridge Avenue, plaintiffs' lot was not "adjacent" to defendants' lot within the meaning of Article III, section 4, and, therefore, that plaintiffs did not have a protected western view.[2] After the ACC approved defendants' plans, they began construction. As expected, their house obstructed plaintiffs' second-floor view of the mountains to the west.

Plaintiffs then filed this action in circuit court, seeking injunctive relief and specific performance of the covenants or monetary damages. The trial court concluded that the ACC had not acted "arbitrarily or unreasonably" in approving defendants' plans, dismissed plaintiffs' complaint, and awarded defendants attorney fees.

---

[2] In a letter to plaintiffs, in the context of an unrelated dispute with another neighbor, the ACC explained its position as follows:

"Previous committees have established ground rules concerning a homeowner's view that are essentially as follows:

"1. Persons with homes on the West side of the street shall have views to the West out the back of their homes.

"2. Persons with homes on the East side of the street shall have views out the back of their homes to the East.

"* * * * *

"Western views, of the Cascade Mountains, are considered the prime views and this is reflected in the fact that lots on the West side of Westridge sell for considerably more than lots on the East side. No one on the East side of the street is guaranteed a Westerly view."

Although plaintiffs argue that the ACC's specific *decision* in their case was "arbitrary, capricious, unfair and unreasonable," they do not argue that the ACC lacked authority *to interpret the covenants.*

The Court of Appeals concluded that it was not required to defer to the ACC's interpretation of the enabling covenant or to its findings on the merits, relying on Hanson v. Salishan Properties, Inc., 267 Ore. 199, 515 P.2d 1325 (1973). The court proceeded to review the trial court's decision *de novo* and concluded that, within the meaning of the covenants, plaintiffs' and defendants' lots were "adjacent" and that plaintiffs were entitled to protection of their view to the west over defendants' lot. The court found that defendants' house materially obstructed plaintiffs' view and concluded that defendants had breached the covenants. Accordingly, the court remanded the case to the trial court to fashion a remedy. We allowed defendants' petition for review to determine the proper role of the courts in reviewing decisions of a contractually created private design committee charged with enforcing a subdivision's restrictive covenants.

This court has referred to restrictive covenants, such as those at issue here, as "contractual obligations imposed upon all lot owners." Ludgate v. Somerville, 121 Ore. 643, 648, 256 P. 1043 (1927). Generally, restrictive covenants such as those found here are enforceable. See Alloway v. Moyer, 275 Ore. 397, 400–01, 550 P.2d 1379 (1976) (the defendant must comply with a reasonable construction of the restriction); Donaldson v. White, 261 Ore. 314, 493 P.2d 1380 (1972) (restrictive covenant enforced); Snashall v. Jewell, 228 Ore. 130, 363 P.2d 566 (1961) (same). As a general rule, the construction of a contract is a question of law. Unambiguous contracts must be enforced according to their terms; whether the terms of a contract are ambiguous is, in the first instance, a question of law. Pacific First Bank v. New Morgan Park Corp., 319 Ore. 342, 347, 876 P.2d 761 (1994).

In Hanson, the plaintiffs sought a permanent injunction prohibiting the defendant, a neighboring leaseholder, from building a specific kind of house on his leased beachfront lot that, the plaintiffs alleged, would interfere with their views of the beach and the ocean. Lease covenants provided that lessees

> "shall restrict the height of improvements * * * to the end that the view of other * * * tenants shall be preserved to the greatest extent reasonably possible."

Hanson, 267 Ore. at 202.

Pursuant to "Architectural Considerations" incorporated into the lease, the defendant submitted construction plans to an architectural committee, which approved them. After the plaintiffs obtained a favorable judgment from the trial court, this court reversed, stating:

> "The more serious restriction is that height will be limited to the end that views 'shall be preserved to the greatest extent reasonably possible.' *The sort of a structure which will so preserve the view is, of course, a matter of opinion* [emphasis added]. The documents in question leave such a decision to the

Architectural Committee. The committee was of the opinion that a few feet of additional height to the [defendants'] house would obstruct less view of consequence than would be the case if the usable square footage in the second story were added to the first floor, thereby creating additional width. * * * Unless this court can find that the decision of the Architectural Committee *did not* [original emphasis] preserve the view of upland owners to the greatest extent reasonably possible, that committee's decision should not be disturbed. From the evidence in this case we cannot say with any conviction that its decision did not so preserve plaintiffs' view." *Id.* at 204.

Hanson did not purport to establish, even in *dictum,* a nondeferential standard of review for decisions of architectural committees charged with applying and enforcing restrictive covenants of a subdivision.

Friberg v. Elrod et al., 136 Ore. 186, 296 P. 1061 (1931), was a suit to foreclose a mechanic's lien for labor performed under a construction contract. The contract provided that "the engineer shall be the sole judge of the * * * quality of the work done by the contractor" and that "all disputes or disagreements between the parties hereto shall be submitted to and decided by the engineer and his decision shall be binding upon both parties." 136 Ore. at 189. The defendant argued that the plaintiff's lien claim already had been decided by the engineer and that the engineer's final estimate of the amount to be paid to the plaintiff under the contract should be accepted. This court agreed, holding:

"Where a contract stipulates that a certain engineer is expressly clothed with the broad authority to determine all questions arising in relation to the work, * * * and provides that after the completion of the work the engineer shall make a final estimate of the amount of work done, and the value thereof to be paid by the builder, * * * the contract does not create a mere naked agreement to submit differences to arbitration, such stipulations are of the very essence of the contract, and such agreement is not subject to revocation by either party, and *an award * * * , in the absence of fraud or of such gross mistake as would imply bad faith or a failure to exercise honest judgment, is binding on both parties to the contract * * * .*"

Id. at 194–95 (emphasis added).

Friberg applied a deferential standard of review to carry out the expressed intention of the parties to avoid costly and time-consuming litigation and to promote finality by upholding the decision of a contractually designated third party. The consistent policy of the law is to encourage the private resolution of disputes.

In this case, plaintiffs argue that the ACC's members are neither "skilled" nor "neutral" and, therefore, that their decision is not entitled to deference under the Friberg standard. We reject that argument. Plaintiffs approved the covenants including the provisions for the creation and authority of the ACC—knowing that the ACC's members would be owners of lots in the subdivision who, like themselves, would not necessarily have any expertise in the matters they might be asked to resolve.

The subdivision's covenants expressly provide that "the [ACC] will be responsible for approval of plans and specifications of private areas and for promulgation and enforcement of its rules and regulations governing the use and maintenance of private areas and improvements thereon." They further provide that "consent of the [ACC] is required for all new construction" and that "the [ACC] may at its discretion withhold consent with respect to any proposal which the [ACC] finds would be inappropriate for the particular lot or would be incompatible with the neighboring homes and terrain within [the subdivision]." The ACC is given broad authority to consider "height, * * * view, effect on other lots * * * and any other factor it reasonably believes to be relevant" in determining whether or not to consent to any proposal. The covenants provide that "the height of improvements * * * on a lot shall not materially obstruct the view of adjacent lot owners," but they further provide that "the [ACC] *shall judge* the suitability of such heights and may impose restrictions." (Emphasis added.) We take the use of the words "shall judge" to mean that in the context of the broad range of authority granted, the ACC is intended to be the final arbiter both as to the applicable law and the facts, with respect to height restrictions.

In summary, the collective wording of the restrictive covenants set out above clearly expresses that the ACC is to make final decisions respecting the relevant issues. We therefore hold that the standard of review articulated in Friberg—review for fraud, bad faith, or failure to exercise honest judgment—is the appropriate standard of review of the ACC's interpretation of the language in the covenants here and of its decision on the merits. Plaintiffs neither have alleged nor proved that the ACC's interpretation of the language in the covenants or its decision on the merits in this case was the result of fraud, bad faith, or a failure to exercise honest judgment.

We hold that the Court of Appeals erred in deciding *de novo* that defendants had breached the covenants. We reverse the decision of the Court of Appeals and remand the case to that court for consideration of defendants' assignment of error concerning attorney fees.

The decision of the Court of Appeals is reversed. The case is remanded to the Court of Appeals for further consideration.

NOTES AND QUESTIONS

1. Suppose the architectural control committee had refused to approve defendants' house plans, and the defendants had brought an action seeking to establish that the committee's decision was inconsistent with the provisions in the declaration. How would the Oregon Supreme Court have resolved the issue?

2. Examine the standard of review articulated by the court. Under what circumstances would the court overturn a decision by the architectural control committee? Consider, in particular, the following hypothetical variations on the facts in *Valenti*:

> a. In two prior cases, the architectural control committee had refused to approve house plans when the plans would obstruct the view of a landowner whose lot was across the street from the applicant's. In the current case, the committee approved plans over the objection of an across-the-street landowner. *See* Chattel Shipping & Inv., Inc. v. Brickell Place Condo. Ass'n, 481 So.2d 29, 30 (Fla. Ct. App. 1985) ("When selective enforcement is demonstrated, the association is 'estopped' from applying a given regulation.").
>
> b. The committee approved neighbor's plans for a house immediately to the west of landowner's home; the committee reasoned that landowner had already planted large trees that obstructed landowner's view, establishing that landowner did not value the view.
>
> c. The committee refused to approve house plans on the ground that any proposed house would obstruct the westerly view of immediate neighbors' from their swimming pool.

In each case, how would you distinguish *Valenti* if you represented the unit owner aggrieved by the committee's determination? How would you respond if you represented the architectural control committee?

3. Did the plaintiff in the *Valenti* case bring an action challenging the determination of the architectural control committee, or did the plaintiff bring an action to enforce the restrictive covenants? Why would plaintiff's lawyer make that choice?

Does the court treat the action as if it were a challenge to the determination of the committee? Why? Would the court's analysis have been different if Article III, Section 4 had restricted the height of improvements and vegetation, but had not given the committee authority to judge the suitability of heights? In the absence of a provision in the declaration giving an association authority to interpret covenants, does the association have exclusive authority to interpret and enforce restrictive covenants? In Morris v. Kadrmas, 812 P.2d 549 (Wyo. 1991), the declaration included a covenant prohibiting use of lots for any purpose other than single family residences. A unit owner sought and obtained from the control committee approval to build a garage and shop building. When a neighboring unit owner brought an action to enforce the covenant, the

Wyoming Supreme Court held that the control committee's approval of the plans did not constitute a defense, despite a provision in the declaration conferring on the committee "sole and exclusive right and authority to determine compliance with the covenants." The court emphasized another provision in the declaration recognizing the right of owners as well as the approval authority to bring an action to remedy violations.

4. In *Valenti,* the declaration provided guidelines for the architectural control committee. Are guidelines necessary? Suppose the declaration simply required every unit owner to obtain the consent of an architectural control committee before beginning any new construction. If the committee refused to consent, what challenges might be available to an aggrieved landowner? *See* Prestwick Landowners Ass'n v. Underhill, 69 Ohio App.2d 45, 429 N.E.2d 1191 (1980) (invalidating restriction requiring consent of architectural control committee because lack of guidelines left owners without notice about what kinds of structures the committee would approve); *see also* Ross v. Newman, 206 Neb. 42, 291 N.W.2d 228 (1980) (court holds restriction invalid for lack of clarity where provision prohibits alteration without consent of majority of owners, and provides that owners consider general appearance, color, and harmony of design). *But see* Normandy Square Ass'n v. Ells, 213 Neb. 60, 327 N.W.2d 101 (1982) (same court, two years later, upholds restriction requiring structures to conform to harmony of external design; court holds that restriction is not ambiguous *per se*).

For other cases upholding broad delegations to architectural control committees, *see, e.g.,* Palmetto Dunes Resort v. Brown, 287 S.C. 1, 336 S.E.2d 15 (1985) (upholding restriction authorizing disapproval for "purely aesthetic considerations"); Rhue v. Cheyenne Homes, Inc., 168 Colo. 6, 449 P.2d 361 (1969).

If you were drafting a declaration, how much detail would you include to provide guidance to the architectural control committee? What risks might there be in providing too much guidance?

5. How do or should public regulatory schemes, such as zoning, and covenants coexist and influence each other? In general, they are deemed to operate independently: Courts have held that zoning laws have no bearing on the validity of private covenants, and private covenants do not affect the administration of zoning laws. There are circumstances, however, where some localities have been authorized to incorporate private agreements into public decision-making. *See, e.g.,* Blakehurst Life Care Community/The Chestnut Real Estate Partnership v. Baltimore County, 146 Md. App. 509, 807 A.2d 179 (2002) (allowing a locality to incorporate a covenant into a county board decision, where the covenant had been incorporated into the public record as part of a consent order ending litigation). Similarly, covenants may factor into rezoning decisions, where the covenant limits some potentially negative impacts of a rezoning decision. *See, e.g.,* Daro Realty, Inc. v. District of Columbia Zoning Comm'n, 581 A.2d 295 (D.C. 1990) (allowing for a rezoning to high-density residential in light of a covenant restricting the use, height, bulk, and setback of the building).

6. How much process does an architectural control committee have to provide to applicants? Must the committee afford applicants an opportunity to appear in person? *Cf.* Europco Mgmt. Co. of Am. v. Smith, 572 So.2d 963 (Fla. Ct. App. 1990) ("The developer is not required to provide a forum at which the applicant can personally appear and be heard.").

7. Municipalities often establish architectural control committees to review building plans for particular projects, or for all projects. Should courts apply the same standard of review to municipal committees as to committees created privately? If not, to which committees should courts be more deferential? Why?

NOTE ON STANDARD OF REVIEW MORE GENERALLY

Community association boards, including architectural control committees, make a variety of decisions about management of the community. As in the *Figure "8"* case, association boards must often decide what repairs and maintenance are necessary, and how best to pay for those expenses. As in *Valenti*, boards must often interpret covenants, and they must also decide whether to devote association resources to enforce covenants when unit owners breach. Moreover, the association's governing documents may also empower an association board to review applications for improvements to individual units to make sure that the improvements do not have an adverse impact on other unit owners. In each situation, a decision by the board has the potential to leave some unit owners unhappy with the board's decision. When a unit owner is sufficiently aggrieved to resort to litigation, how should courts treat the board's decision?

Analytically, courts face two questions: first, did the association board have authority to make the decision it made, and second, was the decision correct? Courts treat the first question as a pure question of law, to be resolved by examination of the association's governing documents, together with any applicable statutes. *See, e.g.,* Johnson v. The Pointe Cmty. Ass'n, Inc., 205 Ariz. 485, 489, 73 P.3d 616, 620 (2003) (association's interpretation of its own restrictive covenants not entitled to deference); Strathmore Ridge Homeowners Ass'n v. Mendicino, 63 A.D.3d 1038, 881 N.Y.S.2d 491 (2009) (applying the business judgment rule to determine an association's authority to pass amendment to bylaws restricting leasing of units).

By contrast, courts do not engage in *de novo* review of every decision of an association board. Although different courts use different formulations to describe the review process, courts agree that the standard should be deferential. In Levandusky v. One Fifth Avenue Apartment Corp., 75 N.Y.2d 530, 537, 554 N.Y.S.2d 807, 553 N.E.2d 1317, 1321 (1990), the New York Court of Appeals held that the standard of review should be "analogous to the business judgment rule applied by courts to determine challenges to decisions made by corporate directors." In the court's words, "[s]o long as the board acts for the purposes of the cooperative, within the scope of its authority and in good faith, courts will not substitute their judgment for the board's." *Id.* at 538, N.E.2d at 1322. In adopting this deferential approach, the court emphasized two factors: first, purchase of a unit in a common interest community "represents a voluntary choice to cede certain of the privileges of single ownership to a governing body." *Id.* at 536, 553 N.E.2d at 1321. Second, "board members will possess experience of the peculiar needs of their building and its residents not shared by the court." *Id.* at 539, 553 N.E.2d at 1322.

The California Supreme Court has framed a standard in similar terms:

"where a duly constituted community association board, upon reasonable investigation, in good faith and with regard for the best interests of the community association and its members, exercises discretion with the scope of its authority under relevant statutes, covenants and restrictions . . . courts should defer to the board's authority and presumed expertise."

Lamden v. La Jolla Shores Clubdominium Homeowners Ass'n, 21 Cal.4th 249, 265, 87 Cal.Rptr.2d 237, 980 P.2d 940, 950 (1999).

NOTES AND QUESTIONS

1. In which of the following cases would the deferential standard articulated in *Levandusky* and *Lamden* be applicable? In each case, what argument would you make for the unit owner who seeks to avoid deferential review? How would you respond if you represented the board?

a. Purchaser of a unit asks the community association board to make all common facilities accessible for persons with disabilities. The board declines to do so after research reveals that the cost would be exorbitant and that neither federal nor state law obligates the board to make the facilities fully accessible. *Cf.* Pelton v. 77 Park Ave. Condo., 38 A.D.3d 1, 825 N.Y.S.2d 28 (2006) (deference to board determination).

b. The association leases three parking spaces for $100 per month each; another unit owner objects, contending that the association could have obtained a better deal.

c. The same lease of parking spaces, but the lessee is the board president. *Cf.* Garcia v. Crescent Plaza Condo. Ass'n, 813 So.2d 975 (Fla. Ct. App. 2002) (no deference to board determination).

d. The community association has 43 residential units and 7 commercial units. The declaration bars leases of all residential units. The association now imposes a fee on leases of commercial units. A commercial user objects. *Cf.* Louis & Anne Abrons Found., Inc. v. 29 E. 64th St. Corp., 297 A.D.2d 258, 746 N.Y.S.2d 482 (2002) (no deference).

2. Consumers concerned about the potential for abusive actions by association boards have several protections that do not involve litigation. First, they can purchase homes that are not restricted by covenants or governed by community associations. Second, they can participate in community association governance, both by voting and by lobbying. Third,

they can sell their units if they become unhappy with association governance. Do these alternatives provide enough protection to justify judicial deference to association decisions? If not, why not? Consider the following:

> Although community associations could promulgate rules that cause significant harm to individual unit owners, institutional constraints substantially reduce the risk of harm. So long as association rules have a similar impact on all units, those rules are not likely to have an adverse impact on the units' market value. A majority of landowners would be unlikely to promulgate a rule that made them all worse off. The principal harm an individual unit owner is likely to suffer when the association promulgates a rule applicable to all unit owners is a loss of the idiosyncratic value she attaches to her unit. That loss, however, will be matched—and generally exceeded—by a gain to other unit owners, and in most cases there will be no way to generate the gain without also imposing the loss. In this instance, the legal system should—and generally does—let the association's decision stand, leaving the dissident owner the option of persuading other members to change the course they have followed. The same considerations and the same result should apply whether the issue before the association is the size of the annual assessment, the wisdom of a restriction on renting individual units, or the merits of a control on unit owner lifestyles.
>
> Three significant exceptions apply. First, when the association's governing documents expressly limit the association's power to regulate particular activities, the association may not promulgate rules inconsistent with those documents. Second, when the context of dealings between the unit owner and association reveals a mutual understanding that the unit owner will engage in particular conduct, and when the unit owner relies on that understanding, the association is effectively estopped from prohibiting the conduct in question. Finally, when the impact of association rules does not fall on all unit owners, but instead redistributes value from some unit owners to others, the association should not be entitled to promulgate the regulation without compensating the adversely affected owners.

Stewart E. Sterk, Minority Protection in Residential Private Governments, 77 B.U. L. Rev. 273, 340–41 (1997).

V. GOVERNANCE: ADAPTING TO CHANGE

Before the emergence of homeowner associations and condominiums, covenants were basically for keeps; once a developer imposed a restrictive covenant on a development, transaction costs made private removal practically impossible. Although statutes and judicial decisions might permit judicial termination of covenants for "changed conditions," courts applied the doctrine sparingly. Moreover, judicial removal required litigation, an expense few individual landowners would be willing to bear.

By contrast, in an era of common interest communities, a well-drafted declaration will make provision for amending the covenants, conditions, and restrictions (CC&Rs), and will also confer rulemaking power on the association. As a result, when conditions change, and make it attractive to strengthen, relax, or remove existing restrictions, or to impose new ones, the association has two basic alternatives: first, the association can amend the CC&Rs, or second, the association can promulgate a rule. Either alternative can provoke a reaction from unit owners who purchased before the association made the change. The following cases illustrate the problems that can arise:

Weldy v. Northbrook Condominium Association, Inc.

Supreme Court of Connecticut, 2006
279 Conn. 728, 904 A.2d 188

■ ZARELLA, J.

The sole issue in this certified appeal is whether a resolution adopted by the board of directors of a condominium association providing that leashes or restraints for household pets shall not exceed twenty feet in length constitutes an illegal amendment of the condominium declaration, which provides that all household pets shall be restrained by leash or other comparable means. The plaintiffs, Thomas P. Weldy and Elizabeth C. Weldy, brought an action to enjoin the defendants, Northbrook Condominium Association, Inc. (association), and the association's five member board of directors (board), from enforcing the resolution. The trial court granted the defendants' motion for summary judgment and rendered judgment thereon, from which the plaintiffs appealed to the Appellate Court, which reversed the trial court's judgment. Weldy v. Northbrook Condominium Ass'n, Inc., 89 Conn. App. 581, 589, 874 A.2d 296 (2005). On appeal to this court, the defendants claim that the board did not act beyond the scope of its authority in adopting the resolution because it constituted a clarification of, rather than an amendment to, the pet restraint provision in the declaration and thus did not require approval by a two-thirds vote of the unit owners and mortgagees. We agree and, accordingly, reverse the judgment of the Appellate Court.

The opinion of the Appellate Court sets forth the following relevant facts and procedural history. "The plaintiffs own a unit in a development known as Northbrook of Monroe, an Expandable Condominium (condominium). . . .

"Article nine of the condominium's declaration governs 'use, purposes and restrictions' of the condominium property. [Article] 9(e) addresses pet ownership and provides in relevant part that all 'dogs, cats or household pets shall be restrained by leash or other comparable means and shall be accompanied by an owner at all times. . . .' [Article] 9(*l*) confers on the board 'the power to make such regulations as may be necessary to carry out the intent of [the] use restrictions. . . .' Pursuant to § 4(b)(5) of the condominium's bylaws, the board possesses the power to adopt and amend 'rules and regulations covering the details of the operation and use of the property, provided, however, that those rules and regulations contained in the [d]eclaration shall be amended in the manner provided for amending the [d]eclaration.' Article eighteen of the declaration provides that the declaration may be amended only on the vote of two thirds of the unit owners and mortgagees of the condominium.

"On June 27, 2003, the board, by letter, informed the condominium's owners and residents of 'new regulations to the pet rules.' The board cited the previously quoted language from [article] 9(e) of the declaration and stated that the word 'leash' was not defined. It further noted 'instances where pets have caused injury to other pets' and the board's 'opinion [that] leashes that exceed twenty feet in length do not permit owners to control their dogs sufficiently to ensure the safety of other pets and/or unit owners.' According to the letter, the board, therefore, had adopted an 'additional clarification pertaining to pets.' The 'clarification' provided in relevant part that '[l]eashes or comparable restraints for dogs, cats or household pets shall not exceed [twenty] feet in length.'

"The plaintiffs own a nine and one-half year old black Labrador retriever. Prior to June 27, 2003, the plaintiffs played ball and Frisbee with and otherwise exercised their dog in a common area behind their unit. To do so, they used a leash that was seventy-five feet in length.

"On July 28, 2003, the plaintiffs filed this action, seeking to enjoin the defendants from enforcing the purported clarification and requesting a finding that the clarification was made without legal authority, is illegal and is of no force or effect."

On appeal, the defendants claim that the trial court properly determined that the board did not exceed the scope of its authority in adopting the leash restriction. The defendants contend that the intent of the policy in article 9 (e) of the declaration is to promote a safe and non-intimidating environment for unit owners and their guests, and that a dog on an excessively long leash cannot be restrained properly in the physically restricted context of a condominium development. Accordingly, the leash restriction gives meaning to, and acts in concert with, the declaration provision. The plaintiffs respond that, because leashes are commonly sold in lengths of thirty to fifty feet, the board in effect illegally amended the declaration by prohibiting leashes more than twenty feet in length. The plaintiffs argue, therefore, that the leash restriction cannot be enforced. We agree with the defendants that the board acted within the scope of its authority in adopting the restriction.

"When a court is called upon to assess the validity of [an action taken] by a board of directors, it first determines whether the board acted within its scope of authority and, second, whether the [action] reflects reasoned or arbitrary and capricious decision making." Beachwood Villas Condominium v. Poor, 448 So. 2d 1143, 1144 (Fla. App. 1984); *cf.* Lamden v. La Jolla Shores Clubdominium Homeowners Ass'n, 21 Cal. 4th 249, 256, 980 P.2d 940, 87 Cal.Rptr.2d 237 (1999). Because the plaintiffs do not contend that the leash restriction itself is unreasonable, the only issue before the court is whether the board exceeded the scope of its authority in adopting the restriction. We therefore turn to an examination of the relevant statutory provisions.

Condominium developments are of relatively recent origin and provide a unique type of shelter that affords some of the benefits of property ownership without the corresponding burdens. Gentry v. Norwalk, 196 Conn. 596, 603, 494 A.2d 1206 (1985). The statutory scheme in Connecticut governing condominium developments is the Common Interest Ownership Act (act). See generally General Statutes § 47–200 et seq. The act "is a comprehensive legislative scheme regulating all forms of common interest ownership that is largely modeled on the Uniform Common Interest Ownership Act." Nicotra Wieler Investment Management, Inc. v. Grower, 207 Conn. 441, 447, 541 A.2d 1226 (1988). See generally Unif. Common Interest Ownership Act of 1994, 7 U.L.A. 835 (2005). The act addresses "the creation, organization and management of common interest communities and contemplates the voluntary participation of the owners. It entails the drafting and filing of a declaration describing the location and configuration of the real property, development rights, and restrictions on its use, occupancy and alienation; General Statutes §§ 47–220, 47–224; the enactment of bylaws; General Statutes § 47–248 ... the establishment of a unit owners' association [to manage the condominium community]; General Statutes § 47–243; and an executive board to act on ... behalf [of the association]. General Statutes § 47–245. It anticipates group decision-making relating to the development of a budget, the maintenance and repair of the common elements, the placement of insurance, and the provision for common expenses and common liabilities. General Statutes §§ 47–244, 47–245, 47–255, 47–249." Wilcox v. Willard Shopping Center Associates, 208 Conn. 318, 326–27, 544 A.2d 1207 (1988).

The standard of review most commonly employed in reviewing a board's authority to adopt rules or regulations is that, "provided ... a board-enacted rule does not contravene either an express provision of the declaration or a right reasonably inferable therefrom, it will be found valid, within the scope of the board's authority. This test . . . is fair and functional; it safeguards the rights of unit owners and preserves unfettered the concept of delegated board management." Beachwood Villas Condominium v. Poor, supra, 448 So. 2d 1145; *cf.* Meadow Bridge Condominium Ass'n v. Bosca, 187 Mich. App. 280, 282, 466 N.W.2d 303 (1990) ("a rule or regulation is a tool to implement or manage existing structural law, while an amendment presumptively changes existing structural law" [internal quotation marks omitted]).

Applying these principles in the present case, we conclude that the twenty foot leash limitation is not more restrictive than the declaration but simply implements the declaration's expressed intent that household pets brought to the common areas of the property be restrained properly and controlled by their owners at all times. An excessively long leash would not achieve this objective within the limited confines of the walkways, parking lots, landscaped and recreational areas that typically comprise the common elements of a condominium development because a pet attached to a seventy-five foot leash would have the ability to stray far from its owner, especially if the owner's attention was diverted from the pet. This could endanger persons walking between the owner and the pet as well as persons and vehicles moving in a parking lot or accessway that must take evasive action to avoid a darting animal. Consequently, the leash restriction does not contravene an express provision of the declaration but is a means of implementing the policy embodied therein by increasing the likelihood that a pet will remain under its owner's control, thereby contributing to "a safe and non-intimidating environment for unit owners and their guests."

This conclusion finds support in other cases in which courts have determined that the board of directors acted within the scope of its authority in regulating an activity specifically addressed in the declaration or bylaws. See, e.g., O'Buck v. Cottonwood Village Condominium Ass'n, Inc., 750 P.2d 813, 815–17 (Alaska 1988) (board acted within scope of authority in banning television antennas on buildings because declaration authorized board to adopt rules and regulations governing use of common areas, including roofs and walls of buildings, and to require action by owners to preserve uniform exterior building appearance); Meadow Bridge Condominium Ass'n v. Bosca, supra, 187 Mich. App. 281–83 (board empowered to adopt regulation prospectively prohibiting new dogs because bylaws provided that no animals could be maintained by owner without specific approval by association, and bylaws authorized association "to adopt such additional rules and regulations with respect to animals as it may deem proper" [internal quotation marks omitted]).

Correspondingly, the present case is distinguishable from cases in which courts have concluded that the board was not empowered to act because the regulation in question conflicted with an express provision in the declaration. *See, e.g.*, In re 560 Ocean Club, L.P., 133 B.R. 310, 317–18 (Bankr. D.N.J. 1991) (board not authorized to adopt regulation requiring minimum of ninety days during summer months and thirty days at other times for short-term leases because declaration merely granted board power to approve or disapprove leases, not to restrict their duration); Mohnani v. La Cancha Condominium Ass'n, Inc., 590 So. 2d 36, 38 (Fla. App. 1991) (board not empowered to adopt regulation that owner could not lease unit for two years following acquisition because regulation contravened declaration provision and rights reasonably inferable therefrom that owners could lease units upon board approval within thirty days following board's receipt of written notice from owner of intent to lease).

The plaintiffs nonetheless argue that the leash restriction is inconsistent with the relevant declaration provision because the twenty foot limitation redefines and changes the everyday meaning of the word "leash," a term applied to restraints sold commercially in lengths of thirty, fifty and even seventy-five feet. We disagree.

Webster's Third New International Dictionary defines the word "leash" as "a thong, cord or chain attached to an animal's collar . . . and held in the hand for the purpose of leading, checking, or controlling the . . . animal or fastened to an object to secure or tether it. . . ." The twenty foot leash restriction does not add to or change the general provision of the declaration that pets must be controlled in the common areas of the property, nor does it redefine the everyday meaning of the word "leash." It merely ensures that a leash will be more likely to achieve its purpose in a high density residential setting because it will prevent a pet from straying more than twenty feet from its owner. See Meadow Bridge Condominium Ass'n v. Bosca, supra, 187 Mich. App. 282 (regulation prospectively prohibiting new dogs on condominium property did not constitute amendment because it was "not inconsistent with the original bylaw and [did] nothing to change the general rule"). The twenty foot leash restriction is therefore consistent with the declaration.

The plaintiffs also argue that the leash restriction deprives unit owners of a right reasonably inferred from the language of the declaration to restrain their pets on a longer leash. See, e.g., Beachwood Villas Condominium v. Poor, supra, 448 So. 2d 1145 (board rule invalid if in contravention of right reasonably inferable from provision of declaration). The plaintiffs argue that the principle that communal living requires individuals to give "fair consideration . . . to the rights and privileges of all owners and occupants" of the community; Dulaney Towers Maintenance Corp. v. O'Brey, 46 Md. App. 464, 466, 418 A.2d

1233 (1980); does not apply in this case because they exercise their dog in a secluded area of the property and thus do not interfere with other persons or animals, even though the leash they use is seventy-five feet in length. This claim has no merit.

We first note the obvious fact that the declaration provision is restrictive in nature because it seeks to protect unit owners from unnecessary inconvenience and annoyance by unrestrained pets through the imposition of a physical restraint *and* by requiring that pets be accompanied by their owners at all times. We also recognize that leashes are sold in varying lengths. The fact that the plaintiffs' dog does not interfere with others has no bearing, however, on whether a reasonable inference may be drawn from the declaration that unit owners have a right to use a leash of virtually any length when permitting their pets to walk, run or otherwise traverse across and exercise within the common areas of the property. At some point, depending on the circumstances, a leash beyond a certain length ceases to function as an effective restraint. Similarly, to the extent that the declaration mandates that a pet be "accompanied" by its owner, a pet that has wandered seventy-five feet from its owner, even if attached to a very long leash, can hardly be said, in most situations, to be "accompanied by" and under the control of the owner. In the present case, the board determined that, in light of the physical limitations of the condominium setting in question, a leash of more than twenty feet could not perform as intended. Accordingly, the plaintiffs' claim must fail because the condominium declaration, which seeks to impose a measure of control over pets on the property, does not support an inference that a leash of any length can fulfill its anticipated purpose merely because one end of the leash is attached to the collar of a pet and the other is held by the owner.

Two cases on which the plaintiffs rely, namely, *In re 560 Ocean Club, L.P.*, and *Mohnani*, are inapposite. These cases are distinguishable because the regulations adopted by the respective boards clearly conflicted with the governing declaration provisions. That is not the situation in the present case for all of the reasons that we previously have discussed. We therefore conclude that the board acted within the scope of its authority in adopting the resolution restricting the length of leashes to no more than twenty feet pursuant to article 9(*l*) of the condominium declaration.

The judgment of the Appellate Court is reversed and the case is remanded to that court with direction to affirm the judgment of the trial court.

NOTES AND QUESTIONS

1. What mechanism did the condominium declaration provide for amendment of the declaration itself? Did the declaration make it easier or

more difficult to promulgate rules or to amend the declaration? What reason would a developer have for differentiating the two processes?

2. In light of the court's conclusion that the board had power to restrict the length of leashes by rule, when would the association ever bother to amend the declaration?

Suppose the Northbrook board, after complaints from residents, wants to prohibit snakes and birds within the development. Would you advise the board to enact a rule prohibiting snakes and birds? If you represented a snake owner, would you advise the owner to challenge the rule? How would the case be different from *Weldy* itself?

3. Would the board have power to promulgate rules on matters not addressed in the declaration itself? Could an association board promulgate a rule banning all pets within the community? *See* Board of Dirs. of 175 E. Delaware Place Homeowners Ass'n v. Hinojosa, 287 Ill.App.3d 886, 223 Ill.Dec. 222, 679 N.E.2d 407 (1997) (upholding restriction). *But see* Granby Heights Ass'n v. Dean, 38 Mass. App. Ct. 266, 647 N.E.2d 75 (1995) (relying on statute to hold invalid an association rule prohibiting pets outside the units; court indicated that such restrictions must be included in declaration or bylaws).

Could an association board promulgate a rule banning alcohol in the association clubhouse? *See* Hidden Harbour Estates v. Norman, 309 So.2d 180 (Fla. App. 1975) (upholding prohibition). Suppose the prohibition had extended to all of the units within the entire common interest community? Consider the question in light of the following excerpt from the Uniform Common Interest Ownership Act (UCIOA):

Section 3–102—Powers of Unit Owners' Association

(a) Except as provided in subsection (b), and subject to the provisions of the declaration, the association may:

    (1) adopt and amend bylaws and rules and regulations; . . .

    (6) regulate the use, maintenance, repair, replacement, and modification of common elements; . . .

    (15) exercise any other powers conferred by the declaration or bylaws; . . .

    (17) exercise any other powers necessary and proper for the governance and operation of the association; . . .

(b) The declaration may not impose limitations on the power of the association to deal with the declarant which are more restrictive than the limitations imposed on the power of the association to deal with other persons.

(c) Unless otherwise permitted by the declaration or this [Act], an association may adopt rules and regulations that affect the use of or behavior in units that may be used for residential purposes only to:

(1)   prevent any use of a unit which violates the declaration;

(2)   regulate any behavior in or occupancy of a unit which violates the declaration or adversely affects the use and enjoyment of other units or the common elements by other unit owners; or

(3)   restrict the leasing of residential units to the extent those rules are reasonably designed to meet underwriting requirements of institutional lenders who regularly lend money secured by first mortgages on units in common interest communities or regularly purchase those mortgages.

Otherwise, the association may not regulate any use of or behavior in units.

If UCIOA were in effect, and if the declaration were silent about the association's rulemaking power, could a homeowner's association prohibit above-ground swimming pools or storage of vehicles on the premises? *Compare* Westfield Homes, Inc. v. Herrick, 229 Ill.App.3d 445, 170 Ill.Dec. 555, 593 N.E.2d 97 (1992) (invalidating rule prohibiting above-ground pools) with Dunlap v. Bavarian Vill. Condo. Ass'n, 780 P.2d 1012 (Alaska 1989) (sustaining rule prohibiting vehicle storage).

Could an association prohibit parking on the development's streets? *Cf.* Martino v. Bd. of Managers of Heron Pointe, 6 A.D.3d 505, 774 N.Y.S.2d 422 (2004); Gillman v. Pebble Cove Home Owners Ass'n, 154 A.D.2d 508, 546 N.Y.S.2d 134 (1989) (upholding parking restrictions imposed by board rule). Could a condominium association, by rule, prohibit washing machines because of the plumbing problems they might create? Could an association prohibit maintenance of tropical fish?

4.   Why does UCIOA impose statutory limits on an association's power to promulgate rules? Should not the limits imposed in the declaration, together with voting power in the association, be sufficient to protect unit owners? Is there any justification for the particular restrictions UCIOA imposes?

5.   *Pet Restrictions More Generally.* Pet restrictions provoke strong reactions from pet owners and their supporters. In Nahrstedt v. Lakeside Village Condominium Ass'n, Inc., 8 Cal.4th 361, 33 Cal.Rptr.2d 63, 878 P.2d 1275 (1994), the declaration itself prohibited unit owners from keeping cats, dogs, and other animals within the development. When the association sought to enforce the restriction against a purchaser who moved in with her three cats, the California Supreme Court upheld the restriction. The California legislature reacted by enacting a statute providing that "[n]o governing documents shall prohibit the owner of a separate interest within a common interest development from keeping at least one pet within the common interest development, subject to reasonable rules and regulations of the association." Cal. Civ. Code § 1360.5(a).

How did the legislature deal with the opposition of common interest communities seeking to preserve their no-pet policies? By "grandfathering" governing documents entered into before January 1, 2001 (and thereby giving existing communities a comparative advantage over communities whose documents were prepared after the statute's effective date)! Cal. Civ. Code § 1360.5(e). The California courts continue to enforce no-pet restrictions in associations created before 2001. *See, e.g.,* Villa De Las Palmas Homeowners Ass'n v. Terifaj, 33 Cal.4th 73, 14 Cal.Rptr.3d 67, 90 P.3d 1223 (2004).

In other states, courts typically enforce no-pet restrictions whether they appear in the declaration or the bylaws, or whether they are promulgated by association rule. *See, e.g.,* Riverside Park Condos. Unit Owners Ass'n v. Lucas, 691 N.W.2d 862 (N.D. 2005) (amendment to declaration upheld); Noble v. Murphy, 34 Mass.App.Ct. 452, 612 N.E.2d 266 (1993) (provision in bylaws upheld); Board of Dirs. of 175 East Delaware Place Homeowners Ass'n v. Hinojosa, 287 Ill.App.3d 886, 223 Ill.Dec. 222, 679 N.E.2d 407 (1997) (board rule upheld).

Why would a common interest community want to ban pets altogether? Why not instead impose a ban on pets which generate excessive noise, or which are aggressive to neighbors? Is a provision like the one upheld in *Weldy* superior to a provision that bans noisy or aggressive pets?

Woodside Village Condominium Association, Inc. v. Jahren

Supreme Court of Florida, 2002
806 So.2d 452

■ ANSTEAD, JUDGE.

At issue is the validity of amendments to the Declaration of Condominium adopted by the condominium owners which restrict the leasing of units in Woodside Village. Woodside Village is a condominium development located in Clearwater, Florida, consisting of 288 units. It was established in 1979 pursuant to Florida's "Condominium Act," chapter 718, Florida Statutes (1977). Petitioner, Woodside Village Condominium Association, Inc. ("Association"), is the condominium association that was formed pursuant to the Declaration of Condominium of Woodside Village ("Declaration"), recorded in the public records of Pinellas County. Respondents, Adolph S. Jahren and Gary M. McClernan, each own residential condominium units in Woodside Village.

The original Declaration of Condominium for Woodside Village included a provision regarding leasing. [W]hile leasing was permitted under the original Declaration, initial leases in excess of one year were subject to board approval. In addition, section 10.3 was amended in 1995 to require that all leases and renewals receive prior approval from the Board of Directors.

In 1997 some owners became concerned that units were increasingly becoming non-owner occupied, and that such a condition would have a negative impact on the quality of life in Woodside Village and on the market value of units. Accordingly, section 10.3 was amended in March of 1997 to limit the leasing of units to a term of no more than nine months in any twelve-month period. A provision was also added prohibiting owners from leasing their units during the first twelve months of ownership. These amendments were adopted by a vote of at least two-thirds of the unit owners as required by the Declaration. The following year the Association notified respondents in writing that two of their respective units were not in compliance with the nine-month lease restriction set out in section 10.3 as amended.

When the respondents failed to come into compliance with the leasing restrictions, the Association filed complaints in circuit court seeking injunctions to enforce compliance with the provisions of the Declaration. Respondents filed essentially identical answers admitting notice of their failure to comply with section 10.3, but denying that compliance could be mandated under Florida law. In addition, respondents filed counterclaims for declaratory and injunctive relief asserting that the lease restriction was unreasonable, arbitrary, and capricious, and had no purpose other than to effectively ban all leasing of units. Respondents also asserted the lease restriction was confiscatory and deprived them of lawful uses which were permissible at the time of purchase. Accordingly, respondents sought an injunction prohibiting the Association from enforcing the lease restriction or, alternatively, requiring the Association to compensate respondents for the fair market value of their units.

Thereafter, the Association and respondents filed separate motions for summary judgment. Following a hearing on the parties' motions, the circuit court granted summary judgment in respondents' favor.

On appeal, the Second District affirmed the trial court's final summary judgment and held that the lease restriction could not be enforced because it was adopted after the respondents acquired their units and no significant lease restrictions existed when respondents purchased their units.

ANALYSIS

Condominiums and the forms of ownership interests therein are strictly creatures of statute. See §§ 718.101–718.622, Fla. Stat. (2000); see also Winkelman v. Toll, 661 So. 2d 102, 105 (Fla. Dist. Ct. App. 1995); Suntide Condominium Ass'n v. Division of Florida Land Sales & Condominiums, 463 So. 2d 314, 317 (Fla. Dist. Ct. App. 1984). In Florida, Chapter 718, Florida Statutes, known as Florida's "Condominium Act," gives statutory recognition to the condominium form of ownership of real property and establishes a detailed scheme for the creation, sale, and operation of condominiums. Pursuant to section 718.104(2), a condominium is created by recording a declaration of condominium in the public records of the county where the land is located. See § 718.104(2), Fla. Stat. (2000).

The declaration, which some courts have referred to as the condominium's "constitution," strictly governs the relationships among the condominium unit owners and the condominium association. As explained by the court in Pepe v. Whispering Sands Condominium Ass'n, Inc., 351 So. 2d 755 (Fla. Dist. Ct. App. 1977):

> A declaration of a condominium is more than a mere contract spelling out mutual rights and obligations of the parties thereto—it assumes some of the attributes of a covenant running with the land, circumscribing the extent and limits of the enjoyment and use of real property. Stated otherwise, it spells out the true extent of the purchased, and thus granted, use interest therein. Absent consent, or an amendment of the declaration of condominium as may be provided for in such declaration, or as may be provided by statute in the absence of such a provision, this enjoyment and use cannot be impaired or diminished.

Id. at 757–58 (footnotes omitted). Hence, because condominiums are a creature of statute courts must look to the statutory scheme as well as the condominium declaration and other documents to determine the legal rights of owners and the association. See §§ 718.101–718.622, Fla. Stat. (2000).

From the outset, courts have recognized that condominium living is unique and involves a greater degree of restrictions upon the rights of the individual unit owners when compared to other property owners. See Seagate Condominium Ass'n, 330 So. 2d at 486 (citing cases). For instance, in White Egret Condominium, Inc. v. Franklin, 379 So. 2d 346 (Fla. 1979), we recognized that [r]easonable restrictions concerning use, occupancy and transfer of condominium units are necessary for the operation and protection of the owners in the condominium concept." *Id.* at 350. Consistent with this analysis of condominium ownership, courts have acknowledged that "increased controls and limitations upon the rights of unit owners to transfer their property are necessary concomitants of condominium living." Aquarian Foundation, Inc. v. Sholom House, Inc., 448 So. 2d 1166, 1167 (Fla. Dist. Ct. App. 1984). Indeed, section 718.104(5), Florida Statutes (2000), expressly recognizes that a declaration of condominium may contain restrictions concerning the use, occupancy, and transfer of units. See § 718.104(5), Fla. Stat. (2000).

Courts have also consistently recognized that restrictions contained within a declaration of condominium should be clothed with a very strong presumption of validity when challenged. The logic behind this presumption was explained in Hidden Harbour Estates, Inc. v. Basso, 393 So. 2d 637 (Fla. Dist. Ct. App. 1981), wherein the court reasoned:

> There are essentially two categories of cases in which a condominium association attempts to enforce rules of

restrictive uses. The first category is that dealing with the validity of restrictions found in the declaration of condominium itself. The second category of cases involves the validity of rules promulgated by the association's board of directors or the refusal of the board of directors to allow a particular use when the board is invested with the power to grant or deny a particular use.

In the first category, the restrictions are clothed with a very strong presumption of validity which arises from the fact that each individual unit owner purchases his unit knowing of and accepting the restrictions to be imposed. *Such restrictions are very much in the nature of covenants running with the land and they will not be invalidated absent a showing that they are wholly arbitrary in their application, in violation of public policy, or that they abrogate some fundamental constitutional right.* See White Egret Condominium, Inc. v. Franklin, 379 So. 2d 346 (Fla. 1979).

Id. at 639–40 (emphasis added).

AMENDMENTS TO DECLARATION

Significantly, section 718.110 also provides broad authority for amending a declaration of condominium. In particular, section 718.110(1)(a) provides:

If the declaration fails to provide a method of amendment, *the declaration may be amended as to all matters* except those listed in subsection (4) or subsection (8) if the amendment is approved by the owners of not less than two-thirds of the units. Except as to those matters described in subsection (4) or subsection (8), no declaration recorded after April 1, 1992, shall require that amendments be approved by more than four-fifths of the voting interests.

§ 718.110(1)(a), Fla. Stat. (2000) (emphasis added). Based upon this broad statutory authority and the provisions for amendment set out in the declaration of condominium, courts have recognized the authority of condominium unit owners to amend the declaration on a wide variety of issues, including restrictions on leasing. Of course, section 718.110(1)(a) itself contains some restrictions on the amendment process. For example, pursuant to subsections (4) and (8), all unit owners must consent to amendments which materially alter or modify the size, configuration or appurtenances to the unit, change the percentage by which the unit owner shares the common expenses and owns the common surplus of the condominium, or permit timeshare estates to be created in any unit of the condominium, unless otherwise provided in the declaration as originally recorded. See § 718.110(4), (8), Fla. Stat. (2000). These provisions are not at issue here.

OTHER JURISDICTIONS

We note that the majority of courts in other jurisdictions have held that a duly adopted amendment restricting either occupancy or leasing is binding upon unit owners who purchased their units before the amendment was effective. See Ritchey v. Villa Nueva Condominium Ass'n, 81 Cal. App. 3d 688, 146 Cal. Rptr. 695, 700 (Cal. Ct. App. 1978); Hill v. Fontaine Condominium Ass'n, Inc., 255 Ga. 24, 334 S.E.2d 690, 691 (Ga. 1985); Apple II Condominium Ass'n v. Worth Bank & Trust Co., 277 Ill. App. 3d 345, 659 N.E. 2d 93, 213 Ill. Dec. 463 (Ill. App. Ct. 1995); Breezy Point Holiday Harbor Lodge-Beachside Apartment Owners' Ass'n v. B.P. P'ship, 531 N.W. 2d 917, 920 (Minn. Ct. App. 1995) (in dicta); McElveen-Hunter v. Fountain Manor Ass'n, Inc., 96 N.C. App. 627, 386 S.E.2d 435, 436 (N.C. Ct. App. 1989), aff'd, 328 N.C. 84, 399 S.E.2d 112 (N.C. 1991); Shorewood West Condominium Ass'n v. Sadri, 140 Wn. 2d 47, 992 P. 2d 1008, 1012 (Wn. 2000); cf. Burgess v. Pelkey, 738 A. 2d 783, 788 (D.C. 1999); but see 560 Ocean Club, L.P. v. Ocean Club Condominium Ass'n (In re 560 Ocean Club, L.P.), 133 B.R. 310, 320 (Bankr. D.N.J. 1991); Breene v. Plaza Tower Ass'n, 310 N.W. 2d 730, 734 (N.D. 1981).

An appellate opinion from Illinois is illustrative of these decisions. In Apple II Condominium Ass'n v. Worth Bank & Trust Co., the Illinois appellate court applied the Fourth District's analysis in *Basso* in upholding the validity of a declaration amendment which restricted leasing of units to no more than once during ownership, with no lease exceeding twelve months. In enforcing the amendment, the court declared:

> The Condominium Property Act specifically states that amendments to the Declaration "shall be deemed effective upon recordation unless the amendment sets forth a different effective date." (765 ILCS 605/17 (West 1994).) In our view, neither the fact that there were no restrictions on the property when the Harmons purchased their unit nor the fact that the Harmons purchased the property for investment purposes is relevant to the proper resolution of the issues presented in this case. As purchasers of the condominium property, the Harmons are charged with knowledge of the Condominium Property Act and that the Declaration governing their unit was subject to amendment. Section 18.4(h) of the Act specifically recognizes that the Board may implement rules governing the "use of the property," so long as the restrictions do not impair those rights guaranteed by the First Amendment to the United States Constitution or the Free Speech provisions of the Illinois Constitution. (See 765 ILCS 605/18.4(h) (West 1994).) In the absence of a provision either in the Amendment or in the original Declaration, condominium owners do not have

vested rights in the *status quo ante*. See Crest Builders, Inc. v. Willow Falls Improvement Association (1979), 74 Ill. App. 3d 420, 30 Ill. Dec. 452, 393 N.E. 2d 107 (party challenging amendment has no vested interest in the Declaration as originally written); McElveen-Hunter v. Fountain Manor Association, Inc. (1989), 96 N.C. App. 627, 386 S.E.2d 435 (noting that most courts have adopted the "sounder view" that changes to a condominium declaration are binding upon both previous and subsequent owners).

Apple II Condominium Ass'n, 659 N.E. 2d at 97. The court further reasoned that the approval of the amendment by the association's membership made the leasing restriction a "category one" restriction under *Basso*, thereby elevating the level of deference given by the court. See *id.* at 98. Accordingly, the court concluded that when an amendment has been passed by an association's membership it would presume the restriction was valid and uphold it unless it was shown that the restriction was arbitrary, against public policy, or in violation of some fundamental constitutional right. See *id.* at 98–99.

We agree with this reasoning. To hold otherwise, we would have to conclude that the right to amend a declaration of condominium is substantially limited, well beyond those limitations imposed by the Legislature in section 718.110(4) and (8). We would also be faced with the difficult task of deciding what subjects could be addressed by the amendment process, a task much better suited for the Legislature, as can be seen by its imposition of restrictions in section 718.110.

THIS CASE

Respondents in this case purchased their units subject to the Declaration which expressly provides that it can be amended and sets forth the procedure for doing so. See Providence Square Ass'n v. Biancardi, 507 So. 2d 1366, 1372 (Fla. 1987) (noting that condominium purchasers are charged with notice of the recorded documents). Section 14 of the Declaration generally provides that an amendment may be adopted by a supermajority of two-thirds of the owners. Further, section 13 expressly states that each owner shall be governed by the Declaration as amended from time to time. In addition, the legal description for each of respondents' units that were allegedly being used in violation of the lease restriction provides that the units are subject to the restrictions contained in the Declaration and subsequent amendments thereto. The legal descriptions for the other three units involved in this case contain similar language.

Thus, we find that respondents were on notice that the unique form of ownership they acquired when they purchased their units in the Woodside Village Condominium was subject to change through the amendment process, and that they would be bound by properly adopted amendments. See Kroop v. Caravelle Condominium, Inc., 323 So. 2d

307, 309 (Fla. Dist. Ct. App. 1975) (upholding restriction limiting leasing to once during ownership where condominium owner acquired unit with knowledge that the declaration might thereafter be lawfully amended); see also Ritchey v. Villa Nueva Condominium Ass'n, 81 Cal. App. 3d 688, 146 Cal. Rptr. 695, 700 (Cal. Ct. App. 1978) (noting that declaration provided bylaws could be amended and that purchaser would be subject to any reasonable amendment properly adopted); McElveen-Hunter v. Fountain Manor Ass'n, Inc., 96 N.C. App. 627, 386 S.E.2d 435, 436 (N.C. Ct. App. 1989), aff'd, 328 N.C. 84, 399 S.E.2d 112 (N.C. 1991) (noting that plaintiff acquired her units subject to the right of other owners to restrict their occupancy through properly enacted amendments to the declaration); Worthinglen Condominium Unit Owners' Ass'n v. Brown, 57 Ohio App. 3d 73, 566 N.E. 2d 1275, 1277 (Ohio Ct. App. 1989) (stating that purchasers of condominium units should realize that the regime in existence at the time of purchase may not continue indefinitely and that changes in the declaration may take the form of restrictions on the unit owners' use of their property); cf. Burgess v. Pelkey, 738 A. 2d 783, 789 (D.C. 1999) (stating unit owner was on notice at time of purchase of the possibility that his rights in the cooperative could be affected by subsequent changes in the cooperative's bylaws and house rules).

It is also uncontradicted that the Association acted within the framework of the Declaration in adopting the amendment at issue. As noted above, the Declaration for Woodside Village specifically provides for amendment and sets forth the procedure for doing so. Further, pursuant to the Declaration, the amendment imposing the nine-month lease restriction was approved by at least two-thirds of the condominium unit owners. Hence, we conclude that the lease restriction amendment was properly enacted under the amendment provisions of the Declaration, and that the respondents took title to their units subject to the amendment provision set out in the Declaration and authorized by statute.

We also conclude that the respondents have failed to demonstrate that the restriction, in and of itself, violates public policy or respondents' constitutional rights, at least as asserted herein. See *Apple II Condominium Ass'n*, 659 N.E. 2d at 98–99. The respondents have simply failed to point out any provision in the statutory scheme for condominiums or any provision in the state or federal constitutions that would bar such lease restrictions. It is apparent from the circumstances giving rise to its adoption that the amendment was intended to promote owner occupancy of the condominium units, a goal certainly consistent with the concept of condominium living as originally contemplated by the legislation authorizing the condominium form of land ownership. Although a different restriction could have been adopted to better promote owner occupancy within the condominium, we cannot conclude that the amendment restricting leases to nine months in any twelve-month period is arbitrary in its attempt to achieve this goal. As discussed above, most such restrictions simply come with the unique territory of condominium ownership. Indeed, it is restrictions such as these that distinguish condominium living from rental apartments or single-family residences. Hence, persons acquiring units in condominiums are on constructive notice of the extensive restrictions that go with this unique, and some would say, restrictive, form of residential property ownership and living. Accordingly, we conclude the amendment is valid and enforceable against respondents.

NOTES AND QUESTIONS

1. Suppose Woodside Village's leasing restrictions had been imposed in an amendment to the association's bylaws or by board rule. Would the Florida Supreme Court have upheld the rule? *See* Shorewood W. Condo. Ass'n v. Sadri, 140 Wash.2d 47, 992 P.2d 1008 (2000) (holding bylaw amendment imposing leasing restrictions cannot be applied to owners who bought before imposition of the restriction).

Why should it make a difference whether the restrictions are imposed by amending the declaration rather than by amendment to the bylaws or by promulgation of a board rule? Note the court's focus on notice in the *Woodside Village* case. Aren't all unit purchasers on notice of the board's rulemaking power? If notice is the critical issue, how would enactment by bylaw amendment or by rule be different from enactment by amendment to the declaration?

Should the procedures for each kind of enactment be relevant? In *Shorewood West*, the bylaws themselves required a favorable vote by owners of 60% of the condominium's ownership interests to amend the bylaws. More than 70% of the ownership interests actually voted in favor of the amendment. Shouldn't those procedures be adequate to protect unit owners?

Would the same protections be available if the board could promulgate leasing restrictions by exercising its rulemaking power?

2. Suppose the leasing restrictions had been included in the original declaration. If a unit owner had approached you about leasing her unit for a two-year period, what advice would you have given to her? In light of the opinion in *Woodside*, do you think it likely that a court would hold that a restriction on leasing of condominium units would constitute an unreasonable restraint on alienation? Should courts be more hostile to absolute prohibitions on leasing? What recourse does a unit owner have if the unit owner's job or other circumstances would make it a hardship to occupy the unit?

3. In *Woodside Village*, the unit owners contended that they had relied on the content of the declaration before the challenged amendment. How does the court respond to the reliance argument? Should a reliance argument ever be sufficient to exempt a unit owner from an amendment to the declaration? Consider the following cases:

a.   A dog owner challenges an amendment to the declaration prohibiting pets. Would it matter whether the unit owner had the dog at the time the amendment was enacted? *Cf.* Villa De Las Palmas Homeowners Ass'n v. Terifaj, 33 Cal.4th 73, 14 Cal.Rptr.3d 67, 90 P.3d 1223 (2004) (upholding amendment against unit owner who purchased the unit and acquired the dog after enactment of the amendment);

b.   A unit owner who has purchased an above-ground swimming pool challenges an amendment prohibiting above-ground pools;

c.   A unit owner who stores three trucks in his back yard challenges an amendment prohibiting vehicle storage on the premises.

How, if at all, are the reliance arguments in these cases different from the reliance arguments in *Woodside*? In which cases (if any) do you think the reliance arguments should prevail?

4.   Is the reliance argument advanced by the unit owners in *Woodside Village* any different from the reliance argument made by a landowner challenging a zoning amendment that restricts his use of land? What does a landowner have to show to escape the application of a newly-enacted zoning restriction? Should the same rules apply to amendments to a community association declaration?

5.   Suppose a condominium board approaches you for advice. A number of unit owners have expressed concern about the high percentage of occupants who are not owners, and also about the number of occupants who park their cars and trucks in backyards and other unpaved areas, leading to a less attractive appearance of the development. The declaration does not address either problem. What advice would you give to the board? If it decides to take action, should the action be prospective or retrospective? Should the board act by amending the declaration, or by promulgating rules?

6.   Another new frontier is the creation of zoning overlays which enable residents of established neighborhoods to obtain many of the benefits of common interest communities. Neighborhood residents seeking to preserve neighborhood character agree on rules, which often place significant restrictions on land use, and then persuade municipal officials to adopt the rules. According to Professor Hannah Wiseman, these zoning overlays are problematic because they are often put into place without much public participation, or even public notice, and because they can be retroactive. *See* Hannah Wiseman, Public Communities, Private Rules, 98 Geo. L.J. 697 (2010). Do you agree with her that there should be a public vote before a common interest community adopts a new zoning overlay? Do you agree with her suggestion that property owners be allowed to go through a process, like a variance in the zoning context, so they can be allowed to deviate from the rules? Should there be a supermajority vote required to retroactively impose rules? Should property owners be able to opt out? Wiseman considers these issues and more in her 2010 article.

VI. PUBLIC POLICY LIMITS ON PRIVATE RESTRICTIONS

When an association acts to amend the declaration or bylaws, or to promulgate rules, the association's action may be in the interest of most members of the community, but it may also frustrate the expectations of individual unit owners who bought without notice of restrictions imposed after purchase. The preceding sections have explored the limits on association power to enact measures that frustrate those expectations.

Suppose, however, a developer imposes restrictions in the original declaration, and that declaration is never amended. Unit owners would appear to have weaker arguments that they lacked notice of the restrictions, or that the restrictions frustrated their expectations. Should there nevertheless be limits on the developer's power to impose restrictions in the original declaration? If so, why? And do those limits, if any, emanate from the constitution, from statutes, or from common law principles? Consider the following case:

Committee for a Better Twin Rivers v. Twin Rivers Homeowners' Association

Supreme Court of New Jersey, 2007
192 N.J. 344, 929 A.2d 1060

■ WALLACE, JR., J.

In this appeal, we determine whether the rules and regulations enacted by a homeowners' association governing the posting of signs, the use of the community room, and access to its newsletter violated our state constitutional guarantees of free expression. The trial court held that the association's rules and regulations were not subject to the right of free speech embodied in our State Constitution. On appeal, the Appellate Division reversed. We granted certification and now reverse the judgment of the Appellate Division.

This case presents us with a hybrid setting to apply the standards set forth in State v. Schmid, 84 N.J. 535, 423 A.2d 615 (1980), appeal dismissed sub nom. Princeton University v. Schmid, 455 U.S. 100, 102 S. Ct. 867, 70 L. Ed. 2d 855 (1982) and New Jersey Coalition Against War in the Middle East v. J.M.B. Realty Corp., 138 N.J. 326, 650 A.2d 757 (1994), cert. denied, 516 U.S. 812, 116 S. Ct. 62, 133 L. Ed. 2d 25 (1995). In applying the *Schmid/Coalition* multi-faceted standard, we conclude that the Association's policies, as set forth in its rules and regulations, do not violate our constitution.

I.

The facts are from the record created in the parties' crossmotions for summary judgment. Twin Rivers is a planned unit development consisting of privately owned condominium duplexes, townhouses, single-family homes, apartments, and commercial buildings located in East Windsor, New Jersey. The community covers approximately one square mile and has a population of approximately 10,000 residents.

The Twin Rivers Homeowners' Association (Association) is a private corporation. The Association maintains the [development's] private residential roads, provides street lighting and snow removal, assigns parking spaces in its parking lots, and collects rubbish in portions of Twin Rivers. By acquiring property in Twin Rivers, the owner automatically becomes a member of the Association and subject to its Articles of Incorporation (Articles) and Bylaws.

The Articles authorize the Association to exercise all of the powers, rights, and privileges provided to corporations organized under the New Jersey Nonprofit Corporation Act, N.J.S.A. 15A:1–1 to–10. The Bylaws additionally authorize the Association to adopt, publish, and enforce rules governing the use of common areas and facilities. The Bylaws may be amended by a majority of a quorum of members present in person or by proxy at a regular or special meeting of the members.

The Association is governed by a Board of Directors (Board), whose members are elected by all eligible voting members of the Association. The Board is responsible for making and enforcing the rules, and for providing services to its members that are financed through mandatory assessments levied against residents pursuant to an annual budget adopted by the Board.

Prior to the commencement of this litigation, various residents of Twin Rivers formed a committee, known as the Committee for a Better Twin Rivers (Committee), for the purpose of affecting the manner in which Twin Rivers was governed. Eventually, the Committee and three individual residents of Twin Rivers (collectively, plaintiffs) filed a nine-count complaint against the Association and Scott Pohl, the president of the Association, seeking to invalidate various rules and regulations. The thrust of the complaint was that the Association had effectively replaced the role of the municipality in the lives of its residents, and therefore, the Association's internal rules and regulations should be subject to the free speech and free association clauses of the New Jersey Constitution.

In count one of the complaint, plaintiffs sought to invalidate the Association's policy relating to the posting of signs. The Association's sign policy provided that residents may post a sign in any window of their residence and outside in the flower beds so long as the sign was no more than three feet from the residence. In essence, the policy limits signs to one per lawn and one per window. The policy also forbids the posting of signs on utility poles and natural features within the community. The stated purpose for the sign policy is to avoid the clutter of signs and to preserve the aesthetic value of the common areas, as well as to allow for lawn maintenance and leaf collection. Plaintiffs sought injunctive relief to permit the posting of political signs on the property of community residents "and on common elements under reasonable regulation," on the basis that the current policy was unconstitutional.

In count two, plaintiffs complained of the Association's policy in respect of the use of its community room. In general, the community room is available to residents of Twin Rivers, as well as clubs, organizations, and committees approved by the Trust who want to rent the room for parties or other events. When the complaint was filed, the community room policy involved a two-tiered rental charge system that differentiated between the uses of the room. However, during the pendency of this action, the Association amended the community room policy to eliminate the tier system in favor of a uniform rental fee of $165 and a refundable security deposit of $250. Additionally, a certificate of insurance naming the Association as an insured was required. The rental fees were intended to cover the costs associated with the maintenance of the room.

Plaintiffs asserted that the community room policy denied them equal protection of the laws and unreasonably and unconstitutionally violated their right to access the community room on a fair and equitable basis. They sought temporary and permanent injunctions "to allow [p]laintiffs to utilize the community room in the same manner as other similarly situated entities." Plaintiffs also urged that the rental fees were excessive because they were not related to the actual rental costs incurred by the Association.

In count three, plaintiffs alleged they were denied equal access to the Association's monthly newspaper, Twin Rivers Today (Today). The purpose of the newspaper is to provide residents with news and information that concerns the community. The editorial committee of Today selects the content of the newspaper. The paper is delivered to all Twin Rivers residents, but not to the general public. Plaintiffs sought a declaration that all Twin Rivers residents should have "equal access" to the pages of Today. Also, plaintiffs sought a permanent injunction enjoining the president of the Board from using Today "as his own personal political trumpet."

The Association filed a motion for summary judgment, and plaintiffs filed a cross-motion for summary judgment. The material facts were not disputed. The trial court issued a comprehensive opinion, granting defendants' motion for summary judgment on the sign claims in count one and on the newspaper claims in count three. The court, however, granted plaintiffs partial relief in respect of the community room claims in count two.

Plaintiffs appealed. In a published opinion, the Appellate Division reversed the trial court, holding that the Association was subject to

state constitutional standards with respect to its internal rules and
regulations.

II.

The Association urges this Court to follow the vast majority of
other jurisdictions that have refused to impose constitutional
obligations on the internal membership rules of private homeowners'
associations. In support of that view, the Association emphasizes that it
does not invite public use of its property, and its members participate in
the decision-making process of the Association. Additionally, its
members are afforded extensive statutory protections, and the business
judgment rule protects members from arbitrary decision-making.
Further, the Association contends that the relationship with its
members is a contractual one, set forth in reasonable and lawful
restrictive covenants that appear in all property deeds.

Defendant Pohl argues that the First Amendment bars a court
from asserting control over the content and editorial policies of the
Association's newspaper, maintaining that the First Amendment gives
the Association discretion to determine the content of its newspaper. He
urges this Court to reinstate the trial court's grant of summary
judgment in favor of the Association dismissing count three.

In contrast, plaintiffs ask this Court to affirm the judgment of the
Appellate Division to find that the New Jersey Constitution limits the
manner in which the Association interacts with its members. They urge
that political speech is entitled to heightened protection and that they
should have the right to post political signs beyond the Association's
restricted sign policy. Plaintiffs further contend that the excessive fees
charged for the use of the community room are not reasonably related
to the actual costs incurred by the Association. Finally, plaintiffs claim
that the State Constitution requires that the Association publish
plaintiffs' views on an equal basis with which the Association's views
are published in its newspaper.

III.

A.

Federal case law has evolved to require that there must be "state
action" to enforce constitutional rights against private entities. Marsh
v. Alabama, 326 U.S. 501, 66 S. Ct. 276, 90 L. Ed. 265 (1946), is
recognized as the leading case in this area of law. In Marsh, a private
company owned and controlled all aspects of the town. *Id.* at 502, 66 S.
Ct. at 277, 90 L. Ed. at 266. The company refused to allow solicitation
and the distribution of religious literature. *Id.* at 503, 66 S. Ct. at 277,
90 L. Ed. at 267. Marsh was arrested for trespassing while distributing
religious literature on company-owned land that was otherwise open to
the public. *Ibid.* The Court explained that "[t]he more an owner, for his
advantage, opens up his property for use by the public in general, the

more do his rights become circumscribed by the statutory and constitutional rights of those who use it." *Id.* at 506, 66 S. Ct. at 278, 90 L. Ed. at 268 (citation omitted). The Court then balanced the constitutional rights of the property owners against the First Amendment rights of Marsh to find that "the latter occupy a preferred position." *Id.* at 509, 66 S. Ct. at 280, 90 L. Ed. at 270 (footnote omitted). The Court concluded that, in those limited circumstances, the property owner's action constituted "state action" and violated the First Amendment. *Id.* at 508–09, 66 S. Ct. at 279–80, 90 L. Ed. at 269–70.

The United States Supreme Court later considered the application of Marsh to shopping centers. In the first case to address the issue, the Court held that the reasoning of Marsh applied to a shopping mall. See Amalgamated Food Employees Union Local 590 v. Logan Valley Plaza, Inc., 391 U.S. 308, 325, 88 S. Ct. 1601, 1612, 20 L. Ed. 2d 603, 616 (1968). However, the Court subsequently retreated from that position and, in a later case, concluded that the First Amendment affords no general right of free speech in privately owned shopping centers. See Pruneyard Shopping Ctr. v. Robins, 447 U.S. 74, 80–81, 100 S. Ct. 2035, 2040, 64 L. Ed. 2d 741, 751–52 (1980) (noting that although First Amendment did not grant right of free expression in shopping centers, states may adopt greater free speech rights); Hudgens v. NLRB, 424 U.S. 507, 520–21, 96 S. Ct. 1029, 1036–37, 47 L. Ed. 2d 196, 207 (1976).

B.

[The court summarized its construction of the New Jersey state constitution. In particular, in *Schmid*, the court had held that even though Princeton University is a private institution, the university violated constitutional rights of speech and assembly by prohibiting distribution of political material. The court emphasized that the university had invited the public to use its facilities, that the distribution of political material was consistent with the public and private uses of Princeton's campus, and that Princeton's regulations contained no standards for governing the exercise of free speech. The court then noted that in the Coalition case, that court had held that a regional shopping center was required to permit leafletting in support of, or in opposition to, causes, candidates and parties.—eds.]

C.

Our review of the case law in other jurisdictions reveals that only a handful of states recognize a constitutional right to engage in free speech, assembly, or electoral activity on privately owned property held open to the public, such as a shopping mall or a college campus. See Robins v. Pruneyard Shopping Ctr., 23 Cal. 3d 899, 153 Cal. Rptr. 854, 592 P.2d 341, 347 (Cal. 1979), aff'd, 447 U.S. 74, 100 S. Ct. 2035, 64 L. Ed. 2d 741 (1980); Batchelder v. Allied Stores Int'l, Inc., 388 Mass. 83, 445 N.E.2d 590, 595 (Mass. 1983). Those courts based their determinations, in part, on the open and public nature of the shopping mall. Further, the Supreme Court of Oregon, which originally found a constitutional right to engage in free speech and related activities, appears to have retreated from that position. Stranahan v. Fred Meyer, Inc., 331 Ore. 38, 11 P.3d 228, 243 (Or. 2000).

Many other states have declined to recognize a constitutional right to free speech in privately owned malls, largely on the ground that malls are not "state actors." See Fiesta Mall Venture v. Mecham Recall Comm., 159 Ariz. 371, 767 P.2d 719, 723–24 (Ariz. Ct. App. 1988); Cologne v. Westfarms Assocs., 192 Conn. 48, 469 A.2d 1201, 1209–10 (Conn. 1984); Citizens for Ethical Gov't, Inc. v. Gwinnett Place Assocs., 260 Ga. 245, 392 S.E.2d 8, 10 (Ga. 1990); Woodland v. Mich. Citizens Lobby, 423 Mich. 188, 378 N.W.2d 337, 348 (Mich. 1985); SHAD Alliance v. Smith Haven Mall, 66 N.Y.2d 496, 488 N.E.2d 1211, 1217–18, 498 N.Y.S.2d 99 (N.Y. 1985); State v. Felmet, 302 N.C. 173, 273 S.E.2d 708, 712 (N.C. 1981); Stranahan, supra, 11 P.3d at 243; W. Pa. Socialist Workers 1982 Campaign v. Conn. Gen. Life Ins. Co., 512 Pa. 23, 515 A.2d 1331, 1333 (Pa. 1986); Charleston Joint Venture v. McPherson, 308 S.C. 145, 417 S.E.2d 544, 548 (S.C. 1992); Southcenter Joint Venture v. Nat'l Democratic Policy Comm., 113 Wn.2d 413, 780 P.2d 1282, 1291 (Wash. 1989); Jacobs v. Major, 139 Wis. 2d 492, 407 N.W.2d 832, 845–46 (Wis. 1987).

We note also that, in the context of an apartment complex, the California Supreme Court modified its position in Robins, supra, and now requires state action before free speech rights will be recognized. Golden Gateway Ctr. v. Golden Gateway Tenants Ass'n, 26 Cal. 4th 1013, 111 Cal. Rptr. 2d 336, 29 P.3d 797, 803 (Cal. 2001). In sum, the vast majority of other jurisdictions that have interpreted a state constitutional provision with language similar to our constitution's free speech provision require "state action" as a precondition to imposing constitutional obligations on private property owners. Those courts recognize either explicitly or implicitly the principle that "the fundamental nature of a constitution is to govern the relationship between the people and their government, not to control the rights of the people vis-a-vis each other." Southcenter Joint Venture, supra, 780 P.2d at 1286 (footnote omitted).

IV.

We concluded in Schmid, supra, that the rights of free speech and assembly under our constitution are not only secure from interference by governmental or public bodies, but under certain circumstances from the interference by the owner of private property as well. 84 N.J. at 559, 423 A.2d 615. Simply stated, we have not followed the approach of other jurisdictions to require some state action before the free speech and assembly clauses under our constitution may be invoked.

This case presents an additional complication: it involves restrictions on conduct both on the private housing association's property and on the homeowners' properties. However, "[i]t is the extent of the restriction, and the circumstances of the restriction that are critical, not the identity of the party restricting free speech." *Coalition*, supra, 138 N.J. at 369, 650 A.2d 757. We conclude that the three-pronged test in *Schmid* and the general balancing of expressional rights and private property interests in Coalition are the appropriate standards to decide this case.

We find that plaintiffs' expressional activities are not unreasonably restricted. As the Association points out, the relationship between it and the homeowners is a contractual one, formalized in reasonable covenants that appear in all deeds. Moreover, unlike the university in *Schmid*, and the shopping center in Coalition, Twin Rivers is not a private forum that invites the public on its property to either facilitate academic discourse or to encourage public commerce. Rather, Twin Rivers is a private, residential community whose residents have contractually agreed to abide by the common rules and regulations of the Association. The mutual benefit and reciprocal nature of those rules and regulations, and their enforcement, is essential to the fundamental nature of the communal living arrangement that Twin Rivers residents enjoy. We further conclude that this factor does not weigh in favor of finding that the Association's rules and regulations violated plaintiffs' constitutional rights.

We are mindful that at least in regard to the signs on the property of the homeowners, it is the private homeowner's property and not that of the Association that is impacted. The private property owner not only is "protected under due process standards from untoward interference with or confiscatory restrictions upon its reasonable use," *Schmid*, supra, 84 N.J. at 561, 423 A.2d 615, but also our constitution affirmatively grants the homeowner free speech and assembly rights that may be exercised on that property. Notably, the Association permits expressional activities to take place on plaintiffs' property but with some minor restrictions. Homeowners are permitted to place a single sign in each window and signs may be placed in the flower beds adjacent to the homes. Those limitations are clearly not an "untoward interference with" or a "confiscatory restriction" on the reasonable use by plaintiffs' on their property to implicate due process standards.

The outcome of the balancing of the expressional rights and the privacy interests is obvious. "We do not interfere lightly with private property rights." *Coalition*, supra, 138 N.J. at 371, 650 A.2d 757. We find that the minor restrictions on plaintiffs' expressional activities are not unreasonable or oppressive, and the Association is not acting as a municipality. The Association's restrictions concerning the placement of the signs, the use of the community room, and access to its newspaper are reasonable "concerning the time, place, and manner of" such restrictions. See *id.* at 362, 650 A.2d 757. Neither singularly nor in combination is the *Schmid/Coalition* test satisfied in favor of concluding that a constitutional right was infringed here. Consequently, we conclude that in balancing plaintiffs' expressional rights against the Association's private property interest, the Association's policies do not violate the free speech and right of assembly clauses of the New Jersey Constitution.

Additionally, plaintiffs have other means of expression beyond the Association's newspaper. Plaintiffs can walk through the neighborhood, ring the doorbells of their neighbors, and advance their views. As found by the trial court, plaintiffs can distribute their own newsletter to residents, and have done so. As members of the Association, plaintiffs can vote, run for office, and participate through the elective process in the decision-making of the Association. Thus, plaintiffs may seek to garner a majority to change the rules and regulations to reduce or eliminate the restrictions they now challenge.

V.

We recognize the concerns of plaintiffs that bear on the extent and exercise of their constitutional rights in this and other similar common interest communities. At a minimum, any restrictions on the exercise of those rights must be reasonable as to time, place, and manner. Our holding does not suggest, however, that residents of a homeowners' association may never successfully seek constitutional redress against a governing association that unreasonably infringes their free speech rights.

Moreover, common interest residents have other protections. First, the business judgment rule protects common interest community residents from arbitrary decision-making. See *Thanasoulis*, supra, 110 N.J. at 666, 542 A.2d 900 (Garibaldi, J., dissenting in part and concurring in part). That is, a homeowners' association's governing body has "a fiduciary relationship to the unit owners, comparable to the obligation that a board of directors of a corporation owes to its stockholders." Siller v. Hartz Mountain Assocs., 93 N.J. 370, 382, 461 A.2d 568, cert. denied, 464 U.S. 961, 104 S. Ct. 395, 78 L. Ed. 2d 337 (1983). Pursuant to the business judgment rule, a homeowners' association's rules and regulations will be invalidated (1) if they are not authorized by statute or by the bylaws or master deed, or (2) if the association's actions are "fraudulent, self-dealing or unconscionable." Owners of the Manor Homes of Whittingham v. Whittingham Homeowners Ass'n, 367 N.J. Super. 314, 322, 842 A.2d 853 (App. Div. 2004) (citation omitted); see, e.g., *Siller*, supra, 93 N.J. at 382, 461 A.2d 568. Our Appellate Division has uniformly invoked the business judgment rule in cases involving homeowners' associations. See, e.g., *Whittingham*, supra, 367 N.J. Super. at 322; Walker v. Briarwood Condo Ass'n, 274 N.J. Super. 422, 426, 644 A.2d 634 (App. Div. 1994); see also Mulligan v. Panther Valley Prop. Owners Ass'n, 337 N.J.

Super. 293, 299–300, 766 A.2d 1186 (App. Div. 2001) (discussing application of the business judgment rule).

Finally, residents are protected under traditional principles of property law—principles that specifically account for the rights afforded under our constitution's free speech and association clauses. Our courts have recognized that restrictive covenants on real property that violate public policy are void as unenforceable. See, e.g., *Clarke*, supra, 123 N.J. Eq. at 178, 196 A. 727 ("The equitable grounds on which restrictions of this nature may be enforced at the instance of a subsequent grantee of the common grantor are well defined. One owning a tract of land may convey a portion of it, and by appropriate covenant or agreement may lawfully restrict the use of the part conveyed for the benefit of the unsold portion, *providing that the nature of the restricted use is not contrary to principles of public policy.*") (quotations omitted) (emphasis added); Courts at Beachgate v. Bird, 226 N.J. Super. 631, 639, 545 A.2d 243 (Ch. Div. 1988) (noting that "[r]estrictions in a master deed" should be enforced "unless those provisions 'are wholly arbitrary in their application, in violation of public policy, or that they abrogate some fundamental constitutional right' " (citation omitted)).

Our constitution and the fundamental rights it protects play a pivotal role in evidencing public policy. See, e.g., Mulhearn v. Fed. Shipbuilding & Dry Dock Co., 2 N.J. 356, 360, 66 A.2d 726 (1949) (noting that public policy is "evidenced" by the New Jersey Constitution and statutes); Vargo v. Nat'l Exch. Carriers Ass'n, 376 N.J. Super. 364, 377, 870 A.2d 679 (App. Div. 2005) ("Sources of public policy include the constitution, statutes, administrative rules, regulations and judicial decisions."); Baylor v. N.J. Dep't of Human Servs., 235 N.J. Super. 22, 46, 561 A.2d 618 (App. Div. 1989) ("Evidentiary sources of public policy include federal and state constitutions and constitutionally valid legislation." (citations omitted)), aff'd, 127 N.J. 286, 604 A.2d 110 (1990). Indeed, in Hennessey v. Coastal Eagle Point Oil Co., 129 N.J. 81, 93, 609 A.2d 11 (1992), we found that in New Jersey, the "highest source of public policy" is our constitution. Thus, restrictive covenants that unreasonably restrict speech—a right most substantial in our constitutional scheme—may be declared unenforceable as a matter of public policy.

VI.

The judgment of the Appellate Division is reversed and we reinstate the judgment of the trial court.

■ CHIEF JUSTICE ZAZZALI and JUSTICES LONG, LAVECCHIA, ALBIN, RIVERA-SOTO, and HOENS join in JUSTICE WALLACE'S opinion.

NOTES AND QUESTIONS

1.   The Twin Rivers sign policy permitted unit owners to place one sign in each window and one sign in the flower beds in front of the unit. Suppose, instead, that the policy had banned signs altogether. Would the court have upheld the ban? Why or why not? Is there any reason a group of home purchasers who are offended by signs and prefer to keep their political activism out of their front yards should not be able to agree to a prohibition on signs?

As the court notes in *Twin Rivers*, most courts have been unwilling to treat community associations as state actors subject to constitutional constraints. But that does not mean that courts cannot use statutes or common law doctrines as a basis for overturning sign prohibitions. Restatement (Third) of Property (Servitudes) § 3.1, provides:

Servitudes that are invalid because they violate public policy include, but are not limited to:

(1)   a servitude that is arbitrary, spiteful, or capricious;

(2)   a servitude that unreasonably burdens a fundamental constitutional right;

(3)   a servitude that imposes an unreasonable restraint on alienation . . . ;

(4)   a servitude that imposes an unreasonable restraint on trade or competition . . . ; and

(5)   a servitude that is unconscionable.

How would Twin Rivers fare under the Restatement formulation? An absolute ban on signs? Should the rules governing private restrictions be different from those governing municipal regulations? If so, why?

2.   In Twin Rivers itself, the sign restriction was not imposed in the declaration, but was instead adopted as a policy by the association board. Because the New Jersey Supreme Court upheld the rule, there is no question that the court would have upheld a similar policy in the declaration. But suppose Twin Rivers had adopted an outright ban. Would there be reasons to uphold the ban if included in the declaration, but not if the ban had been enacted by board rule or policy?

3.   Suppose a condominium declaration forbids display of flags except on defined ceremonial occasions. Should the restriction be enforceable against a veteran who wants to display the American flag? *See* Gerber v. Longboat Harbour North Condo. Inc., 724 F.Supp. 884 (M.D. Fla. 1989) (held, no). If the restriction is unenforceable, is the restriction unenforceable because it is unconstitutional, or because it violates state public policy? Congress has mooted the question by enacting the "Freedom to Display the American Flag Act of 2005," which prohibits community associations from imposing limitations on the right of unit owners to display American flags. 4 U.S.C. § 5. The statute does not explicitly restrict the right of associations to limit display of other flags. Would the *Twin Rivers* court uphold an absolute ban on displaying flags of foreign nations when an association seeks to enforce the ban on residents of Italian descent celebrating a victory in soccer's World Cup by displaying an Italian flag?

4. Would we think differently about the rules at issue in *Twin Rivers* if they were imposed upon renters? As Professor Hannah Wiseman has pointed out, tenants are governed by sometimes intrusive private rules for property use which constrain their use of their premises. Hannah J. Wiseman, Rethinking the Renter/Owner Divide in Private Governance, 2012 Utah L. Rev. 2067. We do not normally consider rental communities to fall within the private community framework, but Wiseman calls the two "nearly identical." *Id.* at 2075. How does landlord-tenant law and common interest community law intersect? Should landlords and community association boards be able (or required) to use similar procedures for enforcing their rules? What about writing them?

5. *Exclusionary Restrictions.* Enforcing restrictions on signs and flags primarily affects the residents of the community. Other restrictions—particularly those that exclude residents who belong to particular groups—have an effect beyond the residents of the community. For that reason, the "contract" argument for enforcing restrictions carries less weight with respect to exclusionary restrictions. Review the following comment for more on this important topic.

Exclusionary Restrictions

All restrictions are exclusionary in some sense. Restrictions on pets exclude pet owners (or at least make residence in a community that precludes pets less attractive). Restrictions on signs make a community less attractive to people who believe it important to display their political identities. But if markets operate smoothly, developers of other communities will find it attractive to permit signs and pets in order to attract a group of potential buyers excluded from restricted communities.

When, however, the persons excluded are members of disadvantaged groups, concerns about exclusion become more significant. In the first half of the twentieth century, racially restrictive covenants became a common way of excluding African-Americans, Jews, Asians, and other groups from subdivisions and neighborhoods, particularly after the Supreme Court outlawed racially restrictive zoning in Buchanan v. Warley, 245 U.S. 60 (1917). (Were these covenants an example of market failure or of the market responding to consumer demand?) By the middle of the century, property ownership in huge sections of major American cities was unavailable to members of these groups. By the late 1940s, 80 percent of the land within the city of Detroit was restricted by racially exclusive covenants. *See* Reynolds Farley et al., Detroit Divided 148 (2000). In Chicago, estimates of restricted property range from 50 to 80 percent of residential parcels. *See* Wendy Plotkin, Hemmed In: The Struggle Against Racial

Restrictive Covenants and Deed Restrictions in Post-WWII Chicago, 94 J. Ill. State Hist. Soc'y 39, 44–45 (2001). In 1948, the Supreme Court held, in Shelley v. Kraemer, 334 U.S. 1 (1948), that racially restrictive covenants violated the Equal Protection clause of the U.S. Constitution. Although the Court observed that "state action" is required to trigger Fourteenth Amendment protection, it argued that judicial enforcement of racially restrictive covenants supplied the necessary state involvement. Subsequent decisions have largely limited *Shelley*'s liberal state action theory to discriminatory covenants. Is this line conceptually or normatively sound? Should state action be found whenever courts enforce covenants of any sort? When they enforce any wishes of private owners? Is there a reason why it is appropriate for the Constitution to prohibit racial restrictions in covenants but not other sorts of restrictions, such as limitations on speech within common-interest communities?

The Fair Housing Act (42 U.S.C. § 3604(a)) makes it unlawful "to make unavailable . . . a dwelling to any person because of race, color, religion, sex, familial status, or national origin." The statute does include some exemptions of importance to common interest communities.

First, 42 U.S.C. § 3607(a) includes a religious organization exemption:

> Nothing in this title shall prohibit a religious organization . . . from limiting the sale, rental or occupancy of dwellings which it owns or operates for other than a commercial purpose to persons of the same religion, or from giving preference to such persons, unless membership in such religion is restricted on account of race, color, or national origin.

Does this exemption enable a developer to limit occupancy to members of the Mormon faith? What advice would you give to a developer who seeks to limit occupancy to Mormons? Suppose an Orthodox Jewish developer included in the declaration a provision prohibiting use of automobiles within the community between sundown Friday and sundown Saturday. If the association sought to enforce the restriction against a resident who does not observe the Orthodox prohibition on driving during the Jewish Sabbath, could the unit owner establish a violation of § 3604? If so, could the association rely on the exemption included in § 3607(a)? *See also* Angela C. Carmella, Religion-Free Environments in Common Interest Communities, 38 Pepp. L. Rev. 57 (2010) (arguing that bans on religious symbols, services, and signs in common interest communities violate public policy and human dignity).

Second, and of greater practical significance, although the statute's prohibition of discrimination based on "familial status" generally prohibits discrimination against families with children, the statute provides that the familial status protection does not apply "with respect to housing for older persons." 42 U.S.C. § 3607(b). The exemption applies to housing "intended and operated for occupancy by persons 55 years of age or older," so long as the housing meets other statutory and regulatory criteria. *See* 24 C.F.R. § 100.304(c)(2) (listing six factors in determining whether an exemption applies, including the manner in which the property owner or manager enforces its age restriction and verifies occupants' age). What rationale would there be for exempting housing for older persons? The exemption makes it extraordinarily attractive for developers to impose "55 and over" restrictions. Can you imagine why?

In addition to the Fair Housing Act, many states impose limitations on exclusionary policies within homeowners associations. Some cases, for instance, hold that a restrictive covenant limiting uses to single-family homes cannot be enforced to prevent operation of a group home created to advance state policies in favor of placing eligible persons within community settings. *See, e.g.,* Crane Neck Ass'n, Inc. v. New York City/Long Island Cnty. Servs. Grp., 61 N.Y.2d 154, 460 N.E.2d 1336, 472 N.Y.S.2d 901 (1984). Other cases stretch the definition of family to hold that a group home does not violate a single-family restriction. *See, e.g.,* Hill v. Community of Damien of Molokai, 121 N.M. 353, 911 P.2d 861 (1996).

How should the law treat covenant restrictions that, while neutral on their face, have disparate impact on different groups? For example, in light of observed racial differences in recreational choices, including a golf course in a private community and forcing residents to pay fees for the upkeep of the course, will predictably attract buyers who are disproportionately white, even when racial correlations with wealth and income are taken into account. *See* Lior Strahilevitz, Exclusionary Amenities in Residential Communities, 92 Va. L. Rev. 437 (2006). For a discussion of "disparate impact" analysis under the federal Fair Housing Act, see Chapter Five.

Should Private Restrictions Replace Zoning and Other Public Controls?

The growth of common interest communities leads to a natural question: should a regime of privately-created restrictions replace much of current zoning law? To some extent, the process has already started. In many areas, common interest communities have assumed many of the functions of municipalities. A developer uses a municipality's planned unit development (PUD) provisions to seek approval for a development that may ignore most of the setback and frontage requirements that would otherwise apply to the development. As one of the terms for obtaining municipal approval, the developer may agree that the developer, and later the community association, will provide many of the services and amenities ordinarily provided by the municipality—such as the construction of maintenance of recreational facilities and trash removal.

Should private regulation replace zoning? Consider two advantages of private regulation by community associations rather than public regulation by zoning. First, private regulation is consensual in nature. By purchasing in a common interest community, the purchaser assents to the restrictions in place within the community. Of course, as we have seen, the purchaser also subjects herself to amendments to those restrictions—amendments to which the purchaser has not assented, and which the purchaser can affect only by making her preferences known through the association's political process. As a result, community associations may be more consensual than municipalities, but the difference is a matter of degree; a purchaser chooses to make her home in a particular municipality, just as she chooses to make her home in a particular common interest community (or in no community). There may be more choice among common interest communities than among municipalities, but in either event, once the purchaser buys, the purchaser has two ways to escape restrictions she doesn't like: she can lobby for change, or she can move. The consensual advantage of private restrictions, then, may be less significant than it seems at first glance.

Second, private regulation typically works on a smaller scale. On many issues, this makes it easier for affected parties to promulgate regulations that generate mutual benefit, and to monitor performance by regulators and service providers. Consider Professor Ellickson's critique of the city as a service provider:

> [I]ncreasing size weakens constituents' incentives to monitor. A city therefore is more vulnerable to being captured by rent-seeking groups such as political machines, municipal unions, public works lobbies, and downtown business interests. These factions favor city policies that deliver largesse to them. To disguise this largesse from voters, these interest groups push for cumbersomely indirect systems for the delivery of favors. Vulnerability to rent-seeking thus leads to substantive city policies that are inherently wasteful. In addition, perhaps to reduce a city's vulnerability to capture by rent seekers, state law and a city's charter may dictate complex procedures for public hiring, bidding for public contracts, sale of public assets, and so on. While these procedural safeguards may stem corruption, they also make municipal bureaucracies relatively sluggish.

Robert C. Ellickson, New Institutions for Old Neighborhoods, 48 Duke L. J, 75, 89 (1998). By contrast, community associations typically involve a greater commonality of interest among members, and fewer interest group pressures. As a result, Ellickson and others have proposed that the legal system should create mechanisms to assist landowners in already-developed areas to create private associations that would assume some of the regulatory and service-providing functions of municipalities. *See also* Robert H. Nelson, Privatizing the Neighborhood: A Proposal to Replace Zoning with Private Collective Property Rights to Existing Neighborhoods, 7 Geo. Mason L. Rev. 827 (1999).

But regulation on a small scale will be inefficient with respect to many issues. The smaller the size of the regulating entity, the larger the number of externalities the entity will not be able to reach. On some issues, therefore, municipal regulation may remain a better choice than private regulation. But the explosive growth of community associations suggests that the alternative (or supplement) of private regulation should not be overlooked as an efficient mechanism for providing many collective benefits. *See generally* Gerald Korngold, The Emergence of Private Land Use Controls in Large-Scale Subdivisions: The Companion Story to Village of Euclid v. Ambler Realty Co., 51 Case W. Res. L. Rev. 617, 641–43 (2001).

VII.   BUSINESS IMPROVEMENT DISTRICTS

So far, the focus in this chapter has been on private regulation of residential development. Private regulation may also affect commercial owners, because many common interest communities are mixed-use developments, with associations that govern both residential and commercial uses. Over the last two decades, however, commercial owners in many municipalities have turned to a new organizational form to improve their business environment: the Business Improvement District (BID). BIDs are a hybrid, created through a public process, but retaining elements of private governance.

In an established business district, creating an association by purely private agreement would be plagued by the usual combination of freerider and holdout problems. In many states, however, legislation authorizes the creation of BIDs without unanimous consent of affected owners. Although the precise process differs from state to state, it is usually property owners themselves who initiate the process of creating a BID and who play a large role in defining its boundaries. Once the BID is established, owners within the BID's area become bound by its decisions. Consider the following:

> BIDs are typically formed by the owners of the property that comprise its territory filing a petition with the city council for approval. They are also created by direct city council action, but opportunity for owner protest ensures that BIDs will have the support of a majority of the owners in the district. Irrespective of statutory procedural requirements, BIDs are rarely, if ever, formed over the objection of a majority of the property owners. Once established, owners of the property

within the BID usually elect their own directors, who in turn are responsible for implementing a budget and supervising the enterprise. Though state law again shows wide variation in the scope of regulatory powers they exercise and services they provide, BIDs are generally authorized to provide a fairly wide range of common services and infrastructure. Though BIDs are used by a large number of municipalities and their popularity appears to be growing, the case law contains only a handful of reported judicial decisions regarding BIDs. In most of the cases, the courts upheld the legality of the BID, rejecting challenges based on the one person, one vote doctrine, uniformity of taxation, the Takings Clause, the Equal Protection Clause, and a variety of state statutory arguments.

BIDs pose a number of difficult questions about accountability, equality, and fairness in local government. For one thing, the typical BID structure does not correspond to one person, one vote principles. As a result, it creates the potential for unchecked intra-BID disparity in treatment and runs counter to well-established notions about democratic representation at the local level. Moreover, its very existence establishes unequal levels of service across the municipality; only those who are willing to pay extra are entitled to the "supplemental" services that BIDs provide. BID supporters note that the results are instrumental in the revival of urban business areas, that BIDs may in some ways stem the exodus of downtown businesses to suburban locations, and that the overall percentage of local revenues BIDs control is still very small. [R]esidents find BIDs attractive precisely because " 'every penny collected for the BID goes back into the BID.' "

Laurie Reynolds, Taxes, Fees, Assessments, Dues and the "Get What You Pay For" Model of Local Government, 56 Fla. L. Rev. 373, 404–06 (2004).

BIDs are just one type of special district, used at the sublocal level to creative incentives and facilitate certain types of development. Other types of special districts, such as municipal utility districts and special development districts, can impose fees upon property owners or users within the district for the delivery of certain services. Each of these types of special districts must be enabled by state statute, and may be further restricted by a state constitution.

NOTES AND QUESTIONS

1.   What powers should a Business Improvement District enjoy? Most statutes authorizing BIDs focus on the BID's power to make improvements and provide for maintenance and other services. See, e.g., N.Y. Gen. Mun. Law § 980–c. Should a BID also be entitled to impose restrictions on the

exterior appearance of buildings within its borders? To regulate the size or appearance of business signs? If not, why not?

2.   In order to pay for improvements and maintenance, a BID must have the power to impose assessments on owners within the district. On what basis should the BID impose assessments? The New York statute requires the district plan, a prerequisite to establishment of the BID, to provide "a statement of the method or methods by which the expenses of a district will be imposed upon benefited real property, in proportion to the benefit received by such property, to defray the cost thereof, including operation and maintenance." N.Y. Gen. Mun. Law § 980–a (b)(8). A BID could choose to assess owners based on the value of property within the district. Is there any other method worth considering? What advantages or disadvantages would another method have?

3.   Why would a commercial landowner support creation of a BID? In the absence of a BID, the municipality has the responsibility to provide maintenance services within the BID. Moreover, if the health of the district is important to the municipality generally, the municipality has incentives to maintain the district. Once a BID is created, municipal officials have incentives to reduce the level of the municipality's maintenance expenditures, and to shift the cost to the BID. Why should owners within a proposed BID take that risk?

4.   *Voting and Governance Procedures.* A BID is typically governed by a board of directors. Who should vote for members of the board? New York's BID statute provides that the BID's certificate of incorporation must provide for voting by owners and tenants, and may provide that owner votes be weighted in proportion to property tax assessments. N.Y. Gen. Mun. Law § 980–m(a). In Kessler v. Grand Central Dist. Mgmt. Ass'n, 158 F.3d 92 (2d Cir. 1998), the Second Circuit upheld the statute against the claim that the voting procedures violated constitutional one-person, one-vote requirements. If BIDs were subject to one-person, one-vote requirements, do you think there would be more or fewer BIDs?

The New York statute also requires that the BID's board "shall be composed of representatives of owners and tenants," that both commercial and residential tenants shall be represented on the board, that a majority of board members shall be owner representatives, and that three board members shall be appointed by public officials. N.Y. Gen. Mun. Law § 980–m(b). The statute requires that in New York City, a fourth board member be appointed by a public official. In light of the statutory requirements, what is the minimum permissible size of the BID board?

If you were drafting a BID statute, would you recommend requiring representation of tenants or public officials? Why or why not? If you were representing a business owner, how would a requirement that tenants be represented on the BID board affect your willingness to support creation of a BID? A requirement that public officials be represented?

5.   If courts have supported the concept of the BID, why don't they support the analogous concept of the neighborhood zoning district, wherein individual neighborhoods are delegated, and exercise, zoning power over a small portion of land within a locality? Professor Kenneth Stahl has explored the distinctions between the BID and the neighborhood zoning district, finding that the only meaningful distinction between the two sublocal forms of government is that the BID actually raises more troubling public policy concerns. Kenneth A. Stahl, Neighborhood Empowerment and the Future of the City, 161 U. Pa. L. Rev. 939 (2013). Consider that neighborhood zoning districts would also be the functional equivalent of common interest communities, which often impose strict architectural controls on a small subset of property owners. What are the concerns created by a neighborhood zoning district when it is located within a city?

CHAPTER NINE

THE PROBLEM OF SCALE IN LAND USE LAWMAKING

One of the most persistent problems in land use law is the question of the proper level and scale of government that should make land use decisions. It is frequently said that land use law has traditionally been the domain of local governments, and this is largely accurate, though with some qualifications we will address later in this chapter. Moreover, local governments by and large mean municipal governments within a larger metropolitan area, as opposed to metropolitan or regional governments.

But these simple statements leave a number of crucial questions unanswered. What is the optimal scale of the government responsible for land use lawmaking? How did the current situation of pervasive local control and jurisdictionally fragmented metropolitan areas come to exist? However it came about, have circumstances changed, at least in certain localities, such that we now ought to allocate primary authority for land use lawmaking to sublocal governmental units—or perhaps to higher level of government, perhaps a regional government, state governments, or even the federal government? If land use decision-making is to remain at the local, sub-metropolitan level, should local governments be obligated to take into consideration the interests of individual sublocal communities, of neighboring localities, or of the state as a whole, in carrying out their land use lawmaking powers?

These are some of the questions we aim to raise in this chapter. In thinking about them, it may help to consider the various factors favoring centralization of land use lawmaking at higher levels of government (or in larger units of local government) as well as the factors favoring decentralization and fragmentation of that authority. Although the literature discussing these issues is immense, most of the discussions boil down to arguments based on considerations of efficiency, democratic participation, and distributive justice. Proponents of allocating substantial land use authority to small, local or sublocal governments argue that such governments are more likely to use resources efficiently and to be responsive and accessible to their constituents.

Proponents of allocating power to regional bodies point to the problem that decisions made about land use within one municipality frequently have effects that spill over into neighboring communities. These theorists argue that such spillovers call into question the efficiency of decisions made by local governments, since those governments do not have the incentive to take into account costs (or benefits) that accrue to neighboring communities. Commentators have also argued that the extraterritorial effects of local government land use decisions undermine claims about the democratic legitimacy of local governments. Finally, they argue that allocating excessive power to local governments undermines redistributive efforts necessary to ensure a just distribution of resources. Keep these arguments and counterarguments in mind as we work through the material in this chapter.

I. MUNICIPAL FORMATION AND THE FRAGMENTED METROPOLIS

The majority of Americans live within the boundaries of the country's largest metropolitan areas. According to the 2000 census, well over half of the country's total population resides in its forty largest metropolitan areas, and 85% of Americans live within the boundaries of one of the country's 381 metropolitan areas. These metropolitan areas are characterized by increasingly fragmented local governments. The largest metropolitan areas in the United States are routinely each governed by local governments numbering in the hundreds, including dozens of municipalities. Governance of the massive New York metropolitan area is divided among roughly 1000 autonomous jurisdictions, including 32 county governments and hundreds of municipalities.

Throughout American history, such fragmented governance of metropolitan areas has been the rule more than the exception, but it has accelerated in recent decades as Americans have spread out into more suburban patterns of living. *See* Jon Teaford, The Political Fragmentation of Metropolitan America, 1850–1970 (1979). Immediately after its 1898 annexation of the outer boroughs, New York City encompassed the entire population of the New York metropolitan area. By 2000, it accounted for only 38% of the area's population. Other cities have experienced similar increases in jurisdictional fragmentation.

There are several complementary explanations for this trend. They include the relative ease of establishing new municipalities in previously unincorporated areas, the increased difficulty (for central cities) of annexing neighboring territories, resistance to annexation by residents of outlying areas, and resistance to the creation of regional governance bodies by residents of cities and suburbs alike.

Nevada Revised Statutes § 266.017. Area suitable for incorporation

The area to be included in a city proposed to be incorporated pursuant to NRS 266.016 to 266.0445, inclusive, must:

1. Be currently used or suitable for residential, commercial, industrial or governmental purposes.

2.   Be contiguous and urban in character, and include all contiguous area used for residential purposes.

3.   In a county whose population is 100,000 or more, have an average population density which is:

(a) Not less than four persons per acre if the proposed city is within 7 miles of the county seat; or

(b) At least equal to the density of any city that is within 7 miles of the proposed boundaries, if the proposed city is not within 7 miles of the county seat.

If the area proposed to be included in the city is more than 7 miles away from the county seat and more than 7 miles away from any existing city, there is no requirement concerning density of population.

4.   Not include any portion of a parcel of privately owned real property that has not been subdivided and is 100 acres or more in area without the written consent of the owner.

5.   Not include any area within the boundaries of an existing incorporated city.

6.   If the area of a city proposed to be incorporated is located in a county whose population is 100,000 or more and includes the area of any unincorporated town, include the entire area of the unincorporated town.

Nevada Revised Statutes § 266.019. Petition for incorporation: Contents; form

1.   The petition for incorporation must include the following information concerning the area proposed to be incorporated:

(a) A description of the area prepared by a professional land surveyor licensed pursuant to chapter 625 of NRS, which need not be made from a current survey nor contain courses and distances measured from fixed points, but may be based upon assessor's parcel maps, existing boundaries of subdivision or parcel maps, visible ground features, extensions of the visible ground features, or by any boundary that coincides with the official boundary of the state, a county, a city, a township, a section or any combination thereof.

(b) The proposed name of the city.

(c) The total acreage of the area.

(d) The number of persons who reside in the area.

(e) The number of owners of record of real property within the area.

(f) A statement that the area meets the requirements of NRS 266.017.

(g) A statement of the committee's plans for providing police and fire protection, maintaining the streets, providing water and sewer services, collecting the garbage and providing administrative services in the proposed city, with an estimate of the costs and sources of revenue.

(h) A map or plat of the area which is prepared from the description required by paragraph (a) and that shows the existing dedicated streets, sewer interceptors and outfalls and their proposed extensions.

NOTES AND QUESTIONS

1. Who should be entitled to vote to approve of a proposed incorporation? All residents within the boundaries of the proposed city? All residents of the county from which the city will be located? Residents of neighboring municipalities?

2. Who should have standing to challenge the validity of a municipal incorporation or annexation? Any resident of the new municipality? Any landowner within its boundaries? Residents of neighboring municipalities? Neighboring municipalities themselves?

3. Are the requirements for petitioning for incorporation in the Nevada statute sufficiently exacting? What other requirements might the state want to include?

4. Should the incorporation decision be subject to environmental quality review? *See* Defreestville Area Neighborhood Ass'n v. Tazbir, 23 A.D.3d 70, 800 N.Y.S.2d 474 (2005).

5. Richard Briffault gives the following account of the law of municipal incorporation in most jurisdictions:

> [G]eneral enabling legislation places municipal incorporation in the hands of local residents or landowners. State laws provide for the initiation of the process by petitions signed by some number or percentage of local residents or landowners. Thereafter, an election is held in which local residents or landowners participate, and if a requisite percentage of the local electorate approves the incorporation goes forward. Neighboring localities, regional entities and residents outside of the boundaries of the territory proposed to be incorporated generally have no role. Judicial or administrative review is usually ministerial and limited to a determination of whether the signature, voting and other formal requirements have been met.
>
> The principal criterion for deciding whether a municipality will be incorporated is whether the local people want it. There are few limits on local discretion. . . . Thus, if a relatively small number of people living on unincorporated land want to create their own municipality, and they can persuade a majority of their neighbors to agree, then they are likely to be able to form that government.

Some states go further and require that the local population be concentrated; that the land be "urban" or suitable for urban development; that the proposed municipality have the need and ability to pay for governmental services; or that the people share a "community of interest.". . . . These additional criteria often prove to be without bite. Courts have treated the local desire for municipal government, as revealed by the incorporation request, as dispositive of the question of local benefit from incorporation. Similarly, the courts have been disinclined to use the "community of interest" requirement as a substantive standard. Courts have sustained proposed incorporations of areas lacking common stores, businesses, schools or social and cultural amenities, in the face of contentions that the lack of such common facilities negated the presence of a "community of interest." In these cases, "community" was often supplied by the common demand for municipal services, as evidenced by the petition for incorporation.

Similarly, courts have found a "community of interest" even when the area proposed for incorporation was only a small piece of a larger area that arguably comprised a true "community" of common economic and social interactions. There is nothing in the incorporation criteria in most states to preclude incorporators from drawing lines that bring in high-tax or elite residential properties and fence out tax-exempt lands or poor or black people. As a general rule, the impact of the incorporation on the well-being and development of the broader "community" outside the proposed municipal borders is not a factor in judicial review of the incorporation or the proposed boundaries.

Richard Briffault, *Our Localism: Part I*, 90 Colum. L. Rev. 1, 74–76 (1990).

6.   In recent years, a number of local governments (particularly in rural areas) have chosen to dissolve due to declining populations and deteriorating fiscal conditions. *See, e.g.*, Jess Bidgood, *In Maine, Local Control is a Luxury Fewer Towns Can Afford*, N.Y. Times, Jan. 16, 2016. According to a survey of state laws by Michelle Wilde Anderson, the procedures for dissolving municipal governments vary dramatically by state. In several (including Pennsylvania, Hawaii and much of New England), it is simply impossible because of the absence of unincorporated territory to which the city can revert. Thirty-seven states permit municipalities to dissolve themselves voluntarily, typically by some combination of petition and election. *See* Michelle Wilde Anderson, *Dissolving Cities*, 121 Yale L.J. 1364, 1375–76 (2012). And states retain the power to dissolve municipal governments, even over the objection of local residents. Should the process for dissolving a municipality be identical to the process for incorporating? Do considerations arise when dissolving a municipality that do not arise when creating one that would justify treating the two processes differently? If a city dissolves, what happens to its outstanding debts?

Village of Barrington Hills v. Village of Hoffman Estates

Supreme Court of Illinois, 1980
81 Ill.2d 392, 43 Ill.Dec. 37, 410 N.E.2d 37

■ UNDERWOOD, J.

Plaintiffs, the village of Barrington Hills (Barrington Hills) and the village of South Barrington (South Barrington), filed a complaint challenging the adoption of particular zoning ordinances and the construction of an open-air theater against defendants, the village of Hoffman Estates (Hoffman Estates); Nederlander Realty Company of Illinois, Performance Properties, Inc., Ned Prop, RKO General, Inc. (Nederlander Group); Pioneer Bank and Trust Company; and Fred and Ethel Hansen.

The facts alleged in the plaintiffs' complaint are adequately set forth in the opinion of the appellate court and need only be summarized here. The subject property consists of approximately 212 acres located in Barrington Township, Cook County, and is included in a larger tract of land bounded by the Northwest Tollway on the south, the Elgin, Joliet and Eastern Railway on the west, Higgins Road on the north, and New Sutton Road on the east. The corporate limits of Barrington Hills, a non-home-rule municipality, and South Barrington, a home rule municipality "are adjacent or in close proximity to the property"; and legal title thereto is held in trust by the Pioneer Bank and Trust Company for Fred and Ethel Hansen, the beneficial owners of the property.

It is alleged in the complaint and admitted by the motion to dismiss (Goodman v. Regional Transportation Authority (1976), 66 Ill. 2d 20, 4 Ill. Dec. 304, 360 N.E.2d 51) that the Nederlander Group plans to develop this real estate for an open-air music theater, to be known as the Poplar Creek Music Theater, which would contain approximately 6,000 seats in an auditorium structure and space in the open for an additional 14,000 persons. The project would also require parking spaces for 6,000 to 7,500 automobiles and would involve commercial and concession activities ancillary to the operation of the theater programs. Among the performances contemplated by the developers are rock concerts, jazz festivals, and country-and-western musical programs, all of which would be electronically amplified.

Following a public hearing pertaining to the annexation of the subject property, Hoffman Estates on August 22, 1979, adopted three ordinances: Ordinance No. 1039–1978 authorized the execution of an annexation agreement between the defendants; Ordinance 1040–1978 authorized annexation of the real estate; and Ordinance No. 1041–1978 rezoned a portion of the property to B–2 central business district and the remainder to F farming district to permit the construction and operation of the theater. Prior to the passage of these ordinances, the real estate was located in an unincorporated area of Cook County and was classified in the R–1 single-family residence district under the Cook County zoning ordinance.

The subject property is located at a substantial distance from the residentially developed area of Hoffman Estates but is in close proximity to residentially developed areas within the corporate limits of Barrington Hills and South Barrington. Pursuant to zoning ordinances, both plaintiffs had adopted comprehensive plans which would restrict the use of the land in the vicinity of the subject property to low-density single-family residences and to agricultural uses.

It was further alleged that the defendant's adoption of the zoning ordinances permitting the construction and operation of the theater denied plaintiffs due process under the Federal and State constitutions, constituted an invalid exercise of police power under the laws of this State, violated the zoning ordinances of Hoffman Estates with respect to the B–2 central business district, and constituted a public nuisance against which temporary and injunctive relief was sought.

Plaintiffs further alleged that the annexation and zoning of the subject property for use and development of the contemplated project would occasion special injury and damage to them in their corporate capacities because of safety hazards on roads and highways within their corporate limits due to traffic congestion; the need to provide additional traffic police at an estimated annual cost to Barrington Hills of at least $42,000 and to South Barrington of not less than $24,000; the diversion of their existing police manpower from their ordinary duties to control theater crowds and to protect their residences from the disorderly activity that might result from persons attending the performances; the cost of purchasing additional squad cars for use only during the period when the proposed music theater would be in operation and of adding additional permanent police officers to their payroll; the expense of clearing from the roads and highways within their corporate limits the litter and debris which would result from crowds arriving or leaving the theater; the exhaust emissions from increased vehicular traffic which would degrade ambient air quality; the substantial increase in sound levels in the vicinity of the subject property resulting from music amplification and traffic; the adverse effects upon property values and hence tax revenues within the corporate limits of both villages; and the general impairment of the health, safety and welfare of residents of both municipalities.

The appellate court affirmance of the trial court's dismissal of plaintiffs' complaint was predicated upon its conclusion that plaintiffs had failed to demonstrate that they were aggrieved parties with standing to challenge Hoffman Estates' zoning of the subject property. Under its interpretation of this court's opinion in City of Hickory Hills

v. Bridgeview (1977), 67 Ill. 2d 399, 10 Ill. Dec. 539, 367 N.E.2d 1305, the appellate court specifically found that Barrington Hills and South Barrington had failed to demonstrate that they had a real interest in the present controversy inasmuch as they could not allege that they had been or would be required to provide services directly to the subject property.

The opinion of the appellate court is predicated on an unduly narrow reading of *Hickory Hills*. Since the complaining municipality in that case was obliged under a previous court order to provide water and sewage services to the subject property, this court concluded that it was an aggrieved person with a real interest in the rezoning ordinances adopted by an adjoining municipality. One ordinance rezoned a portion of the area involved from a limited-industrial district to a single-family-residence district, and the other ordinance reclassified a portion of the subject property to a planned unit development. Our recognition of that municipality's standing to sue was based on its allegations demonstrating that it would be directly injured in its corporate capacity by the challenged ordinances. Nothing in *Hickory Hills*, however, indicates that the "real interest" conferring standing can arise only where the objecting municipality furnishes services directly to the subject property.

Under the rule set forth in *Hickory Hills*, the appellate court in City of West Chicago v. County of Du Page (1979), 67 Ill. App. 3d 924, 926, 24 Ill. Dec. 685, 385 N.E.2d 826, concluded that a municipality's objection to a county ordinance permitting the construction of township offices, a garage, and other facilities within 1 1/2 miles of its single-family-residential district constituted a real interest sufficient to permit its intervention in an action challenging the ordinance. (*See also* Forestview Homeowners Association, Inc. v. County of Cook (1974), 18 Ill. App. 3d 230, 309 N.E.2d 763.) Decisions in other jurisdictions have similarly recognized that a municipality has standing to challenge the zoning ordinances of another municipality upon showing the existence of a real interest in the subject matter of the controversy. *See* Borough of Cresskill v. Borough of Dumont (1954), 15 N.J. 238, 245, 104 A.2d 441, 444; Borough of Allendale v. Township Committee of the Township of Mahwah (1979), 169 N.J. Super. 34, 37, 404 A.2d 50, 51; *see also* Ruegg v. Board of County Commissioners (1978), 32 Or. App. 77, 79, 573 P.2d 740, 742; Annot. 49 A.L.R.3d 1126 et seq. (1973); 3 A. Rathkopf, Zoning and Planning ch. 36, sec. 1.2, at 34 (4th ed. 1979 Supp.); Comment, Standing to Appeal Zoning Determinations: The "Aggrieved Person" Requirement, 64 Mich. L. Rev. 1070, 1082 (1966).

Defendants argue that according plaintiffs standing to sue will invite chaos in the relationships between municipalities and flood the courts with zoning litigation. Our holding, however, is not so broad, since it conditions a municipality's standing to challenge the zoning decisions of other governmental units upon a clear demonstration that it would be substantially, directly and adversely affected in its corporate capacity.

Here, as set forth in greater detail earlier in this opinion, it is admitted for purposes of the motion to dismiss that the development of the proposed project under the challenged zoning ordinances will cause Barrington Hills and South Barrington to suffer special damages in their corporate capacities in the form of a loss of municipal revenues due to a diminution in property values, an increase in municipal expenditures for the hiring of additional police manpower and squad cars to monitor vehicular congestion, the additional expense of clearing litter and debris on their roads and highways that would result from theater crowds, the degradation of ambient air quality due to vehicular exhaust and the increase in sound levels resulting from the electronic amplification of music and traffic flows. While these effects of the rezoning may appear less severe than those in *Hickory Hills*, they nevertheless portend direct, substantial and adverse effects upon the plaintiff municipalities in the performance of their corporate obligations, thus giving them a real interest in the subject matter of the controversy. Their complaint was therefore improperly dismissed.

The judgment of the appellate court affirming the trial court's order dismissing the complaint of the plaintiffs is accordingly reversed, and the cause remanded for further proceedings consistent with this opinion.

Reversed and remanded.

NOTES AND QUESTIONS

1. Did the Nederlander group support annexation of its parcel to the Village of Hoffman Estates? Would incorporation of the 221-acre parcel as a separate village have been preferable from the standpoint of the Nederlander group?

2. Why would the Village of Hoffman Estates have chosen to annex the Nederlander parcel? What motivated Hoffman Estates to rezone the parcel in question?

3. Could the Village of Barrington Hills or the Village of South Barrington have annexed the property, and thereby beaten Hoffman Estates to the punch? Would you have advised those villages to pursue that course? *See* 65 ILCS 5/7–1–2 (limiting power of a village to initiate annexation proceedings over the objection of landowners who own ten acres or more).

4. Did Barrington Hills and South Barrington challenge the annexation or the zoning ordinance enacted once the annexation was complete? Assuming the villages had standing to challenge either the annexation or the ordinance, which challenge is more likely to be successful on the

merits? What standard should the court apply in evaluating a challenge to annexation? To a neighboring municipality's zoning ordinance?

5. What role is the racial breakdown of the respective communities likely to play in the decision whether to annex an outlying, unincorporated area? *See* Michelle Wilde Anderson, *Cities Inside Out: Race, Poverty, and Exclusion at the Urban Fringe,* 55 U.C.L.A. L. Rev. 1095, 1105–06 (2008). Where the failure to annex unincorporated lands leads to significant racially disparate impacts in the delivery of local government services, should there be a legal obligation to annex? Or, put another way, can the failure to annex an outlying community, apparently because of its race, constitute discriminatory state action that violates civil rights statutes or the Fourteenth Amendment's Equal Protection Clause?

6. William Fischel predicts that these kinds of conflicts between municipalities will be relatively rare. Consider his argument:

> Neighboring towns in the same state and same county may not always get along, but a respect-thy-neighbor characterization is surely closer to the truth than the Hobbesian view that sees them perpetually on the prowl to get short-term gains from others. Moreover, even the prisoners' dilemma does not have to result in its tragic ending if there are opportunities for repeat play, as Robert Axelrod (1984) has shown in imaginative experiments and historical accounts. . . . Because local governments are geographically permanent and interact regularly with most of their neighbors, they are unlikely to pursue mutually destructive, beggar-they-neighbor policies. When there is some deviance from neighborly norms, existing legal and legislative institutions seem capable of correcting them without wholesale preemption of local authority.

William Fischel, The Homevoter Hypothesis 203–05 (2001).

If Barrington Hills's legal challenges fail, is there anything it can do to even the score with Hoffman Estates? In other words, are Hoffman Estates and Barrington Hills equally in a position to harm one another?

7. In the *Barrington Hills* case, the Nederlander group was eager for annexation by the Village of Hoffman Estates. Suppose, however, a municipality wants to annex land over the objection of the affected landowners. Almost all state statutes would preclude annexation. Does that make sense? Professor Laurie Reynolds has argued that the principle of self-determination should not invariably apply in annexation cases:

> Those who live on the fringe of a municipality have in fact exercised their right of self-determination; they have chosen to live in and be a part of an urban area. Having made that choice, the municipality's exercise of its annexation power would merely confirm the reality that this land is already urban. The nonresidents on the fringe should no more have the power to opt out of the responsibilities of urban life than should city residents be able to claim an exemption from taxes to support services they

do not use. In many instances, then, the self-determination principle merely provides nonresidents a way to protect themselves from assuming the burdens, while letting them enjoy the benefits, of being part of a municipality.

Laurie Reynolds, *Rethinking Municipal Annexation Powers,* 24 Urb. Law. 247, 266 (1992*).*

8. Richard Briffault has observed that many of the spillovers that result from fragmentation of the metropolitan area are diffuse, with effects that are not limited to neighboring jurisdictions. *See* Richard Briffault, *The Local Government Boundary Problem in Metropolitan Areas*, 48 Stan. L. Rev. 1115, 1133–37 (1996). Briffault's argument raises the possibility that the tit-for-tat dynamic identified by Fischel as constraining the production of interlocal externalities may not be strong enough to prevent significant spillovers from emerging. Which sort of situation do you think is likely to be more common: the localized tit-for-tat spillovers identified by Fischel as constraining interlocal conflict, or the more diffuse spillovers discussed by Briffault?

II. APPROACHES TO THE PROBLEM OF SCALE

Where there is a mismatch in scale between the governmental land use decision-maker and the impact of the issue being addressed, there are a number of possible approaches. First, we can retain the existing decision-making structures but require the participants in those structures to take into account the implications of their decisions for the narrower or wider community. That is, we can try to get existing local governments to think either sublocally or regionally, as the case may be. Second, we can create new governmental structures whose geographic scope matches the scale of the impact of their decisions. These governments can then be assigned either broad or narrow portfolios of authority. Finally, where a regional perspective is in order, we can shift the decision-making authority over certain questions to existing, higher levels of government, such as the state or even federal governments. Which solution is preferable, however, may well differ based on whether the question is approached from a framework that prioritizes efficiency, participation, or justice. In this section, we will take a look at these options in action, and you will have an opportunity to consider their various strengths and weaknesses.

A. GETTING LOCAL GOVERNMENTS TO THINK SUBLOCALLY

Sublocal institutions may help address the problem of scale when the land use issue has discrete, localized impacts. Consider the case of neighborhoods within a large urban municipality like New York City. Where decisions are taken at the municipal level that impose costs on a particular neighborhood in order to generate benefits that are widely shared, residents of the neighborhood may feel short-changed by their local government. Over time, in a well-functioning city, these costs and benefits should even out. And the benefits of being part of a municipality should exceed the costs for every neighborhood. Where things are not going well, however, certain neighborhoods may bear a disproportionate share of costs and reap few benefits from participating in a local government. Such a situation raises serious questions of efficiency, democratic participation, and distributive justice.

Even where a local government does not intentionally mistreat a neighborhood, there may be issues that are more properly left to the sublocal level because of the small scale of the costs and benefits involved. In one study, researchers found that library collections at public library branches in poor neighborhoods did not match the interest of the local residents, because the acquisition decisions were centrally managed. As a consequence, circulation at libraries in those neighborhoods was low. Since acquisition budgets were allocated based on circulation activity, the consequence was that poor neighborhoods received even fewer new books, feeding the cycle. *See* Frank Levy et al., Urban Outcomes: Schools, Streets and Libraries (1974). Some neighborhood activists have responded to concerns that central municipal government can be out of step with neighborhood-level needs by demanding the creation of sublocal units of governance—such as neighborhood or ward councils. *See, e.g.*, Milton Kotler, Neighborhood Government: The Local Foundations of Political Life (1969); Terry L. Cooper & Juliet A. Musso, *The Potential for Neighborhood Council Involvement in American Metropolitan Governance*, 2 Int'l J. Org. Theory & Behav. 199 (1999).

Some theorists have argued that, for some issues, even the neighborhood unit is too large. Robert Ellickson has argued that block improvement districts—private governments built around the same legal structures as common interest communities (covered in Chapter Eight)—offer an attractive mechanism for creating block-level governance within existing municipalities. *See* Robert C. Ellickson, *New Institutions for Old Neighborhoods*, 48 Duke L.J. 75 (1998). Ellickson offered several reasons why (for at least some purposes) block-level governance is superior to governance at the neighborhood or municipal level:

> First, micro-institutions seem to be efficiently scaled to produce the most localized varieties of public goods. . . .
>
> Second, block-level institutions are better able than neighborhood institutions to cater to individuals' tastes for uncommonly provided public goods. . . .
>
> Third, support from a coterminous informal social network helps an institution flourish. A high level of solidarity generally is easier to maintain within a small group than within a large one. . . . As a result, at the block level, social

pressures to pull one's oar tend to be stronger than they are at the neighborhood level.

Fourth and finally, block-level institutions are well scaled to strengthen members' involvement and skills in collective governance. Many commentators seek to revitalize civic life in the United States.

So far, sublocal strategies have been fairly limited to special-purpose groups like the business improvement districts and to requirements in zoning laws that an officially recognized neighborhood group be consulted on specific proposals in their neighborhood. Whether theorists' ideas about expanding and strengthening sublocal institutions take hold remains to be seen.

NOTES AND QUESTIONS

1. Organizing a small town into sublocal decision-making units such as Professor Ellickson's block improvement districts may be silly. The case is stronger for larger cities. Consider the benefits and the disadvantages of sublocal governments, as described above. Should such neighborhood level governance be required for municipalities beyond a certain size?

2. Where a local government persistently abuses a particular neighborhood, what remedy, if any, can a court provide?

3. Does the size of large cities contribute to corruption in the governments of large municipalities? *See* David Schleicher, *I Would, But I Need the Eggs: Why Neither Exit nor Voice Substantially Limits Big City Corruption*, 42 Loy. U. Chi. L.J. 277 (2011).

B. GETTING LOCAL GOVERNMENTS TO THINK REGIONALLY

1. OBLIGATIONS TO ACCOUNT FOR REGIONAL IMPACTS IN ZONING DECISIONS

Associated Home Builders of the Greater Eastbay, Inc. v. City of Livermore

Supreme Court of California, 1976
18 Cal.3d 582, 557 P.2d 473, 135 Cal.Rptr. 41

■ TOBRINER, J.

We face today the question of the validity of an initiative ordinance enacted by the voters of the City of Livermore which prohibits issuance of further residential building permits until local educational, sewage disposal, and water supply facilities comply with specified standards. Plaintiff, an association of contractors, subdividers, and other persons interested in residential construction in Livermore, brought this suit to enjoin enforcement of the ordinance. The superior court issued a permanent injunction, and the city appealed.

[W]e reject plaintiff's suggestion that we sustain the trial court's injunction on the ground that the ordinance unconstitutionally attempts to bar immigration to Livermore. Plaintiff's contention symbolizes the growing conflict between the efforts of suburban communities to check disorderly development, with its concomitant problems of air and water pollution and inadequate public facilities, and the increasing public need for adequate housing opportunities. We take this opportunity, therefore, to reaffirm and clarify the principles which govern validity of land use ordinances which substantially limit immigration into a community; we hold that such ordinances need not be sustained by a compelling state interest, but are constitutional if they are reasonably related to the welfare of the region affected by the ordinance.

Plaintiff contends that the ordinance therefore attempts an unconstitutional exercise of the police power because it exceeds the police power of the municipality.

As we shall explain, the limited record here prevents us from resolving that constitutional issue. We deal here with a case in which a land use ordinance is challenged solely on the ground that it assertedly exceeds the municipality's authority under the police power; the challenger eschews any claim that the ordinance discriminates on a basis of race or wealth. Under such circumstances, we view the past decisions of this court and the federal courts as establishing the following standard: the land use restriction withstands constitutional attack if it is fairly debatable that the restriction in fact bears a reasonable relation to the general welfare. For the guidance of the trial court we point out that if a restriction significantly affects residents of surrounding communities, the constitutionality of the restriction must be measured by its impact not only upon the welfare of the enacting community, but upon the welfare of the surrounding region. We explain the process by which the court can determine whether or not such a restriction reasonably relates to the regional welfare. Since the record in the present case is limited to the pleadings and stipulations, and is devoid of evidence concerning the probable impact and duration of the ordinance's restrictions, we conclude that we cannot now adjudicate the constitutionality of the ordinance. Thus we cannot sustain the trial court judgment on the ground that the ordinance exceeds the city's authority under the police power; that issue can be resolved only after trial.

In deciding whether a challenged ordinance reasonably relates to the public welfare, the courts recognize that such ordinances are presumed to be constitutional, and come before the court with every intendment in their favor. "The courts may differ with the zoning authorities as to the 'necessity or propriety of an enactment,' but so long as it remains a 'question upon which reasonable minds might differ,' there will be no judicial interference with the municipality's determination of policy." (Clemons v. City of Los Angeles (1950) 36 Cal. 2d 95, 98, 222 P.2d 439, 441.) In short, as stated by the Supreme Court in Euclid v. Ambler Co., *supra*, "If the validity . . . be fairly debatable, the legislative judgment must be allowed to control." (272 U.S. 365, 388, 47 S. Ct. 114, 118, 71 L. Ed. 303.)

We reaffirm the established constitutional principle that a local land use ordinance falls within the authority of the police power if it is reasonably related to the public welfare. Most previous decisions applying this test, however, have involved ordinances without substantial effect beyond the municipal boundaries. The present ordinance, in contrast, significantly affects the interests of nonresidents who are not represented in the city legislative body and cannot vote on a city initiative. We therefore believe it desirable for the guidance of the trial court to clarify the application of the traditional police power test to an ordinance which significantly affects nonresidents of the municipality.

When we inquire whether an ordinance reasonably relates to the public welfare, inquiry should begin by asking whose welfare must the ordinance serve. In past cases, when discussing ordinances without significant effect beyond the municipal boundaries, we have been content to assume that the ordinance need only reasonably relate to the welfare of the enacting municipality and its residents. But municipalities are not isolated islands remote from the needs and problems of the area in which they are located; thus an ordinance, superficially reasonable from the limited viewpoint of the municipality, may be disclosed as unreasonable when viewed from a larger perspective.

These considerations impel us to the conclusion that the proper constitutional test is one which inquires whether the ordinance reasonably relates to the welfare of those whom it significantly affects. If its impact is limited to the city boundaries, the inquiry may be limited accordingly; if, as alleged here, the ordinance may strongly influence the supply and distribution of housing for an entire metropolitan region, judicial inquiry must consider the welfare of that region.[24]

We explain the process by which a trial court may determine whether a challenged restriction reasonably relates to the regional welfare. The first step in that analysis is to forecast the probable effect and duration of the restriction. In the instant case the Livermore ordinance posits a total ban on residential construction, but one which terminates as soon as public facilities reach specified standards. Thus

---

[24] In ascertaining whether a challenged ordinance reasonably relates to the regional welfare, the extent and bounds of the region significantly affected by the ordinance should be determined as a question of fact by the trial court.

to evaluate the impact of the restriction, the court must ascertain the extent to which public facilities currently fall short of the specified standards, must inquire whether the city or appropriate regional agencies have undertaken to construct needed improvements, and must determine when the improvements are likely to be completed.

The second step is to identify the competing interests affected by the restriction. We touch in this area deep social antagonisms. We allude to the conflict between the environmental protectionists and the egalitarian humanists; a collision between the forces that would save the benefits of nature and those that would preserve the opportunity of people in general to settle. Suburban residents who seek to overcome problems of inadequate schools and public facilities to secure "the blessing of quiet seclusion and clean air" and to "make the area a sanctuary for people" (Village of Belle Terre v. Boraas, *supra*, 416 U.S. 1, 9, 94 S. Ct. 1536, 1541, 39 L. Ed. 2d 797) may assert a vital interest in limiting immigration to their community. Outsiders searching for a place to live in the face of a growing shortage of adequate housing, and hoping to share in the perceived benefits of suburban life, may present a countervailing interest opposing barriers to immigration.

Having identified and weighed the competing interests, the final step is to determine whether the ordinance, in light of its probable impact, represents a reasonable accommodation of the competing interests. We do not hold that a court in inquiring whether an ordinance reasonably relates to the regional welfare, cannot defer to the judgment of the municipality's legislative body. But judicial deference is not judicial abdication. The ordinance must have a *real and substantial* relation to the public welfare. (Miller v. Board of Public Works, *supra*, 195 Cal. 477, 490, 234 P. 381.) There must be a reasonable basis in fact, not in fancy, to support the legislative determination. (Consolidated Rock Products Co. v. City of Los Angeles (1962) 57 Cal. 2d 515, 522, 20 Cal. Rptr. 638, 370 P.2d 342.) Although in many cases it will be "fairly debatable" (Euclid v. Ambler Co., *supra*, 272 U.S. 365, 388, 47 S. Ct. 114, 71 L. Ed. 303) that the ordinance reasonably relates to the regional welfare, it cannot be assumed that a land use ordinance can *never* be invalidated as an enactment in excess of the police power.

The burden rests with the party challenging the constitutionality of an ordinance to present the evidence and documentation which the court will require in undertaking this constitutional analysis. Plaintiff in the present case has not yet attempted to shoulder that burden. Although plaintiff obtained a stipulation that as of the date of trial the ordinance's goals had not been fulfilled, it presented no evidence to show the likely duration or effect of the ordinance's restriction upon building permits. We must presume that the City of Livermore and appropriate regional agencies will attempt in good faith to provide that community with adequate schools, sewage disposal facilities, and a sufficient water supply; plaintiff, however, has not presented evidence to show whether the city and such agencies have undertaken to construct the needed improvements or when such improvements will be completed. Consequently we cannot determine the impact upon either Livermore or the surrounding region of the ordinance's restriction on the issuance of building permits pending achievement of its goals.

With respect to the competing interests, plaintiff asserts the existence of an acute housing shortage in the San Francisco Bay Area, but presents no evidence to document that shortage or to relate it to the probable effect of the Livermore ordinance. Defendants maintain that Livermore has severe problems of air pollution and inadequate public facilities which make it reasonable to divert new housing, at least temporarily, to other communities but offer no evidence to support that claim. Without an evidentiary record to demonstrate the validity and significance of the asserted interests, we cannot determine whether the instant ordinance attempts a reasonable accommodation of those interests.

In short, we cannot determine on the pleadings and stipulations alone whether this ordinance reasonably relates to the general welfare of the region it affects. The ordinance carries the presumption of constitutionality; plaintiff cannot overcome that presumption on the limited record before us. Thus the judgment rendered on this limited record cannot be sustained on the ground that the initiative ordinance falls beyond the proper scope of the police power.

The judgment of the superior court is reversed, and the cause remanded for further proceedings consistent with the views expressed herein.

■ Mosk, J. (dissenting).

I dissent.

Limitations on growth may be justified in resort communities, beach and lake and mountain sites, and other rural and recreational areas; such restrictions are generally designed to preserve nature's environment for the benefit of all mankind. They fulfill our fiduciary obligation to posterity. As Thomas Jefferson wrote, the earth belongs to the living, but in usufruct.

But there is a vast qualitative difference when a suburban community invokes an elitist concept to construct a mythical moat around its perimeter, not for the benefit of mankind but to exclude all but its fortunate current residents.

The majority, somewhat desultorily, deny that the ordinance imposes an absolute prohibition upon population growth or residential construction. It is true that the measure prohibits the issuance of building permits for single-family residential, multiple residential and trailer residential units until designated public services meet specified standards. But to see such restriction in practicality as something short of total prohibition is to employ ostrich vision.

First of all, the ordinance provides no timetable or dates by which the public services are to be made adequate. Thus the moratorium on permits is likely to continue for decades, or at least until attrition ultimately reduces the present population. Second, it is obvious that no inducement exists for *present* residents to expend their resources to render facilities adequate for the purpose of accommodating *future* residents. It would seem more rational, if improved services are really contemplated for any time in the foreseeable future, to admit the new residents and compel them to make their proportionate contribution to the cost of the educational, sewage and water services. Thus it cannot seriously be argued that Livermore maintains anything other than total exclusion.

The trial court found, *inter alia*, that the ordinance prohibited the issuance of building permits for residential purposes until certain conditions are met, but the measure does not provide that any person or agency is required to expend or commence any efforts on behalf of the city to meet the requirements. Nor is the city itself obliged to act within any specified time to cure its own deficiencies. Thus, in these circumstances procrastination produces its own reward: continued exclusion of new residents.

The significant omissions, when noted in relation to the ordinance preamble, reveal that the underlying purpose of the measure is "to control residential building permits in the City of Livermore"— translation: to keep newcomers out of the city—and not to solve the purported inadequacies in municipal educational, sewage and water services. Livermore concedes no building permits are now being issued and it relates no current or prospective schedule designed to correct its defective municipal services.

A municipal policy of preventing acquisition and development of property by nonresidents clearly violates article I, sections 1 and 7, subdivisions (a) and (b), of the Constitution of California.

Exclusion of unwanted outsiders, while a more frequent phenomenon recently, is not entirely innovative. The State of California made an abortive effort toward exclusivity back in the 1930s as part of a scheme to stem the influx of poor migrants from the dust bowl states of the southwest. The additional burden these indigent new residents placed on California services and facilities was severely aggravated by the great depression of that period. In Edwards v. California (1941) 314 U.S. 160, 62 S. Ct. 164, 86 L. Ed. 119, the Supreme Court held, however, that the nature of the union established by the Constitution did not permit any one state to "isolate itself from the difficulties common to all of them by restraining the transportation of persons and property across its borders." The sanction against immigration of indigents was invalidated.

If California could not protect itself from the growth problems of that era, may Livermore build a Chinese Wall to insulate itself from growth problems today? And if Livermore may do so, why not every municipality in Alameda County and in all other counties in Northern California? With a patchwork of enclaves the inevitable result will be creation of an aristocracy housed in exclusive suburbs while modest wage earners will be confined to declining neighborhoods, crowded into sterile, monotonous, multifamily projects, or assigned to pockets of marginal housing on the urban fringe. The overriding objective should be to minimize rather than exacerbate social and economic disparities, to lower barriers rather than raise them, to emphasize heterogeneity rather than homogeneity, to increase choice rather than limit it.

I realize the easiest course is for this court to defer to the political judgment of the townspeople of Livermore, on a they-know-what's-best-for-them theory (Eastlake v. Forest City Enterprises, Inc. (1976) 426 U.S. 668, 96 S. Ct. 2358, 49 L. Ed. 2d 132; James v. Valtierra (1971) 402 U.S. 137, 91 S. Ct. 1331, 28 L. Ed. 2d 678). But conceptually, when a locality adopts a comprehensive, articulated program to prevent any population growth over the foreseeable future, it places its public policy intentions visibly on the table for judicial scrutiny and constitutional analysis.

Communities adopt growth limits from a variety of motives. There may be conservationists genuinely motivated to preserve general or specific environments. There may be others whose motivation is social exclusionism, racial exclusion, racial discrimination, income segregation, fiscal protection, or just fear of any future change; each of these purposes is well served by growth prevention.

Whatever the motivation, total exclusion of people from a community is both immoral and illegal. (Cal. Const. art. I, §§ 1, 7, subds. (a) & (b).) Courts have a duty to prevent such practices, while at the same time recognizing the validity of genuine conservationist efforts.

The problem is not insoluble, nor does it necessarily provoke extreme results. Indeed, the solution can be relatively simply if municipal agencies would consider the aspirations of society as a whole, rather than merely the effect upon their narrow constituency. (*See, e.g.,* A.L.I. Model Land Development Code, art. 7.) Accommodation between environmental preservation and satisfaction of housing needs can be reached through rational guidelines for land-use decision-making. Ours, of course, is not the legislative function. But two legal inhibitions must be the benchmark of any such guidelines. First, any absolute prohibition on housing development is presumptively invalid. And second, local regulations, based on parochialism, that limit population densities in growing suburban areas may be found invalid unless the community is absorbing a reasonable share of the region's population pressures.

NOTES AND QUESTIONS

1.   The *Livermore* court's suggestion that a municipality should consider the needs of the entire region (at least when its policies would affect the entire region) raises two questions: (1) is it desirable, from a policy perspective, for local officials to consider regional needs, and (2) as a practical matter, can local officials be expected to exalt regional concerns over those of their immediate constituents? The materials that follow address both of those questions.

2.   What incentives are there for officials in the City of Livermore to consider the interests of San Francisco residents when they conflict with the interests of Livermore residents? Who votes in Livermore elections?

Note that in the *Livermore* case itself, the builders attacked an ordinance enacted not by local officials, but by voter initiative. Are the voters more or less likely to consider regional needs than their elected representatives?

3.   Is judicial review likely to provide effective incentives for municipal officials (or voters) to take regional needs into account? Suppose you, as a municipal lawyer, were to advise local officials that courts will strike down ordinances that have exclusionary effects. Would you expect local officials to stop enacting such ordinances, or to enact the ordinances and blame courts when the ordinances are invalidated?

4.   In light of *Livermore*, how likely is it that the California courts will strike down local ordinances as exclusionary? The *Livermore* majority says: "plaintiff asserts the existence of an acute housing shortage in the San Francisco Bay Area, but presents no evidence to document that shortage or to relate it to the probable effect of the Livermore ordinance." Is any plaintiff likely to be able to be able to carry this burden? Is the *Livermore* rule toothless?

5.   *Efficiency.* When it comes to determining to whom to allocate land use lawmaking authority, efficiency concerns simultaneously push in opposing directions. On the one hand, scholars frequently argue that efficiency is enhanced by allocating land use lawmaking power to small units of local government. The foremost statements of this decentralizing position draw heavily on the work of Charles Tiebout. In an influential article, Tiebout famously suggested that, when certain assumptions are satisfied,[3] the jurisdictional fragmentation of a metropolitan area will operate like an efficient market for local government services, with municipalities

---

[3]   The Tiebout Hypothesis assumes that resident-consumers have perfect information, that their mobility is costless, that the region has a large number of localities and people, and that no municipality has the sort of distinctive characteristics (e.g., waterfront) that might give it a unique competitive advantage not related to its policy choices. *See* Tiebout, *supra*, at 418–20.

competing with one another for residents and with residents sorting themselves according to their preferences for particular mixes of taxes, regulations, and services. *See* Charles Tiebout, *A Pure Theory of Local Expenditures*, 64 J. Pol. Econ. 416 (1956); *see also* William Fischel, The Homevoter Hypothesis (2001).

The result, the argument goes, is greater allocative efficiency, that is, greater aggregate satisfaction of preferences for particular mixes of municipal taxes and services than would be possible where one central entity was responsible for making the decisions on behalf of everyone. It also yields more efficient government "production" of the services provided, as governments compete with one another to provide the same level of service for as little (tax) cost as possible. At least as a positive matter, studies have provided some evidence to support this market-based analysis of local governance. One, for example, concluded that metropolitan areas that are more fragmented tended to grow at higher rates than more consolidated metropolitan areas. *See* Dean Stansel, Interjurisdictional Competition and Local Economic Performance, Working Paper (Mar. 2002) (on file with editor). Another study found that interlocal competition enables highly fragmented metropolitan areas to do a better job of holding down expenditures. *See* Mark Schneider, The Competitive City: The Political Economy of Suburbia (1989).

Pushing in the other direction, however, is the problem of spillovers, which we raised at the beginning of the chapter and which was one of the central concerns of the *Livermore* court. One of the assumptions necessary for Tiebout's "market" in local governments to operate efficiently is the absence of externalities between municipalities. *See* Fischel, *supra* at 62, 202–04. Sufficient externalities can distort the operation of that market, mitigating the efficiency it generates by permitting certain municipalities, in effect, to free-ride on the other municipalities in the metropolitan area. If it can find ways to exclude low-income residents, for example, a community can push the expense of educating the children of the poor onto neighboring communities, which may or may not have the same ability to exclude. Although residents of the exclusive community may still enjoy access to low-wage workers afforded by their presence within the larger metropolitan community, they would not share equally in the costs associated with the provision of necessary services to low-income households. The result would be higher taxes or reduced services in the communities where those low-income residents reside. Moreover, if low-income residents end up being concentrated in particular municipalities, there may be consequences of that concentration of poverty that would not arise if the poor were more evenly integrated throughout the metropolitan area. Similarly, a community that zones exclusively for large lot sizes and low-density, single-family dwellings may preserve itself from congestion or unsightly commercial development, but only by contributing to greater automobile usage and congestion in the metropolitan area as a whole. *See, e.g.*, John Carruthers, Growth at the Fringe: The Influence of Political Fragmentation in United States Metropolitan Areas, Papers in Regional Science 82: 472–99 (2003).

6. *Democracy.* Local governments are frequently praised by the supporters of metropolitan fragmentation as more participatory and responsive units of government, which these commentators often see as a direct consequence of local government's small size. Gerald Frug, for example, argues that "[l]imited size seems to be a prerequisite to the ability of ordinary citizens to participate in public life." *See* Gerald F. Frug, City Making 21 (1999). Aaron Saiger concurs that "[v]oice is a vital democratic value, and individual voices are often best heard, and most effective, in their local communities." *See* Aaron J. Saiger, Local Government Without Tiebout, 41 Urb. Law. 93 (2009). In contrast to more distant units of government, participation in which present daunting challenges for all but professional politicians, local governments empower ordinary citizens to become involved in their own governance.

Critics of fragmentation, however, also point to democratic values in support of more centralized metropolitan governance structures. Once again, the crux of the problem is spillovers. The actions taken within one local jurisdiction will, within the metropolitan context, frequently have consequences for those who live outside of it. According to Briffault, this amounts to a form of extraterritorial regulation. A community that zones in order to exclude low-income people from moving into the jurisdiction, for example, limits the residential options of low-income non-residents who might otherwise want to purchase or rent a home in the community. The value of self-governance would therefore seem to call for some mechanism for matching the scale or level of government responsible for land use lawmaking with the scale of the consequences those laws generate. And this, in turn, may argue in favor of delegating at least some land use lawmaking authority to a more regional entity in which those impacted by the land use decisions are able to participate. Does the ease of incorporating a municipality with zoning power adequately protect the interests of metropolitan area residents in participating in decisions that affect their lives? Does the degree of judicial scrutiny of zoning decisions announced by the court in *Livermore* support or impair democratic values?

7. *Distributive Justice.* Although economic analysis of the question often limits itself to positive description of the likely behavior and efficiency of potential land use lawmakers, economic analysts sometimes go farther and endorse the justice of the consequences that result from allocating that power to local decision-makers. Because the threat of exit by the rich makes it difficult for local governments to redistribute from the wealthy to the poor, those whose theories of justice lead them to oppose redistribution on moral grounds are likely to favor empowering local governments over higher levels of government.

But, as with efficiency and democracy, considerations of distributive justice can also point towards consolidating land use decisions at higher levels of government. As Aaron Saiger puts it, "[i]n an efficient market for local government, residents sort themselves not only according to tastes, but also wealth. As a result, the schools of the poor are execrable when those of the rich are excellent; the distribution of policing correlates positively with wealth and inversely with crime; rich neighborhoods enjoy numerous and beautiful parks, while those of the poor feature incinerators and bus depots, and so on. It is not intuitive that the poor as well as the rich are better off as a result." Saiger, *supra*. The incentives for local governments to use land use laws in order to exclude low-income people from enjoying the benefits of local public goods lead to the sorts of distributive consequences that Justice Mosk describes in his *Livermore* dissent. *See also* Michelle J. White, Fiscal Zoning in Fragmented Metropolitan Areas, in Fiscal Zoning and Land Use Controls 31, 35 (Edwin S. Mills & Wallace E. Oates eds., 1975).

Even if these distributive consequences were efficient, they might not be consistent with certain theories of distributive justice. Richard Schragger describes the objection this way: "[C]ertain basic public goods like education, environmental quality, sanitation, housing, and policing should be provided on a relatively equal basis regardless of individuals' private resources." Richard Schragger, *Consuming Government,* 101 Mich. L. Rev. 1824, 1835 (2003). If local control over land use law (in combination with local provision of these sorts of services) predictably limits access to these services on the basis of wealth, then, according to the proponents of the sorts of egalitarian theories of distributive justice that Schragger describes, this would count as a reason to favor changing either the way services are provided or, alternatively, shifting the level of government at which land use law is made.

The academic literature on regionalism, localism, and the costs (and benefits) of metropolitan fragmentation is enormous. In addition to the sources already cited or discussed in this section, the contributions to the symposium on the law and politics of local governance in the Spring 2005 issue of the *Journal of Law and Politics* provide a useful introduction to the various debates. *See also* Peter Calthorpe & William Fulton, The Regional City (2001); Anthony Downs, New Visions for Metropolitan America (1994); Gerald E. Frug, City Making (1999); Myron Orfield, American Metropolitics (2002); David Rusk, Cities Without Suburbs (1993); Gregory R. Weiher, The Fractured Metropolis (1991); Michelle Wilde Anderson, Dissolving Cities, 121 Yale L.J. 1364 (2012); David J. Barron, *Reclaiming Home Rule,* 116 Harv. L. Rev. 2255 (2003); Richard Briffault, *Localism and Regionalism,* 48 Buff. L. Rev. 1 (2000); Sheryll D. Cashin, *Localism, Self-Interest, and the Tyranny of the Favored Quarter,* 88 Geo. L.J. 1985 (2000); Nestor M. Davidson, *Cooperative Localism,* 93 Va. L. Rev. 959 (2007); Nector M. Davidson & Sheila R. Foster, *The Mobility Case for Regionalism,* 47 U.C. Davis L. Rev. 63 (2013); Gerald E. Frug & David J. Barron, *International Local Government Law,* 38 Urb. Law 1 (2006); Nicole Stelle Garnett, *Suburbs as Exit, Suburbs as Entrance,* 106 Mich. L. Rev. 277 (2007); Clayton P. Gillette, *Regionalization and Interlocal Bargains,* 76 N.Y.U. L. Rev. 190 (2001); Katherine J. Jackson, *The Need for Regional Management of Growth,* 37 Urb. Law. 299 (2005); Georgette C. Poindexter, *Collective Individualism,* 145 U. Pa. L. Rev. 607 (1997); Laurie Reynolds, *Home Rule, Extraterritorial Impact, and the Region,* 86 Denv. U. L. Rev. 1271 (2009); Shelley Ross Saxer, *Local Autonomy or Regionalism,* 30 Ind. L. Rev. 659

(1997); David Schleicher, *I Would But I Need the Eggs,* 42 Loy. U. Chi. L.J. 277 (2011); Christopher J. Tyson, *Localism and Involuntary Annexation,* 87 Tul. L. Rev. 297 (2012); Erika K. Wilson, *Toward a Theory of Equitable Federated Regionalism in Public Education,* 61 UCLA L. Rev. 1416 (2015).

8.   In *Livermore,* Justice Mosk says, "[L]ocal regulations, based on parochialism, that limit population densities in growing suburban areas may be found invalid unless the community is absorbing a reasonable share of the region's population pressures." What is a "reasonable share" of regional pressures? What is the appropriate "region" for determining this share? Who will make the determination? If a local government claims that it has attempted to accommodate regional pressures, how much deference is owed by courts to that local government's assertion? Consider these questions as you read the next case.

2.   THE *MT. LAUREL* DOCTRINE

Southern Burlington County N.A.A.C.P. v. Township of Mount Laurel

Supreme Court of New Jersey, 1975
67 N.J. 151, 336 A.2d 713

■ HALL, J.

This case attacks the system of land use regulation by defendant Township of Mount Laurel on the ground that low and moderate income families are thereby unlawfully excluded from the municipality.

The implications of the issue presented are indeed broad and far-reaching, extending much beyond these particular plaintiffs and the boundaries of this particular municipality.

There is not the slightest doubt that New Jersey has been, and continues to be, faced with a desperate need for housing, especially of decent living accommodations economically suitable for low and moderate income families. The situation was characterized as a "crisis" and fully explored and documented by Governor Cahill in two special messages to the Legislature—A Blueprint for Housing in New Jersey (1970) and New Horizons in Housing (1972).

Plaintiffs represent the minority group poor (black and Hispanic) seeking such quarters. But they are not the only category of persons barred from so many municipalities by reason of restrictive land use regulations.

The Facts

Mount Laurel is a flat, sprawling township, 22 square miles, or about 14,000 acres, in area, on the west central edge of Burlington County. In 1950, the township had a population of 2,817, only about 600 more people than it had in 1940. It was then, as it had been for decades, primarily a rural agricultural area with no sizeable settlements or commercial or industrial enterprises. After 1950, as in so many other municipalities similarly situated, residential development and some commerce and industry began to come in. By 1960 the population had almost doubled to 5,249 and by 1970 had more than doubled again to 11,221. These new residents were, of course, "outsiders" from the nearby central cities and older suburbs or from more distant places drawn here by reason of employment in the region. The township is now definitely a part of the outer ring of the South Jersey metropolitan area, which area we define as those portions of Camden, Burlington and Gloucester Counties within a semicircle having a radius of 20 miles or so from the heart of Camden city. And 65% of the township is still vacant land or in agricultural use.

The location and nature of development has been, as usual, controlled by the local zoning enactments.

Under the present ordinance, 29.2% of all the land in the township, or 4,121 acres, is zoned for industry. This amounts to 2,800 more acres than were so zoned by the 1954 ordinance. The industrial districts comprise most of the land on both sides of the turnpike and routes I–295, 73 and 38. Only industry meeting specified performance standards is permitted. The effect is to limit the use substantially to light manufacturing, research, distribution of goods, offices and the like. At the time of trial no more than 100 acres, mostly in the southwesterly corner along route 73 adjacent to the turnpike and I–295 interchanges, were actually occupied by industrial uses. They had been constructed in recent years, mostly in several industrial parks, and involved tax ratables of about 16 million dollars. The rest of the land so zoned has remained undeveloped. If it were fully utilized, the testimony was that about 43,500 industrial jobs would be created, but it appeared clear that, as happens in the case of so many municipalities, much more land has been so zoned than the reasonable potential for industrial movement or expansion warrants. At the same time, however, the land cannot be used for residential development under the general ordinance.

The amount of land zoned for retail business use under the general ordinance is relatively small—169 acres, or 1.2% of the total. Some of it is near the turnpike interchange; most of the rest is allocated to a handful of neighborhood commercial districts. While the greater part of the land so zoned appears to be in use, there is no major shopping center or concentrated retail commercial area—"downtown"—in the township.

The balance of the land area, almost 10,000 acres, has been developed until recently in the conventional form of major subdivisions. The general ordinance provides for four residential zones, designated R–1, R–1D, R–2 and R–3. All permit only single-family, detached dwellings, one house per lot—the usual form of grid development.

Attached townhouses, apartments (except on farms for agricultural workers) and mobile homes are not allowed anywhere in the township under the general ordinance.

The general ordinance requirements, while not as restrictive as those in many similar municipalities, nonetheless realistically allow only homes within the financial reach of persons of at least middle income.

The record thoroughly substantiates the findings of the trial court that over the years Mount Laurel "has acted affirmatively to control development and to attract a selective type of growth" (119 N.J. Super. at 168, 290 A.2d at 467) and that "through its zoning ordinances has exhibited economic discrimination in that the poor have been deprived of adequate housing and the opportunity to secure the construction of subsidized housing, and has used federal, state, county and local finances and resources solely for the betterment of middle and upper-income persons." (119 N.J. Super. at 178, 290 A.2d at 473).

There cannot be the slightest doubt that the reason for this course of conduct has been to keep down local taxes on Property (Mount Laurel is not a high tax municipality) and that the policy was carried out without regard for non-fiscal considerations with respect to People, either within or without its boundaries. This conclusion is demonstrated not only by what was done and what happened, as we have related, but also by innumerable direct statements of municipal officials at public meetings over the years which are found in the exhibits. The trial court referred to a number of them. 119 N.J. Super. at 169–170, 290 A.2d 465. No official testified to the contrary.

This policy of land use regulation for a fiscal end derives from New Jersey's tax structure, which has imposed on local real estate most of the cost of municipal and county government and of the primary and secondary education of the municipality's children. The latter expense is much the largest, so, basically, the fewer the school children, the lower the tax rate. Sizeable industrial and commercial ratables are eagerly sought and homes and the lots on which they are situated are required to be large enough, through minimum lot sizes and minimum floor areas, to have substantial value in order to produce greater tax revenues to meet school costs. Large families who cannot afford to buy large houses and must live in cheaper rental accommodations are definitely not wanted, so we find drastic bedroom restrictions for, or complete prohibition of, multi-family or other feasible housing for those of lesser income.

This pattern of land use regulation has been adopted for the same purpose in developing municipality after developing municipality. Almost every one acts solely in its own selfish and parochial interest and in effect builds a wall around itself to keep out those people or entities not adding favorably to the tax base, despite the location of the municipality or the demand for varied kinds of housing. There has been no effective intermunicipal or area planning or land use regulation. One incongruous result is the picture of developing municipalities rendering it impossible for lower paid employees of industries they have eagerly sought and welcomed with open arms (and, in Mount Laurel's case, even some of its own lower paid municipal employees) to live in the community where they work.

The Legal Issue

The legal question before us, as earlier indicated, is whether a developing municipality like Mount Laurel may validly, by a system of land use regulation, make it physically and economically impossible to provide low and moderate income housing in the municipality for the various categories of persons who need and want it and thereby, as Mount Laurel has, exclude such people from living within its confines because of the limited extent of their income and resources. Necessarily implicated are the broader questions of the right of such municipalities to limit the kinds of available housing and of any obligation to make possible a variety and choice of types of living accommodations.

We conclude that every such municipality must, by its land use regulations, presumptively make realistically possible an appropriate variety and choice of housing. More specifically, presumptively it cannot foreclose the opportunity of the classes of people mentioned for low and moderate income housing and in its regulations must affirmatively afford that opportunity, at least to the extent of the municipality's fair share of the present and prospective regional need therefor. These obligations must be met unless the particular municipality can sustain the heavy burden of demonstrating peculiar circumstances which dictate that it should not be required so to do.

We reach this conclusion under state law and so do not find it necessary to consider federal constitutional grounds urged by plaintiffs. We begin with some fundamental principles as applied to the scene before us.

It is elementary theory that all police power enactments, no matter at what level of government, must conform to the basic state constitutional requirements of substantive due process and equal protection of the laws. These are inherent in Art. I, par. 1 of our Constitution, the requirements of which may be more demanding than those of the federal Constitution. It is required that, affirmatively, a zoning regulation, like any police power enactment, must promote public health, safety, morals or the general welfare. (The last term seems broad enough to encompass the others.) Conversely, a zoning enactment which is contrary to the general welfare is invalid. Indeed these considerations are specifically set forth in the zoning enabling act as among the various purposes of zoning for which regulations must be designed. N.J.S.A. 40:55–32. Their inclusion therein really adds little; the same requirement would exist even if they were omitted.

Frequently the decisions in this state have spoken only in terms of the interest of the enacting municipality, so that it has been thought, at least in some quarters, that such was the only welfare requiring consideration. It is, of course, true that many cases have dealt only with regulations having little, if any, outside impact where the local decision is ordinarily entitled to prevail. However, it is fundamental and not to be forgotten that the zoning power is a police power of the state and the local authority is acting only as a delegate of that power and is restricted in the same manner as is the state. So, when regulation does have a substantial external impact, the welfare of the state's citizens beyond the borders of the particular municipality cannot be disregarded and must be recognized and served.

It is plain beyond dispute that proper provision for adequate housing of all categories of people is certainly an absolute essential in promotion of the general welfare required in all local land use regulation. Further the universal and constant need for such housing is so important and of such broad public interest that the general welfare which developing municipalities like Mount Laurel must consider extends beyond their boundaries and cannot be parochially confined to the claimed good of the particular municipality. It has to follow that, broadly speaking, the presumptive obligation arises for each such municipality affirmatively to plan and provide, by its land use regulations, the reasonable opportunity for an appropriate variety and choice of housing, including, of course, low and moderate cost housing, to meet the needs, desires and resources of all categories of people who may desire to live within its boundaries. Negatively, it may not adopt regulations or policies which thwart or preclude that opportunity.

It is also entirely clear, as we pointed out earlier, that most developing municipalities, including Mount Laurel, have not met their affirmative or negative obligations, primarily for local fiscal reasons. Governor Cahill summed it up in his 1970 special legislative message, A Blueprint for Housing in New Jersey, *supra*, at 10–11:

> We have reached a point in the State where the zoning criteria in many municipalities is two-fold; dwelling units of all kinds must be curtailed; industrial development must be encouraged. This is a far cry from the original concept of municipal zoning and planning.

> The fundamental objective of (the) constitutional amendment and the implementing Municipal Zoning Enabling Act was local control of zoning and planning for the purpose of effecting the public good. The original concept of local planning and zoning never contemplated prohibition in lieu of regulation nor the welfare of the few in place of the general welfare.

In sum, we are satisfied beyond any doubt that, by reason of the basic importance of appropriate housing and the longstanding pressing need for it, especially in the low and moderate cost category, and of the exclusionary zoning practices of so many municipalities, conditions have changed, and judicial attitudes must be altered to require, as we have just said, a broader view of the general welfare and the presumptive obligation on the part of developing municipalities at least to afford the opportunity by land use regulations for appropriate housing for all.

We have spoken of this obligation of such municipalities as "presumptive." The term has two aspects, procedural and substantive. Procedurally, we think the basic importance of appropriate housing for all dictates that, when it is shown that a developing municipality in its land use regulations has not made realistically possible a variety and choice of housing, including adequate provision to afford the opportunity for low and moderate income housing or has expressly prescribed requirements or restrictions which preclude or substantially hinder it, a facial showing of violation of substantive due process or equal protection under the state constitution has been made out and the burden, and it is a heavy one, shifts to the municipality to establish a valid basis for its action or non-action. The substantive aspect of "presumptive" relates to the specifics, on the one hand, of what municipal land use regulation provisions, or the absence thereof, will evidence invalidity and shift the burden of proof and, on the other hand, of what bases and considerations will carry the municipality's burden and sustain what it has done or failed to do. Both kinds of specifics may well vary between municipalities according to peculiar circumstances.

We turn to application of these principles in appraisal of Mount Laurel's zoning ordinance, useful as well, we think, as guidelines for future application in other municipalities.

Without further elaboration at this point, our opinion is that Mount Laurel's zoning ordinance is presumptively contrary to the general welfare and outside the intended scope of the zoning power in the particulars mentioned. A facial showing of invalidity is thus established, shifting to the municipality the burden of establishing valid superseding reasons for its action and non-action. We now examine the reasons it advances.

The township's principal reason in support of its zoning plan and ordinance housing provisions, advanced especially strongly at oral argument, is the fiscal one previously adverted to, i.e., that by reason of New Jersey's tax structure which substantially finances municipal governmental and educational costs from taxes on local real property, every municipality may, by the exercise of the zoning power, allow only such uses and to such extent as will be beneficial to the local tax rate. In other words, the position is that any municipality may zone extensively to seek and encourage the "good" tax ratables of industry and commerce and limit the permissible types of housing to those having the fewest school children or to those providing sufficient value to attain or approach paying their own way taxwise.

We have no hesitancy in now saying, and do so emphatically, that, considering the basic importance of the opportunity for appropriate housing for all classes of our citizenry, no municipality may exclude or limit categories of housing for that reason or purpose. While we fully recognize the increasingly heavy burden of local taxes for municipal governmental and school costs on homeowners relief from the consequences of this tax system will have to be furnished by other branches of government. It cannot legitimately be accomplished by restricting types of housing through the zoning process in developing municipalities.

By way of summary, what we have said comes down to this. As a developing municipality, Mount Laurel must, by its land use regulations, make realistically possible the opportunity for an appropriate variety and choice of housing for all categories of people who may desire to live there, of course including those of low and moderate income. It must permit multi-family housing, without bedroom or similar restrictions, as well as small dwellings on very small lots, low cost housing of other types and, in general, high density zoning, without artificial and unjustifiable minimum requirements as to lot size, building size and the like, to meet the full panoply of these needs. Certainly when a municipality zones for industry and commerce for local tax benefit purposes, it without question must zone to permit adequate housing within the means of the employees involved in such uses. (If planned unit developments are authorized, one would assume that each must include a reasonable amount of low and moderate income housing in its residential "mix," unless opportunity for such housing has already been realistically provided for elsewhere in the municipality.) The amount of land removed from residential use by allocation to industrial and commercial purposes must be reasonably related to the present and future potential for such purposes. In other words, such municipalities must zone primarily for the living welfare of people and not for the benefit of the local tax rate.

We have earlier stated that a developing municipality's obligation to afford the opportunity for decent and adequate low and moderate income housing extends at least to the municipality's fair share of the present and prospective regional need therefore. Some comment on that conclusion is in order at this point. Frequently it might be sounder to have more of such housing, like some specialized land uses, in one municipality in a region than in another, because of greater availability of suitable land, location of employment, accessibility of public transportation or some other significant reason. But, under present

New Jersey legislation, zoning must be on an individual municipal basis, rather than regionally. So long as that situation persists under the present tax structure, or in the absence of some kind of binding agreement among all the municipalities of a region, we feel that every municipality therein must bear its fair share of the regional burden. (In this respect our holding is broader than that of the trial court, which was limited to Mount Laurel-related low and moderate income housing needs.)

The composition of the applicable "region" will necessarily vary from situation to situation and probably no hard and fast rule will serve to furnish the answer in every case. Confinement to or within a certain county appears not to be realistic, but restriction within the boundaries of the state seem practical and advisable. There is no reason why developing municipalities like Mount Laurel, required by this opinion to afford the opportunity for all types of housing to meet the needs of various categories of people, may not become and remain attractive, viable communities providing good living and adequate services for all their residents in the kind of atmosphere which a democracy and free institutions demand. They can have industrial sections, commercial sections and sections for every kind of housing from low cost and multi-family to lots of more than an acre with very expensive homes. Proper planning and governmental cooperation can prevent over-intensive and too sudden development, insure against future suburban sprawl and slums and assure the preservation of open space and local beauty. We do not intend that developing municipalities shall be overwhelmed by voracious land speculators and developers if they use the powers which they have intelligently and in the broad public interest. Under our holdings today, they can be better communities for all than they previously have been.

The Remedy

We see no reason why the entire zoning ordinance should be nullified. Therefore we declare it to be invalid only to the extent and in the particulars set forth in this opinion. The township is granted 90 days from the date hereof, or such additional time as the trial court may find it reasonable and necessary to allow, to adopt amendments to correct the deficiencies herein specified. It is the local function and responsibility, in the first instance at least, rather than the court's, to decide on the details of the same within the guidelines we have laid down. If plaintiffs desire to attack such amendments, they may do so by supplemental complaint filed in this cause within 30 days of the final adoption of the amendments.

The municipality should first have full opportunity to itself act without judicial supervision. We trust it will do so in the spirit we have suggested, both by appropriate zoning ordinance amendments and whatever additional action encouraging the fulfillment of its fair share of the regional need for low and moderate income housing may be indicated as necessary and advisable. (We have in mind that there is at least a moral obligation in a municipality to establish a local housing agency pursuant to state law to provide housing for its resident poor now living in dilapidated, unhealthy quarters.) The portion of the trial court's judgment ordering the preparation and submission of the aforesaid study, report and plan to it for further action is therefore vacated as at least premature. Should Mount Laurel not perform as we expect, further judicial action may be sought by supplemental pleading in this cause.

The judgment of the Law Division is modified as set forth herein. No costs.

NOTES AND QUESTIONS

1. What is the constitutional provision the New Jersey Supreme Court finds Mt. Laurel Township to have violated? Is the case decided on the basis of individual rights enshrined in the New Jersey constitution?

2. Should the New Jersey Supreme Court have left the creation of a doctrine like this to the state's legislative branch? Are there reasons why a state legislature might be unwilling or unable to deal with the problem of local spillovers from exclusionary zoning? What are the interest groups that support leaving such zoning decisions with suburban local governments? What are the interests groups that favor regional doctrines like *Mt. Laurel*? Which groups are more likely to be able to effectively represent their interests in the state legislature?

3. The New Jersey Supreme Court seems to bend over backwards to avoid talking about race. Does that avoidance strengthen or weaken its reasoning? What might one consequence of that avoidance be when it comes to the remedies ultimately adopted? *See* John Charles Boger, *Mount Laurel at 21 Years*, 27 Seton Hall L. Rev. 1450 (1997) (finding that *Mt. Laurel* has had "virtually no" impact on racial diversity in New Jersey's suburbs).

4. What is a "developing municipality"? Does it make sense for the Court to limit its holding to such municipalities? What is the "region" to whose interests a developing municipality must attend, and how is it to be determined? How is a municipality's "fair share" of low-income housing to be calculated within that region?

5. Precisely what must that municipality do to "affirmatively afford" an opportunity for the construction of lower income housing? The NAACP's initial complaint was about Mt. Laurel's zoning practices. Suppose Mt. Laurel had amended its ordinance to zone ten percent of the town's land area (about 1,400 acres) for multi-family housing. Would that have satisfied the town's obligations?

6. Suppose Mt. Laurel had zoned ten percent of its land area for multi-family housing. An owner whose land has been zoned for multi-family housing approaches you and asks whether she can build luxury apartments on the site. What advice would you provide? Is there any guarantee that relaxing Mt. Laurel's zoning restrictions would have generated low or moderate income housing within the township? Would relaxing the restrictions have generated *more* housing? Would that, in itself, have been beneficial to less affluent residents of the area?

7. Who has standing to challenge a municipality's zoning ordinance as excessively exclusionary? Residents? Potential residents? Developers? Residents of neighboring municipalities that do make room for low-income residents? The neighboring municipalities themselves? All of the above?

8. In response to this decision, Mt. Laurel rezoned 20 acres of land (less than 0.25% of its land) for moderate income families. Most other municipalities simply ignored the ruling. A few years later, the NAACP was back in court, trying to force Mt. Laurel to take steps to facilitate the construction of low-income housing in the township. This led to a second New Jersey Supreme Court opinion.

Southern Burlington County N.A.A.C.P. v. Township of Mount Laurel (Mt. Laurel II)

Supreme Court of New Jersey, 1983
92 N.J. 158, 456 A.2d 390

■ WILENTZ, C.J.

This is the return, eight years later, of Southern Burlington County N.A.A.C.P. v. Township of Mount Laurel, 67 N.J. 151, 336 A.2d 713 (1975) (*Mount Laurel I*). We set forth in that case, for the first time, the doctrine requiring that municipalities' land use regulations provide a realistic opportunity for low and moderate income housing. The doctrine has become famous. The *Mount Laurel* case itself threatens to become infamous. After all this time, ten years after the trial court's initial order invalidating its zoning ordinance, Mount Laurel remains afflicted with a blatantly exclusionary ordinance. Papered over with studies, rationalized by hired experts, the ordinance at its core is true to nothing but Mount Laurel's determination to exclude the poor. Mount Laurel is not alone; we believe that there is widespread non-compliance with the constitutional mandate of our original opinion in this case.

To the best of our ability, we shall not allow it to continue. This Court is more firmly committed to the original *Mount Laurel* doctrine than ever, and we are determined, within appropriate judicial bounds, to make it work. The obligation is to provide a realistic opportunity for housing, not litigation. We have learned from experience, however, that unless a strong judicial hand is used, *Mount Laurel* will not result in housing, but in paper, process, witnesses, trials and appeals. We intend by this decision to strengthen it, clarify it, and make it easier for public officials, including judges, to apply it.

This case is accompanied by five others, heard together and decided in this opinion. All involve questions arising from the *Mount Laurel* doctrine. They demonstrate the need to put some steel into that doctrine. The deficiencies in its application range from uncertainty and inconsistency at the trial level to inflexible review criteria at the appellate level. The waste of judicial energy involved at every level is substantial and is matched only by the often needless expenditure of talent on the part of lawyers and experts. The length and complexity of trials is often outrageous, and the expense of litigation is so high that a real question develops whether the municipality can afford to defend or the plaintiffs can afford to sue.

The constitutional basis for the *Mount Laurel* doctrine remains the same. The constitutional power to zone, delegated to the municipalities subject to legislation, is but one portion of the police power and, as such, must be exercised for the general welfare. When the exercise of that power by a municipality affects something as fundamental as housing, the general welfare includes more than the welfare of that municipality and its citizens: it also includes the general welfare—in this case the housing needs—of those residing outside of the municipality but within the region that contributes to the housing demand within the municipality. Municipal land use regulations that conflict with the general welfare thus defined abuse the police power and are unconstitutional. In particular, those regulations that do not provide the requisite opportunity for a fair share of the region's need for low and moderate income housing conflict with the general welfare and violate the state constitutional requirements of substantive due process and equal protection. *Mount Laurel I*, 67 N.J. at 174 and 181, 336 A.2d 713.

That is the constitutional rationale for the *Mount Laurel* doctrine. The doctrine is a corollary of the constitutional obligation to zone only in furtherance of the general welfare. The doctrine provides a method of satisfying that obligation when the zoning in question affects housing.

It would be useful to remind ourselves that the doctrine does not arise from some theoretical analysis of our Constitution, but rather from underlying concepts of fundamental fairness in the exercise of governmental power. The basis for the constitutional obligation is simple: the State controls the use of land, *all* of the land. In exercising that control it cannot favor rich over poor. It cannot legislatively set aside dilapidated housing in urban ghettos for the poor and decent housing elsewhere for everyone else. The government that controls this land represents everyone. While the State may not have the ability to eliminate poverty, it cannot use that condition as the basis for imposing further disadvantages. And the same applies to the municipality, to which this control over land has been constitutionally delegated.

The clarity of the constitutional obligation is seen most simply by imagining what this state could be like were this claim never to be recognized and enforced: poor people forever zoned out of substantial areas of the state, not because housing could not be built for them but because they are not wanted; poor people forced to live in urban slums forever not because suburbia, developing rural areas, fully developed residential sections, seashore resorts, and other attractive locations could not accommodate them, but simply because they are not wanted. It is a vision not only at variance with the requirement that the zoning power be used for the general welfare but with all concepts of fundamental fairness and decency that underpin many constitutional obligations.

No one has challenged the *Mount Laurel* doctrine on these appeals. Nevertheless, a brief reminder of the judicial role in this sensitive area is appropriate, since powerful reasons suggest, and we agree, that the matter is better left to the Legislature. We act first and foremost because the Constitution of our State requires protection of the interests involved and because the Legislature has not protected them. We recognize the social and economic controversy (and its political consequences) that has resulted in relatively little legislative action in this field. We understand the enormous difficulty of achieving a political consensus that might lead to significant legislation enforcing the constitutional mandate better than we can, legislation that might completely remove this Court from those controversies. But enforcement of constitutional rights cannot await a supporting political consensus. So while we have always preferred legislative to judicial action in this field, we shall continue—until the Legislature acts—to do our best to uphold the constitutional obligation that underlies the *Mount Laurel* doctrine. That is our duty. We may not build houses, but we do enforce the Constitution. . . . In the absence of adequate legislative and executive help, we must give meaning to the constitutional doctrine in the cases before us through our own devices, even if they are relatively less suitable. That is the basic explanation of our decisions today.

Our rulings today have several purposes. First, we intend to encourage voluntary compliance with the constitutional obligation by defining it more clearly. We believe that the use of the State Development Guide Plan ("SDGP") and the confinement of all *Mount Laurel* litigation to a small group of judges, selected by the Chief Justice with the approval of the Court, will tend to serve that purpose. Second, we hope to simplify litigation in this area. While we are not overly optimistic, we think that the remedial use of the SDGP may achieve that purpose, given the significance accorded it in this opinion. Third, the decisions are intended to increase substantially the effectiveness of the judicial remedy. In most cases, upon determination that the municipality has not fulfilled its constitutional obligation, the trial court will retain jurisdiction, order an immediate revision of the ordinance (including, if necessary, supervision of the revision through a court appointed master), and require the use of effective affirmative planning and zoning devices. The long delays of interminable appellate review will be discouraged, if not completely ended, and the opportunity for low and moderate income housing found in the new ordinance will be as realistic as judicial remedies can make it. We hope to achieve all of these purposes while preserving the fundamental legitimate control of municipalities over their own zoning and, indeed, their destiny.

The following is a summary of the more significant rulings of these cases:

(1) *Every* municipality's land use regulations should provide a realistic opportunity for decent housing for at least some part of its resident poor who now occupy dilapidated housing. The zoning power is no more abused by keeping out the region's poor than by forcing out the resident poor. In other words, each municipality must provide a realistic opportunity for decent housing for its indigenous poor except where they represent a disproportionately large segment of the population as compared with the rest of the region. This is the case in many of our urban areas.

(2) The existence of a municipal obligation to provide a realistic opportunity for a fair share of the region's present and prospective low and moderate income housing need will no longer be determined by whether or not a municipality is "developing." The obligation extends, instead, to every municipality, any portion of which is designated by the State, through the SDGP as a "growth area." This obligation, imposed as a remedial measure, does not extend to those areas where the SDGP discourages growth—namely, open spaces, rural areas, prime farmland, conservation areas, limited growth areas, parts of the Pinelands and certain Coastal Zone areas. The SDGP represents the conscious determination of the State, through the executive and legislative branches, on how best to plan its future. It appropriately serves as a judicial remedial tool. The obligation to encourage lower income housing, therefore, will hereafter depend on rational long-range land use planning (incorporated into the SDGP) rather than upon the sheer economic forces that have dictated whether a municipality is "developing." Moreover, the fact that a municipality is fully developed does not eliminate this obligation although, obviously, it may affect the extent of the obligation and the timing of its satisfaction. The remedial obligation of municipalities that consist of both "growth areas" and other areas may be reduced, based on many factors, as compared to a municipality completely within a "growth area."

There shall be a heavy burden on any party seeking to vary the foregoing remedial consequences of the SDGP designations.

(3) *Mount Laurel* litigation will ordinarily include proof of the municipality's fair share of low and moderate income housing in terms of the number of units needed immediately, as well as the number needed for a reasonable period of time in the future. "Numberless" resolution of the issue based upon a conclusion that the ordinance provides a realistic opportunity for *some* low and moderate income housing will be insufficient. Plaintiffs, however, will still be able to prove a *prima facie* case, without proving the precise fair share of the municipality, by proving that the zoning ordinance is substantially affected by restrictive devices, that proof creating a presumption that the ordinance is invalid.

The municipal obligation to provide a realistic opportunity for low and moderate income housing is not satisfied by a good faith attempt. The housing opportunity provided must, in fact, be the substantial equivalent of the fair share.

(4) Any future *Mount Laurel* litigation shall be assigned only to those judges selected by the Chief Justice with the approval of the Supreme Court.

(5) The municipal obligation to provide a realistic opportunity for the construction of its fair share of low and moderate income housing may require more than the elimination of unnecessary cost-producing requirements and restrictions. Affirmative governmental devices should be used to make that opportunity realistic, including lower-income density bonuses and mandatory set-asides. Furthermore the municipality should cooperate with the developer's attempts to obtain federal subsidies. For instance, where federal subsidies depend on the municipality providing certain municipal tax treatment allowed by state statutes for lower income housing, the municipality should make a good faith effort to provide it. Mobile homes may not be prohibited, unless there is solid proof that sound planning in a particular municipality requires such prohibition.

(6) The lower income regional housing need is comprised of both low and moderate income housing. A municipality's fair share should include both in such proportion as reflects consideration of all relevant factors, including the proportion of low and moderate income housing that make up the regional need.

(7) Providing a realistic opportunity for the construction of least-cost housing will satisfy a municipality's *Mount Laurel* obligation if, and only if, it cannot otherwise be satisfied. In other words, it is only after *all* alternatives have been explored, *all* affirmative devices considered, including, where appropriate, a reasonable period of time to determine whether low and moderate income housing is produced, only when everything has been considered and tried in order to produce a realistic opportunity for low and moderate income housing that least-cost housing will provide an adequate substitute. Least-cost housing means

what it says, namely, housing that can be produced at the lowest possible price consistent with minimal standards of health and safety.

(8) Builder's remedies will be afforded to plaintiffs in *Mount Laurel* litigation where appropriate, on a case-by-case basis. Where the plaintiff has acted in good faith, attempted to obtain relief without litigation, and thereafter vindicates the constitutional obligation in *Mount Laurel*-type litigation, ordinarily a builder's remedy will be granted, provided that the proposed project includes an appropriate portion of low and moderate income housing, and provided further that it is located and designed in accordance with sound zoning and planning concepts, including its environmental impact.

(9) The judiciary should manage *Mount Laurel* litigation to dispose of a case in all of its aspects with one trial and one appeal, unless substantial considerations indicate some other course. This means that in most cases after a determination of invalidity, and prior to final judgment and possible appeal, the municipality will be required to rezone, preserving its contention that the trial court's adjudication was incorrect. If an appeal is taken, all facets of the litigation will be considered by the appellate court including both the correctness of the lower court's determination of invalidity, the scope of remedies imposed on the municipality, and the validity of the ordinance adopted after the judgment of invalidity. The grant or denial of a stay will depend upon the circumstances of each case. The trial court will appoint a master to assist in formulating and implementing a proper remedy whenever that course seems desirable.

(10) The *Mount Laurel* obligation to meet the prospective lower income housing need of the region is, by definition, one that is met year after year in the future, throughout the years of the particular projection used in calculating prospective need. In this sense the affirmative obligation to provide a realistic opportunity to construct a fair share of lower income housing is met by a "phase-in" over those years; it need not be provided immediately. Nevertheless, there may be circumstances in which the obligation requires zoning that will provide an immediate opportunity—for instance, zoning to meet the region's present lower income housing need. In some cases, the provision of such a realistic opportunity might result in the immediate construction of lower income housing in such quantity as would radically transform the municipality overnight. Trial courts shall have the discretion, under those circumstances, to moderate the impact of such housing by allowing even the present need to be phased in over a period of years. Such power, however, should be exercised sparingly. The same power may be exercised in the satisfaction of prospective need, equally sparingly, and with special care to assure that such further postponement will not significantly dilute the *Mount Laurel* obligation.

We reassure all concerned that *Mount Laurel* is not designed to sweep away all land use restrictions or leave our open spaces and natural resources prey to speculators. Municipalities consisting largely of conservation, agricultural, or environmentally sensitive areas will not be required to grow because of *Mount Laurel*. No forests or small towns need be paved over and covered with high-rise apartments as a result of today's decision.

As for those municipalities that may have to make adjustments in their lifestyles to provide for their fair share of low and moderate income housing, they should remember that they are not being required to provide more than their *fair* share. No one community need be concerned that it will be radically transformed by a deluge of low and moderate income developments. Nor should any community conclude that its residents will move to other suburbs as a result of this decision, for those "other suburbs" may very well be required to do their part to provide the same housing. Finally, once a community has satisfied its fair share obligation, the *Mount Laurel* doctrine will not restrict other measures, including large-lot and open area zoning, that would maintain its beauty and communal character.

Many of these points will be discussed later in this opinion. We mention them now only to reassure all concerned that any changes brought about by this opinion need not be drastic or destructive. Our scenic and rural areas will remain essentially scenic and rural, and our suburban communities will retain their basic suburban character. But there will be *some* change, as there must be if the constitutional rights of our lower income citizens are ever to be protected. That change will be much less painful for us than the status quo has been for them.

NOTES AND QUESTIONS

1. Note the New Jersey Supreme Court's apparent frustration with the lack of legislative response to its decision in *Mt. Laurel I*. Its new opinion in *Mt. Laurel II*, in effect, created out of whole cloth an administrative agency within the state judiciary to carry out the mandate of the *Mt. Laurel* doctrine.

2. In *Mt. Laurel II*, the New Jersey Supreme Court begins to talk about the "rights of our lower income citizens." This sort of "rights talk" was largely absent in *Mt. Laurel I*. What are the rights of "lower income citizens" that are implicated by exclusionary zoning? The right not to be shut out of a suburban lifestyle? The right to access superior public services, especially schools, that are available in suburban communities? Does it make sense to attack these problems through an assault on zoning laws, as opposed to, say, the structures of local government finance that create the incentives for exclusionary zoning that the court discussed in *Mt. Laurel I*?

3. *Affirmative Governmental Devices.* In *Mt. Laurel II,* the court makes it clear that removing government-imposed obstacles to construction of low-cost housing is not enough to meet the *Mt. Laurel* obligation. Instead, New Jersey municipalities must take affirmative steps to provide low-cost housing. Of course, a municipality cannot simply decree that low-cost housing will be built within its borders; so long as the municipality relies on private developers to build housing, the municipality must provide a structure in which developers, pursuing self-interest, are willing to develop low-cost housing. In its opinion, the court discusses two affirmative government devices: *mandatory set-asides* and *density bonuses.*

A mandatory set-aside requires developers to set aside a specified percentage of housing units for low-cost housing. If the developer wants to build, the developer has no choice but to meet the specified percentage.

A density bonus, by contrast, does not require a developer to build low-cost housing, but provides a financial incentive for her to do so: if she builds a specified number of low-cost units, she will be entitled to build additional "market rate" units. Density bonuses, then, are a species of the "incentive zoning" discussed in Chapter Three.

Which affirmative governmental device is more likely to generate low-cost housing? Does the answer depend on market conditions?

4. If the New Jersey Supreme Court's goal in *Mt. Laurel II* was to force the state legislature's hand, it achieved its goal. In 1985, the New Jersey legislature enacted the Fair Housing Act. Among other things, the law transferred authority over affordable housing issues to an administrative agency, the Council on Affordable Housing ("COAH"). COAH would be responsible for establishing regional needs for low-income housing and for allocating to each municipality its "fair share" of that need. Compliance with COAH's regulations is voluntary for municipalities, but those who obtain COAH certification are protected by the FHA from builder's lawsuits. The carrot of this protection led a large number of municipalities to enter the COAH process. The law also allowed municipalities to purchase their way out of meeting up to 50% of their "fair share" by contributing financially to the construction of low-income housing in other municipalities in what are called "Regional Contribution Agreements" ("RCAs"). These RCAs were the subject of a great deal of controversy, with some critics charging that they undermined the purposes of the *Mt. Laurel* doctrine and others taking issue with their "price" and with the lack of oversight as to how the RCA money was spent by the receiving jurisdiction. The New Jersey Supreme Court upheld the FHA in the case of Hills Dev. Co. v. Township of Bernards, 103 N.J. 1, 510 A.2d 621 (1986).

5. The FHA required COAH to publish housing need estimates and compliance regulations every six years. The first two "rounds" of regulations were published in 1986 and 1994, respectively, and these regulations were for the most part upheld by New Jersey courts. In each round, COAH's estimate of New Jersey's need for low-income housing decreased (from 10,849 units per year in the first round, to 6,465 units per year in the second round). It took ten years, and a great deal of litigation, for COAH to release its third round of rules. In 2004, it finally did so. The rules dramatically decreased the agency's estimate of New Jersey's housing needs to 3,515 units per year. The new rules also permitted municipalities to restrict up to half of their "fair share" obligation to senior citizens. Combined with the RCAs, this rule would have permitted municipalities to completely fulfill their fair share obligations without accepting any low-income families into their communities. In In re Adoption of N.J.A.C. 5:94 and 5:95 by the New Jersey Council on Affordable Hous., 390 N.J.Super. 1, 914 A.2d 348 (App. 2007), the New Jersey appellate division struck down the bulk of the third round regulations as inconsistent with the constitutional principles set forth in the *Mt. Laurel* cases. In July of 2008, while COAH was revising its regulations to comply with the court's order, New Jersey's legislature enacted amendments to the FHA prohibiting the use of RCAs to meet a municipality's low-income housing share (although it allowed existing RCAs to remain in place). *See* A–500, July 17, 2008.

COAH reissued its third round regulations in late 2008. Those regulations embraced a "growth share" approach to determining a municipality's obligations to accept low-income housing, seemingly in contradiction to *Mt. Laurel II*. In 2013, the New Jersey Supreme Court affirmed the New Jersey Appellate Division's invalidation of those regulations. *See* In re Adoption of N.J.A.C. 5:96 & 5.97, 416 N.J. Super. 462 (App. Div. 2010); aff'd 215 N.J. 578 (2013). In so doing, however, the New Jersey Supreme Court seemed to close the door on the constitutionalization of the specific *Mt. Laurel* remedies. In place of a judicially administered constitutional scheme, it firmly placed the power to determine the proper ways to implement the *Mt. Laurel* doctrine with the legislature:

> The exceptional circumstances leading this Court to create a judicial remedy thirty years ago, which required a specific approach to the identification and fulfillment of present and prospective need for affordable housing in accordance with housing regions in our state, should not foreclose efforts to assess whether alternative approaches are better suited to modern planning, development, and economic conditions in the Garden State. The policymaking branches may arrive at another approach to fulfill the constitutional obligation to promote ample affordable housing to address the needs of the people of this state and, at the same time, deter exclusionary zoning practices. We hold that our remedy, imposed thirty years ago, should not now be viewed as a constitutional straightjacket to legislative innovation.

> However, unless the Legislature amends the FHA, which tracks the judicial remedy in its operative provisions, the present regulations premised on a growth share methodology cannot be sustained. The changes in the Third Round Rules are beyond the purview of the rulemaking authority delegated to COAH because they conflict with the FHA, rendering the regulations ultra vires. *Id.* at 585.

On April 30, 2014, COAH issued yet another version of its Third Round proposed regulations for public comment. As of this edition's printing, those regulations have not yet been finalized.

There has been a robust debate over the impact of *Mt. Laurel* (and the FHA) on the availability of low-income housing in New Jersey. Although there are few empirical studies, one estimate puts the additional homes attributable to *Mt. Laurel* at 30,000, with an additional 8,000 homes built under RCAs. John M. Payne, The Paradox of Progress: Three Decades of the Mount Laurel Doctrine, 5 J. Plan. Hist. 126, 134 (2006). Whether this number makes *Mt. Laurel* a success or a failure depends on one's perspective. Over that same period of time, within the State of New Jersey, residential building permits were issued for over 700,000 new units. *See* N.J. Housing Opportunity Task Force, Findings and Recommendations 26–27 (2010). For the purposes of comparison, however, it is helpful to keep in mind that the first estimates of the need for low-income housing in the suburbs (by the three-judge panel appointed in *Mt. Laurel II*) estimated that number to be 240,000. COAH's first determination of the need for low-income housing estimated it to be 145,000 in 1986. Some groups have generated much larger numbers for New Jersey's need for low-income housing. One estimate puts the number as high as 600,000. *See id.* Some have argued that the primary beneficiaries of Mt. Laurel have been very young couples with low incomes and the very elderly. *See* John Charles Boger, Mount Laurel at 21 Years, 27 Seton Hall L. Rev. 1450 (1997).

3.   ANTI-SNOB ZONING STATUTES

MASSACHUSETTS GEN. STATUTES, CH. 40B

Section 21. Low or moderate income housing; applications for approval of proposed construction; hearing; appeal

Any public agency or limited dividend or nonprofit organization proposing to build low or moderate income housing may submit to the board of appeals, established under section twelve of chapter forty A, a single application to build such housing in lieu of separate applications to the applicable local boards. The board of appeals shall forthwith notify each such local board, as applicable, of the filing of such application by sending a copy thereof to such local boards for their recommendations and shall, within thirty days of the receipt of such application, hold a public hearing on the same. The board of appeals shall request the appearance at said hearing of such representatives of said local boards as are deemed necessary or helpful in making its decision upon such application and shall have the same power to issue permits or approvals as any local board or official who would otherwise act with respect to such application, including but not limited to the power to attach to said permit or approval conditions and requirements with respect to height, site plan, size or shape, or building materials as are consistent with the terms of this section. The board of appeals, in making its decision on said application, shall take into consideration the recommendations of the local boards and shall have the authority to use the testimony of consultants. The board of appeals shall adopt rules, not inconsistent with the purposes of this chapter, for the conduct of its business pursuant to this chapter and shall file a copy of said rules with the city or town clerk. The provisions of section eleven of chapter forty A shall apply to all such hearings. The board of appeals shall render a decision, based upon a majority vote of said board, within forty days after the termination of the public hearing and, if favorable to the applicant, shall forthwith issue a comprehensive permit or approval. If said hearing is not convened or a decision is not rendered within the time allowed, unless the time has been extended by mutual agreement between the board and the applicant, the application shall be deemed to have been allowed and the comprehensive permit or approval shall forthwith issue. Any person aggrieved by the issuance of a comprehensive permit or approval may appeal to the court as provided in section seventeen of chapter forty A.

Section 22. Appeal to housing appeals committee; procedure; judicial review

Whenever an application filed under the provisions of section twenty-one is denied, or is granted with such conditions and requirements as to make the building or operation of such housing uneconomic, the applicant shall have the right to appeal to the housing appeals committee in the department of housing and community development for a review of the same. Such appeal shall be taken within twenty days after the date of the notice of the decision by the board of appeals by filing with said committee a statement of the prior proceedings and the reasons upon which the appeal is based. The committee shall forthwith notify the board of appeals of the filing of such petition for review and the latter shall, within ten days of the receipt of such notice, transmit a copy of its decision and the reasons therefor to the committee. Such appeal shall be heard by the committee within twenty days after receipt of the applicant's statement. A stenographic record of the proceedings shall be kept and the committee shall render a written decision, based upon a majority vote, stating its findings of fact, its conclusions and the reasons therefor within thirty days after the termination of the hearing, unless such time shall have been extended by mutual agreement between the committee and the applicant. Such decision may be reviewed in the superior court in accordance with the provisions of chapter thirty A.

Section 23. Hearing by housing appeals committee; issues; powers of disposition; orders; enforcement

The hearing by the housing appeals committee in the department of housing and community development shall be limited to the issue of whether, in the case of the denial of an application, the decision of the board of appeals was reasonable and consistent with local needs and, in the case of an approval of an application with conditions and requirements imposed, whether such conditions and requirements make the construction or operation of such housing uneconomic and whether they are consistent with local needs. If the committee finds, in the case of a denial, that the decision of the board of appeals was unreasonable and not consistent with local needs, it shall vacate such decision and shall direct the board to issue a comprehensive permit or approval to the applicant. If the committee finds, in the case of an approval with conditions and requirements imposed, that the decision of the board makes the building or operation of such housing uneconomic and is not consistent with local needs, it shall order such board to modify or remove any such condition or requirement so as to make the proposal no longer uneconomic and to issue any necessary permit or approval; provided, however, that the committee shall not issue any order that would permit the building or operation of such housing in accordance with standards less safe than the applicable building and site plan requirements of the federal Housing Administration or the Massachusetts Housing Finance Agency, whichever agency is financially assisting such housing. Decisions or conditions and requirements imposed by a board of appeals that are consistent with local needs shall not be vacated, modified or removed by the committee notwithstanding that such decisions or conditions and requirements have the effect of making the applicant's proposal uneconomic.

The housing appeals committee or the petitioner shall have the power to enforce the orders of the committee at law or in equity in the superior court. The board of appeals shall carry out the order of the hearing appeals committee within thirty days of its entry and, upon failure to do so, the order of said committee shall, for all purposes, be deemed to be the action of said board, unless the petitioner consents to a different decision or order by such board.

PROBLEM

In light of the Massachusetts statute, consider the following facts:

On July 11, 1977, Cedar Street Associates (Cedar Street), a limited dividend organization, applied for a comprehensive permit to build forty-eight units of low or moderate income housing. After a public hearing, the board, on November 10, 1977, granted Cedar Street a comprehensive permit to build thirty-six units, on condition that at least eighty percent of the units be occupied by the elderly. In addition, the board required evidence, within twelve months, that Cedar Street had received the necessary financing. Later, the board granted Cedar Street's request for a four-month extension of this deadline.

Cedar Street obtained a loan from the Massachusetts Housing Finance Agency. The loan was made subject to several conditions. The development would have to provide only ten rent-subsidized units for the elderly. In addition, the developer would have to include eight rent-subsidized units for families, and eighteen units for rental at market rates. Notified of these conditions, the board required Cedar Street to file a new application for a comprehensive permit.

On June 29, 1979, Cedar Street filed a second application. The board denied this application. The board found that the area of the proposed site was not equipped to provide the facilities necessary for a high density population; that the project was detrimental to the health and safety of the anticipated occupants and their neighbors; and that the planning objections incidental to the development outweighed the need for low or moderate income housing.

1. What is the next step for the Cedar Street Associates?

2. What sorts of arguments should Cedar Street Associates make that their second application should have been granted? To what sort of evidence might they point in support of their position?

3. If the Housing Appeals Committee (HAC) rules in favor of Cedar Street, does the local zoning board have any further recourse?

4. Does the process established by the Massachusetts statute make any provision for hearing from neighbors who might be adversely affected by the HAC's decision?

NOTES AND QUESTIONS

1. In addition to Massachusetts, several other states have also adopted legislation to combat exclusionary zoning, though the statutes operate differently in each state. *See, e.g.*, Cal. Gov't Code §§ 65580—89.8; Conn. Gen. Stat. §§ 8–30g to 8–30h; Or. Rev. Stat. §§ 197.005 to .850; R.I. Gen. Laws §§ 45–53–1 to–8. Does the existence of these statutes suggest that the New Jersey Supreme Court's decision in *Mt. Laurel* was a usurpation of authority more properly left to the state's legislature?

2. Between 1975 and 1982, 101 cases were appealed to the HAC from adverse local zoning board decisions. Of those 101 cases, only 55 had been decided by 1987. Of those 55, the HAC reversed the local zoning board 34 times. *See* Harold A. McDougall, From Litigation to Legislation in Exclusionary Zoning Law, 22 Harv. C.R.–C.L. L. Rev. 623, 646–47 (1987). According to one commentator, "[u]nderstaffing and lack of budgetary support at the [HAC] have been responsible for considerable processing delays." *Id.* HAC rulings favorable to developers are routinely appealed to the Massachusetts Supreme Judicial Court, further delaying the ultimate resolution of these cases. Under these sorts of conditions, is it possible for the Massachusetts statute to have a noticeable impact on exclusionary zoning?

3. By 1999, it was estimated by one study that the Massachusetts statute was responsible for the construction of 18,000 low-income housing units, mostly in suburban communities. *See* Sharon Perlman Krefetz, The Impact and Evolution of the Massachusetts Comprehensive Permit and Zoning Appeals Act, 22 W. New Eng. L. Rev. 381 (2001). Sharon Krefetz concludes that the statute has had a dramatic impact on the geography of low-income housing in Massachusetts, dramatically reducing the number of communities totally lacking low-income units.

4. What sorts of changes might make the Massachusetts statute more effective? How would they impact the fairness of the statute (a) for neighbors of proposed developments, (b) for developers of low-income housing, or (c) for local governments?

C. CREATING REGIONAL GOVERNANCE

Instead of forcing existing local governments to think regionally, some communities have responded to problems of scale by creating new units of government with regional powers and responsibilities. Occasionally, these take the form of general purpose, regional-scale governments. More often, the regional entities are special-purpose governments with a narrow, even technical, focus.

1. REGIONAL GOVERNMENTS

Regional governments are extremely rare in the United States. As we discussed above, the governments of large cities during the nineteenth and early twentieth centuries approximated "regional" governments because easy annexation meant that city governments could contain an entire metropolitan area. Most metropolitan areas today, however, are highly fragmented.

The most significant exception to this general rule is the Portland area's regional land use authority, known as Metro. Metro, which was created by the state legislature, encompasses dozens of municipalities and spans three counties. It is responsible for land use planning for the entire region and is funded by a combination of user fees (especially for garbage collection) and property taxes. It is run by a council of seven elected representatives (six councilors represent districts and the council president is elected from the region at large). For a summary of Metro's history and structure, *see* Keith Aoki, *Democracy in Action*, 21 J.L. & Pol. 347, 427–34 (2005). Similar in certain ways is the Twin Cities Metropolitan Council, a regional entity spanning the cities of Minneapolis and St. Paul, that is vested with significant planning powers. Unlike in Portland, the Metropolitan Council is not directly elected by the voters; its 17 members are appointed by the governor of Minnesota, and its portfolio is less broadly defined. *See* Myron Orfield, Metropolitics, 106–08, 174 (2002).

2.   SPECIAL USE DISTRICTS

Wrestling with MUDs to Pin Down
the Truth About Special Districts

Sara C. Galvan
75 Fordham L. Rev. 3041 (2007)

If you have ever called the fire department, been to an airport, or strolled around a business improvement district, you have likely enjoyed the services of a special district. Special districts handle a wide range of discrete governmental functions—from local matters like emergency services or library maintenance to regional matters like irrigation, flood control, and transportation. Despite having myriad missions, all special districts share the same basic structure: They are board-run, special purpose local government units that are administratively and fiscally independent from general purpose governments. Special districts also share in significant support from policies that encourage their proliferation and empower them with broad capabilities.

Three concepts may explain such [favorable] treatment: democracy, limited power, and efficiency. First, in theory, special districts are among the most democratic forms of governance—closer to the people by virtue of their small size. Second, special districts are limited in purpose, which means that states can tailor districts' powers to solve a specific problem. Finally, special districts can supposedly target a defined geographic area more efficiently than general purpose governments. For these reasons, as a federal commission observed thirty years ago, "[a]ll three levels of government have encouraged the growth of special districts": The federal government provides incentives in its transportation, housing, natural resource, and public facility construction grant programs and policies; the states release special districts from tax and debt restrictions and weaken the powers of other local governments, allowing special districts to operate without having to comply with local rules; and general purpose local governments advocate for special districts as an easy solution for the toughest problems. As a result of these favorable policies, special districts have been the fastest-growing type of local government in the United States (as compared to general purpose local governments, counties, and school districts) since they first came to prominence around World War II. By 1952, 12,340 special districts existed in the United States; fifty years later, they numbered 35,052—a nearly threefold increase. Today, special districts earn approximately $123 billion in revenues annually (and have approximately $217 billion in debt).

QUESTIONS

1. Are special use districts spanning multiple municipalities preferable to general purpose regional governance?

2. What explains the popularity of special use districts as compared with regional governments?

3. Many special districts are located in unincorporated areas, outside of established cities. Developers of unincorporated areas may establish special districts, such as the Texas municipal utility districts on which Professor Bronin (formerly Galvan) focuses in the excerpted piece, to effectively function as local governments. Texas municipality utility districts, for example, can do everything from build roads to operate water supplies to finance fire stations. More importantly, they can bond for these improvements and indebt current and future property owners. Despite all of these powers, these districts often operate under the radar, with minimal democratic processes involved in electing their leaders and limited ongoing oversight. What are some of the issues involving special districts outside of urban areas? Professor Bronin is actually quite critical of special districts in the excerpted piece.

D. POURING NEW WINE INTO OLD WINESKINS

Another way to overcome the problem of parochialism in local decision-making is to shift decision-making authority to existing regional levels of government, such as county governments, state governments, or even the federal government. In different times and on different issues, all three strategies have been used.

1. CITY-COUNTY CONSOLIDATION

In a handful of urban areas, the consolidation of municipal into county governments (as opposed to annexation of outlying areas by municipal governments) has had the effect of creating something that approaches regional governance without the need to resort to a new type of governmental entity. In 1970, for example, the city of Indianapolis merged with Marion County. Although this merger has generated some of the benefits of regional governance for the Indianapolis metropolitan area, its impact has been limited by the powers and services excluded from the consolidation, including schools, police, fire, courts, hospitals, poverty-alleviation services, and local property tax bases. *See* Myron Orfield, Metropolitics 136–37 (2002). In Hawaii, there are no municipalities, just four county governments.

2. STATE LAND USE REGULATION

In several states, state governments have intervened directly into the land-use planning process. Two of the most robust and developed statewide land use regimes are in Hawaii and Oregon.

Hawaii

In Hawaii, Act 187 (enacted in 1961) created a statewide land use system. The system is administered by a state agency, the Land Use Commission (LUC), a nine-member board, seven of whom are appointed by the governor. The LUC periodically classifies land in the state into four categories: agriculture, conservation, urban, and rural. State designations are revisited every 5 years. In the interim, the LUC hears requests for reclassifications on a case by case basis, but such reclassifications must conform to the state land use plan. Counties then create their own plans to regulate uses within urban, rural, and agricultural zones, but these county plans must conform with the state's designation, at least to the extent that they cannot fall below the level of protection of open space provided by the state plan. They can, however, provide for less intensive uses than would be permitted under the state designations. One result of this dual level of regulation is that a landowner seeking a redesignation of her land must proceed through both levels of government, a process that can take several years.

Oregon

Beginning with SB100 in 1973, Oregon has similarly brought land use planning to the state level. SB100 created the Land Conservation and Development Commission ("LCDC"). The LCDC's role is to adopt "goals" or "development standards" with which local planning and zoning must comply. Local planning efforts can be challenged for failing to comply with those goals. The goals include, for example, the creation of urban growth boundaries, beyond which urban development is not permitted, as well as the limitation of municipal services to areas within those urban growth boundaries (Goal 11). Goal 3, which is discussed at length in the case that follows, requires that "[a]gricultural lands shall be preserved and maintained for farm use." Goal 4 requires local governments "[t]o conserve forest lands by maintaining the forest land base." The law also establishes a system of specialized "courts," the Land Use Board of Appeals ("LUBA"), to review local land use decisions. The LUBA is empowered to overrule local planning decisions that conflict with the statewide goals, either by granting approval for projects that local officials have rejected, or withholding approval of projects that local officials have permitted to go forward.

Rudd v. Malheur County

Land Use Board of Appeals, State of Oregon, 1980
LUBA No. 80–056

Appeal from Malheur County

NATURE OF THE PROCEEDINGS

Petitioners appeal the granting of a zone change by Malheur County from F–2 [eds.—farm use] to R–1 (rural residential, one acre minimum lot size) for approximately 32 acres of class 2 and 4 soil located outside of the urban growth boundary for the City of Ontario.

SUMMARY OF ARGUMENT

Petitioners assignments of error are summarized in the following from their Petition for Review:

> In summary, the final order in this case, dated April 23, 1980, should be reversed upon the grounds that: (1) The court below failed to give adequate, timely and meaningful notice as required by the county code, Oregon Statute and the LCDC Goals and Guidelines; (2) The court below improperly applied the LCDC goals and failed to properly apply the exceptions process for agricultural lands as required by LCDC Goals 2 and 3 and the guidelines thereto; (3) The court's findings are noncompelling with respect to the exceptions process, inconsistent and constitutes mere recital of evidence as opposed to findings of fact to support its conclusions of law; (4) The court failed to consider the whole record; (5) The court has participated in a consistent pattern of ex-parte contact which has denied petitioners fundamental fairness.

FACTS

Lem Wilson and Jim Abbe petitioned for a zone change from F–2 to R–1 to allow development of 32 acres of class 2 and 4 soil into approximately 23 rural residential home sites. The property is located approximately 4 miles from the City of Ontario and is outside of the city's urban growth boundary.

Malheur County recognized that Goal 3 was applicable to the zone change request and attempted to take an exception to it. With respect to the question of need for the zone change, the first factor which must be addressed in the exceptions process, the opinion and order of the county provides as follows:

> The petitioners have addressed the question of whether there is a need for the zone change. Lem Wilson has submitted statements of findings of fact by the County Planning Department relating to the urban growth boundary for the City of Ontario. Among those findings, the Planning Department concludes:

> > The urban growth boundary for the City of Ontario is adequate in size if the low development estimates are not exceeded. However, if the high development estimates are met, the urban growth boundary is not large enough. With the possibility that the urban growth boundary will not be large enough, the County must take on the responsibility of allowing room for the needed growth. This could be in the form of rural residential zones.

The realtors in the area confirm that there is a strong market demand for the kind of lots provided in an R–1 zone, and that such lots are in scarce supply in the Ontario area. In a letter contained in Exhibit No. 3 and in testimony to the County Court, Dean Bertalotto, an Ontario realtor, stated that he always has clients looking for a country parcel to build a home or to buy an existing home in the country, and it is almost impossible to find these parcels. Letters from Ontario realtors Gary Goodfellow and Jim Weber, contained in Exhibit No. 3, share the view of Mr. Bertalotto.

In testimony to the Court, a realtor from Village Realty in Ontario testified that there is a special need for rural residential parcels of less than five (5) acres. He testified that many people who are seeking rural housing simply want enough room for a house, a garden and perhaps some animals, and that lots of five (5) acres or more are too large to maintain except as part of an extensive farming or ranching operation. Lem Wilson offered similar testimony.

As set forth in Exhibit No. 3, in a letter from William Buxton, City Engineer for the City of Ontario, to County Planning Director Jon Beal, the Ontario Planning Commission voted on April 9, 1979, to recommend approval of the zone change from F–2 to R–1 to allow one acre sites.

In considering the testimony and exhibits, the County Court finds that, not only is there a need for additional housing in the Ontario area, but there is a need for rural non-farm housing available in an R–1 zone but not in an F–2 zone.

OPINION

Petitioner's first assignment of error is that the county erred in failing to give notice that an exception to Goal 3 was proposed in its notices of public hearing in violation of Goal 2, Part II, Exceptions. The pertinent portion of Goal 2 provides as follows:

> When, during the application of the statewide goals to plans, it appears that it is not possible to apply the appropriate goal to specific property or situations, then each proposed exception to a goal shall be set forth during the plan preparation phases and also specifically noted in the notices of public hearing. The notices of hearing shall summarize the issues in an understandable and meaningful manner.

In its policy paper on the exceptions process, LCDC has described the type of notice required:

> 5.A. Goal number 2 requires that the intent to take an exception should be communicated widely, and should begin as soon as it becomes apparent that a Goal cannot be applied to a particular area. Adequate notice and time to review and comment on the proposed Exception should be provided. The

LCDC Field Representative must also be notified promptly of the intent to take an exception.

B. When the comprehensive plan, plan element or amendment reaches the public hearings stage, Goal 2 requires that the public notices must describe each proposed Exception. At a minimum the notice should indicate that an Exception to a specific Goal is being discussed, and should summarize the location of the Exception and the issues involved. Specific opportunities for comment on the proposed Exception shall be provided at the public hearing(s).

In the present case, the need to take an exception to Goal 3 for the proposed zone change first became apparent to Malheur County when the planning director in a memo dated April 24, 1979, to the Malheur County planning commission, stated the following:

Should this area be rezoned from farm use to rural residential an exception to LCDC Goal 3 (Agricultural Lands) would have to be taken under the procedure set forth in Part II, LCDC Goal 2 (Land Use Planning). I have attached the current LCDC policy paper regarding the "Exceptions Process" for your information. . . .

The notices of public hearing in the present case, both those published in the newspapers and those mailed to property owners in the area, do not mention that an exception is proposed to be taken let alone describe any of the issues involved in the exceptions process. Petitioner's first assignment of error is sustained.

Petitioner's second assignment of error is that the county failed to properly take an exception to Goal 3 in rezoning the parcel from F–2 to R–1. In Wright v. Marion County, ___ Or. LUBA ___, (LUBA No. 80–010, 1980), we concluded that in order for an exception to be valid under Goal 2, the exception must be taken as part of the comprehensive planning process. In other words, the exception and its justification must be included in the county's comprehensive plan either by way of an amendment to an existing comprehensive plan or in the process of adopting a new comprehensive plan. Referring to the LCDC policy paper on the exceptions process we said:

The policy paper states that the only time an exception is not required for Goals 3 and 4 is when findings can be made that the land is: (a) Physically developed or built upon or, (b) irrevocably committed to non-farm or non-forest uses in urban or rural areas. Section 14. The policy paper makes it quite clear, however, that an exception is required when "agricultural and forest lands are available for agricultural and forest uses, [i.e., not committed or built upon] but are needed for use not allowed by Goal 3 and 4."

In the present case, Malheur County attempted to base the exception upon need rather than precommitment to urban uses. There is nothing, however, in the opinion and order of the county which amends the comprehensive plan for Malheur County by incorporating therein the findings contained in the opinion and order. The opinion and order simply grants the zone change without also amending the comprehensive plan. Because it failed to take the exception to the comprehensive plan, we must reverse.

In addition to the procedural failure discussed above, Malheur County's exception is not adequate on substantive grounds. In Still v. Marion County, 42 Or. App. 115, 600 P.2d 433 (1979), the Court of Appeals addressed the validity of an exception taken by Marion County to allow the subdivision of a 99 acre parcel of rural land into 30 lots of various sizes. As in the present case, the property at issue in *Still* was located outside city limits and outside any urban growth boundary. Concerning the county's finding of need, the Court stated:

> The Board's conclusion that there is a need for the proposed development in Marion County is based on its finding that there is a scarcity of similar lots, as indicated by the price and small number of similar lots on the market. This correctly summarizes the evidence, which shows that there is a market for residential lots of the kind in the proposed subdivision. A market demand for rural residential development, however, does not constitute a "need" for it, as that word is used in Goal 2. Goal 3 was enacted to preserve agricultural land from encroachment by urban and suburban sprawl by subordinating the free play of the market place to broader public policy objectives. Land is not excepted from the agricultural goal merely because somebody wants to buy it for a house.

A determination of whether this land is needed for residences should be made in accordance with Goal 10, Housing, which mandates that local government should designate sufficient suitable land within the urban growth boundary to meet residential needs. There is no showing in the record that no suitable land is available inside the urban growth boundary for residential use. The Board's finding regarding need misconstrues the applicable legal standard and is not supported by substantial evidence.

In the present case, Malheur County based its "need" determination upon market demand for one acre rural residential lots and its conclusion that population growth within the Ontario urban growth boundary would soon exhaust the supply of land available for residential home sites. As the court in *Still* correctly points out, the fact that there is a market demand for one acre rural homesite does not satisfy the "need" requirement in Goal 2, Part II, Exceptions. Nor does the fact that Ontario may in the near future exhaust the supply of available land within its urban growth boundary give rise to a "need" to use agricultural land located outside the urban growth boundary for Ontario's housing needs. If the Ontario urban growth boundary is too small to accommodate Ontario's population, then it must be amended to include more land for residential housing needs. A county may not use agricultural land located outside urban growth boundaries to satisfy housing needs because those needs must be satisfied under Goal 10 by using land within urban growth boundaries.

For the foregoing reasons, the opinion and order of Malheur County must be reversed.

NOTES AND QUESTIONS

1.   Was the market demand to which the lower court referred in approving the rezoning a result of the existing urban growth boundary restricting development in the surrounding rural areas? If so, would permitting the trial court to rezone the respondents' property be fair to neighboring landowners who continued to be subject to the more restrictive agricultural zoning regime?

2.   Could a person wanting to purchase a home within the urban growth boundary of the city of Ontario, in Malheur County, bring a lawsuit arguing that Ontario's zoning code did not permit adequately dense development within the urban growth boundary to provide enough housing to meet the rapidly growing city's needs? On which of the statewide goals would the claimant rely?

Hawaii and Oregon are far from alone in imposing statewide land use regimes. Since the 1970s, over a dozen states have created a significant role for the state in the land use planning process. *See* Sara C. Bronin & Dwight Merriam, eds., 3 Rathkopf's The Law of Zoning and Planning §§ 36:11–36:12 (4th ed. 2011).

3.   FEDERAL INVOLVEMENT IN LAND USE PLANNING

Although land use policymaking is often described as a paradigmatic function of local government (*see* Solid Waste Agency of Northern Cook County v. Army Corps of Eng'rs, 531 U.S. 159 (2001)), there is a history of significant federal involvement in the land use arena. For most of the nineteenth century, the federal government was responsible for land use decisions over the large swaths of territory it controlled in the American west. But even as to land within the states, the federal government has played an active, though limited, role.

A great deal of federal involvement has operated through its use of the spending power. In the first half of the 1970s, the Congress considered, but failed to enact, a series of bills, to encourage states to engage in land use planning activities in exchange for federal funds (or the avoidance of federal penalties). Some supporters of these bills sought to insert a degree of substantive federal oversight into the process. *See* Margaret Weir, The Political Failure of National Land Use Legislation, 1970–75, in The American Planning Tradition 193, 199–202 (Robert Fishman ed. 2000). These more ambitious bills never made it out of committee, but the basic elements of the abortive federal land use law (reliance on the federal spending power, encouraging state and local governments to plan) have echoed through subsequent federal forays into land use policy.

a. Coastal Zone Management Act

The Coastal Zone Management Act, for example, makes available federal funding for coastal zone management activities. In exchange for the federal funds, states are required to formulate a coastal zone management plan and to do their planning in accordance with federal standards established by National Oceanic and Atmosphere Administration (NOAA). Of the 35 eligible states, 34 participate in the program. As we have seen in Chapter Five, a number of important regulatory takings cases have emerged from the activities of the Coastal Commissions established in response to the 1972 Act.

b. Urban Renewal

The federal program known as "Urban Renewal" was first created by Congress as part of the 1949 Housing Act. Its ostensible goal was "slum removal," but it was supported by a coalition of city planners, politicians, and downtown business interests who saw it as an opportunity both to remake downtowns according to prevailing ideas about city-planning and to foster their own economic interests. *See* Marc A. Weiss, The Origins and Legacy of Urban Renewal, in Federal Housing Policy and Programs 253 (J. Paul Mitchell, ed. 1985). Although usually associated with the post-war period, its goals and policy preferences had decades-old roots in American planning discussions, where a consensus had formed over the early decades of the twentieth century that the cure for urban ills was the reconstruction of the city on a large scale according to a comprehensive, rational plan. *See* Robert Fishman, Urban Utopias of the Twentieth Century (1977). Urban Renewal provided federal dollars to realize this vision of clearing, planning, and rebuilding on a large scale in "blighted" or "slum" areas. Using federal dollars and applying federal criteria, cities wielded their eminent domain power to acquire and then demolish enormous downtown parcels, which they then made available to private developers.

Although the law required cities to make efforts to provide substitute housing for those displaced by the wrecking ball, this obligation was honored more in the breach. *See* Terry J. Tondro, *Urban Renewal Relocation: Problems in Enforcement of Conditions on Federal Grants to Local Agencies,* 117 U. Pa. L. Rev. 183 (1968). Urban

Renewal's neighborhood clearing caused the dislocation of hundreds of thousands of poor city residents, a disproportionate number of whom were African-American. This led some critics to redub the program "Negro removal." Wendel E. Pritchett, *The "Public Menace" of Blight: Urban Renewal and the Private Uses of Eminent Domain,* 21 Yale L. & Pol'y Rev. 1, 47 (2003). Contemporary observers attributed urban unrest that broke out across the United States in the late 1960s to the dislocations caused by Urban Renewal. *See, e.g.,* Note, Family Relocation in Urban Renewal, 82 Harv. L. Rev. 864, 902 n.224 (1969). By the end of the 1960s, public opposition to large scale demolition had swelled and the federal government ultimately shifted its policy from the subsidization of large-scale "slum clearance" to support for more fine-grained rehabilitation and the provision of community-development block grants.

The experience of Urban Renewal, however, survives as a cautionary tale. We will return to some of the many questions raised by Urban Renewal program in our discussion in Chapter Ten of government as a market participant.

c.   *Transportation Policy*

Perhaps the most important way the federal government has historically influenced land use policy is through its role in shaping national transportation policy. Decisions about transportation infrastructure, which often occur at the federal level, do a great deal to guide and constrain local land use policy. One obvious example is the construction of the Interstate Highway system, which facilitated the spread of automobile-dependent suburban sprawl in the years after the Second World War. Interstate highways dramatically increased the distance over which individuals could commute, and therefore greatly facilitated the decentralization of metropolitan areas that has characterized American cities over the past sixty years. *See* Oliver Gillham, The Limitless City 30–35 (2002). The Intermodal Surface Transportation Efficiency Act (ISTEA) of 1991 empowered Metropolitan Planning Organizations ("MPOs") with quasi-governmental authority over regional transportation policy. Some commentators have argued that MPOs might even constitute the framework for regional governing bodies with broader land use regulatory portfolios.

For more discussions of the connection between transportation policy and land use, see Peter Newman & Jeffrey Kenworthy, *The Land Use-Transport Connection: An Overview,* 13 Land Use Policy 1 (1996); Peter Newman & Jeffrey Kenworthy, Sustainability and Cities ch. 2 (1999).

d.   Environmental Statutes

Clean Water Act ("CWA")

Finally, federal environmental statutes often inject federal policymakers directly into land use debates. Section 404 of the Clean Water Act, for example, empowers the Army Corps of Engineers to regulate the dumping of fill material into "navigable waters," a category that the Corps has traditionally defined quite broadly to include any water whose filling, alone or in conjunction with the filling of other similar waters, might have an impact on interstate commerce. In recent years, the Supreme Court has pushed back against these expansive definitions. Two cases merit particular notice, Solid Waste Agency of Northern Cook County v. Army Corps of Eng'rs, 531 U.S. 159 (2001) & Rapanos v. United States, 547 U.S. 715 (2006).

Applying the so-called "migratory bird rule," under which the Army Corps of Engineers treated as "navigable waters" even isolated, non-navigable waters or wetlands that provided habitat for migratory birds, the Corps denied the Solid Waste Agency of Northern Cook County ("SWANCC") a permit to fill wetlands for the construction of a solid waste disposal facility. The wetlands were an old sand and gravel site in which the sand and gravel pits had filled with water and become the home to several species of migratory birds. Over a vigorous dissent by Justice John Paul Stevens, a five-justice majority of the Supreme Court held that the migratory bird rule exceeded the Army Corps' authority under Section 404 of the Clean Water Act. The Court declined to extend deference to the Corps' reading of the statute under Chevron, U.S.A., Inc. v. Natural Resources Defense Council, 467 U.S. 837 (1984), because, it said, such deference is not appropriate where the interpretation in question would raise serious constitutional questions. Noting that land use is an area traditionally reserved for local control and, normally, with only limited connections to interstate commerce, the Court intimated that, as an interpretation of Section 404, the migratory bird rule might well exceed the limits of Congress's power under the Commerce Clause. After *SWANCC*, lower courts attempted to determine the meaning of the decision for the outer limits of the Corps' authority. Several lower courts held that, under *SWANCC*, the Corps could continue to regulate non-navigable tributaries of actually navigable waters. *See, e.g.*, Treacy v. Newdunn Assoc., 344 F.3d 407, 410 (4th Cir. 2003); United States v. Deaton, 332 F.3d 698, 702 (4th Cir. 2003); Community Ass'n for Restoration of Env't v. Henry Bosma Dairy, 305 F.3d 943, 954–955 (9th Cir. 2002); Headwaters, Inc. v. Talent Irrigation Dist., 243 F.3d 526, 534 (9th Cir. 2001); Save Our Sonoran, Inc. v. Flowers, 408 F.3d 1113, 1118 (9th Cir. 2005); Baccarat Fremont Developers, LLC v. Army Corps of Eng'rs, 425 F.3d 1150, 1152, 1157 (9th Cir. 2005); United States v. Rueth Dev. Co., 189 F. Supp. 2d 874, 877–878 (N.D. Ind. 2001).

In Rapanos v. United States, 547 U.S. 715 (2006), the Court attempted once more to define the limits of the CWA's jurisdictional reach, but may only have succeeded in further muddying the waters. Without seeking a section 404 permit from the Corps, John Rapanos filled 54 acres of wetlands that ultimately drained into actually navigable waters. Rapanos was found to have violated the CWA and appealed, arguing that the Army Corps of Engineers lacked jurisdiction over his wetlands. A fractured U.S. Supreme Court reversed. A plurality of four justices, in an opinion by Justice Scalia, argued that the Corps' jurisdiction under the CWA was limited to "relatively permanent, standing or flowing bodies of water" and specifically excludes "channels through which water flows intermittently or ephemerally." Four justices, led by Justice Stevens, dissented. They would have given *Chevron* deference to the Corps' interpretation of its authority under the CWA and affirmed its assertion of jurisdiction over Rapanos's wetlands. The Corps' interpretation was reasonable, the dissenters argued, because even wetlands with an intermittent connection to navigable water can have a significant impact on water quality. Justice Kennedy agreed with the plurality that the Corps had exceeded its authority in this case, but he favored a more permissive interpretation of the Corps' authority under the CWA. According to Justice Kennedy, "the plurality's opinion is inconsistent with the [CWA's] text, structure and purpose." But Justice Kennedy thought the dissenters went too far in deferring to the Corps' assertion of jurisdiction, which he understood to reach only waters and wetlands with a "significant nexus" to "navigable waters in the traditional sense."

In the wake of these Supreme Court cases, the precise contours of the Corps' authority under the CWA remains somewhat uncertain.

Endangered Species Act ("ESA")

The Endangered Species Act grants extensive authority to the federal government with respect to land that is the habitat of a listed endangered species. Section 9(a)(1)(B) of the ESA makes it unlawful for any person to "take" any endangered species. To "take" a species is defined by the ESA and the associated regulations very broadly, and includes to "harass," "harm," "shoot," or "capture" endangered animals. The Fish and Wildlife Service, which is responsible for administering the ESA, has defined "harm" to include actions like the modification or destruction of habitat, a definition that can impose significant constraints on private owners of endangered species habitat. *See* Babbitt v. Sweet Home Chapter of Communities for a Greater Oregon, 515 U.S. 687 (1995).

Clean Air Act ("CAA")

Finally, the Clean Air Act envisions a substantial federal role in the attainment of National Ambient Air Quality Standards ("NAAQS"). The federal government creates the NAAQS, which set the maximum acceptable concentration of pollutants in the air around us. The CAA then assigns primary responsibility for the attainment of NAAQS to the states. States are required to create state implementation plans ("SIPs") detailing how the NAAQS will be met. But if a state fails to submit a SIP or submit one that is defective or inadequate, the federal government (through the EPA) can step in and promulgate a federal implementation plan ("FIP"). Because of the impact of land use decisions on air quality—through the location of industry and, perhaps more importantly, the relationship between land use and transportation activity (which generates its own pollution)—compliance with the CAA can have significant effects on local land use decision-making, particularly in areas that have not attained the goals established by the NAAQS. For the same reasons, the federal impact on land use through the CAA is likely to grow even more significant if the federal government begins to address the problem of climate change through the regulatory structures established by the CAA.

In thinking about the interplay of federal environmental regulations in the land use context, consider the following case:

Rancho Viejo, LLC v. Norton

United States Court of Appeals, District of Columbia Circuit, 2003
323 F.3d 1062

■ GARLAND, CIRCUIT JUDGE:

Rancho Viejo is a real estate development company that wishes to construct a 202-acre housing development in San Diego County, California. The United States Fish and Wildlife Service determined that Rancho Viejo's construction plan was likely to jeopardize the continued existence of the arroyo southwestern toad, which the Secretary of the Interior has listed as an endangered species since 1994. Rather than accept an alternative plan proposed by the Service, Rancho Viejo filed suit challenging the application of the Endangered Species Act, 16 U.S.C. §§ 1531 *et seq.,* to its project as an unconstitutional exercise of federal authority under the Commerce Clause. The district court dismissed the suit. We conclude that this case is governed by our prior decision in *National Association of Home Builders v. Babbitt,* 130 F.3d 1041 (D.C.Cir. 1997), and therefore affirm.

I

The Endangered Species Act (ESA), 16 U.S.C. §§ 1531 *et seq.,* is "the most comprehensive legislation for the preservation of endangered species ever enacted by any nation." *Tennessee Valley Auth. v. Hill,* 437 U.S. 153, 180, 98 S.Ct. 2279, 2281, 57 L.Ed.2d 117 (1978). Finding that "various species of fish, wildlife, and plants in the United States have been rendered extinct as a consequence of economic growth and development untempered by adequate concern and conservation," 16

U.S.C. § 1531(a)(1), Congress passed the ESA "to provide a means whereby the ecosystems upon which endangered species and threatened species depend may be conserved," *id.* § 1531(b).

The ESA directs the Secretary of the Interior to list fish, wildlife, or plant species that she determines are endangered or threatened. 16 U.S.C. § 1533(a). Section 9 of the Act makes it unlawful to "take" any such listed species without a permit. *Id.* § 1538(a)(1)(B). "The term 'take' means to harass, harm, pursue, hunt, shoot, wound, kill, trap, capture, or collect, or to attempt to engage in any such conduct." *Id.* § 1532(19). The Secretary has promulgated, and the Supreme Court has upheld, a regulation that defines "harm" as including "significant habitat modification or degradation where it actually kills or injures wildlife by significantly impairing essential behavioral patterns, including breeding." 50 C.F.R. § 17.3.

Section 7 of the ESA requires all federal agencies to ensure that none of their activities, including the granting of licenses and permits, will "jeopardize the continued existence of any endangered species . . . or result in the destruction or adverse modification of habitat of such species which is determined by the Secretary . . . to be critical." *Id.* § 1536(a)(2). When an agency concludes that its activities may adversely affect a listed species, it must engage in a formal consultation with the Interior Department's Fish and Wildlife Service (FWS). Where applicable, such consultations result in the issuance of a Biological Opinion that includes a "jeopardy" or "no jeopardy" determination. If the FWS decides that the proposed action is likely to "jeopardize the continued existence of a listed species or result in the destruction or adverse modification of critical habitat," the opinion must set forth "reasonable and prudent alternatives," if any, that will avoid such consequences. 50 C.F.R. § 402.14(h)(3); *see* 16 U.S.C. § 1536(b)(3)(A).

The Secretary listed the arroyo toad as an endangered species on December 16, 1994. The toads live in scattered populations from California's Monterey County in the north to Mexico's Baja California in the south. They breed in shallow, sandy, or gravelly pools along streams, and spend most of their adult lives in upland habitats. The toads range no farther than 1.2 miles from the streams where they breed, and none in the area at issue in this case travel outside the state of California. Habitat destruction has driven the toad from approximately 76% of its former California range.

Plaintiff Rancho Viejo plans to build a 280-home residential development on a 202-acre site in San Diego County. The property is bordered on the south by Keys Creek, a major tributary of the San Luis Rey River, and is just east of Interstate 15. The company's construction plan is to build homes in an upland area of approximately 52 acres, and to use an additional 77 acres of its upland property and portions of the Keys Creek streambed as a "borrow area" to provide fill for the project.

Rancho Viejo wants to remove six feet or more of soil from the surface of the borrow area, amounting to approximately 750,000 cubic yards of material, and to transport that soil to the 52-acre housing site to the north. Joint Stip. Surveys of Keys Creek have confirmed the presence of arroyo toads on and adjacent to the project site.

Because Rancho Viejo's plan would involve the discharge of "fill into waters of the United States, including wetlands," Biological/Conference Opinion at 8, the company was required by section 404 of the Clean Water Act, 33 U.S.C. § 1344, to obtain a permit from the U.S. Army Corps of Engineers (the "Corps"). The Corps determined that the project "may affect" the arroyo toad population in the area, and sought a formal consultation with the FWS pursuant to ESA § 7.

In May 2000, Rancho Viejo excavated a trench and erected a fence, each running parallel to the bank of Keys Creek. Arroyo toads were observed on the upland side of the fence. In the FWS's view, the fence has prevented and may continue to impede movement of the toads between their upland habitat and their breeding habitat in the creek. On May 22, the FWS informed Rancho Viejo that construction of the fence "has resulted in the illegal take and will result in the future illegal take of federally endangered" arroyo toads "in violation of the Endangered Species Act."

In August 2000, the FWS issued a Biological Opinion that determined that excavation of the 77-acre borrow area would result in the taking of arroyo toads and was "likely to jeopardize the continued existence" of the species. [T]he FWS proposed an alternative that would, without jeopardizing the continued existence of the toad, allow Rancho Viejo to complete its development by obtaining fill dirt from off-site sources instead of from the proposed borrow area.

Rancho Viejo neither removed the fence nor adopted the FWS's proposed alternative. Instead, it filed a complaint in the United States District Court for the District of Columbia against the Secretary of the Interior and other federal defendants, alleging that the listing of the arroyo toad as an endangered species under the ESA, and the application of the ESA to Rancho Viejo's construction plans, exceeded the federal government's power under the Commerce Clause.

The parties filed cross motions for summary judgment. [T]he court granted the government's motion.

II

A

In [*United States v.*] *Lopez,* [514 U.S. 549 (1995)], the Supreme Court considered whether a provision of the Gun-Free School Zones Act, 18 U.S.C. § 922(q)(1)(A) (1988 ed., Supp. V), which made it a federal offense to possess a firearm near a school, exceeded Congress' authority under the Commerce Clause. 514 U.S. at 551, 115 S.Ct. at 1626. The Court held that the clause authorizes Congress to regulate "three broad categories of activity":

> First, Congress may regulate the use of the channels of interstate commerce. Second, Congress is empowered to regulate and protect the instrumentalities of interstate commerce, or persons or things in interstate commerce, even though the threat may come only from intrastate activities. Finally, Congress' commerce authority includes the power to regulate those activities having a substantial relation to interstate commerce, *i.e.,* those activities that substantially affect interstate commerce.

Id. at 558–59. With respect to the third category, the Court discussed four factors that led it to conclude that the activities regulated by the Gun-Free School Zones Act did not substantially affect interstate commerce.

First, the Court said, "the possession of a gun in a school zone . . . has nothing to do with 'commerce' or any sort of economic enterprise, however broadly one might define those terms." *Lopez,* 514 U.S. at 560–61. Second, the Court observed that the Act "has no express jurisdictional element which might limit its reach to a discrete set of firearm possessions that additionally have an explicit connection with or effect on interstate commerce." *Id.* at 562. Third, *Lopez* noted that, "[a]lthough as part of our independent evaluation of constitutionality under the Commerce Clause we of course consider legislative findings, and indeed even congressional committee findings, . . . neither the statute nor its legislative history contains express congressional findings regarding the effects upon interstate commerce of gun possession in a school zone." *Id.* the Court determined that the relationship between gun possession and interstate commerce was simply too "tenuous[ ]" to be regarded as substantial, and that if the government's arguments were accepted, the Court would be "hard pressed to posit any activity by an individual that Congress is without power to regulate." *Id.* at 564.

In [*National Association of Home Builders v. Babbitt,* 130 F.3d 1041 (D.C.Cir. 1997) (hereinafter *NAHB*)], this circuit applied *Lopez* in a case challenging the application of the ESA to a construction project in an area that contained the habitat of the Delhi Sands Flower-Loving Fly. The fly, an endangered species, is found in only two counties, both in California. *Id.* One of those counties reported to the FWS that it planned to construct a hospital and power plant on a site occupied by the fly, and to expand a highway intersection in connection with that work. The FWS informed the county that the expansion of the intersection would likely lead to a take of the fly in violation of section 9 of the ESA. Thereafter, the county filed suit against the Secretary of the

Interior, contending that application of the ESA in those circumstances exceeded the authority of the federal government under the Commerce Clause.

A majority of the *NAHB* court held that the take provision of ESA § 9, and its application to the facts of that case, constituted a valid exercise of Congress' commerce power. The court found that application of the ESA fell within the third *Lopez* category, concluding that the regulated activity "substantially affects" interstate commerce. In so holding, the majority agreed upon two rationales: (1) "the loss of biodiversity itself has a substantial effect on our ecosystem and likewise on interstate commerce"; and (2) "the Department's protection of the flies regulates and substantially affects commercial development activity which is plainly interstate." *Id.* at 1058 (Henderson, J., concurring); *see id.* at 1046 n. 3, 1056 (Wald, J.). Examining those two rationales within the context of *Lopez*'s four factors, the *NAHB* court concluded that application of the ESA to the county's proposed construction project was constitutional. *Id.* at 1042, 1057 (Wald, J.); *id.* at 1057 (Henderson, J., concurring). Because the second *NAHB* rationale readily resolves this case, it is the focus of the balance of our discussion.

B

Secretary Norton argues, and the district court concluded, that application of the four *Lopez* factors leads to the same result here as it did in *NAHB*. We agree.

The first *Lopez* factor is whether the regulated activity has anything "to do with 'commerce' or any sort of economic enterprise, however broadly one might define those terms." *Lopez,* 514 U.S. at 561. The regulated activity at issue in *NAHB*—the construction of a hospital, power plant, and supporting infrastructure—was plainly an economic enterprise. . . . The same is true here, where the regulated activity is the construction of a 202 acre commercial housing development.

Second, the court must consider whether the statute in question contains an "express jurisdictional element." Section 9 of the ESA has no express jurisdictional hook that limits its application, for example, to takes "in or affecting commerce." *Lopez* did not indicate that such a hook is required, however, and its absence did not dissuade the *NAHB* court from finding application of the ESA constitutional.

The third *Lopez* factor looks to whether there are "express congressional findings" or legislative history "regarding the effects upon interstate commerce" of the regulated activity. There are no such findings or history with respect to the specific rationale that we rely upon here, the effect of commercial housing construction on interstate commerce. But neither findings nor legislative history is necessary. Rather, such evidence merely "enable[s] [the court] to evaluate the legislative judgment that the activity in question substantially affected interstate commerce, even though no such substantial effect was visible to the naked eye." *Lopez,* 514 U.S. at 563. As we discuss in the remainder of this section, the naked eye requires no assistance here.

The fourth *Lopez* factor is whether the relationship between the regulated activity and interstate commerce is too attenuated to be regarded as substantial. Although Rancho Viejo avers that the effect on interstate commerce of preserving endangered species is too tenuous to satisfy this test, it does not argue that the effect of commercial construction projects is similarly attenuated. Because the rationale upon which we rely focuses on the activity that the federal government seeks to regulate in this case (the construction of Rancho Viejo's housing development), and because we are required to accord congressional legislation a "presumption of constitutionality," United States v. *Morrison,* 529 U.S. 598, 607 (2000), plaintiff's failure to demonstrate (or even to argue) that its project and those like it are without substantial interstate effect is fatal to its cause.

This conclusion is not diminished by the fact that the arroyo toad, like the Flower-Loving Fly, does not travel outside of California, or that Rancho Viejo's development, like the San Bernardino hospital, is located wholly within the state. As Judge Henderson said in *NAHB,* the regulation of commercial land development, quite "apart from the characteristics or range of the specific endangered species involved, has a plain and substantial effect on interstate commerce."

III

Rancho Viejo does not seriously dispute that *NAHB* is indistinguishable from this case. Rather, plaintiff argues that, as a result of subsequent Supreme Court decisions in *United States v. Morrison,* 529 U.S. 598 (2000), and *Solid Waste Agency of Northern Cook County v. U.S. Army Corps of Engineers* ("*SWANCC*"), 531 U.S. 159 (2001), *NAHB* is no longer "good law." Before considering plaintiff's argument in detail, we explain why the nature of the Supreme Court's analysis in those decisions makes it highly unlikely that they undermine our circuit precedent. [B]ecause *NAHB* was based upon *Lopez,* and because *Morrison* made clear that "*Lopez* . . . provides the proper framework for conducting the required analysis," [*Morrison,* 529 U.S. at 609,] it would be quite surprising if *Morrison* undermined our decision in *NAHB.* Rancho Viejo's reliance on *SWANCC* is even further from the mark. In that case, the Supreme Court held, as a matter of statutory construction, that an abandoned gravel pit that provided habitat for migratory birds did not constitute "navigable waters" within the meaning of the Clean Water Act, 33 U.S.C. § 1344(a), and hence was beyond the regulatory authority of the Army Corps of Engineers. 531 U.S. at 167, 171–72. Although the petitioner in *SWANCC* also asked the Court to decide whether Congress *could* exercise such authority under the Commerce Clause if it chose to do so, the Court expressly declined to reach that question. *Id.* at 162. As Rancho Viejo notes, the Court did indicate that if it were to consider the constitutionality of such an exercise, it "would have to evaluate the precise object or activity that, in the aggregate, substantially affects interstate commerce." *Id.* at 173. But as we discuss below, identifying the "precise activity" at issue in Rancho Viejo's case only strengthens the conclusion that the take provision of the ESA can constitutionally be applied to plaintiff's construction project.

In *Morrison,* the Court considered a challenge to a section of the Violence Against Women Act, 42 U.S.C. § 13981, which provided a federal civil remedy for victims of gender-motivated violence. Concluding that the case was "controlled by our decision[ ] in *United States v. Lopez*," the Court held that Congress lacked authority to enact the provision under the Commerce Clause. *Lopez,* of course, is the case that controlled this court's decision in *NAHB.* Accordingly, because *NAHB* was based upon *Lopez,* and because *Morrison* made clear that "*Lopez* . . . provides the proper framework for conducting the required analysis," 529 U.S. at 609, it would be quite surprising if *Morrison* undermined our decision in *NAHB.*

. . . Rancho Viejo draws our attention to *Morrison*'s declaration that "[t]he Constitution requires a distinction between what is truly national and what is truly local." *Id.* at 617–18. Plaintiff argues that the ESA represents an unlawful assertion of congressional power over local land use decisions, which it describes as an area of traditional state regulation. The ESA, however, does not constitute a general regulation of land use.[22] Far from encroaching upon territory that has traditionally been the domain of state and local government, the ESA represents a national response to a specific problem of "truly national" concern.

In making these points, we can do little to improve upon the Fourth Circuit's opinion in *Gibbs* [*v. Babbitt,* 214 F.3d 483 (4th Cir. 2000)], which upheld, as a valid exercise of federal power under the Commerce Clause, an FWS regulation that limited the taking of red wolves. As Chief Judge Wilkinson explained, regulation of the taking of endangered species "does not involve an 'area of traditional state concern,' one to which 'States lay claim by right of history and expertise.'" *Id.* at 499. Rather, as the Supreme Court acknowledged in *Minnesota v. Mille Lacs Band of Chippewa Indians,* "[a]lthough States have important interests in regulating wildlife and natural resources within their borders, this authority is shared with the Federal Government when the Federal Government exercises one of its enumerated constitutional powers." 526 U.S. 172, 204 (1999). Moreover,

---

[22]   *Cf. California Coastal Comm'n v. Granite Rock Co.,* 480 U.S. 572, 587, 107 S.Ct. 1419, 1428, 94 L.Ed.2d 577 (1987) (stating that "the core activity described by" land use planning and environmental regulation "is undoubtedly different," because "environmental regulation . . . does not mandate particular uses of the land but requires only that, however the land is used, damage to the environment is kept within prescribed limits").

while "states and localities possess broad regulatory and zoning authority over land within their jurisdictions, . . . [i]t is well established . . . that Congress can regulate even private land use for environmental and wildlife conservation." *Gibbs,* 214 F.3d at 500. Tracing a hundred-year history of congressional involvement in natural resource conservation, Chief Judge Wilkinson concluded that "it is clear from our laws and precedent that federal regulation of endangered wildlife does not trench impermissibly upon state powers." *Id.* at 500–01.

The Fourth Circuit also recognized the national scope of the problem posed by species conservation. Citing the ESA's legislative history, the court noted Congress' concern that " 'protection of endangered species is not a matter that can be handled in the absence of coherent national and international policies: the results of a series of unconnected and disorganized policies and programs by various states might well be confusion compounded.' " *Gibbs,* 214 F.3d at 502 (quoting H.R.REP. NO. 93–412, at 7 (1973)). As the *Gibbs* court explained: "States may decide to forego or limit conservation efforts in order to lower these costs, and other states may be forced to follow suit in order to compete." *Id.* at 501. *See NAHB,* 130 F.3d at 1055 (Wald, J.) (noting that states may be "motivated to adopt lower standards of endangered species protection in order to attract development"). And the Supreme Court, as the Fourth Circuit observed, "has held that Congress may take cognizance of this dynamic and arrest the 'race to the bottom' in order to prevent interstate competition whose overall effect would damage the quality of the national environment." *Gibbs,* 214 F.3d at 501.

For these reasons, the protection of endangered species cannot fairly be described as a power "which the Founders denied the National Government and reposed in the States." *Morrison,* 529 U.S. at 618, 120 S.Ct. at 1754. Rather, "the preservation of endangered species is historically a federal function," *Gibbs,* 214 F.3d at 505, and invalidating this application of the ESA "would call into question the historic power of the federal government to preserve scarce resources in one locality for the future benefit of all Americans," *id.* at 492. We therefore agree with Chief Judge Wilkinson that to sustain challenges of this nature "would require courts to move abruptly from preserving traditional state roles to dismantling historic federal ones." *Id.* at 504.

■ GINSBURG, CHIEF JUDGE, concurring:

Although I do not disagree with anything in the opinion of the court, I write separately because I do not believe our opinion makes clear, as the Supreme Court requires, that there is a logical stopping point to our rationale for upholding the constitutionality of the exercise of the Congress's power under the Commerce Clause here challenged.

In this case I think it clear that our rationale for concluding the take of the arroyo toad affects interstate commerce does indeed have a logical stopping point, though it goes unremarked in the opinion of the court. Our rationale is that, with respect to a species that is not an article in interstate commerce and does not affect interstate commerce, a take can be regulated if—but only if—the take itself substantially affects interstate commerce. The large-scale residential development that is the take in this case clearly does affect interstate commerce. Just as important, however, the lone hiker in the woods, or the homeowner who moves dirt in order to landscape his property, though he takes the toad, does not affect interstate commerce.

Without this limitation, the Government could regulate as a take any kind of activity, regardless whether that activity had any connection with interstate commerce. With this understanding of the rationale of the case, I concur in the opinion of the court.

QUESTIONS

1. How did the Fish and Wildlife Service become involved in the approval process for the Rancho Viejo project?

2. Would increased federal involvement in land use decision-making constitute a fundamental constitutional transformation? Or is the absence of pervasive federal involvement in land use an anomaly in light of the federal government's extensive involvement in other legal domains?

3. Are you convinced by the D.C. Circuit's argument in its footnote that the Endangered Species Act is not land use regulation?

4. How useful is the distinction that Judge Ginsburg introduces in his concurring opinion between large scale developments and "the homeowner who moves dirt in order to landscape his property"? Applying his distinction, how should we treat the landowner who seeks a permit to fill navigable waters in order to expand her house? Her small home-business?

5. How effective is the D.C. Circuit's treatment of the *SWANCC* case? How might you reframe Rancho Viejo's arguments to sharpen its challenge to *NAHB* on the basis of *SWANCC*'s treatment of the Commerce Clause issue?

6. Is there something "inherently local" about land use regulation that makes federal involvement unwise, even if it is not unconstitutional?

E. LAND USE LAW AND CLIMATE CHANGE

In 2007, the United Nations Intergovernmental Panel on Climate Change stated that evidence of global warming "is unequivocal, as is now evident from observations of increases in global average air and ocean temperatures, widespread melting of snow and ice and rising global average sea level." If left unchecked, the consequences of climate change for human communities may well be catastrophic. They include rising sea levels, increased extreme weather, heat waves, droughts and water shortages, disease, and mass extinctions. In order to stem rising global temperatures, there is a growing consensus that greenhouse gas emissions must be curbed in coming years.

Land use policies can have a dramatic and direct effect on greenhouse gas emissions. The first, and most obvious, connection between land use law and climate change involves the impact of land use law on transportation. Nearly one third of U.S. greenhouse gas emissions come from the transportation sector. *See* Energy Information Administration, Office of Integrated Analysis and Forecasting, U.S. Department of Energy, Emissions of Greenhouse Gases in the United States, 2007. And land use patterns associated with post-World War II American suburbs—low density, separation of uses, and auto-friendly street design—make it hard for people to use public transportation and literally force individuals into private automobiles.

Although more research is clearly necessary, some preliminary evidence suggests that residents within the kinds of higher density, mixed-use developments favored by New Urbanists—which can be very difficult to build under traditional suburban zoning codes—generate fewer greenhouse gas emissions than residents of typical suburban communities. *See, e.g.*, Steve Winkelman et al., Center for Clean Air Policy, Cost-Effective GHG Reductions Through Smart Growth and Improved Transportation Choices, John R. Nolon, Transportation and Climate Change, 8 N.Y. Zoning Laws Practice Report (2007); Wesley E. Marshall & Norman W. Garrick, Effect of Street Network Design on Walking and Biking, Transp. Research Record, No. 2198, at 103 (2010); *But see* Daniel A. Rodriguez et al., *Can New Urbanism Encourage Physical Activity?,* 72 J. Am. Planning Ass'n 43 (2006) (finding no effect of traditional neighborhood development patterns on driving behavior). Denser, mixed-use developments permit residents and employees to replace several automobile trips per day with walking trips, thereby reducing their vehicle miles traveled in a private automobile and the associated greenhouse gas emissions. Residents in the New Urbanist Atlantic Station development in downtown Atlanta, for example, have reported daily vehicle miles traveled that are 59% lower than the typical Atlanta resident. Employees at Atlantic Station similarly report significant reductions in vehicle miles traveled. Writing land use laws and comprehensive plans that facilitate or encourage the development of dense, walkable neighborhoods may contribute in significant ways to the U.S. effort to reduce its carbon footprint.

Land use policy impacts on greenhouse gas emissions go beyond the land use/transportation nexus. Building and rehabilitation codes can be structured to encourage energy efficiency, thereby reducing household carbon emissions.

Some jurisdictions have taken steps to use their land use law to reduce carbon emissions. Massachusetts and California have enacted laws requiring the inclusion of greenhouse gas emissions impacts as part of state environmental impact review. *See, e.g.*, Mass. Gen. Laws Ann. Ch. 30, § 61; Cal. Pub. Res. Code § 21083.05. Under the California law, comprehensive land use plans created at the local level are required to consider greenhouse gas emissions impacts as part of their planning process. Consider the following case.

Cleveland National Forest Foundation v. San Diego Association of Governments

California Court of Appeal, 2014
180 Cal. Rptr. 3d 548, *rev. granted* 184 Cal. Rptr. 3d 725 (2015)

■ McCONNELL, P.J.

After the San Diego Association of Governments (SANDAG) certified an environmental impact report (EIR) for its 2050 Regional Transportation Plan/Sustainable Communities Strategy (transportation plan), CREED–21 and Affordable Housing Coalition of San Diego filed a petition for writ of mandate challenging the EIR's adequacy under the California Environmental Quality Act (CEQA). Cleveland National Forest Foundation and the Center for Biological Diversity filed a similar petition, in which Sierra Club and the People later joined.

The superior court granted the petitions in part, finding the EIR failed to carry out its role as an informational document because it did not analyze the inconsistency between the state's policy goals reflected in Executive Order S–3–05 (Executive Order) and the transportation plan's greenhouse gas emissions impacts after 2020. The court also found the EIR failed to adequately address mitigation measures for the transportation plan's greenhouse gas emissions impacts.

SANDAG appeals, contending the EIR complied with CEQA in both respects.

Background

1

In 2005 then Governor Arnold Schwarzenegger issued the Executive Order establishing greenhouse gas emissions reduction targets for California. Specifically, the Executive Order required reduction of greenhouse gas emissions to 2000 levels by 2010, to 1990 levels by 2020, and to 80 percent below 1990 levels by 2050.

The Legislature subsequently enacted the California Global Warming Solutions Act of 2006, referred to by the parties as Assembly Bill No. 32 (AB 32). Among its provisions, AB 32 tasked the California Air Resources Board (CARB) with determining the state's 1990 greenhouse gas emissions level and approving an equivalent emissions level to be achieved by 2020.

The Legislature intended for the emissions limit to "continue in existence and be used to maintain and continue reductions in emissions of greenhouse gases beyond 2020." The Legislature also intended for the emissions limit to work in concert with other environmental protection laws, expressly stating AB 32 does not "relieve any person, entity, or public agency of compliance with other applicable federal, state, or local laws or regulations, including state air and water quality requirements, and other requirements for protecting public health or the environment." The Legislature further intended for "the Climate Action Team established by the Governor to coordinate the efforts set forth under [the Executive Order] continue its role in coordinating overall climate policy." Thus, the Legislature, through AB 32, effectively endorsed the Executive Order and its overarching goal of ongoing greenhouse gas emissions reductions as state climate policy.

Bolstering this conclusion, the Legislature also enacted the Sustainable Communities and Climate Protection Act of 2008, referred to by the parties as Senate Bill No. 375 (SB 375). In enacting SB 375, the Legislature found automobiles and light trucks are responsible for 30 percent of the state's greenhouse gas emissions. Accordingly, SB 375 directed CARB to develop regional greenhouse gas emission reduction targets for automobiles and light trucks for 2020 and 2035. The targets established by CARB for the San Diego region require a 7 percent per capita reduction in carbon dioxide emissions by 2020 and a 13 percent per capita reduction by 2035 (compared to a 2005 baseline). CARB must update these targets every eight years until 2050, and may update the targets every four years based on changing factors.

2

The transportation plan, which SANDAG must prepare every four years "serves as the long-range plan designed to coordinate and manage future regional transportation improvements, services, and programs among the various agencies operating within the San Diego region." In enacting SB 375, the Legislature found the state's emissions reductions goals cannot be met without improved land use and transportation policy. Consequently, SB 375 mandates the transportation plan include a sustainable communities strategy to, as the EIR states, "guide the San Diego region toward a more sustainable future by integrating land use, housing, and transportation planning to create more sustainable, walkable, transit-oriented, compact development patterns and communities that meet [CARB's greenhouse gas] emissions targets for passenger cars and light-duty trucks." Once the sustainable communities strategy is approved, some transit priority projects consistent with the strategy are exempt from CEQA requirements. Other transit priority projects, residential projects, and mixed-use projects consistent with the strategy are subject to streamlined CEQA requirements.

Greenhouse Gas Emissions Impacts Analysis

The EIR acknowledged the transportation plan's implementation would lead to an overall increase in greenhouse gas emissions levels; however, the EIR did not analyze whether this consequence conflicted with the Executive Order, or would impair or impede the achievement of the Executive Order's goals. As it did in the EIR and below, SANDAG contends on appeal its decision to omit an analysis of the transportation plan's consistency with the Executive Order (consistency analysis) did not violate CEQA because CEQA does not require such a consistency analysis. Whether the EIR's analysis complies with CEQA depends on whether the analysis reflects a reasonable, good faith effort to disclose and evaluate the transportation plan's greenhouse gas emissions impacts. We review the sufficiency of the analysis in light of what is reasonably foreseeable. As the focus of SANDAG's contention is whether the EIR's analysis was reasonable and not whether the EIR violated a specific statute or regulation, the contention presents a predominately factual question and our review is for substantial evidence.

Substantial evidence for CEQA purposes is "enough relevant information and reasonable inferences from this information that a fair argument can be made to support a conclusion, even though other conclusions might also be reached." Substantial evidence includes "facts, reasonable assumptions predicated upon facts, and expert opinion supported by facts." It does not include argument, speculation, unsubstantiated opinion or narrative, clearly erroneous or inaccurate evidence, or evidence of social or economic impacts which do not contribute to or are not caused by physical impacts on the environment.

"In reviewing for substantial evidence, [we] 'may not set aside an agency's approval of an EIR on the ground that an opposite conclusion would have been equally or more reasonable,' for, on factual questions, our task 'is not to weigh conflicting evidence and determine who has the better argument.' " Rather, we must resolve any reasonable doubts and any conflicts in the evidence in favor of the agency's findings and decision.

In this case, SANDAG's decision to omit an analysis of the transportation plan's consistency with the Executive Order did not reflect a reasonable, good faith effort at full disclosure and is not supported by substantial evidence because SANDAG's decision ignored the Executive Order's role in shaping state climate policy. The Executive Order underpins all of the state's current efforts to reduce greenhouse gas emissions. As SANDAG itself noted in its Climate Action Strategy, the Executive Order's 2050 emissions reduction goal "is based on the scientifically-supported level of emissions reduction needed to avoid significant disruption of the climate and *is used as the long-term driver for state climate change policy development.*" (Italics added.)

Indeed, the Executive Order led directly to the enactment of AB 32, which validated and ratified the Executive Order's overarching goal of ongoing emissions reductions, recognized the Governor's Climate Action Team as the coordinator of the state's overall climate policy, and tasked CARB with establishing overall emissions reduction targets for 2020 and beyond. The Executive Order also led directly to the enactment of SB 375, which tasked CARB with establishing regional automobile and light truck emissions reduction targets for 2020 and 2035. CARB is required to revisit these targets every eight years through 2050, or sooner if warranted by changing circumstances. Thus, the Executive Order, with the Legislature's unqualified endorsement, will continue to underpin the state's efforts to reduce greenhouse gas emissions throughout the life of the transportation plan. The EIR's failure to analyze the transportation plan's consistency with the Executive Order, or more particularly with the Executive Order's overarching goal of ongoing greenhouse gas emissions reductions, was therefore a failure to analyze the transportation plan's consistency with state climate policy. As evidence in the record indicates the transportation plan would actually be inconsistent with state climate policy over the long term, the omission deprived the public and decision makers of relevant information about the transportation plan's environmental consequences. The omission was prejudicial because it precluded informed decisionmaking and public participation.

SANDAG contends the EIR cannot analyze the transportation plan's consistency with the Executive Order because there is no statute or regulation translating the Executive Order's goals into comparable, scientifically based emissions reduction targets. However, we do not agree the lack of such targets precludes the EIR from performing a meaningful consistency analysis in this instance. "Drafting an EIR . . . necessarily involves some degree of forecasting. While foreseeing the unforeseeable is not possible, an agency must use its best efforts to find out and disclose all that it reasonably can." Although SANDAG may not know precisely what future emissions reduction targets the transportation plan will be required to meet, it knows from the information in its own Climate Action Strategy the theoretical emissions reduction targets necessary for the region to meet its share of the Executive Order's goals. It also knows state climate policy, as reflected in the Executive Order and AB 32, requires a continual *decrease* in the state's greenhouse gas emissions and the transportation plan after 2020 produces a continual *increase* in greenhouse gas emissions. With this knowledge, SANDAG could have reasonably analyzed whether the transportation plan was consistent with, or whether it would impair or impede, state climate policy.

SANDAG's attempts to disavow its responsibility for performing this analysis are unavailing. The Legislature specifically found reducing greenhouse gas emissions cannot be accomplished without improved land use and transportation policy. Accordingly, the transportation plan plays both a necessary and important role in achieving state climate policy. By failing to adequately inform the public and decision makers the transportation plan is inconsistent with state climate policy, the EIR deterred the decision makers from devising and considering changes to favorably alter the trajectory of the transportation plan's post-2020 greenhouse gas emissions. When the decision makers are inevitably faced with post-2020 requirements aligned with state climate policy, their task of complying with these requirements will be more difficult and some opportunities for compliance may be lost. As SANDAG explained in its Climate Action Strategy, "Once in place, land use patterns and transportation infrastructure typically remain part of the built environment and influence travel behavior and greenhouse gas emissions for several decades, perhaps longer." In this regard, the EIR falls far short of being "an 'environmental "alarm bell" whose purpose it is to alert the public and its responsible officials to environmental changes before they have reach ecological points of no return.' " It also falls far short of " 'demonstrat[ing] to an apprehensive citizenry that the agency has, in fact, analyzed and considered the ecological implications of its actions.' "

. . . We are also unpersuaded by SANDAG's assertion it was not required to analyze the transportation plan's consistency with the state climate policy reflected in the Executive Order because SANDAG has broad discretion to select the criteria it uses to determine the significance of the transportation plan's impacts. While we agree SANDAG has such, SANDAG abuses its discretion if it exercises it in a manner that causes an EIR's analysis to be misleading or without informational value. "A lead agency cannot avoid finding a potentially significant effect on the environment by rotely applying standards of significance that do not address that potential effect."

By disregarding the Executive Order's overarching goal of ongoing emissions reductions, the EIR's analysis of the transportation plan's greenhouse gas emissions makes it falsely appear as if the transportation plan is furthering state climate policy when, in fact, the trajectory of the transportation plan's post-2020 emissions directly contravenes it. "[O]mitting material necessary to informed decisionmaking and informed public participation" subverts the purposes of CEQA and "precludes both identification of potential environmental consequences arising from the project and also thoughtful analysis of the sufficiency of measures to mitigate those consequences." Such an omission is particularly troubling where, as here, the project under review involves long-term, planned expenditures of billions of taxpayer dollars. No one can reasonably suggest it would be prudent to go forward with planned expenditures of this magnitude before the public and decision makers have been provided with all reasonably available information bearing on the project's impacts to the health, safety, and welfare of the region's inhabitants. We, therefore, conclude SANDAG prejudicially abused its discretion by omitting from the EIR an analysis of the transportation plan's consistency with the state climate policy, reflected in the Executive Order, of continual greenhouse gas emissions reductions.

Mitigation of Greenhouse Gas Emissions Impacts

1

Although the EIR did not analyze the transportation plan's consistency with the state climate policy reflected in the Executive Order, the EIR nevertheless, analyzed the transportation plan's greenhouse gas emissions impacts against three significance thresholds for each of the planning years 2020, 2035, and 2050. Under the first threshold, the EIR posited the transportation plan's impacts would be significant if the transportation plan's implementation were to increase greenhouse gas emissions compared to existing, or 2010, conditions. Under the second threshold, the EIR posited the transportation plan's impacts would be significant if the transportation plan's implementation conflicted with CARB's regional automobile and light truck emissions reductions targets. Under the third threshold, the EIR stated the transportation plan's impacts would be significant if the transportation plan's implementation conflicted with either CARB's Climate Change Scoping Plan (Scoping Plan) or SANDAG's own Climate Action Strategy.

The EIR concluded the transportation plan's greenhouse gas emissions impacts would be significant under the first significance threshold for the 2035 and 2050 planning years because the emissions would be higher in those planning years than in 2010. The EIR concluded the greenhouse gas emissions impacts would be less than significant in all other respects analyzed.

2

To mitigate the significant greenhouse gas emissions impacts found under the first threshold, the EIR identified three mitigation measures it deemed feasible. The first mitigation measure required SANDAG to update its future regional comprehensive plans, regional transportation plans, and sustainable communities plans to incorporate policies and measures leading to reduced greenhouse gas emissions. The second mitigation measure encouraged the San Diego region cities and the County of San Diego (County) to adopt and implement climate action plans for reducing greenhouse gas emissions to a level the particular city or the County determined would not be cumulatively considerable. The second mitigation measure also identified various provisions the plans should include and stated SANDAG would assist in the preparation of the plans and other climate strategies through the continued implementation of its own Climate Action Strategy and Energy Roadmap Program. The third mitigation measure stated SANDAG would and other agencies should require the use of best available control technology to reduce greenhouse gas emissions during the construction and operation of projects.

According to the EIR, these mitigation measures encourage reduction in greenhouse gas emissions, but they do not provide a mechanism guaranteeing such reductions. Consequently, the EIR concluded the significant impacts found under the first threshold would remain significant and unavoidable.

The EIR also considered and rejected three other mitigation measures deemed infeasible. These mitigation measures were: (1) requiring all vehicles driven within the region to be zero-emission vehicles or to be powered by renewable energy; (2) requiring all future construction to be net-zero energy use; and (3) requiring all future construction activity to include only equipment retrofitted to significantly reduce greenhouse gas emissions.

3

SANDAG contends the EIR adequately addressed mitigation for the transportation plan's significant greenhouse gas emissions impacts. Given our conclusion, *ante,* this challenge is at least partially moot as the additional analysis necessary to properly address the transportation plan's consistency with the state climate policy reflected in the Executive Order will likely require revisions to related sections of the EIR, including the EIR's discussion of mitigation measures. We, nonetheless, briefly address SANDAG's contention. As this contention is predominately factual, our review is for substantial evidence.

a

"The core of an EIR is the mitigation and alternatives sections." "Section 21002 requires agencies to adopt feasible mitigation measures to substantially lessen or avoid otherwise significant adverse environmental impacts. . . . "For each significant effect, the EIR must identify specific mitigation measures; where several potential mitigation measures are available, each should be discussed separately, and the reasons for choosing one over the others should be stated. If the inclusion of a mitigation measure would itself create new significant effects, these too, must be discussed, though in less detail than required for those caused by the project itself."

For significant greenhouse gas emissions effects, feasible mitigation measures may include: "(1) Measures in an existing plan or mitigation program for the reduction of emissions that are required as part of the lead agency's decision; [¶] (2) Reductions in emissions resulting from a project through implementation of project features, project design, or other measures . . . ; [¶] (3) Off-site measures, including offsets that are not otherwise required, to mitigate a project's emissions; [¶] (4) Measures that sequester greenhouse gases; [¶] [and] (5) In the case of the adoption of a plan, such as a general plan, long range development plan, or plans for the reduction of greenhouse gas emissions, mitigation may include the identification of specific measures that may be implemented on a project-by-project basis. Mitigation may also include the incorporation of specific measures or policies found in an adopted ordinance or regulation that reduces the cumulative effect of emissions." (Guidelines, § 15126.4, subd. (c).)

b

At one extreme, the EIR in this case considered and deemed feasible three measures requiring little to no effort to implement and assuring little to no concrete steps toward emissions reduction. In addition, according to the EIR, many of the suggestions contained in these measures have already been incorporated into the transportation plan and, by implication, the transportation plan's emissions estimates. "A 'mitigation measure' is a suggestion or change that would reduce or minimize significant adverse impacts on the environment caused by the project as proposed." A mitigation measure is not part of the project. Thus, it is questionable whether these measures even qualify as mitigation measures.

At the other extreme, the EIR considered and deemed infeasible three particularly onerous measures. Each of the measures would be difficult, if not impossible, to enforce and each requires implementation resources not readily available. Unrealistic mitigation measures, similar to unrealistic project alternatives, do not contribute to a useful CEQA analysis. As none of these measures had any probability of implementation, their inclusion in the EIR was illusory.

Missing from the EIR is what CEQA requires: a discussion of mitigation alternatives that could both substantially lessen the transportation plan's significant greenhouse gas emissions impacts and feasibly be implemented. A few examples of potential alternatives identified in the Climate Action Strategy include: supporting the planning and development of smart growth areas through transportation investments and other funding decisions; offering incentives for transit-oriented developments in smart growth areas; coordinating the funding of low carbon transportation with smart growth development; and encouraging parking management measures that promote walking and transit use in smart growth areas. Given the absence of any discussion of such mitigation alternatives, we conclude there is not substantial evidence to support SANDAG's determination the EIR adequately addressed mitigation for the transportation plan's greenhouse gas emissions impacts. The error is prejudicial because it precluded informed public participation and decisionmaking.

The judgment is affirmed.

NOTES AND QUESTIONS

1. At what level of government is the impact of land use on climate change most appropriately addressed? At the municipal level? The state level? The federal level? The international level? Does the problem of climate change fundamentally undermine the traditional statement that land use is most properly assessed by local governments?

2. Do existing environmental laws provide adequate means of incorporating climate change concerns into the land use lawmaking process, or are fundamentally new approaches necessary? Should such interventions take the form of substantive regulations of land use or can they be adequately addressed by procedural statutes (e.g., statutes requiring environmental impact statements), open-ended greenhouse gas emissions "performance" standards, or some other sort of regulation?

3. Climate change can also be addressed proactively through zoning regulations. In 2016, the city of Hartford, Connecticut, passed a set of zoning regulations that has as one of its primary aims "responding to the threat of climate change." Hartford, Conn., Zoning Regulations § 2.1.1.A.(2). Among other things, Hartford's regulations: provide height bonuses for green roofs, renewable energy, and cogeneration; require electric vehicle charging stations in large parking garages; promote transit oriented development at designated nodes by, among other things, reducing parking requirements in such nodes by 50%; provide for cistern and rainwater collection systems; adopt Complete Streets principles that put pedestrians and bicyclists on an equal playing field with car drivers; and allow for renewable energy systems (solar and wind) in every district. All of these measures aim to reduce water and energy usage and promote more compact development that reduces vehicle miles traveled. One of the casebook authors, Sara Bronin, chaired the planning and zoning commission during the drafting process and drafted many of the climate change-related provisions—along with her students.

CHAPTER TEN

LOCAL GOVERNMENT AS MARKET PARTICIPANT

Government's traditional role in the development process has been that of a mediator or umpire between the interests of developers and neighbors, primarily through zoning regulation. Euclidean zoning operates by separating uses with the potential to cause conflict with one another. More flexible regulatory mechanisms—planned unit developments, conditional zoning, subdivision controls and site plan review—involve governmental scrutiny of a developer's proposals to minimize the potential harm to neighbors and, in many cases, to ensure that the project adds value to the surrounding community. Other regulatory regimes, such as subdivision regulation, historic preservation law and aesthetic regulation, influence or dictate private decision-making.

Are there circumstances where government should move beyond regulating the land development market, and become an active participant in that market? No matter what combination of incentives and constraints government uses to channel development in particular directions, some markets may not generate some uses. When, if ever, should government step in to affirmatively support development of particular uses that the private market will not support?

Government might choose to subsidize development that redistributes wealth. For instance, during the post-World War II era, Congress expanded the funding available for public housing, and many large cities built high-rise apartment buildings to provide what was intended to be better housing for residents without the means to rent decent private housing. The experience was not uniformly a positive one. Due to a number of factors, including the high-rise design, low quality of materials used, concentration of poverty within the projects, and bureaucratic mismanagement, many of these projects soon became less desirable than the slums they replaced. Although a large number of smaller-scale public housing projects remain relatively successful, Chicago, Philadelphia, Baltimore and other large cities have demolished a number of their largest projects only decades after they were built. The focus of housing policy has shifted from government-built projects to government subsidies that tenants can use to secure private housing.

Government might also want to promote or subsidize development that generates external benefits—jobs, in particular. Municipalities are often willing to make concessions to attract potential employers, or to keep existing employers from leaving the area. Conversely, municipalities may be willing to subsidize new construction in order to stop "urban blight"—which imposes external costs on neighboring buildings and areas.

For the most part, government could address these problems by providing subsidies (in the form of cash or tax benefits) were it not for the problem of holdouts. In an already developed municipality, however, a private developer embarking on a large-scale project will generally have to assemble land owned by a significant number of separate landowners. Assembly is much easier for government, because government can use—or threaten to use—its eminent domain power. As a result, a municipality's use of its eminent domain power may be the most cost-effective way to subsidize development that generates external benefits. What limits, if any, should there be on the government's use of its eminent domain power to promote development?

Consider the following case:

Kelo v. City of New London
Supreme Court of the United States, 2005
545 U.S. 469

■ JUSTICE STEVENS delivered the opinion of the Court.

In 2000, the city of New London approved a development plan that, in the words of the Supreme Court of Connecticut, was "projected to create in excess of 1,000 jobs, to increase tax and other revenues, and to revitalize an economically distressed city, including its downtown and waterfront areas." 268 Conn. 1, 5, 843 A.2d 500, 507 (2004). In assembling the land needed for this project, the city's development agent has purchased property from willing sellers and proposes to use the power of eminent domain to acquire the remainder of the property from unwilling owners in exchange for just compensation. The question presented is whether the city's proposed disposition of this property qualifies as a "public use" within the meaning of the Takings Clause of the Fifth Amendment to the Constitution.

The city of New London (hereinafter City) sits at the junction of the Thames River and the Long Island Sound in southeastern Connecticut. Decades of economic decline led a state agency in 1990 to designate the City a "distressed municipality." In 1996, the Federal Government closed the Naval Undersea Warfare Center, which had been located in the Fort Trumbull area of the City and had employed over 1,500 people. In 1998, the City's unemployment rate was nearly double that of the State, and its population of just under 24,000 residents was at its lowest since 1920.

These conditions prompted state and local officials to target New London, and particularly its Fort Trumbull area, for economic revitalization. To this end, respondent New London Development

Corporation (NLDC), a private nonprofit entity established some years earlier to assist the City in planning economic development, was reactivated. In January 1998, the State authorized a $5.35 million bond issue to support the NLDC's planning activities and a $10 million bond issue toward the creation of a Fort Trumbull State Park. In February, the pharmaceutical company Pfizer Inc. announced that it would build a $300 million research facility on a site immediately adjacent to Fort Trumbull; local planners hoped that Pfizer would draw new business to the area, thereby serving as a catalyst to the area's rejuvenation. After receiving initial approval from the city council, the NLDC continued its planning activities and held a series of neighborhood meetings to educate the public about the process. In May, the city council authorized the NLDC to formally submit its plans to the relevant state agencies for review. Upon obtaining state-level approval, the NLDC finalized an integrated development plan focused on 90 acres of the Fort Trumbull area.

The Fort Trumbull area is situated on a peninsula that juts into the Thames River. The area comprises approximately 115 privately owned properties, as well as the 32 acres of land formerly occupied by the naval facility (Trumbull State Park now occupies 18 of those 32 acres). The development plan encompasses seven parcels. Parcel 1 is designated for a waterfront conference hotel at the center of a "small urban village" that will include restaurants and shopping. This parcel will also have marinas for both recreational and commercial uses. A pedestrian "riverwalk" will originate here and continue down the coast, connecting the waterfront areas of the development. Parcel 2 will be the site of approximately 80 new residences organized into an urban neighborhood and linked by public walkway to the remainder of the development, including the state park. This parcel also includes space reserved for a new U.S. Coast Guard Museum. Parcel 3, which is located immediately north of the Pfizer facility, will contain at least 90,000 square feet of research and development office space. Parcel 4A is a 2.4-acre site that will be used either to support the adjacent state park, by providing parking or retail services for visitors, or to support the nearby marina. Parcel 4B will include a renovated marina, as well as the final stretch of the riverwalk. Parcels 5, 6, and 7 will provide land for office and retail space, parking, and water-dependent commercial uses. App. 109–113.

The NLDC intended the development plan to capitalize on the arrival of the Pfizer facility and the new commerce it was expected to attract. In addition to creating jobs, generating tax revenue, and helping to "build momentum for the revitalization of downtown New London," *id.,* at 92, the plan was also designed to make the City more attractive and to create leisure and recreational opportunities on the waterfront and in the park.

The city council approved the plan in January 2000, and designated the NLDC as its development agent in charge of implementation. See Conn. Gen. Stat. § 8–188 (2005). The city council also authorized the NLDC to purchase property or to acquire property by exercising eminent domain in the City's name. § 8–193. The NLDC successfully negotiated the purchase of most of the real estate in the 90-acre area, but its negotiations with petitioners failed. As a consequence, in November 2000, the NLDC initiated the condemnation proceedings that gave rise to this case.

II

Petitioner Susette Kelo has lived in the Fort Trumbull area since 1997. She has made extensive improvements to her house, which she prizes for its water view. Petitioner Wilhelmina Dery was born in her Fort Trumbull house in 1918 and has lived there her entire life. Her husband Charles (also a petitioner) has lived in the house since they married some 60 years ago. In all, the nine petitioners own 15 properties in Fort Trumbull—4 in parcel 3 of the development plan and 11 in parcel 4A. Ten of the parcels are occupied by the owner or a family member; the other five are held as investment properties. There is no allegation that any of these properties is blighted or otherwise in poor condition; rather, they were condemned only because they happen to be located in the development area.

In December 2000, petitioners brought this action in the New London Superior Court. They claimed, among other things, that the taking of their properties would violate the "public use" restriction in the Fifth Amendment. After a 7-day bench trial, the Superior Court granted a permanent restraining order prohibiting the taking of the properties located in parcel 4A (park or marina support).

After the Superior Court ruled, both sides took appeals to the Supreme Court of Connecticut. That court held, over a dissent, that all of the City's proposed takings were valid. It began by upholding the lower court's determination that the takings were authorized by chapter 132, the State's municipal development statute. See Conn. Gen. Stat. § 8–186 et seq. (2005). That statute expresses a legislative determination that the taking of land, even developed land, as part of an economic development project is a "public use" and in the "public interest." 268 Conn., at 18–28, 843 A. 2d, at 515–521. Next, relying on cases such as Hawaii Housing Authority v. Midkiff, 467 U.S. 229, 81 L. Ed. 2d 186, 104 S. Ct. 2321 (1984), and Berman v. Parker, 348 U.S. 26, 99 L. Ed. 27, 75 S. Ct. 98 (1954), the court held that such economic development qualified as a valid public use under both the Federal and State Constitutions. 268 Conn., at 40, 843 A. 2d, at 527.

III

Two polar propositions are perfectly clear. On the one hand, it has long been accepted that the sovereign may not take the property of A for the sole purpose of transferring it to another private party B, even though A is paid just compensation. On the other hand, it is equally clear that a State may transfer property from one private party to another if future "use by the public" is the purpose of the taking; the condemnation of land for a railroad with common-carrier duties is a familiar example. Neither of these propositions, however, determines the disposition of this case.

Viewed as a whole, our jurisprudence has recognized that the needs of society have varied between different parts of the Nation, just as they have evolved over time in response to changed circumstances. Our earliest cases in particular embodied a strong theme of federalism, emphasizing the "great respect" that we owe to state legislatures and state courts in discerning local public needs. See Hairston v. Danville & Western R. Co., 208 U.S. 598, 606–607, 52 L. Ed. 637, 28 S. Ct. 331 (1908) (noting that these needs were likely to vary depending on a State's "resources, the capacity of the soil, the relative importance of industries to the general public welfare, and the long-established methods and habits of the people"). For more than a century, our public use jurisprudence has wisely eschewed rigid formulas and intrusive scrutiny in favor of affording legislatures broad latitude in determining what public needs justify the use of the takings power.

IV

Those who govern the City were not confronted with the need to remove blight in the Fort Trumbull area, but their determination that the area was sufficiently distressed to justify a program of economic rejuvenation is entitled to our deference. The City has carefully formulated an economic development plan that it believes will provide appreciable benefits to the community, including—but by no means limited to—new jobs and increased tax revenue. As with other exercises in urban planning and development, the City is endeavoring to coordinate a variety of commercial, residential, and recreational uses of land, with the hope that they will form a whole greater than the sum of its parts. To effectuate this plan, the City has invoked a state statute that specifically authorizes the use of eminent domain to promote economic development. Given the comprehensive character of the plan, the thorough deliberation that preceded its adoption, and the limited scope of our review, it is appropriate for us, as it was in *Berman*, to resolve the challenges of the individual owners, not on a piecemeal basis, but rather in light of the entire plan. Because that plan unquestionably serves a public purpose, the takings challenged here satisfy the public use requirement of the Fifth Amendment.

To avoid this result, petitioners urge us to adopt a new bright-line rule that economic development does not qualify as a public use. Putting aside the unpersuasive suggestion that the City's plan will provide only purely economic benefits, neither precedent nor logic supports petitioners' proposal. Promoting economic development is a traditional and long-accepted function of government. There is, moreover, no principled way of distinguishing economic development from the other public purposes that we have recognized.

Petitioners contend that using eminent domain for economic development impermissibly blurs the boundary between public and private takings. Again, our cases foreclose this objection. Quite simply, the government's pursuit of a public purpose will often benefit individual private parties.

It is further argued that without a bright-line rule nothing would stop a city from transferring citizen A's property to citizen B for the sole reason that citizen B will put the property to a more productive use and thus pay more taxes. Such a one-to-one transfer of property, executed outside the confines of an integrated development plan, is not presented in this case. While such an unusual exercise of government power would certainly raise a suspicion that a private purpose was afoot, the hypothetical cases posited by petitioners can be confronted if and when they arise. They do not warrant the crafting of an artificial restriction on the concept of public use.

Alternatively, petitioners maintain that for takings of this kind we should require a "reasonable certainty" that the expected public benefits will actually accrue. Such a rule, however, would represent an even greater departure from our precedent. "When the legislature's purpose is legitimate and its means are not irrational, our cases make clear that empirical debates over the wisdom of takings—no less than debates over the wisdom of other kinds of socioeconomic legislation— are not to be carried out in the federal courts." *Midkiff*, 467 U.S., at 242, 81 L. Ed. 2d 186, 104 S. Ct. 2321.

Just as we decline to second-guess the City's considered judgments about the efficacy of its development plan, we also decline to second-guess the City's determinations as to what lands it needs to acquire in order to effectuate the project. "It is not for the courts to oversee the choice of the boundary line nor to sit in review on the size of a particular project area. Once the question of the public purpose has been decided, the amount and character of land to be taken for the project and the need for a particular tract to complete the integrated plan rests in the discretion of the legislative branch." *Berman*, 348 U.S., at 35–36, 99 L. Ed. 27, 75 S. Ct. 98.

In affirming the City's authority to take petitioners' properties, we do not minimize the hardship that condemnations may entail, notwithstanding the payment of just compensation. We emphasize that nothing in our opinion precludes any State from placing further restrictions on its exercise of the takings power. Indeed, many States already impose "public use" requirements that are stricter than the federal baseline. Some of these requirements have been established as a matter of state constitutional law, while others are expressed in state eminent domain statutes that carefully limit the grounds upon which takings may be exercised. As the submissions of the parties and their *amici* make clear, the necessity and wisdom of using eminent domain to promote economic development are certainly matters of legitimate public debate. This Court's authority, however, extends only to determining whether the City's proposed condemnations are for a "public use" within the meaning of the Fifth Amendment to the Federal Constitution. Because over a century of our case law interpreting that provision dictates an affirmative answer to that question, we may not grant petitioners the relief that they seek.

■ JUSTICE KENNEDY, concurring.

I join the opinion for the Court and add these further observations.

This Court has declared that a taking should be upheld as consistent with the Public Use Clause, U.S. Const., Amdt. 5, as long as it is "rationally related to a conceivable public purpose." Hawaii Housing Authority v. Midkiff, 467 U.S. 229, 241, 81 L. Ed. 2d 186, 104 S. Ct. 2321 (1984); see also Berman v. Parker, 348 U.S. 26, 99 L. Ed. 27, 75 S. Ct. 98 (1954).

A court applying rational-basis review under the Public Use Clause should strike down a taking that, by a clear showing, is intended to favor a particular private party, with only incidental or pretextual public benefits, just as a court applying rational-basis review under the Equal Protection Clause must strike down a government classification that is clearly intended to injure a particular class of private parties, with only incidental or pretextual public justifications.

A court confronted with a plausible accusation of impermissible favoritism to private parties should treat the objection as a serious one and review the record to see if it has merit, though with the presumption that the government's actions were reasonable and intended to serve a public purpose. Here, the trial court conducted a careful and extensive inquiry into "whether, in fact, the development plan is of primary benefit to . . . the developer [*i.e.*, Corcoran Jennison], and private businesses which may eventually locate in the plan area [*e.g.*, Pfizer], and in that regard, only of incidental benefit to the city." App. to Pet. for Cert. 261.

This case, then, survives the meaningful rational basis review that in my view is required under the Public Use Clause.

Petitioners and their *amici* argue that any taking justified by the promotion of economic development must be treated by the courts as *per se* invalid, or at least presumptively invalid. Petitioners overstate the need for such a rule, however, by making the incorrect assumption that review under *Berman* and *Midkiff* imposes no meaningful judicial limits on the government's power to condemn any property it likes. A broad *per se* rule or a strong presumption of invalidity, furthermore, would prohibit a large number of government takings that have the purpose and expected effect of conferring substantial benefits on the public at large and so do not offend the *Public Use Clause.*

My agreement with the Court that a presumption of invalidity is not warranted for economic development takings in general, or for the particular takings at issue in this case, does not foreclose the possibility that a more stringent standard of review than that announced in *Berman* and *Midkiff* might be appropriate for a more narrowly drawn category of takings. There may be private transfers in which the risk of undetected impermissible favoritism of private parties is so acute that a presumption (rebuttable or otherwise) of invalidity is warranted under the *Public Use Clause. Cf.* Eastern Enterprises v. Apfel, 524 U.S. 498, 549–550, 141 L. Ed. 2d 451, 118 S. Ct. 2131 (1998) (Kennedy, J., concurring in judgment and dissenting in part) (heightened scrutiny for retroactive legislation under the Due Process Clause). This demanding level of scrutiny, however, is not required simply because the purpose of the taking is economic development.

This is not the occasion for conjecture as to what sort of cases might justify a more demanding standard, but it is appropriate to underscore aspects of the instant case that convince me no departure from *Berman* and *Midkiff* is appropriate here. This taking occurred in the context of a comprehensive development plan meant to address a serious city wide depression, and the projected economic benefits of the project cannot be characterized as *de minimis*. The identities of most of the private beneficiaries were unknown at the time the city formulated its plans. The city complied with elaborate procedural requirements that facilitate review of the record and inquiry into the city's purposes. In sum, while there may be categories of cases in which the transfers are so suspicious, or the procedures employed so prone to abuse, or the purported benefits are so trivial or implausible, that courts should presume an impermissible private purpose, no such circumstances are present in this case.

■ JUSTICE O'CONNOR, with whom the CHIEF JUSTICE, JUSTICE SCALIA, and JUSTICE THOMAS join, dissenting.

While the Takings Clause presupposes that government can take private property without the owner's consent, the just compensation requirement spreads the cost of condemnations and thus "prevents the public from loading upon one individual more than his just share of the burdens of government." Monongahela Nav. Co. v. United States, 148 U.S. 312, 325, 37 L. Ed. 463, 13 S. Ct. 622 (1893); see also Armstrong v. United States, 364 U.S. 40, 49, 4 L. Ed. 2d 1554, 80 S. Ct. 1563 (1960). The public use requirement, in turn, imposes a more basic limitation, circumscribing the very scope of the eminent domain power: Government may compel an individual to forfeit her property for the *public's* use, but not for the benefit of another private person. This requirement promotes fairness as well as security. *Cf.* Tahoe-Sierra Preservation Council, Inc. v. Tahoe Regional Planning Agency, 535 U.S. 302, 336, 152 L. Ed. 2d 517, 122 S. Ct. 1465 (2002) ("The concepts of 'fairness and justice' . . . underlie the Takings Clause").

Where is the line between "public" and "private" property use? We give considerable deference to legislatures' determinations about what governmental activities will advantage the public. But were the political branches the sole arbiters of the public-private distinction, the Public Use Clause would amount to little more than hortatory fluff. An external, judicial check on how the public use requirement is interpreted, however limited, is necessary if this constraint on government power is to retain any meaning. See Cincinnati v. Vester, 281 U.S. 439, 446, 74 L. Ed. 950, 50 S. Ct. 360 (1930) ("It is well established that . . . the question [of] what is a public use is a judicial one").

This case returns us for the first time in over 20 years to the hard question of when a purportedly "public purpose" taking meets the public use requirement. It presents an issue of first impression: Are economic development takings constitutional? I would hold that they are not.

In moving away from our decisions sanctioning the condemnation of harmful property use, the Court today significantly expands the meaning of public use. It holds that the sovereign may take private property currently put to ordinary private use, and give it over for new, ordinary private use, so long as the new use is predicted to generate some secondary benefit for the public—such as increased tax revenue, more jobs, maybe even esthetic pleasure. But nearly any lawful use of real private property can be said to generate some incidental benefit to the public. Thus, if predicted (or even guaranteed) positive side effects are enough to render transfer from one private party to another constitutional, then the words "for public use" do not realistically exclude *any* takings, and thus do not exert any constraint on the eminent domain power.

The Court protests that it does not sanction the bare transfer from A to B for B's benefit. It suggests two limitations on what can be taken after today's decision. First, it maintains a role for courts in ferreting out takings whose sole purpose is to bestow a benefit on the private transferee—without detailing how courts are to conduct that complicated inquiry. Ante, at 477–478, 162 L. Ed. 2d, at 450. For his part, Justice Kennedy suggests that courts may divine illicit purpose by a careful review of the record and the process by which a legislature arrived at the decision to take—without specifying what courts should look for in a case with different facts, how they will know if they have found it, and what to do if they do not. Ante, at 491–492, 162 L. Ed. 2d, at 459–460 (concurring opinion). Whatever the details of Justice

Kennedy's as-yet-undisclosed test, it is difficult to envision anyone but the "stupid staff[er]" failing it. See Lucas v. South Carolina Coastal Council, 505 U.S. 1003, 1025–1026, n. 12, 120 L. Ed. 2d 798, 112 S. Ct. 2886 (1992). The trouble with economic development takings is that private benefit and incidental public benefit are, by definition, merged and mutually reinforcing. In this case, for example, any boon for Pfizer or the plan's developer is difficult to disaggregate from the promised public gains in taxes and jobs. See App. to Pet. for Cert. 275–277.

Even if there were a practical way to isolate the motives behind a given taking, the gesture toward a purpose test is theoretically flawed. If it is true that incidental public benefits from new private use are enough to ensure the "public purpose" in a taking, why should it matter, as far as the Fifth Amendment is concerned, what inspired the taking in the first place? How much the government does or does not desire to benefit a favored private party has no bearing on whether an economic development taking will or will not generate secondary benefit for the public. And whatever the reason for a given condemnation, the effect is the same from the constitutional perspective—private property is forcibly relinquished to new private ownership.

A second proposed limitation is implicit in the Court's opinion. The logic of today's decision is that eminent domain may only be used to upgrade—not downgrade—property. At best this makes the Public Use Clause redundant with the Due Process Clause, which already prohibits irrational government action. See Lingle, 544 U.S. 528, 161 L. Ed. 2d 876, 125 S. Ct. 2074 (2005). The Court rightfully admits, however, that the judiciary cannot get bogged down in predictive judgments about whether the public will actually be better off after a property transfer. In any event, this constraint has no realistic import. For who among us can say she already makes the most productive or attractive possible use of her property? The specter of condemnation hangs over all property. Nothing is to prevent the State from replacing any Motel 6 with a Ritz-Carlton, any home with a shopping mall, or any farm with a factory.

Any property may now be taken for the benefit of another private party, but the fallout from this decision will not be random. The beneficiaries are likely to be those citizens with disproportionate influence and power in the political process, including large corporations and development firms. As for the victims, the government now has license to transfer property from those with fewer resources to those with more. The Founders cannot have intended this perverse result. "[T]hat alone is a *just* government," wrote James Madison, "which *impartially* secures to every man, whatever is his *own*." For the National Gazette, Property, (Mar. 27, 1792), reprinted in 14 Papers of James Madison 266 (R. Rutland et al. eds. 1983).

I would hold that the takings in both Parcel 3 and Parcel 4A are unconstitutional, reverse the judgment of the Supreme Court of Connecticut, and remand for further proceedings.

NOTES AND QUESTIONS

1. What limits does *Kelo* place on governmental power to condemn land for economic development purposes? Professor Julia Mahoney concludes that "[t]aken together, the majority opinion and the concurrence can be read as signaling a willingness to enjoin condemnations in situations where there is convincing evidence of government favoritism or animus, or where there is no plausible claim that the overall public interest is being served." Julia D. Mahoney, Kelo's Legacy: Eminent Domain and the Future of Property Rights, 2005 Sup. Ct. Rev. 103, 131. How often would you expect the Supreme Court to find such convincing evidence? Is there any reason to believe lower courts will find such evidence more often? Less often?

2. Public reaction to the *Kelo* decision was quick and overwhelmingly negative. In response to the decision, nearly a dozen states amended their constitutions, and many state legislatures enacted statutes purporting to restrict local power to condemn land for economic development purposes. One of the chief attorneys for Mrs. Kelo summarized Kelo's impacts after ten years: "a total of forty-four states changed their laws." Dana Berliner, Looking Back Ten Years After Kelo, 125 Yale L.J. F. 82, 84–86 (2015) (further stating that, among other changes, thirty states tightened their definitions of "public use" or "public purpose," eleven states gave prior owners the right of first refusal to repurchase property not used for the purpose for which it was condemned, and nine states shifted the burden of proof to the government).

Read the following statute, and consider whether it would alter the result in *Kelo* itself:

TEXAS GOVERNMENT CODE

Section 2206.001.   Limitation on Eminent Domain for Private Parties or Economic Development Purposes

(b) A governmental or private entity may not take private property through the use of eminent domain if the taking:

(1) confers a private benefit on a particular private party through the use of the property;

(2) is for a public use that is merely a pretext to confer a private benefit on a particular private party; or

(3) is for economic development purposes, unless the economic development is a secondary purpose resulting from municipal community development or municipal urban renewal activities to eliminate an existing affirmative harm on society from slum or blighted areas . . .

Professor Ilya Somin concludes that most of the statutes enacted by legislatures in response to *Kelo* are likely to be ineffective at constraining governmental exercises of eminent domain, but he suggests that the statutes enacted by referendum have more potential to constrain government action. Ilya Somin, The Limits of Backlash: Assessing the Political Response to Kelo, 93 Minn. L. Rev. 2100 (2009). What might explain the disparity?

3. Will the political process discipline municipal officials who are too aggressive in using eminent domain to promote redevelopment projects? Why wouldn't voter anger be more effective than litigation as a check on abusive use of eminent domain? *See generally* Daniel H. Cole, Why Kelo is Not Good News for Local Planners and Developers, 22 Ga. St. U. L. Rev. 803, 851 (2006) (contending that political backlash against *Kelo* discourages local politicians from engaging in politically sensitive development and redevelopment projects).

Would requiring more public participation in the redevelopment process provide an effective check on municipal abuse? *Compare* Damon Y. Smith, Participatory Planning and Procedural Protections: The Case for Deeper Public Participation in Urban Redevelopment, 29 St. Louis U. Pub. L. Rev. 243 (2009) (advocating greater participation) *with* Nicole Stelle Garnett, Planning as Public Use, 34 Ecology L.Q. 443, 463–64 (2007)(expressing skepticism).

Professor Audrey McFarlane suggests that community benefit agreements (CBAs) might at least assure that community residents adversely affected by a redevelopment project obtain something in return. She describes the CBA and its advantages:

> In the contractual agreement between representatives of communities in which a development project will take place and the developer, the project's developer promises to provide a variety of amenities (for example, open space or physical upgrades to existing buildings or roads) or to take certain beneficial actions (such as first hire agreements, low-income tenant set-asides, or to provide cash). In return, the community gives two things: First, it agrees to publicly support the development project, sometimes a prerequisite for developers getting regulatory approvals. Second, it promises to refrain from entering into litigation against the developer.

Audrey G. McFarlane, Putting the "Public" Back into Public–Private Partnerships for Economic Development, 30 W. New Eng. L. Rev. 39, 58 (2007).

Professor Alejandro Camacho joins others who view CBAs as highly problematic. Alejandro E. Camacho, Community Benefits Agreements: A Symptom, Not the Antidote, of Bilateral Land Use Regulation, 78 Brooklyn L. Rev. 355 (2013). He explains that the weaknesses of CBAs "reflect the continued inadequacy of the existing bilateral-negotiation process in providing for legitimate land use decisions." *Id.* at 357.

4. Even the majority in *Kelo* concedes that the government may not use the eminent domain power to take property from A for the sole purpose of transferring it to B. Suppose, however, government uses the eminent domain power to take property from 40 landowners for the purpose of transferring that property to a single B who faces land assembly problems. Should the eminent domain power be available in that instance? *See generally* Abraham Bell, Private Takings, 76 U. Chi. L. Rev 517, 558 (2009) (arguing for expanded use of private takings to overcome land assembly problems). *But see* Daniel B. Kelly, The "Public Use" Requirement in Eminent Domain Law: A Rationale Based on Secret Purchases and Private Influence, 92 Cornell L. Rev. 1 (2006) (contending that private parties can use secret buying agents to overcome land assembly problems, while government cannot).

5.   Suppose the City of New London had sought to encourage development in the Fort Trumbull area by zoning the area for office use, or by creating a mixed-use district. If Fort Trumbull were suitable for office or mixed-use development, wouldn't rezoning alone have generated that development? If not, why not?

6.   Suppose now that the city had zoned the Fort Trumbull area for office use, and had not permitted continuation of pre-existing non-conforming uses. Would that have accomplished the city's objectives?

If the city had pursued that course of action, what recourse would have been available to Mrs. Kelo? In particular, what remedies would have been available to her? If her primary remedy would be an award of compensation from the city, what does that suggest about the dissenting position in *Kelo*?

7.   What led the city to believe its redevelopment plan for the Fort Trumbull area would accomplish the city's objectives? How confident are you that a municipality can accurately assess the probability that its development plan will succeed? Consider Professor Richard Schragger's account:

> [T]hough it is an empirical question whether current-day subsidies are welfare-enhancing (and the studies are decidedly mixed), what we know from the history of local government is that they have often turned out poorly. Public officials tend to have short time horizons. Even if they are acting honorably, they may engage in giveaways because economically they have little choice or because politically they need to be seen as doing something to enhance local competitiveness. And whether subsidies are welfare-enhancing in the short term does not solve the main problem—the boom and bust cycle. Once mobile capital is attracted it can then leave; this volatility has substantial negative effects given that the city is fixed in place and residents' ability to relocate lags or is limited.

Richard C. Schragger, Mobile Capital, Local Economic Regulation, and the Democratic City, 123 Harv. L. Rev. 482, 495 (2009). See also Steven J. Eagle, *Kelo*, Directed Growth, and Municipal Industrial Policy, 17 Sup. Ct. Econ. Rev 63, 92–103 (2009) (expressing doubts about ability of municipalities to gauge effect of economic development policies).

8.   When a municipality makes a deal in order to present a favored use with the facilities it wants, what recourse does the municipality have if the user can't produce the benefits the municipality expects?

One of the most infamous uses of condemnation to promote economic development came in Detroit, where the city condemned an entire residential neighborhood in order to pave the way for a new General Motors plant. In Poletown Neighborhood Council v. City of Detroit, 410 Mich. 616, 304 N.W.2d 455 (1981), the Michigan Supreme Court upheld the condemnation, but the plant never generated more than a fraction of the 6,000 jobs the city had anticipated.

Subsequently, in County of Wayne v. Hathcock, 471 Mich. 445, 684 N.W.2d 765 (2004), the Michigan Supreme Court overruled its *Poletown* decision. The court wrote:

> To justify the exercise of eminent domain solely on the basis of the fact that the use of that property by a private entity seeking its own profit might contribute to the economy's health is to render impotent our constitutional limitations on the government's power of eminent domain. Poletown's "economic benefit" rationale would validate practically *any* exercise of the power of eminent domain on behalf of a private entity. After all, if one's ownership of private property is forever subject to the government's determination that another private party would put one's land to better use, then the ownership of real property is perpetually threatened by the expansion plans of any large discount retailer, "megastore," or the like.

471 Mich. at 482, 684 N.W.2d at 786.

Centene Plaza Redevelopment Corp. v. Mint Properties

Supreme Court of Missouri, 2007
225 S.W.3d 431

■ PER CURIAM.

The city of Clayton solicited redevelopment plans for one block of Forsyth Boulevard. Centene Plaza Redevelopment Corporation submitted the plan approved by Clayton, which included condemnation authority. When Centene failed to reach agreement with all the property owners to acquire the properties, it filed this condemnation action. Mint Properties and several other defendants resisted the condemnation on the basis that the property was not blighted, as defined by section 353.020, RSMo 2000. The trial court found in favor of Centene. Because the finding of blight was not supported by substantial evidence, the judgment is reversed.

Development of the plan

Centene purchased property located at 7700 Forsyth and 21 Hanley with the intent to expand its current office and parking space. Centene also sought to purchase a garage owned by the city adjacent to Centene's current office building. During discussions about purchasing the garage, Centene discovered that the city was seeking redevelopment of the area.

The city subsequently issued a general request seeking proposals from developers to redevelop the entire block of Forsyth bordered by South Bemiston Avenue, Hanley Road, and Carondelet Avenue. Centene submitted the only response to the request for proposals. Centene proposed a three-phase project that included formation of a redevelopment corporation, tax abatement, and the power of eminent domain.

The city reviewed Centene's response and then commissioned Peckham, Guyton, Albers, & Viets ("PGAV") to conduct an analysis of the area to determine whether it qualified as a blighted area. PGAV's analysis ultimately concluded that the property qualified as a blighted area.

The city subsequently passed an ordinance declaring the area to be blighted and approving Centene's plan. The area included defendants' properties. After approval of the plan, Centene sought to acquire the affected properties. When these efforts failed, condemnation actions were filed.

Standard of review

This Court examines the record to determine whether there is substantial evidence to support the legislative decision. Binger v. City of Independence, 588 S.W.2d 481, 486 (Mo. banc 1979).

Blight requires a showing of "social liability"

Section 353.020 sets forth the definition of "blighted area." A blighted area consists of those portions of the city that "by reason of age, obsolescence, inadequate or outmoded design or physical deterioration have become economic and social liabilities, and that such conditions are conducive to ill health, transmission of disease, crime or inability to pay reasonable taxes...." (Emphasis added.) Centene concedes that the determination of blight must include findings that the area in question is both an economic liability and a social liability.

Although the term "social liability" is not specifically defined by statute or in case law, the historical context suggests the definition of "social liability" focuses upon the health, safety, and welfare of the public. In that regard, it has been noted that the transformation of this country from primarily agricultural to a predominantly industrial society resulted in significant growth in the cities. Tax Increment Financing Com'n of Kansas City v. J.E. Dunn Const. Co., Inc., 781

S.W.2d 70, 78 (Mo. banc 1989). One result of this growth was blighted areas, which constituted a "menace injurious to the public health, safety, morals and welfare" of the residents. Id. The blighted areas also presented economic concerns. *Id.* The need to eliminate these conditions as a "breeding ground for juvenile delinquency, infant mortality, crime and disease," prompted a movement toward redevelopment. *Id.*

The evidence of social liability was insufficient

Based on the foregoing definition of "social liability," the evidence was insufficient. In particular, the evidence before the city concerning fire, police, and emergency services reports did not support a conclusion of social liability. Michael Schoedel, the city manager, testified that he requested information from the Clayton fire and police departments regarding the calls in the area. A memorandum from Mark Thorp, the fire chief, indicated that from 2001 to 2006, there were no fire calls and no emergency services calls at all for most of the properties in the redevelopment area, and collectively, there were only four fire calls and two emergency responses for eight properties in the area over the course of five years.

Tom Burn, the chief of police, also submitted a memorandum to Schoedel, indicating the number of police calls to the properties in the redevelopment area dating back to 1999. There were a total of 143 calls for five properties over approximately seven years, but this was less than half the number of calls for a single property located across the street during that time frame.

Although Schoedel expressed some potential concerns regarding safety, crime, fire hazards, and vandalism due to vacancies in the area, the information he received from the fire and police departments did not validate these concerns. In addition, there was no evidence presented regarding any public health concerns resulting from the condition of the area.

According to Schoedel, the PGAV blighting study commissioned by the city was a critical component in the city's determination of blight. However, while the PGAV study did conclude that the area was an economic liability because of the age, obsolescence, inadequate or outmoded design, and physical deterioration of some of the properties, it did not make any conclusions regarding the social liability of the area. Moreover, the PGAV study did not find that any of these conditions were injurious to the public health or safety. In fact, John Brancaglione, PGAV's employee, testified that the factors existent in the area did not constitute a social liability in the way he "understood that to be applicable to these situations." Instead, Brancaglione testified that the area was a social liability only to the extent that it constituted an economic liability because of its inability to pay reasonable taxes. Nevertheless, Centene argues that the blighting study prepared by PGAV was not the only factor in the city's determination of blight.

However, as noted, Schoedel specifically testified that the PGAV study was a critical component in the determination of blight.

Centene also claims that the determination of blight was supported by substantial evidence by citing the increase in jobs the redevelopment would provide and the "vibrant," pedestrian-friendly atmosphere that would result from the redevelopment. However, this evidence focuses only upon the prospective benefits of redevelopment—not the current state of the properties themselves. The city's ultimate goals for the area cannot serve as probative evidence of social liability in light of the lack of evidence concerning the public health, safety, and welfare in the record. Furthermore, if evidence to support a finding of economic liability could also constitute evidence to support a finding of social liability, the plain language of section 353.020 would be defeated.

Finally, while under section 353.020(1), an "area" may include buildings that are not themselves blighted, but which are deemed necessary for the redevelopment, there is a lack of evidence of social liability as to any portion of the area sought to be condemned. The area, therefore, failed to meet the statutory definition of "blighted area."

Conclusion

The judgment is reversed.

■ WHITE, J., dissenting:

I respectfully dissent. In my view, Centene presented sufficient evidence from which the City of Clayton reasonably could have determined that the redevelopment area had become an "economic and social liability." This phrase demonstrates the legislature's recognition of the causal connection between economics and social welfare. A decline in the former inevitably undermines the latter, and I would interpret the statute as such.

NOTES AND QUESTIONS

1. *Background.* Centene Corporation, a national health care provider, wanted to build a new headquarters. At first, Centene sought to purchase the parcels it wanted on the market. When that strategy proved unsuccessful, Centene formed a redevelopment corporation under Missouri law. A Missouri statute authorized municipalities to confer condemnation authority on redevelopment corporations, but not on ordinary for-profit corporations. As the Missouri Supreme Court indicated, the statute explicitly conditioned condemnation on a finding of blight.

2. How much deference did the *Centene* court give to the ESDC's finding of blight? Note that the Supreme Court in *Kelo* held that, for federal constitutional purposes, a finding of blight is unnecessary to support an exercise of the eminent domain power, but the *Kelo* opinion also indicated that the states had greater latitude to impose more stringent restrictions on condemnation power. As a result, states are free to require a finding of

blight, and to review that finding by any standard the state legislature or courts think appropriate.

Compare *Centene* with Goldstein v. New York State Urban Development Corp., 13 N.Y.3d 511, 893 N.Y.S.2d 472, 921 N.E.2d 164 (2009). In *Goldstein,* the New York Court of Appeals upheld the public authority's exercise of eminent domain power at the behest of private developers seeking to assemble a 22-acre parcel in Brooklyn for a mixed-use development to include a sports arena as well as residential and commercial construction. The Atlantic Yards project certainly encompassed some blighted areas, but also included some ordinary residential neighborhoods. In sustaining a finding of blight, the court's majority wrote:

> It is only where there is no room for reasonable difference of opinion as to whether an area is blighted, that judges may substitute their views as to the adequacy with which the public purpose of blight removal has been made out for that of the legislatively designated agencies; where, as here, "those bodies have made their finding, not corruptly or irrationally or baselessly, there is nothing for the courts to do about it . . . "

Id. at 526, 921 N.E.2d 164 at 172 (quoting from an earlier case). Is the *Centene* court's standard of review consistent with that in *Goldstein*, or is it more consistent with the approach of the *Goldstein* dissent?:

> The whole point of the public use limitation is to prevent takings even when a state agency deems them desirable. To let the agency itself determine when the public use requirement is satisfied is to make the agency a judge in its own cause. I think that it is we who should perform the role of judges, and that we should do so by deciding that the proposed taking in this case is not for public use.

N.Y.3d. at 552, 921 N.E.2d at 190 (Smith, J., dissenting). Reviews of Atlantic Yards' impact on the surrounding neighborhood have been mixed, given the hulking size of the sports arena, delays in constructing all parts of the project, and cost overruns.

3.   Columbia University sought to expand its New York City campus to a neighboring area. Columbia began acquiring property on the market, and simultaneously obtained the support of the New York City Economic Development Corporation (EDC) for redevelopment of the area. In 2002, the EDC issued a master plan for the area, characterizing the current land use as "auto-related or vacant," with several "handsome, mid-rise buildings [. . .] interspersed with parking lots and partially empty industrial buildings." Columbia continued to acquire buildings in the area, but some commercial owners were unwilling to sell. Ultimately, the Empire State Development Corporation (ESDC), a quasi-public entity, condemned the parcels owned by unwilling sellers, who challenged the finding of "blight" on which the condemnation was founded. The New York Court of Appeals, relying on its prior holding in *Goldstein*, upheld the finding of blight. Kaur

v. New York State Urban Development Corp., 15 N.Y.3d 235, 907 N.Y.S.2d 122, 933 N.E.2d 721 (2010).

Professor Ilya Somin has criticized both *Goldstein* and *Kaur*, calling them "the most widely publicized and controversial property rights rulings" since *Kelo*, given their characterization of the condemned properties as blighted and their narrow definition of pretextual takings. Ilya Somin, Let There Be Blight: Blight Condemnations in New York after *Goldstein* and *Kaur*, 38 Fordham Urban L. J. 1193, 1193–94 (2011).

City College of New York (CCNY), a component of the city's public university system, is located several blocks to the north of the Manhattanville area at issue in the *Kaur* case. Suppose CCNY, rather than Columbia, had sought to expand into the area. Would a finding of blight have been necessary to sustain the condemnation?

So long as the ESDC, a quasi-governmental entity, was the actual condemnor, should it matter whether ESDC was condemning the land for a public university or a private university? In Berman v. Parker, 348 U.S. 26, 33–34 (1954), Justice Douglas wrote, in sustaining an exercise of eminent domain to permit a private developer to engage in a slum clearance project, that "[t]he public end may be as well or better served through an agency of private enterprise than through a department of government." If that is true, why should it matter whether New York promotes education by permitting Columbia, rather than CCNY, to benefit from exercise of the eminent domain power?

Suppose Wal-Mart, rather than Columbia, had sought to condemn land in Manhattanville. Would the ESDC have co-operated with Wal-Mart? If the ESDC did co-operate, do you think the Court of Appeals would have voted to uphold the condemnation?

4.   After losing the case, Centene paid $19 million for three disputed properties. St. Louis Bus. J., June 11, 2009. (Perhaps not coincidentally, the City of Clayton offered Centene an $18.9 million tax abatement. CHS Online Globe, Oct. 20, 2009.)

In *Goldstein* (the Atlantic Yards case discussed in note 2, supra), the developer paid the last holdout $3 million for his condominium (purchased in 2003 for $590,000), even after the New York Court of Appeals sustained the use of the eminent domain power to take his apartment. Andy Newman and Charles V. Bagli, Daniel Goldstein, Last Atlantic Yards Holdout, Leaves for $3 Million, N.Y. Times, Apr. 21, 2010.

What do these payments teach us about the wisdom of permitting condemnation for redevelopment purposes? That condemnation is unnecessary because a party interested in redevelopment will ultimately overcome any holdout problems? That condemnation should routinely be permitted because the parties who resist are doing so largely to extract large cash settlements?

5.   *Development of Unproductive or Underproductive Land.* Especially in urban areas, municipalities or quasi-public agencies attempt to use the eminent domain power to assemble land in areas that are already developed. Sometimes, the condemnor contends that the land is underproductive, and therefore blighted. Suppose, however, that a government entity attempts to condemn vacant land to ensure its development. Should courts sustain condemnation?

The New Jersey Supreme Court faced that problem in Gallenthin Realty Development, Inc. v. Borough of Paulsboro, 191 N.J. 344, 924 A.2d 447 (2007). A New Jersey statute authorized condemnation of property "in need of redevelopment" when conditions led to "a stagnant or not fully productive condition of land potentially useful and valuable for contributing to and serving the public health, safety and welfare." The borough relied on the statute to condemn vacant waterfront land used for farming, open space, and occasional dredging. The New Jersey Supreme Court invalidated the condemnation, holding that the statute exceeded the scope of New Jersey's Constitution, which declares that "development or redevelopment of blighted areas shall be a public purpose and public use, for which private property may be taken or acquired." N.J. Const. art. VIII, § 3, par. 1.

The court went on to indicate that municipal redevelopment designations "are entitled to deference provided that they are supported by substantial evidence on the record." The court then concluded that "[t]he substantial evidence standard is not met if a municipality's decision is supported by only the net opinion of an expert." If you represented a municipality seeking to condemn land in New Jersey, how would you build a record to support the condemnation determination?

6.   In *Centene* and in *Gallenthin*, the areas the municipality sought to take were not afflicted by poverty. Condemnation was held invalid. In *Goldstein* and *Kaur* poor people inhabited at least some of the condemned land. Condemnation was upheld. In Berman v. Parker, 348 U.S. 26 (1954), the Supreme Court upheld the use of eminent domain for the purpose of slum clearance or "urban renewal." Almost by definition, urban renewal projects displace more poor people than rich or middle-class people. Should that be a matter of concern? Often, an objective of a redevelopment project is to replace dilapidated housing with habitable housing. Is that process likely to be beneficial or harmful to residents afflicted by poverty?

7.   How much confidence do you have in government's ability to foresee what sort of development will generate economic benefits? Is that question of greater importance when the government is acting as an active participant in the development market than when the government acts as a regulator of private activity?

INDEX

References are to Pages